RAYMOND NE...
20/11/0...

Sommario

Nomenclatura delle località citate e carta della regione
Alphabetisches Ortsverzeichnis und Übersichtskarte

Inhaltsverzeichnis

Shetland Islands

1

Orkney Islands

Aberdeen

SCOTLAND

Dundee

Glasgow

Edinburgh

4

Newcastle

NORTHERN

Belfast 2 IRELAND

Isle of Man

3

REPUBLIC OF IRELAND

Liverpool Manchester

Dublin

Limerick

Birmingham

Norwich

Cork

WALES ENGLAND

Cardiff Bristol Greater London

Southampton

Plymouth Isle of Wight

GREAT BRITAIN : the maps and town plans in the Great Britain Section of this Guide are based upon the Ordnance Survey of Great Britain with the permission of the Controller of Her Majesty's Stationery Office. Crown Copyright reserved.

NORTHERN IRELAND : the maps and town plans in the Northern Ireland Section of this Guide are based upon the Ordnance Survey of Northern Ireland with the sanction of the Controller of H.M. Stationery Office.

REPUBLIC OF IRELAND : the maps and town plans in the Republic of Ireland Section of this Guide are based upon the Ordnance Survey of Ireland by permission of the Government of the Republic, Permit number 4099

ATLANTIC OCEAN

NORTH CHANNEL

Oba

Mull

Colonsay   Lochgilphe

Jura

Port Askaig   Tarbert

Islay

Port Ellen

Campbelto

Liverpool

IRISH

SEA

ST GEORGE'S CHANNEL

CELTIC SEA

Letterkenny

Londonderry

Coleraine   A 2

Waterfoot

A 26

Ballymena

Larne

Donegal

NORTHERN IRELAND

Omagh

Ballygawley

Lough Neagh

Bangor

BELFAST

Strangford Lough

Newcastle

Enniskillen

Sligo

L. Allen

Armagh

Banbridge

Monaghan

A 25

Ballina

Boyle

Cavan

Dundalk

Westport

L. Mask

REPUBLIC

Roscommon

Edgeworthstown

Kells

Drogheda

Clifden

L. Corrib

OF

L. Ree

Mullingar

Boyne

Galway

Athlone

IRELAND

Ballinasloe

Tullamore

DUBLIN

Liverpool

Holyhead

Bray

Lisdoonvarna

River Shannon

Roscrea

Naas

Wicklow

Ennis

Kilkee

Thurles

Carlow

Arklow

LIMERICK

Kilkenny

Cashel

Tralee

Cahir

Enniscorthy

Dingle

Killarney

Carrick on Suir

Wexford

R Blackwater

Fermoy

Lismore

Waterford

Rosslare

Glengarriff

CORK

Cobh

Youghal

Bantry

Fishgua

Abergwau

Milford Have

Aberdaugleddau

Pembro

Penfr

le Havre

Rosslare

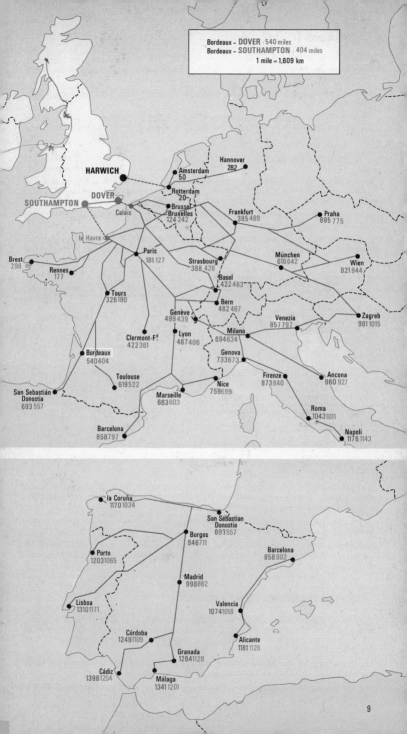

Bordeaux – DOVER : 540 miles
Bordeaux – SOUTHAMPTON : 404 miles
1 mile = 1,609 km

HARWICH
SOUTHAMPTON
DOVER
Calais

Amsterdam 50
Hannover 282
Rotterdam 20
Brussel
Bruxelles 124 242
Frankfurt 385 489
Praha 695 775
le Havre
Paris 181 127
Strasbourg 388 428
München 616 642
Wien 821 944
Brest 298
Rennes 177
Basel 422 463
Tours 326 190
Bern 482 467
Genève 499 439
Venezia 857 797
Zagreb 981 1015
Clermont-Fd 422 361
Lyon 467 406
Milano 694 634
Bordeaux 540 404
Genova 733 673
Toulouse 619 522
Nice 759 699
Firenze 873 840
Ancona 960 927
San Sebastián Donostia 693 557
Marseille 663 603
Roma 1043 1011
Barcelona 858 797
Napoli 1176 1143

la Coruña 1170 1034
San Sebastián Donostia 693 557
Burgos 846 711
Barcelona 858 802
Porto 1203 1065
Madrid 998 862
Valencia 1074 1018
Lisboa 1310 1171
Córdoba 1249 1109
Alicante 1181 1128
Granada 1264 1129
Cádiz 1398 1254
Málaga 1341 1201

DISTANCES

All distances in this edition are quoted in miles. The distance is given from each town to its neighbours and to the capital of each region as grouped in the guide. Towns appearing in the charts are preceded by a lozenge ♦ in text.

To avoid excessive repetition some distances have only been quoted once — you may therefore have to look under both town headings.

The mileages quoted are not necessarily the lowest but have been based on the roads which afford the best driving conditions and are therefore the most practical.

DISTANCES EN MILES

Pour chaque région traitée, vous trouverez au texte de chacune des localités sa distance par rapport à la capitale et aux villes environnantes. Lorsque ces villes sont celles des tableaux, leur nom est précédé d'un losange noir ♦.

La distance d'une localité à une autre n'est pas toujours répétée aux deux villes intéressées : voyez au texte de l'une ou de l'autre.

Ces distances ne sont pas nécessairement comptées par la route la plus courte mais par la plus pratique, c'est-à-dire celle offrant les meilleures conditions de roulage.

```
            Belfast
    250   Cork
    103  154   Dublin                                              133 Miles
     50  200   53   Dundalk
    196  122  135  153   Galway                      Dublin - Sligo
    273   54  189  223  133   Killarney
    204   58  120  154   64   69   Limerick
     70  281  146   98  176  300  231   Londonderry
     68  247  112   64  148  266  197   34   Omagh
    126  200  133  106   90  216  147   86   69   Sligo
    132  118   60   82   82  141   72  163  129   95   Tullamore
    197   73   96  147  141  112   77  242  208  176   81   Waterford
```

DISTANZE IN MIGLIA

Per ciascuna delle regioni trattate, troverete nel testo di ogni località la sua distanza dalla capitale e dalle città circostanti. Quando queste città sono comprese nelle tabelle, il loro nome è preceduto da una losanga ♦.

La distanza da una località all'altra non è sempre ripetuta nelle due città interessate : vedere nel testo dell'una o dell'altra.

Le distanze non sono necessariamente calcolate seguendo il percorso più breve, ma vengono stabilite secondo l'itinerario più pratico, che offre cioè le migliori condizioni di viaggio.

ENTFERNUNGSANGABEN IN MEILEN

Die Entfernungen der einzelnen Orte zur Landeshauptstadt und zu den nächstgrößeren Städten in der Umgebung sind im allgemeinen Ortstext angegeben. Die Namen der Städte in der Umgebung, die auf der Tabelle zu finden sind, sind durch eine Raute ♦ gekennzeichnet.

Die Entfernung zweier Städte voneinander können Sie aus den Angaben im Ortstext der einen oder der anderen Stadt ersehen.

Die Entfernungsangaben gelten nicht immer für den kürzesten, sondern für den günstigsten Weg.

DISTANCES BETWEEN MAJOR TOWNS

DISTANCES ENTRE PRINCIPALES VILLES

DISTANZE TRA LE PRINCIPALI CITTÀ

ENTFERNUNGEN ZWISCHEN DEN GRÖSSEREN STÄDTEN

442 Miles	
Example	Esempio
Example	Beispiel
Edinburgh – Southampton	

Distance chart (triangular mileage table). Cities along the diagonal, in order:

Aberdeen, Ayr, Birmingham, Blackpool, Brighton, Bristol, Cambridge, Cardiff, Carlisle, Coventry, Dover, Dumfries, Dundee, Edinburgh, Glasgow, Inverness, Ipswich, Kingston upon Hull, Leeds, Leicester, Liverpool, London, Manchester, Middlesbrough, Newcastle, Norwich, Nottingham, Oban, Oxford, Plymouth, Portsmouth, Sheffield, Southampton, Stoke on Trent, Swansea, Wick

City	Distances (reading left to right)
Aberdeen	
Ayr	196 292
Birmingham	336 187 129
Blackpool	608 459 172 296
Brighton	526 377 91 214 140
Bristol	500 351 115 222 111 165
Cambridge	545 396 110 233 182 46 199
Cardiff	242 93 200 95 150 96 259 304
Carlisle	461 311 18 148 150 93 93 120 219
Coventry	637 488 201 325 84 203 124 237 396 179
Dover	67 129 375 459 400 318 124 34 175 252 429
Dumfries	130 81 300 467 385 335 219 101 319 394 453 154
Dundee	107 207 268 467 385 335 281 155 189 317 495 80 63
Edinburgh	553 404 275 129 202 54 244 312 146 124 663 570 453 172 46
Glasgow	396 247 144 233 230 138 155 249 141 138 396 255 188 124 79 156
Inverness	365 216 88 254 210 148 229 124 88 229 365 216 146 105 91 174 139
Ipswich	470 320 43 157 157 121 74 149 228 24 186 261 403 293 327 496 579 61 96 131
Kingston upon Hull	368 219 102 56 269 187 209 172 127 121 298 160 301 227 226 394 131 101 75 130 107
Leeds	558 409 246 53 51 252 170 155 317 55 76 350 491 417 584 496 183 204 75 142 219 107
Leicester	363 214 86 51 252 170 297 189 122 105 281 155 222 221 302 70 42 91 160 35 247 219 35
Liverpool	276 182 178 123 123 297 268 202 90 179 319 264 146 189 217 255 89 160 142 202 247 160 276 202
London	235 150 123 224 297 202 220 316 59 208 348 91 105 157 126 283 126 95 119 170 276 109 139 256 161
Manchester	526 377 248 62 175 224 230 258 174 154 173 361 318 261 283 43 174 188 119 110 109 174 72 161 228 120
Middlesbrough	431 282 50 185 224 62 88 88 52 66 214 223 266 289 457 141 94 74 26 130 74 74 258 161 256
Newcastle	180 127 143 185 149 88 166 190 88 190 595 178 364 123 93 511 354 323 428 326 121 516 109 258 484 389
Norwich	509 359 194 566 106 73 81 267 48 419 116 296 574 118 535 146 169 70 169 35 247 153 98
Nottingham	641 492 329 296 93 124 103 400 211 166 438 500 667 331 345 242 285 302 325 412 345 264 467
Oban	604 455 213 48 213 292 161 363 199 253 166 462 499 630 154 272 302 285 236 310 383 248 599
Oxford	418 268 292 100 224 286 135 139 176 123 240 240 463 176 149 41 71 119 252 339 199 183 562 85 182
Plymouth	583 434 271 224 180 342 199 342 112 375 147 244 516 441 609 251 160 227 71 80 134 318 190 106 376 254 160 542
Portsmouth	397 248 61 100 135 156 176 65 241 189 330 256 442 609 423 132 95 162 58 162 179 289 41 113 208 21 289 41
Sheffield	46 212 135 224 149 133 123 189 256 255 186 423 186 160 245 190 162 190 245 208 53 355
Southampton	85 130 212 213 79 130 176 132 275 280 474 567 398 179 155 313 342 318 161 197 245 158 113 245 208 53
Stoke on Trent	136 218 82 235 129 123 212 65 280 474 298 192 186 190 158 197 175
Swansea	228 218 235 149 130 133 112 260 373 548 705 583 678 387 483 678 515 387
Wick	233 333 594 488 652 760 678 613 789 548 260 126 298 517 515 710 622 620

Discover
the guide...

To make the most of the guide know how to use it. The Michelin Guide offers in addition to the selection of hotels and restaurants a wide range of information to help you on your travels.

The key to the guide

...is the explanatory chapters which follow.
Remember that the same symbol and character whether in red or black or in bold or light type, have different meanings.

The selection of hotels and restaurants

This book is not an exhaustive list of all hotels but a selection which has been limited on purpose. The final choice is based on regular on the spot enquiries and visits. These visits are the occasion for examining attentively the comments and opinions of our readers.

Town plans

These indicate with precision pedestrian and shopping streets ; major through routes in built up areas ; exact location of hotels whether they be on main or side streets ; post offices ; tourist information centres ; the principal historic buildings and other tourist sights.

For your car

In the text of many towns is to be found a list of agents for the main car manufacturers with their addresses and telephone numbers. Therefore even while travelling you can have your car serviced or repaired.

Your views or comments concerning the above subjects or any others, are always welcome. Your letter will be answered.

Thank you in advance.

Michelin Tyre Public Limited Company
Tourism Department
81 Fulham Road, LONDON SW3 6RD

Bibendum wishes you a pleasant journey.

Choosing your hotel or restaurant

We have classified the hotels and restaurants with the travelling motorist in mind. In each category they have been listed in order of preference.

CLASS, STANDARD OF COMFORT

🏨🏨🏨	Luxury in the traditional style	XXXXX
🏨🏨	Top class comfort	XXXX
🏨🏨	Very comfortable	XXX
🏨	Good average	XX
🏛	Quite comfortable	X
⌂	Modest comfort	
⌂	Other recommended accommodation, at moderate prices	
without rest.	The hotel has no restaurant	
	The restaurant has bedrooms	with rm

HOTEL FACILITIES

Hotels in categories 🏨🏨🏨, 🏨🏨, 🏨🏨, usually have every comfort and exchange facilities ; details are not repeated under each hotel.

In other categories, we indicate the facilities available, however, they may not be found in each room.

30 rm	Number of rooms
🛗	Lift (elevator)
▤	Air conditioning
TV	Television in room
🛁wc 🛁	Private bathroom with toilet, private bathroom without toilet
🚿wc 🚿	Private shower with toilet, private shower without toilet
☏	Telephone in room : outside calls connected by the operator
☎	Telephone in room : direct dialling for outside calls
♿	Rooms accessible to the physically handicapped
⊿ ⊡	Outdoor or indoor swimming pool
🌳	Garden
⚒	Hotel tennis court
┌₁₈	Golf course and number of holes
🎣	Fishing available to hotel guests. A charge may be made
🏛	Equipped conference hall (minimum seating : 25)
🚗	Garage available (usually charged for)
℗	Car park
🐕	Dogs are not allowed
	Where dogs are allowed, they are generally accepted only in bedrooms
May-October	Dates when open, as indicated by the hotelier
season	Probably open for the season - precise dates not available
	Where no date or season is shown, establishments are open all year round
LL35 0SB	Postal code
(T.H.F.)	Hotel Group *(See list at end of the Guide)*

Choosing your hotel or restaurant

AMENITY

Your stay in certain hotels will be sometimes particularly agreeable or restful.

Such a quality may derive from the hotel's fortunate setting, its decor, welcoming atmosphere and service.

Such establishments are distinguished in the guide by the symbols shown below.

🏨 ... 🏠	Pleasant hotels
XXXXX ... X	Pleasant restaurants
« Park »	Particularly attractive feature
🦘	Very quiet or quiet, secluded hotel
🦘	Quiet hotel
≤ sea	Exceptional view
≤	Interesting or extensive view

By consulting the maps preceding each geographical area you will find it easier to locate them.

We do not claim to have indicated all the pleasant, very quiet or quiet, secluded hotels which exist.

Our enquiries continue. You can help us by letting us know your opinions and discoveries.

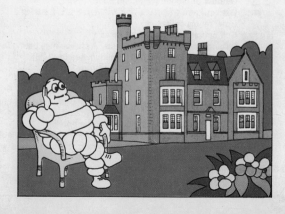

14

CUISINE

The stars for good cooking

We indicate by ❀, ❀❀ or ❀❀❀, establishments where the standard of cooking, whether particular to the country or foreign, deserves to be brought especially to the attention of our readers (see list p. 48 and the maps preceding each geographical area).

In the text of these establishments we show some of the dishes typical of their style of cooking.

❀ **An especially good restaurant in its class**

The star indicates a good place to stop on your journey.

But beware of comparing the star given to a " de luxe " establishment with accordingly high prices, with that of a simpler one, where for a lesser sum one can still eat a meal of quality.

❀❀ **Excellent cooking, worth a detour**

Specialities and wines of first class quality... Do not expect such meals to be cheap.

❀❀❀ **Some of the best cuisine, worth a journey**

Superb food, fine wines, faultless service, elegant surroundings... One will pay accordingly !

M **The red « M »**

Whilst appreciating the quality of the cooking in restaurants with a star, you may, however, wish to find some serving a perhaps less elaborate but nonetheless always carefully prepared meal.

Certain restaurants seem to us to answer this requirement. We bring them to your attention by marking them with a red « M » in the text of the Guide.

Alcoholic beverages-conditions of sale

The sale of alcoholic drinks is governed in Great Britain and Ireland by licensing laws which vary greatly from country to country.

Allowing for local variances, hotel bars and public houses close during the afternoon and after 11 pm. Hotel residents, however, may buy drinks outside the permitted hours at the discretion of the hotelier.

Children under the age of 14 are not allowed in bars.

Choosing your hotel or restaurant

PRICES

Valid for late 1984, the rates shown may be revised if the cost of living changes to any great extent. They are given in the currency of the country. In any event they should be regarded as basic charges.

Your recommendation is self-evident if you always walk into a hotel guide in hand.

Hotels and restaurants whose names appear in bold type have supplied us with their charges in detail and undertaken to abide by them, wherever possible, if the traveller is in possession of this year's guide.

If you think you have been overcharged, let us know. Where no rates are shown it is best to enquire about terms in advance.

Prices are given in £ sterling, except for the Republic of Ireland (Punts)

Where no mention s., t. or st. is shown, prices are subject to the addition of service charge, V.A.T., or both (V.A.T. does not apply in the Channel Islands).

Meals

M 7.00/9.00	**Set meals** — Lunch 7.00, dinner 9.00 — including cover charge, where applicable - served at normal hours (12.30 to 2.30 pm and 7 to 9 pm).
M 11.00/13.00	See page 15.
s. t.	Service only included. — V.A.T. included.
st.	Service and V.A.T. included (net prices).
🍾 4.00	Price of 1/2 bottle or carafe of ordinary wine.
M a la carte 14.00/18.00	**A la carte meals** — The first figure is for a plain meal and includes light entrée, main dish of the day with vegetables and dessert. The second figure is for a fuller meal and includes hors-d'œuvre, a main dish, cheese or dessert. These prices include a cover charge where applicable.
☕ 4.00	Charge for full cooked breakfast (i.e. not included in the room rate). Continental breakfast may be available at a lower rate.

Rooms

rm 21.00/38.00	Lowest price 21.00 for a comfortable single and highest price 38.00 for the best double room (including bathroom when applicable).
rm ☕ 30.00/45.00	Full cooked breakfast is included the price of the room.

Short Breaks (see p. 17)

SB 50.00/60.00	Prices indicated are lowest and highest per person for two nights in high season.

▧ AE ⑩ *VISA*	Principal **credit cards** accepted by establishments : Access — American Express — Diners Club — Visa (Barclaycard).

Choosing your hotel or restaurant

A FEW USEFUL DETAILS

Meals

Ask for menus including set meals and a la carte menus with the prices clearly marked if they are not produced automatically.

Hotels

Breakfast is often included in the price of the room, even if it is not required.

Special Rate for "Short Breaks"

Many hotels now offer a special rate for a stay of two nights which includes dinner, room and breakfast usually for a minimum of two people.

High season rates usually operate between June and September. It is always advisable to agree terms in advance with a hotelier.

Reservations

Hotels : Reserving in advance, when possible, is advised. Ask the hotelier to provide you, in his letter of confirmation, with all terms and conditions applicable to your reservation.

In seaside resorts especially, reservations usually begin and end on Saturdays.

Certain hoteliers require the payment of a deposit. This constitutes a mutual guarantee of good faith. Deposits, except in special cases, may amount to 10 % of the estimated hotel account.

Restaurants : it is strongly recommended always to book your table well ahead in order to avoid the disappointment of a refusal.

Animals

It is forbidden to bring domestic animals (dogs, cats...) into Great Britain and Ireland.

CAR, TYRES

In the text of many towns are to be found the names of garages or motor agents many of which offer a breakdown service.

The wearing of seat belts is obligatory for drivers and front seat passengers in Great Britain and Ireland.

Motoring organisations

The major motoring organisations in Great Britain are the Automobile Association and the Royal Automobile Club. Each provides services in varying degrees for non-resident members of affiliated clubs.

AUTOMOBILE ASSOCIATION
Fanum House
BASINGSTOKE, Hants., RG21 2EA
✆ (0256) 20123

ROYAL AUTOMOBILE CLUB
83-85 Pall Mall
LONDON SW1Y 5HW
✆ (01) 930 4343

Seeing a town and its surroundings

SIGHTS

Star-rating

★★★	Worth a journey
★★	Worth a detour
★	Interesting
AC	Admission charge

Finding the sights

See	Sights in town
Envir.	On the outskirts
Exc.	In the surrounding area
N, S, E, W	The sight lies north, south, east or west of the town
A 22	Go by road A 22, indicated by the same symbol on the Guide map
2 m.	Mileage

TOWNS

⊠ York	Post office serving the town
☢ 0225 Bath	STD dialling code (name of exchange indicated only when different from name of the town). Omit 0 when dialling from abroad
401 M 27, ⑩	Michelin map and co-ordinates or fold
West Country G.	See the Michelin Green Guide England : The West Country
pop. 1,057	Population
ECD : Wednesday	Early closing day (shops close at midday)
BX **A**	Letters giving the location of a place on the town map
▯₁₈	Golf course and number of holes (visitors unrestricted)
⁂,	Panoramic view, viewpoint
✈	Airport
🚗 ☎ 218	Place with a motorail connection ; further information from telephone number listed
▄▄▄▄	Shipping line
⟵	Passenger transport only *see list of companies at the end of the Guide*
ⓘ	Tourist Information Centre

Standard Time

In winter standard time throughout the British Isles is Greenwich Mean Time (G.M.T.). In summer British clocks are advanced by one hour to give British Summer Time (B.S.T.). The actual dates are announced annually but always occur over weekends in March and October.

TOWN PLANS

Roads

Motorway, dual carriageway
Interchange : complete, limited, number
Major through route
One-way street - Unsuitable for traffic
Pedestrian street
Shopping street - Car park
Gateway - Street passing under arch - Tunnel
Station and railway
Car ferry - Lever bridge

Sights — Hotels — Restaurants

Place of interest and its main entrance
Interesting place of worship :
    Cathedral, church or chapel
    Windmill
    Other sights
Castle - Ruins
Reference letter locating a sight
Hotel, restaurant with reference letter

Various signs

Tourist Information Centre
Hospital - Mosque - Synagogue
Garden, park, wood - Cemetery - Cross
Stadium - Golf course
View - Panorama
Airport - Racecourse
Funicular - Cable-car
Monument, statue - Fountain
Pleasure boat harbour - Lighthouse
Ferry services : passengers and cars
Public buildings located by letter :
    County Council Offices
    Town Hall
    Museum - Theatre
    Police (in large towns police headquarters)
    University, colleges
Main post office with poste restante, telephone
Golf course (with restrictions for visitors)
Communications tower or mast
Underground station

London

BRENT SOHO Borough - Area
Borough boundary - Area boundary

19

Découvrez
le guide...

et sachez l'utiliser pour en tirer le meilleur profit. Le Guide Michelin n'est pas seulement une liste de bonnes tables ou d'hôtels, c'est aussi une multitude d'informations pour faciliter vos voyages.

La clé du Guide

Elle vous est donnée par les pages explicatives qui suivent.
Sachez qu'un même symbole, qu'un même caractère, en rouge ou en noir, en maigre ou en gras, n'a pas tout à fait la même signification.

La sélection des hôtels et des restaurants

Ce Guide n'est pas un répertoire complet des ressources hôtelières, il en présente seulement une sélection volontairement limitée. Cette sélection est établie après visites et enquêtes effectuées régulièrement sur place. C'est lors de ces visites que les avis et observations de nos lecteurs sont examinés.

Les plans de ville

Ils indiquent avec précision : les rues piétonnes et commerçantes, comment traverser ou contourner l'agglomération, où se situent les hôtels (sur de grandes artères ou à l'écart), où se trouvent la poste, l'office de tourisme, les grands monuments, les principaux sites, etc.

Pour votre véhicule

Au texte de la plupart des localités figure une liste de représentants des grandes marques automobiles avec leur adresse et leur numéro d'appel téléphonique. En route, vous pouvez ainsi faire entretenir ou dépanner votre voiture, si nécessaire.

Sur tous ces points et aussi sur beaucoup d'autres, nous souhaitons vivement connaître votre avis. N'hésitez pas à nous écrire, nous vous répondrons.

Merci d'avance.

Services de Tourisme Michelin
46, avenue de Breteuil, 75341 PARIS CEDEX 07

Bibendum vous souhaite d'agréables voyages.

Le choix d'un hôtel, d'un restaurant

Notre classement est établi à l'usage de l'automobiliste de passage. Dans chaque catégorie les établissements sont cités par ordre de préférence.

CLASSE ET CONFORT

🏨	Grand luxe et tradition	✗✗✗✗✗
🏨	Grand confort	✗✗✗✗
🏨	Très confortable	✗✗✗
🏨	De bon confort	✗✗
🏤	Assez confortable	✗
✿	Simple mais convenable	
↑	Autre ressource hôtelière conseillée, à prix modérés	
without rest.	L'hôtel n'a pas de restaurant	
	Le restaurant possède des chambres	with rm

L'INSTALLATION

Les hôtels des catégories 🏨, 🏨, 🏨, possèdent tout le confort et assurent en général le change, les symboles de détail n'apparaissent donc pas au texte de ces hôtels.

Dans les autres catégories, les éléments de confort indiqués n'existent le plus souvent que dans certaines chambres.

30 rm	Nombre de chambres
🛗	Ascenseur
▤	Air conditionné
📺	Télévision dans la chambre
🛁wc 🛁	Salle de bains et wc privés, Salle de bains privée sans wc
🚿wc 🚿	Douche et wc privés, Douche privée sans wc
📞	Téléphone dans la chambre relié par standard
☎	Téléphone dans la chambre, direct avec l'extérieur (cadran)
♿	Chambres accessibles aux handicapés physiques
🏊 🏊	Piscine : de plein air ou couverte
🌳	Jardin de repos
🎾	Tennis à l'hôtel
⛳₁₈	Golf et nombre de trous
🎣	Pêche ouverte aux clients de l'hôtel (éventuellement payant)
🏛	Salles de conférences (25 places minimum)
🚗	Garage
🅿	Parc à voitures
🐕	Accès interdit aux chiens
	Lorsque les chiens sont acceptés, ils ne le sont que dans les chambres.
May-October	Période d'ouverture communiquée par l'hôtelier
season	Ouverture probable en saison mais dates non précisées
	Les établissements ouverts toute l'année sont ceux pour lesquels aucune mention n'est indiquée.
LL35 OSB	Code postal de l'établissement
(T.H.F.)	Chaîne hôtelière (voir liste en fin de guide)

L'AGRÉMENT

Le séjour dans certains hôtels se révèle parfois particulièrement agréable ou reposant.

Cela peut tenir d'une part au caractère de l'édifice, au décor original, au site, à l'accueil et aux services qui sont proposés, d'autre part à la tranquillité des lieux.

De tels établissements se distinguent dans le guide par les symboles rouges indiqués ci-après.

🏚️ ... 🏠	Hôtels agréables
⚔️⚔️⚔️ ... ✕	Restaurants agréables
« Park »	Élément particulièrement agréable
🐦	Hôtel très tranquille ou isolé et tranquille
🐦	Hôtel tranquille
⩽ sea	Vue exceptionnelle
⩽	Vue intéressante ou étendue

Consultez les cartes placées au début de chacune des régions traitées dans ce guide, elles faciliteront vos recherches.

Nous ne prétendons pas avoir signalé tous les hôtels agréables, ni tous ceux qui sont tranquilles ou isolés et tranquilles.

Nos enquêtes continuent. Vous pouvez les faciliter en nous faisant connaître vos observations et vos découvertes.

LA TABLE

Les étoiles :

Nous marquons par ❁, ❁❁ ou ❁❁❁ les établissements dont la qualité de la table nous a paru mériter d'être signalée spécialement à l'attention de nos lecteurs, qu'il s'agisse de cuisines propres au pays ou étrangères (voir liste p. 48).

Au texte de ces établissements nous indiquons quelques plats caractéristiques du genre de cuisine de la maison.

❁ **Une très bonne table dans sa catégorie**

L'étoile marque une bonne étape sur votre itinéraire.

Mais ne comparez pas l'étoile d'un établissement de luxe à prix élevés avec celle d'une petite maison où à prix raisonnables, on sert également une cuisine de qualité.

❁❁ **Table excellente, mérite un détour**

Spécialités et vins de choix, attendez-vous à une dépense en rapport.

❁❁❁ **Une des meilleures tables, vaut le voyage**

Table merveilleuse, grands vins, service impeccable, cadre élégant… Prix en conséquence.

M **Le « M » rouge**

Tout en appréciant les tables à « étoiles », on peut souhaiter trouver sur sa route un repas plus simple mais toujours de préparation soignée. Certaines maisons nous ont paru répondre à cette préoccupation.

Un « M » rouge les signale à votre attention dans le texte de ce guide.

La vente de boissons alcoolisées

En Grande-Bretagne et en Irlande, la vente de boissons alcoolisées est soumise à des lois pouvant varier d'une région à l'autre.

D'une façon générale, les bars situés dans les hôtels ainsi que les pubs ferment l'après-midi et après 23 heures, les horaires d'ouverture pouvant varier localement.

Néanmoins, l'hôtelier a toujours la possibilité de servir, à sa clientèle, des boissons alcoolisées en dehors des heures légales.

Les enfants au-dessous de 14 ans n'ont pas accès aux bars.

LES PRIX

Les prix que nous indiquons dans ce guide ont été établis en fin d'année 1984. Ils sont susceptibles d'être augmentés ou modifiés si le coût de la vie subit des variations importantes. Ils doivent, en tout cas, être considérés comme des prix de base.

Entrez à l'hôtel le Guide à la main, vous montrerez ainsi qu'il vous conduit là en confiance.

Les hôtels et restaurants figurent en gros caractères lorsque les hôteliers nous ont donné tous leurs prix et se sont engagés à les appliquer aux touristes de passage porteurs de notre guide.

Prévenez-nous de toute majoration paraissant injustifiée. Si aucun prix n'est indiqué, nous vous conseillons de demander les conditions.

Les prix sont indiqués en livres sterling (1 L = 100 pence), sauf en République d'Irlande (Punts).

Lorsque les mentions s.t., ou st. ne figurent pas, les prix indiqués peuvent être majorés d'un pourcentage pour le service, la T.V.A. ou les deux. (La T.V.A. n'est pas appliquée dans les Channel Islands).

Repas

M 7.00/9.00	**Repas à prix fixe** — Déjeuner 7.00, dîner 9.00 servis aux heures normales (12 h 30 à 14 h 30 et 19 h à 21 h) y compris le couvert éventuellement.
M 11.00/13.00	Voir page 23.
s. t.	Service compris — T.V.A. comprise.
st.	Service et T.V.A. compris (prix nets).
♦ 4.00	Prix de la 1/2 bouteille ou carafe de vin ordinaire.
M a la carte 14.00/18.00	**Repas à la carte** — Le 1er prix correspond à un repas simple mais soigné, comprenant : petite entrée, plat du jour garni, dessert. Le 2e prix concerne un repas plus complet, comprenant : hors-d'œuvre, plat principal, fromage ou dessert. Ces prix s'entendent couvert compris.
⌣ 4.00	Prix du petit déjeuner à l'anglaise, s'il n'est pas compris dans celui de la chambre. Un petit déjeuner continental peut être obtenu à moindre prix.

Chambres

rm 21.00/38.00	Prix minimum 21.00 d'une chambre pour une personne et prix maximum 38.00 de la plus belle chambre occupée par deux personnes.
rm ⌣ 30.00/45.00	Le prix du petit déjeuner à l'anglaise est inclus dans le prix de la chambre.

"Short Breaks" (voir p. 25)

SB 50.00/60.00	Prix minimum et maximum par personne pour un séjour de deux nuits en haute saison.
⟠ AE ⓓ VISA	Principales **cartes de crédit** acceptées par l'établissement : Access (Eurocard) — American Express — Diners Club — Visa (Carte Bleue).

QUELQUES PRÉCISIONS UTILES

Au restaurant

Réclamez les menus à prix fixes et la carte chiffrée s'ils ne vous sont pas présentés spontanément.

A l'hôtel

Le prix du petit déjeuner, même s'il n'est pas consommé, est souvent inclus dans le prix de la chambre.

Conditions spéciales pour ''Short Breaks''

De nombreux hôtels proposent des conditions avantageuses pour un séjour de deux nuits ou ''Short Break''. Ce forfait comprend la chambre, le dîner et le petit déjeuner, en général pour un minimum de deux personnes.

Les prix haute saison sont habituellement pratiqués de juin à septembre.

Réservations

Hôtels : Chaque fois que possible, la réservation préalable est souhaitable. Demandez à l'hôtelier de vous fournir dans sa lettre d'accord toutes précisions utiles sur la réservation et les conditions de séjour. Dans les stations balnéaires en particulier, les réservations s'appliquent généralement à des séjours partant d'un samedi à l'autre.

A toute demande écrite il est conseillé de joindre un coupon-réponse international.

Certains hôteliers demandent parfois le versement d'arrhes. Il s'agit d'un dépôt-garantie qui engage l'hôtelier comme le client. Sauf accord spécial le montant des arrhes peut être fixé à 10 % du montant total estimé.

Restaurants : il est vivement recommandé de réserver sa table aussi longtemps que possible à l'avance, de façon à éviter le désagrément d'un refus.

Animaux

L'introduction d'animaux domestiques (chiens, chats...) est interdite en Grande Bretagne et en Irlande.

LA VOITURE, LES PNEUS

Au texte de la plupart des localités figure une liste des garagistes ou concessionnaires automobiles pouvant, éventuellement, vous aider en cas de panne.

En Grande Bretagne et en Irlande, le port de la ceinture de sécurité est obligatoire pour le conducteur et le passager avant.

Automobile Clubs

Les principales organisations de secours automobile dans le pays sont l'Automobile Association et le Royal Automobile Club, toutes deux offrant certains de leurs services aux membres de clubs affiliés.

AUTOMOBILE ASSOCIATION
Fanum House
BASINGSTOKE, Hants., RG21 2EA
℘ (0256) 20123

ROYAL AUTOMOBILE CLUB
83-85 Pall Mall
LONDON SW1Y 5HW
℘ (01) 930 4343

LES CURIOSITÉS

Intérêt

★★★	Vaut le voyage
★★	Mérite un détour
★	Intéressant
AC	Entrée payante

Situation

See	Dans la ville
Envir.	Aux environs de la ville
Exc.	Excursions dans la région
N, S, E, W	La curiosité est située : au Nord, au Sud, à l'Est, à l'Ouest
A 22	On s'y rend par la route A 22, repérée par le même signe sur le plan du Guide
2 m.	Distance en miles

LES VILLES

✉ York	Bureau de poste dessservant la localité
✆ 0225 Bath	Indicatif téléphonique interurbain suivi, si nécessaire, de la localité de rattachement (De l'étranger, ne pas composer le 0)
401 M 27, ⑩	Numéro des cartes Michelin et carroyage ou numéro du pli
West Country G.	Voir le guide vert Michelin England : The West Country
pop. 1,057	Population
ECD : Wednesday	Jour de fermeture des magasins (après-midi seulement)
BX **A**	Lettres repérant un emplacement sur le plan
⛳ 18	Golf et nombre de trous
☀, ≼	Panorama, point de vue
✈	Aéroport
🚗 ✆ 218	Localité desservie par train-auto. Renseignements au numéro de téléphone indiqué
⛴	Transports maritimes
⛴	Transports maritimes (pour passagers seulement) *Voir liste des compagnies en fin de guide*
🛈	Information touristique

Heure légale

Les visiteurs devront tenir compte de l'heure officielle en Grande Bretagne : une heure de retard sur l'heure française.

LES PLANS

Voirie

Autoroute, route à chaussées séparées
  échangeur : complet, partiel, numéro
Grande voie de circulation
Sens unique - Rue impraticable
Rue piétonne
Pasteur   P   Rue commerçante - Parc de stationnement
Porte - Passage sous voûte - Tunnel
Gare et voie ferrée
F B   Bac pour autos - Pont mobile

Curiosités — Hôtels Restaurants

Bâtiment intéressant et entrée principale
Édifice religieux intéressant :
  Cathédrale, église ou chapelle
  Moulin à vent
  Curiosités diverses
Château - Ruines
B   Lettre identifiant une curiosité
Hôtel, restaurant. Lettre les identifiant

Signes divers

Information touristique
Hôpital - Mosquée - Synagogue
Jardin, parc, bois - Cimetière - Calvaire
Stade - Golf
Aéroport - Hippodrome - Vue - Panorama
Funiculaire - Téléphérique, télécabine
Monument, statue - Fontaine - Port de plaisance - Phare
Transport par bateau :
  passagers et voitures
Bâtiment public repéré par une lettre :
  C   Bureau de l'Administration du comté
  H   Hôtel de ville
  M   T   Musée - Théâtre
  POL.   U   Police (commissariat central) - Université, grande école
Bureau principal de poste restante, téléphone
Golf (réservé)
Tour ou pylône de télécommunications
Station de métro

Londres

BRENT   SOHO   Nom d'arrondissement (borough) - de quartier (area)
Limite de « borough » - d' « area »

Scoprite
la guida...

e sappiatela utilizzare per trarre il miglior van-
taggio. La Guida Michelin è un elenco dei migliori alberghi e ristoranti, naturalmente. Ma
anche una serie di utili informazioni per i Vostri
viaggi !

La '' chiave ''

Leggete le pagine che seguono e comprenderete !
Sapete che uno stesso simbolo o una stessa parola in rosso o in nero, in
carattere magro o grasso, non ha lo stesso significato ?

La selezione degli alberghi e ristoranti

Attenzione ! La guida non elenca tutte le risorse alberghiere. E' il risultato
di una selezione, volontariamente limitata, stabilita in seguito a visite ed
inchieste effettuate sul posto. E, durante queste visite, amici lettori,
vengono tenute in evidenza le Vs. critiche ed i Vs. apprezzamenti !

Le piante di città

Indicano con precisione : strade pedonali e commerciali, il modo migliore
per attraversare od aggirare il centro, l'esatta ubicazione degli alberghi e
ristoranti citati, della posta centrale, dell'ufficio informazioni turistiche,
dei monumenti più importanti e poi altre e altre ancora utili informazioni
per Voi !

Per la Vs. automobile

Nel testo di molte località sono elencati gli indirizzi delle principali
marche automobilistiche. Così, in caso di necessità, saprete dove trovare
il « medico » per la Vs. vettura.

Su tutti questi punti e su altri ancora, gradiremmo conoscere il Vs.
parere. Scriveteci e non mancheremo di risponderVi !

Michelin Tyre Public Limited Company
Tourism Department
81, Fulham Road, GB-LONDON SW3 6RD

Grazie e buon viaggio.

La scelta di un albergo, di un ristorante

La nostra classificazione è stabilita ad uso dell'automobilista di passaggio. In ogni categoria, gli esercizi vengono citati in ordine di preferenza.

CLASSE E CONFORT

🏨	Gran lusso e tradizione	XXXXX
🏨	Gran confort	XXXXX
🏨	Molto confortevole	XXX
🏨	Di buon confort	XX
🏨	Abbastanza confortevole	X
🏠	Semplice ma conveniente	
🏠	Altra risorsa, consigliata per prezzi contenuti	
without rest.	L'albergo non ha ristorante	
	Il ristorante dispone di camere	with rm

INSTALLAZIONI

I 🏨, 🏨, 🏨 offrono ogni confort ed effettuano generalmente il cambio di valute ; per questi alberghi non specifichiamo quindi il dettaglio delle installazioni.

Nelle altre categorie indichiamo gli elementi di confort esistenti, alcune camere possono talvolta esserne sprovviste.

30 rm	Numero di camere
🛗	Ascensore
▤	Aria condizionata
tv	Televisione in camera
⌴wc ⌴	Bagno e wc privati, bagno privato senza wc
⋔wc ⋔	Doccia e wc privati, doccia privata senza wc
☎	Telefono in camera collegato con il centralino
☎	Telefono in camera comunicante direttamente con l'esterno
♿	Camere d'agevole accesso per i minorati fisici
⚓ ▧	Piscina : all'aperto, coperta
🌳	Giardino da riposo
✗	Tennis appartenente all'albergo
⛳	Golf e numero di buche,
⚓	Pesca aperta ai clienti dell'albergo (eventualmente a pagamento)
🏛	Sale per conferenze (minimo 25 posti)
🚗	Garage
Ⓟ	Parcheggio
✗	E' vietato l'accesso ai cani
	Se i cani sono accetati, lo sono soltanto nelle camere.
May-October	Periodo di apertura comunicato dall'albergatore
season	Possibile apertura in stagione, ma periodo non precisato.
	Gli esercizi senza tali indicazioni sono aperti tutto l'anno.
LL35 0SB	Codice postale dell'esercizio
(T.H.F.)	Catena alberghiera (Vedere la lista alla fine della Guida)

AMENITÀ

Il soggiorno in alcuni alberghi si rivela talvolta particolarmente ameno o riposante.

Ciò può dipendere sia dalle caratteristiche dell'edificio, dalle decorazioni non comuni, dalla sua posizione, dall'accoglienza e dai servizi offerti, sia dalla tranquillità dei luoghi.

Questi esercizi sono così contraddistinti :

🏨 ... 🏠	Alberghi ameni
🅇🅇🅇🅇🅇 ... 🍴	Ristoranti ameni
« Park »	Un particolare piacevole
🐾	Albergo molto tranquillo o isolato e tranquillo
🐾	Albergo tranquillo
⩽ sea	Vista eccezionale
⩽	Vista interessante o estesa

Consultate le carte che precedono ciascuna delle regioni trattate nella guida : sarete facilitati nelle vostre ricerche.

Non abbiamo la pretesa di aver segnalato tutti gli alberghi ameni, nè tutti quelli molto tranquilli o isolati e tranquilli.

Le nostre ricerche continuano. Le potrete agevolare facendoci conoscere le vostre osservazioni e le vostre scoperte.

La scelta di un albergo, di un ristorante

LA TAVOLA

Le stelle di ottima tavola

Abbiamo contraddistinto con ❀, ❀❀ o ❀❀❀ quegli esercizi che, a nostro parere, meritano di essere segnalaiti alla vostra attenzione per la qualità della cucina, che può essere tipicamente nazionale o d'importazione (vedere p. 48).

Nel testo di questi esercizi indichiamo alcuni piatti tipici della cucina della casa.

❀   **Un'ottima tavola nella sua categoria.**

La stella indica una tappa gastronomica sul vostro itinerario.

Non mettete però a confronto la stella di un esercizio di lusso, dai prezzi elevati, con quella di un piccolo esercizio dove, a prezzi ragionevoli, viene offerta una cucina di qualità.

❀❀   **Tavola eccellente : merita una deviazione.**

Specialità e vini scelti... Aspettatevi una spesa in proporzione.

❀❀❀   **Una delle migliori tavole : vale il viaggio.**

Tavola meravigliosa, grandi vini, servizio impeccabile, ambientazione accurata... Prezzi conformi.

M   **La « M » rossa**

Pur apprezzando le tavole a « stella », si desidera alle volte consumare un pasto più semplice ma sempre accuratamente preparato.

Alcuni esercizi ci son parsi rispondenti a tale esigenza e sono contraddistinti nella guida da una « M » in rosso.

La vendita di bevande alcoliche

In Gran Bretagna e Irlanda la vendita di bevande alcoliche è soggetta a leggi che possono variare da una regione all'altra.

Generalmente i bar degli alberghi, così come i pubs, chiudono il pomeriggio e dopo le ore 23.00 ; gli orari d'apertura possono variare di località in località.

L'albergatore ha tuttavia la possibilità di servire alla clientela bevande alcoliche anche oltre le ore legali.

Ai ragazzi inferiori ai 14 anni è vietato l'accesso ai bar.

La scelta di un albergo, di un ristorante

I PREZZI

Questi prezzi, redatti alla fine dell'anno 1984, possono venire modificati qualora il costo della vita subisca notevoli variazioni. Essi debbono comunque essere considerati come prezzi base.

Entrate nell'albergo o nel ristorante con la Guida alla mano, dimostrando in tal modo la fiducia in chi vi ha indirizzato.

Gli alberghi e ristoranti figurano in carattere grassetto quando gli albergatori ci hanno comunicato tutti i loro prezzi e si sono impegnati ad applicarli ai turisti di passaggio in possesso della nostra pubblicazione.

Segnalateci eventuali maggiorazioni che vi sembrino ingiustificate. Quando i prezzi non sono indicati, vi consigliamo di chiedere preventivamente le condizioni.

I prezzi sono indicati in lire sterline (1 £ = 100 pence) ad eccezione per la Repubblica d'Irlanda (Punts).

Quando non figurano le lettere s., t., o st. i prezzi indicati possono essere maggiorati per il servizio o per l'I.V.A. o per entrambi. (L'I.V.A. non viene applicata nelle Channel Islands).

Pasti

M 7.00/9.00	**Prezzo fisso** — Pranzo 7.00, cena 9.00 serviti ad ore normali (dalle 12.30 alle 14.30 e dalle 19 alle 21) compreso il coperto se del caso.
M 11.00/13.00	Vedere p. 31.
s. t.	Servizio compreso. — I.V.A. compresa.
st.	Servizio ed I.V.A. compresi (prezzi netti).
⌁ 4.00	Prezzo della mezza bottiglia o di una caraffa di vino.
M a la carte 14.00/18.00	**Alla carta** — Il 1° prezzo corrisponde ad un pasto semplice comprendente : primo piatto, piatto del giorno con contorno, dessert. Il 2° prezzo corrisponde ad un pasto più completo comprendente : antipasto, piatto principale, formaggio e dessert. Questi prezzi comprendono, se del caso, il coperto.
⌕ 4.00	Prezzo della prima colazione inglese se non è compreso nel prezzo della camera. Una prima colazione continentale puó essere ottenuta a minor prezzo.

Camere

rm 21.00/38.00	Prezzo minimo 21.00 per una camera singola e prezzo massimo 38.00 per la camera più bella per due persone.
rm ⌕ 30.00/45.00	Il prezzo della prima colazione inglese è compreso nel prezzo della camera.

"Short Breaks" (vedere p. 33)

SB 50.00/60.00	Prezzo minimo e massimo per persona per un soggiorno di due notti in alta stagione.
▣ ▣ ▣ ▣	Principali **carte di credito** accettate da un albergo o ristorante : Access (MasterCard) — American Express — Diners Club — Visa (BankAmericard).

QUALCHE CHIARIMENTO UTILE

Al ristorante

Chiedete i menu a prezzo fisso e la carta coi relativi prezzi se non vi vengono spontaneamente presentati.

All'albergo

Il prezzo della prima colazione, anche se non viene consumata, è spesso compreso nel prezzo della camera.

Condizioni speciali per "Short Breaks"

Numerosi alberghi propongono delle condizioni vantaggiose per un soggiorno di due notti o "Short Break". Questo forfait comprende la camera, la cena e la colazione del mattino generalmente per un minimo di due persone.

I prezzi di alta stagione vengono generalmente praticati da giugno a settembre.

Le prenotazioni

Alberghi : appena possibile, la prenotazione è consigliabile ; chiedete all'albergatore di fornirvi, nella sua lettera di conferma, ogni dettaglio sulla prenotazione e sulle condizioni di soggiorno. Nelle stazioni balneari in particolar modo, le prenotazioni si applicano generalmente a soggiorni che vanno da un sabato all'altro.

Si consiglia di allegare sempre alle richieste scritte di prenotazione un tagliando risposta internazionale.

Alle volte alcuni albergatori chiedono il versamento di una caparra. E' un deposito-garanzia che impegna tanto l'albergatore che il cliente. Salvo accordi speciali, l'ammontare della caparra può venire fissato nella misura del 10 % dell'ammontare totale previsto.

Ristoranti : è sempre consigliabile prenotare con un certo anticipo per evitare uno spiacevole rifiuto all'ultimo momento.

Animali

Non possono accedere in Gran Bretagna e Irlanda animali domestici (cani, gatti...)

L'AUTOMOBILE, I PNEUMATICI

Nel testo di molte località abbiamo elencato gli indirizzi di garage o concessionari in grado di effettuare, eventualmente, il traino o le riparazioni.

In Gran Bretagna e in Irlanda, l'uso della cintura di sicurezza e' obbligatorio per il guidatore e il passeggero che gli siede accanto.

Soccorso automobilistico

Le principali organizzazioni di soccorso automobilistico sono l'Automobile Association ed il Royal Automobile Club : entrambe offrono alcuni loro servizi ai membri dei club affiliati

AUTOMOBILE ASSOCIATION
Fanum House
BASINGSTOKE, Hants, RG21 2EA
☏ (0256) 20123

ROYAL AUTOMOBILE CLUB
83-85 Pall Mall
LONDON SW1Y 5HW
☏ (01) 930 4343

LE CURIOSITÀ

Grado d'interesse

★★★	Vale il viaggio
★★	Merita una deviazione
★	Interessante
AC	Entrata a pagamento

Situazione

See	Nella città
Envir.	Nei dintorni della città
Exc.	Nella regione
N, S, E, W	La curiosità è situata : a Nord, a Sud, a Est, a Ovest
A 22	Ci si va per la strada A 22 indicata con lo stesso segno sulla pianta
2 m.	Distanza in miglia

LE CITTÀ

✉ York	Sede dell'ufficio postale
☎ 0225 Bath	Prefisso telefonico interurbano (nome del centralino indicato solo quando differisce dal nome della località). Dall'estero non formare lo 0
401 M 27, ⑩	Numero della carta Michelin e del riquadro o numero della piega
West Country G.	Vedere la Guida Verde Michelin England : The West Country.
pop. 1,057	Popolazione
ECD : Wednesday	Giorno di chiusura settimanale dei negozi (solo pomeriggio)
BX A	Lettere indicanti l'ubicazione sulla pianta
🏌 18	Golf e numero di buche (accesso consentito a tutti)
☀, ≤	Panorama, punto di vista
✈	Aeroporto
🚗 ☎ 218	Località con servizio auto su treno. Informarsi al numero di telefono indicato
⛴	Trasporti marittimi
⛴	Trasporti marittimi (solo passeggeri) *Vedere la lista delle compagnie alla fine della Guida*
🛈	Ufficio informazioni turistiche

Ora legale

I visitatori dovranno tenere in considerazione l'ora ufficiale in Gran bretagna : un' ora di ritardo sull'ora italiana.

LE PIANTE

Viabilità

Autostrada, strada a carreggiate separate
    svincolo : completo, parziale, numero
Grande via di circolazione
Senso unico - Via impraticabile
Via pedonale -
Pasteur   P   Via commerciale - Parcheggio
Porta - Sottopassaggio - Galleria
Stazione e ferrovia
F B   Battello per auto - Ponte mobile

Curiosità — Alberghi — Ristoranti

Edificio interessante ed entrata principale
Costruzione religiosa interessante :
    Cattedrale, chiesa o cappella
    Mulino a vento - Curiosità varie
Castello - Ruderi
B   Lettera che identifica una curiosità
⊕   Albergo, Ristorante. Lettera di riferimento che li identifica sulla pianta

Simboli vari

Ufficio informazioni turistiche
Moschea - Sinagoga
Ospedale -
Giardino, parco, bosco - Cimitero - Calvario
Stadio - Golf
Vista - Panorama
Aeroporto - Ippodromo
Funicolare - Funivia, Cabinovia
Monumento, statua - Fontana
Porto per imbarcazioni da diporto - Faro
Trasporto con traghetto :
    passeggeri ed autovetture
Edificio pubblico indicato con lettera :
C   Sede dell' Amministrazione di Contea
H   M   T   Municipio - Museo - Teatro
POL.   Polizia (Questura, nelle grandi città)
U   Università, grande scuola
Ufficio centrale di fermo posta, telefono
Golf riservato - Stazione della Metropolitana
Torre o pilone per telecomunicazione

Londra

BRENT   SOHO   Nome del distretto amministrativo (borough) - del quartiere (area)
Limite del « borough » - di « area »

Der
Michelin-Führer...

Er ist nicht nur ein Verzeichnis guter Restaurants und Hotels, sondern gibt zusätzlich eine Fülle nützlicher Tips für die Reise. Nutzen Sie die zahlreichen Informationen, die er bietet.

Zum Gebrauch dieses Führers

Die Erläuterungen stehen auf den folgenden Seiten.

Beachten Sie dabei, daß das gleiche Zeichen, rot oder schwarz, fett oder dünn gedruckt, verschiedene Bedeutungen hat.

Zur Auswahl der Hotels und Restaurants

Der Rote Michelin-Führer ist kein vollständiges Verzeichnis aller Hotels und Restaurants. Er bringt nur eine bewußt getroffene, begrenzte Auswahl. Diese basiert auf regelmäßigen Überprüfungen durch unsere Inspektoren an Ort und Stelle. Bei der Beurteilung werden auch die zahlreichen Hinweise unserer Leser berücksichtigt.

Zu den Stadtplänen

Sie informieren über Fußgänger- und Geschäftsstraßen, Durchgangsoder Umgehungsstraßen, Lage von Hotels und Restaurants (an Hauptverkehrsstraßen oder in ruhiger Gegend), wo sich die Post, das Verkehrsamt, die wichtigsten öffentlichen Gebäude und Sehenswürdigkeiten u. dgl. befinden.

Hinweise für den Autofahrer

Bei den meisten Orten geben wir Adresse und Telefonnummer der Vertragshändler der großen Automobilfirmen an. So können Sie Ihren Wagen im Bedarfsfall unterwegs warten oder reparieren lassen.

Ihre Meinung zu den Angaben des Führers, Ihre Kritik, Ihre Verbesserungsvorschläge interessieren uns sehr. Zögern Sie daher nicht, uns diese mitzuteilen... wir antworten bestimmt.

**Michelin Tyre Public Limited Company
Tourism Department
81, Fulham Road, GB-LONDON SW3 6RD**

Vielen Dank im voraus und angenehme Reise !

Unsere Auswahl ist für Durchreisende gedacht. In jeder Kategorie drückt die Reihen-
folge der Betriebe eine weitere Rangordnung aus.

KLASSENEINTEILUNG UND KOMFORT

🏰	Großer Luxus und Tradition	XXXXX
🏨	Großer Komfort	XXXX
🏨	Sehr komfortabel	XXX
🏨	Mit gutem Komfort	XX
🏛	Mit ausreichendem Komfort	X
☘	Bürgerlich	
⌂	Preiswerte, empfehlenswerte Gasthäuser und Pensionen	
without rest.	Hotel ohne Restaurant	
	Restaurant vermietet auch Zimmer	with rm

EINRICHTUNG

Für die 🏰, 🏨, 🏨 geben wir keine Einzelheiten über die Einrichtung
an, da diese Hotels im allgemeinen jeden Komfort besitzen. Außerdem
besteht die Möglichkeit, Geld zu wechseln.

In den Häusern der übrigen Kategorien nennen wir die vorhandenen
Einrichtungen, diese können in einigen Zimmern fehlen.

30 rm	Anzahl der Zimmer
🛗	Fahrstuhl
▤	Klimaanlage
📺	Fernsehen im Zimmer
🛁wc 🛁	Privatbad mit wc, Privatbad ohne wc
🚿wc 🚿	Privatdusche mit wc, Privatdusche ohne wc
☎	Zimmertelefon mit Außenverbindung über Telefonzentrale
☎	Zimmertelefon mit direkter Außenverbindung
♿	Für Körperbehinderte leicht zugängliche Zimmer
🏊 🏊	Freibad, Hallenbad
🌳	Liegewiese, Garten
🎾	Hoteleigener Tennisplatz
⛳	Golfplatz und Lochzahl
🎣	Angelmöglichkeit für Hotelgäste, evtl. gegen Gebühr
👥	Konferenzräume (mind. 25 Plätze)
🚗	Garage
℗	Parkplatz
🐕	Das Mitführen von Hunden ist im ganzen Haus unerwünscht
	Falls Hunde dennoch geduldet werden, dann nur in den Zimmern.
May-October	Öffnungszeit, vom Hotelier mitgeteilt
season	Unbestimmte Öffnungszeit eines Saisonhotels
	Die Häuser, für die wir keine Schließungszeiten angeben, sind ganzjährig geöffnet.
LL35 0SB	Angabe des Postbezirks (hinter der Hoteladresse)
(T.H.F.)	Hotelkette (Liste am Ende des Führers)

ANNEHMLICHKEITEN

In manchen Hotels ist der Aufenthalt wegen der schönen, ruhigen Lage, der nicht alltäglichen Einrichtung und Atmosphäre und dem gebotenen Service besonders angenehm und erholsam.

Solche Häuser und ihre besonderen Annehmlichkeiten sind im Führer durch folgende Symbole gekennzeichnet :

🏰 ... 🏠	Angenehme Hotels
XXXXX ... X	Angenehme Restaurants
« Park »	Besondere Annehmlichkeit
🦢	Sehr ruhiges, oder abgelegenes und ruhiges Hotel
🦢	Ruhiges Hotel
≤ sea	Reizvolle Aussicht
≤	Interessante oder weite Sicht

Die Karten in der Einleitung zu den einzelnen Landesteilen geben Ihnen einen Überblick über die Orte, in denen sich mindestens ein angenehmes, sehr ruhiges Haus befindet.

Wir wissen, daß diese Auswahl noch nicht vollständig ist, sind aber laufend bemüht, weitere solche Häuser für Sie zu entdecken ; dabei sind uns Ihre Erfahrungen und Hinweise eine wertvolle Hilfe.

KÜCHE

Die Sterne für gute Küche

Mit ❀, ❀❀ oder ❀❀❀ kennzeichnen wir die Häuser mit landesüblicher oder ausländischer Küche, deren Qualität wir der Aufmerksamkeit der Leser besonders empfehlen möchten (siehe S. 48).

Für diese Häuser geben wir im Text einige typische Gerichte bürgerlicher Küche an.

❀ **Eine sehr gute Küche : verdient Ihre besondere Beachtung**

Der Stern bedeutet eine angenehme Unterbrechung Ihrer Reise. Vergleichen Sie aber bitte nicht den Stern eines teuren Luxusrestaurants mit dem Stern eines kleinen oder mittleren Hauses, wo man Ihnen zu einem annehmbaren Preis eine ebenfalls vorzügliche Mahlzeit reicht.

❀❀ **Eine hervorragende Küche : verdient einen Umweg**

Ausgesuchte Spezialitäten und Weine... angemessene Preise.

❀❀❀ **Eine der besten Küchen : eine Reise wert**

Ein denkwürdiges Essen, edle Weine, tadelloser Service, gepflegte Atmosphäre... entsprechende Preise.

M **Das rote « M »**

Wir glauben, daß Sie neben den Häusern mit Stern auch solche Adressen interessieren werden, die einfache, aber sorgfältig zubereitete Mahlzeiten anbieten.

Auf solche Häuser weisen wir im Text durch das rote « M » hin.

Ausschank alkoholischer Getränke

In Großbritannien und Irland unterliegt der Ausschank alkoholischer Getränke gesetzlichen Bestimmungen, die in den einzelnen Gegenden verschieden sind.

Im allgemeinen schließen die Hotelbars und Pubs nachmittags sowie nach 23 Uhr ; die genauen Öffnungszeiten sind jedoch örtlich verschieden.

Hotelgästen können alkoholische Getränke jedoch auch außerhalb der Ausschankzeiten serviert werden.

Kindern unter 14 Jahren ist der Zutritt zu den Bars untersagt.

PREISE

Die in diesem Führer genannten Preise wurden uns Ende 1984 angegeben. Sie können sich 1985 erhöhen, wenn die allgemeinen Lebenshaltungskosten steigen. Sie können aber in diesem Fall als Richtpreise angesehen werden.

Halten Sie beim Betreten des Hotels den Führer in der Hand. Sie zeigen damit, daß Sie aufgrund dieser Empfehlung gekommen sind.

Die Namen der Hotels und Restaurants, die ihre Preise genannt haben, sind fett gedruckt. Gleichzeitig haben sich diese Häuser verpflichtet, diese Preise den Benutzern des Michelin-Führers zu berechnen.

Informieren Sie uns bitte über jede unangemessen erscheinende Preiserhöhung. Wenn keine Preise angegeben sind, raten wir Ihnen, sich beim Hotelier danach zu erkundigen.

Die Preise sind in Pfund Sterling angegeben (1 £ = 100 pence) mit Ausnahme der Republik Irland (Punts).

Wenn die Buchstaben s., t., oder st. nicht hinter den angegebenen Preisen aufgeführt sind, können sich diese um den Zuschlag für Bedienung und/oder MWSt erhöhen (keine MWSt auf den Channel Islands).

Mahlzeiten

M 7.00/9.00	**Feste Menupreise** — Mittagessen 7.00, Abendessen 9.00 (inklusive Couvert) für die Mahlzeiten, die zu den normalen Tischzeiten serviert werden (12.30 - 14.30 und 19 - 21 Uhr).
M 11.00/13.00	Siehe Seite 39.
s. t.	Bedienung inbegriffen - MWSt inbegriffen.
st.	Bedienung und MWSt inbegriffen (Inklusivpreise).
⌀ 4.00	Preis für 1/2 Flasche oder eine Karaffe Tafelwein.
M a la carte 14.00/18.00	**Mahlzeiten « à la carte »** — Der erste Preis entspricht einer einfachen aber sorgfältig zubereiteten Mahlzeit, bestehend aus kleiner Vorspeise, Tagesgericht mit Beilage und Nachtisch. Der zweite Preis entspricht einer reichlicheren Mahlzeit mit Vorspeise, Hauptgericht, Käse oder Nachtisch (« couvert » ist in den Preisen enthalten).
⌴ 4.00	Preis des Englischen Frühstücks, wenn dieser nicht im Übernachtungspreis enthalten ist. Einfaches, billigeres Frühstück (Continental breakfast) erhältlich.

Zimmer

rm 21.00/38.00	Mindestpreis 21.00 für ein Einzelzimmer und Höchstpreis 38.00 für das schönste Doppelzimmer
rm ⌴ 30.00/45.00	Übernachtung mit Englischem Frühstück.

"Short Breaks" (Siehe Seite 41)

SB 50.00/60.00	Mindest- und Höchstpreis pro Person in der Hochsaison bei einem Aufenthalt von 2 Nächten.
⬛ AE ⑩ *VISA*	Von Hotels und Restaurants angenommene **Kreditkarten :** Access (MasterCard) — American Express — Diners Club — Visa (BankAmericard).

NÜTZLICHE HINWEISE

Im Restaurant

Verlangen Sie die Karte der Tagesmenus zu Festpreisen und die Speise-karte, wenn sie Ihnen nicht von selbst vorgelegt werden.

Im Hotel

Im allgemeinen ist das Frühstück (auch wenn es nicht eingenommen wird) im Zimmerpreis enthalten.

Pauschale für "Short Breaks"

Zahlreiche Hotels bieten Vorzugspreise bei einem Aufenthalt von 2 Nächten ("Short Break"). Diese Pauschalpreise (für mindestens 2 Per-sonen) umfassen Zimmer, Abendessen und Frühstück.

Hochsaisonpreise werden im allgemeinen von Juni bis September berechnet.

Zimmerreservierung

Hotels : Es ist ratsam, wenn irgend möglich, die Zimmer reservieren zu lassen. Bitten Sie den Hotelier, daß er Ihnen in seinem Bestätigungs-schreiben alle seine Bedingungen mitteilt.

Besonders in Seebädern wird Vollpension im allgemeinen nur wochen-weise, von Samstag zu Samstag, gewährt.

Bei schriftlichen Zimmerbestellungen empfiehlt es sich, einen Freium-schlag oder einen internationalen Antwortschein beizufügen.

Einige Hoteliers verlangen eine Anzahlung (etwa 10 % wenn nichts anderes vereinbart wird) auf den voraussichtlichen Endpreis. Sie ist als Garantie für beide Seiten anzusehen.

Restaurant : Es empfiehlt sich, Tische immer und so früh wie möglich vorzubestellen.

Tiere

Das Mitführen von Haustieren (Hunde, Katzen u. dgl.) bei der Einreise in Großbritannien und Irland ist untersagt.

DAS AUTO, DIE REIFEN

Bei den meisten Orten geben wir Adressen von Kfz-Vertragswerkstätten an ; viele davon haben einen Abschlepp- bzw. Reparaturdienst.

In Großbritannien und Irland besteht Gurtanlegepflicht für Fahrer und Beifahrer auf den Vordersitzen.

Automobilclubs

Die wichtigsten Automobilclubs des Landes sind die Automobile Association und der Royal Automobile Club, die den Mitgliedern der der FIA angeschlossenen Auto-mobilclubs Pannenhilfe leisten und einige ihrer Dienstleistungen anbieten.

AUTOMOBILE ASSOCIATION
Fanum House
BASINGSTOKE, Hants., RG21 2EA
✆ (0256) 20123

ROYAL AUTOMOBILE CLUB
83-85 Pall Mall
LONDON SW1Y 5HW
✆ (01) 930 4343

HAUPTSEHENSWÜRDIGKEITEN

Bewertung

★★★	Eine Reise wert
★★	Verdient einen Umweg
★	Sehenswert
AC	Eintritt (gegen Gebühr)

Lage

See	In der Stadt
Envir.	In der Umgebung der Stadt
Exc.	Ausflugsziele
N, S, E, W	Im Norden (N), Süden (S), Osten (E), Westen (W) der Stadt.
A 22	Zu erreichen über die Straße A 22.
2 m.	Entfernung in Meilen

STÄDTE

✉ York	Zuständiges Postamt
✆ 0225 Bath	Vorwahlnummer und evtl. zuständiges Fernsprechamt (bei Gesprächen vom Ausland aus wird die erste Null weggelassen)
101 M 27, ⑩	Nummer der Michelin-Karte und Koordinaten des Gratfeldes oder Faltseite
West Country G.	Siehe auch den grünen Michelinführer "England : The West Country"
pop. 1,057	Einwohnerzahl
ECD : Wednesday	Tag, an dem die Läden nachmittags geschlossen sind
BX **A**	Markierung auf dem Stadtplan
⌐18	Öffentlicher Golfplatz und Lochzahl
⚹, ≼	Rundblick, Aussichtspunkt
✈	Flughafen
🚗 ✆ 218	Ladestelle für Autoreisezüge - Nähere Auskünfte unter der angegebenen Telefonnummer
⛴	Autofähre
⛴	Personenfähre *Liste der Schiffahrtsgesellschaften am Ende des Führers*
🛈	Informationsstelle

Uhrzeit

In Großbritannien ist eine Zeitverschiebung zu beachten und die Uhr gegenüber der deutschen Zeit um 1 Stunde zurückzustellen.

STADTPLÄNE

Straßen

Autobahn, Straße mit getrennten Fahrbahnen

0   0   Anschlußstelle : Autobahneinfahrt und/oder -ausfahrt, Nummer

Hauptverkehrsstraße

Einbahnstraße - nicht befahrbare Straße

Fußgängerzone

Pasteur   **P**   Einkaufsstraße - Parkplatz

Tor - Passage - Tunnel

Bahnhof und Bahnlinie

F B   △   Autofähre - Bewegliche Brücke

Sehenswürdigkeiten — Hotels — Restaurants

Sehenswertes Gebäude mit Haupteingang

Sehenswerter Sakralbau :

Kathedrale, Kirche oder Kapelle

Windmühle

▲   Sonstige Sehenswürdigkeiten

Schloß - Ruine

B   Referenzbuchstabe einer Sehenswürdigkeit

Hotel, Restaurant - Referenzbuchstabe

Sonstige Zeichen

Informationsstelle

Krankenhaus - Moschee — Synagoge

Garten, Park, Wäldchen - Friedhof - Bildstock

Stadion - Golfplatz

Flughafen - Pferderennbahn- Aussicht - Rundblick

Standseilbahn - Seilschwebebahn

Denkmal, Statue - Brunnen - Jachthafen - Leuchtturm

Schiffsverbindungen : Autofähre

Öffentliches Gebäude, durch einen Buchstaben gekennzeichnet :

c   Sitz der Grafschaftsverwaltung

H   M   T   Rathaus - Museum - Theater

POL.   Polizei (in größeren Städten Polizeipräsidium)

U   Universität, Hochschule

Hauptpostamt (postlagernde Sendungen), Telefon

Golfplatz (Zutritt bedingt erlaubt)

Funk-, Fernsehturm

U-Bahnstation

London

BRENT   SOHO   Name des Verwaltungsbezirks (borough) - des Stadtteils (area)

Grenze des „ borough " - des „ area "

MOTORWAY HOTELS

Hotels included in the Guide on, or near the interchanges of motorways and A (M) class roads. See appropriate town for details.

ALBERGHI AUTOSTRADALI

I sottoindicati alberghi, selezionati nella guida, si trovano lungo le autostrade o lungo le strade principali, in prossimità degli svincoli. Per ogni dettaglio vedere la località interessata.

HOTELS D'AUTOROUTE

Les hôtels ci-dessous, sélectionnés dans le guide se trouvent sur les autoroutes ou les routes principales, à proximité des échangeurs. Pour tous détails, voir le nom de la ville.

AUTOBAHN-RASTHÄUSER

Die unten aufgeführten Hotels befinden sich an Autobahnen, Hauptverkehrsstraßen oder in der Nähe von Autobahnauffahrten. Nähere Einzelheiten unter dem Ortstext.

Location	Town	Hotel
M 1		
Scratchwood Service Area	Hendon (L.B. of Barnet)	🏛 TraveLodge
Junction 5 − S : ½ m. on A 41	Watford	🏛 Ladbroke
Junction 6 − NE : 1 m. on A 405 (this hotel also under M 10)	St. Albans	🏛 Noke
Junction 8 − W : ½ m. on A 4147	Hemel Hempstead	🏛 Post House
Junction 9 − NW : 1 m. on A 5	Flamstead	🏛 Hertfordshire Moat House
Junction 11 − E : ¾ m. on A 505	Luton	🏛 Chiltern
Junction 11 − on A 505	Luton	🏛 Crest
Junction 11 − E : 1 ½ m. on A 505	Luton	🏛 Humberstone
Newport Pagnell Service Area 3	Newport Pagnell	🏛 TraveLodge
Junction 18 − E : ¼ m. on A 428	Rugby (at Crick)	🏛 Post House
Junction 21/21A − NE : 2 ½ m. on A 46	Leicester (at Braunstone)	🏛 Post House
Junction 25 − W : ¼ m. on A 52	Nottingham (at Sandiacre)	🏛 Post House
Junction 25 − S : ½ m. on B 6002	Nottingham (at Long Eaton)	🏛 Novotel
Junction 28	South Normanton	🏛 Swallow
Junction 40 − E : ½ m. on A 638	Wakefield	🏛 Post House
A 1 (M)		
Junction 1, A 638 − N : 2 ½ m. on A 1	Wentbridge (at Barnsdale Bar)	🏛 Doncaster TraveLodge
A 1 (M) via A 66 (M) − E : 2 m. on A 66	Darlington	🏛 Blackwell Grange Moat House
A 1 (M) Junction with A 602 and B 197 − W : 1 ¼ m. on A 602	Hitchin	🏛 Blakemore
A 1 (M) via A 167 − S : ¾ m. by A 167	Darlington (at Coatham Mundeville)	🏛 Hall Garth Country House
A 1 (M) Junction with A 1231 − E : ½ m. by A 1231	Washington	🏛 Post House
A 1 (M) Junction A 6 and M 25 (this hotel also under M 25)	South Mimms	🏛 Crest
M 2		
Junction 1 − W : ½ m. on A 2	Shorne	🏛 Inn on the Lake
Junction 3 − N : 1 m. on A 229	Rochester	🏛 Crest
M 3		
Junction 3 − N : 1 m. on A 30	Bagshot	🏛 Cricketer's
Junction 6 − SW : 1 ½ m. at junction A 30 and A 339	Basingstoke	🏛 Crest

M 4

Junction 3 — N : 1 ½ m. off A 312	Heathrow Airport (L.B. of Hillingdon)	Arlington
Junction 4 — S : ½ m. on B 379	Heathrow Airport	Post House
Junction 4 — N : ½ m. on B 379	Heathrow Airport	Holiday Inn
Junction 5 — NW : ¼ m. on A 4	Slough	Holiday Inn
Junction 8-9 — SE : 3 m. by A 308 (M) and A 308	Windsor	Oakley Court
Junction 9 A — NE : ½ m. on Shoppenhangers Rd	Maidenhead	Crest
Junction 11 — N : ½ m. on A 33	Reading	Post House
Junction 15 — N : 2 m. on A 345	Swindon	Post House
Junction 19 — SW : 2 ½ m. by M 32 on A 4174 (this hotel also under M 32)	Bristol (at Hambrook)	Crest
Junction 24 — S : ½ m. on A 48	Newport (Gwent)	Celtic Manor
Junction 24 — E : 1 ½ m. on A 48	Newport (Gwent) (at Langstone)	New Inn Motel
Junction 24 — S : ¼ m. on A 48	Newport (Gwent)	Ladbroke

M 5

Junction 1 — W : 1 m. by A 41	Birmingham (at West Bromwich)	West Bromwich Moat House
Junction 5 — SW : 1 m. on A 38	Droitwich	Château Impney
Junction 11 — E : 1 m. on A 40	Cheltenham	Golden Valley Thistle
Junction 13 — SE : 1 ¾ m. on A 419	Stroud (at Stonehouse)	Stonehouse Court
Junction 14 — SW : 1 ½ m. on A 38 by B 4509	Falfield	Park

M 6

Junction 2 — S : 1 m. on A 46	Coventry (at Walsgrave-on-Sowe)	Crest
Junction 3 — SE : 1 m. on A 444	Coventry (at Longford)	Novotel
Junction 5	Birmingham (at Castle Bromwich)	Bradford Arms
Junction 7 — N : ¼ m. on A 34	Birmingham (at Great Barr)	Post House
Junction 7 — N : 1 ½ m. on A 34	Walsall	Crest
Junction 12 — E : 2 m. on A 5	Cannock	Roman Way
Junction 14 — SE : ½ m. on A 5013	Stafford	Tillington Hall
Junction 15 — N : ¼ m. on A 519	Newcastle-under-Lyme	Post House
Junction 15 — N : ¾ m. on A 519	Newcastle-under-Lyme	Clayton Lodge
Charnock Richard Service Area	Charnock Richard	TraveLodge
Junction 19 — NE : 2 ½ m. on A 556 (this hotel also under M 56)	Knutsford (at Bucklow Hill)	Swan
Junction 23 — N : ½ m. on A 49	Haydock	Post House
Junction 27 — E : ¼ m. on B 5239	Standish	Casinelli's
Junction 28 — W : ¼ m. on B 5256	Leyland	Ladbroke
Junction 31 — W : ¼ m. on A 59	Preston (at Samlesbury)	Tickled Trout
Junction 33 — at Junction of A 6 and M 6	Lancaster	Hampson House
Junction 34 — SW : ¼ m. on A 683	Lancaster	Post House
Junction 36 — N : 1 ¼ m. on A 65	Kendal	Crooklands
Junction 44 — N : ¼ m. on A 7	Carlisle (at Kingstown)	Crest

M 10

Junction 1 — SW : 1 m. on A 405 (this hotel also under M 1)	St. Albans	Noke Thistle

M 11

Junction 14 with A 604 — NW : 1 ¾ m. on A 604	Cambridge (at Bar Hill)	Cunard Cambridge-shire

M 20

Junction 2 A	**Wrotham Heath**	🏨 Post House

M 23

Junction 9 — in Gatwick Airport	**Horley**	🏨 Gatwick Hilton International
Junction 9 — W : 1 m. on A 23	**Horley**	🏨 Gatwick Penta
Junction 9 — W : 1 m. on A 23	**Horley**	🏨 Post House
Junction 9 — W : 1 m. on A 23	**Horley**	🏨 Gatwick Moat House

M 25

Junction 28 — NE : ¾ m. on A 1023	**Brentwood**	🏨 Brentwood Moat House
Junction 28 — NE : ¼ m. on A 1023	**Brentwood**	🏨 Post House
Junction with A 30 — NW : ½ m. on A 308	**Egham**	🏨 Runnymede
Junction A 6 and A 1 (M) (this hotel also under A 1 (M))	**South Mimms**	🏨 Crest

M 26

Junction 2 A	**Wrotham Heath**	🏨 Post House

M 27

Junction 1 — on A 337 at Junction of A 31 and A 336	**Cadnam**	🏨 Bartley Lodge
Junction 12 — N : at junction of A 3 and A 27	**Portsmouth & Southsea (at Cosham)**	🏨 Holiday Inn

M 32

Junction 1 — W : ½ m. on A 4174 (this hotel also under M 4)	**Bristol (at Hambrook)**	🏨 Crest

M 40

Junction 2 — E : 1 ¾ m. by A 355 on A 40	**Beaconsfield**	🏨 Bellhouse
Junction 4 — on Crest Road	**High Wycombe**	🏨 Crest

M 55

Junction 1 — N : ¾ m.	**Preston**	🏨 Broughton Park

M 56

Junction 5 — on Airport Approach Road	**Manchester (at Airport)**	🏨 Excelsior
Junction 6 — N : ¼ m. on A 538	**Altrinchan**	🏨 Four Seasons
Junction 7/8 — SW : 2 m. on A 556 (this hotel also under M 6)	**Knutsford (at Bucklow Hill)**	🏨 Swan Inn
Junction 11 — N : ¼ m. on A 56	**Daresbury**	🏨 Lord Daresbury
Junction 12 — SE : ½ m. by A 557	**Runcorn**	🏨 Crest

M 61

Junction 5 — NE : 1 m. on A 58	**Bolton**	🏨 Crest

M 62

Junction 24 — NE : ½ m. on A 629	**Huddersfield**	🏨 Ladbroke
Junction 26 — NW : ¼ m. M 606 Euroway Trading Estate exit	**Bradford**	🏨 Novotel Bradford
Junction 30 — N : 1 m. on A 639	**Leeds (at Oulton)**	🏨 Crest

M 63

Junction 9 — by approach Rd	**Manchester (at Northenden)**	🏨 Post House

46

MAP OF TOWNS INCLUDED IN THE GUIDE

To keep the full, distinctive flavour of the separate kingdoms, principality, province, republic and islands which go to make up the British Isles, the Guide has been divided into sections each preceded by a separate map.

The maps show the towns and places with establishments included in the Guide, and those particularly selected for their general attractiveness, quiet atmosphere and good food.

A map of Great Britain and the Republic of Ireland at the beginning of the Guide shows major roads and main passenger and car ferry routes.

CARTES DES LOCALITÉS CITÉES

Afin de respecter le caractère propre à chaque Royaume ou Etat composant les Iles Britanniques, ce guide est présenté en six parties, chacune précédée d'une carte de toutes les localités citées.

Ces cartes précisent les lieux où nous recommandons spécialement des établissements hôteliers pour leur agrément, leur tranquillité ou leur bonne cuisine.

Une carte générale de la Grande-Bretagne et de la République d'Irlande figure en outre au début du guide et donne les principales voies de communication terrestres et maritimes.

CARTE DELLE LOCALITÀ COMPRESE NELLA GUIDA

Ogni Reame o Stato che compone le Isole Britanniche mantiene la sua propria personalità; perciò abbiamo ritenuto opportuno presentarli facendo precedere una carta geografica alla nomenclatura di ciascuno di essi.

Queste carte segnalano le località selezionate e, per ognuna di esse, l'eventuale esistenza di esercizi particolarmente raccomandabili per la loro amenità, la loro tranquillità o la loro buona cucina.

Inoltre, una carta generale della Gran Bretagna e della Repubblica d'Irlanda figura all'inizio della Guida ed indica le principali vie di comunicazione terrestri e marittime.

KARTEN MIT DEN ERWÄHNTEN ORTSCHAFTEN

Jedes einzelne der Länder, die unter dem Begriff « Britische Inseln » zusammengefaßt sind, hat seinen eigenen Charakter; wir haben dem Rechnung getragen, indem wir dem Ortsverzeichnis jedes « Landes » eine Übersichtskarte vorangestellt haben.

Auf diesen Karten finden Sie alle im Führer erwähnten Orte, Orte mit besonders angenehmen oder ruhig gelegenen Häusern, sowie solche mit besonders guter Küche.

Eine Gesamtkarte Großbritanniens und der Republik Irland mit den wichtigsten Verkehrsverbindungen (Land- und Seewege) finden Sie in der Einleitung.

TOWNS WITH ESTABLISHMENTS AWARDED 🏵🏵🏵, 🏵🏵, 🏵, M

Localités possédant des établissements à 🏵🏵🏵, 🏵🏵, 🏵, M

Località che possiedono esercizi con 🏵🏵🏵, 🏵🏵, 🏵, M

In folgenden Orten finden sie Häuser mit 🏵🏵🏵, 🏵🏵, 🏵, M

England and Wales

Bray-on-Thames	Waterside Inn	**London**	pages bordered in red

England and Wales

Great Milton	Le Manoir aux Quat'Saisons	**London**	pages bordered in red
Ilkley	Box Tree		

🏵

England and Wales

Canterbury	74	**Reading**	Milton Sandford
Chagford	Gidleigh Park	**Royal Leamington**	
Dartmouth	Carved Angel	**Spa**	Mallory Court
Dedham	Le Talbooth	**Taunton**	Castle
East Grinstead	Gravetye Manor	**Woburn**	Paris House
Great Malvern	Croque-en-Bouche		
Limpsfield	Old Lodge	**Scotland**	
London	pages bordered in red	**Fort William**	Inverlochy Castle
New Milton	Chewton Glen	**Republic of Ireland**	
Oakham	Hambleton Hall	**Kenmare**	Park

M

England and Wales

Abergavenny	Walnut Tree Inn	**St. Just**	Count House
Badminton	Bodkin House	**Shipdham**	Shipdham Place
Bakewell	Fischers	**Stamford**	Manor House
Bath	The Hole in the Wall	**Storrington**	Manley's
Bath	Homewood Park	**Sturminster Newton**	Plumber Manor
Bath	The Priory	**Swansea**	Drangway
Boroughbridge	Fountain House	**Thornbury**	Thornbury Castle
Broadway	Buckland Manor	**Ullswater**	Sharrow Bay Country House
Bromsgrove	Grafton Manor	**Warwick**	Westgate Arms
Chichester	White Horse	**Waterhouses**	Old Beams
Diss	Salisbury House	**Winchester**	Old Chesil Rectory
Earl Stonham	Mr Underhill's	**Windermere**	Miller Howe
Eastbourne	Hungry Monk	**Woodstock**	Feathers
Flitwick	Flitwick Manor	**Worcester**	Brown's
Fressingfield	Fox and Goose	**Wymondham**	Adlard's
Glensford	Weeks		
Grasmere	Michael's Nook	**Scotland**	
	Country House	**Arisaig**	Arisaig House
Grasmere	White Moss House	**Glasgow**	Poacher's
Great Dunmow	Starr	**Gullane**	La Potinière
Harrogate	Russell	**Kilchrenan**	Ardanaisaig
Helford	Riverside	**Peat Inn**	The Peat Inn
Horton	French Partridge	**Port Appin**	Airds
Kintbury	Dundas Arms		
Ledbury	Hope End Country House	**Republic of Ireland**	
London	pages bordered in red	**Cashel**	Chez Hans
Newport	Pantry	**Cork**	Lovetts
Northallerton	McCoys at the Tontine	**Dingle**	Doyle's Seafood Bar
Padstow	Seafood	**Gorey**	Marlfield House
Pateley Bridge	Sportsman's Arms	**Mallow**	Longueville House
Plymouth	Chez Nous	**Navan**	Dunderry Lodge
Pool-in-Wharfedale	Pool Court	**Shanagarry**	Ballymaloe House

48

England
and *Wales*

ENGLAND

Avon	Avon
Bedfordshire	Beds.
Berkshire	Berks.
Buckinghamshire	Bucks.
Cambridgeshire	Cambs.
Cheshire	Cheshire
Cleveland	Cleveland
Cornwall	Cornwall
Cumbria	Cumbria
Derbyshire	Derbs.
Devon	Devon
Dorset	Dorset
Durham	Durham
East Sussex	East Sussex
Essex	Essex
Gloucestershire	Glos.
Greater Manchester	Greater Manchester
Hampshire	Hants.
Hereford and Worcester	Heref. and Worc.
Hertfordshire	Herts.
Humberside	Humberside
Isle of Wight	I. O. W.
Kent	Kent
Lancashire	Lancs.
Leicestershire	Leics.
Lincolnshire	Lincs.
Merseyside	Merseyside
Norfolk	Norfolk
Northamptonshire	Northants.
Northumberland	Northumb.
North Yorkshire	North Yorks.
Nottinghamshire	Notts.
Oxfordshire	Oxon.
Shropshire	Salop
Somerset	Somerset
South Yorkshire	South Yorks.
Staffordshire	Staffs.
Suffolk	Suffolk
Surrey	Surrey
Tyne and Wear	Tyne and Wear
Warwickshire	Warw.
West Midlands	West Midlands
West Sussex	West Sussex
West Yorkshire	West Yorks.
Wiltshire	Wilts.

WALES

Clwyd	Clwyd
Dyfed	Dyfed
Gwent	Gwent
Gwynedd	Gwynedd
Mid Glamorgan	Mid Glam.
Powys	Powys
South Glamorgan	South Glam.
West Glamorgan	West Glam.

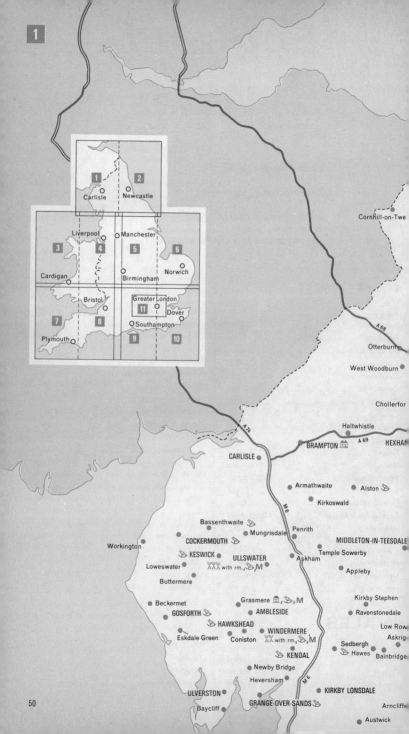

1

Carlisle ○ ○ Newcastle

1 **2**

Liverpool ○ ○ Manchester

3 **4** **5** **6**

Cardigan ○ ○ Norwich

Birmingham ○

7 **8**

Greater London

11 ○ Dover ○

Southampton ○

9 **10**

Plymouth ○

Cornhill-on-Twe

A 68

Otterburn ●

West Woodburn ●

Chollerfor

Haltwhistle ●

BRAMPTON 🏛 A 69 HEXHA

CARLISLE ●

Armathwaite ● Alston 🐟

Kirkoswald ●

A 7 4

M 6

Bassenthwaite 🐟

COCKERMOUTH ● 🐟 ● Mungrisdale Penrith ●

Workington ● 🐟 KESWICK ● Temple Sowerby ● MIDDLETON-IN-TEESDALE ●

Loweswater 🐟 ULLSWATER 🐟 Askham ●

ⅩⅩ with rm., 🐟, M

Appleby ●

Buttermere ●

Grasmere 🏛, 🐟, M

Beckermet ● Kirkby Stephen ●

GOSFORTH ● 🐟 ● AMBLESIDE Ravenstonedale ●

🐟 HAWKSHEAD ● Low Row

Eskdale Green ● Coniston ● WINDERMERE ● Askrig

ⅩⅩ with rm., 🐟, M Sedbergh ●

🐟 KENDAL ● 🐟 Hawes ● Bainbridge ●

● Newby Bridge

Heversham ● M 6

ULVERSTON ● KIRKBY LONSDALE ●

Arncliff

Baycliff ● GRANGE-OVER-SANDS 🐟

● Austwick

50

2

Place with at least :

one hotel or restaurant..................● Durham
one pleasant hotel.................🏠 , ✕ with rm
one quiet, secluded hotel...............🔊
one restaurant with..............❀, ❀❀, ❀❀❀, M
See this town for establishments
located in its vicinity...............MORPETH

Localité offrant au moins :

une ressource hôtelière.............● Durham
un hôtel agréable.................🏠 , ✕ with rm
un hôtel très tranquille, isolé..........🔊
une bonne table à..............❀, ❀❀, ❀❀❀, M
Localité groupant dans le texte
les ressources de ses environs............MORPETH

La località possiede come minimo :

una risorsa alberghiera.............● Durham
un albergo ameno.................🏠 , ✕ with rm
un albergo molto tranquillo, isolato.........🔊
un'ottima tavola con..............❀, ❀❀, ❀❀❀, M
La località raggruppa nel suo testo
le risorse dei dintorni.............MORPETH

Ort mit mindestens :

einem Hotel oder Restaurant.............● Durham
einem angenehmen Hotel.................🏠 , ✕ with rm
einem sehr ruhigen und abgelegenen Hotel.....🔊
einem Restaurant mit..............❀, ❀❀, ❀❀❀, M
Ort mit Angaben über Hotels und Restaurants
in seiner Umgebung.................MORPETH

Berwick-upon-Tweed

Bamburgh
Belford
Seahouses

Wooler

Powburn 🔊
Alnwick ●
Alnmouth

Rothbury ●

MORPETH 🔊
Whitley Bay
Tynemouth
NEWCASTLE-UPON-TYNE
bridge
A 696
South Shields
Gateshead
Cleadon
Washington
Sunderland
anchland
Chester-le-Street ●

Durham ●
Bowburn ●
Hartlepool

Bishop Auckland ●
A 1
Sedgefield ●

nard Castle
STOCKTON-ON-TEES ● Billingham
Greta Bridge ●
Thornaby-on-Tees
MIDDLESBROUGH
Loftus 🔊
Dalton ●
DARLINGTON ● Yarm
Great Ayton
WHITBY
Richmond ●
Moulton
Stokesley
Castleton
Goathland
Rosedale Abbey ● Hartoft End
Kirkby Fleetham 🔊
Leyburn ● NORTHALLERTON M, 🔊
LASTINGHAM 🔊
SCARBOROUGH 🔊
Witton ●
Middleham ● Pickhill
KIRKBYMOORSIDE ●
Appleton-le-Moors
Masham ●
Thirsk
PICKERING
Snainton
HELMSLEY
Ebberston ●
Brompton
lewell ●
A 1
Hovingham
Malton ●
Flamborough
Ripon ●
Bridlington
PATELEY BRIDGE ●
Boroughbridge M
Whitwell-on-the-Hill 🔊

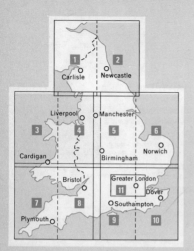

Benllech

Trearddur Bay

Beaumaris

A5

Port Dinorwic · Bar

Caernar

Llanbe

Beddgelert

NEFYN

PORTHMAD

Criccieth

Tudweiliog

ABERSOCH

Harlech

Llanbedr

Barmou

Aberdovey

ABERYSTWYTH

Aberaeron

Aberporth

Lampeter

CARDIGAN

FISHGUARD   NEWPORT M

Newcastle-Emlyn

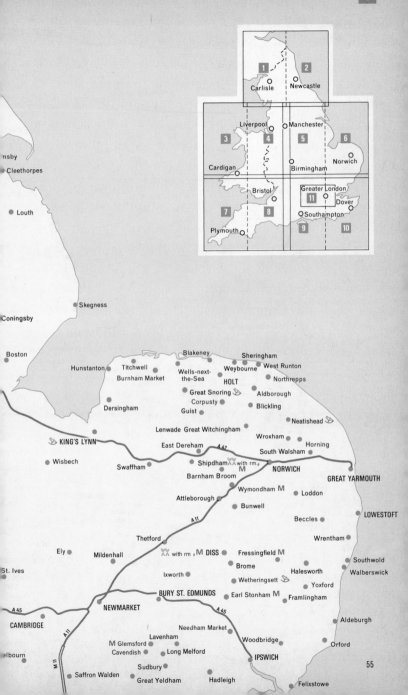

6

1 Carlisle
2 Newcastle

3
Liverpool 4 Manchester
5 6 Norwich
Cardigan Birmingham

Bristol
Greater London
11 Dover
7 8 Southampton
Plymouth 9 10

Cleethorpes

Louth

Coningsby

Skegness

Boston

Blakeney   Sheringham
Hunstanton Titchwell   Weybourne West Runton
Burnham Market Wells-next- Northrepps
the-Sea   HOLT
Great Snoring ✂ Aldborough
Corpusty Blickling
Dersingham Guist
Neatishead ✂
Lenwade Great Witchingham
✂ KING'S LYNN Wroxham
East Dereham A 47 Horning
Wisbech Shipdham ✂✂ with rm › South Walsham
Swaffham M NORWICH
Barnham Broom
Attleborough Wymondham M Loddon GREAT YARMOUTH
Bunwell
A 11 Beccles LOWESTOFT
Thetford Wrentham
Ely Mildenhall ✂✂ with rm › M DISS › Fressingfield M Southwold
St. Ives Ixworth Brome Halesworth Walberswick
Wetheringsett ✂ Yoxford
A 45 BURY ST. EDMUNDS Earl Stonham M Framlingham
NEWMARKET A 45 Aldeburgh
Needham Market Orford
CAMBRIDGE Lavenham Woodbridge
M Glemsford
Cavendish Long Melford
elbourn Sudbury IPSWICH 55
Saffron Walden Great Yeldham Hadleigh Felixstowe

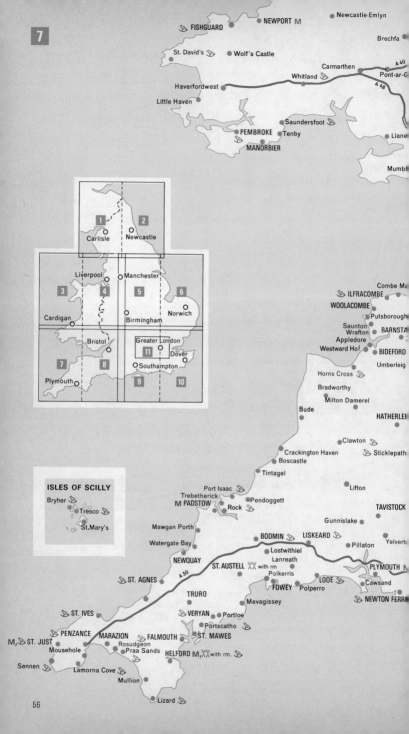

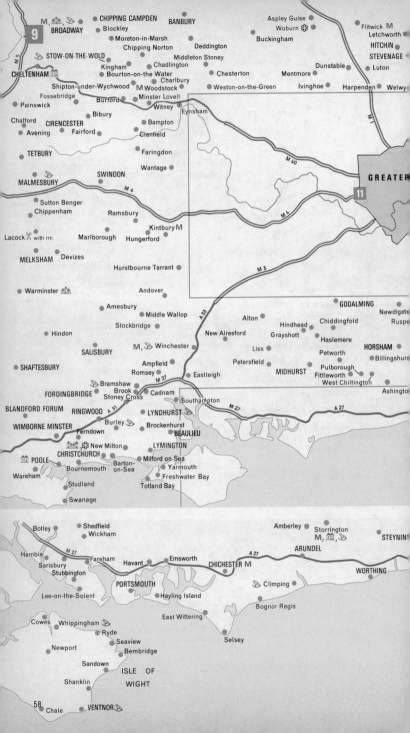

Saffron Walden · Sudbury · Hadleigh · IPSWICH
Baldock
Clavering · Great Bardfield
Bishop's Stortford · Braintree · Coggeshall · Thorpe-le-Soken
Great Dunmow M · Felsted
Witham
CHELMSFORD
Maldon
South Woodham Ferrers
Rochford
Basildon
ONDON ❀❀❀
North Stifford
Gravesend
Shorne · Rochester
Sittingbourne · Faversham
M 2
MAIDSTONE
Hadlow · Charing
PENSHURST
T GRINSTEAD ❀🏛❀🏛⚓
AWLEY · ROYAL TUNBRIDGE WELLS
FOREST ROW · Wadhurst
Crowborough
Cuckfield · Mayfield
UCKFIELD
Hurstpierpoint · Halland · HERSTMONCEUX
Lewes A 27
GHTON AND HOVE
tingdean · Alfriston
Newhaven · EASTBOURNE M,

Great Yeldham
🏛⚓❀ Dedham
East Bergholt
Felixstowe
Harwich and Dovercourt
COLCHESTER
Frinton-on-Sea
Clacton-on-Sea
West Mersea
Burnham-on-Crouch
SOUTHEND-ON-SEA
A 2
BROADSTAIRS
RAMSGATE
WHITSTABLE
Sandwich
❀ CANTERBURY
Wye
ASHFORD ⚓
Goudhurst · Biddenden
Cranbrook 🏛, ⚓
Hawkhurst · Tenterden
Bodiam ⚓
Northiam
Sedlescombe
Rushlake Green · Battle ⚓
Bexhill
Hastings and St.Leonards
A 2
DOVER ⚓
Folkestone
Hythe
New Romney
RYE
A 259

10

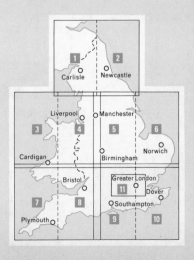

1 Carlisle	2 Newcastle
3 Liverpool	4	5 Manchester	6 Norwich
	Cardigan		Birmingham
7	8 Bristol	Greater London 11	Dover
Plymouth		9 Southampton	10

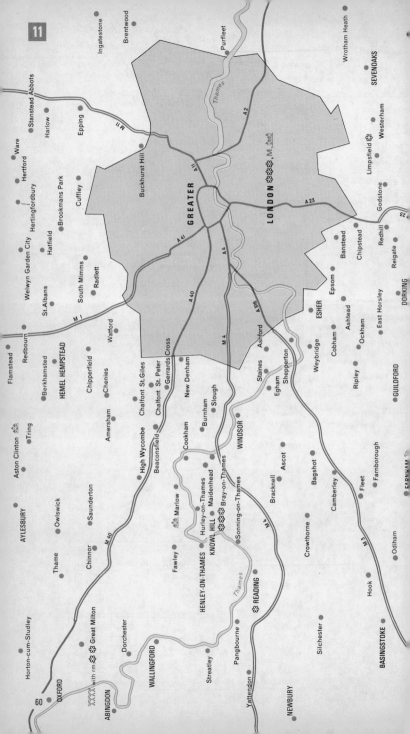

ENGLAND and WALES

Towns

ABBERLEY Heref. and Worc. 🔢 🔢 M 27 – pop. 558 – ECD : Wednesday – ✉ Worcester – ✪ 029 921 Great Witley.
♦ London 137 – ♦Birmingham 27 – Worcester 13.

🏨 **The Elms** ≫, WR6 6AT, W : 2 m. on A 443 ✆ 666, Telex 337105, ≤, ♨, park, ℀ – 📺 ☎ 🅿.
🛆, ⊠ AE ⓪ VISA ℀
M 10.00/15.50 **st.** – **27 rm** ⤢ 41.00/62.00 **st.** – SB 79.50/85.00 **st.**

ABERAERON Dyfed 🔢 H 27 – pop. 1,350 – ECD : Thursday – ✪ 0545.
Envir. : New Quay (site★) SW : 8 m.
🛈 Harbour Car Park, Market St. ✆ 570602 (summer only).
♦ London 237 – Carmarthen 36 – Fishguard 42 – ♦ Swansea 64.

🏠 **Feathers Royal**, SA46 0AQ, ✆ 570214, ⊠ – ➡wc 🛁wc 🅿, 🛆, VISA
M (closed Sunday dinner in winter) 8.00/9.00 **t.** ▯ 4.00 – **14 rm** ⤢ 14.00/25.00 **st.**

FORD, VOLVO ✆ 570312

ABERDOVEY (ABERDYFI) Gwynedd 🔢 H 26 – pop. 927 – ECD : Wednesday – ✪ 065 472.
See : Afon Dovey's mouth (site★★).
Envir. : Llangelynin (church★) N : 8 m. – Dolgoch Falls★ NE : 10 m.
🛈 Snowdonia National Park Centre, The Wharf ✆ 321 (summer only).
♦ London 230 – Dolgellau 25 – Shrewsbury 66.

🏨 **Plas Penhelig** ≫, LL35 0NA, E : 1 m. on A 493 ✆ 676, ≤, ♨, park, ℀ – ➡wc 🛁 🅿. ⊠ AE
⓪ VISA
closed first 2 weeks November – **M** 5.50/9.50 **t.** – **11 rm** ⤢ 25.00/37.75 **t.** – SB (weekends only) 38.00/48.60 **st.**

🏨 **Trefeddian** ≫, LL35 0SB, W : 1 m. on A 493 ✆ 213, ≤ golf course and sea, ⊠, ♨, park, ℀
– 🛗➡wc 🛁 ⊠ 🅿. ⊠
30 March-10 November – **M** 6.00/8.30 **t.** ▯ 2.40 – **44 rm** ⤢ 17.00/42.60 **t.** – SB (spring and autumn only) 36.00 **st.**

🏠 **Penhelig Arms**, LL35 0LT, ✆ 215, ≤ – 📺 ➡wc 🛁wc 🅿. ⊠ AE ⓪ VISA ℀
M (bar lunch) 6.95 **t.** ▯ 1.95 – **11 rm** ⤢ 13.00/36.00 **t.** – SB (winter only) 35.00 **st.**

⚐ **Bodfor,** Bodfor Terrace, LL35 0EA, ✆ 475, ≤ – 🛁wc. VISA
M (bar lunch) 6.00 **t.** ▯ 2.50 – **15 rm** ⤢ 12.50/25.00 **t.** – SB (winter only) 32.00 **st.**

⚐ **Harbour,** 17 Glandovey Terr., LL35 0EB, ✆ 250, ≤ – ➡wc 🛁wc. ⊠ VISA
March-October – **M** a la carte 4.65/7.10 **t.** – **6 rm** ⤢ 18.00/25.00 **st.**

ABERGAVENNY (Y-FENNI) Gwent 🔢 L 28 – pop. 9,401 – ECD : Thursday – ✪ 0873.
Envir. : Llanthony Priory★ N : 10 m. – Bwlch (≤★ of the Usk Valley), NW : 9 ½ m. – Brecon Cathedral★ 13C, NW : 19 ½ m.
📷 Llanfoist, ✆ 3171, S : 2 m.
🛈 Brecon Beacons National Park Centre, 2 Lower Monk St. ✆ 3254 (summer only) – at Brecon : Brecon Beacons National Park, 7 Glamorgan St. ✆ 0874 (Brecon) 4437 (summer only) – Market Car Park ✆ 0874 (Brecon) 2485 (summer only).
♦ London 163 – Gloucester 43 – Newport 19 – ♦Swansea 49.

🏨 **Angel** (T.H.F.), 15 Cross St., NP7 5EN, ✆ 7121 – 📺 ➡wc ☏ 🅿. 🛆. ⊠ AE ⓪ VISA
M (buffet lunch) 8.25 **st.** ▯ 2.65 – ⤢ 4.50 – **29 rm** 32.00/41.00 **st.**

↑ **Park,** 36 Hereford Rd, NP7 5RA, ✆ 3715 – 🅿
7 rm ⤢ 8.50/17.00 **st.**

at Llandewi Skirrid NE : 3 ½ m. by A 465 on B 4521 – ✉ ✪ 0873 Abergavenny :

✗ **Walnut Tree Inn,** NP7 8AW, ✆ 2797 – ▦ rest 🅿
closed Sunday – **M** a la carte 13.00/20.00 **t.** ▯ 3.00.

at Llanwenarth NW : 3 m. on A 40 – ✉ Abergavenny – ✪ 0873 Crickhowell :

🏠 **Llanwenarth Arms,** Brecon Rd, NP8 1EP, ✆ 810550, ≤, ☋ – 📺 ➡wc ☏ 🅿. ⊠ AE ⓪
VISA ℀
M a la carte 6.70/10.45 **st.** ▯ 2.00 – **18 rm** ⤢ 25.00/29.00 **st.**

AUSTIN-ROVER, FORD Brecon Rd ✆ 2126
PEUGEOT, TALBOT Penpergwm, Gobion ✆ 087 385
(Gobion) 287

RENAULT 9 Monmouth Rd ✆ 2323

4

ABERGWAUN = Fishguard.

ABERGWESYN Powys **403** I 27 – see Llanwrtyd Wells.

ABERGYNOLWYN Gwynedd **402 403** I 26 – pop. 231 – ⊠ Twywn – ☎ 065 477.
♦London 228 – Dolgellau 12 – Shrewsbury 63.

  ⋔ **Dolgoch Falls,** SW : 2 ½ m. on B 4405 ℰ 258, ≼, ⟲ – ℗. *VISA*
     January-October and weekends only November-December – **7 rm** ⌿ 10.25/20.50 **t.**

ABERLLYNFI = Three Cocks.

ABERMAW = Barmouth.

ABERMULE (ABER-MIWL) Powys **403** K 26 – see Newtown.

ABERPORTH Dyfed **403** G 27 – pop. 1,618 – ECD : Wednesday – ☎ 0239.
See : Site★.
Envir. : Llangranog (cliffs★) NE : 4 m.
♦ London 249 – Carmarthen 29 – Fishguard 26.

  🏛 **Penrallt,** SA43 2BS, SW : 1 m. by B 4333 ℰ 810227, ⟲, ⤫ – 📺 ⊟wc ⋔wc ☏ ℗. 🔲 ⓪
     VISA
     closed 1 week at Christmas – **M** (bar lunch) 8.00 **st.** ⌖ 2.75 – **16 rm** ⌿ 25.00/37.00 **st.** – SB
     (winter only) 45.00 **st.**

  🏠 **Highcliffe,** SA43 2DA, ℰ 810534 – 📺 ⊟wc ℗. 🔲 *VISA*
     M (bar lunch) 7.00 **st.** ⌖ 2.45 – **16 rm** ⌿ 15.00/44.00 **st.** – SB (except summer) 34.00/38.00 **st.**

  🏠 Morlan Motel, SA43 2EN, ℰ 810611 – 📺 ⊟wc ℗. 🔲 ⒶⒺ ⓪ *VISA*
     March-October – **M** (grill rest. only) – **38 rm** ⌿ 15.50/27.50 **t.**

  ⋔ **Ffynonwen Country** ⟜, SA43 2HT, SE : 1 m. by B 43333 ℰ 810312, ≼ – ℗
     12 rm ⌿ 11.00/22.00 **t.**

ABERSOCH Gwynedd **402 403** G 25 – pop. 800 – ECD : Wednesday – ⊠ Pwllheli – ☎ 075 881.
Envir. : Llanengan (church★ : twin aisles rood screen) W : 2 m. – Hell's Mouth★ W : 3 m. – Aber-
daron (site★) W : 10 m. – Braich y Pwll (≼★★ from 2nd car park) W : 12 m.
🏌 Golf Rd, Pwllheli, ℰ 0758 (Pwllheli) 2520, NE : 7 m. – 🏌 Pwllheli, ℰ 2622.
♦ London 265 – Caernarfon 28 – Shrewsbury 101.

  🏠 **Riverside,** LL53 7HW, ℰ 2419, ≼, 🔲 – ⊟wc ⋔wc ℗. 🔲 *VISA*. ⤫
     March-October – **M** (bar lunch) 14.00 **t.** ⌖ 3.00 – **12 rm** ⌿ 20.00/40.00 **t.**

  🏠 Abersoch Harbour (Best Western), Long Engan, LL53 7HR, ℰ 2406, ≼ – 📺 ⊟wc ⋔wc ℗
     season – **18 rm**.

  ⋔ **Llysfor,** Lôn Garmon, LL53 7AL, ℰ 2248, ⟲ – ℗. *VISA*
     Easter-October – **8 rm** ⌿ 9.00/20.00 **st.**

  ✕✕ **Bronheulog** ⟜ with rm, Lôn Garmon, LL53 7UL, NW : ¾ m. ℰ 2177, ⟲ – ⊟wc ℗. ⤫
     March-October – **M** *(closed Sunday)* (dinner only) (booking essential) a la carte 8.60/10.90 **s.**
     ⌖ 2.40 – **4 rm** ⌿ 12.00/30.00 **st.**

     at Bwlchtocyn S : 2 m. – ⊠ Pwllheli – ☎ 075 881 Abersoch :

  🏛 **Porth Tocyn** ⟜, LL53 7BU, ℰ 2966, ≼ Cardigan Bay and mountains, « Country house
     atmosphere », ⛴ heated, ⟲, ⤫ – ⊟wc ℗. 🔲 ⒶⒺ
     Easter-October – **M** (buffet lunch) 13.50 **st.** ⌖ 3.75 – **18 rm** ⌿ 22.50/52.50 **st.**

ABERTAWE = Swansea.

ABERTEIFI = Cardigan.

ABERYSTWYTH Dyfed **403** H 26 – pop. 10,688 – ECD : Wednesday – ☎ 0970.
See : ≼★ from the National Library.
Envir. : Vale of Rheidol★ SE : 6 m.
🏌 Brynymore, ℰ 615104, N : ½ m.
🚩 Eastgate ℰ 612125 and 617911.
♦ London 238 – Chester 98 – Fishguard 58 – Shrewsbury 74.

  🏛 **The Groves,** 44-46 North Par., SY23 2NF, ℰ 617623 – 📺 ⊟wc ⋔wc ℗. 🔲 ⒶⒺ ⓪ *VISA*. ⤫
     closed 24 December-6 January – **M** *(closed Sunday lunch in summer and Sunday dinner ir
     winter)* (bar lunch) a la carte 5.70/9.50 **t.** ⌖ 2.10 – **12 rm** ⌿ 18.00/32.00 **t.** – SB (except sum-
     mer and Bank Holidays) 35.50/42.50 **st.**

  🍴 **Four Seasons,** 50-54 Portland St., SY23 2DX, ℰ 612120 – ⊟wc ℗. 🔲 *VISA*. ⤫
     closed 24 December-3 January – **M** (bar lunch Monday to Saturday) 7.85/10.50 **t.** ⌖ 2.55 –
     16 rm ⌿ 14.00/31.00 **t.** – SB (except summer) 35.00/40.00 **st.**

at Chancery (Rhydgaled) S : 4 m. on A 487 – ⊠ 🅖 0970 Aberystwyth :

🏨 **Conrah Country** 🦢, SY23 4DF, ☎ 617941, ≼, « 18C country house », 🔲, 🐎, park – 🅿 📺
🖵wc 🛗wc 🅿 🄰 🔌 ⏏ 𝑉𝐼𝑆𝐴 ⬚
closed 1 week at Christmas – **M** 6.75/9.75 t. 🄰 2.45 – **22 rm** ⚌ 26.00/48.00 t. – SB (weekends only) 48.00/54.00 **st.**

AUSTIN-ROVER-JAGUAR Park Av. ☎ 4841   FORD North Parade ☎ 4171
FIAT Llanfarian ☎ 612311

ABINGDON Oxon. 🔢🔢 Q 28 – pop. 18,610 – ECD : Thursday – 🅖 0235.
🄱 8 Market Pl. ☎ 22711.
♦ London 64 – ♦Oxford 6 – Reading 25.

🏨 **Upper Reaches** (T.H.F.), Thames St., OX14 3TA, ☎ 22311 – 📺 🖵wc 🌍 🅿 🄰 🔌 ⏏ ⏏
𝑉𝐼𝑆𝐴
M 6.25/8.95 **st.** 🄰 2.60 – ⚌ 5.00 – **20 rm** 42.00/53.50 **st.**

at Frilford W : 4 m. on A 415 – ⊠ Abingdon – 🅖 0865 Frilford Heath :

XXX **Noah's Ark**, OX13 5NZ, S : ½ m. on A 338 ☎ 391470, 🐎 – 🅿 ⏏ ⏏ 𝑉𝐼𝑆𝐴
closed Sunday dinner and Monday – **M** a la carte 11.05/14.55 **t.** 🄰 2.30.

AUSTIN-ROVER Drayton Rd ☎ 22822

ACOCKS GREEN West Midlands 🔢🔢 ⊛ – see Birmingham.

ADLINGTON Lancs. 🔢🔢 M 23 – see Chorley.

AIGBURTH Merseyside – see Liverpool.

ALBRIGHTON Salop 🔢🔢 L 25 – see Shrewsbury.

ALCESTER Warw. 🔢🔢 O 27 – pop. 5,149 – ECD : Thursday – 🅖 0789.
Envir. : Ragley Hall★★ (17C) *AC*, SW : 2 m.
♦London 104 – ♦Birmingham 20 – ♦Coventry 28 – Gloucester 34.

X **Rossini**, 50 Birmingham Rd, on A 435 ☎ 762764, Italian rest. – 🅿 🔌 ⏏ ⏏ 𝑉𝐼𝑆𝐴
closed Sunday, last 2 weeks August and first 2 weeks September – **M** a la carte 7.40/11.10 **t.**
🄰 2.80.

ALDBOROUGH Norfolk 🔢 X 25 – pop. 461 – ⊠ Norwich – 🅖 0263 Cromer.
♦London 127 – ♦Cambridge 80 – ♦Norwich 18.

X **Old Red Lion**, The Green, NR11 7AA, ☎ 761451 – 🅿 𝑉𝐼𝑆𝐴
closed Sunday dinner, Monday and 26-30 December – **M** 5.95/7.95 t.

ALDEBURGH Suffolk 🔢 Y 27 – pop. 2,791 – ECD : Wednesday – 🅖 072 885.
🄸₈ at Thorpeness ☎ 2176, N : 2 ½ m.
🄱 Festival Office, High St. ☎ 3637 (summer only).
♦ London 97 – ♦Ipswich 24 – ♦Norwich 41.

🏨 **Brudenell** (T.H.F.), The Parade, IP15 5BU, ☎ 2071, ≼ – 🅿 📺 🖵wc 🌍 🅿 🄰 🔌 ⏏ ⏏ 𝑉𝐼𝑆𝐴
M 5.50/7.75 **st.** 🄰 2.85 – ⚌ 5.00 – **47 rm** 28.50/40.00 **st.**

🏨 **Wentworth**, Wentworth Rd, IP15 5BD, ☎ 2312, ≼ – 📺 🖵wc 🛗wc 🅿 ⏏
closed 1 to 14 January – **M** 6.50/8.75 t. 🄰 2.25 – **33 rm** ⚌ 19.50/54.00 **st.** – SB (summer only) 51.00/61.50 **st.**

🏠 **Uplands**, Victoria Rd, IP15 5DX, ☎ 2420, 🐎 – 📺 🖵wc & 🅿 🔌 ⏏ ⏏ 𝑉𝐼𝑆𝐴 ⬚
M (bar lunch) 8.00 **t.** 🄰 2.50 – **20 rm** ⚌ 18.00/38.00 **t.** – SB (weekends only)(except summer) 40.00 **st.**

ALDERLEY EDGE Cheshire 🔢🔢🔢 N 24 – pop. 4,470 – ECD : Wednesday – 🅖 0625.
Envir. : Capesthorne Hall★ (18C) *AC*, S : 4 ½ m.
♦ London 187 – Chester 34 – ♦Manchester 14 – ♦Stoke-on-Trent 25.

🏨 **De Trafford Arms**, London Rd, SK9 7AA, ☎ 583881 – 🅿 📺 🖵wc 🌍 🅿 🔌 ⏏ 𝑉𝐼𝑆𝐴
M (bar lunch) 8.00 **st.** 🄰 3.25 – **37 rm** ⚌ 34.50/45.00 **st.** – SB (weekends only) 43.50 **st.**

🏠 **Milverton House**, Wilmslow Rd, SK9 7QL, N : ¾ m. on A 34 ☎ 583615 – 📺 🖵wc 🅿 ⬚
14 rm ⚌ 12.50/30.00.

XX **Mandarin**, 2-3 The Parade, SK9 7JX, ☎ 584434, Chinese rest. – ⏏
closed Monday except Bank Holidays and 25-26 December – **M** a la carte 7.00/9.00 **t.** 🄰 2.80.

X **Wizard Country**, Macclesfield Rd, Nether Alderley, SK10 4UB, SE : 1½ m. on B 5087
☎ 584000 – 🅿 🔌 ⏏ ⏏ 𝑉𝐼𝑆𝐴
closed Sunday – **M** a la carte 7.50/11.00 **t.** 🄰 2.75.

X **Octobers**, 47 London Rd, SK9 7JT, ☎ 583942 – 🔌 𝑉𝐼𝑆𝐴
closed Sunday – **M** (dinner only) approx. 10.00 t. 🄰 2.90.

AUSTIN-ROVER-JAGUAR London Rd ☎ 582218   VOLVO 77 London Rd ☎ 583912
VAUXHALL-OPEL Knutsford Rd ☎ 582691

ALDRIDGE West Midlands **402 403 404** O 26 – pop. 16,500 – ECD : Thursday – ✉ Walsall – ☎ 0922.

♦London 130 – ♦Birmingham 12 – Derby 32 – ♦Leicester 40 – ♦Stoke-on-Trent 38.

🏨 **Fairlawns,** 178 Little Aston Rd, WS9 0NU, E : 1 m. on A 454 ⌀ 55122 – 📺 ⇔wc 🗍wc 🅿 🏧 🅿 AE ⓪ *VISA*
closed *27 to 30 December* – **M** 7.00/8.50 t. ⌀ 2.40 – **30 rm** ⇆ 32.50/44.00 t. – SB (weekends only) 46.00 **st.**

ALFRISTON East Sussex **404** U 31 – pop. 763 – ECD : Wednesday – ✉ Polegate – ☎ 0323.

♦ London 66 – Eastbourne 9 – Lewes 10 – Newhaven 8.

🏨 **Star Inn** (T.H.F.), High St., BN26 5TA, ⌀ 870495 – 📺 ⇔wc 🗍 🅿 🏧 AE ⓪ *VISA*
M 8.45/9.45 **st.** ⌀ 2.60 – ⇆ 5.00 – **32 rm** 32.50/46.50 **st.**

🏨 **Deans Place,** BN26 5TW, ⌀ 870248, ≼, 🔟 heated, 🚗, park, % – ⇔wc ☎ 🅿
closed *29 December-mid February* – **M** (bar lunch Monday to Saturday) 5.00/8.00 t. ⌀ 2.00 –
43 rm ⇆ 22.00/40.00 t.

✕✕ **Moonrakers,** High St., BN26 5TD, ⌀ 870472
closed *Sunday, Monday and 14 January-13 February* – **M** (dinner only) 11.40 t. ⌀ 2.50.

ALLESLEY West Midlands **403 404** P 26 – see Coventry.

ALLESTREE Derbs. **402 403 404** P 35 – see Derby.

ALNMOUTH Northumb. **401 402** P 17 – pop. 543 – ECD : Wednesday – ☎ 0665.

♦London 314 – ♦Edinburgh 90 – ♦Newcastle-upon-Tyne 37.

⋔ **Marine House,** 1 Marine Rd, NE66 2RW, ⌀ 830349, 🚗 – 🗍wc
8 rm ⇆ 13.50/22.00 **st.**

ALNWICK Northumb. **401 402** O 17 – pop. 7,190 – ECD : Wednesday – ☎ 0665.

See : Castle** (Norman) *AC.*

Envir. : Dunstanburgh Castle 14C-15C (ruins, coastal setting★) *AC*, 1 ¼ m. walk from Craster, no cars, NE : 7 ½ m. – Warkworth (castle★ 12C) *AC*, SE : 7 m. – Rothbury (Cragside gardens★ : rhododendrons) *AC*, SW : 12 m.

🖥 Foxton Hall, Alnmouth ⌀ 066 573 (Alnmouth) 231, SE : 5 m. – 🖥 Swansfield Park, Alnwick – 🖥 Marine Rd, Alnmouth ⌀ 0665 (Alnmouth) 830370, SE : 5 m.

🗓 The Shambles ⌀ 603120 (summer only).

♦ London 320 – ♦Edinburgh 86 – ♦Newcastle-upon-Tyne 34.

🏨 **White Swan** (Swallow), Bondgate Within, NE66 1TD, ⌀ 602109, Group Telex 53168 – 📺 ⇔wc 🗍 🅿 🏧 🅿 AE ⓪ *VISA*
M 4.90/8.00 **st.** ⌀ 3.40 – **41 rm** ⇆ 28.00/45.90 **st.** – SB 52.00 **st.**

🏨 **Hotspur,** Bondgate Without, NE66 1PR, ⌀ 602924 – ⇔wc 🗍 🅿 🏧 *VISA*
M a la carte 5.95/9.75 t. – ⇆ 3.25 – **28 rm** 14.00/28.00 t.

⋔ **Bondgate House,** Bondgate Without, NE66 1PN, ⌀ 602025 – 🅿
8 rm ⇆ 9.00/18.00 **st.**

FORD Langy St. ⌀ 602294

ALRESFORD Hants. **403 404** Q 30 – see New Alresford.

ALSAGER Cheshire **402 403 404** N 24 – pop. 12,000 – ✉ Stoke-on-Trent – ☎ 093 63.

♦ London 180 – Chester 36 – ♦ Liverpool 49 – ♦ Manchester 32 – ♦ Stoke-on-Trent 11.

🏨 **Manor House,** Audley Rd, ST7 2QQ, SE : ½ m. ⌀ 78013 – 📺 🗍wc ☎ 🅿 🏧 AE ⓪ *VISA* . %
M (bar lunch Saturday) a la carte 10.30/14.85 **st.** ⌀ 3.25 – **8 rm** ⇆ 32.00/39.50 **st.**

AUSTIN-ROVER Lawton Rd ⌀ 2146   FORD 52 Sandbach Rd South ⌀ 3241
CITROEN Rode Heath ⌀ 3879

ALSTON Cumbria **401 402** M 19 – pop. 1,916 (inc. Garrigill) – ECD : Tuesday – ☎ 0498.

🖥 Alston Moor ⌀ 81675, N : 2 m.

🗓 Railway Station ⌀ 81696.

♦ London 309 – ♦Carlisle 28 – ♦Newcastle-upon-Tyne 45.

🏨 **Lovelady Shield Country House** ⌁, Nenthead Rd, CA9 3LF, E : 2 ½ m. on A 689 ⌀ 81203, ≼, 🚗, % – ⇔wc 🗍wc 🅿 AE ⓪
April-October – **M** (dinner only and Sunday lunch) 7.00/11.00 t. ⌀ 2.50 – **11 rm** ⇆ 17.00/38.00 t.

🏨 **Lowbyer Manor,** Hexham Rd, CA9 3JX, ⌀ 81230, 🚗 – ⇔wc 🅿 🏧 AE ⓪ . %
M (bar lunch) 8.50 t. ⌀ 2.95 – **11 rm** ⇆ 28.50/31.50 t.

🏨 **High Fell Old Farmhouse** ⌁, CA9 3BP, S : 1 ¾ m. on A 686 ⌀ 81597, ≼ – 🅿
M (booking essential) a la carte 7.30/20.00 **st.** ⌀ 2.70 – **5 rm** ⇆ 15.00/29.00 **st.**

ALTHORPE Humberside **402 404** R 23 – see Scunthorpe.

ALTON Hants. ▨▨▨ R 30 – pop. 9,920 – ECD : Wednesday – ✆ 0420.

🔂 Old Odiham Rd ✆ 82042, N : 2 m.

♦ London 53 – Reading 24 – ♦Southampton 29 – Winchester 18.

🏛 **Swan** (Anchor), High St., GU34 1AT, ✆ 83777, Group Telex 858875 – 📺 ⌂wc 🛁wc ☎ 🅿.
▥ 🔼 𝔸𝔼 ⓞ 𝓥𝓘𝓢𝓐
M (carving rest.) 8.65 **st.** ▯ 2.65 – **38 rm** ⚏ 34.50/45.00 **st.** – SB (weekends only) 46.00 **st.**

🏠 Grange, 17 London Rd, Holybourne, GU34 4EG, ✆ 86565, 🌶 – 📺 ⌂wc 🛁wc ☎ 🅿
13 rm.

AUSTIN-ROVER, VAUXHALL Butts Rd ✆ 84141   PEUGEOT, TALBOT Four Marks ✆ 62354
FORD Ackender Rd ✆ 83993

ALTRINCHAM Greater Manchester ▨▨▨ ▨▨▨ ▨▨▨ N 23 – pop. 40,787 – ECD : Wednesday –
✆ 061 Manchester.

🔂 Stockport Rd, Timperley ✆ 928 0761, E : 1 m. on A 160 – 🔂 Dunham Forest, Oldfield Lane
✆ 928 2605, W : 1 m.

♦ London 191 – Chester 30 – ♦Liverpool 30 – ♦Manchester 8.

🏛 **Cresta Court** (Best Western), Church St., WA14 4DP, on A 56 ✆ 928 8017, Telex 667242 – 📶
📺 ⌂wc ☎ 🅿. ▥ 🔼 𝔸𝔼 ⓞ 𝓥𝓘𝓢𝓐
M a la carte 5.05/8.00 **st.** ▯ 3.00 – **139 rm** ⚏ 31.50/48.00 **t.** – SB (weekends only) 45.00 **st.**

🏛 **George and Dragon,** 22 Manchester Rd, WA14 4PH, on A 56 ✆ 928 9933, Group Telex
629462 – 📶 📺 ⌂wc 🛁wc ☎ 🅿.
closed Christmas and New Year – **M** (closed Sunday dinner) (bar lunch Monday to Saturday)
5.00/8.00 **st.** ▯ 3.50 – **46 rm** ⚏ 35.00/45.00 **st.**

🏠 **Pelican,** Manchester Rd, West Timperley, WA14 5NH, N : 2 m. on A 56 ✆ 962 7414 – 📺
🛁wc ☎ 🅿. ▥ 𝔸𝔼 ⓞ 𝓥𝓘𝓢𝓐. ⁒
M 4.50/6.50 **st.** ▯ 2.50 – **50 rm** ⚏ 31.00/39.00 **st.**

↑ **Bollin,** 58 Manchester Rd, WA14 4PJ, on A 56 ✆ 928 2390 – 🅿
10 rm ⚏ 12.65/21.85 **t.**

XX **Portofino,** The Downs, WA14 1BU, ✆ 928 1511, Italian rest. – 🅿. ▥ 𝔸𝔼 ⓞ 𝓥𝓘𝓢𝓐
closed Saturday lunch and Sunday – **M** a la carte 8.30/15.90 **t.** ▯ 2.60.

at Timperley NE : 2 m. by A 560 on B 5165 – ✉ Altrincham – ✆ 061 Manchester :

XXX **Le Bon Viveur** (at Hare and Hounds H.), Wood Lane, WA15 7LY, on A 560 ✆ 904 0266,
French rest. – 🅿. ▥ 𝔸𝔼 ⓞ 𝓥𝓘𝓢𝓐
closed Saturday lunch, Sunday dinner and Bank Holidays – **M** 8.65/15.50 **t.**

at Hale SE : 1 m. on B 5163 – ✉ Altrincham – ✆ 061 Manchester :

🏛 **Ashley,** Ashley Rd, WA15 9SF, ✆ 928 3794, Group Telex 629462 – 📶 📺 ⌂wc ☎. ▥. 🔼
𝔸𝔼 ⓞ 𝓥𝓘𝓢𝓐
M 5.95/6.75 **st.** ▯ 2.85 – **49 rm** ⚏ 32.00/41.00 **t.** – SB (weekends only) 41.80 **st.**

XX **Evergreen,** 169-171 Ashley Rd, WA15 7EV, ✆ 928 1222, Chinese rest. – 🔼 𝓥𝓘𝓢𝓐
M (dinner only) a la carte 5.75/10.85 **st.**

at Halebarns SE : 3 m. on A 538 – ✉ Altrincham – ✆ 061 Manchester :

🏛 **Four Seasons,** Hale Rd, WA15 8XW, ✆ 904 0301, Telex 665492 – 📶 📺 ⌂wc ☎ ♿ 🅿. ▥.
🔼 𝔸𝔼 ⓞ 𝓥𝓘𝓢𝓐
M a la carte 8.80/14.10 **t.** ▯ 3.00 – **48 rm** ⚏ 39.50/49.50 **st.**

at Bowdon SW : 1 m. – ✉ Altrincham – ✆ 061 Manchester :

🏛 **Bowdon,** Langham Rd, WA14 2HT, ✆ 928 7121, Telex 668208 – 📺 ⌂wc ☎ 🅿. ▥. 🔼 𝔸𝔼
ⓞ 𝓥𝓘𝓢𝓐
M a la carte 9.00/13.40 **st.** ▯ 2.50 – **41 rm** ⚏ 20.00/44.00 **st.** – SB (weekends only) 42.00 **st.**

🏛 **Bowdon Croft** ⌂, Green Walk, WA14 2SN, ✆ 928 1718, ≤, « Period house », 🌶 – 📺
⌂wc ☎ 🅿. ▥ 🔼. ⁒
M (booking essential) 8.50/9.50 **s.** ▯ 3.00 – **6 rm** ⚏ 35.00/42.00 **s.**

ALFA-ROMEO Money Ash Rd, Hale Bridge ✆   NISSAN Manchester Rd ✆ 973 3021
928 5980   SAAB Bancroft Rd, Hale ✆ 980 8004
AUSTIN-ROVER 16 Stockport Rd ✆ 941 4111   TOYOTA Ashley ✆ 928 3112
AUSTIN-ROVER-DAIMLER-JAGUAR Victoria Rd ✆   VAUXHALL-OPEL 276-280 Stockport Rd, Timperley
928 7124   ✆ 980 3212
FORD 44 Hale Rd Bridge ✆ 928 2275   VOLVO Manchester Rd ✆ 928 2384
HONDA, SAAB Bancroft Rd, Hale ✆ 980 8004

ALVESTON Avon ▨▨▨ ▨▨▨ M 29 – pop. 2,776 – ECD : Wednesday – ✉ Bristol – ✆ 0454 Thornbury.

♦London 127 – ♦Bristol 11 – Gloucester 23 – Swindon 42.

🏛 **Post House** (T.H.F.), Thornbury Rd, BS12 2LL, on A 38 ✆ 412521, Telex 444753, ⌇ heated,
🌶 – 📺 ⌂wc ☎ 🅿. ▥. 🔼 𝔸𝔼 ⓞ 𝓥𝓘𝓢𝓐
M 6.95/9.25 **st.** ▯ 2.60 – ⚏ 5.00 – **75 rm** 39.50/47.00 **st.**

🏛 **Alveston House,** BS12 2LJ, on A 38 ✆ 415050, Telex 449212, 🌶 – 📺 ⌂wc 🛁wc ☎ 🅿.
🔼 𝓥𝓘𝓢𝓐. ⁒
M a la carte 7.80/10.90 **st.** ▯ 2.95 – **17 rm** ⚏ 28.50/36.50 **st.** – SB (weekends only) 41.00 **st.**

AMBERLEY West Sussex 🄴🄾🄾 S 31 – pop. 510 – ⊠ Arundel – ☎ 079 881 Bury.
♦London 58 – ♦Brighton 23 – Chichester 12 – Worthing 14.

   ✕   **La Capanna,** Houghton Bridge, BN18 9LR, SW : ¾ m. on B 2139 🖉 790, ≤, Italian rest. – 🄿 ⑩
     closed Sunday and 24 December-mid January – **M** (dinner only) a la carte 8.65/11.25 **t.** 🍷 3.50.

AMBLESIDE Cumbria 🄰🄾🄿 L 20 – pop. 2,657 – ECD : Thursday – ☎ 0966.
Envir. : Tarn Hows★★ (lake) SW : 6 m. by A 593 AY – Langdale Valley★★ W : 7 m. by B 5343 AY.
🄸 Old Courthouse, Church St. 🖉 32582 and 33084 (summer only).
♦London 278 – ♦Carlisle 47 – Kendal 14.

Plan opposite

  🏨 **Kirkstone Foot** ⌂, Kirkstone Pass Rd, LA22 9EH, NE : ¼ m. 🖉 32232, 🐎 – 🖚wc 🄿 🄴
     🄰🄴 ⑩ *VISA*   AZ c
     23 February-9 November – **M** (dinner only) 10.50 **st.** 🍷 2.50 – **18 rm** ⌷ (dinner included)
     37.35/56.00 **st.** – SB 49.00/56.00 **st.**

  🏠 **Elder Grove,** Lake Rd, LA22 0DB, 🖉 32504 – 🖚wc 🄿 🄴 *VISA*   AZ a
     April-mid November – **14 rm** ⌷ 12.50/31.00 **t.**

    at Waterhead S : 1 m. on A 591 – ⊠ ☎ 0966 Ambleside :

  🏨 **Waterhead** (Best Western), Lake Rd, LA22 0ER, 🖉 32566, ≤, 🐎 – 🄣 🖚wc 🍽wc 🕮 🄿
     🄡 🄴 ⑩ *VISA*   BY n
     M 5.00/9.95 **st.** 🍷 2.75 – **30 rm** ⌷ 18.30/36.60 **st.** – SB (winter only) 33.00/40.00 **st.**

  🏩 **Regent,** LA22 0ES, 🖉 32254 – 🄣 🖚wc 🍽wc 🄿 🄡 🄴 ⑩ *VISA*   BY e
     April-December – **M** (bar lunch) 12.50 **t.** 🍷 2.20 – **11 rm** ⌷ 28.00/56.00 **st.** – SB 39.00/45.00 **st.**

  🏩 **Wateredge,** Borrans Rd, LA22 0EP, 🖉 32332, ≤, « Part 17C Fishermans cottages, lakeside
     setting », 🐎 – 🖚wc 🍽wc 🄿 🄡 *VISA*   BY o
     closed 3 December-1 February – **M** (bar lunch residents only) 12.90 **t.** 🍷 2.60 – **20 rm**
     ⌷ 14.00/56.00 **t.** – SB (except summer) 40.00/56.00 **st.**

    at Rothay Bridge S : ½ m. on A 593 – ⊠ ☎ 0966 Ambleside :

  🏨 **Rothay Manor,** LA22 0EH, 🖉 33605, ≤, 🐎 – 🄣 🖚wc ☎ 🄿 🄡 🄴 ⑩ *VISA* ※   BY i
     closed 6 January-8 February – **M** (buffet lunch Monday to Saturday) 8.00/15.50 **t.** 🍷 3.20 –
     16 rm ⌷ 40.00/64.00 **t.** – SB (winter only) 69.00/83.00 **st.**

  🏩 **Riverside H. and Lodge** ⌂, under Loughrigg, LA22 9LJ, N : ¼ m. by A 593 🖉 32395, 🐎 –
     🖚wc 🄿 🄡 *VISA* ※   BY s
     M (bar lunch) 9.50 **t.** 🍷 3.20 – **14 rm** ⌷ 19.00/38.00 **t.** – SB (winter only) 52.00 **st.**

    at Clappersgate W : 1 m. on A 593 – ⊠ ☎ 0966 Ambleside :

  🏩 **Nanny Brow Country House** ⌂, LA23 9NF, 🖉 32036, ≤ Brathay Valley and Langdale,
     « Terraced gardens », 🐎, ※ – 🄣 🖚wc 🄿 🄡 *VISA*   BY u
     M (dinner only) 8.50 **st.** 🍷 2.30 – **12 rm** ⌷ 20.00/40.00 **st.** – SB (weekends only) (win-
     ter only) 42.00 **st.**

    at Skelwith Bridge W : 2 ½ m. on A 593 – ⊠ ☎ 0966 Ambleside :

  🏩 **Skelwith Bridge,** LA22 9NJ, 🖉 32115, ≤, 🐎 – 🖚wc 🄿 🄡 *VISA*   AY v
     M (bar lunch Monday to Saturday) 5.45/10.25 **st.** 🍷 2.80 – **24 rm** ⌷ 13.50/45.00 **st.** – SB (win-
     ter only) 38.00/41.00 **st.**

    at Elterwater W : 4 ½ m. by B 5343 – ⊠ Ambleside – ☎ 096 67 Langdale :

  🏤 **Britannia Inn** ⌂, LA22 9HP, 🖉 210, ≤ – 🄿 🄡 *VISA*   AY x
     closed Christmas – **M** *(closed November-January)* (bar lunch) 10.00 **t.** 🍷 3.50 – **10 rm**
     ⌷ 14.50/30.00 **t.** – SB (not weekends) (spring only) 22.70 **st.**

    at Little Langdale W : 4 ½ m. by A 593 – ⊠ ☎ 096 67 Langdale :

  🏤 **Three Shires Inn** ⌂, LA22 9NZ, 🖉 215, ≤, 🐎 ※   AY z
     M (bar lunch) 4.00/10.00 **st.** 🍷 2.60 – **8 rm** ⌷ 13.50/30.00 **st.**

    at Chapel Stile W : 5 m. on B 5343 – ⊠ Chapel Stile – ☎ 096 67 Langdale :

  🏦 **Pillar** ⌂, LA22 9JB, 🖉 302, Telex 65188, 🏊, ⌂, park, squash – 🍽 rest 🄣 ☎ 🄿 🄡 🄡 🄴
     VISA ※   AY c
     M 7.50/16.50 **t.** 🍷 3.00 – **36 rm** ⌷ 45.00/75.00 **t.** – SB (spring only) 60.00/72.00 **st.**

  🏩 **Langdales** ⌂, Great Langdale, LA22 9JF, 🖉 253, ≤, 🐎 – 🖚wc 🍽wc 🄿   AY a
     closed 6 January-8 February – **M** (bar lunch Monday to Saturday) 5.00/10.00 **t.** 🍷 2.00 – **20 rm**
     ⌷ 19.00/44.00 **t.** – SB (winter only) 56.00 **st.**

    at Rydal NW : 1 ½ m. on A 591 – ⊠ ☎ 0966 Ambleside :

  🏩 **Glen Rothay,** LA22 9LR, 🖉 32524, 🐎 – 🖚wc 🍽wc 🄿 🄡 🄴 ⑩ *VISA*   BY a
     closed 6 to 25 January and 7 to 20 December – **M** (bar lunch) 11.50 **t.** 🍷 3.35 – **11 rm**
     ⌷ 20.00/46.00 **t.** – SB (except summer) 45.00/54.00 **st.**

  🏠 **Rydal Lodge,** Rydal Rd, LA22 9LR, 🖉 33208, 🐎 – 🄿 🄡 *VISA*   BY c
     closed January – **8 rm** ⌷ 17.00/40.00 **t.**

FORD   Millans Park 🖉 33033

AMBLESIDE
GRASMERE

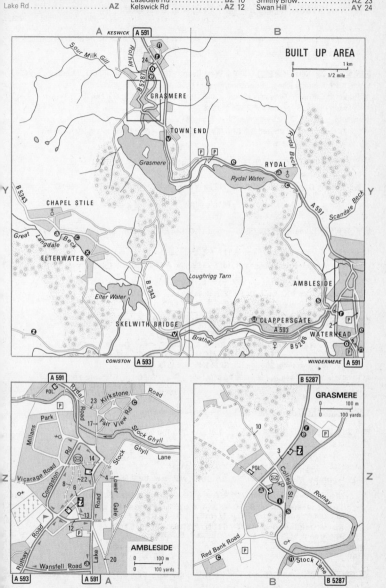

Town plans : roads most used by traffic and those on which guide listed hotels and restaurants stand are fully drawn ; the beginning only of lesser roads is indicated.

67

AMERSHAM (Old Town) Bucks. **404** S 28 – pop. 17,254 – ECD : Thursday – ☏ 024 03.

♦London 29 – Aylesbury 16 – ♦Oxford 33.

🏨 **Crown** (T.H.F.), High St., HP7 0DH, 🖉 21541, 🐎 – 📺 ⌂wc ☎ 🄿 ⚟ AE ⓞ 𝘝𝘐𝘚𝘈
M 8.50/10.50 **st.** ⓗ 2.60 – ⌇ 5.25 – **19 rm** 29.50/46.50 **st.**

XX **King's Arms,** High St., HP7 0DJ, 🖉 6333 – 🄿 ⚟ AE ⓞ 𝘝𝘐𝘚𝘈
closed Sunday dinner, Monday and Tuesday after Bank Holidays – **M** a la carte 8.15/12.25 **t.** ⓗ 3.00.

AUSTIN-ROVER-DAIMLER-JAGUAR   London Rd 🖉 5911
TALBOT   4/8 White Lion Rd 🖉 024 04 (Little Chalfont) 4666
RENAULT   The Broadway 🖉 4656

AMESBURY Wilts. **403 404** O 30 The West Country G. – pop. 5,540 – ECD : Monday – ☏ 0980.
Envir. : Stonehenge (Megalithic Monument)★★★ *AC*, W : 2 m.

🎦 Tidworth Garrison, Tidworth, Hants. 🖉 0980 (Stonehenge) 42321, N : 7 m.

🄴 Redworth House, Flower Lane 🖉 23255 and 22833.

♦London 88 – ♦Bristol 52 – ♦Southampton 31 – Taunton 61.

🏨 Antrobus Arms, Church St., SP4 7EY, 🖉 23163, 🐎 – 📺 ⌂wc ☎ ⟵ 🄿 – **20 rm**.

RENAULT   High St. 🖉 22525

AMMANFORD (RHYDAMAN) Dyfed **403** I 28 – pop. 5,711 – ✉ ☏ 0269 Llandybie.

♦London 208 – Carmarthen 22 – ♦Swansea 19.

🏨 **Mill at Glynhir** ⤷, SA18 2TE, NE : 3 ¼ m. by A 483 and Glynhir Rd 🖉 850672, 🔍, 🐎 – 📺 ⌂wc 🎦wc 🄿
closed 25 and 26 December – **M** a la carte 7.00/13.10 **t.** ⓗ 2.75 – **9 rm** ⌇ 21.00/42.00 **t.** – SB 45.00/54.00 **st.**

AMPFIELD Hants. **403 404** P 30 – pop. 1,460 – ECD : Wednesday – ✉ Romsey – ☏ 0794 Braishfield.

♦London 79 – Bournemouth 31 – Salisbury 19 – ♦Southampton 11 – Winchester 7.

🏨 **Potters Heron,** Winchester Rd, SO5 9ZF, on A 31 🖉 66611 – 📺 ⌂wc ☎ 🄿 ⚟ ⚟ AE ⓞ 𝘝𝘐𝘚𝘈 ⤴
M 6.00/9.00 **t.** – **42 rm** ⌇ 38.00/50.00 **t.** – SB (weekends only) 50.00/60.00 **st.**

XX **Keats,** SO5 9BQ, on A 31 🖉 68252, Italian rest. – 🄿 ⚟ AE ⓞ 𝘝𝘐𝘚𝘈
closed Sunday dinner, Monday and Bank Holidays – **M** a la carte 8.60/13.45 **t.** ⓗ 2.35.

ANDOVER Hants. **403 404** P 30 – pop. 25,881 – ECD : Wednesday – ☏ 0264.

♦London 74 – Bath 53 – Salisbury 17 – Winchester 11.

🏨 **White Hart,** Bridge St., SP10 1BH, 🖉 52266 – 📺 ⌂wc 🎦wc ☎ 🄿 ⚟ AE ⓞ 𝘝𝘐𝘚𝘈
M 9.95 **t.** ⓗ 2.65 – **21 rm** ⌇ 34.50/47.00 **t.** – SB (weekends only) 45.00/47.00 **st.**

X Wood's Brasserie, 90 High St., SP10 1NE, 🖉 64033.

ALFA-ROMEO, FIAT, LANCIA   Salisbury Rd 🖉 61166
AUDI, VW   50 London St. 🖉 52839
AUSTIN-ROVER   278 Weyhill Rd 🖉 3781
AUSTIN-ROVER   94 Charlton Rd 🖉 3603
FORD   West St. 🖉 51811
VAUXHALL   Newbury Rd 🖉 4233

ANDOVERSFORD Glos. **403 404** O 28 – see Cheltenham.

APPLEBY Cumbria **402** M 20 – pop. 1,949 – ECD : Thursday – ☏ 0930.

🎦 🖉 51432, S : 2 m.

🄴 Moot Hall 🖉 51177.

♦London 285 – ♦Carlisle 33 – Kendal 24 – ♦Middlesbrough 58.

🏨 **Appleby Manor,** Roman Rd, CA16 6JD, NE : ½ m. by B 6542 🖉 51571, ≤, 🐎 – ⌂wc 🄿 ⚟ AE ⓞ 𝘝𝘐𝘚𝘈
M (lunch by arrangement) 7.05/9.00 **st.** ⓗ 3.05 – **19 rm** ⌇ 23.50/38.50 **st.** – SB 46.00/50.00 **st.**

🏨 **Tufton Arms,** Market Sq., CA16 6XA, 🖉 51593 – ⌂wc ☎ 🄿 ⚟ ⚟ ⓞ 𝘝𝘐𝘚𝘈
M (buffet lunch) 6.50 **t.** ⓗ 2.50 – **17 rm** ⌇ 15.00/28.00 **t.**

🏠 **Royal Oak Inn,** Bongate, CA16 6UN, 🖉 51463 – 📺 🄿 ⚟ 𝘝𝘐𝘚𝘈
M a la carte 5.50/7.50 **t.** ⓗ 2.00 – **7 rm** ⌇ 11.50/30.00 **t.**

FORD   The Sands 🖉 51133
PEUGEOT-TALBOT 🖉 61227
RENAULT 🖉 51460

APPLEDORE Devon **403** H 30 The West Country G. – pop. 2,172 – ECD : Wednesday – ✉ ☏ 023 72 Bideford.
See : Site★.

♦London 235 – Bideford 4 – Exeter 47 – ♦Plymouth 62.

🏠 **Seagate,** The Quay, EX39 1QS, 🖉 2589 – 📺 ⌂wc 🄿 ⚟ ⓞ
M (bar lunch) 10.00 **t.** ⓗ 2.50 – **9 rm** ⌇ 15.00/40.00 **t.**

APPLETON-LE-MOORS North Yorks. – pop. 715 – ✆ 075 15 Lastingham.
* London 245 – ✦Middlesbrough 37 – ✦Scarborough 27 – York 33.

🏠 **Dweldapilton Hall**, YO6 6TF, ✆ 227, 🍴 – 🖥 📺 ⌂wc ⋔wc 🅿. 🔼 🆎 💳
   M (bar lunch Monday to Saturday) 7.50 **t.** ⓘ 2.85 – **12 rm** ⊑ 18.50/37.00 **t.** – SB (winter only) 40.00 **st.**

ARDSLEY South Yorks. – see Barnsley.

ARMATHWAITE Cumbria **401 402** L 19 – pop. 150 – ✉ Carlisle – ✆ 069 92.
* London 305 – ✦Carlisle 10 – Penrith 12.

🏨 Duke's Head, Front St., CA4 9PB, ✆ 226 – 🅿 – **8 rm**.
🏨 Red Lion, CA4 9PY, ✆ 204, ≤, 🍸 – 🅿 – **10 rm**.

ARMITAGE Staffs. **402 403 404** O 25 – see Rugeley.

ARNCLIFFE North Yorks. **402** N 21 – pop. 71 – ✉ Skipton – ✆ 075 677.
* London 232 – Kendal 41 – ✦Leeds 41 – Preston 50 – York 52.

🏠 **Amerdale House** ⌂, BD23 5QE, ✆ 250, ≤, 🍴 – 🅿. 🔼 💳
   April-October – M (bar lunch) 10.00 **st.** ⓘ 2.00 – **9 rm** ⊑ 13.00/35.00 **st.** – SB 46.00 **st.**

ARUNDEL West Sussex **404** S 31 – pop. 2,434 – ECD : Wednesday – ✆ 0903.
See : Castle★ (keep 12C, ≤★ 119 steps, State apartments★) AC – St. Nicholas' Church (chancel or Fitzalan chapel★ 14C).
Envir. : Bignor (Roman Villa : mosaics★★ AC) NW : 7 m.
🅱 61 High St. ✆ 882268.
* London 58 – ✦Brighton 21 – ✦Southampton 41 – Worthing 9.

🏨 **Norfolk Arms**, 22 High St., BN18 9AD, ✆ 882101 – 📺 ⌂wc 🅿. 🔼 🆎 ⓞ 💳
   M a la carte 4.75/9.45 **t.** – **35 rm** ⊑ 25.00/38.00 **t.** – SB 52.00 **st.**
🏨 **Swan**, 29 High St., BN18 9AG, ✆ 882314 – ⌂wc ⋔wc. 🔼 🆎 ⓞ 💳. 🎊
   M (grill rest. only) 5.00 **t.** ⓘ 2.50 – **11 rm** ⊑ 20.00/30.00 **t.** – SB 35.00/50.00 **st.**
🏨 **Bridge**, 15 Queen St., BN18 9JG, ✆ 882242, 🍴 – ⋔ 🅿. 🔼 🆎 ⓞ 💳
   M (carving rest.) (bar lunch) 6.50 **t.** ⓘ 1.90 – ⊑ 1.50 – **13 rm** 16.00/30.00 **st.**

   at Burpham NE : 3 m. by A 27 – ✉ ✆ 0903 Arundel :

⋔ **Burpham Country** ⌂, Old Down, BN18 9RJ, ✆ 882160, ≤, 🍴 – 🅿. 🔼. 🎊
   6 rm ⊑ 15.00/34.00 **t.**

   at Walberton W : 3 m. by A 27 on B 2132 – ✉ Arundel – ✆ 0243 Yapton :

🏨 **Avisford Park**, Yapton Lane, BN18 0LS, ✆ 551215, ≤, ⌇ heated, 🍴, park, 🎾 – 📺 ⌂wc
   📞 🅿. 🚶. 🔼 🆎 💳
   M 8.25/11.25 **st.** ⓘ 2.75 – **76 rm** ⊑ 33.00/48.00 **st.** – SB (weekends only) 55.00 **st.**

ASCOT Berks. **404** R 29 – pop. 15,630 – ECD : Wednesday – ✆ 0990.
🅱 Downshire, Easthampstead Park ✆ 0344 (Bracknell) 24066, W : 4 m.
* London 36 – Reading 15.

🏨 **Berystede** (T.H.F.), Bagshot Rd, Sunninghill, SL5 9JH, S : 1 ¼ m. on A 330 ✆ 23311, Telex 847707, ⌇ heated, 🍴 – 🖥 📺 🅿. 🚶. 🔼 🆎 ⓞ 💳
   M a la carte 12.50/18.50 **st.** ⓘ 4.00 – ⊑ 5.50 – **90 rm** 42.00/50.50 **st.**

AUSTIN-ROVER Ascot Motor Works ✆ 20324   CITROEN Lyndhurst Rd, South Ascot ✆ 22257

ASHBURTON Devon **403** I 32 The West Country G. – pop. 3,518 – ECD : Wednesday – ✆ 0364.
* London 220 – Exeter 20 – ✦Plymouth 23.

🏠 **Holne Chase** ⌂, Two Bridges Rd, TQ13 7NS, NW : 3 m. on B 3357 ✆ 036 43 (Poundsgate) 471, ≤, 🍸, 🍴, park – ⌂wc ⋔wc 🅿. 🔼 🆎 ⓞ 💳
   M 7.00/11.00 **t.** ⓘ 2.30 – **15 rm** ⊑ 18.40/30.00 **t.** – SB 40.50/55.00 **st.**
🏠 **Dartmoor Motel**, Peartree Cross, TQ13 7JW, W : ½ m. ✆ 52232 – 📺 ⌂wc 🅿. 🔼 🆎 ⓞ
   💳
   closed 25 and 26 December – M 4.00/5.00 **t.** ⓘ 2.00 – **22 rm** ⊑ 20.85/35.45 **t.** – SB 33.85/40.85 **st.**
🍽🍽 **Country Garden**, 22 East St., TQ13 7AZ, ✆ 53431 – 🔼 💳
   closed Sunday, 2 weeks October and 1 week at Christmas – M (dinner only) a la carte 10.50/12.70 **t.** ⓘ 2.35.

COLT 6 East St. ✆ 52215

ASHBY DE LA ZOUCH Leics. **402 403 404** P 25 – pop. 7,490 – ECD : Wednesday – ✆ 0530.
* London 119 – ✦Birmingham 29 – ✦Leicester 18 – ✦Nottingham 22.

🏨 **Royal Crest** (Crest), Station Rd, LE6 5GP, ✆ 412833, 🍴 – 📺 ⌂wc ⋔wc 📞 🅿. 🚶. 🔼 🆎
   ⓞ 💳
   M approx. 11.00 **st.** – ⊑ 5.25 – **31 rm** 38.00/48.00 **st.**

AUSTIN-ROVER, SHERPA Bath St. ✆ 412770

ASHFORD Kent 404 W 30 – pop. 31,240 – ECD : Wednesday – ✆ 0233.

Envir. : Hothfield (St. Margaret's Church : memorial tomb★ 17C) NW : 3 m. – Lenham (St. Mary's Church : woodwork★) NW : 9 ½ m.

🖪 The Civic Centre, Tannery Lane ✆ 37311 ext 316.

♦London 56 – Canterbury 14 – ♦Dover 24 – Hastings 30 – Maidstone 19.

🏰 **Eastwell Manor** ⬥, Eastwell Park, TN25 4HR, N : 3 m. by A 28 on A 251 ✆ 35751, Telex 966281, ≼, « Reconstructed period mansion in formal gardens », ⬥, park, ✗ – 🛎 �📺 ✆ &.
🅿. 🅰. 🔼 AE ⓞ VISA ✗
M 9.50/15.00 st. ≬ 4.50 – **24 rm** ⊑ 43.00/108.00 st. – SB (not weekends) (winter only) 79.50 **st.**

at Kennington NE : 2 m. on A 28 – ✉ ✆ 0233 Ashford :

🏨 **Spearpoint,** Canterbury Rd, TN24 9QR, ✆ 36863, ⟿ – �📺 ⌂wc �🚿wc 🅿. 🔼 AE ⓞ VISA
M a la carte 8.20/10.40 t. ≬ 2.40 – **37 rm** ⊑ 20.00/41.00 st. – SB (weekends only) 41.00 **st.**

⌂ **Downsview,** Willesborough Rd, TN24 9QP, ✆ 21953, ⟿ – �📺 ⌂wc 🅿. 🔼 VISA
M (dinner only) 6.00 **st.** – **16 rm** ⊑ 15.10/28.25 st. – SB 31.70/36.15 **st.**

AUSTIN-ROVER 20-46 New St. ✆ 20334
CITROEN Beaver Rd ✆ 35735
FORD Station Rd ✆ 23451
NISSAN Godinton Road ✆ 38441

RENAULT Maidstone Rd ✆ 34177
SKODA, FIAT Chart Rd ✆ 20624
VAUXHALL Faversham Rd ✆ 23173
VOLVO Chart Rd ✆ 35661

ASHFORD Surrey 404 S 29 – pop. 22,987 – ECD : Wednesday – ✆ 078 42.

♦London 21 – Reading 27.

✗✗ **Terrazza,** 45 Church Rd, TW15 2TY, ✆ 44887, Italian rest. – 🔼 ⓞ VISA
closed Saturday lunch, Sunday and Bank Holidays except Christmas Day lunch – **M** a la carte 10.80/17.90 t. ≬ 3.00.

CITROEN 594 London Rd ✆ 52125
FIAT, LANCIA 445 Staines Rd West ✆ 43591

VAUXHALL Staines Rd ✆ 41901
VW 554 London Rd ✆ 50051

ASHFORD-IN-THE-WATER Derbs – see Bakewell.

ASHINGTON West Sussex 404 S 31 – pop. 1,470 – ECD : Wednesday – ✉ Pulborough – ✆ 0903.

♦London 50 – ♦Brighton 20 – Worthing 9.

🏨 **Mill House** ⬥, Mill Lane, RH20 3BZ, ✆ 892426, ⟿ – �📺 ⌂wc 🚿wc 🅿. 🔼 AE ⓞ VISA
closed 25 December-1 January – **M** (dinner only and Sunday lunch) a la carte 7.50/10.50 t. ≬ 2.20 – ⊑ 3.50 – **10 rm** 17.00/32.00 t. – SB (weekends only) 37.00/42.00 **st.**

ASHTEAD Surrey 404 T 30 – pop. 3,549 – ✆ 037 22.

♦London 19 – Guildford 15.

✗ Snooty Fox, 21 The Street, KT21 1AA, ✆ 76606.

ASKHAM Cumbria 401 402 L 20 – pop. 392 – ECD : Thursday – ✉ Penrith – ✆ 093 12 Hackthorpe.

See : Lowther (Wildlife Park★) *AC* – ♦London 288 – ♦Carlisle 23 – Kendal 28.

⌂ Queen's Head Inn, CA10 2PF, ✆ 225 – 🅿. ✗
6 rm ⊑ 15.50/30.00 **st.**

ASKRIGG North Yorks. 402 N 21 – pop. 384 – ✉ Leyburn – ✆ 0969 Wensleydale.

♦London 251 – Kendal 32 – ♦Leeds 70 – York 63.

⌂ **King's Arms,** Market Pl., DL8 3HQ, ✆ 50258 – �📺 ⌂wc 🚿wc. 🔼 VISA
M (bar lunch) 9.00 t. ≬ 2.50 – **10 rm** ⊑ 19.00/40.00 t. – SB (except summer and Bank Holidays) 34.00/49.00 **st.**

✗ Rowan Tree, DL8 3HT, ✆ 50536.

ASPLEY GUISE Beds. 404 S 27 – pop. 2,296 – ✉ ✆ 0908 Milton Keynes.

♦London 50 – Bedford 12 – Luton 15 – Northampton 22.

🏨 **Holt,** The Square, MK17 8DW, ✆ 583652, ⟿ – �📺 ⌂wc 🚿wc 🅿. 🔼 AE ⓞ VISA
M 8.00/9.00 **st.** ≬ 2.50 – **12 rm** ⊑ 30.00/50.00 **st.** – SB (weekends only) 40.00/70.00 **st.**

ASTON CLINTON Bucks. 404 R 28 – pop. 2,473 – ECD : Wednesday – ✉ ✆ 0296 Aylesbury.

♦London 42 – Aylesbury 4 – ♦Oxford 26.

🏰 **Bell Inn,** HP22 5HP, ✆ 630252, Telex 83252, « Courtyard and gardens » – 🍴 rest �📺 ✆ 🅿.
🅰. 🔼 VISA
M *(closed Sunday dinner from October to March and Monday, except Christmas, to non residents)* a la carte 16.75/31.00 **s.** ≬ 3.50 – **21 rm** 45.00/90.00 **s.**

ATCHAM Salop 402 403 L 25 – see Shrewsbury.

ATTLEBOROUGH Norfolk 404 X 26 – pop. 6,175 – ECD : Wednesday – 🕿 0953.
◆London 94 – ◆Cambridge 47 – ◆Norwich 15.

  🏨 **Griffin,** Church St., NR17 2AH, ℰ 452149 – 📺 🅿. 🛠
    M (bar lunch) a la carte 5.00 **st.** ⓝ 2.00 – **7 rm** ⌖ 13.00/22.00 **st.**

AUSTWICK North Yorks. 402 M 21 – pop. 509 – ⬚ Lancaster (Lancs.) – 🕿 046 85 Clapham.
◆London 237 – Kendal 26 – Lancaster 23 – ◆Leeds 47.

  ⋔ **Traddock** ⟨⟩, LA2 8BY, ℰ 224, � – 🛏wc 🅿. 🛠
    May-October – **11 rm** ⌖ 12.50/26.00 **t.**

AVON Hants. – see Ringwood.

AXBRIDGE Somerset 403 L 30 The West Country G. – pop. 1,097 – 🕿 0934.
See : Site★★ – King John's Hunting Lodge★ – St. John the Baptist Church★.
Envir. : The Cheddar Gorge★★ (The Gorge★★ - Jacob's Ladder ≤★ - The Caves★★).
◆London 142 – ◆Bristol 17 – Taunton 31 – Weston-Super-Mare 10.

  ✗ **Oak House** with rm, The Square, BS26 2AP, ℰ 732444 – 📺 🛏wc. 🔼 🖭 🖽 VISA. 🛠
    M (closed Sunday dinner to non-residents) a la carte 10.60/12.70 **t.** ⓝ 3.00 – **11 rm**
    ⌖ 14.00/29.00 **t.** – SB (weekends only) 45.00 **st.**

AXMINSTER Devon 403 L 31 – pop. 4,515 – ECD : Wednesday – 🕿 0297.
🛈 Old Court House, Church St. ℰ 34386 (summer only).
◆London 156 – Exeter 27 – Lyme Regis 5.5 – Taunton 22 – Yeovil 24.

  🏨 **Woodbury Park Country House** ⟨⟩, Woodbury Cross, EX13 5TL, SE :1½ m. on A 35 ℰ
    33010, ≤, ☒ heated, 🌠, park – 🛏wc 🅿. 🔼 🖭 🖽 VISA
    M (closed Monday to non-residents) a la carte 5.65/9.85 **t.** – **8 rm** ⌖ 11.00/32.00 **t.**

  at Hawkchurch NE : 4 ½ m. by A 35 off B 3165 – ⬚ Axminster – 🕿 029 77 Hawkchurch :

  🏨 **Fairwater Head** ⟨⟩, EX13 5TX, S : ¾ m. ℰ 349, ≤ Axe Vale, 🌠 – 🛏wc 🅿. 🔼 🖭 VISA. 🛠
    closed January – **M** 5.00/8.00 **st.** ⓝ 3.00 – **14 rm** ⌖ 26.00/46.00 **st.** – SB 55.00 **st.**

AYLESBURY Bucks. 404 R 28 – pop. 40,569 – ECD : Thursday – 🕿 0296.
Envir. : Waddesdon Manor (Rothschild Collection★★★) AC, NW : 5 ½ m. – Ascott House★★ (Rothschild Collection★★) and gardens★ AC, NE : 8 ½ m. – Stewkley (St. Michael's Church★ 12C) NE :
12 m.
🏌 Weston Turville, New Rd ℰ 24084, SE : 2 ½ m.
🛈 County Hall, Walton St. ℰ 5000.
◆London 46 – ◆Birmingham 72 – Northampton 37 – ◆Oxford 22.

  🏨 **Bell** (T.H.F.), Market Sq., HP20 1TX, ℰ 82141 – 📺 🛏wc ☎. 🔼 🖭 🖽 VISA
    M approx. 7.50 **st.** ⓝ 2.85 – ⌖ 5.00 – **17 rm** 32.50/41.00 **st.**

  ✗ **Pebbles,** 1 Pebble Lane, HP20 2JH, ℰ 86622 – 🔼
    closed Saturday lunch, Monday dinner and Sunday – **M** a la carte 10.30/12.40 **st.** ⓝ 3.00.

  at Weston Turville SE : 3 ½ m. by A 413 on B 4544 – ⬚ Aylesbury – 🕿 029 661 Stoke
  Mandeville :

  🏨 **Five Bells,** 40 Main St., HP22 5RW, ℰ 3131 – 📺 🛏wc ☎ 🅿. 🔼 VISA. 🛠
    M (closed Sunday dinner and 26 December to 1 January) 7.00/10.00 **t.** – **17 rm** ⌖ 25.00/42.00 **st.**

  ✗✗ **Chequers Inn,** Church Lane, by Bate's Lane, ℰ 3298 – 🅿. 🔼 🖭 VISA
    closed Saturday lunch and Sunday dinner – **M** a la carte 12.50/17.50 **t.** ⓝ 2.50.

  at Stoke Mandeville S : 3 ¼ m. by A 413 on A 4010 – ⬚ Aylesbury – 🕿 029 661 Stoke
  Mandeville :

  🏨 **Belmore,** Risborough Rd, HP22 5UT, ℰ 2258, ☒ heated, 🌠 – 📺 🛏wc 🛈 ♿ 🅿. 🔼 🖭 🖭
    VISA. 🛠
    closed 6 days at Christmas – **M** (dinner only) 6.50 **s.** ⓝ 3.80 – ⌖ 2.80 – **15 rm** 20.00/34.00 **s.**

AUSTIN-ROVER-DAIMLER-JAGUAR Buckingham   VAUXHALL-OPEL 143 Cambridge St. ℰ 82321
Rd ℰ 84071   VOLVO Stocklake ℰ 5344
MERCEDES-BENZ Bicester Rd ℰ 81641
RENAULT Little Kimble ℰ 029 661 (Stoke Mandeville) 2239

BABBACOMBE Devon 403 J 32 – see Torquay.

BACKFORD CROSS Cheshire 402 403 L 24 – see Chester.

BADMINTON Avon 🅓🅓🅓 🅓🅓🅓 N 29 The West Country G. – pop. 280 – ☺ 045 423 Didmarton.

See : Badminton House★.

♦London 114 – ♦Bristol 19 – Gloucester 26 – Swindon 33.

  🏠 Petty France, GL9 1AF, NW : 3 m. on A 46 ℰ 361, 🏤 – 📺 🚽wc 🚿wc ☏ 🅿 – **16 rm**.

  XXX **Bodkin House,** Petty France, GL9 1AF, NW : 3 m. on A 46 ℰ 310, « Tastefully furnished former coaching inn » – 🅿. 🔼 🆎 𝓥𝓘𝓢𝓐
       closed Sunday, Monday, first 2 weeks August, 25-26 December and 1 January – **M** a la carte 11.15/17.35 **t.** 🍷 3.55.

BAE COLWYN = Colwyn Bay.

BAGSHOT Surrey 🅓🅓🅓 R 29 – pop. 21,074 – ECD : Wednesday – ☺ 0276.

♦London 37 – Reading 17 – ♦Southampton 49.

  🏨 Pennyhill Park 🏊, College Ride, GU19 5ET, off A 30 ℰ 71774, Telex 858841, ≤, 🔼 heated, 🎿, 🌳, 🏤, park, 🎾 – 📺 ☎ 🅿. 🅰️ 🔼 🆎 ⓞ 𝓥𝓘𝓢𝓐. 🍴 – **35 rm**.

  🏠 Cricketer's, London Rd, GU19 5HR, N : ½ m. on A 30 ℰ 73196, 🏤 – 📺 🚽wc ☏ 🅿
     26 rm.

BAINBRIDGE North Yorks. 🅓🅓🅓 N 21 – pop. 445 – ECD : Wednesday – ✉ Leyburn – ☺ 0969 Wensleydale.

♦London 249 – Kendal 31 – ♦Leeds 68 – York 61.

  🍴 **Rose and Crown,** DL8 3EE, ℰ 50225 – 📺 🚽wc 🅿. 🔼 𝓥𝓘𝓢𝓐
     M (bar lunch) a la carte 4.70/11.15 **t.** – **13 rm** 🛏 15.50/36.00 **t.**

BAKEWELL Derbs. 🅓🅓🅓 🅓🅓🅓 🅓🅓🅓 O 24 – pop. 4,249 – ECD : Thursday – ☺ 062 981.

Envir. : Chatsworth★★★ : site★★, house★★★ (Renaissance) garden★★★ *AC*, NE : 2 ½ m. – Haddon Hall★★ (14C-16C) *AC*, SE : 3 m.

🎿 Station Rd ℰ 2307.

♦London 160 – Derby 26 – ♦Manchester 37 – ♦Nottingham 33 – ♦Sheffield 17.

  🏠 **Milford House,** Mill St., DE4 1DA, ℰ 2130, 🏤 – 🚽wc 🅿. 🍴
     closed 1 December-mid February – **11 rm** 🛏 14.95/31.05 **t.**

  XX **Fischer's,** Bath St., DE4 1BX, ℰ 2687 – 🔼 🆎
     closed Sunday dinner, Monday, 1 to 22 January, last week August and first week September – **M** (restricted lunch) a la carte 10.05/16.25 **t.** 🍷 2.70.

     at Hassop N : 3 ½ m. by A 619 on B 6001 – ✉ Bakewell – ☺ 062 987 Great Longstone :

  🏨 **Hassop Hall** 🏊, DE4 1NS, ℰ 488, ≤, « Part 16C hall », 🏤, park – 📠 📺 🅿. 🔼 🆎 ⓞ 𝓥𝓘𝓢𝓐. 🍴
     closed 3 days at Christmas – **M** *(closed Sunday dinner)* 7.95/13.95 **st.** 🍷 3.95 – 🛏 5.00 – **10 rm** 40.00/55.00 **st.**

     at Ashford-in-the-Water NW : 1 ¾ m. by A 6 on A 6020 – ✉ ☺ 062 981 Bakewell :

  XX **Riverside Country House** with rm, DE4 1QF, ℰ 4275, 🏤 – 📺 🚽wc 🚿wc 🅿. 🔼 🆎 𝓥𝓘𝓢𝓐. 🍴
     M *(closed Sunday dinner to non-residents)* (bar lunch Monday to Saturday) 15.00 **t.** 🍷 3.50 – **4 rm** 🛏 30.00/45.00 **st.** – SB 58.00/64.00 **st.**

BALA Gwynedd 🅓🅓🅓 🅓🅓🅓 J 25 – pop. 1,578 – ECD : Wednesday – ☺ 0678.

See : Site★.

Envir. : SW : Road ★ from Pandy to Dinas Mawddwy.

🎿 Penlan ℰ 520359.

🅹 Snowdonia National Park Visitor Centre, High St. ℰ 520367 (summer only).

♦London 216 – Chester 46 – Dolgellau 18 – Shrewsbury 52.

  🏨 **Palé Hall** 🏊, Llandderfel, LL23 7PS, E : 4 ¾ m. by A 494 on B 4401 ℰ 067 83 (Llandderfel) 285, ≤, 🏤, park – 📠 ☎ 🅿. 🔼 🆎 ⓞ 𝓥𝓘𝓢𝓐
     M 10.00/14.00 **t.** – **17 rm** 🛏 (dinner included) 45.00/90.00 **t.**

  🏨 **White Lion Royal,** High St., LL23 7AE, ℰ 520314 – 🚽wc ☏ 🅿. 🔼 🆎 ⓞ 𝓥𝓘𝓢𝓐
     closed 2 weeks at Christmas – **M** 3.70/7.00 **st.** – **22 rm** 🛏 23.50/30.00 **st.** – SB 43.50/48.00 **st.**

  🏠 **Bala Lake** 🏊, LL23 7BS, SW : 1 ¼ m. by B 4391 on B 4403 ℰ 520344, ≤, 🔼, 🎿 – 🚿wc 🅿. 🔼 𝓥𝓘𝓢𝓐
     M a la carte 6.50/8.00 **st.** 🍷 2.90 – **12 rm** 🛏 18.00/35.00 **st.** – SB (winter only) (not Christmas) 38.00/40.00 **st.**

  🏠 **Plas Teg,** 45 Tegid St., LL23 7EW, ℰ 520268, 🏤 – 🅿
     8 rm 🛏 8.25/16.50 **s.**

FORD High St. ℰ 520777   VOLVO High St. ℰ 520210

BALDOCK Herts. **404** T 28 – pop. 6,428 – ECD : Thursday – ✆ 0462.

Envir. : Ashwell (St. Mary's Church★ 14C : Medieval graffiti) NE : 4 ½ m.

◆London 42 – Bedford 20 – ◆Cambridge 21 – Luton 15.

🏨 **Butterfield House** without rest., 4 Hitchin St., SG7 6AE, ✆ 892701, ☞ – 📺 ➟wc ☎ ㄴ 🅿.
◼ 🄰🄴 🆅🅸🆂🄰 ⋙
⌸ 1.75 – **11 rm** 21.50/28.00 **s.**

COLT High St. ✆ 893305

BAMBURGH Northumb. **401** **402** O 17 – pop. 458 – ECD : Wednesday – ✆ 066 84.

See : Castle★★ (12C-18C) *AC*.

🏨 Bamburgh Castle ✆ 378.

◆London 337 – ◆Edinburgh 77 – ◆Newcastle-upon-Tyne 51.

🏨 **Lord Crewe Arms**, Front St., NE69 7BL, ✆ 243 – 📺 ➟wc 🅿
April-October – **M** 4.50/8.50 **t.** 🍷 2.50 – **25 rm** ⌸ 17.50/36.00 **t.** – SB 42.00/48.00 **st.**

🏠 **Sunningdale**, 21-23 Lucker Rd, NE69 7BS, ✆ 334 – ➟wc 🅿
March-October – **18 rm** ⌸ 10.00/24.00.

BAMPTON Oxon. **403** **404** P 28 – pop. 1,889 – ✆ 0993 Bampton Castle.

◆London 75 – ◆Oxford 18 – Swindon 18.

🏠 **University Farm**, Lew, OX8 2AU, NE : 2 m. on A 4095 ✆ 850297, ☞ – ➟wc ⋔wc 🅿. ⋙
closed Christmas and New Year – **6 rm** ⌸ 18.50/26.00 **t.**

BANBURY Oxon. **403** **404** P 27 – pop. 29,387 – ECD : Tuesday – ✆ 0295.

Envir. : Upton House (pictures★★★, porcelain★★) *AC*, NW : 7 m. – East Adderbury (St. Mary's Church : corbels★) SE : 3 ½ m. – Broughton Castle (great hall★, white room : 1599 plaster ceiling★★) and St. Mary's Church (memorial tombs★) *AC*, SW : 3 ½ m. – Wroxton (thatched cottages★) NW : 3 m. – Farnborough Hall (interior plasterwork★) *AC*, NW : 6 m.

🏨 Cherwell Edge, Chacombe ✆ 711591, NE : 4 m.

🛈 8 Horsefair ✆ 59855.

◆London 76 – ◆Birmingham 40 – ◆Coventry 25 – ◆Oxford 23.

🏨 **Whately Hall** (T.H.F.), Horsefair, by Banbury Cross, OX16 0AN, ✆ 3451, Telex 837149, « Part 17C hall », ☞ – 🛗 📺 🅿. ♨. ◼ 🄰🄴 🄾 🆅🅸🆂🄰
M 7.50/9.25 **st.** 🍷 4.00 – ⌸ 5.50 – **72 rm** 36.00/43.50 **st.**

🏨 **Lismore**, 61 Oxford Rd, OX16 9AJ, ✆ 62105, ☞ – 📺 ➟wc 🅿. ◼ 🆅🅸🆂🄰. ⋙
M *(closed Sunday)* (dinner only) 7.25 **st.** 🍷 3.00 – **14 rm** ⌸ 16.00/32.00 **st.** – SB (weekends only) (except July-September) 34.00 **st.**

🏨 **White Lion**, 64 High St., OX16 8JW, ✆ 4358 – 📺 ⋔. ◼ 🄰🄴 🄾 🆅🅸🆂🄰
M 5.50/9.00 **st.** 🍷 2.75 – **15 rm** ⌸ 24.00/33.00 **st.** – SB (weekends only) 44.00/48.00 **st.**

🏠 **Tredis**, 15 Broughton Rd, OX16 9QB, ✆ 4632, ☞
6 rm ⌸ 9.00/16.00 **st.**

  at Bloxham SW : 4 ¼ m. on A 361 – ✉ ✆ 0295 Banbury :

🏨 **Olde School**, Church St., OX15 4ET, ✆ 720369 – 📺 ➟wc ⋔wc 🅿. ♨. ◼ 🄰🄴 🄾 🆅🅸🆂🄰
M 6.70/8.70 **t.** 🍷 2.50 – ⌸ 3.50 – **16 rm** 18.00/31.00 **t.** – SB (weekends only) 44.00/52.00 **st.**

  at Wroxton NW : 3 m. by A 41 on A 422 – ✉ Banbury – ✆ 029 573 Wroxton St. Mary :

🏨 Wroxton House, Silver St., OX15 6PZ, ✆ 482, Telex 837921, ☞ – 📺 ➟wc ⋔wc ☜ 🅿
15 rm.

AUSTIN-ROVER Southam Rd ✆ 51551
CITROEN, VAUXHALL-OPEL 8 Middleton Rd ✆ 3551
FIAT Hook Norton ✆ 0608 (Hook Norton) 737641
FIAT, SAAB 21-27 Broad St. ✆ 50733
FORD 98 Warwick Rd ✆ 67711
PEUGEOT, TALBOT Thorpe Rd, Middleton Cheney ✆ 710325

PEUGEOT-TALBOT Southam Rd ✆ 53511
RENAULT 9/16 Southam Rd ✆ 50141
VOLVO Main Rd, Middleton Cheney ✆ 710233
VW, AUDI George St. ✆ 65432

BANGOR Gwynedd **402** **403** H 24 – pop. 14,558 – ECD : Wednesday – ✆ 0248.

Envir. : Bethesda (slate quarries★) SE : 5 m. – Nant Francon Pass★★ SE : 9 m.

🏨 Penlan ✆ 0248 (Llanfairfechan) 680144, 7 m. off A 55.

🛈 Garth Rd ✆ 52786 (summer only) – Town Hall ✆ 2463 (Easter-September).

◆London 247 – Birkenhead 68 – Holyhead 23 – Shrewsbury 83.

🏨 **Ty-Uchaf,** Tal-y-Bont, LL57 3UR, SE : 2 m. on A 55 ✆ 352219 – 📺 ➟wc ⋔wc ☜ 🅿. ◼ 🆅🅸🆂🄰 ⋙
M (bar lunch Monday to Saturday) 7.50 **t.** 🍷 2.50 – **10 rm** ⌸ 15.00/26.00 **t.**

BANSTEAD Surrey 404 T 30 – pop. 45,052 – ECD : Wednesday – ⊠ Tadworth – ☎ 073 73 Burgh Heath.

🖫 Sandy Lane, Kingswood, Tadworth ✆ 0737 (Mogador) 832188, S : 3 m.

♦London 17 – ♦Brighton 39.

 🏨 **Pickard Motor** (Best Western) without rest., Brighton Road, KT20 6BW, S : 1 ½ m. on A 217 ✆ 53355, Telex 929908 – 📺 ⌷wc ☎ 🅿 ⚠ ◪ ⒜ ⓪ 𝗩𝗜𝗦𝗔
 ⊠ 3.00 – **44 rm** 31.00/47.00 t.

BARFORD ST. MARTIN Wilts. 403 404 O 30 – see Salisbury.

BAR HILL Cambs. 404 U 27 – see Cambridge.

BARKSTON Lincs. 402 404 S 25 – see Grantham.

BARMOUTH (ABERMAW) Gwynedd 402 403 H 25 – pop. 2,150 – ECD : Wednesday – ☎ 0341.
See : Site★★ – Panorama walk★★.

🛈 The Old Library ✆ 280787 (summer only).

♦London 231 – Chester 74 – Dolgellau 10 – Shrewsbury 67.

 🏠 **Ty'r Craig Castle,** Llanaber Rd, LL42 1YN, on A 496 ✆ 280470, ≼ – 📺 ⌷wc ⌷wc 🅿 ◪ 𝗩𝗜𝗦𝗔
 April-October – **M** 6.00 t. 🛈 2.95 – **12 rm** ⊠ 14.50/30.00 t. – SB (spring and autumn only) 35.00 st.

 🍴 **Marwyn,** 21 Marine Par., LL42 1NA, ✆ 280185 – 📺 ⌷wc ⌷wc ☎ ◪ 𝗩𝗜𝗦𝗔 ✿
 closed December-January – **M** (closed Thursday lunch) 4.50/7.50 st. 🛈 3.25 – **7 rm**
 ⊠ 13.50/29.00 st. – SB 35.00/38.00 st.

 ↟ **Bryn Melyn** ⌷, Panorama Rd, LL42 1DQ, ✆ 280556, ≼ Mawddach estuary and mountains – ⌷wc 🅿 ◪
 23 March-2 November – **9 rm** ⊠ 15.00/25.00 st.

AUSTIN-ROVER, DAIMLER-JAGUAR Park Rd ✆ COLT ✆ 034 17 (Dyffryn) 279 280449

BARNARD CASTLE Durham 402 O 20 – pop. 5,270 – ECD : Thursday – ☎ 0833 Teesdale.
See : Bowes Museum★★ AC – Castle★ (ruins 12C-14C).
Envir. : Raby Castle★ (14C) AC, NE : 6 m.

🖫 Harmire Rd ✆ 37237.

🛈 43 Galgate ✆ 38481.

♦London 258 – ♦Carlisle 63 – ♦Leeds 68 – ♦Middlesbrough 31 – ♦Newcastle-upon-Tyne 39.

 🏨 **Kings Head,** 14 Market Pl., DL12 8ND, ✆ 38356 – 📺 ⌷wc ☎ 🅿 ◪ ⒜ 𝗩𝗜𝗦𝗔 ✿
 M (bar lunch) 7.50 t. 🛈 2.70 – **19 rm** ⊠ 24.00/33.00 t. – SB (summer only) 43.00 st.

 🍴🍴 **Blagraves House,** 30-32 The Bank, DL12 8PN, ✆ 37668 – ⒜ 𝗩𝗜𝗦𝗔
 closed Sunday and Monday – **M** (dinner only) a la carte 5.50/9.25 t. 🛈 2.50.

FORD, AUSTIN-ROVER 19 Galgate ✆ 37129   VAUXHALL Newgate ✆ 38352

BARNBY MOOR Notts. 402 403 404 Q 23 – pop. 280 – ⊠ ☎ 0777 Retford.

♦London 151 – ♦Leeds 44 – Lincoln 27 – ♦Nottingham 31.

 🏨 **Ye Olde Bell** (T.H.F.), DN22 8QS, ✆ 705121, ☞ – 📺 ⌷wc ☞ 🅿 ◪ ⒜ ◪ ⒜ ⓪ 𝗩𝗜𝗦𝗔
 M 5.95/9.25 st. 🛈 2.60 – ⊠ 5.00 – **55 rm** 28.50/40.00 st.

BARNHAM BROOM Norfolk 404 X 26 – pop. 518 – ⊠ Norwich – ☎ 060 545.

🖫 Barnham Broom Hotel ✆ 393.

♦London 109 – East Dereham 10 – ♦Norwich 10.

 🏨 **Barnham Broom** (Best Western), NR9 4DD, NE : 1 m. ✆ 393, Telex 975568, ≼, ◪, 🖫, ⌷,
 ✿, squash – 📺 ⌷wc ☎ & 🅿 ⚠ ◪ ⒜ ⓪ 𝗩𝗜𝗦𝗔
 M (carving lunch) 8.50 st. 🛈 3.25 – **35 rm** ⊠ 35.00/45.00 st. – SB 53.00/56.00 st.

BARNSDALE BAR West Yorks. 402 404 Q 23 – see Wentbridge.

BARNSLEY South Yorks. 402 404 P 23 – pop. 75,395 – ECD : Thursday – ☎ 0226.

🖫 Wakefield Rd, Staincross ✆ 382856, N : 4 m.

🛈 Civic Hall, Eldon St. ✆ 6757.

♦London 177 – ♦Leeds 21 – ♦Manchester 36 – ♦Sheffield 15.

 🏨 **Queens,** Regent St., S70 2HQ, ✆ 84192 – 📺 ⌷wc ☞ ⚠ ◪ ⒜ ⓪ 𝗩𝗜𝗦𝗔
 M (grill rest. only) approx. 10.00 st. 🛈 2.65 – **37 rm** ⊠ 32.50/40.00 st. – SB (week-ends only) 37.00 st.

 🏠 **Royal,** Church St., S70 2AD, ✆ 203658 – 📺 ⚠ ◪ ⒜ ⓪
 M 5.15/10.05 t. 🛈 2.50 – **17 rm** ⊠ 21.00/35.00 t. – SB (weekends only) 30.00 t.

74

at Ardsley E : 2 ½ m. on A 635 – ⊠ ✆ 0226 Barnsley :

🏨 **Ardsley House** (Best Western), Doncaster Rd, S71 5EH, ✆ 89401, Telex 547762, 🐎 – 📺 🅿 🏛 ᴷ 🅰🄴 ① 𝐕𝐈𝐒𝐀
M 7.00/8.50 t. 🍷 2.40 – ☲ 5.00 – **62 rm** 28.00/38.00 **st.** – SB (weekends only) 44.00 **st.**

AUSTIN-ROVER Claycliff Rd, Barkgreen ✆ 299891
CITROEN The Cross, Silkstone ✆ 790636
FORD Dodworth Rd ✆ 5741
HONDA Doncaster Rd ✆ 87417
LADA Wakefield Rd ✆ 43228

RENAULT Doncaster Rd ✆ 291554
TALBOT, FIAT, PEUGEOT Stairfoot ✆ 6675
VAUXHALL-OPEL New St. ✆ 89181
VW, AUDI Huddersfield Rd ✆ 299494

BARNSTAPLE Devon �403 H 30 **The West Country** G. – pop. 17,317 – ECD : Wednesday – ✆ 0271.

See : Site★★ – The Long Bridge★ – **Envir. :** Arlington Court★★, NE : 8 m. on A 39.

🎫 Holland St. ✆ 72742.

♦London 222 – Exeter 40 – Taunton 51.

🏨 **Imperial** (T.H.F.), Taw Vale Par., EX32 8NB, ✆ 45861 – 📶 📺 ⌂wc 🐎 🅿 🏛 ᴷ 🅰🄴 ① 𝐕𝐈𝐒𝐀
M (bar lunch Monday to Saturday) 8.75 **st.** 🍷 2.60 – ☲ 5.00 – **56 rm** 29.50/40.00 **st.**

🏨 **Royal and Fortescue,** Boutport St., EX31 1HG, ✆ 42289, Telex 42551 – 📶 📺 ⌂wc 🅿 🅺
🄰🄴 ① 𝐕𝐈𝐒𝐀
M 4.00/5.75 **s.** 🍷 2.50 – **61 rm** ☲ 14.50/18.50 **s.** – SB 40.40 **st.**

🏨 **North Devon Motel,** Taw Vale, EX32 8NJ, ✆ 72166 – 📺 ⌂wc 🐎 🅿 🏛 – **26 rm**.

🍴🍴 **Lynwood House,** Bishops Tawton Rd, EX32 9DZ, on A 377 ✆ 43695, Seafood – 🅿 🅺 🅰🄴
① 𝐕𝐈𝐒𝐀
closed Saturday lunch and Sunday – **M** a la carte 7.05/16.70 **t.** 🍷 2.75.

at Bishop's Tawton S : 2 m. on A 377 – ⊠ ✆ 0271 Barnstaple :

🏨 **Downrew House** ⚓, EX32 0DY, SE : 1 ½ m. on Chittlehampton Rd ✆ 42497, ≤, « Country
house atmosphere », 🛱 heated, 🞈 park, 🞐 – 📺 ⌂wc 🅿 🞀
Late March-October – **M** (bar lunch)(residents only) 11.50 🍷 2.20 – **14 rm** ☲ (dinner included)
30.50/73.70 **t.** – SB 54.05/65.80 **st.**

AUSTIN-ROVER-DAIMLER-JAGUAR Boutport St. ✆
73232
BMW Abbey Rd ✆ 74070
DAIHATSU Newport Rd ✆ 45363

FIAT, TOYOTA, VOLVO Pottington Industrial Estate,
Pillandway ✆ 76551
FORD New Rd ✆ 74173
VAUXHALL-OPEL 42 Boutport St. ✆ 74366

BARRY (BARRI) South Glam. �403 K 29 – pop. 41,681 – ECD : Wednesday – ✆ 0446.

🏌 Brynhill, Port Rd, Colcot ✆ 735061.

🎫 Barry Island ✆ 747171 (summer only).

♦London 167 – ♦Cardiff 10 – ♦Swansea 39.

🏨 **Water's Edge,** The Knap, CF6 8YY, ✆ 733392, ≤ – 📶 📺 ⌂wc 🐎 🅿 🞀
32 rm

🏨 **Mount Sorrel,** Porthkerry Rd, CF6 8AY, ✆ 740069 – 📺 ⌂wc 🍴wc 🐎 🅿 🅺 🅰🄴 ① 𝐕𝐈𝐒𝐀 🞀
M 4.25/8.00 **t.** 🍷 2.25 – **37 rm** ☲ 25.00/32.50 **t.** – SB (weekends only) 35.00/37.50 **st.**

AUSTIN-ROVER-DAIMLER-JAGUAR Brook St. ✆ 734365

BARTON Lancs. �402 L 22 – pop. 2,010 – ⊠ Preston – ✆ 0772 Broughton.

♦London 228 – ♦Blackpool 18 – Lancaster 16 – Preston 4.5.

🏨 **Barton Grange** (Best Western), Garstang Rd, PR3 5AA, ✆ 862551, Telex 67392, 🖼, 🐎, 🞐
– 📶 📺 ⌂wc 🍴wc ☎ 🅿 🏛 🅺 🅰🄴 ① 𝐕𝐈𝐒𝐀 🞀
M (bar lunch Monday to Saturday) 5.50/7.50 **st.** 🍷 2.65 – **65 rm** ☲ 20.00/38.00 **st.** – SB
44.00/47.00 **st.**

BARTON ON SEA Hants. �403 �404 P 31 – pop. 3,590 – ✆ 0425 New Milton.

♦London 101 – Bournemouth 11 – ♦Southampton 23.

↰ **Gainsborough,** 39 Marine Drive East, BH25 7DX, ✆ 610541, ≤ – 🅿
9 rm ☲ 13.50/28.00 **st.**

BARWICK Somerset �403 �404 M 31 – see Yeovil.

BASFORD Staffs. – see Stoke-on-Trent.

BASILDON Essex �404 V 29 – pop. 88,000 – ECD : Wednesday – ✆ 0268.

🏌 Kingswood ✆ 3297.

♦London 30 – Chelmsford 17 – Southend-on-Sea 13.

🏨 **Crest** (Crest), Cranes Farm Rd, SS14 3DG, NW : 2 ¼ m. by A 176 off A 1235 ✆ 3955, Telex
995141 – 📶 📺 ⌂wc 🐎 🅿 🏛 🅺 🅰🄴 ① 𝐕𝐈𝐒𝐀 🞀
M approx. 11.00 **st.** – ☲ 4.95 – **116 rm** 42.00/52.00 **st.**

AUSTIN-ROVER Southern Hay ✆ 22661
FORD Cherrydown ✆ 22741

NISSAN Nethermayne ✆ 22261
VAUXHALL-OPEL High Rd, Laindon ✆ 42481

BASINGSTOKE Hants. 403 404 Q 30 – pop. 52,587 – ☎ 0256.

Bishopswood, Bishopswood Lane ☎ 073 56 (Tadley) 5213, N : 6 m. off A 340 Z.

•London 55 – Reading 17 – •Southampton 31 – Winchester 18.

BASINGSTOKE

London Street . . . . Y 19
Upper Church Street . . . . Y 24
Winchester Street . . . . Y 27

Aldermaston Road . . . . Z 2
Beaconsfield Road . . . . Y 3
Buckland Avenue . . . . Z 5
Chequers Road . . . . Y 6
Church Street . . . . Y 7
Churchill Way East . . . . Z 9
Churchill Way West . . . . Z 10
Council Road . . . . Y 12
Cross Street . . . . Y 13
Fairfields Road . . . . Y 14
Houndmills Road . . . . Z 17
New Street . . . . Y 20
Reading Road . . . . Z 22
Southern Ringway . . . . Z 23
Victoria Street . . . . Y 25
Wote Street . . . . Y 28

North is at the top on all town plans.

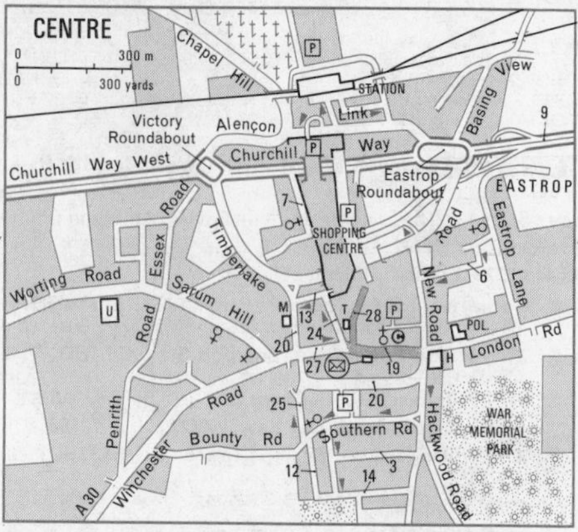

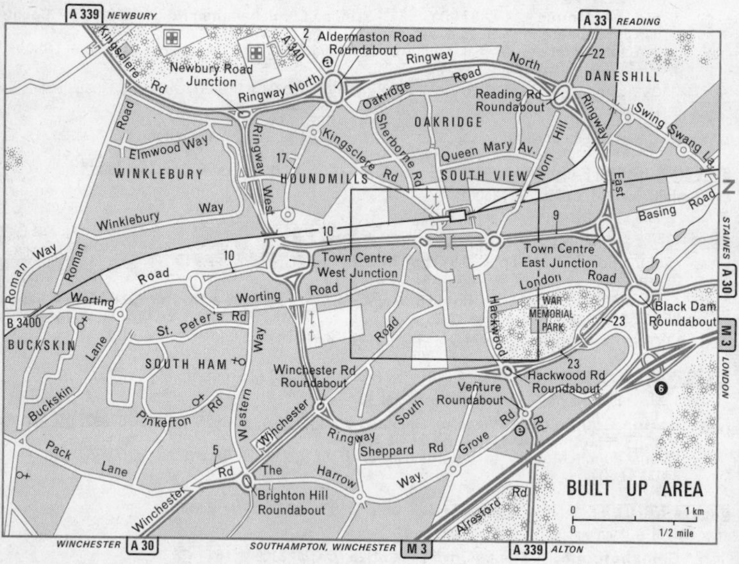

Crest (Crest), Grove Rd, RG21 3EE, SW : 1 m. junction A 339 and A 30 ☎ 468181, Telex 858501 – TV wc ☎ P. AE VISA — Z e
M approx. 11.00 **st.** – 4.75 – **86 rm** 45.75/54.50 **st.**

Ladbroke (Ladbroke), Aldermaston Roundabout, Ringway North, RG24 9NV, N : 2 m. junction A 339 and A 340 ☎ 20212, Telex 858223 – TV wc ☎ P. AE VISA — Z a
M *(closed Saturday lunch)* 8.50/10.50 **st.** 5.95 – 5.50 – **108 rm** 42.00/48.00 **st.** – SB (weekends only) 49.00 **st.**

Red Lion (Anchor) 24 London St., RG21 1NY, ☎ 28525, Telex 859504 – TV wc wc ☎ P. AE VISA — Y c
M (carving lunch) 8.65 **st.** 2.65 – **63 rm** 40.00/47.00 **st.** – SB (weekends only) 45.00 **st.**

at Oakley W : 5 m. on B 3400 – Z – ✉ ☎ 0256 Basingstoke :

Beach Arms, Andover Rd, RG23 7EP, on B 3400 ☎ 780210, – TV wc ☎ P. AE VISA
M (bar lunch Saturday) 7.50 **st.** – **17 rm** 36.00/45.00 **st.**

AUDI, VW London Rd 🖋 24444
AUSTIN-ROVER-DAIMLER Houndmills 🖋 65991
AUSTIN-ROVER-JAGUAR New Rd 🖋 24561
BEDFORD, VAUXHALL-OPEL West Ham 🖋 62551

FIAT, LANCIA, ALFA-ROMEO London Rd 🖋 55221
FORD Lower Wote St. 🖋 3561
TALBOT Eastdrop Roundabout 🖋 65454
VOLVO London Rd 🖋 66111

BASLOW Derbs. **402 403 404** P 24 – pop. 1,166 (inc. Bubnell) – ECD : Wednesday – ⊠ Bakewell – 🟊 024 688.

♦London 161 – Derby 27 – ♦Manchester 35 – ♦Sheffield 13.

🏨 **Cavendish,** DE4 1SP, on A 619 🖋 2311, Telex 547150, ≼, « Tasteful decor », 🦢, 🍽 – 📺
🛁wc ☎ 🅿. 🅰🅴 ⓪ 𝑉𝐼𝑆𝐴 🚲
M a la carte 13.40/22.75 t. – ☐ 4.80 – **23 rm** 37.50/47.50 t.

BASSENTHWAITE Cumbria **401 402** K 19 – pop. 518 – 🟊 059 681 Bassenthwaite Lake.

♦London 300 – ♦Carlisle 24 – Keswick 7.

🏨 **Armathwaite Hall** 🦢, CA12 4RE, W : 1 ½ m. on B 5291 ⊠ Keswick 🖋 551, ≼ Bassenthwaite Lake, « Stately home in extensive grounds », 🏊, 🦢, 🍽, park, 🚲, squash – 🛗 📺 ☎ 🡒
🅿. 🅰 🅰🅴 ⓪ 𝑉𝐼𝑆𝐴
April-December – **M** 7.25/11.50 t. – **37 rm** ☐ 27.00/64.00 t.

🏨 **Castle Inn,** CA12 4RG, W : 1 m. at junction A 591 and B 5291 ⊠ Keswick 🖋 401, ≼,
🏊 heated, 🍽, 🚲 – 📺 🛁wc ☎ 🅟 🅿. 🅰 🅰🅴 ⓪ 𝑉𝐼𝑆𝐴
closed 14 to 19 November and 4 days at Christmas – **M** 6.50/9.50 **st.** 🝙 3.00 – **20 rm**
☐ 20.00/45.00 **st.** – SB (weekends only)(except August-October) 60.00 **st.**

🏨 **Pheasant Inn,** CA13 9YE, SW : 3 ¼ m. by B 5291 off A 66 ⊠ Cockermouth 🖋 234, « 16C
inn », 🍽 – 🛁wc 🅿. 🚲
closed Christmas Day – **M** 5.00/9.50 **st.** 🝙 2.40 – **20 rm** ☐ 21.00/44.00 **st.** – SB (winter only) 46.00/56.00 **st.**

🏨 **Overwater Hall** 🦢, CA5 1HH, NE : 2 ¼ m. on Uldale Rd ⊠ Ireby 🖋 566, ≼, 🍽, park – 📺
🛁wc 🅿. 🅰 𝑉𝐼𝑆𝐴
closed 1 January-22 February – **M** (dinner only) 9.50 t. 🝙 2.60 – **13 rm** ☐ 18.00/30.00 t. – SB (except summer) 38.00/42.00 **st.**

*Es ist empfehlenswert, **in der Hauptsaison** und vor allem*
in Urlaubsorten, Hotelzimmer im voraus zu bestellen.
Benachrichtigen Sie sofort das Hotel, wenn Sie ein bestelltes
Zimmer nicht belegen können.
Wenn Sie an ein Hotel im Ausland schreiben, fügen Sie Ihrem Brief
einen internationalen Antwortschein bei (im Postamt erhältlich).

BATH Avon **403 404** M 29 The West Country G. – pop. 84,670 – ECD : Monday and Thursday – 🟊 0225.

See : The Georgian city★★★ : Royal Crescent★★★ (N° 1 Royal Crescent★★) V – Circus★★★ V – Museum of costume★★★ V **M2** – Roman Baths★★ (Pump Room★) X D – Holburne of Menstrie Museum★★ V **M1** – Pulteney Bridge★ X – Assembly Rooms★ V **M2** – Bath Abbey★ X B – Camden Works Museum★ V **M4** – Bath Carriage Museum★ V **M5**.

Envir. : Lansdown Crescent★★ (Somerset Place★) Y – at Claverton, E : 2 ½ m. Z American Museum★★ - Claverton Pump★ – Camden Crescent★ V – Beckford Tower and Museum (prospect★) Y **M6** – Dyrham Park★, N : 8 m. by A 46 Y.

🖌₈, 🖌 Tracy Park, Bath Rd, Wick 🖋 027 582 (Abson) 2251, N : 5 m. by Lansdown Rd Y – 🖌 Lansdown 🖋 25007, NW : 3 m. by Lansdown Rd Y.

🖪 Abbey Churchyard 🖋 62831/60521.

♦London 119 – ♦Bristol 13 – ♦Southampton 63 – Taunton 49.

Plan on next page

🏨 **The Priory,** Weston Rd, BA1 2XT, 🖋 331922, Telex 44612, ≼, 🏊 heated, 🍽 – 📺 🦢 ☎ 🅿. 🅰
🅰🅴 𝑉𝐼𝑆𝐴 🚲   Y c
closed first 3 weeks January – **M** (buffet lunch Monday to Saturday) 14.50/21.00 **s.** 🝙 3.35 – ☐ 4.00 – **15 rm** 37.50/77.00 **s.** – SB (winter only) 97.00/104.00 **st.**

🏨 **Royal Crescent,** 16 Royal Crescent, BA1 2LS, 🖋 319090, Telex 444251, ≼, « Tastefully restored Georgian town houses », 🍽 – 🛗 📺 ☎ 🅿. 🅰 🅰🅴 ⓪ 𝑉𝐼𝑆𝐴   V u
M 19.00/22.50 **st.** 🝙 4.25 – ☐ 8.00 – **35 rm** 58.00/250.00 **st.** – SB (not weekends) 125.00 **st.**

🏨 **Francis** (T.H.F.), Queen Sq., BA1 2HH, 🖋 24257, Telex 449162 – 🛗 📺 🛗 🅿. 🦢. 🅰 🅰🅴 ⓪
𝑉𝐼𝑆𝐴   X o
M 7.75/10.95 **st.** 🝙 2.60 – ☐ 5.50 – **90 rm** 42.00/52.50 **st.**

🏨 **Ladbroke Beaufort** (Ladbroke), Walcot St., BA1 5BJ, 🖋 63411, Telex 449519 – 🛗 📺 🅿.
🦢. 🅰 🅰🅴 ⓪ 𝑉𝐼𝑆𝐴 🚲   V i
M 7.00/9.00 t. 🝙 3.50 – ☐ 5.50 – **123 rm** 40.00/55.00 t. – SB 48.00 **st.**

77

BATH

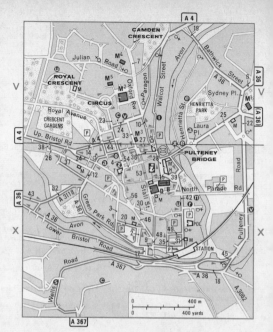

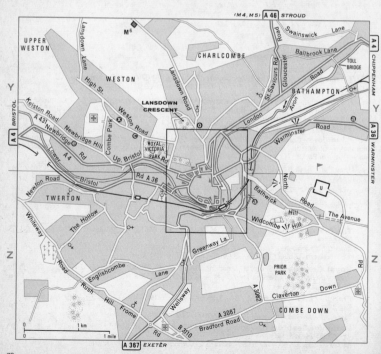

🏨 **Lansdown Grove** (Best Western), Lansdown Rd, BA1 5EH, ℘ 315891, ⚗ – 🛎 📺 🛏wc 🅿 🏫 ▨ 🅰🅴 ⓘ 𝘝𝘐𝘚𝘈
    M 5.50/8.75 t. ▯ 2.65 – **43 rm** � 33.00/52.00 t. – SB (weekends only) 53.00/60.00 **st.**
    Y **o**

🏨 **Redcar,** 27 Henrietta St., BA2 6LR, ℘ 65432 – 📺 🛏wc ☜ 🅿 🏫 ▨ 🅰🅴 ⓘ 𝘝𝘐𝘚𝘈
    M approx. 5.95 t. ▯ 3.70 – **31 rm** ⊏ 24.50/49.00 t. – SB (weekends only) 56.00/60.00 **st.**
    V **a**

🏨 **Pratt's,** South Par., BA2 4AB, ℘ 60441, Telex 47439 – 🛎 📺 🛏wc ☜. 🏫 ▨ 🅰🅴 ⓘ 𝘝𝘐𝘚𝘈
    M (bar lunch Monday to Saturday) 5.25/12.95 **st.** ▯ 3.45 – **46 rm** ⊏ 27.00/42.00 **st.** – SB
    52.00/56.00 **st.**
    X **r**

🏨 **Gainsborough** without rest., Weston Lane, BA1 4AB, ℘ 311380, ⚗ – 📺 🛏wc 🏮wc ☜ 🅿
    ▨ 🅰🅴 𝘝𝘐𝘚𝘈. ⌘
    closed 2 weeks at Christmas – **14 rm** ⊏ 17.00/38.00 t.
    Y **x**

🏨 **Apsley House,** 141 Newbridge Hill, BA1 3PT, ℘ 336966, ⚗ – 📺 🛏wc ☜ 🅿 ▨ 🅰🅴 ⓘ
    𝘝𝘐𝘚𝘈
    M (closed Sunday lunch) (buffet lunch) a la carte 12.95/17.45 **st.** ▯ 3.50 – **7 rm** ⊏ 50.00/68.00 **st.**
    – SB (winter only) 70.00/80.00 **st.**
    Y **e**

🏨 **Number Nine,** 9 Miles Building, George St., BA1 2QS, ℘ 25462 – 📺 🛏wc 🏮wc ☎. 🅰🅴 ⓘ
    𝘝𝘐𝘚𝘈. ⌘
    closed Christmas-mid January – **M** (closed Sunday and Monday) (dinner only) a la carte
    6.40/11.35 t. – **8 rm** ⊏ 25.35/50.00 t. – SB (except Sunday and Monday) (not summer)
    45.00 **st.**
    V **c**

🏨 **Villa Magdala** without rest., Henrietta Rd, BA2 6LX, ℘ 66329, ⚗ – 📺 🛏wc 🏮wc 🅿. ⌘
    closed 15 December-30 January – **17 rm** ⊏ 18.00/35.00 **st.**
    V **e**

🏨 **Paradise House** without rest., 86-88 Holloway, BA2 4PX, ℘ 317723, ≤, ⚗ – 📺 🛏wc. ▨
    𝘝𝘐𝘚𝘈. ⌘
    closed 15 December-15 January – **9 rm** ⊏ 18.00/34.00 **st.**
    X **c**

🏨 **Oldfields** without rest., 102 Wells Rd, BA2 3AL, ℘ 317984, ⚗ – 📺 🏮wc 🅿 ▨ 𝘝𝘐𝘚𝘈. ⌘
    closed 15 December-15 January – **14 rm** ⊏ 14.00/32.50 **st.**
    X **s**

🏨 **North Parade,** 10 North Par., BA2 4AL, ℘ 60007 – 📺 🏮. ▨ 🅰🅴 ⓘ 𝘝𝘐𝘚𝘈
    closed Christmas – **M** (dinner only) 5.65 t. – **17 rm** ⊏ 12.25/35.00 **st.**
    X **n**

⌂ **Holly Villa,** 14 Pulteney Gdns, BA2 4HG, ℘ 310331, ⚗ – ⌘
    5 rm ⊏ 12.00/24.00 t.
    Z **a**

⌂ Lynwood, 6 Pulteney Gdns., BA2 4HG, ℘ 26410 – 📺 🏮
    14 rm
    X **v**

XXX **Popjoy's,** Beau Nash's House, Sawclose, BA1 1EU, ℘ 60494, « Former residence of Beau
    Nash » – ▨ 🅰🅴 ⓘ 𝘝𝘐𝘚𝘈
    closed Sunday, Monday and Bank Holidays – **M** (dinner only) a la carte approx. 11.50 t.
    ▯ 2.70.
    X **z**

XX **The Hole in the Wall** with rm, 16 George St., BA1 2EN, ℘ 25242, « Converted Georgian
    kitchen and coal hole » – 📺 🛏wc ☜. ▨ 🅰🅴 ⓘ 𝘝𝘐𝘚𝘈
    closed 3 weeks after Christmas – **M** (closed Sunday) 17.50 **st.** ▯ 3.00 – ⊏ 2.50 – **8 rm**
    28.00/60.00 **st.**
    V **v**

XX **Rajpoot,** 4 Argyle St., BA2 4BE, ℘ 66833, Indian rest. – ▨ 🅰🅴 ⓘ 𝘝𝘐𝘚𝘈
    closed Monday in winter and Christmas – **M** a la carte 10.25/11.40 t. ▯ 3.10.
    VX **e**

X **Flowers,** 27 Monmouth St, BA1 2AP, ℘ 313774 – ▨ 🅰🅴 ⓘ 𝘝𝘐𝘚𝘈
    closed Saturday lunch, Sunday, Monday, 1 week Easter, 3 weeks August and 3 weeks
    Christmas-New Year – **M** 6.50/11.00 t. ▯ 2.50.
    X **a**

X **Ainslie's,** 12 Pierrepont St., BA1 1LA, ℘ 61745, Bistro – ▨ 🅰🅴 ⓘ 𝘝𝘐𝘚𝘈
    closed Sunday lunch – **M** (bar lunch) a la carte 9.10/11.55 t. ▯ 2.20.
    X **u**

X **Eastern Eye,** 11 Argyle St., BA2 4BQ, ℘ 22323, Indian rest. – ▨ 🅰🅴 ⓘ 𝘝𝘐𝘚𝘈
    M a la carte approx. 8.00 t. ▯ 2.70.
    VX **x**

    at Bathampton E : 2 ½ m. on A 36 – ✉ ☎ 0225 Bath :

🏨 **Orchard House,** Warminster Rd, BA2 6XG, E : 2 ½ m. on A 36 ℘ 66115 – 📺 🛏wc 🅿. ▨
    🅰🅴 ⓘ 𝘝𝘐𝘚𝘈. ⌘
    M (dinner only) 7.00 **st.** ▯ 2.50 – **14 rm** ⊏ 25.00/34.00 **st.** – SB (summer only) 40.00/48.00 **st.**
    Y **a**

    at Bathford E : 3 ½ m. by A 4 off A 363 – Y – ☎ ☎ 0225 Bath :

⌂ **Eagle House,** Church St., BA1 7RS, ℘ 859946, « Georgian house », ⚗ – 📺 🛏wc
    closed 17 February- 4 March – ⊏ 1.65 – **6 rm** 20.00/32.00 **st.**

    at Freshford S : 7 ½ m. on A 36 – Y – ✉ Bath – ☎ 022 122 Limpley Stoke :

XXX **Homewood Park** ⌘ with rm, Hinton Charterhouse, BA1 6BB, on A 36 ℘ 2643, ≤, « Taste-
    fully converted country house », ⚗, park, ⚘ – 📺 🛏wc ☜ 🅿. ▨ 🅰🅴 ⓘ 𝘝𝘐𝘚𝘈. ⌘
    closed 24 December-17 January – **M** a la carte 12.00/16.00 **st.** ▯ 3.50 – ⊏ 3.50 – **15 rm**
    50.00/69.00 **st.** – SB (not weekends) (November-March) 75.00 **st.**

    P.T.O. →

  at Woolverton S : 10 m. on A 36 – Y – ⊠ Bath – ☻ 0373 Frome :

🏠 **Woolverton House,** BA3 6QS, ℰ 830415, 🛥 – 📺 🚿wc 🅿. 🔊 🎗E 𝗩𝗜𝗦𝗔
  closed January and February – **M** *(closed Sunday)* (dinner only) 11.50 **t.** 🍷 2.60 – ⊠ 3.00 –
  8 rm 25.00/36.00 **t.** – SB 25.00/33.00 **st.**

  at Hunstrete W : 8 ½ m. by A 4 – Y – and A 39 off A 368 – ⊠ Pensford – ☻ 076 18
  Compton Dando :

🏰 **Hunstrete House** 🌭, BS18 4NS, ℰ 578, Telex 449540, ≼, « Country house atmosphere
  and gardens », 🏊 heated, park, 🎾 – 📺 ☎ 🅿. 🔊 🎗E ⓄE 𝗩𝗜𝗦𝗔. 🎗
  M (buffet lunch Monday to Saturday) 12.00/20.00 **s.** – ⊠ 3.50 – **20 rm** 48.00/100.00 **s.**

AUSTIN-ROVER-DAIMLER-JAGUAR   Newbridge Rd   FORD 5/10 James St. West ℰ 61636
ℰ 312774   NISSAN Lower Bristol Rd ℰ 25864
BMW Wellsway ℰ 29187   VAUXHALL, BEDFORD Rush Hill ℰ 833338
CITROEN, DAIHATSU Prior Park Rd ℰ 29552   VAUXHALL Upper Bristol Rd ℰ 22131
FIAT, ALFA ROMEO Margarets Buildings, Circus Pl.   VOLVO Bathwick Hill ℰ 65814
ℰ 27328

BATTISBOROUGH CROSS Devon – see Newton Ferrers.

BATTLE East Sussex 404 V 31 – pop. 4,987 – ☻ 042 46.

See : Abbey★ (11C-14C) *AC* (site of the Battle of Hastings 1066).
🛈 88 High St. ℰ 3721.
♦London 55 – ♦Brighton 34 – Folkestone 43 – Maidstone 30.

🏰 **Netherfield Place Country House** 🌭, TN3 3PP, NW : 1 ¾ m. by A 2100 on Netherfield
  Rd ℰ 4455, ≼, « Gardens », park – 📺 🚿wc 🅿. 🔊 🎗E 𝗩𝗜𝗦𝗔. 🎗
  closed last week January and first 2 weeks February – **M** 13.50 **t.** 🍷 3.50 – **12 rm**
  ⊠ 30.00/65.00 **st.**

🏠 **George,** 23 High St., TN33 0EA, ℰ 4466 – 📺 🚿wc 🐾 🅿. 🔊 🎗E ⓄE 𝗩𝗜𝗦𝗔
  M 5.95 **st.** 🍷 3.95 – ⊠ 1.95 – **22 rm** 19.75/28.50 **st.** – SB (weekends only) 38.50 **st.**

XX **Boxers,** 31 Mount St., TN33 0EG, ℰ 2132 – 🅿. 🔊 🎗E ⓄE 𝗩𝗜𝗦𝗔
  closed Sunday dinner, Monday, Tuesday and 2 to 31 January – **M** (dinner only and Sunday
  lunch) 6.50/11.50 **t.** 🍷 2.75.

X **Blacksmiths,** 43 High St., TN33 0EE, ℰ 3200 – 🔊
  closed Monday except Bank Holiday lunch, 2 weeks October and 26-27 December – **M** a la
  carte 9.80/13.30 **t.** 🍷 3.25.

AUSTIN-ROVER High St. ℰ 2425   FORD Upper Lake ℰ 3155
CITROEN Ninfield ℰ 0424 (Ninfield) 892278   RELIANT, SKODA ℰ 0424 (Ninfield) 892286
CITROEN Whatlington ℰ 042 487 (Sedlescombe)   VAUXHALL-OPEL Battle Hill ℰ 2286
307

BAWTRY South Yorks. 402 403 404 Q 23 – pop. 1,497 – ⊠ ☻ 0302 Doncaster.

🏕 Austerfield, Low Common Lane ℰ 710850, NE : 2 m. off A 614.
♦London 158 – ♦Leeds 39 – Lincoln 32 – ♦Nottingham 36 – ♦Sheffield 22.

🏠 **Crown** (Anchor), High St., DN10 6JW, ℰ 710341, Telex 547089, 🛥 – 📺 🚿wc 🐾 🅿. 🏌. 🔊
  🎗E ⓄE 𝗩𝗜𝗦𝗔
  M (bar lunch Saturday) a la carte 7.50/12.00 **st.** 🍷 2.65 – **57 rm** ⊠ 35.00/42.00 **st.** – SB (week-
  ends only) 48.00 **st.**

BAYCLIFF Cumbria 402 K 21 – pop. 150 – ⊠ Ulverston – ☻ 022 988 Bardsea.

♦ London 284 – Kendal 30 – Lancaster 44.

🏠 **Fisherman's Arms,** Coast Rd, LA12 9RJ, ℰ 387 – 🚿wc 🅿. 🔊 🎗E 𝗩𝗜𝗦𝗔
  M a la carte 5.50/9.80 **t.** 🍷 3.00 – **12 rm** ⊠ 17.50/35.00 **t.**

BEACONSFIELD Bucks. 404 S 29 – pop. 12,640 – ECD : Wednesday and Saturday – ☻ 049 46.

♦London 26 – Aylesbury 19 – ♦Oxford 32.

🏰 **Bellhouse** (De Vere), Oxford Rd, HP9 2XE, E : 1 ¾ m. on A 40 ℰ 0753 (Gerrard's
  Cross) 887211, Telex 848719 – 🍴 📺 🚿wc 🅿. 🏌. 🔊 🎗E ⓄE 𝗩𝗜𝗦𝗔
  M 7.75/8.25 **st.** 🍷 3.10 – ⊠ 4.50 – **126 rm** 40.00/44.50 **st.** – SB (weekends only) 51.00 **st.**

🏨 **Crest** (Crest), Aylesbury End, HP9 1LW, ℰ 71211 – 📺 🚿wc 🐾 🅿. 🔊 🎗E ⓄE 𝗩𝗜𝗦𝗔
  M approx. 11.00 **st.** – ⊠ 4.95 – **39 rm** 30.00/52.00 **st.**

XX **Santella,** 43 Aylesbury End, HP9 1LV, ℰ 6806, Italian rest. – 🔊 🎗E ⓄE 𝗩𝗜𝗦𝗔
  closed Sunday, last 3 weeks August and Bank Holidays – **M** a la carte 11.05/14.75 **t.** 🍷 2.50.

XX **La Lanterna,** 57 Wycombe End, HP9 1LX, ℰ 5210, Italian rest. – 🎗E ⓄE 𝗩𝗜𝗦𝗔
  M a la carte 7.95/16.00 **t.** 🍷 3.25.

HONDA Penn Rd ℰ 5272   VAUXHALL-OPEL Penn Rd, Knotty Green ℰ 3730
MERCEDES-BENZ, TOYOTA 55 Station Rd ℰ 2141

BEADLAM North Yorks. – see Helmsley.

BEAMINSTER Dorset 403 L 31 The West Country G. – pop. 2,346 – ECD : Wednesday – ✆ 0308.

♦London 149 – Dorchester 19 – Exeter 40 – Taunton 31.

✗ **Nevitt's Eating House,** 57 Hogshill St., DT8 3AA, ✆ 862600
   M *(closed Sunday dinner and Monday except Bank Holidays)* (dinner only and Sunday lunch)
   a la carte 8.50/11.50 **t.** ⌖ 2.50.

BEAULIEU Hants. 403 404 P 31 – pop. 1,083 – ECD : Tuesday and Saturday – ⌧ Brockenhurst
– ✆ 0590.

See : Beaulieu Abbey* (ruins 13C) : Palace House* 14C, National Motor Museum**, Buckler's
Hard Maritime Museum *AC*.

🛈 John Montagu Building ✆ 612345.

♦London 102 – Bournemouth 24 – ♦Southampton 13 – Winchester 23.

🏛 **Montagu Arms,** Palace Lane, SO4 7ZL, ✆ 612324, « Part 18C inn », 🚗 – 📺 🅿 🔦 🅰🅴 ⓪
   𝑉𝐼𝑆𝐴
   M 8.75/17.75 **st.** ⌖ 2.95 – **26 rm** 🚮 28.50/56.50 **st.** – SB 47.50/67.50 **st.**

   at Bucklers Hard S : 2 ½ m. – ⌧ Brockenhurst – ✆ 059 063 Bucklers Hard :

🏛 Master Builder's House, SO4 7XB, ✆ 253, ≼, 🚗 – 📺 ⌁wc 🕭 🅿 🛁 – **23 rm**.

BEAUMARIS Gwynedd 402 403 H 24 – pop. 2,102 – ECD : Wednesday – ✆ 0248.

See : Castle* (13C) *AC*.

Envir. : Menai Strait* (Channel, Menai Suspension Bridge ≼* SW : 4 ½ m. – Bryn Celli Du (burial
chamber*) SW : 8 m.

🛈 Baron Hill ✆ 810231, NW : 1 m.

♦London 253 – Birkenhead 74 – Holyhead 25.

🏛 **Bulkeley Arms,** 19 Castle St., LL58 8AW, ✆ 810415, ≼ Menai Strait, 🚗 – 📳 📺 ⌁wc 🅿.
   🔦 🅰🅴 ⓪ 𝑉𝐼𝑆𝐴
   M 6.25/9.25 **t.** ⌖ 2.50 – **41 rm** 🚮 14.00/35.00 **t.** – SB 39.50/65.00 **st.**

🏛 **Bishopsgate House,** 54 Castle St., LL58 8AB, ✆ 810302 – 📺 🔦⌁wc 🅿. 🔦 𝑉𝐼𝑆𝐴
   April-October – **M** *(closed Sunday lunch)* 4.50/12.00 **t.** ⌖ 2.50 – **11 rm** 🚮 12.50/27.00 **t.**

✗ **Hobson's Choice,** 13 Castle St., LL58 8AP, ✆ 810323 – 🔦 𝑉𝐼𝑆𝐴
   closed Sunday – **M** a la carte 7.80/13.55 **t.** ⌖ 2.25.

BECCLES Suffolk 404 Y 26 – pop. 8,015 – ECD : Wednesday – ✆ 0502.

♦London 113 – Great Yarmouth 15 – ♦Ipswich 40 – ♦Norwich 18.

🏛 **Waveney House,** Puddingmoor, NR34 9PL, ✆ 712270 – 📺 ⌁wc 🔦wc 🚗 🅿. 🔦 🅰🅴 ⓪
   𝑉𝐼𝑆𝐴
   M 7.00 **t.** ⌖ 3.70 – **13 rm** 🚮 25.00/41.00 **t.** – SB 48.50 **st.**

✗ St. Peter's House with rm, Old Market, NR34 9AF, ✆ 713203, 🚗 – ✗ – **3 rm**.

AUSTIN-ROVER Beccles Rd. Barnby ✆ 050 276   VAUXHALL-OPEL Station Rd ✆ 712268
(Barnby) 204

BECKERMET Cumbria 402 J 20 – ECD : Tuesday and Thursday – ⌧ ✆ 094 684.

♦London 326 – ♦Carlisle 45 – Kendal 62 – Workington 17.

🏛 **Royal Oak** without rest., CA21 2XB, ✆ 551 – 📺 ⌁wc 🕭 🅿
   8 rm 🚮 17.50/36.00 **st.** – SB (weekends only) 36.00/38.00 **st.**

BEDDGELERT Gwynedd 402 403 H 24 – pop. 671 – ECD : Wednesday – ✆ 076 686.

Envir. : NE : Llyn Dinas valley** – Llyn Gwynant valley*.

Exc. : Blaenau Ffestiniog (site : slate quarries*) E : 14 m. by Penrhyndeudraeth.

♦London 249 – Caernarfon 13 – Chester 73.

🏛 **Royal Goat,** LL55 4YE, ✆ 224 – ⌁wc 🕭 🅿. 🔦 🅰🅴 ⓪ 𝑉𝐼𝑆𝐴. ✗
   M (bar lunch) 10.00 **st.** ⌖ 2.75 – **25 rm** 🚮 20.00/40.00 **st.**

🏚 **Tanronen,** LL55 4YB, ✆ 347 – 🅿. 🔦 𝑉𝐼𝑆𝐴
   M (bar lunch Monday to Saturday) 4.50/6.75 **st.** ⌖ 2.30 – **8 rm** 🚮 11.50/23.00 **st.** – SB 34.00 **st.**

BEDFORD Beds. 404 S 27 – pop. 73,229 – ECD : Thursday – ✆ 0234.

See : Embankment* – Cecil Higgins Art Gallery (porcelain* 18C).

Envir. : Elstow (Abbey Church* 11C, Moot Hall : John Bunyan Museum *AC*) S : 1 ¼ m. – Ampthill
(Houghton House : site*, ≼*) S : 5 m. – Old Warden (St. Leonard's Church : woodwork* –
Aeroplane Museum, near Biggleswade Aerodrome : the Shuttleworth collection* *AC*) SE : 7 ½ m.

🛈 Mowsbury, Kimbolton Rd ✆ 771042, N : 3 m.

🛈 10 St. Paul's Sq. ✆ 215226.

♦London 59 – ♦Cambridge 31 – Colchester 70 – ♦Leicester 51 – Lincoln 95 – Luton 20 – ♦Oxford 52 – Southend-
on-Sea 87.

🏨 **Bedford Swan** (Mt. Charlotte), The Embankment, MK40 1RW, ℰ 46565 – 📺 ⇔wc ☎ ℗.
🦽 📶 AE ⓞ VISA.
M 6.75 st. ⓘ 2.45 – **84 rm** ⇌ 32.50/41.50 st. – SB (weekends only) 42.00 **st.**

🏨 **De Parys**, 41 de Parys Av., MK40 2UA, ℰ 52121, 🌫 – 📺 ⇔wc 🍴wc ℗. 🦽 📶 AE ⓞ VISA.
🧩
closed 10 days Christmas – **M** (bar lunch) 7.95 **st.** ⓘ 3.00 – **33 rm** ⇌ 23.00/40.00 st. – SB
(weekends only) 44.00/48.00 **st.**

🏨 **Shakespeare**, 27 Shakespeare Rd, MK40 2DX, ℰ 213147 – 📺 ⇔wc 🍴wc ℗. 📶 AE ⓞ VISA.
M *(closed Saturday lunch)* – **16 rm** ⇌ 22.00/38.50 t.

🛏 **Edwardian House,** 15 Shakespeare Rd, MK40 2DZ, ℰ 45281 – 📺 ⇔wc 🍴wc ℗. AE ⓞ
closed Christmas – **17 rm** ⇌ 16.50/39.50 **st.**

at Houghton Conquest S : 6 ½ m. by A 6 – ✉ ✆ 0234 Bedford :

XX **Knife and Cleaver**, MK45 3LA, ℰ 740387 – ℗. 📶 VISA
closed Saturday lunch, Sunday and Bank Holidays – **M** a la carte 10.70/12.50 **t.** ⓘ 3.00.

at Turvey W : 7 m. on A 428 – ✉ Bedford – ✆ 023 064 Turvey :

XX **Laws** with rm, MK43 8DB, ℰ 213, 🌫 – 📺 ⇔wc ℗. 📶 VISA. 🧩
closed Sunday and 1 week at Christmas – **M** *(closed Monday and Saturday lunch)* a la carte
10.15/13.45 **t.** – **5 rm** ⇌ 29.50/40.00 **st.**

at Clapham NW : 2 m. on A 6 – ✉ ✆ 0234 Bedford :

🏨 **Woodlands Manor**, Green Lane, MK41 6EP, ℰ 63281, Telex 825007, 🌫 – 📺 ☎ ℗. 🦽 📶
AE VISA. 🧩
closed first 2 weeks August and 1 week at Christmas – **M** *(closed lunch Saturday and Bank
Holidays)* 12.50 **t.** ⓘ 4.40 – **21 rm** ⇌ 43.00/61.00 **t.** – SB (weekends only) 54.50 **st.**

MICHELIN Branch, Hammond Rd, Elms Farm Industrial Estate, MK41 0LG, ℰ 213491

AUDI, MERCEDES-BENZ, VAUXHALL Barker's Lane ℰ 50011	FORD 8/10 The Broadway ℰ 58391
	FORD Hudson Rd ℰ 40041
AUSTIN-ROVER-DAIMLER-JAGUAR 120 Golding-ton Rd ℰ 55221	HONDA, VOLVO Windsor Rd ℰ 45454
	NISSAN 180 Goldington Rd ℰ 60121
BMW, ROLLS ROYCE-BENTLEY Shuttleworth Rd, Goldington ℰ 60412	RENAULT 87 High St., Clapham ℰ 54257
	SAAB Station Rd, Oakley ℰ 023 02 (Oakley) 3118

BEESTON Cheshire 402 403 404 L 24 – pop. 221 – ✉ Tarporley – ✆ 0829 Bunbury.
♦London 186 – Chester 15 – ♦Liverpool 40 – Shrewsbury 32.

XXX **Wild Boar Inn** (Embassy) with rm, CW6 9NW, on A 49 ℰ 260309, Telex 61455, 🌫 – 📺
⇔wc ℗. 🦽 📶 AE ⓞ VISA. 🧩
closed 27 to 31 December – **M** a la carte 12.00/20.05 **st.** ⓘ 4.55 – ⇌ 4.25 – **30 rm** 29.25/40.50 **st.**
– SB (weekends only) 42.00/58.00 **st.**

XXX Rembrandt, Whitchurch Road, Spurstow, CW6 9TD, on A 49 ℰ 260281 – ℗.

BEESTON Notts. 402 403 404 Q 25 – see Nottingham.

BELBROUGHTON Heref. and Worc. 403 404 N 26 – see Stourbridge (West Midlands).

BELFORD Northumb. 401 402 O 17 – pop. 960 – ECD : Thursday – ✆ 066 83.
♦London 335 – ♦Edinburgh 71 – ♦Newcastle-upon-Tyne 49.

🏨 **Blue Bell** (Swallow), Market Pl., NE70 7NE, ℰ 543, Group Telex 53168, 🌫 – 📺 ⇔wc ☎ ℗
15 rm.

BELPER Derbs. 402 403 404 P 24 – pop. 24,723 – ✉ ✆ 077 382.
♦London 141 – Derby 8 – ♦Manchester 55 – ♦Nottingham 17.

XX **Remy's**, 84 Bridge St., DE5 1AZ, ℰ 2246, French rest. – AE ⓞ
closed Sunday, Monday, 1 week Easter, 3 weeks August, 2 weeks Christmas and Bank Holidays
– **M** (lunch by arrangement) 9.75 **st.** ⓘ 3.00.

BEMBRIDGE I.O.W. 403 404 Q 31 – see Wight (Isle of).

BENLLECH Gwynedd 402 403 H 24 – pop. 2,554 – ECD : Thursday – ✆ 0248 Tynygongl.
♦London 258 – Caernarfon 17 – Chester 70 – Holyhead 22.

🏨 **Rhostrefor**, Amlwch Rd, LL74 8SR, on A 5025 ℰ 852347, 🌫 – ⇔wc 🍴wc ℗. 📶
M (bar lunch Monday to Friday) 6.00/15.00 **t.** ⓘ 2.60 – **15 rm** ⇌ 13.00/26.00 **st.** – SB (week-ends only) 33.00/46.00 **st.**

BEPTON West Sussex – see Midhurst.

BERKHAMSTED Herts 404 S 28 – pop. 15,539 – ECD : Wednesday and Saturday – ✪ 044 27.

◆London 33 – Luton 16 – ◆Oxford 35.

🏠 **Hamberlin's** 🐾 without rest., Tring Rd, Northchurch, HP4 3TL, NW : 1 ½ m. on A 41 ☞ 75100, ☞ – 📺wc 🅿. 🔼 ⓞ 𝘝𝘐𝘚𝘈
16 rm ☲ 22.00/35.00 t.

BERWICK-UPON-TWEED Northumb. 401 402 O 16 – pop. 11,647 – ECD : Thursday – ✪ 0289.
See : City Walls★ 16C.

Envir. : Norham Castle★ (12C) SW : 7 m..

🔼₈ Goswick, Beal ☞ 87256, S : 5 m. – 🔼₈ Magdalene Fields ☞ 5109.

🔁 Castlegate Car Park ☞ 307187 (summer only).

◆London 349 – ◆Edinburgh 57 – ◆Newcastle-upon-Tyne 63.

🏨 **Turret House,** Etal Rd, TD15 2EG, S : ¾ m. by A 1 on B 6354 ☞ 307344, ☞ – 📺wc ☎ 🅿. 🔼 🅰🅴 ⓞ 𝘝𝘐𝘚𝘈
M 4.75/9.75 st. ¼ 3.25 – **10 rm** ☲ 23.00/39.00 st. – SB 45.00/50.00 st.

🏠 **King's Arms,** 43 Hide Hill, TD15 1EJ, ☞ 307454, Telex 8811232, ☞ – 📺 📺wc 📺wc ☎. 🔼 🅰🅴 ⓞ 𝘝𝘐𝘚𝘈
M (bar lunch) 4.50/9.50 st. ¼ 2.95 – **30 rm** ☲ 26.00/43.00 st. – SB (weekends only) (not summer) 44.00 st.

AUSTIN-ROVER Tweedside Trading Estate ☞ 307561
RENAULT Golden Sq. ☞ 307371

VAUXHALL 12 Silver St. ☞ 307436
VOLVO Tweed St. ☞ 307537
VW, AUDI Spittal ☞ 307214

BETWS-Y-COED Gwynedd 402 403 I 24 – pop. 729 – ECD : Thursday – ✪ 069 02.
Envir. : Fairy Glen and Conway Falls★ AC, SE : 2 m. – Swallow Falls★ AC, NW : 2 m. – Nanty-gwryd valley★ W : by Capel Curig.

🔼₉ ☞ 556, ½ m. off A 5.

🔁 ☞ 426 (summer only).

◆London 226 – Holyhead 44 – Shrewsbury 62.

🏨 **Royal Oak (Best Western),** Holyhead Rd, LL24 0AY, ☞ 219 – 📺 📺wc ☎ 🅿. 🔼 🅰🅴 ⓞ 𝘝𝘐𝘚𝘈. 🍴
closed 3 days at Christmas – **21 rm** ☲ 30.00/37.00 st. – SB 47.00/50.00 st.

🏠 **Waterloo,** LL24 0AR, on A 5 ☞ 411 – 📺 📺wc ☎ 🅿. 🔼 🅰🅴 ⓞ 𝘝𝘐𝘚𝘈. 🍴
closed Christmas – **M** a la carte 8.95/12.60 t. ¼ 2.80 – **28 rm** ☲ 19.50/36.00 t.

🏠 **Craig-y-Dderwen** 🐾, LL24 0AS, SE : ¼ m. on A 5 ☞ 293, ≼, 🐾, ☞ – 📺 📺wc 🅿. 🔼 ⓞ 𝘝𝘐𝘚𝘈
M 5.00/7.50 t. ¼ 3.00 – **21 rm** ☲ 13.50/36.00 t.

↑ **Park Hill,** Llanrwst Rd, LL24 0HD, NE : 1 m. by A 5 on A 470 ☞ 540, ≼ Vale of Conwy, 🔼, ☞ – 📺wc 📺wc 🅿. 🔼 🅰🅴 ⓞ 𝘝𝘐𝘚𝘈
closed January and first 2 weeks October – **11 rm** ☲ 14.00/34.00 t.

↑ **Henllys (Old Court),** LL24 0AL, ☞ 534, « Converted courthouse and jail », ☞ – 📺 📺wc 📺wc 🅿
10 rm ☲ 10.75/31.00 st.

↑ **Fairy Glen,** Dolgellau Rd, LL24 0SH, S : 1 m. on A 470 ☞ 269 – 📺wc 🅿. 🅰🅴
10 rm ☲ 12.00/16.00 st.

at Pont-y-Pant SW : 4 ½ m. on A 470 – ✉ ✪ 069 06 Dolwyddelan :

🏨 **Plas Hall,** LL25 0PJ, ☞ 206, 🐾, ☞ – 📺 📺wc ☎ 👶 🅿. 🔼 🅰🅴 ⓞ 𝘝𝘐𝘚𝘈. 🍴
M 5.95/7.95 st. ¼ 3.00 – **16 rm** ☲ 23.00/46.00 st. – SB (except summer) 42.00/45.00 st.

BEVERLEY Humberside 402 S 22 – pop. 17,132 – ECD : Thursday – ✉ ✪ 0482 Kingston-upon-Hull.
See : Minster★★ 13C-15C – St. Mary's Church★ 14C-15C.

🔼₈ Walkington Rd ☞ 867190.

🔁 30 Market Pl. ☞ 867430.

◆London 188 – ◆Kingston-upon-Hull 8 – ◆Leeds 52 – York 29.

🏨 **Beverley Arms (T.H.F.),** North Bar Within, HU17 8DD, ☞ 869241, Telex 527568 – 🛗 🚻 📺 📺wc ☎ 🅿. 🔼 🅰🅴 ⓞ 𝘝𝘐𝘚𝘈
M 6.50/8.15 st. ¼ 2.60 – ☲ 5.50 – **61 rm** 35.00/45.50 st.

🏠 **Lairgate,** 30 Lairgate, HU17 8EP, ☞ 882141 – 📺 📺wc 📺wc ☎ 🅿. 🔼 𝘝𝘐𝘚𝘈
M 5.50/8.50 t. ¼ 2.50 – **20 rm** ☲ 20.00/34.50 t. – SB (weekends only) (winter only) 24.00/27.00 st.

🏛 King's Head, Market Pl., HH17 9AH, ☞ 868103 – 🅿 – **9 rm**.

at Tickton NE : 3 ½ m. by A 1035 – ✉ Kingston-upon-Hull – ✪ 0401 Leven :

🏨 **Tickton Grange,** HU17 9SH, ☞ 43666, ☞ – 📺 📺wc 📺wc ☎ 🅿. 🔼 🅰🅴 𝘝𝘐𝘚𝘈
M a la carte 8.15/14.85 t. ¼ 3.95 – ☲ 4.25 – **12 rm** ☲ 32.50/43.00 t.

AUSTIN-ROVER 20 Norwood ☞ 867922
FORD Wednesday Market ☞ 868311

VAUXHALL-OPEL Swinemoor Lane ☞ 882207
VOLVO North Bar Within ☞ 881208

BEWDLEY Heref. and Worc. 403 404 N 26 – pop. 7,237 – ECD : Wednesday – ☎ 0299.
🖪 The Library, Load St. ☏ 403303.
♦London 140 – ♦Birmingham 20 – Worcester 16.

🏠 **Black Boy,** Kidderminster Rd, DY12 1AG, ☏ 402119, 🍴 – 📺 🛏wc 🏧 🅿. 🔄 🖭 𝘝𝘐𝘚𝘈
M 4.95/7.25 t. 🍷 3.00 – **25 rm** ☲ 14.50/36.00 t. – SB (weekends only) 35.50/45.00 t.

BEXHILL East Sussex 404 V 31 – pop. 32,898 – ECD : Wednesday – ☎ 0424.
🔟 Cooden Beach ☏ 042 43 (Cooden) 2040.
🖪 De La Warr Pavilion, Marina ☏ 212023.
♦London 66 – ♦ Brighton 32 – Folkestone 42.

🏨 Cooden Beach (Best Western), Cooden Sea Rd, Cooden Beach, TN39 4TT, W : 2 m. on B 2182 ☏ 04243 (Cooden) 2281, Telex 95489, 🏊 heated, 🍴 – 📺 ☎ 🚗 🅿. 🛁. ❄
33 rm

AUDI, VW King Offa Way ☏ 212255
AUSTIN-ROVER-DAIMLER-JAGUAR   Cooden Beach ☏ 2224
AUSTIN-ROVER-DAIMLER-JAGUAR   57-69 London Rd ☏ 212000
FIAT, MAZDA Holliers Hill ☏ 213577

FORD ☏ 212727
HONDA Sackville Rd ☏ 221330
RENAULT London Rd ☏ 210485
TOYOTA Holliers Hill ☏ 213577
VAUXHALL-OPEL Dorset Rd ☏ 211212

BIBURY Glos. 403 404 O 28 – pop. 599 – ECD : Wednesday – ✉ Cirencester – ☎ 028 574.
See : Arlington Row★ 17C.
♦London 86 – Gloucester 26 – ♦Oxford 30.

🏨 **Swan,** GL7 5NW, ☏ 204, « Garden and trout stream », 🍴 – 📺 🛏wc ☎ 🅿. 🔄 𝘝𝘐𝘚𝘈
M 8.75/12.50 t. 🍷 2.50 – **23 rm** ☲ 27.50/47.50 t. – SB 65.00/75.00 st.

BIDDENDEN Kent 404 V 30 – pop. 2,154 – ✉ Ashford – ☎ 0580.
♦London 51 – Folkestone 29 – Hastings 23 – Maidstone 14.

XX **Ye Maydes,** 13-15 High St., TN27 8AL, ☏ 291306 – 🔄
closed Sunday, Monday, 1 week January, 2 weeks August and 1 week October – **M** a la carte 9.10/12.65 t. 🍷 2.80.

XX **West House,** 28 High St., TN27 8AH, ☏ 291341, Italian rest. – 🅿. 🔄 𝘝𝘐𝘚𝘈
closed Sunday, Monday, 1 week April, 2 weeks August and Bank Holidays – **M** a la carte 8.70/13.30 st. 🍷 4.00.

BIDEFORD Devon 403 H 30 The West Country G. – pop. 11,802 – ECD : Wednesday – ☎ 023 72.
See : The Bridge★★ – Burton Art Gallery★.
Envir. : Clovelly★★, W : 11 m. – Great Torrington : Dartington Glass★, SE : 7 m.
🖪 The Quay ☏ 77676 (summer only).
♦London 231 – Exeter 43 – ♦Plymouth 58 – Taunton 60.

🏨 **Durrant House,** Heywood Rd, Northam, EX39 3QB, N : 1 m. on A 386 ☏ 2361, 🏊 heated –
📺 🛏wc ☎ 🅿. 🔄 🖭 ① 𝘝𝘐𝘚𝘈
M 8.25 t. 🍷 2.80 – **52 rm** ☲ 27.50/39.50 t. – SB (weekends only) (winter only) 23.50 st.

🏨 **Yeoldon House** (Best Western) 🐾, Durrant Lane, Northam, EX39 2RL, N : 1 ½ m. by A 386 ☏ 4400, ≤ Torridge estuary, « Country house atmosphere », 🍴 – 📺 🛏wc 🏧wc 🅿. 🔄 🖭 ① 𝘝𝘐𝘚𝘈. ❄
closed 24 December-10 January – **M** (bar lunch) 11.00 st. 🍷 2.90 – **10 rm** ☲ 27.75/48.50 st. – SB (winter only) 45.00/67.50 st.

🏠 **Beaconside House** 🐾, Landcross, EX39 5JL, S : 3 m. by A 386 on A 388 ☏ 77205, ≤, 🏊, 🍴, park, ❄ – 📺 🛏wc 🅿. 🔄 ①. ❄
M (bar lunch Monday to Saturday) 6.50/8.00 st. 🍷 2.20 – **9 rm** ☲ 18.10/34.50 t. – SB 40.00/46.00 st

🏠 **Riversford** 🐾, Limers Lane, Northam, EX39 2RG, N : 1 m. by A 386 ☏ 74239, ≤, 🍴 – 📺 🛏wc 🅿. 🖭 ① 𝘝𝘐𝘚𝘈
closed December and January – **M** (bar lunch Monday to Saturday) 4.70/7.60 st. 🍷 4.75 – **18 rm** ☲ 13.70/37.80 t. – SB (weekends only) 40.50/45.80 st.

⌂ **Rosskerry,** Orchard Hill, EX39 2QY, N : ¾ m. by A 386 ☏ 2872, 🍴 – 🛏wc 🅿. 🔄 🖭 𝘝𝘐𝘚𝘈
10 rm ☲ 9.75/22.50 st.

XX **Gray's,** 4 Fore St., Northam, EX39 1AW, N : 1 ¾ m. by A 386 ☏ 6371 – 🔄 𝘝𝘐𝘚𝘈
closed Sunday, Monday and first 2 weeks October – **M** (dinner only)(booking essential) 11.50 t. 🍷 3.40.

at Instow N : 3 m. on A 39 – ✉ Bideford – ☎ 0271 Instow :

🏨 **Commodore,** Marine Par., EX39 4JN, ☏ 860347, ≤ Taw and Torridge estuaries, 🍴 – 📺 🅿. 🛁. 🔄 🖭 𝘝𝘐𝘚𝘈. ❄
closed Christmas Day – **M** 6.85/9.50 t. 🍷 3.15 – **21 rm** ☲ 27.50/49.50 t.

AUSTIN-ROVER 6 Queen St. ☏ 3304
PEUGEOT-TALBOT Bridgeland St. ☏ 2016
RENAULT Kingsley Rd ☏ 2546

SAAB Meddon St. ☏ 2467
VAUXHALL-OPEL, BEDFORD Handy Cross ☏ 2282

BIDFORD-ON-AVON Warw. 403 404 O 27 – pop. 2,822 – ECD : Thursday – ✉ Alcester – ☎ 0789.

♦London 103 – ♦Birmingham 25 – ♦Coventry 27 – ♦Oxford 50 – Worcester 22.

　🏠 **White Lion,** High St., B50 4BQ, ✆ 773309 – 📺 ⊪wc 🅿 . ◪ 🖃. 🛇
　M (bar lunch)/12.10 **t.** ⓘ 3.00 – ⊊ 1.50 – **15 rm** 17.00/40.00 **t.** – SB 42.00/46.00 **t.**

BIGBURY-ON-SEA Devon 403 I 33 – ✉ Kingsbridge – ☎ 054 881.

♦London 196 – Exeter 42 – ♦Plymouth 17.

　🏠 **Henley,** Folly Hill, TQ7 4AR, ✆ 240, ≤, 🞴 – ⊟wc 🅿
　Mid May-September – **M** (bar lunch)(residents only) 7.00 **st.** ⓘ 2.00 – **9 rm** ⊊ (dinner included) 16.00/36.00 **st.**

BILBROOK Somerset 403 J 30 – pop. 100 – ✉ Minehead – ☎ 0984 Washford.

♦London 181 – Minehead 5 – Taunton 19.

　🏠 Dragon House, TA24 6HQ, ✆ 40215, « Part 18C house with gardens » – 📺 ⊟wc ⊪wc 🅿
　11 rm.

　🏠 **Bilbrook Lawns,** TA24 6HE, ✆ 40331, 🞴 – 📺 ⊟wc 🅿
　M (bar lunch) 8.50 **st.** ⓘ 2.75 – **13 rm** ⊊ 15.00/30.00 **st.**

BILLESLEY Warw. – see Stratford-upon-Avon.

BILLINGHAM Cleveland 402 Q 20 – pop. 38,107 – ✉ ☎ 0642 Stockton-on-Tees.

🏌 Sandy Lane ✆ 554494.

♦London 255 – ♦Middlesbrough 3 – Sunderland 26.

　🏠 Billingham Arms Thistle (Thistle), Town Sq., TS23 2HD, ✆ 553661, Group Telex 587746 – 📺
　⊟wc ⊪wc 🕾 🅿 . 🏂. ◪ 🖃. 🛇
　⊊ 4.75 – **63 rm** 29.00/48.00 **t.** – SB (weekends only) 44.00 **st.**

AUSTIN-ROVER　Wolviston Rd ✆ 553959
FORD　The Green ✆ 550415
RENAULT　Central Garage ✆ 553071

BILLINGSHURST West Sussex 404 S 30 – pop. 4,421 – ECD : Wednesday – ☎ 040 381.

♦London 44 – ♦Brighton 30 – Guildford 20 – ♦Portsmouth 40.

　✕✕ **The Jennie Wren,** Pulborough Rd, RH14 9EU, S : ½ m. on A 29 ✆ 2571 – 🅿 . ◪ 🖃 ⓞ 🖃
　closed Saturday lunch, Sunday, Monday and 2 weeks February – **M** a la carte 7.95/12.50 **t.**
　ⓘ 3.00.

AUSTIN-ROVER-JAGUAR-LAND-ROVER　62 High St.
✆ 2022
FORD　High St. ✆ 2537
MERCEDES-BENZ, PORSCHE, SCIMITAR　High St.
✆ 3341
PEUGEOT-TALBOT　Five Oaks ✆ 2075

BINGLEY West Yorks. 402 O 22 – pop. 20,420 – ECD : Tuesday – ✉ ☎ 0274 Bradford.

♦London 204 – Bradford 6 – Skipton 13.

　🏠 **Bankfield (Embassy),** Bradford Rd, BD16 1TV, SE : 1 ½ m. on A 650 ✆ 567123, 🞴 – 📺
　⊟wc ⊪wc 🕾 🅿 . 🏂. ◪ 🖃 ⓞ 🖃. 🛇
　M (carving rest.) 7.50 **st.** ⓘ 4.50 – ⊊ 4.25 – **69 rm** 33.00/50.00 **st.** – SB (week-
　ends only) 45.00/52.00 **st.**

　at Cullingworth SW : 3 ½ m. on B 6429 – ✉ ☎ 0274 Bradford :

　🏠 Five Flags, Manywell Heights, BD13 5EA, SW : 1 m. by B 6429 on A 629 ✆ 834188 – 📺 ⊟wc
　🕾 🅿 – **26 rm**.

SCIMITAR　Park Rd ✆ 563556

BIRKENHEAD Merseyside 402 403 K 23 – pop. 137,852 – ECD : Thursday – ☎ 051 Liverpool.

🏌 Arrowe Park, Woodchurch ✆ 677 1527 – 🏌 Prenton, Golf Links Rd ✆ 608 1461.

🚢 to Liverpool (Merseyside Transport) frequent services daily (7-8 mn).

🛈 Central Library, Borough Rd ✆ 652 6106/7/8.

♦London 213 – ♦Liverpool 2.

Plan : see Liverpool p. 3

　🏠 **Bowler Hat,** 2 Talbot Rd, Oxton, L43 2HH, ✆ 652 4931, 🞴 – 📺 🅿 . 🏂. ◪ 🖃 ⓞ 🖃
　M 6.95/10.75 **st.** ⓘ 2.75 – ⊊ 5.55 – **29 rm** 38.50/49.00 **st.**
　　AX

ALFA-ROMEO　Watermound ✆ 630 1844
AUSTIN-ROVER　Park Rd North ✆ 647 9445
COLT　New Chester Rd ✆ 608 9121
FIAT　Claughton Firs ✆ 653 8555
FORD　Ronson St. ✆ 608 9121
LANCIA　Watermound ✆ 638 0046
MAZDA　Albion Rd ✆ 638 2234
NISSAN　Hoylake Rd ✆ 678 1060
RENAULT　Borough Rd ✆ 608 9121
VAUXHALL-OPEL　6 Woodchurch Rd ✆ 652 2366

Do not lose your way in Europe, use the Michelin
Main Road maps, scale : 1 inch : 16 miles.

BIRMINGHAM West Midlands 403 404 O 26 – pop. 1,014,670 – ECD : Wednesday – ✪ 021.

See : Museum and Art Gallery★★ JZ **M1** – Museum of Science and Industry★ JY **M2** – Cathedral (stained glass windows★ 19C) KYZ **E**.

🏌 Cocks Moor Woods, Alcester Rd South, King's Heath ✆ 444 2062, S : 6 ½ m. by A 435 FX – 🏌 Edgbaston, Church Rd ✆ 454 1736, S : 1 m. FX – 🏌 Pype Hayes, Eachelhurst Rd, Walmley ✆ 351 1014, NE : 7 ½ m. DT – 🏌 Warley, Lightwoods Hill, ✆ 429 2440, W : 5 m. BU.

✈ Birmingham Airport : ✆ 743 6227, E : 6 ½ m. by A 45 DU.

🛈 2 City Arcade ✆ 643 2514 – National Exhibition Centre ✆ 780 4141.

♦London 122 – ♦Bristol 91 – ♦Liverpool 102 – ♦Manchester 86 – ♦Nottingham 50.

Town plans : Birmingham pp. 2-7
Except where otherwise stated see pp. 6 and 7

🏛 **Albany** (T.H.F.), Smallbrook, Queensway, B5 4EW, ✆ 643 8171, Telex 337031, ≼, ◨ – 🛗 📺 ☎ ⅃. ⌲. ◨ AE ⑪ VISA
M 6.95/15.00 st. ♪ 3.40 – ⌑ 5.50 – **254 rm** 43.00/52.50 st.
JKZ **a**

🏛 **Plough and Harrow** (Crest), 135 Hagley Rd, Edgbaston, B16 8LS, W : 1 ½ m. on A 456 ✆ 454 4111, Telex 338074, ♨ – 🛗 📺 ☎ ⅃. ◨ AE ⑪ VISA
M approx. 15.00 st. – ⌑ 6.00 – **44 rm** 60.50/72.00 st.
p. 4 EX **a**

🏛 **Holiday Inn**, Central Sq., Holiday St., B1 1HH, ✆ 643 2766, Telex 337272, ≼, ◨ – 🛗 📺 ☎ ⅃. ◨ AE ⑪ VISA
M 7.45/7.95 st. ♪ 2.75 – ⌑ 4.25 – **304 rm** 38.00/43.00 s.
JZ **z**

🏛 **Midland** (Best Western), 128 New St., B2 4JT, ✆ 643 2601, Telex 338419 – 🛗 📺 ⅃. ⌲. ◨ AE ⑪ VISA. ⅏
M 10.50/12.50 st. – **114 rm** ⌑ 21.40/55.00 st. – SB (weekends only) 44.00/60.00 st.
KZ **r**

🏛 **Strathallan Thistle** (Thistle), 225 Hagley Rd, Edgbaston, B16 9RY, W : 2 m. on A 456 ✆ 455 9777, Telex 336680 – 🛗 📺 ☎ ⅃. ⌲. ◨ AE ⑪ VISA. ⅏
M 9.00/12.00 t. ♪ 3.45 – **164 rm** 39.00/48.50 t. – SB (weekends only) 52.00 st.
p. 4 EX **i**

🏛 **Grand** (Q.M.H.), Colmore Row, B3 2DA, ✆ 236 7951, Telex 338174 – 🛗 📺 ⅃. ◨ AE ⑪ VISA
closed 4 days at Christmas – **M** 7.95 st. ♪ 2.95 – **145 rm** ⌑ 42.00/52.00 st. – SB (weekends only) 48.00 st.
JKY **c**

🏛 **Royal Angus Thistle** (Thistle), St. Chad's Queensway, B4 6MY, ✆ 236 4211, Telex 336889 – 🛗 📺 ☎ ⅃. ⌲. ◨ AE ⑪ VISA. ⅏
M 8.75/8.90 t. ♪ 3.45 – ⌑ 4.75 – **139 rm** 36.00/48.50 t. – SB (weekends only) 48.00 st.
KY **s**

🏨 **Apollo**, 243-247 Hagley Rd, Edgbaston, B16 9RA, W : 2 ¼ m. on A 456 ✆ 455 0271, Telex 336759 – 🛗 ▤ rest 📺 ⌷wc ☎ ℗. ⅃. ◨ AE ⑪ VISA
M 9.85/11.25 st. ♪ 3.25 – ⌑ 4.50 – **130 rm** 30.75/41.00 s. – SB (weekends only) 61.70/76.20 st.
p. 4 EX **o**

🏨 **Cobden**, 166-174 Hagley Rd, Edgbaston, B16 9NZ, W : 2 m. on A 456 ✆ 454 6621, Group Telex 339715, ♨ – 🛗 📺 ⌷wc 🍽wc ☎ ℗. ⅃. ◨ VISA
closed Christmas – **M** 4.00/7.00 st. – **210 rm** ⌑ 17.00/38.00 st. – SB (weekends only) 41.70/47.70 st.
p. 4 EX **n**

🏨 **Norfolk**, 257-267 Hagley Rd, Edgbaston, B16 9NA, W : 2 ¼ m. on A 456 ✆ 454 8071, Group Telex 339715, ♨ – 🛗 📺 ⌷wc 🍽wc ☎ ⅃ ℗. ⅃. ◨ VISA
closed Christmas – **M** 4.00/7.00 st. (unlicensed) – **175 rm** ⌑ 16.00/36.00 st. – SB (weekends only) 39.70/44.70 st.
p. 4 EX **u**

🏨 **Berrow Court** ⌗, Berrow Drive off Westfield Rd, Edgbaston, B15 3UD, W : 3 m. by A 456 ✆ 454 1488, ♨ – ℗. AE VISA
closed 24 December-2 January – **M** (closed Saturday and Sunday) (dinner only) 5.80 st. ♪ 2.00 – **16 rm** ⌑ 18.50/28.50 st.
p. 4 EX **e**

🏨 **Asquith House**, 19 Portland Rd, off Hagley Rd, Edgbaston, B16 9HN, W : 2 m. by A 456 ✆ 454 5282, ♨ – 📺 ⌷wc 🍽wc ☎ ℗. ◨
closed Christmas – **M** (booking essential) 10.40/11.05 st. ♪ 2.20 – **10 rm** ⌑ 21.75/38.70 st. – SB (weekends only) 57.40/70.20 st.
p. 4 EX **c**

🏨 **Hagley Court**, 229 Hagley Rd, Edgbaston, B16 9RP, W : 2 m. on A 456 ✆ 454 6514 – 📺 ⌷wc 🍽wc ☎ ℗. ◨ VISA. ⅏
closed Christmas – **M** (closed Friday to Sunday) (dinner only) 6.75 st. ♪ 2.20 – **24 rm** ⌑ 19.00/35.00 st.
p. 4 EX **b**

XX **Sloans** ⌗, Chad Sq., off Harborne Rd, Edgbaston, B15 3TQ, ✆ 455 6697, Seafood – ◨ AE ⑪ VISA
closed Saturday lunch, Sunday and Bank Holidays – **M** a la carte 11.00/23.10 t.
p. 4 EX **v**

XX **Rajdoot**, 12-22 Albert St., B4 7UD, ✆ 643 8805, Indian rest. – ◨ AE ⑪ VISA
closed Sunday lunch and 25-26 December – **M** a la carte 8.80/13.30 t. ♪ 2.40.
KZ **c**

XX **Jonathans'**, 16-20 Wolverhampton Rd, B68 0LH, W : 4 m. by A 456 ✆ 429 3757, English rest. – ◨ AE ⑪ VISA
closed Saturday lunch and 26-27 December – **M** a la carte 11.00/13.00 st. ♪ 3.00.
p. 2 BU **e**

XX **Dynasty**, 93-103 Hurst St., B5 4TE, ✆ 622 1410, Chinese rest.. ◨ AE ⑪ VISA
M 5.00/7.00 t. ♪ 2.70.
KZ **e**

XX **Lorenzo**, 3 Park St., Digbeth, B5 5JD, ✆ 643 0541, Italian rest. – ◨ AE ⑪ VISA
closed Saturday lunch, Monday dinner, Sunday, 3 weeks July-August and Bank Holidays – **M** a la carte 7.30/13.20 t. ♪ 3.10.
KZ **o**

✗ **La Capanna,** 43 Hurst St., B5 4BD, ✆ 622 2287, Italian rest. – **☻. ⟡. AE ⓞ VISA** KZ **n**
  closed Sunday, 25 December and Bank Holidays – **M** a la carte 6.60/10.80 t. ⟟ 2.40.

✗ **Pinocchio's,** 8 Chad Sq., off Harborne Rd, B15 3TQ, W : 2¾ m. by A 456 ✆ 454 8672, Italian
  rest. – **⟡ AE ⓞ VISA** p. 4 EX **v**
  closed Sunday – **M** a la carte 7.10/11.00 t. ⟟ 2.50.

MICHELIN Branch, Valepits Rd, Garretts Green, B33 0YD, ✆ 784 7900

AUSTIN-ROVER 9-14 Dozells St. ✆ 643 5111	FORD 156/182 Bristol St. ✆ 622 2777
AUSTIN-ROVER Bristol St. ✆ 622 1122	FORD Long Acre, Aston ✆ 327 4791
AUSTIN-ROVER Essex St. ✆ 622 2851	FORD 221 High St., Digbeth ✆ 632 6756
AUSTIN-ROVER 193-194 Broad St. ✆ 643 4971	MAZDA Rookery Rd, Handsworth ✆ 554 9333
AUSTIN-ROVER-DAIMLER-JAGUAR 22 Berkeley St. ✆ 643 7901	MAZDA 193-194 Broad St. ✆ 643 4971
	MERCEDES-BENZ Charles Henry St. ✆ 622 3031
AUSTIN-ROVER-JAGUAR Aston Hall Rd, Aston ✆ 328 0833	NISSAN 4 Birmingham Rd ✆ 358 7011
	PEUGEOT, TALBOT Summer Lane, Newtown ✆ 359 4848
AUSTIN-ROVER 71 Aston Rd North, Aston ✆ 359 2011	RENAULT 1300 Bristol Rd South ✆ 475 5241
CITROEN Barnes Hill, Weoley Castle ✆ 427 5231	TALBOT, PEUGEOT Charlotte St. ✆ 236 4382
COLT, FORD, VAUXHALL 91-96 Summerhill Rd ✆ 236 9575	TALBOT Old Walsall Rd, Perry Barr ✆ 357 1131
	TOYOTA 138 Soho Hill, Handsworth ✆ 554 6311
COLT 266 Broad St. ✆ 643 6508	VOLVO Bristol St. ✆ 622 4491
COLT, LONSDALE 205 Lozells Rd ✆ 551 7717	VW, AUDI Digbeth ✆ 643 7341

Except where otherwise stated see pp. 2 and 3

at Streetly N : 7 m. on A 452 – ✉ Sutton Coldfield – ☎ 021 Birmingham :

▥ **Parson and Clerk** (Golden Oak) without rest., Chester Rd North, B73 6SP, S : 1 ½ m. on A
  452 ✆ 352 0944 – ▥wc **☻. ⟡. AE VISA. ⁂** CT **s**
  30 rm � 26.00/31.00 t.

at Walmley NE : 6 m. by B 4148 – ✉ Sutton Coldfield – ☎ 021 Birmingham :

▦ **Penns Hall** (Embassy) ⟡, Penns Lane, B76 8LH, ✆ 351 3111, Telex 335789, ⟲, ⟿ – ▤ TV
  ☻. ⟡. AE ⓞ VISA. ⁂ DT **v**
  closed Bank Holidays – **M** *(closed Sunday dinner to non-residents)* (bar lunch Saturday) a la
  carte 11.30/17.50 st. ⟟ 4.25 – � 4.25 – **115 rm** 30.00/49.00 – SB (weekends only) 45.00/50.00 st.

BMW Jockey Rd, Boldmere ✆ 354 8131	NISSAN 504-508 College Rd, Erdington ✆ 373 2542
CITROEN Old Kingsbury Rd, Minworth ✆ 351 4367	SAAB Eachelhurst Rd, Erdington ✆ 351 1027
FIAT, LANCIA 35 Sutton New Rd, Erdington ✆ 350 1301	TALBOT, PEUGEOT Newport Rd, Castle Bromwich ✆ 747 4712
FORD Kingsbury Rd, Erdington ✆ 382 1111	TALBOT, PEUGEOT 103 Goosemoor Lane, Erdington ✆ 382 1919
HONDA Bromford Lane ✆ 328 4211	
HYUNDAI 1016-1018 Kingsbury Rd, Erdington ✆ 747 2065	VAUXHALL 364 Chester Rd, Castle Bromwich ✆ 747 4601

at Castle Bromwich NE : 6 m. by A 47 – ✉ ☎ 021 Birmingham :

▦ **Bradford Arms,** Chester Rd, B36 0AG, ✆ 747 0227 – TV ⟡wc **☎ ☻. ⟡. AE ⓞ VISA**
  closed 3 days at Christmas – **M** (grill rest. only) – **30 rm** ⟹ 27.50/32.00 st. p. 5 HV **a**

at Sutton Coldfield NE : 8 m. by A 38 – ✉ Sutton Coldfield – ☎ 021 Birmingham :

▦ **Belfry** (Best Western) ⟡, Lichfield Rd, Wishaw, B76 9PR, E : 3 m. on A 446 ✆ 0675 (Curdworth) 70301, Telex 338848, ≼, ⟐, ▥, ⟿, park, ⁂, squash – TV **☎ ☻. ⟡. ⟡. AE ⓞ VISA**
  M 8.40/17.35 st. ⟟ 2.80 – **116 rm** ⟹ 44.50/73.00 st. – SB (weekends only) 57.50 st.
  by A 38 DT

▦ **Moor Hall** (Best Western) ⟡, Moor Hall Drive, Four Oaks, B75 6LN, NE : 1 m. by A 453
  ✆ 308 3751, ⟿ – TV ⟡wc ☎ **☻. ⟡. VISA. ⁂** DT **r**
  M 9.95/12.95 t. ⟟ 3.75 – **50 rm** ⟹ 36.00/43.00 t. – SB (weekends only) 42.00/52.00 st.

↑ **Standbridge,** 138 Birmingham Rd, B72 1LY, ✆ 354 3007, ⟿ – ▥ **☻** DT **a**
  closed last week May and 1 week at Christmas – **9 rm** ⟹ 12.25/25.30 st.

✗✗ **La Gondola,** Mere Green Precinct, 304 Lichfield Rd, B74 2UW, N : 2 m. on A 5127 ✆ 308 6782,
  Italian rest. DT **o**

✗✗ **Le Bon Viveur,** 65 Birmingham Rd, B72 1QF, ✆ 355 5836 – ▤ rest. **⟡ AE ⓞ VISA** DT **u**
  closed Saturday lunch, Sunday, Monday and August – **M** a la carte 9.85/13.45 t. ⟟ 2.75.

ALFA-ROMEO 62 Chester Rd ✆ 353 1345	SKODA Coleshill Rd ✆ 354 6783
AUSTIN-ROVER Maney Corner ✆ 354 7601	VOLVO 127 Chester Rd ✆ 353 3191
AUSTIN-ROVER 10 Birmingham Rd ✆ 355 5537	VW, AUDI 45-51 Kings Rd ✆ 355 1261
DAIHATSU 35 Sutton New Rd ✆ 350 1301	

at National Exhibition Centre E : 9 ½ m. on A 45 – DU – ✉ ☎ 021 Birmingham :

▦▦ **Birmingham Metropole,** Blackfirs Lane, Bickenhill, B40 1PP, ✆ 780 4242, Telex 336129, ≼,
  squash – ▤ ▦ ⟡ & **☻. ⟡. ⟡. AE ⓞ VISA**
  M a la carte 7.50/17.50 t. ⟟ 3.00 – ⟹ 3.75 – **501 rm** 45.00/70.00 t. – SB (weekends only) (spring only) 48.00/64.90 st.

▦ **Warwick,** Blackfirs Lane, Bickenhill, B40 1PP, ✆ 780 4242, Telex 336129 – ▤ ▤ TV ⟡wc
  ☎ **☻. ⟡. AE ⓞ VISA**
  Exhibitions only – **M** a la carte 7.50/17.50 t. ⟟ 3.00 – ⟹ 3.75 – **200 rm** 41.00/82.00 t.

▦ **Arden,** Coventry Rd, Bickenhill, B92 0EH, S : ½ m. on A 45 ✉ Solihull ✆ 067 55 (Hampton-
  in-Arden) 3221 – ▤ TV ⟡wc ☎ **☻. ⟡. ⟡. AE ⓞ VISA**
  M 6.95/15.00 st. ⟟ 1.85 – ⟹ 3.50 – **46 rm** 22.00/36.00 st.

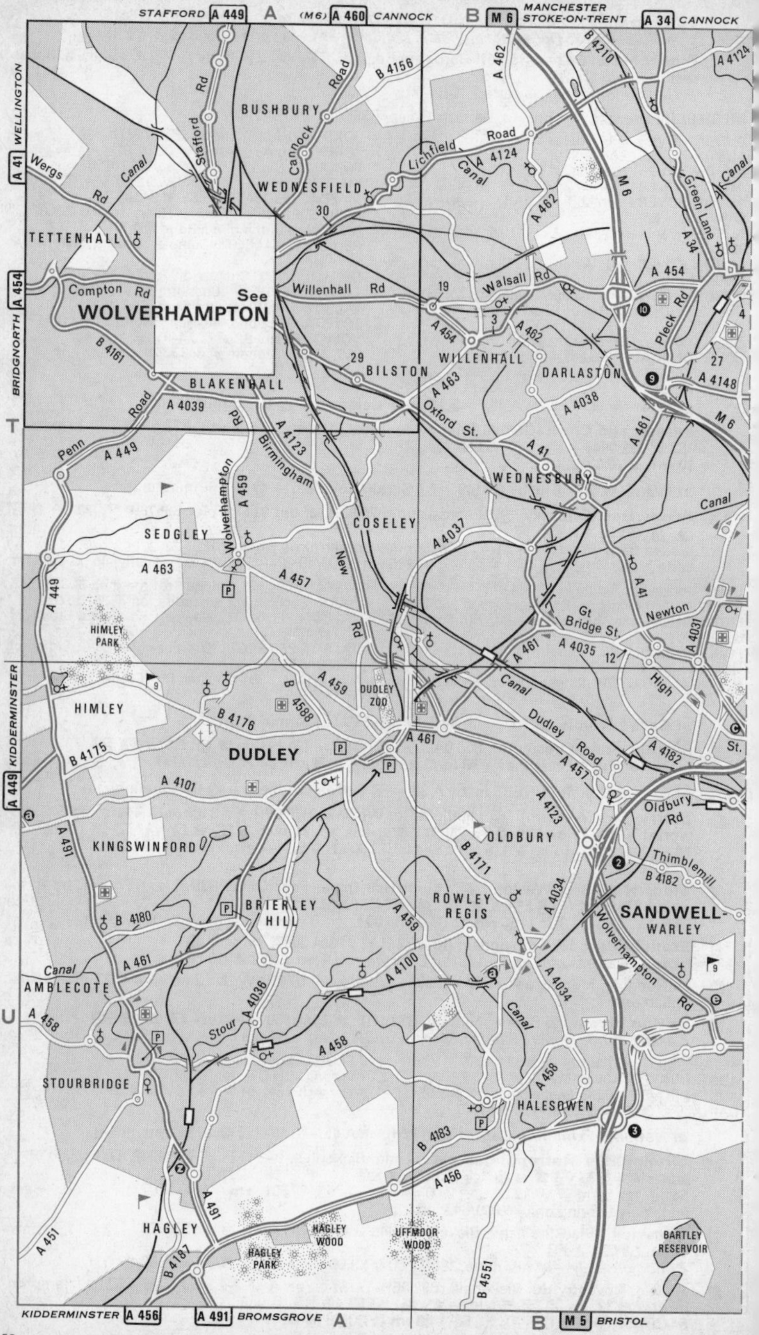

STAFFORD A 449 A (M6) A 460 CANNOCK B M 6 MANCHESTER STOKE-ON-TRENT A 34 CANNOCK

A 41 WELLINGTON

BRIDGNORTH A 454

KIDDERMINSTER A 449

T

U

A 462
B 4156
A 4210
A 4124
BUSHBURY
Stafford Rd
Cannock Road
Lichfield Road
A 4124
Canal
M 6
Green Lane
Canal
Wergs Rd
Canal
WEDNESFIELD
A 462
A 454
Pleck Rd
10
Compton Rd
See
WOLVERHAMPTON
Willenhall Rd
Walsall Rd
3
A 454
A 462
27
B 4161
30
19
9
A 4148
M 6
BLAKENHALL
29
BILSTON
WILLENHALL
DARLASTON
A 4039
A 463
Oxford St.
A 4038
A 461
Road
Penn
A 4123
Birmingham
A 41
WEDNESBURY
A 449
Wolverhampton
A 459
COSELEY
A 4037
Canal
SEDGLEY
A 463
A 457
New
Gt. Bridge St.
Newton
A 4031
P
Rd
A 461
A 4035
12
High
HIMLEY PARK
A 459
DUDLEY ZOO
Canal
Dudley Road
A 4182
St.
9
HIMLEY
B 4176
A 458
P
A 461
A 457
A 449
B 4175
DUDLEY
A 461
Oldbury Rd
A 4101
P
P
A 4123
OLDBURY
2
Thimblemill
KINGSWINFORD
B 4171
A 4034
B 4182
A 491
P
BRIERLEY HILL
A 459
ROWLEY REGIS
SANDWELL WARLEY
B 4180
A 461
A 100
Wolverhampton Rd
9
AMBLECOTE
A 4036
A 034
U
A 458
Stour
Canal
STOURBRIDGE
A 458
B 4183
HALESOWEN
P
3
2
A 456
A 491
HAGLEY
HAGLEY WOOD
UFFMOOR WOOD
BARTLEY RESERVOIR
A 451
B 4187
HAGLEY PARK
B 4551

KIDDERMINSTER A 456 A 491 BROMSGROVE A B M 5 BRISTOL

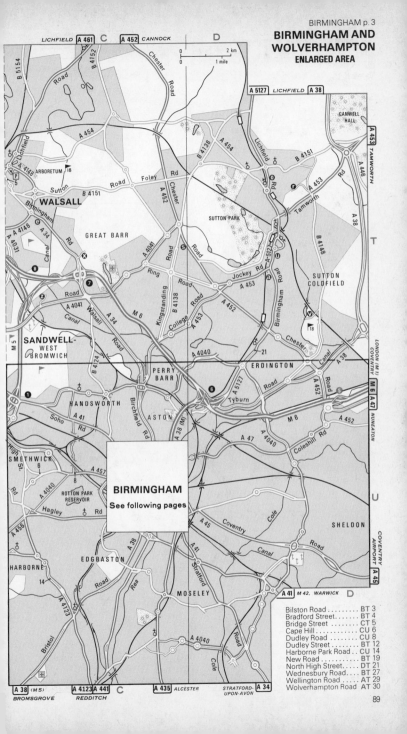

BIRMINGHAM AND WOLVERHAMPTON
ENLARGED AREA

Bilston Road .... BT 3
Bradford Street .... BT 4
Bridge Street .... CT 5
Cape Hill .... CU 6
Dudley Road .... CU 8
Dudley Street .... BT 12
Harborne Park Road .. CU 14
New Road .... BT 19
North High Street..... DT 21
Wednesbury Road.... BT 27
Wellington Road ..... AT 29
Wolverhampton Road AT 30

BIRMINGHAM
See following pages

89

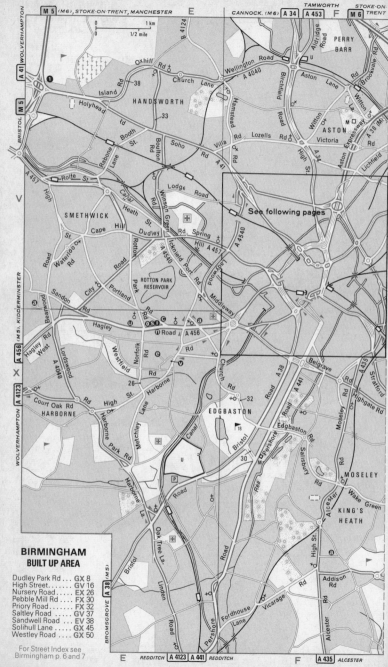

For Street Index see
Birmingham p. 6 and 7

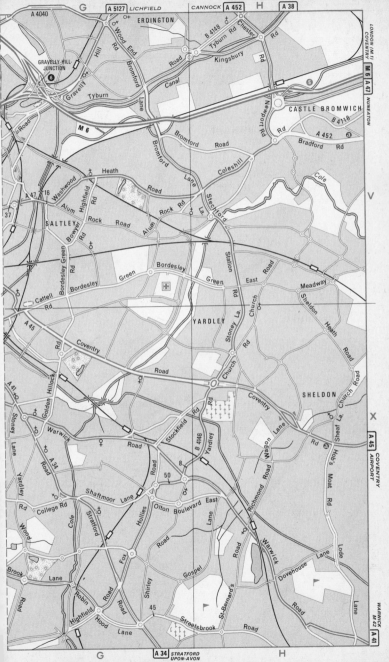

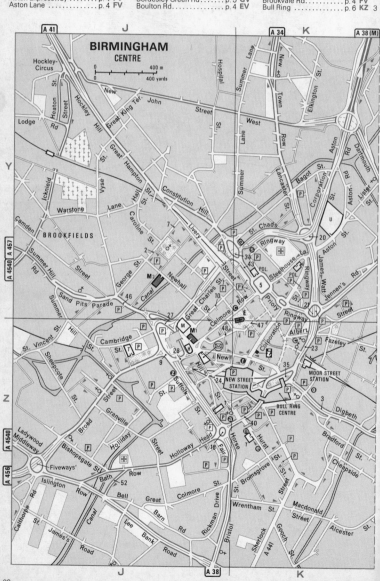

at *Acocks Green* SE : 4 ½ m. on A 41 – DU – ⊠ ✆ 021 Birmingham :

↑ **Kerry House,** 946 Warwick Rd, B27 6QG, ℰ 707 0316 – 🛋wc ℗
  23 rm ⊡ 16.10/23.00 **st.**

ALFA-ROMEO 683 Stratford Rd, Sparkhill ℰ 778 1295

AUSTIN-ROVER 884 Warwick Rd ℰ 706 8271

AUSTIN-ROVER Warwick Rd, Tyseley ℰ 706 4331

CITROEN 2 Warwick Rd ℰ 707 3122

DAIHATSU, SKODA 1520 Stratford Rd, Hall Green ℰ 744 1144

FIAT, LANCIA 979 Stratford Rd, Hall Green ℰ 778 2323

FSO 438 Stratford Rd, Spartihill ℰ 773 8646

LADA 723-725 Stratford Rd, Sparkhill ℰ 777 6164

RENAULT High St., Bordesley ℰ 773 8251

RENAULT 1370 Stratford Rd, Hall Green ℰ 777 1131

TALBOT Coventry Rd, Small Heath ℰ 772 4388

TOYOTA, RELIANT 32-38 Coventry Rd, Bordesley ℰ 772 5916

VAUXHALL 291 Shaftmoor Lane, Hall Green ℰ 777 1074

VAUXHALL-OPEL 870 Stratford Rd, Sparkhill ℰ 777 3361

at *Sheldon* SE : 6 m. on A 45 – HX – ⊠ ✆ 021 Birmingham :

🏨 **Wheatsheaf** (Golden Oak), 2225 Coventry Rd, B26 3EH, ℰ 742 6201 – 📺 🛋wc ☏ ℗. 🅰.
  🔀 🆎 𝘝𝘐𝘚𝘈. ⚘   p. 5 HX **a**
  M *(closed Saturday lunch, Sunday and Bank Holidays)* 6.50/8.50 **t.** ᐟ 2.70 – **84 rm**
  ⊡ 31.50/37.00 **t.**

AUSTIN-ROVER 1652 Coventry Rd ℰ 706 1688

PEUGEOT 2119 Coventry Rd ℰ 742 5533

at *Birmingham Airport* SE : 7 m. on A 45 – DU – ⊠ ✆ 021 Birmingham :

🏨 **Excelsior** (T.H.F.), Coventry Rd, Elmdon, B26 3QW, ℰ 743 8141, Telex 338005 – 📺 ℗. 🅰.
  🔀 🆎 ⓞ 𝘝𝘐𝘚𝘈
  M 6.35/7.95 **st.** ᐟ 2.60 – ⊡ 5.50 – **141 rm** 36.00/45.00 **st.**

AUSTIN-ROVER Station Rd, Marston Green ℰ 779 2261

at *Kings Heath* S : 3 ½ m. on A 435 – ⊠ ✆ 021 Birmingham :

✕ **Giovanni's,** 27 Poplar Rd off High st., B14 7AA, ℰ 443 2391, Italian rest. 🔀 ⓞ 𝘝𝘐𝘚𝘈
  closed Sunday 6 to 20 January and 7 to 21 July – **M** a la carte 8.40/14.00 **t.** ᐟ 3.00.   p. 4 FX **x**

AUSTIN-ROVER 367 Moseley Rd, Balsall Heath ℰ 440 1131

AUSTIN-ROVER Alcester Rd, Moseley ℰ 449 6115

CITROEN Hallan St., Balsall Heath ℰ 440 4606

FORD 82 St. Mary's Row, Moseley ℰ 449 3771

NISSAN 120-126 Alcester Rd, Moseley ℰ 449 4751

SKODA 307 Northfield Rd, Harborne ℰ 427 4050

VAUXHALL 16 Ryland St., Edgbaston ℰ 455 7171

at *Northfield* SW : 6 m. by A 38 – CU – ⊠ ✆ 021 Birmingham :

↑ **Norwood,** 87 Bunbury Rd, B31 2ET, 🚗 – ℗
  closed 1 week at Christmas – **12 rm** ⊡ 14.75/30.50 **st.**

AUSTIN-ROVER 428 Redditch Rd, Kings Norton ℰ 458 4031

NISSAN 57 Walkers Heath Rd ℰ 451 1411

at *Smethwick* W : 3 ½ m. by A 456 – ⊠ ✆ 021 Birmingham :

✕ **Franzl's,** 151 Milcote Rd, Bearwood, B67 5BN, ℰ 429 7920, Austrian rest. – 🔀 𝘝𝘐𝘚𝘈
  closed Sunday, Monday, first 3 weeks August and 25 December-2 January – **M** (dinner only)
  a la carte 6.85/9.70 **t.** ᐟ 3.10.   p. 4 EV **a**

at *West Bromwich* NW : 6 m. on A 41 – ⊠ West Bromwich – ✆ 021 Birmingham :

🏨 **West Bromwich Moat House** (Q.M.H.) Birmingham Rd, B70 6RS, SW : 1 m. by A 41
  ℰ 553 6111, Telex 336232 – 🛗 📺 🛋wc ☎ ℗. 🅰. 🔀 🆎 ⓞ 𝘝𝘐𝘚𝘈   BU **c**
  M 7.65/7.95 **st.** ᐟ 3.40 – **179 rm** ⊡ 36.00/48.00 **st.** – SB (weekends only) 37.00 **st.**

AUSTIN-ROVER High St. ℰ 553 0778

FERRARI, FIAT Birmingham Rd ℰ 553 7509

FORD 377 High St. ℰ 553 1881

VAUXHALL-OPEL Spon Lane ℰ 553 3777

at *Great Barr* NW : 6 m. on A 34 – ⊠ Great Barr – ✆ 021 Birmingham :

🏨 **Post House** (T.H.F), Chapel Lane, B43 7BG, ℰ 357 7444, Telex 338497, ⊿ heated – 📺
  🛋wc ☎ ℗. 🅰. 🔀 🆎 ⓞ 𝘝𝘐𝘚𝘈   CT **x**
  M a la carte 10.15/15.25 **st.** ᐟ 2.60 – ⊡ 5.00 – **204 rm** 34.50/42.00 **st.**

🏨 **Barr,** Pear Tree Drive, Newton Rd, B43 6HS, W : 1 m. by A 4041 ℰ 357 1141, Telex 336406, 🚗
  – 📺 🛋wc ☎ ℗. 🅰. 🔀 🆎 ⓞ 𝘝𝘐𝘚𝘈   CT **z**
  closed 24 to 26 December – **M** 5.50/6.00 **st.** – **111 rm** ⊡ 33.00/43.00 **st.** – SB (weekends only) 76.00 **st.**

BIRTLE Greater Manchester 402 ⑳ 404 ⑩ – pop. 1,989 (inc. Ashworth) – ⊠ Bury – ✆ 061 Manchester – ♦London 217 – Bolton 10 – ♦Manchester 11.

🏨 **Normandie** 🦐, Elbut Lane, BL9 6UT, ℰ 764 3869 – 🛗 📺 🛋wc 🛋wc ☎ ℗. 🔀 🆎 ⓞ 𝘝𝘐𝘚𝘈
  closed 27, 29 and 30 December and 1 January – **M** *(closed Sunday dinner to non-residents and Saturday lunch)* 7.00/13.50 **t.** – **17 rm** ⊡ 26.50/42.50 **t.**

BISHOP AUCKLAND Durham 401 402 P 20 – pop. 32,572 – ECD : Wednesday – ✆ 0388.
♦London 253 – ♦Carlisle 73 – ♦Middlesbrough 24 – ♦Newcastle-upon-Tyne 28 – Sunderland 25.

🏠 **Park Head,** New Coundon, DL14 8AL, ℰ 661727 – 📺 🛋wc ☎ ℗. 🔀 🆎 ⓞ 𝘝𝘐𝘚𝘈
  M a la carte 8.50/13.95 **t.** ᐟ 2.50 – **12 rm** ⊡ 25.00/30.00 **t.** – SB (weekends only) 35.00/45.00 **st.**

BISHOP'S CASTLE Salop 🌢🄾🄸 L 26 – pop. 1,810 – ✆ 0588.

♦London 182 – ♦Birmingham 71 – Shrewsbury 24.

🏤 **Castle,** Market Sq., SD9 5DG, ✆ 638403 – 🄿. 🖂 🄰🄴 🅾
M a la carte 2.95/7.75 st. – **7 rm** ☲ 14.50/23.00 st. – SB 34.00 st.

BISHOP'S STORTFORD Herts. 🄾🄾🄸 U 28 – pop. 20,750 – ECD : Wednesday – ✆ 0279.

✈ Stansted Airport : ✆ 502380, Telex 81102, NE : 3 ½ m.

🛈 The Causeway ✆ 53372.

♦London 34 – ♦Cambridge 27 – Chelmsford 19 – Colchester 33.

🏨 **Foxley,** Foxley Drive, Stanstead Rd, CM23 2EB, N : ¾ m. on A 1184 ✆ 53977, 🚗 – 🆃🆅 🛏wc
🄿 – **12 rm**.

🏠 **Brook House,** 29 Northgate End, CM23 2LD, ✆ 57892, 🚗 – 🆃🆅 🛏wc 🚿wc 🄿. 🕸
M a la carte 4.85/9.50 t. 🍷 3.50 – **24 rm** ☲ 19.50/29.00 t.

AUSTIN-ROVER-DAIMLER-JAGUAR 123-129 South
St. ✆ 58441
CITROEN Dunmow Rd ✆ 54335
DAIHATSU, LANCIA London Rd ✆ 54181
FORD London Rd ✆ 52214

PEUGEOT-TALBOT 26 Northgate End ✆ 53494
RENAULT Northgate End ✆ 53127
VAUXHALL-OPEL, VOLVO The Causeway ✆ 52304
VW, AUDI Dane St. ✆ 54680

BISHOP'S TAWTON Devon 🄾🄾🄸 H 30 – see Barnstaple.

BLACKBURN Lancs. 🄾🄾🄸 M 22 – pop. 101,816 – ECD : Thursday – ✆ 0254.

🇮🇸 Beardwood Brow, ✆ 51122 – 🇮🇸 Pleasington ✆ 21028, W : 3 m.

🛈 Town Hall ✆ 55201 ext 214 and 53277.

♦London 228 – ♦Leeds 47 – ♦Liverpool 39 – ♦Manchester 24 – Preston 11.

🏨 **Blackburn Moat House** (Q.M.H.), Preston New Rd, Yew Tree Drive, BB2 7AJ, NW : 2 m. at
junction A 677 and A 6119 ✆ 64441, Telex 63271, 🛝 heated – 📶 🆃🆅 🛏wc 📺 🄿. 🚶. 🖂 🄰🄴
🅾 🆅🅸🆂🅰
M 6.00/7.00 st. 🍷 3.25 – **96 rm** ☲ 33.00/55.00 st. – SB (weekends only) 43.00/45.00 st.

🏠 **Woodlands,** 363 Preston New Rd, BB2 7AA, NW : 1 ¼ m. on A 677 ✆ 691122 – 🆃🆅 🛏wc 🄿.
🖂 🄰🄴 🅾 🆅🅸🆂🅰
closed 25-26 December and 1 January – M a la carte 6.15/10.20 t. 🍷 2.50 – ☲ 2.95 – **14 rm**
16.00/27.50 t.

AUSTIN-ROVER-DAIMLER-JAGUAR Park Rd ✆
662721
AUSTIN-ROVER Accrington Rd ✆ 57333
CITROEN Whalley New Rd ✆ 661616
FIAT 52/56 King St. ✆ 52981
FORD Montague St. ✆ 57021

RENAULT Gt. Harwood ✆ 886590
TALBOT, PEUGEOT King St. ✆ 52981
VAUXHALL Quarry St., Eanam ✆ 51191
VAUXHALL-OPEL Montague St. ✆ 53885
VW, AUDI 854 Whalley New Rd ✆ 48091

BLACKPOOL Lancs. 🄾🄾🄸 K 22 – pop. 151,860 – ECD : Wednesday – ✆ 0253.

See : Illuminations★★ (late September and early October) – Tower★ (※★) AC AY A.

🇮🇸 Blackpool North Shore, Devonshire Rd ✆ 52054, N : 1 ½ m. from main station BY – 🇮🇸 Blackpool
Park, Stanley Park ✆ 33960, E : 1 ½ m. BY – 🇮🇸 Poulton-le-Fylde, Myrtle Farm, Breck Rd ✆ 0253
(Poulton) 886831, E : 3 m. by A 586 BY.

🛈 1 Clifton St. ✆ 21623 and 25212 (weekdays only) – 87a Coronation St. ✆ 21891.

♦London 246 – ♦Leeds 88 – ♦Liverpool 56 – ♦Manchester 51 – ♦Middlesbrough 123.

Plan on next page

🏩 **Pembroke,** North Promenade, FY1 2JQ, ✆ 23434, Telex 677469, ≼, 🖂 – 📶 🆃🆅 🕿 🕭 🄿. 🚶.
🖂 🄰🄴 🅾 🆅🅸🆂🅰   AY x
M (buffet lunch) 7.20/7.95 st. 🍷 3.30 – **201 rm** ☲ 39.75/56.75 t. – SB 51.00/74.00 st.

🏩 **Imperial,** North Promenade, FY1 2HB, ✆ 23971, Telex 677376, ≼, 🖂 – 📶 🆃🆅 🄿. 🚶. 🖂 🄰🄴
🅾 🆅🅸🆂🅰   AY c
M 7.50/8.00 t. 🍷 3.00 – **150 rm** ☲ 40.00/56.00 t.

🏨 **Savoy,** Queens Promenade, FY2 9SJ, ✆ 52561 – 📶 🆃🆅 🛏wc 🚿wc 🕭 🄿. 🚶. 🖂 🄰🄴 🅾 🆅🅸🆂🅰
M (restricted lunch Monday to Friday) 4.50/6.75 t. – **128 rm** ☲ 17.00/42.00 t. – SB (weekends only) 44.00 st.   AY a

🏨 **New Clifton,** Talbot Sq., FY1 1ND, ✆ 21481, Group Telex 67415 – 📶 🆃🆅 🛏wc 🕿. 🚶. 🖂
🄴 🅾 🆅🅸🆂🅰   AY n
M 4.50/5.50 t. 🍷 2.50 – **78 rm** ☲ 32.00/48.00 st. – SB (weekends only) 21.00/24.00 st.

🏠 **Warwick** (Best Western), 603-609 New South Promenade, FY4 1NG, ✆ 42192, 🖂 – 🆃🆅
🛏wc 🄿. 🚶. 🖂 🄰🄴 🅾 🆅🅸🆂🅰   BZ u
M (bar lunch) 6.00 st. 🍷 2.05 – **52 rm** ☲ 19.00/44.00 st.

🏠 **Mimosa** without rest., 24a Lonsdale Rd, FY1 6EE, ✆ 41906 – 🆃🆅 🛏wc 🄿. 🆅🅸🆂🅰. 🕸   BZ c
closed 23 December-3 January – **15 rm** 16.10/23.00 t.

↑ **Sunray,** 42 Knowle Av., off Queens Promenade, FY2 9TQ, ✆ 51937 – 🆃🆅 🚿wc 🄿   BY c
closed Christmas and New Year – **7 rm** ☲ 10.00/23.00 st.

↑ **Denely,** 15 King Edward Av., FY2 9TA, ✆ 52757 – 🚿 🄿. 🕸   AY e
9 rm ☲ 8.00/13.00.

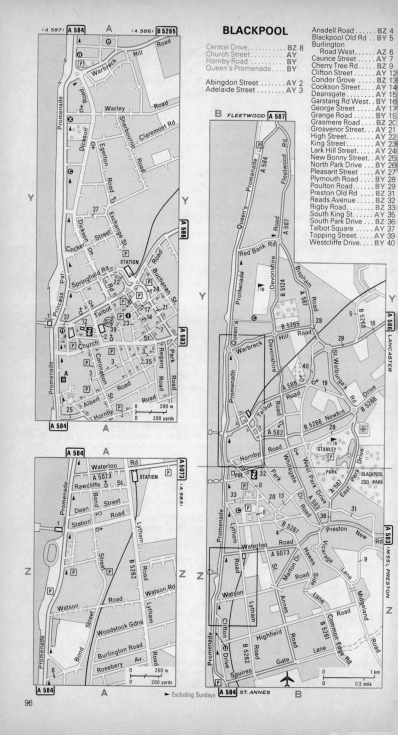

BLACKPOOL

Central Drive........... BZ 8
Church Street........... AY
Hornby Road............ BY
Queen's Promenade..... BY

Abingdon Street .... AY 2
Adelaide Street .... AY 3

Ansdell Road .... BZ 4
Blackpool Old Rd .. BY 5
Burlington
 Road West....... AZ 6
Caunce Street ..... AY 7
Cherry Tree Rd .... BZ 9
Clifton Street ...... AY 12
Condor Grove ..... BZ 13
Cookson Street .... AY 14
Deansgate .... AY 15
Garstang Rd West.. BY 16
George Street ..... AY 17
Grange Road ...... AY 19
Grasmere Road .... BZ 20
Grosvenor Street... AY 21
High Street........ AY 22
King Street........ AY 23
Lark Hill Street..... AY 24
New Bonny Street.. AY 25
North Park Drive ... BY 26
Pleasant Street .... AY 27
Plymouth Road .... BY 28
Poulton Road...... AY 29
Preston Old Rd .... BZ 31
Reads Avenue ..... BZ 32
Rigby Road........ AY 33
South King St. ..... AY 35
South Park Drive .. BZ 36
Talbot Square ..... AY 37
Topping Street .... AY 39
Westcliffe Drive.... BY 40

► Excluding Sundays

96

at Little Thornton NE : 5 m. by A 586 – BY – off A 588 – ⊠ Blackpool – ☎ 0253 Poulton-le-Fylde :

XX **River House** ⟍ with rm, Skippool Creek, Wyre Rd, FY5 5LF, *℘* 883497, ≤, 🐎 – 📺 🅿 🔄 🅰🅴

M (booking essential) a la carte 11.10/19.50 t. ⚬ 2.25 – **4 rm** ⊏⊐ 18.00/32.00 t. – SB (weekends only) 45.00 **st.**

ALFA-ROMEO, DAIHATSU St. Annes Rd *℘* 402671	MERCEDES-BENZ Church St. *℘* 22257
AUSTIN-ROVER Cherry Tree Rd *℘* 67811	MERCEDES Church St. *℘* 28436
AUSTIN-ROVER-DAIMLER-JAGUAR 159 Devonshire Rd *℘* 34301	PEUGEOT 79/83 Breck Rd, Poulton-le-Fylde *℘* 882571
BMW Bloomfield Rd *℘* 402541	PEUGEOT-TALBOT Squires Gate Lane *℘* 45544
COLT 234 Talbot Rd *℘* 26688	TOYOTA 145/147 Dickson Rd *℘* 21469
FORD Whitegate Drive *℘* 63333	VW, AUDI Central Drive *℘* 401228
HONDA Devonshire Rd *℘* 35816	

BLACKWOOD (COED-DUON) Gwent 🔢🔢🔢 K 29 – pop. 12,700 – ECD : Thursday – ☎ 0495.

♦London 158 – ♦Cardiff 15 – Newport 13.

🏛 **Maes Manor** ⟍, Maesruddend, NP2 0AG, N : 1 ¼ m. off A 4048 by Rock Inn *℘* 224551, Telex 497887, 🐎, park – 📺 🚻wc 🍴 🐎 🅿 🔄 🔄 🅰🅴 🆅🆂🅰
M 8.00 **st.** – **24 rm** ⊏⊐ 25.00/38.50 **st.** – SB (weekends only) 35.00 **st.**

BLAGDON Avon 🔢🔢🔢 L 30 – pop. 1,238 – ECD : Saturday – ⊠ Bristol – ☎ 0761.

♦London 138 – Bath 19 – ♦Bristol 17 – Taunton 39.

🏛 **Mendip** ⟍, Street End, BS18 6TS, *℘* 62688, ≤ lake and countryside – 📺 🚻wc 🍴wc 🐎 🅿 🔄 🔄 🅰🅴 ⓞ 🆅🆂🅰
closed Christmas – **M** 8.50/11.95 t. ⚬ 3.75 – **36 rm** ⊏⊐ 25.00/45.00 t. – SB (weekends only) 52.00/70.00 **st.**

BLAKENEY Norfolk 🔢🔢🔢 X 25 – pop. 677 – ECD : Wednesday – ⊠ Holt – ☎ 0263 Cley.

♦London 127 – King's Lynn 37 – ♦Norwich 28.

🏛 **Manor,** The Quay, NR25 7ND, *℘* 740376, 🐎 – 📺 🚻wc & 🅿
closed December – **M** (buffet lunch) 6.35/8.85 **st.** ⚬ 2.90 – **22 rm** ⊏⊐ 20.25/55.65 **st.** – SB (winter and spring only) 40.00/51.00 **st.**

🏛 **Blakeney** (Best Western), The Quay, NR25 7NE, *℘* 740797, ≤, 🔄, 🐎 – 📺 🚻wc 🐎 🅿 🔄 🔄 🅰🅴 ⓞ 🆅🆂🅰
M (buffet lunch Monday to Saturday) 7.00/9.00 t. ⚬ 2.80 – **54 rm** ⊏⊐ 19.00/66.00 t. – SB 62.00/76.00 **st.**

BLANCHLAND Northumb. 🔢🔢🔢 🔢🔢🔢 N 19 – pop. 167 – ECD : Monday – ⊠ Consett (Durham) – ☎ 043 475.

♦London 298 – ♦Carlisle 47 – ♦Newcastle-upon-Tyne 24.

🏛 **Lord Crewe Arms** ⟍, DH8 9SP, *℘* 251, « Part 13C abbey », 🐎 – 🚻wc 🍴wc ☎ 🅿 🔄 🅰🅴 ⓞ 🆅🆂🅰
closed Monday to Thursday from January-mid March – **M** (bar lunch Monday to Saturday) 7.00/10.00 **st.** ⚬ 2.40 – **15 rm** ⊏⊐ 27.00/44.00 **st.** – SB 50.00/58.00 **st.**

BLANDFORD FORUM Dorset 🔢🔢🔢 🔢🔢🔢 N 31 The West Country G. – pop. 6,100 – ECD : Wednesday – ☎ 0258 Blandford.

Envir. : Royal Blandford Signals Museum★, NE : 2 m. off B 3082.

🅱 Parish Church, East St. *℘* 51989 (summer only).

♦London 124 – Bournemouth 17 – Dorchester 17 – Salisbury 24.

XX **La Belle Alliance** with rm, Portman Lodge, Whitecliff, Mill St., DT11 7BP, *℘* 52842 – 📺 🚻wc 🅿 🔄 🅰🅴 ⓞ
closed first 2 weeks January – **M** *(closed Sunday)* (dinner only) a la carte 8.00/11.70 **st.** ⚬ 2.20 – **4 rm** ⊏⊐ 18.00/30.00 **st.**

at Pimperne NE : 2 ½ m. on A 354 – ⊠ ☎ 0258 Blandford Forum :

🏠 **Anvil,** DT11 8UQ, *℘* 53431, 🔄 heated – 🚻wc 🍴wc 🅿 🔄 🅰🅴 ⓞ 🆅🆂🅰
M a la carte 6.70/11.50 t. ⚬ 2.80 – **8 rm** ⊏⊐ 16.00/30.00 t. – SB 44.00 **st.**

at Tarrant Monkton NE : 5 ½ m. by A 354 – ⊠ Blandford Forum – ☎ 025 889 Tarrant Hinton :

XX **Langtons,** DT11 8RX, *℘* 225 – 🅿 🔄 🅰🅴 ⓞ 🆅🆂🅰
M (bar lunch) a la carte 7.00/9.50 t. ⚬ 2.50.

AUSTIN-ROVER Mill St. *℘* 52457	RENAULT St. Leonards Av. *℘* 52311
FERRARI, LANCIA Pimperne *℘* 51211	

BLICKLING Norfolk 🔢🔢🔢 X 25 – pop. 141 – ⊠ ☎ 0263 Aylsham.

See : Blickling Hall★ (Jacobean) – ♦London 125 – Cromer 12 – ♦Norwich 14.

X **Buckinghamshire Arms** with rm, NR11 6NF, *℘* 732133 – 📺 🅿 🔄 🅰🅴 ⓞ 🆅🆂🅰
closed Christmas Day – **M** (bar lunch)/11.50 t. ⚬ 2.75 – **3 rm** ⊏⊐ 23.00/30.00 t. – SB 53.00 **st.**

BLOCKLEY Glos. **403** **404** O 27 – pop. 1,853 – ECD : Thursday – ⊠ Moreton-in-Marsh – ☎ 0386.
♦London 89 – ♦Birmingham 40 – Gloucester 29 – ♦Oxford 33.

🏠 **Lower Brook House** 🦢, Lower St., GL56 9DS, ℰ 700286, 🛏 – 🚪wc 🅿 🔌
closed 8 January-1 February – **M** (bar lunch Monday to Saturday) 5.50/13.50 t. 🍷 2.50 – **8 rm**
🚗 33.00/66.50 t. – SB (weekends only) 60.00/63.00 **st.**

BLOFIELD Norfolk **404** Y 26 – see Norwich.

BLOXHAM Oxon. **403** **404** P 28 – see Banbury.

BLUE ANCHOR Somerset – see Minehead.

BLUNDELLSANDS Merseyside **402** **403** K 23 – see Liverpool.

BLUNSDON Wilts. **403** **404** O 29 – see Swindon.

BLYTH Notts. **402** **403** **404** Q 23 – pop. 1,131 – ECD : Wednesday – ⊠ Worksop – ☎ 090 976.
♦London 154 – ♦Leeds 41 – Lincoln 29 – ♦Nottingham 31 – ♦Sheffield 21.

🏠 **Fourways**, High St., S81 8EW, ℰ 235 – 🅿 🔌 🆎 ⓪ 𝘝𝘐𝘚𝘈
M 8.00/13.00 t. 🍷 3.00 – **9 rm** 🚗 18.70/27.50 t.

BODIAM East Sussex **404** V 30 – pop. 303 – ⊠ Robertsbridge – ☎ 058 083 Staplecross.
See : Castle★ 14C (ruins) *AC*.
♦London 54 – Folkestone 36 – Hastings 12 – Maidstone 23.

🏠 **Justins** 🦢, Sandhurst Rd, TN32 5UJ, ℰ 058 083 (Staplecross) 372, ≤, 🛏 – 🚪wc 🛁wc 🅿
🔌 𝘝𝘐𝘚𝘈
closed December – **M** (dinner only) 7.00 t. 🍷 2.50 – **9 rm** 🚗 16.10/34.20 t. – SB 40.50/41.50 **st.**

BODINNICK-BY-FOWEY Cornwall – see Fowey.

BODMIN Cornwall **403** F 32 The West Country G. – pop. 9,207 – ECD : Wednesday – ☎ 0208.
See : St. Petroc Church★ – Envir. : Lanhydrock★★, S : 3 m.
🅱 Shire House, Mount Folly Sq. ℰ 4159.
♦London 273 – Exeter 63 – Penzance 47 – ♦Plymouth 30.

🏠 **Westberry**, Rhind St., PL31 2EL, ℰ 2772 – 📺 🚪wc 🛁wc 🕾 🅿 🔌 𝘝𝘐𝘚𝘈
M *(closed Saturday and Sunday)* (bar lunch) 6.30 t. 🍷 2.30 – **24 rm** 🚗 14.00/27.00 **st.** – SB
(weekends only) 26.00/30.00 **st.**

at Tredethy N : 5 m. by A 389 off B 3266 – ⊠ Bodmin – ☎ 020 884 St. Mabyn :

🏠 **Tredethy Country** 🦢, PL30 4QS, ℰ 262, ≤, « Country house atmosphere », 🌊 heated,
🛏, park – 🚪wc 🛁wc 🅿 ✗
closed 1 week at Christmas – **M** (lunch by arrangement) 6.50/7.50 t. 🍷 2.00 – **11 rm**
🚗 17.00/30.00 t. – SB (winter only) 40.00 **st.**

BOGNOR REGIS West Sussex **404** R 31 – pop. 39,150 – ECD : Wednesday – ☎ 0243.
🅱 1-2 Place St-Maur des Fossés, Belmont St. ℰ 823140.
♦London 65 – ♦Brighton 31 – ♦Portsmouth 25 – ♦Southampton 37.

🏨 **Royal Norfolk** (Best Western), The Esplanade, PO21 2LH, ℰ 826222, ≤, 🌊 heated, 🛏, ✗
– 🛗 📺 🅿 🌅 🔌 🆎 ⓪ 𝘝𝘐𝘚𝘈
M 7.60/10.25 t. 🍷 2.70 – **52 rm** 🚗 23.00/41.75 t. – SB 59.50 **st.**
🏠 **Steyne House**, 10 West St., PO21 1UF, ℰ 828476 – 📺 🅿
closed 2 weeks at Christmas – **7 rm** 🚗 8.00/24.00 **s.**

AUSTIN-ROVER   65 Aldwick Rd ℰ 864041
AUSTIN-ROVER, FORD   Lennox St. ℰ 864641
PEUGEOT-TALBOT   131 Elmer Rd, Middleton-on-Sea
ℰ 024 369 (Middleton-on-Sea) 2432

VW, AUDI   126 Felpham Way ℰ 024 369 (Middleton-on-Sea) 3185

BOLTON Greater Manchester **402** **404** M 23 – pop. 154,199 – ECD : Wednesday – ☎ 0204.
Envir. : Hall I'Th'Wood★ (16C) *AC*, N : 1 ½ m.
🅱 Bolton Municipal, Links Rd, Lostock ℰ 42336 – 🅱 Dunscar, Longworth Lane, Bromley Cross ℰ
53321, N : 3 m. off A 666 – 🅱 Lostock Park, ℰ 43278, W : 3 ½ m.
🅱 Town Hall, ℰ 22311 ext 211/485 and 384174.
♦London 214 – Burnley 19 – ♦Liverpool 32 – ♦Manchester 11 – Preston 23.

🏨 **Crest** (Crest), Beaumont Rd, BL3 4TA, SW : 2 ½ m. on A 58 ℰ 651511, Telex 635527 – 📺
🚪wc 🅿 🔌 🆎 ⓪ 𝘝𝘐𝘚𝘈
M approx. 11.00 **st.** – 🚗 5.25 – **100 rm** 42.00/53.00 **st.**
🏨 **Pack Horse**, 1 Nelson Sq., BL1 1DP, ℰ 27261, Telex 635168 – 🛗 📺 🚪wc 🕾 🌅 🔌 🆎 ⓪
𝘝𝘐𝘚𝘈
closed 24 December-2 January – **M** (carving rest.) 7.95/8.95 **st.** 🍷 3.50 – **78 rm** 🚗 16.00/48.00 **st.**
– SB (weekends only) 48.00 **st.**

at Egerton N : 3 ½ m. by A 673 on A 666 – ✉ ❂ 0204 Bolton :

⌂⌂ **Egerton House** 🔇, Blackburn Rd, BL7 9PL, on A 666 ☎ 57171, <, 🌳, park – [TV] 🛁wc 📞 [P]. [Access] [AE] [D]. ⊘
M a la carte 9.70/20.00 **t.** – **18 rm** ☕ 38.00/48.00 **st.**

at Bromley Cross N : 4 m. by A 676 – ✉ ❂ 0204 Bolton :

⌂⌂ Last Drop Village, Hospital Rd, PL7 9PZ, ☎ 591131, Telex 635322, 🌳 – [TV] 🛁wc 📞 [P]. 👥. [Access] [AE] [D] [VISA]
closed 26 December – **69 rm** ☕ 36.00/50.00 **st.** – SB (weekends only) 46.00/48.00 **st.**

AUSTIN-ROVER-DAIMLER-JAGUAR Manchester Rd ☎ 32241
COLT 154/160 Crook St. ☎ 24686
FORD 54/56 Higher Bridge St. ☎ 24474
HYUNDAI, SUBARU Thynne St. ☎ 32511
OPEL Halliwell Rd ☎ 26566
PEUGEOT-TALBOT, CITROEN, LANCIA Bradshawgate ☎ 31323
TOYOTA Radcliffe Rd ☎ 382234
VW, AUDI Blackburn Rd ☎ 31464
VW, AUDI St. Helens Rd ☎ 62131

BOLTON ABBEY North Yorks. [402] O 22 – pop. 136 – ✉ Skipton – ❂ 075 671.
See : Bolton Priory★ (ruins) and woods (the Strid★ and nature trails in upper Wharfedale).
♦London 216 – Harrogate 18 – ♦Leeds 23 – Skipton 6.

⌂⌂⌂ **Devonshire Arms** 🔇, BD21 6AJ, Bolton Bridge ☎ 441, Telex 51218, <, 🎣 – [TV] 📞 ♿ [P]. 👥. [Access] [AE] [D] [VISA]
M (buffet lunch) a la carte 9.65/16.00 **st.** 🍷 4.00 – **37 rm** ☕ 48.00/68.00 **st.**

BOLTON BY BOWLAND Lancs. [402] N 22 – pop. 693 – ✉ Clitheroe – ❂ 020 07.
♦London 249 – Kendal 46 – ♦Leeds 41 – ♦Manchester 38 – Preston 25.

⌂ **Harrop Fold Farm** 🔇, Harrop Fold, BB7 4PJ, W : 3½ m. via Lane Ends ☎ 600, <, 🎣 – [TV] 🛁wc [P]
M (dinner only) a la carte 5.80/12.80 **st.** 🍷 2.60 – **7 rm** ☕ 16.00/35.00 **st.** – SB (except Christmas) 44.50/50.00 **st.**

BONCHURCH I.O.W. [403] [404] Q 32 – see Wight (Isle of) : Ventnor.

BONTDDU Gwynedd [402] [403] I 25 – see Dolgellau.

BONT-FAEN = Cowbridge.

BOOTLE Merseyside [402] ㉜ [403] ② – see Liverpool.

BOREHAM STREET East Sussex [404] V 31 – see Herstmonceux.

BOROUGHBRIDGE North Yorks. [402] P 21 – pop. 1,864 – ECD : Thursday – ❂ 090 12.
♦London 216 – ♦Leeds 26 – ♦Middlesbrough 35 – York 17.

⌂⌂⌂ **Crown,** Horsefair, YO5 9LB, ☎ 2328 – ⇅ [TV] ♿ [P]. 👥. [Access] [AE] [D] [VISA]
M 6.95/9.25 **st.** 🍷 3.20 – **43 rm** ☕ 29.75/52.75 **t.** – SB 44.00/51.00 **st.**

⌂⌂ **Three Arrows** (Embassy) 🔇, Horsefair, YO5 9LL, ☎ 2245, 🌳, park – [TV] 🛁wc 📞 [P]. [Access] [AE] [D] [VISA]. ⊘
M 6.75/8.50 **st.** 🍷 4.50 – ☕ 4.25 – **17 rm** 29.00/39.00 **st.** – SB (weekends only) 45.00/52.00 **st.**

🍴🍴 **Fountain House,** St. James Sq., YO5 9AR, ☎ 2241 – [P]. [Access] [AE] [D] [VISA]
closed Sunday, Monday and 11 to 24 June – **M** (dinner only) a la carte 11.35/13.80 **t.** 🍷 2.50.

BORROWDALE Cumbria [402] K 20 – see Keswick.

BOSCASTLE Cornwall [403] F 31 **The West Country G.** – ❂ 084 05.
See : Site★.
♦London 260 – Bude 14 – Exeter 59 – ♦Plymouth 43.

⌂ Riverside, The Harbour, PL35 0HE, ☎ 216 – 🛁wc 🚿wc [P]. ⊘ – **11 rm**.

⌂ **Bottreaux House,** PL35 0BG, on B 3266 ☎ 231 – [TV] 🛁wc 🚿wc [P]. [Access] [VISA]
M (bar lunch) 10.00 **t.** 🍷 2.90 – **10 rm** ☕ 12.00/28.00 **t.**

⌃ **St. Christopher's Country House,** High St., PL35 0BD, S : ½ m. by B 3266 ☎ 412 – 🚿wc [P]
March-November – **8 rm** ☕ 9.00/35.00 **st.**

BOSHAM West Sussex [404] R 31 – see Chichester.

EUROPE on a single sheet
Michelin map no [920].

BOSTON Lincs. 402 404 T 25 – pop. 26,025 – ECD : Thursday – ☎ 0205.

See : St. Botolph's Church★★ 14C.

📷 Cowbridge, Horncastle Rd ℘ 62306, N : 2 m. on B 1183.

🅱 28 South St. ℘ 64601 (summer only).

♦London 122 – Lincoln 35 – ♦Nottingham 55.

🏨 **New England** (Anchor), 49 Wide Bargate, PE21 6SH, ℘ 65255 – 📺 ➰wc ☎. 🔊 🅰🅴 ⓪ 𝗩𝗜𝗦𝗔
   M (carving rest.) 8.65 **st.** ░ 2.65 – **25 rm** ☑ 30.00/40.00 **st.** – SB (weekends only) 45.00 **st.**

AUSTIN-ROVER-DAIMLER Wide Bargate ℘ 66677
AUSTIN-ROVER-JAGUAR Leverton ℘ 226
BMW, NISSAN ℘ 63851
COLT, LADA, RELIANT Frith Rd ℘ 62230
FIAT London Rd ℘ 55500
FORD 57 High St. ℘ 60404
MERCEDES-BENZ 6 Horncastle Rd ℘ 64708

PEUGEOT, TALBOT Grantham Rd ℘ 69020
RENAULT Sleaford Rd ℘ 61901
TOYOTA Tawney St. ℘ 68626
VAUXHALL Butterwick ℘ 760421
VOLVO West St. ℘ 69288
VW, AUDI-NSU ℘ 63867

BOTALLACK Cornwall – see St. Just.

BOTLEY Hants. 403 404 Q 31 – pop. 2,163 – ECD : Thursday – ✉ Hedge End, Southampton – ☎ 048 92.

♦London 83 – ♦Portsmouth 17 – ♦Southampton 6 – Winchester 11.

🏨 **Botleigh Grange** 🦢, Grange Rd, Hedge End, SO3 2GA, W : 1 m. on A 334 ℘ 5611, ≼, 🦢,
   🌳, park – 📦 📺 ➰wc 🚿wc ☎ 🅿 🔊 🅰 𝗩𝗜𝗦𝗔
   M 8.00 **st.** ░ 2.75 – **45 rm** ☑ 28.50/46.00 **st.**

XX **Cobbett's**, 13-15 The Square, SO3 2EA, ℘ 2068 – 🅿 🔊 𝗩𝗜𝗦𝗔
   closed Saturday and Monday lunch, Sunday, 2 weeks in winter and 2 weeks in summer – **M** a
   la carte 12.70/17.00 **t.** ░ 3.30.

AUDI, VW Shamblehurst Lane ℘ 3434

AUSTIN-ROVER-DAIMLER-JAGUAR Southampton
Rd ℘ 5111

BOTTESFORD Leics. 402 404 R 25 – pop. 2,375 – ECD : Wednesday – ☎ 0949.

♦ London 116 – Grantham 75 – Lincoln 26 – ♦ Leicester 32 – ♦ Nottingham 18.

XX **Thatch,** 26 High St., NG13 0AA, ℘ 42330 – 🅿 🔊 🅰🅴 ⓪ 𝗩𝗜𝗦𝗔
   M (closed Sunday) (lunch by arrangement) a la carte 10.20/15.65 **st.** ░ 2.85.

BOURNE Lincs. 402 404 S 25 – pop. 5,420 – ECD : Wednesday – ☎ 077 833 Witham-on-the-Hill.

♦London 101 – ♦Leicester 42 – Lincoln 35 – ♦Nottingham 42.

🏠 **Toft House**, Main Rd, Toft, PE10 0JT, SW : 3 m. on A 6121 ℘ 614, 🌳, squash – 📺 ➰wc
   🚿wc 🅿 𝗩𝗜𝗦𝗔 🍴
   M 4.55/5.55 **t.** ░ 2.40 – **10 rm** ☑ 12.50/26.00.

AUSTIN-ROVER Thurlby Rd ℘ 2892
AUSTIN-ROVER North St. ℘ 2129

NISSAN Rippingale ℘ 07785 (Dowsby) 777

BOURNE END Herts. 404 S 28 – see Hemel Hempstead.

BOURNEMOUTH Dorset 403 404 O 31 The West Country G. – pop. 153,869 – ECD : Wednesday and Saturday – ☎ 0202.

See : Museums★DX, DZ **M.**

📷 Meyrick Park ℘ 20871CY – 📷 Queen's Park, Queen's Park South Drive ℘ 36198, NE : 2 m.CV.

✈ Hurn Airport : ℘ 578646, Telex 41345, N : 5 m. by Hurn RdDV.

🅱 Westover Rd ℘ 291715 and 20883.

♦London 107 – ♦Bristol 76 – ♦Southampton 34.

Plans on following pages

🏨 **Carlton**, Meyrick Rd, East Overcliff, BH1 3DN, ℘ 22011, Telex 41244, ≼, 🌊 heated, 🌳 – 🕴
   📺 ᨃ ➰ 🅿 🔊 🅰🅴 ⓪ 𝗩𝗜𝗦𝗔   EZ **a**
   M 9.50/12.00 **t.** (see also **La Causerie** below) – ☑ 6.00 – **55 rm** 42.50/75.00 **t.** – SB
   88.00/132.00 **st.**

🏨 **Royal Bath** (De Vere), Bath Rd, BH1 2EW, ℘ 25555, Telex 41375, ≼, 🌊 heated, 🌳 – 🕴 📺
   ᨃ ➰ 🅿 🔊 🅰🅴 ⓪ 𝗩𝗜𝗦𝗔 🍴   DZ **a**
   M 8.50/15.00 **t.** ░ 3.25 (see also **The Royal Grill** below) – **133 rm** ☑ 48.00/110.00 **t.** – SB 85.00 **st.**

🏨 **Palace Court,** Westover Rd, BH1 3BZ, ℘ 27681, Telex 418451, ≼ – 🕴 📺 ☎ 🅿 🔊 🅰🅴
   ⓪ 𝗩𝗜𝗦𝗔   DZ **c**
   M 8.00/9.50 **st.** ░ 3.00 (see also **La Taverna** below) – **103 rm** ☑ 36.00/62.00 **st.**

🏨 **Highcliff** (Best Western), 105 St. Michael's Rd, West Cliff, BH2 5DU, ℘ 27702, Telex 417153,
   ≼, 🌊 heated, 🌳, 🍴 – 🕴 📺 ☎ 🅿 🔊 🅰🅴 ⓪ 𝗩𝗜𝗦𝗔   CZ **z**
   M 7.00/10.50 **st.** – **99 rm** ☑ 33.00/47.00 **st.** – SB 60.00/80.00 **st.**

🏨 **Marsham Court** (De Vere), Russell Cotes Rd, East Cliff, BH1 3AB, ℘ 22111, Group Telex
   41420, ≼, 🌊 heated – 🕴 📺 🅿 🔊 🅰🅴 ⓪ 𝗩𝗜𝗦𝗔 🍴   DZ **e**
   M 6.75/8.00 **t.** ░ 3.25 – **80 rm** ☑ 30.00/56.00 **t.** – SB (weekends only) 50.00/59.00 **st.**

🏨 **Cliff End,** Manor Rd, East Cliff, BH1 3EX, ℰ 309711, ⌁ heated, 🚗 – ▮ TV ⌷wc ▥wc ☎ ℗
    CX **v**
M 6.00/7.50 st. – **40 rm** ⌷ 22.50/49.00 st. – SB 41.80/58.00 st.

🏨 **Crest** (Crest), Meyrick Rd, The Lansdowne, BH1 2PR, ℰ 23262, Telex 41232 – ▮ TV ⌷wc
    ☎ ℗ ≜ 🖭 AE ⓞ VISA   DY **a**
M approx. 10.00 st. – ⌷ 5.25 – **102 rm** 36.50/54.50 st.

🏨 **Burley Court,** 29 Bath Rd, BH1 2NP, ℰ 22824, ⌁ heated – ▮ TV ⌷wc ☎ 🖳 ℗ 🖭 VISA
    closed first 2 weeks January – **M** (bar lunch) 7.00 st. ▯ 2.80 – **41 rm** ⌷ 16.50/45.00 st. – SB
    (weekends only) 39.00 st.   DY **i**

🏨 **East Cliff Court,** East Overcliff Drive, BH1 3AN, ℰ 24545, ≼, ⌁ heated – ▮ TV ⌷wc ☎
    ℗ ≜ 🖭 VISA   EZ **e**
M 7.25/9.75 t. ▯ 2.95 – **70 rm** ⌷ 23.00/46.00 t. – SB (weekends only) (not sum-
mer and Bank Holidays) 46.00/51.00 st.

🏨 **Cliffeside,** 32 East Overcliff Drive, BH1 3AQ, ℰ 25724, ≼, ⌁ heated – ▮ TV ⌷wc ☎
    ℗ ≜ 🖭 VISA   EZ **v**
M 5.50/7.50 st. ▯ 2.00 – **64 rm** ⌷ 18.00/53.00 t. – SB 38.00/55.00 st.

🏨 **Chesterwood,** East Overcliff Drive, BH1 3AR, ℰ 28057, ≼, ⌁ heated – ▮ TV ⌷wc ▥wc
    ℗ 🖭 ⓞ VISA   EZ **i**
closed January and February – **M** 5.00/7.50 st. ▯ 2.50 – **54 rm** ⌷ 15.50/43.60 st. – SB (win-
ter only) 38.00/40.00 st.

🏨 **Winterbourne,** Priory Rd, BH2 5GJ, ℰ 24927, ≼, ⌁ heated – ▮ TV ⌷wc ▥wc 🖭 VISA
    CZ **n**
M (bar lunch) 6.75 st. ▯ 1.90 – **41 rm** ⌷ 15.25/43.00 st. – SB (except summer) 34.00/
39.50 st.

🏨 **Bournemouth Moat House** (Q.M.H.), Knyveton Rd, BH1 3QQ, ℰ 293311, ⌁ heated – ▮
    TV ⌷wc ☎ ℗ 🖭 🖭 VISA   CX **e**
M 6.00/8.00 st. – **113 rm** ⌷ 27.00/41.00 st. – SB 46.00/49.50 st.

🏨 **Queens,** Meyrick Rd, Eastcliff, BH1 3DL, ℰ 24415, Group Telex 418297 – ▮ TV ⌷wc ☎ ℗.
    ≜ 🖭 VISA   EYZ **r**
M 4.95/7.95 st. ▯ 2.60 – **110 rm** ⌷ 18.00/42.00 t. – SB 45.00/47.00 st.

🏨 **Ladbroke Savoy** (Ladbroke), West Hill Rd, West Cliff, BH2 5EJ, ℰ 294241, ≼, ⌁ heated, 🚗
    – ▮ TV ⌷wc ☎ 🖳 ℗ ≜   CZ **x**
88 rm

🏨 **Heathlands,** 12 Grove Rd, East Cliff, BH1 3AY, ℰ 23336, Group Telex 418261, ⌁ heated –
    ▮ TV ⌷wc ☎ 🖳 ℗ ≜ 🖭 🖭 VISA   EZ **c**
M 7.00/8.50 st. – **120 rm** ⌷ 20.00/40.00 st. – SB (weekends only) (spring only) 40.00/45.00 st.

🏨 **Durley Hall,** 7 Durley Chine Rd, Westcliff, BH2 5JS, ⌁ heated, 🚗 – ▮ TV
    ⌷wc ☎ ℗ ≜ 🖭 ⓞ VISA   CZ **s**
M 5.00/8.50 t. ▯ 2.25 – **82 rm** ⌷ 14.00/40.00 t. – SB (weekends only) 31.00/50.00 st.

🏨 **Anglo-Swiss,** 16 Gervis Rd, East Cliff, BH1 3EQ, ℰ 24794, Group Telex 418261, ⌁ heated,
    🚗 – ▮ TV ⌷wc ☎ ℗ 🖭 🖭 ⓞ VISA   EY **e**
M (buffet lunch) 6.00/7.50 st. ▯ 2.50 – **63 rm** ⌷ 20.00/56.00 st.

🏠 **Hinton Firs,** 9 Manor Rd, East Cliff, BH1 3HB, ℰ 25409, ⌁ heated – ▮ TV ⌷wc ℗. 🍴
M 5.25/6.25 st. ▯ 2.30 – **56 rm** ⌷ 13.25/42.00 st. – SB (winter only except Christmas and Eas-
ter) 32.00/39.00 st.   EY **n**

🏠 **Miramar,** 19 Grove Rd, East Overcliff, BH1 3AL, ℰ 26581, ≼, 🚗 – ▮ TV ⌷wc ▥wc ☎ ℗.
    🖭 🖭   DZ **u**
M 5.50/8.00 ▯ 3.00 – **42 rm** ⌷ 19.00/42.00 – SB (except summer) 37.00/43.00 st.

🏠 **Cliff House,** 113 Alumhurst Rd, Alum Chine, BH4 8HS, ℰ 763003, ≼ – ▮ TV ⌷wc ▥wc 🖳
    ℗ 🍴   BX **s**
closed 5 January-28 February and 2 November-17 December – **M** (dinner only) 7.50 st. ▯ 2.50
– **10 rm** ⌷ 12.65/41.50 st.

🏠 **Cottonwood,** 79 Grove Rd, East Cliff, BH1 3AP, ℰ 23183, ≼, 🚗 – ▮ TV ⌷wc ▥wc ℗
M (bar lunch) 7.00 t. ▯ 2.75 – **30 rm** ⌷ 14.50/35.00.   EY **s**

🏠 **Chinehead,** 31 Alumhurst Rd, BH4 8EN, ℰ 761693 – ⌷wc ℗. 🖭 VISA   BX **n**
M (bar lunch) 4.50 st. – **27 rm** ⌷ 10.00/28.50 st.

⋔ **Alumcliff,** 121 Alumhurst Rd, Alum Chine, BH4 8HS, ℰ 764777, ≼ – ⌷wc ▥wc ℗. 🖭 🖭
    VISA   BX **a**
16 rm ⌷ 16.70/35.65 t.

⋔ **Valberg,** 1A Wollstonecraft Rd, Boscombe, BH5 1JQ, ℰ 34644, 🚗 – ▥wc ℗. 🍴   CX **s**
closed Christmas – **10 rm** ⌷ 8.50/19.00.

⋔ **Naseby Nye,** 10 Byron Rd, Boscombe Overcliff, BH5 1JD, ℰ 34079, 🚗 – ⌷wc ℗   DX **z**
13 rm ⌷ 10.00/23.50 s.

⋔ **Tudor Grange,** 31 Gervis Rd, BH1 3EE, ℰ 291472, 🚗 – ℗   EY **o**
12 rm ⌷ 10.00/27.00 st.

⋔ **Mariners,** 22 Clifton Rd, Southbourne, BH6 3PA, ℰ 420851 – ℗   EX **c**
March-October – **15 rm** ⌷ 7.50/15.00 st.

⋔ **Wood Lodge,** 10 Manor Rd, East Cliff, BH1 3EY, ℰ 290891, 🚗 – ⌷wc ▥wc ℗. 🍴   EY **z**
April-October – **16 rm** ⌷ 9.75/24.25 t.

⋔ **Southwood Lodge,** 36-38 Southwood Av., Southbourne, BH6 3QB, ℰ 422213 – ▥wc ℗.
    🖭 VISA   DX **r**
31 rm ⌷ 6.50/15.00 st.

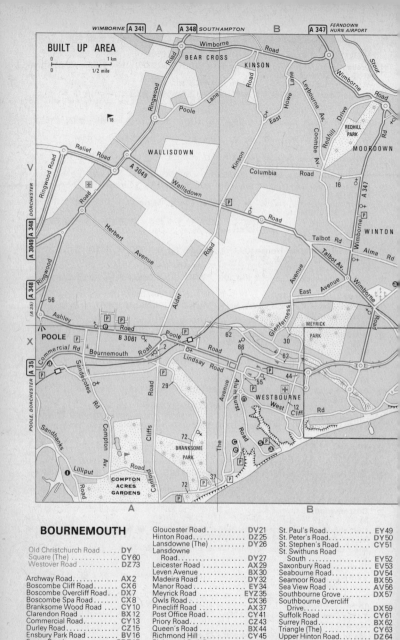

BOURNEMOUTH

Town plans : the names of main shopping streets are indicated in red
at the beginning of the list of streets.

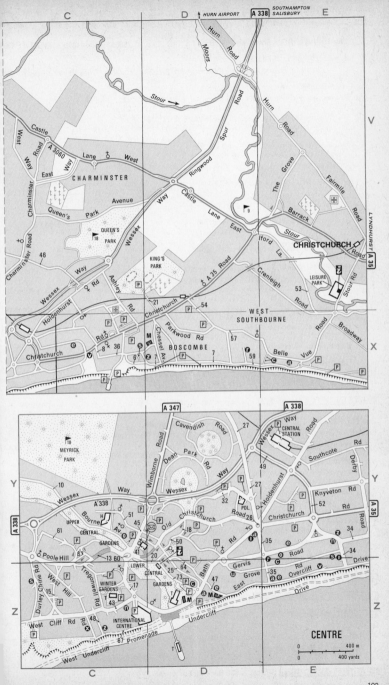

XXX **La Causerie** (at Carlton H.), Meyrick Rd, East Overcliff, BH1 3DN, ℰ 22011, Telex 41244 – ℗
EZ a

XXX **The Royal Grill** (at Royal Bath H.), Bath Rd, BH1 2EW, ℰ 25555, Telex 41375 – ℗. ⬛ AE ⑩ **VISA**
DZ a
M a la carte 14.00/20.50 t. ⓵ 3.25.

XX **La Taverna** (at Palace Court H.), Westover Rd, BH1 3BZ, ℰ 27681, Telex 418451 – ℗. ⬛ AE ⑩ **VISA**
DZ c
closed Sunday – **M** a la carte 11.15/17.75

XX **Provence,** 91 Belle Vue Rd., Southbourne, BH6 3DH, ℰ 424421, French rest. – ⬛ AE ⑩ **VISA**
EX a
closed Sunday, Monday and February – **M** a la carte 11.20/12.50 **st.**

X **Sophisticats,** 43 Charminster Rd, BH8 8UE, ℰ 291019
BV a
M *(closed Sunday, Monday, last 2 weeks January and first week February)* (dinner only) a la carte 9.45/11.00 **t.**

X **Crust,** The Square, ℰ 21430 – ⬛ ⑩ **VISA**
CY o
closed 25 and 26 December – **M** a la carte 6.75/11.50 **t.** ⓵ 2.50.

ALFA-ROMEO, VOLVO 33 R. L. Stephenson Av. ℰ 763344
AUSTIN-ROVER 235 Castle Lane West, Redhill ℰ 510201
AUSTIN-ROVER 14 Carbery Row ℰ 423243
BENTLEY, ROLLS ROYCE 26 Oxford Rd ℰ 25748
BMW Exeter Rd ℰ 24433
CITROEN, PEUGEOT, TALBOT 43 Holdenhurst Rd ℰ 26566

DAIMLER-JAGUAR 38 Poole Hill ℰ 25405
FORD Poole Rd ℰ 762442
LANCIA 318/320 Holdenhurst Rd ℰ 33304
PEUGEOT 25/27 Palmerston Rd, Boscombe ℰ 37206
PORSCHE 382/386 Charminster Rd ℰ 510252
VAUXHALL 521 Christchurch Rd ℰ 35362
VAUXHALL Castle Lane West ℰ 526434
VAUXHALL 984 Christchurch Rd ℰ 423201
VAUXHALL-OPEL Poole Rd ℰ 763361

BOURTON-ON-THE-WATER Glos. 🆊🆊🆊 🆊🆊🆊 O 28 – pop. 2,251 – ECD : Saturday – ✆ 0451 Cotswold.

♦London 91 – ♦Birmingham 47 – Gloucester 24 – ♦Oxford 36.

🏨 **Old Manse,** Victoria St., GL54 2BX, ℰ 20642, 🐾 – ⛝ 📺 🛁wc ℗. ⬛ **VISA** 🐾
closed 6 to 20 January – **M** 5.50/6.85 **t.** ⓵ 3.25 – ☷ 1.95 – **9 rm** 20.50/36.00 **t.** – SB (winter only) 53.00/55.00 **st.**

🏨 **Old New Inn,** High St., GL54 2AF, ℰ 20467, « Bourton model village », 🐾 – 🚗 ℗. ⬛ **VISA**
closed Christmas – **M** 5.50/8.80 **st.** ⓵ 1.80 – **24 rm** ☷ 15.90/34.80 **st.**

🏨 **Brookside,** Riverside, GL54 2BS, ℰ 20371, 🐾 – 📺 🛁wc ⛝wc ℗. ⬛ AE ⑩ **VISA**
M 5.50/10.00 **t.** ⓵ 2.90 – **10 rm** ☷ 13.65/32.00 **t.** – SB 38.00/45.00 **st.**

X **Rose Tree,** Riverside, GL54 2BX, ℰ 20635 – ⬛ AE ⑩ **VISA**
closed Sunday lunch in summer, Sunday dinner, Monday and February – **M** (bar lunch Tuesday to Saturday) 9.00/15.50 **t.** ⓵ 2.95.

FORD Lansdowne Rd ℰ 20366
FORD Station Rd ℰ 20366
SKODA Fossway ℰ 20132

BOVEY TRACEY Devon 🆊🆊🆊 I 32 The West Country G. – pop. 3,834 – ECD : Wednesday – ✉ Newton Abbot – ✆ 0626.

See : St. Peter, St. Paul and St. Thomas of Canterbury Church★.

🛈 Lower Car Park ℰ 832047 (summer only) – ♦London 214 – Exeter 14 – ♦Plymouth 32.

🏨 **Prestbury Country House** 🐾, Brimley Lane, Brimley, TQ13 9JS, SW : 1 m. by A 382 ℰ 833246, ≼, « Country house atmosphere », 🐾 – ⛝wc ⛝wc ℗. ⬛ AE ⑩ **VISA** 🐾
March-October – **M** (bar lunch) 10.00 **st.** ⓵ 2.00 – **8 rm** ☷ 18.00/40.00 **st.**

🏨 **Coombe Cross,** Coombe Cross, TQ13 9EY, ℰ 832476, 🐾 – ⛝wc ℗. AE **VISA** 🐾
closed 1 January-21 February – **M** (buffet lunch) 3.50/8.00 **t.** ⓵ 2.50 – **22 rm** ☷ 24.00/36.00 **t.**

↑ **Front House,** East St., TQ13 9EL, ℰ 832202, ⬛, 🐾 – ⛝wc ℗
April-October – **6 rm** ☷ 10.00/20.00 **st.**

BOWBURN Durham 🆊🆊🆊 🆊🆊🆊 P 19 – pop. 5,060 – ✆ 0385 Durham.

♦London 265 – Durham 3 – ♦Middlesbrough 20.

🏨 **Bowburn Hall,** DH6 5NT, E : 1 m. ℰ 770311, Telex 537681, 🐾 – 📺 🛁wc 🚗 ℗. ⬛ AE
M 5.00/7.50 **st.** ⓵ 3.00 – **20 rm** ☷ 26.00/32.00 **st.**

BOWDON Greater Manchester 🆊🆊🆊 🆊🆊🆊 🆊🆊🆊 M 23 – see Altrincham.

BOWNESS-ON-WINDERMERE Cumbria 🆊🆊🆊 L 20 – see Windermere.

BRACKNELL Berks. 🆊🆊🆊 R 29 – pop. 34,067 – ECD : Wednesday – ✆ 0344.

🛈 Central Library, Town Sq., ℰ 423149 – ♦London 35 – Reading 11.

🏨 **Ladbroke** (Ladbroke), Bagshot Rd, RG12 3QJ, S : 2 m. on A 322 ℰ 424801, Telex 848058 – 📶 📺 ⛝wc ☎ ⓵ ⬛. 🐾. ⬛ AE ⑩ **VISA**
M 9.50 **t.** ⓵ 4.45 – ☷ 5.50 – **115 rm** 46.00/56.00 **st.** – SB (weekends only) 49.00 **st.**

BRADFIELD COMBUST Suffolk – see Bury St. Edmunds.

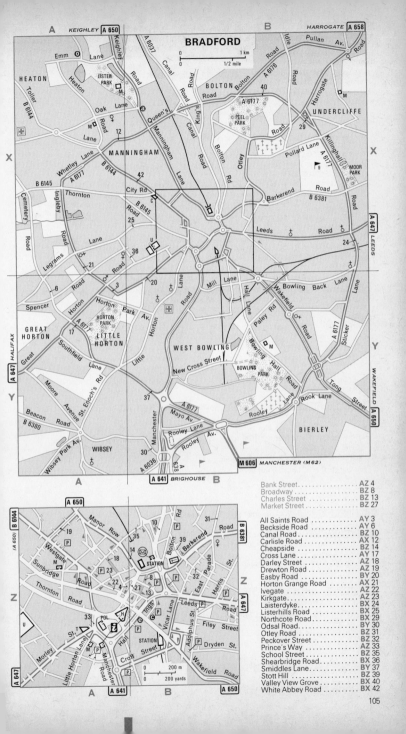

BRADFORD

BRADFORD West Yorks. 402 O 22 – pop. 294,177 – ECD : Wednesday – ✆ 0274.

☞ West Bradford, Chellow Grange, Haworth Rd ℰ 427671, NW : 3 m. by A 6144 AX – ☞ Hawksworth Lane, Guiseley ℰ 0943 (Guiseley) 75570, N : 8 m. by A 6037 BX – ☞ Bradford Moor, Scarr Hall, Pollard Lane ℰ 638313 BX – ☞ East Bierley, South View Rd ℰ 681023, SE : 4 m. on plan of Leeds BX.

✈ Leeds and Bradford Airport : ℰ 0532 (Rawdon) 503431, NE : 6 m. by A 658 BX – **Terminal :** Chester St., Bus Station, Bradford.

🛈 Central Library, Princes Way ℰ 753682 – City Hall ℰ 753682.

♦ London 212 – ♦Leeds 9 – ♦Manchester 39 – ♦Middlesbrough 75 – ♦Sheffield 45.

Plan of Enlarged Area : see Leeds

Plan on preceding page

🏤 **Stakis Norfolk Gardens** (Stakis), Hall Ings, BD1 5SH, ℰ 734734, Telex 517573 – 🛗 📺 ⅃.
🚗 ⚑ AE ⓪ VISA ⅏
M 5.95/8.50 t. ⅃ 3.25 – **123 rm** ⚏ 39.00/44.00 t. – SB 46.00 st.
BZ e

🏛 **Victoria** (T.H.F.), Bridge St., BD1 1JX, ℰ 728706, Telex 517456 – 🛗 📺 ➪wc 🏚wc 🅿.
🚗 ⚑ AE ⓪ VISA
M (carving rest.) 7.45/7.95 st. ⅃ 2.85 – ⚏ 5.25 – **59 rm** 26.00/41.50 st.
BZ c

🏛 **Novotel Bradford,** Euroway Trading Estate, Merrydale Rd, BD4 6SA, S : 3 ½ m. by A 641 and A 6117 off M 606 ℰ 683683, Telex 517312, ⌇ heated – 🛗 📺 ➪wc ☎ ⅃ 🅿. 🚗 ⚑ AE ⓪ VISA
on plan of Leeds AX a
M a la carte 4.95/9.00 st. ⅃ 3.10 – ⚏ 4.00 – **131 rm** 31.50/37.00 st. – SB (weekends only) 41.00 st.

♨ **Cartwright,** 308 Manningham Lane, BD8 7AX, ℰ 499908 – 📺 ➪wc 🅿. VISA ⅏
M 5.50/7.00 t. ⅃ 2.50 – **12 rm** ⚏ 21.00/30.00 t. – SB (weekends only) 36.00/40.00 st.
BX a

⌂ **Maple Hill,** 3 Park Drive, Heaton, BD9 4DP, ℰ 44061, 🍴 – 🅿. ⅏
10 rm ⚏ 10.50/18.50 t.
AX o

at Thornton W : 5 ¼ m. on B 6145 – AX – ⊠ ✆ 0274 Bradford :

XXX **Cottage,** 869 Thornton Rd, BD13 3NW, W : 1 m. on B 6145 ℰ 832752 – 🅿. ⚑ AE ⓪ VISA
closed Saturday lunch and Sunday – **M** a la carte 10.00/14.05 ⅃ 4.00.

AUSTIN-ROVER-DAIMLER-JAGUAR Canal Rd ℰ 733488
AUSTIN-ROVER 38 Manningham Lane ℰ 732444
BMW Oak Lane ℰ 495521
CITROEN Whetley Hill ℰ 495543
COLT St. Enoch's Rd ℰ 722234
FIAT Keighley Rd, Frizinghall ℰ 490031
FORD 44 Bowland St. ℰ 725131
FORD 146/148 Tong St. ℰ 681601
MERCEDES-BENZ Thornton Rd ℰ 494122
NISSAN 88 Thornton Rd ℰ 727302

NISSAN, PORSCHE, VAUXHALL-OPEL Parry Lane ℰ 392321
PEUGEOT-TALBOT 150 Manningham Lane ℰ 727181
POLONEZ, FSO 341 Leeds Rd ℰ 726812
RENAULT Frizinghall Rd ℰ 495711
SAAB Apperley Lane, Yeadon ℰ 0532 (Leeds) 502231
VAUXHALL-OPEL 230 Manningham Lane ℰ 491432
VOLVO 221 Sunbridge Rd ℰ 721720
VW, AUDI-NSU Ingleby Rd ℰ 494100

BRADFORD-ON-AVON Wilts. 403 404 N 29 The West Country G. – pop. 9,250 – ECD : Wednesday – ✆ 022 16.

See : Site★★ – Saxon Church of St. Lawrence★★ – Bridge★.
Envir. : Great Chalfield Manor★ (Church★), NE : 2 m. – Westwood Manor★, SW : 1 ½ m.
🛈 1 Church St. ℰ 2224.
♦London 118 – ♦ Bristol 24 – Salisbury 35 – Swindon 33.

🏠 **Leigh Park,** Leigh Road West, BA15 2RA, NE : 1 m. by A 363 and B 3109 on B 3105 ℰ 3433, 🍴, 🚗 – 🛗 📺 ➪wc 🏚wc 🅿. 🚗 ⚑ VISA ⅏
closed 24 and 25 December – **M** (closed Sunday lunch and Saturday) 4.75/8.50 t. – **20 rm** ⚏ 19.50/33.00 t.

BRADFORD-ON-TONE Somerset 403 K 30 – see Taunton.

BRADWORTHY Devon 403 G 31 – pop. 826 – ECD : Wednesday – ⊠ Holsworthy – ✆ 040 924.
♦London 251 – Barnstaple 27 – Exeter 50 – ♦Plymouth 47.

🏠 **Lake Villa** ⌇, EX22 7SQ, E : ½ m. ℰ 342, 🍴, ⅏ – 📺 ➪wc 🏚wc 🅿. ⅏
M (bar lunch)(booking essential) 8.50 st. ⅃ 2.75 – **7 rm** ⚏ 17.50/31.00 t. – SB (June-September) 42.00/46.00 st.

BRAINTREE Essex 404 V 28 – pop. 22,310 – ECD : Thursday – ✆ 0376.
♦London 45 – ♦Cambridge 38 – Chelmsford 12 – Colchester 15.

🏛 **White Hart,** Bocking End, CM7 6AB, ℰ 21401 – 📺 ➪wc 🚿 🅿. 🚗
35 rm.

ALFA-ROMEO Bocking ℰ 26604
FORD Rayne Rd ℰ 21202
MAZDA Rayne ℰ 42159

VAUXHALL-OPEL 277/281 Rayne Rd ℰ 21456
VOLVO Skitts Hill ℰ 47797

BRAITHWAITE Cumbria 401 402 K 20 – see Keswick.

BRAMBER West Sussex – see Steyning.

BRAMHALL Greater Manchester 402 403 404 N 23 – pop. 39,619 – ECD : Wednesday – © 061 Manchester.

See : Bramhall Hall★ (14C-16C) *AC*.

☖ Ladythorn Rd ☏ 439 4057.

🛈 13 Bramhall Lane South ☏ 440 8400.

♦London 194 – ♦Liverpool 44 – ♦Manchester 10 – ♦Stoke-on-Trent 33.

🏨 **Bramhall Moat House** (Q.M.H.), Bramhall Lane South, SK7 2EB, on A 5102 ☏ 439 8116 –
🌅 📺 ➡wc ☎ 🅿 ♨ 🔥 🅰🅴 ⊙ 𝑉𝐼𝑆𝐴
closed 25 December-2 January – **M** (bar lunch Monday to Saturday) 5.75/8.50 **t**. ◊ 3.15 –
40 rm ⊇ 33.00/44.00 **t**. – SB (weekends only) 47.00/49.00 **st**.

BRAMHOPE West Yorks. 402 P 22 – see Leeds.

BRAMLEY Surrey 404 S 30 – see Guildford.

BRAMPTON Cambs. 404 T 27 – pop. 4,494 – ECD : Tuesday and Saturday – ⊠ © 0480 Huntingdon.

♦London 67 – Bedford 19 – Huntingdon 2.

🏨 **Brampton,** PE18 8NH, W : 1 ½ m. at junction A 1 and A 604 ☏ 810434 – 📺 ➡wc ☎ 🅿 ♨.
🔥 🅰🅴 𝑉𝐼𝑆𝐴
M a la carte 7.80/12.00 **st**. ◊ 3.00 – **17 rm** ⊇ 33.00/48.00 **st**. – SB (weekends only) 46.00 **st**.

CITROEN Huntingdon Rd ☏ 53132

BRAMPTON Cumbria 401 402 L 19 – pop. 3,895 – ECD : Thursday – © 069 77.

Envir. : Lanercost : Priory★ (14C ruins) *AC*, NE : 3 m. – Bewcastle (churchyard Runic Cross★ 8C) N : 12 m.

☖ Talkin Tarn ☏ 2255, SE : 1 m. on B 6413.

🛈 Moot Hall, Market Place ☏ 3433 (summer only).

♦ London 317 – ♦Carlisle 9 – ♦Newcastle-upon-Tyne 49.

🏨 **Farlam Hall** ⬗, CA8 2NG, SE : 2 ¾ m. on A 689 ☏ 069 76 (Hallbankgate) 234, ≼, « Gardens »
– ➡wc 🅿 🔥 🅰🅴 ⊙. 🐾
closed Monday and Tuesday November-January, February and first 2 weeks November – **M**
(dinner only and Sunday lunch) 8.50/12.50 **t**. – **11 rm** ⊇ 32.00/64.00 **t**. – SB (winter only) 60.00 **st**.

at Talkin S : 2 m. by B 6413 – ⊠ © 069 77 Brampton :

✕✕ **Tarn End** ⬗ with rm, Talkin Tarn, CA8 1LS, ☏ 2340, ≼ Talkin Tarn, 🐟, 🌲 – 🅿 🔥 🅰🅴 ⊙.
🐾
closed October and Christmas Day – **M** a la carte 10.60/15.75 **st**. ◊ 2.75 – **6 rm** ⊇ 23.00/40.00 **st**.
– SB (winter only) 50.00/56.00 **st**.

BRAMSHAW Hants. 403 404 P 31 – pop. 602 – ECD : Tuesday – ⊠ Lyndhurst – © 0703 Southampton.

♦London 93 – Salisbury 13 – ♦Southampton 11 – Winchester 21.

🏠 **Bramble Hill** ⬗, Bramble Hill, SO4 7JG, W : ½ m. ☏ 813165, ≼, « Former hunting lodge »,
🌲, park – ➡wc 🅿. 🔥
M *(closed November-March)* (bar lunch Monday to Saturday) 6.00/7.50 **t**. ◊ 2.00 – **16 rm**
⊇ 15.30/33.60 **t**. – SB (summer only) 40.00/44.50 **st**.

BRANDON Warw. 403 404 P 26 – see Coventry.

BRANSCOMBE Devon 403 K 32 The West Country G. – pop. 477 – ECD : Thursday – ⊠ Seaton
– © 029 780.

♦London 167 – Exeter 20 – Lyme Regis 11.

🏨 **Ye Olde Masons Arms,** EX12 3DJ, ☏ 300, « 14C inn », 🌲 – ➡wc 🅿
M (bar lunch Monday to Saturday) 6.50/13.00 **t**. ◊ 2.95 – **20 rm** ⊇ 16.00/46.00 **s**.

BRANSTON Staffs. – see Burton-upon-Trent.

BRAUNSTONE Leics. 402 403 404 Q 26 – see Leicester.

Do not mix up :		
Comfort of hotels	🏨🏨 ... 🏠, 🏡, ⌂	
Comfort of restaurants	✗✗✗✗✗ ..... ✗	
Quality of the cuisine	🌸🌸🌸, 🌸🌸, 🌸, M	

BRAY-ON-THAMES Berks. 404 R 29 – pop. 5,818 – ✉ ☎ 0628 Maidenhead.
◆London 34 – Reading 13.

🏨 **Monkey Island** (Best Western), SL6 2EE, SE : 1 m. by Monkey Island Lane ℰ 23400, ≼, « Island in River Thames », ⚲, 🍴, park – 📺 📞wc 🛗wc ℗ 🏖 🔼 AE ① VISA
closed 25 and 26 December – **M** 12.50 t. ⏳ 4.00 – **25 rm** ⏸ 46.00/58.00 t. – SB 55.00 st.

🏨 **Chauntry House,** High St., SL6 2AB, ℰ 73991, ⚲, 🍴 – 📺 📞wc 🛗wc ℗ 🔼 AE VISA
M (closed Friday, Saturday and Sunday) (bar lunch) 10.50 st. ⏳ 3.50 – **9 rm** ⏸ 39.10/49.50 st.

XXXX ❀❀❀ **Waterside Inn**, Ferry Rd, SL6 2AT, ℰ 20691, Telex 8813079, ≼, French rest. – « Thames-side setting », 🍴 – ℗ 🔼 AE ① VISA
closed Tuesday lunch, Sunday dinner 20 October-21 April, Monday, 26 December-15 February and Bank Holidays – **M** a la carte 20.40/27.30 st.
Spec. Ravioles de homard truffées sauce vierge, Filets de lapereau grillés aux marrons glacés, Panaché de tarte au citron et délice au cassis.

XX **Hind's Head,** High St., SL6 2AB, ℰ 26151, English rest., 🍴 – ℗ 🔼 AE ① VISA
M (closed Sunday dinner) 16.00/17.50 st.

BRECHFA Dyfed 403 H 28 – pop. 175 – ✉ Carmarthen – ☎ 026 789.
◆London 223 – Carmarthen 11 – ◆Swansea 30.

XX **Ty Mawr** 🦢 with rm, Abergorlech Rd, SA32 7RA, ℰ 332, ⚲, 🍴 – 🛗wc ℗ 🔼 ① VISA
M (closed Sunday and Monday to non-residents) (lunch residents only) a la carte 7.35/9.50 st. ⏳ 2.60 – **5 rm** ⏸ 21.00/38.50 st. – SB 50.00 st.

BREDWARDINE Heref. and Worc. 403 L 27 – pop. 172 – ✉ Hereford – ☎ 098 17 Moccas.
◆London 150 – Hereford 12 – Newport 51.

🏨 **Red Lion,** HR3 6BU, ℰ 303, ⚲, 🍴 – 🛗wc ℗ 🔼 AE ① VISA, 🐾
M (bar lunch) 10.50 t. ⏳ 2.50 – **10 rm** ⏸ 12.50/38.00 t. – SB (March-June) 35.00/45.00 st.

BRENDON Devon 403 I 30 – see Lynton.

BRENTWOOD Essex 404 V 29 – pop. 51,330 – ECD : Thursday – ☎ 0277.
🏌 King George's playing fields ℰ 218714.
◆London 22 – Chelmsford 11 – Southend-on-Sea 21.

🏨 **Brentwood Moat House** (Q.M.H.), London Rd, CM14 4NR, SW : 1 ¼ m. on A 1023 ℰ 225252, Telex 995182, ⚲ – 📺 🦮 ℗ 🔼 🔼 AE ① VISA
M a la carte 12.50/17.75 t. ⏳ 2.90 – ⏸ 5.25 – **37 rm** 40.00/48.50 st.

🏨 **Post House** (T.H.F.), Brook St., CM14 5NF, SW : 1 ¾ m. on A 1023 ℰ 210888, Telex 995379, ⏳ heated – 📺 🛗wc ⚲ 🦮 ℗ 🔼 🔼 AE ① VISA
M (closed Saturday lunch and Sunday dinner) 6.95/8.75 st. ⏳ 2.85 – ⏸ 5.00 – **120 rm** 40.00/47.00 st.

AUDI, VW, DAIMLER-JAGUAR 2 Brook St. ℰ 216161
AUSTIN-ROVER Ingrave Rd ℰ 221401
FORD Brook St. ℰ 215544

NISSAN 110 Shenfield Rd, Shenfield ℰ 222424
RENAULT Shenfield ℰ 218686
VAUXHALL-OPEL Brook St. ℰ 233131

BRERETON Cheshire – see Holmes Chapel.

BRIDGEND (PEN-Y-BONT) Mid Glam. 403 J 29 – pop. 14,544 – ECD : Wednesday – ☎ 0656 Pencoed.
◆London 177 – ◆Cardiff 20 – ◆Swansea 23.

🏨 **Heronston,** Ewenny, CF35 5AW, S : 2 m. on B 4265 ℰ 68811, Telex 498232, ⬛ – 📺 🛗wc ☎ ℗ 🦮 – **20 rm.**

at Coychurch E : 2 ¼ m. by A 473 – ✉ ☎ 0656 Bridgend :

XXX **Coed-y-Mwstwr** 🦢 with rm, CF35 6AF, N : 1 m. ℰ 860621, ≼, ⏳ heated, 🍴, park, 🐾 – 📺 📞wc 🛗wc ⚲ ℗ 🔼 🔼 AE ① VISA
closed 25 to 27 December – **M** (closed Saturday lunch and Sunday dinner) a la carte 15.75/21.75 t. ⏳ 3.00 – ⏸ 5.25 – **16 rm** 26.50/45.00 t.

MICHELIN Branch, Brackla Industrial Estate, CF31 2BD, ℰ 62343

BRIDGNORTH Salop 403 404 M 26 – pop. 9,400 – ECD : Thursday – ☎ 074 62.
Envir. : Claverley (Parish church : wall paintings★ 13C-15C) E : 5 m. – Much Wenlock – Wenlock priory★ (ruins 11C) AC, NW : 8 ½ m. – 🏌 Stanley Lane ℰ 3315, N : 1 m.
🅱 Bridgnorth Library, Listley St. ℰ 3358.
◆London 146 – ◆Birmingham 26 – Shrewsbury 20 – Worcester 29.

🏨 **Falcon,** St. John's St., Low Town, WV15 6AG, ℰ 3134 – 📺 📞wc 🛗wc ℗ 🔼 AE ① VISA
M 6.00/7.50 st. ⏳ 3.25 – **16 rm** ⏸ 17.50/30.00 st.

at Worfield NE : 4 m. by A 454 – ✉ Bridgnorth – ☎ 074 64 Worfield :

🏨 **Old Vicarage** 🦢, WV15 5JZ, ℰ 498, 🍴 – 📺 📞wc 🛗wc 🔼 🔼 AE ① VISA
M (booking essential) 7.95/10.00 s. – **10 rm** ⏸ 22.50/30.50 s. – SB 46.00 st.

AUSTIN-ROVER-DAIMLER-JAGUAR-LAND ROVER 52 West Castle St. ℰ 2207

RENAULT ℰ 3332
VW, AUDI Hollybush Rd ℰ 4343

BRIDGWATER Somerset **408** L 30 The West Country G. – pop. 26,642 – ECD : Thursday – ✆ 0278.

See : Castle St.★ – St. Mary's★ – Admiral Blake Museum★.

Envir. : Stogursey Priory Church★★, NW : 14 m. by A 39 – Westonzoyland Church★★, SE : 3 m. – North Petherton Church Tower★★, S : 3 m.

🛈 Enmore Park ✆ 027 867 (Spaxton) 244, W : 3 m.

◆London 160 – ◆Bristol 39 – Taunton 11.

   🏠 **Old Vicarage,** 45-47 St. Mary St., TA6 3EQ, ✆ 58891, 🌲 – 📺 ➾wc 🅿. 🔼 🄰🄴 ⓞ 𝐕𝐈𝐒𝐀. ⋇
      M *(closed Sunday)* a la carte 4.65/8.90 t. – **10 rm** ⊊ 17.50/25.00 t.

   🏠 **Watergate,** 10-11 West Quay, TA6 3DB, ✆ 423847 – 📺 ➾wc. 🔼 🄰🄴 ⓞ 𝐕𝐈𝐒𝐀. ⋇
      M *(closed Sunday to non-residents)* 8.00/10.00 st. ⏐ 2.60 – **8 rm** ⊊ 18.00/26.00 st.

      at West Huntspill N : 6 m. on A 38 – ⊠ Highbridge – ✆ 0278 Burnham-on-Sea :

   🏡 **Sundowner,** 74 Main Rd, TA9 3QU, on A 38 ✆ 784766 – 📺 ➾wc 🍴 🅿. 🔼 🄰🄴 ⓞ 𝐕𝐈𝐒𝐀
      M *(closed Sunday dinner)* 6.50/8.75 t. ⏐ 2.85 – **8 rm** ⊊ 14.00/25.00 t. – SB (winter only) 35.00 st.

   XX **Huntspill Villa** with rm, 82 Main Rd, TA9 3QX, ✆ 782291 – 📺 ➾wc 🅿. 🔼 🄰🄴 𝐕𝐈𝐒𝐀. ⋇
      M *(closed Saturday lunch, Sunday and Monday)* a la carte 10.45/11.95 t. ⏐ 2.45 – **4 rm**
      ⊊ 17.50/30.00 t.

      at Chilton Polden NE : 6 ¼ m. by A 39 – ⊠ Bridgwater – ✆ 0278.

   X Wilton Farmhouse, 9 Goose Lane, TA7 9ED, ✆ 722134 – 🅿
      M (booking essential).

AUSTIN-ROVER Market St. ✆ 422125
BMW High St., Cannington ✆ 652228
FORD 37 Frian St. ✆ 451332
NISSAN Main Rd, Cannington ✆ 0278 (Combwich) 652233

RENAULT 52 Eastover ✆ 422218
VOLVO Bristol Rd ✆ 55333

BRIDLINGTON Humberside **402** T 21 – pop. 26,776 – ECD : Thursday – ✆ 0262.

See : Priory Church★ 12C-15C.

Envir. : Burton Agnes Hall★ (Elizabethan) *AC*, SW : 6 m.

🛈 Belvedere ✆ 72092, S : 1 ½ m. on A 165 – 🛈 Flamborough Head ✆ 850333, NE : 5 m.

🅱 Garrison St. ✆ 73474 and 79626.

◆ London 236 – ◆Kingston-upon-Hull 29 – York 41.

   🏨 **Expanse,** North Marine Drive, YO15 2LS, ✆ 675347, ≼ – 🛗 📺 ➾wc ☎ 🅿. 🔼 🄰🄴 ⓞ 𝐕𝐈𝐒𝐀. ⋇
      M 4.25/7.00 t. ⏐ 2.80 – **50 rm** ⊊ 17.00/36.00 t. – SB 42.00/44.00 st.

   🏠 **Monarch,** South Marine Drive, YO15 3JJ, ✆ 674447, ≼ – 🛗 ➾wc ☎ 🅿. 🔼 🄰🄴 ⓞ 𝐕𝐈𝐒𝐀. ⋇
      April-October – **M** (bar lunch Monday to Saturday) 7.50 **st.** ⏐ 2.80 – **44 rm** ⊊ 15.00/34.00 st. –
      SB 35.00/42.00 st.

   XX **Old Cooperage,** 91-93 High St., Old Town, YO16 4PN, ✆ 675190 – 🔼 𝐕𝐈𝐒𝐀
      closed lunch Saturday and Monday and Sunday dinner – **M** a la carte 9.05/14.20 t. ⏐ 3.25.

FORD Hamilton Rd ✆ 75336
NISSAN Quay Rd ✆ 70331
TALBOT 74 Pessingby Rd ✆ 78141

VAUXHALL-OPEL 52-60 Quay Rd ✆ 72022
VOLVO Pinfold Lane ✆ 70351

BRIDPORT Dorset **408** L 31 The West Country G. – pop. 6,369 – ECD : Thursday – ✆ 0308.

Envir. : Parnham House★★, N : 6 m. on A 3066.

🛈 Bridport and West Dorset, West Bay ✆ 22597, S : 1 ½ m.

🅱 32 South St. ✆ 24901 (summer only).

◆London 150 – Exeter 38 – Taunton 33 – Weymouth 19.

   ↟ **Roundham House,** Roundham Gdns, West Bay Rd, DT6 4BD, ✆ 22753, 🌲 – ➾wc 🍴wc
      🅿. 🔼
      9 rm ⊊ 11.50/27.00 t.

   ↟ **Britmead House,** 154 West Bay Rd, DT6 4EG, S : 1 m. by B 3157 ✆ 22941 – 📺 ➾wc 🅿.
      🔼 𝐕𝐈𝐒𝐀
      8 rm ⊊ 10.50/24.00 st.

      at West Bexington SE : 7 ½ m. by B 3157 – ⊠ Bridport – ✆ 0308 Burton Bradstock :

   🏠 **Manor,** DT2 9DF, ✆ 897616, ≼, 🌲 – 📺 ➾wc 🅿. 🔼 🄰🄴 ⓞ 𝐕𝐈𝐒𝐀
      M 6.95/8.95 t. ⏐ 2.45 – **11 rm** ⊊ 16.50/34.00 t. – SB 45.00/52.00 st.

      at West Bay S : 1 ½ m. on B 3157 – ⊠ ✆ 0308 Bridport :

   🏠 **Haddon House,** DT6 4EN, ✆ 23626 – 📺 ➾wc 🍴wc 🅿. 🔼 🄰🄴 ⓞ 𝐕𝐈𝐒𝐀
      M 7.50/10.25 st. ⏐ 3.45 – **13 rm** ⊊ 23.50/35.00 st.

      at Chideock W : 3 m. on A 35 – ⊠ Bridport – ✆ 029 789 Chideock :

   🏠 **Chideock House,** Main St., DT6 6JN, ✆ 242 – ➾wc 🅿. 🔼 🄰🄴 ⓞ 𝐕𝐈𝐒𝐀
      M *(closed Monday lunch)* a la carte 9.10/11.75 t. ⏐ 2.40 – **9 rm** ⊊ 15.00/28.00 t. – SB
      (except Bank Holidays) 39.00/42.00 st.

BRIGHTON AND HOVE

BRIGHTON
AND HOVE
CENTRE

For names of numbered streets,
see previous page.

0   300 m
0   300 yards

111

BRIGHTON AND HOVE East Sussex 四〇四 T 31 – pop. 234,437 (inc. Hove) – ECD : Wednesday and Thursday – ✪ 0273 – **See** : Royal Pavilion★ (interior★★) *AC* CZ – Aquarium★ *AC* CZ **A** – Booth Museum (bird collection)★ BV **M** – Preston Manor (Chinese collection★) BV **D** – The Lanes CZ.

Envir. : Stanmer Park (site★) N : 3 ½ m. by A 27 CV – Clayton (church of St. John the Baptist : frescoes★ 14C) N : 6 m. by A 23 BV.

🔩 East Brighton, Roedean ✆ 603989 CV – 🔩 Hollingbury Park, Ditchling Rd ✆ 552010 BV – 🔩 Dyke, Dyke Rd ✆ 079 156 (Poynings) 296, N : by Dyke Rd BV – 🔩 Dyke Rd ✆ 556482 BV.

✈ Shoreham Airport : ✆ 079 17 (Shoreham-by-Sea) 2304 W : 8 m. by A 27 A.

🛈 Marlborough House, 54 Old Steine ✆ 23755 or 26450 (weekends) – Sea Front, Kings Rd ✆ 26450 (summer only).

🛈 at Hove : Town Hall, Norton Rd ✆ 775400.

♦London 53 – ♦Portsmouth 48 – ♦Southampton 61.

Plans on preceding pages

🏦 **Wheeler's Sheridan** without rest., 64 King's Rd, BN1 1NA, ✆ 23221, ⇐ – 📶 TV. 🔄 AE ⓪ *VISA*. 🛠 BZ **e**
closed 25 and 26 December – **58 rm** ⇌ 30.00/50.00 st.

🏨 **Old Ship**, King's Rd, BN1 1NR, ✆ 29001, Telex 877101, ⇐ – 📶 TV ⇌wc 🚗 ⇦. 🔄 AE ⓪ *VISA* 🛠 CZ **n**
M 8.50/9.50 t. – **151 rm** ⇌ 39.50/55.00 st. – SB (weekends only) 57.00/60.00 st.

🏨 **Norfolk Resort**, 149 King's Rd, BN1 2PP, ✆ 738201, Telex 877247, ⇐ – 📶 TV ⇌wc ☎ Ⓟ. ⇦. 🔄 AE ⓪ *VISA* BZ **c**
M a la carte 8.50/12.00 t. ⓵ 3.00 – **65 rm** ⇌ 35.00/56.00 st. – SB 46.00/56.00 st.

🏨 **Topps**, 17 Regency Sq., BN1 2FG, ✆ 729334 – 📶 TV ⇌wc ⓶wc 🔄. 🔄 AE ⓪ *VISA*. 🛠 BZ **i**
closed January – **M** (closed Sunday and Wednesday) (dinner only) a la carte 6.20/8.00 st. ⓵ 1.65 – **7 rm** ⇌ 25.00/50.00 st. – SB (weekends only) 55.00/65.00 st.

🏨 **Granville**, 125 King's Rd, BN1 2FA, ✆ 733516, ⇐ – 📶 TV ⇌wc ⓶wc 🔄. 🔄 AE ⓪ *VISA*. 🛠 BZ **n**
closed 24 December-1 January – **M** (closed lunch Friday and Saturday and Bank Holidays) 5.95/10.95 t. – ⇌ 3.70 – **11 rm** 30.80/72.50 t. – SB 49.50/77.00 st.

🏨 **The Twenty One**, 21 Charlotte St., BN2 1AG, ✆ 686450 – 📶 TV ⓶wc. 🔄 🔄 AE ⓪ *VISA* CV **i**
closed January – **M** (closed Sunday)(residents only) 12.00 st. – **6 rm** ⇌ 19.00/30.00 st.

↟ **Marine House**, 8 Charlotte St., BN2 1AG, ✆ 605349 – 📶 TV ⓶wc CV **n**
closed December and January – **10 rm** ⇌ 9.00/24.00 s.

XXX **Le Francais**, 1 Paston Pl., Kemptown, BN2 1HA, ✆ 680716, French rest. – 🔄 AE ⓪ *VISA* CV **a**
M (closed Christmas and Bank Holidays) (dinner only) a la carte 22.50/29.00 t. ⓵ 3.00.

XX **La Marinade**, 77 St. Georges Rd, Kemp Town, BN2 1EF, ✆ 600992 – 🔄 AE ⓪ *VISA* CV **c**
closed Sunday, Monday, last 2 weeks August and 24 December-8 January – **M** a la carte 9.10/11.75 t. ⓵ 2.95.

XX **Wheeler's**, 17 Market St., BN1 5FG, ✆ 25135, Seafood – 🔄 AE ⓪ *VISA* CZ **s**
closed 25-26 December and 1 January – **M** a la carte 9.75/14.25 st. ⓵ 2.25.

XX **Dolce Vito**, 106c Western Rd, Corner of Bedford Pl., BN1 2AA, ✆ 737200, Italian rest. – 🔄 AE ⓪ *VISA* BY **u**
M a la carte 9.30/12.50 t. ⓵ 3.35.

X **Café de Paris**, 40 St. James's St., BN2 1RG, ✆ 603740, French rest. – 🔄 AE ⓪ *VISA* CZ **a**
closed Sunday – **M** (dinner only) a la carte 8.90/16.50 t. ⓵ 2.45.

X **Orchard**, 33 Western St., BN1 2PG, ✆ 776618 – 🔄 AE ⓪ *VISA* BZ **o**
closed Sunday dinner, Monday and 23 to 28 December – **M** (dinner only and Sunday lunch) 5.95/9.95 t. ⓵ 3.00.

X **Foggs**, 5 Little Western St., BN1 2PU, ✆ 735907 – 🔄 AE *VISA* BY **a**
M (dinner only) a la carte 8.20/10.65 t. ⓵ 2.05.

X **Le Grandgousier**, 15 Western St., BN1 2PG, ✆ 772005, French rest. – AE BY **x**
closed Saturday lunch, Sunday and 23 December-1 January – **M** (booking essential) 7.25 (wine included) t.

at Hove – ⌧ Hove – ✪ 0273 Brighton :

🏦 **Dudley** (T.H.F.), Lansdowne Pl., BN3 1HQ, ✆ 736266, Telex 87537 – 📶 TV 🚗 Ⓟ. ⇦. 🔄 AE ⓪ *VISA* AY **o**
M 6.95/9.50 st. ⓵ 2.60 – ⇌ 5.50 – **79 rm** 41.50/55.00 st.

🏦 **Courtlands**, 19-27 The Drive, BN3 3JE, ✆ 731055, Telex 87574 – 📶 TV Ⓟ. 🔄 AE ⓪ *VISA* AY **c**
M 8.00/9.75 t. ⓵ 3.25 – **62 rm** ⇌ 36.50/45.00 st. – SB (weekends only except Bank Holidays) 47.50/52.50 st.

🏨 **Sackville** (Best Western), 189 Kingsway, BN3 4GU, ✆ 736292, Telex 877830, ⇐ – 📶 TV ⇌wc 🚗 ⇦. 🔄. 🔄 AE ⓪ *VISA* AV **n**
M 7.95/9.75 st. ⓵ 3.10 – **48 rm** ⇌ 35.20/65.45 st. – SB (weekends only)(spring and summer only) 60.00 st.

🏨 **St. Catherine's Lodge**, Kingsway, BN3 2RZ, ✆ 778181, Telex 877073 – 📶 TV ⇌wc 🔄. AE ⓪ *VISA* AV **a**
M 5.50/7.50 st. – **55 rm** ⇌ 24.00/44.00 st. – SB 42.00/50.00 st.

🏨 **Whitehaven**, 34 Wilbury Rd, BN3 3JP, ✆ 778355, 🌺 – TV ⇌wc ⓶wc ☎. 🔄 AE ⓪ *VISA*. 🛠 AX **c**
M (bar lunch) 8.00 st. ⓵ 2.25 – **15 rm** ⇌ 27.00/42.00 st. – SB (weekends only) 45.00/48.00 st.

XXX **Eaton,** 13 Eaton Gdns, BN3 3TN, ℰ 738921 – 🅿 ☒ 🅰🅴 ⑩ *VISA*   AX **a**
closed Sunday dinner, Good Friday and Christmas Day – **M** a la carte 9.25/14.50 **t.** 🍷 3.50.

XX Hove Manor, 5 Hove Manor Par., Hove St., ℰ 730850   AV **c**

XX **Peking,** 9 Western Rd, BN3 1AE, ℰ 722090, Chinese rest. – ☒ 🅰🅴 *VISA*   BY **c**
closed 25 and 26 December – **M** a la carte approx. 5.00 **t.**

X **Fig Leaf,** 37 Waterloo St., BN3 1AY, ℰ 732383 – ☒ *VISA*   BY **i**
closed Sunday, Monday, first week September and 1 week at Christmas – **M** (dinner only)
9.75 **t.** 🍷 2.40.

X **Lawrence,** 40 Waterloo St., BN3 1AY, ℰ 772922 – ☒ 🅰🅴 *VISA*   BY **e**
closed Sunday and 25-26 December – **M** (dinner only) a la carte 9.60/12.75 **t.** 🍷 3.25.

at Poynings NW : 8 ½ m. by A 23 – BV – off A 281 – ✉ Brighton – ☎ 079 156 Poynings :

X **Au Petit Normand,** 2 The Street, BN4 7AQ, ℰ 346, French rest. – ☒ 🅰🅴 *VISA*
closed Sunday dinner and Monday – **M** (dinner only and Sunday lunch).

ALFA-ROMEO Old Shoreham Rd, Portslade ℰ 411020	MAZDA 42/43 George St. ℰ 681766	
AUDI, VW Old Shoreham Rd, Portslade ℰ 422552	MAZDA 373 Kingsway, Hove ℰ 413833	
AUSTIN-ROVER-DAIMLER-JAGUAR 200 DYKE Rd ℰ 553061	MERCEDES-BENZ Victoria Rd ℰ 414911	
AUSTIN-ROVER 233 Preston Rd ℰ 553021	NISSAN 21/29 Preston Rd ℰ 685985	
AUSTIN-ROVER 1a Lewes Rd ℰ 604131	RENAULT Stephenson Rd ℰ 692111	
BMW Sillwood St. ℰ 27991	SKODA, TALBOT Longridge Av., Saltdean ℰ 31061	
FIAT, LANCIA 100 Lewes Rd ℰ 603244	TALBOT 270-272 Old Shoreham Rd ℰ 737555	
FORD 90/96 Preston Rd ℰ 550211	VAUXHALL-OPEL Old Shoreham Rd, Portslade ℰ 422552	
	VOLVO Bedford Place ℰ 203487	

BRIMSCOMBE Glos. 🗹🗹🗹 🗹🗹🗹 N 28 – see Stroud.

☞ *Pour aller loin rapidement, utilisez les* **cartes Michelin** *à 1/1 000 000.*

BRISTOL Avon 🗹🗹🗹 🗹🗹🗹 M 29 **The West Country G.** – pop. 426,657 – ECD : **Wednesday and**
Saturday – ☎ 0272.

See : Clifton Suspension Bridge★★★ AY – Cabot Tower Area★★ – The Georgian House★★★ CZ – St.
Nicholas Church Museum★★ DZ **M1** – Theatre Royal★★ DZ **T** – Quakers Friars★★ EZ **K** – St. Mary
Redcliffe Church★★ DZ – S.S. Great Britain★★ AY **A** – Industrial Museum★★ AY **M2** – Bristol
Zoological Garden★★ AY – Clifton Roman Catholic Cathedral of SS Peter and Paul★★ AY **B** –
Cathedral★ DZ – City Museum and Art Gallery★ CZ **M.**

🏌 Carsons Rd, Mangotsfield.

✈ Bristol Airport : ℰ 027 587 (Lulsgate) 4441/6, SW : 7 m. by A 38 AY – **Terminal : Marlborough**
Street Bus Station.

🚗 ℰ 291001 ext 2479.

🛈 Colston House, Colston St. ℰ 293891 – Watershed, 1 Canons Rd ℰ 214272/293891 (summer only).

♦London 121 – ♦Birmingham 91.

Plans on following pages

🏨 **Holiday Inn,** Lower Castle St., Old Market, BS1 3AD, ℰ 294281, Telex 449720, ☒ – 🛗 📺
☎ ૐ 🅿 🛎 ☒ 🅰🅴 ⑩ *VISA*   EZ **s**
M (buffet lunch) 10.50 **st.** 🍷 3.50 – ⅏ 5.65 – **284 rm** 43.50/54.50 **s.** – SB (weekends only) 88.50 **st.**

🏨 Grand (Mt. Charlotte), Broad St., BS1 2EL, ℰ 291645, Telex 449889 – 🛗 📺 ☎ 🅿 🛎 ☒ 🅰🅴
⑩ *VISA*   DZ **a**
179 rm ⅏ 45.65/57.75 **st.**

🏨 **Unicorn** (Rank), Prince St., BS1 4QF, ℰ 294811, Telex 44315 – 🛗 📺 ☎ 🅿 🛎 ☒ 🅰🅴 ⑩ *VISA*
M *(closed Saturday lunch)* 6.25/8.50 **t.** – ⅏ 4.75 – **194 rm** 33.50/46.75 **t.** – SB (week-   DZ **i**
ends only) 27.60 **st.**

🏨 **Ladbroke Dragonara** (Ladbroke), Redcliffe Way, BS1 6NJ, ℰ 20044, Telex 449240 – 🛗 📺
☎ ૐ 🅿 🛎 ☒ 🅰🅴 ⑩ *VISA*   DEZ **n**
M (bar lunch Saturday) 7.25/9.75 **st.** 🍷 3.25 – ⅏ 5.65 – **204 rm** 36.00/54.00 **st.** – SB
54.00/60.00 **st.**

🏨 **St. Vincent Rocks** (Anchor), Sion Hill, Clifton, BS8 4BB, ℰ 739251 – 📺 🛁wc 📵wc ☎ 🅿
☒ 🅰🅴 ⑩ *VISA*   AY **c**
M *(closed Saturday lunch)* a la carte 8.10/12.75 **st.** 🍷 2.65 – **46 rm** ⅏ 37.00/45.00 **st.** – SB
(weekends only) 46.00 **st.**

🏨 **Avon Gorge** (Mt. Charlotte), Sion Hill, Clifton, BS8 4LD, ℰ 738955, Telex 444237, ≤ – 🛗 📺
🛁wc 📵wc ૐ 🛎 ☒ 🅰🅴 ⑩ *VISA*   AY **x**
M approx. 8.25 **st.** 🍷 4.00 – **76 rm** ⅏ 35.75/46.75 **st.** – SB (weekends only) 50.00 **st.**

🏠 **Oakfield,** 52-54 Oakfield Rd, Clifton, BS8 2BG, ℰ 735556 – 🅿   AY **n**
closed 23 December-1 January – **27 rm** ⅏ 12.00/24.00 **st.**

🏠 **Westbury Park,** 37 Westbury Rd, BS9 3AU, ℰ 620465 – 📺 🛁wc 🅿   AX **r**
9 rm ⅏ 15.50/30.50 **t.**

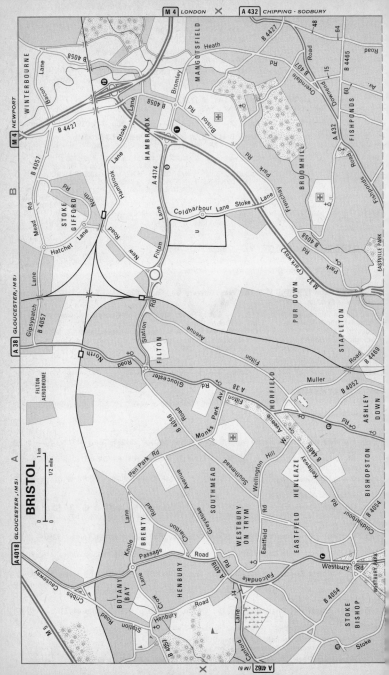

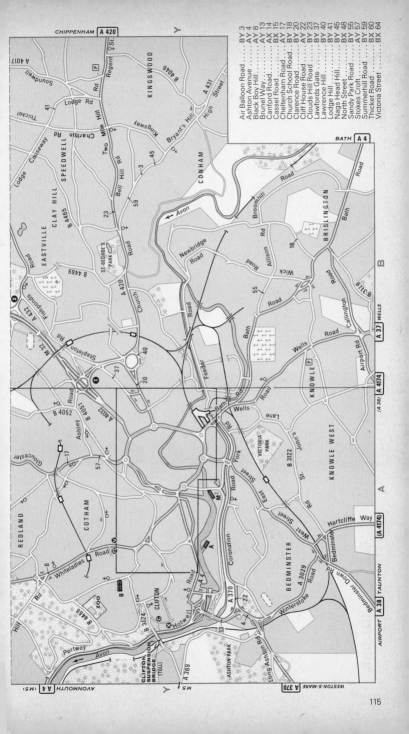

CHIPPENHAM A 420

BATH A 4

AVONMOUTH A 4 (M5)

WESTON-S-MARE A 370

AIRPORT A 38 TAUNTON

A 37 WELLS

A 4174

(A 38)

A 4174

(A 4174)

115

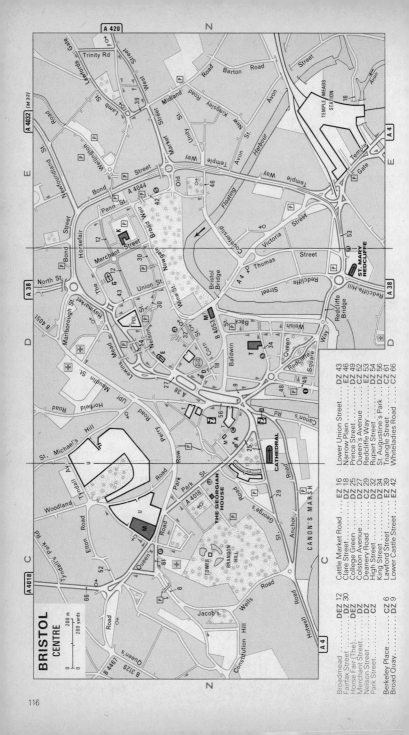

BRISTOL
CENTRE

0 ___ 200 m
0 ___ 200 yards

XXX **Harvey's,** 12 Denmark St., BS1 5DQ, ✆ 277665 – 🖃 AE ⑩ VISA   DZ **c**
closed Saturday lunch, Sunday and Bank Holidays – **M** a la carte 12.45/18.55 **t.** ⑨ 3.50.

XX **Les Semailles,** 9 Druid Hill, Stoke Bishop, BS9 1EW, ✆ 686456, French rest. – AE VISA
closed Sunday, last 2 weeks July, 22 December-5 January and Bank Holidays – **M** (booking
essential) a la carte 16.00/23.00 **st.**   AX **a**

XX **Rajdoot,** 83 Park St., BS1 5PJ, ✆ 28033, Indian rest. – 🖃 AE ⑩ VISA   CZ **u**
closed lunch Sunday and Bank Holidays and 25-26 December – **M** a la carte 8.85/12.00 **t.**
⑨ 3.00.

XX **Du Gourmet,** 43 Whiteladies Rd, BS8 2LS, ✆ 736230 – 🖃 AE ⑩ VISA   AY **v**
*closed Saturday lunch, Sunday and Monday except December, Good Friday and 24 to 30
December* – **M** a la carte 9.60/16.00 **t.** ⑨ 2.70.

X **Masters,** 2 Upper Byron Place, The Triangle, BS8 1JY, ✆ 28314 – 🖃 AE ⑩ VISA   CZ **e**
closed Sunday – **M** a la carte 8.40/13.20 **t.** ⑨ 2.50.

X **La Taverna Dell'Artista,** 33 King St., BS1 4EF, ✆ 297712, Italian rest. – 🖃 VISA   DZ **s**
closed Sunday, Monday and Bank Holidays – **M** a la carte 4.55/10.70 **t.** ⑨ 2.50.

X **Ganges,** 368 Gloucester Rd, Horfield, BS7 8TP, ✆ 45234, Indian rest. – 🖃 🖃 AE ⑩ VISA
closed Christmas Day – **M** a la carte 7.45/9.00 **t.**   AX **e**

at Hambrook NE : 5 ½ m. by M 32 on A 4174 – ✉ ☺ 0272 Bristol :

🏨 **Crest** (Crest), Filton Rd, BS16 1QX, ✆ 564242, Telex 449376, ⚞, park – 🛗 🖃 rest 📺 ➘wc
☎ & 📞 ⚿ 🖃 AE ⑩ VISA ✄   BX **o**
M approx. 10.00 **t.** – ⯑ 5.50 – **151 rm** 47.50/56.00 **st.**

at Winterbourne N : 6 ¾ m. by M 32 on B 4058 – BX – ✉ Bristol – ☺ 0454 Winterbourne :

XXX **Grange** ≫ with rm, Northwoods, BS17 1RP, NW : 2 m. by B 4057 on B 4427 ✆ 777333, ⚞,
park – 📺 ➘wc ☎ 📞 🖃 AE ⑩ VISA
M a la carte 10.15/12.80 **t.** – ⯑ 2.00 – **28 rm** 38.50/48.50 **t.** – SB (weekends only) 30.00 **st.**

MICHELIN Branch, Pennywell Rd, BS5 0UB, ✆ 559802

AUSTIN-ROVER Church Rd ✆ 556381
AUSTIN-ROVER 135 High St. ✆ 670011
AUSTIN-ROVER 74-80 Staple Hill Rd ✆ 654776
AUSTIN-ROVER-DAIMLER-JAGUAR, ROLLS
ROYCE 11/15 Merchants Rd, Clifton ✆ 730361
AUSTIN-ROVER-DAIMLER-JAGUAR 156 Chelten-
ham Rd ✆ 48051
BMW 33 Zetland Rd ✆ 428333
CITROEN, FIAT 724 Fishponds Rd ✆ 657247
FORD 175/185 Muller Rd, Horfield ✆ 513333
FORD College Green ✆ 293881
MAZDA 676 Fishponds Rd ✆ 655439

MERCEDES-BENZ, CITROEN, FIAT, LANCIA 20
Whitehouse St. ✆ 669331
NISSAN 168/176 Coronation Rd ✆ 631101
PEUGEOT-TALBOT 84 Downend Rd ✆ 567088
RENAULT Vale Lane ✆ 665070
RENAULT Station Rd, Kingswood ✆ 569911
RENAULT Marlborough St. ✆ 421816
TOYOTA Gloucester Rd, Patchway ✆ 693704
VAUXHALL-OPEL, BEDFORD Gloucester Rd ✆
694331
VOLVO Berkeley Pl. ✆ 277355

■**BRIXHAM**■ Devon 403 J 32 The West Country G. – pop. 12,000 – ECD : Wednesday – ☺ 080 45.

Envir. : Berry Head★ (≤★★★), E : 2 m.

🖪 The Old Market House, The Quay ✆ 2861 – ◆London 230 – Exeter 30 – ◆Plymouth 32 – Torquay 8.

🏨 **Quayside,** 41-49 King St., TQ5 9TJ, ✆ 55751, ≤ harbour – 📺 ➘wc ☎ 📞 🖃 AE ⑩ VISA
M *(closed for dinner January and February)* (bar lunch Monday to Saturday) 8.85 **t.** ⑨ 3.60 –
32 rm ⯑ 22.50/52.00 **t.** – SB 47.00/59.00 **st.**

🏠 **Smuggler's Haunt,** 1 Church Hill East, TQ5 8HH, ✆ 3050 – ➘wc. 🖃 AE VISA
M a la carte 6.90/9.95 **t.** ⑨ 2.50 – **14 rm** ⯑ 12.50/22.50 **t.**

AUSTIN-ROVER Milton St. ✆ 2474
FORD Churston Ferrers ✆ 0803 (Churston) 842245

RENAULT New Rd ✆ 2266

■**BROADSTAIRS**■ Kent 404 Y 29 – pop. 20,048 (inc. St. Peter's) – ECD : Wednesday – ☺ 0843
Thanet.

See : Bleak House (stayed in by Charles Dickens) *AC*.

🖪 Pierremont Hall, High St. ✆ 68399 – ◆London 77 – ◆Dover 22 – Maidstone 46 – Margate 3.5.

🏨 **Castlemere,** 14 Western Esplanade, CT10 1TD, ✆ 61566, ≤, ⚞ – 📺 ➘wc 🚾wc ☎ 📞 🖃
VISA
M *(closed for lunch November-April)* (bar lunch) 8.80 **st.** ⑨ 2.75 – **38 rm** ⯑ 19.55/41.80 **st.** –
SB (weekends only except Bank Holidays) 43.00/51.00 **st.**

🏠 **Royal Albion,** Albion St., CT10 1LU, ✆ 68071, Telex 965761, ≤, ⚞ – 📺 ➘wc 🚾wc ☜ 📞.
🛗 🖃 AE ⑩ VISA
M *(October-June see* **Marchesi** *rest. below)* (bar lunch) 5.50/6.75 **t.** ⑨ 2.75 – **18 rm**
⯑ 24.00/38.00 **st.** – SB (except summer) 45.00/53.00 **st.**

↟ **Bay Tree,** 12 Eastern Esplanade, CT10 1DR, ✆ 62502, ≤ – 📞
March-October – **9 rm** ⯑ 8.50/19.00 **s.**

↟ **Keston Court,** 14 Ramsgate Rd, CT10 1PS, ✆ 62401 – 📞. 🖃 VISA
9 rm ⯑ 9.00/18.00 **t.**

XX **Marchesi,** 18 Albion St., CT10 1LU, ✆ 62481, ≤ – 📞. 🖃 AE ⑩ VISA
closed 26 to 28 December – **M** a la carte 8.30/12.05 **t.** ⑨ 2.10.

BROADSTAIRS

at Kingsgate N : 2 m. on B 2052 – ⊠ Broadstairs – ☎ 0843 Thanet :

🏰 **Castle Keep,** Joss Gap Rd, CT10 3PQ, ℰ 65222, ≼, 🏊 heated, ✍ – 📺 🅿 🅰 🔊 🄰🄴 ⑩ *VISA*
M 7.00/9.00 t. 🍴 2.75 – **29 rm** ⚏ 30.00/36.00 t. – SB (except July and August) 55.00 **st.**

AUDI, VW   St. Peter's Rd ℰ 62333   RENAULT Oscar Rd ℰ 62568
PEUGEOT-TALBOT Ramsgate Rd ℰ 63531

BROADSTONE Dorset 🈯🈯 O 31 – see Wimbourne Minster.

BROADWATER Herts. – see Stevenage.

BROADWAY Heref. and Worc. 🈯🈯 O 27 – pop. 2,503 – ECD : Thursday – ☎ 0386.
♦London 93 – ♦Birmingham 36 – Cheltenham 15 – Worcester 22.

🏛 **Lygon Arms,** High St., WR12 7DU, ℰ 852255, Telex 338260, « Part 15C inn », ✍, ✗ – 📺
☎ 🍴 ⌑ 🅿 🅰 🔊 🄰🄴 ⑩ *VISA*
M 8.50/15.25 t. 🍴 3.45 – ⚏ 4.50 – **65 rm** 45.00/86.00 t. – SB 92.00/98.00 t.

🏨 **Broadway,** The Green, WR12 7AA, ℰ 852401, ✍ – 📺 ☐wc ☎ 🅿 🔊 🄰🄴 ⑩ *VISA* ✗
M (bar lunch) 8.95 t. 🍴 2.50 – **23 rm** ⚏ 19.00/48.00 t. – SB (winter and spring only) 40.00/96.00 **st.**

🏠 **Collin House** ⌂, Collin Lane, WR12 7PB, NW : 1 ¼ m. by A 44 ℰ 858354, ≼, 🏊, ✍ –
☐wc 🔊 *VISA* ✗
closed 25 and 26 December – **M** (closed Sunday dinner to non-residents) (bar lunch) (booking essential) 12.50 t. – **7 rm** ⚏ 35.00/45.00 t. – SB (winter only) 58.00/63.00 **st.**

⋔ **Halfway House,** 89 High St., WR12 7AL, ℰ 852237 – 🅿. ✗
5 rm ⚏ 15.00/30.00 **s.**

⋔ **Westdon,** Station Rd, WR12 7DE, ℰ 858821, ✍ – 🅿. ✗
March-October – **6 rm** ⚏ 12.00/28.00 **st.**

✗✗ **Hunters Lodge,** High St., WR12 7DT, ℰ 853247, ✍ – 🅿. 🔊 🄰🄴 ⑩ *VISA*
closed Sunday dinner, Monday, first 2 weeks January and first 2 weeks August – **M** a la carte 10.60/15.25 t. 🍴 2.75.

at Willersley N : 2 m. on A 46 – ⊠ ☎ 0386 Broadway :

🏠 **Old Rectory** ⌂ without rest., Church St., WR12 7PM, ℰ 853729, ✍ – 📺 ☐wc �🔔wc 🅿.
🔊 *VISA* ✗
5 rm ⚏ 31.00/41.00 t.

at Willersey Hill (Glos.) E : 2 m. by A 44 – ⊠ ☎ 0386 Broadway :

🏛 **Dormy House,** WR12 7LF, ℰ 852711, Telex 338571, ✍ – 📺 ☎ 🅿 🅰 🔊 🄰🄴 ⑩ *VISA*
M (closed Saturday lunch) 12.00/14.00 t. 🍴 6.00 – **49 rm** ⚏ 36.00/73.00 t. – SB (weekends only) 77.00/86.00 st.

at Buckland (Glos.) SW : 2 ¼ m. by A 46 – ⊠ ☎ 0386 Broadway :

🏛 **Buckland Manor** ⌂, WR12 7LY, ℰ 852626, « Country house atmosphere », 🏊, heated, ✍,
park, ✗ – 📺 🅿. 🔊 🄰🄴 ⑩ *VISA* ✗
closed 3 weeks January-February – **M** a la carte approx. 16.95 t. – **11 rm** ⚏ 68.00/105.00 t.

AUSTIN-ROVER Willersley ℰ 852338

BROADWINDSOR Dorset 🈯 L 31 – pop. 1,021 – ⊠ Beaminster – ☎ 0308.
♦London 148 – Exeter 37 – Taunton 26 – Weymouth 26.

🏠 **Broadwindsor House** ⌂, Beaminster Rd, DT8 3PX, ℰ 68353, ≼, ✍ – ☐wc 🅿
closed February – **M** (dinner only and Sunday lunch) 4.50/8.00 **st.** – **12 rm** ⚏ 10.50/25.00 **st.**

BROCKENHURST Hants. 🈯🈯 P 31 – pop. 2,599 – ECD : Wednesday – ☎ 0590 Lymington.
♦London 99 – Bournemouth 17 – ♦Southampton 14 – Winchester 27.

🏛 **Ladbroke Balmer Lawn** (Ladbroke), Lyndhurst Rd, SO4 7ZB, ℰ 23116, ≼, 🏊 heated, ✍,
✗, squash – ▤ 📺 ☐wc ☎ 🅿. 🅰 🔊 🄰🄴 ⑩ *VISA*
M a la carte 9.85/13.30 st. 🍴 3.00 – **60 rm** ⚏ 35.00/48.00 **st.** – SB (weekends only) 65.00/68.00 **st.**

🏛 **Carey's Manor,** Lyndhurst Rd, SO4 7RH, ℰ 23551, Telex 47442, Dancing Friday and Saturday, ✍ – 📺 ☐wc ☎ ⌑ 🅿. 🅰 🔊 🄰🄴 ⑩ *VISA*
M 7.95/10.95 t. 🍴 2.95 – **57 rm** ⚏ 37.95/59.90 t. – SB 59.70/69.70 **st.**

🏛 **Forest Park,** Rhinefield Rd, SO4 7SG, ℰ 22844, 🏊 heated, ✍, ✗ – ☐wc ☎ 🅿. 🅰
🔊 🄰🄴 ⑩ *VISA*
M 5.95/11.40 t. – **38 rm** ⚏ 28.00/42.00 t. – SB 52.00/54.00 **st.**

🏠 **Whitley Ridge** ⌂, Beaulieu Rd, SO4 7QL, E : 1 m. on B 3055 ℰ 22354, ≼, ✍, ✗ – ☐wc
�🔔wc 🅿. 🔊 *VISA* ✗
M (bar lunch)(residents only) 9.50 t. 🍴 2.75 – **14 rm** ⚏ 27.50/39.50 st. – SB 48.00/52.00 **st.**

🏠 **Watersplash,** The Rise, SO4 7ZP, ℰ 22344, 🏊 heated, ✍ – ☐wc ⌑ 🅿. 🅰 🔊 *VISA*
M 6.00/9.50 t. 🍴 2.40 – **27 rm** ⚏ 17.00/22.00 t. – SB (except summer) 41.00/45.00 **st.**

✗✗ **Le Poussin,** 57-59 Brookley Rd, SO4 7RB, ℰ 23063, French rest. – 🔊 🄰🄴 ⑩ *VISA*
closed first 2 weeks February – **M** (booking essential) a la carte 10.55/13.50 t. 🍴 2.75.

AUSTIN-ROVER Sway Rd ℰ 23344   SAAB, HONDA 24 Brookley Rd ℰ 23464

BROMBOROUGH Merseyside **402** L 24 – pop. 15,800 – ⊠ Wirral – 🕾 051 Liverpool.
◆London 223 – Birkenhead 4 – Chester 13 – ◆Liverpool 6 – ◆Manchester 46.

　　✗　**Raffles,** 914 New Chester Rd, L62 6AU, 🖉 327 2039 – 🖭 ⓪ *VISA*
　　　　closed Saturday and Sunday lunch and 25-26 December – **M** (lunch by arrangement) a la
　　　　carte 8.50/14.00 **t.** 🛢 4.20.

BROME Suffolk **404** X 26 – pop. 267 – ⊠ 🕾 0379 Eye.
◆London 86 – ◆Cambridge 50 – ◆Ipswich 20 – ◆Norwich 22.

　　🏠　**Oaksmere** ◈, IP23 8AJ, 🖉 870326, 🐗, park – 🖭 ⅲwc ℗. 🔼 🖭 ⓪ *VISA*
　　　　M a la carte 9.45/13.45 **t.** 🛢 3.95 – **5 rm** ⊡ 27.00/38.50 **st.** – SB (weekends only except Christ-
　　　　mas and New Year) 58.30 **st.**

BROMLEY CROSS Greater Manchester **402 404** M 23 – see Bolton.

BROMPTON North Yorks. **402** S 21 – pop. 572 – ⊠ 🕾 0723 Scarborough.
◆London 242 – ◆Kingston-upon-Hull 44 – Scarborough 8 – York 31.

　　✗✗　Brompton Forge, YO13 9DP, 🖉 85409 – ℗.

BROMSGROVE Heref. and Worc. **403 404** N 26 – pop. 30,210 – ECD : Thursday – 🕾 0527.
🖪 47/49 Worcester Rd 🖉 31809.
◆London 117 – ◆Birmingham 14 – ◆Bristol 71 – Worcester 13.

　　🏠　Perry Hall (Embassy), 13 Kidderminster Rd, B61 7JN, 🖉 31976, 🐗 – 🖭 ⊟wc ⅲwc ⊛ ℗.
　　　　🔼. ✸ – **53 rm.**
　　🏠　Pine Lodge, 85 Kidderminster Rd, B61 9AB, W : 1 m. on A 448 🖉 33033, 🟰 heated, 🐗 – 🖭
　　　　⊟wc ℗. 🔼 *VISA*
　　　　M (closed Sunday dinner) (carving rest.) 5.20/6.40 **st.** – **21 rm.**
　　✗✗✗　**Grafton Manor** ◈ with rm, Grafton Lane, B61 7HA, SW : 1 ¾ m. by Worcester Rd (A 38)
　　　　🖉 31525, « 16C and 18C manor », ◈, 🐗, park – 🖭 ⊟wc ℗. 🔼 🖭 ⓪ *VISA*. ✸
　　　　closed Bank Holidays – **M** (closed Sunday dinner and Monday) (dinner only and Sunday
　　　　lunch) 9.75/14.95 **t.** 🛢 2.90 – ⊡ 4.75 – **5 rm** 44.50/65.00 **t.**

AUSTIN-ROVER 52 Birmingham Rd 🖉 72212　　　　　　RENAULT 17-21 Worcester Rd 🖉 79898
FORD 184/188 Worcester Rd 🖉 31178　　　　　　　VAUXHALL-OPEL 137 Birmingham Rd 🖉 71244
LADA Windsor St. 🖉 75210
PEUGEOT-TALBOT 12/14 Old Birmingham Rd 🖉
72552

BROOK Hants. **403 404** P 31 – pop. 572 – ECD : Tuesday – ⊠ Lyndhurst – 🕾 0703 Southamp-
ton.
🖪, 🖪 Bramshaw 🖉 813252.
◆London 92 – Bournemouth 24 – ◆Southampton 14.

　　🏠　**Bell,** SO4 7HE, 🖉 812214, 🖪, 🐗 – 🖭 ⊟wc ℗. 🔼 🖭 ⓪ *VISA*
　　　　M 6.50/7.75 **t.** – **12 rm** ⊡ 21.00/46.00 **t.**

BROOKMANS PARK Herts. **404** T 28 – pop. 3,062 – 🕾 0707 Potters Bar.
◆London 21 – Luton 21.

　　✗✗　**Villa Rosa,** 3 Great North Rd, SE : 1 ¾ m. on A 1000 🖉 51444, Italian rest. – ℗. 🔼 🖭 ⓪
　　　　VISA
　　　　closed Saturday lunch and Sunday – **M** a la carte 7.20/11.75 **t.** 🛢 2.95.

BROUGHTON Lancs. **402** L 22 – see Preston.

BRUNDALL Norfolk **404** Y 26 – see Norwich.

BRUSHFORD Somerset **403** J 30 – pop. 475 – ⊠ 🕾 0398 Dulverton.
◆London 195 – Exeter 24 – Minehead 18 – Taunton 24.

　　🏠　**Carnarvon Arms,** TA22 9AE, 🖉 23302, 🟰 heated, ◈, 🐗, park, ✸ – ⊟wc ℗
　　　　M 8.50/14.00 **st.** 🛢 2.45 – **27 rm** ⊡ 19.00/45.00 **st.** – SB (June-September) 52.00/64.00 **st.**
　　🏠　**Three Acres Captain's Country** ◈, TA22 9AR, 🖉 23426, 🐗 – ⊟wc ℗
　　　　closed January and February – **M** 4.15/8.00 **t.** 🛢 1.70 – **7 rm** ⊡ (dinner included) 20.00/44.00 **t.**
　　　　– SB 36.00 **st.**

BRUTON Somerset **403 404** M 30 – pop. 2,248 – 🕾 074 981.
◆London 118 – ◆Bristol 27 – Bournemouth 44 – Salisbury 35 – Taunton 36.

　　✗✗　**Grants** with rm, High St., BA10 0EQ, 🖉 3395 – ⊟wc. 🔼 *VISA*. ✸
　　　　M (closed Tuesday) (dinner only and Sunday lunch) a la carte 9.50/12.00 **t.** 🛢 2.70 – **3 rm**
　　　　⊡ 14.00/24.00 **t.**
　　✗　**Clogs,** 95 High St., 🖉 2255, « Dutch Indonesian »
　　　　closed Sunday dinner, Monday, 1 week April, 1 week September and 25 to 27 December – **M**
　　　　(dinner only and Sunday lunch) (booking essential) 10.85/12.45.

BRYHER Cornwall `403` ㉚ – see Scilly (Isles of).

BRYNBUGA = Usk.

BUCKFASTLEIGH Devon `403` I 32 The West Country G. – pop. 2,656 – ECD : Wednesday – ✆ 0364.
See : Buckfast Abbey (the Sacrament Chapel★).
♦London 223 – Exeter 23 – ♦Plymouth 20.

　↑ **Furzeleigh Mill**, Dart Bridge, TQ11 0JP, NE : ¾ m. on old A 38 ℰ 43476, 🐴 – 🛏wc 🅿
　　closed December – **17 rm** ☲ 8.00/25.00 t.

BUCKHURST HILL Essex `404` ㊸ – pop. 11,683 – ECD : Wednesday – ✆ 01 London.
♦London 13 – Chelmsford 25.

Plan : see Greater London (North-East)

　🏨 **Roebuck** (T.H.F.), North End, IG9 1QY, ℰ 505 4636 – 📺 🛏wc ☎ 🅿 🔏 🔼 AE ① VISA
　　M 6.50/9.00 st. ┇ 2.60 – ☲ 5.00 – **23 rm** 35.50/44.50 st.　　　　　　　　　　　　GU **u**

BUCKINGHAM Bucks. `403` `404` Q 27 – pop. 5,076 – ECD : Thursday – ✆ 0280.
Envir. : Claydon House★ (Rococo interior★★ : Chinese Room★★ staircase★★★, Florence Nightingale Museum) *AC*, SE : 8 m. – Stowe School 18C (south front★, Marble Saloon★, park : monuments★ 18C, ≤★ from the Lake Pavilions) *AC*.
♦London 64 – ♦Birmingham 61 – Northampton 20 – ♦Oxford 25.

　🏨 **White Hart** (T.H.F.), Market Sq., MK18 1NL, ℰ 815151 – 📺 🛏wc ☎ 🅿 🔏 🔼 AE ① VISA
　　M (buffet lunch) 8.50 st. ┇ 2.75 – ☲ 4.75 – **19 rm** 32.50/41.50 st.

AUSTIN-ROVER Motorworks ℰ 812121　　　　　　　　VAUXHALL-OPEL School Lane ℰ 812209

BUCKLAND Glos. `403` `404` O 27 – see Broadway (Heref. and Worc.).

BUCKLAND IN THE MOOR Devon The West Country G. – pop. 79 – ✉ ✆ 0364 Ashburton.
♦London 225 – Exeter 25 – ♦Plymouth 28.

　🏠 **Buckland Hall** ⌁, TQ13 7HL, ℰ 52679, ≤ countryside and Holne Moor, 🐴, park – 🛏wc 🅿
　　April-October – **M** (dinner only) 8.50 st. ┇ 2.50 – **6 rm** ☲ 19.00/34.00 st. – SB 39.00/45.00 st.

BUCKLERS HARD Hants. `403` `404` P 31 – see Beaulieu.

BUCKLOW HILL Cheshire `402` `403` `404` M 24 – see Knutsford.

BUDE Cornwall `403` G 31 The West Country G. – pop. 4,069 – ECD : Thursday – ✆ 0288.
See : The breakwater★★ – ≤ from Compass Point★.
🏌 Burn View ℰ 2006 – 🏌 Holsworthy ℰ 0409 (Holsworthy) 253177, E : 8 ½ m.
🅸 The Castle ℰ 4240 (summer only) – A 39, Stamford Hill, Stratton ℰ 3781.
♦London 252 – Exeter 51 – ♦Plymouth 44 – Truro 53.

　🏨 **Strand** (T.H.F.), The Strand, EX23 8RA, ℰ 3222 – 🛗 📺 🛏wc ☎ 🅿 🔼 AE ① VISA
　　M (bar lunch) 7.00 st. ┇ 2.60 – ☲ 5.00 – **40 rm** 28.50/42.00 st.
　🏨 **Hartland**, Hartland Terr., EX23 8JY, ℰ 2509, ≤, ⩳ heated – 🛗 📺 🛏wc 📺wc 🅿
　　Easter-September – **M** 5.50/6.50 ┇ 2.50 – **30 rm** ☲ 14.00/37.00.
　🏠 **Camelot**, Downs View, EX23 8RS, ℰ 2361 – 🛏wc 📺wc 🅿 🔼 VISA
　　M (carving lunch) 5.00/7.95 st. ┇ 2.95 – **13 rm** ☲ 9.50/24.50 st.
　🏠 **Bude Haven,** Flexbury Av., EX23 8NS, ℰ 2305, 🐴 – 🛏wc 📺wc 🅿 🔼 VISA
　　M (bar lunch) 5.75 st. ┇ 1.95 – **10 rm** ☲ 12.50/26.50 t. – SB 30.00/37.50 st.
　↑ **Meva Gwin,** Upton, EX23 0LY, S : 1 ¼ m. on coast rd ℰ 2347, ≤ – 🛏wc 🅿 ⌁
　　March-mid October – **17 rm** ☲ 9.20/24.15 st.
　↑ **Teeside,** 2 Burn View, EX23 8BY, ℰ 2351 – ⌁
　　closed November and December – **6 rm** ☲ 7.00/15.00 s.

AUSTIN-ROVER Bencoolen Rd ℰ 2146　　　　　　　FORD, POLSKI, FIAT Bencoolen Rd ℰ 4616

BUDLEIGH SALTERTON Devon `403` K 32 The West Country G. – pop. 4,157 – ECD : Thursday – ✆ 039 54.
🅸 Rolle Mews Car Park, Fore St. ℰ 5275 (summer only) – ♦London 215 – Exeter 16 – ♦Plymouth 55.

　🏠 **Southlands**, 9 Marine Par., EX9 6NS, ℰ 3497, ≤ – 🛏wc 🅿 VISA
　　M 4.25/6.25 t. – **20 rm** ☲ 13.50/16.25 st. – SB 32.50/43.00 st.
　↑ **Long Range,** 5 Vales Rd, EX9 6HS, ℰ 3321, 🐴 – 🅿 ⌁
　　closed winter – **10 rm** ☲ 11.00/22.00 t.
　↑ **Park House** ⌁, Park Lane, Little Knowle, EX9 6QT, ℰ 3303, 🐴 – 📺wc 🅿
　　Easter-October – **10 rm** ☲ 13.50/30.00 st.

AUSTIN-ROVER 9 High St. ℰ 2277

120

BUILTH WELLS (LLANFAIR-YM-MUALLT) Powys **403** J 27 – pop. 1,597 – 🕾 0982.

♦London 197 – Brecon 22 – ♦Cardiff 63 – ♦Swansea 63 – Shrewsbury 70.

🏨 **Caer Beris Manor,** Garth Rd, LD2 3NP, W : ¾ m. by A 483 ℰ 552601, ≼, « 19C mock-tudor house », 🔫, park – 🚗wc 🅿. 🔼 🗛🗉 🚾. 🛠
M 5.75/7.20 **st.** – **14 rm** 🖙 14.00/16.00 **st.**

🏠 Llanfair, 1, The Strand, LD2 3BG, ℰ 553253, 🛲 – 📺 🅿 – **8 rm**.

BUNWELL Norfolk **404** X 26 – pop. 738 – ECD : Monday and Wednesday – 🕾 095 389.

♦London 102 – ♦Cambridge 51 – ♦Norwich 16.

🏨 **Bunwell Manor** 🦌, Bunwell St., NR16 1QU, NW : 1 m. ℰ 317, 🛲 – 📺 🚗wc 🛁wc 🅿. 🔼 🗛🗉
M (bar lunch) 7.50 **t.** 🍷 4.40 – **11 rm** 🖙 18.00/28.00 **t.** – SB 40.00 **st.**

BURFORD Oxon. **403 404** P 28 – pop. 1,255 (inc. Upton and Signet) – ECD : Wednesday – 🕾 099 382.

See : St. John's Church★ 12C-14C – Envir. : Swinbrook (church : Fettiplace Monuments★) E : 3 ½ m. – Cotswold Wildlife Park★ *AC*, S : 2 m – Northleach : SS. Peter and Paul's Church : South Porch and the brasses★ (Perpendicular) NW : 7 ½ m.

🛈 The Brewery, Sheep St. ℰ 3590.

♦London 76 – ♦Birmingham 55 – Gloucester 32 – ♦Oxford 20.

🏨 **Bay Tree,** Sheep St., OX8 4LW, ℰ 3137, 🛲 – 📺 🚗wc 🚘 🅿. 🔼 🗛🗉 🚾. 🛠
closed 27 January-14 February – **M** a la carte approx. 9.50 **t.** 🍷 2.95 – **22 rm** 🖙 20.00/52.00 **st.**

🏨 **Inn For All Seasons,** The Barringtons, OX8 4TN, W : 3 ¼ m. on A 40 ℰ 045 14 (Windrush) 324, 🛲 – 📺 🚗wc 🚘 🅿. 🔼 🗛🗉 🚾. 🛠
closed 2 weeks at Christmas – **M** (closed Sunday dinner) (bar lunch) 10.95 **t.** 🍷 3.75 – **9 rm**
🖙 27.50/42.00 **t.** – SB (winter only) 47.00 **st.**

🏠 **Golden Pheasant,** High St., OX8 4RJ, ℰ 3223 – 📺 🚗wc 🛁wc 🚘 🅿. 🔼
M 6.50/10.50 **st.** 🍷 2.90 – **12 rm** 🖙 20.00/37.50 **st.** – SB 49.00/54.00 **st.**

🏨 **Lamb Inn,** Sheep St., OX8 4LR, ℰ 3155, 🛲 – 🚗wc 🅿
M (closed Sunday dinner to non-residents) (bar lunch Monday to Saturday) 13.00 **t.** 🍷 2.75 –
13 rm 🖙 16.50/39.00 **t.** – SB (winter only) 44.00/58.00 **st.**

🏠 **Corner House,** High St., OX8 4RJ, ℰ 3151 – 🚗wc 🛁wc
Mid February-mid November – **M** (closed Sunday lunch) a la carte 4.60/9.10 **t.** 🍷 3.10 – **9 rm**
🖙 17.00/30.00 **t.**

BURGHFIELD Berks. **403 404** Q 29 – see Reading.

BURLEY Hants. **403 404** O 31 – pop. 1,552 – ECD : Wednesday – ✉ Ringwood – 🕾 042 53.
🍸 ℰ 2431.

♦London 102 – Bournemouth 17 – ♦Southampton 17 – Winchester 30.

🏨 **Moorhill House** 🦌, BH24 4AG, ℰ 3285, 🔲, 🛲 – 🚗wc 🛁wc 🅿. 🔼 🗛🗉 🗝 🚾
M (lunch by arrangement) 4.00/10.50 **st.** 🍷 1.95 – **24 rm** 🖙 20.00/40.00 **st.** – SB 48.00/53.00 **st.**

🏨 **Tree House,** The Cross, Ringwood Rd, BH24 4BA, ℰ 3448, 🛲 – 📺 🛁wc 🅿. 🔼 🗛🗉 🗝 🚾.
🛠
March-November – **M** (closed Sunday dinner) 6.55 **st.** 🍷 2.40 – **8 rm** 🖙 16.25/31.90 **st.**

BURN BRIDGE North Yorks. – see Harrogate.

BURNHAM Bucks. **404** S 29 – pop. 17,751 – ECD : Thursday – 🕾 062 86.

♦London 33 – ♦Oxford 37 – Reading 17.

🏨 **Grovefield** 🦌, Taplow Common Rd, SL1 8LP, ℰ 3131, 🛲 – 🔌 📺 🚗wc ☎ 🅿. 🔼. 🔼 🗛🗉
🗝 🚾
M 9.00/11.00 **t.** 🍷 2.75 – **33 rm** 🖙 43.00/50.00 **st.** – SB (weekends only) 103.00 **st.**

CITROEN 46/48 High St. ℰ 5255   VAUXHALL 71 Stomp Rd ℰ 4994

BURNHAM MARKET Norfolk **404** W 25 – pop. 962 – 🕾 0328 Fakenham.

♦London 128 – ♦Cambridge 71 – ♦Norwich 36.

✕ **Fishes,** Market Pl., PE31 8HE, ℰ 738588, Seafood – 🔼 🗛🗉 🗝 🚾
closed Sunday dinner October-June, Monday and 24 to 28 December – **M** a la carte 7.25/12.40 **t.**

BURNHAM-ON-CROUCH Essex **404** W 29 – pop. 4,619 – ECD : Wednesday – 🕾 0621 Maldon.

♦London 52 – Chelmsford 19 – Colchester 32 – Southend-on-Sea 25.

✕✕ **Contented Sole,** 80 High St., CM0 8AA, ℰ 782139
closed Sunday, Monday, 14-27 July and 23 December-19 January – **M** a la carte 9.35/12.25 **s.**
🍷 2.35.

✕ **Boozles,** 4 Station Rd, CM0 8BG, ℰ 783167 – 🔼 🚾
closed Sunday, Monday and 26 to 28 December – **M** (lunch by arrangement in winter)
a la carte 5.65/9.15 **t.** 🍷 2.25.

AUSTIN-ROVER Station Rd ℰ 782130

BURNLEY Lancs. 四〇2 N 22 – pop. 76,513 – ✆ 0282.

Envir. : Towneley Hall★ (16C-18C) SE : 1 m.

🏌 Towneley, Towneley Park ✆ 38473, E : 1 ½ m. – 🏌 Glen View ✆ 21045 – 🏌 Marsden Park, Townhouse Rd, Walton Lane, Nelson ✆ 0282 (Nelson) 67525, N : 4 m – 🏌 Marsden Heights, Brierfield, Nelson ✆ 0282 (Nelson) 64583, N : 2 m.

♦London 236 – Bradford 32 – ♦Leeds 37 – ♦Liverpool 55 – ♦Manchester 25 – ♦Middlesbrough 104 – Preston 22 – ♦Sheffield 68.

🏨 **Oaks,** Colne Rd, Reedley, BB10 2LF, N : 2 m. on A 56 ✆ 414141, 🔲, 🛋, 🌳 – 📺 🚻wc ☎ 🅿.
🏋. 🔄 ㏂ ⑩ 𝗩𝗜𝗦𝗔
M 5.95/10.00 **st.** 🍷 3.25 – **32 rm** ⊃ 36.00/46.00 **st.** – SB (weekends only) 56.00/76.00 **st.**

🏨 **Kierby,** Keirby Walk, BB11 2DH, ✆ 27611, Telex 63119 – 🔌 📺 🚻wc ☜ 🅿. 🏋. 🔄 ㏂ ⑩
M 4.45/6.95 **t.** – ⊃ 2.00 – **49 rm** 27.50/36.50 **t.** – SB (weekends only) 41.90/53.90 **st.**

🏨 **Rosehill House,** Rosehill Av., Manchester Rd, BB11 2PW, ✆ 53931, 🌳 – 📺 🚻wc 🛁wc ☜ 🅿. 🔄 ㏂ 𝗩𝗜𝗦𝗔
M 8.50 **st.** 🍷 3.00 – **20 rm** ⊃ 24.00/35.00 **st.** – SB (weekends only) 44.50 **st.**

AUSTIN-ROVER Todmorden Rd ✆ 36131
FIAT Accrington Rd ✆ 27328
FIAT, FSO Manchester Rd ✆ 26020

RENAULT Trafalgar St. ✆ 33311
VAUXHALL Accrington Rd ✆ 27321

BURNSALL North Yorks. 四〇2 O 21 – pop. 109 – ECD : Tuesday – ✉ Skipton – ✆ 075 672.

♦London 223 – Bradford 26 – ♦Leeds 29.

🛏 **Red Lion,** BD23 6BU, ✆ 204 – 🚻wc 🅿. 🍴
closed Christmas – **M** (bar lunch Monday to Friday) 4.60/8.60 **t.** 🍷 3.00 – **12 rm** ⊃ 15.00/36.00 **t.**

🛏 **Manor House,** BD23 6BW, ✆ 231 – 🅿
7 rm ⊃ 10.00/17.00 **st.**

BURPHAM West Sussex 四〇4 S 30 – see Arundel.

BURRINGTON Devon – ECD : Saturday – ✆ 0769 High Bickington.

♦London 260 – Barnstaple 14 – Exeter 28 – Taunton 50.

🏨 **Northcote Manor** (Best Western) ☜, EX37 9LZ, NW : 1 m. ✆ 60501, ≼, 🌳 – 📺 🚻wc ☜ 🅿. 🔄 ㏂ ⑩ 𝗩𝗜𝗦𝗔. 🍴
March-October – **M** (bar lunch) 10.00 **st.** 🍷 3.00 – **11 rm** ⊃ 22.00/44.00 **st.** – SB (March-October) 53.00/58.00 **st.**

BURTON-UPON-TRENT Staffs. 四〇2 四〇3 四〇4 O 25 – pop. 50,201 – ECD : Wednesday – ✆ 0283.

🅱 Town Hall, King Edward Square ✆ 45454.

♦London 128 – ♦Birmingham 29 – ♦Leicester 27 – ♦Nottingham 27 – Stafford 27.

🛏 **Edgecote,** 179 Ashby Rd, DE15 0LB, SE : 1 m. on A 50 ✆ 68966, 🌳 – 🅿
11 rm ⊃ 10.90/22.50 **t.**

at Rolleston on Dove N : 4 m. by A 38 – ✉ ✆ 0283 Burton-upon-Trent :

XXX **Brookhouse Inn** ☜ with rm, Brookside, DE13 9AA, ✆ 814188, Telex 913001, 🌳 – 📺 🚻wc ☜ 🅿. 🔄 ㏂ ⑩ 𝗩𝗜𝗦𝗔. 🍴
closed 24 December-4 January and Bank Holidays – **M** *(closed Saturday lunch and Sunday)* a la carte 7.05/13.45 **t.** 🍷 2.45 – **16 rm** ⊃ 30.00/50.00 **st.** – SB (weekends only) 54.00 **st.**

at Newton Solney NE : 3 m. by A 50 on B 5008 – ✉ ✆ 0283 Burton-upon-Trent :

🏨 **Newton Park** (Embassy) ☜, DE15 0SS, ✆ 703568, ≼, 🌳 – 📺 🚻wc ☜ 🅿. 🏋. 🔄 ㏂ ⑩ 𝗩𝗜𝗦𝗔. 🍴
closed Christmas – **M** *(closed Saturday lunch and Sunday dinner to non-residents)* 7.15/12.10 **st.** 🍷 4.50 – ⊃ 4.25 – **27 rm** 31.00/37.00 **st.** – SB (weekends only) 41.00/48.00 **st.**

at Branston SW : 1 ½ m. on A 5121 – ✉ ✆ 0283 Burton-upon-Trent :

🏠 **Riverside** ☜, Riverside Dr., off Warren Lane, DE14 3EP, ✆ 63117, 🌳 – 📺 🚻wc ☜ 🅿. 𝗩𝗜𝗦𝗔
closed Christmas Night – **M** *(closed Saturday lunch)* 6.00/8.50 **t.** – **22 rm** ⊃ 27.00/40.00 **t.**

AUSTIN-ROVER-JAGUAR Moor St. ✆ 45353
FORD Horninglow St. ✆ 61081
NISSAN Scalpcliffe Rd ✆ 66677
PEUGEOT, TALBOT Derby Rd ✆ 65432

RENAULT 118 Horninglow Rd ✆ 67811
VAUXHALL-OPEL 12 Lichfield St. ✆ 61655
VOLVO New St. ✆ 31331
VW, AUDI Tutbury Rd ✆ 31336

Pleasant hotels and restaurants
are shown in the Guide by a red sign.

Please send us the names
of any where you have enjoyed your stay.

Your Michelin Guide will be even better.

🏨🏨🏨 … 🏠

XXXXX … X

BURY ST. EDMUNDS Suffolk **404** W 27 – pop. 25,661 – ECD : Thursday – ☎ 0284.

See : St. Mary's Church★ 15C (the Angel roof★★).

Envir. : Ickworth House★ (18C) *AC*, SW : 3 m.

🏌 Lark Valley, Fornham St. Martin ℰ 63426, off A 134 on B 1106.

🎫 Abbey Gardens, Angel Hill ℰ 64667 (summer only).

♦London 79 – ♦Cambridge 27 – ♦Ipswich 26 – ♦Norwich 41.

🏨 **Angel,** 3 Angel Hill, IP33 1LT, ℰ 3926, Telex 81630 – 🔟 🅿 🔌 🔼 🆎 ⓞ 🆅🆂🆁 ⋘
   M a la carte 10.30/15.50 **st.** 🍷 3.10 – **41 rm** 🖃 40.00/50.00 **st.**

🏨 **Suffolk** (T.H.F.), 38 The Buttermarket, IP33 1DC, ℰ 3995 – 🔟 🚿wc ☜. 🔼 🆎 ⓞ 🆅🆂🆁
   M 6.50/7.50 **st.** 🍷 2.60 – 🖃 4.75 – **41 rm** 26.00/31.50 **st.**

✗ **Bradleys,** St. Andrews St. South, ℰ 703825 – 🆅🆂🆁
   closed Sunday, Monday, 2 weeks summer and 1 week winter – **M** (lunch by arrangement) a la
   carte 10.45/17.00 **t.** 🍷 2.55.

   at Bradfield Combust SE : 4 ½ m. on A 134 – ⊠ Bury St. Edmunds – ☎ 028 486 Sickles-
   mere :

✗✗ **Bradfield House,** Sudbury Rd, IP30 0LR, ℰ 301, 🍴 – 🅿 🆎 ⓞ 🆅🆂🆁
   closed Sunday dinner and Monday – **M** (lunch by arrangement) a la carte 9.90/13.70 **t.** 🍷 3.50.

AUSTIN-ROVER 76 Risbygate St. ℰ 31015
FIAT, LANCIA Mildenhall Rd ℰ 3280
FORD 5 Fornham Rd ℰ 2332
RENAULT Bury Rd, Horringer ℰ 028 488 (Horringer)
362

VAUXHALL-OPEL Cotton Lane ℰ 5621
VOLVO, NISSAN Out Risbygate ℰ 62444
VW, AUDI Northern Way ℰ 63441

BUTTERMERE Cumbria **402** K 20 – pop. 257 – ⊠ Cockermouth – ☎ 059 685.

See : Lake★ – ♦London 306 – ♦Carlisle 35 – Kendal 43.

🏨 **Bridge,** CA13 9UZ, ℰ 252, ← – 🚿wc 🛁wc 🅿
   closed December and January – **M** (bar lunch) 9.00 **t.** 🍷 3.25 – **19 rm** 🖃 (dinner included) 27.00/54.00 **t.** – SB (February, March and November only) 48.00 **st.**

BUXTON Derbs. **402 403 404** O 24 – pop. 20,324 – ECD : Wednesday – ⊠ Stockport – ☎ 0298.

Envir. : Tideswell (Parish Church★ 14C) NE : 9 m.

🏌 Buxton and High Peak, Townend ℰ 3453, NE : on A 6 – 🏌 Cavendish, Gadley Lane ℰ 3494, ¾ m.
Buxton Station.

🎫 The Cresent ℰ 5106 – ♦London 172 – Derby 38 – ♦Manchester 25 – ♦Stoke-on-Trent 24.

🏨 **Lee Wood** (Best Western), 13 Manchester Rd, SK17 6TQ, on A 5002 ℰ 3002, 🍴 – ⧉ 🔟
   🚿wc 🛁wc 🅿. 🔌 🔼 🆎 ⓞ 🆅🆂🆁
   M (buffet lunch) 6.00/8.50 **t.** 🍷 2.10 – **40 rm** 🖃 25.50/38.00 **t.** – SB 48.50/50.00 **st.**

🏨 **Hartington,** 18 Broad Walk, SK17 6JR, ℰ 2638 – 🚿wc 🛁wc 🔥 🅿. ⋘
   closed first week November and 24 December-3 January – **M** (dinner only) 5.50 **t.** 🍷 2.50 –
   17 rm 🖃 20.00/28.00 **t.** – SB 28.00/36.00 **st.**

AUDI, VW 3 The Front ℰ 2903
AUSTIN-ROVER Spring Gardens ℰ 2321
FORD 127 London Rd ℰ 3816

HONDA, SAAB Leek Rd ℰ 2494
RENAULT The Old Court House ℰ 3947
VAUXHALL-OPEL Leek Rd ℰ 3466

BWLCHTOCYN Gwynedd **402 403** G 25 – see Abersoch.

CADNAM Hants. **403 404** P 31 – pop. 2,500 – ECD : Wednesday – ☎ 0703 Southampton.

♦London 91 – Salisbury 16 – ♦Southampton 8 – Winchester 19.

🏨 **Bartley Lodge** 🐾, Lyndhurst Rd, SO4 2NR, on A 337 ℰ 812248, ←, 🏊, 🍴 – 🔟 🚿wc 🛁wc
   🅿 🆎 🆅🆂🆁
   M 5.95/8.95 **st.** 🍷 2.00 – **13 rm** 🖃 18.00/35.00 **t.** – SB (except summer) 40.00/50.00 **st.**

CAERDYDD = Cardiff.

CAERFFILI = Caerphilly.

CAERFYRDDIN = Carmarthen.

CAERGYBI = Holyhead.

CAERNARFON Gwynedd **402 403** H 24 – pop. 9,260 – ☎ 0286 Llanwnda.

See : Castle★★★ 13C-14C (Royal Welsh Fusiliers Regimental museum★) *AC* – City walls★.

Envir. : SE : Snowdon (ascent and ✳★★★) 1 h 15 mn by Snowdon Mountain Railway (*AC*) from
Llanberis (Pass★★) SE : 13 m. – Dinas Dindle★ SW : 5 m.

🎫 The Slate Quay ℰ 2232 (summer only).

♦London 249 – Birkenhead 76 – Chester 68 – Holyhead 30 – Shrewsbury 85.

✗✗ **The Stables** with rm, Llanwnda, LL54 5SD, SW : 3 ½ m. by A 487 on A 499 ℰ 830711, 🏊, 🍴
   – 🔟 🚿wc 🛁wc 🅿. ⋘
   M a la carte 9.25/12.35 **st.** 🍷 2.85 – **12 rm** 🖃 26.40/40.00 **st.** – SB (weekends only)(except
   Easter and Christmas) 49.00/52.00 **st.**

CAERPHILLY (CAERFFILI) Mid Glam. **403** K 29 – pop. 29,400 – ECD : Wednesday – ✆ 0222.

See : Castle★★ 13C.

🛈 Park Lane ✆ 863378 (summer only).

◆London 157 – ◆Cardiff 8 – Newport 11.

Hotels and restaurants see : Cardiff S : 8 m., *Newport (Gwent)* E : 11 m.

CAERSWS Powys **403** J 26 – pop. 1,205 – ECD : Thursday – ✉ Newtown – ✆ 068 684.

◆London 202 – Aberystwyth 38 – Newtown 6.

🏡 **Maesmawr Hall** 🦢, SY17 5SF, E : 1 m. on A 489 ✆ 255, ≼, « 16C manor house in large garden », ⚘, park – ⌂wc 📺 🅿 ⚑ ⒜ 🆎 ⓞ *VISA*
M 6.00/8.00 🍷 1.75 – **19 rm** ⥥ 20.25/42.50 **t.** – SB (summer only) 55.00/60.00 **st.**

AUSTIN-ROVER Central Garage ✆ 345   VOLVO Trefeglwys ✆ 055 16 (Trefeglwys) 202

CALCOT Glos. – see Tetbury.

CAMBERLEY Surrey **404** R 29 – pop. 44,967 (inc. Frimley) – ECD : Wednesday – ✆ 0276.

Envir. : Sandhurst (Royal Military Academy : Royal Memorial Chapel★) NW : 1 ½ m.

◆London 40 – Reading 13 – ◆Southampton 48.

🏨 **Frimley Hall** (T.H.F.), off Portsmouth Rd via Lime Av., GU15 2BG, E : ¾ m. by A 325 ✆ 28321, Telex 858446, ⚑ – 📺 🅿 ⚑ ⒜ 🆎 ⓞ *VISA*
M 7.50/10.50 **st.** 🍷 3.40 – ⥥ 5.50 – **66 rm** 36.00/47.00 **st.**

%% **Tithas,** 31 High St., GU15 3RE, ✆ 23279, Indian rest. – ⒜ 🆎 ⓞ *VISA*
M a la carte 6.65/7.45 **t.**

% **Villa Romana,** 20 Park St., GU15 3PL, ✆ 24370, Italian rest. – ⒜ 🆎 ⓞ *VISA*
closed Sunday – **M** a la carte 6.50/12.25 **t.** 🍷 2.25.

AUSTIN-ROVER London Rd ✆ 63443

CAMBRIDGE Cambs. **404** U 27 – pop. 98,840 – ECD : Thursday – ✆ 0223.

See : Colleges Quarter★★★ : King's College★★ (King's Chapel★★★) Z – Queens' College★★ (Cloister Court) Z – St. John's College★★ (Gateway★) Y – Fitzwilliam Museum★★ *AC* Z M1 – Trinity College★★ (Wren Library★★, Chapel★, Great Court and Gate★) Y – Holy Sepulchre★ (12C round church) Y E – Senate House★ Z S – The Backs★ YZ – Jesus College (Chapel★) Y K – Christ's College (Gatehouse) YZ **A.**

Envir. : Anglesey Abbey 12C (interior★★ and park★ *AC*) NE : 6 m. by A 1303 X and B 1102.

🕞 Cambridgeshire Hotel, Bar Hill ✆ 0954 (Crafts Hill) 80555, NW : 5 ½ m. by A 1307 X.

✈ Cambridge Airport : ✆ 61133, E : 2 m. on A 1303 X.

🛈 Wheeler St. ✆ 358977 or 353363 (weekends).

◆London 55 – ◆Coventry 93 – ◆Kingston-upon-Hull 138 – ◆Ipswich 54 – ◆Leicester 74 – ◆Norwich 62 – ◆Nottingham 88 – ◆Oxford 81.

Plan opposite

🏨 **Garden House,** Granta Pl., off Mill Lane, CB2 1RT, ✆ 63421, Telex 81463, ≼, ⚑ – 🛗 📺 ☎
🅿 ⚑ ⒜ 🆎 ⓞ *VISA*, ⚶   Z n
M 6.95/12.50 **t.** 🍷 2.65 – ⥥ 4.25 – **117 rm** 42.00/60.00 **t.** – SB (except Monday to Wednesday) 67.50/93.00 **st.**

🏨 **University Arms,** Regent St., CB2 1AD, ✆ 351241, Telex 817311 – 🛗 📺 ☎ 🅿 ⚑ ⒜ 🆎
ⓞ *VISA*   Z e
M 6.20/7.90 **st.** 🍷 2.00 – **113 rm** ⥥ 30.50/44.50 **st.** – SB (weekends only) 47.00/49.80 **st.**

🏡 **Gonville,** Gonville Pl., CB1 1LY, ✆ 66611 – 🛗 📺 ⌂wc ☎ 🅿 ⚑ ⒜ 🆎 *VISA*   Z r
closed 3 days at Christmas – **M** 6.50/8.95 **st.** 🍷 3.15 – **62 rm** ⥥ 30.50/44.50 **st.** – SB (weekends only) (except summer) 47.00/49.85 **st.**

🏡 **Blue Boar** (T.H.F.), 17 Trinity St., CB2 1TB, ✆ 63121 – 📺 ⌂wc ☎ ⚑ ⒜ 🆎 ⓞ *VISA*   Y s
M 6.95/8.25 **st.** 🍷 2.85 – ⥥ 5.50 – **48 rm** 24.00/44.00 **st.**

🏠 **Arundel House,** 53 Chesterton Rd, CB4 3AN, ✆ 67701 – 📺 ⌂wc ⌂wc ☎ 🅿 ⚑ ⒜ 🆎
VISA   Y u
closed Christmas – **M** 5.50/7.35 **t.** 🍷 1.80 – ⥥ .75 – **72 rm** 15.50/39.50 **t.** – SB (weekends only) (April-October) 44.00/48.25 **st.**

🏠 **Centennial,** 63-69 Hills Rd, CB2 1PG, ✆ 314652 – ⌂wc 📺 🅿 ⒜ 🆎 ⓞ *VISA*. ⚶   X x
closed 25 December-2 January – **M** 6.00 **st.** – **24 rm** ⥥ 15.00/32.00 **t.**

🏠 **Ashley,** 74 Chesterton Rd, CB4 1ER, ✆ 350059, ⚑ – 📺 ⌂wc ☎ 🅿 ⒜ *VISA*   Y o
closed 25 to 26 December – **10 rm** ⥥ 15.00/25.50 **st.**

🏠 **May View,** 12 Park Par., CB5 8AL, ✆ 66018 – ⚶   Y v
6 rm ⥥ 15.00/20.00 **st.**

🏠 **Helen,** 167-169 Hills Rd, CB2 2RJ, ✆ 246465 – 📺 ⌂wc ☎ 🅿 ⒜ ⓞ *VISA*   X c
closed 10 December-10 January – **24 rm** ⥥ 17.00/30.00 **st.**

%% **Cambridge Lodge** with rm, 139 Huntingdon Rd, CB3 0DQ, ✆ 352833, Telex 817438, ⚑ –
📺 ⌂wc ⌂wc 🅿 ⒜ 🆎 ⓞ *VISA*   X i
closed lunch Saturday – **M** a la carte 10.20/16.75 **t.** 🍷 5.25 – **11 rm** ⥥ 28.75/42.25 **t.**

CAMBRIDGE

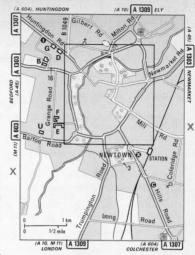

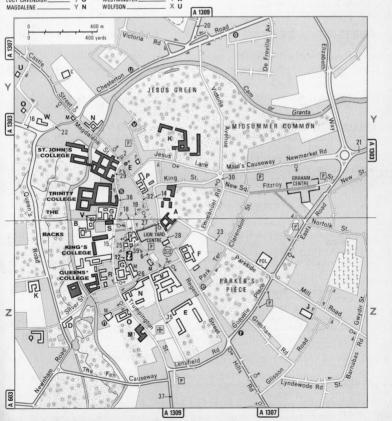

at Impington N : 2 m. on B 1049 at junction of A 45 − X − ⊠ Cambridge − ☻ 022 023 Histon :

🏨 **Post House** (T.H.F.), Lakeview, Bridge Rd, CB4 4PH, ℰ 7000, Telex 817123, 🔍, 🛋 − 🛗 📺
🛎 🕭 ℗. 🏄. 🔄 🖭 ⓪ 🆅🆂🅰
M 8.75/12.95 **st.** 🍷 2.60 − 🛏 5.00 − **120 rm** 42.00/52.50 **st.**

at Fowlmere S : 8 ¾ m. by A 1309 − X − and A 10 on B 1368 − ⊠ Royston − ☻ 076 382 Fowlmere :

✕✕ **Chequers Inn,** High St., SG8 7SR, ℰ 369 − ℗. 🔄 🖭 ⓪ 🆅🆂🅰
closed 25-26 December − **M** a la carte 11.60/18.30 **st.**

✕✕ **Swan House Inn,** High St., SG8 7SR, ℰ 444 − ℗. 🔄 🖭 ⓪ 🆅🆂🅰
M 9.00 **t.** 🍷 2.75.

at Madingley W : 4 ½ m. by A 1303 − X − ⊠ ☻ 0954 Madingley :

✕✕ **Three Horseshoes,** High Street, CB3 8AB, ℰ 210221, 🛋 − ℗. 🔄 🖭 🆅🆂🅰
M a la carte 13.00/16.30 **st.**

at Bar Hill NW : 5 ½ m. by A 1307 − X − on A 604 − ⊠ Bar Hill − ☻ 0954 Crafts Hill :

🏨 **Cambridgeshire Moat House** (Q.M.H.), Huntingdon Rd, CB3 8EU, ℰ 80555, Telex 817141,
🔍, 🕭, 🛋, ✕, squash − 📺 🖰wc ℗. 🏄. 🔄 🖭 ⓪ 🆅🆂🅰
M a la carte 11.45/16.40 **st.** − **100 rm** 🛏 42.50/56.00 **st.** − SB (weekends only) 66.00 **st.**

ALFA-ROMEO, HYUNDAI, SUZUKI Babraham Rd ℰ 247072
AUSTIN-ROVER-DAIMLER-JAGUAR 400 Newmarket Rd ℰ 65111
BEDFORD, OPEL-VAUXHALL 137 Histon Rd ℰ 66751
CITROEN Newmarket Rd, Duxford ℰ 832136
HONDA Cheddars Lane ℰ 59151

MERCEDES-BENZ 121/129 Perne Rd ℰ 247268
NISSAN 315 Mill Rd ℰ 242222
RENAULT 217 Newmarket Rd ℰ 51616
TOYOTA 1 Union Lane ℰ 356225
VAUXHALL-OPEL Elizabeth Way ℰ 321321
VOLVO Harston ℰ 870123
VW, AUDI 383 Milton Rd ℰ 354472

CANNOCK Staffs. 🔢🔢🔢 N 25 − pop. 59,235 − ECD : Thursday − ☻ 054 35 (4 and 5 fig.) 0543 (6 fig.).

♦London 135 − ♦Birmingham 20 − Derby 36 − ♦Leicester 51 − Shrewsbury 32 − ♦Stoke-on-Trent 28.

🏨 **Roman Way,** Watling St., Hatherton, WS11 1SH, SW : 1 ¼ m. by A 460 on A 5 ℰ 72121 − 📺
🖰wc 🖰wc ℗. 🔄 🖭 🆅🆂🅰
M a la carte 7.10/12.35 **t.** − **24 rm**

🏨 **Hollies,** Hollies Av., off Hednesford St., WS11 1DW, ℰ 3151, 🛋 − 📺 ℗. 🔄 🖭 ⓪ 🆅🆂🅰. 🍴
M *(closed Saturday lunch and Sunday dinner)* 6.50/9.00 **st.** 🍷 3.00 − **6 rm** 🛏 18.00/26.00 **st.**

CANTERBURY Kent 🔢 X 30 − pop. 33,176 − ECD : Thursday − ☻ 0227.

See : Christ Church Cathedral★★★ (Norman crypt★★, Bell Harry Tower★★, Great Cloister★★, ≼★ from Green Court) Y − King's School★ Y B − Mercery Lane★ Y − Weavers★ (old houses) Y D.

Envir. : Patrixbourne : St. Mary's Church : south door★) SE : 3 m. by A 2 Z.

🛈 22 St. Peter's St. ℰ 66567.

♦London 59 − ♦Brighton 76 − ♦Dover 15 − Maidstone 28 − Margate 17.

Plan opposite

🏨 **County,** High St., CT1 2RX, ℰ 66266, Telex 965076 − 🛗 ▤ rest 📺 ⟺ ℗. 🏄. 🔄 🖭 ⓪ 🆅🆂🅰. 🍴
                                  Y n
M 7.00/11.50 **t.** − **74 rm** 🛏 37.50/53.50 **t.**

🏨 **Chaucer** (T.H.F.), Ivy Lane, CT1 1TV, ℰ 464427, Telex 965096 − 📺 🖰wc ☎ ℗. 🏄. 🔄 🖭
⓪ 🆅🆂🅰
                                  Z c
M 6.50/8.50 **st.** 🍷 2.60 − 🛏 5.25 − **51 rm** 25.00/42.50 **st.**

🏨 **Slatters** (Q.M.H.), St. Margaret's St., CT1 3TB, ℰ 463271 − 🛗 📺 🖰wc ☎ ℗. 🏄. 🔄 🖭 ⓪ 🆅🆂🅰
                                  Z e
M 5.00/7.00 **st.** 🍷 2.85 − **30 rm** 🛏 35.20/46.00 **st.** − SB 50.00/56.00 **st.**

🏨 **Canterbury,** 71 New Dover Rd, CT1 3DY, ℰ 450551, Telex 965386 − 📺 🖰wc 🖰wc ☎ ℗.
🔄 🖭 ⓪ 🆅🆂🅰
closed 27 to 30 December − **M** (bar lunch) 12.00 **t.** 🍷 2.25 − **30 rm** 🛏 28.00/35.00 **st.** − SB (weekends only)(not summer) 32.50/36.50 **st.**
                                  Z u

🏨 **Victoria,** 59 London Rd, CT2 7HG, ℰ 459333, 🛋 − 📺 🖰wc 🖰wc ☎ ℗. 🔄 🖭 ⓪ 🆅🆂🅰
closed 1 week at Christmas − **M** *(closed Sunday dinner)* (bar lunch) 12.00 **t.** 🍷 3.60 − **24 rm** 🛏 15.00/35.00 **t.**
                                  Y i

🏨 **Falstaff,** 8-12 St. Dunstan's St., CT2 8AF, ℰ 462138 − 📺 🖰wc ☎ ℗. 🍴
16 rm.
                                  Y a

🏨 **Ebury,** 65-67 New Dover Rd, CT1 3DX, ℰ 68433, 🛋 − 📺 🖰wc 🖰wc ☎ ℗. 🔄 🖭 🆅🆂🅰. 🍴
closed 1 to 16 January − **M** *(closed Sunday)* (dinner only) 7.50 **t.** 🍷 2.20 − **15 rm** 🛏 23.00/34.00 **t.**
                                  Z r

🏨 **Ann's** without rest., 63 London Rd, CT2 8JZ, ℰ 68767, 🛋 − 📺 🖰wc 🖰wc ℗. 🍴
19 rm 🛏 20.00/24.00 **st.**
                                  Y r

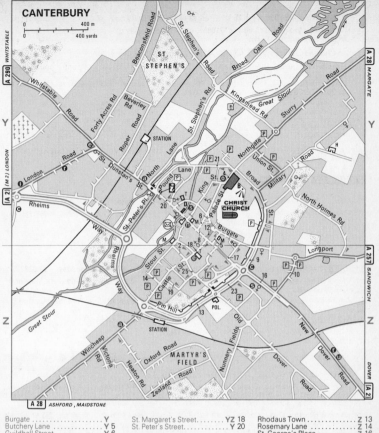

🏠 **Pointers,** 1 London Rd, CT2 8LR, 𝒫 456846 – 📺 🛏wc ⋔ 🕾 🅿. 🔼 AE ① VISA   Y **e**
closed Christmas-mid January – **M** (dinner only) 7.50 **t.** ⎓ 2.70 – **14 rm** ⊇ 14.00/28.00 **t.** – SB 36.00/38.00 **st.**

🏠 **Red House,** London Rd, CT2 8NB, 𝒫 463578, ⇗ – 🛏wc ⋔wc 🅿. 🔼 VISA. ⌘
M *(closed Sunday)* (dinner only) 7.50 **t.** ⎓ 2.40 – **14 rm** ⊇ 12.65/28.00 **t.** – SB 35.00/42.00 **st.**
by London Rd   Y.

⌂ **Highfield,** Summer Hill, Harbledown, CT2 8NH, 𝒫 462772, ⇗ – ⋔wc 🅿. 🔼 VISA   Y **c**
closed Christmas and New Year – **10 rm** ⊇ 10.00/21.00 **t.**

XXX ❀ **Seventy-Four,** 74 Wincheap, CT1 3RS, 𝒫 67411 – 🅿. 🔼 AE VISA   X **a**
closed Sunday, 2 weeks mid August and Bank Holidays – **M** a la carte 12.80/15.45 **t.** ⎓ 3.80
Spec. Chicken and lobster 'sausage' on a creamy spring onion sauce. Fillet of lamb with a scallop mousseline and fresh scallops (spring). Brandy snap biscuit filled with a rhubarb sorbet (January-March).

XX **Waterfield's,** 5A Best Lane, CT1 2JB, 𝒫 450276 – 🔼 AE   Y **s**
closed Monday lunch, Sunday, Christmas and early January – **M** a la carte 10.00/13.50 **t.** ⎓ 2.25.

XX **Beehive,** 52 Dover St., CT1 3MD, 𝒫 61126, Italian rest. – 🔼 AE ① VISA   Z **s**
closed Sunday – **M** a la carte 8.60/12.75 **t.** ⎓ 2.50.

XX **Tuo e Mio,** 16 The Borough, CT1 2DB, 𝒫 61471, Italian rest. – 🔼 AE ① VISA   Y **o**
closed Tuesday lunch, Monday, 15 to 28 February and 18 August-4 September – **M** a la carte 7.65/13.20 **t.** ⎓ 3.00.

CANTERBURY

   at Fordwich NE : 3 m. by A 28 – Y – ⊠ ☺ 0227 Canterbury :

🏠 George and Dragon, CT2 0BX, ℰ 710661, 🍴 – 📺 ⌷wc ☎ 🅿
   M (grill rest. only) – **13 rm**.

   at Chartham Hatch W : 3 ¼ m. by A 28 – Z – ⊠ ☺ 0227 Canterbury :

🏠 **Howfield Manor,** Howfield Lane, CT4 7HQ, SE : 1 m. ℰ 738294, « Country house atmosphere », 🍴 – ⌷wc 🏠wc 🅿. 🔼 🅰🅴 𝘝𝘐𝘚𝘈. 🞨
   closed mid December-mid January – **M** (dinner only, residents only) 12.00 **st.** ᐤ 4.00 – **5 rm**
   ⊐ 25.00/38.00 **st.** – SB (winter only) 52.00 **st.**

AUSTIN-ROVER-DAIMLER-JAGUAR 5 Rose Lane
and 28/30 St. Peters St. ℰ 66161
BMW Vauxhall Rd ℰ 54341
COLT 1/3 Park Rd ℰ 75114
FIAT, CITROEN, ROLLS ROYCE 41 St. Georges Pl. ℰ 66131
FORD 23 Lower Bridge St. ℰ 51777
NISSAN Island Rd ℰ 710431

PEUGEOT, TALBOT The Pavillon ℰ 51791
RENAULT Northgate ℰ 65561
SUBARU Castle Row ℰ 53810
TOYOTA Union St. ℰ 61993
VAUXHALL-OPEL Ashford Rd, Chartham ℰ 731331
VOLVO Mill Rd, Sturry ℰ 710481
VW-AUDI Vauxhall Rd Industrial Estate ℰ 57611

CARBIS BAY Cornwall 🄰🄾🄱 D 33 – see St. Ives.

   En saison, surtout dans les stations fréquentées, il est prudent de retenir à l'avance.
   Cependant, si vous ne pouvez pas occuper la chambre que vous avez retenue,
   prévenez immédiatement l'hôtelier.
   Si vous écrivez à un hôtel à l'étranger, joignez à votre lettre
   un coupon-réponse international (disponible dans les bureaux de poste).

CARDIFF (CAERDYDD) South Glam. 🄰🄾🄱 K 29 – pop. 290,500 – ECD : Wednesday – ☺ 0222.

See : National Museum★★ BY **M** – Llandaff Cathedral★ AY **B** – St. Fagan's Castle (Folk Museum)★
AC, by St. Fagans Rd AY.

🛫 Cardiff-Wales Airport ℰ 0446 (Rhoose) 711211, SW : 8 m. by A 48 AZ – Terminal : Central Bus
Station.

🚉 3 Castle St. ℰ 27281.

♦London 155 – ♦Birmingham 110 – ♦Bristol 46 – ♦Coventry 124.

Plans on following pages

🏨 Park (Mt. Charlotte), Park Pl., CF1 3UD, ℰ 23471, Telex 497195 – 🛗📺☎🅿. 🛆. 🔼 🅰🅴 ⓞ
   𝘝𝘐𝘚𝘈   BZ c
   108 rm ⊐ 43.45/54.45 **st.** – SB (weekends only) 49.50 **st.**

🏨 Inn on the Avenue, Circle Way East, Llanedeyrn, CF4 7XF, NE : 3 m. on A 48 ℰ 732520,
   Telex 497582, 🔲 – 🛗 ▤ rest 📺 ☎ 🅿. 🛆. 🔼 🅰🅴 ⓞ 𝘝𝘐𝘚𝘈. 🞨   AY n
   M 8.00/9.50 **st.** ᐤ 2.85 – **150 rm** ⊐ 38.00/49.50 **st.** – SB (weekends only) 52.00 **st.**

🏨 Angel (Norfolk Cap.), Castle St., CF1 2QZ, ℰ 32633, Telex 498132 – 🛗 ▤ rest 📺 ☎ 🅿. 🛆.
   🔼 🅰🅴 ⓞ 𝘝𝘐𝘚𝘈   BZ a
   M 8.50 t. ᐤ 2.50 – **97 rm** ⊐ 40.00/75.00 **t.** – SB 53.00/58.00 **st.**

🏨 Post House (T.H.F.), Church Rd, Pentwyn, CF2 7XA, NE : 4 m. on A 48 ℰ 731212, Telex
   497633 – 🛗 📺 ⌷wc ☎ 🅿. 🛆. 🔼 🅰🅴 ⓞ 𝘝𝘐𝘚𝘈   on A 48 AY
   M (closed Saturday lunch and Sunday dinner) 6.95/8.50 **st.** ᐤ 2.60 – ⊐ 5.00 – **150 rm**
   34.50/42.00 **st.**

🏨 Crest (Crest), Westgate St., CF1 1JB, ℰ 388681, Telex 497258 – 🛗 📺 ⌷wc ☎ 🅿. 🛆. 🔼
   🅰🅴 ⓞ 𝘝𝘐𝘚𝘈   BZ i
   M approx. 10.00 **st.** – ⊐ 5.25 – **160 rm** 41.00/52.00 **st.**

🏨 Beverley, 75 Cathedral Rd, CF1 9PG, ℰ 43443 – 📺 ⌷wc 🏠wc ☎ 🅿   AZ o
   18 rm.

🏠 Ferrier's, 130-132 Cathedral Rd, CF1 9LQ, ℰ 383413 – 📺 🏠 🅿. 🔼 🅰🅴 ⓞ 𝘝𝘐𝘚𝘈   AY e
   closed 1 week at Christmas – **M** (closed Friday, Saturday, Sunday and Bank Holidays) (dinner
   only) a la carte 3.70/7.50 **t.** – **27 rm** ⊐ 15.00/28.00 **t.**

🛏 Abbey, 151 Cathedral Rd, CF1 9PJ, ℰ 390896   AY o
   14 rm ⊐ 11.50/30.00 **t.**

🛏 Tane's, 148 Newport Rd, CF2 1DJ, ℰ 491755 – 🅿   AY s
   9 rm

🛏 Princes, 10 Princes St., Roath, CF2 3PR, ℰ 491732 – 🞨   AY r
   6 rm ⊐ 10.00/17.00 **t.**

XX La Chaumière, Ely Rd, Llandaff (behind Maltsters Arms), ℰ 555319 – 🅿. 🔼 🅰🅴 ⓞ 𝘝𝘐𝘚𝘈
   M a la carte 9.55/12.45 **t.** ᐤ 3.00.   AY a

X Gibson's, 8 Romilly Crescent, Canton, CF1 9NR, ℰ 41264, Bistro – 🔼 🅰🅴 ⓞ 𝘝𝘐𝘚𝘈   AZ a
   closed Sunday, 1 week Christmas and Bank Holidays – **M** 11.60/12.60 **t.** ᐤ 3.00.

X Waldo's Positano, 9 Church St., CF1 2BG, ℰ 35810, Italian rest. – 🔼 🅰🅴 𝘝𝘐𝘚𝘈   BZ e
   closed Sunday and 2 weeks August – **M** a la carte 8.60/11.55 **t.** ᐤ 2.80.

128

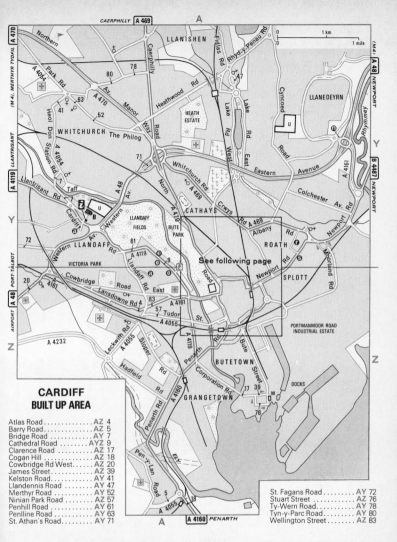

CARDIFF
BUILT UP AREA

Atlas Road.............AZ 4
Barry Road.............AZ 5
Bridge Road ....AY 7
Cathedral Road ....AYZ 9
Clarence Road ....AZ 17
Cogan Hill ....AZ 18
Cowbridge Rd West....AZ 20
James Street...........AZ 39
Kelston Road...........AY 41
Llandennis Road ....AY 47
Merthyr Road ....AY 52
Ninian Park Road ......AZ 57
Penhill Road ....AY 61
Penlline Road ....AY 63
St. Athan's Road........AY 71

St. Fagans Road.........AY 72
Stuart Street ....AZ 76
Ty-Wern Road..........AY 78
Tyn-y-Parc Road........AY 80
Wellington Street.......AZ 83

---

at Castleton (Cas-Bach) (Gwent) NE : 7 m. on A 48 – AY – ⊠ Cardiff – ☎ 0633 Castleton :

🏨 **Ladbroke Wentloog Castle** (Ladbroke), CF3 8UO, ℰ 680591 – 📺 🛏️wc ╢wc ☎ 🅿. 🅰️.
🆎 🆎 🔘 *VISA*
closed 1 week at Christmas – **M** a la carte 8.20/11.40 **t.** ╢ 2.00 – **54 rm** ⊊ 32.00/42.00 **t.** – SB
(weekends only) 45.00/70.00 **st.**

AUSTIN-ROVER-JAGUAR 52 Penarth Rd ℰ 43571
AUSTIN-ROVER Rhiwbina ℰ 63232
AUSTIN-ROVER-DAIMLER-JAGUAR 501 Newport
Rd ℰ 495591
BMW 325 Penarth Rd ℰ 23122
FORD 505 Newport Rd ℰ 490511
FORD 281 Penarth Rd ℰ 21071
MERCEDES-BENZ 14 Station Rd ℰ 566260

NISSAN 516 Cowbridge Rd ℰ 561212
PORSCHE, ROLLS ROYCE Cowbridge Road West
ℰ 592363
RENAULT Llantrisant Rd ℰ 562345
SAAB Crwys Rd ℰ 485725
VAUXHALL-OPEL, HONDA, CITROEN Sloper Rd ℰ
387221
VOLVO Newport Rd, St. Mellons ℰ 77183

*Plans de ville : Les noms des principales voies commerçantes
sont inscrits en rouge au début des légendes rues.*

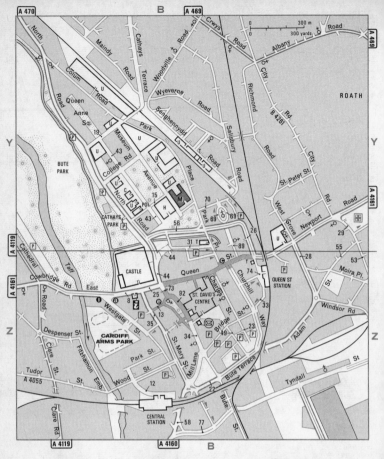

CARDIFF
CENTRE

CARDIGAN (ABERTEIFI) Dyfed **403** G 27 – pop. 3,810 – ECD : Wednesday – ☎ 0239.

Envir. : Mwnt (site★) N : 6 m. – Gwbert-on-Sea (cliffs ≼★) NW : 3 m. – Cilgerran (castle★ 13C) *AC* SE : 4 m.

☗ Gwbert-on-Sea ☎ 612035, NW : 3 m.

🛈 3 Heathfield, Pendre ☎ 613230 (summer only).

♦London 250 – Carmarthen 30 – Fishguard 19.

   ✗ **Rhyd-Garn-Wen** 🦢 with rm, SA43 3NW, SW : 2 ¾ m. by A 487 on Cilgerran rd ☎ 612742, ☛ – ⅷwc **ⓟ**. **🖂**. **🆑**. ✸
   Mid March-mid October – **M** *(closed lunch to non-residents)* (booking essential) 7.50/11.50 **t**. ⓵ 3.00 – **3 rm** ⇌ (dinner included) 29.50/54.00 **t**.

   at Gwbert-on-Sea NW : 3 m. on B 4548 – ✉ ☎ 0239 Cardigan :

   🏨 **Cliff** 🦢, SA43 1PP, ☎ 613241, Telex 48440, ≼ bay and countryside, ⏋ heated, ▮₅, 🦢, ☛, squash – ⓣⓥ ⌁wc ⅷwc **☏** **ⓟ**. **🖾**. **🆑** **🆎** **⑩** **VISA**
   M a la carte 6.75/10.15 **st**. ⓵ 2.70 – **70 rm** ⇌ 22.00/58.00 **st**. – SB (except summer) 52.00/58.00 **st**.

AUSTIN-ROVER Aberystwyth Rd ☎ 612365   FIAT St. Dogmaels ☎ 612025

CARLISLE Cumbria **401** **402** L 19 – pop. 71,582 – ECD : Thursday – ☎ 0228.

See : Castle★ (12C) *AC* AY – Cathedral★ 12C-14C AY E.

☗ Aglionby ☎ 022 872 (Scotby) 303 E : 2 m. by A 69 BY – ☗ Stoneyholme ☎ 34856 E : 1 m. by St. Aidan's Rd BY.

🚗 ☎ 44711.

🛈 The Old Town Hall, Greenmarket ☎ 25517.

♦London 317 – ♦Blackpool 95 – ♦Edinburgh 101 – ♦Glasgow 100 – ♦Leeds 124 – ♦Liverpool 127 – ♦Manchester 122 – ♦Newcastle-upon-Tyne 59.

Plan on next page

   🏨 **Cumbrian Thistle** (Thistle), Court Sq., CA1 1OY, ☎ 31951, Telex 64287 – 🛗 ⓣⓥ ⌁wc ☏ **ⓟ**. **🖾**. **🆑** **🆎** **⑩** **VISA**
                                               BZ **u**
   ⇌ 4.75 – **70 rm** 29.00/45.00 **t**. – SB (weekends only) 48.00 **st**.

   🏨 **Swallow Hilltop** (Swallow), London Rd, CA1 2PQ, SE : 1 m. on A 6 ☎ 29255, Telex 64292 – 🛗 ⓣⓥ ⌁wc ☏ **ⓟ**. **🖾**. **🆑** **🆎** **⑩** **VISA**
                                         by A 6 BZ
   M 7.00/8.00 **st**. ⓵ 3.00 – **110 rm** ⇌ 23.50/48.50 **st**. – SB (weekends only) 50.00/54.00 **st**.

   🏨 **Crown and Mitre**, English St., CA3 8HZ, ☎ 25491, Telex 64183 – 🛗 ⓣⓥ ⌁wc ☏ **ⓟ**. **🖾**. **🆑** **🆎** **⑩** **VISA**. ✸
                                           BY **a**
   closed 4 days at Christmas – **M** *(closed Sunday lunch)* (bar lunch) 6.25 **st**. – ⇌ 3.50 – **94 rm** 29.50/38.50 **st**.

   🏨 **Cumbria Park**, 32 Scotland Rd, CA3 9DG, N : 1 m. on A 7 ☎ 22887 – ⌁wc ⅷwc **ⓟ**. **🖾** **VISA**. ✸
                                       by A 7 BY
   closed 24 to 26 December – **M** (bar lunch) 7.30 **st**. ⓵ 2.50 – **35 rm** ⇌ 19.00/30.00 **st**.

   at Kingstown N : 3 m. at junction 44 of A 7 – BY – and M 6 – ✉ ☎ 0228 Carlisle :

   🏨 **Crest** (Crest), Kingstown, CA4 0HR, ☎ 31201, Telex 64201 – ⓣⓥ ⌁wc ☏ **ⓟ**. **🖾**. **🆑** **🆎** **⑩** **VISA**. ✸
   M 11.00 **st**. – ⇌ 5.25 – **100 rm** 41.00/52.00 **st**.

   at Crosby-on-Eden NE : 4 ½ m. by A 7 – BY – on B 6264 – ✉ Carlisle – ☎ 022 873 Crosby-on-Eden :

   ✗✗ **Crosby Lodge** 🦢 with rm, CA6 4QZ, ☎ 618, ≼, « 18C country mansion », ☛ – ⌁wc ⅷwc **ⓟ**. **🆎** **⑩**. ✸
   closed 24 December-21 January – **M** *(closed Sunday dinner)* a la carte 12.00/17.25 **t**. ⓵ 3.00 – **11 rm** ⇌ 32.00/48.00 **t**. – SB (weekends only)(winter only) 55.00 **st**.

   at Faugh E : 8 ¼ m. by A 69 – BY – ✉ Carlisle – ☎ 022 870 Hayton :

   🏠 **String of Horses Inn**, Heads Nook, CA4 9EG, ☎ 297, « Elaborately furnished 17C inn », ⏋ heated – 🍽 rest ⓣⓥ ⌁wc ⅷwc ☏ **ⓟ**. **🖾** **🆎** **⑩** **VISA**. ✸
   M a la carte 7.15/11.90 **t**. ⓵ 2.75 – **13 rm** ⇌ 34.00/58.00 **t**.

   at Wetheral SE : 6 ¼ m. by A 6 – BZ – on B 6233 – ✉ Carlisle – ☎ 0228 Wetheral :

   🏨 **Crown** (Best Western), CA4 8ES, ☎ 61888, Telex 64175, ☛ – ⓣⓥ ⌁wc ☏ **ⓟ**. **🖾**. **🆑** **🆎** **⑩** **VISA**
   M (bar lunch Saturday) 5.50/10.50 **st**. ⓵ 3.25 – **50 rm** ⇌ 37.50/57.50 **st**. – SB (weekends only) 48.00/50.00 **st**.

   🏠 **Killoran** 🦢, The Green, CA4 8ET, ☎ 60200, ☛ – ⅷ **ⓟ**. **🆑** **⑩** **VISA**
   M (bar lunch) 7.00 **st**. ⓵ 2.30 – **9 rm** ⇌ 17.50/35.00 **st**. – SB (weekends only) 38.00 **st**.

   ✗✗ **Fantails**, The Green, CA4 8ET, ☎ 60239 – **ⓟ**. **🖾** **🆎** **⑩** **VISA**
   closed Sunday, Monday and February – **M** (dinner only November-March) a la carte 6.00/11.90 **t**. ⓵ 2.60.

CARLISLE

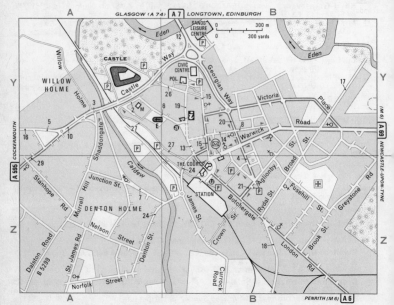

ALFA, MAZDA Kingstown Estate ℰ 38444
AUSTIN-ROVER-DAIMLER-JAGUAR Rosehill Estate
ℰ 24387
BMW, VAUXHALL-OPEL Viaduct Estate ℰ 29401
CITROEN, SAAB Willowholme Estate ℰ 26617
COLT ℰ 27287
FIAT Church St., Caldewgate ℰ 25092
FORD Warwick Circus ℰ 24234

LADA Cecil St. ℰ 25051
MERCEDES-BENZ, VOLVO Victoria Viaduct ℰ 28234
NISSAN Lowther St. ℰ 31469
RENAULT Church St. ℰ 22423
VAUXHALL Viaduct Estate ℰ 29401
VOLVO Victoria Viaduct ℰ 28234
VW, AUDI-NSU Lowther St. ℰ 26104

CARLYON BAY Cornwall **403** F 33 — see St. Austell.

CARMARTHEN (CAERFYRDDIN) Dyfed **403** G 28 — pop. 13,081 — ECD : Thursday — ✆ 026 723 (4 and 5 fig.) or 0267 (6 fig.) — ⛳ Blaenycoed Rd ℰ 87214, NW : 4 m.

🛈 Lammas St. ℰ 231557 (summer only) — ♦London 220 — Fishguard 45 — ♦Swansea 27.

🏨 **Ivy Bush Royal** (T.H.F.), 11-13 Spilman St., SA31 1LG, ℰ 235111, Telex 48520 — ▯ 📺 🚻wc
🛏wc ⇄ 🅿 🚗 🔄 AE ⓞ VISA
M 7.00/9.00 **st.** ⅃ 2.60 — 🖙 5.50 — **80 rm** 27.00/35.50 **st.**

AUSTIN-ROVER-DAIMLER-JAGUAR Pensarn Rd ℰ
5252
FIAT Pensarn ℰ 6633
FORD The Bridge ℰ 6482

HONDA, TOYOTA Priory St. ℰ 4171
NISSAN Glasfryn, Portmyrhyd ℰ 026 786 (Llandda-rog) 370
NISSAN Penguin Court ℰ 7356

CARTMEL Cumbria **402** L 21 — see Grange-over-Sands.

CAS-BACH = Castleton.

CAS-BLAIDD = Wolf's Castle.

CASNEWYDD-AR-WYSG = Newport.

CASTELL NEWYDD EMLYN = Newcastle Emlyn.

CASTERTON Cumbria — see Kirkby Lonsdale.

132

CASTLE ACRE Norfolk 404 W 25 – pop. 955 – ☎ 076 05.

See : Priory★★ (ruins 11C - 14C) *AC*.

♦London 101 – King's Lynn 20 – ✦Norwich 31.

   Hotels see : King's Lynn NW : 20 m., *Swaffam* S : 4 m.

CASTLE BROMWICH West Midlands 403 404 O 26 – see Birmingham.

CASTLE CARY Somerset 403 404 M 30 – pop. 1,754 – ECD : Thursday – ☎ 0963.

♦London 125 – ✦Bristol 28 – Taunton 31 – Yeovil 13.

   🏨 **George,** Market Pl., BA7 7AH, ℰ 50761 – 📺 ➙wc ⓜwc ⚙ 🅿. 🔼 🆎 ⑩ *VISA*
       closed 24 to 26 December – **M** a la carte 5.65/8.00 **t.** 🍷 2.45 – **17 rm** � 25.00/35.00 **st.** – SB
       55.00/70.00 **st.**

CASTLE COMBE Wilts. 403 404 N 29 The West Country G. – pop. 414 – ✉ Chippenham –
☎ 0249.

See : Site ★ – ♦London 110 – ✦Bristol 23 – Chippenham 6.

   🏨 **Manor House** (Best Western) ♨, SN14 7HR, ℰ 782206, « Part 14C manor house in park »,
       ▨ heated, ⚓, ⚔, ✎ – 📺 ☎ 🅿. 🔼 🆎 ⑩ *VISA*
       M 7.50/13.50 **t.** – **33 rm** ⊑ 35.00/78.00 **st.** – SB (November-March) 72.00 **st.**

   🏨 **Castle,** SN14 7HN, ℰ 782461 – ➙wc ⓜwc. 🔼 🆎 ⑩ *VISA*
       M (bar lunch Monday to Saturday) 6.50/9.50 **t.** 🍷 2.30 – **9 rm** ⊑ 25.00/44.00 **st.** – SB (win-
       ter only) 40.50/47.50 **st.**

CASTLE DONINGTON Leics. 402 403 404 P 25 – pop. 5,113 – ✉ ☎ 0332 Derby.

🛫 East Midlands, ℰ 810621, Telex 37543.

♦London 123 – ✦Birmingham 38 – ✦Leicester 23 – ✦Nottingham 13.

   🏨 **Donington Manor,** High St., DE7 2PP, ℰ 810253, Telex 377208 – 📺 ➙wc ⓜwc ☎ 🅿. 🛁.
       🔼 🆎 ⑩ *VISA*. ✂
       closed 26 to 31 December – **M** 4.50/6.00 **st.** 🍷 3.25 – **38 rm** ⊑ 27.85/41.20 **st.**

VAUXHALL-OPEL Station Rd ℰ 810221

CASTLETON Derbs. 402 403 404 O 23 – pop. 729 – ECD : Wednesday – ✉ Sheffield (South
Yorks.) – ☎ 0433 Hope Valley.

Envir. : Blue John Caverns★ *AC*, W : 1 m – ♦London 173 – ✦Manchester 27 – ✦Sheffield 16.

   🏠 **Ye Olde Nag's Head,** Cross St., S30 2WH, ℰ 20248 – 🅿. 🔼 🆎 ⑩ *VISA*. ✂
       M 6.45/7.25 **t.** – **7 rm** ⊑ 13.50/25.00 **t.**

CASTLETON (CAS-BACH) Gwent 403 K 29 – see Cardiff (South Glam.).

CASTLETON North Yorks. 402 R 20 – pop. 1,460 (inc. Danby) – ✉ Whitby – ☎ 0287.

♦London 258 – ✦Middlesbrough 18 – York 61.

   🏠 **Moorlands,** High St., YO21 2DB, ℰ 60206, ← – ⓜwc 🅿
       Easter-October – **M** (bar lunch Monday to Saturday) 4.75/8.50 **st.** 🍷 2.25 – **10 rm**
       ⊑ 12.75/27.50 **st.** – SB (except July and August) 39.50/41.50 **st.**

CAVENDISH Suffolk 404 V 27 – pop. 701 – ✉ Sudbury – ☎ 0787 Glemsford.

♦London 66 – ✦Cambridge 29 – ✦Ipswich 28.

   ✖✖ **Alfonso's** with rm, The Green, CO10 8BB, ℰ 280372, Italian rest. – ⓜwc 🅿. 🆎 ⑩. ✂
       M a la carte 7.90/11.50 **st.** 🍷 3.50 – **5 rm** ⊑ 17.00/29.00 **st.**

CAWSAND Cornwall 403 H 33 – pop. 600 – ✉ ☎ 0752 Plymouth.

♦London 253 – ✦Plymouth 10 – Truro 53.

   🏠 **Criterion** ♨, Garrett St., PL10 1PD, ℰ 822244, ← Plymouth Sound, « Converted fishermen's
       cottages » – 📺 ⓜwc
       M (bar lunch) 9.00 **t.** 🍷 2.65 – **8 rm** ⊑ 13.50/32.00 **t.**

CERNE ABBAS Dorset 403 404 M 31 The West Country G. – pop. 650 – ☎ 030 03.

See : Site★.

♦ London 137 – Dorchester 8 – Salisbury 49 – Yeovil 16.

   ✖✖ **Old Market House,** 25 Long St., DT2 7JG, ℰ 680 – 🔼 🆎 ⑩
       closed Sunday dinner, Monday and January – **M** (lunch by arrangement Tuesday to Saturday)
       a la carte 9.50/13.50 **t.** 🍷 4.55.

CHADLINGTON Oxon. 403 404 P 28 – pop. 717 – ☎ 060 876.

♦London 74 – Cheltenham 32 – ✦Oxford 18 – Stratford-upon-Avon 25.

   🏠 **Chadlington House,** OX7 3LZ, ℰ 437, ⚓ – ➙wc ⓜwc 🅿. 🔼 🆎 ⑩ *VISA*. ✂
       closed January – **M** (dinner only) 10.00 **t.** 🍷 2.50 – **10 rm** ⊑ 15.00/36.00 **t.** – SB 45.00/50.00 **st.**

CHAGFORD Devon [403] I 31 The West Country G. – pop. 1,250 – ECD : Wednesday – ☏ 064 73.
Envir. : Castle Drogo★, NE : 2 m.
♦London 218 – Exeter 17 – ♦Plymouth 28.

🏨 ✿ **Gidleigh Park** 🐦, TQ13 8HH, NW : 2 m. by Gidleigh Rd ✆ 2367, <, « Country house atmosphere », 🌳, park – [TV] ☎ [P]. [AE]
M (booking essential) a la carte 14.25/17.25 **s.** 🍷 3.50 – ☕ 3.50 – **12 rm** 60.00/95.00 **s.**
Spec. Sautéed monkfish with cucumber and Dijon mustard sauce, Roast duck breast with wild mushrooms, Raspberries in puff pastry with Devon cream and raspberry purée.

🏨 **Teignworthy Country House** 🐦, Frenchbeer, TQ13 8EX, SW : 2 ½ m. by Fernworthy Rd, off Thornworthy Rd ✆ 3355, <, « Country house atmosphere », 🌳, park, 🎾 – [TV] 🛁wc ☎ [P]. 🚫🐕
M a la carte 10.00/16.50 **st.** 🍷 3.50 – **9 rm** ☕ (dinner included) 55.00/92.00 **st.** – SB (winter only) 78.00/88.00 **st.**

at Sandypark NE : 1 ½ m. – ✉ ☏ 064 73 Chagford :

🏨 **Mill End** 🐦, TQ13 8JN, on A 382 ✆ 2282, « Country house with water mill », 🎣, 🌳 – [TV] 🛁wc ☎ 🚗 [P]. 💳 [AE] [D] [VISA]
closed 9 to 24 January and 10 to 27 December – **M** (lunch by arrangement) 8.50/11.50 **st.** 🍷 3.00 – **16 rm** ☕ 32.50/50.00 **st.** – SB 55.00/67.00 **st.**

🏨 **Great Tree** 🐦, Sandy Park, TQ13 8JS, on A 382 ✆ 2491, <, « Country house atmosphere », 🌳, park – [TV] 🛁wc [P]. 💳 [AE] [D] [VISA]
closed 28 December-1 February – **M** 6.50/9.50 **t.** 🍷 2.75 – **14 rm** 24.15/52.90 **t.** – SB (winter only) 50.00 **st.**

at Easton Cross NE : 1 ½ m. – ✉ ☏ 064 73 Chagford :

🏨 **Easton Court,** TQ13 8JL, on A 382 ✆ 3469, « 15C thatched house », 🌳 – 🛁wc 🚿wc [P]. 💳 [AE] [D] [VISA]
M (bar lunch) 11.00 **st.** 🍷 2.50 – **8 rm** ☕ 15.00/32.00 **st.** – SB (winter only) 24.50/27.00 **st.**

RENAULT New St. ✆ 2226

CHALE I.O.W. – see Wight (Isle of).

CHALFONT ST. GILES Bucks. [404] S 29 – pop. 8,500 – ☏ 024 07.
See : Milton's Cottage *AC*.
♦London 26 – Aylesbury 18.

XX Le Relais, London Rd, HP8 4NJ, ✆ 2590 – [P].

AUSTIN-ROVER London Rd ✆ 3045

CHALFONT ST. PETER Bucks. [404] S 29 – pop. 18,760 – ☏ 024 07 Chalfont St. Giles.
♦London 22 – ♦Oxford 37.

🏠 **Greyhound Inn,** High St., SL9 9QL, ✆ 0753 (Gerrard's Cross) 883404 – [TV] [P]. [AE] [D] [VISA]. 🚫🐕
M (bar lunch Monday to Saturday) a la carte approx. 7.60 **t.** 🍷 2.00 – **7 rm** ☕ 17.50/27.30 **t.**

NISSAN High St. ✆ 028 13 (Gerrards Cross) 885581

CHALFORD Glos. [403] [404] N 28 – pop. 2,928 – ✉ Stroud – ☏ 0453 Brimscombe.
♦London 105 – ♦Bristol 40 – Gloucester 14 – Swindon 22.

🏨 **Springfield House,** London Rd, GL6 8NW, on A 419 ✆ 883555, 🌳 – [TV] 🛁wc ☎ [P]. [AE] [D] [VISA]
closed January – **M** 5.50/7.75 **st.** 🍷 3.00 – **8 rm** ☕ 25.00/38.00 **st.** – SB 22.00 **st.**

CHANCERY (RHYDGALED) Dyfed [403] H 26 – see Aberystwyth.

CHAPEL-EN-LE-FRITH Derbs. [402] [403] [404] O 24 – pop. 8,122 – ✉ Stockport (Cheshire) – ☏ 0298.
⛳18 Cockyard ✆ 2118.
♦ London 176 – ♦ Manchester 22 – Derby 42 – ♦ Sheffield 24.

🏠 King's Arms, Market Place, SK12 6EN, ✆ 812105 – [TV] [P]. 💳 [AE] [VISA]
M (bar lunch Monday to Saturday) a la carte 4.50/7.60 🍷 1.25 – **11 rm** – SB (except Bank Holidays) 25.00/30.00 **st.**

CHAPEL STILE Cumbria [402] K 20 – see Ambleside.

CHARD Somerset [403] L 31 The West Country G. – pop. 10,146 – ECD : Wednesday – ☏ 046 06.
♦London 180 – Exeter 31 – ♦Southampton 85 – Taunton 16.

🏨 **George,** 15 Fore St., TA20 1PH, ✆ 3413 – [TV] 🛁wc 🚿wc [P]. 👥. 💳 [AE] [D] [VISA]
M a la carte 6.95/8.60 **t.** 🍷 2.50 – **20 rm** ☕ 16.00/30.00 **t.** – SB 33.00/37.00 **st.**

CHARING Kent 404 W 30 – pop. 2,700 – © 023 371.
♦London 49 – Canterbury 15 – Folkestone 20 – Maidstone 15.

   X **Wishing Well,** 19 High St., ☎ 2170 – 🅿 AE VISA
      closed Sunday, Monday, 2 weeks summer and 1 week winter – **M** (dinner only) 11.50 **t.** ◊ 2.50.

CHARLBURY Oxon. 403 404 P 28 – pop. 2,249 – © 0608.
♦London 72 – ♦Birmingham 50 – ♦Oxford 15.

   🏛 **Bell at Charlbury** (Best Western), Church St., OX7 3AP, ☎ 810278 – TV ⇔wc ☏ 🅿 AE
      OD VISA
      M 8.50/9.75 **t.** ◊ 3.00 – **13 rm** ⇆ 25.00/38.00 **t.** – SB 48.00 **st.**

CHARLECOTE Warw. – see Stratford-upon-Avon.

CHARLESTOWN Cornwall 403 F 33 – see St. Austell.

CHARLTON West Sussex 404 R 31 – see Chichester.

CHARMOUTH Dorset 403 L 31 – pop. 1,017 – ECD : Thursday – ✉ Bridport – © 0297.
♦London 157 – Dorchester 22 – Exeter 31 – Taunton 27.

   🏛 **White House,** 2 Hillside, The Street, DT6 6PJ, ☎ 60411 – TV ⇔wc 🅿 VISA
      M a la carte 8.15/12.25 **st.** ◊ 2.40 – **7 rm** ⇆ 29.00/33.00 **st.** – SB 42.00/45.00 **st.**
   🏛 **Fernhill,** Fernhill, DT6 6BX, W : ¾ m. by A 35 on A 3052 ☎ 60492, ⌂ heated, 🐎 – ⇔wc
      🗠wc 🅿 VISA
      M (bar lunch) 8.95 **t.** – **15 rm** ⇆ 17.00/38.00 **t.** – SB (except summer) 43.00/49.00 **st.**
   ↑ **Newlands House,** Stonebarrow Lane, DT6 6RA, ☎ 60212, 🐎 – TV ⇔wc 🗠wc 🅿
      March-19 October – **9 rm** ⇆ 11.00/25.00 **st.**
   ↑ **Sea Horse,** Higher Sea Lane, DT6 6BB, ☎ 60414, <, 🐎 – ⇔wc 🅿
      closed November and February – **10 rm** ⇆ 17.00/28.00 **t.**

CHARNOCK RICHARD Lancs. 402 404 M 23 – pop. 1,684 – ECD : Wednesday – © 0257
Coppull.
🏌 Duxbury Park, Chorley ☎ 025 72 (Chorley) 65380, E : 2 m.
♦London 215 – ♦Liverpool 26 – ♦Manchester 24 – Preston 10.

   🏛 **TraveLodge** (T.H.F.) without rest., Mill Lane, PR7 5LR, on M 6 ☎ 791746, Telex 67315 – TV
      ⇔wc ☏ & 🅿 AE OD VISA – **105 rm** 25.00/33.00 **st.**

CHARTHAM HATCH Kent 404 X 30 – see Canterbury.

CHEDINGTON Dorset – pop. 96 – ✉ Beaminster – © 093 589 Corscombe.
♦ London 148 – Dorchester 17 – Taunton 25.

   🏛 **Chedington Court** ⌂, DT8 3HY, ☎ 093 589 (Corscombe) 265, < countryside, « Country
      house in landscaped gardens », park – TV ⇔wc ☏ 🅿 AE ⌧
      M (bar lunch residents only) 15.50 **t.** ◊ 3.00 – **8 rm** ⇆ 32.00/52.00 **t.** – SB 58.00/76.00 **st.**

CHELMSFORD Essex 404 V 28 – pop. 58,194 – ECD : Wednesday – © 0245.
♦London 33 – ♦Cambridge 46 – ♦Ipswich 40 – Southend-on-Sea 19.

   🏛 **South Lodge** (Best Western), 196 New London Rd, CM2 0AR, ☎ 264564, Telex 99452, 🐎 –
      TV ⇔wc 🅿 & AE OD VISA
      M 8.00/8.50 **t.** ◊ 2.80 – ⇆ 4.50 – **41 rm**.
   🏛 **County,** 29 Rainsford Rd, CM1 2QA, ☎ 266911 – TV ⇔wc 🗠wc ☏ 🅿 AE OD VISA
      closed 1 week after Christmas – **M** 6.00/7.00 **t.** ◊ 3.00 – **52 rm** ⇆ 22.00/48.00 **t.**
   ↑ Oaklands, 240 Springfield Rd, CM2 6BP, ☎ 352004, 🐎 – 🗠wc 🅿 ⌧ – **8 rm**.
   ↑ **Tanunda,** 217-219 New London Rd, CM2 0AJ, ☎ 354295, 🐎 – TV ⇔wc 🗠wc 🅿
      closed 1 week at Christmas – **20 rm** ⇆ 12.95/28.25 **st.**

     at Great Baddow SE : 3 m. by A 130 – ✉ © 0245 Chelmsford :

   XXX **Pontlands Park** ⌂ with rm, West Hanningfield Rd, CM2 8HR, ☎ 76444, Telex 995411, <,
      ⌂, 🐎, park – TV ⇔wc ☏ 🅿 & AE OD VISA ⌧
      closed 2 to 6 January – **M** *(closed Saturday lunch, Sunday dinner and Bank Holidays)* a la
      carte 7.50/16.50 **t.** ◊ 3.00 – ⇆ 4.75 – **8 rm** 35.00/65.00 **t.** – SB (weekends only) 77.00 **st.**

     at High Easter NW : 10 m. by A 414 and A 1060 – ✉ Chelmsford – © 024 531 Good Easter :

   XX **Punch Bowl,** CM1 4QW, ☎ 222 – 🅿 AE OD VISA
      closed Sunday dinner and Monday – **M** (lunch by arrangement Tuesday to Saturday) a la
      carte 11.10/14.60 **t.** ◊ 2.50.

AUSTIN-ROVER, RENAULT   74 Main Rd, Broomfield
☎ 440571
CITROEN, LANCIA   Galley Wood ☎ 268366
FORD   39 Robjohns Rd ☎ 264111
NISSAN, PEUGEOT-TALBOT   Bridge St. ☎ 421233

RENAULT   Southend Rd, Sandon ☎ 71113
VAUXHALL   Eastern Approach ☎ 466333
VAUXHALL-OPEL   Moulsham Lodge ☎ 351611
VOLVO   Colchester Rd, Springfield ☎ 468151

CHELTENHAM

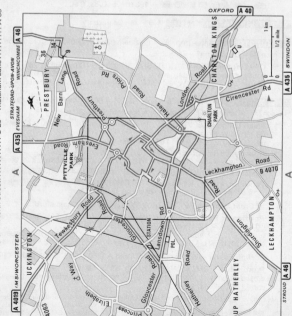

CENTRE

See : Pittville Park★ A – Municipal Art Gallery and Museum★ B **M.**

Envir. : Elkstone (Parish Church : doorway★ and arches★ 12C) SE : 7 m. by A 435 A – Sudeley Castle★ (12C - 15C) *AC*, NE : 6 m.

🏌 Cleeve Hill ♟ 024 267 (Bishop's Cleeve) 2025, N : 3 m. by A 46 A.

🛈 The Promenade ♟ 522878.

♦London 99 – ♦Birmingham 48 – ♦Bristol 40 – Gloucester 9 – ♦Oxford 43.

Plan opposite

🏨 **Queen's** (T.H.F.), Promenade, GL50 1NN, ♟ 514724, Telex 43381, 🛤 – 🕮 📺 📞 🚗 🔝 🆎
  🚗 🆅🆂🅰   B **n**
  M 9.75/12.50 **st.** ⅜ 3.15 – ☲ 5.50 – **77 rm** 42.00/52.50 **st.**

🏨 **Golden Valley Thistle** (Thistle), Gloucester Rd, GL51 0TS, W : 2 m. on A 40 ♟ 32691, Telex
  43410, 🛤 – 🕮 📺 📞 🚗 🔝 🆎 ⓪ 🆅🆂🅰   by A 40   A
  ☲ 4.95 – **103 rm** 39.50/55.50 **t.** – SB 58.00 **st.**

🏨 **Carlton**, Parabola Rd, GL50 3AQ, ♟ 514453, 🛤 – 🕮 📺 🖼wc 📞 🚗 🔝 🆎 ⓪ 🆅🆂🅰
  M 6.75/8.00 **st.** ⅜ 2.25 – **49 rm** ☲ 30.50/42.00 **st.** – SB 45.00 **st.**   B **r**

🏨 **Wyastone**, Parabola Rd, GL50 3BG, ♟ 45549 – 📺 🖼wc 🚾wc 📞 🚗 🔝 🆎 ⓪ 🛎   B **e**
  M 8.50 **st.** ⅜ 2.25 – ☲ 3.00 – **13 rm** 28.00/42.00 **st.** – SB (weekends only) 56.00 **st.**

🏠 **Abbottslee**, Priory Walk, GL52 6DU, ♟ 515255 – 📞 🛎   C **a**
  6 rm ☲ 11.00/22.00 **st.**

🏠 **Willoughby**, 1 Suffolk Sq., GL50 2DR, ♟ 522798, 🛤 – 🖼wc 📞   B **o**
  closed 2 weeks Christmas and New Year – **9 rm** ☲ 10.50/24.00 **t.**

XX **Twelve,** 12 Suffolk Par., GL50 2AB, ♟ 584544 – 🔝 🆅🆂🅰   B **i**
  closed Sunday dinner and Monday – **M** a la carte 9.20/11.40.

X **La Ciboulette**, 24 Suffolk St., GL50 2AQ, ♟ 573449 – 🔝 🆎 🆅🆂🅰   B **c**
  closed Sunday, Monday, Easter week, 5 to 26 August and 25 December-2 January – **M** a la
  carte 10.30/14.90 **t.** ⅜ 4.00.

X **Mayflower**, 32 Clarence St., GL50 3NX, ♟ 522426, Chinese rest. – 🆎 ⓪   C **e**
  closed Sunday lunch and 25 to 28 December – **M** a la carte 6.00/10.60 **t.**

  at Southam NE : 3 m. on A 46 – A – ✉ ☎ 0242 Cheltenham :

🏨 **De La Bere** (Best Western), GL52 3NH, ♟ 37771, Telex 43232, « Tudor manor house »,
  ⅃ heated, 🛤, park, 🛎, squash – 📺 📞 🚗 🔝 🆎 ⓪ 🆅🆂🅰
  M 7.25/11.75 **t.** ⅜ 2.90 – ☲ 3.75 – **31 rm** 29.50/58.00 **st.** – SB 63.00/70.00 **st.**

  at Cleeve Hill NE : 4 m. on A 46 – A – ✉ Cheltenham – ☎ 024 267 Bishop's Cleeve :

🏨 **Rising Sun**, GL52 3PX, ♟ 2002, ≤, 🛤 – 📺 🖼wc 🚾wc 📞 🔝 🆎 ⓪ 🆅🆂🅰 🛎
  M a la carte 4.70/10.00 **st.** ⅜ 3.00 – **13 rm** ☲ 25.00/35.00 **st.** – SB (weekends only) 22.50/24.00 **st.**

XXX **Malvern View** with rm, GL52 3PR, ♟ 2017, ≤ Malvern hills, 🛤 – 📺 🖼wc 🚾wc 📞 🆅🆂🅰 🛎
  closed 3 weeks at Christmas – **M** *(closed Sunday to non - residents)* (dinner only) 12.00 **st.**
  ⅜ 3.50 – **6 rm** ☲ 25.00/35.00 **st.**

  at Andoversford SE : 6 m. on A 40 – A – ✉ ☎ 0242 Cheltenham :

🏠 **Cold Comfort Farm,** Kilkenny, GL54 4LR, SW : 1 ½ m. on A 436 ♟ 820349, 🛤 – 📞 🛎
  6 rm ☲ 12.00/17.00 **st.**

  at Shurdington SW : 3 ¾ m. on A 46 – A – ✉ ☎ 0242 Cheltenham :

🏨 **Greenway** ⅏, GL51 5UG, ♟ 862352, Telex 437216, ≤, « Country house, gardens », park –
  📺 🖼wc ☎ 📞 🔝 🆎 ⓪ 🆅🆂🅰 🛎
  M *(closed lunch Saturday and Bank Holiday Mondays)* (Sunday dinner residents only) 16.00 **st.**
  – ☲ 3.00 – **11 rm** 50.00/100.00 **t.** – SB (winter only) 77.50/112.00 **st.**

ALFA-ROMEO High St, Prestbury ♟ 44247
AUSTIN-ROVER Princess Elizabeth Way ♟ 520441
CITROEN, PEUGEOT-TALBOT 16/28 Bath Rd ♟ 515391
DAIHATSU Swindon Rd ♟ 37016
FIAT Bishops Cleeve ♟ 674851
FORD 71/93 Winchcombe St. ♟ 527061
HONDA 172 Leckhampton Rd ♟ 524348
LADA, YUGO Stoke Orchard ♟ 024 268 (Combe Hill) 428
LANCIA Swindon Rd ♟ 32167
MAZDA Bath Rd ♟ 23879

NISSAN 60/66 Fairview Rd ♟ 513880
PEUGEOT-TALBOT Charlton Kings ♟ 521131
RENAULT Montpellier Spa Rd ♟ 521651
RENAULT Montpellier Spa Rd ♟ 521121
ROLLS ROYCE-BENTLEY Manor Rd Industrial Estate ♟ 515374
SUBARU Andoversford ♟ 04515 (Guiting Power) 274
TOYOTA 38 Suffolk Rd ♟ 527778
VAUXHALL-OPEL 379 High St. ♟ 522666
VAUXHALL-OPEL Albion St. ♟ 525252
VW, AUDI North St ♟ 515301

CHENIES Bucks. **404** S 28 – pop. 1,099 – ECD : Thursday – ✉ Rickmansworth – ☎ 092 78 Chorleywood.

♦London 30 – Aylesbury 18 – Watford 7.

🏨 **Bedford Arms Thistle** (Thistle), WB3 6EQ, ♟ 3301, Telex 893939, « 16C inn », 🛤 – 📺 📞
  🔝 🆎 ⓪ 🆅🆂🅰 🛎
  M a la carte 17.85/21.50 **t.** ⅜ 3.45 – ☲ 5.95 – **10 rm** 42.50/59.50 **t.**

CHEPSTOW Gwent **403 404** M 29 – pop. 8,480 – ECD : Wednesday – ☎ 029 12.

See : Castle★ (stronghold) *AC*.

🛈 The Gatehouse, High St. ☎ 3772 (summer only).

♦London 131 – ♦Bristol 17 – ♦Cardiff 28 – Gloucester 34.

  🏠 **Castle View,** 16 Bridge St., NP6 5EZ, ☎ 70349, 🚍 – 📺 ⇌wc 🅿 🕾. 🔄 ⒜Ⓔ *VISA*
    M 8.50/12.00 **st.** ◊ 3.00 – **10 rm** ⇌ 23.00/39.00 **st.** – SB 48.00/52.00 **st.**

  🏠 **George** (T.H.F.), Moor St., NP6 5DB, ☎ 2365 – 📺 ⇌wc 🕾. 🅿. 🔄 ⒜Ⓔ ⓪ *VISA*
    M (buffet lunch) a la carte 8.20/12.15 **st.** ◊ 2.60 – ⇌ 5.00 – **19 rm** 26.50/38.50 **st.**

AUSTIN-ROVER Station Rd ☎ 3159
FORD Newport Rd ☎ 2861

PEUGEOT, TALBOT Tutshill ☎ 3131
VAUXHALL-OPEL St. Lawrence Rd ☎ 3889

If you write to a hotel abroad,
enclose an International Reply Coupon
(available from Post Offices).

CHESTER Cheshire **402 403** L 24 – pop. 62,911 – ECD : Wednesday – ☎ 0244.

See : Cathedral★★ 14C-16C (choir stalls and misericords★★) – St. John's Church★ 12C **D** – The Rows★ – City Walls★ – Grosvenor Museum (Roman gallery★) **M1**.

Envir. : Upton (Chester Zoo★★) *AC*, N : 3 m. by A 5116.

🏌 Upton-by-Chester, Upton Lane ☎ 381183, by A 5116 – 🏌 Vicars Cross ☎ 35174, E : 2 m. by A 51 – 🏌 Helsby, Tower's Lane ☎ 092 82 (Helsby) 2021, NE : 8 m. by A 56 – 🏌 Ellesmere Port, Chester Rd ☎ 051 (Liverpool) 339 7502, N : 9 m. by A 5116 on A 41.

🛈 Town Hall, Northgate St. ☎ 40144 ext 2111/2250.

♦London 198 – Birkenhead 15 – ♦Birmingham 81 – ♦Liverpool 17 – ♦Manchester 40 – Preston 52 – ♦Sheffield 76 – ♦Stoke-on-Trent 38.

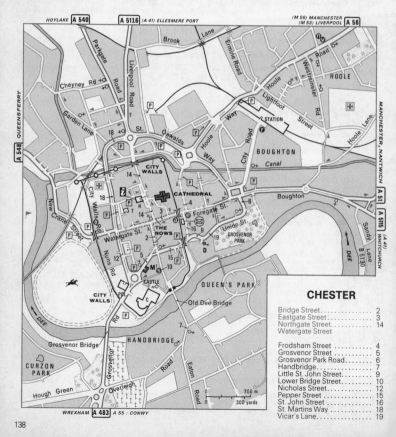

CHESTER

Chester Grosvenor, Eastgate St., CH1 1LT, ℰ 24024, Telex 61240 – 🛗 📺 🖵 ᴄ ⅄ ℗ 🛗 🔊
ᴀᴇ ⓞ 𝘝𝘐𝘚𝘈
closed 25 and 26 December – **M** 7.25/12.00 **t.** 🍷 3.00 – ⊡ 5.50 – **98 rm** 43.00/100.00 **t.** – SB
85.00/115.00 **st.**

Queen (T.H.F.), City Rd, CH1 3AH, ℰ 28341, Telex 617101, 🚗 – 🛗 📺 ℗ ⅄ 🔊 ᴀᴇ ⓞ 𝘝𝘐𝘚𝘈 r
M (bar lunch Saturday) 6.95/8.60 **st.** 🍷 2.60 – ⊡ 5.25 – **91 rm** 33.00/43.50 **st.**

Mollington Banastre (Best Western), Parkgate Rd, CH1 6NN, NW : 2 m. on A 540
ℰ 851471, Telex 61686, 🚗 – 🛗 📺 ᴄwc 🅟 ℗ ⅄ 🔊 ᴀᴇ ⓞ 𝘝𝘐𝘚𝘈
M a la carte 8.90/11.50 **st.** 🍷 3.50 – **47 rm** ⊡ 40.00/55.00 **st.** – SB 64.00 **st.**

Post House (T.H.F.), Wrexham Rd, CH4 9DL, S : 2 m. on A 483 ℰ 674111, Telex 61450, 🚗 –
📺 ᴄwc ᴄ ⅄ ℗ ⅄ 🔊 ᴀᴇ ⓞ 𝘝𝘐𝘚𝘈
M (buffet lunch) 8.25 **st.** 🍷 2.60 – ⊡ 5.00 – **62 rm** 34.00/41.50 **st.**

Blossoms, St. John St., CH1 1HL, ℰ 23186, Telex 61113 – 🛗 📺 ᴄwc ᴄ ⅄ 🔊 ᴀᴇ ⓞ 𝘝𝘐𝘚𝘈
M (carving lunch) a la carte 9.35/14.95 **t.** 🍷 2.75 – **70 rm** ⊡ 38.00/54.00 **st.** – SB (winter only) 54.00/59.00 **st.**   e

City Walls, 14 Stanley Pl., CH1 2LU, ℰ 313416 – 🛗 📺 ᴄwc ᴄ 🔊 𝘝𝘐𝘚𝘈   o
M *(closed Sunday dinner)* (carving lunch) 5.00/9.00 **st.** – ⊡ 2.75 – **17 rm** 20.00/29.00 **t.**

Gloster Lodge without rest., 44 Hoole Rd, CH2 3NP, ℰ 48410 – 📺 ᴄwc ℗   n
closed 24 to 27 December – **8 rm** ⊡ 17.00/29.50 **t.**

Ye Olde King's Head, 48-50 Lower Bridge St., CH1 1RS, ℰ 24855, « 16C inn » – 🔊 ᴀᴇ ⓞ
𝘝𝘐𝘚𝘈 ✻   s
closed 25 and 26 December – **M** 4.00/6.00 **t.** 🍷 2.75 – **11 rm** ⊡ 18.00/25.00 **t.** – SB 36.00/38.00 **st.**

Redland, 64 Hough Green, CH4 8JY, SW : 1 m. on A 549 ℰ 671024 – 🛗wc ℗ ✻
closed December and January – **10 rm** ⊡ 12.00/25.00 **st.**

Green Bough, 60 Hoole Rd, CH2 3NL, ℰ 26241 – 📺 ᴄwc 🛗wc ℗ 🔊 𝘝𝘐𝘚𝘈   i
closed 24 December-2 January – **11 rm** ⊡ 18.00/26.00 **t.**

Chester Court, 48 Hoole Rd, ℰ 20779 – 📺 ᴄwc 🛗wc ℗ 🔊 ᴀᴇ ⓞ 𝘝𝘐𝘚𝘈   v
19 rm ⊡ 17.00/28.00 **st.**

at Backford Cross N : 4 ½ m. by A 5116 junction A 41 and A 5117 – ✉ Chester – ☎ 0244
Great Mollington :

Ladbroke (Ladbroke), CH1 6PE, ℰ 851551, Telex 61552 – 📺 ᴄwc ☎ ᴄ ℗ ⅄ 🔊 ᴀᴇ ⓞ
𝘝𝘐𝘚𝘈
M 7.95/9.75 **st.** 🍷 3.50 – ⊡ 5.50 – **122 rm** 39.00/49.50 **st.** – SB (weekends only) 51.00/54.00 **st.**

at Christleton E : 2 m. on A 41 – ✉ ☎ 0244 Chester :

Abbots Well (Embassy), Whitchurch Rd, CH3 5QL, ℰ 332121, Telex 61561, 🚗 – 📺 ᴄwc
ᴄ ℗ ⅄ 🔊 ᴀᴇ ⓞ 𝘝𝘐𝘚𝘈 ᴄ
M (bar lunch Saturday) 6.25/9.00 **st.** 🍷 4.75 – ⊡ 4.25 – **127 rm** 35.00/47.00 **st.** – SB (weekends only) 49.00/58.00 **st.**

MICHELIN Branch, Sandycroft Industrial Estate, Glendale Av., Sandycroft, Deeside, CH5 2QP, ℰ
537373

AUSTIN-ROVER Victoria Rd ℰ 381246
BMW Chester Rd ℰ 311404
CITROEN Border House ℰ 672977
COLT Chester Rd ℰ 534347
DAIMLER-JAGUAR, ROLLS ROYCE 8 Russell St. ℰ
25262
FIAT Sealand Rd ℰ 374440
FORD Bridge Gate ℰ 20444
NISSAN Hamilton Pl. ℰ 317661

PEUGEOT-TALBOT The Highway ℰ 532362
SAAB Western Av. ℰ 375744
TOYOTA Welsh Rd ℰ 813633
VAUXHALL-OPEL Hoole Lane, Broughton ℰ 24611
VAUXHALL-OPEL 21/25 Garden Lane ℰ 46955
VAUXHALL-OPEL Parkgate Rd ℰ 372666
VOLVO, MERCEDES-BENZ 36 Tarvin Rd ℰ 47441
VW, AUDI Saughall Rd ℰ 377363

CHESTERFIELD Derbs. 🆘 🆘 🆘 P 24 – pop. 70,169 – ECD : Wednesday – ☎ 0246.
Envir. : Chatsworth✻✻✻ : site✻✻, house✻✻✻ (Renaissance), garden✻✻✻ *AC*, W : 7 m. – Hardwick
Hall✻✻ 16C (Tapestries and embroideries✻✻) *AC*, SE : 8 m. – Bolsover Castle✻ (17C) *AC*, E : 6 m. –
Worksop (Priory Church : Norman nave✻) NE : 14 m.
🏌 Chesterfield Municipal, Murray house, Crow Lane, Tapton ℰ 73887.
🚩 The Peacock Tourist Information and Heritage Centre, Low Pavement ℰ 207777 and 207778.
♦London 152 – Derby 24 – ♦Nottingham 25 – ♦Sheffield 12.

Chesterfield (Best Western), Malkin St., S41 7UA, ℰ 71141, Telex 547492 – 🛗 📺 ᴄwc ☎
🚗 ℗ ⅄ 🔊 ᴀᴇ ⓞ 𝘝𝘐𝘚𝘈
M 7.45 **st.** 🍷 2.65 – **61 rm** ⊡ 33.00/45.00 **st.** – SB (weekends only) 47.00 **st.**

Portland, West Bars, S40 1AY, ℰ 34502 – 📺 ᴄwc ℗ ⅄ 🔊 ⓞ 𝘝𝘐𝘚𝘈
M 7.20/10.75 **t.** 🍷 2.75 – **23 rm** ⊡ 20.50/38.50 **t.** – SB 38.50 **st.**

AUSTIN-ROVER Park Rd ℰ 73428
AUSTIN-ROVER 221 Sheffield Rd ℰ 77241
CITROEN, HONDA, AUDI Sheffield Rd ℰ 451611
DAIHATSU, SAAB Pottery Lane, Whittington Moor
ℰ 451611
FIAT Soresby St. ℰ 34351
FORD Barker Lane ℰ 76341

NISSAN Ringwood Rd ℰ 77386
OPEL, FIAT Chesterfield Rd, Staveley ℰ 473286
PEUGEOT-TALBOT, SIMCA 361 Sheffield Rd ℰ
450383
PORSCHE, AUDI-VW Broombank Rd ℰ 451611
VAUXHALL 464 Chatsworth Rd ℰ 79201
VOLVO Whittington Moor ℰ 453655

Envir. : Lumley Castle★ (14C) *AC*, E : 1 ½ m. – Beamish (North of England open Air Museum★) *AC*, NW : 3 m.

♦London 275 – Durham 7 – ♦Newcastle-upon-Tyne 8.

🏛 **Lumley Castle,** DH3 4NX, E : 1 m. on B 1284 ℰ 891111, Telex 537433, « 13C castle », 🐎, park – 📺 🛏wc ⋔wc ☎ ℗. 🚗. 🔼 AE ① VISA
  closed 25 and 26 December – **M** 7.95/9.95 t. ⓵ 3.60 – **50 rm** ⊊ 35.00/64.50 t. – SB (week-ends only) 70.00 **st.**

MICHELIN Branch, Drum Rd, DH3 2AF, ℰ 091 (Tyneside) 410 7762

AUSTIN-ROVER Newcastle Rd ℰ 882267
FIAT Petton Rd ℰ 881813
FORD 187 Front St. ℰ 884221

RENAULT Durham Rd, Birtley ℰ (091) 4103485
VAUXHALL Hopgarth ℰ 886111

CHESTERTON Oxon. **403** **404** Q 28 – pop. 990 – ⊠ ✆ 0869 Bicester.

♦London 65 – Northampton 33 – ♦Oxford 13.

XX **Woods,** Bignell View, OX6 8UE, on A 4095 ℰ 241444, 🐎 – ℗. 🔼 AE ① VISA
  closed Saturday lunch, Sunday dinner, Monday and 1 January – **M** a la carte 6.95/13.50 t.
  ⓵ 2.50.

CHICHESTER West Sussex **404** R 31 – pop. 20,649 – ECD : Thursday – ✆ 0243.

See : Cathedral★ 11C-15C BZ **A** – Market Cross★ BZ **B**.

Envir. : Fishbourne Roman Palace (mosaics★) *AC* W : 2 m. AZ **R** – Goodwood House★ (18C) *AC*, NE : 4 m. by A 27 AY and A 285.

🛈 The Council House, St. Peter's Market, West St. ℰ 775888.

♦London 69 – ♦Brighton 31 – ♦Portsmouth 18 – ♦Southampton 30.

CHICHESTER

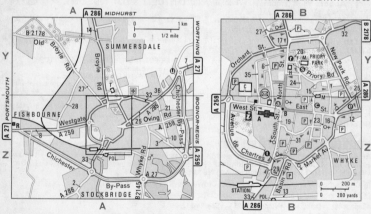

🏛 **Dolphin and Anchor** (T.H.F.), West St., PO19 1QE, ℰ 785121 – 📺 🛏wc ☎. 🚗. 🔼 AE ①
  VISA
  M 6.95/10.25 **st.** ⓵ 2.70 – ⊊ 5.00 – **54 rm** 35.00/46.00 **st.**
  BZ **a**

🏛 **Chichester Lodge,** Westhampnett Roundabout, PO19 4UL, on A 27 ℰ 786351, 🐎 – 📺
  🛏wc ℗. 🚗. 🔼 AE ① VISA
  M 6.75/9.25 t. ⓵ 2.75 – **43 rm** ⊊ 35.00/46.00 t. – SB 51.00/58.00 **st.**
  AY **u**

🏠 **Bedford** without rest., Southgate, PO19 1DP, ℰ 785766 – 📺 ⋔. 🔼 AE ① VISA. ⋘
  27 rm ⊊ 15.00/32.50 **st.**
  BZ **i**

🏠 **Ship,** North St., PO19 1NH, ℰ 782028, Telex 957141 – 🛗 📺 🛏wc ☎ ℗. 🔼 AE ① VISA. ⋘
  M (carving lunch) 6.00/7.50 t. ⓵ 2.45 – **36 rm** ⊊ 17.50/40.00 t. – SB 48.00/50.00 **st.**
  BY **r**

XX **Clinchs'** with rm, 4 Guildhall St., PO19 1NJ, ☞ 789915, « Tastefully furnished town house »
– 🔟 ⌷wc ⋔wc ☎ 🅿. 🔼 🔤 ⑩ 𝘝𝘐𝘚𝘈 🛇   BY **s**
closed 1 week at Christmas – **M** *(closed Sunday dinner)* (dinner only) 14.00 **t.** 🍴 2.90 – **7 rm**
⊊ 33.00/45.00 **t.**

XX **Christopher's,** 149 St. Pancras, PO19 1SH, ☞ 788724 – 🔼 🅰🅴 ⑩ 𝘝𝘐𝘚𝘈   BZ **e**
closed Sunday, Monday, 3 weeks October and 1 week at Christmas – **M** a la carte 8.20/9.85 **t.**
🍴 2.95.

XX **Little London,** 38 Little London, PO19 1PL, ☞ 784899 – 🔼 🅰🅴 ⑩ 𝘝𝘐𝘚𝘈   BZ **c**
closed Sunday and Monday – **M** a la carte 10.40/13.30 **t.** 🍴 3.10.

   at Chilgrove N : 6 ½ m. by A 286 – AY – on B 2141 – ✉ Chichester – ☏ 024 359 East
Marden :

XX **White Horse Inn,** 1 High St., PO18 9HX, ☞ 219 – 🅿. 🔼 🅰🅴 ⑩ 𝘝𝘐𝘚𝘈
closed Sunday dinner, Monday and 4 weeks January-February – **M** 11.95/13.95 **t.** 🍴 2.50.

   at Charlton N : 6 ¼ m. by A 286 – AY – ✉ Chichester – ☏ 024 363 Singleton :

🏡 **Woodstock House,** PO18 0HU, ☞ 666, 🌳, – ⌷wc ⋔wc 🅿. 🛇
mid February-mid November – **M** (dinner only) 8.00 **t.** 🍴 2.50 – **11 rm** ⊊ 13.00/35.00 **t.** – SB
39.00/46.00 **st.**

   at Bosham W : 4 m. by A 27 – AZ – ✉ ☏ 0243 Chichester :

🏨 **Millstream** (Best Western), Bosham Lane, PO18 8HL, ☞ 573234, « Tasteful decor », 🌳 –
🔟 ⌷wc ☏ 🅿. 🔼 🅰🅴 ⑩ 𝘝𝘐𝘚𝘈
M 7.00/10.00 **t.** 🍴 2.50 – **22 rm** ⊊ 30.00/48.00 **t.** – SB 52.00/64.00 **st.**

AUSTIN-ROVER-DAIMLER-JAGUAR   Westhamp-
nett Rd ☞ 781331
FIAT, LANCIA Northgate ☞ 784844
FORD The Hornet ☞ 788100
NISSAN Delling Lane, Bosham ☞ 573271

RENAULT 113 The Hornet ☞ 782293
VAUXHALL-OPEL, CITROEN, TOYOTA, VOLVO 55
Fishbourne Rd ☞ 782241
VW, AUDI 51/54 Bognor Rd ☞ 787684

CHIDDINGFOLD Surrey �404 S 30 – pop. 2,449 – ☏ 042 879 Wormley.

◆London 45 – ◆Brighton 40 – Guildford 12.

XXX **Crown Inn** with rm, The Green, Petworth Rd, RU8 4TS, ☞ 2255, « 13C inn » – 🔟 ⌷wc ☏
🅿. 🔼 🅰🅴 ⑩ 𝘝𝘐𝘚𝘈
closed Christmas Night – **M** a la carte 9.20/14.00 **t.** 🍴 3.20 – ⊊ 3.00 – **5 rm** 30.00/40.00 **st.**

CHIDDINGSTONE Kent 404 U 30 – see Penshurst.

CHIDEOCK Dorset 403 L 31 – see Bridport.

CHILGROVE West Sussex 404 R 31 – see Chichester.

CHILLINGTON Devon 403 I 33 – see Kingsbridge.

CHILTON POLDEN Somerset – see Bridgwater.

CHINNOR Oxon. 404 R 28 – pop. 6,040 – ☏ 0844 Kingston Blount.

◆London 45 – ◆Oxford 19.

XX **Cricket's,** 4 Keen's Lane, OX9 4PF, ☞ 53566 – ⅙ 🅿. 🔼 🅰🅴 ⑩ 𝘝𝘐𝘚𝘈
closed Sunday dinner, Monday, 2 weeks August, 25 to 30 December and January – **M** (dinner
only) a la carte 10.75/15.70 **t.** 🍴 2.95.

XX **Peaches,** 59-61 Lower Rd, OX9 4DU, ☞ 53752 – 🅿. 🔼 🅰🅴 ⑩ 𝘝𝘐𝘚𝘈
closed Sunday and mid January-mid February – **M** (dinner only) a la carte 11.10/14.00 **st.**
🍴 2.60.

CHIPPENHAM Wilts. 403 404 N 29 The West Country G. – pop. 18,696 – ECD : Wednesday –
☏ 0249.

See : Yelde Hall★.

Envir. : Biddestone★, W : 4 ½ m. – Sheldon Manor★, W : 1 ½ m. – Bowood House★ (Library ⩽★ of
the Park), SE : 5 m..

🅱 Malmesbury Rd ☞ 2040, N : 1 m.

🅱 The Neeld Hall, High St. ☞ 657733.

◆London 106 – ◆Bristol 27 – ◆Southampton 64 – Swindon 21.

🏨 **Angel** (Norfolk Cap.), 8 Market Pl., SN15 3HD, ☞ 652615, Group Telex 23241 – 🔟 ⌷wc ☎
🅿. 🛆. 🔼 🅰🅴 ⑩ 𝘝𝘐𝘚𝘈. 🛇
M a la carte 7.80/12.40 **st.** – **46 rm** ⊊ 19.00/29.00 **st.** – SB (summer only) 44.60/52.80 **st.**

AUSTIN-ROVER Station Hill ☞ 652215
FORD Cocklebury Rd ☞ 653255
RENAULT London Rd ☞ 6551131

VAUXHALL 16/17 The Causeway ☞ 654321
VOLVO Malmesbury Rd ☞ 652016

CHIPPERFIELD Herts. 404 @ – pop. 1,660 – ⊠ ✪ 092 77 Kings Langley.
♦ London 27 – Hemel Hempstead 5 – Watford 6.

⭐ **Two Brewers Inn** (T.H.F.), The Common, WD4 9BS, ⌖ 65266 – 📺 ⊟wc ® 🅿. 🔼 AE ①
VISA
M 7.50/9.95 **st.** ⌖ 2.50 – ⌕ 5.50 – **20 rm** 35.50/46.50 **st.**

CHIPPING Lancs. 402 M 22 – pop. 1,376 – ⊠ Preston – ✪ 099 56.
♦London 233 – Lancaster 30 – ♦Leeds 54 – ♦Manchester 40 – Preston 12.

⭐ **Gibbon Bridge** ⋟, PR3 2TQ, SE : 1 ¼ m. ⌖ 277, ≤, ≉ – 📺 ⍟wc 🅿 – **6 rm**.

CHIPPING CAMPDEN Glos. 403 404 O 27 – pop. 1,956 – ECD : Thursday – ✪ 0386 Evesham.
See : High Street★.
Envir. : Hidcote Manor Garden★ AC, NE : 2 ½ m.
🗿 Woolstaplers Hall Museum, High St. ⌖ 840289 (summer only).
♦London 93 – Cheltenham 21 – ♦Oxford 37 – Stratford-upon-Avon 12.

⭐ **King's Arms,** The Square, GL55 6AW, ⌖ 840256, ≉ – ⊟wc. 🔼 AE ① VISA
closed weekdays January-February – **M** (closed Tuesday lunch, Sunday dinner and Monday
during November-December (bar lunch Monday to Saturday) 9.45/10.95 **st.** ⌖ 3.20 – **14 rm**
⌕ 17.75/44.30 **st.** – SB (weekends only)(winter only) 47.25/52.50 **st.**

⭐ **Noel Arms,** High St., GL55 6AT, ⌖ 840317 – ⊟wc ⍟wc 🅿. 🔼. ≉
M 6.50/8.50 **t.** ⌖ 2.85 – **19 rm** ⌕ 30.50/39.50 **t.** – SB 42.00/52.50 **st.**

✕ **Caminetto,** Wool Market House, High St., GL55 6AG, ⌖ 840934, Italian rest. – 🔼 ① VISA
closed Sunday, 1 week January and 3 weeks September – **M** (dinner only) a la carte 5.85/13.30 **t.**
⌖ 2.85.

at Mickleton N : 3 ¼ m. by B 4035 and B 4081 on A 46 – ⊠ Chipping Campden – ✪ 038 677
Mickleton :

⭐ **Three Ways,** Chapel Lane, GL55 6SB, ⌖ 231, ≉ – 📺 ⊟wc & 🅿. 🔼 🔼 AE ① VISA
closed 2 and 3 January – **M** (bar lunch) 9.50 **t.** ⌖ 2.75 – **39 rm** ⌕ 26.00/42.00 **t.**

AUSTIN-ROVER High St. ⌖ 840213
CITROEN Sheep St. ⌖ 840221
FORD Mickleton ⌖ 038 677 (Mickleton) 270

CHIPPING NORTON Oxon. 403 404 P 28 – pop. 4,767 – ECD : Thursday – ✪ 0608.
🗿 22 New St. ⌖ 41320.
♦London 77 – ♦Birmingham 44 – Gloucester 36 – ♦Oxford 21.

⭐ **White Hart** (T.H.F.), High St., OX7 5AD, ⌖ 2572 – 📺 ⊟wc ® 🅿. 🔼 AE ① VISA
M (bar lunch Monday to Saturday) 6.50/8.50 **st.** ⌖ 2.60 – ⌕ 5.00 – **22 rm** 26.00/38.50 **st.**

✕✕ **La Madonette,** 7 Horse Fair, OX7 5AL, ⌖ 2320 – 🔼 VISA
closed Sunday and mid August-mid September – **M** (dinner only) a la carte 11.05/13.85 **t.**
⌖ 2.50.

AUSTIN-ROVER London Rd ⌖ 2014
VAUXHALL-OPEL Burford Rd ⌖ 2461

CHIPSTEAD Surrey 404 T 30 – pop. 4,129 (inc. Hooley) – ✪ 073 75 Downland.
♦London 15 – Reigate 6.

✕✕✕ **Dene Farm,** Outwood Lane, CR3 3NP, on B 2032 ⌖ 52661, ≉ – 🅿. 🔼 AE ① VISA
closed Saturday lunch, Sunday dinner, Monday, first 2 weeks August, 2 weeks after Christmas
and Bank Holidays – **M** a la carte 12.50/14.75 **t.** ⌖ 3.00.

BMW Outwood Lane ⌖ 56221

CHIRK (Y WAUN) Clwyd 403 K 25 – pop. 3,440 – ECD : Saturday – ⊠ Wrexham – ✪ 0691.
See : Castle★ (gates★) AC.
Envir. : W : Vale of Ceiriog★.
♦London 188 – Chester 22 – Shrewsbury 24 – Welshpool 21.

⭐ **Hand,** Church St., LL14 5EY, on A 5 ⌖ 773472, ≉ – ⍟wc 🅿. 🔼 AE ① VISA. ≉
M (closed Sunday dinner to non-residents) 5.50/7.50 **t.** ⌖ 2.80 – **11 rm** ⌕ 14.75/29.00 **t.** – SB
(weekends only) 36.00/42.00 **st.**

CHITTLEHAMHOLT Devon 403 I 31 – pop. 146 – ⊠ Umberleigh – ✪ 076 94.
♦London 216 – Barnstaple 14 – Exeter 28 – Taunton 45.

⭐ **Highbullen** ⋟, EX37 9HD, ⌖ 248, ≤, ⌕ heated, 🔼, ⌕⊽, ⋧, ≉, park, ✕, squash – 📺
⊟wc 🅿. ≉
M (bar lunch) 9.50 **st.** ⌖ 2.95 – ⌕ 1.50 – **30 rm** 27.50/44.00 **st.** – SB 45.00/59.00 **st.**

CHOLLERFORD Northumb. 401 402 N 18 – ⊠ Hexham – ✪ 043 481 Humshaugh.
♦London 303 – ♦Carlisle 36 – ♦Newcastle-upon-Tyne 21.

⭐ **George** (Swallow), NE46 4EW, ⌖ 205, Group Telex 53168, ≤, « Riverside gardens », ⋧ –
📺 ⊟wc ® 🅿. 🔼 AE ① VISA
M 6.50/9.00 **st.** ⌖ 2.50 – **54 rm** ⌕ 30.00/46.00 **st.** – SB 52.00 **st.**

142

CHORLEY Lancs. 402 404 M 23 – pop. 34,777 – ECD : Wednesday – © 025 72.
♦London 222 – ♦Blackpool 30 – ♦Liverpool 32 – ♦Manchester 26.

🏛 **Shaw Hill Country Club** ⅍, Preston Rd, Whittle-le-Woods, PR6 7PP, N : 2 ½ m. on A 6
 🖋 69221, ≤, 🔭 – 🔟 🚾🚾 ☎ 🅿. ⚎. 🔼 🄰🄴 ⓞ 𝐕𝐈𝐒𝐀
 M (bar lunch Saturday) 7.70/8.70 **st.** ⏐ 2.50 – **17 rm** 🖵 40.00/65.00 **st.** – SB 80.00/90.00 **st.**

 at Adlington S : 3 m. on A 6 – ⊠ Chorley – © 0257 Adlington :

🏠 **Gladmar** ⅍, Railway Rd, PR6 9RH, 🖋 480398, 🌿 – 🔟 🚾🚾 🕯🚾 ☎ 🅿. ⚘
 M (bar lunch) 8.50 **st.** ⏐ 2.80 – **13 rm** 🖵 20.00/28.00 **st.**

CHRISTCHURCH Dorset 403 404 O 31 – pop. 31,463 – ECD : Wednesday – © 0202.
See : Site★ – Priory ★ – Envir. : Hengistbury Head★ (≤★★), SW : 4 m. by B 3059.
🄸 30 Saxon Sq. 🖋 471780.
♦London 111 – Bournemouth 6 – Salisbury 26 – ♦Southampton 24 – Winchester 39.

🏛 **King's Arms Crest** (Crest), Castle St., BH23 1DT, 🖋 484117 – 🕮 🔟 🚾🚾 🕯🚾 ☎ 🅿. ⚎. ⚘
 32 rm.

🏠 **Park House,** 48 Barrack Rd, BH23 1PF, 🖋 482124, 🌿 – 🅿. 🔼 𝐕𝐈𝐒𝐀. ⚘
 closed Christmas and New Year – **9 rm** 🖵 11.00/30.00 **s.**

🍴 **Splinters,** 12 Church St., BH23 1BW, 🖋 483454 – 🄰🄴 ⓞ 𝐕𝐈𝐒𝐀
 closed Sunday and 25-26 December – **M** (dinner only) a la carte 10.45/13.00 **t.** ⏐ 2.35.

 at Mudeford SE : 2 m. – ⊠ © 0202 Christchurch :

🏛 **Avonmouth** (T.H.F.), BH23 3NT, 🖋 483434, ≤ Christchurch harbour, ⊒ heated, 🌿 – 🔟
 🚾🚾 ☎ 🅿. ⚎ 🔼 🄰🄴 ⓞ 𝐕𝐈𝐒𝐀
 M (buffet lunch Monday to Saturday) 7.00/9.25 **st.** ⏐ 3.00 – 🖵 5.00 – **41 rm** 31.00/50.00 **st.**

🏠 **The Pines,** 39 Mudeford, BH23 3NQ, 🖋 475121 – 🔟 🕯🚾 🅿
 13 rm 🖵 10.00/25.00 **s.**

CITROEN Barrack Rd 🖋 479351
FIAT Highcliffe 🖋 042 52 (Highcliffe) 72333

FORD Lyndhurst Rd 🖋 042 52 (Highcliffe) 71371
VW, AUDI 105 Summerford Rd 🖋 476871

CHRISTLETON Cheshire 402 403 L 24 – see Chester.

CHURCH STRETTON Salop 403 L 26 – pop. 3,346 – ECD : Wednesday – © 069 42 (4 fig.) or
0694 (6 fig.).
🔭 Links Rd 🖋 722281.
🄸 Church St. 🖋 722535 (summer only).
♦London 166 – ♦Birmingham 46 – Hereford 39 – Shrewsbury 14.

🏛 **Stretton Hall** ⅍, Old Shrewsbury Rd, All Stretton, SY6 6HG, NE : 1 m. on B 4370 🖋 723224,
 🌿 – 🔟 🚾🚾 ☎ 🅿. 🔼 🄰🄴 ⓞ 𝐕𝐈𝐒𝐀
 M a la carte 8.35/10.95 **t.** – **12 rm** 🖵 20.00/32.00 **t.** – SB 35.50/40.00 **st.**

🏠 **Sandford,** Watling St. South, SY6 7BG, 🖋 722131, 🌿 – 🚾🚾 🕯🚾 🅿. 🔼 𝐕𝐈𝐒𝐀
 M (bar lunch Monday to Saturday) 4.50/5.75 **t.** ⏐ 3.00 – **24 rm** 🖵 14.50/29.00 **t.** – SB
 35.00/38.00 **st.**

🏠 **Mynd House,** Ludlow Rd, Little Stretton, SY6 6RB, SW : 1 m. on B 4370 🖋 722212, ≤, 🌿 –
 🚾🚾 🕯 🅿. 🔼 𝐕𝐈𝐒𝐀
 closed 16 December-1 February – **13 rm** 🖵 11.00/28.00 **t.**

CHURT Surrey 404 R 30 – see Farnham.

CIRENCESTER Glos. 403 404 O 28 – pop. 11,990 – ECD : Thursday – © 0285.
See : Parish Church★ (Perpendicular) – Corinium Museum★.
Envir. : Chedworth (Roman Villa ★) AC, N : 7 m.
🔭 Cheltenham Rd 🖋 3939, N : 1 ½ m.
🄸 Corn Hall, Market Pl. 🖋 4180.
♦London 97 – ♦Bristol 37 – Gloucester 19 – ♦Oxford 37.

🏛 **King's Head** (Best Western), 24 Market Pl., GL7 2NR, 🖋 3322, Telex 43470 – 🕮 🔟 🅿. ⚎.
 🔼 🄰🄴 ⓞ 𝐕𝐈𝐒𝐀
 closed 28 and 29 December – **M** 7.25/9.35 **st.** ⏐ 3.50 – **70 rm** 🖵 32.00/52.00 **st.** – SB
 52.00/62.00 **st.**

🏛 **Fleece,** Market Pl., GL7 4NZ, 🖋 68507 – 🔟 🚾🚾 ☎ 🅿. 🔼 🄰🄴 ⓞ 𝐕𝐈𝐒𝐀
 closed 25 to 27 December – **M** 12.50/15.00 **t.** ⏐ 2.50 – 🖵 4.75 – **19 rm** 32.50/45.00 **t.** – SB
 (January-May) 49.00/51.00 **st.**

🏠 Corinium Court, 12 Gloucester St., GL7 2DG, 🖋 4499 – 🔟 🚾🚾 🕯🚾 🅿 – **8 rm**.

🏠 **La Ronde,** 52-54 Ashcroft Rd, GL7 1QX, 🖋 4611 – ⚘
 10 rm 🖵 16.50/24.50 **t.**

 at Ewen SW : 3 ¼ m. by A 429 – ⊠ Cirencester – © 028 577 Kemble :

🍴 **Wild Duck Inn,** GL7 6BY, 🖋 364, 🌿 – 🔟 🚾🚾 🅿. 🔼 🄰🄴 ⓞ 𝐕𝐈𝐒𝐀
 M 6.50/9.50 **t.** ⏐ 2.75 – **8 rm** 🖵 27.00/38.00 **t.** – SB 55.00/62.50 **st.**

at Stratton NW : 1 ¼ m. on A 417 – ⊠ ۞ 0285 Cirencester :

🏛 **Stratton House,** Gloucester Rd, GL7 2LE, ℰ 61761, ⌂ – 📺 🛏wc �🛏wc ☎ 🅿 🧺 🔳 🅰🅴
🅥🅘🅢🅐

M 6.75/8.60 **st.** ⅃ 3.00 – **26 rm** ⊏⊐ 23.75/39.75 **st.** – SB 30.75/33.00 **st.**

AUSTIN-ROVER Tetbury Rd ℰ 2614
CITROEN Perrotts Brook ℰ 028 583 (North Cerney) 219
COLT Love Lane ℰ 5799

NISSAN Chesterton Lane ℰ 2196
PEUGEOT-TALBOT Victoria Rd ℰ 3460
RENAULT 27 Victoria Rd ℰ 3020
VAUXHALL Lovelane Trading Estate ℰ 3314

CLACTON-ON-SEA Essex 🔢🔢 X 28 – pop. 38,070 – ECD : Wednesday – ۞ 0255.
See : Sea front (gardens)★.
🇮 Town Hall, Station Rd ℰ 425501 ext 200 – Central Seafront, Marine Parade ℰ 423400 (summer only).
♦London 71 – Chelmsford 38 – Colchester 16.

🏕 **Kings Cliff,** 55 Kings Par., Esplanade, Holland-on-Sea, CO15 5JB, NE : 1 ½ m ℰ 812343, ≼ – 📺 🛏wc 🅿 🔳 🅥🅘🅢🅐 🛇
M 3.95/5.50 **st.** ⅃ 1.75 – **13 rm** ⊏⊐ 16.50/35.00 **st.** – SB (winter only) 45.00/53.50 **st.**

⌂ **York House,** 19 York Rd, Holland-on-Sea, CO15 5NS, NE : 1 ½ m. ℰ 814333, ⌂ – 🔳 🅰🅴
🅥🅘🅢🅐
6 rm ⊏⊐ 9.50/19.00 **st.**

AUSTIN-ROVER 107 Old Rd ℰ 424128
BEDFORD, OPEL-VAUXHALL 65 High St. ℰ 420444
CITROEN 67 Frinton Rd ℰ 812205

CITROEN 67 Frinton Rd ℰ 812205
FORD St John's Rd ℰ 425487

CLANFIELD Oxon. 🔢🔢 🔢🔢 P 28 – pop. 607 – ECD : Wednesday and Saturday – ۞ 036 781.
♦London 76 – ♦Oxford 20 – Swindon 17.

✗✗ **Plough** with rm, Bourton Rd, OX8 2RB, on A 4095 ℰ 222, ⌂ – 📺 🅿 🔳 🅰🅴 🅞 🅥🅘🅢🅐
closed Sunday and Monday from January-April – **M** a la carte 11.05/15.25 **t.** ⅃ 2.95 – **6 rm** ⊏⊐ 22.50/37.50 **t.** – SB 36.00/42.00 **st.**

CLAPHAM Beds. 🔢🔢 S 27 – see Bedford.

CLAPPERSGATE Cumbria – see Ambleside.

CLAVERING Essex 🔢🔢 U 28 – pop. 1,003 – ۞ 079 985.
♦London 44 – ♦Cambridge 25 – Colchester 44 – Luton 29.

✗ **Cricketers,** CB11 4QT, ℰ 442 – 🅿 🔳 🅥🅘🅢🅐
M (bar lunch) 11.00 **t.** ⅃ 2.00.

CLAWTON Devon 🔢🔢 H 31 – pop. 303 – ⊠ Holsworthy – ۞ 040 927 North Tamerton.
♦London 240 – Exeter 39 – ♦Plymouth 36.

🏰 **Court Barn** 🛇, EX22 6PS, W : ½ m. ℰ 219, « Gardens » – 🛏wc ⚑🛏wc 🅿
closed 10 to 24 December and 27 December-11 January – **M** (booking essential)(bar lunch) a la carte 6.20/8.70 **t.** ⅃ 2.10 – **8 rm** ⊏⊐ 14.00/40.00 **t.** – SB (except summer) 31.00/35.00 **st.**

CLAYWORTH Notts. 🔢🔢 🔢🔢 R 23 – pop. 275 – ⊠ ۞ 0777 Retford.
♦London 150 – ♦Leeds 49 – Lincoln 26 – ♦Nottingham 38 – ♦Sheffield 29.

🏰 **Royston Manor** 🛇, St. Peters Lane, DN22 9AA, ℰ 817484, ≼, ⌂ – 📺 🛏wc ⚑🛏wc ☎ 🅿
🔳 🅰🅴 🅞 🅥🅘🅢🅐
M *(closed Saturday lunch)* (bar lunch) 10.75 **st.** ⅃ 2.90 – ⊏⊐ 3.50 – **12 rm** 18.00/30.00 **st.** – SB (weekends only) 50.00 **st.**

CLEADON Tyne and Wear 🔢🔢 🔢🔢 P 19 – pop. 4,494 – ۞ 0783 Bolden.
♦London 285 – ♦Newcastle-upon-Tyne 10 – Sunderland 4.

✗ **French Blackboard,** 61 Front St., SR6 7PG, ℰ 367397 – 🔳 🅰🅴 🅞 🅥🅘🅢🅐
M (dinner only and Sunday lunch) 6.90/10.25 **st.** ⅃ 2.25.

CLEETHORPES Humberside 🔢🔢 🔢🔢 U 23 – pop. 35,837 – ECD : Thursday – ۞ 0472.
🇮 43 Alexandra Rd ℰ 697472.
♦London 171 – Boston 49 – Lincoln 38 – ♦Sheffield 77.

Plan : see Grimsby

🏛 **Kingsway,** Kingsway, DN35 0AE, ℰ 601122, ≼, ⌂ – 📶 📺 🛏wc ☎ ⟷ 🅿 🧺 🔳 🅰🅴 🅞
🅥🅘🅢🅐 🛇
BZ **a**
closed 25 and 26 December – **M** 6.25/7.50 **st.** ⅃ 3.00 – **53 rm** ⊏⊐ 24.00/45.00 **st.** – SB (weekends only) 44.00 **st.**

🏰 **Wellow,** Kings Rd, DN35 0AQ, ℰ 695589 – 📺 🛏wc ☎ 🅿 🔳 🅰🅴 🅥🅘🅢🅐
Y
M 4.95/8.95 **t.** ⅃ 2.65 – **10 rm** ⊏⊐ 18.00/33.00 **t.** – SB (weekends only) 28.90/38.90 **st.**

CITROEN 76-80 Brereton Av. ℰ 55558

LANCIA 421 Grimsby Rd ℰ 698991

CLEEVE HILL Glos. 🔢🔢 🔢🔢 N 28 – see Cheltenham.

CLEOBURY MORTIMER Salop 408 404 M 26 – pop. 1,892 – ✪ 0299.
♦London 147 – ♦Birmingham 29 – Shrewsbury 35.

🏠 **Redfern,** Lower St., DY14 8AA, ☏ 270395, Telex 335176 – 📺 ⌷wc �𝄂wc ☎ 🅿. ◱ 🆎 ⑩ 𝘝𝘐𝘚𝘈
M 4.00/7.75 **st.** ⌷ 2.50 – **11 rm** ⌷ 21.00/32.00 **st.** – SB 40.00/44.00 **st.**

CLEVEDON Avon 408 L 29 The West Country G. – pop. 13,070 – ECD : Wednesday – ✪ 0272.
See : Site★ (⩽ from park benches★★) – Clevedon Court★.
♦London 138 – ♦Bristol 15 – Taunton 34.

🏠 **Walton Park,** 1 Wellington Terr., BS21 7BL, ☏ 874253, ⩽, 🏤 – 🕭 📺 ⌷wc ⟻ 🅿. ◱. ◱
🆎 ⑩ 𝘝𝘐𝘚𝘈
M 6.75/9.40 **t.** – **35 rm** ⌷ 26.50/41.95 **t.** – SB (weekends only) 45.00/50.00 **st.**

AUSTIN-ROVER Old Church Rd ☏ 872201

CLIMPING West Sussex 404 S 31 – pop. 800 – ⊠ ✪ 090 64 Littlehampton.
♦London 64 – Bognor Regis 5 – ♦ Brighton 23.

🏠 **Bailiffscourt** ⌖, Climping St., BN17 5RW, ☏ 723511, « Reconstructed medieval house »,
◱, 🏤, park, ⚒ – 📺 ⌷wc ☎ 🅿. ◱. ◱ 🆎 ⑩ 𝘝𝘐𝘚𝘈
closed 4 January-6 February – **M** 12.00/15.00 **st.** ⌷ 3.50 – **18 rm** ⌷ 40.00/95.00 **st.**

CLITHEROE Lancs. 402 M 22 – pop. 13,194 – ECD : Wednesday – ✪ 0200.
🖈 Whalley Rd, ☏ 22618, SW : 2 m.
🛈 Council Offices, Church Walk ☏ 25566.
♦London 236 – ♦Blackpool 35 – Burnley 12 – Kendal 53 – ♦Leeds 47 – ♦Manchester 31.

🏠 **Fairway,** 48 King St., BB7 2EU, ☏ 22025 – ⟻wc 🅿. ◱ 🆎 𝘝𝘐𝘚𝘈
9 rm ⌷ 8.00/19.00 **s.**

CLOWNE Derbs. 402 403 404 Q 24 – pop. 6,847 – ✪ 0246 Chesterfield.
♦London 156 – Derby 40 – Lincoln 35 – ♦Nottingham 30 – ♦Sheffield 12.

🏠 **Van Dyk,** Worksop Rd, S43 4TD, N : ¾ m. on A 619 ☏ 810219 – 📺 ⌷wc ⟻wc ⟻ 🅿. ◱ 🆎
𝘝𝘐𝘚𝘈
M (closed Sunday dinner) 6.50/7.15 **t.** – ⌷ 3.25 – **16 rm** 24.00/41.00 **t.** – SB (week-
ends only) 38.50 **st.**

CLUN Salop 403 KL 26 – pop. 817 – ⊠ Craven Arms – ✪ 058 84.
♦London 178 – ♦Birmingham 60 – Shrewsbury 29.

⚓ **Sun Inn,** High St., SY7 8JB, ☏ 559 – ⟻wc 🅿. ◱. ⚘
M (bar lunch) 6.50 **st.** ⌷ 3.00 – **7 rm** ⌷ 10.00/26.00 **st.**

COATHAM-MUNDEVILLE Durham 402 P 20 – see Darlington.

COBHAM Surrey 404 S 30 – pop. 14,580 – ECD : Wednesday – ✪ 093 26.
Envir. : Wisley gardens★★ *AC*, SW : 4 m. by A 3 AZ.
🖈 Silvermere, Redhill Rd ☏ 6007, by A245 AZ.
♦London 24 – Guildford 10.

Plan : see Greater London (South-West)

🏠 **Ladbroke Seven Hills** (Ladbroke), Seven Hills Rd South, KT11 1EW, W : 1 ½ m. by A 245
☏ 4471, Telex 929196, ◱ heated, 🏤, park, ⚒, squash – 🕭 📺 ⌷wc ☎ 🅿. ◱. ◱
𝘝𝘐𝘚𝘈. ⚘
M 8.75/10.00 **t.** – ⌷ 5.50 – **92 rm** 41.00/60.00 **t.**   by A 3   AZ

XX **San Domenico,** Portsmouth Rd, KT11 1EL, SW : 1 m. on A 3 ☏ 3006, Italian rest., 🏤 – 🅿.
◱ 🆎 ⑩ 𝘝𝘐𝘚𝘈   by A 3   AZ
closed Sunday dinner – **M** a la carte 10.60/15.45 **t.** ⌷ 2.50.

ALFA-ROMEO, VW-AUDI 42 Portsmouth Rd ☏ 4493   BMW 22 Portsmouth Rd ☏ 7141
AUSTIN-ROVER Stoke Rd ☏ 4244

COCKERMOUTH Cumbria 401 402 J 20 – pop. 5,750 – ECD : Thursday – ✪ 0900.
🛈 Riverside Car Park, Market St. ☏ 822634 (summer only).
♦London 306 – ♦Carlisle 25 – Keswick 13.

🏠 **Trout,** Crown St., CA13 0EJ, ☏ 823591, 🏤 – 📺 ⌷wc ⟻wc 🅿. 𝘝𝘐𝘚𝘈
closed Christmas Day – **M** 6.00/10.50 **t.** ⌷ 2.80 – **16 rm** ⌷ 22.00/35.00 **t.** – SB (weekends only) 41.00 **st.**

🏠 **Wordsworth,** Main St., CA13 9JS, ☏ 822757 – 📺 ⌷wc 🅿. ◱ 𝘝𝘐𝘚𝘈. ⚘
closed Christmas Day – **M** (bar lunch) 7.50 **st.** – **18 rm** ⌷ 16.00/32.00 **st.** – SB (weekends only) 38.00 **st.**

X **Old Court House,** 2 Main St., ☏ 823871
closed Sunday and Bank Holidays – **M** approx. 9.80 **st.** ⌷ 3.60.

at Great Broughton W : 2 ¾ m. by A 66 – ⊠ ✆ 0900 Cockermouth :

🏛 **Broughton Craggs** ⟨, CA13 0XW, ✆ 824400, 🍴 – 📺 ⇔wc ☎ 🅿 🔄 AE VISA ⚘
M 5.50/9.25 **t.** ⌂ 2.75 – **10 rm** ⇆ 23.00/32.00 **t.** – SB (weekends only) 35.00/40.00 **st.**

BMW, VOLVO Derwent St. ✆ 823666   PEUGEOT-TALBOT Gote Rd ✆ 823017
FORD Lorton St. ✆ 822033

COED-DUON = Blackwood.

COGGESHALL Essex 📖📖 W 28 – pop. 3,643 – ECD : Wednesday – ⊠ Colchester – ✆ 0376.
♦London 49 – Braintree 6 – Chelmsford 16 – Colchester 9.

🏛 **White Hart,** Market End, CO6 1NH, ✆ 61654, « Part 14C Guild Hall » – 📺 ⇔wc ⽘wc ☎
🅿 🔄 AE ⓞ VISA ⚘
closed 1 week Christmas and August – **M** *(closed Sunday)* a la carte 10.45/15.45 **t.** ⌂ 3.25 –
24 rm ⇆ 30.00/50.00 **t.**

COLCHESTER Essex 📖📖 W 28 – pop. 76,531 – ECD : Thursday – ✆ 0206.
See : Roman Walls★.
Envir. : Layer Marney (Marney Tower★ 16C) SW : 7 m.
🏌 Birch Grove, Layer Rd ✆ 020 634 (Layer-de-la-Haye) 276, S : 2 m.
🛈 Town Hall, High St. ✆ 46379 and 576071.
♦London 52 – ♦Cambridge 48 – ♦Ipswich 18 – Luton 76 – Southend-on-Sea 41.

🏛 **George** (Q.M.H.), 116 High St., CO1 1TD, ✆ 578494 – 📺 ⇔wc ☎ 🅿 🔄 AE ⓞ VISA
M (carving rest.) 7.25 **st.** ⌂ 2.50 – **47 rm** ⇆ 31.00/43.00 **st.** – SB 21.50 **st.**

🏛 **Rose and Crown,** East Gates, CO1 2TZ, ✆ 866677, « Part 15C inn » – 📺 ⇔wc ⽘wc ☎ 🅿
🔄 AE ⓞ VISA
M 8.50 **st.** ⌂ 2.75 – **28 rm** ⇆ 22.50/36.50 **st.**

✕ **Wm. Scraggs,** 2 North Hill, CO1 1DZ, ✆ 41111, Seafood – 🔄 AE VISA
closed Sunday and Bank Holidays – **M** a la carte 8.20/20.30 **st.** ⌂ 3.00.

✕ **Bistro 9,** 9 North Hill, CO1 1OZ, ✆ 576466 – 🔄 VISA
closed Sunday, Monday and 25 December-3 January – **M** a la carte 7.20/9.50 **t.** ⌂ 2.60.

at Marks Tey W : 5 m. by A 12 on B 1408 – ⊠ ✆ 0206 Colchester :

🏛 Marks Tey (Mt. Charlotte), London Rd, CO6 1DU, ✆ 210001, Telex 987176 – 📺 ⇔wc ☎ 🅿
🏊 – **106 rm**.

at Nayland (Suffolk) NW : 6 m. by A 134 – ⊠ Colchester – ✆ 0206 Nayland :

✕✕ **Bear Country House** with rm, Bear St., CO6 4HX, ✆ 262204, 🏊, 🍴 – 📺 ⇔wc 🅿 🔄 AE
ⓞ VISA
closed Sunday dinner, last week January, last week March and Christmas Day – **M** (dinner
only and Sunday lunch) 13.00 **t.** ⌂ 3.50 – **4 rm** ⇆ 18.00/35.00 **t.**

MICHELIN Branch, Clarenden Way, Anglia Trading Estate, CO1 1XB, ✆ 578451

AUDI, FERRARI, PORSCHE, MERCEDES-BENZ, VW
Auto Way, Ipswich Rd ✆ 48141
AUSTIN-ROVER East Gates ✆ 867484
AUSTIN-ROVER Cowdray Av. ✆ 76291
AUSTIN-ROVER-DAIMLER-JAGUAR Elmstead Rd
✆ 862811
CITROEN Butt Rd ✆ 76803
FIAT, TOYOTA Gosbecks Rd ✆ 76455

FORD Magdalen St. ✆ 71171
HONDA, LADA, RELIANT ✆ 867298
NISSAN 78 Military Rd ✆ 77295
RENAULT Ipswich Rd ✆ 68555
TALBOT, PEUGEOT, ALFA-ROMEO Wimpole Rd ✆
570197
VAUXHALL-OPEL Ipswich Rd ✆ 844422
VOLVO, BMW 10 Osborne St. ✆ 77287

COLEBROOK Devon – see Plymouth.

COLEFORD Glos. 📖📖 📖📖 M 28 – pop. 3,627 – ECD : Thursday – ⊠ Gloucester – ✆ 0594
Dean.
🏌 Coalway Rd ✆ 0594 (Dean) 32583, ½ m. on Parkend Rd.
♦London 143 – ♦ Bristol 28 – Gloucester 19 – Newport 29.

🏛 **Speech House** (T.H.F.), Forest of Dean, GL16 7EL, NE : 3 m. on B 4226 ✆ 22607, 🍴 – 📺
⇔wc ☎ 🅿 🔄 AE ⓞ VISA
M a la carte 10.30/12.75 **st.** ⌂ 2.60 – ⇆ 4.75 – **14 rm** 29.50/41.50 **st.**

🏛 **Lambsquay** ⟨, Perrygrove Rd, GL16 8QB, S : 1 m. on B 4228 ✆ 33127, 🍴 – 📺 ⇔wc 🅿
M *(closed Sunday)* a la carte 5.45/9.15 **t.** ⌂ 2.70 – **10 rm** ⇆ 15.50/39.00 **t.**

AUSTIN-ROVER-LAND ROVER Market Pl. ✆ 32468   NISSAN ✆ 33517
FORD High St ✆ 32747

Pour parcourir l'Europe,
utilisez les cartes Michelin **Grandes Routes** à 1/1 000 000.

COLESHILL Warw. 408 404 O 26 – pop. 6,297 – ECD : Monday and Thursday – ✉ Birmingham – ☎ 0675.

🛦, 🛦 The Belfry, Wishaw ℰ 0675 (Curdworth) 70301, N : 4 m.

◆London 113 – ◆Birmingham 8 – ◆Coventry 11.

🏦 **Swan** (Golden Oak), High St., B46 3BL, ℰ 62212 – 📺 🏬wc ☎ 🅿. 🍴. 🅭 AE VISA. 🍴
M *(closed Saturday lunch)* a la carte 8.15/10.45 **t.** 🍷 2.50 – **35 rm** ☷ 24.50/34.50 **t.** – SB (weekends only) 40.50/46.50 **st.**

🏦 **Coleshill,** 152 High St., B46 3BG, ℰ 65527 – 📺 🛏wc ☎ 🅿. 🅭 AE ⓘ VISA. 🍴
M 5.95/7.95 **t.** 🍷 2.85 – ☷ 3.00 – **15 rm** 27.00/30.00 **t.**

✕ **Blythe's,** 19 High St., B46 1AY, ℰ 62266 – 🅿. 🅭 ⓘ VISA
closed Saturday lunch, Monday dinner, Sunday, first week January, last 2 weeks August and Bank Holidays – **M** 6.10/13.75 **t.** 🍷 2.80.

COLLYWESTON Northants. 402 404 S 26 – see Stamford (Lincs.).

COLWALL Heref. and Worc. – see Great Malvern.

COLWYN BAY (BAE COLWYN) Clwyd 402 403 I 24 – pop. 25,564 – ECD : Wednesday – ☎ 0492.
See : Zoo★.

Envir. : Bodnant gardens★★ *AC*, SW : 6 m.

🛦 Abergele and Pensarn, Tan-y-Goppa Rd, Abergele ℰ 0745 (Abergele) 824034, E : 6 m. – 🛦 Old Colwyn, Woodland Av. ℰ 55581.

🅱 Prince of Wales Theatre ℰ 30478 – Colwyn Bay Hotels and Guest Houses Association ℰ 55719 (summer only).

◆London 237 – Birkenhead 50 – Chester 42 – Holyhead 41.

🏦 **Norfolk House,** 39 Princes Drive, LL29 8PF, ℰ 31757, 🚗 – ⬛ 📺 🛏wc 🏬wc ☎ 🅿. 🅭 AE ⓘ VISA
M (bar lunch) 8.50 **t.** 🍷 3.50 – **30 rm** ☷ 28.50/38.00 **t.** – SB (weekends only except Easter) 67.00 **t.**

🏠 **Hopeside,** 63-67 Prince's Drive, West End, LL29 8PW, ℰ 33244, Telex 61254 – 📺 🛏wc 🏬wc ☎ 🅿. 🅭 AE ⓘ VISA
closed 2 weeks Christmas and New Year – **M** *(closed Sunday lunch)* (bar lunch) 9.00 **t.** 🍷 1.40 – **17 rm** ☷ 20.50/38.00 **st.** – SB 42.00/53.00 **st.**

🏠 **Lyndale,** 410 Abergele Rd, LL29 9AB, ℰ 515429 – 📺 🛏wc 🏬wc 🅿. 🅭 VISA
M 4.50/6.50 **st.** 🍷 2.95 – **14 rm** ☷ 16.00/28.00 **st.** – SB 34.00/41.00 **st.**

↑ Clevedon, 18-20 Hawarden Rd, LL29 8NA, ℰ 2368 – **17 rm**.

at Penmaenhead E : 2 m. on A 55 – ✉ ☎ 0492 Colwyn Bay :

🏨 **Hotel 70°** (Best Western), LL29 9LD, ℰ 516555, Telex 61362, ≼ – 📺 ☎ 🅿. 🍴. 🅭 AE ⓘ VISA
closed 24 December-3 January – **M** 9.50/16.00 **st.** 🍷 3.50 – **43 rm** ☷ 31.00/50.00 **st.** – SB 51.50/57.50 **st.**

at Rhos-on-Sea (Llandrillo-yn-Rhos) NW : 1 m. – ✉ ☎ 0492 Colwyn Bay :

🏠 **Ashmount,** College Av., LL28 4NT, ℰ 45479 – 📺 🛏wc 🏬wc 🅿. 🅭 ⓘ VISA
M 3.95/5.80 **st.** 🍷 2.75 – **14 rm** ☷ 15.40/26.40 **t.** – SB 32.00 **st.**

↑ **Cabin Hill,** 12 College Av., LL28 4NT, ℰ 44568 – 🏬wc. 🍴
March-October – **10 rm** ☷ 9.50/24.00 **st.**

AUSTIN-ROVER 394 Abergele Rd ℰ 55292
FORD Conwy Rd ℰ 2201
PEUGEOT 268 Conwy Rd ℰ 44278

PORSCHE, MERCEDES-BENZ Abergele Rd ℰ 30456
VAUXALL Conwy Rd ℰ 30271
VW, AUDI Penrhyn Av. ℰ 46722

COLYFORD Devon – see Colyton.

COLYTON Devon 403 K 31 The West Country G. – pop. 2,112 – ☎ 0297.
See : Site★ – St. Andrew's Church★.

◆London 160 – Exeter 23 – Lyme Regis 7.

↑ **Grove,** South St., EX13 6ER, ℰ 52438, 🚗 – 🏬wc 🅿
closed 20 December-14 January – **7 rm** ☷ 8.75/20.00 **st.**

at Colyford S : 1 m. by B 3161 on A 3052 – ✉ ☎ 0297 Colyton :

🏡 **Old Manor** 🍴, Swan Hill Rd, EX13 6QQ, ℰ 52862, ≼, « Converted 15C manor house », 🚗, 🍴 – 🅿. 🍴
March-mid October and Christmas – **M** (bar lunch) 8.50 **t.** 🍷 2.40 – **11 rm** ☷ 15.50/40.00 **t.**

COMBEINTEIGNHEAD Devon – pop. 400 – ✉ Newton Abbot – ☎ 062 687 Shaldon.

◆London 219 – Exeter 19 – ◆Plymouth 34 – Torquay 10.

🏠 **Netherton House** 🍴, TQ12 4RN, W : ¾ m. by B 3195 ℰ 3251, ⌧ heated, 🚗, park – 📺 🛏wc 🅿. 🅭 AE VISA
M (bar lunch) 11.50 **t.** 🍷 2.50 – **10 rm** ☷ 15.00/44.00 **t.** – SB (except summer) 48.00/59.00 **st.**

147

COMBE MARTIN Devon 403 H 30 **The West Country G. – pop. 2,207 – ECD : Wednesday – ✉ Ilfracombe – ☎ 027 188.**

ℹ Sea Cottage, Cross St. ℘ 3319 (summer only).

♦London 218 – Exeter 56 – Taunton 58.

- **Coulsworthy Country House** ⛰, EX34 0PD, SE : 2 ½ m. by A 399 on road to Hunters Inn ℘ 2463, ←, heated, 🌳, 🏸 – TV wc wc P
  closed mid December-January – **M** *(closed for dinner to non-residents)* (bar lunch) 10.25 **t.** 2.30 – **10 rm** 20.00/64.00 **st.**

AUSTIN-ROVER Borough Rd ℘ 2391 — VAUXHALL-OPEL Borough Rd ℘ 3257

COMPTON Surrey 404 **S 30 – see Guildford.**

CONINGSBY Lincs. 402 404 **T 24 – pop. 3,029 – ☎ 0526.**

♦London 134 – ♦Leicester 61 – Lincoln 29 – ♦Nottingham 54.

- XX **Ratty's,** 43 High St., LN4 4RB, ℘ 42285, 🌳 – P. VISA
  closed Sunday and Monday – **M** (lunch by arrangement) 10.00 **t.** 3.50.

CONISTON Cumbria 402 **K 20 – pop. 1,063 – ☎ 0966.**

ℹ 1 Yewdale Rd ℘ 41533.

♦London 285 – ♦Carlisle 55 – Kendal 22 – Lancaster 42.

- **Sun** ⛰, LA21 8HQ, ℘ 41248, ←, 🌳 – wc P. VISA
  March-October – **M** (bar lunch) 11.50 **t.** 3.30 – **10 rm** 16.00/35.00 **t.**

AUSTIN-ROVER Broughton Rd ℘ 253

CONSTANTINE BAY Cornwall 403 **E 32 – see Padstow.**

CONWY Gwynedd 402 403 **I 24 – pop. 12,206 – ECD : Wednesday – ☎ 049 263.**

See : Site★★ – Castle★★ (13C) *AC* **– St. Mary's Church★ 14C.**

Envir. : Sychnant Pass★ W : 2 ½ m.

⛳9 **Penmaenmawr ℘ 0492 (Penmaenmawr) 623330 W : 4 m.**

ℹ Snowdonia National Park, Visitor Centre, Castle St. ℘ 2248.

♦London 241 – Caernarfon 22 – Chester 46 – Holyhead 37.

- **Bryn Cregin Garden,** Ty Mawr Rd, Deganwy, LL31 9UR, NE : 2 m. by A 55 on A 546 ℘ 85266, ←, 🌳 – TV wc wc ☎ P. AE VISA
  closed January-mid February – **M** *(closed Monday and lunch to non-residents in winter)* (bar lunch) 7.50 **t.** 3.10 – **16 rm** 15.00/40.00 **t.** – SB 44.95/49.90 **st.**
- **Castle** (T.H.F.), High St., LL32 8DB, ℘ 2324 – TV wc ☎ P. AE VISA
  M (buffet lunch) 8.50 **st.** 2.85 – 4.75 – **25 rm** 29.50/41.00 **st.**
- **Sychnant Pass,** Synchnant Pass Rd, LL32 8BJ, SW : 1 ¾ m. ℘ 6868, 🌳 – TV wc wc ☎ P. AE VISA
  closed January – **M** 8.00/13.00 **st.** 3.00 – **10 rm** 33.00/48.00 **st.** – SB (summer only) 53.00/63.00 **st.**
- **Castle Bank,** Mount Pleasant, LL32 8NY, ℘ 3888, ← – TV wc P.
  closed January and February – **M** (lunch by arrangement) 5.50/8.00 **t.** 3.50 – **9 rm** 13.00/30.00 **t.** – SB (except summer) 35.00/37.00 **st.**
- **Llys Gwilym,** 3 Mountain Rd (off Cadnant Park), LL32 8PU, ℘ 2351 –
  6 rm 8.00/15.00 **s.**

at Roewen **S : 3 m. by B 5106 – ✉ Conwy – ☎ 049 267 Twyn-y-Groes :**

- **Tir-y-Coed** ⛰, LL32 8TP, ℘ 219, ←, 🌳 – TV wc wc P
  March-October – **8 rm** 13.50/30.00 **t.**

at Tal-y-Bont **S : 5 ¼ m. on B 5106 – ✉ Conwy – ☎ 049 269 Dolgarrog :**

- XX **Lodge** with rm, LL32 8YX, ℘ 534 – TV wc P. AE VISA
  M 5.50/10.00 **t.** 3.00 – **10 rm** 25.00/36.00 **t.** – SB 42.50/47.50 **st.**

COOKHAM Berks. 404 **R 29 – pop. 5,500 – ECD : Wednesday and Thursday – ✉ Maidenhead – ☎ 062 85 Bourne End.**

Envir. : Cliveden House★ 19C (Park★★) *AC* **SE : 2 m.**

⛳18 **Winter Hill, Grange Lane ℘ 27613.**

♦London 36 – High Wycombe 7 – Reading 16.

- X **Cookham Tandoori,** High St., SL6 9SL, ℘ 22584 – AE VISA
  closed 25 and 26 December – **M** a la carte 7.40/16.40 **t.**

CITROEN High St. ℘ 22984

COPDOCK Suffolk 404 **X 27 – see Ipswich.**

COPTHORNE West Sussex 404 **T 30 – see Crawley.**

CORBRIDGE Northumb. 401 402 N 19 – pop. 3,177 – ECD : Thursday – ✆ 043 471.

Envir. : Corstopitum Roman Fort★ *AC*, NW : 1 ½ m.

🆔 Vicar's Pele Tower, Market Pl. ✆ 2815 (summer only).

◆London 300 – Hexham 3 – ◆Newcastle-upon-Tyne 18.

🏛 **Riverside,** Main St., NE45 5LE, ✆ 2942 – 🅿
Mid February-mid November – **M** (dinner only) 8.45 **st.** ⅄ 2.85 – **10 rm** ⌸ 14.75/26.00 **st.**

🏛 **Angel Inn,** Main St., NE45 5LA, ✆ 2119 – 📺 🅿. 🔼 🖭 ⓪ 𝑉𝐼𝑆𝐴
M *(closed Sunday dinner)* 5.00/7.00 **st.** ⅄ 2.45 – **6 rm** ⌸ 15.00/19.80 **st.**

XXX **Ramblers Country House,** Tinklers Bank, Farnley, NE45 5RN, S : 3 ¾ m. on A 68 ✆ 2424,
German rest. – 🅿. 🔼 🖭 ⓪ 𝑉𝐼𝑆𝐴
closed Sunday and Monday – **M** (dinner only) a la carte 11.05/12.45 **t.** ⅄ 2.25.

AUSTIN-ROVER Main St. ✆ 2068

HYUNDAI, SUBARU Stagshaw ✆ 043 472 (Great Whittington) 216

CORNHILL-ON-TWEED Northumb. 401 402 N 17 – pop. 320 – ECD : Thursday – ✆ 0890 Cold-stream.

◆London 345 – ◆Edinburgh 49 – ◆Newcastle-upon-Tyne 59.

🏛 Collingwood Arms, Main St., TD12 4UH, ✆ 2424, 🐎 – 🛁wc 🛏wc ☎ 🅿 – **17 rm**.

BMW, DAIHATSU, SAAB Station Garage ✆ 2146

CORPUSTY Norfolk 404 X 25 – pop. 1,234 – ✉ Heydon – ✆ 026 387 Saxthorpe.

◆London 134 – ◆Cambridge 77 – ◆Norwich 16.

🏛 **Cropton Hall** ⌘, WR11 6RX, S : 1 m. ✆ 869, 🏊, 🐎 – 📺 🛁wc 🛏wc 🅿. 🔼
M (bar lunch) 6.95 **t.** ⅄ 3.50 – **8 rm** ⌸ 15.00/39.00 **t.** – SB 31.00/39.00 **st.**

CORRIS Gwynedd 402 403 I 26 – see Machynlleth (Powys).

CORSE LAWN Heref. and Worc. – see Tewkesbury (Glos.).

CORSHAM Wilts. 403 404 N 29 The West Country G. – pop. 6,360 – ECD : Wednesday – ✆ 0249.

See : Corsham Court★★★.

◆London 110 – ◆Bristol 22 – Swindon 25.

🏛 **Rudloe Park,** Leafy Lane, SN13 0PA, ✆ 810555, ≤, 🐎 – 📺 🛁wc ☎ 🅿. 🔼. 🔼 🖭 ⓪ 𝑉𝐼𝑆𝐴.
⌘
M 6.75/10.50 **t.** ⅄ 3.50 – **8 rm** ⌸ 35.00/60.00 **st.** – SB (weekends only) 68.10/78.10 **st.**

X **Weavers Loft,** 1 High St., SN13 0ES, ✆ 713982 – 🔼 ⓪ 𝑉𝐼𝑆𝐴
closed Sunday dinner, Monday and 2 weeks November – **M** (dinner only and Sunday lunch) a
la carte 8.95/12.55 **st.** ⅄ 3.25.

CORWEN Clwyd 402 403 J 25 – pop. 784 – ✆ 0490.

◆London 202 – Aberystwyth 64 – Chester 32 – Holyhead 67 – Shrewsbury 41.

X **Valentine's,** London Rd, LL21 0DR, ✆ 2838 – 🔼 𝑉𝐼𝑆𝐴
closed Sunday lunch, Tuesday, 2 weeks February and 1 week October – **M** a la carte
12.50/18.70 **t.** ⅄ 2.75.

COSHAM Hants. 403 404 Q 31 – see Portsmouth and Southsea.

COVENTRY West Midlands 403 404 P 26 – pop. 335,238 – ECD : Thursday – ✆ 0203.

See : St. Michael's Cathedral★★★ (1962) : tapestry★★★ AV – Old Cathedral★ (ruins) AV **A** – St. John's Church★ 14C-15C AV **B** – Old houses★ 16C-17C AV DEF.

🏌 City of Coventry, Brandon Lane ✆ 0203 (Wolston) 543141, SE : 6 m – 🏌 Sphinx, Siddeley Av. ✆ 458890 BY.

✈ Coventry Airport : ✆ 301717, S : 3 ½ m. by Coventry Rd BZ.

🆔 36 Broadgate ✆ 20084 and 51717.

◆London 100 – ◆Birmingham 18 – ◆Bristol 96 – ◆Nottingham 52.

Plans on following pages

🏨 **De Vere** (De Vere), Cathedral Sq., CV1 5RP, ✆ 51851, Telex 31380 – 📶 📺. 🔼. 🔼 🖭 ⓪ 𝑉𝐼𝑆𝐴
M a la carte 7.75/15.90 **st.** ⅄ 2.80 – ⌸ 5.00 – **215 rm** 42.00/52.00 **st.**
AV **n**

🏨 **Leofric** (Embassy), Broadgate, CV1 1LZ, ✆ 21371, Telex 311193 – 📶 📺. 🔼. 🔼 🖭 ⓪ 𝑉𝐼𝑆𝐴.
⌘
M *(closed Saturday lunch)* 7.75/8.75 **st.** ⅄ 4.75 – ⌸ 4.25 – **90 rm** 39.00/49.00 **st.** – SB (week-
ends only) 45.00/52.00 **st.**
AV **c**

🏠 **Fairlight,** 14 Regent St., CV1 3EP, ✆ 24215 – 🅿
AV **i**
11 rm ⌸ 9.00/16.00 **s.**

🏠 **Croft,** 23 Stoke Green, off Binley Rd, CV3 1FP, ✆ 457846, 🐎 – 🅿. ⌘
BY **x**
12 rm ⌸ 13.00/27.00 **st.**

149

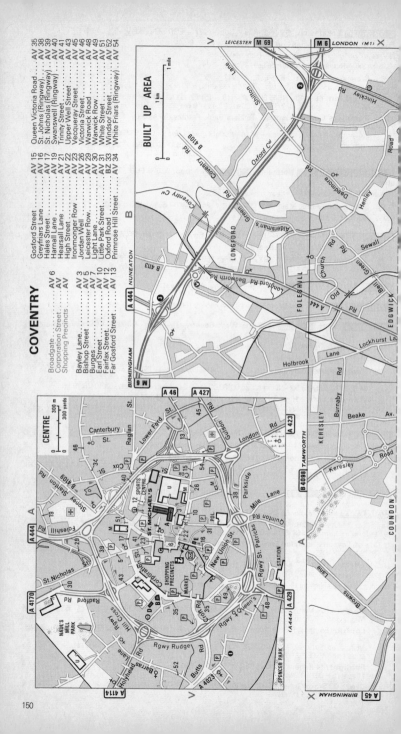

COVENTRY

Broadgate	AV 6
Corporation Street	AV
Shopping Precincts	AV
Bayley Lane	AV 3
Bishop Street	AV 5
Burges	AV 7
Earl Street	AV 10
Fairfax Street	AV 12
Far Gosford Street	AV 13

Gosford Street	AV 15
Greyfriars Lane	AV 16
Hales Street	AV 18
Harnall Lane	AV 19
Hearsall Lane	AV 21
High Street	AV 22
Ironmonger Row	AV 23
Jordan Well	AV 26
Leicester Row	AV 29
Light Lane	AV 30
Little Park Street	AV 31
Oxford Road	BZ 33
Primrose Hill Street	AV 34

Queen Victoria Road	AV 35
St. Nicholas (Rignway)	AV 38
St. Nicholas (Ringway)	AV 39
Swanswell (Ringway)	AV 40
Trinity Street	AV 41
Upper Well Street	AV 43
Vecqueray Street	AV 45
Victoria Street	AV 46
Warwick Road	AV 48
Warwick Row	AV 49
White Street	AV 51
Windsor Street	AV 52
White Friars (Ringway)	AV 54

150

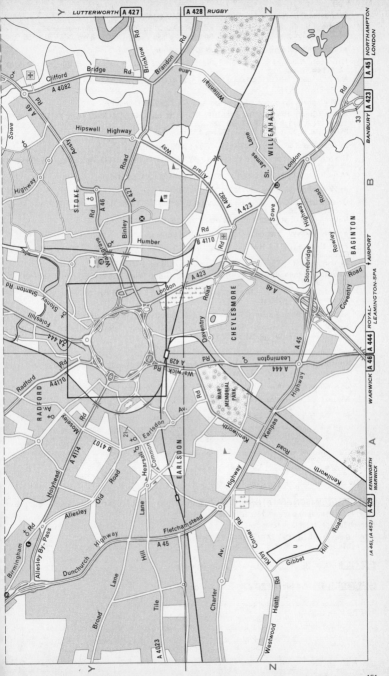

XX **Grandstand**, Coventry F.C., King Richard St., CV2 4FW, ℰ 27053 – 🅿

BY **a**

X **Herbs** with rm, 28 Lower Holyhead Rd, CV1 3AU, ℰ 555654, Vegetarian rest. – ⌖   AV **o**
M *(closed Sunday dinner)* (dinner only) a la carte 5.45/7.50 **t.** ₳ 2.00 – **8 rm** ⊊ 11.50/18.50 **t.**

at Longford N : 4 m. on A 444 – ✉ ✪ 0203 Coventry :

🏨 **Novotel**, Wilsons Lane, CV6 6HL, ℰ 365000, Telex 31545, ⊒ heated – 🛗 📺 🛁wc ☎ 🕭 🅿
🛔 🔌 AE ⓞ VISA   BV **v**
M a la carte 10.00/12.00 **st.** ₳ 3.50 – ⊊ 4.00 – **99 rm** 35.00/42.00 **st.** – SB (week-ends only) 41.00 **st.**

at Walsgrave on Sowe NE : 3 m. on A 46 – ✉ ✪ 0203 Coventry :

🏨 **Crest** (Crest), Hinckley Rd, CV2 2HP, NE : ½ m. on A 46 ℰ 613261, Telex 311292 – 🛗 📺
🛁wc 📾 🕭 🅿 🛔 🔌 AE ⓞ VISA ⌖   BX **e**
M approx. 11.00 **st.** – ⊊ 5.25 – **160 rm** 42.00/53.00 **st.**

at Brandon E : 6 m. by A 428 – BZ – ✉ ✪ 0203 Coventry :

🏨 **Brandon Hall** (T.H.F.), Main St., CV8 3FW, ℰ 542571, Telex 31472, 🐎, park – 📺 🛁wc 📾
🅿 🛔 🔌 AE ⓞ VISA
M (buffet lunch) 9.50 **st.** ₳ 2.85 – ⊊ 5.00 – **68 rm** 21.50/41.50 **st.**

at Willenhall SE : 3 m. on A 423 – ✉ ✪ 0203 Coventry :

🏨 **Chace Crest** (Crest), London Rd, CV3 4EQ, ℰ 303398, Telex 311993, 🐎 – 📺 🛁wc 📾 🅿
🛔 🔌 AE ⓞ VISA   BZ **u**
M approx. 11.00 **st.** – ⊊ 4.95 – **68 rm** 38.50/48.50 **st.**

at Allesley NW : 3 m. on A 4114 – ✉ ✪ 0203 Coventry :

🏨 **Post House** (T.H.F.), Rye Hill, CV5 9PH, ℰ 402151, Telex 31427 – 🛗 📺 🛁wc ☎ 🅿 🛔 🔌
AE ⓞ VISA   AXY **s**
M (carving rest.) 5.75/6.50 **st.** ₳ 2.60 – ⊊ 5.00 – **196 rm** 35.00/42.50 **st.**

🏨 **Allesley**, Birmingham Rd, CV5 9GT, ℰ 403272, Group Telex 312549 – 📺 🛁wc 🍴 📾 🅿 🛔
🔌 AE ⓞ VISA 🕭   AY **r**
closed Christmas Day – **M** (bar lunch) 7.50/8.75 **t.** ₳ 3.45 – **37 rm** ⊊ 18.70/38.50 **st.** – SB (weekends only) 49.80 **st.**

at Keresley NW : 3 m. on B 4098 – AX – ✉ Coventry – ✪ 0203 Keresley :

🏨 **Royal Court**, Tamworth Rd, CV7 8JG, ℰ 334171, Group Telex 312549, 🐎, ⌖ – 🛗 📺
🛁wc 🍴wc 🕭 🅿 🛔 🔌 AE ⓞ VISA ⌖
closed Christmas Day – **M** 7.50/8.20 ₳ 3.45 – **99 rm** ⊊ 25.00/44.00 **st.** – SB (week-ends only) 40.40 **st.**

🏩 **Beechwood**, Sandpits Lane, CV6 2FR, ℰ 334243, 🐎 – 📺 🍴wc 🅿 🔌 AE ⓞ VISA
M approx. 8.50 **t.** ₳ 1.90 – **27 rm.**

at Meriden NW : 6 m. by A 45 on B 4102 – AX – ✉ Coventry – ✪ 0676 Meriden :

🏨 **Manor** (De Vere), Main Rd, CV7 7NH, ℰ 22735, Telex 311011, ⊒ heated, 🐎 – 📺 🛁wc 📾
🅿 🛔 🔌 AE ⓞ VISA
M 7.50/8.50 **st.** ₳ 2.45 – ⊊ 5.00 – **32 rm** 34.00/44.00 **st.** – SB (weekends only) 50.00/56.00 **st.**

AUSTIN-ROVER Lockhurst Lane ℰ 88851
AUSTIN-ROVER-DAIMLER-JAGUAR-LAND ROVER
Kenpas Highway ℰ 411515
BMW 138 Sutherland Av. ℰ 461441
CITROEN 105 Foleshill Rd ℰ 26417
FIAT 324 Station Rd Balsall Common ℰ 0676
(Berkswell) 33145
HONDA 207 Wheelwright Lane, Exhall ℰ 364004

NISSAN 149 Far Gosford St. ℰ 24552
PEUGEOT-TALBOT 136 Daventry Rd ℰ 503522
RELIANT, SKODA 142 Lower Ford St. ℰ 20475
RENAULT 181-6 Walsgrave Rd ℰ 458600
TOYOTA Bennetts Rd, Keresley ℰ 334204
VAUXHALL-OPEL Raglan St. ℰ 25361
VW, AUDI Spon End ℰ 56325

COWBRIDGE (BONT-FAEN) South Glam. 𝟰𝟬𝟯 J 29 – pop. 1,224 – ECD : Wednesday – ✪ 044 63.
Envir. : Old Beaupré Castle★ 14C, SE : 3 m.
♦London 169 – ♦Cardiff 12 – ♦Swansea 27.

🏨 **Bear**, High St., CF7 7AF, ℰ 4814 – 📺 🛁wc ☎ 🅿 🛔 🔌 AE VISA
M (bar lunch) 6.95 **st.** ₳ 3.00 – **31 rm** ⊊ 19.50/32.00 **t.** – SB (weekends only) 21.00/25.00 **st.**

COWES I.O.W. 𝟰𝟬𝟯 𝟰𝟬𝟰 PQ 31 – see Wight (Isle of).

COYCHURCH Mid Glam. 𝟰𝟬𝟯 J 29 – see Bridgend.

CRACKINGTON HAVEN Cornwall [403] G 31 **The West Country G.** – pop. 380 – ECD : Tuesday – ✉ Bude – ☎ 084 03 St. Gennys.

♦London 262 – Bude 11 – Truro 42.

- 🏨 **Crackington Manor** 🌙, EX23 0JG, ☎ 397, 🏊 heated, 🌳 – 🛁wc Ⓟ. [AE] [VISA]
  closed January-mid March – **M** (bar lunch Monday to Saturday) 9.50 **t.** 🍷 1.70 – **15 rm** ☕ 22.50/23.50 **t.** – SB (except summer) 32.00 **st.**
- 🏨 Coombe Barton, EX23 0JG, ☎ 345, ≤ – 🛁wc Ⓟ – **10 rm**.

CRANBROOK Kent [404] V 30 – pop. 5,326 – ECD : Wednesday – ☎ 058 04 (4 fig.) or 0580 (6 fig.).

Envir. : Sissinghurst : castle★ 16C (≤★, 78 steps), gardens★★ *AC* NE : 1 ½ m.

⛳ Benenden Rd ☎ 712833.

ℹ Vestry Hall, Stone St. ☎ 712538 (summer only).

♦London 53 – Hastings 19 – Maidstone 15.

- 🏨 **Willesley,** Angley Rd, TN17 2LE, N : ¾ m. on B 2189 at junction with A 229 ☎ 713555, 🌳 – [TV] 🛁wc ☎ Ⓟ. [AE] [VISA]
  closed first week February – **M** 6.00/9.50 **st.** 🍷 2.75 – **16 rm** ☕ 27.50/44.00 **st.** – SB 58.00/62.00 **st.**
- 🏨 **Kennel Holt** 🌙, Flishinghurst, TN17 2PT, NW : 2 ¼ m. by A 229 on A 262 ☎ 712032, ≤, « Country house atmosphere and gardens » – [TV] 🛁wc Ⓟ. 🚫🐕
  closed 3 to 28 January – **M** (restricted lunch residents only) (booking essential) 10.50 **t.** – **7 rm** ☕ 17.00/53.00 **st.** – SB (winter only) 51.00/57.00 **st.**

AUSTIN-ROVER Cranbrook Rd, Staplehurst ☎ 892093
FORD Stone St. ☎ 712121
RENAULT Wisley Pound ☎ 713262

CRANTOCK Cornwall [403] E 32 – see Newquay.

During the season, particularly in resorts, it is wise to book in advance. However, if you find you cannot take up a hotel booking you have made, please let the hotel know immediately.
If you are writing to a hotel abroad enclose an International Reply Coupon (available from Post Offices.)

CRAWLEY West Sussex [404] T 30 – pop. 73,000 – ECD : Wednesday – ☎ 0293.

⛳ Cottesmore, Buchan Hill ☎ 28256, S : 4 m. AZ – ⛳ Gatwick Manor ☎ 24470, N : 5 m. AY.

ℹ Arrivals Concourse, 2nd Floor Terminal Building ☎ 502042.

♦London 33 – ♦Brighton 21 – Lewes 23 – Royal Tunbridge Wells 23.

Plans on following pages

- 🏨 **George** (T.H.F.), High St., RH10 1BS, ☎ 24215, Telex 87385 – [TV] 🛁wc ☎ Ⓟ. 🏛 [AE] [VISA] — BZ **o**
  M 6.95/9.00 **st.** 🍷 2.60 – ☕ 5.50 – **76 rm** 37.50/45.00 **st.**
- 🏨 **Crest** (Crest), Langley Drive, Tushmore Roundabout, RH11 7SX, ☎ 29991, Telex 877311 – [lift] [TV] 🛁wc ☎ Ⓟ. 🏛 [AE] [VISA]. 🚫🐕 — BY **n**
  M approx. 11.00 **st.** – ☕ 5.25 – **230 rm** 43.00/53.00 **st.**
- 🏨 Goffs Park, 45 Goffs Park Rd, RH11 8AX, ☎ 35447, 🌳 – [TV] 🛁wc 🚿wc ☎ Ⓟ. [AE] [VISA] **47 rm**. — BZ **s**
- 🏨 **Grange,** 15 Brighton Rd, RH10 6AE, ☎ 35191 – [TV] 🚿wc ☎ Ⓟ. [AE] [VISA]. 🚫🐕 — BZ **a**
  M (dinner only) 7.50 **t.** 🍷 3.00 – **40 rm** ☕ 23.00/35.00.

at Lowfield Heath N : 2 m. by A 23 – ✉ ☎ 0293 Crawley :

- 🏨 **Gatwick Concorde** (Q.M.H.), Church Lane, RH11 0PQ, ☎ 33441, Telex 87287 – [lift] [TV] ♿ Ⓟ. [AE] [VISA] — AY **i**
  M 6.50/8.95 **st.** 🍷 3.00 – ☕ 4.25 – **92 rm** 38.50/49.50 **st.** – SB (weekends only) 29.50/31.50 **st.**

at Copthorne NE : 4 ½ m. on A 264 – AY – ✉ Crawley – ☎ 0342 Copthorne :

- 🏨 **Copthorne,** Copthorne Rd, RH10 3PG, ☎ 714971, Telex 95500, 🌳, park, squash – [TV] ☎ ♿ Ⓟ. 🏛 [AE] [VISA]
  M a la carte 15.55/24.35 **t.** 🍷 3.75 – ☕ 5.00 – **221 rm** 45.25/57.00 – SB (weekends only) 51.00 **st.**

at Pound Hill E : 3 m. by A 264 on B 2036 – ✉ ☎ 0293 Crawley :

- 🏨 **Barnwood,** Balcombe Rd, RH10 4RU, ☎ 882709, Telex 877005, 🌳 – [TV] 🚿wc ☎ Ⓟ. [AE] [VISA]. 🚫🐕 — AZ **a**
  M (grill rest. only)(bar lunch) 4.85/7.80 🍷 1.50 – **30 rm** ☕ 24.00/38.00 **t.**

AUSTIN-ROVER Copthorne ☎ 713933
BEDFORD, OPEL-VAUXHALL Fleming Way ☎ 29771
CITROEN 163/165 Three Bridges Rd ☎ 25533
FORD Worth Park Av., Three Bridges ☎ 28381
PEUGEOT-TALBOT Barton ☎ 543232
RENAULT Orchard St. ☎ 23323
SAAB Turners Hill ☎ 715467
SKODA Balcombe Rd ☎ 882620
VW, AUDI Overdene Way ☎ 515551

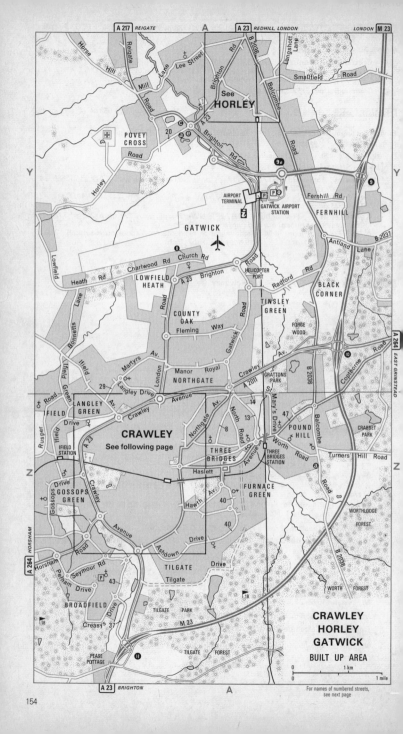

CRAWLEY
HORLEY
GATWICK

BUILT UP AREA

For names of numbered streets,
see next page

154

CRAWLEY
HORLEY
GATWICK

Broad Walk............. **BZ** 2
High Street............. **BYZ**
Queens Square......... **BZ** 22
The Broadway.......... **BZ**
The Martlets........... **BZ**

Buckmans Road .... **BY** 3
Caffins Close .... **BY** 4
College Road .... **BZ** 6
Crossways .... **AZ** 8
Drake Road .... **BZ** 10
Exchange Road .... **BY** 12
Hazelwick Avenue .... **AZ** 13
Hazelwick Mill Lane ...... **AZ** 14
Hunter Road............. **BZ** 15
Livingstone Road .... **BZ** 18
Orchard Street........... **BZ** 19
Povey Cross Road........ **AY** 20

Queensway .... **BZ** 24
Southgate Road .... **BZ** 28
Stagelands................ **AY** 29
Station Road .... **BZ** 30
The Boulevard .... **BZ** 32
Titmus Drive............. **BZ** 34
Tollgate Hill .... **AZ** 37
Weald Drive............. **AZ** 40
West Street .... **BZ** 42
Woodmans Hill .... **AZ** 43
Woolborough Road .... **BY** 45
Worth Park Avenue........ **AZ** 47

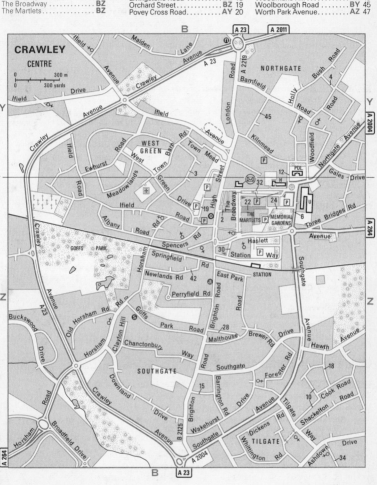

CREWE Cheshire 402 403 404 M 24 – pop. 51,421 – ECD : Wednesday – ✆ 0270.
Envir. : Sandbach (Two Crosses★ 7C, in Market Place) NE : 10 m.
🚗 ✆ 214343.
🅷 Delamere House, Delamere St., ✆ 583191.
♦London 174 – Chester 24 – ♦Liverpool 49 – ♦Manchester 36 – ♦Stoke-on-Trent 15.

🏨 **Crewe Arms** (Embassy), Nantwich Rd, CW1 1DW, ✆ 213204 – 📺 🛏wc 🕿 🅿 🚗 🅰🅴
   ⑴ 𝚅𝙸𝚂𝙰 ⚡
   M a la carte 8.35/15.00 **st.** ⑂ 4.00 – ☲ 4.25 – **36 rm** 29.50/38.00 **st.**

ALFA-ROMEO Newcastle Rd ✆ 665138
AUSTIN-ROVER Hough ✆ 841320
AUSTIN-ROVER High St. ✆ 256521
CITROEN Woolstanwood ✆ 213495
FORD Macon Way ✆ 583511
LADA Stewart St. ✆ 67560
MAZDA West St. ✆ 214317

NISSAN Cross Green ✆ 583437
PEUGEOT, TALBOT 613 Crewe Rd, Wistaston ✆ 664111
RENAULT Nantwich Rd ✆ 257392
VOLVO Earle St. ✆ 587711
VW, AUDI Oak St. ✆ 213241

CREWKERNE Somerset 403 L 31 The West Country G. – pop. 4,821 – ECD : Thursday – ✆ 0460.
♦London 145 – Exeter 38 – ♦Southampton 81 – Taunton 20.

🏨 **Old Parsonage,** 55-59 Barn St., TA18 8BP, ✆ 73516 – 📺 🛏wc 🕸wc 🅿 🚗 🅰🅴 ⑴ 𝚅𝙸𝚂𝙰
   M (closed Sunday to non-residents) 6.50/10.50 **t.** ⑂ 2.00 – **10 rm** ☲ 16.00/34.00 **t.** – SB (week-ends only) 33.50/38.50 **st.**

   at Haselbury Plucknett NE : 2 ¾ m. by A 30 on A 3066 – ✉ ✆ 0460 Crewkerne :

↑ **Oak House,** North St., TA18 7RB, ✆ 73625, « 16C thatched cottage », 🌧 – 🅿
   April-October – **7 rm** ☲ 11.00/22.00 **st.**

CRICCIETH Gwynedd 402 403 H 25 – pop. 1,505 – ECD : Wednesday – ✆ 076 671.
See : Castle ≤★★ AC.
🅷 Ednyfed Hill ✆ 2154.
♦London 249 – Caernarfon 17 – Shrewsbury 85.

🏨 **Bron Eifion Country House** 🦢, LL52 0SA, W : ½ m. on A 497 ✆ 2385, ≤, « 19C country house in large garden », park – 🛏wc 🕸wc 🕿 🅿 🚗
   closed first 3 weeks February – **M** 6.50/11.00 **st.** ⑂ 3.50 – **24 rm** ☲ (dinner included) 31.50/73.00 **st.** – SB (winter only) 44.00/60.00 **st.**

🏨 **Plas Isa,** Porthmadog Rd, LL52 0HP, ✆ 2443 – 📺 🛏wc 🕿 🅿 🚗 🅰🅴 ⑴ 𝚅𝙸𝚂𝙰 ⚡
   M (bar lunch) 6.20 **t.** ⑂ 2.75 – **12 rm** ☲ 16.75/33.50 **t.** – SB (except summer) 42.00 **st.**

↑ **Glyn-y-Coed,** Portmadoc Rd, LL52 0HL, ✆ 2870 – 🅿
   closed Christmas and New Year – **10 rm** ☲ 10.00/20.00 **t.**

❌❌ **Moelwyn** with rm, 27-29 Mona Terr., LL52 0HG, ✆ 2500, ≤ – 🚗 𝚅𝙸𝚂𝙰 ⚡
   April-December – **M** (closed Sunday lunch) a la carte 6.80/11.10 **t.** ⑂ 2.75 – **7 rm** ☲ 8.50/17.00 **t.** – SB (September-December) 28.00/35.00 **st.**

AUDI, MERCEDES-BENZ, VW Caernarfon Rd ✆ 2516
FIAT Ala Rd, Pwllheli ✆ 612827

VOLVO Llanystumdwy ✆ 2733

CRICK Northants. 403 404 Q 26 – see Rugby.

CRICKHOWELL Powys 403 K 28 – pop. 1,286 – ECD : Wednesday – ✆ 0873.
Envir. : Tretower Court and Castle★, NW : 2 ½ m.
♦London 169 – Abergavenny 6 – Brecon 14 – Newport 25.

🏨 **Gliffaes Country House** 🦢, NP8 1RH, W : 3 ¾ m. by A 40 ✆ 0874 (Bwlch) 730371, ≤, « Garden », 🏞, park, ⚹ – 🛏wc 🕸wc 🅿 🚗 🅰🅴 𝚅𝙸𝚂𝙰 ⚡
   closed January-mid March – **M** (bar lunch) 8.50 **st.** ⑂ 2.50 – **19 rm** ☲ 17.30/46.20 **st.** – SB 52.50/72.40 **st.**

🏨 **Bear,** High St., NP8 1BW, ✆ 810408, 🌧 – 🛏wc 🕸wc 🅿 🚗
   M (bar lunch) a la carte 9.45/11.65 **t.** ⑂ 3.40 – **12 rm** ☲ 16.00/27.00.

AUSTIN-ROVER 16 Church St. ✆ 512203
FORD 2 Beach Rd ✆ 513181

RENAULT Cabbell Rd ✆ 512557

CROOKLANDS Cumbria 402 L 21 – see Kendal.

CROSBY-ON-EDEN Cumbria 401 402 L 29 – see Carlisle.

CROWBOROUGH East Sussex 404 U 30 – pop. 11,540 – ECD : Wednesday – ✆ 089 26.
♦London 45 – ♦Brighton 25 – Maidstone 26.

🏨 **Crest,** Beacon Rd, TN6 1AD, on A 26 ✆ 2772 – 🔀 📺 🛏wc 🕸wc 🕿 🅿 🚗 🅰🅴 ⑴ 𝚅𝙸𝚂𝙰
   M 7.00/8.00 **t.** ⑂ 2.75 – **30 rm** ☲ 22.00/46.20 **st.** – SB 48.00/52.00 **st.**

AUSTIN-ROVER Beacon Rd ✆ 2777
FORD Crowborough Hill ✆ 2175

TALBOT Church Rd ✆ 3424

CROWTHORNE Berks. 404 R 29 – pop. 7,964 – ✉ 🕲 0344.
♦London 42 – Reading 15.

🏨 **Waterloo** (Anchor), Dukes Ride, RG11 7NW, on B 3348 ☎ 777711, Telex 848139, 🐎 – 📺
⌂wc 🛁wc ☎ ℗ 🏥 🅰 🆎 ⓪ 𝘝𝘐𝘚𝘈
M (bar lunch Saturday) a la carte 8.10/12.75 **st.** ⓭ 2.65 – **54 rm** ⌚ 40.00/47.00 – SB (weekends only) 46.00 **st.**

CRUDWELL Wilts. 403 404 N 29 – see Malmesbury.

CRUG-Y-BAR Dyfed 403 I 27 – pop. 200 – ECD : Saturday – ✉ Llanwrda – 🕲 055 83 Talley.
♦London 213 – Carmarthen 26 – ♦Swansea 36.

🏚 **Glanrannell Park** ⬙, SA19 8SA, SW : ½ m. by B 4302 ☎ 230, ≼, 🐟, 🐎, park – ⌂wc ℗
April-October – **M** (bar lunch) 8.50 **t.** ⓭ 2.80 – **8 rm** ⌚ 14.00/31.00 **t.**

CUCKFIELD West Sussex 404 T 30 – pop. 2,694 – ECD : Wednesday – 🕲 0444 Haywards
Heath – ♦London 40 – ♦Brighton 15.

🏨 **Ockenden Manor,** Ockenden Lane, RH17 5LD, ☎ 416111, « Part 16C manor », 🐎 – 📺
⌂wc ☎ ℗ 🏥 🅰 ⓪ 𝘝𝘐𝘚𝘈 🌂
M 8.50/12.50 **t.** ⓭ 3.25 – ⌚ 5.50 – **10 rm** 35.00/75.00 **t.** – SB (weekends only) 77.00 **st.**

CUFFLEY Herts. 404 T 28 – pop. 4,450 – ECD : Thursday – 🕲 0707 Potter's Bar.
♦London 16 – ♦Cambridge 44 – Luton 26.

🏩 **Ponsbourne** ⬙, Ponsbourne Park, Newgate St., SG13 8QZ, N : 3 m. by B 157 ☎ 875221,
Telex 299912, ≼, ⬛, 🐎, park, ⬤ – 📺 ℗ 🏥 🅰 🆎 ⓪ 𝘝𝘐𝘚𝘈
closed 5 April – **M** *(closed Sunday dinner)* 10.00/15.00 **t.** – **32 rm** ⌚ 33.00/44.00 **t.**

CULLINGWORTH West Yorks. 402 O 22 – see Bingley.

CUMNOR Oxon. 403 404 P 28 – see Oxford.

CWMBRAN Gwent 403 K 29 – pop. 45,000 – ECD : Wednesday – 🕲 063 33.
🏌₉ Greenmeadow, Treherbert Rd ☎ 69321 – ♦London 149 – ♦Bristol 35 – ♦Cardiff 17 – Newport 5.

🏨 **Commodore,** Mill Lane, Llan-yr-Afon, NP44 8SN, ☎ 4091 – 🛗 📺 ⌂wc 🛁wc ☎ ℗ 🏥 🅰
🆎 ⓪ 𝘝𝘐𝘚𝘈
M (carving rest.)(bar lunch Monday to Saturday) 3.25/7.60 **st.** ⓭ 3.50 – **60 rm** ⌚ 19.50/37.50 **st.**
– SB 37.00/40.50 **st.**

DALLINGTON East Sussex 404 V 31 – pop. 286 – ✉ Heathfield – 🕲 042 482 Brightling.
♦London 59 – ♦Brighton 26 – Hastings 14 – Maidstone 34.

✗ **Little Byres** with rm, Christmas Farm, Battle Rd, TN21 9LE, on B 2096 ☎ 230 – 📺 🛁wc ♿
℗ 🏥 🌂
closed January – **M** *(closed Sunday dinner)* (dinner only and Sunday lunch) 7.25/10.00 **t.** ⓭ 2.50
– **5 rm** 24.00 **t.** – SB 33.00/40.00 **st.**

DALTON North Yorks. 402 P 31 – pop. 120 – ✉ Richmond – 🕲 0833 Teesdale.
♦London 250 – ♦Carlisle 66 – ♦Leeds 60 – ♦Middlesbrough 31 – ♦Newcastle-upon-Tyne 48.

✗ **Traveller's Rest,** DL11 7HU, ☎ 21225 – ℗ 🏥 𝘝𝘐𝘚𝘈
closed Sunday – **M** (dinner only) a la carte 5.60/11.05 **t.** ⓭ 2.95.

DARESBURY Cheshire 402 403 404 M 23 – pop. 330 – ✉ 🕲 0925 Warrington.
♦London 197 – Chester 16 – ♦Liverpool 22 – ♦Manchester 25.

🏨 **Lord Daresbury,** Chester Rd, WA4 4BB, on A 56 ☎ 67331, Telex 629330 – 🛗 📺 ⌂wc ☎
♿ ℗ 🏥 🅰 🆎 ⓪ 𝘝𝘐𝘚𝘈
M 8.50 **st.** ⓭ 3.00 – **141 rm** ⌚ 36.00/46.00 **st.** – SB (weekends only) 50.00 **st.**

DARLINGTON Durham 402 P 20 – pop. 85,938 – ECD : Wednesday – 🕲 0325.
🏌₁₈ Blackwell Grange, Briar Close ☎ 64464 S : 1 m. on A 66 – 🏌 Stressholme, Snipe Lane, ☎ 53073,
S : 2 m – ✈ Tees-side Airport : ☎ 332811, E : 6 m. by A 67.
🛈 Branch Library, Crown St. ☎ 469858.
♦London 251 – ♦Leeds 61 – ♦Middlesbrough 14 – ♦Newcastle-upon-Tyne 35.

🏩 **Blackwell Grange Moat House** (Q.M.H.) ⬙, Blackwell Grange, DL3 8QH, SW : 2 m. on
A 66 ☎ 460111, Telex 587272, 🐎 – 🛗 📺 ⌂wc ☎ ℗ 🏥 🅰 🆎 ⓪ 𝘝𝘐𝘚𝘈
M 7.25/8.95 **st.** ⓭ 2.80 – **96 rm** ⌚ 32.00/47.00 **st.** – SB (weekends only) 44.00 **st.**

🏨 **King's Head** (Swallow), Priestgate, DL1 1NW, ☎ 467612, Group Telex 53168 – 🛗 📺 ⌂wc
☎ ℗ 🏥 🅰 🆎 ⓪ 𝘝𝘐𝘚𝘈

🏨 **Stakis White Horse** (Stakis), Harrowgate Hill, DL1 3AD, N : 2 ¼ m. on A 167 ☎ 487111 – 🛗
📺 ⌂wc ☎ ℗ 🏥 🅰 🆎 ⓪ 𝘝𝘐𝘚𝘈
M 8.00/9.00 **t.** ⓭ 2.70 – **40 rm** ⌚ 32.00/40.00 **t.** – SB 50.00/60.00 **st.**

✗✗ **Bishop's House,** 38 Coniscliffe Rd, DL3 7RG, ☎ 286666 – 🏥 🆎 𝘝𝘐𝘚𝘈
*closed Saturday lunch, Sunday, last week May, first week June, 15 December-3 January and
Bank Holidays* – **M** 5.95/11.50 **t.** ⓭ 3.50.

at Coatham Mundeville N : 4 m. by A 167 – ✉ Darlington – ☺ 0325 Aycliffe :

🏛 Hall Garth Country House ⌕, DL1 3LU, ☎ 313333, « Country house atmosphere », ⅃ heated, 🎇 – 🖵 ➩wc ⋔wc ☏ **P**. 🖾 AE ⓪ **VISA**
closed 5 and 6 May – **19 rm**.

at Tees-side Airport E : 5 ½ m. by A 67 – ✉ ☺ 0325 Darlington :

🏛 St. George (Mt. Charlotte), DL2 1RH, ☎ 332631, Telex 58664, ✵, squash – 🖵 ➩wc ☏ **P**.
🖄. 🖾 AE ⓪ **VISA** – **58 rm**.

at Neasham SE : 6 ½ m. by A 66 off A 167 – ✉ ☺ 0325 Darlington :

🏛 **Newbus Arms** ⌕, DL2 1PE, W : ½ m. ☎ 721071, 🐎, squash – 🖵 ➩wc ☏ **P**. 🖄. 🖾 AE
⓪ **VISA** ⌕.
M a la carte 10.00/13.30 **st.** 🍷 3.00 – **15 rm** ⌑ 30.00/38.00 **st.**

AUSTIN-ROVER-DAIMLER-JAGUAR Croft Rd ☎ 62728	SAAB Grange Rd. ☎ 465343
CITROEN, COLT 163 Northgate ☎ 68753	TOYOTA Neasham Rd. ☎ 482141
FIAT Woodland Rd ☎ 483251	VAUXHALL Chestnut St. ☎ 66155
FORD St. Cuthberts Way ☎ 67581	VAUXHALL-OPEL Whessoe Rd ☎ 66044
LADA Albert Rd ☎ 485759	VW, AUDI 28/56 West Auckland Rd, Faverdale ☎ 53737
PEUGEOT-TALBOT Feethams ☎ 481948	YUGO Haughton Rd ☎ 63384
RENAULT Chestnut St. ☎ 485141	

DARRINGTON West Yorks. 🗚🗚🗚 Q 22 – pop. 1,095 – ☺ 0977 Pontefract.
♦London 184 – Doncaster 12 – ♦Leeds 18.

🏛 **Darrington,** Great North Rd, WF8 3BL, on A 1 ☎ 791458 – 🖵 ➩wc ⋔wc ☏ **P**. 🖄. 🖾 AE
⓪ **VISA**
M a la carte 6.40/10.50 **t.** 🍷 2.85 – **29 rm** ⌑ 21.00/36.00 – SB (weekends only) 39.50/49.50 **st.**

DARTINGTON Devon 🗚🗚🗚 I 32 – see Totnes.

DARTMOUTH Devon 🗚🗚🗚 J 32 The West Country G. – pop. 5,707 – ECD : Wednesday and Saturday – ☺ 080 43.
See : Site** (≤*) – Dartmouth Castle (≤***).
🗓 The Guildhall, Victoria St. ☎ 2281.
♦London 236 – Exeter 36 – ♦Plymouth 35.

🏛 **Dart Marina** (T.H.F.), Sandquay, TQ6 9PH, ☎ 2580, ≤ – 🖵 ➩wc ☏ **P**. 🖾 AE ⓪ **VISA**
M 8.80/13.00 **st.** 🍷 2.85 – ⌑ 5.00 – **35 rm** 22.50/44.00 **st.**

🏛 Royal Castle, 11 The Quay, TQ6 9PS, ☎ 2397 – 🖵 ➩wc ⟜
20 rm.

🏛 **Gunfield,** Castle Rd, TQ6 9JN, ☎ 2896, ≤ Dart estuary, 🐎 – ➩wc 🖾 AE ⓪ **VISA**
M 4.00 **t.** 🍷 3.00 – **11 rm** ⌑ 15.00/30.00 **t.** – SB (winter only) 40.00 **st.**

⌂ **Townstal Farm,** Townstal Rd, N : 1 m. on A 379 ☎ 2300, 🐎 – ☏
7 rm ⌑ 16.00/19.00.

XX ☺ **Carved Angel,** 2 South Embankment, TQ6 9BB, ☎ 2465, ≤ – 🖾 **VISA**
closed Sunday dinner, Monday and January – **M** a la carte 11.00/13.00 **st.** 🍷 3.50
Spec. Fish tart with a soufflé sauce, Salmon with Samphire and champagne (April-August), Fruit in a honey saffron custard.

at Strete SW : 6 m. on A 379 – ✉ Dartmouth – ☺ 080 427 Stoke Fleming :

X **Laughing Monk,** TQ6 0RN, ☎ 770639 – ☏. 🖾 AE ⓪ **VISA**
closed Sunday to Tuesday during winter and 3 to 17 January – **M** (dinner only)(booking essential in winter) a la carte 8.30/9.90 **t.** 🍷 2.25.

DAWLISH Devon 🗚🗚🗚 J 32 The West Country G. – pop. 9,519 – ECD : Thursday and Saturday – ☺ 0626.
🎱 Warren ☎ 862255, E : 1 ½ m.
🗓 The Lawn ☎ 863589 and 865985.
♦London 215 – Exeter 13 – ♦Plymouth 40 – Torquay 11.

🏛 **Langstone Cliff** ⌕, Dawlish Warren, EX7 0NA, N : 2 m. by A 379 ☎ 865155, ⅃ heated, 🖾,
🐎, ✵ – 🍴 🖵 ➩wc ☏ ⚿ **P**. 🖄. 🖾 AE ⓪ **VISA**
March-October – **M** 6.00/8.00 **st.** 🍷 2.80 – **70 rm** ⌑ 15.00/44.00 **st.**

⌂ **Lynbridge,** 8 Barton Villas, The Bartons, EX7 9QJ, ☎ 862352, 🐎 – ☏. ✾
April-September – **8 rm** ⌑ 8.00/16.00 **st.**

DEDDINGTON Oxon. 🗚🗚🗚 🗚🗚🗚 Q 28 – pop. 1,464 – ☺ 0869.
♦London 72 – ♦Birmingham 46 – ♦Coventry 33 – ♦Oxford 18.

⌂ **Maunds Farm,** High St., OX5 4SL, ☎ 38569, 🐎 – ☏. ✾
closed Christmas – **8 rm** ⌑ 8.50/17.00 **st.**

DEDHAM Essex **404** X 28 – pop. 1,641 – ECD : Wednesday – ✉ ✆ 0206 Colchester.

🛈 Countryside Centre, Duchy Barn, The Drift ✆ 323447 (summer only).

♦London 63 – Chelmsford 30 – Colchester 8 – ♦Ipswich 12.

🏨 **Maison Talbooth** ⌖ without rest., Stratford Rd, CO7 6HN, W : ½ m. ✆ 322367, ≤, 🐾 –
📺 🅿 🔁 *VISA*
⊑ 3.50 – **10 rm** 45.00/90.00 **st.**

🏛 ❀ **Le Talbooth**, Gun Hill, CO7 6HP, W : 1 m. ✆ 323150, ≤, « Tudor house on riverside », 🐾
– 🅿 🔁 ⁑ ⓪ *VISA*
M a la carte 13.00/17.45 **t.** ▌2.75
Spec. Soufflé Talbooth, Salmon with sole and Lobster wrapped in puff pastry-chive butter sauce, Brandy snaps
with cognac cream.

🏛 **Dedham Vale** with rm, Stratford Rd, CO7 6HW, W : ¾ m. ✆ 322273, ≤, 🐾 – 📺 ➱wc ☎ 🅿.
🔁 ⁑ ⓪ *VISA*
closed Sunday dinner in winter – **M** (dinner only and Sunday lunch) – ⊑ 3.50 – **6 rm**
40.00/65.00 **st.**

DENBIGH Clwyd **402** **403** J 24 – pop. 7,948 – ECD : Thursday – ✆ 074 578 Llanynys.

♦London 217 – Chester 29 – Shrewsbury 55.

🏨 **Bryn Morfydd** ⌖, LL16 4NP, SE : 3 ¼ m. by A 525 ✆ 280, ≤ Vale of Clwyd, ☄ heated, ⌂,
🐾, park, ⁑, squash – 📺 ➱wc ⁂wc ☎ 🅿. 🔁 ⁑ ⓪ *VISA*. ⌖
M 5.50/9.50 **t.** ▌2.50 – **25 rm** ⊑ 25.00/35.00 **t.** – SB 35.00/45.00 **st.**

Annex : 🏨 Llanrhaeadr Hall ⌖, on A 525 ✆ 313, ≤, 🐾 – 🅿
M (see Bryn Morfydd H.) – **12 rm.**

DENTON Greater Manchester **402** **403** **404** N 23 – pop. 38,154 – ECD : Tuesday – ✉ ✆ 061
Manchester.

♦London 204 – ♦Manchester 6 – ♦Sheffield 34.

🏨 **Old Rectory** ⌖, Meadow Lane, Haughton Green, M34 1GD, S : 2 m. by A 6017 ✆ 336 7516,
Telex 668615, 🐾 – 📺 ➱wc ☎ 🅿. ⌖
closed 1 week at Christmas and Bank Holidays – **M** *(closed Saturday lunch and Sunday)* a la
carte 7.85/9.20 **st.** ▌2.15 – **26 rm** ⊑ 30.00/40.00 **st.**

DERBY Derbs. **402** **403** **404** P 25 – pop. 219,582 – ECD : Wednesday – ✆ 0332.

Envir. : Kedleston Hall★★ (18C) *AC*, NW : 5 m. by Kedleston Rd X – Melbourne (St. Michael's
Church : Norman nave★) S : 8 m. by A 514 X.

🏌 Allestree Park, ✆ 550616, N : 2 m. on A 6 X – 🏌 Sinfin Lane ✆ 766462 X – 🏌 Mickleover
✆ 513339, W : 3 m. by A 38 X – 🏌 Breadsall Priory, Moor Rd, Morley ✆ 832273, NE : 3 m. off A 38 X.

✈ East Midlands, Castle Donington ✆ 810621, SE : 12 m. by A 6 X.

🛈 Central Library, Warwick ✆ 31111 ext 2185/6 or 46124 (evenings and Saturday).

♦London 132 – ♦Birmingham 40 – ♦Coventry 49 – ♦Leicester 29 – ♦Manchester 62 – ♦Nottingham 16 – ♦Sheffield
47 – ♦Stoke-on-Trent 35.

Plan on next page

🏨 **Midland,** Midland Rd, DE1 2SQ, ✆ 45894, 🐾 – 📺 ➱wc ☎ 🅿. 🔁 ⁑ ⓪ *VISA*. ⌖
M a la carte 4.30/7.00 **st.** – **63 rm** ⊑ 22.00/41.00 **st.** Z i

🏨 **Pennine,** Macklin St., DE1 1LF, ✆ 41741, Telex 377545 – 🕭 📺 ➱wc ⁂wc ☎. 🔁 ⁑ ⓪
VISA Z e
closed 24 December-1 January – **M** *(closed lunch Saturday, Sunday and Bank Holidays* (buffet
lunch) 7.00 **st.** ▌3.10 – **100 rm** ⊑ 33.50/42.00 **st.**

🏠 **Gables,** 119 London Rd, DE1 2QR, ✆ 40633 – 📺 ⁂wc 🅿. 🔁 *VISA*. ⌖ Z o
closed 1 week at Christmas – **M** 4.95/6.95 **t.** – **54 rm** ⊑ 16.00/33.00 **t.** – SB (weekends only) 39.50/49.50 **st.**

🏛 **524,** 524 Burton Rd, DE3 6FN, SW : 1 ½ m. on A 5250 ✆ 371524, French rest. – 🅿. 🔁 ⁑ ⓪
VISA X a
closed Sunday, Monday and Tuesday after Bank Holidays – **M** a la carte 14.15/19.00 **s.** ▌2.90.

🏛 **La Gondola,** 220 Osmaston Rd, DE3 8JX, ✆ 32895, Italian rest. Dancing (Saturday) – 🅿. 🔁
⁑ ⓪ *VISA* X c
closed Sunday dinner – **M** a la carte 8.85/11.55 **t.** ▌2.30.

at Allestree N : 2 m. on A 6 – X – ✉ ✆ 0332 Derby :

🏛 **Palm Court,** Duffield Rd, DE3 1ET, ✆ 558107 – 🅿. 🔁 ⁑ ⓪ *VISA*
closed Sunday dinner – **M** a la carte 10.95/22.65 **t.** ▌3.25.

at Shelton Lock S : 3 ½ m. on A 514 – X – ✉ ✆ 0332 Derby :

🏛 **Golden Pheasant,** 221 Chellaston Rd, DE9 9EE, ✆ 700112 – 🅿. 🔁 ⁑ ⓪ *VISA*
closed Sunday dinner and Bank Holidays – **M** a la carte 8.50/16.75 **st.** ▌3.20.

at Littleover SW : 2 ½ m. on A 5250 – ✉ ✆ 0332 Derby :

🏨 **Crest** (Crest), Pasture Hill, DE3 7BA, ✆ 514933, Telex 377081, 🐾 – 📺 ➱wc ☎ 🅧 🅿. 🔁
🔁 ⁑ ⓪ *VISA* X a
M approx. 12.00 **st.** – ⊑ 5.25 – **66 rm** 42.00/53.00 **st.**

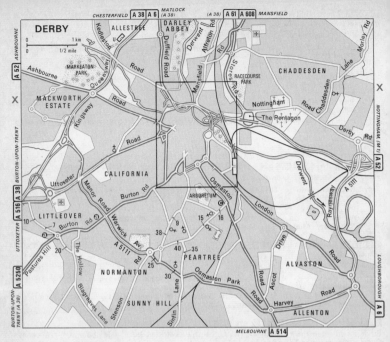

DERBY

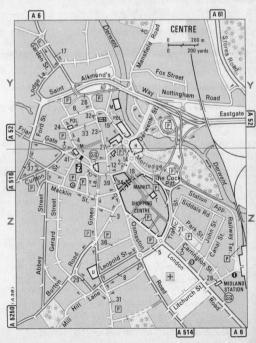

CENTRE

ALFA-ROMEO Walbrook Rd ✆ 767920
AUDI, VW 29-33 Ashbourne Rd ✆ 31282
AUSTIN-ROVER 152/160 Burton Rd ✆ 43224
BMW King St. ✆ 369511
CITROEN Alfreton Rd ✆ 381502
FIAT London Rd ✆ 71198
FORD Normanton Rd ✆ 40271

NISSAN Burton Rd ✆ 369723
RENAULT 1263 London Rd, Alvaston ✆ 71847
SAAB Uttoxeter Rd ✆ 513943
VAUXHALL-OPEL Pentagon Island, Nottingham Rd ✆ 362661
VOLVO Kedleston Rd ✆ 32625

DERSINGHAM Norfolk **402 404** V 25 – pop. 3,279 – ✆ 0485.

♦London 110 – ♦Cambridge 53 – ♦Norwich 46.

⚲ **Westdene House,** 60 Hunstanton Rd, PE31 6HQ, ✆ 40395, 🚗 – 🅿. ⚘
closed February and November – **5 rm** ⊑ 10.00/25.00 **st.**

DEVERON Cornwall – see Truro.

DEVIL'S BRIDGE (PONTARFYNACH) Dyfed **403** I 26 – pop. 150 – ✉ Aberystwyth – ✆ 097 085 Ponterwyd.

See : Nature Trail (Mynach Falls and Devil's Bridge)★★.

♦London 230 – Aberystwyth 12 – Shrewsbury 66.

Hotels see : Aberystwyth W : 12 m.

DEVIZES Wilts. **403 404** O 29 The West Country G. – pop. 10,179 – ECD : Wednesday – ✆ 0380.

See : Site★ – St. John's Church★★ – Market Place★ – Devizes Museum★.

Envir. : Potterne : Porch House★★, S : 2 m. on A 360.

🏌 North Wilts., Bishop's Cannings ✆ 038 086 (Cannings) 257, N : 5 m.

🛈 Canal Centre, Couch Lane ✆ 71069 (summer only).

♦London 98 – ♦Bristol 38 – Salisbury 25 – Swindon 19.

🏠 **Bear,** Market Pl., SN10 1HS, ✆ 2444 – 📺 ⌂wc 🕿 🅿. 🔼 AE VISA
M 6.00/7.50 **t.** ⏐ 2.95 – **26 rm** ⊑ 24.00/38.00 **t.** – SB (weekends only) 45.00/48.00 **st.**

FORD New Park St. ✆ 3456   PEUGEOT ✆ 038 081 (Lavington) 2336

DIDDLEBURY Salop **403** L 26 – ✉ Craven Arms – ✆ 058 476 Munslow.

♦ London 169 – ♦ Birmingham 46.

⚲ **Glebe Farm** ⏎, SY7 9DH, ✆ 221, 🚗 – 🅿. ⚘
March-November – **7 rm** ⊑ 12.00/30.00 **st.**

DINBYCH-Y-PYSGOD = Tenby.

DISLEY Cheshire **402 403 404** N 23 – pop. 3,986 – ECD : Wednesday – ✉ Stockport – ✆ 066 32.

🏌 Stanley Hall Lane ✆ 2071.

♦London 187 – Chesterfield 35 – ♦Manchester 12.

🏠 **Moorside** ⏎, Mudhurst Lane, Higher Disley, SK12 2AP, SE : 2 m. ✆ 4151, Telex 665170, ≼
– 📺 ⌂wc 🕿 🛂. AE ⓄVISA
M 6.75/11.50 **t.** ⏐ 3.00 – **25 rm** ⊑ 28.50/38.00 **t.** – SB (weekends only, except Christmas) 45.00 **st.**

MAZDA Fountain Sq. ✆ 2327   RENAULT 159 Buxton Rd ✆ 2105

DISS Norfolk **404** X 26 – pop. 4,470 – ECD : Tuesday – ✉ ✆ 0379.

♦London 98 – ♦Ipswich 25 – ♦Norwich 21 – Thetford 17.

XX **Salisbury House** with rm, 84 Victoria Rd, IP22 3JG, ✆ 4738, « Victorian house with period furniture, garden » – 📺 ⌂wc ⌂wc 🅿
closed 1 week spring, 1 week autumn and 2 weeks at Christmas – **M** *(closed Sunday and Monday)* (lunch by arrangement) 15.50 **t.** ⏐ 3.50 – **3 rm** ⊑ 35.00/40.00 **t.**

at Scole E : 2 m. by A 1066 on A 143 – ✉ ✆ 0379 Diss :

🏠 **Scole Inn** (Best Western), Main St., IP21 4DR, ✆ 740481, « 17C inn » – 📺 ⌂wc 🅿. 🔼 AE Ⓞ VISA
M a la carte 8.40/11.90 **t.** ⏐ 2.00 – **20 rm** ⊑ 21.00/36.00 **t.** – SB 44.00/46.00 **st.**

AUSTIN-ROVER Victoria Rd ✆ 3141   VAUXHALL-OPEL 142/144 Victoria Rd ✆ 2241
FORD Park Rd ✆ 2311

DITTON PRIORS Salop **403 404** M 26 – pop. 693 – ✉ Bridgnorth – ✆ 074 634.

♦London 154 – ♦Birmingham 34 – Ludlow 13 – Shrewsbury 21.

XX **Howard Arms** ⏎ with rm, WV16 6SQ, ✆ 200, 🚗 – 🅿. ⚘
closed 1 week July and 2 weeks August – **M** *(closed Sunday dinner and Monday)* (bar lunch Tuesday to Saturday) 10.00/14.50 **t.** ⏐ 3.20 – **2 rm** ⊑ 18.00/28.00 **t.**

DODDISCOMBSLEIGH Devon – see Exeter.

DOLGELLAU Gwynedd 402 403 I 25 – pop. 2,340 – ECD : Wednesday – ☎ 0341.

Envir. : N : Precipice walk★★, Torrent walk★, Rhaiadr Ddu (Black waterfalls★), Coed-y-Brenin Forest★ – E : Bwlch Oerddrws★ on road★ from Cross Foxes Hotel to Dinas Mawddwy – S : Cader Idris (road★★ to Cader Idris : Cregennau lakes) – Tal-y-Llyn Lake★★.

🛐 Pencefn Rd ✆ 422603.

🅱 Snowdonia National Park Visitor Centre, The Bridge ✆ 422888 (summer only).

◆London 221 – Birkenhead 72 – Chester 64 – Shrewsbury 57.

🏨 **Golden Lion Royal,** Lion St., LL40 1DG, ✆ 422579, 🏄 – 📺 📟wc 🅿. 🔼 🆎 ⓪ 𝚅𝙸𝚂𝙰
  M 4.90/8.50 **st.** – **22 rm** ☲ 12.00/36.00 **st.** – SB 29.00/39.00 **st.**

🏨 **Royal Ship,** Queen Sq., LL40 1AR, ✆ 422209 – 🛗 📟wc 🅿. 🔼 𝚅𝙸𝚂𝙰
  M 4.50/7.75 **t.** – **23 rm** ☲ 12.00/32.00 **t.** – SB 36.50/42.00 **st.**

🏥 **Gwernan Lake** 🦢, Cader Idris Rd, LL40 1TL, SW : 2 m. ✆ 422488, ≼, 🦢, 🏄 – 🅿. 🛁
  Easter-September – **M** (bar lunch) 8.00 **t.** 🍷 2.50 – **11 rm** ☲ 12.60/25.20 **t.**

✗ **La Petite Auberge,** 2 Smithfield St., LL40 1BS, ✆ 422870, French rest.
  March-September – **M** *(closed Monday)* (dinner only) (booking essential) a la carte 7.60/10.20 **st.** 🍷 2.70.

  at Penmaenpool W : 2 m. on A 493 – ✉ ☎ 0341 Dolgellau :

✗ **George III** with rm, LL40 1YD, ✆ 422525, ≼ Mawddach estuary and mountains – 📺 📟wc 🅿. 🔼 🆎 𝚅𝙸𝚂𝙰
  closed Christmas – **M** *(closed Sunday dinner to non - residents)* (bar lunch Monday to Saturday) a la carte 7.85/10.55 **t.** – **12 rm** ☲ 18.50/44.00 **t.** – SB (November-April) 41.80/52.80 **st.**

  at Bontddu W : 5 m. on A 496 – ✉ Dolgellau – ☎ 034 149 Bontddu :

🏰 **Bontddu Hall,** LL40 2SU, ✆ 661, ≼ Mawddach estuary and mountains, « Victorian mansion in large gardens » – 📺 📟wc ⋔wc 🅿 ☎. 🔼 🆎 ⓪ 𝚅𝙸𝚂𝙰
  Easter-mid October – **M** (buffet lunch) 12.95 **t.** – **23 rm** ☲ 23.00/52.00 **t.** – SB 70.00/76.00 **st.**

🏥 **Halfway House,** LL40 2UE, ✆ 635 – 🅿
  M *(closed Sunday dinner in winter)* (bar lunch) 8.75 **t.** 🍷 2.50 – **4 rm** ☲ 11.50/25.00 **t.**

AUSTIN-ROVER-LAND ROVER Arran Rd ✆ 422631   PEUGEOT-TALBOT Bontddu ✆ 49278
NISSAN Bala Rd ✆ 422681

DOLWYDDELAN Gwynedd 402 403 I 24 – ECD : Thursday – ☎ 069 06.

◆London 232 – Holyhead 51 – Dolgellau 24 – LLandudno 27.

🏨 **Elen's Castle,** LL25 0EJ, on A 470 ✆ 207, ≼, 🦢, 🏄 – 📟wc ⋔wc 🅿
  April-September – **M** (bar lunch) 7.50 **t.** 🍷 1.35 – **10 rm** ☲ 12.70/31.40 **t.** – SB 30.80/33.00 **st.**

DONCASTER South Yorks. 402 403 404 Q 23 – pop. 82,668 – ECD : Thursday – ☎ 0302.

🛐 Wheatley, Armthorpe Rd ✆ 831 203, E : 3 m. – 🛐 Crookhill Park, Conisbrough ✆ 0709 (Rotherham) 862979, W : 3 m. on A 630.

🅱 Central Library, Waterdale ✆ 69123.

◆London 173 – ◆Kingston-upon-Hull 46 – ◆Leeds 30 – ◆Nottingham 46 – ◆Sheffield 19.

🏰 **Earl of Doncaster** (Anchor), Roman Rd, Bennethorpe, DN2 6AD, SE : ½ m. on A 638 ✆ 61371, Telex 547932 – 🛗 📺 📟wc 🍽 🅿. 🏊 🔼 🆎 ⓪ 𝚅𝙸𝚂𝙰
  M (carving rest.) 8.65 **st.** 🍷 2.65 – **39 rm** ☲ 35.00/42.00 – SB (weekends only) 43.00 **st.**

🏰 **Punch's** (Embassy), Bawtry Rd, Bessacarr, DN4 7BS, SE : 3 m. on A 638 ✆ 535235 – 📺 📟wc ☎ 🅿. 🏊 🔼 🆎 ⓪ 𝚅𝙸𝚂𝙰 🛁
  M *(closed Saturday lunch and Sunday dinner to non-residents)* (carving rest.) 7.00/7.25 **st.** 🍷 4.75 – ☲ 4.25 – **25 rm** 23.00/47.00 **st.** – SB (weekends only) 37.00/44.00 **st.**

🏰 **Danum** (Swallow), High St., DN1 1DN, ✆ 62261, Telex 547533 – 🛗 📺 📟wc 🅿 🏊 🔼 🆎 ⓪ 𝚅𝙸𝚂𝙰
  M 7.50/9.50 **st.** 🍷 1.40 – **66 rm** ☲ 24.00/45.00 **st.** – SB 38.50 **st.**

🏨 **Grand St. Leger,** Bennethorpe, DN3 6AX, ✆ 64111 – 📺 📟wc ⋔wc ☎ 🅿. 🏊 🔼 🆎 ⓪ 𝚅𝙸𝚂𝙰
  M *(closed Saturday lunch)* 5.70/7.50 **st.** 🍷 3.40 – **14 rm** ☲ 28.00/38.00 **st.** – SB (weekends only) 31.00/49.00 **st.**

  at Rossington S : 6 m. on A 638 – ✉ ☎ 0302 Doncaster :

🏨 **Mount Pleasant,** Great North Rd, DN11 0HP, on A 638 ✆ 868219, 🏄 – 📺 📟wc ☎ 🅿. 🛁
  closed Christmas Day – **M** 8.00/9.00 **t.** 🍷 2.40 – **26 rm** ☲ 14.50/40.00 **t.**

  at Sprotbrough W : 3 ½ m. by A 630 – ✉ ☎ 0302 Doncaster :

✗ **Edelweiss,** 4 Main St., DN5 7PJ, ✆ 853923 – 🔼 🆎 ⓪ 𝚅𝙸𝚂𝙰
  closed Monday – **M** (dinner only) a la carte 7.95/13.00 **t.** 🍷 2.50.

BMW Wheatley Hall Rd ✆ 69191
COLT 8 Wood St. ✆ 64766
LANCIA Springwell Lane ✆ 854674
RENAULT Selby Rd, Thorne ✆ 0405 (Thorne) 8121100
TOYOTA Thorne Rd, Hatfield ✆ 840348
VW, AUDI York Rd Roundabout ✆ 64141

DONHEAD ST. ANDREW Wilts. – see Shaftesbury (Dorset).

DONYATT Somerset 🔢🔢🔢 L 37 – pop. 342 – ⊠ ◎ 046 05 Ilminster.

♦London 147 – Exeter 33 – Taunton 11 – Yeovil 17.

    ✗ **Thatchers Pond,** TA19 0RG, ✆ 3210, 🚗 – ℗
        closed Sunday dinner, Monday and 24 December-7 February – **M** (cold buffet only) a la carte
        8.50/9.80 **t.**

DORCHESTER Dorset 🔢🔢🔢 🔢🔢🔢 M 31 The West Country G. – pop. 13,736 – ECD : Thursday –
◎ 0305.

See : Site★ – Dorset Country Museum★.

Envir. : Bere Regis : St. John the Baptist Church★★★, NE : 11 m. by A 35 – Maiden Castle★★, SW :
2 m. by A 354 – Puddletown Church★, NE : 5 m. by A 35 – Athelhampton★, NE : 6 m. on A 35.

🏌 Came Down ✆ 030 581 (Upwey) 2531, S : 2 m.

🛈 Antelope Yard, South St. ✆ 67992.

♦London 135 – Bournemouth 27 – Exeter 53 – ♦Southampton 53.

    🏠 **King's Arms,** 30 High East St., DT1 1HF, ✆ 65353 – 📺 📶wc 🐾 ℗. 🅰. 🔼 🆎 𝘝𝘐𝘚𝘈
        M a la carte 5.65/9.00 **t.** ◊ 2.50 – **27 rm** ⌐ 20.50/42.50 **t.** – SB 40.00/45.00 **st.**

    🏠 **Casterbridge** without rest., 49 High East St., ✆ 64043 – 📺 📶wc 🚿wc. 🔼 🆎 ⓞ 𝘝𝘐𝘚𝘈. �
        closed 25 and 26 December – **15 rm** ⌐ 17.00/32.00 **t.**

    at Owermoigne SE : 7 m. by A 352 – ⊠ Dorchester – ◎ 0305 Warmwell :

    🏠 **Owermoigne Moor Country House** 🌲, 32 Moreton Rd, DT2 8DX, N : 1 ½ m. ✆ 852663,
        ⟨, 🚗, park – ℗
        M (bar lunch) 8.50 **st.** ◊ 2.25 – **7 rm** ⌐ 15.00/25.00 **st.**

AUSTIN-ROVER 21/26 Trinity St. ✆ 63031   FORD Prince of Wales Rd ✆ 62211
BMW North Sq. ✆ 67411   NISSAN London Rd ✆ 66066
CITROEN, PEUGEOT, TALBOT Puddletown ✆ 84456   VAUXHALL 6 High East St. ✆ 63913
FIAT, MERCEDES-BENZ Trinity St. ✆ 64494   VOLVO Bridport Rd ✆ 65555

DORCHESTER Oxon. 🔢🔢🔢 🔢🔢🔢 Q 29 – pop. 905 – ◎ 0865 Oxford.

See : Abbey Church★ 14C.

♦London 51 – Abingdon 6 – ♦Oxford 8 – Reading 17.

    🏛 **White Hart,** 26 High St., OX9 8HN, ✆ 340074, « Tastefully converted 17C coaching inn » –
        📺 📶wc ℗. 🔼 🆎 ⓞ 𝘝𝘐𝘚𝘈. �
        M 13.00/17.50 **st.** ◊ 3.75 – **16 rm** ⌐ 45.00/60.00 **st.** – SB (weekends only) 75.00/80.00 **st.**

    🏠 **George,** High St., OX9 8HH, ✆ 340404 – 📺 📶wc 🐾 ℗. 🔼 🆎 ⓞ 𝘝𝘐𝘚𝘈. �
        closed Christmas – **M** 7.00/9.00 **st.** ◊ 5.35 – **17 rm** ⌐ 28.00/59.00 **st.** – SB (week-
        ends only) 49.50/55.50 **st.**

DORKING Surrey 🔢🔢🔢 T 30 – pop. 22,530 – ECD : Wednesday – ◎ 0306.

Envir. : Box Hill ⟨★★ NE : 2 ½ m. – Polesden Lacey★★ (19C) *AC*, NW : 4 ½ m.

♦London 26 – ♦Brighton 39 – Guildford 12 – Worthing 33.

    🏛 **Burford Bridge** (T.H.F.), Box Hill, RH5 6BT, N : 1 ½ m. on A 24 ✆ 884561, Telex 859507,
        🏊 heated, 🚗 – 📺 ℗. 🅰. 🔼 🆎 ⓞ 𝘝𝘐𝘚𝘈
        M 11.50/14.50 **st.** ◊ 2.75 – ⌐ 5.50 – **50 rm** 44.00/58.50 **st.**

    🏛 **White Horse** (T.H.F.), High St., RH4 1BE, ✆ 881138, 🏊 heated – 📺 📶wc 🐾 ℗. 🅰. 🔼 🆎
        ⓞ 𝘝𝘐𝘚𝘈
        M a la carte 9.15/12.45 **st.** ◊ 2.55 – ⌐ 5.00 – **70 rm** 34.00/45.00 **st.**

    🏠 **Punch Bowl** (Anchor), Reigate Rd, RH4 1QB, ✆ 889335 – 📺 📶wc 🐾 ℗. 🔼 🆎 ⓞ 𝘝𝘐𝘚𝘈
        M (carving rest.) 8.65 **st.** ◊ 2.65 – **29 rm** ⌐ 36.00/44.00 **st.** – SB (weekends only) 45.00 **st.**

    ✗ **Le Bistro,** 84 South St., RH4 2EZ, ✆ 883239, French rest. – 🔼 🆎 ⓞ 𝘝𝘐𝘚𝘈
        closed lunch Saturday and Bank Holidays, Sunday, 25 to 27 December and 1 to 3 January – **M**
        a la carte 6.40/15.90 **t.** ◊ 2.50.

    at Peaslake SW : 8 m. by A 25 – ⊠ Guildford – ◎ 0306 Dorking :

    🏠 **Hurtwood Inn** (T.H.F.), Walking Bottom, GU5 9RR, ✆ 730851, 🚗 – 📺 📶wc 🐾 ℗. 🔼 🆎
        ⓞ 𝘝𝘐𝘚𝘈
        M a la carte 8.80/13.35 **st.** ◊ 2.60 – ⌐ 4.75 – **18 rm** 26.00/41.00 **st.**

    at Gomshall W : 5 ½ m. on A 25 – ⊠ Guildford – ◎ 048 641 Shere :

    🍴 **Black Horse Inn,** GU5 9NP, on A 25 ✆ 2242, 🚗 – ℗. ⓞ 𝘝𝘐𝘚𝘈. �
        M *(closed Sunday dinner and Monday)* (bar lunch Tuesday to Saturday) a la carte 5.25/13.25 **t.**
        ◊ 2.70 – **6 rm** ⌐ 16.10/32.20 **t.**

    at Shere W : 6 ¼ m. by A 25 – ⊠ Guildford – ◎ 048 641 Shere :

    ✗✗ **La Chaumiere,** Gomshall Lane, GU5 9HE, ✆ 2168 – ℗. 🔼 🆎 ⓞ 𝘝𝘐𝘚𝘈
        M a la carte 9.95/12.70 **t.** ◊ 2.95.

AUSTIN-ROVER 105 South St. ✆ 882244   VAUXHALL-OPEL Reigate Rd ✆ 885022
RENAULT 40 West St ✆ 886080

DORMINGTON Heref. and Worc. – see Hereford.

DORRINGTON Salop 402 403 L 26 – see Shrewsbury.

DOVER Kent 404 Y 30 – pop. 34,395 – ECD : Wednesday – ✪ 0304.

See : Castle★★ 12C (≤★) *AC* Y.

Envir. : Barfreston (Norman Church★ 11C : carvings★★) NW : 6 ½ m. by A 2 Z – Bleriot Memorial E : 1½ m. Z **A**.

🚢 Shipping connections with the Continent : to France (Boulogne) (P & O Ferries : Channel Services) (Hoverspeed) – to France (Calais) (Sealink) (Hoverspeed) (Townsend Thoresen) – to France (Dunkerque West) (Sealink) – to Belgium (Oostende) (Sealink) – to Belgium (Zeebrugge) (Townsend Thoresen).

🚢 to Belgium (Oostende) (Sealink, Jetfoil).

🛈 Townwall St. ℰ 205108 – Town Hall, High St. ℰ 206941.

♦London 76 – ♦Brighton 84.

DOVER

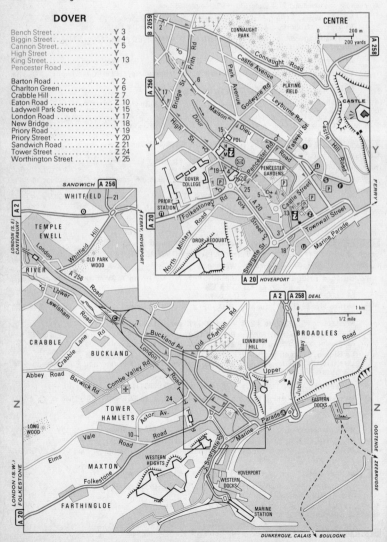

🏨🏨 **Holiday Inn,** Townwall St., CT16 1SZ, ℰ 203270, Telex 96458, 🖾 – 📶 📼 ☎ 🕭 **P** 🖾 – 🔄 🖾 ᴬᴱ ⑪ 𝗩𝗜𝗦𝗔　Ｙ　**z**
M (buffet lunch) a la carte approx. 15.60 **t.** 🍷 3.50 – ⊇ 4.25 – **80 rm** 38.00/51.50 **st.**

🏨 **White Cliffs,** Marine Par., Seafront, CT17 9BW, ℰ 203633 – 📶 📼 ⇔wc 🛏wc ☜ ☜. 🔄
ᴬᴱ ⑪ 𝗩𝗜𝗦𝗔　Ｙ　**a**
closed 25 and 26 December – **M** 5.85/6.00 **t.** 🍷 3.75 – **62 rm** ⊇ 20.00/40.00 **t.**

🏠 **Mildmay,** 78 Folkestone Rd, CT17 9SF, ℰ 204278 – 📼 ⇔wc **P**. 🔄 ᴬᴱ ⑪ 𝗩𝗜𝗦𝗔. 🍴　Ｙ　**n**
closed January – **21 rm** ⊇ 24.00/32.00 **st.** – SB 42.00/45.00 **st.**

🏠 **Cliffe Court,** 25-26 East Cliff, Marine Par., CT16 1LU, ℰ 211001, ≤ – 📼 ⇔wc 🛏wc **P**. 🔄 ᴬᴱ
⑪ 𝗩𝗜𝗦𝗔. 🍴　Ｚ　**a**
24 rm ⊇ 17.00/27.50 **st.** – SB 44.00 **st.**

🏠 **St. James,** 2 Harold St., CT16 1SF, ℰ 204579 – 📼 ⇔wc 🛏wc ☜. 🔄 ᴬᴱ ⑪ 𝗩𝗜𝗦𝗔　Ｙ　**i**
M (lunch by arrangement) a la carte 4.50/11.50 **t.** 🍷 2.00 – **16 rm** ⊇ 13.00/28.00 **st.** – SB
(winter only) 36.00 **st.**

🏡 **Hubert House,** 9 Castle Hill Rd, CT16 1QW, ℰ 202253 – 📼 🛏 **P**. 🔄 ⑪ 𝗩𝗜𝗦𝗔. 🍴　Ｙ　**s**
closed first 2 weeks April and October – **M** (closed Sunday) (dinner only) 6.50 **t.** 🍷 2.00 – **8 rm**
⊇ 16.00/22.00 **st.**

↰ **Number One,** 1 Castle St., CT16 1QH, ℰ 202007 – 📼 🛏wc. 🍴　Ｙ　**u**
6 rm ⊇ 12.00/18.00 **s.**

↰ **Beulah House,** 94 Crabble Hill, London Rd, CT17 0SA, ℰ 824615, ☞ – ☜ **P**. 🍴　Ｚ　**c**
7 rm ⊇ 12.00/20.00 **s.**

↰ **St. Martins,** 17 Castle Hill Rd, CT16 1QW, ℰ 205938 – 📼 🛏. 🍴　Ｙ　**r**
6 rm ⊇ 9.00/18.00 **s.**

　　at Whitfield N : 3 ½ m. on A 256 – ✉ ☯ 0304 Dover :

🏨 **Dover Motel,** Singledge Lane, CT16 3LF, ℰ 821222, Telex 965866 – 📼 ⇔wc ☎ 🕭 **P**. 🔄
🔄 ᴬᴱ ⑪ 𝗩𝗜𝗦𝗔　Ｚ　**o**
M a la carte 11.25/13.85 **t.** 🍷 3.35 – ⊇ 3.45 – **67 rm** 33.00/42.00 **st.** – SB (weekends only) (spring only) 55.00/70.00 **st.**

　　at St. Margaret's Bay NE : 4 m. by A 258 – Ｚ – and B 2058 – ✉ ☯ 0304 Dover :

🏠 **Granville** 🏊, Hotel Rd, off Granville Rd, CT15 6OX, ℰ 852212, ≤ sea and coastline, ☞ –
⇔wc ☜ **P**. 🔄 ᴬᴱ ⑪ 𝗩𝗜𝗦𝗔
M 5.75/6.60 **st.** 🍷 2.50 – ⊇ 3.30 – **21 rm** 11.00/25.50 **st.**

AUSTIN-ROVER Woolcomber St. ℰ 201904　　　　RENAULT 6/12 Folkestone Rd ℰ 201760
NISSAN Woolcomber St. ℰ 206518　　　　　　　TOYOTA Eric Rd, Buckland ℰ 201235
NISSAN Cherry Tree Av. ℰ 206682　　　　　　　VAUXHALL Castle St. ℰ 203001
RELIANT South Rd ℰ 206160　　　　　　　　　VW, AUDI 1 Crabble Hill ℰ 206710
RENAULT London Rd, River ℰ 74155

DOWNTON Wilts. 🔢🔢 O 31 – see Salisbury.

DRAYTON Norfolk 🔢 X 25 – see Norwich.

DRENEWYDD = Newtown.

DRENEWYDD YN NOTAIS (NOTTAGE) Mid Glam. – see Porthcawl.

DRIFFIELD Humberside 🔢 S 21 – see Great Driffield.

DROITWICH Heref. and Worc. 🔢🔢 N 27 – pop. 12,748 – ECD : Thursday – ☯ 0905.
🛈 Heritage Way ℰ 774312.
♦London 129 – ♦Birmingham 20 – ♦Bristol 66 – Worcester 6.

🏨🏨 **Château Impney,** WR9 0BN, NE : 1 m. on A 38 ℰ 774411, Group Telex 336673, « Reproduction 16C French château », ☞, park, 🎾 – 📶 📼 **P**. 🔄 🔄 ᴬᴱ ⑪ 𝗩𝗜𝗦𝗔
closed Christmas – **M** 8.00/10.00 **st.** 🍷 3.25 – ⊇ 5.95 – **67 rm** 54.95/59.95 **st.**

🏨🏨 **Raven,** St. Andrews Rd, WR9 8DV, ℰ 772224, Group Telex 336673, ☞ – 📶 📼 **P**. 🔄 🔄 ᴬᴱ
⑪ 𝗩𝗜𝗦𝗔
closed Christmas – **M** 8.00/9.00 **st.** 🍷 3.25 – ⊇ 5.95 – **55 rm** 39.95/49.95 **st.**

AUSTIN-ROVER St. Georges Sq. ℰ 775123　　　RENAULT Cutnall Green ℰ 029 923 (Cutnall Green)
FORD 141-149 Worcester Rd ℰ 772132　　　　344

DRONFIELD Derbs. 🔢🔢🔢 P 24 – pop. 13,980 – ECD : Wednesday – ✉ Sheffield (South
Yorks) – ☯ 0246.
♦ London 158 – Derby 30 – ♦ Nottingham 31 – ♦ Sheffield 6.

🏠 **Manor,** 10-15 High St., S18 6PY, off Lea Rd and Church St. ℰ 413971 – 📼 🛏wc **P**
10 rm.

DULVERTON Somerset 408 J 30 **The West Country G.** – pop. 1,288 – ECD : Thursday – 🕿 0398.
See : Site★.
Envir. : Tarr Steps★★, NW : 6 m. by B 3223.
♦London 198 – Barnstaple 27 – Exeter 26 – Minehead 18 – Taunton 27.

  🏠 **Ashwick House** 📎, TA22 9QD, NW : 4 ¼ m. by B 3223 ℰ 23868, ≼, « Country house atmosphere », 🚗 – 📺 🚽wc 🅿. **M** *(closed Sunday and Monday to non-residents)* (dinner only) 7.25 **t.** 🍷 2.50 – **6 rm** � 23.00/40.00 **t.** – SB (except Bank Holidays) 42.00/48.00 **st.**

DUNCHURCH Warw. 408 404 Q 26 – pop. 2,859 – ✉ 🕿 0788 Rugby.
♦London 90 – ♦Coventry 12 – ♦Leicester 24 – Northampton 26.

  🏠 **Dun Cow,** The Green, CV22 6NJ, ℰ 810233 – 📺 🚽wc 🅿. 🔥 🔼 AE ⓿ VISA
  M 6.95/7.95 **st.** 🍷 3.50 – **21 rm** ⊇ 25.00/55.00 **st.** – SB (weekends only) 63.00/93.00 **st.**

VW, AUDI Coventry Rd ℰ 815044

DUNSTABLE Beds. 404 S 28 – pop. 31,828 – ECD : Thursday – 🕿 0582.
See : Priory Church of St. Peter (West front★).
Envir. : Whipsnade Park★ (zoo) ≼★★ *AC*, S : 3 m.
🏌 Tilsworth, Dunstable Rd ℰ 0525 (Leighton Buzzard) 210721, N : 2 m. on A 5.
🎟 Queensway Hall, Vernon Pl. ℰ 603326.
♦London 40 – Bedford 24 – Luton 4.5 – Northampton 35.

  🏨 **Old Palace Lodge,** Church St., LU5 4RT, ℰ 62201 – 📶 🗐 rest 📺 🅿. 🔥 🔼 AE ⓿ VISA 🍴
  M a la carte 10.80/18.00 **t.** 🍷 2.50 – ⊇ 4.50 – **33 rm** 33.00/37.00 **st.**

  🏠 **Highwayman,** London Rd, LU6 3DX, SE : 1 m. on A 5 ℰ 61999 – 📺 🚽wc 🚽wc 🕿 🅿. 🔼 AE ⓿ VISA
  closed 4 days at Christmas – **26 rm** ⊇ 24.00/34.00 **st.**

AUSTIN-ROVER London Rd ℰ 696111
FORD 55 London Rd ℰ 67811

RENAULT 3 Tring Rd ℰ 63231
VW, AUDI Common Rd, Kensworth ℰ 872182

Wenn Sie an ein Hotel im Ausland schreiben,
fügen Sie Ihrem Brief einen internationalen Antwortschein bei
(im Postamt erhältlich).

DUNSTER Somerset 408 J 30 – pop. 815 – ECD : Wednesday – ✉ Minehead – 🕿 064 382.
See : Site★★ – Castle★★ (upper rooms ≼★ from window) – Dunster Castle Water Mill★ – Dovecote★ – St. Georges Church★.
Envir. : Cleeve Abbey★★, SE : 5 m. on A 39.
♦London 184 – ♦Bristol 61 – Exeter 40 – Taunton 22.

  🏨 **Luttrell Arms** (T.H.F.), 36 High St., TA24 6SG, ℰ 555, 🚗 – 📺 🚽wc 🕿. 🔼 AE ⓿ VISA
  M 6.50/9.00 **st.** 🍷 2.60 – ⊇ 5.00 – **21 rm** 33.50/44.50 **st.**

  🏠 **Exmoor House,** 12 West St., TA24 6SN, ℰ 821268, 🚗 – 📺 🚽wc. 🔼 AE ⓿ VISA 🍴
  closed January – **M** *(closed Saturday lunch)* 3.45/8.75 **t.** 🍷 2.60 – **6 rm** ⊇ 16.50/33.00 **t.** – SB (except August and September) 42.80/46.80 **st.**

DURHAM Durham 401 402 P 19 – pop. 24,776 – ECD : Wednesday – 🕿 0385.
See : Cathedral★★★ (Norman) (Chapel of the Nine Altars★★) B – University (Gulbenkian Museum of Art and Archaeology★★ *AC*) by Elvet Hill Rd A – Castle★ (Norman chapel★) *AC* B.
🏌 Low Job's Hill, Crook ℰ 0388 (Bishop Auckland) 762429, SW : 10 m. by A 690 A – 🏌 South Moor, The Middles, Craghead ℰ 0207 (Stanley) 32848, NW : 8 m. by Framwelgate Peth A and B 6532 – 🏌 Durham City, Littleburn, Langley Moor ℰ 780069 by Potters Bank A.
🎟 13 Claypath ℰ 43720.
♦London 267 – ♦Leeds 77 – ♦Middlesbrough 23 – Sunderland 12.

Plan opposite

  🏨 **Royal County** (Swallow), Old Elvet, DH1 3JN, ℰ 66821, Group Telex 538238 – 📶 📺 🅿. 🔥
  🔼 AE ⓿ VISA
  M 6.00/8.50 **st.** 🍷 4.75 – **120 rm** ⊇ 38.00/48.75 **st.** – SB (weekends only) 53.00 **st.**
  B **a**

  🏨 **Three Tuns** (Swallow), New Elvet, DH1 3AQ, ℰ 64326, Group Telex 538238 – 📺 🚽wc 🕿
  🅿. 🔥 🔼 ⓿ VISA
  M 6.00/12.50 **st.** 🍷 3.40 – **51 rm** ⊇ 27.50/39.50 **st.** – SB (weekends only) 45.00/47.50 **st.**
  B **e**

ALFA-ROMEO, NISSAN 81 New Elvet ℰ 47777
AUSTIN-ROVER 74 New Elvet ℰ 47278
AUSTIN-ROVER Gilesgate Moor ℰ 67231
CITROEN Croxdale ℰ 0388 (Spennymoor) 814671
HONDA Bearpark ℰ 43266
HYUNDAI Langley Moor ℰ 780438

PEUGEOT-TALBOT Abbey Rd ℰ 46363
RENAULT Langley Moor ℰ 69666
VAUXHALL Claypath ℰ 42511
VOLVO Sawmills Lane ℰ 780866
VW, AUDI 20 Alma Rd, Gilesgate Moor ℰ 67215
YUGO Pity Me ℰ 44000

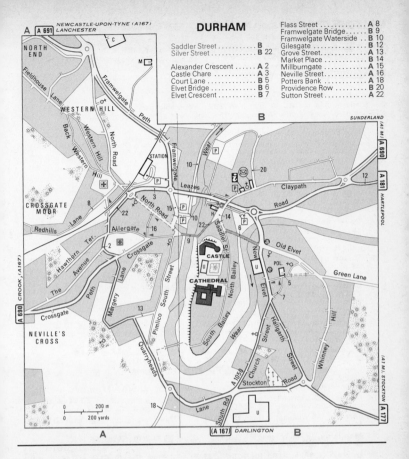

DURHAM

DURSLEY Glos. **403 404** M 28 – pop. 27,207 – ☎ 0453.

Envir. : Berkeley Castle★★ (12C) *AC*, NE : 5 ½ m.

☗ Stinchcombe Hill ✆ 2015, W : 1 m.

♦London 124 – ♦Bristol 26 – Gloucester 17.

   🏠 Stinchcombe Manor ⤳, Stinchcombe Village, GL11 6BQ, NW : 2 ½ m. by A 4135 off B 4060
   ✆ 2538, ⬓ heated, ☞, ⁂ – ☎ ⌷wc ⃒⃥wc ☏ 🅿
   16 rm.

FORD 2 May Lane ✆ 2270   VAUXHALL Cam ✆ 3681

EAGLESCLIFFE Cleveland **402** P 20 – see Stockton-on-Tees.

EARL SHILTON Leics. **403 404** Q 26 – ECD : Wednesday – ✉ Leicester – ☎ 0455.

♦London 107 – ♦Birmingham 35 – ♦Coventry 16 – ♦Leicester 9 – ♦Nottingham 35.

   🏠 **Fernleigh,** 32 Wood St., LE9 7ND, ✆ 47011 – ☎ ⃒⃥wc ☏ 🅿 ⃒⃥ *VISA*. ⁂
   closed 25 December-1 January – **M** *(closed Monday lunch and Sunday dinner)* 9.50 **t.** – **12 rm**
   ⊡ 23.00/30.00 **t.**

EARL STONHAM Suffolk **404** X 27 – pop. 528 – ✉ Stowmarket – ☎ 044 971 Stonham (from
January 0449 Stowmarket).

♦London 81 – ♦Cambridge 47 – ♦Ipswich 10 – ♦Norwich 33.

   ✗✗ **Mr. Underhill's,** IP14 5DW, Junction of A 140 and A 1120 ✆ 711206 – 🅿 *VISA*
   closed Saturday lunch, Sunday, Monday and Bank Holidays – **M** (lunch by arrangement)
   (booking essential) 13.00/16.95 **st.** ⃒ 4.00.

167

EAST BERGHOLT Suffolk **404** X 28 – pop. 2,746 – ⊠ ✆ 0206 Colchester (Essex).
♦London 59 – Colchester 9 – ♦Ipswich 8.5.

XX **Fountain House,** The Street, CO7 6TB, ℰ 298232 – **P**. **△** **VISA**
closed Sunday dinner, Monday and 4 to 18 January – **M** 6.95/8.95 t.

EASTBOURNE East Sussex **404** U 31 – pop. 70,921 – ECD : Wednesday – ✆ 0323.
See : Grand Parade★ X.

Envir. : Beachy Head★ (cliff), ⋇★ SW : 3 m. Z – Seven Sisters★ (cliffs) from Birling Gap, SW : 5 m.
Z – Charleston Manor★ AC, W : 8 m. by A 259 Z – W : scenic road★ from Eastdean by A 259 Z up to
Wilmington by Westdean – Wilmington : The Long Man★ : prehistoric giant figure, NW : 7 m. by A
27 Y.

🏌, 🏌 Royal Eastbourne, Paradise Drive ℰ 30412 Z.

🛈 3 Cornfield Terr. ℰ 27474 – Seafront, Grand Parade ℰ 27474 (summer only) – Town Kiosk, Terminus Rd ℰ
27474 – at Pevensey, Castle Car Park, High St. ℰ 0323 (Eastbourne) 761444.
♦London 68 – ♦Brighton 25 – ♦Dover 61 – Maidstone 49.

Plan opposite

🏨 **Grand** (De Vere), King Edward's Par., BN21 4EQ, ℰ 22611, Telex 87332, ≼, 🔲 heated, 🚗 –
🔟 📺 🅿 **△** **AE** **⑩** **VISA**
M 10.00/13.50 st. 🍷 2.95 – **178 rm** � 50.00/80.00 st. – SB (weekends only)(except sum-
mer) 90.00/110.00 st.
Z x

🏨 **Cavendish** (De Vere), 37-40 Grand Par., BN21 4DH, ℰ 27401, Telex 87579, ≼ – 🔟 📺 🕭 🅿.
△ **AE** **⑩** **VISA**
M (dinner only and Sunday lunch) 11.50/13.00 st. 🍷 3.00 – **115 rm** ⊠ 42.00/89.00 st. – SB
66.00 st.
X r

🏨 **Queen's** (De Vere), Marine Par., BN21 3DY, ℰ 22822, Telex 877736, ≼ – 🔟 📺 🅿. **△**. **△**. **AE**
VISA
M 8.50/10.00 st. 🍷 2.75 – **112 rm** ⊠ 34.00/60.00 st. – SB 64.00/72.00 st.
V e

🏨 **Lansdowne** (Best Western), King Edward's Par., BN21 4EE, ℰ 25174, ≼ – 🔟 📺 ⊟wc 🛁wc
🍽 🕭 🚗. **△**. **△**. **AE** **⑩** **VISA**
closed 1 to 17 January – **M** (bar lunch) 7.75 st. 🍷 2.75 – **137 rm** ⊠ 20.00/50.00 st. – SB
(except summer) 33.00/46.00 st.
Z z

🏨 **Chatsworth,** Grand Par., BN21 3YR, ℰ 30327, ≼ – 🔟 📺 ⊟wc 🛁wc 🍽. **△**. **△**. **AE** X n
closed January and February – **M** (dinner only in winter) 6.60/7.70 t. 🍷 2.45 – **45 rm**
⊠ 21.85/46.00 t. – SB 47.15/49.45 st.

🏨 **Sandhurst,** Grand Par., BN21 4DJ, ℰ 27868, ≼ – 🔟 📺 ⊟wc 🛁wc 🍽. **AE** **⑩** X o
M 5.50/7.00 t. 🍷 2.75 – **64 rm** ⊠ 18.50/55.00 st. – SB 41.00/60.00 st.

🏨 **Wish Tower** (T.H.F.), King Edward's Par., BN21 4EB, ℰ 22676, ≼ – 🔟 📺 ⊟wc 🍽 🕭. **△**. **AE**
VISA
M (buffet lunch Monday to Saturday) 6.95/7.45 st. 🍷 2.85 – ⊠ 5.00 – **73 rm** 21.00/40.00 st.
Z r

🏨 **Princes,** 12-20 Lascelles Terr., BN21 4BL, ℰ 22056 – 🔟 📺 ⊟wc 🕿. **△**. **△**. **AE** **⑩** **VISA** X z
closed January and February – **M** 6.25/8.25 st. 🍷 2.65 – **51 rm** ⊠ 15.50/52.50 st.

🏨 **Farrar's,** 3-5 Wilmington Gdns, BN21 4JN, ℰ 23737, 🚗 – 🔟 📺 ⊟wc 🛁wc 🅿. **△**. **AE** **VISA**
M 4.50/6.50 t. 🍷 2.00 – **42 rm** ⊠ 16.50/44.00 t.
X s

🏨 **Mandalay,** 16 Trinity Trees, BN21 3LE, ℰ 29222 – 📺 🛁wc 🅿. **△**. **VISA**. ⋇
M (chinese rest.)(bar lunch) 10.00 t. 🍷 3.40 – **12 rm** 14.40/32.20 t. – SB 27.00/30.00 st.
V v

🏨 **Downland,** 37 Lewes Rd, BN21 2BU, ℰ 32689 – 🔟 📺 ⊟wc 🛁wc 🅿. **△**. **VISA**. ⋇
closed December-February except Christmas – **M** (bar lunch) 7.50 st. 🍷 2.75 – **16 rm**
⊠ 20.00/36.00 t. – SB 42.00/47.50 st.
V r

🛖 **Oban,** King Edward's Par., BN21 4DS, ℰ 31581 – 🔟 📺 ⊟wc 🛁wc. **VISA**
May-October – **M** 4.50/6.50 t. 🍷 2.50 – **28 rm** ⊠ 12.50/25.00 t.
X a

↟ **Traquair,** 25 Hyde Gdns, BN21 4PX, ℰ 25198 – 📺 🛁wc
11 rm ⊠ 10.00/28.00 t.
V x

↟ **Hanburies,** 4 Hardwick Rd, BN21 4NY, ℰ 30698 – ⊟wc. ⋇
14 rm ⊠ 10.50/26.50 t.
X c

↟ **Orchard House,** 10 Old Orchard Rd, BN21 1DB, ℰ 23682 – ⊟wc 🛁wc. ⋇
7 rm ⊠ 12.00/24.00 t.
X o

↟ **Nirvana,** 32 Redoubt Rd, BN22 7DL, ℰ 22603 – ⋇
8 rm ⊠ 7.50/17.00 st.
V n

XX **Crimples,** 42-44 Meads St., BN20 7RG, ℰ 26805 – **△** **VISA**
closed Sunday dinner, Monday, 1 week March, 2 weeks October and 25-26 December – **M** a la
carte 9.10/11.10 t. 🍷 2.70.
Z a

X **Byron's,** 6 Crown St., Old Town, BN21 1NX, ℰ 20171 – **AE** **⑩** **VISA**
closed Saturday lunch, Sunday, 1 week at Christmas and Bank Holidays – **M** a la carte
6.05/12.10 t. 🍷 2.20.
Z s

X **Brown's,** 17 Carlisle Rd, BN21 4BT, ℰ 28837, Bistro – **△**. **AE** **⑩** **VISA**
closed Sunday except lunch in Summer and Monday – **M** a la carte 7.70/12.40 t. 🍷 2.80.
X e

at Willingdon N : 2 ¾ m. on A 22 – ⊠ ✆ 0323 Eastbourne :

🏨 **Chalk Farm** ⋟, Coopers Hill, BN20 9JD, ℰ 53800, ≼, 🚗 – ⊟wc 🛁wc. ⋇
M (closed Sunday dinner and Monday to non-residents) 5.50/8.95 t. 🍷 2.75 – **8 rm**
⊠ 14.00/30.00 t.
Y a

168

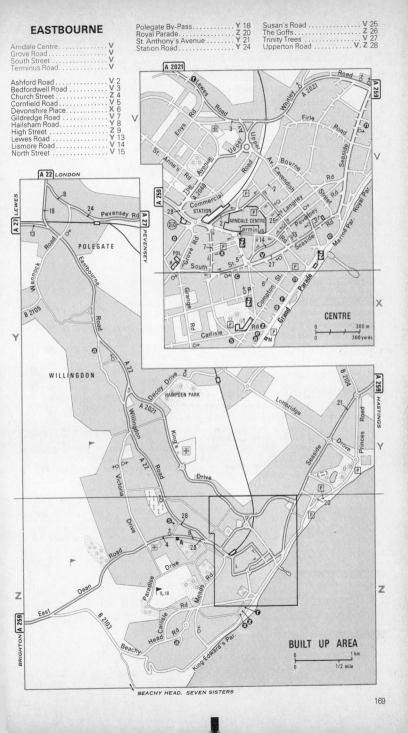

EASTBOURNE

Arndale Centre.................. V
Grove Road...................... V
South Street..................... V
Terminus Road.................. V

Ashford Road.................... V 2
Bedfordwell Road............... V 3
Church Street.................... Z 4
Cornfield Road................... V 5
Devonshire Place............... X 6
Gildredge Road................. V 7
Hailsham Road.................. Y 8
High Street....................... Z 9
Lewes Road...................... Y 13
Lismore Road.................... V 14
North Street..................... V 15

CENTRE

0 —————— 300 m
0 —————— 300 yards

BUILT UP AREA

0 —————— 1 km
0 —————— 1/2 mile

BEACHY HEAD. SEVEN SISTERS

169

at Stone Cross N : 4 m. by A 259 on B 2104 (Hailsham Rd) – Y – ✉ Pevensey – ⊛ 0323 Hailsham :

🏨🏨 **Glyndley Manor** 🐚, Hailsham Rd, BN24 5BS, NW : 1 3/4 m. on B 2104 ☎ 843737, <, 🏊 heated, 🏊, ⛱, park, 🎾 – [TV] 🛁wc 🚿wc ☎ [P]. 🎤. [A] [AE] (D) [VISA]
M 9.00/10.00 **st.** – **20 rm** ☕ 33.00/55.00 **t.** – SB 64.00 **st.**

at Pevensey NE : 5 m. by A 259 – Y – on A27 – ✉ ⊛ 0323 Eastbourne :

🏨 **Priory Court,** High St., BN24 5LG, ☎ 763150, ⛱ – [TV] 🛁wc [P]. [A] [AE] (D) [VISA]. 🚫🐕
M 6.95/7.50 **t.** – ☕ 2.50 – **12 rm** 19.00/39.00 **st.** – SB (weekends only) 23.50/26.50 **st.**

at Jevington NW : 6 m. by A 259 – Z – on B 2105 – ✉ ⊛ 032 12 Polegate :

🍴🍴 **Hungry Monk,** The Street, BN26 5QF, ☎ 2178 – [P]
closed 24 to 26 December – **M** (dinner only and Sunday lunch) (booking essential) 8.25/8.95 🍷 2.30.

at Wilmington NW : 6 1/2 m. by A 22 on A 27 – Y – ✉ ⊛ 032 12 Polegate :

⌂ Crossways, BN26 5SG, ☎ 2455, ⛱ – [P]
10 rm ☕ 10.00/22.00.

AUSTIN-ROVER, ROLLS ROYCE Meads Rd ☎ 30201
CITROEN, SAAB 8-14 Seaside ☎ 640139
FIAT Ashford Rd ☎ 640101
FORD Lottbridge Drove ☎ 37171
LADA, SUBARU Susans Rd ☎ 639589
NISSAN 46 Pevensey Rd ☎ 37339
PEUGEOT-TALBOT East Dean ☎ 3053
RELIANT, SKODA Pevensey Bay Rd ☎ 761150
RENAULT 18 Lottbridge Drove ☎ 37233
VAUXHALL, RELIANT 336/8 Seaside ☎ 30663
VW, AUDI Burlington Rd ☎ 640114

EAST BUCKLAND Devon [403] I 30 – see South Molton.

EAST CHINNOCK Somerset – see Yeovil.

EAST DEREHAM Norfolk [404] W 25 – pop. 8,060 – ⊛ 0362 Dereham.
♦London 109 – ♦Cambridge 57 – King's Lynn 27 – ♦Norwich 16.

🏨🏨 **Phoenix** (T.H.F.), Church St., NR19 1DL, ☎ 2276 – [TV] 🛁wc ☎ [P]. 🎤. [A] [AE] (D) [VISA]
M 5.30/8.00 **st.** 🍷 2.60 – ☕ 4.75 – **28 rm** 25.50/40.00 **st.**

🏨 **King's Head,** 42 Norwich St., NR19 1AD, ☎ 3842 – [TV] 🛁wc 🚿wc [P]. [A] [AE] (D) [VISA]
M 6.75/7.50 **t.** 🍷 2.15 – **15 rm** ☕ 18.50/30.00 **t.** – SB (weekends only) 43.00/47.00 **st.**

AUSTIN-ROVER Two Oaks Garage Beetley ☎ 860219
AUSTIN-ROVER Norwich Rd ☎ 2293
FORD High St. ☎ 2281

EAST GRINSTEAD West Sussex [404] T 30 – pop. 16,560 – ECD : Wednesday – ⊛ 0342.
Envir. : Hever Castle★ (13C-20C) and gardens★★ *AC*, NE : 10 m.
♦London 32 – ♦Brighton 29 – Eastbourne 33 – Lewes 21 – Maidstone 32.

🏨🏨 **Felbridge,** London Rd, RH19 2BH, NW : 1 1/2 m. on A 22 ☎ 26992, Telex 95156, 🏊 heated, 🏊, ⛱ – [TV] 🛁wc ☎ [P]. 🎤. [A] [AE] (D) [VISA]
M *(closed Saturday lunch)* (carving lunch) 8.00/9.25 **st.** – **48 rm** ☕ 37.50/50.00 **st.** – SB (weekends only) 51.00 **st.**

🍴🍴 **Woodbury House** with rm, Lewes Rd, RH19 3UD, SE : 1/2 m. on A 22 ☎ 25684, ⛱ – [TV] 🛁wc 🚿wc. [A] [AE] (D) [VISA]
M *(closed Sunday dinner)* a la carte 11.45/12.50 **t.** 🍷 2.40 – **7 rm** ☕ 19.00/35.00 **t.**

at Gravetye SW : 4 1/2 m. by B 2110 – ✉ East Grinstead – ⊛ 0342 Sharpthorne :

🏨🏨🏨 ✿ **Gravetye Manor** 🐚, RH19 4LJ, ☎ 810567, Telex 957239, <, « 16C Manor house with gardens and grounds by William Robinson », 🏊, park – [TV] [P]. 🚫🐕
M (booking essential) a la carte 16.30/24.05 **s.** 🍷 5.50 – ☕ 6.00 – **14 rm** 42.00/84.00 **s.**
Spec. Roulade of smoked salmon with avocado sauce, Roast venison with Juniper berry sauce, Poached sea bass with caviare.

AUSTIN-ROVER King St. ☎ 24666
FORD 220 London Rd ☎ 24344

EAST HORSLEY Surrey [404] S 30 – pop. 1,455 – ✉ Leatherhead – ⊛ 048 65.
♦London 29 – Guildford 7.

🏨🏨 **Thatchers** (Best Western), Epsom Rd, KT24 6TB, on A 246 ☎ 4291, 🏊 heated, ⛱ – [TV] 🛁wc ☎ [P]. 🎤. [A] [AE] (D) [VISA]
M 6.50/10.75 **st.** 🍷 5.50 – ☕ 4.75 – **28 rm** 33.50/44.50 **st.** – SB (weekends only) 50.00/60.00 **st.**

EASTLEIGH Hants. [403] P 31 – pop. 25,900 – ⊛ 0703.
[i] Town Hall Centre, Leigh Rd ☎ 614646 ext 3067.
♦London 74 – Winchester 8 – ♦Southampton 4.

🏨🏨🏨 **Crest** (Crest), Leigh Rd, SO5 5PG, ☎ 619700, Telex 47606 – [lift] ▤ rest [TV] ☎ ♿ [P]. 🎤. [A] [AE] (D) [VISA]. 🚫🐕
M approx. 10.00 **st.** – ☕ 5.25 – **120 rm** 45.50/56.00 **st.**

EAST MOLESEY Surrey 404 ⑫ – see Esher.

EASTON CROSS Devon 403 I 31 – see Chagford.

EASTON GREY Wilts. 403 404 N 29 – see Malmesbury.

EAST PRESTON West Sussex 404 S 31 – see Worthing.

EAST WITTERING West Sussex 404 R 31 – pop. 2,869 – ❸ 0243 Chichester.
◆London 74 – ◆Brighton 37 – ◆Portsmouth 25.

  ✗ **Clifford's Cottage**, Bracklesham Lane, Bracklesham Bay, PO20 8JF, E : ¼ m. by B 2179 on B 2198 ℰ 670250 – ❷. ⃟ ⓘ *VISA*
    closed Sunday dinner, Monday October-Easter, second week February and second week October – **M** a la carte 8.65/16.70 **st.** ⋔ 2.80.

EBBERSTON North Yorks. 402 S 21 – pop. 430 – ✉ ❸ 0723 Scarborough.
◆London 243 – Scarborough 9 – York 31.

  ⭒ **Foxholm**, YO13 9NJ, off A 170 ℰ 85550, ☞ – 🏠wc ❷
    March-October and Christmas – **10 rm** ⫢ 11.00/30.00 **t.**

ECCLESHALL Staffs. 402 403 404 N 25 – pop. 3,630 – ECD : Wednesday – ❸ 0785.
See : Parish Church★ 12C.
◆London 160 – ◆Birmingham 38 – Newport 8.5 – ◆Stoke-on-Trent 11.

  ✗✗ La Corbière, 8-12 Castle St., ST21 6OS, ℰ 850180 – ❷.

EDWALTON Notts. 402 403 404 Q 25 – see Nottingham.

EDWINSTOWE Notts. 402 403 404 Q 24 – pop. 4,839 – ✉ ❸ 0623 Mansfield.
◆London 154 – Derby 31 – Lincoln 26 – ◆Nottingham 21 – ◆Sheffield 25.

  ✗✗ **Maid Marian**, 8-10 Church St., NG21 9QA, ℰ 822266 – ❷. ⃟ ⒶⒺ ⓘ *VISA*
    closed Sunday dinner, Monday and 25 to 30 December – **M** a la carte 6.65/9.55 **t.** ⋔ 3.40.

EGERTON Greater Manchester 402 ㉑ 403 ② 404 ⑨ – see Bolton.

EGHAM Surrey 404 S 29 – pop. 30,609 – ECD : Thursday – ❸ 0784.
◆London 29 – Reading 21.

  🏨🏨🏨 **Runnymede**, Windsor Rd, TW20 0AG, on A 308 ℰ 36171, Telex 934900, ≼ – 🛗 ⓉⓋ ☎ ❷. 🕭.
    ⃟ ⒶⒺ ⓘ *VISA*
    M 7.75/9.00 **st.** ⋔ 3.15 – ⫢ 2.00 – **90 rm** 41.00/53.00 **st.** – SB (weekends only) 52.00/56.00 **st.**

  🏨🏨 **Great Fosters**, Stroude Rd, TW20 9UR, S : 1 m. by B 388 ℰ 33822, ≼, « Elizabethan mansion with extensive gardens », ⛉ heated, park, ✗✗ – ⓉⓋ ❷. 🕭. ⃟ ⒶⒺ ⓘ *VISA*. ✾
    M 9.75/13.00 **t.** ⋔ 2.75 – **44 rm** ⫢ 34.50/67.50 **t.**

  ✗✗✗ **Bailiwick**, Wick Rd, Englefield Green, TW20 0HN, SW : 2 ½ m. by A 30 ℰ 32223 – ⃟ ⒶⒺ ⓘ *VISA*
    closed Sunday dinner – **M** a la carte 10.80/16.05 **t.**

  ✗✗ **La Bonne Franquette**, 5 High St., TW20 9EA, ℰ 33206 – ❷. ⃟ ⒶⒺ ⓘ *VISA*
    closed Saturday lunch and Bank Holidays – **M** a la carte 12.80/17.00 **t.** ⋔ 4.00.

  ✗ **Trattoria il Borgo**, 15 The Precinct, ℰ 33544, Italian rest. – ⃟ ⒶⒺ *VISA*
    closed Sunday, Christmas and Bank Holidays – **M** a la carte 7.25/13.40 **t.** ⋔ 2.50.

AUSTIN-ROVER The Causeway ℰ 36191   PEUGEOT-TALBOT 186 High St. ℰ 38787
FERRARI Egham-by-pass ℰ 36431

EGLWYSFACH Dyfed 403 I 26 – see Machynlleth (Powys).

ELLESMERE Salop 402 403 L 25 – pop. 2,474 – ECD : Thursday – ❸ 069 171.
◆London 181 – Chester 24 – Shrewsbury 17 – ◆Stoke-on-Trent 33.

  🏠 **Grange**, Grange Rd, SY12 9DE, on A 528 ℰ 2735, ☞ – ⓉⓋ 🏠wc ❷. ⃟ ⓘ *VISA*
    M (bar lunch Monday to Saturday) 6.50/7.50 **t.** ⋔ 2.50 – **15 rm** ⫢ 12.00/29.00 **t.** – SB 38.00/42.00 **st.**

ELTERWATER Cumbria – see Ambleside.

ELY Cambs. **404** U 26 – pop. 9,020 – ECD : Tuesday – 🕿 0353.

See : Cathedral★★ 11C-16C (Norman nave★★★, lantern★★★).

🗽 Ely City, Cambridge Rd ℰ 2751.

🛈 24 St. Mary's St. ℰ 3311 and 2894 ext 253.

♦London 74 – ♦Cambridge 16 – ♦Norwich 60.

　🏠　**Lamb** (Q.M.H.), 2 Lynn Rd, CB7 4EJ, ℰ 3574 – 📺 ⌷wc ☜ 🅿. ♨. 🔌 AE ⓪ VISA
　　　M 7.50 **st.** ▮ 2.50 – **31 rm** ⊇ 28.00/37.00 **st.** – SB (weekends only) 44.00 **st.**

　✗　**Old Fire Engine House,** 25 St. Mary's St., CB7 4ER, ℰ 2582, English rest. – 🅿
　　　closed Sunday dinner, 2 weeks at Christmas and Bank Holidays – **M** a la carte 7.00/10.00 **st.**

AUSTIN-ROVER　Lynn Rd ℰ 2981
CITROEN, PEUGEOT, TALBOT　St. Mary's St. ℰ 2952
FORD　Station Rd ℰ 61181

NISSAN　64 St. Mary's St. ℰ 2300
VOLVO　The Slade, Witcham ℰ 778403

EMBOROUGH Somerset **403 404** M 30 – pop. 168 – ✉ Bath (Avon) – 🕿 0761 Stratton-on-the-Fosse.

♦London 127 – ♦Bristol 15 – Taunton 33.

　🏠　**Court,** Lynch Hill, BA3 4SA, E : ¼ m. on B 3139 ℰ 232237, ☞, ✗ – 📺 ⌷wc 🗇wc 🅿. 🔌
　　　VISA
　　　closed 25 December-11 January – **M** (closed Monday lunch) 7.00/9.25 **t.** ▮ 2.25 – **10 rm**
　　　⊇ 22.00/35.00 **t.** – SB (weekends only except Bank Holidays) 42.50/45.50 **st.**

EMSWORTH Hants. **404** R 31 – pop. 9,016 – ECD : Wednesday – 🕿 024 34.

♦London 75 – ♦Brighton 37 – ♦Portsmouth 10.

　🏠　**Brookfield,** Havant Rd, PO10 7LF, ℰ 3363, ☞ – 📺 ⌷wc 🗇wc ☎ 🅿. 🔌 AE ⓪ VISA 🛇.
　　　M (closed Sunday lunch) 9.50/11.00 ▮ 2.00 – **17 rm** ⊇ 22.00/30.00 **s.**

ENBORNE Berks. – see Newbury.

EPPING Essex **404** U 28 – pop. 10,830 – ECD : Wednesday – 🕿 0378.

See : Forest★.

Envir. : Waltham Abbey (Abbey★) W : 6 m.

♦London 20 – ♦Cambridge 40 – Chelmsford 18.

　🏨　**Post House** (T.H.F.), High Rd, Bell Common, CM16 4DG, S : ¾ m. on B 1393 ℰ 73137, Telex
　　　81617, ☞ – 📺 ⌷wc ☎ 🅿. 🔌 AE ⓪ VISA
　　　M 6.75/8.75 **st.** ▮ 2.85 – ⊇ 5.00 – **82 rm** 38.50/45.50 **st.**

RENAULT　High Rd ℰ 72266

EPSOM Surrey **404** ⑳ – pop. 72,301 (inc. Ewell) – ECD : Wednesday – 🕿 037 27.

Envir. : Chessington Zoo★ AC, NW : 3 ½ m.

🗽 ℰ 23363.

♦London 17 – Guildford 16.

　↟　**White House,** Downshill Rd, KT18 5HW, ℰ 22472, ☞ – ⌷wc 🅿. 🛇
　　　10 rm ⊇ 14.50/27.50.

AUSTIN-ROVER　4 Church St. ℰ 26611
CITROEN　Walton-on-the-Hill ℰ 073 781 (Tadworth)
3811
FORD　East St. ℰ 26246
MAZDA　5 Ruxley Lane, Ewell ℰ 01 393 0202

PEUGEOT, TALBOT　38 Upper High St. ℰ 25611
RENAULT　1/3 Dorking Rd ℰ 28391
VAUXHALL　48 Upper High St. ℰ 25920
VW, AUDI　Reigate Rd ℰ 073 73 (Burgh Heath) 60111

ESHER Surrey **404** S 29 – pop. 64,414 – ECD : Wednesday – 🕿 0372.

🗽 Moore Place, Portsmouth Rd ℰ 63533 BZ – 🗽 Sandown Park, More Lane ℰ 65921 BZ.

♦London 20 – ♦Portsmouth 58.

Plan : see Greater London (South-West)

　✗✗　**Good Earth,** 14-16 High St., KT10 9RT, ℰ 62489, Chinese rest. – 🍽. 🔌 AE ⓪ VISA　　BZ　**e**
　　　M a la carte 9.00/13.50 **t.** ▮ 2.30.

　✗✗　**Le Pierrot,** 63 High St., KT10 9RQ, ℰ 63191, French rest. – 🍽. 🔌 AE ⓪ VISA　　　　BZ　**o**
　　　closed Saturday lunch and Sunday – **M** a la carte 9.95/11.25 **t.** ▮ 3.00.

　　　at East Molesey N : 2 m. by A 309 – ✉ East Molesey – 🕿 01 London :

　✗✗　**Vecchia Roma,** 55-57 Bridge Rd, KT8 9ER, ℰ 979 5490, Italian rest. – 🔌 ⓪ VISA　　　BZ　**n**
　　　closed Saturday lunch – **M** a la carte 10.80/15.65 **t.** ▮ 3.45.

　✗✗　**Le Chien Qui Fume,** 107 Walton Rd, KT8 0DR, ℰ 979 7150, French rest. – 🔌 AE ⓪ VISA
　　　closed Sunday and Bank Holidays – **M** a la carte 8.90/14.65 **t.** ▮ 2.75.　　　　　　BZ　**c**

　✗✗　**Lantern,** 20 Bridge Rd, KT8 9AH, ℰ 979 1531, French rest. – 🔌 AE ⓪ VISA　　　　　BZ　**i**
　　　closed Sunday, August and Bank Holidays – **M** (lunch by arrangement) a la carte 11.65/15.25 **t.**
　　　▮ 2.40.

AUSTIN-ROVER　94 Hare Lane, Claygate ℰ 62996

VAUXHALL　Kingston By-Pass, Hinchley Wood ℰ 01
(London) 398 0123

[ESKDALE GREEN] Cumbria [402] K 20 – pop. 450 – ECD : Wednesday and Saturday – ✉ Holmrook – ☎ 094 03.
♦London 312 – ♦Carlisle 59 – Kendal 60.

- **Bower House Inn** 🌿, Holmrook, CA19 1TD, W : ¾ m. ☎ 244, 🌳 – [TV] 🛁wc [P]
closed 24 to 26 December – **M** (bar lunch) 9.50 **t.** 🍷 3.00 – **13 rm** ☕ 17.50/45.00 **t.**

[ETON] Berks. [404] S 29 – see Windsor.

[ETTINGTON] Warw. [403] [404] P 27 – see Stratford-upon-Avon.

[EVERSHOT] Dorset [403] [404] M 31 – pop. 217 – ✉ Dorchester – ☎ 093 583.
♦London 149 – Bournemouth 39 – Dorchester 12 – Salisbury 53 – Taunton 30 – Yeovil 10.

- **Summer Lodge** 🌿, Summer Lane, DT2 0JR, ☎ 424, « Country house atmosphere », 🏊 heated, 🌳 – 🛁wc [P]. [AE] [VISA]
closed December-January – **M** (dinner only) 12.50 **t.** 🍷 2.35 – **9 rm** ☕ 25.00/60.00 **t.** – SB (except summer) 31.50/35.00 **st.**

[EVESHAM] Heref. and Worc. [403] [404] O 27 – pop. 13,855 – ECD : Wednesday – ☎ 0386.
[i] The Almonry Museum, Abbey Gate ☎ 6944.
♦London 99 – ♦Birmingham 30 – Cheltenham 16 – ♦Coventry 32.

- **Evesham,** Coopers Lane, off Waterside (A 44), WR11 6DA, ☎ 49111, Telex 339342, 🌳 – [TV] 🛁wc 🚿wc ☎ [P]. ♿. [AE] [DC] [VISA]
closed 25 and 26 December – **M** (buffet lunch) a la carte 8.55/11.15 **st.** 🍷 2.90 – **34 rm** ☕ 34.00/47.00 **st.** – SB (weekends only) 50.00/64.00 **st.**

AUSTIN-ROVER Abbey Rd ☎ 6173
BEDFORD, VAUXHALL-OPEL 70 High St. ☎ 2614
BMW, VW, AUDI Harvington ☎ 870612
COLT Bretforton ☎ 830278
FIAT 3 Cheltenham Rd ☎ 2301
FORD Market Pl. ☎ 2525
LOTUS High St., Pershore ☎ 555433
NISSAN Cheltenham Rd ☎ 47103
PEUGEOT-TALBOT Broadway Rd ☎ 6441
RENAULT Pershore ☎ 0386 (Pershore) 2167
RENAULT 123 Pershore Rd, Hampton ☎ 45072
SKODA Sedgeberrow ☎ 881208

[EWEN] Glos. [403] [404] O 28 – see Cirencester.

[EXETER] Devon [403] J 31 **The West Country G.** – pop. 95,729 – ☎ 0392.
See : Site★★ – **Cathedral**★★ AZ **A** – **Maritime Museum**★★ AZ – **Royal Albert Memorial Museum**★ AZ **M2** – **Envir. :** Killerton House★★, N : 7 m. by B 3181 BY.
⛳18 Downes Crediton ☎ 036 32 (Crediton) 3991, NW : 7 ½ m. by A 377 AY.
✈ Exeter Airport : ☎ 67433, Telex 42648, E : 5 m. by A 30 BY – **Terminal :** St. David's and Central Stations.
[i] Civic Centre, Dix's Field ☎ 72434 – Exeter Services Area (M 5) Sandygate, ☎ 37581 (summer only).
♦London 201 – Bournemouth 83 – ♦Bristol 83 – ♦Plymouth 46 – ♦Southampton 110.

Plan on next page

- **Buckerell Lodge** (Crest), Topsham Rd, EX2 4SQ, SE : 1 m. on B 3182 ☎ 52451, Telex 42410, 🌳 – [TV] 🛁wc ☎ ♿ [P]. [AE] [DC] [VISA]. 🐕 BY **a**
M approx. 12.50 **st.** – ☕ 5.25 – **54 rm** 41.00/52.00 **st.**
- **White Hart,** 65-66 South St., EX1 1EE, ☎ 79897, « Part 14C inn » – [lift] [TV] 🛁wc 🚿wc ☎ [P]. ♿. [AE] [DC] [VISA]. 🐕 AZ **n**
closed 24 and 25 December – **M** a la carte 10.00/16.00 **t.** 🍷 3.20 – **62 rm** ☕ 19.00/44.00 **t.** – SB (weekends only) 41.00/52.00 **st.**
- **Royal Clarence** (Norfolk Cap.), Cathedral Yard, EX1 1HD, ☎ 58464, Group Telex 23241 – [lift] [TV] 🛁wc 🚿wc ☎. ♿. [AE] [DC] [VISA]. 🐕 AZ **z**
M 6.00/8.00 **t.** 🍷 2.25 – **62 rm** ☕ 32.50/49.00 **st.** – SB (May-October) 55.00 **st.**
- Rougemont (Mt. Charlotte), Queen St., EX4 3SP, ☎ 54982, Telex 42455 – [lift] [TV] 🛁wc ☎ [P]. ♿. [AE] [DC] [VISA] AZ **x**
63 rm ☕ 32.45/43.45 **st.** – SB (weekends only) 55.00 **st.**
- **Exeter Moat House** (Q.M.H.), 398 Topsham Rd, EX2 6HE, S : 2 ½ m. at junction of A 379 and B 3182 ☎ 039 287 (Topsham) 5441 – [TV] 🛁wc ☎ [P]. ♿. [AE] [DC] [VISA] BY **o**
M 5.95/6.50 **t.** 🍷 2.55 – **44 rm** ☕ 29.45/37.00 **st.** – SB 41.00/43.00 **st.**
- **Imperial,** St. David's Hill, EX4 4JX, ☎ 211811, Telex 42551, 🌳 – [TV] 🛁wc 🚿wc ☎ 🚗 [P]. ♿. [AE] [DC] [VISA] AZ **v**
M 7.45/10.25 **t.** 🍷 2.60 – **25 rm** ☕ 17.00/40.00 **t.** – SB (weekends only)(except summer) 40.00/45.00 **st.**
- **Great Western,** St. David's Station Approach, EX4 4LS, ☎ 74039 – [TV] 🛁wc ☎ [P]. [AE] [DC] [VISA] AZ **c**
M 4.25/6.95 **t.** – **44 rm** ☕ 17.50/30.00 **t.** – SB (weekends only) 38.00/44.00 **st.**
- **Red House,** 2 Whipton Village Rd, EX4 8AR, ☎ 56104 – [TV] 🛁wc 🚿wc [P]. [AE] [DC] [VISA]
M a la carte 4.40/10.35 🍷 2.10 – **13 rm** ☕ 12.00/27.00 **st.** – SB (weekends only) 35.00/50.00 **st.** BY **r**
- **St. Andrews,** 28 Alphington Rd, EX2 8HN, ☎ 76784 – [TV] 🛁wc [P]. [AE] [VISA] AY **a**
closed 1 week at Christmas – **M** (bar lunch) 6.50 **st.** – **16 rm** ☕ 16.00/30.00 **st.**
- **Bystock,** 6-8 Bystock Terr., EX4 4HY, ☎ 72709 – [TV] 🛁wc. [VISA] AZ **a**
M *(closed Sunday lunch)* (bar lunch) 5.60/8.10 **t.** 🍷 2.45 – **24 rm** ☕ 12.50/26.00 **t.**

EXETER

Bedford Street .... **AZ** 3
Fore Street .... **AZ**
High Street .... **AZ**
Shopping Precinct .... **AZ**

Alphington Road .... **AZ** 2
Blackall Road .... **AZ** 4
Butts Road .... **BY** 5
Commins Road .... **BZ** 8

Edmund Street .... **AZ** 9
East Wonford Hill .... **BY** 10
Frog Street .... **AZ** 12
Ladysmith Road .... **BZ** 16
Little John's Cross Hill ..... **AY** 17
Magdalen Street .... **AZ** 20
Mount Pleasant Road ...... **BY** 21
New Bridge Street .... **AZ** 22
North Street .... **AZ** 23
North Street HEAVITREE .... **BY** 24
Okehampton Road .... **AZ** 26
Old Tiverton Road .... **BZ** 27

Paris Street .... **BZ** 28
Prince Charles Road .... **BY** 30
Prince of Wales Road ...... **AY** 31
Richmond Road .... **AZ** 32
St. Andrew's Road .... **AZ** 33
Southernhay East ...... **ABZ** 34
Southernhay West .... **AZ** 35
Sweetbriar Lane .... **BY** 36
Union Road .... **AY** 37
Western Way .... **AZ** 38
Whipton Lane .... **BY** 39
Wonford Street .... **BY** 40

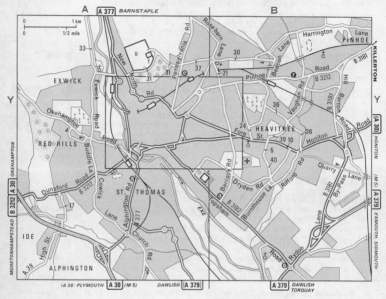

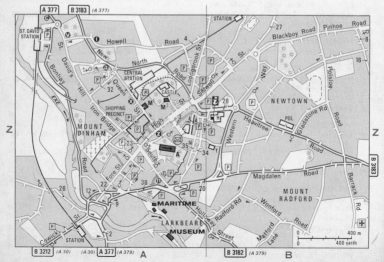

174

⌂ **Sylvania House,** 64 Pennsylvania Rd, EX4 6DF, ☎ 75583 – ⫙wc [P]. VISA. ✗ AY **e**
closed 15-31 December – **8 rm** ☕ 10.00/22.50 **t.**

⌂ **Park View,** 8 Howell Rd, EX4 4LG, ☎ 71772 – [TV] ⛀wc ⫙wc [P]. [S] VISA AZ **i**
closed 21-30 December – **15 rm** ☕ 9.80/23.00 **t.**

at Huxham N : 5 m. by A 377 – AY – off A 396 – ✉ Exeter – ☎ 039 284 Stoke Canon :

🍴🍴 **Barton Cross,** EX5 4EJ, ☎ 245, « Part 16C thatched cottage », 🌳 – [P]. [S] VISA
closed Sunday, Monday and 3 weeks January – **M** (booking essential) 10.40/13.10 **t.** 🍷 2.85.

at Pinhoe NE : 3 m. by B 3212 on B 3181 – BY – ✉ ☎ 0392 Exeter :

🏨 **Gipsy Hill** 🐦, Gipsy Hill Lane, via Station Rd, EX1 3RN, ☎ 65252, 🌳 – [TV] ⛀wc ☎ [P]. 🎤. [S] [AE] VISA. ✗
M 5.50/7.50 **t.** 🍷 2.50 – **19 rm** ☕ 26.50/37.00 **t.** – SB 45.00 **st.**

at Whimple NE : 9 m. by A 30 – BY – ✉ Exeter – ☎ 0404 Whimple :

🏨 **Woodhayes** 🐦, EX5 2TD, ☎ 822237, « Country house atmosphere », 🌳 – [TV] ⛀wc ☎ 🚗 [P]. [S] [AE] [O] VISA. ✗
M (lunch by arrangement)(booking essential) 10.00/15.00 – **6 rm** ☕ 30.00/60.00 **st.** – SB (weekends only)(winter only) 59.50 **st.**

at Kennford S : 5 m. on A 38 – AY – ✉ ☎ 0392 Exeter :

🏨 **Ladbroke Mercury Motor Inn** (Ladbroke), Kennford Services, EX6 7UX, ☎ 832121 – [TV] ⛀wc ☎ ♿ [P]. 🎤. [S] [AE] [O] VISA
M (grill rest. only) a la carte 7.30/10.45 **t.** 🍷 3.85 – **61 rm** ☕ 31.00/41.00 **t.** – SB (weekends only) 33.00 **st.**

🏨 **Fairwinds,** EX6 7UD, ☎ 832911 – [TV] ⛀wc ⫙wc [P]. ✗
closed 14 to 31 December – **M** (residents only)(bar lunch) 5.00/8.15 **t.** 🍷 2.00 – **8 rm** ☕ 17.00/32.00 **t.** – SB 34.00/38.00 **st.**

at Doddiscombsleigh SW : 7 ½ m. by A 38 – AY – ✉ Exeter – ☎ 0647 Christow :

🏠 **Nobody Inn** 🐦, EX6 7PS, ☎ 52394, « 16C inn », 🌳 – ⛀wc ⫙wc [P]. [S] VISA. ✗
closed Christmas Day – **M** *(closed dinner Sunday and Monday except Bank Holidays)* (bar lunch) a la carte 6.90/10.00 **t.** 🍷 1.75 – **7 rm** ☕ 10.00/28.00 **t.**

MICHELIN Branch, Kestrel Way, Sowton Industrial Estate, EX2 7LH, ☎ **77246/7/8/9**

ALFA-ROMEO, SUZUKI Hennock Rd, Marsh Barton ☎ 37337
AUSTIN-ROVER 55 Sidwell St. ☎ 78342
AUSTIN-ROVER 84-88 Sidwell St. ☎ 54923
AUSTIN-ROVER-DAIMLER-JAGUAR, ROLLS ROYCE Marsh Barton Rd ☎ 37152
BMW Pinhill, Pinhoe ☎ 69595
CITROEN, FIAT, MERCEDES-BENZ Trusham Rd, Marsh Barton ☎ 77311
COLT 66 Polsloe Rd ☎ 57990
FORD 9 Marsh Barton Rd ☎ 50141
MAZDA Alphinbrook Rd ☎ 57737
NISSAN Honiton Rd ☎ 68187
RENAULT Summerland St. ☎ 77225
TOYOTA 37 Marsh Green Rd, Marsh Barton ☎ 34761
VAUXHALL-OPEL, BEDFORD Marsh Baxton Trading Estate ☎ 34851
VOLVO Longbrook Terr. ☎ 215691
VW, AUDI Haven Rd ☎ 30321

EXFORD Somerset [403] J 30 **The West Country G.** – **pop. 452** – **ECD : Tuesday** – ✉ **Minehead** – ☎ **064 383.**

See : Exmoor National Park★★ – **Church**★ – **Envir. : Dunkery Beacon**★★★ (≤★★★), **N : 4 ½ m.**

♦London 194 – Exeter 35 – Minehead 13 – Taunton 32.

🏨 **Crown,** TA24 7PP, ☎ 554 – [TV] ⛀wc [P]. [S] [AE] [O] VISA
M 5.75/12.75 **t.** 🍷 2.85 – **18 rm** ☕ 26.00/68.00 **t.** – SB (May to July) 56.00 **st.**

EXMOUTH Devon [403] J 32 **The West Country G.** – **pop. 21,030** – **ECD : Wednesday** – ☎ **039 52 (4 and 5 fig.) or 0395 (6 fig.).**

Envir. : A La Ronde★, **N : 2 m.**

[i] Alexandra Terr. ☎ 263744 (summer only).

♦London 210 – Exeter 11.

🏨 **Imperial** (T.H.F.), The Esplanade, EX8 2SW, ☎ 274761, ≤, 🏊 heated, 🌳, 🎾 – [lift] [TV] [P]. [S] [AE] [O] VISA
M (bar lunch Monday to Saturday) 7.95 **st.** 🍷 2.85 – ☕ 5.00 – **60 rm** 29.50/57.50 **st.**

🏨 **Royal Beacon,** The Beacon, EX8 2AF, ☎ 264886, ≤ – [lift] ▤ rest [TV] ⛀wc 🚗 [P]. [S] [AE] [O] VISA
M 5.00/7.00 **t.** 🍷 2.75 – **35 rm** ☕ 17.00/44.00 **t.** – SB (October to May except Easter and Christmas) 21.50 **st.**

🏨 **Balcombe House** 🐦, 7 Stevenstone Rd, EX8 2EP, NE : 1 m. by A 376 ☎ 266349, 🌳 – [TV] ⫙wc ♿ [P]. ✗
April-October – **M** (bar lunch) 6.50 **t.** 🍷 1.80 – **12 rm** ☕ 13.00/30.00 **t.**

at Lympstone N : 3 m. by A 376 – ✉ ☎ 0395 Exmouth

🍴🍴🍴 **River House,** The Strand, EX8 5EY, ☎ 265147, ≤ Exe Estuary – [S] [AE] VISA
closed Sunday dinner and Monday – **M** (booking essential) a la carte 10.80/13.85 **t.** 🍷 3.45.

AUSTIN-ROVER The Parade ☎ 72258
RENAULT 4 Church Rd ☎ 263888
VAUXHALL-OPEL Salterton Rd ☎ 264366

EYAM Derbs. **403 404** O 24 – pop. 915 – ⊠ Sheffield (South Yorks.) – ☎ 0433 Hope Valley.
See : Celtic Cross★ 8C.

♦London 163 – Derby 29 – ♦Manchester 32 – ♦Sheffield 12.

  ✗ **Miners Arms** with rm, Water Lane, S30 1RG, ℰ 30853 – **P**. ℀
    M *(closed Monday lunch)* 3.75/11.00 **t.** 🍴 2.90 – **4 rm** ☲ 12.00/18.00 **st.**

EYNSHAM Oxon. **403 404** P 28 – ☎ 0865 Oxford.

♦London 65 – ♦Birmingham 65 – Gloucester 40 – Northampton 43.

  ✗✗ **Edward's,** 4 Lombard St., OX8 1HT, ℰ 880777 – 🅐 VISA
    closed Saturday lunch, Sunday dinner, 24-26 December and first 2 weeks January – **M** a la
    carte 7.00/11.10 **t.** 🍴 2.00.

FADMOOR North Yorks. – see Kirkbymoorside.

FAIRFORD Glos. **403 404** O 28 – pop. 1,840 – ECD : Saturday – ☎ 0285.
See : St. Mary's Church (stained glass windows★★ 15C-16C).

♦London 99 – ♦Bristol 46 – Gloucester 28 – ♦Oxford 27.

  🏠 Bull, Market Pl., GL7 4AA, ℰ 712535, ✎, 🚗 – 📺 🚻wc **P** – **17 rm**.
AUSTIN-ROVER The Bridge ℰ 712222   RENAULT ℰ 712219

FALFIELD Avon **403 404** M 29 – pop. 658 – ☎ 0454.

♦London 129 – ♦Bristol 16 – Gloucester 18 – Newport 30.

  🏠 **Park,** GL12 8DR, S : 1 m. on A 38 ℰ 260550, 🚗 – 📺 🚻wc 🛏wc **P**. 🅐 AE ⓪ VISA
    M *(closed Sunday)* a la carte 7.75/20.00 **st.** 🍴 3.25 – ☲ 4.00 – **10 rm** 18.50/35.00 **st.**

FALLOWFIELD Greater Manchester **402** ⑱ **403** ③ **404** ⑩ – see Manchester.

FALMOUTH Cornwall **403** E 33 The West Country G. – pop. 18,041 – ECD : Wednesday – ☎ 0326.
See : Site★★ – Pendennis Castle★ (⩤★★) B.
Envir. : Glendurgan Garden★★, S : 3 ½ m. by Swanpool Rd A.

🏌 Swanpool Rd ℰ 311262 A – 🏌 Budock Vean Hotel ℰ 0326 (Mawnan Smith) 288, SW : 7 m. by
Trescobeas Rd A.

🛈 Town Hall, The Moor ℰ 312300 – ♦London 308 – Penzance 26 – ♦Plymouth 65 – Truro 11.

Plan opposite

  🏨 **Falmouth,** TR11 4NZ, ℰ 312671, Telex 45262, ⩤, ⌇ heated, 🚗 – 🛗 📺 **P**. 🔬 🅐 AE ⓪ VISA
    closed Christmas and New Year – **M** (bar lunch Monday to Saturday) 6.00/10.50 **st.** 🍴 2.45 –
    73 rm ☲ 22.55/68.00 **st.** – SB 56.00/73.00 **st.**   B **x**

  🏨 Royal Duchy, Cliff Rd, TR11 4NX, ℰ 313042, ⩤, 🚗 – 🛗 📺 **P**. 🅐 AE ⓪ VISA   B **a**
    M 4.60/6.35 **t.** – **38 rm**.

  🏨 **Green Lawns,** Western Terr., TR11 4QJ, ℰ 312734, Telex 45169 – 📺 🚻wc 🛏wc 🕾 **P**. 🔬
    🅐 AE ⓪ VISA   A **i**
    M 6.00/8.50 **t.** 🍴 2.50 – **43 rm** ☲ 13.80/46.00 **t.** – SB (except summer) 41.00/55.95 **st.**

  🏨 **St. Michaels,** Sea Front, Gyllyngvase Beach, TR11 4NB, ℰ 312707, Telex 45540, ⩤, ⌇, ✎,
    🚗 – 📺 🚻wc 🛏wc 🕾 **P**. 🅐 AE ⓪ VISA   A **z**
    M 5.00/9.00 **t.** 🍴 2.40 – **75 rm** ☲ 22.50/52.00 **t.** – SB (except summer) 42.00/46.00 **st.**

  🏨 **Falmouth Beach,** Gyllyngvase Beach, Seafront, TR11 4NA, ℰ 318084, Telex 45540, ⩤ – 🛗
    📺 🚻wc 🛏wc 🕾 **P**. 🅐 AE ⓪ VISA   A **r**
    closed January and February – **M** (bar lunch) 9.00 **t.** 🍴 2.25 – **67 rm** ☲ 19.50/41.00 **t.**

  🏨 **Greenbank,** Harbourside, TR11 4SR, ℰ 312440, Telex 45240, ⩤ harbour – 🛗 📺 🚻wc 🕾
    ⇦ **P**. 🅐 AE ⓪ VISA   A **a**
    closed 24 December-1 February – **M** 7.00/9.00 **t.** – **40 rm** ☲ 25.00/42.50 **t.** – SB (week-
    ends only) 50.00/73.00 **st.**

  🏠 **Penmere Manor** (Best Western) ⅍, Mongleath Rd, TR11 4PN, ℰ 314545, ⌇ heated, 🚗 –
    📺 🚻wc 🛏wc 🕾 **P**. 🅐 AE ⓪ VISA   A **e**
    M (bar lunch) 9.00 **t.** – **29 rm** ☲ 22.50/42.00 **t.** – SB 49.00/59.00 **st.**

  🏠 **Crill House** ⅍, Golden Bank, TR11 5BL, SW : 2 ½ m. by Swanpool Rd ℰ 312994, ⌇ heated,
    🚗 – 🚻wc **P**. 🅐 VISA   by Boslowick Rd A
    April-mid October – **M** (bar lunch) 8.00 **t.** 🍴 3.30 – **11 rm** ☲ 14.00/44.00 **t.**

  🏠 **Carthion,** Cliff Rd, TR11 4AP, ℰ 313669, ⩤, 🚗 – 🚻wc 🛏wc **P**. 🅐 AE ⓪ VISA B **v**
    March-October – **M** (bar lunch) 8.00 **t.** 🍴 2.60 – **14 rm** ☲ 12.10/36.30 **t.**

  🏠 **Broadmead,** 68 Kimberley Park Rd, TR11 2DD, ℰ 315704 – 📺 🚻wc ☎. 🅐 VISA A **u**
    M (bar lunch) (booking essential) 7.50 **st.** 🍴 3.00 – **13 rm** ☲ 13.00/30.00 **st.** – SB 30.00/50.00 **st.**

  🏠 **Rosemullion,** Gyllyngvase Hill, TR11 4DF, ℰ 314690 – 🛏wc **P**. ℀   B **c**
    May-October – **14 rm** ☲ 11.50/23.00 **st.**

  🏠 **Gyllyngvase House,** Gyllyngvase Rd, TR11 4DJ, ℰ 312956, 🚗 – 🚻wc **P**. VISA. ℀ B **s**
    16 rm ☲ 10.35/25.30 **st.**

  🏠 **Cotswold House,** 49 Melvill Rd, TR11 4DF, ℰ 312077 – 🚻wc 🛏 **P**. ℀   B **o**
    April-October – **11 rm** ☲ 7.95/22.00 **st.**

  🏠 **Tresillian House,** 3 Stracey Rd, TR11 4DW, ℰ 312425 – 📺 🚻wc 🛏wc **P**. ℀   A **n**
    Mid March-October – **12 rm** ☲ 12.15/28.30 **t.**

FALMOUTH

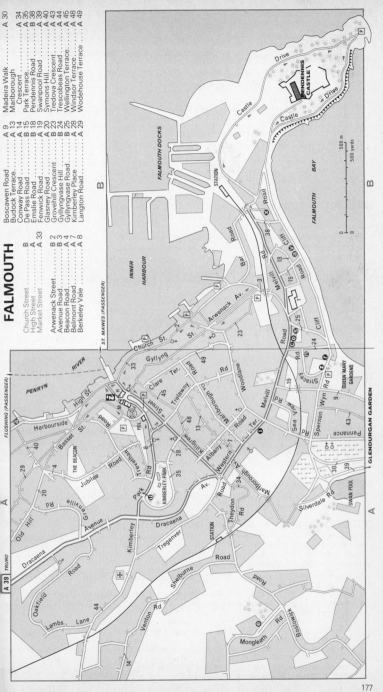

at Mawnan Smith SW : 5 m. by Trescobeas Rd – A – off B 3291 – ⊠ ✪ 0326 Falmouth :

🏨 **Meudon** 🦕, TR11 5HT, E : ½ m. 𝒫 250541, « ≤ Terraced gardens » – 📺 ☎ 🅿 🔼 🅰 ⓞ **VISA**
closed December-mid February – **M** 8.00/12.00 **t.** 🍷 2.95 – **30 rm** ⤶ 22.00/68.00 **t.** – SB 56.00/66.00 **st.**

🏨 **Budock Vean** 🦕, TR11 5LG, 𝒫 250288, ≤, 🔲, 🗗, 🐎, park, 🎾 – 🛁🅿 🔼 🅰 ⓞ **VISA**
🦕
closed Monday to Thursday January-February – **M** 6.00/12.75 **t.** 🍷 3.75 – **50 rm** ⤶ (dinner included) 29.00/80.00 **t.**

🏨 **Nansidwell Country House** 🦕, TR11 5HU, E : ¼ m. on Mawnan Church rd 𝒫 250340, ≤, « Gardens », park, 🎾 – 🚺wc 🅿 🔼 ⓞ **VISA**
closed January and February – **M** (bar lunch) 8.00 **t.** 🍷 2.00 – **20 rm** ⤶ (dinner included) 19.30/60.00 **t.** – SB (except summer) 38.60/54.00 **st.**

🏠 **Trelawne** 🦕, Maenporth Rd, TR11 5HS, E : ¾ m. 𝒫 250226, 🔲, 🐎 – 📺 🚺wc 🚿wc 🔼 🅰 ⓞ **VISA**
closed January and December – **M** (bar lunch) 9.50 **t.** 🍷 2.50 – **16 rm** ⤶ 18.00/40.00 **t.**

AUSTIN-ROVER The Moor 𝒫 312316
BMW Falmouth Rd, Penryn 𝒫 032 67 (Penryn) 2641
FORD Ponsharden 𝒫 72011
NISSAN Dracaena Av. 𝒫 311616
TOYOTA North Parade 𝒫 313029

FAREHAM Hants. 🆘🆗 Q 31 – pop. 80,403 – ECD : Wednesday – ✪ 0329.
Envir. : Porchester castle★ (ruins 3C - 12C), Keep ≤★ *AC*, SE : 2 ½ m.
🛈 Ferneham Hall, Osborn Rd 𝒫 236100.
♦London 77 – ♦Portsmouth 9 – ♦Southampton 13 – Winchester 19.

🏛 Red Lion, East St., PO16 0BP, 𝒫 239611 – 📺 🚺wc ☎ 🅿 🔼 🎾 – **33 rm**
AUSTIN-ROVER West St. 𝒫 231511   PEUGEOT-TALBOT Newgate Lane 𝒫 282811

FARINGDON Oxon. 🆘🆗 P 29 – pop. 3,898 – ECD : Thursday – ✪ 0367.
🛈 Car Park, Southampton Rd 𝒫 22191 (summer only).
♦London 79 – ♦Bristol 55 – ♦Oxford 17 – Reading 34.

🏠 **Bell,** Market Pl., SN7 7HP, 𝒫 20534 – 📺 🚺wc 🅿 🔼 🅰 ⓞ **VISA**
M a la carte 7.80/12.05 **st.** – ⤶ 3.25 – **11 rm** 19.75/31.75 **st.**

✕ **Restaurant 1645,** Market Pl., SN7 7HP, 𝒫 20678 – ⓞ **VISA**
closed Sunday, 2 weeks Easter and last week August – **M** (dinner only) a la carte 8.60/11.20 **t.** 🍷 3.00.

AUSTIN-ROVER Church St. 𝒫 22070   PEUGEOT, TALBOT Marlborough St. 𝒫 21212

FARNBOROUGH Hants. 🆗 R 30 – pop. 41,474 – ECD : Wednesday – ✪ 0252.
See : St. Michael's Abbey church★ 19C (Imperial crypt *AC*).
🗗 Southwood, Ively Rd 𝒫 48700, W : 1 m.
🛈 County Library, Pinehurst Av. 𝒫 513838 ext 24.
♦London 41 – Reading 17 – ♦Southampton 44 – Winchester 33.

🏨 **Queens** (Anchor), Lynchford Rd, GU14 6AZ, S : 1 ½ m. on Farnborough Rd (A 325) 𝒫 545051, Group Telex 858875 – 📺 🚺wc ☎ 🅿 🔼 🔼 🅰 ⓞ **VISA**
M (bar lunch Saturday) a la carte 8.10/12.75 **st.** 🍷 2.65 – **83 rm** ⤶ 39.50/46.00 **st.** – SB (weekends only) 46.00 **st.**

FORD Elles Rd 𝒫 544344

FARNE ISLANDS Northumb. 🆘🆗 P 17.
See : Islands★★ (Sea Bird Sanctuary and grey seals, by boat from Seahouses *AC*).
Hotels see : Bamburgh.

FARNHAM Surrey 🆗 R 30 – pop. 21,110 – ECD : Wednesday – ✪ 0252.
See : Castle keep 12C (square tower★) *AC* – **Envir. :** Birdworld★ (zoological bird gardens) *AC*, SW : 3 ½ m.
🛈 Locality Office, South St. 𝒫 048 68 (Godalming) 4104 ext 554.
♦London 45 – Reading 22 – ♦Southampton 39 – Winchester 28.

🏛 **Bush** (Anchor), The Borough, GU9 7NN, 𝒫 715237, Group Telex 858764, 🐎 – 📺 🚺wc 🚃 🅿 🔼 🅰 ⓞ **VISA**
M a la carte 8.10/12.75 **st.** 🍷 2.65 – **62 rm** ⤶ 39.50/47.50 **st.** – SB (weekends only) 50.00 **st.**

🏠 **Bishop's Table** (Best Western), 27 West St., GU9 7DR, 𝒫 715545, 🐎 – 📺 🚺wc 🚿wc 🚃 🔼 🅰 ⓞ **VISA**
M 9.00 **st.** – **16 rm** ⤶ 28.00/41.00 **st.** – SB (weekends only) 42.00 **st.**

🏠 **Trevena House** 🦕, Alton Rd, GU10 5ER, SW : 1 ¾ m. on A 31 𝒫 716908, ≤, 🔲 heated, 🐎, 🎾 – 📺 🚺wc 🚃 🅿 🔼 🅰 ⓞ **VISA**
closed Christmas and first 2 weeks January – **M** (closed Sunday dinner to non-residents) (dinner only) a la carte 8.00/10.50 **t.** 🍷 2.75 – **19 rm** ⤶ 27.50/44.00 **st.** – SB 45.00 **st.**

✕ **Vienna Stüberl,** 101 West St., GU9 7EN, 𝒫 722978 – 🔼
closed Sunday – **M** a la carte 4.75/9.00 **t.** 🍷 2.80.

at Seale E : 4 m. on A 31 – ⊠ Farnham – ✪ 025 18 Runfold :

🏨 **Hog's Back** (Embassy), GU10 1EX, on A 31 ℰ 2345, ≤, 🐾 – 📺 🛏wc ☎ & 🅟 🏃 🔼 AE ⓪ VISA ℀
M 9.00 st. – ⎓ 4.25 – **50 rm** 36.00/44.00 st. – SB (weekends only) 44.00/50.00 st.

at Churt S : 5 ¾ m. on A 287 – ⊠ Farnham – ✪ 025 125 Frensham :

🏨 **Frensham Pond** ⌇, GU10 2QB, N : 1 ½ m. by A 287 ℰ 3175, Telex 858610, ≤, 🐾 – 📺 ☎ 🅟 🏃 🔼 AE ⓪ VISA ℀
M a la carte 10.35/15.55 t. – **19 rm** ⎓ 40.00/52.00 t. – SB (weekends only except Bank Holidays) 60.00 st.

🏩 **Pride of the Valley Inn** (Best Western) ⌇, GU10 2LE, E : 1 ½ m. by A 287 via Hale House Lane ℰ 042 873 (Hindhead) 5799, 🐾 – 📺 🛏wc ☜ 🅟 🔼 AE ⓪ VISA
M (bar lunch) 7.50 t. 🍷 2.50 – **10 rm** ⎓ 25.50/37.00 st. – SB 47.00/50.00 st.

AUSTIN-ROVER East St. ℰ 716201   VW, AUDI West St. and Crondall Lane ℰ 715616
MERCEDES-BENZ 48/50 Shortheath Rd ℰ 716266

FARRINGTON GURNEY Avon 403 404 M 30 – pop. 647 – ⊠ Bristol – ✪ 0761 Temple Cloud.
♦London 132 – Bath 13 – ♦Bristol 12 – Wells 8.

🏠 **Country Ways,** Marsh Lane, BS18 5TT, ℰ 52449, 🐾 – 📺 🛏wc ☜ 🅟 🔼 ⓪ VISA ℀
closed Christmas – **M** (bar lunch) 9.50 t. 🍷 2.55 – **6 rm** ⎓ 19.55/38.00 t. – SB 44.80/52.00 st.

XX **Old Parsonage** with rm, Main St., BS18 5UB, ℰ 52211, 🐾 – 🛏wc 🅟. ℀
closed 5 April and 25-26 December – **M** *(closed Sunday dinner and Monday to non-residents)* (booking essential) a la carte 8.60/11.65 🍷 2.05 – **2 rm** ⎓ 17.50/35.00 st.

at Ston Easton S : 1 ¼ m. on A 37 – ⊠ Bath – ✪ 076 121 Chewton Mendip :

🏰 **Ston Easton Park** ⌇, BA3 4DF, ℰ 631, Telex 444738, ≤, « Palladian country house », 🐾, park – 📺 ☎ 🅟 🔼 AE ⓪ VISA ℀
M a la carte 17.25/20.50 t. 🍷 3.25 – ⎓ 4.50 – **17 rm** 45.00/125.00 st.

FAUGH Cumbria – see Carlisle.

FAVERSHAM Kent 404 W 30 – pop. 16,300 – ✪ 0795.
♦London 52 – ♦Dover 26 – Maidstone 21 – Margate 25.

XX **Reads,** Painters Forstal, ME13 0EE, SW : 2 ¼ m. off A 2 ℰ 535344 – 🅟. AE ⓪ VISA
closed Sunday – **M** a la carte 10.35/13.85 t. 🍷 2.25.

FAWLEY Bucks. 404 R 29 – pop. 398 – ECD : Wednesday – ⊠ Henley-on-Thames (Oxon.) – ✪ 049 163 Turville Heath.
♦London 45 – ♦Oxford 25 – Reading 12.

X **Walnut Tree,** Fawley Green, RG9 6JE, ℰ 360 – 🅟. 🔼 VISA
closed Christmas Day – **M** a la carte 7.00/9.50 t.

FELINDRE FARCHOG (VELINDRE) Dyfed 403 F 27 – see Newport (Dyfed).

FELINHELI = Port Dinorwic.

FELIXSTOWE Suffolk 404 Y 28 – pop. 18,925 – ECD : Wednesday – ✪ 0394.
🚢 Shipping connections with the Continent : to Belgium (Zeebrugge) (Townsend Thoresen).
🚢 to Harwich (Orwell & Harwich Navigation Co.) 5-7 daily (15 mn).
🛈 91 Undercliffe Rd West ℰ 282126 and 282122 – ♦London 84 – ♦Ipswich 11.

🏨 **Orwell Moat House** (Q.M.H.), Hamilton Rd, IP11 7DX, ℰ 285511, 🐾 – 🛗 📺 ☎ 🅟 🏃 🔼 AE ⓪ VISA
M 8.00/10.00 st. 🍷 4.00 – ⎓ 5.00 – **58 rm** 35.00/45.00 st. – SB (weekends only) 50.00/80.00 st.

AUSTIN-ROVER Crescent Rd ℰ 283221   NISSAN Garrison Lane ℰ 285591

FELSTED Essex 404 V 28 – pop. 2.814 – ✪ 0371 Great Dunmow.
♦London 44 – ♦Cambridge 30 – Colchester 18 – Chelmsford 11.

XX **Boote House,** Chelmsford Rd, CM6 3DH, ℰ 820279 – 🔼 AE ⓪ VISA
closed Sunday dinner, Monday, Tuesday, 2 weeks January and 2 weeks August – **M** (dinner only and Sunday lunch) a la carte 9.60/15.95 t. 🍷 2.90.

FERNDOWN Dorset 403 404 O 31 – pop. 11,752 – ECD : Wednesday – ✪ 0202.
♦London 108 – Bournemouth 6 – Dorchester 27 – Salisbury 23.

🏨 **Dormy** (De Vere), New Rd, BH22 8ES, on A 347 ℰ 872121, Telex 418301, 🔲, 🐾, ℀ – 🛗 🍽 rest 📺 & 🅟 🏃 🔼 AE ⓪ VISA
M 7.50/8.50 st. 🍷 3.50 – **95 rm** ⎓ 35.00/60.00 t. – SB (weekends only) 70.00 st.

🏩 **Coach House Motel,** Wimbourne Rd, Tricketts Cross, BH22 9NW, on A 31 ℰ 871222 – 📺 🛏wc 🅟. 🔼 AE ⓪ VISA
M 6.50 t. 🍷 3.00 – **44 rm** ⎓ 23.00/38.00 st. – SB (weekends only) 45.00/65.00 st.

AUSTIN-ROVER 553 Ringwood Rd ℰ 872212   TOYOTA Ringwood Rd ℰ 872201
COLT Victoria Rd ℰ 871131   VAUXHALL-OPEL Wimborne Rd East ℰ 872055

FINDON West Sussex 𝟒𝟎𝟒 S 31 – see Worthing.

FISHBOURNE I.O.W. 𝟒𝟎𝟑 𝟒𝟎𝟒 Q 31 Shipping Services : see Wight (Isle of).

FISHGUARD (ABERGWAUN) Dyfed 𝟒𝟎𝟑 F 28 – pop. 2,810 – ECD : Wednesday – ✆ 0348.
Envir. : Porthgain (cliffs ❄***) SW : 10 m. – Goodwick (≤**) NW : 1 ½ m. – Strumble Head
(≤** from the lighthouse) NW : 5 m. – Trevine (≤**) SW : 8 m. – Bryn Henllan (site*) NE : 5 m.
⚓ to Ireland (Rosslare) (Sealink) 1-2 daily (3 h 30 mn).
🛈 Town Hall ℘ 873484 (summer only).
♦London 266 – ♦Cardiff 115 – Gloucester 164 – Holyhead 169 – Shrewsbury 136 – ♦Swansea 76.

🏠 Cartref, High St., SA65 9AW, ℘ 872430 – ⃞wc 🅕wc. ❄ – **14 rm**.

🏠 **Blair Athol,** Windy Hall, SA65 9DP, ℘ 873147 – ❶. ❄
closed 2 weeks February – **M** *(closed Sunday to non-residents)* (dinner only)(booking essential)
a la carte 4.90/7.15 t. ⟘ 3.50 – **9 rm** ⊐ 8.65/17.25 **st.**

at Llanychaer SE : 2 ¼ m. on B 4313 – ⊠ Fishguard – ✆ 034 882 Puncheston :

✕ **Penlan-Oleu** 🌿 with rm, SA65 9TL, SE : 2 m. by B 4313 off Puncheston rd ℘ 314, ≤,
« Converted farmhouse », ⚞ – ⃞wc ❶. ⟁ 𝘝𝘐𝘚𝘈. ❄
M (booking essential) a la carte 10.00/11.00 **st.** ⟘ 2.50 – **3 rm** ⊐ 14.00/28.00 **st.**

at Goodwick (Wdig) NW : 1 ½ m. – ⊠ ✆ 0348 Fishguard :

🏨 **Fishguard Bay,** Quay Rd, SA64 0BT, ℘ 873571, ⅀ heated, park – 🛗 ⃞wc ♿ ❶. 🅰. ⟁ ⟁⟁
⓪ 𝘝𝘐𝘚𝘈
M (bar lunch) 7.50 **t.** – **62 rm** ⊐ 21.00/50.00 **t.**

AUSTIN-ROVER West St. ℘ 872253

FITTLEWORTH West Sussex 𝟒𝟎𝟒 S 31 – pop. 895 – ECD : Wednesday – ⊠ Pulborough –
✆ 079 882.
♦London 52 – ♦Brighton 28 – Chichester 15 – Worthing 17.

🏠 **Swan,** Lower St., RH20 1EN, ℘ 429, ⚞ – 🍴 ❶. ⟁ ⟁⟁ ⓪
M 5.00/8.00 **st.** ⟘ 2.95 – **7 rm** ⊐ 16.00/34.00 **st.** – SB 50.00 **st.**

FLAMBOROUGH Humberside 𝟒𝟎𝟐 T 21 – pop. 1,762 – ✆ 0262 Bridlington.
♦London 240 – ♦Kingston-upon-Hull 34 – Scarborough 18 – York 45.

🏠 **Timoneer Country Manor** 🌿, South Landing, YO15 1AG, ℘ 850219, ⚞ – 📺 ⃞wc 🅕wc
❶. ⟁ ⟁⟁ ⓪ 𝘝𝘐𝘚𝘈
M (bar lunch Monday to Saturday) 5.25/6.95 **st.** ⟘ 2.50 – **10 rm** ⊐ 19.50/35.00 – SB
42.00/52.00 **st.**

FLAMSTEAD Herts. 𝟒𝟎𝟒 S 28 – pop. 1,350 – ⊠ St. Albans – ✆ 0582 Luton.
♦London 32 – Luton 5.

🏨 **Hertfordshire Moat House** (Q.M.H.), London Rd, AL3 8HH, on A 5 ℘ 840840 – 📺 ⃞wc
⚞ ❶. 🅰. ⟁ ⟁⟁ ⓪ 𝘝𝘐𝘚𝘈
M (bar lunch Saturday) 8.00/9.50 **st.** ⟘ 3.30 – **97 rm** ⊐ 28.00/43.00 **st.** – SB (except weekdays mid September-mid June) 50.00 **st.**

FLEET Hants. 𝟒𝟎𝟒 R 30 – pop. 17,260 – ECD : Wednesday – ✆ 025 14.
♦London 46 – Guildford 14 – Reading 16 – ♦Southampton 42.

🏨 **Lismoyne,** Church Rd, GU13 8NA, ℘ 28555, ⚞ – 📺 ⃞wc 🅕wc ⚞ ❶. 🅰. ⟁ ⟁⟁ ⓪ 𝘝𝘐𝘚𝘈
M 5.80/6.35 **st.** ⟘ 3.10 – **40 rm** ⊐ 22.00/40.00 **st.**

AUSTIN-ROVER 66 Albert St. ℘ 3303   VW, AUDI 42 Reading Rd South ℘ 3425

FLEETWOOD Lancs. 𝟒𝟎𝟐 K 22 – pop. 28,599 – ECD : Wednesday – ✆ 039 17.
🏌, 🏌 Fleetwood, Princes Way ℘ 3114, W : from Promenade.
⚓ to the Isle of Man : Douglas (Isle of Man Steam Packet Co.) June-September. 2-3 weekly (3 h).
🛈 Marine Hall, The Esplanade ℘ 71141.
♦London 245 – ♦Blackpool 10 – Lancaster 28 – ♦Manchester 53.

🏨 **North Euston,** The Esplanade, FY7 6BN, ℘ 6525 – 🛗 📺 ⃞wc 🅕wc ⚞ ❶. 🅰. ⟁ ⟁⟁ ⓪ 𝘝𝘐𝘚𝘈
M *(closed lunch Saturday)* 5.00/8.00 **t.** – **57 rm** ⊐ 18.00/35.00 **t.**

FORD West View ℘ 2292

FLITWICK Beds. 𝟒𝟎𝟒 S 27 – pop. 8,441 – ✆ 0525.
♦London 45 – Bedford 13 – Luton 12 – Northampton 28.

✕✕✕ **Flitwick Manor,** Church Rd, off Dunstable Rd, MK45 1AE, ℘ 712242, Telex 825562, « 18C
manor house », ⚞ – ❶. ⟁ ⟁⟁ ⓪ 𝘝𝘐𝘚𝘈
closed 25 and 26 December – **M** *(closed Sunday dinner)* a la carte 10.50/15.20 **t.** ⟘ 3.20.

FOLKESTONE Kent 404 X 30 – pop. 43,801 – ECD : Wednesday and Saturday – ☎ 0303 –
See : Site★.

Envir. : The Warren★ (cliffs) E : 2 m. by A 20 X – Acrise Place★ AC, NW : 6 m. by A 260 X – 📷
Sene Valley, Folkestone and Hythe, Sene, ℰ 66726, N : 2 m. from Hythe on B 2065, W : byA 259 X.

⚓ Shipping connections to France (Boulogne, Calais) and Belgium (Oostende) (Sealink).

🄵 Harbour St. ℰ 58594 – Pedestrian Precinct, Sandgate Rd ℰ 53840 (summer only).

♦London 69 – ♦Brighton 76 – ♦Dover 8 – Maidstone 33.

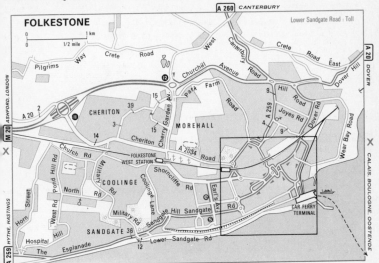

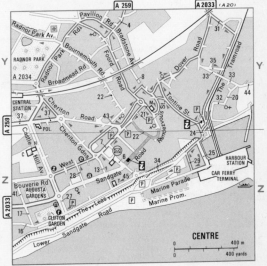

Guildhall Street . . . . Y 22
Rendezvous Street . . . . YZ
Sandgate Road . . . . Z
Tontine Street . . . . Y

Ashford Road . . . . X 2
Ashley Avenue . . . . X 3
Black Bull Road . . . . X, Y 4
Bouverie Place . . . . Z 6
Bouverie Road East . . . . . Z 7
Bradstone Road . . . . Y 8
Canterbury Road. . . . . X 9
Castle Road . . . . X 12
Cheriton Place . . . . X 13
Cheriton High Street . . . . . X 14
Cherry Garden Lane . . . . . X 15
Clifton Crescent. . . . . Z 16
Clifton Road. . . . . Y 17
Dunlocks (The) . . . . Y 21
Grace Hill . . . . Y 20
Harbour Street. . . . . Z 24
Harbour App. Road . . . . . . Z 25
Langhorn Gardens . . . . . . Z 27
Manor Road . . . . Z 28
Marine Terrace . . . . Z 29
Morrison Street. . . . . Y 31
North Street . . . . Y 32
Radnor Bridge Road. . . . . Y 33
Remembrance (Road of). . Z 34
Ryland Place . . . . Y 35
Sandgate Hill Street. . . . . X 36
Shorncliffe Road . . . . Y 37
Tilekiln Lane . . . . Z 41
Trinity Gardens . . . . Y 43
Victoria Grove . . . . Y 44
Wear Bay Road . . . . Y 45
West Terrace . . . . Z 45

🏛 **Burlington,** Earl's Av., CT20 2HR, ℰ 55301, ≤, 🐜 – 📳 📺 🛏wc 📞 🅿. 🕹. 🔼 🄰🄴 ⓘ 𝑉𝐼𝑆𝐴.
   🦌   X s
   M 7.75/9.00 t. 🍷 4.00 – **57 rm** ⊇ 30.00/47.00 t. – SB 45.00/57.00 st.

🏛 **Clifton** (T.H.F.), The Leas, CT20 2EB, ℰ 41231, ≤, 🐜 – 📳 📺 🛏wc 📞. 🕹. 🔼 🄰🄴 ⓘ 𝑉𝐼𝑆𝐴   Z r
   M a la carte 9.60/13.15 st. 🍷 2.85 – ⊇ 5.00 – **59 rm** 19.00/39.00 st.

181

🏛 **Banque** without rest., 4 Castle Hill Av., CT20 2QT, ℘ 53797 – 📺 🛏wc. 🅼 🅰🅴 ⓓ *VISA*
12 rm ⊊ 14.50/29.00 st.
Z z

🏛 **Chilworth Court**, 39-41 Earl's Av., CT20 2HB, ℘ 41583, 🛤 – 📺 🛏wc 🍴wc ☜ Ⓟ
21 rm
X e

XX **Emilio's Portofino**, 124a Sandgate Rd, CT20 2BT, ℘ 55762, Italian rest. – 🅼 🅰🅴 ⓓ *VISA*
closed Monday and Bank Holidays – **M** a la carte 8.40/12.40 t. ♟ 2.40.
Z a

XX **La Tavernetta**, Leaside Court, Clifton Gdns, CT20 2EY, ℘ 54955, Italian rest. – 🅼 🅰🅴 ⓓ
VISA
closed Sunday and Bank Holidays – **M** a la carte 8.75/12.35 t. ♟ 2.85.
Z n

X **Paul's**, 2a Bouverie Rd West, CT20 2RX, ℘ 59697 – 🅼 🅰🅴 ⓓ *VISA*
closed Sunday, 1 week summer, 1 week winter and 25-26 December – **M** a la carte
approx. 9.25 t. ♟ 2.50.
Z e

AUSTIN-ROVER 141/143 Sandgate Rd ℘ 55101
CITROEN, FIAT, ROLLS ROYCE, VAUXHALL Caesars
Way, Cheriton ℘ 76431
COLT 1/3 Park Rd ℘ 75114
FORD 104 Foord Rd ℘ 41234

NISSAN Shorncliffe Industrial Estate ℘ 39656
PEUGEOT, TALBOT Cheriton Rd ℘ 76959
RENAULT Sandgate Rd ℘ 55331
VAUXHALL Sandgate Rd ℘ 53103
VOLVO Park Farm Industrial Estate ℘ 42027

FONTMELL MAGNA Dorset 🔢🔢 N 30 – see Shaftesbury.

FORDINGBRIDGE Hants. 🔢🔢 O 31 – pop. 5,432 – ECD : Thursday – ☎ 0425.
See : St. Mary's Church★ 13C.
Envir. : Breamore House★ (Elizabethan) *AC*, N : 2 m.
◆London 101 – Bournemouth 17 – Salisbury 11 – Winchester 30.

XX **Hour Glass**, Salisbury Rd, Burgate, SP6 1LX, N : 1 m. on A 338 ℘ 52348, « 14C thatched
cottage » – Ⓟ. 🅼 🅰🅴 ⓓ *VISA*
closed Sunday and Monday – **M** (dinner only) a la carte 10.45/14.90 st. ♟ 3.35.

at Stuckton SW : 1 m. by B 3078 – ✉ ☎ 0425 Fordingbridge :

X **Three Lions Inn**, Stuckton Rd, SP6 2HF, ℘ 52489 – Ⓟ
closed February, 8-15 April, 2 weeks July-August, 1 week September-October and 24
December-2 January – **M** (closed Tuesday lunch, Sunday dinner and Monday) (booking
essential) a la carte 7.50/15.50 t. ♟ 2.40.

FORDWICH Kent 🔢 X 30 – see Canterbury.

FOREST ROW East Sussex 🔢 U 30 – pop. 4,484 – ECD : Wednesday – ☎ 034 282.
🏌 Royal Ashdown Forest ℘ 2018 – 🏌 Royal Ashdown New, Chapel Lane ℘ 2010 and 2751.
◆London 35 – ◆Brighton 26 – Eastbourne 30 – Maidstone 32.

🏛 **Chequers Inn**, The Square, RH19 5EF, ℘ 4394 – 📺 🛏wc ☜ Ⓟ. 🅼 🅰🅴 ⓓ *VISA*. ⌘
M a la carte 8.45/17.10 t. ♟ 3.00 – **16 rm** 17.00/25.00 t.

🏛 **Brambletye**, The Square, RH18 5EZ, ℘ 4144, Telex 8952645 – 📺 🛏wc ☎ Ⓟ
13 rm.

at Wych Cross S : 2 ½ m. on A 22 – ✉ ☎ 034 282 Forest Row :

🏛 **Roebuck** (Embassy), RH18 5JL, ℘ 3811, Telex 957088, 🛤 – 📺 🛏wc ☜ Ⓟ. 🅰. 🅼 🅰🅴 ⓓ
VISA ⌘
M 7.50 st. – ⊊ 4.25 – **31 rm** 23.00/38.00 st. – SB (weekends only) 44.00/50.00 st.

AUDI, VW 92-93 Hartfield Rd ℘ 3055

FOSSEBRIDGE Glos. 🔢🔢 O 28 – pop. 1,706 – ✉ ☎ 028 572.
◆London 88 – Gloucester 23 – ◆Oxford 31 – Swindon 21.

🏕 **Fossebridge Inn**, GL54 3JS, ℘ 310, 🛤 – 🛏wc Ⓟ. 🅼 *VISA*. ⌘
closed Christmas Day – **M** a la carte 6.50/9.70 t. ♟ 3.00 – **10 rm** ⊊ 18.75/39.50 t.

FOWEY Cornwall 🔢 G 32 The West Country G. – pop. 2,369 – ECD : Wednesday – ☎ 072 683.
See : Site★★.
🗓 Albert Quay ℘ 3320.
◆London 277 – Newquay 24 – ◆Plymouth 34 – Truro 22.

🏛 **Fowey** ⌘, The Esplanade, PL23 1HX, ℘ 2551, ≼ Fowey estuary and Polruan, 🛤 – ᛘ 📺
🛏wc ☜ Ⓟ. 🅼 🅰🅴 ⓓ *VISA* ⌘
M (bar lunch Monday to Saturday) approx. 7.50 t. ♟ 2.90 – **20 rm** ⊊ 19.80/46.20 t. – SB 55.00 st.

🏛 **Marina**, The Esplanade, PL23 1HY, ℘ 3315, ≼ Fowey river and harbour – 🛏wc. 🅼 🅰🅴 ⓓ
VISA ⌘
M (dinner only April to October) 8.00 t. ♟ 2.25 – **13 rm** ⊊ 15.00/39.00 t.

XX **Food for Thought,** 4 Town Quay, PL23 1AT, ✆ 2221, ≼ – ◪ *VISA*
closed weekdays November-February and Sunday – **M** (dinner only) (booking essential) a la carte 10.00/14.70 **t.** ⬧ 2.50.

XX **Cordon Bleu,** 3 The Esplanade, PL23 1HY, ✆ 2359 – ◪ Æ ⓞ *VISA*
closed Monday to Wednesday during winter and Sunday – **M** (dinner only) (booking essential) a la carte 8.00/11.95 **t.** ⬧ 2.40.

at Golant N : 3 m. by B 3269 – ✉ ✿ 072 683 Fowey :

🏠 **Cormorant** ⤳, PL23 1LL, ✆ 3426, ≼ river Fowey, ◪, 🐎, – ▣ ⌂wc ☎ ℗. *VISA*
M (bar lunch) 12.00 **t.** ⬧ 3.45 – **10 rm** ⚏ 23.00/40.00 **t.** – SB (except summer) 52.00 **st.**

at Bodinnick-by-Fowey E : ¼ m. via car ferry – ✉ Fowey – ✿ 072 687 Polruan :

🏠 **Old Ferry Inn,** PL23 1LY, ✆ 237, ≼ Fowey estuary and town, « Part 16C inn » – ⌂wc ℗.
VISA
M *(closed November-February)* (bar lunch) 9.50 **t.** ⬧ 2.75 – **12 rm** ⚏ 15.50/34.00 **t.**

FOWLMERE Cambs. 404 U 27 – see Cambridge.

FOWNHOPE Heref. and Worc. 403 404 M 27 – pop. 1,362 – ✉ Hereford – ✿ 043 277.
♦London 132 – ♦Cardiff 46 – Hereford 6 – Gloucester 27.

🏠 **Bowens Farmhouse,** HR1 4PS, on B 4224 ✆ 430, 🐎 – ⌂wc 🍴 ℗. ⊗
closed January – **10 rm** ⚏ 13.00/28.00 **t.**

FRAMFIELD East Sussex 404 U 31 – see Uckfield.

FRAMLINGHAM Suffolk 404 X 27 – pop. 2,258 – ECD : Wednesday – ✉ Woodbridge – ✿ 0728.
See : Castle ramparts★ (Norman ruins) *AC*.
♦London 92 – ♦Ipswich 19 – ♦Norwich 42.

🏠 **Crown** (T.H.F.), Market Hill, IP13 9AN, ✆ 723521, « 16C inn » – ▣ ⌂wc ⊕ ℗. ◪ Æ ⓞ
VISA
M 6.00/10.75 **st.** ⬧ 2.85 – ⚏ 4.75 – **17 rm** 26.00/40.00 **st.**

X **Market Place,** 18 Market Hill, IP13 9BB, ✆ 724275. ◪ *VISA*
closed Sunday, Monday and last 2 weeks January – **M** (restricted lunch) a la carte 7.00/10.20 **st.**
⬧ 2.20.

FORD Market Hill ✆ 723215

FRANT Kent 404 U 30 – see Royal Tunbridge Wells.

FRESHFORD Avon – see Bath.

FRESHWATER BAY I.O.W. 403 404 P 31 – see Wight (Isle of).

FRESSINGFIELD Suffolk 404 X 26 – pop. 730 – ✉ Diss – ✿ 037 986.
♦London 103 – ♦Ipswich 30 – ♦Norwich 23.

X **Fox and Goose,** IP21 5PB, ✆ 247 – ℗. ◪ Æ ⓞ *VISA*
closed Tuesday and 21 to 28 December – **M** (booking essential) a la carte 11.50/19.50 **st.**

FRIETH Bucks. – see Henley-on-Thames (Oxon.).

FRILFORD Oxon. 403 404 P 28 – see Abingdon.

FRINTON-ON-SEA Essex 404 X 28 – pop. 12,475 (inc. Walton) – ECD : Wednesday – ✿ 025 56.
♦London 72 – Chelmsford 39 – Colchester 17.

🏨 **Frinton Lodge** (Best Western), 32 Esplanade, CO13 9HL, ✆ 4391, ≼, Dancing (Saturday) –
🍴 ▣ ⌂wc ⊕ ℗. ◪ Æ ⓞ *VISA*
M 8.75 **t.** ⬧ 3.95 – **24 rm** ⚏ 21.00/53.00 **t.** – SB 49.00/58.00 **st.**

🏠 **Maplin,** Esplanade, CO13 9EL, ✆ 3832, ≼, ⚏ heated – ▣ ⌂wc ⊕ ℗. ◪ Æ ⓞ *VISA*
closed January – **M** 8.25/11.25 **st.** ⬧ 2.60 – **12 rm** ⚏ 20.00/43.00 **st.**

🏠 **Uplands,** 41 Hadleigh Rd, CO13 9HQ, ✆ 4889, 🐎 – ℗
closed January – **8 rm** ⚏ 9.90/19.80 **st.**

AUSTIN-ROVER Connaught Av. ✆ 4311
FIAT, VOLVO 132 Connaught Av. ✆ 4341
FORD Connaught Av. ✆ 77137

PEUGEOT, TALBOT ✆ 4383
TOYOTA Frinton Rd, Kirby Cross ✆ 4141

FRODSHAM Cheshire 402 403 404 L 24 – pop. 8,980 – ✉ Warrington – ✿ 0928.
♦London 203 – Chester 11 – ♦Liverpool 21 – ♦Manchester 29 – Stoke on Trent 42.

🏠 **Old Hall,** Main St., WA6 7AB, ✆ 32052 – ▣ ⌂wc ⊕ ◪ Æ ⓞ *VISA*
M a la carte 6.40/11.00 **t.** ⬧ 2.85 – **17 rm** ⚏ 17.50/38.50 **st.**

FROME Somerset 403 404 N 30 **The West Country G.** – pop. 12,310 – ECD : Thursday – 🎯 0373.
Envir. : Farleigh Hungerford Castle★, N : 11 m. by A 361 and A 36 – Longleat House★★★ SE : 7 m.
ℹ Cattle Market Car Park ℘ 67271 (summer only).
♦London 115 – ♦Bristol 28 – ♦Southampton 51 – Taunton 43.

- **Mendip Lodge,** Bath Rd, BA11 2HP, N : ½ m. on A 361 ℘ 63223, ←, 🐎 – 📺 ⛀wc ☎ Ⓟ. 🅰 Access AE Diners VISA
  M (buffet lunch) 8.95 **st.** 🍾 4.25 – ☕ 3.50 – **40 rm** 30.00/42.00 **st.** – SB (weekends only) (October to May) 29.00 **st.**

GAINSBOROUGH Lincs. 402 404 R 23 – pop. 18,110 – ECD : Wednesday – 🎯 0427.
See : Old Hall★★ (15C) *AC*.
♦London 150 – Lincoln 19 – ♦Nottingham 42 – ♦Sheffield 34.

Hotels and Restaurant see : ***Bawtry*** NW : 12 m., ***Scunthorpe*** NE : 17 m.

AUSTIN-ROVER North St. ℘ 2251
FORD Trinity St. ℘ 3146
TALBOT North St. ℘ 2505
VAUXHALL-OPEL 35 Trinity St. ℘ 611570

GARFORTH West Yorks. 402 P 22 – see Leeds.

GARGRAVE North Yorks. 402 N 22 – pop. 1,426 – ECD : Tuesday – ✉ 🎯 075 678.
♦London 222 – ♦Leeds 30 – Preston 37.

- **Anchor Inn,** BD23 3NA, W : ½ m.on A 65 ℘ 666, 🐎 – 📺 ⛀wc 🚿wc Ⓟ. Access AE Diners VISA. ✗
  M (bar lunch) a la carte 7.30/10.45 **st.** 🍾 2.80 – **8 rm** ☕ 20.00/32.00 **st.**

GATESHEAD Tyne and Wear 401 402 P 19 – pop. 94,469 – ECD : Wednesday – 🎯 0632 (from Spring 1985 091 Tyneside).
golf 18 Ravensworth, Mossheaps ℘ 0632 (Low Fell) 876014 – golf 18 Whickham, Hollinside Park ℘ 887309, SW : 5 m.
ℹ Central Library, Prince Consort Rd ℘ 773478.
♦London 282 – Durham 16 – ♦Middlesbrough 38 – ♦Newcastle-upon-Tyne 1 – Sunderland 11.

Plan : see Newcastle-upon-Tyne

- **Springfield** (Embassy), Durham Rd, NE9 5BT, S : ½ m. on A 6127 ℘ 774121 (from spring 1985 477 4121) – 📺 ⛀wc ☎ Ⓟ. 🅰 Access AE Diners VISA. ✗ BX **s**
  M a la carte 7.80/11.50 **st.** 🍾 4.00 – ☕ 4.25 – **40 rm** 31.50/39.50 **st.** – SB (weekends only) 40.00/46.00 **st.**
- **Five Bridges** (Swallow), High West Street, NE8 1PE, ℘ 771105 (from spring 1985 477 1105), Telex 53534 – 🛗 📺 ⛀wc ☎ Ⓟ. 🅰 Access AE Diners VISA CZ **r**
  M a la carte 5.25/10.00 **st.** 🍾 3.40 – **106 rm** ☕ 20.00/38.00 **st.** – SB 40.00 **st.**
- **Eslington Villa,** Station Rd, Low Fell, NE9 1DR, ℘ 091 (Tyneside) 487 6017 – 📺 ⛀wc 🚿wc ☎ Ⓟ. Access AE Diners VISA by A 6127 BX
  M *(closed lunch Saturday to Monday and Sunday dinner)* 4.75/12.50 **st.** – **8 rm** ☕ 24.50/30.50 **st.**

AUDI, VW Bensham Rd ℘ 784545
AUSTIN-ROVER Low Fell ℘ 872118
FORD Eslington Park ℘ 607464
TOYOTA St. James Sq. ℘ 784333
VAUXHALL 106/108 Lobley Hill Rd ℘ 0632 (Dunston) 604691

GATWICK AIRPORT West Sussex 404 T 30 – see hotels at Crawley and Horley.
✈ ℘ 0293 (Crawley) 28822 and ℘ 01 (London) 668 4211.

GERRARDS CROSS Bucks. 404 S 29 – pop. 6,524 – ECD : Wednesday – 🎯 0753.
♦London 22 – Aylesbury 22 – ♦Oxford 36.

- **Bull** (De Vere), Oxford Rd, SL9 7PA, on A 40 ℘ 885995, Group Telex 847747, 🐎 – 📺 ⛀wc ☎ Ⓟ. 🅰 Access AE Diners VISA. ✗
  M 10.20/11.50 **st.** 🍾 3.30 – ☕ 5.00 – **40 rm** 44.00/55.00 **st.** – SB (weekends only) 60.00 **st.**
- Ethorpe, Packhorse Rd, FL9 8HX, ℘ 882039, 🐎 – 📺 ⛀wc ☎ Ⓟ – **28 rm.**

BMW 31-33 Station Rd ℘ 888321
TALBOT Oxford Rd ℘ 882545

GIGGLESWICK North Yorks. – see Settle.

GILLAN Cornwall 403 E 33 **The West Country G.** – see Helford.

GISBURN Lancs. 402 N 22 – pop. 433 – ECD : Wednesday – ✉ Clitheroe – 🎯 020 05.
golf 9 Ghyll, Ghyll Brow, Barnoldswick ℘ 0282 (Earby) 842466, SE : 5 ½ m.
♦London 243 – ♦Manchester 37 – Preston 25.

- **Stirk House,** BB7 4LJ, SW : 1 m. on A 59 ℘ 581, Telex 635238, 🏊, 🐎, squash – 📺 ⛀wc ☎ Ⓟ. 🅰 Access AE Diners VISA. ✗
  M a la carte 8.80/12.75 **st.** 🍾 3.25 – **50 rm** ☕ 27.75/45.00 **st.** – SB (weekends only) 45.00/48.00 **st.**

GITTISHAM Devon 403 K 31 – pop. 220 – ECD : Thursday – ⊠ ✿ 0404 Honiton.
♦London 164 – Exeter 14 – Sidmouth 9 – Taunton 21.

🏛 **Combe House** ♨, EX14 0AD, ℘ 2756, ≼, « Country house atmosphere », ⚞, park – 📺
🛏wc flwc ℗. 🔼 🅰🅴 ⓪ 𝕍𝕀𝕊𝔸
M (bar lunch Monday to Saturday) 10.85/15.00 **st.** – **12 rm** ⊑ 23.50/80.00 **st.**

GLASTONBURY Somerset 403 L 30 The West Country G. – pop. 6,558 – ECD : Wednesday –
✿ 0458.
See : Site★★★ – Abbey★★★ – St. John the Baptist Church★★ – Somerset Rural Life Museum★★ –
Glastonbury Tor★ (≼★★★).
Envir. : at Street : Shoe Museum★, SW : 2 m. on A 39.
🅱 1 Marchant's Buildings, Northload St. ℘ 32954 (summer only).
♦London 136 – ♦Bristol 26 – Taunton 22.

🏛 **George and Pilgrims,** 1 High St., BA6 9DP, ℘ 31146, « Part 15C inn » – 🛏wc. 🔼 🅰🅴 ⓪
𝕍𝕀𝕊𝔸. ♨
M (buffet Sunday dinner) 5.00/10.00 **t.** 🍷 2.95 – **14 rm** ⊑ 27.00/48.00 **t.** – SB (except summer) 46.00/54.00 **st.**

🏛 **Hawthorns,** Northload St., BA6 9JJ, ℘ 31255 – flwc. 🔼 🅰🅴 ⓪ 𝕍𝕀𝕊𝔸. ♨
M (buffet lunch) 6.50 **st.** 🍷 3.00 – **12 rm** ⊑ 12.00/16.50 **st.** – SB 30.00/35.00 **st.**

XX **No 3,** 3 Magdalene St., BA6 9EW, ℘ 32129, ⚞ – ℗. 🅰🅴 ⓪ 𝕍𝕀𝕊𝔸
closed Sunday dinner, Monday and first 2 weeks February – **M** (dinner only and Sunday lunch) (booking essential) 18.00 **t.**

AUSTIN-ROVER Street Rd ℘ 32137   RENAULT Mill Lane ℘ 32741

GLEMSFORD Suffolk 404 W 27 – pop. 2,423 – ⊠ ✿ 0787.
♦London 145 – ♦Cambridge 32 – Colchester 21 – ♦Ipswich 28.

XX **Weeks,** 31 Egremont St., CO10 7SA, ℘ 281573 – ℗
closed Sunday, Monday and 2 weeks late October – **M** (dinner only) (booking essential) 13.25 **t.** 🍷 2.10.

GLENRIDDING Cumbria 402 L 20 – see Ullswater.

GLOUCESTER Glos. 403 404 N 28 – pop. 90,232 – ECD : Thursday – ✿ 0452.
See : Cathedral★★ 12C-14C (Great Cloister★★★ 14C) Y – Bishop Hooper's Lodging (Folk Museum)★
15C Y M.
🅸ｓ, 🅸ｓ Gloucester Hotel and Country Club, Matson Lane ℘ 25653, S : 2 m. Z.
🅱 6 College St. ℘ 421188.
♦London 105 – ♦Birmingham 52 – ♦Bristol 38 – ♦Cardiff 66 – ♦Coventry 57 – Northampton 83 – ♦Oxford 48 –
♦Southampton 98 – ♦Swansea 92 – Swindon 35.

Plan on next page

🏛 **Crest** (Crest), Crest Way, Barnwood, GL4 7RX, E : 3 m. on A 417 ℘ 63311, Telex 437273 – 📺
🛏wc ☎ 🅖 ℗. 🔼 🅰🅴 ⓪ 𝕍𝕀𝕊𝔸. ♨   by A 417   Z
M approx. 10.50 **st.** – ⊑ 5.25 – **100 rm** 43.50/54.00 **st.**

🏛 **Gloucester Hotel and Country Club** (Embassy), Robinswood Hill, Matson Lane, GL4 9AE
SE : 3 m. by B 4073 ℘ 25653, 🅸ｓ – 📺 🛏wc ☎ 🅖 ℗. 🔼   Z c
74 rm.

⌂ **Montieth,** 127 Stroud Rd, GL1 5JL, ℘ 25369 – 📺 🛏wc ℗. ♨   Z a
8 rm ⊑ 9.00/23.00 **st.**

X **College Green,** 7-11 College St., GL1 2NE, ℘ 20739 – 🔼 🅰🅴 ⓪ 𝕍𝕀𝕊𝔸   Y a
closed dinner Monday and Tuesday, Sunday and Bank Holidays – **M** a la carte 8.00/12.60 **st.**
🍷 2.00.

at Upton St. Leonards SE : 3 ½ m. on B 4073 – ⊠ ✿ 0452 Gloucester :

🏛 **Tara,** Upton Hill, GL4 8DE, ℘ 67412, ≼ Severn Valley, 🛁 heated, ⚞ – 📺 🛏wc flwc ☎ ℗.
🔼 🔼 🅰🅴 ⓪ 𝕍𝕀𝕊𝔸. ♨   by B 4073   Z
M a la carte 10.00/18.95 **t.** 🍷 2.85 – **22 rm** ⊑ 23.50/49.50 **t.** – SB (weekends only) 25.00/40.00 **st.**

at Minsterworth W : 5 m. by A 40 on A 48 – Z – ⊠ Gloucester – ✿ 045 275 Minsterworth :

⌂ **Severn Bank,** Main Rd, GL2 8JH, ℘ 357, ⚞ – ℗. ♨
closed Christmas Day – **6 rm** ⊑ 8.50/17.00 **st.**

AUDI, VW Eastern Av. ℘ 25177
AUSTIN-ROVER Mercia Rd ℘ 416565
BEDFORD, PANTHER LIMA, VAUXHALL Shepherd
Rd, Cole Av. ℘ 26711
BMW Kingsholm Rd ℘ 23456
CITROEN, FIAT 143 Westgate St. ℘ 23252
FORD Bristol Rd ℘ 21731
LADA Painswick Rd ℘ 29866
LANCIA, DAIHATSU, FIAT Bristol Rd ℘ 29755

NISSAN Eastern Av. ℘ 423691
PEUGEOT, TALBOT London Rd ℘ 24081
RENAULT St. Oswalds Rd ℘ 35051
SAAB Montpelier ℘ 22404
TOYOTA London Rd ℘ 21555
VAUXHALL-OPEL Cole Av. ℘ 26711
VAUXHALL-OPEL Priory Rd ℘ 24912
VOLVO 100 Eastgate St. ℘ 25291
VW, AUDI Eastern Av. ℘ 25177

GLOUCESTER

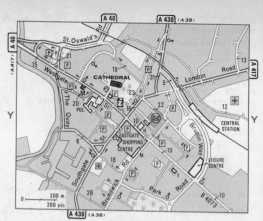

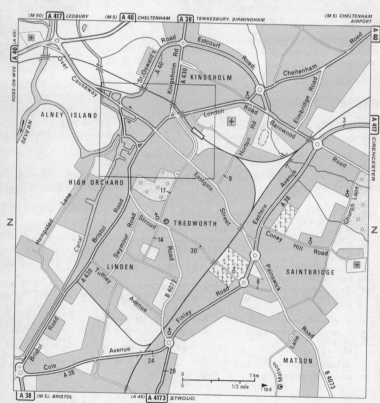

GOATHLAND North Yorks. 402 R 20 – pop. 458 – ECD : Wednesday and Saturday – ⊠ ☎ 0947 Whitby.

♦London 248 – ♦Middlesbrough 36 – York 38.

🏠 **Mallyan Spout** ⌖, YO22 5AN, 𝒫 86206, ☞ – 📺 ⌂wc 🅿. AE ① VISA
closed December and January – **M** (bar lunch) 9.00 t. ⏐ 2.10 – **22 rm** ⊇ 14.00/36.00 t. – SB (summer only) 38.00/48.50 **st.**

⋔ **Heatherdene** ⌖, The Common, YO22 5AN, 𝒫 86334, ≼, ☞ – ⌂wc 🅿
6 rm ⊇ 12.00/25.00 **st.**

⋔ **Whitfield House** ⌖, Darnholm, YO22 5LA, NW : ¾ m. 𝒫 86215, ☞
12 rm ⊇ 10.75/21.00 t.

GODALMING Surrey 404 S 30 – pop. 18,669 – ECD : Wednesday – ☎ 048 68.

♦London 38 – Guildford 5 – ♦Southampton 51.

⋔ **Meads**, 65 Meadrow, GU7 3HS, N : ½ m. on A 3100 𝒫 21800 – ⋔wc 🅿. AE VISA
14 rm ⊇ 12.00/24.00 t.

at Hascombe SE : 3 ½ m. on B 2130 – ⊠ Godalming – ☎ 048 632 Hascombe :

✗ White Horse, GU8 4JA, 𝒫 258, Bistro, ☞ – 🅿.

NISSAN The Wharf 𝒫 5201   VAUXHALL Ockford Rd 𝒫 5666
TALBOT Farncombe 𝒫 7743

GODSTONE Surrey 404 T 30 – pop. 5,568 – ☎ 0342 South Godstone.

♦London 22 – ♦Brighton 36 – Maidstone 28.

✗✗ **La Bonne Auberge**, Tilburstow Hill, South Godstone, RH9 8JY, S : 2 ¼ m. 𝒫 892318, French rest., ☞ – 🅿. ◪ AE ① VISA
closed Sunday dinner and Monday – **M** a la carte 11.90/17.00 **st.**

VAUXHALL Eastbourne Rd 𝒫 842000

GOLANT Cornwall 403 G 32 – see Fowey.

GOLCAR West Yorks. – see Huddersfield.

GOMSHALL Surrey 404 S 30 – see Dorking.

GOODRICH Heref. and Worc. 403 404 M 28 – see Ross-on-Wye.

GOODWICK (WDIG) Dyfed 403 F 27 – see Fishguard.

GORLESTON-ON-SEA Norfolk 404 Z 26 – see Great Yarmouth.

GOSFORTH Cumbria 402 J 20 – pop. 1,076 – ⊠ Seascale – ☎ 094 05.

Envir. : E : Wast Water★, Wasdale Head (site★).

🏌 Seascale, The Banks 𝒫 0940 (Seascale) 28202 or 28800, SW : 3 m. by B 5344.

♦London 314 – Kendal 62 – Workington 20.

⌂ **Gosforth Hall**, CA20 1AZ, 𝒫 322, ◪, ☞ – ⌂wc 🅿. ✂
closed Christmas and New Year – **M** a la carte 7.65/8.00 t. ⏐ 1.95 – **10 rm** ⊇ 17.00/27.50 t. – SB (weekends only) 40.00 **st.**

at Wasdale Head NE : 9 m. – ⊠ Gosforth – ☎ 094 06 Wasdale :

🏠 **Wasdale Head Inn** ⌖, CA20 1EX, 𝒫 229, ≼ Wasdale Head – ⌂wc ⋔wc 🅿. ◪ VISA
closed 10 November-26 December – **M** (bar lunch) 8.25 t. ⏐ 2.50 – **10 rm** ⊇ 16.25/36.50 t.

GOSFORTH Tyne and Wear 401 402 P 18 – see Newcastle-upon-Tyne.

GOUDHURST Kent 404 V 30 – pop. 2,950 – ECD : Wednesday – ⊠ Cranbrook – ☎ 0580.

♦London 45 – Hastings 22 – Maidstone 13.

🏠 **Star and Eagle**, High St., TN17 1AB, 𝒫 211512 – 📺 ⌂wc 🅿. ◪ AE ① VISA
M (bar lunch Monday) 6.50/8.50 t. – **11 rm** ⊇ 26.00/35.00 t. – SB (winter only) 45.00 **st.**

GOVETON Devon 403 I 33 – see Kingsbridge.

GRANGE-IN-BORROWDALE Cumbria 402 K 20 – see Keswick.

Per viaggiare in Europa, utilizzate le Carte Michelin
Le Grandi Strade scala 1/1 000 000.

GRANGE-OVER-SANDS Cumbria 402 L 21 – pop. 3,474 – ECD : Thursday – ✆ 044 84.

Envir. : Cartmel (Priory Church★ 12C chancel★★) NW : 3 m.

🏌 Meathop Rd ☎ 3180, ½ m. Grange Station – 🏌 Grange Fell, Cartmell Rd ☎ 2536.

🛈 Council Offices, Main St. ☎ 4331 (summer only).

♦London 268 – Kendal 13 – Lancaster 24.

🏛 **Graythwaite Manor** 🗤, Fernhill Rd, LA11 7JE, ☎ 2001, ≼ gardens and sea, « Extensive
flowered gardens », park, ※ – 📺wc ⇔ 🅿 🔼 *VISA* ※
M *(closed 25 and 26 December to non-residents)* 4.50/9.50 **st.** ¼ 2.25 – **24 rm** ⯑ (dinner included) 26.00/60.00 **st.** – SB 48.00/60.00 **st.**

🏛 **Cumbria Grand** 🗤, Lindale Rd, LA11 6EN, ☎ 2331, ≼, ⚘, park, ※ – ▌☰▐ 📺 📺wc ⇔ 🕭 🅿
🏃 – **90 rm.**

🏠 **Netherwood** 🗤, Lindale Rd, LA11 6ET, ☎ 2552, ≼, ⚘ – 📺wc ⇔ 🅿 🏃
M 4.50/7.00 **st.** ¼ 2.30 – **23 rm** ⯑ 16.00/36.00 **st.** – SB 21.00/23.00 **st.**

🏠 **Hardcragg Hall,** Grange Fell Rd, LA11 6BJ, ☎ 3353, « Renovated 16C manor », ⚘ –
📺wc 🅿 🔼 *VISA*
M 6.95 **t.** ¼ 2.00 – **7 rm** ⯑ 13.25/28.50 **t.**

↑ **Somerset House,** Kents Bank Rd, LA11 7EY, ☎ 2631 – ※
March-October – **8 rm** ⯑ (dinner included) 11.95/20.00.

at Witherslack NE : 5 m. by B 5277 off A 590 – ✆ 044 852 Witherslack :

※※ **Old Vicarage** 🗤 with rm, Church Rd, LA11 6RS, ☎ 381, ⚘ – 📺 📺wc ▥wc 🅿 🔼 *AE*
VISA ※
closed 1 week at Christmas – **M** (dinner only)(booking essential) 14.50 **t.** ¼ 2.70 – **7 rm**
⯑ 40.00/64.00 **t.** – SB (winter only) 79.00/82.00 **st.**

at Kents Bank SW : 1 ¾ m. by B 5277 – ✉ ✆ 044 84 Grange-over-Sands :

↑ **Kents Bank,** Kentsford Rd, LA11 7BB, ☎ 2054, ≼ – 📺wc 🅿 🔼 *VISA*
8 rm ⯑ 13.75/26.00 **t.**

at Cartmel NW : 3 m. – ✉ Grange-over-Sands – ✆ 044 854 Cartmel :

🏠 **Aynsome Manor** 🗤, LA11 6HH, NE : ½ m. ☎ 276, « Country house atmosphere », ⚘ –
📺wc 🅿 🔼 *AE* *VISA*
closed 2 to 18 January – **M** (dinner only and Sunday lunch) 5.95/10.00 **t.** ¼ 2.80 – **14 rm**
⯑ 25.50/28.50 **t.** – SB (except summer) 38.00/42.00 **st.**

🏨 **Grammar,** NW : ¼ m. ☎ 367 – 📺wc 🅿
closed January and February – **M** (bar lunch) 6.50/7.50 **t.** ¼ 2.20 – **11 rm** ⯑ 11.00/26.00 **t.** – SB
(weekends only) 37.00/43.00 **st.**

BMW Lindale Corner ☎ 3751   VW, AUDI Lindale ☎ 4242
FORD, SUBARU, HYUNDAI Lindale Corner ☎ 2282

GRANTHAM Lincs. 402 404 S 25 – pop. 27,943 – ECD : Wednesday – ✆ 0476.

See : St. Wulfram's Church★ 13C.

Envir. : Belton House★ (Renaissance) *AC* NE : 2 m. – Belvoir Castle 19C (interior★) W : 8 m.

🏌 Belton Park, Belton Lane, Londonthorpe Rd ☎ 3355, N : 2 m. – 🏌 Stoke Rochford, Great North
Rd ☎ 045 683 (Great Ponton) 275, S : 6 m. on A 1.

🛈 The Guildhall, St. Peters Hill ☎ 66444 (summer only).

♦London 113 – ♦Leicester 31 – Lincoln 29 – ♦Nottingham 24.

🏛 **George** (Best Western), High St., NG31 6NN, ☎ 63286, Telex 378121 – 📺 📺wc ▥wc ☎ 🅿.
🏃 🔼 *AE* 🕦 *VISA*
M 6.50/9.95 **t.** ¼ 3.00 – **43 rm** ⯑ 28.00/50.00 **t.** – SB (weekends only) 42.50/50.00 **st.**

🏛 **Angel and Royal** (T.H.F.), 4 High St., NG31 6PN, ☎ 65816, « 13C walled restaurant
and bar » – 📺 📺wc ⇔ 🅿 🏃 🔼 *AE* 🕦 *VISA*
M 5.25/7.50 **st.** ¼ 5.00 – ⯑ 5.00 – **32 rm** 26.00/41.00 **st.**

🏠 **King's,** 130 North Par., NG31 8AU, ☎ 65881 – 📺 📺wc ▥wc ⇔ 🅿 🔼 *AE* 🕦 *VISA*
M 5.55/6.85 **st.** ¼ 2.45 – **17 rm** ⯑ 17.50/31.00 **st.** – SB (weekends only) 35.00/40.00 **st.**

※※ **Premier,** 2-6 North Par., NG31 8AW, ☎ 77855 – 🔼 *AE* 🕦 *VISA*
closed Tuesday lunch, Sunday dinner and Monday – **M** a la carte 9.50/17.15 **t.**

at Barkston N : 3 ¾ m. on A 607 – ✉ Grantham – ✆ 0400 Loveden :

※※ **Barkston House** with rm, NG32 2NH, ☎ 50555, ⚘ – 📺 📺wc ☎ 🅿 🔼 *AE* 🕦 *VISA*
closed Sunday dinner, Monday and Christmas Day – **M** (bar lunch) a la carte approx. 10.75 **st.**
– **2 rm** ⯑ 24.00/36.00 **st.**

AUSTIN-ROVER 12 North St. ☎ 61066   TOYOTA Great Ponton ☎ 047 683 261
FORD 30/40 London Rd ☎ 5195   VAUXHALL Watergate ☎ 3267
NISSAN Barrowby High Rd ☎ 4443   VOLVO Barrowby Rd ☎ 4114
PEUGEOT-TALBOT 66 London Rd ☎ 2595   VW, AUDI, SUBARU Spittlegate ☎ 66416
RENAULT London Rd ☎ 61338

GRAPPENHALL Cheshire – see Warrington.

188

7 Broadgate News Agency ✆ 245.

♦London 282 – ♦Carlisle 43 – Kendal 18.

Plans : see Ambleside

🏨 **Wordsworth,** LA22 9SW, ✆ 592, Telex 65329, 🔲, 🐎 – 🔄 📺 ⅘ 🅿. 🏛. 🔼 AE ⓪ VISA. 🎇
M a la carte 13.25/16.90 t. 🍷 2.75 – **35 rm** 🛏 36.00/76.00 t. – SB (winter only) 75.00/79.00 t.
BZ **s**

🏨 **Swan** (T.H.F.), LA22 9RF, ✆ 551, ≼, 🐎 – 📺 ➜wc 🕾 🅿. 🔼 AE ⓪ VISA
M 7.50/11.00 st. 🍷 2.85 – 🛏 5.00 – **41 rm** 29.50/47.50 st.
AY **r**

🏨 **Michaels Nook Country House** ﴾, LA22 9RP, ✆ 496, Group Telex 65329, ≼ mountains and countryside, « Antiques and gardens » – 📺 ➜wc 🕾 🅿. 🎇
M (booking essential) 15.75/21.00 t. 🍷 2.60 – **10 rm** 🛏 (dinner included) 58.00/124.00 t.
AY **n**

🏨 **Gold Rill** ﴾, Langdale Rd, LA22 9PU, ✆ 486, ≼, 🛁 heated, 🐎 – ➜wc 🅿. 🔼 AE ⓪ VISA.
M (bar lunch) 12.00 st. 🍷 2.20 – **21 rm** 🛏 32.00/64.00 t.
BZ **c**

🏨 **Grasmere Red Lion,** Red Lion Sq., LA22 9SS, ✆ 456, 🐎 – 🔄 📺 ➜wc 🕾 🅿. 🔼 AE ⓪ VISA
closed late November-mid February – M (bar lunch Monday to Saturday) a la carte 8.20/13.20 st. 🍷 3.10 – **36 rm** 🛏 21.50/45.00 st. – SB 52.00/56.00 st.
BZ **a**

🏠 **White Moss House,** Rydal Water, LA22 9SE, S : 1 ½ m. on A 591 ✆ 295, 🐎 – ➜wc 🅿.
21 March-4 November – M (dinner only) (booking essential) 13.95 t. 🍷 2.75 – **6 rm** 🛏 (dinner included) 42.00/82.00 st. – SB (weekdays only in March, April, July, August and November) 75.00 st.
BY **e**

🏠 **Oak Bank,** Broadgate, LA22 9TA, ✆ 217, 🐎 – ➜wc 🔟wc 🔼 VISA
closed mid November-mid February – M (bar lunch) 10.00 st. – **14 rm** 🛏 14.00/36.00 st. – SB (winter only) 24.00/50.00 st.
BZ **e**

🏠 **Grasmere,** Broadgate, LA22 9TA, ✆ 277, 🐎 – 🔟wc 🅿
March-November – M (bar lunch) 10.00 t. 🍷 2.20 – **11 rm** 🛏 22.00/36.00 t.
BZ **r**

🏠 **Rothay Bank,** Broadgate, LA22 9RH, ✆ 334, 🐎 – 🔟wc 🅿. 🔼 AE VISA
closed 3 January-15 February – M (bar lunch to residents only) 5.00/9.50 t. 🍷 2.25 – **15 rm** 🛏 12.75/24.95 t.
AY **e**

🏠 **Moss Grove,** LA22 9SW, ✆ 251 – 🔟wc 🅿. 🎇
April-October – **15 rm** 🛏 12.00/30.00 st.
BZ **i**

🏠 **Bridge House** ﴾, Stock Lane, LA22 9SN, ✆ 425, 🐎 – ➜wc 🅿. 🔼 VISA. 🎇
March-November – **12 rm** 🛏 (dinner included) 18.00/44.00 t.
BZ **n**

🏠 **Rothay Lodge** ﴾, White Bridge, LA22 9RH, ✆ 341, 🐎 – 🅿. 🎇
closed December – **6 rm** 🛏 10.75/21.50 st.
AY **o**

🏠 **How Foot Lodge,** Town End, LA22 9SQ, ✆ 366, ≼, 🐎 – ➜wc 🔟wc 🅿. 🎇
March-November – **6 rm** 🛏 14.00/28.00 st.
AY **v**

♦London 240 – Bradford 30 – Burnley 28 – ♦Leeds 37.

🏨 **Wilson Arms** (Best Western), Station Rd, Threshfield, BD23 5EL, SW : ½ m. on B 6265 ✆ 752666, Telex 51564, 🐎 – 🔄 ▤ rest 📺 ➜wc 🕾 ➜ 🅿. 🔼 AE ⓪ VISA
M 7.00/10.00 t. 🍷 2.75 – **28 rm** 🛏 28.50/57.00 t.

⛴ to Tilbury (Sealink) frequent services daily (5 mn).

♦London 25 – ♦Dover 54 – Maidstone 16 – Margate 53.

🏨 **Tollgate Moat House** (Q.M.H.), Watling St., DA13 9RA, S : 2 m. at junction A 2 and A 227 ✆ 57655, Telex 966227 – 📺 ➜wc 🕾 ⅘ 🅿. 🏛. 🔼 AE ⓪ VISA
M a la carte 8.70/11.40 st. 🍷 2.35 – **122 rm** 🛏 27.50/40.00 st. – SB (weekends only) 40.00 st.

🏨 **Overcliffe,** 16 The Overcliffe, DA11 0EF, ✆ 22131 – 📺 🔟wc 🕾 🅿. 🔼 AE ⓪ VISA. 🎇
M (closed lunch Saturday and Sunday) 5.25/7.50 st. 🍷 3.50 – **19 rm** 🛏 26.00/32.50 st. – SB (weekends only) 30.00 st.

GRAVETYE East Sussex – see East Grinstead.

♦London 47 – Chichester 23 – Farnham 9 – Guilford 14 – ♦Portsmouth and Southsea 31.

✗ **Woods,** Headley Rd, GU26 6LB, ✆ 5555 – 🔼 ⓪ VISA
closed Sunday and Monday – M (dinner only) a la carte 14.05/16.70 t. 🍷 2.10.

GREAT AYTON North Yorks. 402 Q 20 – pop. 4,816 – ✉ ✆ 0642 Middlesbrough.
♦London 245 – ♦Leeds 63 – ♦Middlesbrough 7 – York 48.

XXX **Ayton Hall** ⚘ with rm, Low Green, TS9 6PS, ✆ 723595, « Tasteful decor », 🐎, ❀ – 📺 🛏wc ☎ ⇔ 🅿 🔊 AE VISA ✆
M a la carte 14.95/19.95 t. ⓘ 3.80 – � 4.95 – **5 rm** 33.00/66.00 t. – SB (weekends only) 65.00/75.00 **st.**

GREAT BADDOW Essex 404 V 28 – see Chelmsford.

GREAT BARDFIELD Essex 404 V 28 – pop. 944 – ✉ Braintree – ✆ 0371 Great Dunmow.
♦London 49 – ♦Cambridge 30 – Chelmsford 24 – Colchester 26.

X **Corn Dolly,** High St., CM7 4SP, ✆ 810554, English rest. – 🔊 AE ① VISA
closed Sunday dinner, Monday except Bank Holidays, Tuesday and January – **M** a la carte 6.50/8.80 t. ⓘ 3.05.

GREAT BARR West Midlands 403 404 O 26 – see Birmingham.

GREAT BROUGHTON Cumbria 401 402 J 19 – see Cockermouth.

GREAT DRIFFIELD Humberside 402 S 21 – pop. 7,040 – ECD : Wednesday – ✉ York – ✆ 0377.
🖪 Driffield, Sunderlandwick ✆ 43116.
♦London 201 – ♦Kingston-upon-Hull 21 – Scarborough 22 – York 29.

🏠 **Bell,** 46 Market Pl., YO25 7AP, ✆ 46661, squash – 📺 🛏wc ☎ ♿ 🅿 🔊 AE ① VISA ✆
M (buffet lunch) a la carte 7.70/10.70 st. ⓘ 2.75 – **14 rm** ⊆ 25.00/35.00 st. – SB (weekends only) 52.00 **st.**

at Nafferton NE : 2 ½ m. on A 166 – ✉ ✆ 0377 Great Driffield :

🏠 **Wold House** ⚘, Wold Rd, YO25 0LD, ✆ 44242, 🔊 heated, 🐎 – 🛏wc 🚻wc 🅿 ✆
M (bar lunch) 5.75/7.50 st. ⓘ 3.50 – **14 rm** ⊆ 17.50/30.00 st. – SB 34.00/37.00 **st.**

GREAT DUNMOW Essex 404 V 28 – pop. 3,827 – ECD : Wednesday – ✆ 0371.
♦London 42 – ♦Cambridge 27 – Chelmsford 13 – Colchester 24.

🏠 **Saracen's Head** (T.H.F.), High St., CM6 1AG, ✆ 3901 – 📺 🛏wc ⇔ 🅿 🔊 🔊 AE ① VISA
M approx. 8.50 **st.** ⓘ 2.85 – ⊆ 5.00 – **24 rm** 35.50/46.50 **st.**

XXX **Starr,** Market Pl., CM6 1AX, ✆ 4321 – 🅿 🔊 🔊 AE ① VISA
closed Sunday dinner, Monday, first 3 weeks August and 25 December-9 January – **M** (dinner only and Sunday lunch) a la carte 13.55/19.50 t. ⓘ 3.25.

BMW The Downs, 81 High St. ✆ 2884

GREAT MALVERN Heref. and Worc. 403 404 N 27 – pop. 30,340 – ECD : Wednesday – ✆ 068 45.
See : Priory Church★ 11C B B – 🛈 Winter Gdns, Grange Rd ✆ 2700.
♦London 127 – ♦Birmingham 34 – ♦Cardiff 66 – Gloucester 24.

Plan opposite

🏠 **Mount Pleasant,** Belle Vue Terr., WR14 4PZ, ✆ 61837, 🐎 – 📺 🛏wc 🅿 🔊 🔊 AE ①
VISA ✆   B e
M (bar lunch) 8.50 **st.** ⓘ 2.00 – **8 rm** ⊆ 30.00/40.00 **st.** – SB 40.00/48.00 **st.**

🏠 **Foley Arms** (Best Western), Worcester Rd, WR14 4QS, ✆ 3397, Telex 437269, ≤, 🐎 – 📺
🛏wc 🚻wc 🅿 🔊 🔊 AE ① VISA   B a
M 5.15/6.25 **st.** ⓘ 2.75 – **26 rm** ⊆ 29.50/44.00 **st.** – SB 42.00/46.00 **st.**

🏠 **Cotford,** Graham Rd, WR14 2JW, ✆ 2427, 🐎 – 🛏wc 🚻wc 🅿 ✆   B o
closed 3 weeks November – **M** (lunch by arrangement) 6.50/7.00 t. ⓘ 2.30 – **15 rm**
⊆ 14.00/30.00 t.

🏠 **Montrose,** 23 Graham Rd, WR14 2HU, ✆ 2335, 🐎 – 🚻wc 🅿 🔊 VISA   B i
M (dinner only) 6.00 **st.** ⓘ 2.40 – **14 rm** ⊆ 15.50/27.00 **st.** – SB (January-March) 31.50/35.00 **st.**

🏠 **Fromefield,** 147 Barnards Green Rd, WR14 3LT, ✆ 62466, 🐎 – ✆   B r
7 rm ⊆ 12.50/27.00 **st.**

X **Walmer Lodge** with rm, 49 Abbey Rd, WR14 3HH, ✆ 4139, ≤, 🐎 – 🛏wc 🚻wc 🅿 ✆
closed Christmas and New Year – **M** (closed Sunday) (dinner only) (booking essential) a la   A n
carte 7.70/9.10 ⓘ 2.80 – **9 rm** ⊆ 14.95/27.60 t.

at Welland SE : 4 ½ m. by A 449 on A 4104 – ✉ Great Malvern – ✆ 0684 Hanley Swan :

🏠 **Holdfast Cottage** ⚘, WR13 6NA, W : ¾ m. ✆ 310288, 🐎 – 🛏wc 🚻wc 🅿   A x
M (dinner only) 9.50 **st.** ⓘ 3.75 – **9 rm** ⊆ 17.00/36.00 t. – SB 48.00/54.00 **st.**

at Malvern Wells S : 2 m. on A 449 – ✉ ✆ 068 45 Great Malvern :

🏠 **Cottage in the Wood** ⚘, Holywell Rd, WR14 4LG, ✆ 3487, ≤ Severn and Evesham Vales,
🐎 – 📺 🛏wc ⇔ 🅿 🔊 VISA ✆   A z
M 7.50/13.50 **st.** ⓘ 3.20 – ⊆ 3.50 – **21 rm** 35.00/55.00 **st.** – SB 49.50/69.50 **st.**

XX ❀ **Croque-en-Bouche,** 221 Wells Rd, WR14 4NF, ✆ 65612 – 🔊 VISA   A u
closed Sunday to Tuesday – **M** (dinner only) (booking essential) 17.00 **st.** ⓘ 3.10
Spec. Turbot on a bed of leeks beurre blanc, Medallions of Venison Francatelli, Tarte tatin (September-February).

GREAT MALVERN

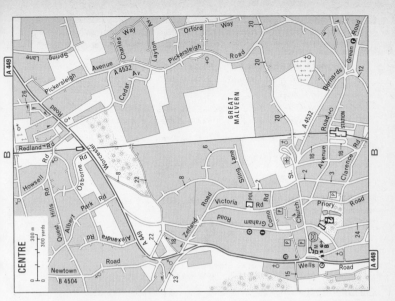

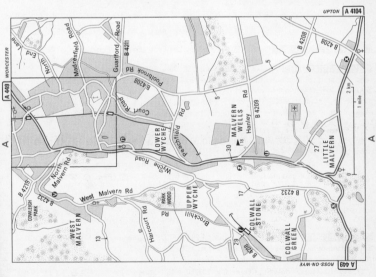

Town plans
roads most used
by traffic and those
on which guide listed
hotels and restaurants
stand are fully drawn ;
the beginning only
of lesser roads
is indicated.

191

at Colwall S : 3 ¼ m. by A 449 on B 4218 – ⊠ Great Malvern – ☎ 0684 Colwall :

🏨 **Colwall Park,** Walwyn Rd, WR13 6QG, ℰ 40206 – 📺 ⌨wc ᛜwc ☎ 🅿. ☷. ◪ 𝘝𝘐𝘚𝘈   A r
M approx. 8.50 t. ▯ 2.25 – **14 rm** ⚏ 25.75/42.50 t.

at Wynds Point S : 4 m. on A 449 – ⊠ Great Malvern – ☎ 0684 Colwall :

🏨 **Malvern Hills,** British Camp, WR13 6DW, ℰ 40237, 🚅 – 📺 ⌨wc 🅿. ◪ 𝘈𝘌 ⓪ –   A s
M (bar lunch) 6.95 **st.** ▯ 2.50 – **15 rm** ⚏ 18.00/38.00 **st.** – SB (except Bank Holi-days) 50.00/65.00 **st.**

at West Malvern W : 2 m. on B 4232 – ⊠ ☎ 068 45 Great Malvern :

⌂ **Broomhill,** West Malvern Rd, WR14 4AY, ℰ 64367, ≤ hills and countryside, 🚅 – ⌨wc   A v
ᛜwc 🅿
March-October – **M** (bar lunch) 7.00 t. – **10 rm** ⚏ 13.50/28.50 t. – SB (except sum-mer) 31.50/37.80 st.

AUSTIN-ROVER-DAIMLER-JAGUAR-LAND ROVER
Worcester Rd ℰ 3301
CITROEN   62 Court Rd ℰ 3391
FORD   203-5 Worcester Rd ℰ 69111

SKODA ℰ 64646
VAUXHALL-OPEL   Linktop ℰ 3336
VOLVO   Pickersleigh Rd ℰ 61498
VW, AUDI   Worcester Rd ℰ 3601

GREAT MILTON Oxon. 403 404 Q 28 – pop. 800 – ⊠ Oxford – ☎ 084 46.
♦London 49 – ♦Oxford 11.

XXXX ❀❀ **Le Manoir aux Quat' Saisons** ⅏ with rm, OX9 7PD, ℰ 230, ≤, « 15C and 16C manor house », ⌓ heated, 🚅, park, ⅍ – 📺 ⌨wc 🅿. ☎ 🅿. ◪ 𝘝𝘐𝘚𝘈. ⅍
closed 24 December-21 January – **M** *(closed Sunday dinner and Monday)* a la carte 27.25/35.30 st. ▯ 6.00 – **10 rm** ⚏ 95.00/150.00 **st.** – SB (not weekends)(winter only) 95.00/150.00 st.
Spec. Tartare de saumon sauvage à la croque de concombres (May-September), Pigeonneau de Bresse en croûte de sel au fumet de truffes, Pomme soufflée au coulis d'abricots et glace vanille.

GREAT SNORING Norfolk 404 W 25 – pop. 199 – ⊠ Fakenham – ☎ 032 872 Walsingham.
♦London 115 – ♦Cambridge 68 – ♦Norwich 28.

🏨 **Old Rectory** ⅏, Barsham Rd, NR21 0HP, ℰ 597, « Country house atmosphere », 🚅 –
⌨wc 🅿. 𝘈𝘌 ⓪. ⅍
closed 24 to 26 December – **M** (lunch by arrangement) 9.75 t. – **6 rm** ⚏ 26.00/38.00 t.

GREAT WITCHINGHAM Norfolk 404 X 25 – see Lenwade - Great Witchingham.

GREAT YARMOUTH Norfolk 404 Z 26 – pop. 50,236 – ECD : Thursday – ☎ 0493.
⛴ Shipping connections with the Continent : to The Netherlands (Scheveningen) (Norfolk Line).
🄳 1 South Quay ℰ 4313/4 – Marine Parade ℰ 2195 (summer only).
♦London 126 – ♦Cambridge 81 – ♦Ipswich 53 – ♦Norwich 20.

🏥 Carlton (Mt. Charlotte), 1-5 Kimberley Terr., Marine Par., NR30 3JE, ℰ 855234, Telex 97249 –
🛗 📺 ⇔ 🅿. ☷. ◪ 𝘈𝘌 ⓪ 𝘝𝘐𝘚𝘈
92 rm ⚏ 32.45/43.45 st.

🏨 Star (Q.M.H.), 24 Hall Quay, NR30 1HG, ℰ 842294 – 🛗 📺 ⌨wc ☎ 🅿. ☷. ◪ 𝘈𝘌 ⓪ 𝘝𝘐𝘚𝘈
M 6.00/7.00 st. ▯ 2.95 – **42 rm** ⚏ 25.00/44.00 **st.** – SB (weekends only) 40.00 **st.**

at Gorleston-on-Sea S : 3 m. on A 12 – ⊠ ☎ 0493 Great Yarmouth :

🏨 Cliff (Best Western), Cliff Hill, NR31 6DH, ℰ 662179, 🚅 – 📺 ⌨wc 🅿. ☷. ◪ 𝘈𝘌 ⓪ 𝘝𝘐𝘚𝘈
M 5.75/6.90 t. ▯ 2.50 – **28 rm** ⚏ 26.00/45.00 **st.** – SB (weekends only) 40.00/48.00 **st.**

AUSTIN-ROVER   North Quay ℰ 4266
CITROEN   Main Rd, Repps ℰ 069 27 (Potter Heigh-ham) 271/256
FORD   South Gates Rd ℰ 4922

FORD   134 Lowestoft Rd, Gorleston-on-Sea ℰ 664151
PEUGEOT, TALBOT   Drudge Rd ℰ 664158
VW, AUDI-NSU   South Denes Rd ℰ 57711

GREAT YELDHAM Essex 404 V 27 – pop. 1,290 – ECD : Wednesday – ⊠ Halstead – ☎ 0787.
Envir. : Hedingham Castle (Norman Keep★) *AC*, SE : 2 ½ m.
♦London 56 – ♦Cambridge 27 – Chelmsford 23 – Colchester 21.

XX **White Hart,** Poole St., CO9 4HJ, ℰ 237250, « 15C timbered inn », 🚅 – 🅿. ☷. ◪ 𝘈𝘌 ⓪ 𝘝𝘐𝘚𝘈
M a la carte 9.30/12.80 t. ▯ 2.95.

GRETA BRIDGE Durham 402 O 20 – pop. 85 – ⊠ Barnard Castle – ☎ 0833 Teesdale.
♦London 253 – ♦Carlisle 63 – ♦Leeds 63 – ♦Middlesbrough 32.

🏨 **Morritt Arms,** DL12 9SE, ℰ 27232, ⅏, – ⌨wc 🅿. ☷. ◪ ⓪ 𝘝𝘐𝘚𝘈
M 8.00/13.00 st. ▯ 3.00 – **23 rm** ⚏ 20.00/42.00 **st.** – SB (winter only) 40.00/42.00 **st.**

L'EUROPE en une seule feuille
Carte Michelin n° 920.

GRIMSBY Humberside **402 404** T 23 – pop. 95,540 – ECD : Thursday – ☎ 0472.

Envir. : Thornton Curtis (St. Lawrence's Church★ : Norman and Gothic) NW : 16 m. by A 18 Y and B 1211 – Thornton Abbey (ruins 14C) : the Gatehouse★ *AC*, NW : 18 m. by A 18 Y and B 1211.

✈ Humberside Airport : ℰ 0652 (Barnetby) 688456, W : 13 m. by A 8 Y.

🅱 Central Library, Town Hall Square ℰ 53123.

♦London 172 – Boston 50 – Lincoln 36 – ♦Sheffield 75.

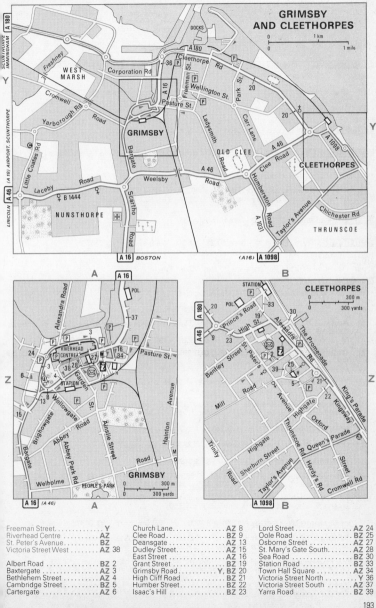

🏨 **Humber Royal** (Crest), Littlecoates Rd, DN34 4LX, ☎ 50295, Telex 527776 – 🛗 📺 ⅃ 🅟 🚗
🆘 ☒ ① 🆅🆂🅰 ᖡ
M approx. 10.00 **st.** – ⚌ 5.50 – **52 rm** 46.50/55.00 **st.**
Y c

🏨 **Crest** (Crest), St. James Sq., DN31 1EP, ☎ 59771, Telex 527741 – 🛗 📺 ▱wc 🚗 ⅃ 🅟 ᖡ
🆘 ☒ ① 🆅🆂🅰
M approx. 11.00 **st.** – ⚌ 5.25 – **132 rm** 41.00/51.00 **st.**
AZ n

ALFA-ROMEO, HONDA Alexandra Rd ☎ 58625	NISSAN 210/212 Victoria St. ☎ 53572
AUSTIN-ROVER 166/168 Hainton Av. ☎ 52461	RENAULT Chelmsford Av. ☎ 70111
AUSTIN-ROVER 415 Victoria St. ☎ 56161	SAAB Heneage Rd ☎ 48527
FIAT Wellowgate ☎ 55951	SKODA Rendel St. ☎ 57362
FORD Corporation Rd ☎ 58941	VAUXHALL-OPEL 123 Cromwell Rd ☎ 46066
MERCEDES-BENZ Bradley Cross Rd ☎ 79274	VAUXHALL-OPEL Brighowgate ☎ 58486

GRIMSTHORPE Lincs. 🄒🄒🄒 🄒🄒🄒 S 25 – pop. 313 – ✉ Bourne – ☻ 077 832 Edenham.

♦London 105 – Lincoln 43 – ♦Nottingham 38.

%% **Black Horse Inn** with rm, PE10 0LY, ☎ 247, English rest. – ▱wc 🅟 🆘 ☒ 🆅🆂🅰
closed Sunday and 24 December to 10 January – **M** 9.95 **t.** ↥ 3.00 – **4 rm** ⚌ 16.50/33.00 **t.** –
SB 48.00/58.00 **st.**

GRIMSTON Norfolk – see Kings Lynn.

GRINDLEFORD Derbs. 🄒🄒🄒 🄒🄒🄒 🄒🄒🄒 P 24 – pop. 1,200 – ✉ Sheffield (South Yorks.) – ☻ 0433
Hope Valley.

♦London 165 – Derby 31 – ♦Manchester 34 – ♦Sheffield 10.

🏨 **Maynard Arms,** Main Rd, S30 1HP, ☎ 30321, ◿, 🐎 – 📺 ▱wc 🅟 ᖡ 🆘 ☒ ① 🆅🆂🅰
M 6.25/8.95 **t.** ↥ 2.50 – **13 rm** ⚌ 26.00/35.00 **t.** – SB 42.00/46.00 **st.**

GRIZEDALE Cumbria 🄒🄒🄒 K 20 – see Hawkshead.

GUILDFORD Surrey 🄒🄒🄒 S 30 – pop. 57,213 – ECD : Wednesday – ☻ 0483.

See : Cathedral★ (1961) Z A.

Envir. : Clandon Park★★ (Renaissance House) *AC*, E : 3 m. by A 246 Z.

🅉 Civic Hall, London Rd ☎ 67314.

♦London 33 – ♦Brighton 43 – Reading 27 – ♦Southampton 49.

Plan opposite

🏨 **Angel** (T.H.F.), High St., GU1 3DR, ☎ 64555, « 16C coaching inn » – 📺 ▱wc 🚗 ⟸ ᖡ
🆘 ☒ ① 🆅🆂🅰
Y a
M *(closed Sunday dinner)* 10.50/12.50 **st.** ↥ 2.85 – ⚌ 5.00 – **25 rm** 35.50/46.00 **st.**

🏩 **Quinns** without rest., 78 Epsom Rd, GU1 2BX, ☎ 60422, 🐎 – 📺 ▱wc ᖡwc 🅟 🆘 ☒ ①
🆅🆂🅰
Z e
11 rm ⚌ 19.50/40.25 **st.**

%% **Three Kingdoms,** 14 Park St., GU1 4XB, ☎ 61458, Chinese rest. – 🆘 ☒ ① 🆅🆂🅰
Y u
closed 25 to 27 December – **M** a la carte 8.55/15.00 **t.**

% **Café de Paris,** 35 Castle St., GU1 3UQ, ☎ 34896, French rest. – 🆘 ☒ ① 🆅🆂🅰
Y c
closed Saturday lunch, Monday dinner and Sunday – **M** a la carte 10.80/17.30 **t.** ↥ 2.70.

at West Clandon NE : 5 m. by A 246 on A 247 – Z – ✉ ☻ 0483 Guildford :

%%% Onslow Arms Inn, The Street, GU4 7TE, ☎ 222447 – 🅟.

at Bramley S : 3 m. on A 281 – Z – ✉ ☻ 0483 Guildford :

🏨 **Bramley Grange,** High St., GU5 0BL, ☎ 893434, 🐎 – 📺 ▱wc 🚗 🅟 🆘 ☒ ① 🆅🆂🅰 ᖡ
M a la carte 11.50/16.50 **t.** ↥ 4.00 – ⚌ 4.25 – **21 rm** 23.00/50.00 **t.**

%% **La Baita,** High St., GU5 0HB, ☎ 893392, Italian rest. – 🅟 🆘 ☒ ① 🆅🆂🅰
closed Sunday – **M** a la carte 10.30/16.30 **t.** ↥ 2.50.

at Compton SW : 4 m. by A 3100 on B 3000 – Z – ✉ Guildford – ☻ 048 68 Godalming :

%% **Withies Inn,** Withies Lane, GU3 1JA, ☎ 21158, 🐎 – 🅟 🆘 ☒ ① 🆅🆂🅰
closed Sunday dinner – **M** a la carte 11.75/15.00 **t.** ↥ 2.75.

BEDFORD, VAUXHALL-OPEL Woking Rd ☎ 37731	MERCEDES-BENZ Aldershot Rd ☎ 60751
AUSTIN-ROVER, ROLLS ROYCE Woodbridge Rd –	RENAULT Walnut Tree Close ☎ 577371
☎ 69231	TALBOT By-Pass Rd ☎ 76931
BMW Moorfield Rd ☎ 502211	TOYOTA Pitch Pl. Worplesdon ☎ 234242
FORD Woodbridge Meadow ☎ 60601	

GUILDFORD

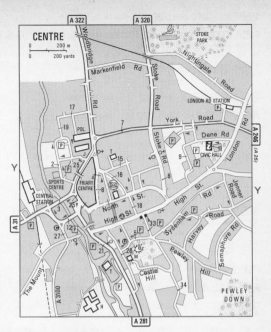

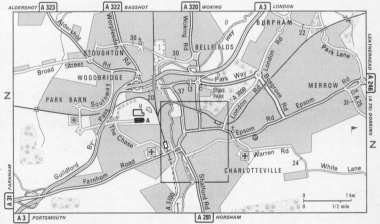

GUIST Norfolk **404** W 25 – pop. 205 – ⊠ Fakenham – ✿ 036 284 Foulsham.

♦London 119 – ♦Cambridge 67 – King's Lynn 29 – ♦Norwich 20.

XX **Tollbridge,** Dereham Rd, NR20 5NU, S : ½ m. on B 1110 ℰ 359, « Attractive setting on
banks of River Wensum », 🐟 – ℗ 𝘝𝘐𝘚𝘈
closed Sunday, Monday, 3 weeks January and first week October – **M** (booking essential) a la
carte 8.35/10.40 **t.** ≬ 2.25.

AUSTIN-ROVER Hempton Rd ℰ 0328 (Fakenham)
2277
NISSAN Norwich Rd ℰ 0328 (Fakenham) 2266
OPEL Greenway Lane ℰ 0328 (Fakenham) 2200

PEUGEOT, VAUXHALL Hempton Rd ℰ 0328 (Fakenham) 3331
TALBOT Sandgate Rd ℰ 0328 (Fakenham) 55331

GULWORTHY Devon 403 H 32 – see Tavistock.

GUNNISLAKE Cornwall 403 H 32 The West Country G. – pop. 4,079 (inc. Calstock) – ECD : Wednesday – ☺ 0822 Tavistock.
Envir. : Cotehele House★★, SW : 2 ½ m.
◆London 244 – Bude 37 – Exeter 43 – ◆Plymouth 20 – Tavistock 5.

   ♤ Cornish Inn, The Square, PL18 9BW, ℰ 832475 – ⇌wc 🅿 – **9 rm**.

GWBERT-ON-SEA Dyfed 403 F 27 – see Cardigan.

HACKNESS North Yorks. 402 S 21 – see Scarborough.

HADLEIGH Suffolk 404 W 27 – pop. 5,620 – ☺ 0473.
◆London 72 – ◆Cambridge 49 – Colchester 17 – ◆Ipswich 10.

   ✕ **Weavers,** 25-27 High St., IP7 5AG, ℰ 827247 – 🔼 𝘝𝘐𝘚𝘈
       closed Sunday, Monday, 7 to 23 July and 25 December-2 January – **M** (dinner only) a la carte 6.55/11.05 **t.** ⓦ 2.50.

AUSTIN-ROVER 115 High St. ℰ 823286   RENAULT 272 London Rd ℰ 554563
PEUGEOT, TALBOT 132 High St. ℰ 823525

HADLOW Kent 404 V 30 – pop. 3,365 – ✉ Tonbridge – ☺ 0732.
◆London 34 – Maidstone 10 – Royal Tunbridge Wells 9.

   ✕✕ **La Cremaillère,** The Square, TN11 0DD, ℰ 851489, French rest. – 🔼 𝔸𝔼 𝘝𝘐𝘚𝘈
       closed Saturday lunch, Sunday, 1 week March, 1 week May, 1 week September and 1 week December – **M** (booking essential) 9.00 **t.** ⓦ 3.80.

HALE Greater Manchester 402 403 404 M 23 – see Altrincham.

HALEBARNS Greater Manchester – see Altrincham.

HALESWORTH Suffolk 404 Y 26 – pop. 3,236 – ECD : Thursday – ☺ 098 67.
◆London 103 – ◆Ipswich 30 – ◆Norwich 25.

   ✕ **Bassett's,** 84 London Rd, IP19 8LS, on A 144 ℰ 3154, ☆ – 🔼 𝘝𝘐𝘚𝘈
       closed Saturday lunch, Sunday, Monday, 1 week February and 1 week October – **M** (buffet lunch) 9.50 **t.** ⓦ 2.55.

AUSTIN-ROVER Market Place ℰ 3213   VAUXHALL-OPEL London Rd ℰ 2138
MAZDA Holton Rd ℰ 3129

HALIFAX West Yorks. 402 O 22 – pop. 91,272 – ECD : Thursday – ☺ 0422.
📵 Halifax Bradley Hall, Holywell Green ℰ 0422 (Elland) 74108 – 📵 West End, Highroad Well ℰ 53608, N : 3 m. – 📵 Ryburn, Norland ℰ 831355, S : 3 m.
🅸 The Piece Hall ℰ 68725 – ◆London 205 – Bradford 8 – Burnley 21 – ◆Leeds 15 – ◆Manchester 28.

   🏠 **Holdsworth House,** Holmfield, HX2 9TG, N : 3 m. by A 629 ℰ 244270 – 📺 🅿 ⚲ 🔼 𝔸𝔼 ⓪ 𝘝𝘐𝘚𝘈
       closed 1 week at Christmas – **M** *(closed Saturday lunch and Sunday)* a la carte 12.00/13.50 **st.** ⓦ 4.00 – **30 rm** ⊡ 24.00/56.00 **st.** – SB (except Christmas) 56.00 **st.**

AUSTIN-ROVER-DAIMLER-JAGUAR Huddersfield   RENAULT Hope St. ℰ 52087
Rd ℰ 65944   VAUXHALL Northgate ℰ 62851
FIAT, CITROEN, LANCIA Queens Rd ℰ 67711   VAUXHALL-OPEL 7 Horton St. ℰ 65846
FIAT, POLSKI Rochdale Rd ℰ 65036   VOLVO 354 Pellon Lane ℰ 61961
FORD Skircoat Rd ℰ 65790   VW, AUDI Denholme Gate Rd. Hipperholme ℰ
HONDA Boothtown ℰ 67516   205611
PEUGEOT-TALBOT Skircoat Rd ℰ 53701

HALLAND East Sussex 404 U 31 – pop. 762 – ECD : Wednesday – ✉ Lewes – ☺ 082 584.
◆London 48 – ◆Brighton 16 – Eastbourne 16 – Royal Tunbridge Wells 19.

   🏠 **Halland Forge,** BN8 6PW, on A 22 ℰ 456, ☆ – 📺 ⇌wc ⇌wc ☎ 🅿 🔼 𝔸𝔼 ⓪ 𝘝𝘐𝘚𝘈 ✼
       M 7.50/9.50 **t.** ⓦ 2.75 – ⊡ 5.00 – **20 rm** 25.00/35.00 **t.** – SB 48.50/53.00 **st.**

HALSE TOWN Cornwall 403 D 33 – see St. Ives.

HALTWHISTLE Northumb. 401 402 M 19 – pop. 3,522 – ☺ 0498.
◆London 335 – ◆Carlisle 22 – ◆Newcastle 37.

   ↑ **Ashcroft,** NE49 0DA, ℰ 20213, ☆ – 🅿 ✼
       closed Christmas and New Year – **8 rm** ⊡ 7.00/14.00.

HAMBLE Hants. 403 404 Q 31 – pop. 3,045 – ☺ 0703 Southampton.
◆London 88 – ◆Portsmouth 20 – ◆Southampton 7 – Winchester 22.

   ✕✕ Beth's, The Quay, ℰ 454314, ≤.
PEUGEOT-TALBOT Hamble Lane ℰ 453757

HAMBLETON Leics. – see Oakham.

HAMBROOK Avon **403 404** M 29 – see Bristol.

HANDFORTH Cheshire **402 403 404** N 23 – see Wilmslow.

HANLEY Staffs. **402 403 404** N 24 – see Stoke-on-Trent.

HARBERTONFORD Devon **403** I 32 – pop. 974 – ⊠ Totnes – 🕾 080 423.
♦London 228 – Exeter 28 – ♦Plymouth 24 – Torquay 13.

　XX　**Hungry Horse,** Old Rd, TQ9 7TA, 𝒫 441 – **🅿** ⚠ ⚑ ⓐ *VISA*
　　　closed Sunday, Monday, 3 weeks February, 1 week June and 1 week Christmas – **M** (dinner only) a la carte 11.65/13.50 **t.**

HARLECH Gwynedd **402 403** H 25 – pop. 1,405 – ECD : Wednesday – 🕾 0766.
See : Castle** (13C) *AC*, site and ≤ from the castle* – Envir. : Llanbedr (Cwm Bychan*) S : 3 ½ m. – Vale of Ffestiniog* NE : 9 m. – ₦ Royal St. David's 𝒫 780203.
🛈 Snowdonia National Park Visitor Centre, High St. 𝒫 780658 (summer only).
♦London 241 – Chester 72 – Dolgellau 21.

　🏛　**Maes-y-Neuadd** 🦢, Talsarnau, LL47 6YA, NE : 3 m. by B 4573 𝒫 780200, ≤, « Part 14C country house », 🍃, 🐾, park – 📺 ⌷wc **🅿** ⚠ ⚑ ⓐ *VISA*
　　　closed 3 to 24 January – **M** (lunch by arrangement Monday to Saturday) 6.00/12.00 **st.** – **11 rm** 🖙 18.00/50.00 **st.** – SB 45.50/52.50 **st.**

　🏠　**Noddfa,** Lower Rd, LL46 2UB, 𝒫 780043, ≤ – ⌷wc **🅿** ⚠ *VISA*
　　　March-October – **M** (bar lunch) 6.00 **t.** 🍷 2.25 – **7 rm** 🖙 13.50/24.00 **t.** – SB (except summer) 29.00/33.00 **st.**

　X　**The Cemlyn,** High St., LL46 2YA, 𝒫 780425, ≤ Harlech Castle, Cardigan Bay and Lleyn Peninsula – ⚠ ⓐ
　　　March-September – **M** *(closed Sunday to Thursday March-Easter)* (lunch by arrangement) a la carte 8.00/10.75 **t.** 🍷 2.80.

HARLOW Essex **404** U 28 – pop. 79,521 – ECD : Wednesday – 🕾 0279.
♦London 22 – ♦Cambridge 37 – ♦Ipswich 60.

　🏛　**Green Man** (Anchor), Mulberry Green, Old Harlow, CM17 0ET, E : 2 ¼ m. by A 414 and B 183 𝒫 442521, Group Telex 817972 – 📺 ⌷wc ☎ **🅿** ⚠ ⚑ ⓐ *VISA*
　　　M (bar lunch Saturday) a la carte 8.55/16.50 **t.** 🍷 2.70 – **55 rm** 🖙 36.50/45.00 **t.** – SB (weekends only September-June) 45.00 **st.**

HARNHAM Wilts. **403 404** O 30 – see Salisbury.

HARPENDEN Herts. **404** S 28 – pop. 21,230 – ECD : Wednesday – 🕾 058 27.
♦London 32 – Luton 6.

　🏛　**Harpenden Moat House** (Q.M.H.), 18 Southdown Rd, AL5 1PE, 𝒫 64111, 🐾 – 📺 **🅿** ⚐ ⚠ ⚑ ⓐ *VISA*
　　　M 9.00/13.00 **t.** 🍷 4.50 – 🖙 5.00 – **35 rm** 37.00/50.00 **t.**

　🏛　**Glen Eagle,** 1 Luton Rd, AL5 2PX, 𝒫 60271 – 🛗 📺 ⌷wc ☎ **🅿** ⚐ ⚠ ⚑ ⓐ *VISA*
　　　M a la carte approx. 17.85 **t.** – 🖙 4.50 – **51 rm** 36.00/41.00 **t.**

DAIHATSU, SAAB 74 High St. 𝒫 4545　　　　　VAUXHALL-OPEL 17 Luton Rd 𝒫 67776
FORD, RENAULT Southdown Rd 𝒫 5217　　　　VOLVO Station Rd 𝒫 64311

HARROGATE North Yorks. **402** P 22 – pop. 62,427 – ECD : Wednesday – 🕾 0423.
See : Harlow Car gardens** by B 6162 Z – Envir. : Fountains Abbey*** (ruins 12C-13C, floodlit in summer), Studley Royal Gardens** – Fountains Hall* (17C) *AC*, NW : 9 m. by A 61 Y.
₦ Starbeck, nr. Harrogate 𝒫 863158, E : 2 m. by A 59 YZ – ₦ Oakdale, off Kent Rd 𝒫 502806 Y – ₦ Crimple Valley, Hookstone Wood Rd 𝒫 883485 by A 661 Z.
🛈 Royal Baths Assembly Rooms, Crescent Rd 𝒫 65912.
♦London 211 – Bradford 18 – ♦Leeds 15 – ♦Newcastle-upon-Tyne 76 – York 22.

Plan on next page

　🏛🏛　**Majestic** (T.H.F.), Ripon Rd, HG1 2HU, 𝒫 68972, Telex 57918, ⬛, 🐾, ✗ – 🛗 📺 **🅿** ⚠ ⚑ ⓐ *VISA*　　　Y　c
　　　M a la carte 11.05/16.05 **st.** 🍷 3.40 – 🖙 5.50 – **151 rm** 40.00/48.00 **st.**

　🏛🏛　**Old Swan** (Best Western), Swan Rd, HG1 2SR, 𝒫 504051, Telex 57922, 🐾, park, ✗ – 🛗 📺 🖕 **🅿** ⚠ ⚑ ⓐ *VISA*　　　Y　e
　　　M (carving rest.) 8.50 **st.** – **138 rm** 🖙 27.00/65.00 **st.** – SB 52.00 **st.**

　🏛🏛　**Crown** (T.H.F.), Crown Pl., HG1 2RZ, 𝒫 67755, Telex 57652 – 🛗 📺 **🅿** ⚠ ⚑ ⓐ *VISA*　　　Z　i
　　　M 5.50/10.00 **st.** 🍷 2.60 – 🖙 5.50 – **120 rm** 38.50/45.50 **st.**

　🏛🏛　**Granby** (Norfolk Cap.), Granby Rd, HG1 4SR, 𝒫 56151, Telex 57423 – 🛗 📺 **🅿** ⚠ ⚑ ⓐ *VISA*, ✗　　　Y　x
　　　M 6.25/7.75 **st.** – **90 rm** 🖙 43.00/61.50 **st.** – SB (summer only) 58.30 **st.**

197

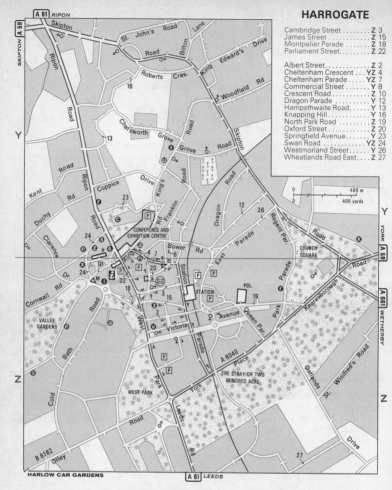

🏨 **Studley,** Swan Rd, HG1 2SE, ℰ 60425, Telex 57506 – 🛗 📺 ⌁wc ☎. 🖭 AE ① VISA. 🛠
M a la carte 9.55/12.60 t. ▯ 2.60 – **40 rm** ⌂ 38.50/54.00 st. – SB (weekends only)
50.00 st.   Z **x**

🏨 **Grants,** 3-7 Swan Rd, HG1 2SS, ℰ 60666 – 🛗 📺 ⌁wc �📶wc ☎ ⌖ ₽. 🖭 AE ① VISA. 🛠
M a la carte 7.65/14.60 t. ▯ 2.65 – **17 rm** ⌂ 32.50/48.50 t. – SB 47.00/54.00 st.   Y **s**

🏨 Hospitality Inn (Mt. Charlotte), West Park, Prospect Pl., HG1 1LB, ℰ 64601, Telex 57530 – 🛗
📺 ⌁wc ⏎ ₽. 🖭 AE ① VISA – **68 rm** ⌂ 38.50/49.50 st. – SB (weekends only) 60.50 st. Z **v**

🏨 **St. George** (Swallow), 1 Ripon Rd, HG1 2SY, ℰ 61431, Telex 57995 – 🛗 📺 ⌁wc ⏎ ₽. 🖓
🖭 AE ① VISA
M (buffet lunch) 6.25/8.75 st. – **82 rm** ⌂ 40.00/56.00 st. – SB 46.50 st.   Y **o**

🏨 **Russell,** 29-35 Valley Drive, HG2 0JP, ℰ 509866 – 🛗 📺 ⌁wc �📶wc ⏎. 🖭 AE ① VISA
M Hodgeson's rest. *(closed Sunday and Monday)* (bar lunch) a la carte 12.75/16.50 t. ▯ 3.00 –
34 rm ⌂ 25.95/42.95 t. – SB 50.50/53.50 st.   Z **e**

🏨 **White House,** 10 Park Par., HG1 5AF, ℰ 501388, 🚗 – 📺 ⌁wc �📶wc ⏎ ₽. 🖭 AE ① VISA
M (dinner only) 8.00 t. ▯ 2.35 – **15 rm** ⌂ 22.50/39.00 t. – SB (weekends only) 38.00 st.   Z **r**

🏨 **Fern,** Swan Rd, HG1 2SS, ℰ 523866, Telex 57583 – 📺 ⌁wc ☎. 🖭 AE ① VISA 🛠
M (lunch residents only) 6.00/14.95 st. ▯ 2.55 – **28 rm** ⌂ 25.95/42.95 st.   Y **z**

🏨 **Italia,** 53 King's Rd, HG1 5HJ, ℰ 67404 – 📺 ⌁wc ₽. AE ① VISA
M *(closed Sunday dinner)* (bar lunch) 13.75 st. ▯ 2.70 – **25 rm** ⌂ 19.25/35.20 st. – SB
49.00/51.00 st.   Y **u**

↑ **Wessex,** 22-23 Harlow Moor Drive, HG2 0JY, ℰ 65890 – 🗐wc   Z s
  14 rm ➘ 15.75/31.50 **t.**

↑ **Gables,** 2 West Grove Rd, HG1 2AD, ℰ 55625, ⇗ – 📺 ⇔wc 🗐wc. ✿   Y i
  9 rm ➘ 18.50/35.00 **st.**

↑ **Ambleside,** 5-7 St. Mary's Walk, HG1 0LW, ℰ 69127   Z a
  9 rm ➘ 9.50/17.00 **st.**

XXX **Oliver,** 24 King's Rd, HG1 5JW, ℰ 68600 – 🖪 🖭 𝘝𝘐𝘚𝘈   Y a
  closed Sunday and Bank Holidays – **M** (dinner only) a la carte 11.30/14.55 **t.**

XXX **Number Six,** 6 Ripon Rd, HG1 2JB, ℰ 502908 – 🖪 🖭 𝘝𝘐𝘚𝘈   Y r
  closed Monday, 3 weeks August and Bank Holidays – **M** (dinner only) 13.95 **t.**

XX **Shabab,** 1 John St., HG1 1JZ, ℰ 500250, Indian rest. – 🖪 🖭 ⓄD 𝘝𝘐𝘚𝘈   Z z
  closed Sunday lunch and Christmas Day.

X **Burdekins,** 21 Cheltenham Cres., HG1 1DH, ℰ 502610 – 🖪 🖭 𝘝𝘐𝘚𝘈   YZ n
  M (dinner only) a la carte 7.90/10.10 **t.** 🍴 2.40.

  at Burn Bridge S : 4 m. by A 61 – Z – ✉ ✆ 0423 Harrogate :

XX **Roman Court,** 55 Burn Bridge Rd, HG3 1PB, ℰ 879933, Italian rest. – 🅿 🖪 🖭 𝘝𝘐𝘚𝘈
  closed Sunday – **M** (dinner only) a la carte 7.50/13.30 **t.** 🍴 3.15.

  at Markington NW : 8 ¾ m. by A 61 – Y – ✉ ✆ 0423 Harrogate :

🏛 **Hob Green** ⌘, HG3 3PJ, SW : ½ m. ℰ 770031, Telex 57780, ≼, « Country house in extensive
  parkland », ⇗, park – 📺 ⇔wc ☎ 🅿 🖪 🖭 ⓄD 𝘝𝘐𝘚𝘈 ✿
  M (buffet lunch) 7.50/14.00 **t.** 🍴 4.00 – **11 rm** ➘ 32.50/52.50 **t.** – SB (except summer) 65.00/70.00 **st.**

AUSTIN-ROVER-DAIMLER-JAGUAR,   ROLLS
ROYCE 91 Leeds Rd ℰ 871263
CITROEN, FIAT Leeds Rd, Panna ℰ 879236
DAIHATSU, LANCIA Cheltenham Mount ℰ 68151
FORD Station Par. ℰ 61061

PEUGEOT-TALBOT, VAUXHALL-OPEL West Park ℰ
504601
RENAULT Pannal ℰ 879231
VOLVO East Parade ℰ 64567
VW, AUDI-NSU Ripon Rd ℰ 55141

HARTFORD Cheshire 402 403 404 M 24 – pop. 3,587 – ✆ 0606 Northwich.

🏌 Delamere Forest ℰ 0606 (Sandiway) 882807, SW : 2 m.

♦London 188 – Chester 15 – ♦Liverpool 31 – ♦Manchester 25.

🏛 **Hartford Hall,** School Lane, CW8 1PW, ℰ 75711, ⇗ – 📺 ⇔wc ☎ 🅿 🖪 🖭 ⓄD 𝘝𝘐𝘚𝘈
  M 5.50/9.50 **t.** 🍴 2.70 – **21 rm** ➘ 31.00/41.00 **t.** – SB (weekends only) 44.80 **st.**

AUDI, VW Station Rd, Northwich ℰ 0606 (North-
wich) 6061
CITROEN Manchester Rd, Northwich ℰ 0606
(Northwich) 3816
FORD Chesterway, Northwich ℰ 0606 (Northwich)
6141
FSO 141 Runcorn Rd, Barnton, Northwich ℰ 0606
(Northwich) 74293

RENAULT Runcorn Rd, Barnton ℰ 1616 (Northwich)
77137
PEUGEOT-TALBOT 322 Chester Rd ℰ 0606 (Sandi-
way) 888188
VAUXHALL-OPEL 9 London Rd, Northwich ℰ 0606
(Northwich) 3434

HARTLEPOOL Cleveland 402 Q 19 – pop. 97,094 – ECD : Wednesday – ✆ 0429.

🏌 Seaton Carew, Tees Rd ℰ 66249.

✈ Teesside Airport ℰ 0325 (Darlington) 332811, SW : 20 m.

🛈 Leisure and Amenities Dept., Civic Centre ℰ 66522 ext 375 – Victoria Terr., Hartlepool Docks ℰ 74922
(summer only).

♦London 263 – Durham 19 – ♦Middlesbrough 9 – Sunderland 21.

🏛 Grand, Swainson St., TS24 8AA, ℰ 66345 – 📶 📺 ⇔wc 📞 🦽 – **44 rm**.

AUSTIN-ROVER 128/130 York Rd ℰ 66393
AUSTIN-ROVER York Rd ℰ 74431
CITROEN Casebourne Rd ℰ 33031

FORD Stockton Rd ℰ 64311
LADA York Rd ℰ 73047

HARTOFT END North Yorks. 402 R 21 – ✉ Pickering – ✆ 075 15 Lastingham.

♦London 243 – Scarborough 26 – York 32.

🏛 **Blacksmith's Arms,** YO18 8EN, ℰ 331 – 🗐wc 🅿 𝘝𝘐𝘚𝘈
  M (bar lunch) a la carte 8.00/12.70 **t.** 🍴 2.80 – **12 rm** ➘ 18.00/36.00 **t.** – SB (except summer) 45.00 **st.**

HARWICH and DOVERCOURT Essex 404 X 28 – pop. 14,926 – ECD : Wednesday – ✆ 025 55
(4 fig.) or 0255 (6 fig.).

🏌 Parkeston Rd ℰ 3616.

🚢 Shipping connections with the Continent : to Germany (Hamburg) (DFDS Prins Ferries) – to
Denmark (Esbjerg) (DFDS Seaways) – from Parkeston Quay to The Netherlands (Hoek van Holland)
(Sealink) – to Sweden (Göteborg) (DFDS Tor Line).

⇔ to Felixstowe (Orwell & Harwich Navigation Co.) 5-7 daily (15 mn).

🛈 Parkeston Quay ℰ 6139 (summer only).

♦London 72 – Chelmsford 41 – Colchester 20 – ♦Ipswich 23.

  🏠   **Tower,** Main Road, CO12 3PJ, ℰ 504952 – 📺 ⋔wc 🅿. 🔃 🆀 ⑩ 𝗩𝗜𝗦𝗔
       M a la carte 6.85/10.70 **t.** ⅃ 2.00 – **17 rm** ⌷ 17.00/34.00 **t.**

  🏠   **Cliff,** Marine Par., CO12 3RD, ℰ 503345, Telex 987372, ≼ – 📺 ⇔wc ⋔wc 🅿. ⚖. 🔃 🆀 ⑩
       𝗩𝗜𝗦𝗔
       M a la carte 7.85/10.85 **st.** ⅃ 2.25 – **33 rm** ⌷ 17.50/43.00 **st.**

  XX   **Pier at Harwich,** The Quay, CO12 4HH, ℰ 503363, ≼, Seafood – 🔃 🆀 ⑩ 𝗩𝗜𝗦𝗔
       M a la carte 8.75/16.25 **t.** ⅃ 2.95.

AUSTIN-ROVER   Main Rd ℰ 3191

HASCOMBE Surrey – see Godalming.

HASELBURY PLUCKNETT Somerset ⅾⅾⅾ L 31 – see Crewkerne.

HASLEMERE Surrey ⅾⅾⅾ R 30 – pop. 10,920 – ECD : Wednesday – 🕲 0428.

Envir. : Petworth House★★★ 17C (paintings★★★ and carved room★★★) *AC*, SE : 11 m.

🖈 Old Thorns, Longmoor Rd, Liphook ℰ 724956, W : 6 m.

♦London 47 – ♦Brighton 46 – ♦Southampton 44.

  🏨   **Lythe Hill** ⅁, Petworth Rd, GU27 3BQ, E : 1 ½ m. on B 2131 ℰ 51251, Telex 858402, ≼, 🦢,
       🌴, park, 🎾 – 📺 ☎ 🅿. ⚖. 🔃 🆀 ⑩ 𝗩𝗜𝗦𝗔
       M 9.00/12.00 **st.** ⅃ 3.85 – ⌷ 3.50 – **36 rm** 36.00/50.00 **st.** – SB 75.50/80.50 **st.**

  XXX   **Auberge de France** (at Lythe Hill H.), Petworth Rd, GU27 3BQ, E : 1 ½ m. on B 2131
       ℰ 51251, Telex 858402, ≼, French rest., 🌴 – 🅿. 🔃 🆀 ⑩ 𝗩𝗜𝗦𝗔
       closed Tuesday lunch and Monday – **M** a la carte 16.10/21.50 **st.** ⅃ 3.85.

  XX   **Morels,** 25 Lower St., GU27 2NY, ℰ 51462 – 🔃 🆀 ⑩ 𝗩𝗜𝗦𝗔
       *closed Saturday lunch, Sunday, Monday, 2 weeks February, 3 weeks September and Bank
       Holidays –* **M** (dinner only and lunch in December) a la carte 15.30/16.70 **t.** ⅃ 2.60.

  X   **Shrimptons,** 2 Grove Cottages, Midhurst Rd, Kingsley Green, GU27 3AL, SW : 1 ¼ m. on A
       286 ℰ 3539 – 🔃 🆀 ⑩ 𝗩𝗜𝗦𝗔
       *closed Sunday, Monday, 24 June-7 July, last week September-first week October, 25-26
       December and 1 January –* **M** (lunch by arrangement) a la carte 8.20/15.00 **t.** ⅃ 2.50.

AUSTIN-ROVER   Grayswood Rd ℰ 2303   VAUXHALL-OPEL   West St. ℰ 3333
FORD   Farnham Lane ℰ 3222   VW, AUDI   Hindhead Rd ℰ 53811
PEUGEOT-TALBOT   High St. ℰ 52552

HASSOP Derbs. – see Bakewell.

---

    *During the season, particularly in resorts, it is wise to book in advance.
    However, if you find you cannot take up a hotel booking you have made,
    please let the hotel know immediately.
    If you are writing to a hotel abroad enclose an International Reply Coupon
    (available from Post Offices.)*

HASTINGS and ST. LEONARDS East Sussex ⅾⅾⅾ V 31 – pop. 72,410 – 🕲 0424.

See : Norman Castle (ruins) ⋇★★ *AC* BZ – Alexandra Park★ AY – White Rocks gardens ≼★ ABZ –
Public Museum and Art Gallery (Pottery★, Durbar Hall★) BZ **M.**

🖈 Beauport Park, St. Leonards, ℰ 52977, NW : 3 m. by B 2159 AY.

🅸 4 Robertson Terr. ℰ 424242.

♦London 65 – ♦Brighton 37 – Folkestone 37 – Maidstone 34.

Plan opposite

  🏨   **Beauport Park** ⅁, Battle Rd, TN38 8EA, NW : 3 ½ m. on A 2100 ℰ 51222, ≼, « Formal
       garden », ⅃ heated, park, ⋇ – 📺 ⇔wc ☎ 🅿. 🔃 🆀 ⑩ 𝗩𝗜𝗦𝗔   on B 2159   AY
       M 6.95/8.50 **st.** ⅃ 2.50 – **23 rm** ⌷ 29.50/44.00 **st.** – SB 44.50/52.50 **st.**

  🛏   **Chimes,** 1 St. Matthews Gdns, Silverhill, TN38 0TS, ℰ 434041, 🌴 – 📺 ⇔wc   AY   **a**
       10 rm ⌷ 10.00/22.00 **st.**

  X   **Coach House,** 60a All Saints St., Old Town, TN34 3BN, ℰ 428080 – 🆀 𝗩𝗜𝗦𝗔   BY   **e**
       closed Saturday lunch, Sunday, Monday and 14 April-2 May – **M** a la carte 10.50/15.00 **t.**
       ⅃ 2.00.

AUSTIN-ROVER   Sedlescombe Rd North ℰ 754444   NISSAN   Bexhill Rd ℰ 431276
CITROEN   London Rd ℰ 427746   PEUGEOT, TALBOT   Sedlescombe Rd North ℰ
DAF, VOLVO   100 Battle Rd ℰ 423451   440511
FIAT, COLT, LANCIA, MAZDA   West Marina ℰ   RENAULT   109/111 Sedlescombe Rd North ℰ 432982
433533   VAUXHALL   36/39 Western Rd, St. Leonards ℰ
FORD   Bohemia Rd ℰ 422727   424545

HASTINGS
AND ST. LEONARDS

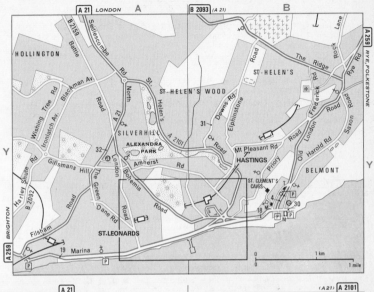

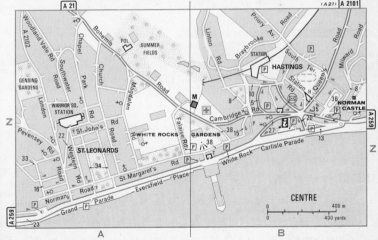

Pour les ⛫⛫⛫⛫ , ⛫⛫⛫ , ⛫⛫ , nous ne donnons pas
le détail de l'installation,
ces hôtels possédant, en général, tout le confort.

⛫wc 🚻wc

☎

201

HATCH BEAUCHAMP Somerset ⁴⁰⁸ K 30 – see Taunton.

HATFIELD Herts. ⁴⁰⁴ T 28 – pop. 26,000 – ECD : Monday and Thursday – ☎ 070 72.
See : Hatfield House★★★ *AC* (gardens★ and Old Palace★).
🇫🇮 Bedwell Park, Essendon ℰ 0707 (Potters Bar) 42624, E : 3 m.
♦London 27 – Bedford 38 – ♦Cambridge 39.

🏨 **Comet** (Embassy), 301 St. Albans Rd West, AL10 9RH, SW : 1 m. by A 1057 at junction with
A 1 and A 414 ℰ 65411 – 🔲 ⇔wc ⊛ 🅿 🔽 🆔 𝑉𝐼𝑆𝐴
M (carving rest.) 7.00 **st.** 🍷 2.20 – ⬚ 4.25 – **57 rm** 32.00/38.00 **st.** – SB (week-
ends only) 40.00/43.00 **st.**

✗✗✗ **Salisbury,** 15 The Broadway, Old Hatfield, AL9 5JB, ℰ 62220 – 🔽 🆔 ⓪ 𝑉𝐼𝑆𝐴
closed Saturday lunch, Sunday dinner and Bank Holidays – **M** a la carte 10.15/14.95 **t.**

ALFA-ROMEO, HONDA, TALBOT, PEUGEOT By-   FIAT North Parade, Barnet by pass ℰ 64698
Pass ℰ 64521   LANCIA, NISSAN 42 Beaconsfield Rd ℰ 71226
AUSTIN-ROVER 1 Great North Rd ℰ 64366

HATHERLEIGH Devon ⁴⁰⁸ H 31 – pop. 915 – ECD : Wednesday – ✉ ☎ 0837 Okehampton.
🇫🇮 at Okehampton ℰ 0837 (Okehampton) 2113, SE : 7 m – ♦London 230 – Exeter 29 – ♦Plymouth 38.

🏨 **George,** Market St., EX20 3JN, ℰ 810454, « 15C inn », ⩩ heated – ⇔wc 🛖wc 🅿 𝑉𝐼𝑆𝐴
closed 11 to 25 November and 3 days at Christmas – **M** (closed Sunday dinner to non-residents)
a la carte 7.35/10.50 **t.** 🍷 1.75 – ⬚ 3.75 – **12 rm** 11.00/24.00 **t.**

at *Sheepwash* NW : 4 ½ m. by A 3072 – ✉ Beaworthy – ☎ 040 923 Black Torrington :

🏨 **Half Moon Inn,** The Square, EX21 5NE, ℰ 376, « 17C inn », ⩩ – 🔲 ⇔wc 🅿 🔽 𝑉𝐼𝑆𝐴
M (bar lunch) 8.50 **t.** 🍷 2.75 – **14 rm** ⬚ 16.50/36.00 **t.** – SB (except summer) 47.00/52.00 **st.**

FORD The Industrial Estate ℰ 810661

HATHERSAGE Derbs. ⁴⁰² ⁴⁰⁸ ⁴⁰⁴ P 24 – pop. 1,458 – ECD : Wednesday – ✉ Sheffield
(South Yorks.) – ☎ 0433 Hope Valley.
♦London 165 – ♦Manchester 33 – ♦Sheffield 10.

🏨 **George,** Main Rd, S30 1BB, ℰ 50436 – 🔲 ⇔wc ⊛ 🅿 🔽 🆔 𝑉𝐼𝑆𝐴
M a la carte 7.65/13.30 **t.** – **18 rm** ⬚ 31.00/41.00 **st.**

AUSTIN-ROVER Main Rd ℰ 50341

HAVANT Hants. ⁴⁰⁴ R 31 – pop. 7,544 – ECD : Wednesday – ☎ 0705.
♦London 70 – ♦Brighton 39 – ♦Portsmouth 9 – ♦Southampton 22.

🏨 **Bear,** 15 East St., PO9 1AA, ℰ 486501 – 🖥 🔲 ⇔wc 🛖wc ☎ 🅿 🔺 🔽 🆔 ⓪ 𝑉𝐼𝑆𝐴 🛇
M 5.95/7.50 **st.** 🍷 4.25 – **35 rm** ⬚ 33.00/45.00 **st.** – SB (weekends only) 48.00/56.00 **st.**

FORD New Rd ℰ 482161

HAVERFORDWEST (HWLFFORDD) Dyfed ⁴⁰⁸ F 28 – pop. 9,104 – ECD : Thursday – ☎ 0437.
Envir. : SW : Martin's Haven ✳︎★★ – St. Ann's Head★★ by Dale ⇐★.
🎑 Pembrokeshire Coast National Park Centre, 40 High St. ℰ 3110 (summer only).
♦London 250 – Fishguard 15 – ♦Swansea 57.

🏨 **Mariners,** Mariners Sq., SA61 2DU, ℰ 3353 – 🔲 ⇔wc 🛖wc ⊛ 🅿 🔽 🆔 ⓪ 𝑉𝐼𝑆𝐴
M (bar lunch Monday to Saturday) 5.50/7.00 **st.** 🍷 2.60 – **29 rm** ⬚ 18.00/36.00 **st.** – SB
(weekends only) 40.00 **st.**

🏨 **Pembroke House,** Spring Gdns, SA61 2EN, ℰ 3652 – 🔲 ⇔wc 🛖wc ⊛ 🅿 🔽 🆔 ⓪ 𝑉𝐼𝑆𝐴
M (lunch by arrangement) 10.00 **st.** 🍷 2.95 – **25 rm** ⬚ 15.85/26.00 **st.** – SB 35.00/38.00 **st.**

🕏 Elliotts Hill 🌭, SA62 6HT, NW : 1 ½ m. on B 4330 ℰ 2383, 🌳, 🛇 – 🅿 🛇 – **20 rm**.

AUSTIN-ROVER-DAIMLER-JAGUAR Salutation Sq.   FORD Dew St. ℰ 3772
ℰ 4511   SAAB Johnston ℰ 0437 (Johnston) 890 377
BMW, NISSAN Rhos ℰ 251   TALBOT, COLT Old Hakin Rd ℰ 2468
FIAT Portfield Rd ℰ 3414   VAUXHALL-OPEL Bridgend Sq. ℰ 2717

HAWES North Yorks ⁴⁰² N 21 – pop. 1,177 – ☎ 09697.
♦London 253 – Kendal 27 – ♦Leeds 72 – ♦York 65.

🏨 **Simonstone Hall** 🌭, Simonstone, DL8 3LY, N : 1 ½ m. ℰ 255, ⇐, « Country house atmosphere », 🌳 – ⇔wc 🅿 🔽 ⓪
M (lunch by arrangement) 9.75 **t.** 🍷 3.00 – **9 rm** ⬚ 18.00/43.00 **t.** – SB (except summer) 44.50/49.50 **st.**

🕏 **Stone House,** Sedbusk, DL8 3PT, N : 1 m. by Mucker rd on Askrigg rd ℰ 571, 🌳 – 🔲 🛖wc
🅿
closed Monday to Thursday in winter – **12 rm** ⬚ 16.50/32.00 **t.**

✗✗ **Cockett's** with rm, Market Place, DL8 3RD, ℰ 312 – 🔲 🛖wc, 🔽 ⓪ 𝑉𝐼𝑆𝐴 🛇
closed last 2 weeks November, January and February – **M** (dinner only)(booking essential)
14.50 **t.** 🍷 3.00 – **5 rm** ⬚ 17.00/29.50 **t.**

HAWKCHURCH Devon ⁴⁰⁸ L 31 – see Axminster.

HAWKHURST Kent 404 V 30 – pop. 4,107 – ECD : Wednesday – ☎ 058 05.

Envir. : Bedgebury Pinetum★ *AC*, NW : 2 m.

☐ High St. ✆ 2396.

◆London 47 – Folkestone 34 – Hastings 14 – Maidstone 19.

🏠 **Tudor Arms** (Best Western), Rye Rd, TN18 5DA, E : 1 ½ m. on A 268 ✆ 2312, Telex 945003, ≼, « Gardens » – ⌷wc fflwc **P**, ☒ **AE** ⓪ **VISA**
M 7.00/7.50 **st.** ░ 3.00 – **13 rm** ⚏ 17.00/56.00 **st.** – SB 48.00/56.00 **st.**

AUSTIN-ROVER Horns Rd ✆ 2020   TALBOT, PEUGEOT Rye Rd ✆ 3151
FORD Winchester Rd ✆ 3313

HAWKRIDGE Somerset 403 J 30 – ✉ Dulverton – ☎ 064 385 Winsford.

◆London 203 – Exeter 32 – Minehead 17 – Taunton 32.

🏠 **Tarr Steps** ≽, TA22 9PY, NE : 1 ½ m. ✆ 293, ≼, ⬀, ☎, park, – ⌷wc **P**, **AE** **VISA**
March-November – **M** (bar lunch Monday to Saturday) 6.50/8.50 **t.** ░ 2.00 – **15 rm**
⚏ 17.50/37.50 **t.**

HAWKSHEAD Cumbria 402 L 20 – pop. 684 – ECD : Thursday – ✉ Ambleside – ☎ 096 66.

☐ Brown Cow Laithe ✆ 525 (summer only).

◆London 283 – ◆Carlisle 52 – Kendal 19.

🏠 **Tarn Hows** ≽, LA22 0PR, NW : 1 ½ m. ✆ 330, ≼, ⎓ heated, ⬀, ☎, park, ✗ – ⌷wc ☎
P, ☒ **AE** **VISA**
M (bar lunch) 10.50 **t.** ░ 1.80 – **20 rm** ⚏ 28.50/60.00 **t.**

⌂ **Highfield House** ≽, Hawkshead Hill, LA22 0PN, W : ½ m. on B 5285 ✆ 344, ≼, ☎ – **P**
12 rm ⚏ 12.00/28.00 **st.**

at Grizedale SW : 2 ¾ m. – ✉ Ambleside – ☎ 096 66 Hawkshead :

XX **Ormandy** ≽ with rm, LA22 0QH, ✆ 532 – fflwc **P**
closed January and February – **M** *(closed Wednesday)* (restricted lunch) (booking essential) a
la carte 5.65/10.35 ░ 2.50 – **5 rm** ⚏ 15.65/25.00 **st.**

HAWORTH West Yorks. 402 O 22 – pop. 3,540 – ECD : Tuesday – ✉ Keighley – ☎ 0535.

See : Brontë Parsonage Museum★ *AC*.

☐ 2/4 West Lane ✆ 42329.

◆London 213 – Burnley 22 – ◆Leeds 22 – ◆Manchester 34.

🏠 **Old White Lion,** 6 West Lane, BD22 8DU, ✆ 42313 – ⌷wc fflwc **P**, ☒ **AE** ⓪ **VISA**
M (bar lunch) 4.55/6.75 **st.** ░ 3.30 – **11 rm** ⚏ 16.00/28.50 **st.** – SB (weekends only) 24.00/30.00 **st.**

HAYDOCK Merseyside 402 403 404 M 23 – pop. 14,900 – ✉ Newton-Le-Willows – ☎ 0942
Ashton-in-Makerfield.

◆London 198 – ◆Liverpool 17 – ◆Manchester 18.

🏠 **Post House** (T.H.F.), Lodge Lane, Newton-le-willows, WA12 0GJ, NE : 1 m. on A 49
✆ 717878, Telex 677672 – ▦ ▣ ☎ ⌷ **P**, ▤ ☒ **AE** ⓪ **VISA**
M 8.50 **st.** ░ 2.60 – ⚏ 5.00 – **98 rm** 39.50/46.50 **st.**

HAYLING ISLAND Hants. 404 R 31 – pop. 10,560 – ECD : Wednesday – ☎ 0705.

☐ 32 Seafront ✆ 67111 (summer only).

◆London 77 – ◆Brighton 45 – ◆Southampton 28.

🏠 **Post House** (T.H.F.), Northney Rd, PO11 0NQ, ✆ 465011, Telex 86620, ≼, ⎓ heated – ▣
⌷wc ☎ **P**, ▤ ☒ **AE** ⓪ **VISA**
M 6.95/8.95 **st.** ░ 2.60 – ⚏ 5.50 – **96 rm** 37.00/44.50 **st.**

🏠 **Newtown House,** Manor Rd, PO11 0QR, ✆ 466131, ⎓ heated, ☎, ✗ – ▣ ⌷wc fflwc ☎
P, ☒ **AE** ⓪ **VISA**
closed 24 December-3 January – **M** 5.50/7.95 **t.** ░ 3.00 – **28 rm** ⚏ 27.50/44.00 **t.** – SB
(weekends only) 48.00/54.00 **t.**

HAY-ON-WYE Powys 403 K 27 – pop. 1,344 – ECD : Tuesday – ☎ 0497.

☐ Chamber of Trade, Car Park (summer only).

◆London 154 – Brecon 16 – Hereford 21 – Newport 62.

🏠 **Old Black Lion,** 26 Lion St., HR3 5AD, ✆ 820841 – ▣ ⌷wc fflwc **P**, ☒
M a la carte 6.25/9.45 **t.** ░ 3.00 – **10 rm** ⚏ 13.00/31.20 **t.** – SB (not weekends) 46.50 **st.**

AUSTIN-ROVER Church St. ✆ 820404

HEALD GREEN Greater Manchester 402 403 404 N 23 – see Manchester.

HEATHROW AIRPORT – see Hillingdon (Greater London).

HEDDONS MOUTH Devon 403 I 30 – see Lynton.

203

HELFORD Cornwall 408 E 33 – pop. 289 (inc. Manaccan) – ⊠ Helston – ☎ 032 623 Manaccan.
♦London 324 – Falmouth 15 – Penzance 22 – Truro 27.

XX **Riverside** with rm, TR12 6JU, ℰ 443, ≼, « Converted cottages in picturesque setting », ☞
– ⊡ ⊟wc ℗. ℅
April-October – **M** *(closed lunch to non-residents)* (booking essential) 20.00 **st.** ⚄ 3.50 – **6 rm**
30.00/53.00 **st.**

at Gillan S : 3 m. – ⊠ Helston – ☎ 032 623 Manaccan :

⌂ **Tregildry** ⅏, TR12 6HG, ℰ 378, ≼, ☞ – ℗
Easter-October – **M** (bar lunch) 7.20 **st.** ⚄ 2.00 – **15 rm** ⊊ (dinner included) 16.00/36.00 **st.**

HELMSLEY North Yorks. 402 Q 21 – pop. 1,278 – ECD : Wednesday – ☎ 0439.
See : Castle★ (ruins 12C) *AC* – Envir. : Rievaulx Abbey★★ (ruins 12C-13C) *AC*, NW : 2 ½ m. –
Byland Abbey★ (ruins 12C) SW : 6 m. by Ampleforth.
🖪 9 Church St. ℰ 70401 – ♦London 234 – ♦Middlesbrough 29 – York 24.

🏤 **Black Swan** (T.H.F.), Market Pl., YO6 5BJ, ℰ 70466, ☞ – ⊡ ℗. ◪ ⒶⒺ ⓪ 𝘝𝘐𝘚𝘈
M 4.75/9.50 **st.** ⚄ 3.15 – ⊊ 4.75 – **38 rm** 35.50/49.50 **st.**

🏨 **Feversham Arms** (Best Western), 1 High St., YO6 5AG, ℰ 70766, ☞, ℅ – ⊡ ⊟wc ☏
℗. ◮ ◪ ⒶⒺ 𝘝𝘐𝘚𝘈
M 6.00/10.00 **t.** – **15 rm** ⊊ 30.00/40.00 **t.** – SB 40.00/54.00 **st.**

⌂ **Crown,** Market Sq., YO6 5BJ, ℰ 70297, ☞ – ⋔wc ⇦ ℗
M 4.20/8.00 **t.** ⚄ 1.85 – **15 rm** ⊊ 16.00/36.00 **t.** – SB (except summer) 37.00/42.00 **st.**

⌂ **Feathers,** Market Pl., YO6 5BH, ℰ 70275 – ⊟wc ⋔wc ℗. ◪ ⒶⒺ ⓪ 𝘝𝘐𝘚𝘈
closed Christmas Day – **M** 6.50/11.00 **st.** ⚄ 2.85 – **18 rm** ⊊ 15.00/36.00 **st.** – SB (except summer) 38.00/42.00 **st.**

at Beadlam E : 3 m. on A 170 – ⊠ York – ☎ 0439 Helmsley :

⌃ **Omega Barn,** High Lane, YO6 5SY, ℰ 71254 – ⋔ ℗. ℅
8 rm ⊊ 10.00/17.00 **t.**

at Nawton E : 3 ¼ m. on A 170 – ⊠ York – ☎ 0439 Helmsley :

⌃ **Plumpton Court,** High St., YO6 5TT, ℰ 71223, ☞ – ℗. ℅
closed December and January – **6 rm** ⊊ 10.00/16.00 **st.**

at Nunnington SE : 6 ¼ m. by A 170 off B 1257 – ⊠ York – ☎ 043 95 Nunnington :

XX **Ryedale Lodge** ⅏ with rm, YO6 5XB, W : 1 m. ℰ 246, ≼, « Converted railway station »,
⬩, ☞ – ⊡ ⊟wc ℗. ◪ ⒶⒺ 𝘝𝘐𝘚𝘈. ℅
M (dinner only) 12.95 **t.** ⚄ 2.75 – **5 rm** ⊊ 27.00/43.00 **t.** – SB (except summer) 54.00/59.00 **st.**

HEMEL HEMPSTEAD Herts. 404 S 28 – pop. 76,000 – ECD : Wednesday – ☎ 0442.
🖪ᵥ Little Hay, Little Hay Farm, Bovingdon ℰ 832674, off A 41 at Box Lane.
🖪 Pavilion, Marlowes ℰ 64451 – ♦London 30 – Aylesbury 16 – Luton 10 – Northampton 46.

🏨 **Post House** (T.H.F.), Breakspear Way, HP2 4UA, E : 2 ½ m. by A 414 on A 4147 ℰ 51122,
Telex 826902, ☞ – ⬗ ⊡ ⊟wc ☏ ℗. ◮ ◪ 𝘝𝘐𝘚𝘈
M 6.95/16.00 **st.** ⚄ 2.60 – ⊊ 5.50 – **107 rm** 37.50/45.00 **st.**

X **Casanova,** 75 Waterhouse St., HP2 1AT, ℰ 47482, Italian rest. – ◪ ⒶⒺ ⓪ 𝘝𝘐𝘚𝘈
closed Saturday lunch, Sunday and Bank Holidays – **M** a la carte 9.40/13.20 **t.** ⚄ 2.60.

at Bourne End W : 2 ¼ m. on A 41 – ⊠ Hemel Hempstead – ☎ 044 27 Berkhamsted :

🏨 **Hemel Hempstead Moat House** (Q.M.H.), London Rd, HP1 2RJ, ℰ 71241 – ⊡ ⊟wc ☏
℗. ◮ ◪ ⒶⒺ ⓪ 𝘝𝘐𝘚𝘈
M 5.50/6.50 **st.** – **40 rm** ⊊ 32.50/39.00 **st.** – SB (weekends only) 36.00/38.00 **st.**

AUSTIN-ROVER-JAGUAR London Rd ℰ 42841
BEDFORD, FIAT, VAUXHALL-OPEL Two Waters Rd
ℰ 51212
FORD Redbourne Rd ℰ 63013
PEUGEOT-TALBOT High St. ℰ 54561
TOYOTA Queensway ℰ 51466

HENDY-GWYN = Whitland.

HENLADE Somerset – see Taunton.

HENLEY-IN-ARDEN Warw. 408 404 O 27 – pop. 1,577 – ECD : Thursday – ☎ 056 42.
♦London 104 – ♦Birmingham 15 – Stratford-upon-Avon 8 – Warwick 8.5.

🏨 **Yew Trees,** 154 High St., B95 5BN, ⊠ Solihull ℰ 4636, ⌧ heated, ☞ – ⊡ ⊟wc ☏ ℗. ◪
ⒶⒺ ⓪ 𝘝𝘐𝘚𝘈
M 8.50 **t.** ⚄ 2.75 – ⊊ 3.75 – **8 rm** 33.00/60.00 **t.** – SB (weekends only) 45.00/57.00 **st.**

⌃ **Ashleigh House,** Whitley Hill, B95 5DL, E : 1 ¾ m. on B 4095 ℰ 2315, ☞ – ⊡ ℗. ℅
8 rm ⊊ 12.00/25.00 **st.**

XX **Beaudesert,** Birmingham Rd, B95 5QR, ⊠ Solihull N : 1 m. on A 34 ℰ 2675 – ℗. ◪ ⒶⒺ ⓪
𝘝𝘐𝘚𝘈
closed Sunday dinner and Monday – **M** (dinner only and Sunday lunch) 7.50/a la carte
11.40/15.65 **t.** ⚄ 2.50.

XX **Le Filbert Cottage,** 64 High St., B95 5BX, ⊠ Solihull ℰ 2700, French rest. – ◪ ⒶⒺ ⓪ 𝘝𝘐𝘚𝘈
closed Sunday, 26 December and Bank Holiday Mondays – **M** a la carte 12.70/16.00 **t.**

HENLEY-ON-THAMES Oxon. 404 R 29 – pop. 11,431 – ECD : Wednesday – ✆ 0491.

Envir. : Greys Court★ *AC*, NW : 2 ½ m – ⛳ Huntercombe, Nuffield ℰ 049 18 (Nettlebed) 641472, W : 6 m. on A 423.

🎫 Town Hall, Market Place ℰ 576982 – ◆London 42 – ◆Oxford 23 – Reading 9.

🏨 **Red Lion,** Hart St., RG9 2AR, ℰ 572161, ≼ – 📺 ➾wc ☎ 🅿. ⬛ 𝘝𝘐𝘚𝘈 ﹠
M 5.00/7.50 **st.** 🍴 2.50 – **28 rm** ⚏ 25.00/50.00 **st.** – SB (weekends only)(winter only) 50.00/55.00 **st.**

⌂ **Thamesmead House,** Remenham Lane, RG9 2LR, E : ½ m. by A 423 ℰ 574745 – ⛮wc 🅿.
⬛ ⓞ 𝘝𝘐𝘚𝘈
8 rm ⚏ 17.50/40.00 **t.**

✕✕ **Hamlyn's** with rm, 15 Northfield End, RG9 2JG, ℰ 573412 – ⬛ ⬛ ⓞ 𝘝𝘐𝘚𝘈
M *(closed Sunday dinner and Monday)* a la carte 8.25/12.20 **t.** 🍴 3.40 – **8 rm** ⚏ 11.50/30.00 **t.**

✕✕ Gaylord Tandoori, 60 Bell St., RG9 2BN, ℰ 575157, Indian rest..

at Frieth (Bucks.) NE : 7 ½ m. by A 4155 – ⊠ Henley-on-Thames – ✆ 0494 High Wycombe :

✕ **Yew Tree,** RG9 6RJ, ℰ 882330 – 🅿 ⬛ ⓞ 𝘝𝘐𝘚𝘈
M (booking essential) a la carte 10.70/14.55 **t.**

AUSTIN-ROVER-DAIMLER-JAGUAR-LAND ROVER FIAT 66 Bell St. ℰ 573077
49 Station Rd ℰ 577933   VW 47 Station Rd ℰ 573555

HENSTRIDGE Somerset 403 404 M 31 – pop. 1,040 – ECD : Thursday – ⊠ Templecombe – ✆ 0963 Stalbridge – ◆London 125 – Bournemouth 33 – Dorchester 20 – Salisbury 32 – Yeovil 11.

⌂ **Keyham House** ⑆, BA8 0QZ, ℰ 62253, ☞ – ⛮wc 🅿
March-October – **6 rm** ⚏ 8.00/25.00 **st.**

HEREFORD Heref. and Worc. 403 L 27 – pop. 46,503 – ECD : Thursday – ✆ 0432.

See : Cathedral★★ 12C-13C (the Mappa Mundi★ 13C) A A – The Old House★ 17C A B – **Envir. :** Abbey Dore★ (12C-17C) SW : 12 m. by A 465 B.

⛳ Herefordshire, Raven's Causeway, Wormsley ℰ 71219, NW : 6 m. by A 438 B.

🎫 Shirehall, 1a St. Owen St. ℰ 268430 – ◆London 133 – ◆Birmingham 51 – ◆Cardiff 56.

HEREFORD

Broad Street . . . . A 7
Commercial Street . . . . . . A 13
High Street . . . . A 19
High Town . . . . A 20

Bath Street . . . . A 2
Belmont Road . . . . B 5
Blue School Street . . . . . . A 6
Castle Street . . . . A 9

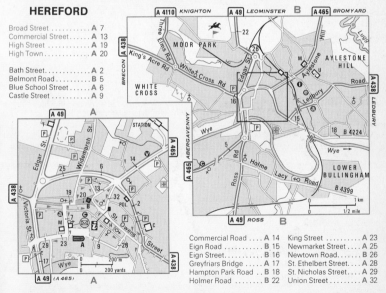

Commercial Road . . . . A 14
Eign Road . . . . B 15
Eign Street . . . . B 16
Greyfriars Bridge . . . . . A 17
Hampton Park Road . . B 18
Holmer Road . . . . B 22

King Street . . . . A 23
Newmarket Street . . . . A 25
Newtown Road . . . . B 26
St. Ethelbert Street . . . . A 28
St. Nicholas Street . . . . A 29
Union Street . . . . A 32

🏨🏨 **Green Dragon** (T.H.F.), Broad St., HR4 9BG, ℰ 272506, Telex 35491 – ▐≣┃ 📺 ➾ 🛎 ⬛ ⬛
⬛ ⓞ 𝘝𝘐𝘚𝘈   A **a**
M (bar lunch Monday to Saturday) 6.50/10.50 **st.** 🍴 2.60 – ⚏ 5.50 – **88 rm** 34.50/41.00 **st.**

🏨 **Hereford Moat House** (Q.M.H.), Belmont Rd, HR2 7BP, SW : 1 ½ m. on A 465 ℰ 54301 –
📺 ➾wc ☎ 🔥 🅿. 🍴 ⬛ ⓞ 𝘝𝘐𝘚𝘈   B **c**
M *(closed lunch Saturday and Bank Holidays)* 6.25/7.50 **st.** 🍴 3.25 – **32 rm** ⚏ 33.00/40.00 **st.** –
SB (weekends only) 45.00 **st.**

🏨 **Merton,** 28 Commercial Rd, HR1 2BD, ℰ 265925 – 📺 ➾wc 🔥 ☎. ⬛ ⓞ 𝘝𝘐𝘚𝘈 ﹠ A **v**
closed 25 December-1 January – **M** (restricted dinner Sunday) 8.00/9.00 **t.** 🍴 2.00 – **14 rm**
⚏ 22.50/38.00 **t.**

☎ **Litchfield Lodge,** 32 Bodenham Rd, HR1 2TS, ℰ 273258 – 📺 🖚wc 🖚wc 🅿. 🖾 AE VISA. ⋘
closed 1 week at Christmas – **M** *(closed Sunday)* a la carte 6.50/8.20 **st.** 🍴 2.80 – **14 rm**
� 17.05/31.90 **st.**   B **e**

⋔ **Somerville,** 12 Bodenham Rd, HR1 2TS, ℰ 273991, 🖛 – 📺 🖚wc 🅿   B **i**
10 rm � 11.00/28.00 **st.**

⋔ **Ferncroft,** 144 Ledbury Rd, HR1 2TB, ℰ 265538, 🖛 – 🅿. 🖾 VISA. ⋘   B **a**
closed mid December-mid January – **11 rm** � 12.50/27.00 **st.**

✗ **Effy's,** 96 East St., HR1 2LW, ℰ 59754 – 🖾 AE ①   A **c**
closed Sundays and Bank Holidays – **M** a la carte 7.50/12.00 **t.** 🍴 3.00.

at Lugwardine E : 2 ½ m. on A 438 – B – ✉ ✆ 0432 Hereford :

🏠 **Newcourt Park** ⋟., HR1 4DP, ℰ 850752, ⋖, « Country house atmosphere », 🖛 – 🖚wc
🅿
April-October – **M** (residents only) (meals by arrangement) 5.00/8.00 **st.** 🍴 2.45 – **9 rm**
� 10.50/30.00 **st.**

at Dormington E : 5 ¼ m. on A 438 – B – ✉ ✆ 0432 Hereford :

☎ **Dormington Court,** HR1 4DA, ℰ 850370, ⟍, 🖛 – 📺 🅿. 🖾 VISA
M 9.00 **t.** 🍴 2.75 – **6 rm** � 12.50/25.00 **t.** – SB 31.00/35.00 **st.**

at Much Birch S : 5 ½ m. on A 49 – B – ✉ Hereford – ✆ 0981 Golden Valley :

🏨 **Pilgrim,** HR2 8HJ, on A 49 ℰ 540742, 🖛 – 📺 🖚wc 🖚wc ☎ 🅿. 🖾 AE ① VISA
closed 26 December-8 January – **M** a la carte 9.75/11.60 **st.** 🍴 2.95 – **15 rm** � 28.50/42.00 **st.**
– SB (weekends only) 49.00/52.00 **st.**

ALFA ROMEO, SUBARU Conningsby St. ℰ 253471
AUSTIN-ROVER-DAIMLER-JAGUAR-LAND ROVER
91/97 Widemarsh St. ℰ 267611
AUSTIN-ROVER Callow G 92 ℰ 273074
BEDFORD, OPEL-VAUXHALL Blackfriars St. ℰ
267441
BMW White Cross Rd ℰ 272589
CITROEN 38 St. Martin St. ℰ 272545
DAF, LADA, SAAB Kings Acre Rd ℰ 266974
FIAT Bath St. ℰ 274134
FORD Commercial Rd ℰ 276494

LANCIA, HYUNDAI Whitestone ℰ 850464
NISSAN Muchgowarne ℰ 053186 (Bosbury) 605
PEUGEOT 101/105 St. Owen St. ℰ 276268
RELIANT Bridge St. ℰ 272341
RENAULT Whitecross Rd ℰ 272589
SKODA ℰ 272341
TALBOT Blue School St. ℰ 272354
TOYOTA Mill St. ℰ 269255
VOLVO 14-15 Commercial Rd ℰ 276275
VW, AUDI Harrow Rd ℰ 59234

HERNE BAY Kent 🆘 X 29 – pop. 24,350 – ECD : Thursday – ✆ 022 73.
Envir. : Reculver (church twin towers★ *AC*) E : 3 m.
♦London 63 – ♦Dover 24 – Maidstone 32 – Margate 13.

✗ **L'Escargot,** 22 High St., CT6 5LH, ℰ 2876 – 🖾 VISA
closed Saturday lunch, Sunday dinner and Bank Holidays – **M** a la carte 7.30/11.70 **t.** 🍴 2.45.

HERSTMONCEUX East Sussex 🆘 U 31 – pop. 2,036 – ✆ 032 181 (4 fig.) or 0323 (6 fig.).
See : Castle 15C (home of the Royal Greenwich Observatory) site and grounds★★ *AC*.
Envir. : Michelham Priory (site★) *AC*, SW : 6 m.
♦London 63 – Eastbourne 12 – Hastings 14 – Lewes 16.

✗✗ **Sundial,** Gardner St., BN27 4LA, ℰ 832217, French rest., « Converted 16C cottage », 🖛 –
🅿. 🖾 AE ① VISA
closed Sunday dinner, Monday, last 2 weeks August and 25 December-22 January – **M** a la
carte 13.70/15.35 **t.** 🍴 3.00.

at Boreham Street SE : 2 m. on A 271 – ✉ ✆ 0323 Herstmonceux :

🏨 **White Friars** (Best Western), Boreham St., BN27 4SE, ℰ 832355, 🖛 – 📺 🖚wc ☎ 🅿. 🖾
AE ① VISA
closed 20 January – **M** *(closed Monday lunch)* 9.75 **st.** 🍴 2.30 – **20 rm** � 19.00/46.00 **st.** – SB
42.00/66.00 **st.**

AUSTIN-ROVER Boreham St. ℰ 832353   FIAT Cowbeech ℰ 833321

HERTFORD Herts. 🆘 T 28 – pop. 21,412 – ECD : Thursday – ✆ 0992.
♦London 24 – ♦Cambridge 35 – Luton 26.

✗✗ **Marquee,** 1 Bircherley Green, SG14 1BN, ℰ 58999, ⋖ – 🖾 AE ① VISA
closed Good Friday and Christmas Day – **M** a la carte 11.65/15.20 **t.** 🍴 3.50.

ALFA ROMEO Templefields Industrial Estate ℰ
21215
AUSTIN-ROVER First Av. ℰ 27541
CITROEN Elizabeth Way ℰ 412161

PEUGEOT-TALBOT North Rd ℰ 53044
SUBARU Fore St. ℰ 52581
VW, AUDI Wych Elm ℰ 21461

HERTINGFORDBURY Herts. 🆘 T 28 – pop. 703 – ✉ ✆ 0992 Hertford.
♦London 26 – Luton 18.

🏨 **White Horse Inn** (T.H.F.), Hertingfordbury Rd, SG14 2LB, ℰ 56791, 🖛 – 📺 🖚wc ☎ 🅿.
M 7.00/10.50 **st.** 🍴 2.60 – � 5.00 – **30 rm** 35.50/45.00 **st.**

HESWALL Merseyside 402 403 K 24 – pop. 16,315 – ⊠ Wirral – ✿ 051 Liverpool.
♦London 223 – Birkenhead 6.5 – Chester 12 – ♦Liverpool 9 – ♦Manchester 48.

✗　**Les Bougies,** 106 Telegraph Rd, L60 0AQ, ☎ 342 6673 – ❷. ↖ AE VISA
　　closed Sunday, Monday, 24-26 December and August – **M** (dinner only) a la carte 8.00/10.65 **t.**
　　↑ 2.00.

HETHERSETT Norfolk 404 X 26 – see Norwich.

HEVERSHAM Cumbria 402 L 21 – pop. 703 – ECD : Thursday and Saturday – ⊠ ✿ 044 82
Milnthorpe.
♦London 259 – Kendal 6 – Lancaster 15.

🏠　**Blue Bell,** The Princes' Way, LA7 7EF, on A 6 ☎ 3159 – ⇌wc �fflwc ❷. ↖ VISA. ⨯
　　M 5.50/10.00 **st.** ↑ 3.00 – **28 rm** ⊊ 19.00/37.00 **st.** – SB (except summer) 42.00/44.00 **st.**

HEXHAM Northumb. 401 402 N 19 – pop. 9,270 – ECD : Thursday – ✿ 0434.
See : Abbey Church★ 13C – **Envir.** : Hadrian's Wall★★ with its forts and milecastles (Chesters
Fort★, museum AC) NW : 5 ½ m. – Housesteads Fort★★, museum AC, NW : 14 m. – Derwent
Reservoir (site★) SE : 7 m. – Vindolanda★ (fort and town) AC, NW : 14 ½ m.

🔟 Spital Park ☎ 602057 – 🅱 The Manor Office, Hallgates ☎ 605225.

♦London 304 – ♦Carlisle 37 – ♦Newcastle-upon-Tyne 21.

🏠　**County,** Priestpopple, NE46 1PS, ☎ 602030 – 📺 �ff̱lwc. ↖ AE VISA
　　M 6.00/10.00 **t.** ↑ 2.40 – **10 rm** ⊊ 16.00/28.00 **t.** – SB (weekends only)(November-
　　Easter) 43.00/56.00 **st.**

🏠　**Beaumont,** Beaumont St., NE46 3LZ, ☎ 602331 – 📺 ⇌wc �f̱flwc. ↖ AE ① VISA
　　M (closed Monday lunch and Bank Holidays) a la carte 5.40/8.65 **t.** ↑ 2.50 – **22 rm**
　　⊊ 17.50/30.00 **st.** – SB (weekends only) 36.50 **st.**

✗　**Pine Kitchen,** Battle Hill, NE46 1BB, ☎ 606688 – ↖ AE ① VISA
　　closed Sunday dinner – **M** a la carte 9.00/12.75 **t.** ↑ 3.00.

　　at Wall N : 4 m. on A 6079 – ⊠ Hexham – ✿ 043 481 Humshaugh :

🏠　**Hadrian,** NE46 4EE, ☎ 232, 🚗 – ❷
　　M 6.00/10.00 **st.** ↑ 2.85 – **8 rm** ⊊ 15.00/28.00 **st.** – SB (weekends only) 42.00 **st.**

AUSTIN-ROVER Alemouth Rd ☎ 605151
CITROEN Priestpopple ☎ 603615
FIAT Tyne Mills ☎ 603013
FORD Priestpopple ☎ 603516
MAZDA Tynemills ☎ 605544
NISSAN Haugh Lane ☎ 604527

RENAULT West Rd ☎ 603861
SAAB ☎ 602184
VAUXHALL Parkwell ☎ 602411
VOLVO Gilesgate ☎ 605825
VW, AUDI Station Garage ☎ 602170

HEYSHAM Lancs. 402 L 21 – pop. 41,908 (inc. Morecambe) – ECD : Wednesday – ✿ 0524.
🚢 to the Isle of Man : Douglas (Sealink) summer 1-2 daily; winter 6-7 weekly (3 h 45 mn day) (7 h
5 mn night).
♦London 251 – ♦Blackpool 33 – ♦Carlisle 74 – Lancaster 8.

　　Hotels see : **Lancaster** E : 8 m., **Morecambe** NE : 3 m.

HIGHAM Derbs. 402 403 404 P 24 – pop. 4,909 (inc. Shirland) – ⊠ ✿ 0773 Alfreton.
♦London 147 – Derby 16 – ♦Nottingham 20 – ♦Sheffield 20.

🏠　**Higham Farm,** Main Rd, DE5 6EH, on B 6013 ☎ 833812, ↖, ⤵ – 📺 ⇌wc �f̱flwc 🐾 ❷ –
　　12 rm.

HIGH EASTER Essex 404 V 28 – see Chelmsford.

HIGH WYCOMBE Bucks. 404 R 29 – pop. 59,340 – ECD : Wednesday – ✿ 0494.
Envir. : Hughenden Manor★ (site★, Disraeli Museum) AC, N : 1 m. – West Wycombe (Manor
House★ 18C, AC, St. Lawrence's Church : from the tower 74 steps, AC, ⨯★) NW : 2 ½ m.
🅱 Council Offices, Queen Victoria Rd ☎ 26100 – ♦London 34 – Aylesbury 17 – ♦Oxford 26 – Reading 18.

🏠　**Crest** (Crest), Crest Rd, HP11 1TL, SW : 1 ½ m. by A 404 ☎ 442100, Telex 83626 – 📺 ⇌wc
　　🕿 ⟨ ❷. ▵ ↖ AE ① VISA. ⨯
　　M approx. 11.50 **st.** – ⊊ 5.25 – **108 rm** 47.50/57.00 **st.**

MICHELIN Branch, Thomas Rd, Wooburn Green, HP10 0PE, ☎ 06285 **(Bourne End)** 27472

AUSTIN-ROVER Main Rd, Naphill ☎ 024 024
(Naphill) 3270
AUSTIN-ROVER, DAIMLER, JAGUAR 111/121
London Rd ☎ 26180

FORD Oxford Rd ☎ 23111
NISSAN, VAUXHALL London Rd ☎ 30021
TOYOTA Littleworth Rd, Downley ☎ 35811
VAUXHALL-OPEL West Wycombe Rd ☎ 32545

HINDHEAD Surrey 404 R 30 – pop. 3,342 – ECD : Wednesday – ✿ 042 873.
See : Devil's Punch Bowl (⩽★).
♦London 46 – Guildford 12 – ♦Portsmouth 28.

🏠　**Hindhead Motor** (Best Western) without rest., GU26 6TF, on A 3 Portsmouth Rd ☎ 6666 –
　　📺 ⇌wc 🐾 ❷. ▵ ↖ AE ① VISA
　　⊊ 2.95 – **16 rm** 25.00/35.00 **st.**

HINDON Wilts. 🔢🔢 N 30 — pop. 534 — ECD : Saturday — ✉ Salisbury — ☎ 074 789.
♦London 107 — Bath 28 — Bournemouth 40 — Salisbury 15.

  🏠 **Lamb at Hindon,** SP3 6DP, ✆ 225, 🍴 — ⬜wc 🅿 🔺 ✖
  M 7.00/10.00 t. 🍷 2.80 — **16 rm** 🛏 15.00/38.00 st. — SB (winter only) 38.00/50.00 st.

HITCHIN Herts. 🔢 T 28 — pop. 25,610 — ECD : Wednesday — ☎ 0462.
🅱, 🅶 Beadlow Manor, Shefford ✆ 0525 (Silsoe) 60800, NW : 9 m.
🅱 Library, Paynes Park ✆ 34738 and 50133.
♦London 40 — Bedford 14 — ♦Cambridge 26 — Luton 9.

  ⌂ **Lord Lister,** Park St., SG4 9AH, ✆ 32712 — 📺 📶 🅿 🔺 AE VISA
  15 rm 🛏 16.00/28.00 t.

  at Little Wymondley SE : 2 ½ m. on A 602 — ✉ Hitchin — ☎ 0438 Stevenage :

  🏨 **Blakemore,** SG4 7JJ, ✆ 355821, Telex 825479, 🔥 heated, 🍴 — ▯ 📺 ⬜wc 🅿 🔺 🔺
  AE ① VISA
  M 7.50 st. 🍷 2.75 — **70 rm** 🛏 35.00/45.00 st.

  XX **Redcoats Farmhouse** 🌳 with rm, Redcoats Green, SG4 7JL, S : ½ m. by A 602 ✆ 729500,
  🍴 — 📺 ⬜wc 🅿 🔺 AE ① VISA
  closed 1 week Christmas and Bank Holidays — **M** *(closed Sunday)* a la carte 11.70/14.50 t.
  🍷 2.50 — **10 rm** 🛏 17.50/34.00 st.

AUSTIN-ROVER Queen St. ✆ 50311   CITROEN High St., Graveley ✆ 0438 (Stevenage)
                                                   316177

HOLFORD Somerset 🔢🔢 K 30 — pop. 283 — ✉ Bridgwater — ☎ 027 874.
Envir. : Stogursey Priory Church★★, W : 4 ½ m..
♦London 171 — ♦Bristol 48 — Minehead 15 — Taunton 22.

  🏠 **Combe House** 🌳, TA5 1RZ, SW : 1 m. ✆ 382, « Country house atmosphere », 🔺, 🍴, ✖
  — 📺 ⬜wc 🅿 🔺 AE VISA
  Mid February-mid November — **M** (bar lunch) 7.50 t. 🍷 2.85 — **16 rm** 🛏 15.50/32.00 t. — SB
  37.00/39.50 st.

  🏠 **Alfoxton Park** 🌳, TA5 1SG, W : 1 ½ m. ✆ 211, ≼, 🔥 heated, 🍴, park, ✖ — 📺 ⬜wc 🅿
  🔺 VISA ✖
  April-October — **M** (bar lunch) 9.00 t. — **18 rm** 🛏 27.00/46.00 t. — SB
  (spring and autumn only) 50.00 st.

HOLMES CHAPEL Cheshire 🔢🔢🔢 M 24 — pop. 4,153 — ✉ Crewe — ☎ 0477.
♦London 181 — Chester 25 — ♦Liverpool 41 — ♦Manchester 24 — ♦Stoke-on-Trent 20.

  🏨 **Holly Lodge,** 70 London Rd, CW4 7AS, ✆ 37033 — 📺 ⬜wc 🅿 🔺 🔺 ① VISA
  M *(closed Saturday lunch and Sunday dinner)* 4.25/8.50 t. 🍷 3.10 — **30 rm** 🛏 25.50/31.50 t.

  🏠 **Old Vicarage,** Knutsford Rd, Cranage, CW4 8EF, NW : ½ m. on A 50 ✆ 32041 — 📺 ⬜wc
  ☎ 🅿 🔺 AE VISA ✖
  M *(closed Bank Holidays)* (bar lunch Saturdays) 6.00/10.50 t. 🍷 3.20 — **7 rm** 🛏 27.00/33.00 t. —
  SB (weekends only) 42.00/50.00 st.

  at Twemlow Green NE : 1 ¾ m. on A 535 — ✉ ☎ 0477 Holmes Chapel :

  XXX **Yellow Broom,** CW4 8BL, ✆ 33289 — 🅿 🔺 VISA
  closed Sunday dinner, Monday and 4 to 20 August — **M** (dinner only and Sunday lunch)
  (booking essential) 7.00/15.00 t. 🍷 3.50.

  at Brereton SE : 2 m. on A 50 — ✉ Sandbach — ☎ 0477 Holmes Chapel :

  🏨 **Bear's Head,** Newcastle Rd, CW11 9RS, ✆ 35251, 🍴, ✖ — 📺 ⬜wc 📶wc ☎ 🅿 🔺 AE
  ① VISA ✖
  M *(closed Sunday dinner to non-residents)* 6.95/8.95 t. 🍷 3.75 — **21 rm** 🛏 28.50/39.00 st.

HOLT Norfolk 🔢 X 25 — pop. 2,532 — ECD : Thursday — ☎ 026 371.
♦London 124 — King's Lynn 34 — ♦Norwich 22.

  ⌂ **Lawns,** 26 Station Rd, NR25 6BS, ✆ 3390, 🍴 — 🅿
  closed January — **10 rm** 🛏 9.00/26.00 t.

  at Thornage SW : 2 ¾ m. on B 1110 — ✉ Thornage — ☎ 0263 Melton Constable :

  X **Black Boys,** NR25 7QG, ✆ 861218 — 🅿 🔺 AE ① VISA
  closed Sunday, Monday and 15 January-February — **M** (dinner only) a la carte 8.90/15.20 t.
  🍷 3.00.

HOLYHEAD (CAERGYBI) Gwynedd 🔢🔢🔢 G 24 — pop. 11,530 — ECD : Tuesday — ☎ 0407.
Envir. : South Stack (cliffs★) W : 3 ½ m. — Rhosneigr (site★) SE : 13 m.
⛴ to Ireland (Dun Laoghaire) (Sealink) summer 2-4 daily; winter 2 daily (3 h 30 mn) — to Ireland
(Dublin) (B & I Line) 1 daily (3 h 30 mn).
🅱 Marine Sq., Salt Island Approach ✆ 2622 (summer only).
♦London 269 — Birkenhead 94 — ♦Cardiff 217 — Chester 87 — Shrewsbury 105 — ♦Swansea 190.

  Hotel see : Trearddur Bay S : 2 ½ m.

HOLY ISLAND Northumb. [401] [402] O 16 – pop. 200 – ☎ 0289 Berwick-upon-Tweed.
See : Castle (16C) ≤★★ *AC* – Priory★ (ruins 12C) *AC*.
♦London 342 – Berwick-upon-Tweed 13 – ♦Newcastle-upon-Tyne 59.

Hotels see : Berwick-upon-Tweed NW : 13 m.

HOLYWELL (TREFFYNNON) Clwyd [402] [403] K 24 – pop. 8,905 – ECD : Wednesday – ☎ 0352.
♦London 217 – Chester 19 – ♦Liverpool 34.

🏨 **Stamford Gate,** Halkyn Rd, CH8 7SJ, ✆ 712942 – [TV] 🛁wc [P]. [CB] [AE] [D] [VISA]. ✂
M 4.50/6.50 **t.** 🍷 2.60 – **12 rm** ☕ 18.00/32.00 **st.**

HONITON Devon [403] K 31 – pop. 6,567 – ☎ 0404.
[i] Angel Hotel Carpark, High St. ✆ 3716.
♦London 186 – Exeter 17 – ♦Southampton 93 – Taunton 18.

🏨 **Deer Park** 🐕, EX14 0PG, ✆ 2064, ≤, 🏊 heated, 🎣, 🌳, park, 🎾, squash – ▤ rest [TV] 🛁wc ☎ [P]. 🏕. [CB] [AE] [D] [VISA]. ✂
M a la carte 10.60/17.00 **st.** 🍷 2.25 – ☕ 5.00 – **31 rm** 24.00/60.00 **st.** – SB 50.00/65.00 **st.**

at Stockland NE : 8 ½ m. by A 30 – pop. 6,627 – ✉ Honiton – ☎ 040 486 Upottery :

🏠 Snodwell Farm 🐕, Stockland Hill, EX14 9HZ, ✆ 263, 🏊, 🌳 – 🛁wc 🚿wc [P] – **11 rm**.

at Wilmington E : 3 ½ m. on A 35 – ✉ Honiton – ☎ 040 483 Wilmington :

🏠 **Home Farm,** EX14 9JR, on A 35 ✆ 278, « Converted 16C thatched farm house », 🌳 – 🛁wc [P]. [CB] [VISA]
closed January and February – **M** 6.50/9.50 **st.** 🍷 2.75 – **14 rm** ☕ 15.00/35.00 **st.** – SB 46.00/50.00 **st.**

HOOK Hants [404] R 30 – pop. 2,912 – ECD : Wednesday – ☎ 025 672.
♦London 47 – Reading 13 – ♦Southampton 35.

🏡 **Oaklea,** London Rd, RG27 9LA, ✆ 2673, 🌳 – [P]
10 rm ☕ 15.75/30.00 **st.**

HOPE COVE Devon [403] I 33 – see Salcombe.

HOPTON WAFERS Salop [403] [404] M 26 – pop. 948 – ✉ Kidderminster – ☎ 0299 Cleobury Mortimer

🍴 **Crown Inn,** DY14 0NB, on A 4117 ✆ 270372 – 🏕. [CB] [VISA]
closed Sunday lunch April-September, Sunday dinner and Monday except Bank Holidays – **M** a la carte 7.25/11.70 **t.** 🍷 2.50.

☞ *Use this year's Guide.*

HORLEY Surrey [404] T 30 – pop. 13,700 – ECD : Wednesday – ☎ 029 34 (4 and 5 fig.) or 0293 (6 fig.).
♦London 27 – ♦Brighton 26 – Royal Tunbridge Wells 22.

Plan of built up area : see Crawley

🏨 **Gatwick Hilton International,** Gatwick Airport, ✉ West Sussex, RH6 0LL, ✆ 518080, Telex 877021, 🏊 – 🛗 ▤ [TV] ☎ ♿ [P]. 🏕. [CB] [AE] [D] [VISA]. ✂
M (buffet lunch Saturday) a la carte 9.05/14.85 **st.** 🍷 4.75 – ☕ 5.25 – **333 rm** 48.65/74.50 **t.**
see plan of Crawley AY **o**

🏨 **Gatwick Penta,** Povey Cross Rd, RH6 0BE, ✆ 5533, Telex 87440 – 🛗 [TV] ☎ [P]. 🏕. [CB] [AE] [D] [VISA]
M 7.50/9.95 **st.** 🍷 3.95 – ☕ 4.95 – **260 rm** 44.00/62.00 **st.**
see plan of Crawley AY **a**

🏨 **Post House** (T.H.F.), Povey Cross Rd, RH6 0BA, ✆ 71621, Telex 877351, 🏊 heated – 🛗 [TV] ♿ [P]. 🏕. [CB] [AE] [D] [VISA]
M *(closed Saturday lunch)* 7.25/9.75 **st.** 🍷 2.60 – ☕ 5.50 – **149 rm** 41.00/52.50 **st.**
see plan of Crawley AY **c**

P.T.O. →

HORLEY
CENTRE

High Street	
Massetts Road	
Victoria Road	39
Charlesfield Road	5
Ladbroke Road	17
Queens Road	21
Rosemary Lane	26
Russell Crescent	27
Station Road	31

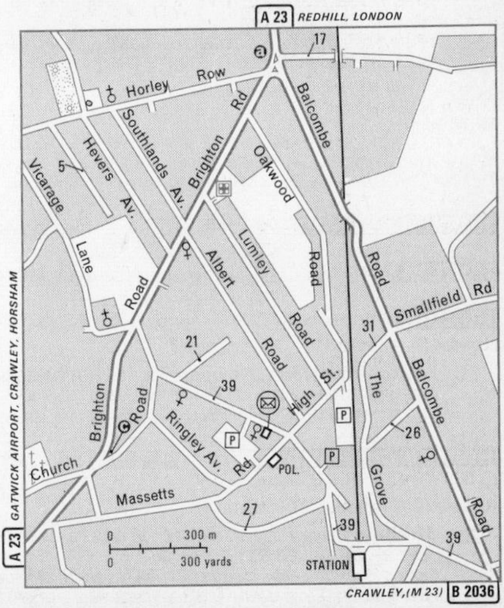

🏨 **Gatwick Moat House** (Q.M.H.), Longbridge Roundabout, RH6 0AB, ℰ 5599, Telex 877138 – 📶
🗺 ⌷wc 🕿 🕭 🅿 🛆   see plan of Crawley AY **e**
122 rm.

🏨 **Chequers Thistle** (Thistle), Brighton Rd, RH6 8PH, ℰ 6992, Telex 877550, 🛝 heated – 📺
⌷wc 🕭 🅿 🛆 🖭 AE 𝖵𝖨𝖲𝖠 ❀   **a**
M 8.50/9.25 t. ⏸ 3.45 – ⌸ 4.50 – **78 rm** 36.00/48.00 t. – SB (weekends only) 54.00 **st.**

⌂ **White House**, 24 Brighton Rd, RH6 7HD, on A 23 ℰ 4322, 🌳 – 📺 🅿 ❀   **c**
closed February – **15 rm** ⌸ 17.50/26.50 **st.**

AUSTIN-ROVER Massetts Rd ℰ 5176
FORD Hookwood Rd ℰ 2257
PEUGEOT Keppers Corner, Burstow ℰ 0342 (Cop-
thorne) 712017

RENAULT 61 Brighton Rd ℰ 72566

HORNCASTLE Lincs. 402 404 T 24 – pop. 4,102 – ECD : Wednesday – ✆ 065 82.
♦London 140 – Lincoln 21.

XX **Magpies**, 73 East St., LN9 6AA, on A 158 ℰ 7004 – 🖭
closed Sunday dinner, Monday, August and Bank Holidays – **M** (lunch by arrangement Tuesday
to Saturday) 5.40/10.00 t. ⏸ 2.80.

AUSTIN-ROVER Spilsby Rd ℰ 2391
FORD Lincoln Rd ℰ 7667

RENAULT Lincoln Rd ℰ 2451

HORNING Norfolk 404 Y 25 – pop. 975 – ECD : Wednesday – ✉ Norwich – ✆ 0692.
♦London 122 – Great Yarmouth 17 – ♦Norwich 11.

🏨 **Petersfield House** ⌂, Lower St., NR12 8PF, ℰ 630741, 🌳 – 📺 ⌷wc 🕿 🅿 🛆 AE ⓞ
𝖵𝖨𝖲𝖠
M 6.50/8.50 t. ⏸ 2.95 – **16 rm** ⌸ 24.00/38.00 t. – SB 49.00 **st.**

HORNS CROSS Devon 403 H 31 – pop. 170 – ECD : Wednesday – ✉ Bideford – ✆ 023 75.
♦London 237 – Barnstaple 15 – Exeter 48.

🏨 **Foxdown Manor** ⌂, Foxdown, EX39 5PJ, S : 1 m. ℰ 325, ≼, « Country house atmosphere »,
🛝 heated, ⛳, park, ❀ – 📺 ⌷wc ⍔wc 🅿 🛆 AE ⓞ 𝖵𝖨𝖲𝖠
M 5.50/10.00 t. – **8 rm** ⌸ (dinner included) 25.00/64.00 t. – SB (except summer) 44.00 **st.**

🏠 **Hoops Inn**, EX39 5DJ, W : ¾ m. on A 39 ℰ 222, 🌳 – 📺 ⌷wc 🕿 🅿
M (bar lunch) 8.35 t. ⏸ 2.75 – **14 rm** ⌸ 12.25/33.00 **st.** – SB (except summer) 40.00/45.00 **st.**

HORSFORTH West Yorks. 402 P 22 – see Leeds.

HORSHAM West Sussex 404 T 30 – pop. 25,800 – ECD : Monday and Thursday – ✆ 0403.
♦London 39 – ♦Brighton 23 – Guildford 20 – Lewes 25 – Worthing 20.

🏠 **Ye Olde King's Head**, 35 Carfax, RH12 1EG, ℰ 53126 – 📺 ⌷wc ⍔wc 🕿 🅿 🛆 AE 𝖵𝖨𝖲𝖠
M 5.25/7.25 t. ⏸ 2.25 – **28 rm** ⌸ 27.50/54.00 t. – SB (weekends only) 39.00 **st.**

at **Lower Beeding** SE : 3 ½ m. on A 281 – ✉ Horsham – ✆ 040 376 Lower Beeding :

XXX **Cisswood House** with rm, Sandygate Lane, RH13 6NF, ℰ 216, 🌳 – 📺 ⌷wc 🕿 🅿 🛆 AE
ⓞ 𝖵𝖨𝖲𝖠 ❀
closed Christmas and New Year – **M** (closed Saturday lunch, Sunday and Monday) a la carte
11.15/14.35 t. – ⌸ 3.00 – **6 rm** 30.00/45.00 **st.**

AUSTIN-ROVER Springfield Rd ℰ 54311
CITROEN Guildford Rd ℰ 61393
FIAT Brighton Rd ℰ 65637
FORD The Bishopric ℰ 54331
PEUGEOT-TALBOT North St. ℰ 62655
RENAULT 108 Crawley Rd ℰ 61146

TOYOTA Slinfold ℰ 790766
VAUXHALL-OPEL, VW, AUDI Plummers Plain ℰ
76466
VAUXHALL-OPEL Broadbridge Heath ℰ 56464
VOLVO Guildford Rd ℰ 56381

HORSHAM ST. FAITH Norfolk 404 X 25 – see Norwich.

HORTON Dorset 403 404 O 31 – see Wimborne Minster.

HORTON Northants. 404 R 27 – pop. 424 – ✉ ✆ 0604 Northampton.
♦London 66 – Bedford 18 – Northampton 6.

XX **French Partridge**, Newport Pagnell Rd, NN7 2AP, ℰ 870033 – 🅿
closed Sunday, Monday, 2 weeks Easter, 3 weeks July-August and 2 weeks at Christmas – **M**
(dinner only) (booking essential) 13.50 **st.** ⏸ 3.20.

HORTON-CUM-STUDLEY Oxon. 403 404 Q 28 – pop. 432 – ECD : Wednesday – ✉ Oxford –
✆ 086 735 Stanton St. John.
♦London 57 – Aylesbury 23 – ♦Oxford 7.

🏨 **Studley Priory** ⌂, OX9 1AZ, ℰ 203, « Converted priory in park », 🌳, ❀ – 📺 ⌷wc
⍔wc 🕿 🅿 🛆 🖭
closed first 2 weeks January – **M** (closed Monday lunch) a la carte 16.70/25.00 **st.** ⏸ 2.90 –
19 rm ⌸ 36.00/80.00 **st.** – SB (except summer) 76.55/98.00 **st.**

HOUGHTON CONQUEST Beds. **404** S 27 – see Bedford.

HOVE East Sussex **404** T 31 – see Brighton and Hove.

HOVINGHAM North Yorks. **402** R 21 – pop. 305 – ECD : Thursday – ⊠ York – ☎ 065 382.
◆London 235 – ◆Middlesbrough 36 – York 25.

🏨 **Worsley Arms,** YO6 4LA, ℰ 234, 宗 – ⇔wc ⇐ ℗ **⚠ VISA**
closed 25 and 26 December – **M** approx. 9.50 **st.** ⬧2.95 – **14 rm** � 24.00/44.50 **st.** – SB 24.50/26.50 **st.**

HOWDEN Humberside **402** R 22 – pop. 2,651 – ECD : Thursday – ☎ 0430.
See : St. Peter's Church* 12C-14C.
◆London 196 – ◆Kingston-upon-Hull 23 – ◆Leeds 37 – York 22.

🏨 **Bowmans,** Bridgegate, DN14 7JG, ℰ 30805 – 📺 ⇔wc ☎ ℗ **⚠ AE ⓞ VISA**
M (closed Saturday lunch and Sunday dinner) a la carte 6.95/13.95 **st.** ⬧3.00 – **13 rm**
⊏ 19.95/35.95 **st.**

HOWEY Powys – see Llandrindod Wells.

Sie suchen ein angenehmes, ruhiges Hotel ?
Blättern Sie nicht wahllos im Führer, sondern benutzen Sie die Karten,
die den verschiedenen Regionen vorangestellt sind.

HUDDERSFIELD West Yorks. **402 404** O 23 – pop. 131,190 – ECD : Wednesday – ☎ 0484.
¶ᵦ Thick Hollins Hall, Meltham ℰ 850227, SW : 5 m. – ¶ᵦ Crosland Heath ℰ 653216, W : 3 m. – ¶₉ Longley Park, Maple St., off Somerset Rd ℰ 22304.
🛈 3-5 Albion St. ℰ 22133 ext 313/685 and 32177 (Saturday only).
◆London 191 – Bradford 11 – ◆Leeds 15 – ◆Manchester 25 – ◆Sheffield 26.

🏨 **Ladbroke** (Ladbroke), Ainley Top, HD3 3RH, NW : 2 ½ m. at junction A 629 and M 62, exit 24 ℰ 0422 (Elland) 75431, Telex 517346 – ⬚📺 ⇔wc ℗ **⚠ AE ⓞ VISA**
M 9.75/10.25 **st.** – ⊏ 5.50 – **110 rm** 40.00/50.00 **t.** – SB (weekends only) 49.00 **st.**

🏨 **George** (T.H.F.), St. George's Sq., HD1 1JA, ℰ 25444 – ⬚📺 ⇔wc ☎. **⚠ AE ⓞ VISA**
M a la carte 9.75/18.30 **st.** ⬧2.85 – ⊏ 5.00 – **62 rm** 22.50/36.50 **st.**

🏨 **Cote Royd,** 7 Halifax Rd, HD3 3AN, ℰ 47588, 宗 – 📺 ⇔wc ⫸wc ℗ **⚠ AE ⓞ VISA** 🐾
closed 25 December-1 January – **M** (dinner only) a la carte 6.65/8.15 **st.** ⬧2.80 – **21 rm**
⊏ 27.00/35.00 **st.**

XX **Shabab,** 37-39 New St., HD1 2BG, ℰ 49514, Indian rest. – **⚠ AE ⓞ VISA**
closed Sunday lunch and Christmas Day.

at Golcar W : 3 ½ m. by A 62 on B 6111 – ⊠ ☎ 0484 Huddersfield :

X **Weaver's Shed,** Knowl Rd, HD7 4AN, via Scar Lane ℰ 654284, « Converted 18C woollen mill » – ℗
closed Saturday lunch, Sunday dinner, Monday, first 2 weeks January and last 2 weeks July –
M a la carte 8.50/13.00 **t.** ⬧2.70.

at Outlane NW : 4 m. on A 640 – ⊠ Huddersfield – ☎ 0422 Elland :

🏨 **Old Golf House,** New Hey Rd, HD3 3YP, ℰ 79311 – 📺 ⇔wc ☎ ℗. **⚠ AE ⓞ VISA**. 🐾
closed Christmas Day – **M** (closed Saturday lunch) 7.00/9.50 **t.** ⬧3.10 – **29 rm** ⊏ 24.00/30.00 **t.**

ALFA-ROMEO, PEUGEOT, TALBOT Northgate ℰ 20822
AUSTIN-ROVER-DAIMLER-JAGUAR Southgate ℰ 35341
AUSTIN-ROVER Scar Lane ℰ 656164
BMW Somerset Rd ℰ 515515
FORD Southgate ℰ 29675

RENAULT 4 Queensgate ℰ 39351
RENAULT Northgate ℰ 35251
SAAB Kirkheaton ℰ 29754
TOYOTA Fartown ℰ 514514
VAUXHALL-OPEL 386 Leeds Rd ℰ 23191
VOLVO Northgate ℰ 31362
VW, AUDI Bradford Rd ℰ 42001

HULL Humberside **402** S 22 – see Kingston-upon-Hull.

HUNGERFORD Berks. **403 404** P 29 – pop. 4,083 – ECD : Thursday – ☎ 048 86 (from March 0488).
Envir. : Littlecote House*, NW : 3 ½ m..
¶ᵦ West Berkshire, Chaddleworth ℰ 048 82 (Chaddleworth) 574, N : 2 ½ m.
◆London 74 – ◆Bristol 57 – ◆Oxford 28 – Reading 26 – ◆Southampton 46.

🏨 **Bear** (Best Western), 17 Charnham St., RG17 0EL, on A 4 ℰ 82512, Telex 477575, 宗 – 📺 ⇔wc ⫸wc ☎ ℗. **⚠ AE ⓞ VISA**
M (closed 25 and 26 December) 14.95/15.95 **t.** – ⊏ 4.25 – **28 rm** 27.50/39.50 **st.** – SB (week-ends only) 47.50/50.50 **st.**

BMW Bath Rd ℰ 82772

PEUGEOT-TALBOT Bath Rd ℰ 82033

211

HUNSTANTON Norfolk 402 404 V 25 – pop. 3,911 – ECD : Thursday – 🕿 048 53.

🛏₁₈ ✆ 2811, E : ½ m.

🅸 The Green ✆ 2610.

◆London 120 – ◆Cambridge 60 – ◆Norwich 45.

🏨 **Le Strange Arms,** Golf Links Lane, PE36 6JJ, N : 1 m. by A 149 ✆ 2810, ≼, 😨 – 🛌wc
🛗wc ⟺ 🅿 🔼 🆎 ⓞ 𝘝𝘐𝘚𝘈
M 7.50 t. ▮ 3.50 – **28 rm** ⚌ 27.50/42.50 **st.** – SB 48.00 **st.**

⌂ **Claremont,** 35 Greevegate, PE36 6AF, ✆ 33171 – 🛞
February-October – **7 rm** ⚌ 9.00/18.00 **st.**

AUSTIN-ROVER 12 Lynn Rd ✆ 33435   CITROEN, FORD Westgate ✆ 2508

HUNSTRETE Avon 403 404 M 29 – see Bath.

HUNTINGDON Cambs. 404 T 26 – pop. 16,557 (inc. Godmanchester) – ECD : Wednesday –
🕿 0480.

See : Cromwell Museum – All Saint's Church (interior★).

Envir. : Hinchingbrooke House★ (Tudor mansion-school) W : 1 m. – Ramsey (Abbey Gatehouse★
15C) NE : 11 ½ m.

🛏₁₅ St. Ives ✆ 64459, E : 5 m.

◆London 69 – Bedford 21 – ◆Cambridge 16.

🏨 **Old Bridge,** 1 High St., PE18 6TQ, ✆ 52681, Telex 32706 – 📺 🛌wc ☎ 🅿 🔼 🆎 ⓞ 𝘝𝘐𝘚𝘈
M a la carte 13.45/18.90 **st. – 22 rm** ⚌ 37.50/55.00 **st.**

🏨 **George** (T.H.F.), George St., PE18 6AB, ✆ 53096 – 📺 🛌wc ☎ 🅿 🔼 🔼 🆎 ⓞ 𝘝𝘐𝘚𝘈
M 6.50/8.25 **st.** ▮ 2.85 – ⚌ 4.75 – **25 rm** 29.50/41.00 **st.**

AUSTIN-ROVER-LAND ROVER 1-3 Hartford Rd ✆   BMW, VAUXHALL-OPEL Ring Rd ✆ 52694
56441

HURLEY-ON-THAMES Berks. 404 R 29 – pop. 2,203 – ECD : Wednesday – ✉ Maidenhead –
🕿 062 882 Littlewick Green.

◆London 38 – ◆Oxford 26 – Reading 12.

🏨 **Ye Olde Bell,** High St., SL6 5LX, ✆ 4244, Telex 847035, 😨 – 📺 🛌wc ☎ 🅿 🔼 🆎 ⓞ 𝘝𝘐𝘚𝘈.
🛞
M 12.50/13.50 **t.** ▮ 3.75 – ⚌ 4.50 – **24 rm** 27.50/55.00 **st.**

HURSTBOURNE TARRANT Hants. 403 404 P 30 – pop. 709 – ✉ Andover – 🕿 026 476.

◆London 77 – ◆Bristol 77 – ◆Oxford 38 – ◆Southampton 33.

XX **Esseborne Manor** 🛞 with rm, SP11 0ER, NE : 1 ½ m. on A 343 ✆ 444, 😨, 🍴 – 📺 🛌wc
☎ 🅿 🔼 🆎 ⓞ 𝘝𝘐𝘚𝘈. 🛞
closed 3 weeks February – **M** (closed Sunday dinner to non-residents) (dinner only) 16.65 **t.**
▮ 3.25 – **6 rm** ⚌ 32.50/45.00 **st.**

HURST GREEN Lancs. 402 M 22 – pop. 1,100 – ✉ Whalley – 🕿 025 486 Stonyhurst.

◆London 236 – Blackburn 12 – Burnley 13 – Preston 12.

🏨 Shireburn Arms 🛞, BB6 9QJ, ✆ 208, « Tastefully furnished part 18C house », 😨 – 📺
🛌wc ☎ 🅿 – **10 rm.**

HURSTPIERPOINT West Sussex 404 T 31 – pop. 5,539 – ✉ Hassocks – 🕿 0273 Brighton.

◆London 45 – ◆Brighton 8.

X **Barron's,** 120 High St., BN6 9PX, ✆ 832183 – 🔼 🆎 𝘝𝘐𝘚𝘈
closed lunch Saturday and Monday and Sunday – **M** a la carte 3.20/6.90 **t.** ▮ 2.35.

HUSBANDS BOSWORTH Leics. 403 404 Q 26 – pop. 820 – ✉ Lutterworth – 🕿 0858 Market
Harborough.

◆London 88 – ◆Birmingham 40 – ◆Leicester 14 – Northampton 17.

XX **Fernie Lodge,** Berridges Lane, LE17 6LE, ✆ 880551 – 🅿. 🔼
closed Saturday lunch, Sunday, Monday, and Bank Holidays – **M** (booking essential)
7.25/11.75 **t.** ▮ 4.25.

HUTTON-LE-HOLE North Yorks. 402 R 21 – see Lastingham.

HUXHAM Devon – see Exeter.

HWLFFORDD = Haverfordwest.

Ensure that you have up to date **Michelin maps** in your car.

HYTHE Kent **404** X 30 – pop. 11,959 – ECD : Wednesday – ✆ 0303.

See : St. Leonard's Church (≤★ from the churchyard) – Canal.

☍ Hythe Imperial, Princes Parade ✎ 67441.

◆London 68 – Folkestone 6 – Hastings 33 – Maidstone 31.

⬛ **Imperial** (Best Western) ♨, Princes Par., CT21 6AE, ✎ 67441, Telex 965082, ≤, 🔲, ☍, 🚗,
✂ – 🛗 📺 🅿️ ▲ 🄰🄴 ⓞ 𝑽𝑰𝑺𝑨 ✂
M 7.50/10.50 **st.** 🛢 2.80 – **83 rm** ⬜ 32.00/65.00 **st.** – SB (weekends only) 60.00/85.00 **st.**

🏠 **Stade Court** (Best Western), West Par., CT21 6DT, ✎ 68263, Telex 965082, ≤ – 🛗 📺 🚻wc
🕅wc ☏ 🅿️ ▲ 🄰🄴 ⓞ 𝑽𝑰𝑺𝑨
M 6.00/9.50 **st.** 🛢 3.00 – **32 rm** ⬜ 20.00/46.00 **st.** – SB (weekends only) 49.00 **st.**

AUSTIN-ROVER   6/12 East St. ✎ 69335
FORD   Stade St. ✎ 67726

PEUGEOT-TALBOT   The Green ✎ 60511
SAAB   215 Seabrook Rd ✎ 38467

IBSLEY Hants. **403 404** O 31 – see Ringwood.

IDE HILL Kent – see Sevenoaks.

IGHTHAM Kent – see Wrotham Heath.

ILFRACOMBE Devon **403** H 30 The West Country G. – pop. 8,360 – ECD : Thursday – ✆ 0271.

See : Capstone Hill★ (≤★) – Hillsborough (≤★★) – St. Nicholas' Chapel (≤★).

☍ Hele Bay ✎ 62176, E : 1 m.

Access to Lundy Island from Hartland Point by helicopter ✎ 062 882 (Littlewick Green) 3431.

⛴ to Isle of Lundy (Lundy Co.) 1-3 weekly (2 h 30 mm).

🛈 The Promenade ✎ 63001.

◆London 223 – Exeter 54 – Taunton 61.

🏠 **St. Helier,** Hillsborough Rd, EX34 9QQ, ✎ 64906, 🚗 – 🚻wc 🅿️
May-September – **M** (bar lunch) 6.50 **st.** 🛢 2.80 – **29 rm** ⬜ 9.50/21.00 **st.**

🏠 **Torrs,** Torrs Park, EX34 8AY, ✎ 62334 – 🚻wc 🕅wc 🅿️ ▲ 🄰🄴 ⓞ 𝑽𝑰𝑺𝑨
April-October – **M** (lunch by arrangement) 8.00 **st.** – **17 rm** ⬜ 12.00/17.50 **t.**

at Lee W : 3 ¼ m. by B 3231 – ✉ ✆ 0271 Ilfracombe :

🏠 **Lee Bay** (Best Western) ♨, EX34 8LP, ✎ 63503, ≤, 🛏 heated, 🦆, 🚗, park – 📺 🚻wc 🈂
🅿️ ▲ 🄰🄴 ⓞ 𝑽𝑰𝑺𝑨
closed January – **M** 6.00/9.00 **t.** – **50 rm** ⬜ 26.75/44.00 – SB 29.50/34.25 **st.**

🏠 Lee Manor ♨, Fuschia Valley, EX34 8LR, ✎ 63920, 🚗, park – 📺 🚻wc 🕅wc 🅿️ – **12 rm**.

PEUGEOT, TALBOT   West Down ✎ 63104

RENAULT   Northfield Rd ✎ 62075

ILKLEY West Yorks. **402** O 22 – pop. 10,930 – ECD : Wednesday – ✆ 0943.

☍ Myddleton ✎ 607277 and 600214 – ☍ Ben Rhydding, High Wood ✎ 608759.

🛈 Station Rd ✎ 602319.

◆London 210 – Bradford 13 – Harrogate 17 – ◆Leeds 16 – Preston 46.

⬛ **Craiglands** (T.H.F.), Cowpasture Rd, LS29 8RQ, ✎ 607676, Telex 51137, 🚗, ✂ – 🛗 📺
🚻wc 🈂 🅿️ ▲ 🄰🄴 ⓞ 𝑽𝑰𝑺𝑨
M 6.95/7.75 **st.** 🛢 2.85 – ⬜ 5.00 – **73 rm** 24.50/43.00 **st.**

⬛ **Rombalds,** 11 West View, Wells Rd, LS29 9JG, ✎ 603201, Telex 51593 – 📺 🚻wc 🕅wc ☏
🅿️ ▲ 🄰🄴 ⓞ 𝑽𝑰𝑺𝑨
M *(closed Saturday lunch to non-residents)* (buffet lunch) 15.00 **t.** 🛢 3.25 – **18 rm**
⬜ 30.00/49.50 **t.** – SB (weekends only) 54.00/61.00 **st.**

🏠 Grove, The Grove, LS29 9PA, ✎ 600298 – 📺 🚻wc 🕅wc 🅿️ – **6 rm**.

✗✗✗ ✿✿ **Box Tree,** 35-37 Church St., LS29 9DR, ✎ 608484, « Ornate decor » – ▲ 🄰🄴 ⓞ 𝑽𝑰𝑺𝑨
closed Sunday, Monday, 25 December and 1 January – **M** (dinner only) (booking essential) a
la carte 13.00/19.50 **t.**
Spec. Boudin blanc aux girolles, Fricassée de homard au gingembre et sa petite garniture, Timbale de fraises
"Box Tree" (seasonal).

AUSTIN-ROVER, ROLLS ROYCE-BENTLEY   Ben
Rhydding ✎ 603261
AUSTIN-ROVER   Skipton Rd ✎ 607606

PEUGEOT-TALBOT   Skipton Rd ✎ 608966
VAUXHALL-OPEL   Bradford Rd, Menston ✎ 0943
(Menston) 76122

IMPINGTON Cambs. – see Cambridge.

INGATESTONE Essex **404** V 28 – pop. 5,420 – ECD : Wednesday – ✆ 0277.

◆London 27 – Chelmsford 6.

✗✗✗ **Furze Hill,** Ivy Barn Lane, Margaretting, CM4 0EW, NE : 2 ¼ m. by A 12 ✎ 353040, Dancing
(Saturday), 🛏 heated, 🚗, ✂ – 🅿️ ▲ 🄰🄴 ⓞ 𝑽𝑰𝑺𝑨
closed Monday lunch and Sunday dinner – **M** a la carte 10.40/18.00 **st.** 🛢 2.55.

INSTOW Devon **403** H 30 – see Bideford.

IPSWICH Suffolk **404** X 27 – pop. 123,312 – ECD : Monday and Wednesday – ☺ 0473.

See : St. Margaret's Church (the roof★) X **A** – Christchurch Mansion (museum★) X **B** – Ancient House★ 16C X **D** – Pykenham House★ 16C X **E** – ⛳ Rushmere Heath 🎣 77109 Y

🅿 Town Hall, Princes St. 🎣 58070 — ◆London 70 — ◆Norwich 43.

IPSWICH

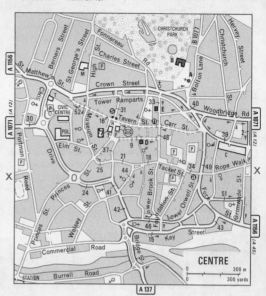

CENTRE

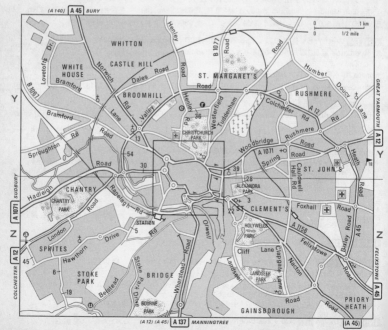

🏨🏨 **Belstead Brook** ⌂, Belstead Rd, IP2 9HB, SW :2 ½ m. ℰ 684241, Telex 987674, ⌖, park –
📺 🅿 ⏚ 🄰🄴 🄾 𝘝𝘐𝘚𝘈 ⚘ Z u
M a la carte 13.00/18.35 **st.** – ⊆ 4.95 – **32 rm** 39.00/52.00 **st.** – SB (weekends only) 35.00 **st.**

🏨🏨 **Marlborough,** Henley Rd, IP1 3SP, ℰ 57677, ⌖ – 📺 🅿 ⏚ 🄰🄴 🄾 𝘝𝘐𝘚𝘈 Y e
M a la carte 10.90/16.55 **t.** 🛇 4.15 – **22 rm** ⊆ 39.00/48.00 **t.** – SB (weekends only) 54.00 **st.**

🏨 **Post House** (T.H.F.), London Rd, IP2 0UA, SW : 2 ¼ m. on A 12 ℰ 212313, Telex 987150,
⤸ heated – 📺 ⇌wc 🕿 🅿 ⏚ 🄰🄴 🄾 𝘝𝘐𝘚𝘈 Z a
M 6.95/9.50 **st.** 🛇 2.85 – ⊆ 5.25 – **118 rm** 37.00/44.50 **st.**

🏛 **Great White Horse** (T.H.F.), Tavern St., IP1 3AH, ℰ 56558 – 📺 ⇌wc 🕿 ⏚ 🄰🄴 🄾
𝘝𝘐𝘚𝘈 X n
M (carving rest.) 7.50 **st.** 🛇 2.60 – ⊆ 5.00 – **54 rm** 26.00/38.00 **st.**

🏠 **Crown and Anchor,** Westgate St., IP1 3EQ, ℰ 58506 – 📺 ⇌wc 🕿 🅿 ⏚ 🄰🄴 🄾 𝘝𝘐𝘚𝘈
M (grill rest. only) a la carte 4.95/8.40 **t.** 🛇 3.00 – **55 rm** ⊆ 27.00/48.00 **t.** – SB (week- X s
ends only) 50.00/60.00 **st.**

🏠 **Gables,** 17 Park Rd, IP1 3SX, ℰ 54252, ⌖ – 🅿 Y r
12 rm ⊆ 11.50/20.70 **st.**

XX **Rajasthan,** 6 Orwell Pl., IP4 1BB, ℰ 51397, Indian rest. – 🄰🄴 🄾 𝘝𝘐𝘚𝘈 X a
M a la carte 6.65/8.50 **t.** 🛇 2.45.

at Copdock SW : 4 m. on A 12 – Z – ✉ Ipswich – ✆ 047 386 Copdock :

🏨 **Ipswich Moat House** (Q.M.H.), London Rd, IP8 3JD, ℰ 444, Telex 987207, ⌖ – 📺 ⇌wc
🕿 🅿 ⏚ 🄰🄴 🄾 𝘝𝘐𝘚𝘈 ⚘
M (carving rest.) 8.50/12.50 **t.** 🛇 2.80 – ⊆ 4.50 – **47 rm** 21.00/50.00 **t.**

AUDI, VW 88 Princes St. ℰ 214231
AUSTIN-ROVER 935 Woodbridge Rd ℰ 76929
AUSTIN-ROVER Barrack Lane ℰ 54202
AUSTIN-ROVER-DAIMLER-JAGUAR,   ROLLS
ROYCE-BENTLEY Majors Corner ℰ 52271
AUSTIN-ROVER Felixstowe Rd ℰ 75431
CITROEN, VOLVO, ALFA-ROMEO Derby Rd ℰ 70101

FIAT, LANCIA Burrel Rd ℰ 210321
FORD Princes St. ℰ 55401
MAZDA, POLSKI Fuchsia Lane ℰ 74535
RENAULT 301/305 Norwich Rd ℰ 43021
SAAB Dales Rd ℰ 42547
TOYOTA 301/5 Woodbridge Rd ℰ 76927
VAUXHALL-OPEL Knightsdale Rd ℰ 43044

IVINGHOE Bucks. 🄜🄾🄜 S 28 – pop. 949 – ✉ Leighton Buzzard – ✆ 0296 Cheddington.
🛉9 ℰ 668696.
♦London 42 – Aylesbury 9 – Luton 11.

XXX **King's Head** (T.H.F.), Station Rd, LU7 9EB, ℰ 668388 – ▤ rest 🅿 ⏚ 🄰🄴 🄾 𝘝𝘐𝘚𝘈
M a la carte 11.45/18.45 **t.** 🛇 3.50.

IXWORTH Suffolk 🄜🄾🄜 W 27 – pop. 2,121 – ✉ Bury St. Edmunds – ✆ 0359 Pakenham.
♦London 85 – ♦Cambridge 35 – ♦Ipswich 25 – ♦Norwich 36.

X **Theobalds,** 68 High St., IP31 2HJ, ℰ 31707 – 🄰🄴 𝘝𝘐𝘚𝘈
*closed Saturday lunch, Sunday dinner, Monday, 1 week spring, 1 week autumn, 25-26 December
and 1 January* – **M** a la carte 8.45/11.40 **t.** 🛇 2.60.

JAMESTON Dyfed 🄜🄾🄷 F 29 – see Manorbier.

JEVINGTON East Sussex 🄜🄾🄜 U 31 – see Eastbourne.

KENDAL Cumbria 🄜🄾🄝 L 21 – pop. 21,596 – ECD : Thursday – ✆ 0539.
See : Abbot Hall Art Gallery (Museum of Lakeland Life and Industry★) *AC*.
Envir. : Levens Hall★ (Elizabethan) *AC* and Topiary Garden★ *AC*, SW : 5 ½ m.
🛉 The Riggs, Sedbergh, E : 9 m.
🛈 Town Hall, Highgate ℰ 25758.
♦London 270 – Bradford 64 – Burnley 63 – ♦Carlisle 49 – Lancaster 22 – ♦Leeds 72 – ♦Middlesbrough 77 –
♦Newcastle-upon-Tyne 104 – Preston 44 – Sunderland 88.

🏨 **Woolpack** (Swallow), Stricklandgate, LA9 4ND, ℰ 23852, Group Telex 53168 – 📺 ⇌wc
▥wc 🕿 ♿ 🅿 ⏚ 🄰🄴 🄾 𝘝𝘐𝘚𝘈
M 5.50/8.95 **st.** 🛇 3.40 – **58 rm** ⊆ 35.50/46.00 **st.** – SB 56.00 **st.**

🏨 **County Thistle** (Thistle), Station Rd, LA9 6BT, ℰ 22461 – 🔌 📺 ⇌wc 🕿 🄰🄴 🄾 𝘝𝘐𝘚𝘈 ⚘
31 rm ⊆ 28.50/43.00 **t.** – SB (weekends only) 52.00 **st.**

🏠 **Garden House** ⌂, Fowling Lane, LA9 6PH, by A 685 ℰ 31131, ⌖ – 📺 ⇌wc ▥wc 🕿 🅿
🄰🄴 𝘝𝘐𝘚𝘈 ⚘
M *(closed lunch Sunday and Monday)* (Sunday dinner residents only)(bar lunch) 9.75 **st.** 🛇 2.90
– **5 rm** ⊆ 23.50/32.00 **st.** – SB 30.00/48.00 **st.**

at Crooklands S : 6 ¼ m. on A 65 – ✉ Milnthorpe – ✆ 04487.

🏨 **Crooklands** (Best Western), LA7 7NW, N : 1 ¼ m. on A 65 ℰ 432, ⌦ – 📺 ⇌wc 🕿 🅿 ⏚
🄰🄴 🄾 𝘝𝘐𝘚𝘈
M *(closed Saturday lunch)* 5.00/11.00 **t.** 🛇 3.40 – **15 rm** ⊆ 32.00/47.00 **t.** – SB 49.00/60.00 **st.**

at Underbarrow W : 3 ½ m. via Allhallows Lane on Crosthwaite rd – ✉ Kendal – ☏ 044 88
Crosthwaite :

🏠 **Greenriggs Country House** ⌚, LA8 8HF, E : ½ m. ℰ 387, ≼, « Country house atmosphere », ☞ – ⌂wc ℗
   M (bar lunch) 10.50 **st.** ₰ 1.95 – **11 rm** ⚏ 14.00/34.00 **st.** – SB (weekends only)(winter only) 46.00 **st.**

ALFA-ROMEO, FORD, MERCEDES BENZ lngs ℰ
0539 (Staveley) 821442
AUSTIN-ROVER Sandes Av. ℰ 28800
FIAT 113 Stricklandgate ℰ 20967
FORD Mintsfeet Rd South ℰ 23534

PEUGEOT Kirkland ℰ 28822
RENAULT Kirklands ℰ 22211
VAUXHALL Sandes Av. ℰ 24420
VW, AUDI-NSU, PORSCHE Longpool ℰ 24331

KENILWORTH Warw. **403 404** P 26 – pop. 19,670 – ECD : Monday and Thursday – ☏ 0926.
See : Castle★ (12C) *AC*.
🐎 Crew Lane ℰ 54296.
🛈 11 Smalley Pl. ℰ 52595.
♦London 102 – ♦Birmingham 19 – ♦Coventry 5 – Warwick 5.

🏨 **De Montfort** (De Vere), The Square, CV8 1ED, ℰ 55544, Telex 311012 – 🛗 📺 ℗ 🅰 🔼 🆎
   ① *VISA*
   M 7.50/8.00 **t.** – **95 rm** ⚏ 40.50/55.50 **t.** – SB (weekends only)(except summer) 50.00 **st.**

🏠 **Clarendon House,** 6-8 High St., Old Town, CV8 1LZ, ℰ 54694 – 📺 ⌂wc ℍwc ℗ 🔼 *VISA*
   M (bar lunch Monday to Saturday) 6.80/12.35 **st.** ₰ 3.25 – **23 rm** ⚏ 23.00/36.50 **t.** – SB (summer and weekends only in winter) 45.00 **st.**

⌂ **Enderley,** 20 Queens Rd, CV8 1JQ, ℰ 55388
   6 rm ⚏ 8.50/16.00 **st.**

XX **Diment,** 121-123 Warwick Rd, CV8 1HP, ℰ 53763, French rest. – ℗ 🔼 🆎 ① *VISA*
   closed Saturday lunch, Sunday, Monday, 3 weeks August and Bank Holidays – **M** a la carte
10.95/13.65 **t.** ₰ 2.85.

XX **Bosquet,** 97a Warwick Rd, CV8 1HP, ℰ 52463 – 🆎 *VISA*
   closed Sunday, 3 weeks July, 1 week at Christmas – **M** (lunch by arrangement) a la carte
12.30/13.90 **t.** ₰ 3.20.

X **Ana's Bistro,** 121-123 Warwick Rd, CV8 1HP, ℰ 53763 – ℗ 🔼 🆎 ① *VISA*
   closed Sunday, Monday, first 3 weeks August and Bank Holidays – **M** (dinner only) a la carte
4.75/7.75 **t.** ₰ 2.00.

ALFA-ROMEO, LANCIA Station Rd ℰ 53073

KENNFORD Devon **403** J 32 – see Exeter.

KENNINGTON Kent **404** W 30 – see Ashford.

KENTS BANK Cumbria **402** L 21 – see Grange-over-Sands.

KERESLEY West Midlands **403 404** P 26 – see Coventry.

KESWICK Cumbria **402** K 20 – pop. 5,183 – ECD : Wednesday – ☏ 0596.
See : Derwent Water★★ Y – Envir. : Castlerigg (stone circle) ※★ E : 2 m. Y A.
🐎 Threlkeld Hall ℰ 059 683 (Threlkeld) 324, E : 4 m. by A 66 Y.
🛈 Moot Hall, Market Sq. ℰ 72645.
♦London 294 – ♦Carlisle 31 – Kendal 30.

Plan opposite

🏨 **Keswick** (T.H.F.) ⌚, Station Rd, CA12 4NQ, ℰ 72020, Telex 64200, ☞ – 🛗 📺 ⇦ ℗ 🅰
   🔼 🆎 ① *VISA*   Z a
   closed January and February – **M** (bar lunch Monday to Saturday) 4.00/5.50 **st.** ₰ 2.60 – ⚏
5.00 – **64 rm** 28.50/41.00 **st.**

🏨 **Royal Oak** (T.H.F.), Station St., CA12 5HH, ℰ 72965 – 🛗 📺 ⌂wc 🐕 ℗ 🅰 🔼 🆎 ① *VISA*
   M (bar lunch) a la carte 10.70/15.55 **st.** ₰ 2.35 – ⚏ 5.25 – **66 rm** 15.50/34.00 **st.**   Z i

🏨 **Underscar** ⌚, Applethwaite, CA12 4PH, N : 1 ½ m. by A 591 ℰ 72469, ≼ Derwent Water
   and mountains, ☞, park – 📺 ⌂wc ℍwc ℗ 🔼 *VISA*   by A 591   Y
   closed December and January – **M** (bar lunch) 9.00 **t.** ₰ 2.40 – ⚏ 3.00 – **18 rm** 20.00/55.00 **st.**
– SB (winter only) 40.00/54.00 **st.**

🏠 **Walpole,** Station Rd, CA12 4NA, ℰ 72072 – 📺 ⌂wc ℍwc ℗   Z o
   M 5.00/6.95 **t.** ₰ 2.50 – **17 rm** ⚏ 12.95/29.90 **t.**

🏠 **Grange Country House** ⌚, Manor Brow, Ambleside Rd, CA12 4BA, ℰ 72500, ≼, ☞ –
   🍽 rest 📺 ⌂wc ℍwc ℗ ✻   Y u
   M 4.50/9.00 **st.** ₰ 1.60 – **10 rm** ⚏ 14.00/28.00 **st.** – SB 20.00/21.50 **st.**

🛖 **Lyzzick Hall** ⌚, Under Skiddaw, CA12 4PY, NW : 2 ½ m. on A 591 ℰ 72277, ≼, ⌇ heated, ☞
   – ℍ ℗ ✻   by A 591   Y
   April-October – **M** (dinner only) 7.50 **s.** – **18 rm.**

KESWICK

*North is at the top
on all town plans.*

*Les plans de villes
sont disposés
le Nord en haut.*

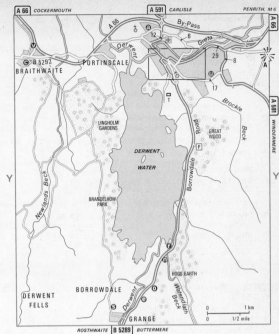

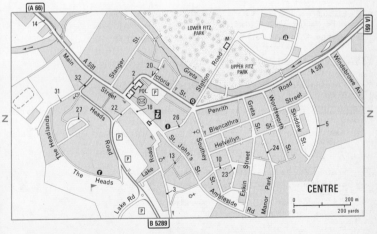

CENTRE

↑ **Lairbeck** ⌂, Vicarage Hill, CA12 5QB, ℰ 73373, 🍴 – 🛏wc 🅿. ⚶   Y **a**
   12 rm ⌷ 11.00/29.00 **t.**

↑ **Highfield,** The Heads, CA12 5ER, ℰ 72508, ≤ – 🛏wc 🅿   Z **r**
   Easter-mid November – **15 rm** ⌷ 9.90/25.20 **t.**

↑ **Gale** ⌂, Applethwaite, CA12 4PL, NW : 1 ¾ m. by A 591 ℰ 72413, ≤, 🍴 – 🅿. ⚶   Y
   April-October – **13 rm** ⌷ 10.00/20.00 **st.**   by A 591

at Borrowdale S : 3 ¼ m. on B 5289 – ✉ Keswick – ☎ 059 684 Borrowdale :

🏨 **Lodore Swiss** ⌂, CA12 5UX, ℰ 285, Group Telex 64305, ≤ Derwent Water and mountains,
   ⛲ heated, 🔲, 🍴, park, ⚶, squash – 🛗 📺 ☎ ⇔ 🅿. 🅰🅴. ⚶   Y **n**
   April-October – **M** 7.00/10.50 **t.** ⫯ 2.80 – **72 rm** ⌷ 29.00/58.00 **t.**

217

🏨 **Borrowdale,** CA12 5UY, ☎ 224, ⩽, 🌳 – [TV] 🛁wc [P]. [EN] — Y **o**
closed 22 December-8 February – **M** (bar lunch Monday to Saturday) 9.95 **t.** 🛈 2.70 – **35 rm** ☕ 14.00/56.00 **t.**

🏨 **Mary Mount Country House** 🐦, CA12 5UU, ☎ 223, Telex 64305, ⩽ Derwent Water and mountains, 🌳, park – [TV] 🛁wc 📞 [P]. [AE]. 🚫🐕 — Y **r**
closed 20 November-28 December – **M** (bar lunch) 9.00 **t.** 🛈 2.50 – **15 rm** ☕ 25.00/40.00 **t.** – SB (3 January-24 March) 43.00/51.00 **st.**

⌂ **Leathes Head** 🐦, CA12 5UY, ☎ 247, ⩽, 🌳 – 🛁wc 🚿wc [P]. 🚫🐕 — Y **e**
23 March-1 November – **13 rm** ☕ 12.00/25.00 **st.**

at Grange-in-Borrowdale **S : 4 ¾ m. by B 5289 – ✉ Keswick – ☎ 059 684 Borrowdale :**

🏨 **Borrowdale Gates Country House** 🐦, CA12 5UQ, ☎ 204, ⩽, 🌳 – [TV] 🛁wc [P] — Y **s**
M (bar lunch) 9.00 **st.** 🛈 2.00 – **20 rm** ☕ 12.50/24.00 **st.** – SB 20.70/24.00 **st.**

at Rosthwaite **S : 6 m. on B 5289 – Y – ✉ Keswick – ☎ 059 684 Borrowdale :**

🏨 **Scafell** 🐦, CA12 5XB, ☎ 208, 🌳 – 🛁wc [P]
April-October and weekends in winter – **M** (bar lunch Monday to Saturday) 9.75 **t.** 🛈 2.00 – **20 rm** ☕ 15.40/30.80 **t.** – SB (weekends only)(winter only) 55.00 **st.**

⌂ **Royal Oak** 🐦, CA12 5XB, ☎ 214 – 🛁wc [P]. [EN]
closed 1 to 27 December – **12 rm** ☕ 14.00/28.00 **t.**

at Braithwaite **W : 2 m. on A 66 – ✉ Keswick – ☎ 059 682 Braithwaite :**

🏨 **Ivy House,** CA12 5SY, ☎ 338 – [TV] 🛁wc [P]. ◑ [VISA]. 🚫🐕 — Y **c**
April-October – **M** (dinner only) 9.75 **st.** 🛈 2.00 – **8 rm** ☕ 14.00/35.00 **st.**

🏨 **Middle Ruddings,** CA12 5RY, on A 66 ☎ 436, 🌳 – [TV] 🛁wc [P]. 🚫🐕 — Y **v**
March-November, Christmas and New Year – **M** (bar lunch Monday to Saturday) 8.50 **t.** 🛈 3.00 – **15 rm** ☕ 15.00/40.00 **t.**

AUSTIN-ROVER High Hill ☎ 72768
FIAT Lake Rd ☎ 72064
FORD Tithe Barn St. ☎ 72386
RENAULT Keswick ☎ 72606

KETTLEWELL North Yorks. [402] N 21 – pop. 333 (inc. Starbotton) – ECD : Tuesday – ✉ Skipton – ☎ 075 676.
♦London 237 – Bradford 33 – ♦Leeds 40.

🏨 **Racehorses,** Town Foot, BD23 5QZ, ☎ 233 – 🛁wc 🚿wc [P]. [EN]
M (bar lunch Monday to Saturday) 5.60/10.25 **t.** 🛈 2.60 – **15 rm** ☕ 18.00/38.00 **t.** – SB 44.00/48.00 **st.**

KEYNSHAM Avon [403] [404] M 29 – pop. 13,370 – ECD : Wednesday – ✉ Bristol – ☎ 027 56.
⛳18 Manor Rd, Saltford ☎ 022 17 (Saltford) 3220, SE : 2 m – ♦London 127 – Bath 8 – ♦Bristol 4.

🏨 **Grange,** 42 Bath Rd, BS18 1SL, ☎ 69181 – [TV] 🛁wc [P]. [EN] [VISA]. 🚫🐕
M 4.00/10.00 **t.** 🛈 3.00 – **30 rm** ☕ 19.00/33.00 **t.**

KEYSTON Cambs. [404] S 26 – pop. 259 (inc. Bythorn) – ✉ Huntingdon – ☎ 080 14 Bythorn.
♦London 75 – ♦Cambridge 29 – Northampton 24.

XX **Pheasant Inn,** Village Loop Rd, PE18 0RE, ☎ 241 – [P]. [EN] [AE] ◑ [VISA]
M 3.25/9.75 **st.** 🛈 4.00.

KIDDERMINSTER Heref. and Worc. [403] [404] N 26 – pop. 47,326 – ECD : Wednesday – ☎ 0562.
[i] Library, Market St. ☎ 752832 – ♦London 139 – ♦Birmingham 17 – Shrewsbury 34 – Worcester 15.

🏨 **Gainsborough House** (Best Western), Bewdley Hill, DY11 6BS, SW : 1 m. on A 456 ☎ 754041, Telex 335672, 🌳 – [TV] 🛁wc 📞 [P]. 🏛. [EN] [AE] ◑ [VISA]
closed 24 December-2 January – **M** 5.00/12.00 **st.** 🛈 3.00 – **42 rm** ☕ 28.25/38.75 **st.** – SB (weekends only) 40.00 **st.**

at Stone **SE : 2 ½ m. on A 448 – ✉ Kidderminster – ☎ 056 283 Chaddesley Corbett :**

🏨 **Stone Manor,** DY10 4PJ, ☎ 555, Telex 335661, ⩽, 🏊 heated, 🌳, park, 🎾 – [TV] [P]. 🏛. [EN] [AE] ◑ [VISA]. 🚫🐕
M a la carte 9.10/18.45 **t.** 🛈 3.50 – ☕ 4.50 – **22 rm** 34.00/46.00 **st.**

ALFA-ROMEO Mill St. ☎ 3708
AUSTIN-ROVER Churchfields ☎ 69159
BMW Mustow Green ☎ 056 283 (Chaddesley Corbett) 435
CITROEN, PEUGEOT, TALBOT Worcester Rd ☎ 2202
FORD Worcester Rd ☎ 752661
LADA Plimsoll St. ☎ 2145
RENAULT Church St. ☎ 0299 (Cleobury Mortimer) 270352
VOLVO Stourport Rd ☎ 515832
VW, AUDI Worcester Rd ☎ 745056

KIDLINGTON Oxon. [403] [404] Q 28 – see Oxford.

KILDWICK North Yorks. [402] O 22 – pop. 131 – ✉ Keighley – ☎ 0535 Cross Hills.
♦London 226 – Burnley 15 – ♦Leeds 23.

🏨 **Kildwick Hall** 🐦, BD20 9AE, ☎ 32244, ⩽, « Jacobean manor house », 🌳 – [TV] [P]. [EN] [AE] ◑ [VISA]
M 7.95/13.95 **st.** 🛈 3.55 – **12 rm** ☕ 30.00/75.00 **st.** – SB 65.50 **st.**

KILSBY Northants. [403] [404] Q 26 – see Rugby (Warw.).

KINGHAM Oxon. [403] [404] P 28 – pop. 831 – ECD : Wednesday – ☏ 060 871.
♦London 81 – Gloucester 32 – ♦Oxford 25.

🏨 **Mill** 🔇, OX7 6UH, ☎ 8188, 🌳 – [TV] 🛁wc 🚿wc ☎ [P]. 💳 [AE] [DC] [VISA]. 🚫🐕
M 6.50/8.50 **t.** 🍷 3.40 – **20 rm** ☕ 24.00/38.00 **t.** – SB 23.00/25.00 **st.**

⌂ **Conygree Gate,** Church St., OX7 6YA, ☎ 389, 🌳 – [P]. 🚫🐕
March-October – **6 rm** ☕ 10.00/20.00 **st.**

KINGSBRIDGE Devon [403] I 33 **The West Country G.** – pop. 3,545 – ECD : Thursday – ☏ 0548.
See : Site★ – Boat Trip to Salcombe★★.
[i] The Quay ☎ 3195 (summer only).
♦London 236 – Exeter 36 – ♦Plymouth 20 – Torquay 21.

🏨 **Crabshell Motor Lodge** without rest., Embankment Rd, TQ7 1JZ, ☎ 3301, ← – [TV] 🛁wc [P]. 💳 [AE] [DC] [VISA]
☕ 3.00 – **24 rm** 18.50/27.50 **t.**

🏨 **Vineyard,** Embankment Rd, TQ7 1JN, ☎ 2520, 🌳 – 🛁wc 🚿wc [P]. 💳 [VISA]
Mid April-October – **M** (bar lunch) 8.00 **t.** – **11 rm** ☕ 13.50/31.50 **t.**

at Loddiswell N : 3 ½ m. by B 3196 – ✉ Kingsbridge – ☏ 054 855 Loddiswell :

XX **Lavinia's,** TQ7 4ED, N : 1 m. ☎ 306, 🌳 – [P]. 💳 [VISA]
Easter-October – **M** *(closed Sunday and Monday)* (lunch by arrangement) a la carte 18.00/20.00 **st.**

at Goveton NE : 2 ½ m. by A 381 – ✉ ☏ 0548 Kingsbridge :

🏨 **Buckland-Tout-Saints** (Best Western) 🔇, TQ7 2DS, ☎ 3055, Telex 42513, ←, « Queen Anne mansion », 🌳, park – [TV] 🛁wc 🚿wc ☎ [P]. 💳 [AE] [DC] [VISA]
closed January – **M** (lunch by arrangement) 12.00/20.00 **st.** 🍷 4.70 – **13 rm** ☕ 27.50/65.00 **st.** – SB (weekends only) 56.00/76.00 **st.**

at Chillington SE : 5 m. on A 379 – ✉ ☏ 0548 Kingsbridge :

🏨 **Oddicombe House,** TQ7 2JD, ☎ 234, 🏊, 🌳 – 🛁wc [P]
April-November – **M** (bar lunch residents only) 8.50 **t.** 🍷 3.00 – **10 rm** ☕ 14.00/40.00 **t.** – SB 42.00/54.00 **st.**

at Thurlestone W : 4 m. by A 381 – ✉ ☏ 0548 Kingsbridge :

🏨 **Thurlestone** (Best Western) 🔇, TQ7 3NN, ☎ 560382, ←, 🏊 heated, 🏊, ⛳9, 🌳, park, 🎾, squash – [lift] [TV] 🛁wc ☎ [P]. 👥. 💳 [AE] [DC] [VISA]
closed 3 to 11 January – **M** 3.75/9.50 **st.** – **74 rm** ☕ 16.00/80.00 **st.** – SB 60.00/96.00 **st.**

🏨 Furzey Close 🔇, TQ7 3NP, ☎ 560333, ←, 🌳 – [TV] 🛁wc 🚿wc [P]
10 rm.

AUSTIN-ROVER The Quay ☎ 2323
FORD Bridge St. ☎ 2305
SAAB Torcross ☎ 580205

KINGSGATE Kent [404] Y 29 – see Broadstairs.

KING'S HEATH West Midlands [403] [404] O 26 – see Birmingham.

KING'S LYNN Norfolk [402] [404] V 25 – pop. 30,107 – ECD : Wednesday – ☏ 0553.
See : St. Margaret's Church★ (17C, chancel 13C) – St. Nicholas' Chapel★ (Gothic).
Envir. : Houghton Hall★★ (18C) *AC*, NE : 15 m. – Sandringham House★ and park★★ *AC*, NE : 6 m.
[i] Saturday Market Place ☎ 63044.
♦London 103 – ♦Cambridge 45 – ♦Leicester 75 – ♦Norwich 44.

🏨 **Duke's Head** (T.H.F.), Tuesday Market Pl., PE30 1JS, ☎ 4996, Telex 817349 – [lift] [TV] 🛁wc ☎ [P]. 👥. 💳 [AE] [DC] [VISA]
M a la carte 11.15/15.05 **st.** 🍷 2.60 – ☕ 5.00 – **72 rm** 33.00/42.50 **st.**

🏨 **Stuart House,** 35 Goodwins Rd, PE30 5QX, ☎ 772169, 🌳 – [TV] 🛁wc [P]. 💳 [DC]. 🚫🐕
closed 24 December-2 January – **M** (bar lunch) 6.25 **t.** 🍷 2.60 – **15 rm** ☕ 14.50/36.00 **t.** – SB 33.00/40.00 **st.**

⌂ **Runcton House,** 53 Goodwins Rd, PE30 5PE, ☎ 773098, 🌳 – [P]
7 rm ☕ 14.50/22.00 **t.**

at Grimston NE : 6 ¼ m. by A 148 – ✉ Kings Lynn – ☏ 0485 Hillington :

🏨 **Congham Hall** 🔇, PE32 1AH, ☎ 600250, Telex 817209, « Country house atmosphere », 🏊 heated, 🌳, park, 🎾 – [TV] 🛁wc ☎ [P]. 💳 [AE] [DC] [VISA]. 🚫🐕
closed 23 December-10 January – **M** *(closed Saturday lunch and Sunday to non-residents)* 8.50/23.50 **t.** 🍷 2.75 – ☕ 2.00 – **9 rm** 42.00/62.00 **t.** – SB (weekends only) 85.00 **st.**

AUSTIN-ROVER-DAIMLER-JAGUAR, ROLLS ROYCE-BENTLEY Church St. ☎ 63133
PEUGEOT-TALBOT Lynn Rd, Heacham ☎ 0485 (Heacham) 70243
RELIANT, MAZDA Valingers Rd ☎ 2255
RENAULT Hardwick Rd ☎ 2644
TOYOTA Tottenhill ☎ 810306
VAUXHALL-OPEL North St. ☎ 3861

KINGSTON-UPOR-HULL

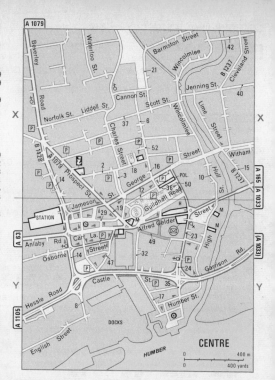

CENTRE

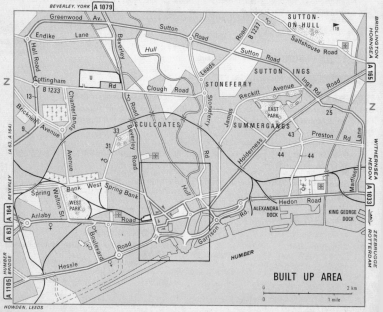

BUILT UP AREA

Envir. : Burton Constable Hall★ (16C) *AC*, NE : 8 m. by A 165 Z.

🛆 Kirk Ella ✆ 658919, W : 5 m. by A 164 Z – 🛆 Springhead Park, Willerby Rd ✆ 656309, W : by Spring Bank West Z – 🛆 Sutton Park, Salthouse Rd ✆ 74242, E : 3 m. Z.

✈ Humberside Airport : ✆ 0652 (Barnetby) 688456, S : 19 m. by A 63 Z and A 15 via Humber Bridge – **Terminal :** Coach Service.

⚓ Shipping connections with the Continent : to The Netherlands (Rotterdam) and Belgium (Zeebrugge) (North Sea Ferries).

🖪 Central Library, Albion St. ✆ 223344 – Corporation Rd, King George Dock, Hedon Rd ✆ 702118.

♦London 183 – ♦Leeds 61 – ♦Nottingham 94 – ♦Sheffield 68.

Plan opposite

🏨 **Crest** (Crest), Paragon St., HU1 3PJ, ✆ 26462, Telex 52431 – 🕴 📺 🛏wc ☏ 🅿. 🏄. 🔼 🖭 ⓪ *VISA*. ❄
Y e
M approx. 11.00 **st.** – ⚏ 4.95 – **125 rm** 39.00/49.50 **st.**

✕✕ **Cerutti's,** 10 Nelson St., HU1 1XE, ✆ 28501, Seafood – 🔼
Y o
closed Saturday lunch, Sunday and 24 December-2 January – **M** a la carte 9.10/13.20 **t.** 🍷 3.45.

at Willerby NW : 5 m. by A 63 – Z – off A 164 – ⊠ Kingston-upon-Hull – ✆ 0482 Hull :

🏨 **Willerby Manor,** Well Lane, HU10 6ER, ✆ 652616, Telex 52659, 🐎 – 📺 🛏wc 🎣wc ☏ 🅿. 🏄. 🔼 🖭 ⓪ *VISA*. ❄
M *(closed Saturday and Sunday dinner)* 6.00/7.00 **st.** 🍷2.50 – ⚏ 3.50 – **41 rm** 29.50/39.75 **st.** – SB (weekends only) 36.00 **st.**

at Little Weighton NW : 11 m. by A 164 – Z – ⊠ Kingston-upon-Hull – ✆ 0482 Hull :

🏨 **Rowley Manor** 🦢, HU20 3XR, SW : ½ m. by Rowley Rd ✆ 848248, ≤, 🐎 – 📺 🛏wc ☏ 🅿. 🔼 🖭 ⓪ *VISA*. ❄
M (dinner only and Sunday lunch) a la carte 8.25/11.50 **st.** 🍷 2.50 – **15 rm** ⚏ 25.00/48.00 **st.** – SB (weekends only) 46.50/60.00 **st.**

at North Ferriby W : 7 m. on A 63 – Z – ⊠ Kingston-upon-Hull – ✆ 0482 Hull :

🏨 **Crest** (Crest), Ferriby High Rd, HU14 3LG, ✆ 645212, Telex 52558 – 📺 🛏wc ☏ 🅿. 🏄. 🔼 🖭 ⓪ *VISA*. ❄
M approx. 11.00 **st.** – ⚏ 5.50 – **102 rm** 43.00/53.00 **st.**

ALFA-ROMEO, LANCIA Calvert Lane ✆ 572444
AUSTIN-ROVER Boothferry Rd ✆ 506911
BMW 54 Anlaby Rd ✆ 25071
COLT 32 Princes Av. ✆ 42739
DAIHATSU, SAAB Anlaby Rd ✆ 23773
FIAT Holderness High Rd ✆ 701785
FIAT 96 Boothferry Rd ✆ 506976
FORD 172 Anlaby Rd ✆ 25732
LADA Holderness Rd ✆ 226611

HONDA 576 Springbank West ✆ 51250
MAZDA 300/2 Boothferry Rd, Hessle ✆ 645 283
MERCEDES-BENZ 170 Aulaby Rd ✆ 20370
NISSAN Witham ✆ 24131
TALBOT Anlaby Rd ✆ 23631
TOYOTA Clarence St. ✆ 20039
VAUXHALL-OPEL 230/6 Anlaby Rd ✆ 23681
VW, AUDI 1/13 Boothferry Rd ✆ 649124

KINGSTOWN Cumbria – see Carlisle.

KINGSWINFORD West Midlands 403 404 N 26 – pop. 14,065 (inc. Wallheath) – ECD : Thursday – ✆ 0384.

♦London 135 – ♦Birmingham 14 – Stafford 22 – Worcester 32.

Plan : see Birmingham p. 2

🏨 **Summerhill House** (Golden Oak), Swindon Rd, DY6 9XA, ✆ 295254, 🐎 – 🛏wc ☏ 🅿. 🔼 🖭 *VISA*. ❄
AU a
M (closed Saturday lunch and Sunday dinner) 5.75/6.35 **st.** 🍷 2.50 – **10 rm** ⚏ 19.50/25.00 **st.**

KINTBURY Berks. 403 404 P 29 – pop. 2,060 – ⊠ Newbury – ✆ 0488.

♦London 73 – Newbury 6 – Reading 23.

✕✕ **Dundas Arms** with rm, Station Rd, RG15 0UT, ✆ 58263, ≤, 🐎 – 📺 🛏wc ☎ 🅿. 🔼 🖭 ⓪ *VISA*. ❄
closed 24 December-1 January – **M** (closed Sunday, Monday and Bank Holidays) (bar lunch) a la carte 13.00/17.75 **t.** 🍷 3.00 – **6 rm** ⚏ 30.00/35.00 **t.**

KINVER Staffs. 403 404 N 26 – see Stourbridge (West Midlands).

KIRKBY Merseyside 402 403 L 23 – pop. 58,360 – ECD : Wednesday – ✆ 051 Liverpool.

🛆 Liverpool Municipal, Ingoe Lane ✆ 546 5435.

🖪 Municipal Buildings, Cherryfield Drive ✆ 548 6555.

♦London 214 – ♦ Blackpool 54 – ♦Liverpool 7 – ♦Manchester 31.

🏨 **Crest** (Crest), East Lancs Rd, Knowsley, Prescot, L34 9HA, S : 1 ½ m. at Junction A 580 and A 5207 ✆ 546 7531, Telex 629769 – 📺 🛏wc ☏ 🅿. 🏄. 🔼 🖭 ⓪ *VISA*. ❄
M 10.00 **st.** – ⚏ 4.95 – **50 rm** 37.00/47.00 **st.**

KIRKBY FLEETHAM North Yorks. – pop. 410 – ⊠ ✪ 0609 Northallerton.

♦London 236 – ♦Leeds 46 – ♦Middlesbrough 31 – ♦Newcastle-upon-Tyne 51 – York 37.

  🏛 **Kirkby Fleetham Hall** ⑤, DL7 0SU, N : 1 m. ☎ 748226, ≼, « Georgian country house », ╦, park – 📺 ⌷wc ☎ 🅿 𝐕𝐈𝐒𝐀 ⅏
    M *(closed lunch Monday to Saturday to non-residents)* 6.95/12.95 **st.** – **13 rm** ⇌ 39.00/59.00 **st.**

KIRKBY LONSDALE Cumbria 𝟒𝟎𝟐 M 21 – pop. 1,506 – ECD : Wednesday – ⊠ Carnforth – ✪ 0468.

🖝 Casterton Rd ☎ 71429, 1 m. on Sedbergh Rd.

🖪 18 Main St. ☎ 71603.

♦London 259 – ♦Carlisle 62 – Kendal 13 – Lancaster 17 – ♦Leeds 58.

  🏛 **Royal,** Main St., Market Sq., LA6 2AE, ☎ 71217 – 📺 ⌷wc 🅿 : ◪ AE ⍟ 𝐕𝐈𝐒𝐀
    M 6.00/9.90 **st.** 🄰 2.95 – **22 rm** ⇌ 20.00/40.00 **t.** – SB (winter only) 40.00/45.00 **st.**

    at Casterton NE : 1 ¼ m. on A 683 – ⊠ ✪ 0468 Kirkby Lonsdale :

  🏠 **Pheasant Inn,** LA6 2SD, ☎ 71230 – ⌷wc 🅿. ◪ AE ⍟ 𝐕𝐈𝐒𝐀
    M (bar lunch) 9.00 **t.** – **6 rm** ⇌ 13.00/33.00 **t.** – SB (winter only) 30.00/38.50 **st.**

KIRKBYMOORSIDE North Yorks. 𝟒𝟎𝟐 R 21 – pop. 1,880 – ECD : Thursday – ✪ 0751.

🖝 Manor Vale ☎ 31525.

♦London 244 – Scarborough 26 – York 33.

  🏠 **George and Dragon,** 17 Market Pl., YO6 6AA, ☎ 31637 – 📺 ⌷wc ⍬wc 🅿. ◪ 𝐕𝐈𝐒𝐀 ⅏
    closed 24 to 26 December – **M** 4.25/12.00 🄰 3.00 – **23 rm** ⇌ 16.00/28.00 – SB (except summer) 22.00/28.00 **st.**

    at Fadmoor N : 2 ½ m. – ⊠ York – ✪ 0751 Kirkbymoorside :

  ✗ **Plough Inn,** YO6 6HY, ☎ 31515 – 🅿
    closed Sunday, Monday, 1 week February, 1 week May and 1 week October – **M** (dinner only) (booking essential) a la carte 8.90 **st.**

NISSAN Pickering Rd ☎ 31551
RENAULT New Rd ☎ 31401
                  VAUXHALL-OPEL Piercy End ☎ 31434

KIRKBY STEPHEN Cumbria 𝟒𝟎𝟐 M 20 – pop. 1,539 – ECD : Thursday – ✪ 0930.

Envir. : Brough (Castle ruins 12C-14C : keep ※ * *AC*) N : 4 m.

🖪 22 Market St. ☎ 71804.

♦London 285 – ♦Carlisle 48 – Kendal 24.

  🏠 **King's Arms,** Market Sq., CA17 4QN, ☎ 71378, ╦ – ◪ 𝐕𝐈𝐒𝐀
    closed Christmas Day – **M** (bar lunch Monday to Saturday) approx. 8.75 **t.** 🄰 3.00 – **9 rm** ⇌ 14.00/32.00 **t.** – SB (except summer)(not Bank Holidays) 36.00 **st.**

KIRKOSWALD Cumbria 𝟒𝟎𝟏 𝟒𝟎𝟐 L 19 – pop. 659 – ⊠ Penrith – ✪ 076 883 Lazonby.

♦London 300 – ♦Carlisle 23 – Kendal 41 – Lancaster 58.

  🏠 **Prospect Hill** ⑤, CA10 1ER, N : ¾ m. ☎ 500, ≼, « Converted 18C farm buildings », ╦ – ⍬wc 🅿. ◪ AE ⍟ 𝐕𝐈𝐒𝐀 ⅏
    closed February – **M** *(closed Monday lunch and Tuesday)* 6.20/7.70 **t.** 🄰 2.80 – **10 rm** ⇌ 12.40/36.00 **t.**

KNARESBOROUGH North Yorks. 𝟒𝟎𝟐 P 21 – pop. 10,640 – ECD : Thursday – ✪ 0423 Harrogate.

🖝 Boroughbridge Rd ☎ 863219, N : 1 ½ m.

🖪 Market Place ☎ 866886 (summer only).

♦London 217 – Bradford 21 – Harrogate 3 – ♦Leeds 18 – York 18.

  🏛 **Dower House,** Bond End, HG5 9AL, ☎ 863302, ╦ – 📺 ⌷wc ⍬wc ☎ 🅿. ◪ 𝐕𝐈𝐒𝐀 ⅏
    closed 25 and 26 December – **M** 6.50/9.50 **t.** 🄰 3.25 – **20 rm** ⇌ 25.00/60.00 **t.** – SB (weekends only)(winter only) 47.50 **st.**

  ✗✗ **Schwallers,** 6-8 Bond End, HG5 9AQ, ☎ 863899 – ◪ 𝐕𝐈𝐒𝐀
    closed Tuesday and 25 to 30 December – **M** (dinner only and Sunday lunch) a la carte 11.70/13.15 **t.** 🄰 2.70.

FORD York Place ☎ 862291
                  VAUXHALL-OPEL Bond End ☎ 862191

KNIGHTWICK Heref. and Worc. 𝟒𝟎𝟑 𝟒𝟎𝟒 M 27 – pop. 114 – ECD : Wednesday – ⊠ Worcester – ✪ 0886.

♦London 132 – Hereford 20 – Leominster 18 – Worcester 8.

  🏠 **Talbot,** WR6 5PH, on B 4197 ☎ 21235, ⍉, squash – ⌷wc ⍬wc 🅿. ◪ 𝐕𝐈𝐒𝐀 ⅏
    M *(closed dinner Sunday and Monday to non-residents)* (bar lunch Monday to Saturday) 7.50/8.75 **st.** 🄰 2.25 – **10 rm** ⇌ 12.50/35.00 **st.** – SB 37.50/42.00 **st.**

KNOWLE West Midlands [403] [404] O 26 – pop. 7,676 – ECD : Thursday – ✉ Solihull – ☎ 056 45.
♦London 108 – ♦Birmingham 9 – ♦Coventry 10 – Warwick 11.

🏨 **Greswolde Arms** (Golden Oak), High St., B93 0LL, ✆ 2711 – [TV] 🚿wc ☏ [P]. [S] [AE] [VISA]. 🚫
M *(closed Saturday lunch and Sunday dinner)* a la carte 6.55/10.80 **st.** 🍷 2.50 – **18 rm** 🛏 30.00/35.00 **t.**

🍴🍴 **Florentine,** 15 Kenilworth Rd, B93 0JB, ✆ 6449, Italian rest. – [S] [AE] [D] [VISA]
closed Monday lunch, Sunday, August and Bank Holidays – **M** a la carte 7.60/10.60 **t.**

AUSTIN-ROVER 25 Station Rd ✆ 4221
NISSAN Four Ashes Rd ✆ 560 5118
VAUXHALL Grange Rd, Dorridge ✆ 6131

KNOWL HILL Berks. [404] R 29 – pop. 495 – ✉ Twyford – ☎ 062 882 Littlewick Green.
♦London 38 – Maidenhead 5 – Reading 8.

🍴🍴 **Bird in Hand,** Bath Rd, RG10 9UP, ✆ 2781, 🌳 – [P]. [S] [AE] [D] [VISA]
M 10.00/14.50 **t.** 🍷 2.65.

at Warren Row NW : 1 m. – ✉ Knowl Hill – ☎ 062 882 Littlewick Green :

🍴🍴 **Warrener,** Wargrave, RG10 8QS, ✆ 2803 – [P]. [S] [AE] [D] [VISA]
closed Saturday lunch, Sunday dinner, Monday, first 2 weeks January, last week April and last week August – **M** a la carte 12.50/19.50 **t.**

KNUTSFORD Cheshire [402] [403] [404] M 24 – pop. 10,050 – ECD : Wednesday – ☎ 0565.
Envir. : Tatton Hall★ (Georgian) and gardens★★ *AC*, N : 2 m. – Jodrell Bank (Concourse building-radiotelescope *AC*) SE : 8 ½ m.
⛳18 Mere Golf ✆ 0565 (Bucklow Hill) 830155, NW : 3 m. on A 50 – [i] Council Offices, Toft Rd ✆ 2611.
♦London 187 – Chester 25 – ♦Liverpool 33 – ♦Manchester 18 – ♦Stoke-on-Trent 30.

🏨 **Royal George,** King St., WA16 6EE, ✆ 4151 – ⇅ [TV] 🛁wc ☏ [P]. ♿. [S] [AE] [D] [VISA]. 🚫
closed 25 and 26 December – **M** (grill rest. only) a la carte 4.65/10.35 **t.** – **30 rm** 🛏 30.00/40.50 **t.** – SB (weekends only) 24.00 **st.**

🏠 **Longview,** 55 Manchester Rd, WA16 0LX, ✆ 2119 – 🚿wc [P]
closed Christmas and New Year – **14 rm** 🛏 13.50/29.00 **st.**

🍴🍴🍴 **La Belle Epoque** with rm, 60 King St., WA16 2DT, ✆ 3060, « Art nouveau » – [TV] [P]. [S] [AE] [D] [VISA]. 🚫
closed Sunday and 1 to 8 January – **M** (dinner only) (booking essential) a la carte 9.25/14.00 **t.** 🍷 2.50 – 🛏 3.50 – **5 rm** 25.00/35.00 **st.**

🍴 **David's Place,** 10 Princess St., WA16 6DD, ✆ 3356 – [S] [AE] [D] [VISA]
closed Sunday and Bank Holidays – **M** a la carte 11.45/15.95 **t.** 🍷 3.00.

at Lower Peover S : 3 ½ m. by A 50 on B 5081 – ✉ Knutsford – ☎ 056 581 Lower Peover :

🍴 Bells of Peover, The Cobbles, ✆ 2269, 🌳 – [P].

at Bucklow Hill NW : 3 ½ m. at junction A 556 and A 5034 – ✉ Knutsford – ☎ 0565 Bucklow Hill :

🏨 **Swan Inn,** Chester Rd, WA14 6RN, ✆ 830295, Telex 666911 – [TV] 🛁wc 🚿wc ☏ [P]. [S] [AE] [D] [VISA]
closed Christmas and New Year – **M** 6.50/14.75 **st.** 🍷 3.10 – **74 rm** 🛏 38.00/50.00 **st.** – SB (weekends only)(except July and August) 50.00 **st.**

ALFA-ROMEO, LANCIA London Rd, Allostock ✆ 056 581 (Lower Peover) 2899
AUSTIN-ROVER Bucklow Hill ✆ 830041
FORD Garden Rd ✆ 4141
RENAULT Toft Rd ✆ 4294
VOLVO Park Lane, Pickmere ✆ 056 589 (Pickmere) 3254

LACOCK Wilts. [403] [404] N 29 The West Country G. – pop. 1,318 – ✉ Chippenham – ☎ 024 973.
See : Site★ – Lacock Village : High St.★, St. Cyriac Church★, Fox Talbot Museum of Photography★ – Lacock Abbey★ – ♦London 109 – Bath 16 – ♦Bristol 30 – Chippenham 3.

🍴 **Sign of the Angel** with rm, 6 Church St., SN15 2LA, ✆ 230, English rest., « 14C inn in National Trust village », 🌳 – 🛁wc
closed 23 December-1 January – **M** *(closed Saturday lunch, Sunday dinner and Bank Holidays)* (booking essential) 12.50/15.00 **st.** 🍷 3.00 – **6 rm** 🛏 30.00/50.00 **st.** – SB (winter only) 65.00 **st.**

LAKE VYRNWY Powys [402] [403] J 25 – pop. 324 – ✉ ☎ 069 173 Llanwddyn.
♦London 204 – Chester 52 – Llanfyllin 10 – Shrewsbury 40.

🏨 **Lake Vyrnwy** 🔇, SY10 0LY, ✆ 244, < Lake Vyrnwy, « Country house atmosphere », 🎣, 🌳, park, 🎾 – ⇅ 🛁wc 🚗 [P]. 🚫
closed February – **M** (buffet lunch Monday to Saturday) 8.00/8.40 **st.** 🍷 2.50 – **28 rm** 🛏 15.00/50.00 **st.** – SB (winter only)(except Christmas, New Year and Easter) 50.00/54.00 **st.**

LAMORNA COVE Cornwall [403] D 33 – ECD : Thursday – ✉ ☎ 0736 Penzance.
Envir. : Land's End★★ W : 7 ½ m – ♦London 323 – Penzance 5 – Truro 31.

🏨 **Lamorna Cove** 🔇, TR19 6XH, ✆ 731411, <, 🏊 heated, 🌳 – ⇅ [TV] 🛁wc 🚿wc ☏ [P]. [S] [AE] [D] [VISA]
closed December and January – **M** 5.95/8.95 **t.** 🍷 3.20 – **23 rm** 🛏 20.00/38.90 **t.** – SB (except summer) 45.00/60.00 **st.**

LAMPETER (LLANBEDR PONT STEFFAN) Dyfed 🅐🅞🅑 H 27 – pop. 2,189 – ECD : Wednesday – ☎ 0570.

🎏 Cilgwyn, Llangybi 🖉 057 045 (Llangybi) 286, NE : 4 m. off A 485.
🚹 Town Hall 🖉 422426 (summer only).
♦London 223 – Brecon 41 – Carmarthen 22 – ♦Swansea 50.

🏨 Black Lion Royal, High St., SA48 7BG, 🖉 422172 – 📺 🛏wc 🅟
18 rm.

LAMPHEY Dyfed – see Pembroke.

LANCASTER Lancs. 🅐🅞🅑 L 21 – pop. 49,584 – ECD : Wednesday – ☎ 0524.

🏌 Lancaster Golf and Country Club, Ashton Hall 🖉 0524 (Galgate) 752090, S : 3 m. on A 588.
🚹 7 Dalton Sq. 🖉 32878.
♦London 252 – ♦Blackpool 26 – Bradford 62 – Burnley 44 – ♦Leeds 71 – ♦Middlesbrough 97 – Preston 26.

🏨 **Post House** (T.H.F.), Waterside Park, Caton Rd, LA1 3RA, NE : 1 ¼ m. on A 683 🖉 65999, Telex 65363, 🔄, 🍴 – 🍽 📺 ☎ 🔥 🅟. 🔆. 🔺 🅰🅴 🅾 🆅🆂🆁
M 8.05/12.55 **st.** ◊ 2.85 – ♀ 5.00 – **120 rm** 40.00/50.50 **st.**

🏨 **Hampson House,** Hampson Green, LA2 0JB, S : 5 m. by A 6, 🅰 Galgate 🖉 751158, 🎠 – 📺 🛏wc 🅟. 🎣
M (closed lunch Monday and Tuesday) (lunch by arrangement) 8.00/12.50 **st.** ◊ 3.20 – **13 rm** ♀ 16.00/30.00 **t.**

FORD Parliament St. 🖉 63553
HYUNDAI, PONY Brookhouse 🖉 0524 (Caton) 770501

TALBOT Bulk Rd 🖉 63373

LANGSTONE Gwent 🅐🅞🅑 L 29 – see Newport.

LANREATH Cornwall 🅐🅞🅑 G 32 – pop. 352 – ✉ Looe – ☎ 0503.
♦London 269 – ♦Plymouth 26 – Truro 34.

🏨 **Punch Bowl Inn,** PL13 2NX, 🖉 20218, 🎠 – 📺 🛏wc 🍴 🅟. 🔺 🆅🆂🆁
April-October – **M** (buffet lunch) a la carte 5.05/8.90 **t.** ◊ 1.90 – **18 rm** ♀ 11.00/30.45 **t.**

LAPFORD Devon 🅐🅞🅑 I 31 – pop. 875 – ✉ Crediton – ☎ 036 35.
♦London 218 – Exeter 17 – ♦Plymouth 63 – Taunton 54.

↑ **Nymet Bridge House** 🏡, EX17 6QX, NW : 1 ½ m. by A 377 🖉 334, 🎠 – 🍴wc 🅟. 🎣
5 rm ♀ 10.00/22.00.

LARKFIELD Kent 🅐🅞🅒 V 30 – see Maidstone.

LASTINGHAM North Yorks. 🅐🅞🅑 R 21 – pop. 88 – ECD : Wednesday – ✉ York – ☎ 075 15.
♦London 244 – Scarborough 26 – York 32.

🏨 **Lastingham Grange** 🏡, YO6 6TH, 🖉 345, ≤, « Country house atmosphere », 🎠 – 🛏wc 🅟. 🅰🅴 🅾. 🎣
closed January-mid February and Christmas – **M** 6.75/10.25 **t.** ◊ 2.00 – **12 rm** ♀ 28.00/55.50 **t.** – SB 67.00/77.00 **st.**

at Hutton-Le-Hole W : 2 m. – ✉ York – ☎ 075 15 Lastingham :

↑ **Barn,** YO6 6UA, 🖉 311 – 🅟. 🎣
May-October – **9 rm** ♀ 10.00/20.00 **t.**

LAVENHAM Suffolk 🅐🅞🅒 W 27 – pop. 1,480 – ECD : Wednesday – ✉ Sudbury – ☎ 0787.
See : SS. Peter and Paul's Church : the Spring Parclose★ (Flemish).
♦London 66 – ♦Cambridge 39 – Colchester 22 – ♦Ipswich 19.

🏨 **Swan** (T.H.F.), High St., CO10 9QA, 🖉 247477, « Part 14C timbered inn », 🎠 – 📺 🅟. 🔆. 🔺 🅰🅴 🅾 🆅🆂🆁
M 9.70/10.80 **st.** ◊ 2.60 – ♀ 5.50 – **42 rm** 35.50/47.50 **st.**

PEUGEOT, TALBOT Sudbury Rd 🖉 247228

LEAMINGTON SPA Warw. 🅐🅞🅑 🅐🅞🅒 P 27 – see Royal Leamington Spa.

LEDBURY Heref. and Worc. 🅐🅞🅑 🅐🅞🅒 M 27 – pop. 3,911 – ECD : Wednesday – ☎ 0531.
See : Church Lane★.
Envir. : Birtsmorton Court★ (15C) AC, SE : 7 m.
🚹 St. Katherine's, High St. 🖉 2461.
♦London 119 – Hereford 14 – Newport 46 – Worcester 16.

224

🏠 **Feathers,** High St., HR8 1DS, ✆ 2600, « Heavily timbered 16C inn », squash – 📺 📧wc 🅿.
🔼 🏧 –
M (lunch by arrangement) a la carte 8.10/12.05 **st.** 🍷 2.50 – **11 rm** � 28.00/39.50 **st.**

🏠 **Royal Oak,** The Southend, HR8 2EY, ✆ 2110 – 🅿. 🔼 VISA. ✖
M *(closed Christmas Day)* (buffet lunch) 6.25 **st.** 🍷 1.75 – **8 rm** ⊑ 13.00/30.00 **st.** – SB (winter only) 33.50 **st.**

at Wellington Heath N : 2 m. by B 4214 – ✉ ✆ 0531 Ledbury :

🏠 **Hope End Country House** ⚘, Hope End, HR8 1DS, N : ¾ m. ✆ 3613, « Country house atmosphere », 🌸, park – 📧wc 🅿. 🔼 🏧 ⓪ VISA. ✖
March-November – **M** (dinner only) (booking essential) 15.00 **st.** 🍷 3.00 – **7 rm** ⊑ (dinner included) 44.00/84.00 **st.** – SB (March and November) 64.00/71.00 **st.**

AUSTIN-ROVER New St. ✆ 2233   FORD New St. ✆ 2261

LEE Devon 🗾 H 30 – see Ilfracombe.

LEEDS West Yorks. 🗾 P 22 – pop. 496,009 – ECD : Wednesday – ✆ 0532.
See : St. John's Church★ 17C DZ **A.**
Envir. : Temple Newsam House★ 17C (interior★★) *AC*, E : 4 m. CX **D** – Kirkstall Abbey★ (ruins 12C) *AC*, NW : 3 m. BV.
🏌, 🏌 The Lady Dorothy Wood, The Lord Irwin, Temple Newsam Rd, Halton ✆ 645624, E : 3 m. CX –
🏌 Gotts Park, Armley Ridge Rd, ✆ 638232, W : 2 m. BV – 🏌 Horsforth, Layton Rise ✆ 586819, NW :
6 m. BV – 🏌 Middleton Park, Town St., Middleton ✆ 700449, S : 3 m. CX.
✈ Leeds and Bradford Airport : ✆ 0532 (Rawdon) 503431, NW : 8 m. by A 65 and A 658 BV –
Terminal : Vicar Lane, Bus Station, Leeds.
🛈 Central Library, Calverley St. ✆ 462454.
♦London 204 – ♦Liverpool 75 – ♦Manchester 43 – ♦Newcastle-upon-Tyne 95 – ♦Nottingham 74.

Plans on following pages

🏨 **Ladbroke Dragonara** (Ladbroke), Neville St., LS1 4BX, ✆ 442000, Telex 557143 – 📶 📺 ☎
🔥 🅿. 🏊 🔼 🏧 ⓪ VISA   DZ **r**
M 7.25/10.75 **st.** 🍷 4.45 – ⊑ 5.50 – **234 rm** 44.00/58.00 **st.**

🏨 **Queen's** (T.H.F.), City Sq., LS1 1PL, ✆ 431323, Telex 55161 – 📶 📺 📧wc 📺. 🏊 🔼 🏧 ⓪
VISA   DZ **a**
M (carving lunch Saturday and Sunday) 4.95/6.50 **st.** 🍷 3.70 – ⊑ 5.50 – **197 rm** 29.50/52.50 **st.**

🏨 **Metropole** (T.H.F.), King St., LS1 2HQ, ✆ 450841, Telex 557755 – 📶 📺 📧wc 📺 🅿. 🏊 🔼
🏧 ⓪ VISA   CZ **o**
M (carving rest.) 7.95 **st.** 🍷 2.95 – ⊑ 5.25 – **110 rm** 27.00/41.50 **st.**

🏨 **Merrion,** Merrion Centre, 17 Wade Lane, LS2 8NH, ✆ 439191, Telex 55459 – 📶 📺 📧wc
☎ 🅿. 🏊 🔼 🏧 ⓪ VISA. 🔥   DZ **x**
M 5.95/7.75 **st.** 🍷 3.00 – **120 rm** 39.00/55.00 **st.** – SB 46.00 **st.**

🔼 **Aragon** ⚘, 250 Stainbeck Lane, LS7 2PS, ✆ 759306, 🌸 – 📧wc 🅿. 🔼 ⓪ VISA   CV **c**
closed Christmas – **11 rm** ⊑ 12.10/24.00 **s.**

🔼 **Highfield,** 79 Cardigan Rd, LS6 1EB, ✆ 752193 – 🅿   AY **x**
10 rm ⊑ 10.00/18.00.

🔼 **Oak Villa,** 57 Cardigan Rd, LS6 1DW, ✆ 758439, 🌸 – 🅿   AY **a**
10 rm ⊑ 11.00/20.00 **st.**

🔼 **Pinewood,** 78 Potternewton Lane, LS7 3LW, ✆ 622561, 🌸 – 🏠. 🔼. 🔥   AY **s**
closed 24 to 31 December – **11 rm** ⊑ 14.50/29.50 **t.**

🗙🗙🗙 **Gardini's Terrazza,** Minerva House, 16 Greek St., LS1 5RU, ✆ 432880, Italian rest. – 🔼 🏧
                                                                                      CDZ **n**
closed Saturday lunch, Sunday and Bank Holidays – **M** a la carte 9.30/12.60 **t.** 🍷 2.90.

🗙🗙🗙 **Mandalay,** 8 Harrison St., LS1 6PA, ✆ 446453, Indian rest. – 🔼 🏧 ⓪ VISA   DZ **e**
closed Saturday lunch, Sunday, Easter Monday and 25-26 December – **M** a la carte 9.15/10.00 **t.**
🍷 3.50.

🗙🗙 **Embassy,** 333 Roundhay Rd, LS8 4HT, NE : 2 ½ m. by A 58 ✆ 490562 – 🅿. 🔼 🏧 ⓪ VISA
closed Sunday – **M** (dinner only) 11.80 **t.** 🍷 2.50.   BY **v**

🗙🗙 **Shabab,** 2 Eastgate, LS2 7JL, ✆ 468988, Indian rest. – 🔼 🏧 ⓪ VISA   DZ **v**
closed Sunday lunch and 25 December – **M** a la carte 8.70/12.25 **t.**

🗙 **Rules,** 188 Selby Rd, LS15 0LF, ✆ 604564 – 🅿. 🔼 🏧 ⓪ VISA   CV **u**
M (dinner only and Sunday lunch) a la carte 7.95/11.00 **st.** 🍷 3.15.

at Seacroft NE : 5 ½ m. at junction of A 64 and A 6120 – ✉ ✆ 0532 Leeds :

🏨 **Stakis Windmill** (Stakis), Ring Rd, LS14 5QP, ✆ 732323 – 📶 📺 📧wc 📺 🔥 🅿. 🏊 🔼 🏧
⓪ VISA   CV **a**
M (grill rest. only) a la carte 5.70/11.25 **st.** 🍷 2.80 – **40 rm** ⊑ 28.00/44.00 **st.** – SB 46.00 **st.**

at Garforth E : 6 m. at junction of A 64 and A 642 – CV – ✉ ✆ 0532 Leeds :

🏨 **Ladbroke Mercury** (Ladbroke), Wakefield Rd, LS25 1LH, ✆ 866556, Telex 556324 – 📺
📧wc 🔥 🅿. 🏊 🔼 🏧 ⓪ VISA
M (carving rest.) 7.95/9.50 **t.** 🍷 2.95 – ⊑ 5.50 – **143 rm** 36.00/44.00 **t.** – SB (weekends only) 47.00/49.00 **st.**

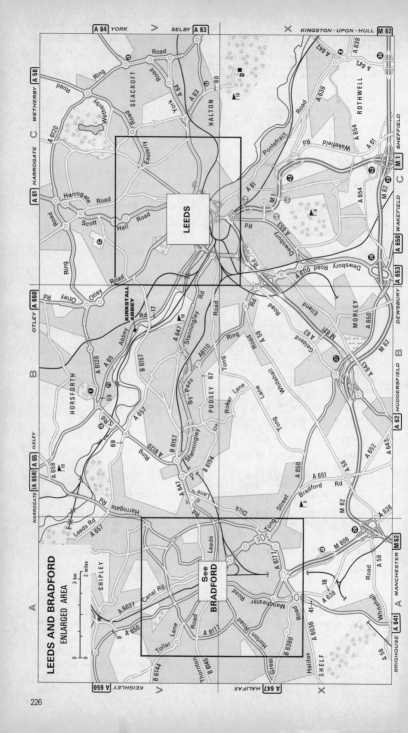

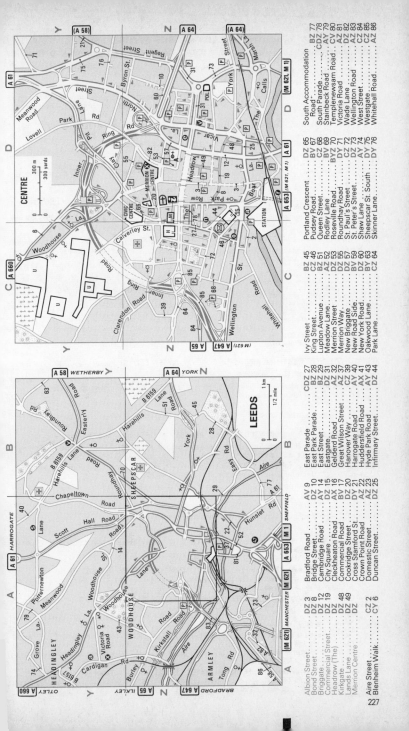

LEEDS

CENTRE

300 m
300 yards

227

at Oulton SE : 6 ¼ m. at junction of A 639 and A 642 – ⊠ ☯ 0532 Leeds :

🏛 **Crest** (Crest), The Grove, LS26 8EJ, ℰ 826201, Telex 557646 – 📺 ⇔wc ⊛ ৬ 🅿 🄰🅴 ⓪ VISA ⚬
CX z
M approx. 11.00 **st.** – ⚏ 5.25 – **40 rm** 42.00/53.00 **st.**

at Horsforth NW : 5 m. by A 65 off A 6120 – ⊠ ☯ 0532 Leeds :

XXX **Low Hall,** Calverley Lane, LS18 4EF, ℰ 588221, « Elizabethan manor », 🖈 – 🅿 🄰 VISA
closed Saturday lunch, Sunday, Monday, 25 to 30 December and Bank Holidays – **M** a la carte
7.70/13.75 **st.** ⅃ 2.50. BV **a**

XX **Roman Garden,** Hall Lane, Hall Park, LS18 5JY, ℰ 587962, <, Italian rest. – 🅿 🄰 VISA
closed Saturday lunch, Sunday and Monday – **M** a la carte 5.00/9.40 **t.** ⅃ 2.75. BV **i**

XX Morty's, 141-145 New Road Side, LS18 4QD, ℰ 580293, Seafood – 🅿 BV **n**

at Bramhope NW : 8 m. on A 660 – BV – ⊠ ☯ 0532 Leeds :

🏛 **Post House** (T.H.F.), Otley Rd, LS16 9JJ, ℰ 842911, Telex 556367, < – ▣ 📺 ⇔wc ⊛ ৬ 🅿
🄰 🄰 🅴 ⓪ VISA
M a la carte 10.40/13.95 **st.** ⅃ 2.50 – ⚏ 5.00 – **120 rm** 40.00/47.00 **st.**

🏛 **Parkway** (Embassy), Otley Rd, LS16 8AG, S : 2 m. on A 660 ℰ 672551, 🖈 – 📺 ⇔wc ⊛
🅿 🄰 🄰 🅴 ⓪ VISA ⚬
M (closed Saturday lunch) (Sunday dinner residents only) 8.00 **st.** ⅃ 4.75 – ⚏ 4.25 – **39 rm**
30.00/45.00 **st.** – SB (weekends only) 41.00/48.00 **st.**

MICHELIN Branch, Gelderd Rd, LS12 6EU, ℰ 793911

AUSTIN-ROVER Town St., Stanningley ℰ 571811
AUSTIN-ROVER Water Lane ℰ 438091
AUSTIN-ROVER-DAIMLER-JAGUAR, ROLLS ROYCE-BENTLEY Roseville Rd ℰ 432731
AUSTIN-ROVER Breary Lane, Bramhope ℰ 0532 (Arthington) 842696
BMW Sheepscar Way ℰ 620641
FORD 83 Roseville Rd ℰ 455955
FORD Aberford Rd ℰ 863261
FORD Whitehall Rd ℰ 634222
LADA, ALFA-ROMEO Domestic St. ℰ 468141
MAZDA York Rd ℰ 480093
NISSAN Meadow Rd ℰ 444531

NISSAN, PORSCHE, SAAB Apperley Lane, Yeadon ℰ 0532 (Rawdon) 502231
PEUGEOT South Milford ℰ 0977 (South Milford) 682714
PEUGEOT-TALBOT, CITROEN Regent St. ℰ 431914
PEUGEOT-TALBOT Wike Ridge Lane ℰ 661129
RENAULT Regent St. ℰ 430837
TOYOTA Low Rd ℰ 702341
TOYOTA Regent St. ℰ 444223
VAUXHALL 123 Hunslet Rd ℰ 439911
VAUXHALL-OPEL Armley Rd ℰ 434554
VOLVO Wellington Rd ℰ 436412
VW, AUDI Gelderd Rd ℰ 633431

LEE-ON-THE-SOLENT Hants. 🄼🄾🄳 🄼🄾🄴 Q 31 – pop. 6,266 – ECD : Thursday – ☯ 0705.
♦London 81 – ♦Portsmouth 13 – ♦Southampton 15 – Winchester 23.

🏠 **Belle Vue,** 39 Marine Par. East, PO13 2BW, ℰ 550258 – 📺 ⇔wc ৠwc 🅿 🄰 VISA
closed 25 and 26 December – **M** (carving rest.) a la carte 3.85/11.40 **t.** – **32 rm** ⚏ 21.45/36.30 **t.**
– SB (weekends only) 39.65 **st.**

NISSAN High St. ℰ 551785

LEICESTER Leics. 🄼🄾🄴 🄼🄾🄳 🄼🄾🄴 Q 26 – pop. 284,208 – ECD : Monday and Thursday – ☯ 0533.
See : Museum of local archaeology, Jewry Wall and baths★ AC BY M1 – Museum and Art Gallery★
CY M2 – St. Mary de Castro's Church★ 12C BY A.

🎣 Leicestershire, Evington Lane ℰ 736035, E : 2 m. AY – 🎣 Western Park, Scudamore Rd ℰ 872339,
W : 4 m. AY – 🎣 Cambridge Rd, Whetstone ℰ 862399 by A 426 AZ.

✈ East Midlands Airport : Castle Donington ℰ 0332 (Derby) 810621, NW : 22 m. by A 50 AX and
M1.

🚹 12 Bishop St. ℰ 556699.

♦London 107 – ♦Birmingham 43 – ♦Coventry 24 – ♦Nottingham 26.

Plans on following pages

🏨 **Holiday Inn,** 129 St. Nicholas Circle, LE1 5LX, ℰ 531161, Telex 341281, 🔲 – ▣ ▤ 📺 ☎ ৬
🅿 🄰 🄰 🅴 ⓪ VISA
BY **c**
M a la carte 8.00/13.00 **st.** – ⚏ 4.75 – **190 rm** 34.00/39.00 **s.**

🏨 **Grand** (Embassy), 73 Granby St., LE1 6ES, ℰ 555599 – ▣ 📺 🅿 🄰 🄰 🅴 ⓪ VISA ⚬
closed 25 and 26 December – **M** (carving rest.) 7.25 **st.** ⅃ 4.50 – ⚏ 4.25 – **93 rm** 40.00/52.00 **st.**
– SB (weekends only) 45.00/52.00 **st.** CY **o**

🏛 **Eaton Bray,** Abbey St., LE1 3TE, ℰ 50666, Telex 342434 – ▣ 📺 ⇔wc ৠwc ⊛ 🄰 🄰
🅴 ⓪ VISA ⚬
CX **a**
M (closed Sunday dinner) a la carte 8.00/14.00 **t.** ⅃ 4.50 – **72 rm** ⚏ 15.00/34.95 **st.** – SB
(weekends only) 15.00/20.00 **st.**

🏛 **Belmont** (Best Western), De Montfort St., LE1 7GR, ℰ 544773, Telex 34619 – ▣ 📺 ⇔wc ☎
🅿 🄰 🅴 ⓪ VISA
CY **c**
M (closed Saturday lunch and Sunday dinner) 6.50/7.50 **st.** ⅃ 3.00 – **61 rm** ⚏ 22.00/50.00 **st.** –
SB (weekends only) 45.00 **st.**

🏛 **Leicester International,** Humberstone Rd, LE5 3AT, ℰ 20471, Telex 341460 – ▣ 📺 ⇔wc
☎ 🄰 🄰 🅴 ⓪ VISA ⚬
CX **n**
M 8.75 **t.** ⅃ 2.20 – ⚏ 3.50 – **220 rm** 29.50/38.50 **st.**

LEICESTER
BUILT UP AREA

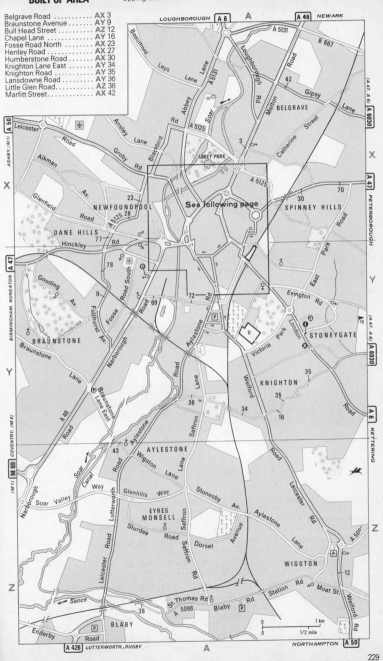

See following page

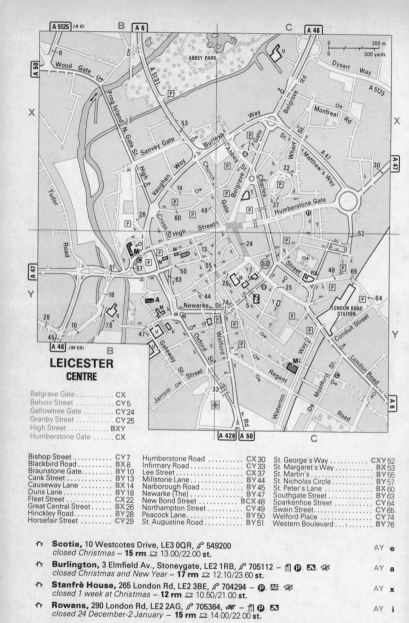

LEICESTER
CENTRE

Belgrave Gate	**CX**
Belvoir Street	**CY** 5
Gallowtree Gate	**CY** 24
Granby Street	**CY** 25
High Street	**BXY**
Humberstone Gate	**CX**

↑ **Scotia,** 10 Westcotes Drive, LE3 0QR, ☏ 549200
closed Christmas – **15 rm** ⌂ 13.00/22.00 **st.**

AY **e**

↑ **Burlington,** 3 Elmfield Av., Stoneygate, LE2 1RB, ☏ 705112 – 🍴 **P**. 🔊. 🛇
closed Christmas and New Year – **17 rm** ⌂ 12.10/23.60 **st.**

AY **a**

↑ **Stanfrè House,** 265 London Rd, LE2 3BE, ☏ 704294 – **P**. 🅰🅴 🛇
closed 1 week at Christmas – **12 rm** ⌂ 10.50/21.00 **st.**

AY **x**

↑ **Rowans,** 290 London Rd, LE2 2AG, ☏ 705364, 🛲 – 🍴 **P**. 🔊
closed 24 December-2 January – **15 rm** ⌂ 14.00/22.00 **st.**

AY **i**

at Rothley N : 5 m. by A 6 – AX – on B 5328 – ✉ ☺ 0533 Leicester :

🏨 **Rothley Court** (Best Western), Westfield Lane, LE7 7LG, W : ½ m. on B 5328 ☏ 374141,
Telex 341995, ≼, « Part 12C house and chapel », 🛲 – 📺 **P**. 🔌 🔊 🅰🅴 ⓪ 𝗩𝗜𝗦𝗔
closed 25 and 26 December – **M** (closed Saturday lunch, Sunday dinner and Bank Holidays to
non-residents) 9.50/12.55 **s.** ⬧ 7.60 – **34 rm** ⌂ 34.50/42.00 – SB (weekends only) 58.30 **st.**

↑ **Rothley,** 35 Mount Sorrel Lane, LE7 7PS, ☏ 302531 – **P**. 🛇
10 rm ⌂ 11.00/21.50.

at Oadby SE : 3 ¼ m. by A 6 on A 5096 – AY – ⊠ 🕲 0533 Leicester :

🏨 **Leicestershire Moat House** (Q.M.H.), Wigston Rd, LE2 5QE, ℰ 719441 – 📳 📺 ⇔wc🅿️
🅿️ 🚗 🔼 🆎 ⓪ 𝗩𝗜𝗦𝗔
M *(closed Saturday lunch)* 6.50/7.50 t. ╢ 2.65 – **29 rm** ⊊ 33.00/41.00 t. – SB (weekends only) 42.00/48.00 **st.**

at Whetstone S : 5 ½ m. by A 426 – AZ – ⊠ – 🕲 0533 Leicester :

💥 **Old Vicarage,** 123 Enderby Rd, LE8 3JH, ℰ 771195 – 🅿️
closed Saturday lunch, Sunday and Bank Holidays – **M** a la carte 7.60/11.45 ╢ 2.25.

at Braunstone SW : 2 m. on A 46 – ⊠ 🕲 0533 Leicester :

🏨 **Post House** (T.H.F.), Braunstone Lane East, LE3 2FW, ℰ 896688, Telex 341009 – 📳 📺
⇔wc 🅿️ 🛆 🅿️ 🚗 🔼 🆎 ⓪ 𝗩𝗜𝗦𝗔
M 6.95/8.95 **st.** ╢ 2.85 – ⊊ 5.00 – **172 rm** 35.50/42.50 **st.**   AY u

at Narborough SW : 6 m. by A 46 – AZ – on B 4114 – ⊠ 🕲 0533 Leicester :

🏚 **Charnwood,** 48 Leicester Rd, LE9 5DF, ℰ 862218, 🚗 – 📺 ⇔wc 🅿️ 🔼 🛠
closed 26 December-2 January – **M** *(closed Saturday lunch, Sunday dinner and Bank Holidays)*
4.35/8.95 t. ╢ 2.30 – **23 rm** ⊊ 17.50/29.00 t.

at Leicester Forest East W : 3 m. on A 47 – AY – ⊠ 🕲 0533 Leicester :

🏨 **Leicester Forest Moat House** (Q.M.H.), Hinckley Rd, LE3 3GH, ℰ 394661 – 📺 ⇔wc 🅿️
🅿️ 🚗 🔼 🆎 𝗩𝗜𝗦𝗔
closed 25 to 31 December – **M** (bar lunch Saturday) a la carte 9.40/11.15 **st.** ╢ 2.75 – **30 rm**
⊊ 33.00/38.00 **st.** – SB (weekends only) 45.00 **st.**

ALFA-ROMEO   2 Saxby St. ℰ 543300
AUDI, VW   Dover St. ℰ 556262
AUSTIN-ROVER   Leicester Rd ℰ 881601
AUSTIN-ROVER   Parker Drive ℰ 352587
AUSTIN-ROVER   Stoughton Drive North ℰ 736362
AUSTIN-ROVER   60/62 North Gate St. ℰ 28612
CITROEN   135/137 Queens St ℰ 709523
CITROEN, SUZUKI   Lee Circle ℰ 25285
FIAT, LANCIA, VW-AUDI   47 Blackbird Rd ℰ 52137
FORD   Belgrave Gate ℰ 50111
FORD   Welford Rd ℰ 706215
HONDA   7 Pike St. ℰ 56281

LADA   Uppingham Rd ℰ 418544
NISSAN   Abbey Lane ℰ 666861
NISSAN   Conduit St. ℰ 544301
PEUGEOT, TALBOT   Stoneygate Rd ℰ 700521
PORSCHE, ALFA-ROMEO   Coventry Rd at Narborough ℰ 848270
RENAULT, ROLLS ROYCE   Welford Rd ℰ 548757
TALBOT   91 Abbey Lane ℰ 61501
VAUXHALL-OPEL   Evington ℰ 730421
VAUXHALL-OPEL   Aylestone Rd ℰ 547515
VOLVO   459 Aylestone Rd ℰ 831052

LEIGH Greater Manchester 402 403 404 M 23 – pop. 46,181 – ECD : Wednesday – 🕲 0942.
🖼 Kenyon Hall, Culcheth ℰ 092 576 (Culcheth) 3130, S : by A 574.
◆London 205 – ◆Liverpool 25 – ◆Manchester 12 – Preston 25.

🏨 **Greyhound** (Embassy), Warrington Rd, WN7 3XQ, S : 1 m. at junction A 580 and A 574
ℰ 671256 – 📳 📺 ⇔wc 🅿️ 🛆 🅿️ 🚗 🔼 🆎 ⓪ 𝗩𝗜𝗦𝗔 🛠
M *(closed Sunday dinner)* 6.95 **st.** ╢ 4.50 – ⊊ 4.25 – **56 rm** 35.50/40.50 **st.** – SB (weekends only) 36.00/42.00 **st.**

AUSTIN-ROVER   Wigan Rd ℰ 676236
FIAT   Small Brook Lane, Atherton ℰ 882201
FORD   Brown St. Nth ℰ 673401

NISSAN   39 Plank Lane ℰ 673334
VAUXHALL-OPEL   Wigan Rd ℰ 602931
VAUXHALL-OPEL   196 Chapel St. ℰ 671326

LENWADE-GREAT WITCHINGHAM Norfolk 404 X 25 – ECD : Wednesday – ⊠ Norwich –
🕲 060 544 Great Witchingham – ◆London 121 – Fakenham 14 – ◆Norwich 10.

🏠 **Lenwade House** 🏊, Fakenham Rd, NR9 5QP, ℰ 288, ≼, 🏊 heated, 🎣, 🚗, park, 🎾,
squash – 📺 ⇔wc 🎞wc 🅿️ 🔼 🆎 ⓪ 𝗩𝗜𝗦𝗔
M a la carte 8.50/11.25 t. – ⊊ 3.00 – **13 rm** 21.80/30.75 t. – SB (winter only) 44.00 **st.**

LEOMINSTER Heref. and Worc. 403 L 27 – pop. 7,079 – ECD : Thursday – 🕲 0568.
See : Priory Church★ 14C (the north aisle★ 12C) – **Envir. :** Berrington Hall★ (Georgian) AC, N : 3 m. – Croft Castle★ (15C) AC, NW : 6 m.
🅱 3 The Grange ℰ 2291 ext 212 – ◆London 141 – ◆Birmingham 47 – Hereford 13 – Worcester 26.

🏠 **Talbot** (Best Western), West St., HR6 8EP, ℰ 2121 – 📺 ⇔wc 🎞wc 🅿️ 🛆 🔼 🆎 𝗩𝗜𝗦𝗔
M 7.50/8.50 t. ╢ 2.80 – **31 rm** ⊊ 24.50/39.50 t. – SB 51.00/54.00 st.

🏠 **Royal Oak,** South St., HR6 8JA, ℰ 2610 – 📺 ⇔wc 🅿️ 🔼 🆎 ⓪ 𝗩𝗜𝗦𝗔
M a la carte 6.60/11.95 **st.** ╢ 2.90 – **16 rm** ⊊ 20.00/45.00 **st.** – SB (weekends only) 36.00/54.00 **st.**

AUSTIN-ROVER   South St. ℰ 2545
FORD   3-4 Etnam St. ℰ 2060

RENAULT   West St. ℰ 2562
TALBOT, VAUXHALL-OPEL   The Bargates ℰ 2337

LETCHWORTH Herts. 404 T 28 – pop. 27,150 – ECD : Wednesday – 🕲 046 26.
◆London 40 – Bedford 22 – ◆Cambridge 22 – Luton 14.

🏨 **Letchworth Hall** 🏊, Letchworth Lane, SG6 3NP, S : 1 m. by A 505 ℰ 693747, ≼, Dancing
(Saturday), 🚗 – 📺 ⇔wc 🅿️ 🛠 – **44 rm**

🏨 **Broadway,** The Broadway, SG6 3NZ, ℰ 5651 – 📳 📺 ⇔wc 🅿️ 🅿️ 🛆 🔼 🆎 ⓪ 𝗩𝗜𝗦𝗔
closed 1 week at Christmas – **M** (bar lunch) (carving rest.) 6.10 t. ╢ 2.40 – **37 rm** ⊊ 25.00/36.00 t.

AUSTIN-ROVER   Works Rd ℰ 73161
FORD   18/22 Station Rd ℰ 3722

HONDA   Norton Way North ℰ 78191
VW, AUDI   Norton Way North ℰ 6341

LEWES East Sussex **404** U 31 – pop. 14,159 – ECD : Wednesday – ✆ 079 16 (4 and 5 fig.) or 0273(6 fig.).

See : Norman Castle (ruins) site and ≼★, 45 steps, *AC* – Anne of Cleves' House (1559) *AC*.

Envir. : Glynde Place (pictures★) *AC*, E : 3 ½ m. – Firle Place★ (mansion 15C-16C) *AC*, SE : 4 ½ m. – Ditchling Beacon ≼★ W : 7 ½ m. – Glyndebourne Opera Festival (May-August) *AC*, E : 3 m..

🔝 Chapel Hill ℰ 3245, Opp. Junction Cliffe High/South St.

🛈 Lewes House, 32 High St. ℰ 71600.

♦London 53 – Brighton 8 – Hastings 29 – Maidstone 43.

🏨 **Shelleys (Mt. Charlotte)**, High St., BN7 1XS, ℰ 2361, ☞ – 📺 ⌂wc ╗wc ☜ 🅿. ☒ 🆎 ⓞ **VISA**
21 rm ⊇ 35.75/57.75 **st.** – SB (weekends only)(except summer) 48.50 **st.**

✗✗ **Trumps**, 19-20 Station St., BN7 2DB, ℰ 473906 – ☒ 🆎 ⓞ **VISA**
closed Monday and 26 to 30 December – **M** a la carte 8.70/15.15 **t.** ♟ 3.50.

✗ **Kenwards**, Pipe Passage, 151a High St., BN7 1XU, ℰ 472343 – 🆎
closed Saturday lunch, Sunday, Monday, 1 week spring and 1 week November – **M** (lunch by arrangement) a la carte 9.55/12.00 **st.**

✗ **Pelham Arms (Sussex Kitchen)**, High St., St. Annes' Hill, BN7 1XL, ℰ 6149 – 🅿
closed Sunday, Monday and Bank Holidays – **M** a la carte 5.60/7.30 **t.** ♟ 2.05.

AUSTIN-ROVER Brooks Rd ℰ 3186
BMW Western Rd ℰ 3221

FORD Station St. ℰ 4461
RENAULT 96/106 Malling St. ℰ 77131

LEYBURN North Yorks. **402** O 21 – pop. 1,680 – ECD : Wednesday – ✆ 0677 Bedale.

🛈 Commercial Sq. ℰ 0969 (Wensleydale) 23069 (summer only).

♦London 248 – Kendal 43 – ♦Leeds 54 – York 47.

✗ **Wyvill Arms**, Constable Burton, E : 3 ½ m. by A 684 ℰ 50581 – 🅿
M (bar lunch) a la carte 7.90/11.50 **t.** ♟ 2.75.

LEYLAND Lancs. **402** L 22 – pop. 14,000 – ECD : Wednesday – ✆ 077 44.

♦London 220 – ♦Liverpool 31 – ♦Manchester 32 – Preston 6.

🏨 **Ladbroke (Ladbroke)**, Leyland Way, PR5 2JX, E : ¾ m. on B 5256 ℰ 22922, Telex 677651 – 📺 ⌂wc ☎ ♟ 🅿. ☒
93 rm.

AUSTIN-ROVER Preston Rd ℰ 52311
FORD Towngate ℰ 21766

PEUGEOT, TALBOT Golden Hill Lane ℰ 23416
SKODA Wigan Rd ℰ 21546

LICHFIELD Staffs. **402 403 404** O 25 – pop. 22,660 – ECD : Wednesday – ✆ 054 32.

See : Cathedral★★ 12C-14C.

🛈 9 Breadmarket St. ℰ 52109.

♦London 128 – ♦Birmingham 16 – Derby 23 – ♦Stoke-on-Trent 30.

🏨 **George (Embassy)**, Bird St., WS13 6PR, ℰ 58822 – 📺 ⌂wc ╗wc ☎ 🅿. ♟ ☒ ☒ ⓞ **VISA**. ✽
M 6.75/7.75 **st.** ♟ 4.35 – ⊇ 4.25 – **40 rm** 29.50/38.00 **st.** – SB (weekends only) 43.00/49.00 **st.**

🏨 **Swan (Embassy)** without rest., Bird St., WS13 6PW, ℰ 55851 – 📺 ⌂wc ☜ 🅿. ♟ ☒ ☒
ⓞ **VISA**. ✽
closed Friday, Saturday and Sunday – ⊇ 4.25 – **31 rm** 28.50/37.50 **st.**

🏨 **Little Barrow**, Beacon St., WS13 7AR, ℰ 53311 – 📺 ⌂wc ☜ 🅿. ☒ 🆎 ⓞ **VISA**. ✽
M *(closed Sunday dinner)* 5.50/8.00 **t.** ♟ 3.25 – **24 rm** ⊇ 28.75/36.80 **t.**

🏛 **Oakleigh House**, 25 St. Chad's Rd, WS13 7LZ, ℰ 22688, ☞ – 📺 ⌂wc ╗wc 🅿. ✽
closed 2 weeks at Christmas – **M** *(closed Sunday and Monday)* (dinner only) 12.00 **t.** ♟ 3.00 –
11 rm ⊇ 16.00/30.00 **st.**

🏛 **Angel Croft**, 3 Beacon St., WS13 7AA, ℰ 23147, ☞ – 📺 ╗wc 🅿. ☒ **VISA**. ✽
closed 25 and 26 December – **M** *(closed Sunday dinner)* 9.00/9.50 **st.** ♟ 2.80 – **13 rm**
⊇ 21.50/42.00 **st.**

⌂ **Gaialands** ✈, 9 Gaiafields Rd, off Bulldog Lane, WS13 7LT, ℰ 23764, ☞ – 🅿. ✽
5 rm ⊇ 10.50/17.00 **st.**

✗✗ **Champs Elysées**, Minster House, Minster Pool Walk, ℰ 53788, French rest. – ☒ **VISA**
closed lunch Saturday and Monday and Sunday dinner – **M** a la carte 12.50/21.60 **t.** ♟ 3.50.

✗ Thrales, 40-44 Tamworth St. (corner of Backcester Lane), ℰ 55091.

AUSTIN-ROVER St. John St. ℰ 51451
FORD Birmingham Rd. ℰ 53566

MAZDA Birmingham Rd ℰ 53571

LIFTON Devon **403** H 32 – pop. 820 – ECD : Tuesday – ✆ 0566.

🔝 Launceston, St. Stephen ℰ 0566 (Launceston) 3442, W : 5 m.

♦London 238 – Bude 24 – Exeter 37 – Launceston 4 – ♦Plymouth 32.

🏨 **Arundell Arms (Best Western)**, Fore St., PL16 0AA, on A 30 ℰ 84666, ⬔, ☞ – 📺 ⌂wc
╗wc ☎ 🅿. ☒ 🆎 ⓞ **VISA**
closed 6 days at Christmas – **M** 7.25/12.00 **st.** ♟ 3.25 – **27 rm** ⊇ 21.00/49.00 **st.** – SB
56.00/68.00 **st.**

LILLIPUT Dorset – see Poole.

LIMPSFIELD Surrey 404 U 30 – pop. 2,350 – ⊠ ✪ 088 33 Oxted.
◆London 24 – ◆Brighton 40 – Maidstone 25.

XX ✿ **Old Lodge,** High St., RH8 0DR, ☎ 2996 – ℗ 🔄 AE ⓪ VISA
closed Saturday lunch, Sunday dinner, Monday and first 2 weeks January – **M** 16.25/18.50 **st.**
♦ 3.75
Spec. Quenelles de St. Pierre aux poivres roses, Les abats, Soufflé glacé à la crème de cacao.

Benachrichtigen Sie sofort das Hotel,
wenn Sie ein bestelltes Zimmer nicht belegen können.

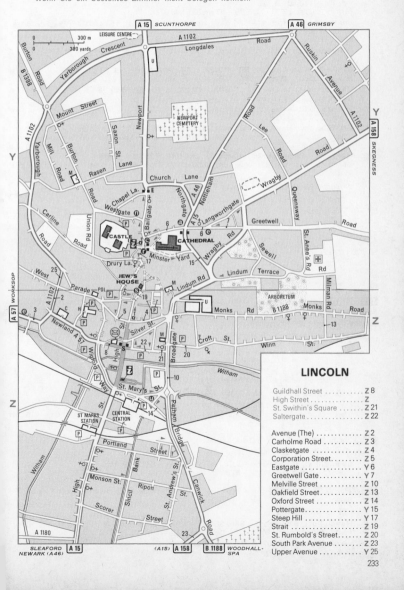

LINCOLN

LINCOLN Lincs. 402 404 S 24 – pop. 74,269 – ECD : Wednesday – ✪ 0522.

See : Cathedral★★★ 11C-15C (Angel Choir★★, Library : Magna Carta *AC*) Y – Jew's House★★ 12C Y – Castle★ (11C) *AC* Y – Newport Arch★ (Roman) Y E – Stonebow and Guildhall★ 15C-16C Z S.

Envir. : Doddington Hall★ (Elizabethan) *AC*, SW : 7 m. by A 15 Z and A 46.

🚉 Carholme 🖉 23725, 1 m. from town centre.

✈ Humberside Airport : 🖉 0652 (Barnetby) 688456, N : 32 m. by A 15 Y.

🛈 9 Castle Hill 🖉 29828 – 21 The Cornhill 🖉 32151 ext 505/6.

♦London 140 – Bradford 81 – ♦Cambridge 94 – ♦Kingston-upon-Hull 44 – ♦Leeds 73 – ♦Leicester 53 – ♦Norwich 104 – ♦Nottingham 38 – ♦Sheffield 48 – York 82.

Plan on preceding page

🏰 **White Hart** (T.H.F.), Bailgate, LN1 3AR, 🖉 26222, Telex 56304, « Antique furniture » – 🛗 📺 ⟲ 🅿 🔥 🔼 🆎 ⓪ *VISA*   Y **c**
M 6.75/10.00 **st.** ﹐ 3.00 – ⟷ 5.75 – **57 rm** 38.50/48.00 **st.**

🏰 **Eastgate Post House** (T.H.F.), Eastgate, LN2 1PN, 🖉 20341, Telex 56316 – 🛗 📺 ♿ 🅿 🔥 🔼 🆎 ⓪ *VISA*   Y **a**
M 6.75/7.55 **st.** ﹐ 2.85 – ⟷ 5.25 – **71 rm** 38.00/45.50 **st.**

🏠 **D'Isney Place** without rest., Eastgate, LN2 4AA, 🖉 38881, 🌳 – 📺 ⟶wc ☎ 🔼   Y **e**
12 rm ⟷ 27.50/37.50 **t.**

🏠 **Grand,** St. Mary's St., LN5 7EP, 🖉 24211 – 📺 ⟶wc ⟦wc ☎ 🅿 🔼 🆎 ⓪ *VISA*   Z **u**
M 5.80/7.00 **st.** – **49 rm** ⟷ 27.00/40.00 **st.** – SB (weekends only) 23.00 **st.**

🏠 **Castle,** Westgate, LN1 3AS, 🖉 38801 – 📺 ⟶wc ⟦wc 🅿 🔼 🆎 ⓪ *VISA*   Y **n**
M 8.50 **st.** – **21 rm** ⟷ 26.50/37.50 **st.** – SB 35.00/40.00 **st.**

🏠 **Hollies,** 65 Carholme Rd, LN1 1RT, 🖉 22419 – 🅿   Z **e**
12 rm ⟷ 12.50/22.00 **st.**

XX **White's,** Jews House, 15 The Strait, LN2 1JD, 🖉 24851, « 12C town house » – 🔼 🆎   YZ **s**
closed Monday lunch, Sunday, 1 week at Christmas and Bank Holidays – **M** (booking essential) a la carte 11.80/17.75 **t.**

XX **Harveys,** 1 Exchequer Gate, Castle Sq., LN2 1LU, 🖉 21886 – 🔼 *VISA*   Y **r**
closed Saturday lunch January-April, Sunday and 1 to 4 January – **M** a la carte 5.65/7.95 **t.** ﹐ 2.75.

at North Hykeham SW : 3 ½ m. by A 15 – Z – on A 46 – ✉ ✪ 0522 Lincoln :

🏠 Loudor, 37 Newark Rd, LN6 8RB, 🖉 680333 – ⟦wc 🅿 🍴 – **12 rm**.

MICHELIN Branch, Tritton Rd, LN6 7RX, 🖉 684023

AUSTIN-ROVER   Outer Circle Rd. 🖉 35771
AUSTIN-ROVER-DAIMLER-JAGUAR-LAND ROVER
St. Rumbold St. 🖉 27117
BMW   South Park Av. 🖉 21345
CITROEN   300 Wragby Rd 🖉 31195
FORD   Wragby Rd 🖉 30101
HONDA, LANCIA   Wragby Rd 🖉 31735
LADA, COLT   Newark Rd 🖉 20216
MAZDA   Newark Rd, North Hykeham 🖉 618242

RENAULT   134 High St. 🖉 21252
NISSAN   148 Newark Rd 🖉 42281
SAAB   247 Lincoln Rd 🖉 681463
TALBOT, PEUGEOT   477 High St. 🖉 29131
TOYOTA   Newark Rd 🖉 692805
VAUXHALL   Wragby Rd 🖉 27127
VOLVO   314 Wragby Rd 🖉 29462/3
VW, AUDI   223 Newark Rd 🖉 31881

LISKEARD Cornwall 403 G 32 The West Country G. – pop. 5,930 – ECD : Wednesday – ✪ 0579.

See : Church★.

♦London 261 – Exeter 59 – ♦Plymouth 18 – Truro 37.

🏠 **Country Castle** ⟨, Station Rd, PL14 4EB, SW : ¾ m. by B 3254 🖉 42694, 🔥, 🌳 – 📺 ⟶wc ⟦wc ☎ 🅿 🔼 *VISA*
closed 1 to 20 November – **M** (bar lunch) 8.50 **t.** ﹐ 2.75 – **11 rm** ⟷ 19.00/38.50 **t.** – SB (except summer) 39.00/48.00 **st.**

🏠 **Lord Eliot,** Castle St., PL14 3AU, 🖉 42717 – ⟶wc ⟦wc 🅿
M (restricted lunch) a la carte 5.70/11.00 **st.** ﹐ 2.60 – **16 rm** ⟷ 15.50/27.50 **st.**

at St. Keyne S : 3 ½ m. on B 3254 – ✉ ✪ 0579 Liskeard :

🏠 **Old Rectory** ⟨, PL14 4RL, 🖉 42617, 🌳 – ⟦wc 🅿 🔼 *VISA*
March-October – **M** (bar lunch)(booking essential for non-residents) 8.50 **t.** – **9 rm** ⟷ 13.00/44.50 **t.**

LISS Hants. 404 R 30 – pop. 5,094 – ✪ 0730.

♦London 57 – ♦Portsmouth 22 – Reading 34.

XX **Le Papillon,** 94 Station Rd., GU33 7AQ, 🖉 893363 – 🔼 🆎 ⓪ *VISA*
closed Sunday and Monday – **M** (lunch by arrangement) 13.00 **t.** ﹐ 2.50.

LITTLE HAVEN Dyfed 403 E 28 – pop. 150 – ECD : Thursday – ✉ Haverfordwest – ✪ 043 783 Broad Haven.

♦London 258 – Haverfordwest 8.

🏠 **Haven Fort,** Settlands Hill, SA62 3LA, 🖉 401, ⬗ St. Brides Bay, 🌳 – ⟶wc ⟦wc 🅿 ⟨
March-mid October – **M** (bar lunch) 8.95 **t.** ﹐ 4.00 – **15 rm** ⟷ 16.50/34.00 **t.**

🏠 **Pendyffryn,** SA62 3LA, 🖉 337, ⬗ – 📺 🅿 ⟨
May-mid October – **7 rm** ⟷ 10.00/16.00.

234

LITTLE KELYNACK Cornwall – see St. Just.

LITTLE LANGDALE Cumbria 402 K 20 – see Ambleside.

LITTLEOVER Derbs. 402 403 404 P 25 – see Derby.

LITTLE THORNTON Lancs. 402 L 22 – see Blackpool.

LITTLE WEIGHTON Humberside 402 S 22 – see Kingston-upon-Hull.

LITTLE WYMONDLEY Herts. 404 T 28 – see Hitchin.

LIVERPOOL Merseyside 402 403 L 23 – pop. 610,113 – ECD : Wednesday – ✆ 051.

See : Walker Art Gallery★★ CY M1 – City of Liverpool Museums★ CY M2 – Anglican Cathedral★ (1904) CZ A – Roman Catholic Cathedral★ (1967) DZ B – **Envir. :** Knowsley Safari Park★★ AC, NE : 8 m. by A 57 BX – Speke Hall★ (16C) AC, SE : 7 m. by A 561 BX.

🏌 Dunnings Bridge Rd, Bootle ℰ 928 6196, N : 5 m. by A 5036 AV – 🏌 Allerton Park ℰ 428 1046, S : 5 m. by B 5180 BX – 🏌 Childwall, Naylor's Rd, Gateacre ℰ 487 9982, E : 7 m. by 5178 BX.

✈ Liverpool Airport : ℰ 494 0066, Telex 629323, SE : 6 m. by A 561 BX – **Terminal :** Pier Head and Lime St.

🚢 to Ireland (Dublin) (B & I Line) 1 nightly (8 h 45 mn) – to Belfast (Belfast Car Ferries) 1 daily (9 h) – to the Isle of Man : Douglas (Isle of Man Steam Packet Co.) 1-5 daily (4 h 15 mn).

🚢 to Birkenhead (Merseyside Transport) frequent services daily (7-8 mn) – to Wallasey (Merseyside Transport) frequent services daily (7-8 mn).

🛈 29 Lime St. ℰ 709 3631 and 8681.

♦London 219 – ♦Birmingham 102 – ♦Leeds 75 – ♦Manchester 35.

Town plans : Liverpool pp. 2-5

🏨 **Holiday Inn,** Paradise St., L1 8JD, ℰ 709 0181, Telex 627270, ⊠ – 🛗 🖳 📺 ☎ 🕭 🅿 🏧 📼
CZ **n**
AE ① VISA
M 5.00/7.50 t. – **258 rm** ⊆ 45.00/60.00 st. – SB (weekends only) 50.00 st.

🏨 **Atlantic Tower Thistle** (Thistle), 30 Chapel St., L3 9RE, ℰ 227 4444, Telex 627070, ← – 🛗
CY **r**
📺 ☎ 🅿 🏧 🔊 AE ① VISA ⚓
M 8.00/12.00 🍷 3.45 – ⊆ 5.25 – **226 rm** 45.00/66.00 st. – SB (weekends only) 54.00 st.

🏨 **St. George's** (T.H.F.), St. John's Precinct, Lime St., L1 1NQ, ℰ 709 7090, Telex 627630 – 🛗
CY **v**
📺 🕭 🏧 🔊 AE ① VISA
M (carving rest.) 5.95/7.95 st. 🍷 2.60 – ⊆ 5.50 – **155 rm** 37.50/48.00 st.

🏨 **Crest** (Crest), Lord Nelson St., L3 5QB, ℰ 709 7050, Telex 627954 – 🛗 📺 ⇌wc ☎ 🅿 🏧
CY **i**
🔊 AE ① VISA ⚓
M approx. 11.00 st. – ⊆ 5.25 – **160 rm** 40.00/51.00 st.

🏨 **Green Park,** 4-6 Green Bank Drive, L17 1AN, SE : 2 ½ m. by A 562 ℰ 733 3382, ⚖ – 📺 ⇌
BX **u**
🍴wc ⚏ 🅿 🔊 AE VISA
M 7.50 st. 🍷 2.00 – **24 rm** ⊆ 16.50/28.00.

XXX Ristorante del Secolo, First Floor, 36-40 Stanley St., L2 6AL, ℰ 236 4004, Italian rest. CY **x**
closed Saturday, Sunday and 2 weeks August.

XXX **Oriel,** 14 Water St., L2 8TH, ℰ 236 4664 – 🔊 AE ① VISA CY **s**
closed Saturday lunch, Sunday and Bank Holidays – **M** a la carte 10.70/26.25 st. 🍷 3.15.

XXX **Churchill's,** Churchill House, Tithebarn St., L2 2PB, ℰ 227 3877. 🔊 AE ① VISA CY **a**
closed Saturday lunch, Sunday and Bank Holidays – **M** a la carte 10.20/14.60 t. 🍷 2.50.

XX **Jenny's Seafood,** Old Ropery, Fenwick St., L2 7NT, ℰ 236 0332, Seafood – 🔊 AE ① VISA
closed Saturday lunch, Monday dinner, Sunday and Bank Holidays – **M** a la carte 8.95/13.75 t.
🍷 2.50. CZ **e**

at Bootle N : 5 m. by A 565 – AV – ⊠ ✆ 051 Liverpool :

🏨 **Park,** Park Lane West, L30 3SU, on A 5036 ℰ 525 7555, Telex 629772 – 🛗 📺 ⇌wc 🍴wc ⚏
🕭 🅿 🏧 🔊 AE ① VISA
M (buffet lunch) a la carte 8.40/11.95 st. 🍷 3.50 – **60 rm** ⊆ 32.00/40.00 st.

at Waterloo N : 5 ¾ m. by A 565 – ⊠ ✆ 051 Liverpool :

🏨 **Royal,** 30 Bath St., L22 5PS, ℰ 928 2332 – 📺 ⇌wc 🍴wc ⚏ 🅿 AV **a**
20 rm.

at Blundellsands N : 6 ½ m. by A 565 – AV – ⊠ ✆ 051 Liverpool :

🏨 **Blundellsands,** Serpentine, L23 6TN, ℰ 924 6515 – 🛗 📺 ⇌wc ⚏ 🅿 🏧 🔊 AE ① VISA
M 8.50/9.50 st. 🍷 2.60 – **44 rm** ⊆ 25.00/45.00 st. – SB (weekends only) 55.00 st.

at Aigburth SE : 4 m. by A 561 – BX – ⊠ ✆ 051 Liverpool :

🏨 **Grange,** 14 Holmefield Rd, L19 3PG, ℰ 427 2950, ⚏ – 📺 ⇌wc 🅿 🔊 VISA ⚓
M (dinner only and Sunday lunch) 6.50/9.50 t. 🍷 3.00 – **25 rm** ⊆ 19.50/34.50 t.

X **L'Alouette,** 2 Lark Lane, L17, ℰ 727 2142, French rest. BX **n**
closed Sunday and Monday – **M** (dinner only) a la carte 8.60/14.75 t. 🍷 3.00.

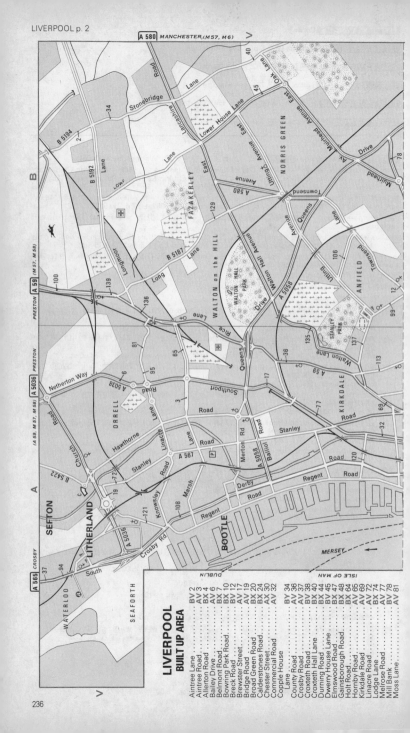

A 580 MANCHESTER, (M57, M6)

LIVERPOOL
BUILT UP AREA

Aintree Lane	BV 2
Aintree Road	AV 3
Allerton Road	AV 4
Bailey Drive	AV 6
Belmont Road	BX 7
Bowring Park Road	BX 10
Breck Road	BV 12
Brewster Street	AV 17
Bridge Road	AV 19
Broad Green Road	BX 20
Calderstones Road	BX 24
Chester Street	AX 30
Commercial Road	AV 32
Copple House	
Lane	BY 34
County Road	AV 36
Crosby Road	AV 37
Croxteth Road	BX 38
Croxteth Hall Lane	BX 40
Durning Road	BX 44
Dwerry House Lane	AV 45
Elmswood Road	BX 47
Gainsborough Road	BX 48
Holt Road	BX 64
Hornby Road	AV 65
Kirkdale Road	AV 69
Linacre Road	AV 72
Lodge Lane	BX 74
Melrose Road	AV 77
Mill Bank	AV 78
Moss Lane	AV 81

236

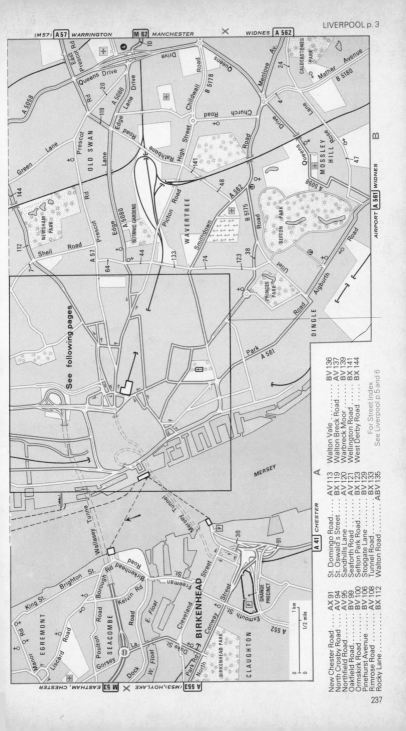

237

LIVERPOOL
CENTRE

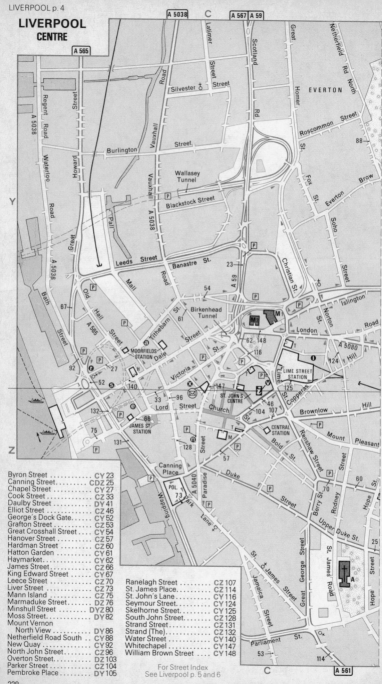

For Street Index
See Liverpool p. 5 and 6

238

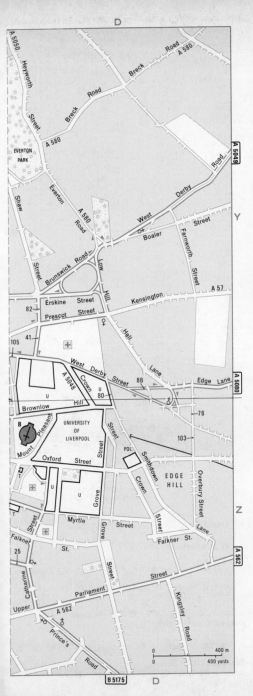

STREET INDEX

Concluded on next page

239

STREET INDEX TO LIVERPOOL TOWN PLANS (concluded)

Hall Lane .... p. 5 **DY**
Hanover St. .... p. 4 **CZ** 57
Hardman St. .... p. 4 **CZ** 60
Hatton Garden .... p. 4 **CY** 61
Haymarket............. p. 4 **CY** 62
Hawthorne Rd.......... p. 2 **AV**
Heyworth St. .... p. 5 **DY**
High St. .... p. 3 **BX**
Holt Rd................ p. 3 **BX** 64
Hope St................ p. 4 **CZ**
Hornby Rd .... p. 2 **AV** 65
Islington.............. p. 4 **CY**
Jamaica St. .... p. 4 **CZ**
James St............... p. 4 **CZ** 66
Kelvin Rd .... p. 3 **AX**
Kensington .... p. 5 **DY**
King St................ p. 3 **AX**
King Edward St. .... p. 4 **CY** 67
Kingsley Rd .... p. 5 **DZ**
Kingsway.............. p. 3 **AX**
Kirkdale Rd .... p. 2 **AV** 69
Knowsley Rd .... p. 2 **AV**
Latimer St............. p. 4 **CY**
Leece St............... p. 4 **CZ** 70
Leeds St. .... p. 4 **CY**
Lime St. .... p. 4 **CY**
Linacre Rd .... p. 2 **AV** 72
Linacre Lane .... p. 2 **AV**
Liscard Rd .... p. 3 **AX**
Liver St. .... p. 4 **CZ** 73
Lodge Lane .... p. 3 **BX** 74
London Rd.............. p. 4 **CY**
Long Lane .... p. 2 **BV**
Longmoor Lane .... p. 2 **BV**
Lord St................ p. 4 **CZ**
Lower House Lane....... p. 2 **BV**
Lower Lane .... p. 2 **BV**
Low Hill .... p. 5 **DY**
Manor Rd............... p. 3 **AX**
Mann Island .... p. 4 **CZ** 75
Marmaduke St........... p. 5 **DZ** 76
Marsh Lane .... p. 2 **AV**
Mather Av.............. p. 3 **BX**
Melrose Rd .... p. 2 **AV** 77
Menlove Av. .... p. 3 **BX**
Merton Rd .... p. 2 **AV**
Mill Bank .... p. 2 **BV** 78
Minshull St............ p. 5 **DY** 80
Moss Lane.............. p. 2 **AV** 81
Moss St................ p. 5 **DY** 82
Mount Pleasant .... p. 4 **CZ**
Mount Vernon
North View .... p. 5 **DY** 86
Muirhead Av. .... p. 2 **BV**
Muirhead Av. E. .... p. 2 **BV**
Myrtle St. .... p. 5 **DZ**
Netherfield Rd N. ..... p. 4 **CY**
Netherfield Rd S. ..... p. 4 **CY** 88
Netherton Way......... p. 2 **AV**
New Chester Rd......... p. 3 **AX** 91
New Quay .... p. 4 **CY** 92
North Crosby Rd........ p. 2 **AV** 94
Northfield Rd .... p. 2 **AV** 95
North John St.......... p. 4 **CZ** 96
Norton St. .... p. 4 **CY**
Oakfield Rd............ p. 2 **BV** 99
Oak Lane .... p. 2 **BV**
Old Hall St. .... p. 4 **CY**
Ormskirk Rd .... p. 2 **BV** 100
Overbury St. .... p. 5 **DZ**
Overton St. .... p. 5 **DZ** 103
Oxford St. .... p. 5 **DZ**
Pall Mall.............. p. 4 **CY**
Paradise St............ p. 4 **CZ**
Parker St.............. p. 4 **CZ** 104
Park Lane.............. p. 4 **CZ**
Park Rd................ p. 3 **AX**
Park Rd North .... p. 3 **AX**
Parliament St.......... p. 4 **CZ**
Pembroke Pl............ p. 5 **DY** 105
Picton Rd.............. p. 3 **BX**
Pinehurst Av........... p. 2 **BV** 106
Poulton Rd............. p. 3 **AX**
Prescot Rd............. p. 3 **BX**
Prescot St............. p. 5 **DY**
Prince's Rd .... p. 5 **DZ**
Queens Drive .... p. 3 **BX**
Queensway.............. p. 3 **AX**
Ranelagh St. .... p. 4 **CZ** 107
Rathbone Rd............ p. 3 **BX**
Regent Rd .... p. 2 **AV**
Renshaw St. .... p. 4 **CZ**
Rice Lane.............. p. 2 **AV**
Rimrose Rd .... p. 2 **AV** 108
Rocky Lane .... p. 3 **BX** 112
Rodney St.............. p. 4 **CZ**
Roscommon St. .... p. 4 **CY**
Rose Lane .... p. 3 **BX**
St. Domingo Rd .... p. 2 **AV** 113
St. James Pl. .... p. 4 **CZ** 114
St. James Rd........... p. 4 **CZ**
St. James St........... p. 4 **CZ**
St. John's Lane........ p. 4 **CY** 116
St. Johns Centre....... p. 4 **CY**
St. Oswald's St. ...... p. 3 **BX** 119
Sandhills Lane .... p. 2 **AV** 120
Scotland Rd .... p. 4 **CY**
Seaforth Rd............ p. 2 **AV** 121
Sefton Park Rd .... p. 3 **BX** 123
Seymour St. .... p. 4 **CY** 124
Shaw St................ p. 5 **DY**
Sheil Rd .... p. 3 **BX**
Silvester St........... p. 4 **CY**
Skelhorne St. .... p. 4 **CY** 125
Smithdown Lane .... p. 5 **DZ**
Smithdown Rd .... p. 3 **BX**
Soho St................ p. 4 **CY**
South Crosby Rd .... p. 2 **AV**
South John St. .... p. 4 **CZ** 128
Southport Rd .... p. 2 **AV**
Stanley Rd............. p. 2 **AV**
Stonebridge Lane ...... p. 2 **BV**
Stopgate Lane .... p. 2 **BV** 129
Strand St.............. p. 4 **CZ** 131
Strand (The) .... p. 4 **CZ** 132
Tithebarn St. .... p. 4 **CY**
Townsend Av............ p. 2 **BV**
Townsend Lane .... p. 2 **BV**
Tunnel Rd .... p. 3 **BX** 133
Ullet Rd .... p. 3 **BX**
Upper Duke St.......... p. 4 **CZ**
Upper Parliament St. .. p. 5 **DZ**
Utting Av.............. p. 2 **BV**
Utting Av. E. .... p. 2 **BV**
Vauxhall Rd............ p. 4 **CY**
Victoria St............ p. 4 **CY**
Walton Lane .... p. 2 **AV**
Walton Rd .... p. 2 **AV** 135
Walton Vale............ p. 2 **BV** 136
Walton Breck Rd .... p. 2 **AV** 137
Walton Hall Av......... p. 2 **BV**
Wapping .... p. 4 **CZ**
Warbreck Moor .... p. 2 **BV** 139
Water St. .... p. 4 **CY** 140
Waterloo Rd .... p. 4 **CY**
Wellington Rd.......... p. 3 **BX** 141
West Derby Rd .... p. 3 **BX** 144
West Derby St. .... p. 5 **DY**
Whitechapel .... p. 4 **CY** 147
William Brown St. ..... p. 4 **CY** 148

ALFA-ROMEO Prescot Rd ☏ 259 1303
AUSTIN-ROVER 72/74 Coronation Rd ☏ 924 6411
AUSTIN-ROVER 84/88 Rose Lane ☏ 724 2377
AUSTIN-ROVER Edge Lane ☏ 228 4737
BMW Scotland Rd ☏ 207 7213
CITROEN Speke Rd ☏ 427 6464
CITROEN 607 West Derby Rd ☏ 228 3670
FIAT East Prescot Rd ☏ 228 9151
FORD Linacre Lane ☏ 922 0070
FORD Prescot St. ☏ 260 9898
FORD Speke Hall Rd ☏ 486 2233
HONDA Berry St. ☏ 709 4207
LADA Prescot Rd ☏ 259 1303
NISSAN Coronation Rd ☏ 924 6575
PEUGEOT-TALBOT Edge Lane ☏ 924 4210
RENAULT, NISSAN Queen's Drive ☏ 523 9779
SAAB 574 Aigburth Rd ☏ 427 3500
SKODA Dorning Rd ☏ 263 7374
TOYOTA Gale Rd ☏ 546 8228
TOYOTA 1 Aigburth Rd ☏ 727 2204
VAUXHALL-OPEL 215 Knowsley Rd ☏ 922 7585
VAUXHALL-OPEL Speke Hall Rd ☏ 486 8846
VAUXHALL-OPEL Derby Rd ☏ 933 7575
VOLVO Fox St. ☏ 207 4364
VW, AUDI Moor Lane, Thornton ☏ 931 2861
VW, AUDI Edge Lane ☏ 228 0919
YUGO Longmoor Lane ☏ 523 3699

To go a long way quickly, use ***Michelin maps*** *at a scale of 1:1 000 000.*

LIVERSEDGE West Yorks. **402** O 22 – ☎ **0924 Heckmondwike.**

♦London 197 – Bradford 7 – ♦Leeds 9 – ♦Manchester 37.

XX **Lillibet's** with rm, Ashfield House, 64 Leeds Rd, WF15 6HX, ☏ **404911**, – TV wc wc ☎ P. AE VISA.
closed 2 weeks August, 25 December-2 January and Bank Holidays – **M** *(closed Sunday)* (dinner only) 9.00/11.95 **t.** 3.00 – **6 rm** 23.50/45.00 **t.**

LIZARD Cornwall **403** E 34 **The West Country G.** – **pop. 1,000** – ☎ **0326 The Lizard.**

See : Lizard Peninsula★★ – Envir. : Kynance Cove★★★, NW : 1 ½ m.

♦London 326 – Penzance 24 – Truro 29.

Housel Bay, Housel Cove, TR12 7PG, ☏ **290417**, < Housel Cove, – wc wc P. AE
M (bar lunch) 9.00 **st.** 2.60 – **22 rm** 18.00/44.00 **st.**

Park Brawse House, Penmenner Rd, TR12 7NR, ☏ **290466**, <, – P
March-October – **6 rm** 10.00/19.00.

LLANARMON DYFFRYN CEIRIOG Clwyd 402 403 K 25 – pop. 161 – ✉ Llangollen – ☎ 069 176.
♦London 196 – Chester 33 – Shrewsbury 32.

   ⋔ **West Arms**, LL20 7LD, 🎱 665, 🔌, 🚗 – 🛏wc ⋔ 🅿. 🔁 🆎 ① 𝘝𝘐𝘚𝘈 🏊
     M (bar lunch Monday to Saturday) 7.50/8.50 **st.** 🍴 2.90 – **13 rm** 🛏 16.50/36.00 **t.**

   ⋔ **Hand**, LL20 7LD, 🎱 666, 🔌, 🚗, 🍴 – 🛏wc 🅿. 🔁 𝘝𝘐𝘚𝘈
     M (bar lunch Monday to Saturday) 7.95/10.50 **t.** – **14 rm** 🛏 23.00/40.00 **t.** – SB 55.00 **st.**

LLANBEDR Gwynedd 402 403 H 25 – pop. 379 – ☎ 034 123.
♦London 262 – Holyhead 54 – Shrewsbury 100.

   ⋔ **Pensarn Hall** 🦢, LL45 2HS, N : ¾ m. on A 496 🎱 236, ≤, 🚗 – 📺 🛏wc 🅿. 🏊
     M (dinner only) 7.50 **st.** 🍴 2.00 – **7 rm** 🛏 12.00/28.00 **st.**

   ⌂ **Ty Mawr** 🦢, LL45 2PX, 🎱 440, 🚗 – 📺 🛏wc ⋔wc 🅿
     M a la carte 7.40/11.75 **t.** – **10 rm** 🛏 13.00/32.00 **t.**

LLANBEDR PONT STEFFAN = Lampeter.

LLANBERIS Gwynedd 403 H 24 – pop. 2,044 – ☎ 0286.
♦London 243 – Caernarfon 7 – Chester 65 – Shrewsbury 78.

   ⌂ **Pen y Gwryd** 🦢, Nant Gwynant, LL55 4NT, SE : 6 m. via Pass of Llanberis 🎱 870211, ≤ –
     🅿
     closed mid November-1 January and weekends only January-February – **M** (buffet lunch) 7.50
     🍴 2.25 – **21 rm** 🛏 9.90/10.90.

   ✗ **Y Bistro**, 45 High St., LL55 4EU, 🎱 871278 – 🔁 🆎 ① 𝘝𝘐𝘚𝘈
     M (closed Sunday and 3 weeks January) (dinner only) (booking essential) 12.50 **t.**

LLANDEILO Dyfed 403 I 28 – pop. 1,799 – ECD : Thursday – ☎ 0558.
Envir. : Talley (abbey and lakes★) N : 7 m.
🏌 Glynhir, Llandybie nr. Ammanford 🎱 0269 (Llandybie) 850472.
♦London 218 – Brecon 34 – Carmarthen 15 – ♦Swansea 25.

   🏨 **Cawdor Arms**, Rhosmaen St., SA19 6EN, 🎱 823500, « Tasteful decor » – 📺 🛏wc ⋔wc
     🐾 🅿. 🔁 🆎 ① 𝘝𝘐𝘚𝘈
     M (closed Sunday dinner) approx. 13.50 **t.** 🍴 3.75 – **18 rm** 🛏 27.50/45.00 **t.** – SB 52.00/55.00 **st.**

     at Rhosmaen N : 1 m. on A 40 – ✉ ☎ 0558 Llandeilo :

   ✗ **Plough Inn**, SA19 6NP, 🎱 823431, Italian rest. – 🅿. 𝘝𝘐𝘚𝘈
     closed Sunday, first week November and Christmas Day – **M** a la carte 8.00/14.25 **t.**

AUSTIN-ROVER   28 Rhosmaen St. 🎱 823221

LLANDEWI SKIRRID Gwent – see Abergavenny.

LLANDOGO Gwent 403 404 L 28 – pop. 290 – ECD : Thursday – ✉ Monmouth – ☎ 0594 Dean.
♦London 140 – ♦Bristol 26 – Gloucester 43 – Newport 25.

   ⋔ **Old Farmhouse**, NP5 4TL, on A 466 🎱 530303 – 📺 🛏wc 🅿. 🔁 🆎 ① 𝘝𝘐𝘚𝘈
     M 4.95/5.95 **st.** 🍴 3.00 – **24 rm** 🛏 16.00/30.00 **st.**

LLANDRILLO-YN-RHOS (RHOS-ON-SEA) Clwyd – see Colwyn Bay.

LLANDRINDOD WELLS Powys 403 J 27 – pop. 4,150 – ECD : Wednesday – ☎ 0597.
🏌 🎱 2010, E : 1 m.
🅱 Rock Park Spa 🎱 4307.
♦London 204 – Brecon 29 – Carmarthen 60 – Shrewsbury 58.

   ⌂ **Griffin Lodge**, Temple St., LD1 5DH, 🎱 2432 – ⋔wc 🅿
     M (bar lunch)(booking essential) 6.00 **t.** 🍴 2.50 – **8 rm** 🛏 10.50/21.00 **t.**

     at Howey S : 1 ½ m. on A 483 – ✉ ☎ 0597 Llandrindod Wells :

   ⋒ **Corven Hall** 🦢, LD1 5RE, S : ½ m. by A 483 on Hundred House rd 🎱 3368, 🚗 – ⋔wc 🅿.
     🏊
     7 rm 🛏 7.50/16.00 **st.**

LLANDUDNO Gwynedd [402] [403] I 24 – pop. 15,890 – ECD : Wednesday except summer – ☎ 0492.

See : Great Orme's Head (≤★★ from the summit) by Ty-Gwyn Rd A – Tour of the Great Orme's Head★★.

⛳18 Rhos-on-Sea Residential, Penryn Bay ☎ 49641 by A 546 B.

[i] Chapel St. ☎ 76413 – Arcadia Theatre ☎ 76413 ext 264 (summer only) – Kiosk, North Promenade ☎ 76572 (summer only).

♦London 243 – Birkenhead 55 – Chester 47 – Holyhead 43.

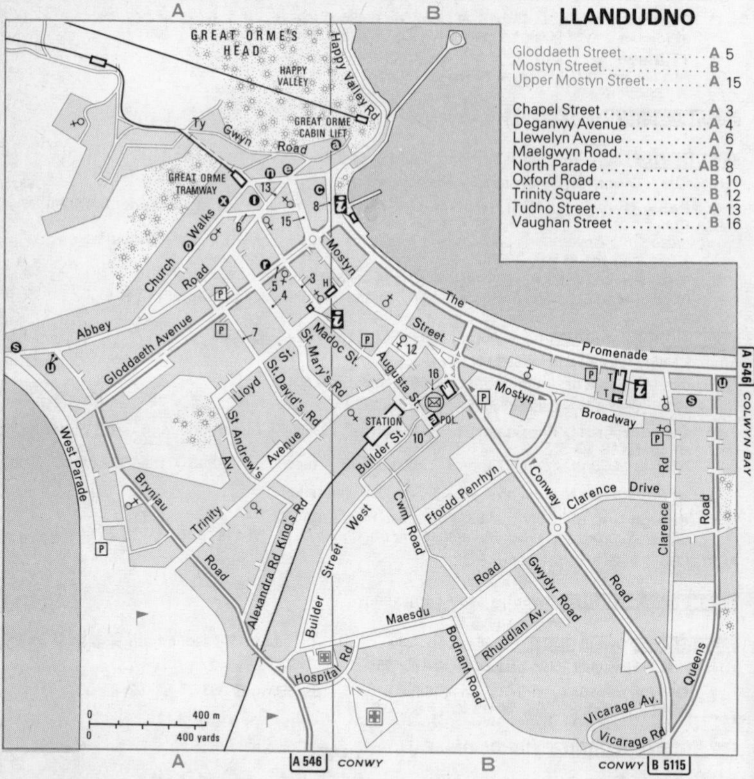

LLANDUDNO

Gloddaeth Street . . . . A 5
Mostyn Street . . . . B
Upper Mostyn Street . . . . A 15

Chapel Street . . . . A 3
Deganwy Avenue . . . . A 4
Llewelyn Avenue . . . . A 6
Maelgwyn Road . . . . A 7
North Parade . . . . AB 8
Oxford Road . . . . B 10
Trinity Square . . . . B 12
Tudno Street . . . . A 13
Vaughan Street . . . . B 16

Bodysgallen Hall 🐎, LL30 1RS, SE : 4 m. by B 5115 ☎ 0492 (Deganwy) 84466, Telex 617163, ≤ gardens and mountains, « Part 17 C and 18 C hall with terraced gardens », 🎾 – [TV] ☎ [P]. [S] [AE] [O] [VISA]. 🐕 by B 5115 B
M 8.30/13.50 **t.** – ☕ 3.50 – **28 rm** 40.00/70.00 **st.** – SB (winter and spring only) 81.00 **st.**

Empire, 73 Church Walks, LL30 2HE, ☎ 79955, Telex 617161, 🏊 – [lift] [TV] [P]. [S] [AE] [O] [VISA]
closed 2 weeks at Christmas and New Year – **M** 7.00/9.45 **st.** 🍷 3.25 – **56 rm** ☕ 22.00/55.00 **st.** – SB 46.00/68.00 **st.** A **e**

Gogarth Abbey, West Shore, LL30 2QY, ☎ 76211, ≤, 🏊, 🌳 – [TV] 🛁wc [P]. [S] [AE] [VISA]. 🐕
closed first 2 weeks January – **M** (bar lunch Monday to Saturday in winter) 12.00 **t.** 🍷 2.75 – **42 rm** ☕ 15.00/40.00 **t.** – SB 40.00/60.00 **st.** A **s**

St. Tudno, North Par., LL30 2LP, ☎ 74411, « Tasteful decor » – [lift] [TV] 🛁wc 🚿wc ☎. [S] [AE] [O] [VISA] A **c**
closed January and Christmas – **M** (bar lunch Monday to Saturday) 7.25/10.50 **t.** 🍷 2.75 – **21 rm** ☕ 25.00/50.00 **t.** – SB 52.00/65.00 **st.**

Bryn-y-Bia Lodge, Bryn-y-Bia Rd, Craigside, LL30 3AS, E : 1 m. on A 546 ☎ 49644, 🌳 – [TV] 🛁wc 🚿wc [P] by A 546 B
closed January – **M** (bar lunch) 10.00 **t.** 🍷 4.00 – **18 rm** ☕ 15.00/36.00 **t.** – SB 38.00/48.00 **st.**

Dunoon, Gloddaeth St., LL30 2DW, ☎ 77078 – [lift] [TV] 🛁wc [P] A **r**
March-October – **M** 4.50/6.00 **st.** 🍷 2.50 – **59 rm** ☕ 16.00/32.00 **st.** – SB 30.00/45.00 **st.**

🏠 **Headlands,** Hill Terr., LL30 2LS, ☎ 77485, ≤ Llandudno and Ormes Bay – [TV] 🛁wc 🚿wc [P]. [S] VISA AB **a**
closed January and February – **M** (bar lunch) 8.00 **t.** – **17 rm** ☕ 13.50/33.00 **t.** – SB (September-May) 42.00/47.00 **st.**

🏠 **Bromwell Court,** Promenade, 6 Craig-y-Don Par., LL30 1BG, ☎ 78416 – [TV] 🛁wc 🚿wc. [S] VISA B **u**
closed 20 December-February – **M** (bar lunch) 8.00 **t.** 🍷 3.00 – **12 rm** ☕ 14.50/30.50 **t.** – SB (except summer) 34.00/38.00 **st.**

🏠 **Plas Fron Deg,** 48 Church Walks, LL30 2HL, ☎ 77267, ≤, 🌳 – 🚿wc [P]. [S] [AE] [O] VISA
M 6.00/10.00 **st.** 🍷 2.50 – **9 rm** ☕ 12.00/28.00 **st.** A **o**

🏡 **Clontarf,** 1 Great Orme's Rd, West Shore, LL30 2AS, ☎ 77621 – 🚿wc [P]. 🐕 A **u**
February-October – **10 rm** ☕ 11.75/23.50 **t.**

🏡 **Cranleigh,** Great Orme's Rd, West Shore, LL30 2AR, ☎ 77688 – 🚿wc [P] A **u**
April-October – **13 rm** ☕ 9.50/28.50 **t.**

🏡 **Bron Orme,** 54 Church Walks, LL30 2HL, ☎ 76735, ≤, 🌳 – 🐕 A **x**
April-October – **11 rm** ☕ 7.50/16.00 **t.**

🍴 **Floral,** Victoria St., Craig y Don, LL30 1LJ, ☎ 75735 B **s**
closed lunch Saturday to Tuesday, Monday, 2 weeks March and 2 weeks September – **M** (booking essential) a la carte 8.70/12.20 **t.** 🍷 2.70.

🍴 **No. 1,** 1 Old Rd, LL30 2HA, ☎ 75424 A **i**
closed Sunday – **M** a la carte 4.70/7.70 **t.** 🍷 2.60.

CITROEN Herkomer Rd ☎ 77607
PEUGEOT-TALBOT Conwy Rd ☎ 77461

LLANELLI Dyfed [403] H 29 – pop. 26,383 – ECD : Tuesday – ☎ 0554.
Envir. : Kidwelly (Castle★★) *AC*, NW : 9 m.
♦London 206 – Carmarthen 20 – ♦Swansea 11.

🏨 **Stradey Park** (T.H.F.), Furnace, SA15 4HA, N : ¾ m. on B 4309 ☎ 758171, Telex 48521 – [lift] [TV] 🛁wc ☎ [P]. 🏛. [S] [AE] [O] VISA
M 6.95/7.95 **st.** 🍷 2.60 – ☕ 5.50 – **77 rm** 27.00/35.50 **st.**

🏠 Diplomat, Felinfoel Rd, SA15 3PJ, NE : 1 m. on A 276 ☎ 56156 – [lift] [TV] 🛁wc 🚿 ☎ [P]. [S] [AE] [O] VISA. 🐕
12 rm ☕ 22.55/37.50 **st.**

AUSTIN-ROVER Vauxhall St. ☎ 3371
AUSTIN-ROVER Pwll ☎ 3666
FORD Sandy Rd ☎ 3285

LLANELWY = St. Asaph.

LLANFAIR-YM-MUALLT = Builth Wells.

LLANFYLLIN Powys [402] [403] K 25 – pop. 1,118 – ECD : Friday – ☎ 069 184.
♦London 188 – Chester 42 – Shrewsbury 24 – Welshpool 11.

🏠 **Bodfach Hall** 🐦, SY22 5HS, NW : 1 m. on B 4391 ☎ 272, ≤, « Country house in extensive gardens », park, 🎾 – [TV] 🛁wc [P]. [O]
closed January and February – **M** (bar lunch) 7.70 **t.** – **9 rm** ☕ 17.50/35.00 **t.** – SB (winter only) 35.00 **st.**

LLANGAMMARCH WELLS Powys [403] J 27 – ECD : Wednesday – ☎ 059 12.
♦London 200 – Brecon 17 – Builth Wells 8.

🏨 **Lake** 🐦, LD4 4BS, E : ¾ m. ☎ 202, ≤, ⛳9, 🎣, 🌳, park, 🎾 – [TV] 🛁wc 🚿wc [P]. [S] VISA
M (bar lunch Monday to Friday) 6.50/10.50 **st.** 🍷 2.90 – **25 rm** ☕ 13.75/39.00 **st.** – SB 49.00/57.00 **st.**

LLANGOLLEN Clwyd [402] [403] K 25 – pop. 3,080 – ECD : Thursday – ☎ 0978.
See : Plas Newydd★★ (the house of the Ladies of Llangollen) *AC*.
Envir. : Horseshoe Pass★, NW : 4 ½ m.
⛳18 Vale of Llangollen, Holyhead Rd ☎ 860040, E : 1 ½ m.
[i] Town Hall, ☎ 860828 (summer only).
♦London 194 – Chester 23 – Holyhead 76 – Shrewsbury 30.

🏨 **Bryn Howel,** LL20 7UW, E : 2 ¾ m. on A 539 ☎ 860331, ≤, 🎣, 🌳 – [TV] 🛁wc ☎ [P]. 🏛. [S] [AE] VISA
closed Christmas day – **M** 6.00/8.00 **st.** 🍷 2.70 – **34 rm** ☕ 17.00/38.00 **st.**

🏨 **Royal** (T.H.F.), Bridge St., LL20 8PG, ☎ 860202, ≤, 🎣 – [TV] 🛁wc ☎ [P]. 🏛. [S] [AE] [O] VISA
M (bar lunch) 8.50 **st.** 🍷 2.60 – ☕ 5.00 – **33 rm** 29.50/41.00 **st.**

🏨 Hand (Mt. Charlotte), Bridge St., LL20 8PL, ☎ 860303, Telex 61160 – [TV] 🛁wc 🚿wc ☎ [P]. 🏛. [S] [AE] [O] VISA
58 rm ☕ 27.50/41.25 **st.** – SB 55.00 **st.**

🍴 **Caesars,** Deeside Lane, ☎ 860133, ≤ – [S] VISA
M (dinner only) 9.95 **st.** 🍷 2.95.

FORD ☎ 860270

LLANGURIG Powys 408 J 26 – pop. 620 – ⊠ Llanidloes – ✆ 055 15.
♦London 188 – Aberystwyth 25 – Carmarthen 75 – Shrewsbury 53.

⌂ **Old Vicarage,** SY18 6RN, ✆ 280 – 🅿
4 rm ⛱ 10.50/21.00 t.

LLANILLTUD FAWR = Llantwit Major.

LLANNEFYDD Clwyd 402 408 J 24 – pop. 565 – ⊠ Denbigh – ✆ 074 579.
♦London 225 – Chester 37 – Shrewsbury 63.

🏨 **Hawk and Buckle Inn,** LL16 5ED, ✆ 249 – 📺 ⛱wc 🅿. 🔼 AE ① VISA. ✂
M *(closed lunch Monday to Friday during winter)* (bar lunch) 8.50 t. 🍷 2.60 – **10 rm**
⛱ 19.00/29.00 t. – SB 39.50/46.00 st.

AUSTIN-ROVER Denbigh Rd ✆ 227

LLANRWST Gwynedd 402 408 I 24 – pop. 2,610 – ECD : Thursday – ✆ 0492.
See : Gwydir Castle★ – Envir. : Capel Garmon (Burial Chamber★) SE : 6 m.
♦London 230 – Holyhead 50 – Shrewsbury 66.

🏨 **Gwesty Plas Maenan** ⌂, LL26 0YR, N : 4 m. on A 470 ✆ 049 269 (Dolgarrog) 232, ≤, ✿,
park – 📺 ⛱wc ☎ 🅿. 🅰 🔼 AE ① VISA. ✂
M 5.35/9.00 t. – **15 rm** ⛱ 24.00/37.50 t. – SB (summer only) 25.00/29.00 st.

🏨 **Maenan Abbey,** N : 2 ½ m. on A 470, LL26 0UL, ✆ 049 269 (Dolgarrog) 247, ⚲, ✿ – ⛱wc
🎞wc ☎ 🅿. 🔼 AE ① VISA
M 4.95/8.75 t. 🍷 2.55 – **12 rm** ⛱ 13.80/30.00 t. – SB (except summer) 34.50 st.

XX **Meadowsweet** with rm, Station Rd, LL26 0DS, ✆ 640732, ≤ – 📺 🎞wc ☎ 🅿. 🔼 AE VISA
M (closed lunch November-February) 6.00/17.50 t. 🍷 2.75 – **10 rm** ⛱ 17.00/38.00 st. – SB
48.00/55.00 st.

AUSTIN-ROVER Kerry Garage ✆ 640381

LLANWENARTH Gwent – see Abergavenny.

LLANTWIT MAJOR (LLANILLTUD FAWR) South Glam. 408 J 29 – pop. 8,740 – ✆ 044 65.
♦London 175 – ♦Cardiff 18 – ♦Swansea 33.

🏨 **West House,** West St., CF6 9SP, ✆ 2406, ✿ – 📺 ⛱wc 🅿. 🔼 AE VISA
M a la carte 8.50/11.00 t. 🍷 2.50 – **19 rm** ⛱ 15.00/30.00 t. – SB 38.50 st.

XX **Quaintways,** Colhugh St., CF6 9RE, ✆ 2321 – 🅿. 🔼
closed Sunday, 26 December-7 January and Bank Holidays – **M** (lunch by arrangement) a la
carte 7.40/12.80 t. 🍷 2.70.

TOYOTA 2 Colhugh St. ✆ 3466

LLANWRTYD WELLS Powys 408 J 27 – pop. 488 – ECD : Wednesday – ✆ 059 13.
See : Cambrian Mountains : road★★ from Llanwrtyd to Tregaron.
Envir. : Rhandir-mwyn (≤★ of Afon Tywi Valley) SW : 12 m.
♦London 214 – Brecon 32 – Carmarthen 39.

⌂ **Lasswade House,** Station Rd, LD5 4RW, ✆ 515, ≤, ⬜, ✿ – 🅿
7 rm ⛱ 12.50/25.00 s.

at Abergwesyn NW : 5 m. – ⊠ Builth Wells – ✆ 059 13 Llanwrtyd Wells :

🏠 **Llwynderw** ⌂, LD5 4TW, ✆ 238, ≤ countryside and hills, ✿ – ⛱wc 🅿
March-October – **M** (lunch by arrangement) 15.00 t. – **10 rm** ⛱ (dinner included) 43.00/106.00.

LLANYCHAER Dyfed 408 F 28 – see Fishguard.

LLWYNMAWR Clwyd 402 408 K 25 – pop. 740 – ⊠ Llangollen – ✆ 069 172 Glyn Ceiriog.
♦London 192 – Shrewsbury 28 – Wrexham 15.

🏨 **Golden Pheasant** ⌂, LL20 7BB, ✆ 281, ≤, ✿ – ⛱wc 🎞wc 🅿. 🔼 AE VISA
M 5.50/9.00 st. 🍷 3.00 – **19 rm** ⛱ 22.00/40.00 st. – SB 58.00 st.

LODDISWELL Devon – see Kingsbridge.

LODDON Norfolk 404 Y 26 – pop. 1,435 – ECD : Wednesday – ✆ 0508.
♦London 121 – Great Yarmouth 16 – ♦Ipswich 48 – ♦Norwich 11.

⌂ **Rackham's Stubbs House** ⌂, Stubbs Green, NR14 6EA, SW : ¾ m. ✆ 20231, ✿ – 🅿.
✂
closed January and December – **9 rm** ⛱ 12.00/27.00 t.

LOFTUS Cleveland 402 R 20 – pop. 6,850 – ECD : Wednesday – ⊠ Saltburn by the Sea –
✆ 0287 Guisborough – ♦London 264 – ♦Leeds 73 – ♦Middlesbrough 17 – Scarborough 36.

🏨 **Grinkle Park** ⌂, Easington, TS13 4UB, SE : 3 ½ m. by A 174 ✆ 40515, ≤, ✿, park – 📺
⛱wc ☎ 🅿. 🔼 VISA
M 6.90/11.75 st. – **20 rm** ⛱ 15.45/42.75 st.

244

LONDON

LONDON (Greater) **404** folds ⑫ to ⑭ — **London G.** — pop. 7,452,346 — ✪ 01.

✈ Heathrow, ℰ 759 4321, Telex 934892, p. 8 AY — **Terminal** : Airbus (A1) from Victoria, Airbus (A2) from Paddington — Underground (Piccadilly line) frequent service daily — Helicopter service to Gatwick Airport.

✈ Gatwick, ℰ 0293 (Crawley) 28822 and ℰ 01 (London) 668 4211, Telex 877725, p. 9 : by A 23 EZ and M 23 — **Terminal** : Coach service from Victoria Coach Station (Flightline 777) — Railink (Gatwick Express) from Victoria (24 h service) — Helicopter service to Heathrow Airport.

✈ Stansted, at Bishop's Stortford, ℰ 0279 (Bishop's Stortford) 502380, Telex 81102, NE : 34 m. off M 11 and A 120.

BA Air Terminal : Victoria Station, ℰ 834 2323, p. 30 BX.

British Caledonian Airways, Victoria Air Terminal : Victoria Station, SW1, ℰ 834 9411, p. 30 BX.

🚄 Euston ℰ 387 8541 — King's Cross ℰ 837 4200 ext 4700 — Paddington ℰ 723 7000 ext 3148.

🖪 London Tourist Board, Head Office, 26 Grosvenor Gardens, SW1W 0DU, ℰ 730 3450, Telex 919041.
National Tourist Information Centre, Victoria Station Forecourt, SW1, ℰ 730 0791.
British Tourist Authority, 64 St. James's St., SW1, ℰ 499 9325.
Telephone Information Service ℰ 730 0791 or Teletourist ℰ 246 8041 (English), 246 8043 (French), 246 8045 (German).

The maps in this section of the Guide are based upon the Ordnance Survey of Great Britain with the permission of the Controller of Her Majesty's Stationery Office. Crown Copyright reserved.

SIGHTS

CURIOSITÉS
LE CURIOSITÀ
SEHENSWÜRDIGKEITEN

■ HISTORIC BUILDINGS AND MONUMENTS

Palace of Westminster*** : House of Lords**, Westminster Hall** (hammerbeam roof***), Robing Room*, Central Lobby*, House of Commons*, Big Ben*, Victoria Tower* p. 19 NX — Tower of London*** (Crown Jewels***, White Tower or Keep***, St. John's Chapel**, Beauchamp Tower*) p. 20 QU.

Banqueting House** p. 19 NV — Buckingham Palace** (Changing of the Guard**, Royal Mews**) p. 30 BV — Kensington Palace** p. 18 JV — Lincoln's Inn** p. 31 FV — London Bridge** p. 20 QV — Royal Hospital Chelsea** p. 29 FU — St. James's Palace** p. 27 EP — South Bank Arts Centre** (Royal Festival Hall*, National Theatre*, County Hall*) p. 19 NV — The Temple** (Middle Temple Hall*) p. 15 NU — Tower Bridge** p. 20 QV.

Albert Memorial* p. 28 CQ — Apsley House* p. 26 BP — Bloomsbury* p. 15 NT — Burlington House* p. 27 EM — Charterhouse* p. 16 PT — Commonwealth Institute* p. 17 HX — Design Centre* p. 27 FM — George Inn*, Southwark p. 20 QV — Gray's Inn* p. 15 NT — Guildhall* (Lord Mayor's Show**) p. 16 PT — Imperial College of Science and Technology* p. 28 CR — Dr Johnson's House* p. 16 PTU A — Lancaster House* p. 27 EP — Leighton House* p. 17 GX — Linley Sambourne House* p. 17 HX — Mansion House* (plate and insignia**) p. 16 QU P — The Monument* (⚊*) p. 16 QU G — Royal Opera Arcade* (New Zealand House) p. 27 FGN — Old Admiralty* p. 19 MV — Royal Exchange* p. 16 QU V — Royal Opera House* (Covent Garden) p. 31 EV — Somerset House* p. 31 EV — Staple Inn* p. 15 NT Y — Stock Exchange* p. 16 QTU — Westminster Bridge* p. 19 NX.

■ CHURCHES

The City Churches

St. Paul's Cathedral*** (Dome ⩽***) p. 16 PU.

St. Bartholomew the Great** (vessel*) p. 16 PT K — St. Dunstan-in-the-East** p. 16 QU F — St. Mary-at-Hill** (plan*, woodwork**) p. 16 QU B — Temple Church** p. 15 NU.

All Hallows-by-the-Tower (font cover**, brasses*) p. 16 QU Y — Christ Church* p. 16 PT E — St. Andrew Undershaft (monuments*) p. 16 QU A — St. Bride* (steeple**) p. 16 PU J — St. Clement Eastcheap (panelled interior**) p. 16 QU E — St. Edmund the King and Martyr (tower and spire*) p. 16 QU D — St. Giles Cripplegate* p. 16 PT N — St. Helen Bishopsgate* (monuments**) p. 16 QTU R — St. James Garlickhythe (tower and spire*, sword rests*) p. 16 PU R — St. Katherine Cree (sword rest*) p. 16 QU J — St. Magnus the Martyr (tower*, sword rest*) p. 16 QU K — St. Margaret Lothbury* (tower and spire*, woodwork*, screen*, font*) p. 16 QT S — St. Margaret Pattens (woodwork*) p. 16 QU N — St. Martin Ludgate (tower and spire*, door cases*) p. 16 PU B — St. Mary Abchurch* (tower and spire*, dome*, reredos*) p. 16 QU X — St. Mary-le-Bow (tower and steeple**) p. 16 PU G — St. Michael Paternoster Royal (tower and spire*) p. 16 PU D — St. Nicholas Cole Abbey (tower and spire*) p. 16 PU F — St. Olave* p. 16 QU S — St. Peter upon Cornhill (screen*) p. 16 QU L — St. Stephen Walbrook* (tower and steeple*, dome*) p. 16 QU Z — St. Vedast (tower and spire*, ceiling*) p. 16 PTU E.

Other Churches

Westminster Abbey*** (Chapel of Edward the Confessor**, Henry VII Chapel***, Chapter House**) p. 19 MX.

Southwark Cathedral** p. 20 QV.

Queen's Chapel* p. 27 EP — St. Clement Danes* p. 31 FV — St. James's* p. 27 EM — St. Margaret's* p. 19 NX A — St. Martin-in-the-Fields* p. 31 DX — St. Paul's* (Covent Garden) p. 31 DV — Westminster Roman Catholic Cathedral* p. 19 MX B.

■ PARKS

Regent's Park*** p. 14 KS (terraces**), Zoo***.

Hyde Park** p. 18 JU — St. James's Park** p. 19 MV

Kensington Gardens* p. 18 JV (Orangery* A).

■ STREETS AND SQUARES

The City*** p. 16 PU.

Bedford Square** p. 15 MT — Belgrave Square** p. 30 AV — Burlington Arcade** p. 27 DM — The Mall** p. 27 FP — Piccadilly** p. 27 EM — The Thames** pp. 18-20 — Trafalgar Square** p. 31 DX — Whitehall** (Horse Guards*) p. 19 MV.

Barbican* p. 16 PT — Bond Street* pp. 26-27 CK-DM — Canonbury Square* p. 16 PR — Carlton House Terrace* p. 27 GN — Charing Cross* p. 31 DX — Cheyne Walk* p. 18 JZ — Fitzroy Square* p. 15 LT — Jermyn Street* p. 27 EN — Merrick Square* p. 20 PX — Montpelier Square* p. 29 EQ — Piccadilly Arcade* p. 27 DEN — Portman Square* p. 26 AJ — Queen Anne's Gate* p. 19 MX — Regent Street* p. 27 EM — St. James's Square* p. 27 FN — St. James's Street* p. 27 EN — Shepherd Market* p. 26 CN — Strand* p. 31 DX — Trinity Church Square* p. 20 PX — Victoria Embankment* p. 31 EX — Waterloo Place* p. 27 FN.

■ MUSEUMS

British Museum*** p. 15 MT — National Gallery*** p. 27 GM — Science Museum*** p. 28 CR — Tate Gallery*** p. 19 MY — Victoria and Albert Museum*** p. 29 DR.

Courtauld Institute Galleries** p. 15 MT M — Museum of London** p. 16 PT M — National Portrait Gallery** p. 27 GM — Natural History Museum** p. 28 CS — Queen's Gallery** p. 30 BV — Wallace Collection** p. 26 AH.

Clock Museum* (Guildhall) p. 16 PT — Geological Museum* p. 28 CR — Imperial War Museum* p. 20 PX — London Transport Museum* p. 31 EV — Madame Tussaud's* p. 14 KT M — Museum of Mankind* p. 27 DM — National Army Museum* p. 29 FU — Percival David Foundation of Chinese Art* p. 15 MS M — Sir John Soane's Museum* p. 15 NT M — Wellington Museum* p. 26 BP.

■ OUTER LONDON

Hampton Court p. 8 BZ (The Palace***, gardens***) — Kew p. 9 CY Royal Botanic Gardens*** : Palm House**, Temperate House*, Kew Palace or Dutch House**, Orangery*, Pagoda*, Japanese Gateway* — Windsor (Castle***) by A 4, M 4 AX.

Blackheath p. 11 GY terraces and houses*, Eltham Palace* A — Brentford p. 8 BY Syon Park**, gardens* — Chiswick p. 9 CX Chiswick Mall**, Chiswick House* D, Hogarth's House* E — Greenwich pp. 10 and 11 : Cutty Sark** FX F, National Maritime Museum** (Queen's House**) FX M, Royal Naval College** (Painted Hall*, the Chapel*) FX G, Old Royal Observatory* (Meridian Building : collection**) GX K, Ranger's House* FY N — Hampstead Kenwood House** (Adam Library**, paintings**) p. 5 EV P, Fenton House* p. 13 GR — Hendon p. 5 CU Royal Air Force Museum** M — Hounslow p. 8 BX Osterley Park** — Lewisham p. 10 FY Horniman Museum* M — Richmond pp. 8 and 9 : Richmond Park**, ⛲*** CY, Richmond Bridge** BY R, Richmond Green** BY S (Maids of Honour Row**, Trumpeter's House*), Asgill House* BY B, Ham House** BY V.

Dulwich p. 10 FY Dulwich College Picture Gallery* X — Shoreditch p. 6 FV Geffrye Museum* M — Tower Hamlets p. 6 FX St. Katharine Dock* (HMS Discovery*) Y — Twickenham p. 8 BY Marble Hill House* Z, Strawberry Hill* A.

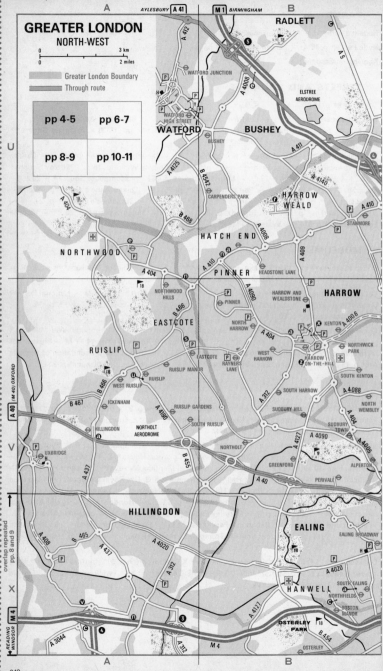

GREATER LONDON
NORTH-WEST

0 — 3 km
0 — 2 miles

Greater London Boundary
Through route

pp 4-5	pp 6-7
pp 8-9	pp 10-11

AYLESBURY A 41 · M 1 BIRMINGHAM

RADLETT

A 472
WATFORD JUNCTION
A 4008
ELSTREE AERODROME
WATFORD HIGH STREET
WATFORD · BUSHEY
BUSHEY
A 4125
B 4562
A 411
A 4140
CARPENDERS PARK
HARROW WEALD
A 410
STANMORE
B 468
HATCH END
A 4008
A 409
A 404
NORTHWOOD
NORTHWOOD HILLS
A 410 HEADSTONE LANE
PINNER
HARROW AND WEALDSTONE
HARROW
PINNER
A 4090
EASTCOTE
NORTH HARROW
A 404
KENTON A 400 6
RUISLIP
EASTCOTE
RAYNERS LANE
WEST HARROW
HARROW ON-THE-HILL
NORTHWICK PARK
SOUTH KENTON
RUISLIP MANOR
B 466
WEST RUISLIP
RUISLIP
B 467
ICKENHAM
RUISLIP GARDENS
A 4090
SOUTH HARROW
A 4088
A 312
SUDBURY HILL
NORTH WEMBLEY
HILLINGDON
NORTHOLT AERODROME
SOUTH RUISLIP
SUDBURY TOWN
A 404
A 406
UXBRIDGE
A 437
NORTHOLT
B 455
A 4127
A 4090
GREENFORD
PERIVALE
A 40
ALPERTON

overlap repeated pp. 8 and 9
A 40 (M 40) OXFORD

HILLINGDON
A 408
B 465
A 437
A 4020
EALING
EALING BROADWAY
A 4020
A 312
HANWELL
SOUTH EALING
NORTHFIELDS
BOSTON MANOR
A 4127
OSTERLEY PARK
B 454
A 3044
M 4
A 312
OSTERLEY

READING WINDSOR
M 4

248

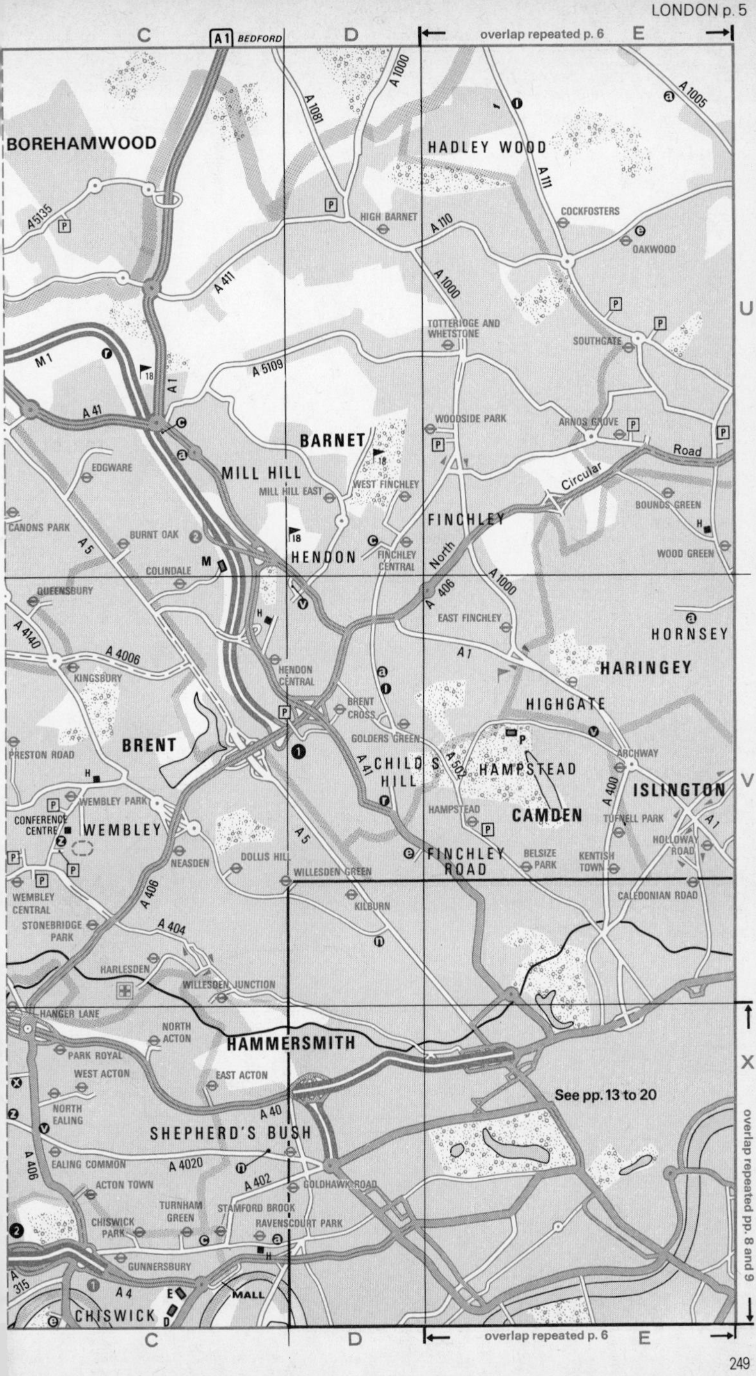

C A1 BEDFORD D ← overlap repeated p. 6 E →

A 1000

A 1005

BOREHAMWOOD

A 1081

HADLEY WOOD

A 5135

A 411

P

HIGH BARNET

A 110

COCKFOSTERS

A 111

OAKWOOD

A 1000

TOTTERIDGE AND WHETSTONE

SOUTHGATE

P

U

M 1

18

A1

A 5109

WOODSIDE PARK

P

ARNOS GROVE

P

Road

A 41

C

BARNET

Circular

A 411

EDGWARE

a

MILL HILL

WEST FINCHLEY

BOUNDS GREEN

H

MILL HILL EAST

FINCHLEY

CANONS PARK

A 5

BURNT OAK

2

18

North

WOOD GREEN

QUEENSBURY

COLINDALE

M

HENDON

FINCHLEY CENTRAL

A 406

A 1000

A 4140

A 4006

V

HENDON CENTRAL

EAST FINCHLEY

A 1

HORNSEY

KINGSBURY

P

BRENT CROSS

a

HARINGEY

HIGHGATE

a

PRESTON ROAD

BRENT

GOLDERS GREEN

CHILD'S HILL

A 41

HAMPSTEAD

ARCHWAY

H

A 5

A 502

CAMDEN

A 400

ISLINGTON

V

WEMBLEY PARK

P

CONFERENCE CENTRE

2

WEMBLEY

NEASDEN

A 5

DOLLIS HILL

HAMPSTEAD

P

TUFNELL PARK

A 1

P

FINCHLEY ROAD

BELSIZE PARK

KENTISH TOWN

HOLLOWAY ROAD

WEMBLEY CENTRAL

P

WILLESDEN GREEN

STONEBRIDGE PARK

A 406

A 404

KILBURN

CALEDONIAN ROAD

HARLESDEN

WILLESDEN JUNCTION

HANGER LANE

NORTH ACTON

HAMMERSMITH

X

PARK ROYAL

WEST ACTON

EAST ACTON

See pp. 13 to 20

X

NORTH EALING

SHEPHERD'S BUSH

A 40

overlap repeated pp. 8 and 9

A 406

EALING COMMON

A 4020

ACTON TOWN

A 402

GOLDHAWK ROAD

CHISWICK PARK

TURNHAM GREEN

STAMFORD BROOK

RAVENSCOURT PARK

2

GUNNERSBURY

A 315

A 4

E

MALL

CHISWICK

D

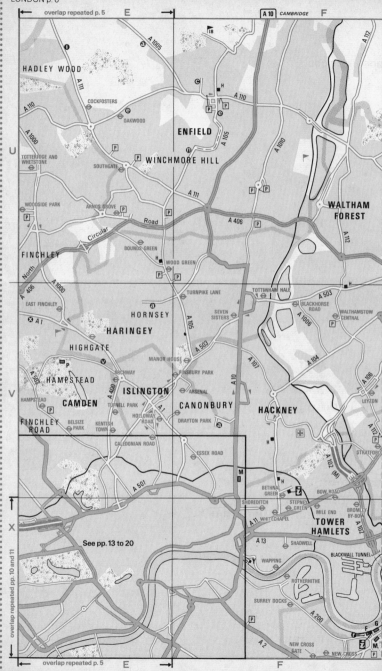

overlap repeated p. 5

E

A 10 CAMBRIDGE F

HADLEY WOOD

COCKFOSTERS

OAKWOOD

ENFIELD

A 110

A 105

WINCHMORE HILL

WALTHAM FOREST

TOTTERIDGE AND WHETSTONE

SOUTHGATE

A 111

WOODSIDE PARK

ARNOS GROVE

Circular Road

A 406

FINCHLEY

North

BOUNDS GREEN

WOOD GREEN

TURNPIKE LANE

TOTTENHAM HALE

A 503

BLACKHORSE ROAD

WALTHAMSTOW CENTRAL

EAST FINCHLEY

A 1

HORNSEY

SEVEN SISTERS

A 1006

HARINGEY

HIGHGATE

A 105

A 503

MANOR HOUSE

A 107

A 104

HAMPSTEAD

ARCHWAY

FINSBURY PARK

A 400

ISLINGTON

ARSENAL

A 10

HACKNEY

LEYTON

HAMPSTEAD

CAMDEN

TUFNELL PARK

A 1

CANONBURY

FINCHLEY ROAD

BELSIZE PARK

KENTISH TOWN

HOLLOWAY ROAD

DRAYTON PARK

CALEDONIAN ROAD

ESSEX ROAD

A 501

A 102 (M)

STRATFORD

BETHNAL GREEN

BOW ROAD

See pp. 13 to 20

SHOREDITCH

STEPNEY GREEN

MILE END

BROMLEY BY-BOW

A 11 WHITECHAPEL

TOWER HAMLETS

A 13

SHADWELL

BLACKWALL TUNNEL

WAPPING

ROTHERHITHE

SURREY DOCKS

A 200

A 2

NEW CROSS GATE

NEW CROSS

overlap repeated pp. 10 and 11

overlap repeated p. 5

E

F

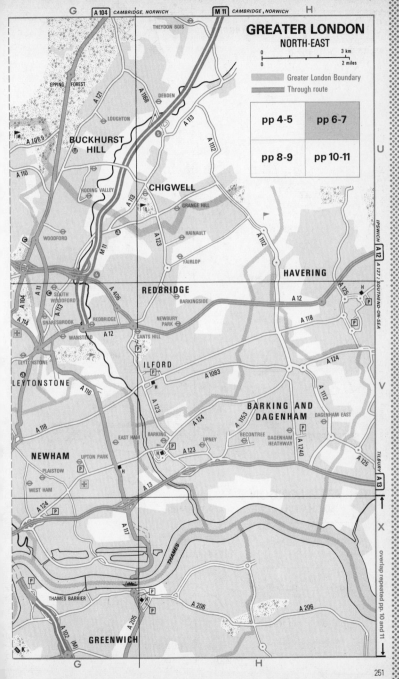

GREATER LONDON
NORTH-EAST

pp 4-5	pp 6-7
pp 8-9	pp 10-11

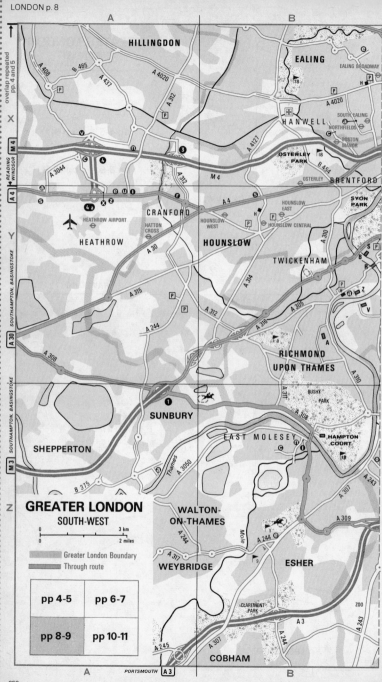

GREATER LONDON
SOUTH-WEST

0 ———— 3 km
0 ———— 2 miles

▒ Greater London Boundary
━━ Through route

pp 4-5	pp 6-7
pp 8-9	pp 10-11

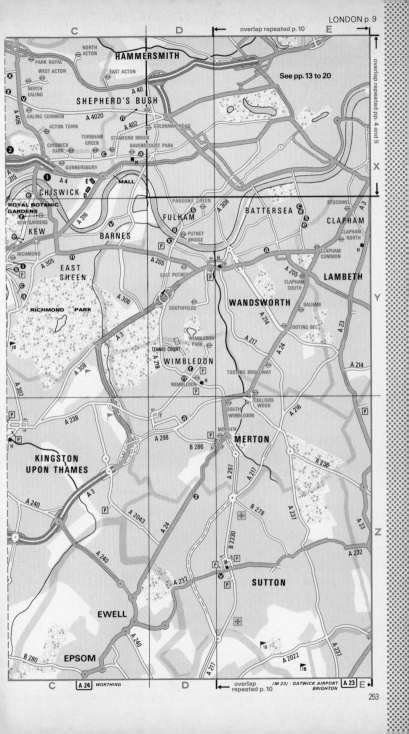

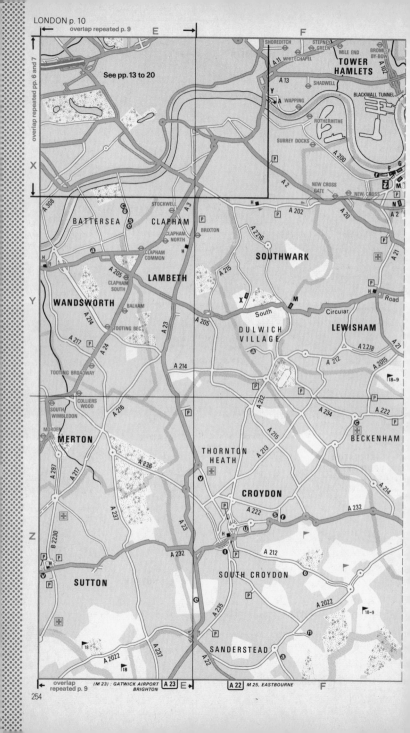

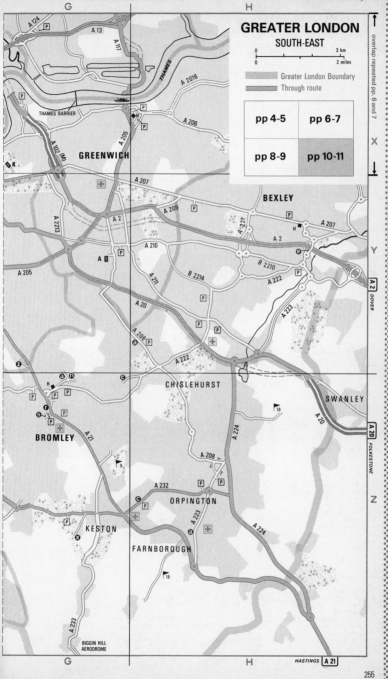

GREATER LONDON
SOUTH-EAST

0 — 3 km
0 — 2 miles

▦ Greater London Boundary
▦ Through route

pp 4-5	pp 6-7
pp 8-9	pp 10-11

overlap repeated pp. 6 and 7

X

Y

A 2 DOVER

A 20 FOLKESTONE

Z

A 124
A 13
A 111
THAMES
A 2016
A 206
THAMES BARRIER
GREENWICH
A 205
A 102 (M)
K

A 207
BEXLEY
A 209
A 2213
A 2 2
A 221
A 207
A 2
B 2210
A 205
A 210
A 1
A 211
B 2214
A 222
B 2223
A 20
A 208
a
A 222
CHISLEHURST
SWANLEY
A 223
A 20
18
H
BROMLEY
A 21
9
A 224
A 208
A 232
ORPINGTON
A 223
Z
KESTON
A 224
x
FARNBOROUGH
18
A 233
BIGGIN HILL
AERODROME

Continued p. 21

Carriage Drive North .... SW11 p. 18 KZ 75
Castle Lane .... SW1 p. 30 CV
Cavendish Square .... W1 p. 26 CJ
Central Street .... EC1 p. 16 PS
Chalk Farm Road .... NW1 p. 14 KR
Chamberlayne Road .... NW10 p. 13 GS
Chancery Lane .... WC2 p. 31 FV 78
Chandos Place .... WC2 p. 31 DX
Chandos Street .... W1 p. 26 CH
Chapel Market .... N1 p. 15 NS
Chapel Street .... SW1 p. 30 AV
Charlbert Street .... NW8 p. 14 KS 79
Charles II Street .... SW1 p. 27 FN
Charles Street .... W1 p. 26 CN
Charing Cross .... SW1 p. 31 DX
Charing Cross Road .... WC2 p. 27 GJ
Charterhouse Square .... EC1 p. 16 PT 81
Charterhouse Street .... EC1 p. 16 PT 83
Cheapside...................... EC2 p. 16 PU
Chelsea Bridge .... SW1, SW8 p. 19 LZ
Chelsea Bridge Road............ SW1 p. 18 KZ
Chelsea Embankment .... SW3 p. 18 KZ
Chelsea Manor Street .... SW3 p. 29 EU
Chelsea Square .... SW3 p. 29 DU
Cheltenham Terrace .... SW3 p. 29 FT
Chepstow Crescent .... W11 p. 30 AZ 84
Chepstow Place .... W2 p. 30 AY
Chepstow Road .... W2 p. 30 AY
Chesham Place .... SW2 p. 29 FR
Chesham Street .... SW1 p. 29 FS
Chester Road .... NW1 p. 14 KS
Chester Row .... SW1 p. 30 AX
Chester Square .... SW1 p. 30 AX 88
Chester Street .... SW1 p. 30 AV
Chesterton Road................ W10 p. 13 GT
Cheval Place .... SW3 p. 29 ER
Cheyne Walk .... SW3, SW10 p. 18 JZ
Chilworth Street .... W2 p. 30 CY 90
Chippenham Road .... W9 p. 13 HS
Chiswell Street .... EC1 p. 16 PT
Church Row .... NW3 p. 13 GR
Church Street .... NW8, NW2 p. 14 JT
Churton Street .... SW1 p. 19 LY 92
Circus Road .... NW8 p. 14 JS
City Road .... EC1 p. 16 PS
Clapham Road .... SW9 p. 19 NZ
Clarendon Place .... W2 p. 31 EY 93
Clarendon Road .... W11 p. 13 GU
Claverton Street .... SW1 p. 19 LZ
Clayton Street.................. SE11 p. 19 NZ
Clerkenwell Road .... EC1 p. 16 PT
Cleveland Gardens .... W2 p. 30 CY 94
Cleveland Square .... W2 p. 30 CY
Cleveland Street .... W1 p. 15 LT
Cleveland Terrace .... W2 p. 30 CY
Clifford Street .... W1 p. 27 DM
Cliveden Place .... SW1 p. 29 FS
Cockspur Street .... SW1 p. 27 GN
Colet Gardens .... W14 p. 17 GY
Collingham Gardens .... SW5 p. 28 AT 99
Collingham Road .... SW5 p. 28 AT 101
Commercial Street .... E1 p. 16 QT
Conduit Street .... W1 p. 27 DL
Connaught Square .... W2 p. 31 FY 103
Connaught Street .... W2 p. 31 EY
Constantine Road .... NW3 p. 13 GR 106
Constitution Hill .... SW1 p. 30 AV
Copenhagen Street .... N1 p. 15 NR
Cork Street..................... W1 p. 27 DM
Cornwall Crescent .... W11 p. 13 GU 107
Cornwall Gardens .... SW7 p. 28 AR
Cornwall Road .... SE1 p. 19 NV 108
Corporation Row .... EC1 p. 16 PS 110
Courtfield Gardens .... SW5 p. 28 AT
Courtfield Road .... SW7 p. 28 BS
Coventry Street .... W1 p. 27 FM
Cowcross Street .... EC1 p. 16 PT 113
Crabtree Lane .... SW6 p. 17 GZ
Cranbourn Street .... WC2 p. 31 DV 115
Cranley Gardens .... SW7 p. 28 CT
Craven Hill .... W2 p. 30 CZ
Craven Road .... W2 p. 31 DY
Craven Street .... WC2 p. 31 DX
Craven Terrace .... W2 p. 31 DZ
Crawford Place .... W1 p. 14 KT 116
Crawford Street .... W1 p. 14 KT
Cromwell Crescent .... SW5 p. 17 HY 119
Cromwell Place .... SW7 p. 28 CS
Cromwell Road .... SW7, SW5 p. 28 CS
Crowndale Road .... NW1 p. 15 LR
Crucifix Lane .... SE1 p. 20 QV 125
Culross Street .... W1 p. 26 AM
Curtain Road................... EC2 p. 16 QS 126

Curzon Street................... W1 p. 26 BN
Cut (The) .... SE1 p. 20 PV
Dante Road.................... SE11 p. 20 PY 129
D'Arblay Street .... W1 p. 27 EK
Davies Street .... W1 p. 26 BK
Dawes Road .... SW6 p. 17 GZ
Dawson Place .... W2 p. 30 AZ
Deanery Street .... W1 p. 26 BN 132
Dean Street .... W1 p. 27 FJ
Delancey Street .... NW1 p. 15 LR
Delaware Road .... W9 p. 13 HS
Denbigh Street .... SW1 p. 19 LZ
Denman Street .... W1 p. 27 FM 133
Denmark Street .... WC2 p. 27 GJ 134
De Vere Gardens .... W8 p. 28 BQ
Devonshire Street .... W1 p. 14 KT
Devonshire Terrace .... W2 p. 30 CY 136
Dewhurst Road .... W14 p. 17 GX 137
Dorset Road .... SW8 p. 19 NZ
Dorset Street .... W1 p. 26 AH
Dovehouse Street .... SW3 p. 29 DU
Dover Street.................... W1 p. 27 DM
Downing Street .... SW1 p. 19 MV 138
Downshire Hill .... NW3 p. 13 GR 139
Draycott Avenue .... SW3 p. 29 ET
Draycott Place.................. SW3 p. 29 ET
Drayton Gardens .... SW10 p. 28 BT
Druid Street .... SE1 p. 20 QX
Drury Lane..................... WC2 p. 31 EV
Dufferin Street .... EC1 p. 16 PS 141
Duke of Wellington Place .... SW1 p. 30 AV 142
Duke of York Street .... SW1 p. 27 EN 143
Duke's Place .... EC3 p. 16 QU 145
Duke Street .... W1 p. 26 BK
Duke Street SW1
    ST. JAMES .... p. 27 EN 146
Duncannon Street .... WC2 p. 31 DX 147
Dunraven Street .... W1 p. 26 AL 149
Durham Street .... SE11 p. 19 NZ 150
Eardley Crescent .... SW5 p. 17 HZ 151
Earlham Street .... WC2 p. 31 DV 153
Earl's Court Road .... W8, SW5 p. 17 HY
Eastbourne Terrace .... W2 p. 31 DY
Eastcastle Street .... W1 p. 27 EJ
Eastcheap .... EC3 p. 16 QU 154
East Heath Road .... NW3 p. 13 GR
East Road .... N1 p. 16 QS
Eaton Gate .... SW1 p. 29 FS 155
Eaton Place .... SW1 p. 30 AV
Eaton Square .... SW1 p. 30 AV
Ebury Bridge .... SW1 p. 19 LZ 156
Ebury Street................... SW1 p. 30 AX
Ebury Bridge Road............. SW1 p. 18 KZ
Eccleston Bridge .... SW1 p. 30 BX 157
Eccleston Square .... SW1 p. 30 BX
Eccleston Street .... SW1 p. 30 AX
Edgware Road .... W2 p. 14 JT
Edith Grove .... SW10 p. 18 JZ
Edith Road .... W14 p. 17 GY
Edwardes Square .... W8 p. 17 HX 158
Egerton Gardens .... SW3 p. 29 DS 160
Egerton Terrace .... SW3 p. 29 DR 161
Egerton Gardens Mews .... SW3 p. 29 ER 162
Elephant and Castle .... SE11 p. 20 PX
Elephant Road .... SE17 p. 20 PY 163
Elgin Avenue .... W9 p. 13 HS
Elizabeth Street................ SW1 p. 30 AX
Elm Park Gardens .... SW10 p. 28 CU
Elm Park Road .... SW3 p. 28 CU
Elsworthy Road .... NW3 p. 14 JR
Elvaston Place................. SW7 p. 28 BR
Elystan Place .... SW3 p. 29 ET
Elystan Street .... SW3 p. 29 DT
Endell Street .... WC2 p. 31 DV
England's Lane .... NW3 p. 29 DQ
Ennismore Gardens .... SW7 p. 29 DQ
Essex Street .... WC2 p. 31 FV
Estcourt Road .... SW6 p. 17 GZ
Eton Avenue .... NW3 p. 14 JR
Euston Road .... NW1 p. 15 MS
Evelyn Gardens .... SW7 p. 28 CU
Eversholt Street .... NW1 p. 15 LS
Exeter Street .... WC2 p. 31 EV
Exhibition Road .... SW7 p. 28 CQ
Fairfax Road .... NW6 p. 14 JR
Fairhazel Gardens .... NW6 p. 14 JR
Falmouth Road .... SE1 p. 20 PX
Farm Street W1
    MAYFAIR..................... p. 26 BM
Fann Street .... W1 p. 16 PT 166
Farringdon Road .... EC1 p. 15 NS

Continued on next page

265

TOWN PLANS (continued)

12

A

H

Dorset St.

Gloucester

Montagu
Square

Baker

Manchester

St.

Aybrook St.

New   Cavendish   St.

Welbeck

Harley   Street

Portland   Place

Blandford

Place

St.

WALLACE
COLLECTION

281

287

413

Queen   Anne   St.

Wimpole

Street

Chandos

REGENT'S PARK
AND MARYLEBONE

Cavendish
Sq.

George   Street

J

Portman
Square

Wigmore

James

Street

287

Street

Henrietta

Vere St.

Pl.

Holles   St.

Seymour   Street

Bryanston   St.

Portman   Street

Orchard   Street

188

Oxford

Duke

Street

Street

314

Street

BOND ST.

35

175

South Molton Street

Davies

New   Bond

210

St.

MARBLE ARCH

North   Street

Row

Weighhouse St.

35   175

Brook

Street

C   Street

Brook's Mews

12

St.

Green   Street

Park

Lees   Pl.

CITY OF
WESTMINSTER

149

Woods Mews

Street

Grosvenor
Square

Grosvenor

Street

Upper   Brook   Street
Culross   St.

Upper   Grosvenor   St.

Reeves   Mews

Carlos   Pl.

Mount Row

MAYFAIR

Berkeley
Square

Bruton

St.

M

Adam's   Row

Mount

Aldford   St.

South Street

South   Audley

Farm   Street

Hay's   Mews

Charles   Street

Curzon

Bolton St.

N

HYDE   PARK

132

422

Hill

Waverton St.

Curzon

Street

Street

Shepherd
Market

Half   Moon   St.

HYDE PARK AND KNIGHTSBRIDGE

Shepherd   Street

220

Brick   Street

Serpentine   Road

205

Old   Park   Lane

Piccadilly

GREEN PARK

P

0   200 m
0   200 yards

APSLEY HOUSE
WELLINGTON MUSEUM

A   B   C

270

Oxford Street is closed to private traffic, Mondays to Saturdays :
from 7 am to 7 pm between Portman Street and St. Giles Circus

271

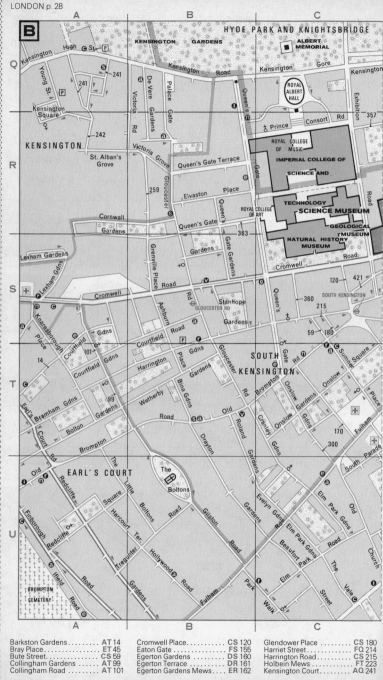

B

HYDE PARK AND KNIGHTSBRIDGE

KENSINGTON GARDENS

ALBERT MEMORIAL

Kensington High St.

Kensington Road

Kensington Gore

Kensington

ROYAL ALBERT HALL

Prince Consort Rd

357

Young St.

241

241

De Vere Gardens

Palace Gate

Queen's Gate

Exhibition Road

242

KENSINGTON

Kensington Square

St. Alban's Grove

Victoria Rd

ROYAL COLLEGE OF MUSIC

IMPERIAL COLLEGE OF SCIENCE AND

Victoria Grove

Queen's Gate Terrace

259

Gloucester Road

Elvaston Place

ROYAL COLLEGE OF ART

TECHNOLOGY

SCIENCE MUSEUM

Cornwall Gardens

Queen's Gate

363

GEOLOGICAL MUSEUM

NATURAL HISTORY MUSEUM

Lexham Gardens

Grenville Place

Gate Gardens

Gardens

Cromwell Road

Lexham Gdns

Cromwell Road

Queen's Gate

120 — 421

Knaresborough Place

Ashburn Road

Stanhope Gardens

GLOUCESTER RD

360

215

SOUTH KENSINGTON

Courtfield Gdns

Courtfield Road

Gardens

Queen's

59 — 180

14

Courtfield Gdns

101

Harrington Place

Gloucester Rd

Gate Rd

Sumner Square

SOUTH KENSINGTON

Onslow Square

Bramham Gdns

Earl's Court

Gardens

Harrington

Bina Gdns

Wetherby

Brompton Road

Onslow Gardens

Onslow Gdns

170

Bolton Gardens

Old Road

Drayton Gardens

Roland Gardens

Cranley Gdns

Fulham Road

South Parade

300

Brompton Rd

EARL'S COURT

The Boltons

Evelyn Gdns

Elm Park Gdns

Old Redcliffe

Square

Little Boltons

Harcourt Ter.

Gilston Road

Elm Park Gardens

Elm Park Road

Beaufort

Old Church Street

Finborough Road

Redcliffe Gardens

Tregunter Road

Hollywood Road

Fulham Road

Park

Elm

The Vale

BROMPTON CEMETERY

Ifield Road

Walk

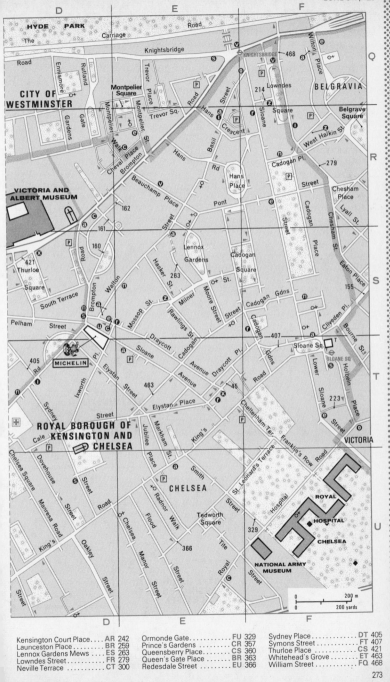

273

C

WELLINGTON ARCH

GREEN PARK

QUEEN VICTORIA MEMORIAL

The Mall

ST. JAMES'S

St. James's Park Lake

ST. JAMES'S PARK

142

Constitution Hill

Grosvenor Cres.

BUCKINGHAM PALACE GARDENS

BUCKINGHAM PALACE

Birdcage Walk

Halkin St.

Grosvenor

Grosvenor Place

Chapel St.

QUEEN'S GALLERY

56

CITY OF WESTMINSTER

56

Petty France

Palmer St.

Belgrave Square

Chester St.

Upper Belgrave St.

Wilton St.

ROYAL MEWS

Palace

Castle La.

56

St.

Victoria St.

BELGRAVIA

Belgrave Place

Belgrave Square

Hobart Pl.

274

Grosvenor Gdns.

Street

H Victoria St.

Eaton Place

Lower Belgrave St.

Victoria

Street

Howick Pl.

7

Eaton Square

88

412

Ashley Pl.

416

Street Row

Eaton Square

Elizabeth

88

Eccleston

VICTORIA STATION

Carlisle Place

WESTMINSTER CATHEDRAL

Francis

VICTORIA

Chester Row

389

Ebury

St.

157

Wilton

Vauxhall

Bridge

Rochester

Vincent Square

389

Street

Buckingham Palace Rd

High Street

Belgrave Rd

Gillingham St.

201

Tachbrook

Way

ck St.

Road

Eccleston Square

0   200 m
0   200 yards

E

Chepstow Rd

Hereford Rd

Newton Road

Bishop's Bridge Rd

Cleveland Ter.

90

Gloucester

Artesian Road

Grove

Queensway

CITY OF WESTMINSTER

94

Cleveland Square

BAYSWATER

136

Westbourne

Chepstow Villas

Leinster Square

Garway Road

Porchester

Inverness

Leinster Gdns

Road

243

362

84

Pembridge Road

Queensway

Queensborough Terrace

Porchester Terrace

Craven Hill

NORTH KENSINGTON

Dawson Place

Moscow Road

Bark Pl.

BAYSWATER

Leinster Ter.

256

Portobello Rd

Pembridge Square

Palace Court

St.Petersburgh Place

Terrace

V

Kensington Park Rd

Pembridge Gdns

328

Bayswater

Road

Pembridge Rd

Gate

The Queensway

ROYAL BOROUGH OF KENSINGTON AND CHELSEA

KENSINGTON GARDENS

Hill

Kensington Palace Gardens

Broad Walk

Notting

238

335

NOTTING HILL GATE

KENSINGTON GARDENS

Kensington Place

KENSINGTON

0   200 m
0   200 yards

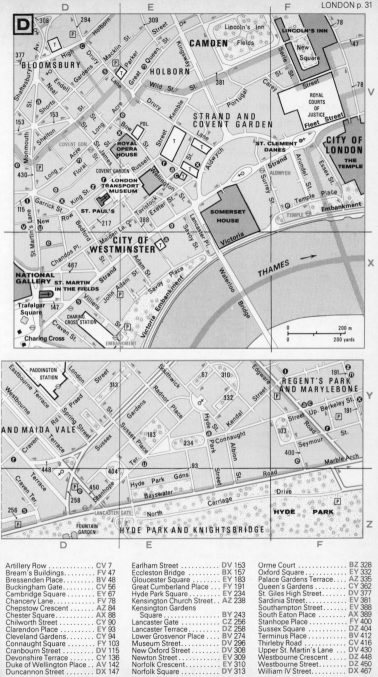

275

ALPHABETICAL LIST OF HOTELS AND RESTAURANTS
LISTE ALPHABÉTIQUE DES HOTELS ET RESTAURANTS
ELENCO ALFABETICO DEGLI ALBERGHI E RISTORANTI
ALPHABETISCHES HOTEL- UND RESTAURANTVERZEICHNIS

STARRED ESTABLISHMENTS IN LONDON
LES ÉTABLISSEMENTS A ÉTOILES DE LONDRES
GLI ESERCIZI CON STELLE A LONDRA
DIE STERN-RESTAURANTS LONDONS

	Area	Page
XXXX Le Gavroche	Mayfair	63

❀❀

	Area	Page
XXX La Tante Claire	Chelsea	55
XX Chez Nico	Battersea	61

❀

	Area	Page			Area	Page
Connaught	Mayfair	63		Le Soufflé	Mayfair	63
Capital	Chelsea	55		L'Arlequin	Battersea	61
The Terrace	Mayfair	63		Lichfield's	Richmond	60
Chelsea Room	Chelsea	55		Ma Cuisine	Chelsea	56
Waltons	Chelsea	55		Tiger Lee	Earl's Court	57

FURTHER ESTABLISHMENTS WHICH MERIT YOUR ATTENTION
AUTRES TABLES QUI MÉRITENT VOTRE ATTENTION
ALTRE TAVOLE PARTICOLARMENTE INTERESSANTI
WEITERE EMPFEHLENSWERTE HÄUSER

M

	Area	Page			Area	Page
XXX Odins	Regent's Park and Marylebone	65		XX Ken Lo's Memories of China	Victoria	68
XXX Suntory	St. James's	66		XX Lampwick's	Battersea	61
XX Bagatelle	Chelsea	56		XX Le Poulbot	City	50
XX Eatons	Victoria	68		X Bubb's	City	50
XX Gavvers	Chelsea	56				

RESTAURANTS CLASSIFIED ACCORDING TO TYPE

RESTAURANTS CLASSÉS SUIVANT LEUR GENRE

RISTORANTI CLASSIFICATI SECONDO IL LORO GENERE

RESTAURANTS NACH ART UND EINRICHTUNG GEORDNET

Borough	Area	Restaurant	Page

BISTRO

Borough	Area	Restaurant	Page
Camden	Regent's Park	✗ Chalcot's Bistro	50
Islington	Islington	✗ M'sieur Frog	55
Wandsworth	Clapham	✗ Pollyanna's	61
Westminster (City of)	Regent's Park & Marylebone	✗ Langan's Bistro	66
—	Victoria	✗ Bumbles	68

DANCING

Borough	Area	Restaurant	Page
Hammersmith	Fulham	✗✗ Barbarella	52
Westminster (City of)	Bayswater & Maida Vale	✗✗ Concordia Notte	62
—	Mayfair	✗✗✗ Tiberio	63
—	St. James's	✗✗✗✗✗ Maxim's de Paris	66

SEAFOOD

Borough	Area	Restaurant	Page
Barnet	Finchley	✗✗ Fogareiro	47
City of London	City of London	✗✗✗ Wheeler's	50
—	—	✗✗ Bill Bentley's Bishopsgate	50
Kensington & Chelsea (Royal Borough of)	Chelsea	✗✗ Poissonnerie de l'Avenue	56
—	—	✗✗ Suquet (Le)	56
—	Earl's Court	✗✗ Croisette (La)	57
—	—	✗✗ ❀ Tiger Lee	57
—	Kensington	✗✗ Quai St. Pierre (Le)	57
Westminster (City of)	Mayfair	✗✗✗✗ Scott's	63
—	—	✗✗ Golden Carp	64
—	Regent's Park & Marylebone	✗✗ Bill Bentley's	65
—	Strand & Covent Garden	✗✗ Frère Jacques	67
—	—	✗✗ Sheekey's	67
—	—	✗ Grimes	67

Borough	Area		Restaurant	Page

CHINESE

Borough	Area		Restaurant	Page
Barnet	Mill Hill	XX	Good Earth	47
–	–	XX	Taicoon	47
Ealing	Ealing	X	Maxim	51
–	Hanwell	X	Happiness Garden	51
Enfield	Winchmore Hill	XX	Dragon Garden	51
Harrow	Hatch End	X	Swan	53
Kensington & Chelsea (Royal Borough of)	Chelsea	XXX	Zen	55
–	–	XX	Good Earth	56
–	–	XX	Good Earth	56
–	Earl's Court	XX	❀ Tiger Lee	57
–	–	X	Crystal Palace	57
–	Kensington	XX	Junk Two	57
–	–	XX	Mama San	57
–	–	XX	Sailing Junk	57
–	–	X	I Ching	58
–	South Kensington	XX	Zen Too	59
Redbridge	South Woodford	XX	Ho-Ho	59
Richmond-upon-Thames	Richmond	XX	Evergreen	60
–	–	XX	Kew Rendezvous	60
–	–	X	Red Lion	60
Westminster (City of)	Bayswater & Maida Vale	XXX	Bombay Palace	62
–	–	X	Fortune Cookie	62
–	Hyde Park & Knightsbridge	XX	Mr. Chow	62
–	Mayfair	XX	Mr Kai	64
–	Regent's Park & Marylebone	XX	Lords Rendezvous	65
–	Soho	X	Galley Rendezvous	66
–	Strand & Covent Garden	X	Poons of Covent Garden	67
–	Victoria	XX	Hunan	68
–	–	XX	Ken Lo's Memories of China	68

ENGLISH

Borough	Area		Restaurant	Page
Camden	Hampstead	X	Turpin's	49
Kensington & Chelsea (Royal Borough of)	Chelsea	XX	English Garden	56
–	–	XX	English House	56
Westminster (City of)	Strand & Covent Garden	XXX	Simpson's-in-the-Strand	67
–	Victoria	XXX	Lockets	68
–	–	X	Tate Gallery Rest.	68

FRENCH

Borough	Area		Restaurant	Page
Barnet	Finchley	X	Aubergade (L')	47
Bromley	Beckenham	XX	Bon Bec (Le)	48
–	Orpington	XXX	Oven d'Or	48
Camden	Bloomsbury	XXX	Etoile (L')	49
–	–	XX	Les Halles	49
–	–	XX	Porte de la Cité	49
–	–	X	Mon Plaisir	49
–	Hampstead	XXX	Keats	49

Borough	Area		Restaurant	Page

			FRENCH (continued)	
City of London	City of London	XX	**Poulbot (Le)** (basement)	50
–	–	X	**Bubb's**	50
–	–	X	**Gamin (Le)**	50
Kensington & Chelsea (Royal Borough of)	Chelsea	XXX	**Français (Le)**	55
–	–	XXX	✿✿ **Tante Claire (La)**	55
–	–	XX	**Bagatelle**	56
–	–	XX	**Gavvers**	56
–	–	XX	✿ **Ma Cuisine**	56
–	–	XX	**St. Quentin**	56
–	–	XX	**Suquet (Le)**	56
–	–	X	**Brasserie (La)**	56
–	Earl's Court	XX	**Croisette (La)**	57
–	Kensington	XX	**Pomme d'Amour (La)**	57
–	–	XX	**Quai St. Pierre (Le)**	57
–	–	X	**Ark (The)**	58
–	–	X	**Résidence (La)**	58
–	North Kensington	XX	**Chez Moi**	58
–	–	XX	**Monsieur Thompsons**	58
Richmond-upon-Thames	Barnes	X	**Barnaby's**	60
Wandsworth	Battersea	XX	✿✿ **Chez Nico**	61
–	–	XX	✿ **Arlequin (L')**	61
Westminster (City of)	Mayfair	XXXXX	✿ **Terrace (The)**	63
–	–	XXXX	✿✿✿ **Gavroche (Le)**	63
–	Regents Park & Marylebone	XX	**Artagnan (D')**	65
–	–	X	**Aventure (L')**	66
–	–	X	**Bois St. Jean (Au)**	65
–	–	X	**Muscadet (Le)**	65
–	St. James's	XXXXX	**Maxims de Paris**	66
–	Soho	XX	**Jardin des Gourmets (Au)**	66
–	–	XX	**Chez Solange**	67
–	–	XX	**Interlude de Tabaillau**	67
–	Strand & Covent Garden	X	**Magnos Brasserie**	67
–	Victoria	XX	**Ciboure**	68
–	–	XX	**Restaurant (The)**	68
–	–	X	**Poule au Pot (La)**	68
–	–	X	**Villa Medici**	68

			GREEK	
Camden	Bloomsbury	XXX	**White Tower**	49
Westminster (City of)	Bayswater & Maida Vale	X	**Kalamaras Taverna**	62

			HUNGARIAN	
Westminster (City of)	Soho	XX	**Gay Hussar**	66

			INDIAN & PAKISTANI	
Brent	Kilburn	X	**Vijay**	47
Camden	Bloomsbury	XX	**Lal Qila**	49
–	Holborn	X	**Last Days of the Raj**	49
Croydon	Croydon	X	**Khyber**	50

Borough	Area	Restaurant		Page

INDIAN & PAKISTANI (continued)

Borough	Area		Restaurant	Page
Hammersmith	Hammersmith	X	Aziz	52
—	—	X	Rajdoot	52
—	Shepherd's Bush	XX	Shireen	52
Kensington & Chelsea (Royal Borough of)	Earl's Court	X	Naraine	57
	South Kensington	XXX	Bombay Brasserie	59
—	—	XX	Memories of India	59
—	—	X	Star of India	59
Westminster (City of)	Bayswater & Maida Vale	XXX	Bombay Palace	62
—	Belgravia	XX	Salloos	62
—	Hyde Park & Knightsbridge	XXX	Shezan	62
—	Mayfair	XX	Gaylord	64
—	Regent's Park & Marylebone	XX	Gaylord	65
—	—	XX	Viceroy of India	65
—	Soho	XX	Red Fort	66
—	—	X	Trusha	66
—	Strand & Covent Garden	X	Taste of India	67
—	Victoria	XXX	Kundan	68

ITALIAN

Borough	Area		Restaurant	Page
Barnet	Finchley	XX	Luigi's '' Belmont ''	47
Bromley	Bromley	XX	Chariot Wheel	48
—	—	X	Capisano	48
—	Chislehurst	XX	Mario	48
—	Farnborough	XX	Ombrello (L')	48
—	Keston	XX	Giannino's	48
Camden	Hampstead	X	Villa Bianca	49
City of London	City of London	XXX	City Tiberio	50
—	—	XX	Villa Augusta	50
Croydon	Sanderstead	X	Elio	51
Ealing	Ealing	XX	Gino's	51
Hammersmith	Fulham	XX	Barbarella	52
—	—	XX	Mio Sogno	52
Haringey	Highgate	XX	San Carlo	52
Harrow	Hatch End	XX	Canaletto 2	53
Hillingdon	Eastcote	X	Sambuca	53
—	Northwood	XX	Martini	54
Islington	Islington	XX	Portofino	55
Kensington & Chelsea (Royal Borough of)	Chelsea	XX	Beccofino	56
—	—	XX	Don Luigi	56
—	—	XX	Eleven Park Walk	55
—	—	XX	Flavio	56
—	—	XX	Mario	55
—	—	XX	Meridiana	56
—	—	XX	Ponte Nuovo	56
—	—	XX	San Frediano	56
—	—	XX	San Ruffillo	56
—	—	XX	Toto	56
—	—	XX	Villa Puccini	56
—	Earl's Court	XX	Pontevecchio	57

Borough	Area	Restaurant	Page

RESTAURANTS OPEN ON SUNDAY (L : lunch - D : dinner) AND RESTAU-RANTS TAKING LAST ORDERS AFTER 11.30 p.m.

RESTAURANTS OUVERTS LE DIMANCHE (L : déjeuner - D : dîner) ET RES-TAURANTS PRENANT LES DERNIÈRES COMMANDES APRÈS 23 h 30

RISTORANTI APERTI LA DOMENICA (L : colazione - D : pranzo) E RISTO-RANTI CHE ACCETTANO ORDINAZIONI DOPO LE 23. 30

RESTAURANTS, DIE SONNTAGS GEÖFFNET SIND (L : Mittagessen - D : Abendessen), BZW. BESTELLUNGEN AUCH NACH 23. 30 UHR ANNEHMEN

Borough	Area	Restaurant	Sunday	11.30 p. m.	Page
Barnet	Child's Hill	✗ Quincy's 84	L		47
—	Finchley	✗✗ Luigi's « Belmont »	L D		47
—	—	✗✗ Fogareiro		x	47
—	Mill Hill	✗✗ Good Earth	L D		47
—	—	✗✗ Taicoon	L D	x	47
Brent	Kilburn	✗ Vijay (11.45)	L D	x	47
Camden	Bloomsbury	✗✗ Lal Qila	L D		49
—	Finchley Road	✗✗ Capability Brown		x	49
—	Hampstead	✗✗✗ Keats		x	49
—	—	✗ Chateaubriand (11.45)		x	49
—	—	✗ Turpin's	L	x	49
—	Holborn	✗✗✗ Opera (L') (12.00)		x	49
—	Regents Park	✗✗ Pratts	L	x	50
—	—	✗ Chalcot's Bistro	L		50
—	Swiss Cottage	✗✗ Peter's	L	x	50
Croydon	Croydon	✗✗✗ Chateau Napoleon	L D		50
—	—	✗ Khyber	L D	x	50
Ealing	Ealing	✗✗ Gino's		x	51
—	—	✗ Maxim (12.00)	D	x	51
—	Hanwell	✗ Happiness Garden		x	51
Enfield	Southgate	✗✗ L'Oiseau Noir	L		51
—	Winchmore Hill	✗✗ Dragon Garden	L D	x	51
Greenwich	Greenwich	✗ Mean Time	L		52
Hammersmith	Fulham	✗✗ Barbarella (1.00)		x	52
—	—	✗ Carlo's Place		x	52

Borough	Area	Restaurant	Sunday	11.30 p. m.	Page
–	Hammersmith	✗ **Aziz (11.45)**		x	52
–	–	✗ **Rajdoot (11.45)**	L D	x	52
–	Sheperd's Bush	✗✗ **Shireen**	L D	x	52
Haringey	Highgate	✗✗ **San Carlo (12.00)**	L D	x	52
Harrow	Hatch End	✗ **Swan**	L D		53
Hillingdon	Eastcote	✗ **Sambuca**	L D	x	53
Islington	Finsbury	✗✗ **Café St. Pierre**	L	x	54
–	Islington	✗✗ **Frederick's**		x	55
–	–	✗✗ **Portofino**		x	55
–	–	✗ **M'sieur Frog**		x	55
Kensington & Chelsea (Royal Borough of)	Chelsea	🏠 ❀ **Capital**	L D		55
–	–	✗✗✗✗ ❀ **Chelsea Room**	L D	x	55
–	–	✗✗✗✗ ❀ **Waltons**	L D	x	55
–	–	✗✗✗ **Zen (12.00)**	L D	x	55
–	–	✗✗ **Beccofino**		x	56
–	–	✗✗ **Bewick's**	D		56
–	–	✗✗ **Daphne's**		x	55
–	–	✗✗ **Don Luigi (12.00)**	L D	x	56
–	–	✗✗ **Eleven Park Walk (12.00)**		x	55
–	–	✗✗ **English Garden**	L D		56
–	–	✗✗ **English House**	L D	x	56
–	–	✗✗ **Good Earth**	L D	x	56
–	–	✗✗ **Good Earth**	L D	x	56
–	–	✗✗ **Ménage à Trois (12.15)**		x	56
–	–	✗✗ **Meridiana (12.00)**	L D	x	56
–	–	✗✗ **Poissonnerie de l'Avenue**		x	56
–	–	✗✗ **Ponte Nuovo (11.45)**	L D	x	56
–	–	✗✗ **St. Quentin (12.00)**	L D	x	56
–	–	✗✗ **Suquet (Le)**	L D	x	56
–	–	✗✗ **Toto**	L D	x	56
–	–	✗✗ **Villa Puccini**	L D	x	56
–	–	✗ **Brasserie (La) (12.00)**	L D	x	56
–	–	✗ **Thierry's (11.45)**		x	56
–	Earl's Court	✗✗✗ **Martin's**		x	57
–	–	✗✗ **Brinkley's**		x	57
–	–	✗✗ **Croisette (La)**	L D	x	57
–	–	✗✗ **L'Olivier**		x	57
–	–	✗✗ **Pontevecchio (11.45)**	L D	x	57
–	–	✗✗ ❀ **Tiger Lee**	D		57
–	–	✗ **Naraine (11.45)**	D	x	57
–	–	✗ **Crystal Palace**	L D	x	57
–	Kensington	🏠 **Royal Garden** (Royal Roof 12.30)		x	57
–	–	✗✗ **Al Gallo d'Oro (11.45)**	L D	x	57
–	–	✗✗ **Franco Ovest**		x	57
–	–	✗✗ **Hiroko**	L D		57
–	–	✗✗ **Junk Two**	D	x	57
–	–	✗✗ **Mama San**	L D		57

Borough	Area	Restaurant		Sunday	11.30 p. m.	Page
–	–	XX	Quai St. Pierre (Le)		x	57
–	–	XX	Sailing Junk	D	x	57
–	–	XX	Topo d'Oro	L D	x	57
–	–	XX	Trattoo	L D	x	57
–	–	X	Ark (The)	D		58
–	–	X	Barbino (Il) (11.45)		x	58
–	–	X	Paesana (La) (11.45)		x	58
–	–	X	Residence (La)	L D		58
–	North Kensington	XXX	Leith's (11.45)	D	x	58
–	–	XX	Chez Moi		x	58
–	–	X	192	L	x	58
–	South Kensington	XXX	Bombay Brasserie (12.00)	L D	x	59
–	–	XX	Reads	L		59
–	–	XX	Zen Too	L D	x	59
–	–	X	Chanterelle (12.00)	L D	x	59
–	–	X	Star of India	L D	x	59
Merton	Wimbledon	XX	San Lorenzo Fuoriporta	L D		59
Redbridge	South Woodford	XX	Ho Ho	L D	x	59
Richmond-upon-Thames	Richmond	XX	Kew Rendezvous	L D		60
–	–	X	Red Lion	L D		60
Southwark	Dulwich Village	XX	Luigi's		x	60
Waltham Forest	Leytonstone	X	Trattoria Parmigiana		x	61
Wandsworth	Battersea	XX	Alonso's		x	61
–	Clapham	X	Pollyanna's (12.00)	L D	x	61
Westminster (City of)	Bayswater & Maida Vale	XX	Concordia Notte (2.00)		x	62
		XX	San Marino		x	62
–	–	XX	Trat West	L D		62
–	–	X	Concordia (11.45)		x	62
–	–	X	Fortune Cookie	L D	x	62
–	–	X	Kalamaras Taverna (12.00)		x	62
–	Belgravia	⌂⌂⌂	Berkeley (Restaurant)	L D		62
–	–	XX	Salloos		x	62
–	Hyde Park & Knightsbridge	XX	Mr Chow (11.45)	L D	x	62
–	Mayfair	⌂⌂⌂	Claridges (Causerie)	L D		63
–	–	⌂⌂⌂	Dorchester (Grill)	L D		63
–	–	⌂⌂⌂	Inn on the Park (Four Seasons)	L D		63
			(Lanes 12.00)	L D	x	63
–	–	XXXXX ✿	Terrace (The)		x	63
–	–	XXXX ✿	Soufflé (Le)	L D		63
–	–	XXXX	Scott's	D		63

Borough	Area	Restaurant	Sunday	11.30 p. m.	Page
–	–	XXX Tiberio (1.00)		x	63
–	–	XX Apicella 81 (11.45)		x	64
–	–	XX Gaylord	L D		64
–	–	XX Golden Carp		x	64
–	–	XX Langan's Brasserie (11.45)		x	64
–	–	XX Mr Kai	L D		64
–	–	XX One Two Three	D		64
–	–	XX Shogun	D		64
–	–	X Ikeda	D		64
–	Regent's Park & Marylebone	XXX Odins		x	65
–	–	XX Gaylord	L D	x	65
–	–	XX Loggia (La)		x	65
–	–	XX Lords Rendezvous	L D		65
–	–	XX Viceroy of India	L D	x	65
–	–	X Bois St. Jean (Au)	L D	x	65
–	–	X Barbino (Il) (11.45)		x	66
–	–	X Biagi's	L D		66
–	–	X Langan's Bistro		x	66
Westminster (City of)	St. James's	XXXXX Maxim's de Paris (11.45)		x	66
–	–	XX Caprice (Le) (12.00)	L D	x	66
–	Soho	XXX Leonis Quo Vadis	D		66
–	–	XX Chesa (Swiss Centre)	L D	x	66
–	–	XX Escargot (L')		x	66
–	–	XX Fuji	D		66
–	–	XX Red Fort	L D		66
–	–	XX Rugantino		x	66
–	–	XX Terrazza (La)	L D		66
–	–	X Frith's		x	66
–	–	X Gallery Rendezvous	L D		66
–	–	X Trattoria Imperia		x	66
–	–	X Trusha		x	66
–	Strand & Covent Garden	Savoy (River)	L D	x	67
–	–	XXX Inigo Jones		x	67
–	–	XX Chez Solange (12.15)		x	67
–	–	XX Grange		x	67
–	–	XX Interlude de Tabaillau		x	67
–	–	XX Luigi's		x	67
–	–	X Colosseo		x	67
–	–	X Grimes		x	67
–	–	X Laguna	L D		67
–	–	X Magnos Brasserie		x	67
–	–	X Poons of Covent Garden		x	67
–	–	X Taste of India (12.00)	L D	x	67
–	Victoria	XXX Kundan		x	68
–	–	XX Ciboure		x	68
–	–	XX Ken Lo's Memories of China	L D		68
–	–	XX Restaurant (The)		x	68
–	–	X Fontana (La)	L D	x	68
–	–	X Mimmo d'Ischia		x	68
–	–	X Tapas		x	68
–	–	X Villa Medici (11.45)		x	68

289

ALPHABETICAL LIST OF AREAS INCLUDED
LISTE ALPHABÉTIQUE DES QUARTIERS CITÉS
ELENCO ALFABETICO DEI QUARTIERI CITATI
LISTE DER ERWÄHNTEN BEZIRKE

BOROUGHS and AREAS

Greater London is divided, for administrative purposes, into 32 boroughs plus the City ; these sub-divide naturally into minor areas, usually grouped around former villages or quarters, which often maintain a distinctive character.

❂ of Greater London : 01 except special cases.

BARNET pp. 4 and 5.

Child's Hill – ✉ NW2.

✗ **Quincy's 84,** 675 Finchley Rd, NW2 2JP, ✆ 794 8499 – 🔄 _VISA_   DV **r**
   closed Saturday lunch, Sunday dinner and Monday – **M** (restricted lunch) 9.50/12.50 **t.** ⅋ 3.00.

Finchley – ✉ N3/N12/NW11.
  ☗ Nether Court, Frith Lane ✆ 346 2436.

✗✗ **Luigi's Belmont,** 2-4 Belmont Par., Finchley Rd, NW11 6XP, at Temple Fortune ✆ 455 0210,
   Italian rest. – 🔄 ᴁᴇ ⓪ _VISA_   DV **a**
   closed Monday – **M** a la carte 11.40/15.10 **st.** ⅋ 3.00.

✗✗ **Fogareiro,** 16-18 Hendon Lane, N 3, ✆ 346 0315, Seafood – 🔄 ᴁᴇ ⓪ _VISA_   DU **c**
   closed Sunday and Bank Holidays – **M** a la carte 12.50/15.00 ⅋ 2.45.

✗ **L'Aubergade,** 816 Finchley Rd, NW11 6XL, at Temple Fortune ✆ 455 8853, French rest.
   closed Sunday – **M** 7.95/9.95 **t.** ⅋ 2.70.   DV **i**

Hendon – ✉ NW4/NW7.
  ☗ off Sanders Lane ✆ 346 7810.

🏛 **Hendon Hall,** Ashley Lane, NW4 1HF, ✆ 203 3341, Telex 8956088, ♨ – 🛗 📺 🅿 🏛 🔄 ᴁᴇ
   ⓪ _VISA_   DV **v**
   M 8.00/8.50 **t.** ⅋ 3.00 – **52 rm** ⊡ 39.00/52.50 **t.** – SB (except Christmas) 46.00/48.00 **st.**

🏛 **Scratchwood TraveLodge** (T.H.F.) without rest., NW7 3HB, at Scratchwood Service Area
   on M 1 ✆ 906 0611, Telex 8814796 – 📺 ⇱wc ☎ ⅋ 🅿 🏛 🔄 ᴁᴇ ⓪ _VISA_   CU **r**
   97 rm 29.00/50.00 **st.**

Mill Hill – ✉ NW7.
  ☗ 100 Barnet Way ✆ 959 2282.

✗✗ **Good Earth,** 143-145 The Broadway, NW7 4RN, ✆ 959 7011, Chinese rest. – 🔄 ᴁᴇ ⓪ _VISA_
   M a la carte 9.00/13.50 **t.** ⅋ 2.30.   CU **a**

✗✗ **Taicoon,** 655 Watford Way, NW7 3JR, at Apex Corner ✆ 959 5037, Chinese rest. – 🔄 ᴁᴇ
   ⓪ _VISA_   CU **c**
   M a la carte 10.00/12.50 **t.**

BEXLEY pp. 10 and 11.

Bexley – ✉ Kent – ❂ 0322 Crayford.

🏛 **Crest** (Crest), Black Prince Interchange, Southwold Rd, DA5 1ND, on A 2 ✆ 526900, Telex
   8956539 – 🛗 📺 ⇱wc ⅋ 🅿 🏛 🔄 ᴁᴇ ⓪ _VISA_   HY **e**
   M approx. 11.00 **st.** – ⊡ 5.25 – **78 rm** 42.00/52.00 **st.**

BRENT pp. 4 and 5.

Kilburn .

✗ **Vijay,** 49 Willesden Lane, NW6 7RF, ✆ 328 1087, South Indian rest. – ▦ 🔄 ᴁᴇ ⓪ _VISA_
   closed 25 and 26 December – **M** a la carte 5.00/8.50 **t.**   DV **n**

Wembley – ✉ Middx.
  ☗ Horsenden Hill, Whitton Av. ✆ 902 4555.

🏛 **Wembley International,** Empire Way, HA9 8DS, ✆ 902 8839, Telex 24837 – 🛗 📺 ⅋ 🅿
   🏛 🔄 ᴁᴇ ⓪ _VISA_   CV **z**
   closed Christmas Day – **M** (closed Saturday lunch) 6.50/8.25 **st.** ⅋ 2.20 – ⊡ 3.25 – **324 rm**
   37.50/47.50 **st.**

BROMLEY pp. 10 and 11.

Beckenham – ✉ Kent.
🏌, 🏌 Beckenham Place Park ✆ 650 2292.

XX **Le Bon Bec,** 189a High St., BR3 1AH, ✆ 650 0593, French rest. – 🍽 rest. 🆓 AE ① VISA
closed Saturday lunch, Sunday, 20 August-5 September and Bank Holidays – **M** 10.50/12.00 t.
🛏 2.40.   FZ **c**

Bromley – ✉ Kent.
🏌 Magpie Hall Lane ✆ 462 7014.

🏨 **Bromley Court** ⑤, Bromley Hill, BR1 4JD, ✆ 464 5011, Telex 896310, 🐎 – 🛗 TV ☎ 🅿. 🅰.
🆓 AE ① VISA   GY **z**
M 6.45/7.75 t. 🛏 2.75 – **130 rm** ⊠ 34.00/42.00 t. – SB (weekends only) 43.75 **st.**

⤴ **Grianan,** 23 Orchard Rd, BR1 2PR, ✆ 460 1795 – 🚰wc 🅿. 🛠   GYZ **n**
12 rm ⊠ 10.35/23.00 **st.**

⤴ **Bromley Continental,** 56-58 Plaistow Lane, BR1 3JE, ✆ 464 2415, 🐎 – 🚰 🅿. 🆓 VISA. 🛠
21 rm ⊠ 11.20/22.50 t.   GZ **a**

XX **Chariot Wheel,** 21-22 Westmoreland Pl., Bromley South Shopping Centre, BR1 1DS, ✆
460 8477, Italian rest. – 🆓 AE ① VISA   GZ **r**
closed Sunday, Monday and Bank Holidays – **M** a la carte 8.10/15.10 t.

X **Capisano,** 9 Simpsons Rd, BR2 9AP, ✆ 464 8036, Italian rest. – 🆓 AE VISA   GZ **s**
closed Sunday, Monday, 18 August-9 September and Bank Holidays – **M** a la carte 8.10/13.10 t.
🛏 2.50.

Chislehurst – ✉ Kent.

XX **Foxes,** 43 High St., BR7 5AF, ✆ 467 2094 – 🆓 AE ① VISA   HY **a**
closed Saturday lunch, Sunday and Bank Holidays – **M** a la carte 9.20/12.25 t. 🛏 2.50.

XX **Mario,** 53 Chislehurst Rd, BR7 5NP, ✆ 467 1341, Italian rest. – 🆓 AE ① VISA   GZ **c**
closed Sunday and Monday – **M** a la carte 8.45/11.25.

Farnborough – ✉ Kent – 🕿 0689 Farnborough.
🏌 High Elms, High Elms Rd ✆ 58175, off A 21 via Shire Lane.

XX **L'Ombrello,** 360 Crofton Rd, Locksbottom, BR6 7XX, ✆ 52286, Italian rest. – 🆓 AE ① VISA
closed Sunday – **M** a la carte 8.30/13.10 t. 🛏 2.50.   HZ **c**

Keston – ✉ Kent – 🕿 0689 Farnborough.

XX Giannino's, 6 Commonside, BR4 2TS, ✆ 56410, Italian rest.   GZ **x**

Orpington – ✉ Kent – 🕿 0689 Orpington.
🏌 Cray Valley, St. Paul's Cray ✆ 37909.

XXX **Oven d'Or,** 4a Crescent Way, BR6 6BL, ✆ 52170, French rest. – 🆓 AE ① VISA   HZ **a**
closed Sunday, Monday, 3 weeks in summer, 1 to 7 January and Bank Holidays – **M** a la carte
10.80/15.10 **st.** 🛏 2.60.

Le Grand Londres (GREATER LONDON) *est composé de la City et de 32 arrondisse-
ments administratifs (Borough) eux-mêmes divisés en quartiers ou villages ayant
conservé leur caractère propre (Area).*

CAMDEN Except where otherwise stated see pp. 13-16.

Bloomsbury – ✉ NW1/W1/WC1.

🏨 **Russell** (T.H.F.), Russell Sq., WC1B 5BE, ✆ 837 6470, Telex 24615 – 🛗 TV ☎. 🅰. 🆓 AE ①
VISA   NT **o**
M (carving rest.) 8.95 **st.** 🛏 2.60 – ⊠ 6.00 – **318 rm** 44.50/55.00 **st.**

🏨 **Grafton,** 130 Tottenham Court Rd, W1P 9HP, ✆ 388 4131, Telex 297234 – 🛗 TV ☎. 🅰. 🆓 AE
① VISA. 🛠   LT **n**
M 10.50 t. 🛏 3.00 – ⊠ 6.50 – **171 rm** 55.90/73.90 **st.**

🏨 **Kenilworth,** 97 Great Russell St., WC1B 3LB, ✆ 637 3477 – 🛗 TV ☎. 🅰. 🆓 AE ① VISA
M 10.00 **st.** – ⊠ 5.50 – **182 rm** 44.90/59.90 **st.**   MT **a**

🏨 **Bonnington,** 92 Southampton Row, WC1B 4BH, ✆ 242 2828, Telex 261591 – 🛗 TV 🚰wc
🕿. 🆓 AE ① VISA   NT **s**
M (grill rest. only) (buffet lunch) 8.00 **st.** 🛏 2.60 – **245 rm** ⊠ 25.50/49.50 **st.**

🏨 **Kingsley** (Mt. Charlotte), Bloomsbury Way, WC1A 2SD, ✆ 242 5881, Telex 21157 – 🛗 TV
🚰wc ☎. 🅰. 🆓 AE ① VISA. 🛠   NT **r**
M (closed Saturday lunch) (carving rest.) 8.75 t. – ⊠ 3.00 – **146 rm** 39.00/60.50 **st.**

⤴ **Harlingford,** 61-63 Cartwright Gdns, WC1H 9EL, ✆ 387 1551 – 🆓 VISA. 🛠   MS **n**
40 rm ⊠ 17.00/36.00 t.

⤴ **Crescent,** 49 Cartwright Gdns, WC1H 9EL, ✆ 387 1515 – 🛠   MS **a**
30 rm ⊠ 14.00/26.00 t.

XXX **White Tower,** 1 Percy St., W1P 0ET, ℰ 636 8141, Greek rest. – ⚡ AE ⓪ VISA — MT u
closed Saturday, Sunday, 3 weeks August, 1 week Christmas and Bank Holidays – **M** a la carte 12.50/23.00 t. ⓷ 3.00.

XXX **Rue St. Jacques,** 5 Charlotte St., W1P 1HD, ℰ 637 0222 – ▤. ⚡ AE ⓪ VISA — MT c
closed Saturday, Sunday, Easter, 3 weeks August, Christmas, New Year and Bank Holidays – **M** a la carte 13.95/26.30 t.

XXX **L'Etoile,** 30 Charlotte St., W1P 1HJ, ℰ 636 7189, French rest. – AE ⓪ VISA — LT e
closed Saturday, Sunday, August and Bank Holidays – **M** a la carte approx. 18.00 t.

XX **Porte de la Cité,** 65 Theobalds Rd, WC1 8TA, ℰ 242 1154, French rest. – ⚡ AE ⓪ VISA — NT c
closed Saturday, Sunday and Bank Holidays – **M** (lunch only) 14.50 t. ⓷ 2.85.

XX **Lal Qila,** 117 Tottenham Court Rd, W1P 9HL, ℰ 387 4570, Indian rest.. ⚡ AE ⓪ VISA — LT u
M a la carte 4.45/6.95 t.

XX **Les Halles,** 57 Theobald's Rd, WC1X 8SP, ℰ 242 6761, French rest. – ⚡ AE ⓪ VISA — NT e
closed Saturday lunch and Sunday – **M** a la carte 10.10/13.40 t. ⓷ 3.50.

X **Mon Plaisir,** 21 Monmouth St., WC2H 9DD, ℰ 836 7243, French rest. — p. 31 DV a
closed Saturday lunch, Sunday, Easter, Christmas-New Year and Bank Holidays – **M** a la carte 5.90/11.60 t. ⓷ 3.50.

Euston – ✉ NW1.

🏨 **Kennedy** (Mt. Charlotte), 43 Cardington St., NW1 2LP, ℰ 387 4400, Telex 28250 – 🛗 📺
⌂wc ☎. 🅰. ⚡ AE ⓪ VISA. ❄ — LS r
M 6.75/7.50 st. ⓷ 2.90 – ⌷ 2.50 – **320 rm** 41.25/52.25 st.

Finchley Road – ✉ NW1/NW3.

🏨 **Charles Bernard,** 5 Frognal, NW3 6AL, ℰ 794 0101, Telex 23560 – 🛗 📺 ⌂wc ☎ 🅿. ⚡
⓪ VISA — GR s
M (dinner only) a la carte 6.25/10.00 st. ⓷ 2.60 – **57 rm** ⌷ 34.50/49.00 st.

↑ **Dawson House,** 72 Canfield Gdns, NW6 3ED, ℰ 624 0079, 🌳 – ❄ — HR a
15 rm ⌷ 10.00/19.00 st.

XX **Capability Brown,** 351 West End Lane, NW6 1LT, ℰ 794 3234 – ⚡ AE ⓪ VISA — DV e
closed Saturday lunch, Sunday and Bank Holidays – **M** a la carte 9.00/16.00 st. ⓷ 2.55.
pp. 4 and 5

Hampstead – ✉ NW3.

🏨 **Ladbroke Clive** (Ladbroke), Primrose Hill Rd, NW3 3NA, ℰ 586 2233, Telex 22759 – 🛗 📺.
🅰. ⚡ AE ⓪ VISA. ❄ — KR a
M *(closed Saturday and Bank Holiday lunch)* 9.00 t. ⓷ 3.25 – ⌷ 5.50 – **84 rm** 42.00/52.00 t.

🏨 **Swiss Cottage,** 4 Adamson Rd, NW3 3HP, ℰ 722 2281, Telex 297232, « Antique furniture collection » – 🛗 📺 ⌂wc ♨wc ☎. 🅰. ⚡ AE ⓪ VISA. ❄ — JR n
M 5.50/8.00 t. ⓷ 2.00 – **65 rm** ⌷ 30.00/60.00 t.

🏨 **Post House** (T.H.F.), 215 Haverstock Hill, NW3 4RB, ℰ 794 8121, Telex 262494 – 🛗 📺
⌂wc ☜ 🅿. ⚡ AE ⓪ VISA — GR r
M 8.00 st. ⓷ 2.85 – ⌷ 5.50 – **140 rm** 41.00/48.50 st.

↑ **Sandringham** ⚶, 3 Holford Rd, NW3 1AD, ℰ 435 1569, <, 🌳 – 🅿. ❄ — GR u
13 rm ⌷ 14.00/29.00 st.

↑ **Frognal Lodge,** 14 Frognal Gdns (off Church Row), NW3 6UX, ℰ 435 8238, Telex 8812714 –
🛗 ⌂wc ☜. ⚡ AE ⓪ VISA — GR v
17 rm ⌷ 19.00/38.50 st.

XXX **Keats,** 3-4 Downshire Hill, NW3 1NR, ℰ 435 3544, French rest. – ⚡ AE ⓪ VISA — GR i
closed Sunday and 3 weeks August – **M** (dinner only) a la carte 17.50/23.00 st. ⓷ 8.00.

X **Villa Bianca,** 1 Perrin's Court, NW3 1QR, ℰ 435 3131, Italian rest.. ⚡ AE ⓪ VISA — GR c
closed last 3 weeks August – **M** a la carte 12.40/14.35 t. ⓷ 2.95.

X **Chateaubriand,** 48 Belsize Lane, NW3 5AR, ℰ 435 4882 – ⚡ AE ⓪ VISA — GR n
closed Sunday – **M** (dinner only) a la carte 9.25/12.30 t.

X **Turpin's,** 118 Heath St., NW3 1DR, ℰ 435 3791, English rest. – ⚡ AE ⓪ VISA — GR a
closed for lunch Monday to Friday and Sunday dinner – **M** a la carte 5.95/14.65 st. ⓷ 3.50.

Holborn – ✉ WC2.

🏨 **Drury Lane Moat House** (Q.M.H.), 10 Drury Lane, High Holborn, WC2B 5RE, ℰ 836 6666,
Telex 8811395 – 🛗 ▤ 📺 🅰. ⚡ AE ⓪ VISA. ❄ — p. 31 DV c
M 9.75 st. ⓷ 3.25 – ⌷ 6.25 – **128 rm** 55.00/73.00 st. – SB 67.00/73.00 st.

XXX **L'Opera,** 32 Great Queen St., WC2B 5AA, ℰ 405 9020 – ⚡ AE ⓪ VISA — p. 31 EV n
closed Saturday lunch and Sunday – **M** a la carte 11.70/15.60 t. ⓷ 2.50.

X **Last Days of the Raj,** 22 Drury Lane, WC2, ℰ 836 1628, Indian rest. — p. 31 DV s

---

King's Cross – ✉ N1.

🏨 **Great Northern,** N1 9AN, ℰ 837 5454, Telex 299041 – 🛗 📺 ⌂wc ☜. 🅰. ⚡ AE ⓪ VISA.
❄ — MNS s
closed Christmas – **M** (carving rest.) 6.25 st. – **79 rm** ⌷ 29.50/59.50 st. – SB (weekends only) 49.00/56.00 st.

Regent's Park – ✉ NW1.

🏨 **White House** (Rank), Albany St., NW1 3UP, ℰ 387 1200, Telex 24111 – 🛗 📺 ☎ ⅙. ⅍. 🔟
AE ⓪ VISA ⅙
                                                                   LS o
M a la carte 7.30/19.25 t. ⅙ 3.50 – ⌸ 5.75 – **587 rm** 48.00/70.00 t.

XX **Pratts,** Commercial Pl., Camden Lock, NW1 8AF, ℰ 485 9987 – 🔟 AE ⓪ VISA   LR a
closed Sunday dinner and 25-26 Decmber – **M** a la carte 11.90/14.90 t. ⅙ 2.50.

X **Chalcot's Bistro,** 49 Chalcot Rd, Primrose Hill, NW1 8LS, ℰ 722 1956 – 🔟 ⓪ VISA   KR u
closed Saturday lunch, Sunday dinner, Monday, Easter, Christmas and Bank Holidays – **M** a la carte 8.45/15.75 t. ⅙ 3.50.

Swiss Cottage – ✉ NW3.

🏨 **Holiday Inn,** 128 King Henry's Rd, NW3 3ST, ℰ 722 7711, Telex 267396, 🔟 – 🛗 📺 ☎ ⅙ ℗.
⅍. 🔟 AE ⓪ VISA   JR a
M 11.75 (wine included)/12.00 t. – ⌸ 5.75 – **291 rm** 54.00/68.00 s.

XX **Peter's,** 65 Fairfax Rd, NW6 4EE, ℰ 624 5804 – 🔟 AE ⓪ VISA   JR i
closed Saturday lunch and Sunday dinner – **M** a la carte 10.20/13.15 t. ⅙ 2.35.

CITY OF LONDON Except where otherwise stated see p. 16.

🛈 St. Paul's Churchyard, EC4, ℰ 606 3030 ext 2456.

XXX **Wheeler's,** 33 Foster Lane, EC2V 6HD, ℰ 606 0896, Seafood   PT o

XXX **City Tiberio,** 8-11 Lime St., EC3M 7AA, ℰ 623 3616, Italian rest. – 🔟 AE ⓪ VISA   QU i
closed Saturday, Sunday and Bank Holidays – **M** (lunch only) a la carte 9.50/14.30 t. ⅙ 2.50.

XX **Le Poulbot** (basement), 45 Cheapside, EC2V 6AR, ℰ 236 4379, French rest. – 🗐. 🔟 AE ⓪
VISA   PU i
closed Saturday, Sunday and Bank Holidays – **M** (lunch only) 24.50 st.

XX **Bill Bentley's,** Swedeland Court, 202-204 Bishopsgate, EC2M 4NR, ℰ 283 1763, Seafood –
🔟 ⓪ VISA   QT e
closed Saturday, Sunday and Bank Holidays – **M** (lunch only) a la carte 12.70/19.05 t. ⅙ 2.85.

XX **Shares,** 12-13 Lime St., EC3M 7AA, ℰ 623 1843 – 🔟 AE ⓪ VISA   QU s
closed Saturday, Sunday and Bank Holidays – **M** (lunch only) 18.50 t.

XX **Villa Augusta,** Bucklersbury House, Queen Victoria St., EC4 9XX, ℰ 248 0095, Italian rest.
– 🔟 AE ⓪ VISA   PQU x
closed Saturday, Sunday and Bank Holidays – **M** (lunch only) a la carte 9.50/14.30 t. ⅙ 2.50.

X **La Bourse Plate,** 78 Leadenhall St., EC3, ℰ 623 5159 – 🔟 AE ⓪ VISA   QU v
closed Saturday and Sunday – **M** (lunch only) 14.50 st. ⅙ 2.95.

X **Bubb's,** 329 Central Market, Farringdon St., EC1A 9NB, ℰ 236 2435, French rest.   PT a
closed Saturday, Sunday, August and Bank Holidays – **M** (booking essential) a la carte
11.75/13.60 t. ⅙ 3.50.

X **Le Gamin,** 32 Old Bailey, EC4M 7HS, ℰ 236 7931, French rest. – 🔟 AE ⓪ VISA   PU a
closed Saturday, Sunday and Bank Holidays – **M** (lunch only) 16.75 st.

X **Ginnan,** 5 Cathedral Pl., St. Paul's, EC4M 7EA, ℰ 236 4120, Japanese rest. – 🔟 AE ⓪ VISA
closed Saturday dinner, Sunday and Bank Holidays – **M** a la carte 7.50/13.90 t. ⅙ 3.50.   PT e

CROYDON pp. 10 and 11.

Croydon – ✉ Surrey.

🖪, 🖪, 🖪 Addington Court, Featherbed Lane ℰ 657 0281, E : 3 m. – 🖪 Coulsdon Court
Municipal ℰ 660 0486, S : 5 m.

🛈 Central Library, Katherine St. ℰ 688 3627/5810.

🏨 Holiday Inn, 7 Altyre Rd, CR9 5AA, ℰ 680 9200, 🔟 – 🛗 📺 ⌸wc ☎ ⅙ ℗. ⅍.   FZ u
214 rm.

🏨 **Aerodrome** (Anchor), Purley Way, CR9 4LT, ℰ 688 5185, Telex 893814, ⋨ – 📺 ⌸wc ☎
℗. ⅍. 🔟 AE ⓪ VISA. ⅙   FZ e
M a la carte 8.10/12.75 st. ⅙ 2.65 – **85 rm** ⌸ 39.50/46.00 st. – SB (weekends only) 45.00 st.

🏠 **Oakwood,** 69-71 Outram Rd, CR0 6XJ, ℰ 654 2835, ⋨ – 📺 ⌸wc ⋔wc ℗. 🔟 AE ⓪ VISA
M (bar lunch) 5.50 st. ⅙ 2.25 – **15 rm** ⌸ 24.00/30.00 st.   FZ s

🏠 **Briarley,** 8-10 Outram Rd, CR0 6XE, ℰ 654 1000, ⋨ – 📺 ⌸wc ⋔wc ☎ ℗. 🔟 AE ⓪ VISA
closed 2 weeks at Christmas – **M** (lunch by arrangement) 7.50 t. ⅙ 2.75 – **19 rm** ⌸ 18.00/37.00 t.
– SB (weekends only) 24.50 st.   FZ r

XXX **Chateau Napoleon,** Coombe Lane, CR0 5RE, ℰ 686 1244 – ℗. 🔟 AE ⓪ VISA   FZ o
M a la carte 13.25/17.50 st. ⅙ 2.75.

X **Khyber,** 284 High St., CR0 1NG, ℰ 686 1729, Indian rest. – 🔟 AE ⓪ VISA   FZ i
M a la carte 5.55/10.50 st. ⅙ 2.50.

Sanderstead – ⊠ Surrey.
🛇 Selsdon Park Hotel, Addington Rd 🏌 657 3127.

🏰 **Selsdon Park** (Best Western), Addington Rd, CR2 8YA, 🏌 657 8811, Telex 945003, ≼, ⤓ heated, 🛇, ↝, park, ✵ – 🕻 🖵 🕭 🅿. 🏛 🖂 🆎 ⓞ 𝘝𝘐𝘚𝘈   FZ **n**
M 10.00/11.50 **st.** 🛝 4.25 – **160 rm** ⚏ 48.00/78.00 **st.** – SB (weekends only) (not Easter) 70.00/100.00 **st.**

✗ **Elio,** 17 Limpsfield Rd, CR2 9LA, 🏌 657 2953, Italian rest. – 🖂 ⓞ 𝘝𝘐𝘚𝘈   FZ **a**
closed Sunday and Bank Holidays – **M** a la carte 8.60/11.10 **t.** 🛝 2.50.

Thornton Heath – ⊠ Surrey.

↑ **Dunheved,** 639-641 London Rd, CR4 6AZ, 🏌 684 2009, ↝ – 🅿. ✵   FZ **v**
closed Christmas Day – **15 rm** ⚏ 15.00/32.00 **st.**

EALING pp. 4 and 5.

Ealing – ⊠ W5.

🏛 **Carnarvon,** Ealing Common, W5 3HN, 🏌 992 5399, Telex 935114 – 🕻 🖵 🖂wc 🕭 🅿. 🏛. ✵
145 rm.   CX **v**

🏛 **Kenton House,** 5 Hillcrest Rd, Hanger Hill, W5 2JL, 🏌 997 8436, Telex 8812544 – 🖵 🖂wc
🏮wc 🕭 🅿. 🖂 🆎 ⓞ 𝘝𝘐𝘚𝘈. ✵   CX **x**
M (bar lunch) a la carte 6.65/9.95 **st.** 🛝 1.90 – **51 rm** ⚏ 35.75/42.75 **st.** – SB (weekends only) 37.00 **st.**

🏛 **Montpelier** ⤓, 9 Montpelier Av., W5 2XP, 🏌 991 1508, ↝ – 🖵 🖂wc 🏮wc 🕭 🅿. 🆎 𝘝𝘐𝘚𝘈.
✵   BX **e**
M (dinner only, residents only) 8.50 **st.** – **9 rm** ⚏ 27.50/38.50 **st.**

✗✗ **Gino's,** 4 The Mall, W5 2PJ, 🏌 567 3681, Italian rest. – 🖂 🆎 ⓞ 𝘝𝘐𝘚𝘈   CX **z**
closed Sunday and Bank Holidays – **M** a la carte 7.00/15.80 **t.**

✗ **Maxim,** 153-155 Northfield Av., W13 9QT, 🏌 567 1719, Chinese-Peking rest. – 🖂 🆎 ⓞ 𝘝𝘐𝘚𝘈
closed Sunday lunch and 25 to 28 December – **M** a la carte 7.00/14.50 **t.** 🛝 2.00.   BX **a**

Hanwell – ⊠ W7.
🛇 Brent Valley, Church Rd, Hanwell 🏌 567 4230.

✗ **Happiness Garden,** 22 Boston Par., Boston Rd, W7 2DG, 🏌 567 9314, Chinese rest. – 🖂
🆎 ⓞ 𝘝𝘐𝘚𝘈   BX **c**
closed lunch Saturday and Monday, Sunday and 25 to 28 December – **M** a la carte 7.60/11.60 **t.**
🛝 2.15.

ENFIELD pp. 6 and 7.

Enfield – ⊠ Middx.
🛇 White Webbs, Enfield Municipal, Whitewebbs Park 🏌 363 4458, N : 1 m.

🏰 **Royal Chace,** 162 The Ridgeway, EN2 8AR, 🏌 366 6500, Telex 266628, ≼, ⤓, ↝ – 🖵 🕭 🅿.
🏛. 🖂 🆎 ⓞ 𝘝𝘐𝘚𝘈. ✵   EU **a**
M 13.75 **t.** 🛝 3.50 – ⚏ 3.75 – **92 rm** 29.25/38.50 **t.**

🏛 **Holtwhites,** 92 Chase Side, EN2 0QN, 🏌 363 0124, Telex 299670 – 🖵 🖂wc 🏮wc 🕭 🅿. 🖂
🆎 ⓞ 𝘝𝘐𝘚𝘈. ✵   FU **c**
M *(closed dinner Friday, Saturday and Sunday)* (bar lunch) a la carte 7.35/14.10 **t.** 🛝 4.00 –
28 rm ⚏ 27.50/45.50 **t.**

✗✗✗ **Norfolk,** 80 London Rd, EN2 6HU, 🏌 363 0979 – 🖂 🆎 ⓞ 𝘝𝘐𝘚𝘈   FU **e**
closed Saturday lunch, Monday dinner, Sunday, first 3 weeks August and Bank Holidays – **M**
a la carte 9.60/16.40 **t.** 🛝 2.60.

Hadley Wood – ⊠ Herts.

🏰 **West Lodge Park** ⤓, off Cockfosters Rd, ⊠ Barnet, EN4 0PY, 🏌 440 8311, Telex 24734, ≼,
↝, park – 🕻 🖵 🕭 🅿. 🏛. 🖂 🆎 ⓞ 𝘝𝘐𝘚𝘈. ✵   EU **i**
M a la carte 8.15/13.00 **st.** – **52 rm** ⚏ 40.00/54.00 **st.**

Southgate – ⊠ N 14.

✗✗ **L'Oiseau Noir,** 163 Bramley Rd, N14, 🏌 367 1100 – 🖂 🆎 ⓞ 𝘝𝘐𝘚𝘈   EU **e**
closed Sunday dinner and Monday – **M** a la carte 9.25/12.00 **t.** 🛝 2.75.

Winchmore Hill – ⊠ N21.

✗✗ **Dragon Garden,** 869 Green Lanes, N21 2QS, 🏌 360 9125, Chinese rest. – 🖂 🆎 ⓞ 𝘝𝘐𝘚𝘈
M approx. 8.80 **t.** 🛝 3.00.   FU **n**

MICHELIN Branch, Eley's Estate, Angel Rd, N18 3DQ, 🏌 803 7341/2/3/4

GREENWICH pp. 10 and 11.

Greenwich – ⊠ SE10.

🛈 Cutty Sark Gardens, near Greenwich Pier, SE10, ℰ 858 6376 (summer only).

XX **Le Papillon,** 57 Greenwich Church St., SE10 9BL, ℰ 858 2668 – ◪ ◭ ⓪ 𝘝𝘐𝘚𝘈   FX **r**
closed Saturday lunch, Sunday, 25 to 31 December and Bank Holidays – **M** a la carte
10.25/14.50 **t.**

X **Mean Time,** 47-49 Greenwich Church St., SE10 9BL, ℰ 858 8705 – ◪ ◭ ⓪ 𝘝𝘐𝘚𝘈   FX **r**
closed Saturday lunch, Sunday dinner and first 2 weeks January – **M** a la carte 11.00/15.65 **st.**
⌀ 3.50.

HAMMERSMITH Except where otherwise stated see pp. 17-20.

Fulham – ⊠ SW6.

XX **Barbarella,** 428 Fulham Rd, SW6 1DU, ℰ 385 9434, Italian rest., Dancing – ◪ ◭ ⓪ 𝘝𝘐𝘚𝘈
closed Sunday and Bank Holidays – **M** (dinner only) a la carte 12.50/13.50 **t.** ⌀ 2.80.   HZ **x**

XX Mio Sogno, 871-873 Fulham Rd, SW6, ℰ 736 3910, Italian rest.   pp. 8 and 9   DY **o**

X **Carlo's Place,** 855 Fulham Rd, SW6 5HJ, ℰ 736 4507 – ▤ ◭ ⓪ 𝘝𝘐𝘚𝘈   pp. 8 and 9   DY **s**
closed Saturday lunch, Sunday, 24 to 30 December and Bank Holidays – **M** a la carte
10.10/15.35 **st.** ⌀ 2.95.

Hammersmith – ⊠ W6/W12/W14.

X **Aziz,** 116 King St., W6, ℰ 748 1826, Indian rest. – ◭ ⓪ 𝘝𝘐𝘚𝘈   pp. 8 and 9   CX **a**
closed Sunday and 25-26 December – **M** approx. 6.35 **t.** ⌀ 3.20.

X **Rajdoot,** 291 King St., W6 9NH, ℰ 748 7345, Indian rest. – ◪ ◭ ⓪ 𝘝𝘐𝘚𝘈
M approx. 5.90 **t.** ⌀ 2.85.   pp. 8 and 9   CX **c**

Shepherd's Bush – ⊠ W 12.

XX **Shireen,** 270 Uxbridge Rd, W12 8NR, ℰ 749 5927, Indian rest. – ◪ ◭ ⓪ 𝘝𝘐𝘚𝘈
closed 25 and 26 December – **M** a la carte 7.35/9.65 **t.**   pp. 8 and 9   CX **n**

West Kensington – ⊠ SW6/W14.

🏨 **London West,** Lillie Rd, SW6 1UQ, ℰ 385 1255, Telex 917728 – 📶 ▉ 📺 🛁wc ☏ 🅿 ♨ ◪
◭ ⓪ 𝘝𝘐𝘚𝘈 ⍓   HZ **e**
M (carving rest.) 9.25 **t.** ⌀ 3.50 – ⌨ 5.50 – **497 rm** 35.00/43.00 **st.**

🏨 **Lily,** 23-33 Lillie Rd, SW6 1UG, ℰ 381 1881, Telex 918922 – 📶 ▉ rest 📺 🛁wc ☏ 🅿 ♨ ◪
◭ ⓪ 𝘝𝘐𝘚𝘈 ⍓   HZ **o**
M (dinner only) 5.50 **st.** ⌀ 1.25 – **99 rm** ⌨ 29.00/35.00 **st.** – SB (weekends only) 60.00/75.00 **st.**

HARINGEY pp. 6 and 7.

Highgate – ⊠ N6.

XX **San Carlo,** 2 High St., N6 5JL, ℰ 340 5823, Italian rest. – ◪ ◭ ⓪ 𝘝𝘐𝘚𝘈   EV **v**
closed Monday, Easter Day, Christmas Day and Bank Holidays – **M** a la carte 10.75/20.25 **st.**
⌀ 2.75.

Hornsey – ⊠ N8.

X M'sieur Frog, 36 The High St., N8 7NX, ℰ 340 2116   EV **u**

*Groß-London (GREATER LONDON) besteht aus der City und 32 Verwaltungsbezirken
(Borough). Diese sind wiederum in kleinere Bezirke (Area) unterteilt, deren Mittelpunkt
ehemalige Dörfer oder Stadtviertel sind, die oft ihren eigenen Charakter bewahrt
haben.*

HARROW pp. 4 and 5.

Central Harrow – ⊠ Middx.

🏛 **Harrow,** 12-22 Pinner Rd, HA1 4HZ, ℰ 427 3435, Telex 917898 – 📺 🛏wc 🛁wc ☎ 🅿. 🔀.
🔼 ⅍ ⑩ 🆅🆂🅰 ⅍   BV **a**
M 9.50 **st.** ⅃ 3.00 – **76 rm** ⊏⊐ 35.00/51.00 **st.** – SB (weekends only) 71.50/77.50 **st.**

🏛 **Cumberland,** 1 St. John's Rd, HA1 2EF, ℰ 863 4111 – 📺 🛏wc 🛁wc ☎ 🅿. 🔼 🔼 ⑩ 🆅🆂🅰.
⅍   BV **x**
M 7.50/8.50 **st.** ⅃ 2.80 – **77 rm** ⊏⊐ 27.00/42.00 **t.** – SB (weekends only) 57.00/61.00 **st.**

✕ **Old Etonian,** 38 High St., Harrow Hill, HA1 3LL, ℰ 422 8482 – 🔼 🔼 ⑩ 🆅🆂🅰   BV **z**
closed Saturday lunch, Sunday and Bank Holidays – **M** a la carte 10.75/12.15 **t.** ⅃ 2.50.

Harrow Weald – ⊠ Middx.

🏛 **Grims Dyke** ⅍, Old Redding, HA3 6SH, ℰ 954 4227, ⅍, park – 📺 🛏wc ☎ 🅿. 🔀. 🔼 🔼
⑩ 🆅🆂🅰   BU **r**
closed 25 to 29 December – **M** 11.00 – ⊏⊐ 5.75 – **48 rm** 40.00/66.00 **st.** – SB (weekends only) 72.00/80.00 **st.**

Hatch End – ⊠ Middx.

✕✕ **Canaletto 2,** 302 Uxbridge Rd, HA5 4HR, ℰ 428 4232, Italian rest. – 🔼 ⑩ 🆅🆂🅰   BU **a**
closed Saturday lunch, Sunday and Bank Holidays – **M** a la carte 10.40/16.25 **t.** ⅃ 2.90.

✕ **Swan,** 322 Uxbridge Rd, ℰ 428 8821, Chinese-Peking rest. – 🔼 🔼 ⑩ 🆅🆂🅰   BU **n**
M a la carte 8.50/11.00 **st.**

Pinner – ⊠ Middx.

✕ **La Giralda,** 66-68 Pinner Green, HA5 2AB, ℰ 868 3429 – 🔼 🔼 ⑩ 🆅🆂🅰   AUV **n**
closed Sunday, Monday and August – **M** 5.50/8.00 **t.**

HAVERING pp. 6 and 7.

Hornchurch by A 12 – HU – on A 127 – ⊠ Essex – ✆ 040 23 Ingrebourne.

🏛 **Ladbroke** (Ladbroke), Southend Arterial Rd (A 127), RM11 3UJ, ℰ 46789, Telex 897315 – 📺
🛏wc ☎ 🕭 🅿. 🔀. 🔼 🔼 ⑩ 🆅🆂🅰
M (closed Saturday lunch) 7.50/9.50 **t.** – ⊏⊐ 5.50 – **140 rm** 41.80/49.50 **t.**

Romford by A 118 – HV – ⊠ Essex – ✆ 0708.

⋔ **Coach House,** 48 Main Rd, RM1 3DB, on A 118 ℰ 751901 – 📺 🅿. 🔼 ⅍
14 rm ⊏⊐ 18.50/33.50 **st.**

HILLINGDON pp. 4 and 8.

Eastcote – ⊠ Middx.

✕ **Sambuca,** 113 Field End Rd, HA5 1QG, ℰ 866 7500, Italian rest.. 🔼 🔼 ⑩ 🆅🆂🅰   AV **s**
closed Christmas Day and Bank Holidays – **M** (dinner only) 13.50 **t.** ⅃ 2.30.

Heathrow Airport – ⊠ Middx.
🛈 Heathrow Central Station, London Airport ℰ 730 0791.

🏨 **Sheraton Skyline,** Bath Rd, Harlington, Hayes, UB3 5BP, ℰ 759 2535, Telex 934254, « Exotic
indoor garden with 🔲 » – ⌷ 🔳 📺 ☎ 🕭 🅿. 🔀. 🔼 🔼 ⑩ 🆅🆂🅰 ⅍   AY **u**
M 14.95 **st.** ⅃ 4.95 – ⊏⊐ 6.10 – **354 rm** 55.00/74.00 **s.**

🏨 **Excelsior** (T.H.F.), Bath Rd, West Drayton, UB7 0DU, ℰ 759 6611, Telex 24525, 🔲 heated –
⌷ 🔳 📺 ☎ 🕭 🅿. 🔀. 🔼 🔼 ⑩ 🆅🆂🅰   AY **x**
M 8.95 **st.** ⅃ 2.60 – ⊏⊐ 5.50 – **609 rm** 49.50/56.50 **st.**

🏨 **Heathrow Penta,** Bath Rd, Hounslow, TW6 2AQ, ℰ 897 6363, Telex 934660, ≤, 🔲 – ⌷ 🔳
📺 🕭 🅿. 🔀. 🔼 🔼 ⑩ 🆅🆂🅰   AY **z**
M 9.50/10.50 **st.** ⅃ 2.50 – ⊏⊐ 5.50 – **670 rm** 58.65/73.60 **st.**

🏨 **Holiday Inn,** Stockley Rd, West Drayton, UB7 9NA, ✆ 0895 (West Drayton) 445555, Telex
934518, 🔄, ※ – ⇔ 🔟 ☎ ᒼ 🅿. ⚠. 🔟 🅰🅴 ⑩ 𝑽𝑰𝑺𝑨   AX **v**
🖃 4.20 – **400 rm** 48.30/56.75 **st.**

🏨 **Sheraton Heathrow,** Colnbrook by-pass, West Drayton, UB7 0HJ, ✆ 759 2424, Telex
934331, 🔄 – ⇔ 🔟 📺 ☎ ᒼ 🅿. ⚠. 🔟 🅰🅴 ⑩ 𝑽𝑰𝑺𝑨. ※   AXY **a**
M a la carte 10.40/14.80 **st.** ᑐ 3.00 – 🖃 5.25 – **440 rm** 37.00/58.50 **s.**

🏨 **Skyway** (T.H.F.), 140 Bath Rd, Hayes, UB3 5AW, ✆ 759 6311, Telex 23935, 🔄 heated – ⇔ 🔳
🔟 ☎ ᒼ 🅿. ⚠. 🔟 🅰🅴 ⑩ 𝑽𝑰𝑺𝑨   AY **e**
M *(closed Saturday lunch)* 7.95 **st.** ᑐ 2.60 – 🖃 5.50 – **440 rm** 40.00/47.00 **st.**

🏨 **Post House** (T.H.F.), Sipson Rd, West Drayton, UB7 0JU, ✆ 759 2323, Telex 934280 – ⇔ 🔳
🔟 ☎ ᒼ 🅿. ⚠. 🔟 🅰🅴 ⑩ 𝑽𝑰𝑺𝑨   AX **c**
M a la carte 11.20/12.95 **st.** ᑐ 3.50 – 🖃 5.00 – **580 rm** 45.00/52.00 **st.**

🏨 **Crest** (Crest), Bath Rd, Longford, West Drayton, UB7 0EQ, ✆ 759 2400, Telex 934093 – 🔳
🔟 ☎ 🅿. ⚠. 🔟 🅰🅴 ⑩ 𝑽𝑰𝑺𝑨   AY **s**
M approx. 11.00 **st.** – 🖃 5.25 – **360 rm** 45.00/55.00 **st.**

🏨 **Ariel** (T.H.F.), Bath Rd, Hayes, UB3 5AJ, ✆ 759 2552, Telex 21777 – ⇔ 🔟 ⇔wc ☎ ᒼ 🅿. ⚠.
🔟 🅰🅴 ⑩ 𝑽𝑰𝑺𝑨   AY **i**
M 7.95/8.95 **st.** ᑐ 2.75 – 🖃 5.25 – **178 rm** 42.00/48.00 **st.**

🏨 **Arlington,** Shepiston Lane, Hayes, UB3 1LP, ✆ 573 6162 – 🔟 ⇔wc 🖝wc ☎ 🅿. ⚠. 🔟 🅰🅴
⑩ 𝑽𝑰𝑺𝑨   AX **n**
M *(closed Saturday lunch)* 7.00/17.00 **t.** – 🖃 3.50 – **80 rm** 32.00/40.00 **st.** – SB (weekends only) 42.00/47.00 **st.**

🔲 **Hillingdon** – ✉ Middx. – 🕿 0895 Uxbridge.
🏌 Civic Centre, Uxbridge ✆ 50600.

🏨 **Master Brewer Motel,** Western Av., Hillingdon Circus, UB10 9BR, ✆ 51199 – 🔟 ⇔wc ☎
🅿. ⚠. 🔟 🅰🅴 ⑩ 𝑽𝑰𝑺𝑨   AV **a**
M a la carte 6.10/8.95 **st.** ᑐ 4.00 – 🖃 3.50 – **64 rm** 36.50/43.00 **st.** – SB (weekends only) 47.00.

🔲 **Northwood** – ✉ Middx. – 🕿 092 74 Northwood.
🏌 Haste Hill, The Drive ✆ 26485.

🍴🍴 **Martini,** 27 Green Lane, ✆ 27052, Italian rest. – 🔟 🅰🅴 ⑩ 𝑽𝑰𝑺𝑨   AU **e**
closed Sunday and Bank Holidays – **M** a la carte 8.20/17.30 **t.** ᑐ 2.20.

🔲 **Ruislip** – ✉ Middx. – 🕿 089 56 Ruislip.
🏌 Ickenham Rd ✆ 32004.

🏡 **Barn,** West End Rd, HA4 6JB, ✆ 36057, Telex 892514, 🌲 – 🔟 ⇔wc ☎ 🅿. 🔟 🅰🅴 𝑽𝑰𝑺𝑨
closed 23 to 31 December – **M** *(closed Saturday lunch and Sunday dinner)* 7.95 **st.** ᑐ 3.15 –
56 rm 🖃 29.50/47.50 **st.** – SB (weekends only) 46.00/59.00 **st.**   AV **u**

🔳 **HOUNSLOW** pp. 8 and 9.
🏌 Wyke Green, Syon Lane, Isleworth ✆ 560 8777, ½ m. from Gillettes Corner (A 4).

🔲 **Cranford** – ✉ Middx.

🏨 **Berkeley Arms** (Embassy), Bath Rd, TW5 9QE, ✆ 897 2121, Telex 935728, 🌲 – ⇔ 🔟
⇔wc ☎ 🅿. ⚠. 🔟 🅰🅴 ⑩ 𝑽𝑰𝑺𝑨. ※   AY **r**
M 7.50 **st.** ᑐ 4.50 – 🖃 4.25 – **41 rm** 40.00/50.00 **st.** – SB (weekends only) 44.00/50.00 **st.**

🔲 **Hounslow** – ✉ Middx.

🏨 **Master Robert Motel,** 366 Great West Rd, TW5 0BD, ✆ 570 6261 – 🔟 ⇔wc 🖝wc ☎ 🅿.
⚠. 🔟 🅰🅴 ⑩ 𝑽𝑰𝑺𝑨   BY **s**
M 9.50 **t.** ᑐ 4.00 – 🖃 3.50 – **63 rm** 36.50/43.00 **st.** – SB (weekends only) 47.00 **st.**

🔳 **ISLINGTON** pp. 13-16.

🔲 **Canonbury** – ✉ N1.

🍴 **Anna's Place,** 90 Mildmay Park, N1, ✆ 249 9379   pp. 6 and 7   FV **a**
closed Sunday, Monday, 2 weeks at Easter, August and 2 weeks at Christmas – **M** (booking
essential) (dinner only) a la carte 11.60/15.75 **t.**

🔲 **Finsbury** – ✉ WC1/EC1.

🏨 **Royal Scot Thistle** (Thistle), 100 King's Cross Rd, WC1X 9QT, ✆ 278 2434, Telex 27657 – ⇔
🔳 🔟 ⇔wc ☎ 🅿. ⚠. 🔟 🅰🅴 ⑩ 𝑽𝑰𝑺𝑨   NS **n**
M 9.00 **t.** ᑐ 3.45 – 🖃 4.95 – **349 rm** 37.50/40.50 **t.** – SB (weekends only) 36.00 **st.**

🏨 **London Ryan** (Mt. Charlotte), Gwynne Pl., King Cross Rd, WC1X 9QN, ✆ 278 6628, Telex
27728 – ⇔ 🔟 ⇔wc ☎ 🅿. 🔟 🅰🅴 ⑩ 𝑽𝑰𝑺𝑨. ※   NS **a**
201 rm 🖃 41.50/52.50.

🍴🍴 **Café St. Pierre,** 29 Clerkenwell Green (1st floor), EC1, ✆ 251 6606 – 🔟 🅰🅴 ⑩ 𝑽𝑰𝑺𝑨   PT **c**
closed Sunday dinner, 25 December-1 January and Bank Holidays – **M** a la carte 15.40/20.55 **t.**
ᑐ 4.50.

Islington – ⊠ N1.

XX **Frederick's,** Camden Passage, N1 8EG, ℰ 359 2888, « Conservatory and walled garden » – 🔊 🖭 ① 𝘝𝘐𝘚𝘈   PR **a**
closed Sunday, 26 December and 1 January – **M** a la carte 10.95/17.30 **t.** ⌀ 3.10.

XX **Portofino,** 39 Camden Passage, N1 8EA, ℰ 226 0884, Italian rest. – 🔊 🖭 ① 𝘝𝘐𝘚𝘈   PR **o**
closed Sunday and Bank Holidays – **M** a la carte 9.25/16.80 **t.** ⌀ 2.45.

XX **Julius's,** 39 Upper St., N1 0PN, ℰ 226 4380   PR **i**

X **M'sieur Frog,** 31a Essex Rd, N1 2SE, ℰ 226 3495, Bistro – 🔊 𝘝𝘐𝘚𝘈   PR **n**
closed Sunday, 3 weeks August and 1 week at Christmas – **M** (dinner only) a la carte 10.05/11.90 **t.** ⌀ 2.25.

KENSINGTON and CHELSEA (Royal Borough of).

Chelsea – ⊠ SW1/SW3/SW10 – Except where otherwise stated see pp. 28 and 29.

🏰🏰🏰 **Hyatt Carlton Tower,** 2 Cadogan Pl., SW1X 9PY, ℰ 235 5411, Telex 21944, ≤, 🛋, 🎾 – 🛗 📺 ☎ ➅ 🅿, ♨. 🔊 🖭 ① 𝘝𝘐𝘚𝘈 ✻   FR **n**
M (see Chelsea Room below) – Rib Room – ⊒ 7.25 – **228 rm** 110.00/145.00 **t.**

🏰🏰 **Sheraton Park Tower,** 101 Knightsbridge, SW1X 7RN, ℰ 235 8050, Telex 915899 – 🛗 ☰ 📺 ☎ ➅ 🅿. ♨. 🔊 🖭 ① 𝘝𝘐𝘚𝘈 ✻   FQ **v**
M a la carte 15.00/22.00 **t.** – ⊒ 6.75 – **293 rm** 95.00/116.00 **s.**

🏰🏰 ❀ **Capital,** 22-24 Basil St., SW3 1AT, ℰ 589 5171, Telex 919042 – 🛗 ☰ 📺 ☎. 🔊 🖭 ① 𝘝𝘐𝘚𝘈. ✻   ER **a**
M 14.50/16.50 **st.** ⌀ 5.00 – ⊒ 5.95 – **60 rm** 79.35/105.80 **st.**
Spec. Salade de pigeon rosé aux deux choux, Médaillons de veau à la dariole niçoise, Marquise au chocolat blanc - sauce au café.

🏰🏰 **Cadogan Thistle** (Thistle), 75 Sloane St., SW1X 9SG, ℰ 235 7141, Telex 267893 – 🛗 📺 ☎. 🔊 🖭 ① 𝘝𝘐𝘚𝘈. ✻   FR **e**
M a la carte 7.50/9.50 **t.** ⌀ 3.45 – ⊒ 5.25 – **68 rm** 53.00/79.00 **t.** – SB (weekends only) 62.00 **st.**

🏰🏰 **Holiday Inn,** 17-25 Sloane St., SW1X 9NU, ℰ 235 4377, Telex 919111, 🔲 – 🛗 📺 ☎. ♨. 🔊 🖭 ① 𝘝𝘐𝘚𝘈.   FR **r**
M a la carte 11.50/18.50 **st.** ⌀ 4.00 – ⊒ 6.00 – **206 rm** 81.65/98.90 **st.**

🏰🏰 **Basil Street,** 8 Basil St., SW3 1AH, ℰ 581 3311, Telex 28379 – 🛗 📺 ☎ ♨. 🔊 🖭 ① 𝘝𝘐𝘚𝘈 ✻   FQ **o**
M a la carte 12.50/16.45 **st.** ⌀ 3.75 – ⊒ 4.85 – **96 rm** 33.00/72.50 **st.** – SB (weekends only)(winter only) 97.70 **st.**

🏰🏰 **Royal Court** (Norfolk Cap.), Sloane Sq., SW1W 8EG, ℰ 730 9191, Telex 296818 – 🛗 📺 ☎. ♨. 🔊 🖭 ① 𝘝𝘐𝘚𝘈. ✻   FST **a**
M a la carte 13.85/18.05 **st.** ⌀ 3.00 – ⊒ 6.40 – **98 rm** 55.00/71.50 **t.** – SB (May-October) 72.60 **st.**

🏰 **L'Hotel** without rest., 28 Basil St., SW3 1AT, ℰ 589 6286, Telex 919042 – 🛗 📺 📺 ⇌wc ☎ 🅿. 🖭. ✻   ER **i**
12 rm 60.00 **st.**

🏰 **Wilbraham,** 1-5 Wilbraham Pl., Sloane St., SW1X 9AE, ℰ 730 8296 – 🛗 ⇌wc ☎. ✻   FS **n**
M *(closed Sunday and Bank Holidays)* (bar lunch) a la carte 4.50/8.15 **t.** ⌀ 2.60 – ⊒ 3.00 – **56 rm** 22.00/40.00.

🏰 **Fenja** without rest., 69 Cadogan Gdns, SW3 2RB, ℰ 589 1183 – 🛗 ⇌wc ☎. 🔊 🖭 ① 𝘝𝘐𝘚𝘈. ✻   FS **r**
16 rm ⊒ 20.00/60.00 **st.** – SB (weekends only)(except summer) 53.00 **st.**

🏰 **Willett** without rest., 32 Sloane Gdns, Sloane Sq., SW1W 8DJ, ℰ 730 0634 – 📺 ⇌wc. ✻   FT **s**
17 rm ⊒ 21.00/32.00 **t.**

XXXX ❀ **Chelsea Room** (at Hyatt Carlton Tower H.), 2 Cadogan Pl., SW1X 9PY, ℰ 235 5411 – ➅. 🔊 🖭 ① 𝘝𝘐𝘚𝘈. ✻   FR **n**
closed Easter Monday and 1 to 3 January – **M** a la carte 19.00/28.00 **t.** ⌀ 4.70
Spec. Foie gras frais Richelieu, Fricassée de turbot et homard aux concombres, Filet d'agneau au basilic et tomate fraîche.

XXXX ❀ **Waltons,** 121 Walton St., SW3 2HP, ℰ 584 0204 – ☰. 🔊 🖭 ① 𝘝𝘐𝘚𝘈   DS **a**
closed Christmas, 4 days at Easter and Bank Holidays – **M** a la carte 8.00/22.00 **t.**
Spec. A cushion of Scotch smoked salmon, Steamed sea bass with lobster-butter sauce, Praline mousse surprise.

XXX ❀❀ **La Tante Claire,** 68 Royal Hospital Rd, SW3 2HP, ℰ 352 6045, French rest. – 🖭 ①
closed Saturday, Sunday, 10 days at Easter, 10 August-3 September, 24 December-2 January and Bank Holidays – **M** a la carte 22.00/25.20 **st.**   EU **c**
Spec. La terrine de poireaux et de langoustines, Le pied de cochon aux morilles, La croustade aux pommes.

XXX **Le Français,** 257-259 Fulham Rd, SW3 6HY, ℰ 352 4748, French rest. – 🖭 𝘝𝘐𝘚𝘈   CU **a**
closed Sunday, Christmas and Bank Holidays – **M** 12.00 **s.** ⌀ 4.20.

XXX **Zen,** Chelsea Cloisters, Sloane Av., SW3 3DW, ℰ 589 1781, Chinese rest. – 🔊 🖭 ① 𝘝𝘐𝘚𝘈   ET **a**
M a la carte 8.70/16.25 **t.**

XX **Daphne's,** 112 Draycott Av., SW3 3AE, ℰ 589 4257 – 🔊 🖭 ① 𝘝𝘐𝘚𝘈   DS **e**
closed Sunday and Bank Holidays – **M** (dinner only) a la carte 11.40/17.50 **t.** ⌀ 3.25.

XX **Eleven Park Walk,** 11 Park Walk, SW10, ℰ 352 3449, Italian rest. – 🖭   CU **r**
closed Sunday and Bank Holidays – **M** a la carte 10.80/15.10 **t.** ⌀ 2.50.

XX Mario, 260-262a Brompton Rd, SW3 2AS, ℰ 584 1724, Italian rest.   DS **n**

13

XX **Gavvers,** 61-63 Lower Sloane St., SW1W 8DH, ℰ 730 5983, French rest. – ⑩   FT **e**
closed Sunday, July, August, 23 December-2 January and Bank Holidays – **M** (dinner only)
17.75 (wine included) **st.**

XX **Bagatelle,** 5 Langton St., SW10 0JL, ℰ 351 4185, French rest. – 🖭 AE ⑩ VISA
closed Sunday and Bank Holidays – **M** a la carte 13.30/17.50 **t.** ⓐ 2.90.   pp. 17-20   JZ **u**

XX **Bewick's,** 87-89 Walton St., SW3 2HP, ℰ 584 6711 – 🖭 AE ⑩ VISA   ES **n**
closed lunch Saturday and Sunday, Easter and 24 December-2 January – **M** a la carte
15.70/20.95 **t.**

XX **Meridiana,** 169 Fulham Rd, SW3 6SP, ℰ 589 8815, Italian rest. – 🖭 AE ⑩ VISA   DT **i**
closed 25 December and Bank Holidays – **M** a la carte 12.85/17.50 **t.** ⓐ 3.00.

XX ✿ **Ma Cuisine,** 113 Walton St., SW3 2JY, ℰ 584 7585, French rest. – AE ⑩   DS **a**
closed Saturday, Sunday, 13 July-12 August and Bank Holidays – **M** a la carte 12.00/16.20 **t.**
ⓐ 3.75
Spec. Brouillade de langoustines à la menthe fraîche, Emincé d'agneau aux rognons et celeri, Mousse brûlée.

XX **Toto,** Walton House, Walton St., SW3 2JH, ℰ 589 0075, Italian rest. – 🖭 AE VISA   ES **a**
closed Christmas – **M** a la carte 14.00/17.50 **t.** ⓐ 2.50.

XX **Good Earth,** 233 Brompton Rd, SW3 2EP, ℰ 584 3658, Chinese rest. – 🖭 AE ⑩ VISA   DR **c**
M a la carte 7.00/14.35 **t.**

XX **Good Earth,** 91 King's Rd, SW3, ℰ 352 9231, Chinese rest. – 🖭 AE ⑩ VISA   EU **a**
M a la carte 9.00/13.50 **t.** ⓐ 2.30.

XX **Ponte Nuovo,** 126 Fulham Rd, SW3, ℰ 370 6656, Italian rest. – 🖭 AE ⑩ VISA   CU **e**
closed Bank Holidays – **M** a la carte 11.50/15.00 **t.** ⓐ 3.20.

XX **Ménage à Trois,** 15 Beauchamp Pl., SW3 1NQ, ℰ 589 4252 – 🖭 AE ⑩ VISA   ER **v**
closed Saturday, Sunday and 25-26 December – **M** a la carte 8.65/23.00 **t.** ⓐ 3.00.

XX **English Garden,** 10 Lincoln St., SW3 2TS, ℰ 584 7272, English rest. – 🖭 AE ⑩ VISA   ET **x**
closed Christmas Day – **M** a la carte 12.50/17.75 **st.** ⓐ 3.25.

XX **English House,** 3 Milner St., SW3 2QA, ℰ 584 3002, English rest. – 🖭 AE ⑩ VISA   ES **z**
closed 25-26 December – **M** a la carte 15.25/19.75 **st.** ⓐ 3.50.

XX **Poissonnerie de l'Avenue,** 82 Sloane Av., SW3 3DZ, ℰ 589 2457, Seafood – 🖭 AE ⑩
VISA   DS **u**
closed Sunday, 2 weeks Christmas and Bank Holidays – **M** a la carte 10.50/16.30 **t.** ⓐ 3.50.

XX **St. Quentin,** 243 Brompton Rd, SW3 2EP, ℰ 589 8005, Telex 8814322, French rest. – 🖭 AE
⑩ VISA   DR **a**
closed 1 week at Christmas – **M** a la carte 10.00/15.30 **t.** ⓐ 4.20.

XX **Flavio,** 1a Langton St., SW10, ℰ 352 7414, Italian rest.   JZ **a**

XX **Don Luigi,** 316 King's Rd, SW3, ℰ 352 0025, Italian rest. – 🖭 AE ⑩ VISA   CU **i**
closed Bank Holidays – **M** a la carte 8.80/12.60 **t.** ⓐ 2.50.

XX **San Ruffillo,** 8 Harriet St., SW1 9JW, ℰ 235 3969, Italian rest. – 🖭 AE ⑩ VISA   FQ **z**
closed Sunday, Christmas and Bank Holidays – **M** a la carte 9.95/15.50 **t.** ⓐ 2.25.

XX **Villa Puccini,** 5 Draycott Av., SW3, ℰ 584 4003, Italian rest. – 🖭 AE ⑩ VISA   ET **r**
M a la carte 7.85/12.35 **t.** ⓐ 2.85.

XX **San Frediano,** 62-64 Fulham Rd, SW3 6HH, ℰ 584 8375, Italian rest. – 🖭 AE ⑩ VISA   DT **n**
closed Sunday and Bank Holidays – **M** a la carte 9.70/11.20 **t.**

XX **Beccofino,** 100 Draycott Av., SW3, ℰ 584 3600, Italian rest. – 🖭 AE VISA   ES **r**
closed Sunday and Bank Holidays – **M** a la carte 9.90/12.60 **t.**

XX **Le Suquet,** 104 Draycott Av., SW3 3AE, ℰ 581 1785, French rest., Seafood – AE   DS **c**
closed Monday and 2 weeks at Christmas – **M** a la carte 12.30/17.80 **t.**

X **Dan's,** 119 Sydney St., SW3 6NR, ℰ 352 2718 – AE ⑩ VISA   DU **s**
closed Saturday, Sunday and Bank Holidays – **M** a la carte 23.40/30.00 **t.** ⓐ 3.00.

X **Thierry's,** 342 King's Rd, SW3, ℰ 352 3365 – AE ⑩ VISA   CU **c**
closed Sunday, Easter, 19 August-2 September, Christmas and Bank Holidays – **M** (restricted
lunch) a la carte 10.75/13.85 **t.** ⓐ 2.75.

X **La Brasserie,** 272 Brompton Rd, SW3 2AW, ℰ 584 1668, French rest. – 🖭 AE ⑩ VISA   DS **s**
closed 25-26 December – **M** a la carte 9.10/12.30 **t.** ⓐ 2.70.

Earl's Court – ✉ SW5/SW10 – Except where otherwise stated see pp. 28 and 29.

🏨 **Barkston,** 34-44 Barkston Gdns, SW5 0EW, ℰ 373 7851, Telex 8953154 – 🛗 📺 ⇔wc ☎.
🔊 🖭 AE ⑩ VISA   AT **c**
M (buffet lunch) a la carte 11.15/11.90 **st.** ⓐ 2.85 – ⚌ 4.75 – **76 rm** 34.00/40.00 **st.**

🏨 **Hogarth,** 27-35 Hogarth Rd, SW5 0QQ, ℰ 370 6831, Telex 8951994 – 🛗 ▤ rest 📺 ⇔wc ☏
🅿 🖭 AE ⑩. ⋇   AS **a**
closed 24 to 27 December – **M** 6.50/8.00 **st.** ⓐ 3.00 – ⚌ 2.60 – **86 rm** 29.00/38.00 **st.**

🏨 **Town House,** 44-48 West Cromwell Rd, SW5 9QL, ℰ 373 4546, Telex 918554, ☛ – 📺 ⇔wc
🅿. 🖭 AE ⑩. ⋇   HY **o**
M 6.50 **st.** ⓐ 2.75 – **40 rm** ⚌ 24.00/39.00 **st.** – SB 48.00/74.00 **st.**

XXX **Martin's,** 88 Ifield Rd, SW10 9AD, ✆ 352 5641 – 🔃 *VISA*   AU **e**
closed Sunday, last 2 weeks August, 24 to 31 December and Bank Holidays – **M** (dinner only)
17.50 **t.** ⅃ 4.00.

XX ✿ **Tiger Lee,** 251 Old Brompton Rd, SW5 9HP, ✆ 370 2323, Chinese rest., Seafood – 🍽 🄰🄴
⓪ *VISA*   AU **n**
closed Christmas Day – **M** (dinner only) a la carte 20.80/27.00 **t.**
Spec. Stuffed baby quail, Homard orientale, Tiger Lee sesame chicken.

XX **La Croisette,** 168 Ifield Rd, SW10 9AF, ✆ 373 3694, French rest., Seafood – 🄰🄴   AU **a**
closed Tuesday lunch, Monday and 2 weeks at Christmas – **M** 18.00 **t.**

XX **Pontevecchio,** 254-258 Old Brompton Rd, SW5 9HP, ✆ 373 9082, Italian rest. – 🔃 🄰🄴 ⓪
VISA   AU **i**
M a la carte 9.90/12.10 **t.** ⅃ 2.50.

XX **L'Artiste Affamé,** 243 Old Brompton Rd, SW5 9HP, ✆ 373 1659 – 🔃 🄰🄴 ⓪ *VISA*   AU **r**
closed Sunday and 24 to 26 December – **M** a la carte 9.45/13.25 **t.** ⅃ 2.55.

XX **Brinkley's,** 47 Hollywood Rd, SW10 9HY, ✆ 351 1683 – 🔃 🄰🄴 ⓪ *VISA*   BU **a**
closed Sunday and Bank Holidays – **M** (dinner only) a la carte 11.60/16.00 **t.** ⅃ 2.75.

XX **L'Olivier,** 116 Finborough Rd, SW10, ✆ 370 4183 – 🄰🄴   AU **c**
closed Monday lunch, Sunday and 2 weeks at Christmas – **M** a la carte 13.90/16.90 **t.** ⅃ 2.50.

X **Crystal Palace,** 10 Hogarth Pl., Hogarth Rd, SW5, ✆ 373 0754, Chinese rest. – 🔃 🄰🄴 ⓪
VISA   pp. 17-20 HY **r**
closed Sunday before Bank Holidays and Christmas Day – **M** a la carte 5.70/9.00 **st.**

X **Naraine,** 10 Kenway Rd, SW5 0RR, ✆ 370 3853, Indian rest.. 🔃 ⓪ *VISA*   pp. 17-20 HY **i**
M (dinner only) a la carte 7.50/7.70 **t.** ⅃ 2.75.

Kensington – ✉ SW7/W8/W11/W14 – Except where otherwise stated see pp. 17-20.

🏨 **Royal Garden** (Rank), Kensington High St., W8 4PT, ✆ 937 8000, Telex 263151, ≼ – 🛗 🍴 📺
🖥 🅿. 🕿. 🔃 ⓪ *VISA*. 🛳   pp. 28 and 29 AQ **c**
M Royal Roof *(closed Sunday and Bank Holidays)* (Dancing) a la carte 18.70/24.25 **st.** ⅃ 6.50 –
☐ 6.75 – **411 rm** 69.50/87.50 **st.**

🏨 **Kensington Palace Thistle** (Thistle), De Vere Gdns, W8 5AF, ✆ 937 8121, Telex 262422 –
🛗 📺 🕿. 🔃 🄰🄴 ⓪ *VISA*   pp. 28 and 29 BQ **a**
M 9.00/10.50 **t.** ⅃ 3.45 – ☐ 5.25 – **316 rm** 49.50/69.50 **t.** – SB (weekends only) 100.00 **st.**

🏨 **Hilton International,** 179-199 Holland Park Av., W11 4UL, ✆ 603 3355, Telex 919763 – 🛗 🍽
📺 🕿 ⅃ 🅿. 🔃 🄰🄴 ⓪ *VISA*. 🛳   GV **s**
M a la carte 11.90/15.60 **t.** ⅃ 2.80 – ☐ 5.55 – **606 rm** 45.00/78.00 **t.**

🏨 **London Tara** (Best Western), Scarsdale Pl., W8 5SR, ✆ 937 7211, Telex 918834 – 🛗 🍽 📺
🕿 ⅃ 🅿. 🔃 🄰🄴 ⓪ *VISA*. 🛳   HX **u**
M 7.80 **t.** ⅃ 3.30 – ☐ 5.10 – **840 rm** 43.00/62.00 **st.** – SB (weekends only) 70.00 **st.**

🏨 **Kensington Close** (T.H.F.), Wrights Lane, W8 5SP, ✆ 937 8170, Telex 23914, 🔃 – 🛗 📺
⊂⊃. ⅃. 🔃 🄰🄴 ⓪ *VISA*   HX **c**
M 5.95/9.45 **st.** ⅃ 2.60 – ☐ 5.25 – **530 rm** 40.00/49.00 **st.**

↑ One-Two-Eight, 128-130 Holland Rd, W14 8BD, ✆ 602 3395, 🍴 – 🛗 🚿wc 🕿. 🛳   GX **x**
28 rm.

XX **La Pomme d'Amour,** 128 Holland Park Av., W11 4UE, ✆ 229 8532, French rest. – 🔃 🄰🄴 ⓪
VISA   GV **e**
closed Saturday lunch, Sunday and Bank Holidays – **M** a la carte 9.40/14.60 **t.** ⅃ 2.60.

XX **Al Gallo d'Oro,** 353 Kensington High St., W8 6NW, ✆ 603 6951, Italian rest. – 🍽 🔃 🄰🄴 ⓪
VISA   GX **a**
closed Saturday lunch and Bank Holidays – **M** a la carte 9.45/13.30 **t.** ⅃ 2.45.

XX **Mama San,** 11 Russell Gdns, W14, ✆ 602 0312, Chinese rest. – 🔃 🄰🄴 ⓪ *VISA*   GX **e**
closed Saturday lunch and Bank Holidays – **M** a la carte 9.50/13.80.

XX **Trattoo,** 2 Abingdon Rd, W8 6AF, ✆ 937 4448, Italian rest. – 🔃 🄰🄴 ⓪ *VISA*   HX **e**
closed Bank Holidays – **M** a la carte 8.80/11.20 **t.** ⅃ 2.50.

XX **Topo d'oro,** 39 Uxbridge St., W8, ✆ 727 5813, Italian rest. – 🔃 🄰🄴 ⓪ *VISA*. 🛳
closed 25-26 December and Bank Holidays for lunch – **M** a la carte 7.30/13.20 **t.** ⅃ 2.20.
pp. 30 and 31 AZ **a**

XX **Le Quai St. Pierre,** 7 Stratford Rd, W8, ✆ 937 6388, French rest., Seafood   HX **r**
closed Monday lunch, Sunday and 2 weeks at Christmas – **M** a la carte 12.30/17.30 **t.**

XX **Hiroko** (at Hilton International H.), 179-199 Holland Park Av., W11 4UL, ✆ 603 5003, Japanese
rest. – 🅿. 🔃 🄰🄴 ⓪ *VISA*   GV **s**
closed Monday lunch, 1 May, 26 August, January and February – **M** 7.00/17.50 **t.** ⅃ 4.50.

XX **Franco Ovest,** 3 Russell Gdns, W14 8EZ, ✆ 602 1242, Italian rest. – 🔃 🄰🄴 ⓪ *VISA*   GX **u**
closed Saturday lunch, Sunday and August – **M** a la carte 9.05/12.05 **t.**

XX **Junk Two,** 2-4 Thackeray St., W8 5ET, ✆ 937 8508, Chinese rest. – 🔃 🄰🄴 ⓪ *VISA*
closed 25-26 December and Bank Holidays – **M** (dinner only) a la carte 5.90/9.90 **t.** ⅃ 2.80.
pp. 28 and 29 AR **a**

XX **Sailing Junk,** 59 Marloes Rd, W8 6LE, ✆ 937 5833, Chinese rest. – 🔃 🄰🄴 ⓪ *VISA*   HX **x**
closed Bank Holidays – **M** (dinner only) 12.00 **t.** ⅃ 2.80.

※ **La Résidence,** 148 Holland Park Av., W11, ℰ 221 6090, French rest. – 🔲 🔲 ⓞ 𝘝𝘐𝘚𝘈   GV z
closed Saturday lunch and Monday – **M** a la carte 9.20/12.40 **st.** ⓵ 2.50.

※ **La Paesana,** 30 Uxbridge St., W8 7TA, ℰ 229 4332, Italian rest. – 🔲 ⓞ 𝘝𝘐𝘚𝘈
closed Sunday, 5 and 8 April and 25-26 December – **M** a la carte 7.70/9.55 **t.** ⓵ 2.00.
pp. 30 and 31   AZ i

※ **Il Barbino,** 32 Kensington Church St., W8, ℰ 937 8752, Italian rest. – 🔲 🔲 ⓞ 𝘝𝘐𝘚𝘈   HV o
closed Saturday lunch, Sunday and Bank Holidays – **M** a la carte 7.80/12.10 **t.** ⓵ 2.30.

※ **The Ark,** Kensington Court, 35 Kensington High St., W8 5BA, ℰ 937 4294, French rest. – 🔲
ⓞ 𝘝𝘐𝘚𝘈   pp. 28 and 29   AQ s
closed Sunday lunch, 4 days at Easter and 4 days at Christmas – **M** a la carte 9.70/13.80 **t.**
⓵ 2.25.

※ I Ching, 40 Earls Court Rd, W8 6EJ, ℰ 937 7047, Chinese rest.   HX a

North Kensington – ✉ W2/W10/W11 – Except where otherwise stated see pp. 13-16.

🏠 **Portobello,** 22 Stanley Gdns, W11 2NG, ℰ 727 2777, Telex 21879 – 🕽 📺 ⌁wc 🕽wc ☎.
🔲 ⓞ 𝘝𝘐𝘚𝘈   GU u
closed 1 week at Christmas – **M** a la carte 7.30/11.00 **s.** ⓵ 2.45 – ⌑ 4.50 – **25 rm** 32.00/90.00 **s.**

🏠 **Pembridge Court,** 34 Pembridge Gdns, W2 4DX, ℰ 229 9977, Telex 298363 – ▤ rest 📺
⌁wc 🕽wc ☜. 🔲 🔲 ⓞ 𝘝𝘐𝘚𝘈   pp. 30 and 31   AZ n
M (closed Sunday and Bank Holidays) (dinner only) a la carte 6.25/9.35 **t.** ⓵ 2.50 – **35 rm**
27.50/39.50 **s.**

※※※ **Leith's,** 92 Kensington Park Rd, W11 2PN, ℰ 229 4481 – ▤. 🔲 🔲 ⓞ 𝘝𝘐𝘚𝘈   GU e
closed 26-27 August and 4 days at Christmas – **M** (dinner only) 24.00 **st.**

※※ **Chez Moi,** 1 Addison Av., Holland Park, W11 4QS, ℰ 603 8267, French rest. – 🔲 🔲 ⓞ 𝘝𝘐𝘚𝘈
closed Sunday, Easter, 2 weeks August and 2 weeks at Christmas – **M** (dinner only) a la carte
12.00/18.00 **t.** ⓵ 4.00.   pp. 17-20   GV n

※※ **Monsieur Thompsons,** 29 Kensington Park Rd, W11, ℰ 727 9957, French rest. – 🔲 🔲 ⓞ
𝘝𝘐𝘚𝘈   GU a
closed Sunday, Christmas-New Year and Bank Holidays – **M** a la carte 15.80/24.00 **t.**

※ **192,** 192 Kensington Park Rd, W11 2JF, ℰ 229 0482 – 🔲 🔲 𝘝𝘐𝘚𝘈   GU c
closed Sunday dinner – **M** a la carte 7.60/13.20 **t.**

PARIS-BORDEAUX 1895   1ère VOITURE sur PNEUS MICHELIN

South Kensington – ✉ SW5/SW7/W8 – pp. 28 and 29.

🏨 **Gloucester** (Rank), 4-18 Harrington Gdns, SW7 4LH, ℰ 373 6030, Telex 917505 – 🕽 ▤ 📺 ☎
⅏ 🅿. 🔊. 🔲 🔲 ⓞ 𝘝𝘐𝘚𝘈. 🛇   BS r
M a la carte 14.00/18.45 **st.** ⓵ 3.15 – ⌑ 6.75 – **531 rm** 80.00/90.00 **t.**

🏨 **John Howard** without rest., 4 Queen's Gate, SW7 5EH, ℰ 581 3011, Telex 8813397 – 🕽 ▤
📺 ☎. 🔲 🔲 ⓞ 𝘝𝘐𝘚𝘈. 🛇   BQ i
⌑ 6.50 – **44 rm** 45.00/82.50 **st.**

🏨 London International (Swallow), 147c Cromwell Rd, SW5 0TH, ℰ 370 4200, Telex 27260 – 🕽
📺 ☎ 🅿. 🔊   AS c
415 rm.

🏨 **Vanderbilt,** 76-86 Cromwell Rd, SW7 5BT, ℰ 589 2424, Telex 919867 – 🕽 📺 ⌁wc 🕽wc ☎.
🔲 🔲 ⓞ 𝘝𝘐𝘚𝘈   BS v
M 7.25 **t.** ⓵ 3.00 – ⌑ 5.50 – **230 rm** 39.90/55.90 **st.**

🏨 **Embassy House** (Embassy), 31-33 Queen's Gate, SW7 5JA, ℰ 584 7222, Telex 8813387 – 🕽
📺 ⌁wc 🕽wc ☜. 🔲 🔲 ⓞ 𝘝𝘐𝘚𝘈. 🛇   BR e
M (closed lunch Saturday and Sunday) (restricted lunch) 4.75/8.75 **st.** ⓵ 4.50 – **69 rm**
⌑ 38.00/50.00 **st.**

🏨 Elizabetta, 162 Cromwell Rd, SW5 0TT, ℰ 370 4282, Telex 918978 – 🕽 📺 ☎ 🅿. 🛇   AS r
84 rm.

🏨 **Gore,** 189 Queen's Gate, SW7 5EX, ℰ 584 6601, Telex 296244 – 🕽 📺 ⌁wc 🕽wc ☎. 🔲 🔲
ⓞ 𝘝𝘐𝘚𝘈. 🛇   BR n
M (coffee shop) a la carte 7.50/11.50 **t.** ⓵ 2.50 – ⌑ 5.00 – **57 rm** 42.00/56.00 **st.** – SB (week-
ends only) (winter only) 72.00 **st.**

🏨 **Rembrandt,** 11 Thurloe Pl., SW7 2RS, ☎ 589 8100, Telex 295828 – 🛗 ▤ rest 📺 ⇨wc ☎. 🔥
🏊 🕮 🕮 **VISA** ☒   DS **x**
190 rm.

🏨 **Regency,** 100-105 Queen's Gate, SW7 5AG, ☎ 370 4595, Telex 267594 – 🛗 📺 ⇨wc ⋔wc
☎. 🔥 🕮 🕮 🕮 **VISA** ☒   CT **e**
M 6.50 st. ⌐ 3.10 – ⊊ 4.50 – **205 rm** 33.00/45.00 st.

🏨 **Eden Plaza,** 68-69 Queen's Gate, SW7 5JT, ☎ 370 6111, Telex 916228 – 🛗 📺 ⇨wc ⋔wc
☎. 🕮 🕮 🕮 **VISA**   CS **o**
M a la carte 5.35/7.10 t. ⌐ 2.35 – **65 rm** ⊊ 35.00/48.00 st.

🏨 **Number Sixteen** without rest., 16 Sumner Pl., SW7 3EG, ☎ 589 5232, Telex 266638, 🚗 –
⇨wc ⋔wc ☎. 🕮 🕮 🕮 **VISA** ☒   CT **c**
⊊ 3.00 – **24 rm** 29.00/70.00 st.

🏨 **Alexander** without rest., 9 Sumner Pl., SW7 3EE, ☎ 581 1591, Telex 917133, 🚗 – 🛗 📺 ⇨wc
⋔wc ☎   CT **a**
36 rm.

↑ **Concord,** 155-157 Cromwell Rd, SW5 0TQ, ☎ 370 4151 – ⇨wc ☎. 🕮   AS **n**
40 rm ⊊ 12.50/25.00 s.

XXX **Bombay Brasserie,** Courtfield Close, 140 Gloucester Rd, SW7 4QH, ☎ 370 4040, Indian
rest. – 🔥 🕮 🕮 **VISA**   BS **a**
M a la carte 12.10/15.65 t. ⌐ 3.95.

XX **Reads,** 152 Old Brompton Rd, SW5 0BE, ☎ 373 2445 – 🔥 🕮 🕮 **VISA**   BT **a**
closed Sunday dinner, 2 weeks Christmas-New Year and Bank Holidays – **M** a la carte
13.00/16.10 t.

XX **Hilaire,** 68 Old Brompton Rd, SW7, ☎ 584 8993 – 🔥 🕮 🕮 **VISA**   CT **n**
closed Saturday lunch and Sunday – **M** 9.50/17.50 t. ⌐ 3.50.

XX **Memories of India,** 18 Gloucester Rd, SW7 4RB, ☎ 589 6450, Indian rest.   BR **s**

XX **Zen Too,** 53 Old Brompton Rd, SW7, ☎ 225 1609, Chinese rest. – ▤. 🔥 🕮 🕮 **VISA**   CST **r**
M a la carte 10.10/14.80 t. ⌐ 2.75.

X **Chanterelle,** 119 Old Brompton Rd, SW7 3RN, ☎ 373 5522 – 🔥 🕮 🕮 **VISA**   BT **v**
closed 24-27 December – **M** 7.00/10.00 t. ⌐ 2.95.

X **Star of India,** 154 Old Brompton Rd, SW5 0BE, ☎ 373 2901, Indian rest. – 🔥 🕮 🕮 **VISA**
closed Bank Holidays – **M** a la carte 7.55/10.40 t. ⌐ 3.95.   BT **s**

KINGSTON UPON THAMES – ✉ Surrey p. 9.

Surbiton – ✉ Surrey.

XX **Chez Max,** 85 Maple Rd, KT6 4AW, ☎ 399 2365 – 🔥 🕮 🕮 **VISA**   BZ **o**
*closed Saturday lunch, Sunday, Monday, 2 weeks August, 25 to 28 December and first week
January* – **M** (booking essential) a la carte 12.40/16.15 t.

LONDON HEATHROW AIRPORT – see Hillingdon, London p. 51.

MERTON pp. 8 and 9.

Merton – ✉ SW19.

X **Les Amoureux,** 156 Merton Hall Rd, SW19 3PZ, ☎ 543 0567 – 🔥 🕮   DZ **a**
closed Sunday – **M** (lunch by arrangement) a la carte 8.85/10.40 t. ⌐ 2.25.

Wimbledon – ✉ SW19.

↑ **Worcester House,** 38 Alwyne Rd, SW19 7AE, ☎ 946 1300 – 📺 ⋔wc. ☒   DY **r**
9 rm ⊊ 19.00/34.00 s.

XX **San Lorenzo Fuoriporta,** 38 Worple Rd Mews, SW19 4DB, ☎ 946 8463, Italian rest. – 🔥
🕮 🕮 **VISA**   DY **n**
closed Bank Holidays – **M** a la carte 14.50/18.00 t. ⌐ 3.50.

MICHELIN Branch, Deer Park Rd, Merton, SW19 3UD, ☎ 540 9034/7

REDBRIDGE pp. 6 and 7.

South Woodford – ✉ Essex.

XX **Ho-Ho,** 20 High Rd, E18 2QL, ☎ 989 1041, Chinese rest. – 🔥 🕮 🕮 **VISA**   GV **c**
M a la carte 9.60/14.70 t.

Woodford – ✉ Essex.

🏨 **Woodford Moat House** (Q.M.H.), Oak Hill, Woodford Green, IG8 9NY, ☎ 505 4511 – 🛗 📺
⇨wc ⋔wc ☎ 🅿 🔥 🔥 🕮 🕮 **VISA**   GU **c**
M (bar lunch Saturday) 8.35 t. – **99 rm** ⊊ 38.50/48.50 st. – SB (weekends only) 48.00 st.

XX **Prince Regent** with rm, Manor Rd, Woodford Bridge, IG8 8AE, E : ¾ m. ☎ 504 7635, 🚗 –
▤ 📺 ⇨wc ⋔wc ☎ 🅿 🔥 🕮 🕮 **VISA** ☒   GU **a**
M *(closed Saturday lunch)* a la carte 12.80/20.25 t. ⌐ 3.00 – **10 rm** ⊊ 33.00/44.00 t.

LONDON p. 60

RICHMOND-UPON-THAMES pp. 8 and 9.

Barnes – ⊠ SW13.

✗ **Barnaby's,** 39b High St., SW13 9LN, ℘ 878 4750, French rest. – ☒ ☒ ☒ ☒   CY **v**
closed lunch Saturday and Monday, Sunday, Easter, 3 weeks September, Christmas and Bank Holidays – **M** a la carte 8.85/11.35 **st.** ⌗ 2.60.

East Sheen – ⊠ Surrey.

✗✗ **Crowther's,** 481 Upper Richmond Rd West, SW14 7PU, ℘ 876 6372 – ☒ ☒   CY **n**
closed Saturday lunch, Sunday, Monday and 2 weeks August-September – **M** (booking essential) 13.75 **t.** ⌗ 3.00.

Kew – ⊠ Surrey.

✗✗ **Le Mange Tout,** 3 Royal Par. (Station Approach), TW9 3QB, ℘ 940 9304 – ☒, ☒ ☒ ☒ ☒
closed Sunday, Christmas Day and 1 January – **M** a la carte 7.65/17.45 **t.** ⌗ 2.55.   CY **r**

✗ **Jasper's Bun in the Oven,** 11 Kew Green, TW9 3AA, ℘ 940 3987 – ☒ ☒ ☒ ☒   CX **e**
closed Sunday and Bank Holidays – **M** a la carte 6.75/12.85 **t.** ⌗ 2.45.

Richmond – ⊠ Surrey.

☖, ☖ Richmond Park ℘ 876 3205.
🛈 Central Library, Little Green ℘ 940 9125.

🏨 **Richmond Gate,** Richmond Hill, TW10 6RP, ℘ 940 0061, Telex 928556, 🐎 – ☒ ➪wc ☎
Ⓟ. ⚘. ☒ ☒. ☒   CY **a**
M (restricted lunch Monday to Saturday) 6.00/11.50 **st.** ⌗ 3.25 – **49 rm** ☲ 45.00/55.00 **st.** – SB (weekends only) 60.00 **st.**

🏨 **Petersham,** Nightingale Lane, Richmond Hill, TW10 6RP, ℘ 940 7471, Telex 948556, ⩽ – 🛗
☒ ➪wc Ⓟ. ⚘. ☒ ☒. ☒   CY **c**
closed 23 December-3 January – **M** (closed Saturday and Sunday) 9.00 **t.** ⌗ 3.50 – **52 rm**
☲ 45.00/55.00 **st.** – SB (weekends only) 60.00 **st.**

✗✗ ❀ **Lichfield's,** 13 Lichfield Terr., Sheen Rd, TW9 1DP, ℘ 940 5236 – ☒ ☒   CY **i**
closed Saturday lunch, Sunday, Monday, 3 weeks August-September and Bank Holidays – **M** (booking essential) a la carte 15.50/27.00 **t.** ⌗ 3.50
Spec. Nage of Lobster and Langoustines with ginger butter, Fillets of hare with beetroot and orange, Variations on an apple theme.

✗✗ **Kew Rendezvous,** 110 Kew Rd, TW9 2PQ, ℘ 948 4343, Chinese-Peking rest. – ☒, ☒ ☒
☒ ☒   CY **e**
closed 25-26 December – **M** 9.00 **t.**

✗✗ **Evergreen,** 102-104 Kew Rd, TW9 2PQ, ℘ 940 9044, Chinese rest. ☒   CY **e**

✗ **Red Lion,** 18 Red Lion St., TW9 1RW, ℘ 940 2371, Chinese-Peking rest. – ☒ ☒ ☒ ☒
closed 24 and 25 December – **M** a la carte 5.00/8.20 **t.** ⌗ 2.80.   CY **s**

Twickenham – ⊠ Middx..

✗✗ **Cézanne,** 68 Richmond Rd, TW1 3BE, ℘ 892 3526 – ☒ ☒ ☒   BY **a**
closed Saturday lunch, Sunday, 1 week at Christmas and Bank Holidays – **M** a la carte 7.65/12.30 **t.** ⌗ 2.00.

SOUTHWARK pp. 10 and 11.

Dulwich Village – ⊠ SE21.

✗✗ **Luigi's,** 129 Gipsy Hill, SE19 1QS, ℘ 670 1843, Italian rest. – ☒ ☒ ☒ ☒   FY **a**
closed Saturday lunch, Sunday, August and Bank Holidays – **M** a la carte 10.70/13.60 **t.** ⌗ 3.50.

SUTTON pp. 8 and 9.

☖ Oak Sports Centre, Woodmansterne Rd, Carshalton ℘ 642 9608.

Sutton – ⊠ Surrey.

⭫ **Dene,** 39 Cheam Rd, SM1 2AT, ℘ 642 3170, 🐎 – ☒ ➪wc 🛁wc Ⓟ. ☒   EZ **v**
17 rm ☲ 12.65/34.50 **t.**

✗✗ **Partners 23,** 23 Stonecot Hill, SM3 9HB, ℘ 644 7743 – ☒ ☒ ☒   DZ **z**
closed Saturday lunch, Sunday, Monday and 25 December-7 January – **M** (booking essential) 11.25/14.50 **t.** ⌗ 2.60.

Do not mix up :

Comfort of hotels   : 🏨🏨 ... 🏠, �, ⭫
Comfort of restaurants   : ✗✗✗✗✗ ..... ✗
Quality of the cuisine   : ❀❀❀, ❀❀, ❀, **M**

304

WALTHAM FOREST pp. 6 and 7.

ʜ₈ at Chingford, 158 Station Rd ℰ 529 2107.

Leytonstone – ✉ E11.

✗ **Trattoria Parmigiana,** 715 High Rd, E11 4RD, ℰ 539 1700, Italian rest. – ☒ 🄰🄴 ① 𝓥𝓘𝓢𝓐
closed Sunday and Bank Holidays – **M** a la carte approx. 11.15 **t.** ⋀ 2.90.   GV **a**

WANDSWORTH pp. 8 and 9.

Battersea – ✉ SW8/SW11.

✗✗ ⊛⊛ **Chez Nico,** 129 Queenstown Rd, SW8 3RH, ℰ 720 6960, French rest. – ☒ 𝓥𝓘𝓢𝓐   EY **c**
*closed Monday lunch, Sunday, 1 week Easter, 3 weeks July-August, 1 week Christmas and
Bank Holidays* – **M** (booking essential) a la carte 22.25/29.00 **st.** ⋀ 5.85
Spec. Parfait fondant de foies de volailles, Suprême de canard au fumet de cèpes, Marquise au chocolat crème
anglaise orangée.

✗✗ **Alonso's,** 32 Queenstown Rd, SW8 3RX, ℰ 720 5986 – 🄰🄴 ① 𝓥𝓘𝓢𝓐   EY **e**
closed Saturday lunch, Sunday and Bank Holidays – **M** 7.95/12.50 **t.**

✗✗ **Lampwicks,** 24 Queenstown Rd, SW8 3RX, ℰ 622 7800 – ☒ 🄰🄴 ① 𝓥𝓘𝓢𝓐   EY **s**
closed Saturday lunch, Sunday, 2 weeks August, 1 week Christmas and Bank Holidays – **M**
10.50/16.50 **t.** ⋀ 3.00.

✗✗ ⊛ **L'Arlequin,** 123 Queenstown Rd, SW8, ℰ 622 0555, French rest. – ☒ ① 𝓥𝓘𝓢𝓐   EY **o**
closed Saturday, Sunday, 3 weeks August and Bank Holidays – **M** a la carte 16.20/23.75 **st.**
Spec. Persillé de ris de veau et homard, Papillote de saumon sauvage au gingembre (seasonal), Chaud froid de
framboises (seasonal).

Clapham – ✉ SW11.

✗ **Pollyanna's,** 2 Battersea Rise, SW11 1ED, ℰ 228 0316, Bistro – ☒ 🄰🄴 ① 𝓥𝓘𝓢𝓐   EY **a**
closed 24 to 27 December and 1 January – **M** (dinner only and Sunday lunch) a la carte
9.70/13.65 **t.** ⋀ 2.50.

WESTMINSTER (City of).

Bayswater and Maida Vale – ✉ W2/W9 – Except where otherwise stated see pp. 30
and 31.

🏨 **Royal Lancaster** (Rank), Lancaster Terr., W2 2TY, ℰ 262 6737, Telex 24822, ⪉ – 🛗 📺 ☎ ⅙
🅿 🄰 📺 🄰🄴 ① 𝓥𝓘𝓢𝓐 🛠   DZ **e**
M 11.50/13.95 (wine included) **st.** ⋀ 4.75 – ⌷ 6.50 – **435 rm** 75.00/97.00 **st.** – SB (weekends only) 42.55/45.55 **st.**

🏨 **London Metropole,** Edgware Rd, W2 1JU, ℰ 402 4141, Telex 23711, ⪉ – 🛗 🖿 📺 ☎ 🅿
🄰 ☒ 🄰🄴 ① 𝓥𝓘𝓢𝓐 🛠   pp. 13-16   JT **c**
M a la carte 11.50/18.50 **t.** ⋀ 3.60 – ⌷ 3.50 – **586 rm** 52.50/60.00 **t.** – SB (weekends only) 54.50 **st.**

🏨 Hospitality Inn (Mt. Charlotte), 104 Bayswater Rd, W2 3HL, ℰ 262 4461, Telex 22667, ⪉ – 🛗
📺 ☎ 🅿 ☒ 🄰🄴 ① 𝓥𝓘𝓢𝓐   CZ **o**
⌷ 5.50 – **175 rm** 43.45/57.75 **st.**

🏨 **London Embassy** (Embassy), 150 Bayswater Rd, W2 4RT, ℰ 229 1212, Telex 27727 – 🛗 📺
⇋wc ☎ ⅙ 🅿 🄰 ☒ 🄰🄴 ① 𝓥𝓘𝓢𝓐 🛠   BZ **o**
M (carving lunch) 7.75/8.75 **st.** ⋀ 4.75 – ⌷ 3.50 – **192 rm** 48.00/68.00 **st.** – SB (weekends only) 60.00/66.00 **st.**

🏨 White's (Mt. Charlotte), Bayswater Rd, 90-92 Lancaster Gate, W2 3NR, ℰ 262 2711, Telex
23922 – 🛗 📺 ⇋wc ☎ 🅿 🄰 ☒ 🄰🄴 ① 𝓥𝓘𝓢𝓐   CZ **v**
61 rm 46.50/58.50 **st.**

🏨 **Coburg** (Best Western), 129 Bayswater Rd, W2 4RJ, ℰ 229 3654, Telex 268235 – 🛗 📺
⇋wc ⊛. 🄰. ☒ 🄰🄴 ① 𝓥𝓘𝓢𝓐   BZ **a**
M 7.50/8.50 **st.** ⋀ 3.50 – **125 rm** ⌷ 25.00/56.00 **st.** – SB (weekends only) 39.00/56.00 **st.**

🏨 **Colonnade,** 2 Warrington Cres., W9 1ER, ℰ 286 1052, Telex 298930 – 🛗 📺 ⇋wc ⋔wc ⊛.
☒ 🄰🄴 ① 𝓥𝓘𝓢𝓐   pp. 13-16   JT **e**
M (dinner only) 7.95 **st.** ⋀ 2.50 – **53 rm** ⌷ 25.50/55.00 **t.**

🏨 **Mornington Lancaster** without rest., 12 Lancaster Gate, W2 3LG, ℰ 262 7361, Telex 24281
– 🛗 📺 ⇋wc 🄰🄴 ① 𝓥𝓘𝓢𝓐   DZ **s**
closed Christmas-New Year – ⌷ 3.00 – **65 rm** 28.00/48.00 **st.**

↥ **Dylan,** 14 Devonshire Terr., Lancaster Gate, W2 3DW, ℰ 723 3280 – ⇋wc ⋔wc. 🄰🄴 ① 𝓥𝓘𝓢𝓐.
🛠   CY **c**
18 rm ⌷ 16.00/32.00 **t.**

↥ **Parkwood,** 4 Stanhope Pl., W2 2HB, ℰ 402 2241, Group Telex 8812714 – 📺 ⇋wc ☎. ☒ 🄰🄴
① 𝓥𝓘𝓢𝓐. 🛠   FY **e**
18 rm ⌷ 20.00/38.50 **st.**

↥ **Allandale,** 3 Devonshire Terr., Lancaster Gate, W2 3DN, ℰ 723 8311 – ⇋wc ⋔wc. ☒ ①
𝓥𝓘𝓢𝓐. 🛠   CY **a**
18 rm ⌷ 18.00/27.00 **s.**

XXX Bombay Palace, 50 Connaught St., Hyde Park Sq., W2, ☎ 723 8855, North Indian   EY **a**

XX **San Marino,** 26 Sussex Pl., W2 2TH, ☎ 723 8395, Italian rest. – ⬛ AE ⓪ VISA   EY **u**
closed Sunday – **M** a la carte 9.40/23.90 **t.** 🍷 3.50.

XX **Trat West,** 143 Edgware Rd, W2 2HR, ☎ 723 8203, Italian rest. – ⬛ AE ⓪ VISA
closed Bank Holidays – **M** a la carte 8.00/10.60 **t.** 🍷 2.50.   pp. 13-16   KT **i**

XX **Concordia Notte,** 29-31 Craven Rd, W2 3BX, ☎ 723 3725, Italian rest., Dancing – ⬛ AE ⓪
VISA   DY **r**
closed Sunday, August and Bank Holidays – **M** (dinner only) a la carte 15.25/19.25 **t.** 🍷 4.00.

XX **Canaletto da Leo,** 451 Edgware Rd, W2 1TH, ☎ 262 7027, Italian rest. – ⬛ AE ⓪ VISA
closed Saturday lunch, Sunday and Bank Holidays – **M** a la carte 10.00/16.00 **t.** 🍷 3.50.
    pp. 13-16   JT **v**

X **Concordia,** 29-31 Craven Rd, W2 3BX, ☎ 402 4985, Italian rest. – ⬛ AE ⓪ VISA   DY **r**
closed Sunday and Bank Holidays – **M** a la carte 9.80/13.30 **t.** 🍷 2.10.

X Fortune Cookie, 1 Queensway, W2 4QJ, ☎ 727 7260, Chinese rest. – ⬛ VISA   BZ **e**

X **Kalamaras Taverna,** 76-78 Inverness Mews, W2 3JQ, ☎ 727 9122, Greek rest. – ⬛ AE ⓪
VISA   BY **a**
closed Sunday and Bank Holidays – **M** (dinner only) a la carte 6.90/10.90 **t.** 🍷 2.60.

Belgravia – ✉ SW1 – Except where otherwise stated see pp. 28 and 29.

🏛️ Berkeley, Wilton Pl., SW1X 7RL, ☎ 235 6000, Telex 919252, 🔲 – 🛗 📺 ☎ 👥 🍽️ 🐕 🖼️. ⬛ AE
VISA 🍴   FQ **e**
M Restaurant *(closed Saturday)* a la carte 12.00/27.00 **st.** – **Buttery** *(closed Sunday)* a la carte
11.75/18.75 **st.** – **153 rm.**

🏛️ **Lowndes Thistle** (Thistle), 21 Lowndes St., SW1X 9ES, ☎ 235 6020, Telex 919065 – 🛗 📺
☎. ⬛ AE ⓪ VISA 🍴   FR **i**
M 12.50 **t.** 🍷 3.45 – ⬜ 6.00 – **80 rm** 69.00/95.00 **t.** – SB (weekends only) 83.50 **st.**

XX **Salloos,** 62-64 Kinnerton St., SW1 8ER, ☎ 235 4444, Indian and Pakistani rest. – 🍽️. ⬛ AE
⓪ VISA   FQ **a**
closed Sunday and Bank Holidays – **M** a la carte 11.90/15.90 **t.** 🍷 2.50.

XX **Motcombs,** 26 Motcomb St., SW1X 8JU, ☎ 235 6382 – ⬛ AE ⓪ VISA   FR **z**
closed Saturday lunch, Sunday and Bank Holidays – **M** a la carte 11.35/16.70 **t.** 🍷 3.50.

Hyde Park and Knightsbridge – ✉ SW1/SW7 – pp. 28 and 29.
🏨 Fourth Floor, Harrods, Knightsbridge, SW1 ☎ 730 0791.

🏛️ **Hyde Park** (T.H.F.), 66 Knightsbridge, SW1Y 7LA, ☎ 235 2000, Telex 262057, ≼ – 🛗 📺 🖼️.
⬛ AE ⓪ VISA   EQ **v**
M *(closed Saturday lunch)* 12.00/13.50 **st.** 🍷 4.50 – ⬜ 6.75 – **179 rm** 102.00/115.50 **st.**

XXX Shezan, 16-22 Cheval Pl., Montpelier St., SW7 1ES, ☎ 589 7918, Indian and Pakistani rest.
    ER **c**

XX **Mr Chow,** 151 Knightsbridge, SW1X 7PA, ☎ 589 7347, Chinese rest. – ⬛ AE ⓪ VISA   EQ **s**
closed Christmas – **M** a la carte 12.40/21.90 **t.** 🍷 3.00.

XX Montpeliano, 13 Montpelier St., SW7 1HQ, ☎ 589 0032, Italian rest.   ER **e**

*La Grande Londra (GREATER LONDON) è composta dalla City e da 32 distretti
amministrativi (Borough) divisi a loro volta in quartieri o villaggi che hanno conservato
il loro proprio carattere (Area).*

Mayfair – ⊠ W1 – pp. 26 and 27.

🏛🏛 **Dorchester,** Park Lane, W1A 2HJ, ℰ 629 8888, Telex 887704 – 🛗 🗐 TV ☎ ᗧ 📞, 🚗 ᗧ, 🔼 AE
① VISA 🍽
BN z
M (see **The Terrace** below) – **Grill** a la carte 16.00/23.20 **st.** ⬧ 3.50 – ⬜ 7.75 – **280 rm** 95.00/135.00 **st.**

🏛🏛 **Claridge's,** Brook St., W1A 2JQ, ℰ 629 8860, Telex 21872 – 🛗 TV ☎ ᗧ, 🔼 AE VISA 🍽
M a la carte 18.00/28.00 **st.** ⬧ 2.80 – **Causerie** – ⬜ 8.00 – **205 rm** 80.00/135.00 **st.**
BL c

🏛🏛 **Inn on the Park,** Hamilton Pl., Park Lane, W1A 1AZ, ℰ 499 0888, Telex 22771 – 🛗 TV ☎ ᗧ,
🚗 ᗧ, 🔼 AE ① VISA 🍽
BP a
M **Four Seasons** a la carte 22.50/27.75 **st.** ⬧ 5.25 – **Lanes** a la carte 16.30/18.10 **st.** ⬧ 5.25 – ⬜ 7.25 – **228 rm** 108.00/128.00 **s.**

🏛🏛 **Grosvenor House** (T.H.F.), Park Lane, W1A 3AA, ℰ 499 6363, Telex 24871, 🔼 – 🛗 TV ☎ ᗧ,
📞 ᗧ, 🔼 AE ① VISA 🍽
AM a
M (see **90 Park Lane** below) – ⬜ 6.50 – **470 rm** 92.50/103.00 **st.**

🏛 ❀ **Connaught,** 16 Carlos Pl., W1Y 6AL, ℰ 499 7070 – 🛗 TV ☎. 🔼 🍽
BM e
M (booking essential) – **90 rm**
Spec. Pâté de turbot froid au homard, sauce pudeur, Rendez-vous du pêcheur, sauce légère au parfum d'Armorique, Salmis de canard strasbourgeoise en surprise.

🏛 **Inter-Continental** (Inter-Con.), 1 Hamilton Pl., Hyde Park Corner, W1V 0QY, ℰ 409 3131,
Telex 25853 – 🛗 🗐 TV ☎ ᗧ 📞, 🚗 ᗧ, 🔼 AE ① VISA 🍽
BP o
M (see also **Le Souffle** below) a la carte approx. 14.50 **st.** ⬧ 5.50 – ⬜ 7.50 – **491 rm** 110.00/128.00.

🏛 **Athenaeum** (Rank), 116 Piccadilly, W1V 0BJ, ℰ 499 3464, Telex 261589 – 🛗 TV ☎ ᗧ,
AE VISA
CP s
M a la carte 18.10/24.70 **st.** ⬧ 4.00 – ⬜ 7.00 – **112 rm** 97.00/140.00 **st.** – SB (weekends only) 121.00/146.00 **st.**

🏛 **Brown's** (T.H.F.), 29-34 Albemarle St., W1A 4SW, ℰ 493 6020, Telex 28866 – 🛗 TV ☎. ᗧ,
🔼 AE ① VISA
DM e
M 18.75/20.75 **st.** ⬧ 4.50 – ⬜ 7.00 – **125 rm** 76.50/101.00 **st.**

🏛 **May Fair** (Inter-Con.), Stratton St., W1A 2AN, ℰ 629 7777, Telex 262526 – 🛗 TV ☎. ᗧ,
AE ① VISA 🍽
DN z
M 15.00/16.00 **t.** ⬧ 6.00 – ⬜ 7.00 – **327 rm** 77.00/125.00.

🏛 **Westbury** (T.H.F.), New Bond St., W1A 4UH, ℰ 629 7755, Telex 24378 – 🛗 TV ☎ ᗧ 📞,
🔼 AE ① VISA
DM a
M 11.25/17.00 **t.** ⬧ 4.25 – ⬜ 7.00 – **242 rm** 75.50/88.00 **st.**

🏛 **Hilton International,** 22 Park Lane, W1A 2HH, ℰ 493 8000, Telex 24873, ≤ London – 🛗 🗐
TV ☎ 📞, ᗧ, 🔼 AE ① VISA – ⬜ 6.50 – **501 rm** 95.00/130.00 **t.**
BP e
M a la carte 13.50/34.00 **t.** ⬧ 4.00 – ⬜ 6.50 – **501 rm** 95.00/130.00 **t.**

🏛 **Holiday Inn,** 3 Berkeley St., W1X 6NE, ℰ 493 8282, Telex 24561 – 🛗 🗐 TV ☎ 🚗, ᗧ, 🔼
AE ① VISA 🍽
DN r
M a la carte 10.50/20.00 **st.** ⬧ 4.00 – ⬜ 7.00 – **186 rm** 78.00/106.00 **st.** – SB (weekends only) 84.00 **st.**

🏛 **Chesterfield** (Forum), 35 Charles St., W1X 8LX, ℰ 491 2622, Telex 269394 – 🛗 TV ☎. 🍽
87 rm
CN c

🏛 **Washington,** 5-7 Curzon St., W1Y 8DT, ℰ 499 7030, Telex 24540 – 🛗 TV 🚻wc ☎. ᗧ, 🔼
AE ① VISA 🍽
CN n
M 10.00 **st.** ⬧ 3.60 – ⬜ 5.50 – **164 rm** 46.50/64.00 **st.**

XXXXX **Mirabelle** (De Vere), 56 Curzon St., W1Y 8DL, ℰ 499 4636, 🌳
CN a

XXXXX ❀ **The Terrace,** (at Dorchester H.), Park Lane, W1A 2HJ, ℰ 629 8888, Telex 887704, French
rest. – 🔼 AE ① VISA
BN z
closed Sunday – **M** (dinner only) a la carte approx. 28.00 **st.**
Spec. Parfait de foies de volailles aux truffes, Délice de turbot gratiné au basilic, sauce aux poivrons jaunes, Rosette de bœuf aux échalotes.

XXXXX **90 Park Lane,** (at Grosvenor House H.), Park Lane, W1A 3AA, ℰ 499 6363 – 📞. 🔼 AE ①
VISA
AM a
closed Saturday lunch and Sunday – **M** a la carte 19.00/35.25 **st.** ⬧ 5.00.

XXXX ❀❀❀ **Le Gavroche,** 43 Upper Brook St., W1P 1PS, ℰ 408 0881, French rest. – 🔼 AE ① VISA
closed Saturday, Sunday, 21 December-2 January and Bank Holidays – **M** (booking essential)
a la carte 26.70/37.40 **st.**
AM c
Spec. Soufflé suissesse, Assiette du boucher, Sablé aux fraises.

XXXX ❀ **Le Soufflé** (at Inter-Continental H.), 1 Hamilton Pl., Hyde Park Corner, W1V 0QY, ℰ
409 3131, Telex 25853 – 📞. 🔼 AE ① VISA
BP o
M 16.80/20.60 **t.** ⬧ 5.50
Spec. Les paupiettes de turbot aux langoustines, La caille « comme chez nous », Le magret de canard au foie gras en cage.

XXXX **Scott's,** 20 Mount St., W1Y 5RB, ℰ 629 5248, Seafood – 🔼 AE ① VISA
BM r
closed Sunday lunch and Bank Holidays – **M** a la carte 16.10/24.40 **t.** ⬧ 3.00.

XXX **Cecconi's,** 5a Burlington Gdns, W1Y 5DT, ℰ 434 1500, Italian rest.
DM c

XXX **Tiberio,** 22 Queen St., W1X 7PJ, ℰ 629 3561, Italian rest., Dancing – 🔼 AE ① VISA
CN z
closed Saturday lunch, Sunday and Bank Holidays – **M** a la carte 13.25/16.50 **t.** ⬧ 2.50.

XX **Greenhouse,** 27a Hay's Mews, W1X 7RJ, 🕾 499 3331 – ⊠ AE ⓪ *VISA* BN **a**
closed Saturday lunch, Sunday, 25 December-7 January and Bank Holidays – **M** a la carte
11.80/17.25 **t.** 🍷 2.75.

XX **Langan's Brasserie,** Stratton St., W1X 5FD, 🕾 493 6437 – ⊠ AE ⓪ *VISA* DN **e**
closed Saturday lunch, Sunday and Bank Holidays – **M** (booking essential) a la carte
12.40/13.85 **t.** 🍷 3.95.

XX **Miyama,** 38 Clarges St., W1Y 7PJ, 🕾 499 2443, Japanese rest. – ▤ ⊠ AE ⓪ *VISA* CN **e**
closed Saturday lunch, Sunday, Easter, Christmas-New Year and Bank Holidays – **M** a la carte
12.50/31.00 **t.** 🍷 3.10.

XX **Apicella 81,** 4a Mill St., W1R 9TE, 🕾 499 1308, Italian rest. – ⊠ AE ⓪ *VISA* DL **x**
closed Saturday lunch, Sunday, Easter, Christmas and Bank Holidays – **M** a la carte
11.00/14.20 **t.** 🍷 2.80.

XX **Shogun** (at Britannia H.), Adams Row, W1, 🕾 493 1255, Telex 8813271, Japanese rest. – ⊠
AE ⓪ *VISA* BM **i**
closed Monday – **M** (dinner only) a la carte 11.00/16.50 **s.** 🍷 3.50.

XX **One Two Three,** 27 Davies St., W1, 🕾 409 0750, Japanese rest. – ⊠ AE ⓪ *VISA* BM **s**
closed Sunday lunch, Saturday and Bank Holidays – **M** a la carte 8.30/16.40 **t.**

XX **Mr. Kai,** 65 South Audley St., W1, 🕾 493 8988, Chinese-Peking rest. – ⊠ AE ⓪ *VISA* BM **v**
closed 25-26 December, 1 January and Bank Holidays – **M** a la carte 16.25/22.25 **t.** 🍷 3.95.

XX **Marquis,** 121a Mount St., W1Y 5HB, 🕾 499 1256 – ⊠ AE ⓪ *VISA* BM **u**
closed Sunday and Bank Holidays – **M** a la carte 10.25/14.40 **t.** 🍷 3.00.

XX **Golden Carp,** 8a Mount St., W1Y 5AD, 🕾 499 3385, Seafood – ⊠ AE ⓪ *VISA* BM **x**
closed Saturday lunch, Sunday, 3 weeks August and Bank Holidays – **M** a la carte 6.55/13.65 **t.**
🍷 3.50.

XX **Gaylord,** 16 Albemarle St., W1 3HA, 🕾 629 9802, Indian rest. – ⊠ AE ⓪ *VISA* DM **u**
M approx. 10.00 **t.** 🍷 3.40.

X **Ikeda,** 30 Brook St., W1Y 1AG, 🕾 629 2730, Japanese rest. – ⊠ AE ⓪ *VISA* CKL **a**
closed Sunday lunch, Saturday and Bank Holidays – **M** a la carte 11.20/18.00 **t.** 🍷 2.50.

X **Trattoria Fiori,** 87-88 Mount St., W1Y 5HG, 🕾 499 1447, Italian rest. – ⊠ AE ⓪ *VISA* BM **o**
closed Sunday and Bank Holidays – **M** a la carte 8.80/11.55 **t.** 🍷 2.50.

Regent's Park and Marylebone – ⊠ NW1/NW6/NW8/W1 – Except where otherwise
stated see pp. 26 and 27.
🎟 Ground Floor, Selfridges, Oxford St., W1 🕾 730 0791.

🏨🏨🏨 **Churchill,** 30 Portman Sq., W1A 4ZX, 🕾 486 5800, Telex 264831 – ▤ ▤ 📺 🕾 & �ⓟ ▦ ⊠
AE ⓪ *VISA* ⌘ AJ **x**
M a la carte 12.30/24.70 **st.** 🍷 2.85 – ⊊ 7.00 – **489 rm** 84.00/97.00.

🏨🏨 **Portman Inter-Continental** (Inter-Con.), 22 Portman Sq., W1H 9FL, 🕾 486 5844, Telex
261526 – ▤ ▤ 📺 🕾 & ⓟ ▦ ⊠ AE ⓪ *VISA* ⌘ AJ **o**
M 8.10/14.50 **t.** 🍷 4.60 – ⊊ 7.55 – **276 rm** 94.00/105.00.

🏨🏨 **Montcalm,** Great Cumberland Pl., W1A 2LF, 🕾 402 4288, Telex 28710 – ▤ ▤ 📺 🕾 ▦ ⊠
⓪ *VISA* pp. 30 and 31 FY **x**
M (*closed Saturday lunch and Sunday*) a la carte 14.20/17.60 **st.** 🍷 2.70 – ⊊ 7.00 – **116 rm**
73.00/83.00.

🏨🏨 **Holiday Inn,** 134 George St., W1H 6DN, 🕾 723 1277, Telex 27983, 🔲 – ▤ ▤ 📺 🕾 & ⓟ
▦ ⊠ AE ⓪ *VISA* pp. 30 and 31 FY **i**
M 12.50 **t.** 🍷 4.25 – ⊊ 7.00 – **241 rm** 85.10/103.50 **st.**

🏨🏨 **Selfridge Thistle** (Thistle), 400 Orchard St., W1H 0JS, 🕾 408 2080, Telex 22361 – ▤ ▤ 📺
🕾 & ⓟ ⊠ AE ⓪ *VISA* ⌘ AK **e**
M 15.00/17.00 **t.** 🍷 3.45 – ⊊ 6.00 – **298 rm** 76.00/90.00 **t.** – SB (weekends only) 62.00 **st.**

🏨 **Ladbroke Westmoreland** (Ladbroke), 18 Lodge Rd, NW8 7JT, 🕾 722 7722, Telex 23101 –
▤ ▤ 📺 🕾 ⓟ ▦ ⊠ AE ⓪ *VISA* pp. 13-16 JS **v**
M 18.00 **st.** 🍷 3.15 – ⊊ 6.25 – **350 rm** 50.00/68.00 **t.** – SB (weekends only) 53.95/61.95 **st.**

🏨🏨 **St. George's** (T.H.F.), Langham Pl., W1N 8QS, 🕾 580 0111, Telex 27274, ⇐ – ▤ 📺 🕾 ⊠ AE
⓪ *VISA* pp. 13-16 LT **a**
M a la carte 11.15/17.75 **st.** 🍷 4.50 – ⊊ 6.00 – **85 rm** 57.50/74.50 **st.**

🏨🏨 **Cumberland** (T.H.F.), Marble Arch, W1A 4RF, 🕾 262 1234, Telex 22215 – ▤ 📺 🕾 & ▦ ⊠
AE ⓪ *VISA* ⌘ AK **n**
M (carving rest.) 9.25 **t.** 🍷 3.00 – ⊊ 6.00 – **910 rm** 55.50/72.00 **st.**

Durrants, 26-32 George St., W1H 6BJ, ☎ 935 8131, Telex 894919 – 🛋 📺 ➚wc ☜. 🏋. 🔝
AH e
🕮 ① *VISA* 🕸
M 15.00/20.00 **st.** 🛈 3.75 – ⬄ 4.00 – **103 rm** 28.00/58.00 **st.**

Londoner, 57-59 Welbeck St., W1M 8HS, ☎ 935 4442, Telex 894630 – 🛋 📺 ➚wc ☜. 🔝 🕮
BJ v
① *VISA* 🕸
M a la carte 7.80/10.10 **t.** 🛈 2.75 – **142 rm** 42.00/55.00 **t.** – SB (weekends only) 55.00 **st.**

Berners, 10 Berners St., W1A 3BE, ☎ 636 1629, Telex 25759 – 🛋 📺 ➚wc ☎ ♿. 🏋. 🔝 🕮
FJ r
① *VISA* 🕸
M (carving rest.) 10.75 **st.** 🛈 3.60 – ⬄ 5.95 – **236 rm** 63.00/84.00 **st.**

Regent Crest (Crest), Carburton St., W1P 8EE, ☎ 388 2300, Telex 22453 – 🛋 📺 ➚wc ☜
pp. 13-16 LT i
🅿. 🏋. 🔝 🕮 ① *VISA* 🕸
M approx. 12.00 **st.** – ⬄ 5.25 – **320 rm** 51.00/62.00 **st.**

Stratford Court, 350 Oxford St., W1N 0BY, ☎ 629 7474, Telex 22270 – 🛋 📺 ➚wc ☜. 🔝
BK n
🕮 ① *VISA*
M (carving rest.) 9.25 **t.** 🛈 3.50 – ⬄ 5.50 – **137 rm** 48.90/65.90 **st.**

Clifton Ford (Forum), 47 Welbeck St., W1M 8DN, ☎ 486 6600, Telex 22569 – 🛋 📺 ➚wc ☜.
BH a
🏋
M (grill rest. only) – **227 rm**.

Harewood, Harewood Row, NW1 6SE, ☎ 262 2707, Telex 297225 – 🛋 📺 ➚wc ☜. 🔝 🕮
pp. 13-16 KT x
① *VISA* 🕸
M (grill rest. only) 10.00 **st.** 🛈 2.00 – **92 rm** ⬄ 38.50/49.50 **st.**

Bryanston Court, 56-60 Great Cumberland Pl., W1H 7FD, ☎ 262 3141, Group Telex 262076
– 🛋 📺 ➚wc 📶wc ☜. 🔝 🕮 ① *VISA*   pp. 30 and 31   FY z
M *(closed Saturday and Sunday)* 9.00 **t.** 🛈 2.50 – ⬄ 2.50 – **53 rm** 33.00/44.00 **st.**

Concorde without rest., 50 Great Cumberland Pl., W1H 7FD, ☎ 402 6169, Group Telex
262076 – 🛋 📺 ➚wc 📶wc ☜. 🔝 🕮 ① *VISA* 🕸   pp. 30 and 31   FY n
⬄ 3.00 – **28 rm** 30.00/38.00 **st.**

Hallam without rest., 12 Hallam St., W1N 5LJ, ☎ 580 1166 – 🛋 ➚wc 📶wc ☜. 🔝 🕮 ①
pp. 13-16 LT r
VISA 🕸
23 rm ⬄ 25.00/35.00 **st.**

Portman Court, 28-30 Seymour St., W1H 5WD, ☎ 402 5401 – ➚wc ☜. 🔝 🕮 ① *VISA*. 🕸
AK a
⬄ 1.00 – **30 rm** 18.00/35.00 **st.**

XXX **Odins,** 27 Devonshire St., W1N 1RS, ☎ 935 7296 – 🕮   pp. 13-16 KT n
closed Saturday lunch, Sunday and Bank Holidays – **M** a la carte 13.15/19.40 **t.**

XX **D'Artagnan,** 19 Blandford St., W1H 3AD, ☎ 935 1023, French rest. – 🔝 🕮 ① *VISA*   AH a
closed Saturday lunch, Sunday, August and Bank Holidays – **M** a la carte 13.55/15.75 **t.**

XX **La Loggia,** 68 Edgware Rd, W2 2EG, ☎ 723 0554, Italian rest. – 🔝 🕮 ① *VISA*
closed Sunday and Bank Holidays – **M** a la carte 9.80/17.50 **t.** 🛈 2.65.   pp. 30 and 31   FY a

XX **Asuka,** Berkeley Arcade, 209a Baker St., NW1 6AB, ☎ 486 5026, Japanese rest. – 🔝 🕮 ①
pp. 13-16 KT u
VISA
closed Saturday lunch, Sunday, 24 December-2 January and Bank Holidays – **M** a la carte
17.60/21.00 **st.**

XX **Tonino,** Berkeley Court, 12 Glentworth St., NW1 5PG, ☎ 935 4220, Italian rest. – 🔝 🕮 ①
pp. 13-16 KT c
VISA
closed Saturday lunch, Sunday and Bank Holidays – **M** a la carte 7.95/13.50 🛈 2.50.

XX **Bill Bentley's,** 239 Baker St., NW1 6XE, ☎ 935 3130, Seafood – 🔝 ① *VISA*
closed Sunday and Bank Holidays – **M** a la carte 11.60/18.40 **t.** 🛈 2.15.   pp. 13-16 KST a

XX **Viceroy of India,** 3-5 Glentworth St., NW1 5PG, ☎ 486 3401, Indian rest. – 🔝 🕮 ① *VISA*
pp. 13-16 KT o
M a la carte 8.10/13.65 **t.**

XX **Gaylord,** 79-81 Mortimer St., W1N 7TB, ☎ 580 3615, Indian and Pakistani rest. – 🔝 🕮 ①
pp. 13-16 LT c
M a la carte 7.15/8.00 **t.** 🛈 2.95.

XX **Masako,** 6-8 St. Christopher's Pl., W1M 5HB, ☎ 935 1579, Japanese rest. – 🔝 🕮 ① *VISA*
closed Sunday, Easter, 1 May, 26 August and 25-26 December – **M** a la carte 9.40/17.90 **t.**
BJ e
🛈 4.50.

XX **La Pavona,** 5-7 Blandford St., W1H 3AF, ☎ 486 9696, Italian rest. – ▤. 🔝 🕮 ① *VISA*   BH c
closed Saturday lunch, Sunday and Bank Holidays – **M** a la carte 12.25/18.50 **t.** 🛈 3.00.

XX **Lords Rendezvous,** 24 Finchley Rd, NW8 6ES, ☎ 586 4280, Chinese rest. – 🔝 🕮 ① *VISA*
closed 25-26 December and Bank Holidays – **M** a la carte 9.50/14.00 **t.** 🛈 2.50.
pp. 13-16 JR r

X **Le Muscadet,** 25 Paddington St., W1, ☎ 935 2883, French rest. – 🔝 *VISA*   KT e
closed Saturday lunch, Sunday, 1 week Easter, 2 weeks August and 23 December-10 January
– **M** a la carte 8.15/13.40 🛈 2.40.

X **Au Bois St. Jean,** 122 St. John's Wood High St., NW8 7SG, ☎ 722 0400, French rest. – 🔝
pp. 13-16 JS n
🕮 ① *VISA*
closed Saturday lunch and Bank Holidays – **M** 9.00/11.00 **t.** 🛈 2.75.

X **Mikado,** 110 George St., W1H 6DJ, ☎ 935 8320, Japanese rest. – 🕮 ① *VISA*   AH s
closed Saturday lunch, Sunday, 1 week August-September and Bank Holidays – **M** a la carte
14.50/24.50 **t.** 🛈 4.75.

XX **Langan's Bistro,** 26 Devonshire St., W1, ☎ 935 4531 – AE   pp. 13-16 KT **r**
 closed Saturday lunch, Sunday, Christmas and Bank Holidays – **M** a la carte 8.55/12.40 **t.**

XX **Biagi's,** 39 Upper Berkeley St., W1H 7PG, ☎ 723 0394, Italian rest. – AE VISA
 closed Bank Holidays – **M** a la carte 6.50/12.70 **t.** 2.65.   pp. 30 and 31 FY **c**

XX **L'Aventure,** 3 Blenheim Terr., NW8 4JS, ☎ 624 6232, French rest. – AE
 closed lunch Saturday and Bank Holidays, Sunday, 3 days Easter and 23 to 30 December – **M**
 a la carte 10.80/14.05 **t.** 2.50.   pp. 13-16 JR **s**

XX **Il Barbino,** 64 Seymour St., W1H 5AF, ☎ 402 6866, Italian rest. – AE VISA
 closed Saturday, Sunday and Bank Holidays – **M** a la carte 8.00/13.10 **t.** 2.30.
    pp. 30 and 31 FY **r**

St. James's – ✉ W1/SW1/WC2 – pp. 26 and 27.

mêmê **Ritz,** Piccadilly, W1V 9DG, ☎ 493 8181, Telex 267200 – TV ☎ AE VISA DN **a**
 M a la carte 25.45/33.65 **st.** 5.25 – 7.00 – **139 rm** 80.00/130.00 **st.**

mêmê **Stafford** , 16-18 St. James's Pl., SW1A 1NJ, ☎ 493 0111, Telex 28602 – TV ☎ AE
 .   DN **u**
 M 14.50/16.00 **st.** – 4.50 – **60 rm** 89.00/120.00 **st.**

mêmê **Dukes** , 35 St. James's Pl., SW1A 1NY, ☎ 491 4840, Telex 28283 – TV ☎ AE ① VISA.
    EP **x**
 M a la carte 21.00/25.00 **st.** – 7.50 – **53 rm** 82.00/123.00 **st.**

mêmê **Cavendish** (T.H.F.), Jermyn St., SW1Y 6JF, ☎ 930 2111, Telex 263187 – TV ☎ P .
 AE ① VISA   EN **i**
 M 10.75/12.75 3.85 – 6.00 – **253 rm** 66.50/85.50 **st.**

mêmê **Royal Trafalgar Thistle** (Thistle), Whitcomb St., WC2H 7HG, ☎ 930 4477, Telex 298564 –
 TV wc ☎ AE ① VISA   GM **r**
 M 11.00/14.00 3.45 – 5.25 – **107 rm** 47.50/59.80 **t.** – SB (weekends only) 67.00 **st.**

mê **Pastoria,** 3-6 St. Martin's St., WC2H 7HL, ☎ 930 8641, Telex 25538 – TV wc . AE
 ① VISA.   GM **v**
 M *(closed Saturday lunch, Sunday and Bank Holidays)* 10.75 **t.** 2.50 – 3.25 – **54 rm**
 29.90/56.35 **t.** – SB (weekends only) 50.00/60.00 **st.**

XXXXX **Maxim's de Paris,** 32-34 Panton St., SW1, ☎ 839 4809, French rest., Dancing – . AE
 ① VISA.   GM **a**
 closed Saturday lunch, Sunday and Bank Holidays – **M** a la carte 15.00/25.50 **st.** 3.75.

XXX **Suntory,** 72-73 St. James's St., SW1A 1PH, ☎ 409 0201, Japanese rest. – . AE ① VISA
 closed Sunday and Bank Holidays – **M** a la carte 12.20/22.50.   EP **z**

XX **Le Caprice,** Arlington House, Arlington St., SW1A 1RT, ☎ 629 2239 – AE VISA DN **c**
 closed Saturday lunch and 24 December-2 January – **M** a la carte 10.00/14.50 **t.** 3.25.

Soho – ✉ W1/WC2 – pp. 26 and 27.

XXX **Leonis Quo Vadis,** 26-29 Dean St., W1V 6LL, ☎ 437 9585, Italian rest. – AE ① VISA
 closed lunch Saturday, Sunday and Bank Holidays and 25 December – **M** a la carte
 10.70/12.85 **t.** 2.45.   FK **u**

XX **La Terrazza,** 19 Romilly St., W1V 5TG, ☎ 437 8991, Italian rest. – AE ① VISA FL **i**
 closed Christmas Day and Bank Holidays – **M** a la carte 9.85/14.10 **t.** 2.50.

XX **L'Escargot,** 48 Greek St., W1V 5LQ, ☎ 437 2679 – AE ① VISA   GK **e**
 closed Saturday lunch, Sunday and Bank Holidays – **M** a la carte 8.85/15.50 **t.** 2.50.

XX **Chesa (Swiss Centre),** 2 New Coventry St., W1V 3HG, ☎ 734 1291 – AE ① VISA GM **n**
 closed Christmas Day – **M** a la carte 12.40/17.80 **st.**

XX **Gay Hussar,** 2 Greek St., W1V 6NB, ☎ 437 0973, Hungarian rest.   GJ **c**
 closed Sunday and Bank Holidays – **M** a la carte 13.50/17.00 **t.** 3.00.

XX **Au Jardin des Gourmets,** 5 Greek St., Soho Sq., W1V 5LA, ☎ 437 1816, French rest. GJ **a**

XX **Venezia,** 21 Great Chapel St., W1V 3AQ, ☎ 437 6506, Italian rest. – AE ① VISA FJ **a**
 closed Saturday lunch, Sunday and Bank Holidays – **M** a la carte 9.45/14.15 **t.** 2.40.

XX **Red Fort,** 77 Dean St., W1V 5HA, ☎ 437 2525, Indian rest. – AE ① VISA FJK **r**
 M a la carte 8.45/10.80 **t.**

XX **Rugantino,** 26 Romilly St., W1V 5TQ, ☎ 437 5302, Italian rest. – AE ① VISA GK **u**
 closed Saturday lunch, Sunday and Bank Holidays – **M** a la carte 8.60/11.10 **t.** 2.65.

XX **Fuji,** 36-40 Brewer St., W1R 3HP, ☎ 734 0957, Japanese rest. – AE ① VISA FL **c**
 closed lunch Saturday and Sunday and 1 week at Christmas – **M** a la carte 10.10/19.30 **st.**
 3.80.

X **Frith's,** 14 Frith St., W1, ☎ 439 3370 – AE ① VISA   FGK **s**
 closed Saturday lunch and Sunday – **M** a la carte 9.80/15.50 **t.** 2.50.

X **Romeo e Giulietta,** 11 Sutton Row, W1V 5FE, ☎ 734 4914, Italian rest. – AE ① VISA
 closed Saturday lunch, Sunday and Bank Holidays – **M** a la carte 7.50/12.50 2.20. GJ **e**

X **Gallery Rendezvous,** 53-55 Beak St., ☎ 734 0445, Chinese-Peking rest. – . AE ① VISA
 M a la carte 6.50/11.50 **t.** 3.50.   EL **a**

X **Trusha,** 11-12 Dean St., W1V 5AH, ☎ 437 3559, Indian rest. – AE ① VISA FJ **e**
 closed Sunday and Bank Holidays – **M** a la carte 4.40/10.65 **t.**

X **Trattoria Imperia,** 19 Charing Cross Rd, WC2H 0ES, ☎ 930 8364, Italian rest. – AE ①
 VISA   GM **z**
 closed Saturday lunch, Sunday, 25-26 December and Bank Holidays – **M** a la carte 7.50/12.30 **t.**
 2.20.

Strand and Covent Garden – ✉ WC2 – p. 31.

Savoy, Strand, WC2R 0EU, ✆ 836 4343, Telex 24234 – ... **M Grill** *(closed Sunday lunch, Saturday, August and Bank Holidays)* a la carte 17.50/24.50 **st.** 5.50 – **River** a la carte 16.70/25.50 **st.** 5.50 – ☕ 6.50 – **200 rm** 90.00/150.00 **st.** – SB (weekends only)(summer only) 148.00 **st.** EX **a**

Waldorf (T.H.F.), Aldwych, WC2B 4DD, ✆ 836 2400, Telex 24574 – ... VISA EV **x**
M *(closed lunch Saturday and Sunday)* a la carte 12.95/37.40 **st.** 3.20 – ☕ 6.00 – **310 rm** 57.50/74.50 **st.**

Howard, 12 Temple Pl., WC2R 2PR, ✆ 836 3555, Telex 268047 – ... VISA. FV **e**
M a la carte 14.20/22.40 **st.** – **136 rm**.

Charing Cross, Strand, WC2N 5HX, ✆ 839 7282, Telex 261101 – ... wc wc ... VISA DX **s**
closed Christmas – **M** (carving rest.) 8.75 **st.** – ☕ 5.75 – **206 rm** 37.00/50.00 **st.**

Inigo Jones, 14 Garrick St., WC2E 9BJ, ✆ 836 6456 – ... VISA DV **o**
closed Saturday lunch, Sunday, 1 week Christmas and Bank Holidays – **M** a la carte 23.00/27.00 **t.** 3.30.

Ivy, 1-5 West St., WC2H 9NE, ✆ 836 4751 – ... VISA DV **e**
closed Saturday lunch, Sunday, 25-26 December and Bank Holidays – **M** a la carte 11.00/17.70 **t.** 2.75.

Simpson's-in-the-Strand, 100 Strand, WC2R 0EW, ✆ 836 9112, English rest. – ... VISA EV **o**
closed Sunday, Easter, 25-26 December and Bank Holidays – **M** a la carte 7.70/17.30 **st.** 2.75.

Thomas de Quincey's, 36 Tavistock St., WC2E 7PB, ✆ 240 3972 – ... VISA EV **c**
closed Saturday lunch, Sunday, 22 July-12 August and Bank Holidays – **M** a la carte 18.95/21.30 **t.** 3.30.

Interlude de Tabaillau, 7-8 Bow St., WC2, ✆ 379 6473, French rest. – ... VISA
closed Saturday lunch, Sunday, 10 days at Easter, 3 weeks August-September, 10 days at Christmas and Bank Holidays – **M** 17.50/22.00 **st.** DEV **x**

Grange, 39 King St., WC2E 8JS, ✆ 240 2939 – AE DV **z**
closed Saturday lunch, Sunday, 5 August-4 September and Bank Holidays – **M** (booking essential) 13.50 (wine included) **t.**

Chez Solange, 35 Cranbourn St., WC2H 7AD, ✆ 836 5886, French rest. – ... VISA DV **i**
closed Sunday and Bank Holidays – **M** a la carte 9.50/15.10 **t.** 3.25.

Sheekey's, 28-32 St. Martin's Court, WC2N 4AL, ✆ 240 2565, Seafood – ... VISA DV **v**
closed Sunday and Bank Holidays – **M** a la carte 9.30/11.30 **t.**

Luigi's, 15 Tavistock St., WC2E 7PA, ✆ 240 1795, Italian rest. – ... VISA EV **a**
closed Sunday and Bank Holidays – **M** a la carte 12.00/17.40 **t.** 2.50.

Azami, 13-15 West St., WC2H 9BL, ✆ 240 0634, Japanese rest. pp. 26 and 27 GK **z**

Frère Jacques, 38 Longacre, WC2, ✆ 836 7823, Seafood – ... DV **n**

Taste of India, 25 Catherine St., WC2B 5JS, ✆ 836 6591, Indian rest. – ... VISA EV **r**
M a la carte 6.95/9.45 **t.**

Poons of Covent Garden, 41 King St., WC2E 8JS, ✆ 240 1743, Chinese rest. – ... VISA DV **r**
closed Sunday – **M** a la carte 7.75/16.25 **t.** 3.50.

Magnos Brasserie, 65A Long Acre, WC2E 9JH, ✆ 836 6077, French rest. – ... VISA
closed Saturday lunch, Sunday, 24 December-2 January and Bank Holidays – **M** a la carte 10.15/13.15 **t.** 3.75. EV **e**

Laguna, 50 St. Martin's Lane, WC2N 4EA, ✆ 836 0960, Italian rest. – ... VISA DV **u**
M a la carte 9.10/11.20 **t.** 3.95.

Colosseo, 12 May's Court, St. Martin's Lane, WC2N 4BS, ✆ 836 6140, Italian rest. – ... VISA DX **e**
closed Saturday lunch, Sunday and Bank Holidays – **M** a la carte 9.65/12.60 **t.** 2.10.

Grimes, 6 Garrick St., WC2R 9BH, ✆ 836 7008, Seafood – ... VISA DV **x**
closed Sunday, Christmas and Bank Holidays – **M** a la carte approx. 11.20 **t.** 2.40.

Victoria – ✉ SW1 – Except otherwise stated see p. 30.

By British Rail Ticket Office, near Platform 15, Victoria Station ✆ 730 0791.

Goring, 15 Beeston Pl., Grosvenor Gdns, SW1W 0JW, ✆ 834 8211, Telex 919166 – ... VISA. BV **a**
M 11.50/13.50 **t.** 4.50 – **100 rm** 60.00/80.00 **st.**

Royal Horseguards Thistle (Thistle), 2 Whitehall Court, SW1A 2EJ, ✆ 839 3400, Telex 917096 – ... rest ... VISA. pp. 17-20 NV **a**
M 9.75 **t.** 3.45 – ☕ 5.25 – **280 rm** 49.50/55.00 **t.** – SB (weekends only) 69.50 **st.**

St. Ermin's (Forum), Caxton St., SW1H 0QW, ✆ 222 7888, Telex 917731 – ... CV **a**
229 rm.

Royal Westminster Thistle (Thistle), Buckingham Palace Rd, SW1W 0QT, ✆ 834 1821, Telex 916821 – ... VISA. BV **z**
M 9.25/9.85 **t.** 3.45 – ☕ 5.50 – **135 rm** 49.50/55.00 **t.** – SB (weekends only) 69.70 **st.**

Grosvenor, 101 Buckingham Palace Rd, SW1W 0SJ, ℰ 834 9494, Telex 916006 – 🛗 📺
wc 📺wc 📞 🛗 🅰🅴 ⓞ 𝐕𝐈𝐒𝐀
BV **e**
closed 1 week at Christmas – **M** 9.50 **t.** ♦ 3.00 – ⌂ 5.25 – **350 rm** 42.00/50.00 **t.**

Ebury Court, 24-32 Ebury St., SW1W 0LU, ℰ 730 8147 – 🛗 wc 📞 𝐕𝐈𝐒𝐀
AV **i**
M a la carte 6.25/10.45 **t.** ♦ 2.10 – **39 rm** ⌂ 28.00/52.00 **t.**

Hamilton House, 60-64 Warwick Way, SW1V 1SA, ℰ 821 7113 – 📺 wc 📞 𝐕𝐈𝐒𝐀
M (grill rest. only) (dinner only) a la carte approx. 4.00 **t.** ♦ 2.10 – **41 rm** ⌂ 19.00/36.00 **t.**
BX **n**

Elizabeth, 37 Eccleston Sq., SW1V 1PB, ℰ 828 6812 – 🍽 🕱
pp. 17-20 LY **c**
24 rm ⌂ 18.00/40.00 **st.**

XXX **Lockets**, Marsham Court, Marsham St., SW1P 4JY, ℰ 834 9552, English rest. – 🅰 🅰🅴 ⓞ
𝐕𝐈𝐒𝐀
pp. 17-20 MY **z**
closed Saturday and Sunday – **M** a la carte 11.40/15.65 **t.** ♦ 2.50.

XXX **Kundan**, 3 Horseferry Rd, SW1P 2AN, ℰ 834 3434, Indian and Pakistani rest. – 🅰 🅰🅴 ⓞ 𝐕𝐈𝐒𝐀
closed Sunday and Bank Holidays.
pp. 17-20 NXY **a**

XX **Ken Lo's Memories of China**, 67-69 Ebury St., SW1W 0NZ, ℰ 730 7734, Chinese rest. –
🅰 🅰🅴 ⓞ 𝐕𝐈𝐒𝐀
AX **u**
M a la carte approx. 15.50 **t.**

XX **The Restaurant**, Dolphin Square, Chichester St., SW1, ℰ 828 3207, French rest., « Art
deco » – 🅰 🅰🅴 ⓞ 𝐕𝐈𝐒𝐀
pp. 17-20 LZ **e**
closed Sunday, 3 days Christmas, 3 days New Year and Bank Holidays – **M** a la carte
12.00/14.50 **t.** ♦ 3.50.

XX **Pomegranates**, 94 Grosvenor Rd, SW1V 3LG, ℰ 828 6560 – 🅰 🅰🅴 ⓞ 𝐕𝐈𝐒𝐀
closed Saturday lunch, Sunday and Bank Holidays – **M** a la carte 11.75/18.45 **t.** ♦ 3.00.
pp. 17-20 LMZ **a**

XX **Eatons**, 49 Elizabeth St., SW1W 9PP, ℰ 730 0074 – 🅰 🅰🅴 ⓞ 𝐕𝐈𝐒𝐀
AX **a**
closed Saturday, Sunday and Bank Holidays – **M** a la carte 9.50/12.90 **s.** ♦ 2.70.

XX **Ciboure**, 21 Eccleston St., SW1W 9LX, ℰ 730 2505, French rest. – 🅰 🅰🅴 ⓞ 𝐕𝐈𝐒𝐀
AX **z**
closed Saturday lunch, Sunday and Bank Holidays – **M** a la carte 14.20/16.40 **s.**

XX **Hunan**, 51 Pimlico Rd, SW1W 8WE, ℰ 730 5712, Chinese rest.
pp. 17-20 KZ **a**

XX **Gran Paradiso**, 52 Wilton Rd, SW1V 1DE, ℰ 828 5818, Italian rest. – 🅰 🅰🅴 ⓞ 𝐕𝐈𝐒𝐀
BX **a**
closed Saturday lunch, Sunday, Easter, Christmas and Bank Holidays – **M** a la carte 9.10/10.30 **t.**
♦ 2.00.

X **Tapas**, 30 Winchester St., SW1, ℰ 828 3366 – 🅰 🅰🅴 ⓞ 𝐕𝐈𝐒𝐀
pp. 17-20 LZ **i**
closed Sunday and Bank Holidays – **M** (dinner only) a la carte 8.95/15.85 **t.** ♦ 3.00.

X **La Fontana**, 101 Pimlico Rd, SW1W 8PH, ℰ 730 6630, Italian rest. – 🅰🅴 ⓞ 𝐕𝐈𝐒𝐀
pp. 28 and 29 FT **o**
M a la carte 9.15/13.35 **t.** ♦ 2.50.

X **La Poule au Pot**, 231 Ebury St., SW1W 8UT, ℰ 730 7763, French rest.
pp. 17-20 KY **n**

X **Mimmo d'Ischia**, 61 Elizabeth St., SW1W 9PP, ℰ 730 5406, Italian rest. – 🅰 🅰🅴 ⓞ 𝐕𝐈𝐒𝐀
closed Sunday and Bank Holidays – **M** a la carte 11.00/16.00 **t.** ♦ 3.50.
AX **o**

X **Bumbles**, 16 Buckingham Palace Rd, SW1W 0QP, ℰ 828 2903, Bistro – 🅰 🅰🅴 ⓞ 𝐕𝐈𝐒𝐀
closed Saturday lunch, Sunday and Bank Holidays – **M** a la carte 8.55/10.50 **t.**
BV **c**

X **Tate Gallery Rest.**, Tate Gallery, Millbank, SW1P 4RG, ℰ 834 6754, English rest., « Rex
Whistler murals
pp. 17-20 NY **c**
M (lunch only).

X **Villa Medici**, 35 Belgrave Rd, SW1, ℰ 828 3613, Italian rest. – 🅰 🅰🅴 ⓞ 𝐕𝐈𝐒𝐀
BX **c**
closed Saturday lunch, Sunday and Bank Holidays – **M** a la carte 7.30/10.40 **t.** ♦ 2.30.

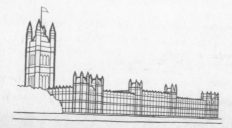

CAR REPAIRS IN LONDON

RÉPARATION DE VOITURES A LONDRES

RIPARAZIONE DI VETTURA A LONDRA

KFZ-REPARATUR IN LONDON

In the event of a breakdown in London, the location of the nearest dealer for your make of car can be obtained by calling the following numbers between 9am and 5pm.

En cas de panne à Londres, vous pouvez obtenir l'adresse du plus proche concessionnaire de votre marque d'automobile en appelant les numéros suivants entre 9 heures et 17 heures.

In caso di guasto a Londra, Vi sara' possibile ottenere l'indirizzo del concessionario della vostra marca di automobile, chiamando i seguenti numeri dalle ore 9.00 alle ore 17.00.

Im Pannenfall können sie die Adresse der nächstgelegenen Reparaturwerkstatt ihrer Automarke zwischen 9 Uhr und 17 Uhr unter folgenden Telefon-Nr. erfahren.

ALFA ROMEO	Alfa Romeo (GB) Ltd Edgware Rd London NW2 6LX (01) 450 9191 ext 281	**AUSTIN ROVER**	(includes Morris, Triumph, MG, Vanden Plas, Landrover, Rangerover) Kennings Northern Welsh Harp West Hendon Broadway Edgware Rd London NW9 7AR (01) 202 6500
BMW	BMW (GB) Ltd Ellesfield Av. Bracknell Berks. RG12 4TA (0344) 26565	**CITROEN**	Citroen Cars Ltd Mill St. Slough Berks. SL2 5DE (0753) 23808
COLT-MITSUBISHI	Colt Car Co. Ltd Watermore Cirencester Glos. GL7 1LS (0285) 5777	**DATSUN-NISSAN**	Datsun (UK) Ltd New Rd Durrington Worthing West Sussex (0903) 68561
FIAT	Fiat Motor Sales Great West Rd Brentford Middx TW8 9DT (01) 560 4111	**FORD**	Ford Motor Co. Ltd Becket House Chapel High Brentwood Essex CM14 4BY (0277) 238502
HONDA	Honda (UK) Ltd Power Rd Chiswick London W4 5YT (01) 995 9381	**JAGUAR**	H.R. Owen Ltd Lyttleton Rd Barnet London (01) 458 7111
MAZDA	Mazda Cars (UK) Ltd Mount Ephraim Tunbridge Wells Kent TN5 8BS (0892) 40123	**MERCEDES BENZ**	Mercedes Benz (UK) Ltd Great West Rd Brentford Middx TW8 9HH (01) 560 2151

313

PORSCHE Porsche Cars (GB) Ltd
23-30 Richfield Av.
Reading
Berks. RG1 8PH
(0734) 595411

RENAULT Renault Ltd
Western Av.
Acton
London W3 ORZ
(01) 992 3481

SKODA Skoda (GB) Ltd
150 Goswell Rd
London EC1
(01) 253 7441

TOYOTA Toyota (GB) Ltd
The Quadrangle
Redhill
Surrey RH1 1PS
(0737) 68585

VOLKSWAGEN-AUDI V.A.G. (UK) Ltd
Yeomans Drive
Blakelands
Milton Keynes
Bucks. MK14 5AN
(0908) 679121

RELIANT Chequered Flag
(Engineering) Ltd
548/580 High Rd
Chiswick
London W4
(01) 995 0022

SAAB Saab (GB) Ltd
Saab House
Fieldhouse Lane
Marlow
Bucks.
(06284) 6977

TALBOT-PEUGEOT Warwick Wright Motors
Ltd
Chiswick Roundabout
North Circular Rd
Chiswick
London W4
(01) 994 6741

VAUXHALL-OPEL Hamilton Motors Ltd
466-490 Edgware Rd
London W2 1EL
(01) 723 0022

VOLVO Volvo Concessionnaires
Ltd
Lancaster Rd
Cressex Industrial Estate
High Wycombe
Bucks. HP12 3QE
(0494) 33444

LONGBRIDGE Warw. – see Warwick.

LONG EATON Derbs. 402 403 404 Q 25 – see Nottingham (Notts.).

LONGFORD West Midlands 403 404 P 26 – see Coventry.

LONGHORSLEY Northumb. 401 402 O 18 – see Morpeth.

LONG MELFORD Suffolk 404 W 27 – pop. 2,870 – ECD : Thursday – ✆ 0787 Sudbury.
See : Holy Trinity Church★ 15C.
♦ London 62 – ♦Cambridge 34 – Colchester 18 – ♦Ipswich 24.

🏨 Bull (T.H.F.), Hall St., CO10 9JG, ☎ 78494, « Part 15C coaching inn » – 📺 ➘wc ☎ 🅿. 🔼 🆎 ⓪ VISA
M 6.45/8.95 **st.** 2.85 – **27 rm**.

LONGNOR Staffs. 402 403 404 O 24 – pop. 352 – ✉ Buxton – ✆ 029 883.
♦ London 161 – Derby 29 – ♦Manchester 31 – ♦Stoke-on-Trent 22.

🏠 **Ye Olde Cheshire Cheese,** High St., SK17 0NS, ☎ 218 – 🅿. 🔼 🆎 ⓪ VISA
M *(closed Sunday dinner and Monday)* 6.00/11.00 **t.** – **5 rm** ⌿ 12.00/20.00 **st.**

LOOE Cornwall 403 G 32 The West Country G. – pop. 4,090 – ECD : Thursday – ✆ 050 36.
🚠 Looe Bin Down ☎ 050 34 (Widegates) 247, E : 3 m.
🎫 The Guildhall, Fore St. ☎ 2072 and 2255 (summer only).
♦ London 264 – ♦Plymouth 21 – Truro 39.

🏨 **Hannafore Point** (Best Western), Marine Drive, West Looe, PL13 2DG, ☎ 3273, ⩽ Looe Bay, 🔼 heated – 📺 ➘wc ☎ 🅿. 🔼 🆎 ⓪ VISA
15 March-6 November – **M** (bar lunch) 9.25 **t.** 2.60 – **40 rm** ⌿ 26.50/61.00 **t.** – SB 59.00/70.00 **st.**

🏠 **Rock Towers,** Marine Drive, Hannafore Rd, West Looe, PL13 2DQ, ☎ 2140, ⩽ Looe Bay and harbour – ➘wc 🅿. VISA ⅜
M (bar lunch) 6.50 **st.** 3.00 – **20 rm** ⌿ 15.00/35.80 **t.**

🏠 **Klymiarven** ⅍, Barbican Hill, East Looe, PL13 1BH, ☎ 2333, ⩽ Looe and harbour, 🔼 heated, 🌲 – 📺 ➘wc 🅿. 🔼
closed January and December – **M** (bar lunch) 7.50 **t.** 2.30 – **14 rm** ⌿ 13.50/31.00 **t.**

🏠 **Fieldhead,** Portruan Rd, Hannafore, PL13 2DR, ☎ 2689, ⩽ Looe Bay, 🔼 heated, 🌲 – ➘wc 🍴 🅿. 🔼 🆎 ⓪ VISA ⅜
Mid March-mid November – **M** (bar lunch) 12.50 **st.** 2.95 – **13 rm** ⌿ 15.50/21.00 **st.**

❌❌ **Trelaske Country** ⅍ with rm, Polperro Rd, Trelaske, PL13 2JS, W : 2 ¼ m. by A 387 ☎ 2159, ⩽, 🌲 – 🍴wc 🅿. VISA ⅜
M (dinner only and Sunday lunch) a la carte 9.10/14.00 **t.** 2.95 – **4 rm** ⌿ 26.00/44.00 **t.** – SB (except summer) 44.00/50.00 **st.**

at Sandplace N : 2 ¼ m. on A 387 – ✉ ✆ 050 36 Looe :

🏠 **Polraen Country House,** PL13 1PJ, ☎ 3956, 🌲 – 🍴wc 🅿. 🔼 VISA
closed 15 December-1 February – **M** (bar lunch) 7.00 **t.** 2.75 – **6 rm** ⌿ 17.50/30.00 **t.** – SB (except Easter and summer) 37.00 **st.**

at Talland Bay SW : 4 m. by A 387 – ✉ Looe – ✆ 0503 Polperro :

🏨 **Talland Bay** ⅍, PL13 2JB, ☎ 72667, ⩽, « Country house atmosphere », 🔼 heated, 🌲 – 📺 ➘wc ☎ 🔥 🔼 🆎 ⓪ VISA ⅜
February-mid December – **M** (bar lunch) 9.50 **t.** 2.80 – **20 rm** ⌿ (dinner included) 26.50/80.00 **t.** – SB (except summer) 53.00/56.00 **st.**

🏠 **Allhays Country House** ⅍, PL13 2JB, ☎ 72434, ⩽, 🌲 – 📺 ➘wc 🅿. 🔼 VISA
April-December – **M** (bar lunch) 7.50 **st.** 2.75 – **9 rm** ⌿ 14.00/32.00 **st.**

LOSTWITHIEL Cornwall 403 G 32 – pop. 1,905 – ECD : Wednesday – ✆ 0208 Bodmin.
Envir. : Restormel Castle★ (⅜★), N : 1 ½ m.
♦ London 273 – ♦Plymouth 30 – Truro 23.

🏠 **Carotel Motel,** 17 Castle Hill, PL22 0DD, on A 390 ☎ 872223 – 📺 ➘wc 🍴wc ☎ 🅿. 🔼 🆎 ⓪ VISA
M (bar lunch) 7.00 **st.** 2.80 – ⌿ 2.50 – **32 rm** 18.00/26.00 **st.**

❌ **Trewithen,** 3 Fore St., PL22 0AD, ☎ 872373 – 🔼 ⓪ VISA
closed Monday in winter, Sunday and 3 weeks May – **M** (dinner only) a la carte 8.35/11.25 **t.** 3.95.

Do not lose your way in Europe, use the Michelin
Main Road maps, scale : 1 inch : 16 miles.

LOUGHBOROUGH Leics. 402 403 404 Q 25 – pop. 45,875 – ECD : Wednesday – ☎ 0509.

🏌 Lingdale, Joe Moores Lane ℰ 0509 (Woodhouse Eaves) 890035, S : 6 m.

🛈 John Storer House, Wards End ℰ 230131.

♦ London 117 – ♦Birmingham 41 – ♦Leicester 11 – ♦Nottingham 15.

🏨 **King's Head** (Embassy), High St., LE11 2QL, ℰ 214893 – 🛗 📺 ⇔wc ☎ 🅿 🏧 🖃 AE ⓪ VISA ⚯
M (carving rest.) 6.50/6.95 **st.** ⓵ 4.50 – ⌸ 4.25 – **83 rm** 32.00/38.00 **st.** – SB (weekends only) 43.00/48.00 **st.**

🏨 **Cedars,** Cedar Rd, LE11 2AB, ℰ 214459, ⌂ heated, ♠ – 📺 ⇔wc 🛗wc ☎ 🅿 ⚯
M (buffet lunch Monday to Saturday and Sunday dinner) 5.50/a la carte approx. 9.50 **t.** ⓵ 2.60 – **37 rm** ⌸ 15.50/36.00 **t.** – SB (weekends only) 78.00 **st.**

at Quorn SE : 3 m. on A 6 – 🖃 ☎ 0509 Loughborough :

🏨 **Quorn Country,** Charnwood House, 66 Leicester Rd, LE12 8BB, ℰ 415050, ♠ – 📺 ☎ 㐧 🅿 🏧 🖃 AE ⓪ VISA
M 7.50/9.95 **st.** ⓵ 4.00 – **19 rm** ⌸ 41.00/54.00 **st.** – SB 50.00/60.00 **st.**

AUSTIN-ROVER-JAGUAR Woodgate ℰ 262710
FIAT Station Rd ℰ 05097 (Kegworth) 2523
VOLVO Derby Rd ℰ 217777
VW, AUDI 28 Market St. ℰ 217080

LOUTH Lincs. 402 404 U 23 – pop. 11,170 – ☎ 0507.

See : St. James' Church★ 15C.

🏌 Crowtree Lane ℰ 2554.

♦ London 155 – Boston 33 – Grimsby 17 – Lincoln 26.

🏨 **Priory,** Eastgate, ℰ 602930, ♠, ⚯ – ⇔wc 🛗wc 🅿 🖃 VISA ⚯
M *(closed Sunday to non-residents)* (dinner only) 7.50 **t.** – **12 rm** ⌸ 22.00/38.50 **t.** – SB (weekends only) 45.00/59.00 **st.**

LOWER BEEDING West Sussex 404 T 30 – see Horsham.

LOWER PEOVER Cheshire 402 403 404 M 24 – see Knutsford.

LOWER SLAUGHTER Glos. 403 404 O 28 – see Stow-on-the-Wold.

LOWER SWELL Glos. 403 404 O 28 – see Stow-on-the-Wold.

LOWESTOFT Suffolk 404 Z 26 – pop. 52,267 – ECD : Thursday – ☎ 0502.

🛈 The Esplanade ℰ 65989.

♦ London 116 – ♦Ipswich 43 – ♦Norwich 30.

🏨 **Victoria,** Kirkley Cliff, NR33 0BZ, ℰ 4433, ≤, ⌂ heated – 🛗 📺 ⇔wc 🛗wc ☎ 㐧 🅿 🏧 🖃 AE ⓪ VISA
M (buttery lunch) 7.75 **t.** – **47 rm** ⌸ 29.50/45.00 **st.** – SB (weekends only) (except Easter and Christmas) 42.00 **st.**

↑ **Rockville,** 6 Pakefield Rd, NR33 0HS, ℰ 81011 – 🖃 VISA ⚯
6 rm ⌸ 7.50/19.50 **st.**

at Oulton NW : 2 m. by B 1074 – 🖃 ☎ 0502 Lowestoft :

🏨 **Parkhill,** Parkhill, NR32 5DQ, N : ½ m. on A 1117 ℰ 730322, ♠ – 📺 ⇔wc ☎ 🅿 🏧 🖃 VISA
M *(closed Sunday lunch)* 9.00 **st.** ⓵ 3.00 – **8 rm** ⌸ 25.00/45.00 **st.**

AUSTIN-ROVER-DAIMLER-JAGUAR 97/99 London Rd South ℰ 61711
FORD Whapload Rd ℰ 653553
NISSAN High St. ℰ 65301
RENAULT 50-58 Long Rd ℰ 2783
TALBOT, PEUGEOT Beccles Rd, Oulton Broad ℰ 63622
VAUXHALL-OPEL London Rd South ℰ 3512
VW, AUDI Cooke Rd, South Lowestoft Industrial Estate ℰ 2583

LOWESWATER Cumbria 402 K 20 – pop. 202 – ECD : Thursday – 🖃 Cockermouth – ☎ 090 085 Lorton.

♦ London 305 – ♦Carlisle 33 – Keswick 12.

🏨 **Scale Hill** ⚯, CA13 9UX, ℰ 232, ≤, ♠ – ⇔wc 㐧 🅿
closed January – **M** (bar lunch) 9.50 **st.** – **13 rm** ⌸ 18.00/39.00 **st.**

LOWFIELD HEATH West Sussex – see Crawley.

LOWICK GREEN Cumbria 402 K 21 – see Ulverston.

LOW LAITHE North Yorks. – see Pateley Bridge.

LOW ROW North Yorks. – pop. 350 (inc. Melbeck) – 🖃 ☎ 0748 Richmond.

♦ London 256 – ♦ Carlisle 64 – ♦ Leeds 66 – ♦ Middlesbrough 39.

🏠 **Punch Bowl Inn,** DL11 6PF, ℰ 86233, ≤ – 🅿 AE ⓪
April-October – **M** (bar lunch) 9.00 **t.** ⓵ 2.30 – **15 rm** ⌸ 15.00/30.00 **st.**

LUDLOW Salop 🄰🄾🄱 L 26 – pop. 6,780 – ECD : Thursday – 🕻 0584.

See : Castle★ (ruins 11C-16C) *AC* – Parish Church★ 13C – Feathers Hotel★ early 17C – Broad Street★ 17C.

Envir. : Stokesay Castle★ (13C) *AC*, NW : 6 ½ m.

🏌 Bromfield ⌀ 058 477 (Bromfield) 285, N : 2 m. on A 49.

🛈 Castle St. ⌀ 3857 (summer only).

♦ London 162 – ♦Birmingham 39 – Hereford 24 – Shrewsbury 29.

🏛 **Feathers,** Bull Ring, SY8 1AA, ⌀ 5261, Telex 35637, « Part Elizabethan house » – 🛗 📺 ☎
🄿. 🛁. 🄰🄴 ⓞ 🆅🅸🆂🄰. ❀
M 7.50/12.50 t. 🍷 2.75 – **35 rm** ⇌ 35.00/58.00 **st.** – SB 74.00/86.00 **st.**

🏛 **Overton Grange** 🐾, Hereford Rd, SY8 4AD, S : 1 ¾ m. on old A 49 ⌀ 3500, 🚗 – 📺 ⌂wc
🎞wc 🅿 🔥 🄰🄴 ⓞ 🆅🅸🆂🄰
M 8.00 t. 🍷 3.25 – **17 rm** ⇌ 15.95/42.35 **st.** – SB 42.65/51.45 **st.**

🏠 **Cecil,** Sheet Rd, SY8 1LR, ⌀ 2442, 🚗 – 🄿
11 rm ⇌ 8.75/17.50 **st.**

🏠 **Croft,** 12 Dinham, SY8 1EJ, ⌀ 2076
8 rm ⇌ 8.00/18.00 **s.**

AUSTIN-ROVER Corve St. ⌀ 2301
FIAT St. John's Lane ⌀ 4531

FORD Ludford Bridge ⌀ 3521
VOLVO, SUBARU Bromfield Rd ⌀ 4666

LUDWELL Wilts. – see Shaftesbury (Dorset).

LUGWARDINE Heref. and Worc. – see Hereford.

LUNDY (Isle of) Devon 🄰🄾🄱 FG 30 The West Country G.

See : Site ★★.

Helicopter service to Ilfracombe (Hartland Point) ⌀ 062 882 (Littlewick Green) 3431.

⛴ to Ilfracombe (Lundy Co.) 1-3 weekly (2 h 30 mn).

Hotels see : Ilfracombe.

LUTON Beds. 🄰🄾🄴 S 28 – pop. 161,405 – ECD : Wednesday – 🕻 0582.

See : Luton Hoo★ (Wernher Collection★★) and park★ *AC*.

🏌 Stockwood Park, London Rd ⌀ 31421, S : 1 m. on A 6.

✈ Luton International Airport : ⌀ 25140, Telex 826409, E : 1 ½ m.

🛈 Central Library, St. George's Sq. ⌀ 32629.

♦ London 35 – ♦Cambridge 36 – ♦Ipswich 94 – ♦Oxford 45 – Southend-on-Sea 63.

🏛 **Chiltern** (Crest), Waller Av., Dunstable Rd, LU4 9RU, NW : 2 m. on A 505 ⌀ 575911, Telex 825048 – 🛗 📺 🛁 🄿. 🔥 🄰🄴 ⓞ 🆅🅸🆂🄰. ❀
M approx. 10.00 **st.** – ⇌ 5.50 – **99 rm** 45.00/53.50 **st.**

🏛 **Strathmore Thistle** (Thistle), Arndale Centre, LU1 2TR, ⌀ 34199, Telex 825763 – 🛗 📺 ☎
🄿. 🛁. 🄰🄴 ⓞ 🆅🅸🆂🄰. ❀
M 9.25/11.50 t. 🍷 3.45 – ⇌ 4.95 – **151 rm** 39.00/48.00 t. – SB (weekends only) 54.00 **st.**

🏛 **Crest** (Crest), 641 Dunstable Rd, LU4 8RQ, NW : 2 ¾ m. on A 505 ⌀ 575955, Telex 826283 –
🛗 📺 ⌂wc 🎞 🅿. 🛁 🄰🄴 ⓞ 🆅🅸🆂🄰. ❀
M approx. 10.50 **st.** – ⇌ 5.25 – **139 rm** 40.50/49.00 **st.**

🏚 **Leaside,** 72 New Bedford Rd, LU3 1BT, ⌀ 417643 – 📺 🎞wc 🎞 🛁 🄰🄴 ⓞ 🆅🅸🆂🄰. ❀
closed 24 December-1 January – **M** *(closed Sunday)* 10.50 t. 🍷 2.75 – **12 rm** ⇌ 25.30/36.80 **st.**

🏚 Red Lion, Castle St., LU1 3AA, ⌀ 27337 – 📺 ⌂wc 🎞 🄿 – **48 rm**.

🏠 **Humberstone,** 618 Dunstable Rd, LU4 8BT, NW : 2 ½ m. on A 505 ⌀ 574399 – 📺 🎞wc 🄿.
❀
closed 25 and 26 December – **14 rm** ⇌ 14.90/33.00 **st.**

AUSTIN-ROVER-DAIMLER-JAGUAR Latimer Rd ⌀ 411311
AUSTIN-ROVER Leagrave Rd ⌀ 51221
BMW 80-88 Marsh Rd ⌀ 56622
FORD 326/340 Dunstable Rd ⌀ 31133

NISSAN 619 Hitchin Rd ⌀ 35332
VAUXHALL-OPEL 15 Hitchin Rd ⌀ 22268
VAUXHALL-OPEL 540/550 Dunstable Rd ⌀ 55944
VAUXHALL Memorial Rd ⌀ 52577
RENAULT, VW-AUDI Castle St. ⌀ 417505

LYDDINGTON Leics. – see Uppingham.

LYME REGIS Dorset 🄰🄾🄱 L 31 The West Country G. – pop. 3,403 – ECD : Thursday – 🕻 029 74.

See : Site ★ – The Cobb ★.

🏌 Timber Hill ⌀ 2043.

🛈 The Guildhall, Bridge St. ⌀ 2138.

♦London 160 – Dorchester 25 – Exeter 31 – Taunton 27.

🏦 **Mariners,** Silver St., DT7 3HS, ℰ 2753, Telex 46491, 🚗 – 🔟 ⌷wc ⌷wc 🅿. 🆘 🆎 ⓞ 💳. ❄
8 March-October – **M** (bar lunch) 11.50 t. ♦ 2.75 – **16 rm** ⬚ 20.00/46.00 t. – SB (except summer) 49.50 **st.**

🏦 **Alexandra,** Pound St., DT7 3HZ, ℰ 2010, ≤, 🚗 – 🔟 ⌷wc ⌷wc 🅿. 🆘 🆎 ⓞ 💳
closed December and January – **M** 5.75/8.50 t. ♦ 3.20 – **26 rm** ⬚ 16.00/66.00 t. – SB (winter and spring only) 38.00/48.00 **st.**

⌂ **Kersbrook,** Pound Rd, DT7 3HX, 🚗 – ⌷wc ⌷wc 🅿. 🆘 🆎 💳
March-10 November – **13 rm** 13.50/29.00 t.

✗ **Toni's,** 14-15 Monmouth St., DT7 3PX, ℰ 2079 – 🆎 ⓞ 💳
Easter-September – **M** *(closed Sunday and Monday)* (dinner only) a la carte 6.50/10.50 t. ♦ 2.75.

at Rousdon (Devon) W : 3 m. on A 3052 – ✉ ☎ 029 74 Lyme Regis :

🏦 **Dower House,** DT7 3RB, ℰ 0297 (Seaton) 21047, 🚗 – ⌷wc ⌷wc 🅿. 🆘 🆎 ⓞ 💳. ❄
closed January-mid February – **M** (bar lunch) 7.95 t. ♦ 2.25 – **10 rm** ⬚ 16.00/50.00 t. – SB 37.00/50.00 st.

🏠 **Orchard Country,** DT7 3XW, ℰ 2972, 🚗 – ⌷wc ⌷wc 🅿. 🆘 🆎 ⓞ. ❄
March-October – **M** (dinner only) 8.00 t. ♦ 2.25 – **15 rm** ⬚ 10.00/24.00 t. – SB 30.00/40.00 **st.**

at Uplyme (Devon) NW : 1 ¼ m. on A 3070 – ✉ ☎ 029 74 Lyme Regis :

🏦 **Devon** (Best Western), Lyme Rd, DT7 3TQ, ℰ 3231, ≤, ⌷ heated, 🚗, park – ⌷wc 🅿. 🆘 🆎 ⓞ 💳
April-October and Christmas – **21 rm** ⬚ (dinner included) 23.00/53.00 t.

LYMINGTON Hants. 🗺️🗺️ P 31 – pop. 35,733 – ECD : Wednesday – ☎ 0590.

🚢 to the Isle of Wight : Yarmouth (Sealink) 24-30 daily (30 mn).

♦London 104 – Bournemouth 18 – ♦Southampton 19 – Winchester 32.

🏦 **Stanwell House,** 15 High St., SO4 9AA, ℰ 77123, 🚗 – 🔟 ⌷wc ☎. 🆘 🆎 ⓞ 💳
closed Christmas – **M** (rest. see **Railings** below) – **21 rm** ⬚ 17.50/42.00 **st.** – SB (except summer) 48.00/52.00 **st.**

✗✗ **Railings,** (at Stanwell House H.) 15 High St., SO4 9AA, ℰ 77124 – 🆘 🆎 ⓞ 💳
closed Christmas – **M** 8.25/a la carte 9.50/11.50 st. ♦ 2.25.

✗ **Limpets,** 9 Gosport St., SO4 9BG, ℰ 75595 – 🆘 🆎
closed Sunday and Monday in winter, November and Christmas – **M** (dinner only) a la carte 8.95/11.50 t. ♦ 2.50.

at Mount Pleasant NW : 2 m. by A 337 – ✉ ☎ 0590 Lymington :

🏨 **Passford House** ❧, Mount Pleasant Lane, SO4 8LS, ℰ 682398, ≤, ⌷ heated, 🚗, park, ❧ – 🔟 🅿. 🏊 🆎 ❄
M 7.50/10.50 t. ♦ 2.50 – **53 rm** ⬚ 31.00/61.00 t. – SB (except summer) 52.00/64.00 **st.**

at Sway NW : 4 m. by A 337 on B 3055 – ✉ ☎ 0590 Lymington :

🏠 **White Rose,** Station Rd, SO4 0BA, ℰ 682754, ⌷, 🚗, park – 📶 🔟 ⌷wc 🅿. 🆘 💳
M 6.00/7.00 st. ♦ 3.00 – **13 rm** ⬚ 14.00/42.00 **st.** – SB 45.00/50.00 **st.**

FIAT Sway ℰ 059 068 (Sway) 2212

LYMM Cheshire 🗺️🗺️🗺️ M 23 – pop. 8,450 – ECD : Wednesday – ☎ 092 575.

🏌️ Whitbarrow Rd ℰ 2177.

♦ London 193 – Chester 24 – ♦Liverpool 23 – ♦Manchester 15.

🏦 **Lymm,** Whitbarrow Rd, WA13 9AQ, ℰ 2233, Telex 629455, 🚗 – 🔟 ⌷wc ⌷wc ☎ 🅿. 🏊. 🆘 🆎 ⓞ 💳
M *(closed Saturday lunch)* 5.65/6.65 t. ♦ 3.10 – **51 rm** ⬚ 32.50/38.50 t. – SB 47.50 **st.**

LYMPSTONE Devon 🗺️ J 32 – see Exmouth.

LYNDHURST Hants. 🗺️🗺️ P 31 – pop. 2,948 – ECD : Wednesday – ☎ 042 128.

See : New Forest★.

🏌️ New Forest ℰ 2450.

🅱 Main Car Park ℰ 2269 (summer only).

♦London 95 – Bournemouth 20 – ♦Southampton 10 – Winchester 23.

🏦 **Parkhill** ❧, Beaulieu Rd, SO4 7FZ, SE : 1 ¼ m. by B 3056 ℰ 2944, ≤, « Tastefully furnished country house », ⌷ heated, 🚗, park – 🔟 ⌷wc ☎ 🅿. 🆘 🆎 ⓞ 💳. ❄
closed first two weeks January – **M** 6.25/9.25 t. ♦ 3.25 – **22 rm** ⬚ 30.00/65.00 t. – SB 68.00/80.00 st.

🏦 **Crown,** 9 High St., SO4 7NF, ℰ 2722 – 📶 🔟 ⌷wc ☎ 🅿. 🆘 🆎 ⓞ 💳
M (buffet lunch Saturday) 8.50 **st.** ♦ 3.00 – **42 rm** ⬚ 31.00/50.00 **st.** – SB (weekends only) 55.00 **st.**

🏨 **Pikes Hill Forest Lodge,** Pikes Hill, Romsey Rd, SO4 7AS, ℰ 3677, ⌛ heated, 🚗 – 📺
🚪wc 🏧wc ☜ ৬ 🅿
M 6.95/9.50 **st.** ╏ 2.75 – **20 rm** ⌚ 20.00/40.00 **st.** – SB 25.00/27.50 **st.**

🏨 **Evergreens,** Romsey Rd, SO4 7AR, ℰ 2175, ⌛ heated, 🚗 – 🏧wc 🅿
M a la carte 6.25/9.10 **st.** ╏ 2.40 – **17 rm** ⌚ 18.00/34.00 **st.**

🏨 **Forest Point,** Romsey Rd, SO4 7AR, ℰ 2420 – 🅿. 🔼 🆎 ⓪ 𝗩𝗜𝗦𝗔. ⌀
closed January – **M** (bar lunch Monday to Saturday) 5.50/7.25 **t.** ╏ 3.00 – ⌚ 3.00 – **10 rm**
11.00/35.00 **t.** – SB (except summer) 40.00 **st.**

⋔ **Whitemoor House,** Southampton Rd, SO4 7BU, ℰ 2186 – 🅿 – **5 rm.**

⋔ **Ormonde House,** Southampton Rd, SO4 7BT, ℰ 2806, 🚗 – 📺 🚪wc 🏧wc 🅿. 🔼 🆎 𝗩𝗜𝗦𝗔.
14 rm ⌚ 11.80/29.00 **t.**

at Woodlands NE : 3 ½ m. by A 35 – ✉ ✪ 042 129 Ashurst :

🏨 **Woodlands Lodge** ⌂, Bartley Rd, SO4 2GN, ℰ 2257, 🚗 – 📺 🚪wc 🏧wc 🅿. 🙇. 🔼 𝗩𝗜𝗦𝗔. ⌀
closed Christmas – **M** (bar lunch) 8.00 **t.** – **11 rm** ⌚ 14.00/38.00 **t.** – SB (except summer) 34.00/40.00 **st.**

AUSTIN-ROVER 77 High St. ℰ 2861   VAUXHALL-OPEL Romsey Rd ℰ 2609

LYNMOUTH Devon 📓📓📓 I 30 – see Lynton.

LYNTON Devon 📓📓📓 I 30 The West Country G. – pop. 1,981 – ECD : Thursday – ✪ 0598.
See : Site ★ (≼★★) – Envir. : Valley of the Rocks ★, W : 1 m – Watersmeet ★, E : 1 ½ m.
🛈 Lee Rd ℰ 2225.
♦London 206 – Exeter 59 – Taunton 44.

🏨 **Lynton Cottage** ⌂, North Walk, EX35 6ED, ℰ 52342, ≼ bay and Countisbury hill, 🚗 –
🚪wc 🏧wc 🅿. 🔼 𝗩𝗜𝗦𝗔
M 5.95/7.50 **st.** ╏ 2.15 – **21 rm** ⌚ 13.50/34.60 **st.** – SB 18.90/24.40 **st.**

🏨 **Hewitt's** ⌂, North Walk, EX35 6HJ, ℰ 52293, ≼ bay and Countisbury hill, 🚗, park – 📺
🚪wc 🅿. 🔼 🆎 ⓪ 𝗩𝗜𝗦𝗔. ⌀
March-October – **M** *(closed Sunday and Monday to non-residents)* (bar lunch residents only)
8.50 **st.** ╏ 2.50 – **12 rm** ⌚ (dinner included) 18.00/26.00 **st.**

🏨 **Crown,** Sinai Hill, EX35 6AG, ℰ 52253 – 📺 🚪wc 🅿. 🔼 🆎 ⓪ 𝗩𝗜𝗦𝗔
M (bar lunch) 7.50 **st.** ╏ 2.80 – **16 rm** ⌚ 18.75/34.50 **st.** – SB 43.00/48.00 **st.**

🏦 **Chough's Nest** ⌂, North Walk, EX35 6HJ, ℰ 53315, ≼ – 🚪wc. ⌀
Easter-mid October – **M** (dinner only) 6.00 **st.** ╏ 2.30 – **11 rm** ⌚ 11.50/24.00 **st.** – SB
37.00/40.00 **st.**

⋔ **Seawood** ⌂, North Walk, EX35 6HJ, ℰ 52272, ≼ – 🏧wc 🅿
Mid March-November – **12 rm** ⌚ 15.60/38.20 **t.**

⋔ **Combe Park** ⌂, Hillsford Bridge, EX35 6LE, S : 3 ½ m. by A 39 ℰ 52356, 🚗 – 🚪wc 🏧wc
🅿
Easter-October – **9 rm** ⌚ 13.20/26.45 **t.**

⋔ **Neubia House,** Lydiate Lane, EX35 6AH, ℰ 52309 – 🚪wc 🏧wc 🅿
closed January and December – **12 rm** ⌚ 12.60/26.40 **t.**

⋔ **Pine Lodge** ⌂, Lynway, EX35 6AX, ℰ 53230, ≼, 🚗 – 🅿
Easter-September – **9 rm** ⌚ 9.00/19.00 **st.**

at Lynmouth – ✉ Lynmouth – ✪ 059 85 Lynton :

🏛 **Tors** ⌂, EX35 6NA, ℰ 53236, ≼ Lynmouth and bay, ⌛ heated, 🚗 – 🛗 🚪wc 🅿. 🔼 🆎 ⓪
𝗩𝗜𝗦𝗔
March-mid November – **M** 5.00/9.50 **st.** ╏ 2.90 – **39 rm** ⌚ 15.00/56.00 **st.** – SB (except summer) 46.00/50.00 **st.**

🏨 **Bath,** EX35 6EL, ℰ 52238 – 🚪wc 🅿. 🔼 🆎 ⓪ 𝗩𝗜𝗦𝗔
weekends only in March and April-October – **M** 4.25/7.50 **st.** ╏ 3.00 – **24 rm** ⌚ 10.00/35.00 **st.**
– SB 30.00/45.00 **st.**

🏦 **Beacon** ⌂, Countisbury Hill, EX35 6ND, E : ½ m. on A 39 ℰ 53268, ≼, 🚗 – 📺 🚪wc 🏧wc
🅿. ⌀
closed December and January – **M** 4.95/7.90 **st.** ╏ 2.10 – **7 rm** ⌚ 14.75/31.50 **st.** – SB
36.50/45.00 **st.**

⋔ **Heatherville** ⌂, Tors Park, EX35 6NB, ℰ 52327 – 🏧wc 🅿. ⌀
closed January and December – **8 rm** ⌚ 10.50/24.00 **st.**

at Brendon E : 4 m. by A 39 – ✉ Lynton – ✪ 059 87 Brendon :

🏨 **Stag Hunters** ⌂, High St., EX35 1PS, ℰ 222, ≼, ⌕, 🚗 – 🚪wc 🅿. 🔼 ⓪ 𝗩𝗜𝗦𝗔
Late March-December – **M** (bar lunch) 7.00 **t.** ╏ 2.75 – **18 rm** ⌚ 15.00/32.00 **t.** – SB
37.00/42.00 **st.**

at Woody Bay W : 3 ¼ m. via Coast Road – ✉ ✪ 059 83 Parracombe :

🏨 **Woody Bay** ⌂, Parracombe, EX31 4QX, ℰ 264, ≼ bay – 🚪wc 🅿. 🔼 🆎 ⓪ 𝗩𝗜𝗦𝗔
M (bar lunch) 5.00/12.00 **t.** ╏ 2.70 – **13 rm** ⌚ 16.00/41.00 **t.** – SB (except July-August) 41.00/49.00 **st.**

at Martinhoe W : 4 ¼ m. via Coast Road – ⊠ ⊛ 059 83 Parracombe :

🏠 **Old Rectory** ⏍, EX31 4QT, 𝒫 368, 🍴 – ➡wc 🅿
Mid March-October – **M** (dinner only) 10.50 t. ⫶ 2.75 – **11 rm** ⟷ 9.00/26.00 t. – SB (October only) 36.00/40.00 st.

at Heddon's Mouth W : 5 ¾ m. by B 3234 off A 39 – ⊠ ⊛ 059 83 Parracombe :

🏨 **Heddon's Gate** ⏍, Parracombe, EX31 4PZ, 𝒫 313, ≤, 🍴 – 📺 ➡wc 🕴wc ☜ 🅿. 🔌 🆎
Easter-October – **M** (bar lunch) 10.50 t. ⫶ 2.50 – **13 rm** ⟷ 11.00/32.00 t. – SB (May and October) 37.00/46.00 st.

LYTHAM ST ANNE'S Lancs. 🔟🔟🔟 L 22 – pop. 40,299 – ECD : Wednesday – ⊛ 0253 St. Anne's.
🛇 Fairhaven, Lytham Hall Park 𝒫 736741, E : 2 m. – 🛇 St. Annes Old Links, Highbury Rd 𝒫 723597 and 721826.
🇿 St. Anne's Rd West 𝒫 725610 and 721222 ext 416.
♦London 237 – ♦Blackpool 7 – ♦Liverpool 44 – Preston 13.

🏨 **Grand Crest** (Crest), 77 South Promenade, FY8 1NB, 𝒫 721288, Telex 67481 – 🛗 📺 ➡wc
☎ 🅿. 🔌. 🔌 🆎 ⓞ 𝘝𝘐𝘚𝘈. ✻
M approx. 10.50 st. – ⟷ 4.95 – **40 rm** 38.00/49.00 st.

at Lytham SE : 3 m. – ⊠ ⊛ 0253 Lytham :

🏰 **Clifton Arms** (Best Western), West Beach, FY8 5QJ, 𝒫 739898, Telex 677463 – 🛗 📺 🅿. 🔌.
🔌 🆎 ⓞ 𝘝𝘐𝘚𝘈. ✻
46 rm.

AUSTIN-ROVER-DAIMLER Kings Rd 𝒫 728051	RENAULT Heyhouse Lane 𝒫 726821
CITROEN, FIAT Henry St. 𝒫 736670	VAUXHALL Heeley Rd 𝒫 726714
FORD Preston Rd 𝒫 733261	VOLVO St. Georges Rd 𝒫 722241
RENAULT Heyhouse Lane 𝒫 726799	

MACCLESFIELD Cheshire 🔟🔟🔟 N 24 – pop. 28,210 – ECD : Wednesday – ⊛ 0625.
🇿 Town Hall, Market Pl. 𝒫 21955 ext 115.
♦London 186 – Chester 38 – ♦Manchester 18 – ♦Stoke-on-Trent 21.

🛖 **Fourways Diner Motel,** Clenlow Cross, Wincle, SK11 0QL, SE : 4 ½ m. on A 54
𝒫 026 07 (Wincle) 228, ≤ – 📺 🕴wc 🅿. 🔌 𝘝𝘐𝘚𝘈
7 rm ⟷ 14.00/24.00 t.

✕ **Olivers Bistro,** 101-103 Chestergate, SK11 6DU, 𝒫 32003 – 🔌 𝘝𝘐𝘚𝘈
closed Sunday and 25-26 December – **M** (dinner only) a la carte 7.60/11.10 t. ⫶ 2.85.

AUSTIN-ROVER-DAIMLER-JAGUAR Hobson St. 𝒫 615555	PEUGEOT, TALBOT Waters Green 𝒫 22226
	RENAULT Daveport St. 𝒫 23677
FIAT London Rd 𝒫 28866	VAUXHALL, OPEL 98 Chestergate 𝒫 22909
FORD Hibel Rd 𝒫 27766	VW-AUDI Crossall St. 𝒫 23036
HONDA Beech Lane 𝒫 23592	

MACHYNLLETH Powys 🔟🔟 I 26 – pop. 2,030 – ECD : Thursday – ⊛ 0654.
Envir. : NW : Cader Idris (road★★ to Cader Idris : Cregenneu lakes) – Aberangell Clipiau (site★)
NE : 10 m. – SE : Llyfnant Valley ★ via Glaspwll.
🇿 Canolfan Owain Glyndwr 𝒫 2401.
♦London 220 – Shrewsbury 56 – Welshpool 37.

🏨 **Wynnstay** (T.H.F.), Maengwyn St., SY80 8AE, 𝒫 2003 – 📺 ➡wc ☜ 🅿. 🔌 🆎 ⓞ 𝘝𝘐𝘚𝘈
M 6.50/8.50 st. ⫶ 2.60 – ⟷ 4.75 – **31 rm** 26.00/38.00 st.

✕ **Janie's,** 57 Maengwyn St., SY20 8EE, 𝒫 2126
closed Mondays except Bank Holidays – **M** (booking essential) a la carte 7.00/10.55 t. ⫶ 2.95.

at Corris (Gwynedd) N : 5 ¼ m. on A 487 – ⊠ Machynlleth (Powys) – ⊛ 065 473 Corris :

♨ **Braich Goch,** SY20 9RD, on A 487 𝒫 229, ≤, 🍴 – 🅿. 🔌
M 5.25/6.00 st. ⫶ 3.05 – **6 rm** ⟷ 13.00/26.00 st. – SB (winter only) 26.00/28.00 st.

at Eglwysfach (Dyfed) SW : 6 m. on A 487 – ⊠ Machynlleth (Powys) – ⊛ 065 474 Glandyfi :

🏨 **Ynyshir Hall** ⏍, SY20 8TA, 𝒫 209, ≤, « Country house in large gardens », park – ➡wc
🅿. 🔌 🆎 ⓞ 𝘝𝘐𝘚𝘈
closed 1 to 14 January – **M** 8.50/14.95 t. ⫶ 2.50 – **11 rm** ⟷ 33.00/73.00 t. – SB 73.00 t.

AUSTIN-ROVER Station Garage 𝒫 2108 ⟶ FORD 𝒫 065 04 (Dinas Mawddwy) 326

MADINGLEY Cambs. 🔟🔟 U 27 – see Cambridge.

MAENORBYR = Manorbier.

MAIDENCOMBE Devon 🔟🔟 J 32 – see Torquay.

MAIDENHEAD Berks. 🗟🗟🗟 R 29 − pop. 45,288 − ECD : Thursday − ☼ 0628.
🛈 Central Library, St. Ives Rd ✆ 25657.
London 35 − ♦Oxford 32 − Reading 13.

🏨 **Crest** (Crest), Manor Lane, SL6 2RA, ✆ 23444, Telex 847502, 🚗 − 📺 🚻wc ☎ & 🅿. 🚗. 🗟 🗟🗟 ⓞ 🆅🆂🅰. 🐾
M (rest. see **Shoppenhangers Manor** below) − 🍽 5.50 − **190 rm** 47.50/57.00 **st.**

🏨 **Fredrick's,** Shoppenhangers Rd, SL6 2PZ, ✆ 35934, 🚗 − 📺 🚻wc ⋔wc ☎ 🅿. 🚗. 🗟 🗟🗟 ⓞ 🆅🆂🅰.
M (rest. see **Fredrick's** below) − **30 rm** 🍽 52.00/65.00 **t.**

🏠 Bear, 8-10 High St., SL6 1QJ, ✆ 25183 − 📺 ⋔ ☎ − **12 rm.**

XXX **Fredrick's** (at Fredrick's H.), Shoppenhangers Rd, SL2 6PZ, ✆ 24737, 🚗 − 🔳 🅿. 🗟 🗟🗟 ⓞ 🆅🆂🅰
closed Saturday lunch − **M** 15.50/20.50 **t.**

XXX **Shoppenhangers Manor** (Crest) (at Crest H.), Manor Lane, SL6 2RA, ✆ 23444, Telex 847502, 🚗 − 🅿. 🗟 🗟🗟 ⓞ 🆅🆂🅰
closed Sunday − **M** approx. 15.00 **st.**

XX **Franco's,** Ray Mead Rd, SL6 8NJ, ✆ 33522, Italian rest. − 🅿. 🗟 🗟🗟 ⓞ 🆅🆂🅰
closed Saturday lunch, Sunday and Bank Holidays − **M** a la carte 8.50/13.80 **t.** ♨ 3.50.

XX **Jasmine Peking,** 29 High St., SL6 1JG, ✆ 20334, Chinese rest. − 🗟 🗟🗟 ⓞ 🆅🆂🅰
M a la carte 6.65/7.50 **t.** ♨ 2.85.

XX **Chez Michel et Valérie,** 7 Glynwood House, Bridge Av., SL6 1RS, ✆ 22450, French rest. − 🗟 🗟🗟 ⓞ 🆅🆂🅰
closed Saturday lunch, Sunday, Monday, 11 to 27 August and 24 December -7 January − **M** a la carte 10.70/15.50 **t.**

X Maidenhead Chinese, 45-47 Queen St., SL6 1LT, ✆ 24545, Chinese rest.

BMW 84 Altwood Rd ✆ 37611
FIAT Woodlands Park ✆ 062 882 (Littlewick Green) 3211
FORD Bath Rd, Taplow ✆ 29711

HONDA, MAZDA 14/20 Bath Rd ✆ 21331
ROLLS ROYCE 128 Bridge Rd ✆ 33188
VAUXHALL Braywick Rd ✆ 25321

MAIDSTONE Kent 🗟🗟🗟 V 30 − pop. 70,987 − ECD : Wednesday − ☼ 0622.
See : All Saints' Church★ − Carriage Museum★ *AC* − Chillington Manor (Museum and Art Gallery★).
Envir. : Leeds Castle★ *AC*, SE : 4 ½ m. − Aylesford (The Friars carmelite priory : great courtyard★) NW : 3 ½ m. − Coldrum Long Barrow (prehistoric stones) site★ : NE : 1 m. from Trottiscliffe plus 5 mn walk, NW : 12 m.
🏌 Leeds Castle ✆ 062 780 (Hollingbourne) 467, E : 5 m.
🛈 The Gatehouse, Old Palace Gardens, Mill St. ✆ 671361 and 673581.
♦London 36 − ♦Brighton 50 − ♦Cambridge 84 − Colchester 70 − Croydon 36 − ♦Dover 45 − Southend-on-Sea 49.

🏨 **Royal Star** (Embassy), 15 High St., ME14 1JA, ✆ 55721 − 📺 🚻wc ⋔wc ☎ 🅿. 🚗. 🗟 🗟🗟 ⓞ 🆅🆂🅰. 🐾
M (grill rest. only) approx. 8.00 **st.** ♨ 4.00 − **32 rm** 🍽 25.00/40.00 **st.**

🏤 **Grange Moor,** St. Michael's Rd (off Tonbridge Rd), ME16 8BS, ✆ 677623 − 📺 ⋔wc 🅿. 🗟 🆅🆂🅰
M 6.00 **st.** ♨ 2.75 − **23 rm** 🍽 16.00/30.00 **st.**

↑ **Rock House,** 102 Tonbridge Rd, ME16 8SL, ✆ 51616 − 🅿. 🗟 🆅🆂🅰. 🐾
closed 24 December-1 January − **10 rm** 🍽 12.65/21.15 **st.**

↑ **Carval,** 56-58 London Rd, ME16 8QL, ✆ 62100 − 🅿. 🗟 🗟🗟 ⓞ 🆅🆂🅰. 🐾
8 rm 🍽 11.00/18.00 **st.**

at Larkfield W : 3 ¼ m. on A 20 − ✉ Larkfield − ☼ 0732 West Malling :

🏨 **Larkfield** (Anchor), London Rd, ME60 6HJ, ✆ 846858, Telex 957420 − 📺 🚻wc ☎ & 🅿. 🚗. 🗟 🗟🗟 ⓞ 🆅🆂🅰
M (carving rest.) 8.65 **st.** ♨ 2.65 − **52 rm** 🍽 36.00/45.00 **st.** − SB (weekends only) 45.00 **st.**

XXX **Wealden Hall,** 773 London Rd, ✆ 840259 − 🅿. 🗟 🗟🗟 ⓞ 🆅🆂🅰
M a la carte 11.25/15.25 **st.** ♨ 2.95.

MICHELIN Branch, St. Michaels Close, Forstal Trading Estate, Aylesford, ME20 7HR, ✆ 76228

AUSTIN-ROVER-DAIMLER-JAGUAR Bircholt Rd ✆ 65461
BMW Broadway ✆ 686666
CITROEN Bow Rd, Wateringbury ✆ 812358
COLT Forstal Rd, Aylesford ✆ 76421
FIAT, LANCIA 29 Union St. ✆ 52439
FORD Ashford Rd ✆ 56781
HONDA Upper Stone St. ✆ 53096
LADA Loose Rd ✆ 52584
NISSAN Ashford Rd, Harrietsham ✆ 859363

PEUGEOT, TALBOT Mill St. ✆ 53333
RENAULT Ashford Rd ✆ 54744
SAAB Linton Rd, Loose ✆ 46629
VAUXHALL-OPEL, MERCEDES-BENZ Park Wood, Sutton Rd ✆ 55531
VAUXHALL London Rd, Ditton ✆ 0732 (West Malling) 844922
VOLVO Bearsted ✆ 39531
VW, AUDI Upper Stone St. ✆ 50821

Une voiture bien équipée, possède à son bord
des **cartes** Michelin à jour.

MALDON Essex **404** V 28 – pop. 13,891 – ECD : Wednesday – ☎ 0621.
🛈 2 High St. ☎ 56503.
♦London 42 – Chelmsford 9 – Colchester 17.

🏨 **Blue Boar** (T.H.F.), Silver St., CM9 7QE, ☎ 52681 – 📺 ⏹️wc ☏ 🅿 🍴 📶 AE ⓞ 𝘝𝘐𝘚𝘈
M 6.75/7.50 **st.** ⓝ 2.60 – ⌤ 4.50 – **25 rm** 29.50/41.00 **st.**

✗ **Francine's,** 1a High St., CM9 7PB, ☎ 56605 – 🅿 📶 𝘝𝘐𝘚𝘈
closed Sunday, Monday, 2 weeks August and 1 week Christmas – **M** (dinner only) (booking essential) a la carte 9.55/11.20 **t.** ⓝ 3.00.

AUSTIN-ROVER Heybridge ☎ 52468
BMW Spital Rd ☎ 52131

FORD 1 Spital Rd ☎ 52345
VAUXHALL-OPEL 127/131 High St. ☎ 52424

MALMESBURY Wilts. **403 404** N 29 – pop. 2,527 – ECD : Thursday – ☎ 066 62.
See : Site ★ – Market Cross ★★ – Abbey ★.
🛈 Town Hall, Cross Hayes ☎ 2143.
♦London 108 – ♦Bristol 28 – Gloucester 24 – Swindon 19.

🏨 **Old Bell,** Abbey Row, SN16 0BW, ☎ 2344, ☞ – 📺 ⏹️wc ⏹️wc ☏ 🅿 🍴 📶 AE ⓞ 𝘝𝘐𝘚𝘈
closed 25 December-1 January – **M** 7.50/10.50 **t.** ⓝ 3.00 – **19 rm** ⌤ 20.00/48.00 **t.** – SB (weekends only) 42.00/56.00 **st.**

at Crudwell N : 4 m. on A 429 – ✉ ☎ 066 67 Crudwell :

🏨 **Mayfield House,** SN16 9EW, ☎ 409, ☞ – ⏹️wc 🅿 📶 𝘝𝘐𝘚𝘈 ✂️
M 5.50/9.00 **t.** ⓝ 2.30 – **21 rm** ⌤ 14.50/33.00 **t.** – SB 28.00/36.00 **st.**

at Easton Grey W : 2 m. on B 4040 – ✉ ☎ 066 62 Malmesbury :

🏨 **Whatley Manor** ⬍, SN16 0RB, E : ½ m. on B 4040 ☎ 2888, ≼, « 18C Manor house », ⬍, heated, ➘, ☞, park – 📺 ☏ 🅿 📶 AE ⓞ 𝘝𝘐𝘚𝘈
M 7.50/12.95 **t.** ⓝ 3.50 – **15 rm** ⌤ 42.00/67.50 **t.** – SB (weekends only) 69.00/75.00 **st.**

PEUGEOT-TALBOT Gloucester Rd ☎ 3434

MALPAS Cheshire **402 403** L 24 – pop. 1,493 – ☎ 0948.
♦London 77 – ♦Birmingham 60 – Chester 15 – Shrewsbury 26 – ♦Stoke-on-Trent 30.

✗✗ **Market House,** Church St., SY14 8NU, ☎ 860400, ☞ – 📶 𝘝𝘐𝘚𝘈
closed Sunday dinner, Monday, 12 to 19 August and 14 to 28 October – **M** (lunch by arrangement) a la carte 6.55/11.40 **t.** ⓝ 2.85.

MALTON North Yorks. **402** R 21 – pop. 3,986 – ECD : Thursday – ☎ 0653.
Envir. : Castle Howard★★ (18C) *AC*, SW : 6 m. – Flamingo Park Zoo★ *AC*, N : 4 ½ m.
🏌 Malton and Norton, Welham Park ☎ 2959.
♦London 229 – ♦Kingston-upon-Hull 36 – Scarborough 24 – York 17.

🏨 **Talbot** (T.H.F.), Yorkersgate, YO17 0AA, ☎ 4031 – 📺 ⏹️wc ☏ ⮾ 🅿 🍴 📶 AE ⓞ 𝘝𝘐𝘚𝘈
M (bar lunch) 9.00 **st.** ⓝ 2.60 – ⌤ 4.75 – **24 rm** 26.00/39.00 **st.**

AUSTIN-ROVER Wintringham ☎ 09442 (Rillington)
242
BMW Church St., Norton ☎ 5151
VOLVO Horse Market Rd ☎ 3019

MALVERN Heref. and Worc. **403 404** N 27 – see Great Malvern.

MALVERN WELLS Heref. and Worc. **403 404** N 27 – see Great Malvern.

MANCHESTER Greater Manchester **402 403 404** N 23 – pop. 543,650 – ECD : Wednesday –
☎ 061.
See : Town Hall★ 19C DZ – City Art Gallery★ DZ **M** – Whitworth Art Gallery★ BY **M** – Cathedral 15C (chancel★) DZ **B** – John Ryland's Library (manuscripts★) CZ **A**.
Envir. : Heaton Hall★ (18C) *AC*, N : 5 m. AX **M**.
🏌 Heaton Park, ☎ 773 1085, N : by A 576 ABX – 🏌 Fairfield Golf and Sailing, Booth Rd, Audenshaw, ☎ 370 1641, E : by A 635 BY – 🏌 Brookdale, Woodhouses ☎ 681 4534, N : 5 m. BX.
✈ ☎ (061) 489 3717 or 489 2404 (British Airways), S : 10 m. by A 5103AY and M 56 – **Terminal** : Coach service from Victoria Station.
🛈 Magnum House, Portland St., Piccadilly ☎ 247 3694 and 3712/3 – Town Hall Extension, Lloyd St. ☎ 236 1606/2035 – Manchester International Airport, Concourse and Arrivals Hall ☎ 437 5233.
♦London 202 – ♦Birmingham 86 – ♦Glasgow 221 – ♦Leeds 43 – ♦Liverpool 35 – ♦Nottingham 72.

Plans on following pages

🏨 **Piccadilly** (Embassy), Piccadilly Plaza, M60 1QR, ☎ 236 8414, Telex 668765, ≼ – 📶 📺 ☏ 🅿
📶 📶 AE ⓞ 𝘝𝘐𝘚𝘈 ✂️
DZ **s**
closed 25-28 December – **M** a la carte 9.40/14.90 **st.** ⓝ 5.05 – ⌤ 5.25 – **250 rm** 49.00/65.00 **st.**
– SB (weekends only) 55.00/62.00 **st.**

🏨 **Midland,** Peter St., M60 2DS, ☎ 236 3333, Telex 667797 – 📶 📺 🍴 📶 AE ⓞ 𝘝𝘐𝘚𝘈   CDZ **n**
M 17.50 **st.** – ⌤ 5.25 – **296 rm** 28.50/55.00 **st.** – SB (weekends only) 67.50 **st.**

Grand (T.H.F.), Aytoun St., M1 3DR, ℰ 236 9559, Telex 667580 – ⌘ ⊡ ⏫ 🔲 🄰🄴 ⑩ 𝘝𝘐𝘚𝘈 **u**
M (carving rest.) 7.95 **st.** ⏦ 2.60 – **146 rm** ⊇ 42.00/50.50 **st.**   DZ **u**

Portland Thistle (Thistle), Piccadilly Gdns., M1 6DP, ℰ 228 3400, Telex 669157 – ⌘ ⊡ ☎
🔲 🄰🄴 ⑩ 𝘝𝘐𝘚𝘈 ⋘ DZ **v**
M 8.50/11.00 ⏦ 3.45 – ⊇ 5.50 – **221 rm** 45.00/70.00 **t.** – SB (weekends only) 54.00 **st.**

Sabre d'Or, 392 Wilbraham Rd, Chorlton-cum-Hardy, M21 1UH, S : 5 m. by A 5103 on A
6010 ℰ 881 5055 – ℗ AY **c**
8 rm ⊇ 12.00/21.00 **st.**

Terrazza, 14 Nicholas St., M1 4FE, ℰ 236 4033, Italian rest. – 🔲 🄰🄴 ⑩ 𝘝𝘐𝘚𝘈 DZ **r**
closed Saturday lunch, Sunday and Bank Holidays – **M** a la carte 10.30/15.30 **t.** ⏦ 2.90.

Isola Bella, 6a Booth St., M2 4AW, ℰ 236 6417, Italian rest. – 🔲 ⑩ 𝘝𝘐𝘚𝘈 DZ **z**
closed Sunday and Bank Holidays – **M** a la carte 9.90/14.40 **st.** ⏦ 3.40.

Leen Hong, 35 George St., ℰ 228 0926, Chinese rest. DZ **z**

Rajdoot, St. James' House, South King St., M2 6DW, ℰ 834 2176, Indian rest. CZ **c**

Gaylord, Amethyst House, Marriott's Court, Spring Gardens, M2 1EA, ℰ 832 6037, Indian
rest. – 🔲 🄰🄴 ⑩ 𝘝𝘐𝘚𝘈 DZ **c**
M 3.50/10.00 **t.** ⏦ 3.50.

323

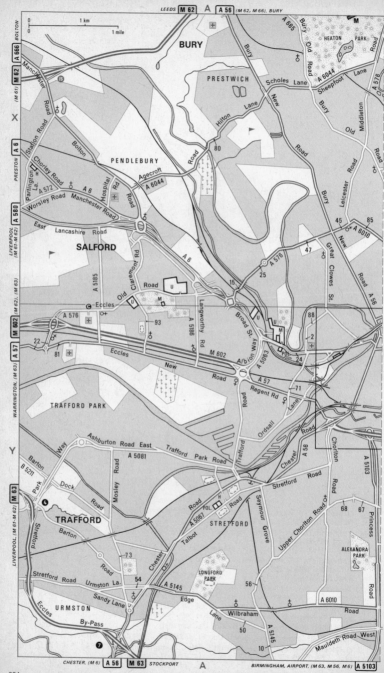

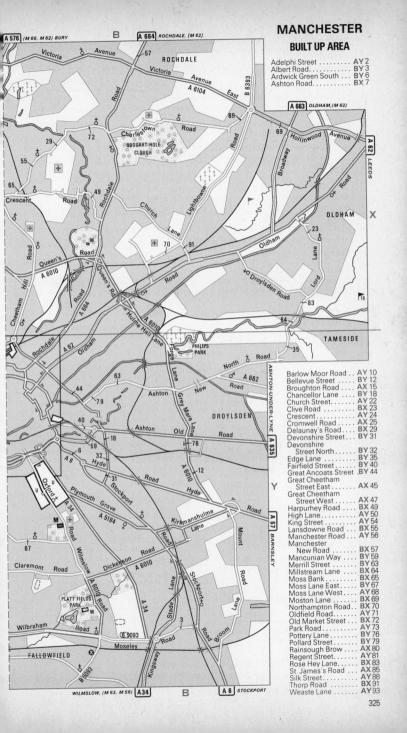

MANCHESTER
BUILT UP AREA

A 576 (M 66, M 62) BURY
A 664 ROCHDALE. (M 62)
A 663 OLDHAM. (M 62)
A 62 LEEDS
A 635
A 57 BARNSLEY
A 6 STOCKPORT
A 34
WILMSLOW. (M 63, M 56)

ROCHDALE
OLDHAM
TAMESIDE
DROYLSDEN
ASHTON-UNDER-LYNE
FALLOWFIELD
PLATT FIELDS PARK
PHILIPS PARK
BOGGART HOLE CLOUGH
Charlestown

325

✗ **Truffles**, 63 Bridge St., M3 6BQ, ℰ 832 9393 – 🔄 AE ⓪ VISA   CZ **a**
closed Sunday, Monday. first 2 weeks August and Bank Holidays – **M** a la carte 11.15/14.70 t.
🍷 3.00.

✗ **Danish Food Centre** (Copenhagen Room), Cross St., M2 7BY, ℰ 832 9924, Smörrebrod. 🔄
AE ⓪ VISA   DZ **n**
closed Sunday and Bank Holidays – **M** a la carte 16.00/21.00 st.

✗ **Market**, 30 Edge St., M4 1HN, ℰ 834 3743   DZ **o**
closed Sunday, Monday, 1 week spring, August and 1 week at Christmas – **M** (dinner only) a
la carte 5.00/9.60 t. 🍷 2.75.

✗ **Yang Sing**, 17 George St., M1 4HE, ℰ 236 2200, Chinese rest. – 🔄 AE   DZ **a**
M a la carte 8.35/11.75 t.

at Fallowfield S : 3 m. on B 5093 – ✉ 🛠 061 Manchester :

🏛 **Willow Bank,** 340 Wilmslow Rd, M14 6AF, ℰ 224 0461, Telex 668222 – 📺 ➾wc ⊛ ℗ 🔄
AE ⓪ VISA 🖧   BY **x**
M *(closed lunch Saturday and Sunday)* 3.50/6.00 st. 🍷 3.00 – ⚏ 3.75 – **123 rm** 26.00/32.00 st.
– SB (weekends only) 39.50/51.50 st.

at Northenden S : 6 ½ m. by A 5103 – AY – and M 56 – ✉ 🛠 061 Manchester :

🏛 **Post House** (T.H.F.), Palatine Rd, M22 4FH, ℰ 998 7090, Telex 669248 – 🖫 📺 ➾wc ⊛ ♿
℗ 🅰 🔄 AE ⓪ VISA
M *(closed Sunday dinner)* 6.95/8.95 st. 🍷 2.60 – ⚏ 5.00 – **201 rm** 39.50/46.50 st.

at Manchester Airport S : 9 m. by A 5103 – AY – and M 56 – ✉ 🛠 061 Manchester :

🏛 **Excelsior** (T.H.F.), Ringway Rd, Wythenshawe, M22 5NS, ℰ 437 5811, Telex 668721, 🔄 heated – 🖫 📺 ➾wc ♿ ℗ 🅰 🔄 AE ⓪ VISA
M 6.25/8.25 st. 🍷 2.85 – ⚏ 5.50 – **304 rm** 46.50/54.00 st.

✗✗✗ **Moss Nook**, Ringway Rd, Moss Nook, M22 5NA, ℰ 437 4778 – ℗. 🔄 AE ⓪ VISA
closed lunch Saturday and Monday, Sunday, 2 weeks Christmas and Bank Holidays – **M** a la
carte 14.20/17.45 t.

at Heald Green S : 10 m. by A 5103 – AY – and M 56 – ✉ 🛠 061 Manchester :

✗✗ **La Bonne Auberge**, 224 Finney Lane, SK8 3QA, ℰ 437 5701, French rest. – ℗. 🔄 AE ⓪
closed Monday dinner, Sunday and Bank Holidays – **M** a la carte 10.60/13.40 t.

MICHELIN Branch, Ferris St., off Louisa St., Openshaw, M11 1BS, ℰ 223 2010 and 3274

ALFA-ROMEO 123 a/b Jersey St. ℰ 205 2213
AUSTIN-ROVER Gill St. ℰ 205 2792
AUSTIN-ROVER 208 Bury New Rd ℰ 792 4343
BMW 325/327 Deansgate ℰ 832 8781
BMW Gt Bridgewater St. ℰ 832 8781
CITROEN, FIAT, LANCIA Ashton Old Rd ℰ 273 4411
DAIHATSU 845 Manchester Rd ℰ 766 3089
FORD 292 Bury New Rd ℰ 792 6161
FORD 391 Palatine Rd ℰ 998 3427
FORD Oxford Rd ℰ 224 7301
FORD 660 Chester Rd ℰ 872 2201
FORD 3/5 New Wakefield St. ℰ 236 4168
HONDA Peter St. ℰ 834 7230
LOTUS, MORGAN, RELIANT, RENAULT Ashley Rd,
Hale ℰ 941 1916
MAZDA Oldham Rd, Ashton ℰ 330 8135
MAZDA 54. Sackville St. ℰ 228 6727
MERCEDES-BENZ Upper Brook St. ℰ 273 8123
NISSAN Victoria Rd ℰ 330 3840

NISSAN Regent Rd, Salford ℰ 832 6041
PEUGEOT, TALBOT Chester Rd ℰ 834 6677
PORSCHE, BMW Bury New Rd at Whitefield ℰ
796 7414
RENAULT Blackfriars Rd ℰ 832 6121 770 Chester
Rd ℰ 865 1151
SAAB Water St. ℰ 832 6566
TALBOT, PEUGEOT 119 Wilmslow Rd ℰ 224 7282
TOYOTA Greenside Lane ℰ 370 2145
TOYOTA Moseley Rd ℰ 224 6265
VAUXHALL-OPEL Middleton Rd ℰ 740 2812
VAUXHALL-OPEL 141 Waterloo Rd ℰ 792 4321
VAUXHALL-OPEL Blackfriars Rd ℰ 834 8200
VAUXHALL-OPEL 80/90 Port St., Gt Ancoats St.
ℰ 236 4311
VAUXHALL-OPEL 799 Chester Rd ℰ 872 2141
VOLVO Rowsley St. ℰ 223 7272
VW, AUDI Ashton Old Rd ℰ 273 4361
VW, AUDI Stamford Rd ℰ 320 5454

MANORBIER (MAENORBYR) Dyfed **403** F 29 – pop. 1,168 – ECD : Saturday – 🛠 083 482.
See : Castle★ (13C) *AC* – ♦London 253 – Carmarthen 33 – Haverfordwest 18.

🏠 **Castle Mead** 🍃, SA70 7TA, ℰ 358, ≤ Manorbier Bay, 🎄 – ➾wc ℗. AE. 🖧
Easter-October – **M** (bar lunch) approx. 7.00 t. 🍷 2.35 – **11 rm** ⚏ 16.00/44.00 st.

at Jameston W : 2 m. on A 4139 – ✉ 🛠 083 482 Manorbier :

🏠 **Tudor Lodge** 🍃, SA70 7SS, ℰ 320, 🎄 – 📺 ➾wc 🚿wc ℗. 🔄
M (bar lunch Monday to Saturday) 5.50/6.50 t. 🍷 2.50 – **10 rm** ⚏ 14.00/32.00 t.

MARAZION Cornwall **403** D 33 The West Country G. – pop. 1,475 – ECD : Wednesday – ✉ Penzance – 🛠 0736.
♦London 318 – Penzance 3 – Truro 26.

🏠 **Mount Haven**, TR17 0DQ, on A 394 ℰ 710249, ≤ St. Michael's Mount and Mount's Bay –
📺 ➾wc ℗ 🔄 VISA 🖧
M (bar lunch) a la carte 7.40/11.90 t. 🍷 3.00 – **15 rm** ⚏ 15.50/33.00 t. – SB 42.00/44.00 st.

at Perranuthnoe SE : 1 ¾ m. by A 394 – ✉ 🛠 0736 Penzance :

↟ **Ednovean House** 🍃, TR20 9LZ, ℰ 711071, ≤ St. Michael's Mount and Mount's Bay, 🎄 –
🚿wc ℗.
8 rm ⚏ 14.95/33.65 st.

MARKET DEEPING Lincs. 🟦🟦🟦 T 25 – pop. 2,816 – ✆ 0778.
♦London 94 – ♦Cambridge 44 – ♦Leicester 41 – Lincoln 42.

🏠 **Deeping Stage,** Market Pl., PE6 8EA, ✆ 343234 – 🅿. 🆅🆂🅰. 🛥
   M *(closed Sunday dinner)* (Dancing Saturday) 5.50/12.00 t. – **8 rm** ⊊ 12.00/20.00 st.

MARKET DRAYTON Salop 🟦🟦🟦 🟦🟦🟦 🟦🟦🟦 M 25 – pop. 5,890 – ECD : Thursday – ✆ 0630.
♦London 161 – ♦Birmingham 44 – Chester 33 – Shrewsbury 19 – ♦Stoke-on-Trent 16.

🏠 **Corbet Arms,** 8 High St., TF9 1PY, ✆ 2037 – 📺 ➖wc 🅿. 🆅🆂🅰. 🅰🅴 🅾 🆅🆂🅰
   M (bar lunch) 4.50/6.50 t. 🍷 2.00 – **9 rm** ⊊ 18.00/30.00 t. – SB (weekends only) 35.00/43.00 **st.**

PEUGEOT-TALBOT Shrewsbury Rd ✆ 2027   VAUXHALL, VOLVO Cheshire St. ✆ 2444
RENAULT Shrewsbury Rd ✆ 4257

MARKET HARBOROUGH Leics. 🟦🟦🟦 R 26 – pop. 13,130 – ECD : Wednesday – ✆ 0858.
🗐 Pen Lloyd Library, Adam and Eve St. ✆ 62649.
♦London 88 – ♦Birmingham 47 – ♦Leicester 15 – Northampton 17.

🏛 **Three Swans,** 21 High St., LE16 7NG, ✆ 66644 – 📺 ➖wc 🎗wc 🕾 🅿. 🆅🆂 🅰🅴 🅾 🆅🆂🅰
   M *(closed Sunday dinner)* a la carte 9.65/12.75 t. 🍷 3.50 – **18 rm** ⊊ 27.50/36.00 t.

   at Marston Trussell (Northants.) W : 3 1/4 m. by A 427 – ✉ ✆ 0858 Market Harborough :

🏠 **Sun Inn** 🏡, Main St., LE16 9TY, ✆ 65531 – 📺 ➖wc 🕾 🅿. 🆅🆂 🅰🅴 🅾 🆅🆂🅰. 🛥
   M 8.95 t. – **10 rm** ⊊ 21.00/28.00 t.

VW Northampton Rd ✆ 65511   FORD Leicester Rd ✆ 66688

MARKET RASEN Lincs. 🟦🟦🟦 🟦🟦🟦 T 23 – pop. 2,433 – ECD : Thursday – ✆ 0673.
♦London 159 – Grimsby 20 – Lincoln 16.

🏠 **Limes,** Gainsborough Rd, LN8 3JW, ✆ 842357, 🚗, 🛥 – 📺 ➖wc 🎗wc 🕾 🅿. 🆅🆂 🅰🅴 🆅🆂🅰
   M 7.00/8.00 t. 🍷 2.70 – **15 rm** ⊊ 28.00/38.00 t. – SB (weekends only) 42.00 **st.**

✗ Carafe, 5 King St., LN8 3BB, ✆ 843427 – 🆅🆂 🅰🅴
   closed Sunday and Monday.

MARKET WEIGHTON Humberside 🟦🟦🟦 S 22 – pop. 2,584 – ECD : Thursday – ✉ York – ✆ 0696.
♦London 208 – ♦Kingston-upon-Hull 18 – ♦Leeds 40 – York 19.

🏠 **Londesborough Arms,** High St., YO4 3AH, ✆ 72219 – 📺 ➖wc 🎗wc 🕾 🅿. 🆅🆂 🅰🅴 🅾 🆅🆂🅰
   M *(closed Sunday dinner)* (buffet lunch) 7.00 t. 🍷 2.70 – **14 rm** ⊊ 18.00/28.00 t.

MARKINGTON North Yorks. 🟦🟦🟦 P 21 – see Harrogate.

MARKS TEY Essex 🟦🟦🟦 W 28 – see Colchester.

MARLBOROUGH Wilts. 🟦🟦🟦 🟦🟦🟦 O 29 The West Country G. – pop. 6,108 – ECD : Wednesday –
✆ 0672.
See : Site ✳.
Envir. : Savernake Forest✳✳ (Grand Avenue✳✳✳), SE : 2 m. off A 346 – Wilton Windmill ✳, S : 9 m.
by A 346 on A 338 – Pewsey : Vale of Pewsey ✳, S : 7 m. on A 3455 – Avebury ✳, W : 7 m.
🛆 The Common ✆ 52147, N : 1 m.
🗐 St. Peter's Church, High St. ✆ 53989 (summer only).
♦London 84 – ♦Bristol 47 – ♦Southampton 40 – Swindon 12.

🏠 **Castle and Ball** (T.H.F.), High St., SN8 1LZ, ✆ 52002 – 📺 ➖wc 🕾 🅿. 🆅🆂 🅰🅴 🅾 🆅🆂🅰
   M 6.50/8.75 **st.** 🍷 2.60 – ⊊ 4.50 – **30 rm** 29.50/41.00 **st.**

AUSTIN-ROVER 80/83 High St. ✆ 52076   PORSCHE London Rd ✆ 52381

MARLOW Bucks. 🟦🟦🟦 R 29 – pop. 10,350 – ECD : Wednesday – ✆ 062 84.
♦London 35 – Aylesbury 22 – ♦Oxford 29 – Reading 14.

🏨 **Compleat Angler** (T.H.F.), Marlow Bridge, Bisham Rd, SL7 1RG, ✆ 4444, Telex 848644, ◁
   River Thames, « Riverside setting and gardens », 🎣, 🛥 – 📺 & 🅿. 🏌 🆅🆂 🅰🅴 🅾 🆅🆂🅰
   M a la carte 15.40/31.95 **st.** – ⊊ 7.00 – **42 rm** 57.50/68.00 **st.**

✗ **Hare and Hounds,** Henley Rd, SL7 2DF, SW : 3/4 m. on A 4155 ✆ 3343 – 🅿. 🆅🆂 🅰🅴
   closed Saturday lunch and Sunday – **M** a la carte 10.00/13.15 t. 🍷 3.80.

AUSTIN-ROVER Oxford Rd ✆ 2215

MARSTON TRUSSELL Northants. – see Market Harborough (Leics.).

MARTINHOE Devon – see Lynton.

MARTON Cleveland – see Middlesbrough.

MARY TAVY Devon 🟦🟦🟦 H 32 – see Tavistock.

MASHAM North Yorks. [402] P 21 – pop. 830 – ECD : Thursday – ✉ Ripon – ☎ 0677 Bedale.

♦London 231 – ♦Leeds 38 – ♦Middlesbrough 37 – York 32.

🏠 **Jervaulx Hall** 🔇, HG4 4PH, NW : 5 ½ m. on A 6108 ✆ 60235, <, « Country house atmosphere », 🌳, park – 🛁wc [P]. [Access] [VISA]
closed 20 December-February – **M** (dinner only) 10.50 **t.** 🍷 3.00 – **8 rm** ☕ 26.00/40.00 **t.**

🏡 **Bank Villa,** HG4 4DB, on A 6108 ✆ 89605, 🌳 – 🚿
March-October – **7 rm** ☕ 12.00/20.00 **st.**

MATLOCK Derbs. [402] [403] [404] P 24 – pop. 19,588 – ECD : Thursday – ☎ 0629.

See : Site★.

Envir. : Riber Castle (ruins) <★ (Fauna Reserve and Wildlife Park *AC*) SE : 2 ½ m.

[i] The Pavilion ✆ 55082.

♦London 153 – Derby 17 – ♦Manchester 46 – ♦Nottingham 24 – ♦Sheffield 24.

🏠 **Riber Hall** 🔇, Riber, DE4 5JU, SE : 3 m. by A 615 ✆ 2795, <, « Elizabethan manor house », 🌳 – [TV] 🛁wc 📞 [P]. [Access] [AE] [DC] [VISA]. 🚫🐕
M a la carte 9.25/14.05 **t.** 🍷 3.75 – ☕ 3.75 – **8 rm** 40.00/55.00 **t.** – SB (winter only) 75.00 **st.**

at Matlock Bath S : 1 ½ m. on A 6 – ✉ ☎ 0629 Matlock :

🏠 **New Bath** (T.H.F.), New Bath Rd, DE4 3PX, ✆ 3275, 🏊 heated, [🏊], 🌳, 🎾 – [TV] 🛁wc 📞 [P]. 👥. [Access] [AE] [DC] [VISA]
M 7.50/10.50 **st.** 🍷 2.85 – ☕ 5.00 – **56 rm** 31.50/43.00 **st.**

AUSTIN-ROVER Bakewell Rd ✆ 3291 FORD 41 Causeway Lane ✆ 2231

MATLOCK BATH Derbs. [402] [403] [404] P 24 – see Matlock.

MAWGAN PORTH Cornwall [403] E 32 – pop. 530 – ECD : Wednesday – ✉ Newquay – ☎ 0637 St. Mawgan.

♦London 293 – Newquay 7 – Truro 20.

🏠 **Tredragon,** TR8 4DQ, ✆ 860213, < Mawgan Porth, [🏊], 🌳 – 🛁wc 🚿wc [P]. [Access]
Easter-October and Christmas – **M** (bar lunch Monday to Saturday) 6.50 **t.** 🍷 1.75 – **30 rm** ☕ 12.00/34.00 **t.**

MAWNAN SMITH Cornwall [403] E 33 – see Falmouth.

MAYFIELD East Sussex [404] U 30 – pop. 1,700 – ECD : Wednesday – ☎ 0435.

♦London 46 – ♦Brighton 25 – Eastbourne 22 – Lewes 17 – Royal Tunbridge Wells 9.

🍴 **Old Brew House,** High St., TN20 6AG, ✆ 872342 – [AE] [DC] [VISA]
closed Sunday, Monday, Tuesday after Bank Holidays and 2 weeks Autumn – **M** (dinner only and Saturday lunch) 11.60 **t.** 🍷 2.80.

MEASHAM Leics. [402] [403] [404] P 25 – pop. 4,220 – ECD : Wednesday – ☎ 0530.

♦London 122 – ♦Birmingham 25 – ♦Leicester 21 – ♦Nottingham 26.

🏠 **Measham Inn,** Tamworth Rd, DE12 7DY, ✆ 70095 – [TV] 🛁wc 📞 [P]. [Access] [AE] [DC] [VISA]
M *(closed Saturday lunch, Sunday dinner to non-residents and Bank Holidays)* 5.50 **st.** 🍷 3.30 – **31 rm** ☕ 24.75/30.50 **t.** – SB (April-September) (not weekends) 41.50 **st.**

MELBOURN Cambs. [404] U 27 – pop. 2,851 – ✉ ☎ 0763 Royston (Herts.).

♦London 44 – ♦Cambridge 10.

🍴🍴 **Pink Geranium,** 25 Station Rd, SG8 6DX, ✆ 60215, 🌳 – [P]. [Access] [AE] [DC] [VISA]
closed Sunday, Monday and last 2 weeks August – **M** a la carte 9.00/10.25 **st.** 🍷 2.50.

🍴🍴 **Sheen Mill** with rm, Station Rd, SG8 6DH, ✆ 61393, <, Dancing (Saturday), 🌳 – [TV] 🚿wc [P]. [Access] [AE] [DC] [VISA]. 🚫🐕
M *(closed Sunday dinner)* a la carte 8.70/12.65 **t.** 🍷 2.50 – **3 rm** ☕ 23.00/39.00 **st.**

MELKSHAM Wilts. [403] [404] N 29 – pop. 15,280 – ECD : Wednesday – ☎ 0225.

[i] Round House, Church St. ✆ 707424.

♦London 113 – ♦Bristol 25 – Salisbury 35 – Swindon 28.

🍴🍴🍴 **Beechfield House** with rm, Beanacre, SN12 7PU, N : 1 m. by A 350 ✆ 703700, <, « Country house and gardens », 🏊 heated, 🎣, park, 🎾 – [TV] 🛁wc 📞 [P]. [Access] [AE] [DC] [VISA]. 🚫🐕
M a la carte 13.75/17.70 **t.** – **16 rm** ☕ 33.50/65.00 **t.** – SB (except summer) 74.25 **st.**

🍴 **Chikako's,** 26 Church St., SN12 6LS, ✆ 705242, Japanese rest.
closed Monday – **M** (dinner only) a la carte 6.50/8.00 **t.** 🍷 1.95.

at Shaw NW : 1 ¼ m. on A 365 – ✉ Melksham – ☎ 0225 Shaw :

🏡 **Shaw Farm,** Bath Rd, SN12 8EF, on A 365 ✆ 702836, 🏊 heated, 🌳 – 🚿wc [P]. 🚫🐕
closed 24 to 26 December – **12 rm** ☕ 13.00/27.50 **st.**

AUSTIN-ROVER Lancaster Rd ✆ 702256

MELTHAM West Yorks. 402 404 O 23 – pop. 6,619 – ✉ ☯ 0484 Huddersfield.

🏌 Thick Hollins Hall 🕭 850227, E : 1 m.

♦London 192 – ♦Leeds 21 – ♦Manchester 23 – ♦Sheffield 26.

🏨 **Durker Roods,** Bishops Way, HD7 3AG, 🕭 851413, 🍴 – 🖵 ⌷wc ☏ 🅿. 🛦. 🔊 A̲E̲ ⓪ 𝘝𝘐𝘚𝘈
closed Christmas night – **M** (closed Sunday dinner) 6.25/9.00 **st.** ▮3.00 – **32 rm**
⛻ 28.00/40.00 **st.** – SB (weekends only) 45.00 **st.**

MELTON MOWBRAY Leics. 402 404 R 25 – pop. 17,810 – ECD : Thursday – ☯ 0664.

🏌 Thorpe Arnold 🕭 62118, NE : 2 m.

🛈 Carnegie Museum, Thorpe End, 🕭 69946.

♦London 113 – ♦Leicester 15 – Northampton 45 – ♦Nottingham 18.

🏨 **George,** High St., LE13 0TR, 🕭 62112 – 🖵 ⌷wc 🏛wc ☏ 🅿. 🔊 A̲E̲ ⓪ 𝘝𝘐𝘚𝘈
M 4.95/9.75 **t.** ▮2.55 – **19 rm** ⛻ 33.00/47.50 **st.**

🏨 **Harboro** (Anchor), Burton St., LE13 1AF, 🕭 60121, Group Telex 858875 – 🖵 ⌷wc 🏛wc ☎
🅿. 🔊 A̲E̲ ⓪ 𝘝𝘐𝘚𝘈
M a la carte 8.10/11.75 **st.** ▮2.65 – **27 rm** ⛻ 32.00/42.50 **st.** – SB (weekends only) 45.00 **st.**

🏤 **King's Head,** Nottingham St., LE13 1NW, 🕭 62110 – 🖵 ⌷wc 🏛wc 🚗 🅿. 🔊 𝘝𝘐𝘚𝘈
M 4.95 **st.** ▮2.30 – **15 rm** ⛻ 21.00/32.00. **st.** – SB (weekends only) 37.00 **st.**

FIAT Mill St. 🕭 60141
TALBOT 26 Victoria St. 🕭 62235

VOLVO 56 Scalford Rd 🕭 63241

MENTMORE Bucks. 404 R 28 – pop. 208 – ✉ Leighton Buzzard – ☯ 0296 Cheddington.

♦London 46 – Aylesbury 10 – Luton 15.

XX **Stag Inn,** The Green, LU7 0QF, 🕭 668423 – 🅿. 🔊 A̲E̲ ⓪ 𝘝𝘐𝘚𝘈
closed Monday – **M** a la carte 9.50/15.45 **t.** ▮2.25.

MERE Wilts. 403 404 N 30 – pop. 2,085 – ECD : Wednesday – ☯ 0747.

Envir. : Stourhead House★★★, NW : 3 m.

🛈 The Square, Church St. 🕭 860341.

♦London 113 – Exeter 65 – Salisbury 26 – Taunton 40.

🏠 **Old Ship,** Castle St., BA12 6JE, 🕭 860258 – 🖵 ⌷wc ☏ 🅿. 🔊 𝘝𝘐𝘚𝘈
M a la carte 6.50/11.25 **t.** ▮2.85 – **22 rm** ⛻ 20.50/38.00. **t.** – SB 46.00/48.00 **st.**

AUSTIN-ROVER Salisbury St. 🕭 860244

CITROEN Castle St. 🕭 860404

MERE BROW Lancs. 402 L 23 – pop. 400 – ✉ Preston – ☯ 077 473 Hesketh Bank.

♦London 221 – ♦Liverpool 22 – Preston 11 – Southport 6.

X **Crab and Lobster,** behind the Leigh Arms, Tarlton, PR4 6LA, 🕭 2734, Seafood – 🅿
closed Sunday, Monday and Christmas-late January – **M** (dinner only) a la carte 7.50/12.50 **t.**

MERIDEN West Midlands 403 404 P 26 – see Coventry.

MERTHYR TYDFIL Mid Glam. 403 J 28 – pop. 55,317 – ECD : Thursday – ☯ 0685.

Envir. : Road★ from Merthyr Tydfil to Brecon – Road★ from Brecon to Hirwaun – Craig-y-Nos
(Dan-yr-Ogof Caves★ AC), W : 17 m.

🏌 Cilsanws Mountain 🕭 3308 – 🏌 Tredegar and Rhymney 🕭 0685 (Rhymney) 840732, NE : 6 m.

🛈 Brecon Mountain Railway, Pant Station 🕭 71491 (summer only).

♦London 181 – Brecon 17 – ♦Cardiff 24 – ♦Swansea 30.

🏨 **Baverstock's,** Heads of the Valley Rd, CF44 0LX, W : 3 m. by A 4102 on A 465 ✉Aberdare
🕭 6221 – 🖵 ⌷wc ☏ 🅿. 🛦. 🔊 A̲E̲ ⓪ 𝘝𝘐𝘚𝘈. 🐾
M (closed Saturday lunch and Sunday dinner) a la carte 10.20/12.45 **st.** ▮4.05 – **43 rm**
⛻ 19.00/41.00 **st.** – SB (weekends only) 46.30 **st.**

FORD Pentrebach Rd 🕭 74111

MEVAGISSEY Cornwall 403 F 33 The West Country G. – pop. 2151 – ECD : Thursday – ☯ 0726.

See : Site ★★.

♦London 287 – Newquay 21 – ♦Plymouth 44 – Truro 20.

🏠 **Trevalsa Court** 🕭, School Hill, Polstreath, PL26 6TH, 🕭 842468, ≤, 🍴 – ⌷wc 🏛wc 🅿.
🔊 A̲E̲ ⓪ 𝘝𝘐𝘚𝘈
closed Christmas and New Year – **M** (bar lunch) approx. 10.95 **t.** ▮2.20 – **9 rm** ⛻ 18.00/24.00 **t.**
– SB 38.00 **st.**

🏠 **Spa** 🕭, Polkirt Hill, Portmellon, PL26 6UY, 🕭 842244, 🍴, 🐾 – ⌷wc 🅿. 🔊 A̲E̲ ⓪ 𝘝𝘐𝘚𝘈. 🐾
M (bar lunch) 8.00 **t.** ▮1.60 – **12 rm** ⛻ 13.00/34.00 **t.** – SB (summer only) 40.00 **st.**

MICKLETON Glos. 403 404 O 27 – see Chipping Campden.

MIDDLEHAM North Yorks. 📖🗂 O 21 — pop. 724 — ECD : Thursday — ☎ 0969 Wensleydale.
♦London 233 — Kendal 45 — ♦Leeds 47 — York 45.

🏠 **Miller's House,** Market Pl., Leyburn, DL8 4NR, ☎ 22630, 🛋 — 📺 ⌁wc 🅿. ⓦ. 🛁
closed January — **M** (bar lunch) a la carte 8.10/10.40 **st.** ⓙ 2.00 — **6 rm** ⌁ 25.00/35.00 **st.** — SB
(except summer) 44.00/46.00 **st.**

During the season, particularly in resorts, it is wise to book in advance.

MIDDLESBROUGH Cleveland 📖🗂 Q 20 — pop. 157,740 — ECD : Wednesday — ☎ 0642.
🖈 Brass Castle Lane ☎ 316430, S : 3 m. by A 172 BZ — 🖈 Middlesbrough Municipal, Ladgate Lane
☎ 315533, S : by Acklam Rd AZ.

✈ Teesside Airport : ☎ 0325 (Darlington) 332811, SW : 13 m. by A 66 AZ and A 19 on A 67.

🛈 125 Albert Rd ☎ 245750/245432 ext 3580.

♦London 247 — ♦Kingston-upon-Hull 89 — ♦Leeds 67 — ♦Newcastle-upon-Tyne 41.

MIDDLESBROUGH

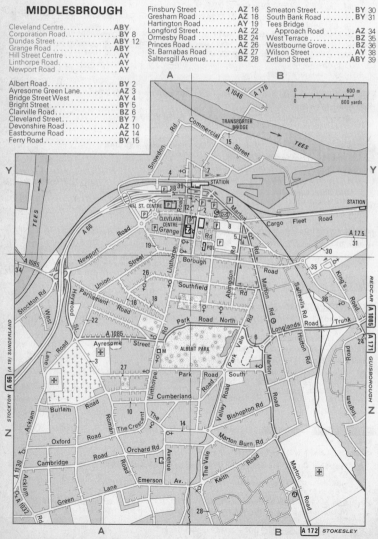

🏨 **Ladbroke Dragonara** (Ladbroke), Fry St., TS1 1JH, ☎ 248133, Telex 58266 – 🛗 🖭 rest 📺
☎ 🅿. 🚗 🔼 🆎 ⓪ 𝗩𝗜𝗦𝗔
BY **c**
M (bar lunch Saturday and Sunday) 6.75/9.50 **t.** 🍷 3.65 – � 5.25 – **140 rm** 25.00/44.00 **st.** – SB
(weekends only) 47.00/49.00 **st.**

🏨 Baltimore, 250 Marton Rd, TS4 2EZ, ☎ 224111 – 📺 ⌂wc ☎ 🅿. ⌘ – **30 rm**.
BZ **e**

🏨 **Marton Way,** Marton Rd, TS4 3BS, S : 2 m. on A 172 ☎ 817651, Telex 587783 – 📺 ⌂wc
☎ 🅿. 🚗 🔼 🆎 ⓪ 𝗩𝗜𝗦𝗔
BZ **a**
M 5.00 **t.** – **53 rm** ⊏⊐ 29.00/38.00 **st.**

at Marton SE : 4 m. on A 172 – BZ – ✉ ☎ 0642 Middlesbrough :

🏨 **Blue Bell Motor Inn** (Swallow), Acklam Rd, TS5 7HL, W : 1 ¾ m. by A 174 ☎ 593939, Group
Telex 53168 – 🛗 📺 ⌂wc ☎ 🅿. 🚗 🔼 🆎 ⓪ 𝗩𝗜𝗦𝗔
M (bar lunch) 8.50 **st.** 🍷 3.40 – **60 rm** ⊏⊐ 32.50/42.00 **st.** – SB (weekends only) 45.00 **st.**

🏨 **Marton Hotel and Country Club,** Stokesley Rd, TS7 8DS, ☎ 317141 – 📺 ⌂wc ☎ 🅿.
🚗 🔼 🆎 𝗩𝗜𝗦𝗔
M 4.50/6.75 **st.** 🍷 4.00 – **52 rm** ⊏⊐ 21.50/30.00 **st.** – SB (weekends only) 35.50/39.50 **st.**

AUSTIN-ROVER 336 Stokesley Rd. Marton ☎ 317171
CITROEN Linthorpe Rd ☎ 822884
COLT Oxford Rd ☎ 89732
FIAT Marton Rd ☎ 243415
FORD North Ormesby Rd ☎ 242451
HONDA South Bank Rd ☎ 247934
LADA Granville Rd ☎ 219151
MAZDA St. Barnabas Rd ☎ 816706

RENAULT Newport Rd ☎ 249346
SKODA Eston Grange ☎ 452436
TALBOT Marton Rd ☎ 242873
TOYOTA Eastbourne Rd ☎ 816658
VAUXHALL-OPEL ☎ 593333
VOLVO Longlands Rd ☎ 244651
VW, AUDI Park End ☎ 317971

MIDDLETON-IN-TEESDALE Durham � �Ⓡ �Ⓒ N 20 – pop. 1,412 – ECD : Wednesday – ☎ 0833
Teesdale.

Envir. : High Force** (waterfalls) *AC*, NW : 5 m. – 🅱 1 Market Pl. ☎ 40806.

♦London 268 – ♦ Carlisle 40 – ♦Leeds 68 – ♦Middlesbrough 41 – ♦Newcastle-upon-Tyne 49.

🏠 **Teesdale,** Market Pl., DL12 0QG, ☎ 40264 – ⌂wc 🅿. 𝗩𝗜𝗦𝗔
M (bar lunch Monday to Saturday) 5.50/7.95 **t.** 🍷 – **14 rm** ⊏⊐ 16.00/32.00 **t.**

at Romaldkirk SE : 4 m. on B 6277 – ✉ Barnard Castle – ☎ 0833 Teesdale :

🏨 **Rose and Crown,** DL12 9EB, ☎ 50213 – 📺 ⌂wc 🍴wc ☎ 🅿. 🔼 🆎 ⓪ 𝗩𝗜𝗦𝗔
M (bar lunch) 10.00 **st.** 🍷 2.70 – **14 rm** ⊏⊐ 18.00/37.00 **st.** – SB (except summer) 44.00/48.00 **st.**

MIDDLETON-STONEY Oxon. 🇒 🇔 Q 28 – pop. 196 – ECD : Saturday – ✉ Bicester –
☎ 086 989.

♦London 66 – Northampton 30 – ♦Oxford 12.

🏠 **Jersey Arms Inn,** Ardley Rd, OX6 8SE, ☎ 234 – 📺 ⌂wc 🅿. 🔼 🆎 𝗩𝗜𝗦𝗔. ⌘
M (closed Sunday dinner to non-residents) a la carte 7.00/10.20 **t.** 🍷 2.90 – **9 rm** ⊏⊐ 25.00/36.00 **t.**
– SB 42.50 **st.**

MIDDLE WALLOP Hants. 🇒 🇔 P 30 – pop. 2,800 – ✉ Stockbridge – ☎ 0264 Andover.

♦London 80 – Salisbury 11 – ♦Southampton 21.

🏨 **Fifehead Manor,** SO20 8EG, on A 343 ☎ 781565, « 16C converted manor house », 🌳 – 📺
⌂wc 🍴wc ☎ 🅿. 🔼 🆎 ⓪ 𝗩𝗜𝗦𝗔
closed 2 weeks at Christmas – **M** 13.00 **st.** 🍷 2.70 – ⊏⊐ 2.50 – **12 rm** 30.00/55.00 **st.**

XX **Old Drapery Stores** with rm, Station Rd, SO20 8HN, ☎ 781301, 🌳 – 🅿. 🆎 ⓪ 𝗩𝗜𝗦𝗔 ⌘
closed 26 December – **M** (closed Sunday) a la carte approx. 9.35 **t.** – **2 rm** ⊏⊐ 12.50/25.00 **st.**

MIDHURST West Sussex 🇔 R 31 – pop. 2,169 – ECD : Wednesday – ☎ 073 081.

See : Cowdray House (Tudor ruins)* *AC* – Envir. : Uppark* (17C-18C) *AC*, SW : 12 m.
🏌 Cowdray Park ☎ 2088, NE : 1 m. on A 272 – 🏌 at Petersfield ☎ 0730 (Petersfield) 3725, W : 10 m.

♦London 57 – ♦Brighton 38 – Chichester 12 – ♦Southampton 41.

🏨 **Spread Eagle** (Best Western), South St., GU29 9NH, ☎ 2211, Telex 86853, « 15C hostelry »
– 📺 ⌂wc ☎ 🅿. 🚗 🔼 🆎 ⓪ 𝗩𝗜𝗦𝗔
M 8.50/11.50 **st.** 🍷 3.95 – **27 rm** ⊏⊐ 37.50/50.00 **st.**

XX **Mida,** Wool Lane, GU29 0ET, ☎ 3284
closed Sunday, Monday, 1 week spring and 1 week autumn – **M** (booking essential) a la carte
13.00/15.50 **t.**

at Bepton SW : 2 ¼ m. by A 286 – ✉ ☎ 073 081 Midhurst :

↑ **Park House** 🌿, GU29 0JB, ☎ 2880, 🏊 heated, 🌳, ⌘ – ⌂wc 🅿.
11 rm ⊏⊐ 20.00/45.00.

at Trotton W : 3 ¼ m. on A 272 – ✉ Petersfield (Hants.) – ☎ 073 080 Rogate :

🏠 **Southdowns** 🌿, GU31 5JN, S : 1 m. ☎ 521, 🌳 – 📺 ⌂wc ☎ 🅿. 🔼 𝗩𝗜𝗦𝗔
M 12.00 **t.** 🍷 2.75 – **8 rm** ⊏⊐ 27.00/45.00 **t.**

AUSTIN-ROVER Petersfield Rd ☎ 2443

RENAULT Rumbolds Hill ☎ 2162

MILDENHALL Suffolk **404** V 26 – pop. 6,780 – ECD : Thursday – ☎ 0638.

♦London 73 – ♦Cambridge 22 – ♦Ipswich 38 – ♦Norwich 41.

🏨 **Bell** (Best Western), High St., IP28 7EA, ℘ 712134 – 📺 🛏wc 🅿. 🔼 AE 🔘 VISA
M (buffet lunch) a la carte 6.95/9.80 t. – **18 rm** ⬜ 20.00/34.00 st. – SB (weekends only) 44.00 st.

MILFORD-ON-SEA Hants. **403** **404** P 31 – pop. 3,625 – ECD : Wednesday – ✉ Lymington – ☎ 0590.

♦London 109 – Bournemouth 15 – ♦Southampton 24 – Winchester 37.

🏨 **South Lawn,** Lymington Rd, SO4 0RF, ℘ 43911, ☛ – 📺 🛏wc 🕿 🅿. 🔼 AE 🔘 VISA. ℀
closed mid December-mid January – **M** (dinner only and Sunday lunch) 6.75/8.50 t. 🍷 3.60 –
17 rm ⬜ 24.00/41.00 t. – SB (winter only) 50.00 t.

🏨 **Westover Hall,** Park Lane, SO4 0PT, ℘ 43044, ⩽ Solent and the Needles, « Restored
Victorian mansion » – 📺 🛏wc 🝙wc 🅿. 🔼 AE 🔘 VISA. ℀
M 5.75/8.00 t. 🍷 3.00 – **11 rm** ⬜ 12.00/50.00 t. – SB (July and August) 50.00/60.00 t.

🏠 **Seaspray,** 8 Hurst Rd, SO4 0PY, ℘ 42627, ⩽ Solent and the Needles – 📺 🝙wc 🅿. ℀
March-October – **6 rm** ⬜ 15.00/24.00 st.

AUSTIN-ROVER High St. ℘ 0590 (Lymington) 42161

MILNROW Greater Manchester **402** **404** N 23 – pop. 10,346 – ✉ Rochdale (Lancs.) – ☎ 045 77
Saddleworth.

♦London 222 – ♦Manchester 14 – Rochdale 2.

XXX **Moorcock,** Huddersfield Rd, OL16 3TJ, SE : 3 m. on A 640 ℘ 2659, ⩽ – 🅿. 🔼 AE 🔘 VISA.
℀
closed Saturday lunch, Sunday dinner and 1 to 11 January – **M** a la carte 12.25/25.25 t. 🍷 3.50.

MILTON ABBAS Dorset **403** **404** N 31 The West Country G. – pop. 788 – ✉ Blandford –
☎ 0258.

See : Village★.

♦London 127 – Bournemouth 23 – Weymouth 19.

🏨 **Milton Manor** ⌂, DT11 0AZ, ℘ 880254, ⩽, « Country house atmosphere », 🞈, park –
🛏wc 🝙wc 🅿. ℀
April-October – **M** (bar lunch) 7.00 st. 🍷 2.75 – **12 rm** ⬜ 18.00/32.00 st.

MILTON DAMEREL Devon **403** H 31 – pop. 409 – ✉ Holsworthy – ☎ 040 926.

♦London 249 – Barnstaple 21 – ♦Plymouth 48.

🏨 **Woodford Bridge,** EX22 7LL, N : 1 m. on A 388 ℘ 481, « Part 15C inn », 🔲, 🞈, 🞈, ℀,
squash – 📺 🕿 🅿. 🚗. ℀
M (bar lunch Monday to Saturday) 6.75/12.00 t. 🍷 1.40 – **22 rm** ⬜ 35.00/58.00 t. – SB
68.00/80.00 t.

MILTON KEYNES Bucks. **404** R 27 – pop. 106,974 – ✉ Stony Stratford – ☎ 0908.

♦London 56 – ♦Birmingham 72 – Bedford 16 – Northampton 18 – ♦Oxford 37.

at Stony Stratford – ✉ ☎ 0908 Milton Keynes :

XX **Stratfords,** St. Paul's Court, 118 High St., ℘ 566577 – 🅿. 🔼 VISA
closed Saturday lunch, Sunday, Monday, 4 to 19 August and 22 December-13 January – **M**
8.50/14.50 t. 🍷 2.50.

MILTON ON STOUR Dorset **403** **404** N 30 – pop. 4,050 (inc. Gillingham) – ECD : Thursday –
☎ 074 76 Gillingham.

♦London 115 – Shaftesbury 6 – Taunton 42.

🏨 **Milton Lodge** ⌂, SP8 5QD, ℘ 2262, 🔼 heated, 🞈 – 📺 🛏wc 🝙 🅿. 🔼
M 6.50/10.50 t. 🍷 2.65 – **10 rm** ⬜ 20.00/50.00 t. – SB 50.00/80.00 st.

MINEHEAD Somerset **403** J 30 The West Country G. – pop. 7,370 – ECD : Wednesday – ☎ 0643.

See : Site ★ – Higher Town : Church Steps ★ – St. Michael's Church ★ – West Somerset Railway ★.

Envir. : Selworthy ★ : Church ★★, W : 4 ½ m.

🏌 Warren Rd ℘ 2057.

🛈 Market House, The Parade ℘ 2624.

♦London 187 – ♦Bristol 64 – Exeter 43 – Taunton 25.

🏨 **Northfield** (Best Western) ⌂, Northfield Rd, TA24 5PU, ℘ 5155, Telex 42513, « ⩽ gardens »
– 📺 🛏wc 🝙wc 🔥 🅿. 🔼 AE 🔘 VISA
Mid February-mid November – **M** 5.50/8.25 t. 🍷 2.60 – **27 rm** ⬜ 24.25/63.50 st. – SB
(except summer) 44.30/51.30 st.

🏨 **Beach** (T.H.F.), The Avenue, TA24 5AP, ℘ 2193, 🔼 heated – 📺 📺 🛏wc 🝙 🅿. 🔼 AE 🔘 VISA
M (bar lunch) 12.00 st. 🍷 2.85 – ⬜ 5.00 – **35 rm** 30.50/37.50 st.

🏛 **Benares** 🦢, Northfield Rd, TA24 5PT, 🖉 2340, 🚗 – 📺 🛏wc **🅟**. 🔄 AE ① VISA
closed last 2 weeks October and 2 weeks Christmas – **M** (bar lunch) 7.00 **t.** 🍷 2.10 – **21 rm**
🖙 22.05/49.70 **t.** – SB (winter only) (except Christmas) 32.00/50.00 **st.**

🏛 **Merton,** Western Lane, The Parks, TA24 8BZ, 🖉 2375, 🚗 – 🛏wc 🛏wc 🕭 **🅟**. 🔄
Easter-October – **M** (bar lunch) 7.50 **st.** – **12 rm** 🖙 9.95/38.35 **st.** – SB (except summer) 31.05/34.05 **st.**

🏠 **York,** 48 The Avenue, TA24 5AN, 🖉 5151 – 🛏wc 🛏wc **🅟**. 🔄 AE ① VISA. 🍴
M a la carte 6.00/9.45 **st.** 🍷 2.70 – **21 rm** 🖙 11.00/30.00 **st.** – SB (except summer) 32.00/37.00 **st.**

🏠 **Mentone,** The Parks, TA24 8BS, 🖉 5229, 🚗 – 📺 🛏wc 🛏wc **🅟**. 🔄 AE VISA
March-October – **9 rm** 🖙 9.50/21.00 **st.**

🏠 **Woodbridge,** The Parks, TA24 8BS, 🖉 3130 – 🛏wc **🅟**. 🔄 AE VISA
10 rm 🖙 12.00/22.20 **st.**

at Blue Anchor SE : 5 m. by A 39 on B 3191 – 📧 ✆ 064 382 Dunster :

🏠 **Langbury,** TA24 6LB, 🖉 821375, 🏊, 🚗 – 🛏wc **🅟**
March-October – **9 rm** 🖙 9.50/25.00 **st.**

FIAT, VAUXHALL Townsend Rd 🖉 3379
RENAULT Blue Anchor 🖉 064 382 (Dunster) 571

VW, AUDI-NSU Mart Rd 🖉 2108

MINSTER-IN-THANET Kent ⬛⬛⬛ Y 29 – see Ramsgate.

MINSTER LOVELL Oxon. ⬛⬛⬛ ⬛⬛⬛ P 28 – pop. 1,085 – 📧 ✆ 0993 Witney.
♦London 72 – Gloucester 36 – ♦Oxford 16.

🏛 **Old Swan** 🦢, Main St., OX8 5RN, 🖉 75614, 🚗 – 📺 🛏wc ✆ **🅟**. 🔄 AE ① VISA. 🍴
M 8.75/11.50 **t.** 🍷 2.75 – **10 rm** 🖙 29.50/44.00 **t.**

MINSTERWORTH Glos. ⬛⬛⬛ ⬛⬛⬛ N 28 – see Gloucester.

MITHIAN Cornwall ⬛⬛⬛ E 33 – see St. Agnes.

MODBURY Devon ⬛⬛⬛ I 32 – pop. 1,131 – ECD : Wednesday – 📧 Ivybridge – ✆ 0548.
♦London 237 – Exeter 37 – ♦Plymouth 12.

🏛 **Ermewood House,** Totnes Rd, Ermington, PL21 9NS, NW : 2 ½ m. by A 379 on B 3210
🖉 830741, 🚗 – 📺 🛏wc 🛏wc **🅟**. 🔄 AE ① VISA
closed 23 to 31 December – **M** (bar lunch) a la carte 9.20/11.75 **t.** 🍷 2.75 – **9 rm** 🖙 25.00/45.00 **st.**
– SB 52.00/54.00 **st.**

MOLD (YR WYDDGRUG) Clwyd ⬛⬛⬛ ⬛⬛⬛ K 24 – pop. 8,465 – ECD : Thursday – ✆ 0352.
🏌 Pantmywyn 🖉 318, W : 4 m. – 🏌 Old Padeswood, Station Rd 🖉 0244 (Buckley) 547401, E : 2 m.
on A 5118 – 🅱 Town Hall, Earl St. 🖉 59331 (summer only).

♦ London 211 – Chester 12 – ♦ Liverpool 29 – Shrewsbury 45.

🏛 **Bryn Awel,** Denbigh Rd, CH7 1BL, on A 541 🖉 3285 – 📺 🛏wc 🚐 **🅟**. 🔄 ① VISA. 🍴
closed 26 December-3 January – **M** a la carte 7.20/12.00 **t.** 🍷 2.60 – **19 rm** 🖙 18.00/32.00 **t.**

MONK FRYSTON North Yorks. ⬛⬛⬛ Q 22 – pop. 539 – 📧 Lumby – ✆ 0977 South Milford.
♦London 190 – ♦Kingston-upon-Hull 42 – ♦Leeds 13 – York 20.

🏛 **Monk Fryston Hall,** LS25 5DU, 🖉 682369, « Italian garden », park – 📺 🛏wc 🖉 **🅟**. 🏌.
🔄 AE VISA
M 6.55/9.75 **st.** 🍷 3.75 – **24 rm** 🖙 32.00/46.00 **st.** – SB (weekends only) 48.00/53.00 **st.**

🏛 **Selby Fork** (Anchor), LS25 5LP, W : 2 ¼ m. by A 63 on A 1 🖉 682711, Group Telex 557074,
🔄, 🍴 – 📺 🛏wc 🛏wc 🕭 **🅟**. 🔄 ① VISA
M a la carte 8.10/12.75 **st.** 🍷 2.65 – **109 rm** 🖙 35.00/42.00 **st.** – SB (weekends only) 48.00 **st.**

MONMOUTH (TREFYNWY) Gwent ⬛⬛⬛ L 28 – pop. 6,570 – ECD : Thursday – ✆ 0600.
Envir. : SE : Wye Valley★ – Raglan (castle★ 15C) SW : 7 m. – Skenfrith (castle and church★) NW :
6 m – 🏌 Leasebrook Lane 🖉 2212 – 🅱 National Trust Visitor Centre, Church St. 🖉 3899.

♦London 147 – Gloucester 26 – Newport 24 – ♦Swansea 64.

🏛 **King's Head,** Agincourt Sq., NP5 3DY, 🖉 2177, Telex 497294 – 📺 🛏wc 🛏wc ✆ **🅟**. 🏌. 🔄
AE ① VISA
M 8.50/12.00 **t.** 🍷 3.95 – 🖙 5.00 – **28 rm** 25.00/40.00 **t.** – SB 54.00 **st.**

🏠 **Leasbrook** 🦢, Dixton, NP5 5JN, NE : ¾ m. on A 40 🖉 2831, 🚗 – 🛏 🕭 **🅟**. 🔄. 🍴
M (dinner only) 8.00 **st.** – **7 rm** 🖙 15.50/28.00 **st.** – SB 35.00/38.00 **st.**

at Whitebrook S : 8 ½ m. by A 466 – 📧 ✆ 0600 Monmouth :

❌❌ **Crown at Whitebrook** 🦢 with rm, NP5 4TX, 🖉 860254, 🚗 – 🛏wc 🛏wc **🅟**. 🔄 AE ① VISA
closed 1 to 20 January – **M** 9.25/17.50 **st.** – **8 rm** 🖙 25.00/40.00 **st.** – SB 65.00/75.00 **st.**

AUSTIN-ROVER St. James Sq. 🖉 2773
FORD 77/79 Monnow St. 🖉 2366
MERCEDES-BENZ Dixton Rd 🖉 3118

VAUXHALL-OPEL, BEDFORD, CITROEN Wonastow
Rd 🖉 2896

MONTACUTE Somerset **408** L 31 – see Yeovil.

MORECAMBE Lancs. **402** L 21 – pop. 41,908 (inc. Heysham) – ECD : Wednesday – ☎ 0524.
See : Marineland★ *AC* – , 🏌 Clubhouse ♟ 418050, on sea front.
🛈 Marine Rd Central ♟ 414110.
♦London 248 – ♦Blackpool 29 – ♦Carlisle 66 – Lancaster 4.

🏨 **Elms,** Princess Crescent, Bare, LA4 6DD, ♟ 411501, ☞ – 🛗 📺 ⌖wc ☎ 🅿 🔼 🅰🅴 💳 ※
   M 4.50/7.00 t. 🍷 2.50 – **39 rm** ⬚ 18.50/38.00 t. – SB (weekends only) 39.50/42.00 st.

🏨 **Strathmore,** Marine Rd East, LA4 5AP, ♟ 411314, Group Telex 57515 – 🛗 📺 ⌖wc 🛁wc
   🅿 🔼 🅰🅴 ⓞ 💳 ※
   M 6.00/7.00 st. 🍷 2.75 – **54 rm** ⬚ 15.00/36.00 st. – SB (weekends only) 34.00/38.00 st.

🏨 **Midland,** Marine Rd, LA4 4BZ, ♟ 417180, ← – 🛗 📺 ⌖wc 🛁wc ☎ 🅿 🔼 🔼 🅰🅴 ⓞ 💳
   M 6.50/9.00 t. 🍷 2.50 – **46 rm** ⬚ 32.50/48.00 t. – SB (weekends only) 44.00 st.

↑ **Prospect,** 363 Marine Rd, East Promenade, LA4 5AQ, ♟ 417819 – ⌖wc
   Easter-October – **14 rm** ⬚ 12.00/18.50 st.

AUSTIN-ROVER Marine Rd Central ♟ 410134   VAUXHALL Bare Lane ♟ 410205
FORD Clarke St. ♟ 415061   VOLVO Marlborough Rd ♟ 417437
TOYOTA West Gate ♟ 413891   VW, AUDI Heysham Rd ♟ 415833

MORETONHAMPSTEAD Devon **408** I 32 The West Country G. – pop. 1,440 – ECD : Thursday –
✉ Newton Abbot – ☎ 064 74 (3 fig.) or 0647 (5 fig.).
🏌 Manor House Hotel ♟ 355.
♦London 213 – Exeter 12 – ♦Plymouth 38.

🏨 **Manor House** ♨, TQ13 8RE, SW : 2 m. on B 3212 ♟ 40355, Telex 42794, ←, 🏌, ♒, ☞,
   park, ※, squash – 🛗 📺 & 🅿 🔼 🔼 🅰🅴 ⓞ 💳 ※
   M (buffet lunch) 16.00 st. 🍷 3.75 – **66 rm** ⬚ 45.00/75.00 st. – SB 40.00/50.00 st.

↑ **Wray Barton Manor** ♨, TQ13 8SE, SE : 1½ m. on A 382 ♟ 40246, ←, ☞ – 📺 ⌖wc 🅿.
   🔼 💳
   March-November – **8 rm** ⬚ 9.50/21.50 st.

MORETON-IN-MARSH Glos. **408 404** O 28 – pop. 2,477 – ECD : Wednesday – ☎ 0608.
Envir. : Chastleton House★ (Elizabethan) *AC*, SE : 3½ m.
🛈 Council Offices ♟ 50881.
♦London 86 – ♦Birmingham 40 – Gloucester 31 – ♦Oxford 29.

🏨 **Manor House,** High St., GL56 0LJ, ♟ 50501, Telex 837151, « 17C manor house, gardens »,
   ⟍ – 🛗 📺 ⌖wc 🛁wc ☎ 🅿 🔼 🔼 🅰🅴 ⓞ 💳 ※
   M 6.00/12.00 t. – **40 rm** ⬚ 19.50/49.50 st. – SB 46.00/58.50 st.

🏨 **White Hart Royal** (T.H.F.), High St., GL56 0BA, ♟ 50731 – 📺 ⌖wc ☎ 🅿 🔼 🔼 🅰🅴 ⓞ
   💳
   M (bar lunch) 10.00 st. 🍷 2.60 – ⬚ 4.50 – **27 rm** 29.50/41.00 st.

AUSTIN-ROVER London Rd ♟ 50585   RENAULT Little Compton ♟ 74202
BMW High St. ♟ 50323

MORFA NEFYN Gwynedd **402 408** G 25 – see Nefyn.

MORPETH Northumb. **401 402** O 18 – pop. 14,054 – ECD : Thursday – ☎ 0670.
Envir. : Brinkburn Priory (site★, church★) *AC*, NW : 10 m.
🏌 Newbiggin-by-the-Sea ♟ 817344, E : 9 m.
♦London 301 – ♦Edinburgh 93 – ♦Newcastle-upon-Tyne 15.

🏨 **Queen's Head,** Bridge St., NE61 1NB, ♟ 512083 – 📺 ⌖wc 🛁 ☎ 🅿 🔼 🅰🅴 ⓞ 💳 ※
   closed 25 and 26 December – **M** a la carte 6.65/12.00 st. 🍷 2.45 – **23 rm** ⬚ 16.00/29.00 t.

   at Longhorsley NW : 7½ m. by A 192 on A 697 – ✉ ☎ 0670 Morpeth :

🏨 **Linden Hall** ♨, NE65 8XF, N : 1 m. on A 697 ♟ 56611, Telex 538224, ←, « Country house in
   extensive grounds », ☞, park, ※ – 🛗 📺 & 🅿 🔼 🔼 🅰🅴 ⓞ 💳 ※
   M a la carte 11.90/19.15 st. 🍷 3.75 – **45 rm** ⬚ 41.50/58.50 st. – SB (weekends only) 59.50 st.

AUSTIN-ROVER Hillgate ♟ 57441   RENAULT Clifton ♟ 512538
DATSUN Oldgate ♟ 514669   VAUXHALL Bridge End ♟ 512115
FORD 53/55 Bridge St. ♟ 519611   VW, AUDI Castle Sq. ♟ 519011
PEUGEOT, TALBOT Ellington ♟ 860327

MORTEHOE Devon **408** H 30 – see Woolacombe.

MOULTON Northants. **404** R 27 – see Northampton.

MOULTON North Yorks. **402** P 20 – pop. 198 – ✉ Richmond – ☎ 032 577 Barton.
♦London 243 – ♦Leeds 53 – ♦Middlesbrough 25 – ♦Newcastle-upon-Tyne 43.

✗✗ **Black Bull Inn,** DL10 6QJ, ♟ 289, « Brighton Belle Pullman coach » – 🅿
   closed Sunday and 23 December-1 January – **M** a la carte 10.00/16.25 t.

334

MOUNT PLEASANT Hants. 403 404 P 31 – see Lymington.

MOUSEHOLE Cornwall 403 D 33 The West Country G. – pop. 1,079 – ECD : Wednesday except summer – ⊠ ✆ 0736 Penzance.
♦London 321 – Penzance 3 – Truro 29.

🏠 **Lobster Pot,** South Cliff, TR19 6QX, ✆ 731251, ≤ – 🛏wc 📶wc
   closed late December-mid March – **M** 3.50/8.50 t. 🍷 3.00 – **24 rm** ⊇ 9.90/25.30 **st.**

🏠 **Carn Du** ॐ, Raginnis Hill, TR19 6SS, ✆ 731233, ≤ Mount's Bay, 🌳 – 📶wc 🅿 🄰 🄰🄴 ⱺ *VISA*
   February-October – **M** (bar lunch) 8.00 **st.** 🍷 2.25 – **7 rm** ⊇ 16.00/36.00 **st.** – SB (except summer) 40.00 **st.**

MUDEFORD Dorset 403 404 O 31 – see Christchurch.

MUCH BIRCH Heref. and Worc. – see Hereford.

MULLION Cornwall 403 E 33 The West Country G. – pop. 1,346 – ECD : Wednesday – ⊠ Helston – ✆ 0326.
See : Mullion Cove ★★★.
♦London 323 – Falmouth 21 – Penzance 21 – Truro 26.

🏠 **Polurrian** ॐ, TR12 7EN, SW : ½ m. ✆ 240421, ≤ Mounts Bay, 🎿 heated, 🌳, ⅋, squash – 📺 🛏wc 🅿 🄰 🄰🄴 ⱺ *VISA*
   Mid April-mid October – **M** a la carte 4.45/9.55 **st.** 🍷 2.25 – **43 rm** ⊇ 19.00/27.50 **st.**

MUMBLES West Glam. 403 I 29 – pop. 13,712 – ECD : Wednesday – ⊠ ✆ 0792 Swansea.
See : Mumbles Head★ – **Envir. :** Cefn Bryn (💥★★★ from the reservoir) W : 12 m. – Rhosili (site and ≤ ★★★) W : 18 m. – W : Oxwich Bay★.
♦London 202 – ♦Swansea 6.

🏠 **Osborne** (Embassy), Rotherslade Rd, Langland Bay, SA3 4QL, W : ¾ m. ✆ 66274, ≤ – ⧈ 📺 🛏wc ☎ 🅿 🄰 🄰🄴 ⱺ *VISA* ⅋
   M *(closed Sunday to non-residents)* 4.75/6.75 **st.** 🍷 4.00 – **41 rm** ⊇ 24.00/40.00 **st.** – SB (weekends only) 42.00/50.00 **st.**

🏠 **Langland Court** (Best Western) ॐ, 31 Langland Court Rd, Langland Bay, SA3 4TD W : 1 m. ✆ 61545, 🌳 – 📺 🛏wc 📶wc ☎ 🅿 🄰 🄰🄴 ⱺ *VISA*
   closed 24 to 27 December – **M** *(closed Sunday dinner)* (bar lunch) 6.50 t. 🍷 3.00 – **21 rm** ⊇ 25.00/45.00 **t.** – SB 50.00/55.00 **st.**

🏠 **Old School House,** 37 Nottage Rd, Newton, SA3 4SU, W : 1 m. ✆ 61541 – 📺 📶wc ☎ 🅿 🄰 🄰🄴 ⱺ *VISA* ⅋
   closed 25-27 December – **M** *(closed Sunday dinner)* (dinner only and Sunday lunch) 8.50 **t.** – **8 rm** ⊇ 23.00/38.00 **t.** – SB (weekends only) 49.50 **st.**

↑ **Wittemberg,** 2 Rotherslade Rd, Langland, SA3 4QN, W : ¾ m. ✆ 69696 – 📶wc 🅿 ⅋
   closed Christmas – **11 rm** ⊇ 12.00/26.00 **st.**

XXX **Norton House** with rm, 17 Norton Rd, SA3 5TQ, ✆ 404891 – 📺 🛏wc 📶wc ☎ 🅿 🄰 *VISA* ⅋
   closed 2 weeks August and 2 weeks Christmas – **M** *(closed Sunday)* (dinner only) a la carte 10.25/16.20 **t.** 🍷 4.50 – ⊇ 4.50 – **16 rm** 26.00/45.00 **st.**

AUSTIN-ROVER 54 Mumbles Rd, Blackpill ✆ 23451

MUNGRISDALE Cumbria 401 402 L 19 20 – pop. 256 – ⊠ Penrith – ✆ 059 683 Threlkeld.
♦London 301 – ♦Carlisle 33 – Keswick 8.5 – Penrith 13.

↑ **Mill** ॐ, CA11 0XR, ✆ 659, 🌳 – 🅿 ⅋
   Mid March-mid November – **8 rm** ⊇ 12.00/34.00 **t.**

↑ **Mill Inn** ॐ, CA11 0XR, ✆ 83632 – 🅿
   April-October – **8 rm** ⊇ 9.00/18.00 **s.**

NAFFERTON Humberside 402 S 21 – see Great Driffield.

NANTWICH Cheshire 402 403 404 M 24 – pop. 11,210 – ECD : Wednesday – ✆ 0270.
🄳 Council Offices, Beam St. ✆ 623914.
♦London 176 – Chester 20 – ♦Liverpool 45 – ♦Stoke-on-Trent 17.

🏰 **Rookery Hall** ॐ, Worleston, CW5 6DQ, N : 2 ½ m. by A 51 on B 5074 ✆ 626866, Telex 367169, ≤, « 19C country house », 🌳, park, ⅋ – 📺 🅿 🄰 🄰🄴 ⱺ *VISA* ⅋
   M (booking essential) 12.95/19.95 **t.** 🍷 5.50 – **12 rm** ⊇ 45.00/110.00 **t.** – SB (weekends only)(winter only) 100.00/130.00 **st.**

XX **Churche's Mansion,** 150 Hospital St., CW5 5RY, ✆ 625933, « 16C half-timbered house », 🌳 – 🅿
   closed Sunday dinner, 25 to 28 December and 1 January – **M** 5.50/10.50 **t.** 🍷 3.60.

AUSTIN-ROVER London Rd ✆ 623151   SAAB Welsh Rd ✆ 627678
HONDA Whitchurch Rd ✆ 780300   VAUXHALL-OPEL Station Rd ✆ 624027

335

NARBOROUGH Leics. 403 404 Q 26 – see Leicester.

NASSINGTON Northants. 404 S 26 – see Peterborough (Cambs.).

NATIONAL EXHIBITION CENTRE West Midlands 403 404 O 26 – see Birmingham.

NAWTON North Yorks. – see Helmsley.

NAYLAND Suffolk 404 W 28 – see Colchester (Essex).

NEASHAM Durham 402 P 20 – see Darlington.

NEATISHEAD Norfolk 404 Y 25 – ☎ 0692 Horning.
◆London 122 – North Walsham 8.5 – ◆Norwich 11.

   ☂ **Barton Lodge** ⬡ , Irstead Rd, Wroxham, NR12 8XP, E : ¾ m. *℘* 630740, *☞* – 📺 🍴wc ℗.
    🔼 AE *VISA*
    M 5.75/11.00 **st.** 🍷 2.50 – **8 rm** ⇌ 14.50/29.50 **st.** – SB (winter only) 42.00/48.00 **st.**

NEEDHAM MARKET Suffolk 404 X 27 – pop. 3473 – ECD : Tuesday – ✉ ☎ 0449.
◆ London 77 – ◆ Cambridge 47 – ◆ Ipswich 8.5 – ◆ Norwich 38.

   🏠 **Limes,** High St., IP6 8DQ, *℘* 720305 – 📺 🍴wc ℗. 🔼 AE ⑩. ☒
    closed 25 and 26 December – **M** 7.75/8.50 **t.** 🍷 2.50 – **11 rm** ⇌ 29.50/45.00 **t.** – SB (week-ends only) 48.50 **st.**

NEFYN Gwynedd 402 403 G 25 – pop. 2,086 – ECD : Wednesday – ☎ 0758.
See : Site ★ – 📷 *℘* 720218, W : 1 ½ m. – ◆London 265 – Caernarfon 20.

   ☂ **Caeau Capel** ⬡ , Rhodfa'r Mor, LL53 6EB, *℘* 720240, *☞* – 🚪wc ℗. 🔼 *VISA*
    Easter and May-September – **M** (bar lunch) 6.35 **t.** 🍷 1.40 – **21 rm** ⇌ 9.20/29.90 **t.**

    at Morfa Nefyn W : 1 ¼ m. on B 4417 – ✉ ☎ 0758 Nefyn :

   🏠 **Linksway,** Lon Las, LL53 6BG, *℘* 720258, *☞* – 🚪wc 🔥 ℗. ☒
    M 4.95/8.95 🍷 2.35 – **26 rm** ⇌ 10.95/25.40 – SB (not weekends) (except summer) 34.45 **st.**

AUSTIN-ROVER Church St. *℘* 720206

NEW ALRESFORD Hants. 403 404 Q 30 – pop. 3,684 – ECD : Wednesday – ☎ 096 273.
📷 Cheriton Rd *℘* 3153, S : 1 m. – ◆London 61 – ◆Southampton 19 – Winchester 8.

   🏠 **Swan,** West St., SO24 9AG, *℘* 2302 – 📺 🚪wc ℗. 🔼 *VISA*. ☒
    M (buffet lunch) a la carte 7.50/11.60 **st.** 🍷 3.50 – **13 rm** ⇌ 18.00/30.00 **st.**

AUSTIN-ROVER 47 West St. *℘* 2601   SAAB, SUBARU New Cheriton *℘* 096 279 (Bram-
FORD The Dene, Ropley *℘* 096 277 (Ropley) 2416   dean) 400

NEWARK-ON-TRENT Notts. 402 404 R 24 – pop. 24,646 – ECD : Thursday – ☎ 0636.
🅱 The Ossington, Beast Market Hill, Castlegate *℘* 78962.
◆London 127 – Lincoln 16 – ◆ Nottingham 20 – ◆ Sheffield 42.

   🏨 **Robin Hood** (Anchor), Lombard St., NG24 1XB, *℘* 703858, Group Telex 858875 – 📺 🚪wc
    🔼 AE ⑩ *VISA*
    M 8.65 **st.** 🍷 2.65 – **20 rm** ⇌ 31.00/42.00 **st.** – SB (weekends only) 42.00 **st.**

   🏠 **Clinton Arms,** 44 Market Pl., NG24 1EG, *℘* 72299 – 📺 🚪wc 🍴wc. 🔼 *VISA*. ☒
    M a la carte 5.45/9.15 **t.** 🍷 2.80 – **18 rm** ⇌ 18.50/33.00 **t.**

   ☂ **Grange,** 73 London Rd, Charles St. Corner, NG24 1RZ, *℘* 703399, *☞* – 📺 🚪wc ℗. 🔼 *VISA*.
    ☒
    closed Christmas – **M** (lunch by arrangement) a la carte 6.05/9.25 **st.** 🍷 2.95 – **6 rm**
    ⇌ 15.95/25.95 **st.**

AUSTIN-ROVER 69 Northgate *℘* 703413   SAAB North Muskham *℘* 703232
FIAT Sleaford Rd *℘* 703405   TALBOT 23/25 London Rd *℘* 705335
FORD Farndon Rd *℘* 704131   VAUXHALL-OPEL 116 Farndon Rd *℘* 705431
LADA London Rd *℘* 704937   VW, AUDI Northern Rd *℘* 704484
RENAULT 36/40 Albert St. *℘* 704619

NEWBRIDGE Cornwall – see Penzance.

NEWBURY Berks. 403 404 Q 29 – pop. 23,634 – ECD : Wednesday – ☎ 0635.
🅱 The Wharf *℘* 30267.
◆London 67 – ◆ Bristol 66 – ◆ Oxford 28 – Reading 17 – ◆ Southampton 38.

   🏨 **Chequers** (T.H.F.), 7-8 Oxford St., RG13 1JB, *℘* 43666, Telex 849205, *☞* – 📺 🚪wc 📶 ℗.
    🔼 AE ⑩ *VISA*
    M 6.95/8.75 **st.** 🍷 2.85 – ⇌ 4.75 – **69 rm** 29.50/46.50 **st.**

   🏨 **Elcot Park Country House** (Best Western) ⬡ , RG16 8NJ, W : 5 m. by A 4 *℘* 0488 (Kint-
    bury) 58100, ≼, *☞*, park, ☒ – 📺 🚪wc ☎ ℗. 🔼 AE ⑩ *VISA*
    M 7.50/12.50 **st.** 🍷 3.60 – **20 rm** ⇌ 40.00/65.00 **t.** – SB (summer only) 65.00/85.00 **st.**

✗ **Sapient Pig,** 29 Oxford St., RG13 1JG, ✆ 47425 – ▨ 𝑉𝐼𝑆𝐴
closed Sunday and Bank Holidays – **M** a la carte 6.70/11.50 **t.**

at Enborne SW : 4 ½ m. by A 343 – ⊠ Enborne – ✪ 0635 Newbury :

✗ **Enborne,** Essex St., RJ15 0JS, ✆ 41237 – **℗.** ▨ 𝐴𝐸 ⓞ 𝑉𝐼𝑆𝐴
closed Saturday lunch, Sunday, 25 to 30 December and Bank Holidays – **M** 8.25 **t.** 🍷 2.30.

AUSTIN-ROVER-TRIUMPH Kings Rd ✆ 49444
AUSTIN-ROVER London Rd ✆ 41100
CITROEN 22 Newtown Rd ✆ 41911

RENAULT London Rd ✆ 41020
VW, AUDI The Broadway ✆ 40678

NEWBY BRIDGE Cumbria **402** L 21 – pop. 200 – ECD : Saturday – ⊠ Ulverston – ✪ 0448.
♦London 270 – Kendal 16 – Lancaster 27.

🏛 **Swan,** LA12 8NB, ✆ 31681, ≤, ⌙, 🚗 – ▥ ⇨wc ☏ **℗.** ▵. ▨ 𝐴𝐸 ⓞ 𝑉𝐼𝑆𝐴. ❄
closed 2 to 11 January – **M** (bar lunch Monday to Saturday) a la carte 11.00/14.00 **t.** 🍷 3.30 –
36 rm ⟷ 25.00/48.00 **st.** – SB (winter only) 50.00/60.00 **st.**

🏛 **Whitewater,** The Lakeland Village, LA12 8PX, SW : 1 ½ m. by A 590 ✆ 31133 – 🛗 ▥ ⇨wc
☎ ⅙. **℗.** ▨ 𝐴𝐸 ⓞ 𝑉𝐼𝑆𝐴. ❄
M 6.50/9.95 **t.** – **34 rm** ⟷ 39.00/49.00 **t.** – SB (weekends only) 40.00/50.00 **st.**

NEWBY WISKE North Yorks. – see Northallerton.

NEWCASTLE EMLYN (CASTELL NEWYDD EMLYN) Dyfed **403** G 27 – pop. 651 – ECD : Wednesday – ✪ 0239.
Envir. : Cenarth Falls★ W : 3 m. – **Exc.** : E : Teifi Valley★.
♦London 240 – Carmarthen 20 – Fishguard 29.

🏛 Emlyn Arms, Bridge St., SA38 9DU, ✆ 710317 – ▥ ⇨wc ☏ **℗** – **38 rm.**

FORD New Rd ✆ 710245

NEWCASTLE-UNDER-LYME Staffs. **402 403 404** N 24 – pop. 77,126 – ECD : Thursday – ✪ 0782
Stoke-on-Trent.
🏌 Newcastle Municipal, Keele Rd ✆ 627596, NW : 2 m. on A 525 V.
🛈 Area Reference Library, Ironmarket ✆ 618125.
♦London 161 – ♦Birmingham 46 – ♦Liverpool 56 – ♦Manchester 43.

Plan of Built up Area : see Stoke-on-Trent

🏛 **Crest** (Crest), Liverpool Rd,
Cross Heath, ST5 9DX, N : 2 m.
on A 34 ✆ 612431, Telex 36681
– 🍽 rest ▥ ⇨wc ☏ ⅙ **℗.**
▵. ▨ 𝐴𝐸 ⓞ **℗**   U **a**
M approx. 10.50 **st.** – ⟷ 5.25
– **75 rm** 37.00/44.50 **st.**

🏛 **Clayton Lodge** (Embassy),
Clayton Rd, Clayton, ST5 4AF,
S : 1 ¼ m. on A 519 ✆ 613093
– ▥ ⇨wc ☎ **℗.** ▵. ▨ 𝐴𝐸
ⓞ 𝑉𝐼𝑆𝐴. ❄   V **e**
M *(closed Saturday lunch)*
6.75 **st.** 🍷 4.50 – ⟷ 4.25 – **50 rm**
21.50/39.00 **st.** – SB (weekends only) 48.00/52.00 **st.**

🏛 **Post House** (T.H.F.), Clayton
Rd, Clayton, ST5 4DL, S : 2 m.
on A 519 ✆ 625151, Telex 36531
– ▥ ⇨wc ☏ **℗.** ▵. ▨ 𝐴𝐸
ⓞ 𝑉𝐼𝑆𝐴   V **n**
M 7.70/8.25 **st.** 🍷 2.40 – ⟷ 5.00
– **126 rm** 35.50/43.00 **st.**

↰ **Grove Court,** 100 Lancaster
Rd, ST5 1DS, ✆ 614406, 🚗 –
▥ ⇨wc ℼwc **℗.** ▨ 𝑉𝐼𝑆𝐴   **c**
11 rm ⟷ 11.50/23.00 **t.**

AUSTIN-ROVER Brook Lane ✆ 618461
BMW Pool Dam ✆ 620811
CITROEN, PEUGEOT-TALBOT Hassell St.
✆ 614621
COLT Brunswick St. ✆ 614791
DATSUN Talke Rd, Chesterton ✆ 563711
FIAT Higherland ✆ 622141
FORD London Rd ✆ 621199
MAZDA North St. ✆ 612274
RENAULT High St., Wolstanton ✆ 626284
SKODA Shelton New Rd ✆ 615106

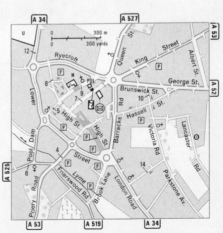

**NEWCASTLE-
UNDER-LYME
CENTRE**

High Street

Blackfriars Road	4
Church Street	6
Iron Market	8
Merrial Street	10
Upper Green	12
Vessey Terrace	14

VAUXHALL-OPEL Higherland ✆ 610941
VOLVO Knutton Rd, Wolstanton ✆ 625333
VW, AUDI Brunswick St. ✆ 617321

NEWCASTLE-UPON-TYNE

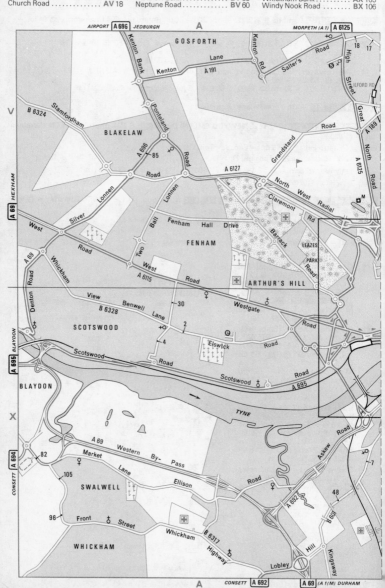

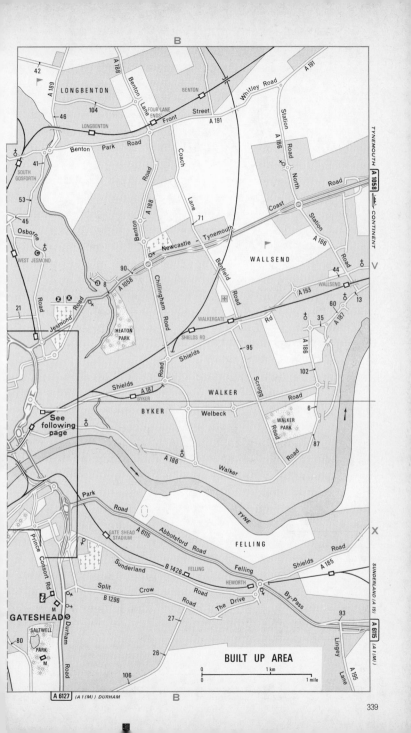

BUILT UP AREA

0   1 km
0   1 mile

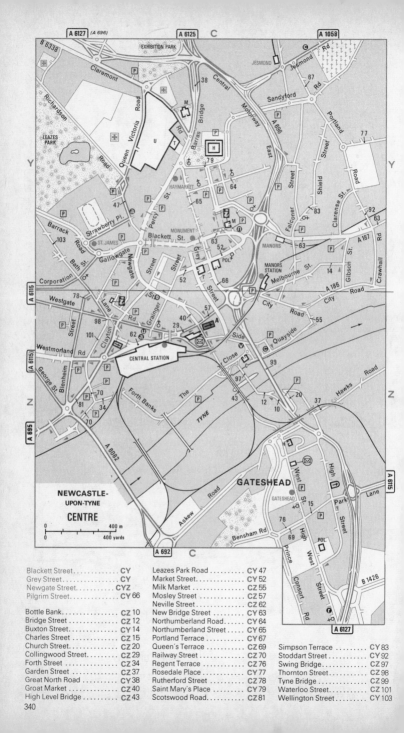

NEWCASTLE-UPON-TYNE CENTRE

Blackett Street	**CY**	Leazes Park Road	**CY** 47
Grey Street	**CY**	Market Street	**CY** 52
Newgate Street	**CYZ**	Milk Market	**CZ** 55
Pilgrim Street	**CY** 66	Mosley Street	**CZ** 57
		Neville Street	**CZ** 62
Bottle Bank	**CZ** 10	New Bridge Street	**CY** 63
Bridge Street	**CZ** 12	Northumberland Road	**CY** 64
Buxton Street	**CY** 14	Northumberland Street	**CY** 65
Charles Street	**CZ** 15	Portland Terrace	**CY** 67
Church Street	**CZ** 20	Queen's Terrace	**CY** 69
Collingwood Street	**CZ** 29	Railway Street	**CZ** 70
Forth Street	**CZ** 34	Regent Terrace	**CY** 76
Garden Street	**CZ** 37	Rosedale Place	**CY** 77
Great North Road	**CY** 38	Rutherford Street	**CZ** 78
Groat Market	**CZ** 40	Saint Mary's Place	**CY** 79
High Level Bridge	**CZ** 43	Scotswood Road	**CZ** 81
		Simpson Terrace	**CY** 83
		Stoddart Street	**CY** 92
		Swing Bridge	**CZ** 97
		Thornton Street	**CZ** 98
		Tyne Bridge	**CZ** 99
		Waterloo Street	**CZ** 101
		Wellington Street	**CY** 103

340

See : Cathedral★ 14C CZ A.

🔟 Three Mile Bridge, Gosforth ℰ 851775, N : 3 m. by A 6125 AV – 🔟 Broadway East, Gosforth, ℰ 856710, N : 3 m. by Kenton Rd AV – 🔟 Whorlton Grange, Westerhope, ℰ 869125, W : 5 m. by B 6324 AV.

✈ Newcastle Airport : ℰ 860966, NW : 5 m. by A 696 AV – **Terminal** : Bus Assembly : Central Station Forecourt.

🚗 ℰ 611234 ext 2621.

⚓ Shipping connections with the Continent : to Norway (Bergen, Stavanger) (Fred Olsen-Bergen Line) – to Denmark (Esbjerg) (DFDS Seaways) – to Sweden (Göteborg) (DFDS Tor Line).

🛈 Central Library, Princess Sq. ℰ 610691 ext 29 – Blackfriars, Monk St. ℰ 615367.

♦London 276 – ♦Edinburgh 105 – ♦Leeds 95.

Plans on preceding pages

🏨 **Crest** (Crest), New Bridge St., NE1 8BS, ℰ 326191, Telex 53467 – 🛗 ▤ rest 📺 🛏wc ☎ ὅ. 🅿. 🔼. 🔼 AE ⓞ 𝘝𝘐𝘚𝘈. ✄
    CY **n**
    M approx. 10.50 st. – ⊡ 5.25 – **178 rm** 42.00/51.00 st.

🏨 **County Thistle** (Thistle), Neville St., NE99 1AH, ℰ 322471, Telex 537873 – 🛗 📺 🛏wc ☎. 🔼. 🔼 AE ⓞ 𝘝𝘐𝘚𝘈. ✄
    CZ **a**
    ⊡ 4.75 – **115 rm** 32.50/43.00 t. – SB (weekends only) 48.00 st.

🏨 **Swallow** (Swallow), Newgate Arcade, Newgate St., NE1 5SX, ℰ 325025, Group Telex 538230 – 🛗 📺 🛏wc ☎ 🅿. 🔼. 🔼 AE ⓞ 𝘝𝘐𝘚𝘈
    CZ **o**
    M 5.00/7.00 st. – **92 rm** ⊡ 36.00/47.50 st.

🏨 **Imperial** (Swallow), Jesmond Rd, NE2 1PR, ℰ 815511, Telex 537972, 🔲 – 🛗 📺 🛏wc ☎ 🅿. 🔼. 🔼 AE ⓞ 𝘝𝘐𝘚𝘈
    CY **c**
    M 5.00/7.50 st. ▯ 3.40 – **130 rm** ⊡ 34.00/42.00 st.

🏨 **New Kent,** 127 Osborne Rd, Jesmond, NE2 2TB, ℰ 817711 – 📺 🛏wc ☎ 🅿. 🔼. 🔼 AE ⓞ 𝘝𝘐𝘚𝘈. ✄
    BV **c**
    M *(closed Sunday dinner)* (dinner only and Sunday lunch) 5.85/9.90 s. ▯ 3.25 – **40 rm** ⊡ 20.90/38.90 t. – SB (weekends only) 21.80/48.80 st.

⌂ **Avenue,** 2 Manor House Rd, Jesmond, NE2 2LU, ℰ 091 (Tyneside) 2811396 – 🔼 ⓞ. ✄
    BV **x**
    9 rm ⊡ 14.50/29.00 s.

⌂ **Westland,** 27 Osborne Av., Jesmond, NE2 1JR, ℰ 810412
    BV **z**
    15 rm ⊡ 14.50/25.50 st.

⌂ **Clifton Cottage,** Dunholme Rd, NE4 6XE, ℰ 091 (Tyneside) 2737347 – 📺 🅿
    AX **e**
    6 rm ⊡ 9.00/15.00 st.

XX **Fisherman's Lodge,** Jesmond Dene, Jesmond, NE7 7BQ, ℰ 091 (Tyneside) 2813281, Seafood – 🅿. 🔼 AE ⓞ 𝘝𝘐𝘚𝘈
    BV **a**
    closed Saturday lunch, Sunday, 25 December-2 January and Bank Holidays – **M** a la carte 13.00/18.10 t. ▯ 3.10.

XX **Fisherman's Wharf,** 15 The Side, NE1 3JE, ℰ 321057, Seafood – 🔼 AE ⓞ 𝘝𝘐𝘚𝘈
    CZ **v**
    closed Saturday lunch, Sunday, 10 days at Christmas and Bank Holidays – **M** a la carte 14.60/23.00 t. ▯ 3.30.

XX **Michelangelo,** 25 King St., Quayside, NE1 3UQ, ℰ 614415 – 🔼 AE ⓞ 𝘝𝘐𝘚𝘈
    CZ **c**
    closed Saturday lunch, Sunday and Bank Holidays – **M** a la carte 8.70/16.65 t. ▯ 2.75.

X Mario, 59 Westgate Rd, ℰ 320708, Italian rest.
    CZ **u**

X **La Toscana,** 22 Leazes Park Rd, NE1 4PG, ℰ 325871, Italian rest. – 🔼 AE ⓞ 𝘝𝘐𝘚𝘈
    CY **a**
    closed Saturday lunch, Sunday and Bank Holidays – **M** a la carte 4.50/13.25 t. ▯ 2.40.

at Gosforth N : 4 ¾ m. on A 6125 – AV – ✉ ✪ 0632 Newcastle-upon-Tyne :

🏨 **Gosforth Park Thistle** (Thistle), High Gosforth Park, NE3 5HN, on B 1318 ℰ 0632 (Wideopen) 364111, Telex 53655, ≮, 🔲, 🔼, park – 🛗 📺 ☎ ὅ 🅿. 🔼 AE ⓞ 𝘝𝘐𝘚𝘈. ✄
    M 10.00/12.00 t. ▯ 3.45 – ⊡ 5.25 – **178 rm** 46.00/80.00 st. – SB (weekends only) 62.00 st.

⌂ **Western House,** 1 West Av., NE3 4ES, ℰ 091 (Tyneside) 2856812 – 𝘝𝘐𝘚𝘈
    AV **s**
    14 rm ⊡ 11.50/18.40 st.

at Seaton Burn N : 8 m. on A 6125 – AV – ✉ Newcastle-upon-Tyne – ✪ 0632 Wideopen :

🏨 **Holiday Inn,** Great North Rd, NE13 6BP, N : ¾ m. ℰ 365432, Telex 53271, 🔲 – 📺 ☎ ὅ 🅿. 🔼. 🔼 AE ⓞ 𝘝𝘐𝘚𝘈
    M 10.25/10.50 st. – ⊡ 5.65 – **150 rm** 42.50/51.00 s.

at Newcastle Airport NW : 6 m. on A 696 – AV – ✉ Woolsington – ✪ 0661 Ponteland :

🏨 **Stakis Airport** (Stakis), NE13 8DJ, ℰ 24911, Telex 537121 – 🛗 📺 🛏wc ☎ ὅ 🅿. 🔼. 🔼 AE ⓞ 𝘝𝘐𝘚𝘈
    M 4.40/10.95 st. ▯ 2.80 – **100 rm** ⊡ 37.50/44.00 st. – SB (weekends only) 46.00 st.

NEWCASTLE-UPON-TYNE

LADA Warwick St. ☎ 321355
LAND ROVER Comington ☎ 676271
PORSCHE Melbourne St. ☎ 612591
RENAULT Shiremoor ☎ 532318
RENAULT Scotswood Rd ☎ 730101
SAAB Whitley Rd, Longbenton ☎ 668223
SKODA Forth St. ☎ 322617

TALBOT Benton Rd ☎ 666361
VAUXHALL Two Ball Lonnen ☎ 741000
VAUXHALL Great North Rd ☎ 363176
VAUXHALL, PEUGEOT Dunn St. ☎ 735211
VOLVO Brunton Lane ☎ 867111
VOLVO Jesmond Rd ☎ 815151
VW, AUDI Fossway ☎ 657121

NEW DENHAM Bucks. 404 @ – pop. 7,543 – ⊠ ✿ 0895 Uxbridge.
♦London 20 – Aylesbury 25 – ♦Oxford 40.

XXX **Giovanni's,** at Denham Lodge, Oxford Rd, UB9 4AA, on A 4020 ☎ 31568, Italian rest. – 🅿.
◪ ▥ ⑩ VISA
closed Saturday lunch, Sunday, last 2 weeks August, last 2 weeks December and Bank Holidays
– **M** a la carte 9.20/14.90 **t.** ⱡ 2.45.

NEWDIGATE Surrey 404 T 30 – pop. 1,404 – ✿ 030 677.
♦London 32 – ♦Brighton 32 – Guildford 18.

XX **Forge,** Parkgate Rd, RH5 5DZ, N : 1 m. ☎ 582 – 🅿. ◪ ▥ ⑩ VISA
closed Saturday lunch, Sunday dinner, Monday and 3 weeks summer – **M** a la carte
12.45/18.30 **st.** ⱡ 4.80.

NEWHAVEN East Sussex 404 U 31 – pop. 9,710 – ECD : Wednesday – ✿ 0273.
☷ Peacehaven, Brighton Rd ☎ 514049.
⌁ Shipping connections with the Continent : to France (Dieppe) (Sealink).
🄸 Car Ferry Terminal Car Park, The Harbour (summer only).
♦London 63 – ♦Brighton 9 – Eastbourne 14 – Lewes 7.

🏨 **Ladbrook Mercury Motor Inn** (Ladbroke), Station Rd, BN25 2RB, SE : 1 ½ m. on A 259
☎ 0323 (Seaford) 891055, ≼ – ⊡ ➟wc ☏ 🅿. 🏧. ◪ ▥ ⑩ VISA
M (dinner only) 5.40 **st.** – **68 rm** ⊊ 27.00/35.00 **st.**

FORD Drove Rd ☎ 515303
VAUXHALL-OPEL Avis Way ☎ 5941

NEWLYN Cornwall 403 D 33 – see Penzance.

NEWMARKET Suffolk 404 V 27 – pop. 9,900 – ECD : Wednesday – ✿ 0638.
☷ Links, Cambridge Rd ☎ 662708, SW : 1 m.
♦London 64 – ♦Cambridge 13 – ♦Ipswich 40 – ♦Norwich 48.

🏨 **Newmarket Moat House** (Q.M.H.), Moulton Rd, CB8 8DY, ☎ 667171 – 🎭 ⊡ 🅿. 🏧. ◪ ▥
⑩ VISA
M (closed Saturday lunch) 7.95 **t.** ⱡ 3.00 – **49 rm** ⊊ 33.00/45.00 **st.** – SB 50.00 **st.**

🏨 **White Hart,** High St., CB8 8JP, ☎ 663051 – ⊡ ➟wc ☏ 🅿. 🏧. ◪ VISA
M 6.50/7.50 **st.** – **21 rm** ⊊ 20.00/37.00 **st.**

at Six Mile Bottom (Cambs.) SW : 6 m. on A 1304 – ⊠ Newmarket – ✿ 063 870 Six Mile
Bottom :

🏨 **Swynford Paddocks,** CB8 0UQ, ☎ 234, « Country house, stud farm », 🐎, park, ⋇ – ⊡
☏ 🅿. ◪ ▥ VISA
M a la carte 9.10/12.40 **t.** ⱡ 3.25 – **12 rm** ⊊ 36.00/68.00 **t.**

TOYOTA Bury Rd ☎ 662130
VAUXHALL-OPEL All Saints Rd ☎ 663121

VOLVO Dullingham ☎ 063 876 (Stetchworth) 244

NEW MILTON Hants. 403 404 P 31 – pop. 4,373 – ECD : Wednesday – ⊠ Bournemouth (Dorset)
– ✿ 0425.
♦London 106 – Bournemouth 12 – ♦Southampton 21 – Winchester 34.

🏨 ✿ **Chewton Glen** 🏡, Christchurch Rd, BH25 6QS, W : ¾ m. on A 337 ☎ 042 52 (Highcliffe) 5341, Telex 41456, ≼, ⊒ heated, 🐎, park, ⋇ – ⊡ ☏ 🅿. 🏧. ◪ ▥ ⑩ VISA. ⋇
M 10.00/23.00 **st.** ⱡ 3.75 – ⊊ 4.00 – **44 rm** 50.00/101.00 **st.** – SB (winter only) 102.00/121.00 **st.**
Spec. Cassoulet d'escargots à l'ail doux, Loup de mer mouginoise (April-September), Aiguillettes de poulet
fermier en pot au feu.

AUSTIN-ROVER Old Milton Rd ☎ 614665
COLT Christchurch Rd ☎ 611198
FORD Fernhill Lane ☎ 612121

NISSAN 25 Station Rd ☎ 610034
RENAULT 53 Lymington Rd ☎ 612296

NEWPORT I.O.W. 403 404 Q 31 – see Wight (Isle of).

NEWPORT (CASNEWYDD-AR-WYSG) Gwent 403 L 29 – pop. 112,286 – ECD : Thursday – ✿ 0633.
Envir. : Caerleon : Roman Amphitheatre★ AC, NE : 3 m.
☷ Llanwern ☎ 412380, E : 3 m.
🄸 John Frost Sq. ☎ 842962.
♦London 145 – ♦Bristol 31 – ♦Cardiff 12 – Gloucester 48.

342

🏨 **Celtic Manor**, Coldra Woods, NP6 2YA, E : 3 m. by A 48 ℰ 413000, ≤ – 📺 ☎ 🅿 🏖 🔼 🅰🅴
🅾 📼 ✆
M a la carte 12.00/20.70 **t.** 🛈 3.25 – **17 rm** 🖵 52.00/67.00 **t.**

🏨 **Ladbroke** (Ladbroke), The Coldra, Chepstow Rd, NP6 2YG, E : 3 m. on A 48 ℰ 412777, Telex
497205 – 📺 🛏wc ☎ 🅿 🏖 – **125 rm**.

🏨 **Queens**, 19 Bridge St., NPT 4RN, ℰ 62992 – 📺 🛏wc 🛁wc ⊛ 🅿 🏖 🔼 🅰🅴 🅾 📼
M (carving rest.) 6.95/11.95 **t.** 🛈 2.45 – **43 rm** 🖵 22.50/39.00 **t.** – SB (July-August) 39.00 **st.**

at Langstone E : 4 ½ m. on A 48 – ✉ Newport – ✆ 0633 Llanwern :

🏨 **New Inn Motel** (Golden Oak), Chepstow Rd, NP6 2JN, ℰ 412426 – 📺 🛏wc ☎ 🅿 🏖 🔼
🅰🅴 📼 ✆
M (closed Sunday dinner) 4.75/11.20 **st.** 🛈 2.50 – **34 rm** 🖵 26.00/32.00 **st.**

AUSTIN-ROVER	Shaftesbury St. ℰ 858451	FORD Lee Way Industrial Estate ℰ 278020	
AUSTIN-ROVER	Bassaleg Rd ℰ 63717	NISSAN ℰ 273414	
AUSTIN-ROVER	Cardiff Rd ℰ 63847	VAUXHALL Turner St. ℰ 59771	
AUSTIN-ROVER	Bassaleg Rd ℰ 53771		

NEWPORT (TREFDRAETH) Dyfed 📟 F 27 – pop. 1,062 – ECD : Wednesday – ✆ 0239.
See : Site★ – Envir. : Pentre Ifan (burial chamber★) SE : 4 ½ m. – 🎣 Newport Sands ℰ 820244.
🛈 Pembrokeshire Coast National Park Centre, East St. ℰ 820912 (summer only).
♦London 258 – Fishguard 7.

🍴 **Pantry**, Market St., SA42 0PH, ℰ 820420 – 🅿 🔼 📼
closed Sunday and Monday – **M** (dinner only) (booking essential) a la carte 8.90/14.10 **t.**
🛈 2.75.

at Velindre (Felindre Farchog) E : 2 ¾ m. on A 487 – ✉ Cardigan – ✆ 0239 Newport :

🏠 **Salutation Inn**, SA41 3UY, ℰ 820564, ☞ – 📺 🛏wc 🅿 🔼 🅰🅴 🅾 📼
M (bar lunch) 7.50 **st.** 🛈 2.50 – **8 rm** 🖵 14.85/22.90 **st.** – SB 33.00/35.00 **st.**

NEWPORT Salop 📟 📟 📟 M 25 – pop. 5,230 – ECD : Thursday – ✆ 0952.
🛈 9 St. Mary's St. ℰ 814109.
♦London 150 – ♦Birmingham 33 – Shrewsbury 18 – ♦Stoke-on-Trent 21.

🏨 **Royal Victoria**, St. Mary's St., TF10 7AB, ℰ 810831 – 📺 🛏wc 🛁wc 🅿 ✆ – **21 rm**.
PEUGEOT-TALBOT High St. ℰ 811076

NEWPORT PAGNELL Bucks. 📟 R 27 – pop. 5,120 – ECD : Thursday – ✆ 0908.
♦London 57 – Bedford 13 – Luton 21 – Northampton 15.

🏨 **TraveLodge** (T.H.F.) without rest., M 1 Service Area 3, MK16 8DS, W : 1 ½ m. by A 422 on M
1 ℰ 610878, Telex 826186 – 📺 🛏wc ⊛ 🅿 🏖 🔼 🅰🅴 🅾 📼
98 rm 26.00/36.00 st.

🏠 **Swan Revived**, High St., MK16 8AR, ℰ 610565 – 🛗 📺 🛏wc 🛁wc ☎ 🅿 🏖 🔼 🅰🅴 🅾 📼
closed 24 December-3 January – **M** 7.25 **st.** 🛈 2.75 – **31 rm** 🖵 30.00/40.00 **st.** – SB
35.00/75.00 **st.**

PEUGEOT High St. ℰ 611715

NEWQUAY Cornwall 📟 E 32 The West Country G. – pop. 12,240 – ECD : Wednesday – ✆ 063 73.
🎣 Perranporth ℰ 087 257 (Perranporth) 2454, SW : 6 m. by A 3075 Y.
✈ Newquay Civil Airport : ℰ 063 74 (St. Mawgan) 551, NE : 6 m. by A 3059 Y.
🛈 Cliff Rd ℰ 71345.
♦London 291 – Exeter 83 – Penzance 34 – ♦Plymouth 48 – Truro 14.

Plan on next page

🏨 **Bristol**, Narrowcliff, TR7 2PQ, ≤, 🔼, – 🛗 📺 🅾 🔼 🅰🅴 🅾 📼   Z r
M 6.00/8.25 **st.** 🛈 2.25 – **100 rm** 🖵 19.00/50.00 **st.** – SB 25.00/32.50 **st.**

🏨 **Riviera** (Best Western), Lusty Glaze Rd, TR7 3AA, ℰ 4251, ≤, 🔼 heated, ☞, squash – 🛗 📺   Z o
🅿 🔼 🅰🅴 📼
M (buffet lunch) 7.00 **t.** 🛈 3.00 – **50 rm** 🖵 21.00/54.00 **t.** – SB (weekends only) 43.00/60.00 **st.**

🏨 **Trebarwith**, Island Estate, TR7 1BZ, ℰ 2288, ≤ bay and coast, 🔼, ☞ – 📺 🛏wc 🛁wc 🅿   Z a
🔼 📼 ✆
Easter-early October – **M** (bar lunch) 9.00 **t.** 🛈 2.00 – **44 rm** 🖵 (dinner included) 25.50/55.00 **t.**

🏨 **Windsor**, Mount Wise, TR7 2AY, ℰ 5188, 🔼 heated, 🔼, ☞, squash – 📺 🛏wc 🅿 🔼 📼   Z n
✆
Easter-October – **M** (bar lunch) 8.00 **st.** 🛈 2.40 – **45 rm** 🖵 17.00/55.00 **st.**

🏨 **Kilbirnie**, Narrowcliff, TR7 2RS, ℰ 5155, 🔼 – 📺 🛏wc ⊛ 🅿 🔼 📼   Z e
closed 1 week at Christmas – **M** (bar lunch) 8.00 **st.** 🛈 2.30 – **73 rm** 🖵 11.50/45.00 **st.** – SB
42.50/51.50 **st.**

🏨 **Mordros**, 4 Pentire Av., TR7 1PA, ℰ 6700, 🔼 heated – 🛏wc 🅿 🔼 📼 ✆   Y x
Easter-mid October – **M** (closed Saturday lunch) (bar lunch) 9.20 **t.** 🛈 2.00 – **30 rm** 🖵 20.70/41.40 **t.**

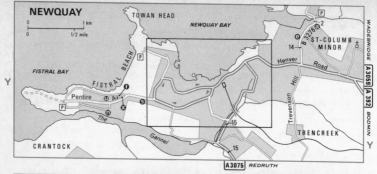

NEWQUAY

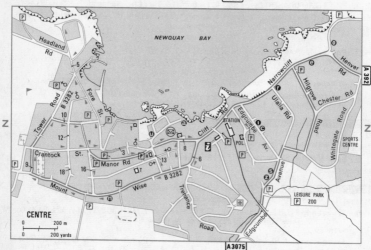

CENTRE

🏚 **Porth Veor Manor,** 56 Porth Way, TR7 3LW, ℘ 3274, ✿ – 📺 🛏wc 🛏wc 🅿 ⚡ AE VISA.
⠿
closed November – **M** 4.50/6.00 t. ▮ 2.50 – **14 rm** ☲ 22.50/43.00 t.   Y e

🏚 **Corisande Manor** ⍋, Riverside Av., Pentire, TR7 1PL, ℘ 2042, ⩽ Gannel Estuary, ✿ – 🛏wc 🛏wc 🅿
May-October – **M** (bar lunch) 6.00 t. ▮ 2.25 – **19 rm** ☲ 10.50/38.00 t. – SB 32.00/34.00 st.   Y n

🏚 **Water's Edge,** Esplanade Rd, Pentire, TR7 1QA, ℘ 2048, ⩽ Fistral Bay, ✿ – 🛏wc 🛏wc 🅿. ⠿
Easter and 16 May-5 October – **M** (bar lunch) 7.95 st. ▮ 2.25 – **20 rm** ☲ (dinner included) 13.25/41.40 t.

🏚 **Bewdley,** Pentire Rd, TR7 1NX, ℘ 2883, ⩽, ⌇ heated – 🛏wc 🛏wc 🅿. ⚡ VISA   Y s
March-October – **M** 3.50/6.00 st. ▮ 1.85 – **30 rm** ☲ 9.00/27.00 st. – SB 24.00/38.00 st.

⌂ **Porth Enodoc,** 4 Esplanade Rd, Pentire, TR7 1PY, ℘ 2372, ⩽ Fistral Bay – 🛏wc 🅿. ⠿
Easter-October – **9 rm** ☲ 9.00/20.00 t.   Y i

⌂ Island House, Island Cres., TR7 1DZ, ℘ 78411, ⩽ – 🛏wc 🅿
9 rm.   Z u

⌂ Pasadera, 15 Edgcumbe Av., TR7 2NJ, ℘ 3235 – 🛏 🅿. ⠿   Z i
Easter-October – **18 rm** ☲ 6.00/14.00 s.

⌂ **Wheal Treasure,** 72 Edgcumbe Av., TR7 2NN, ℘ 4136 – 🛏wc 🅿. ⠿   Z z
May-September – **10 rm** ☲ 7.00/28.00 st.

↑ **Copper Beech,** 70 Edgcumbe Av., TR7 2NN, ℰ 3376 – 🏛 **P.** 𝗩𝗜𝗦𝗔 ⌘   Z **s**
Easter-October – **16 rm** ⌷ 7.50/18.40 **st.**

↑ **Hepworth,** 27 Edgcumbe Av., TR7 2NJ, ℰ 3686, 🚲 – 🏛wc **P.** ⌘   Z **c**
Easter-September – **13 rm** ⌷ 7.00/20.00.

↑ **Pendeen,** 7 Alexandra Rd, Porth, TR7 3ND, ℰ 3521, 🚲 – 🛏wc 🏛wc **P.** ⌘   Y **a**
March-October – **15 rm** ⌷ 9.00/25.00.

  at St. Columb Minor NE : 3 m. by A 3059 – Y – ✉ 🕿 063 73 Newquay :

🏛 **Cross Mount,** 60 Church St., TR7 3EX, ℰ 2669 – 🛏wc 🏛wc **P.** 🔼 𝗩𝗜𝗦𝗔 ⌘
closed Christmas and Christmas – **M** (bar lunch Monday to Saturday) 6.50 **t.** ⌁ 2.00 – **12 rm**
⌷ 10.00/35.00 **t.** – SB 29.00/31.00 **st.**

  at Crantock SW : 4 m. by A 3075 – Y – ✉ Newquay – 🕿 0637 Crantock :

🏛 **Fairbank,** West Pentire Rd, TR8 5SA, ℰ 830424, ⩽, 🚲 – 📺 🛏wc 🏛wc **P.** ⌘
April-October – **M** (bar lunch) 6.85 **t.** ⌁ 2.00 – **29 rm** ⌷ 14.00/45.00 **t.** – SB 38.40/49.15 **st.**

🏛 **Crantock Bay** ⌂, West Pentire, TR8 5SE, W : ¾ m. ℰ 830229, ⩽ Crantock Bay, 🚲 –
🛏wc **P.** 𝗩𝗜𝗦𝗔
April-October – **M** (buffet lunch) 6.95 **st.** ⌁ 2.15 – **30 rm** ⌷ 12.60/40.70.

AUSTIN-ROVER Quintrell Downs ℰ 2410   VOLVO Newlyn East ℰ 087 251 (Mitchell) 347
COLT, VOLVO Summercourt ℰ 087 251 (Mitchell)
386

■ NEW ROMNEY Kent **404** W 31 – pop. 3,447 – ECD : Wednesday – 🕿 0679.
Envir. : Lydd (All Saints' Church tower : groined vaulting★) SW : 3 ½ m. – Brookland (St. Augustine's
Church : belfry★ 15C, Norman font★) W : 6 m.

♦London 71 – Folkestone 14 – Hastings 23 – Maidstone 33.

🏛 **Blue Dolphins,** Dymchurch Rd, TN28 8BE, ℰ 63224 – 🏛 **P.** 🔼 𝗩𝗜𝗦𝗔 ⌘
M *(closed Sunday)* (dinner only) 10.25 **t.** ⌁ 2.40 – **8 rm** ⌷ 11.50/23.50 **t.**

FORD The Avenue, Littlestone ℰ 62184   RENAULT Sussex Rd ℰ 2404

During the season, particularly in resorts, it is wise to book in advance.
However, if you find you cannot take up a hotel booking you have made,
please let the hotel know immediately.
If you are writing to a hotel abroad enclose an International Reply Coupon
(available from Post Offices.)

■ NEWTON ABBOT Devon **403** J 32 The West Country G. – pop. 19,130 – ECD : Thursday –
🕿 0626.
🚂 ℰ 66490 (to Stirling) – ℰ 01 (London) 723 7000 ext. 3148.
🛈 8 Sherborne Rd ℰ 67494.

♦London 216 – Exeter 16 – ♦Plymouth 31 – Torquay 7.

🏛 **Queen's,** Queen St., TQ12 2EZ, ℰ 63133 – 📺 🛏wc 🏛wc **P.** ⌂. 🔼 ① 𝗩𝗜𝗦𝗔
M 5.00/6.00 **st.** ⌁ 2.50 – **25 rm** ⌷ 18.00/34.00 **st.**

ALFA-ROMEO, VOLVO Wolborough St. ℰ 2545
AUSTIN-ROVER-LAND ROVER 64/72 Wolborough
St. ℰ 4141
FIAT The Avenue ℰ 2526
FORD Wolborough St. ℰ 65081
PEUGEOT-TALBOT 174 Exeter Rd, Kingsteignton
ℰ 3545

PEUGEOT-TALBOT, RENAULT Kingsteignton Rd ℰ
68322
TOYOTA Highweek ℰ 4702
VAUXHALL-OPEL 177/187 Queen St. ℰ 3838
VW, AUDI The Avenue ℰ 2641

■ NEWTON FERRERS Devon **403** H 33 The West Country G. – pop. 1,815 – 🕿 0752 Plymouth.

♦London 242 – Exeter 42 – ♦Plymouth 11.

🏛 **Court House** ⌂, Court Rd, PL8 1AQ, ℰ 872324, ⌇ heated, 🚲 – 🛏wc **P.** 𝗩𝗜𝗦𝗔
M 6.00/9.00 **st.** ⌁ 3.25 – **12 rm** ⌷ 20.00/60.00 **t.** – SB 28.00/30.00 **st.**

  at Battisborough Cross E : 3 m. – ✉ Newton Ferrers – 🕿 075 530 Holbeton :

🏛 **Alston Hall** ⌂, PL8 1HN, ℰ 259, ⩽, ⌇ heated, 🚲, ⌘ – 📺 🛏wc 🕿 **P.** 🔼 ⚏ ① 𝗩𝗜𝗦𝗔 ⌘
M 6.50/13.50 **t.** ⌁ 2.95 – **9 rm** ⌷ 31.00/52.00 **st.**

■ NEWTON SOLNEY Derbs. **402 403 404** P 25 – see Burton-upon-Trent (Staffs.).

■ NEWTOWN (DRENEWYDD) Powys **403** K 26 – pop. 5,450 – ECD : Thursday – 🕿 0686.
🛈 Town Council Buildings, The Cross ℰ 25580.

♦London 196 – Aberystwyth 44 – Chester 56 – Shrewsbury 32.

🏛 **The Bear,** Broad St., SY16 2LU, ℰ 26964, Telex 35205 – 📺 🛏wc 🏛wc 🕿 **P.** 🔼 ⚏ ① 𝗩𝗜𝗦𝗔
M 7.00 **st.** – **33 rm** ⌷ 18.00/32.00 **st.** – SB (weekends only) 30.00/39.50 **st.**

at Abermule (Aber-Miwl) NE : 4 ½ m. on A 483 – ⊠ 🟢 068 686 Abermule :

🏛 **Dolforwyn Hall** 🍴, Dolforwyn, SY15 6JG, N : ½ m. on A 483 🅿 221 – 📺 ⌂wc 🛁wc 🄿.
🅰 🄰🄴 🚫
  M a la carte 6.85/14.25 t. ▯ 1.85 – **7 rm** 🛏 16.00/28.00 **st.** – SB (weekends only) 45.00 **st.**

AUDI, VW Abermule 🅿 068 686 (Abermule) 615   FORD Pool Rd 🅿 25514
AUSTIN-ROVER Pool Rd 🅿 25942

NORMAN CROSS Cambs. 🖪🖪🖪 T 26 – see Peterborough.

NORTHALLERTON North Yorks. 🖪🖪🖪 P 20 – pop. 9,300 – ECD : Thursday – 🟢 0609.
Envir. : Bedale, Leyburn Rd (Parish church★ 13C-14C) SW : 7 ½ m.
🏌 at Bedale 🅿 0677 (Bedale) 22568, SW : 7 ½ m.
◆London 238 – ◆Leeds 48 – ◆Middlesbrough 24 – York 33.

🏛 **Golden Lion** (T.H.F.), High St., DL7 8PP, 🅿 2404 – 📺 ⌂wc 🕿 🄿. 🅰. 🅰 🄰🄴 🄾 *VISA*
  M 6.50/8.25 **st.** ▯ 2.60 – 🛏 4.50 – **29 rm** 29.00/39.00 **st.**

✕✕ **McCoys at the Tontine**, Staddlebridge, DL6 3JB, NE : 8 ½ m. by A 684 on A 19
  🅿 060 982 (East Harlsey) 207, « 1930's decor » – 🄿. 🅰 🄰🄴 🄾 *VISA*
  closed 24-26 December – **M** (dinner only) a la carte 15.35/18.40 **t.** ▯ 3.75.

✕✕ **Romanby Court**, 5 Romanby Court, High St., DL7 8PG, 🅿 774918 – 🅰 *VISA*
  closed Sunday and Monday – **M** a la carte 4.65/8.50 **t.** ▯ 2.25.

✕ McCoy's Bistro, Staddlebridge, DL6 3JB, NE : 8 ½ m. by A 684 on A 19 🅿 207 – 🄿.

at Newby Wiske S : 2 ½ m. by A 167 – ⊠ 🟢 0609 Northallerton :

🏛 **Solberge Hall** (Best Western) 🍴, DL7 9ER, 🅿 779191, 🦌, park – 📺 ⌂wc 🕿 🄿. 🅰 🄰🄴
  🄾 *VISA*
  closed January – **M** 5.50/10.50 **st.** ▯ 3.00 – **15 rm** 🛏 28.00/52.00 **st.** – SB 53.00/70.00 **st.**

AUSTIN-ROVER Brompton Rd 🅿 3891   HONDA, SAAB East Rd 🅿 3921
FIAT North End 🅿 6346   RENAULT Leeming Bar 🅿 2388

Prices	For full details of the prices quoted in the guide, consult p. 16.

NORTHAMPTON Northants. 🖪🖪🖪 R 27 – pop. 151,000 – 🟢 0604.
See : Church of the Holy Sepulchre★ 12C ✕ A – Central Museum and Art Gallery (collection of footwear★) ✕ M.
Envir. : Brixworth (All Saints Church★ 7C Saxon) N : 7 m. by A 508 Y – Earls Barton (All Saints Church : 10C Saxon tower★) NE : 5 m. by A 45 Y – Castle Ashby★ (16C-17C) *AC*, NE : 8 m. by A 428 Z.
🏌 Delapre, Eagle Drive 🅿 64036 Z.
🛈 21 St. Giles St. 🅿 22677 and 34881 ext 404.
◆London 69 – ◆Cambridge 53 – ◆Coventry 34 – ◆Leicester 42 – Luton 35 – ◆Oxford 41.

Plan opposite

🏨 Northampton Moat House (Q.M.H.), Silver St., NN1 2TA, 🅿 22441, Telex 311142 – 🛗 📺 🄿.
  🅰. 🅰 🄰🄴 🄾 *VISA*   X n
  M 4.95/6.95 **st.** ▯ 2.95 – 🛏 4.50 – **134 rm**.

✕ **Napoleon's Bistro**, 9-11 Welford Rd, Kingsthorpe, NN2 8AE, N : 1 ¾ m. by A 508 on A 50
  🅿 713899 – 🅰 🄰🄴 🄾 *VISA*   Y c
  closed Sunday, Monday and 25 December-2 January – **M** 8.05/12.25 **t.** ▯ 2.85.

✕ **Ca d'Oro**, 334 Wellingborough Rd, NN1 4ES, 🅿 32660, Italian rest. – 🅰 🄰🄴 🄾 *VISA*   Z e
  closed Sunday and Bank Holidays – **M** a la carte 7.70/14.80 **st.** ▯ 2.90.

at Weston Favell NE : 3 ½ m. by A 4500 – ⊠ 🟢 0604 Northampton :

🏛 **Westone Moat House** (Q.M.H.), Ashley Way, NN3 3EA, 🅿 406262, Telex 312587, 🦌 – 🛗
  📺 ⌂wc 🕿 🄿. 🅰. 🅰 🄰🄴 🄾 *VISA*   Y a
  M *(closed Saturday lunch)* 6.25/7.25 **s.** ▯ 2.85 – **64 rm** 🛏 33.00/42.00 **st.** – SB (weekends only) 46.00/50.00 **st.**

at Moulton NE : 4 ½ m. by A 43 – Y – ⊠ 🟢 0604 Northampton :

🏠 **Poplars**, 33 Cross St., NN3 1RZ, 🅿 43983, 🦌 – 📺 ⌂wc 🛁wc 🄿. 🅰
  21 rm 🛏 15.00/35.00 **st.**

ALFA-ROMEO 78 St. Michaels Rd 🅿 30771   NISSAN 159/185 Abington Av. 🅿 714303
AUSTIN-ROVER Weedon Rd 🅿 54041   RENAULT Bedford Rd 🅿 39645
AUSTIN-ROVER 46/50 Sheep St. 🅿 35471   TOYOTA 348 Wellingborough Rd 🅿 31086
AUSTIN-ROVER-DAIMLER-JAGUAR-LAND ROVER   VOLVO Bedford Rd 🅿 21363
592 Wellingborough Rd 🅿 401141   VW, AUDI, MERCEDES-BENZ 42/50 Harborough Rd
CITROEN 194/200 Kingsthorpe Grove 🅿 713202   🅿 716716
FIAT, LANCIA 74 Kingsthorpe Rd 🅿 714555

NORTHAMPTON

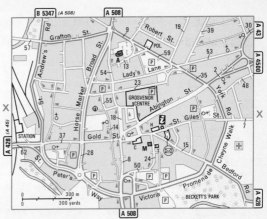

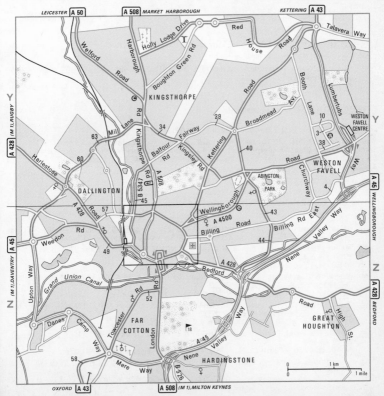

347

NORTH BOVEY Devon 🗺️403 I 32 – ✉ Newton Abbot – ☎ 0647 Moretonhampstead.
♦London 214 – Exeter 13 – ♦Plymouth 31 – Torquay 21.

🏠 **Glebe House** ≫, TQ13 8RA, 𝒫 40544, ≼, 🚗, park – 🚪wc 🛏️wc 🅿 – **9 rm**

🏠 **Blackaller House** ≫, TQ13 8QY, 𝒫 40322, ≼, 🚗 – 🚪wc 🅿 💳 AE VISA
March-mid November – **M** (dinner only) 11.50 **t.** 🍷 2.80 – **6 rm** ⟷ 13.75/35.00 **t.** – SB 24.25/26.50 **st.**

NORTHENDEN Greater Manchester 🗺️402 ㉝ 🗺️403 ③ 🗺️404 ⑩ – see Manchester.

NORTH FERRIBY Humberside 🗺️402 S 22 – see Kingston-upon-Hull.

NORTHFIELD West Midlands 🗺️403 ㉒ 🗺️404 ⑳ – see Birmingham.

NORTH HYKEHAM Lincs. 🗺️402 🗺️404 S 24 – see Lincoln.

NORTHIAM East Sussex 🗺️404 V 31 – pop. 1,500 – ECD : Wednesday – ✉ Rye – ☎ 079 74.
♦London 55 – Folkestone 36 – Hastings 12 – Maidstone 27.

🏨 **Hayes Arms**, Village Green, TN31 6NN, 𝒫 3142, « Part Tudor and Georgian country house », 🚗 – 🚪wc 🅿 💳 AE VISA
M (restricted lunch) 4.50/9.75 **t.** 🍷 2.25 – **7 rm** ⟷ 18.00/40.00 **t.** – SB 51.00/55.00 **st.**

NORTH PETHERTON Somerset 🗺️403 K 30 – pop. 3,792 – ECD : Thursday and Saturday – ☎ 0278.
♦London 161 – ♦Bristol 43 – Taunton 8.

🏠 **Walnut Tree Inn**, TA6 6QA, 𝒫 662255 – 📺 🚪wc 🅿 🦽 💳 AE ① VISA 🐾
M a la carte 7.50/10.45 **t.** 🍷 1.75 – **11 rm** ⟷ 24.00/34.00 **t.** – SB (weekends only) 28.00 **st.**

NORTHREPPS Norfolk 🗺️404 Y 25 – pop. 664 – ✉ Cromer – ☎ 026 378 Overstrand.
♦London 131 – ♦Norwich 22.

XX **Church Barn**, Church St., NR27 0LG, 𝒫 558 – 🅿 💳 VISA
closed Sunday dinner, Monday, first 2 weeks January and 26-27 December – **M** a la carte 8.20/13.45 **t.**

NORTH STIFFORD Essex 🗺️404 ㊹ – ✉ Grays – ☎ 0375 Grays Thurrock.
♦London 22 – Chelmsford 24 – Southend-on-Sea 20.

🏨 **Stifford Moat House** (Q.M.H.), High Rd, RM16 1UE, 𝒫 71451, 🚗, ✂ – 📺 🚪wc ☎ 🅿
🦽 💳 AE ① VISA
closed 27 to 31 December – **M** *(closed Saturday lunch)* 8.30/12.50 **t.** 🍷 3.00 – ⟷ 4.00 – **64 rm** 20.00/40.00 **st.** – SB (weekends only) 43.00 **st.**

NORTH STOKE Oxon. – see Wallingford.

NORWICH Norfolk 🗺️404 Y 26 – pop. 122,083 – ☎ 0603.
See : Cathedral⋆⋆ 11C-12C (bosses⋆⋆ of nave vaulting) Y – Castle (museum⋆⋆) *AC* Z M – St. Peter Mancroft's Church⋆ (Perpendicular) Z B – Sainsbury Centre for Visual Arts⋆ (University of East Anglia) *AC*, by B 1108 X – Envir. : Norfolk Wildlife Park⋆ *AC*, NW : 12 m. by A 1067 V.
🏌️ Barnham Broom 𝒫 060 545 (Barnham Broom) 437, W : 7 m. off A 47 V.
✈ 𝒫 411923, Telex 97209, N : 3 ½ m. by A 140 V.
🚹 Augustine Steward House, 14 Tombland 𝒫 666071/2.
♦London 109 – ♦Kingston-upon-Hull 148 – ♦Leicester 119 – ♦Nottingham 120.

Plan opposite

🏰 **Maid's Head** (Q.M.H.), Tombland, NR3 1LB, 𝒫 28821 – 📶 📺 🅿 🦽 💳 AE ① VISA   Y **u**
M 6.00/7.75 **t.** 🍷 2.80 – **82 rm** ⟷ 37.25/48.80 **t.** – SB (weekends only) 48.00/56.00 **st.**

🏨 **Nelson** (Best Western), Prince of Wales Rd, NR1 1DX, 𝒫 28612, Telex 975203, ≼ – 📶 📺
🚪wc ☎ 🦽 🅿 🦽 💳 AE ① VISA 🐾   Z **a**
M 8.00 **st.** 🍷 2.40 – **94 rm** ⟷ 39.00/46.50 **st.** – SB 53.00 **st.**

🏨 **Norwich** (Best Western), 121-131 Boundary Rd, NR3 2BA, on A 1047 𝒫 410431, Telex 975337 – 📺 🚪wc ☎ 🦽 🅿 🦽 💳 AE ① VISA 🐾   V **r**
M 8.00 **st.** 🍷 2.40 – **102 rm** ⟷ 36.50/44.00 **st.** – SB 46.00/50.00 **st.**

🏨 **Post House** (T.H.F.), Ipswich Rd, NR4 6EP, S : 2 ¼ m. on A 140 𝒫 56431, Telex 975106, 🌊 heated – 📺 🚪wc 🦽 🅿 🦽 💳 AE ① VISA 🐾   on A 140 X
M 6.25/8.95 **st.** 🍷 2.60 – ⟷ 5.00 – **120 rm** 35.00/43.50 **st.**

🏨 **Castle** (De Vere), Castle Meadow, NR1 3PZ, 𝒫 611511, Telex 975582 – 📶 📺 🚪wc ☎ 🦽
💳 AE ① VISA 🐾   Z **n**
M 7.50 **st.** 🍷 2.50 – **78 rm** ⟷ 24.00/38.00 **st.** – SB (weekends only) 34.00/41.00 **st.**

🏨 **Lansdowne** (Embassy), 116 Thorpe Rd, NR1 1RU, 𝒫 20302 – 📶 📺 🚪wc ☎ 🅿 🦽 💳 AE
① VISA 🐾   X **i**
closed 25 and 26 December – **M** 6.25 **st.** 🍷 4.50 – ⟷ 4.25 – **44 rm** 22.00/38.00 **st.** – SB (weekends only) 38.00/46.00 **st.**

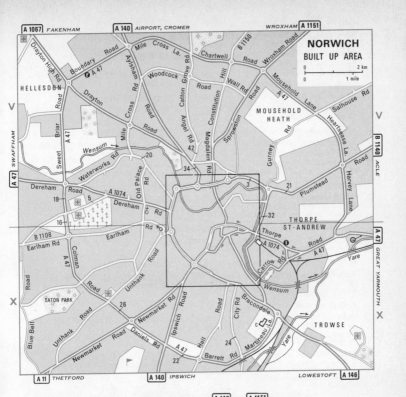

NORWICH
BUILT UP AREA

0   1 mile   2 km

A 1067 FAKENHAM   A 140 AIRPORT, CROMER   WROXHAM A 1151

HELLESDON

MOUSEHOLD HEATH

THORPE ST-ANDREW

EATON PARK

TROWSE

A 11 THETFORD   A 140 IPSWICH   LOWESTOFT A 146

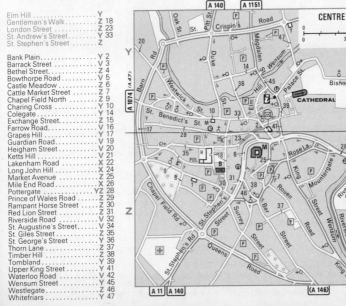

CENTRE

0   300 yards
0   300 m

A 140   A 1151

CATHEDRAL

Bishopgate

NORWICH STATION

A 11   A 140   (A 146)   A 146

↟ **Riverside,** 11-12 Riverside Rd, NR1 1SQ, ☏ 23978　　　　　　　Z **s**
　10 rm ⊠ 10.00/18.00 **st.**

↟ **Conway,** 2 Aspland Rd, NR1 1SH, ☏ 24761 – ⊡. ◪ ◭ 𝘝𝘐𝘚𝘈. ⚬⚬　　　Z **v**
　8 rm ⊠ 12.00/32.00 **t.**

XX **Marco's,** 17 Pottergate, NR2 1DS, ☏ 24044, Italian rest – ◪ ◭ ⓪ 𝘝𝘐𝘚𝘈　YZ **e**
　closed Saturday, Sunday and August – **M** a la carte 9.10/17.00 **t.**

　at Horsham St. Faith N : 4 ½ m. by A 140 – V – ⊠ ✆ 0603 Norwich :

↟ **Elm Farm Chalet,** 55 Norwich Rd, NR10 3HH, ☏ 898366, ⚘, ⟲ – ⊡ �🛏wc ⓟ. ⚬⚬
　14 rm ⊠ 12.50/24.00 **st.**

　at Thorpe St. Andrew E : 2 ½ m. on A 47 – X – ⊠ ✆ 0603 Norwich :

🏛 **Town House,** 18-22 Yarmouth Rd, NR7 0EF, ☏ 37717, ≼, ⚘, ⟲ – ⊡ �🛏wc ☜ ⓟ. ◪ 𝘝𝘐𝘚𝘈. ⚬⚬　X **e**
　M *(closed Sunday dinner)* 5.25/7.95 **st.** ⓙ 2.75 – **22 rm** ⊠ 17.50/30.50 **st.**

🏛 **Oaklands,** 89 Yarmouth Rd, NR7 0HH, ☏ 34471, ⚘ – ⊡ �🛏wc ⓟ. ◪ 𝘝𝘐𝘚𝘈
　M 4.25/6.25 **st.** ⓙ 2.10 – **42 rm** ⊠ 17.50/31.50 **st.** – SB (weekends only) 42.00 **st.**

　at Brundall E : 5 ½ m. by A 47 – X – ⊠ ✆ 0603 Norwich :

XX **Old Beams,** 39 The Street, NR13 5AA, ☏ 712215 – ⓟ. ◪ 𝘝𝘐𝘚𝘈
　closed Sunday dinner, Monday, 1 week February and 2 weeks mid-October – **M** (dinner only
　and Sunday lunch) a la carte 8.70/14.55 **t.** ⓙ 3.25.

　at Blofield E : 7 ½ m. by A 47 – X – ⊠ ✆ 0603 Norwich :

XX **La Locanda,** Fox Lane, NR13 4LW, ☏ 713787, Italian rest. – ⓟ. ◪ ◭ ⓪ 𝘝𝘐𝘚𝘈
　closed Saturday lunch and Sunday – **M** a la carte 10.10/17.15 **t.** ⓙ 2.50.

　at Hethersett SW : 6 m. on A 11 – V – ⊠ ✆ 0603 Norwich :

🏛 **Park Farm** ⚲, NR9 3DL, ☏ 810264, ◪, ⚘, ⚬ – ⊡ ⌐wc �🛏wc ⓟ. ◪ ◭ 𝘝𝘐𝘚𝘈. ⚬⚬
　M *(closed Sunday dinner)* 5.00/8.00 **t.** ⓙ 2.60 – **21 rm** ⊠ 26.00/38.00 **st.** – SB (week-
　ends only) (spring only) 29.40 **st.**

　at Drayton NW : 5 m. on A 1067 – V – ⊠ ✆ 0603 Norwich :

XXX **Drayton Wood** ⚲ with rm, Drayton High Rd, NR8 6BL, SW : 1 ½ m. on A 1067 ☏ 409451,
　⚘, park – ⊡ ⌐wc ☜ ◪ ◭ ⓪ 𝘝𝘐𝘚𝘈. ⚬⚬
　closed 25 to 31 December – **M** *(closed Sunday dinner)* a la carte 10.35/13.35 **t.** ⓙ 2.75 – **4 rm**
　⊠ 27.00/45.00 **t.**

ALFA-ROMEO, MERCEDES-BENZ, VW, AUDI Heig-
ham Causeway, Heigham St. ☏ 612111
ASTON-MARTIN, AUSTIN-ROVER Ipswich Rd, Long
Stratton ☏ 0508 (Long Stratton) 30491
AUSTIN-ROVER Earlham Rd ☏ 21393
AUSTIN-ROVER 162 Cromer Rd ☏ 46946
AUSTIN-ROVER Norwich Rd, Stoke Holy Cross ☏
05086 (Framingham Earl) 2218
AUSTIN-ROVER Mile Cross Lane ☏ 483001
AUSTIN-ROVER 5 Prince of Wales Rd ☏ 28383
BMW 26/29 Cattlemarket St. ☏ 21471
FIAT, LANCIA Aylsham Rd ☏ 45345
FORD 39 Palace St. ☏ 24144

HONDA 36 Duke St. ☏ 29825
NISSAN Constitution Hill ☏ 43944
NISSAN 79 Mile Cross Lane ☏ 410661
PORSCHE Vulcan Rd South ☏ 401814
RENAULT 22 Heigham St. ☏ 28911
ROLLS ROYCE-BENTLEY King St. ☏ 28383
TALBOT, VW, AUDI, PEUGEOT 116 Prince of Wales
Rd ☏ 28811
TOYOTA Rouen Rd ☏ 29655
VAUXHALL-OPEL Aylsham Rd, Mile Cross ☏ 414321
VAUXHALL-OPEL Mountergate ☏ 23111
VOLVO Westwick St. ☏ 26192

☞　*Michelin puts no plaque or sign*
　　on the hotels and restaurants mentioned in this Guide.

▇**NOTTAGE**▇ **(DRENEWYDD YN NOTAIS)** Mid Glam. ❹❶❸ I 29 – see Porthcawl.

▇**NOTTINGHAM**▇ Notts. ❹❷ ❹❸ ❹❹ Q 25 – pop. 300,630 – ECD : Thursday – ✆ 0602.

See : Castle★ (Renaissance) and museum★ *AC* CZ **M**.

Envir. : Newstead Abbey★★ 16C and gardens★★*AC*, N : 9 m. by B 683 AY – Wollaton Hall★ (16C)
AC, W : 3 ½ m. AZ **M**.

🅱 Wollaton Park ☏ 787572, W : 2 m. AZ – 🅱 Bulwell Hall Park Links ☏ 278021, N : 5 m. AY – 🅱
Beeston Fields, Beeston ☏ 257062, S : 4 m. by A 52 AZ.

✈ East Midlands Airport : Castle Donington ☏ 0332 (Derby) 810621, SW : 15 m. by A 453 AZ.

🛈 18 Milton St. ☏ 470661 – Castle Gatehouse, Castle Rd ☏ 470661 (summer only).

🛈 at Long Eaton : Central Library, Tamworth Rd ☏ 0602 735426 – at West Bridgford : County Hall ☏ 823823.

♦London 135 – ♦Birmingham 50 – ♦Leeds 74 – ♦Manchester 72.

Plans on following pages

🏨 **Albany** (T.H.F.), St. James's St., NG1 6BN, ☏ 470131, Telex 37211 – 🛗 🍽 ⊡ ☎ ♿ ◭ ◪
　◭ ⓪ 𝘝𝘐𝘚𝘈　　　　　　　　　　　　　　　　　　　　　　　　　　　　　　CYZ **a**
　M 6.95/7.95 **st.** – ⊠ 5.50 – **160 rm** 41.00/51.50 **st.**

🏨 **Royal,** Wollaton St., NG1 5RH, ☏ 414444, Telex 37101, squash – 🛗 🍽 ⊡ ☎. ♿ ◪ ◭ ⓪
　𝘝𝘐𝘚𝘈. ⚬⚬　　　　　　　　　　　　　　　　　　　　　　　　　　　　　　　　CY **e**
　closed Christmas Day – **M** 5.50/6.50 **t.** ⓙ 2.40 – ⊠ 3.50 – **201 rm** 35.00/42.00 **t.**

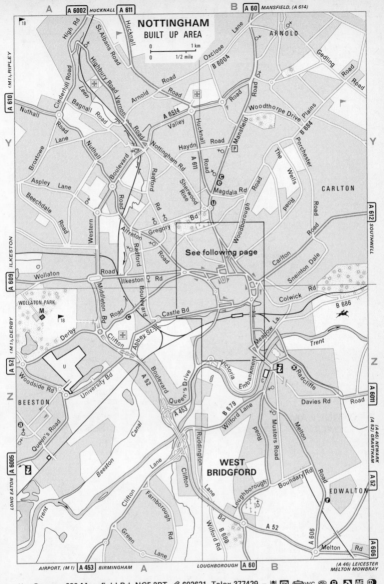

NOTTINGHAM
BUILT UP AREA

0		1 km	
0	1/2 mile		

See following page

🏨 **Savoy,** 296 Mansfield Rd, NG5 2BT, ℰ 602621, Telex 377429 – 🛗 📺 ➥wc ☎ 🅿 . 🔼 AE ⑩
VISA . 🛠
   M 4.75/6.85 t. 🍴 2.50 – ☲ 3.25 – **125 rm** 27.50/35.00 t.   BY **u**

🏨 **Stakis Victoria** (Stakis), Milton St., NG1 3PZ, ℰ 419561, Telex 37401 – 🛗 📺 ➥wc ☎ . 🔼
   🔼 AE ⑩ VISA . 🛠
   M (buffet lunch) 9.00 t. – **167 rm** ☲ 36.00/43.00 t. – SB 46.00/60.00 st.   DY **a**

🏨 **Strathdon Thistle** (Thistle), 44 Derby Rd, NG1 5FT, ℰ 418501, Telex 377185 – 🛗 📺 ➥wc
   🍴wc ☎ . 🔼 🔼 AE ⑩ VISA . 🛠
   M 8.60/9.80 🍴 3.45 – ☲ 4.75 – **64 rm** 32.00/42.50 t. – SB (weekends only) 50.00 st.   CY **c**

🏠 **Lucieville** without rest., 349 Derby Rd, NG7 2DZ, ℰ 787389, 🚗 – 🍴wc 🅿 – **9 rm.**   AZ **c**

351

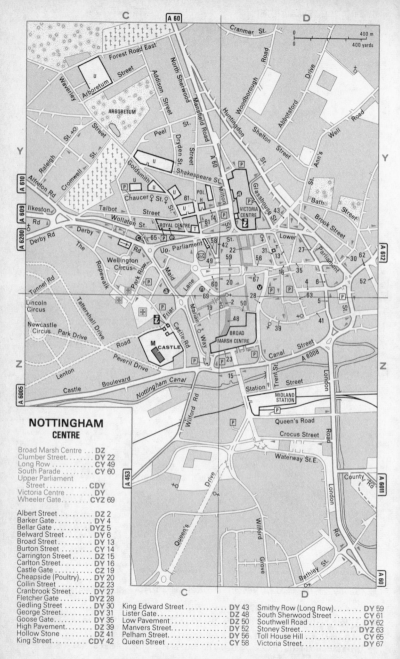

NOTTINGHAM
CENTRE

Broad Marsh Centre ... **DZ**
Clumber Street .... **DY** 22
Long Row .... **CY** 49
South Parade .... **CY** 60
Upper Parliament
  Street .... **CDY**
Victoria Centre .... **DY**
Wheeler Gate .... **CYZ** 69

Albert Street .... **DZ** 2
Barker Gate.......... **DY** 4
Bellar Gate .... **DYZ** 5
Belward Street .... **DY** 6
Broad Street .... **DY** 13
Burton Street .... **CY** 14
Carrington Street ..... **DZ** 15
Carlton Street .... **DY** 16
Castle Gate .... **CZ** 19
Cheapside (Poultry) ... **DY** 20
Collin Street .... **DZ** 23
Cranbrook Street...... **DY** 27
Fletcher Gate .... **DYZ** 28
Gedling Street .... **DY** 30
George Street .... **DY** 31
Goose Gate .... **DY** 35
High Pavement .... **DZ** 39
Hollow Stone .... **DZ** 41
King Street.......... **CDY** 42

King Edward Street .... **DY** 43
Lister Gate .... **DZ** 48
Low Pavement .... **DZ** 50
Manvers Street .... **DY** 52
Pelham Street .... **DY** 56
Queen Street .... **CY** 58

Smithy Row (Long Row) .... **DY** 59
South Sherwood Street .... **CY** 61
Southwell Road .... **DY** 62
Stoney Street .... **DYZ** 63
Toll House Hill .... **CY** 65
Victoria Street .... **DY** 67

If you find you cannot take up a hotel booking you have made,
please let the hotel know immediately.

352

⋔ **Royston,** 326 Mansfield Rd, NG5 2EF, ℰ 622947 – 📺 ⋔wc 🅿. ◪. ⋘   BY **e**
  15 rm ⊑ 17.50/35.00 st.

⋔ **Cotswold,** 332 Mansfield Rd, NG5 2EF, ℰ 623547 – 📺 ⋔wc 🅿. ◪ AE ⓞ VISA   BY **c**
  18 rm ⊑ 13.95/28.00 st.

XX **Trattoria Conti,** 14-16 Wheeler Gate, NG1 2NB, ℰ 474056, Italian rest. – ◪ AE ⓞ VISA
   closed Sunday, 23 July-21 August and Bank Holidays – **M** a la carte 7.15/13.60 t. ◊ 2.50.
                                                                              CY **n**

XX **Rhinegold,** 10 King John's Chambers, Fletcher Gate, NG1 2HD, ℰ 501294 – ◪ AE   DY **v**
   closed Sunday and Bank Holidays – **M** a la carte 7.50/9.95 ◊ 2.75.

   at West Bridgford SE : 2 m. on A 52 – ✉ ✆ 0602 Nottingham :

🏛 **Windsor Lodge,** 116 Radcliffe Rd, NG2 5HG, ℰ 813773 – 📺 ⋔wc 🅿. ◪ VISA. ⋘   BZ **x**
  M *(closed Friday to Sunday)* (dinner only) 6.00 ◊ 2.50 – **43 rm** ⊑ 14.00/28.00.

   at Edwalton S : 3 m. on A 606 – ✉ ✆ 0602 Nottingham :

🏛 **Edwalton Hall,** NG12 4AE, ℰ 231116, 🌳 – ⇔wc ⋔ ☎ 🅿. ◪ AE ⓞ VISA   BZ **r**
  M 6.00/8.50 t. ◊ 3.00 – **12 rm** ⊑ 14.50/35.00.

   at Beeston SW : 4 ¼ m. by A 52 on B 6006 – ✉ ✆ 0602 Nottingham :

X **Les Artistes Gourmands,** NG9 2NG, 61 Wollaton Rd ℰ 228288, French rest.   AZ **a**
   closed Sunday and 1 to 23 January – **M** (dinner only) 6.60/12.90 st.

   at Toton SW : 6 ½ m. on A 6005 – AZ – ✉ Nottingham – ✆ 0602 Long Eaton :

⋔ **Manor,** Nottingham Rd, NG9 6EF, junction with B 6003 ℰ 733487 – ⇔wc 🅿
   closed Christmas – **17 rm** ⊑ 15.50/28.00.

   at Long Eaton (Derbs.) SW : 8 m. by A 52 on B 6002 – AZ – ✉ Nottingham – ✆ 0602 Long
   Eaton :

🏨 **Novotel,** Bostock Lane, NG10 4EP, ℰ 720106, Telex 377585, ⅃ heated, 🌳 – 🛏 🍽 📺 ⇔wc
   ☎ ᵫ 🅿. 🏋. ◪ AE ⓞ VISA
   M a la carte 9.45/11.70 t. ◊ 3.50 – **112 rm** ⊑ 35.90/44.00 st. – SB (weekends only) 41.00 st.

   at Sandiacre (Derbs.) SW : 8 m. on A 52 – AZ – ✉ ✆ 0602 Nottingham :

🏨 **Post House** (T.H.F.), Bostocks Lane, NG10 5NJ, ℰ 397800, Telex 377378 – 📺 ⇔wc ☎ 🅿.
   🏋. ◪ AE ⓞ VISA
   M *(closed Saturday lunch and Sunday dinner)* 4.20/5.95 st. ◊ 2.60 – ⊑ 5.00 – **106 rm**
   39.00/46.00 st.

ALFA-ROMEO Lortas Rd, New Basford ℰ 705555
AUSTIN-ROVER 136 Burton Rd, Carlton ℰ 617111
AUSTIN-ROVER-DAIMLER-JAGUAR,   ROLLS
ROYCE-BENTLEY Derby Rd ℰ 787701
BMW 165 Huntington St. ℰ 582831
CITROEN, FIAT, LANCIA 333 Mansfield Rd ℰ 621000
COLT 61a Mansfield Rd ℰ 45635
DATSUN Woodborough Rd ℰ 623324
DATSUN Main St., Bulwell ℰ 272226
FIAT Melton Rd West, Bridgford ℰ 812269
FIAT Wilford Rd, Ruddington ℰ 844114
FORD Lower Parliament St. ℰ 56282
MERCEDES-BENZ Loughborough Rd ℰ 822333
PEUGEOT-TALBOT Lenton Lane ℰ 863301

PEUGEOT-TALBOT 134/138 Loughborough Rd ℰ
814320
RENAULT Ilkestone Rd ℰ 781938
RENAULT Sawley, Long Eaton ℰ 060 76 (Long
Eaton) 3121
RENAULT Clifton Lane, Clifton ℰ 211228
SAAB 499/509 Woodborough Rd ℰ 606674
VAUXHALL-OPEL 5 Haywood Rd, Mapperley ℰ
603231
VAUXHALL-OPEL Main St., Bulwell ℰ 277031
VOLVO 50 Plains Rd ℰ 266336
VOLVO 131 Alfreton Rd ℰ 708181
VW, AUDI 180 Loughborough Rd ℰ 813813

NUNEATON Warw. 🅰🅾🅱 🅰🅾🅰 P 26 – pop. 67,027 – ECD : Thursday – ✆ 0203.

Envir. : Arbury Hall★ (Gothic house 18C) *AC*, SW : 4 m.

🚠 Burbage Common, Leicester Rd, Hinckley ℰ 0455 (Hinckley) 615124, NE : 6 m.

🖪 Public Library, Church St. ℰ 384027.

♦London 107 – ♦Birmingham 25 – ♦Coventry 10 – ♦Leicester 18.

🏨 **Chase (Golden Oak), Higham Lane,** CV11 6AG, NE : 1 m. by A 47 ℰ 341013, 🌳 – 📺 ⇔wc
   ☎ 🅿. 🏋. ◪ AE VISA – **28 rm**.

🏨 **Longshoot Motel,** Watling St., CV11 6JH, NE : 2 ½ m. on A 47 at junction with A 5 ℰ
   329711, Telex 311100 – 📺 ⇔wc ☎ ᵫ 🅿. ◪ AE ⓞ VISA. ⋘
   M (carving rest.) 4.75 – **47 rm** ⊑ 26.50/33.50 t.

AUSTIN-ROVER-JAGUAR Weddington Rd ℰ
383471
FIAT Haunchwood Rd ℰ 382807
RENAULT Nuneaton Rd, Bulkington ℰ 383344

TALBOT 208/214 Edward St. ℰ 383339
TOYOTA 45 Attleborough Rd ℰ 382241
VOLVO Watling St. ℰ 385757

NUNNINGTON North Yorks. 🅰🅾🅱 R 21 – see Helmsley.

OADBY Leics. 🅰🅾🅱 🅰🅾🅱 🅰🅾🅱 Q 26 – see Leicester.

OAKFORDBRIDE Devon – see Tiverton.

OAKHAM Leics. 402 404 R 25 – pop. 6,414 – ECD : Thursday – ☎ 0572.
🛈 Public Library, Catmos St. ☎ 2918.
♦London 103 – ♦Leicester 26 – Northampton 35 – ♦Nottingham 28.

 🏨 **Crown** (Best Western), 16 High St., LE15 6AL, ☎ 3631 – 📺 ⌦wc ☎ 🅿 🏛 🛺 AE ① VISA
 M 6.00/8.50 t. ♪ 2.85 – **25 rm** ⚡ 24.00/44.00 t. – SB (weekends only) 38.00/41.00 st.

 at Hambleton E : 3 m. by A 606 – ⊠ ☎ 0572 Oakham :

 🏰 ※ **Hambleton Hall** ⌖, LE15 8TH, ☎ 56991, Telex 342888, ≼ Rutland water, ↖, 🐎, park, ※
 – 🕭 📺 ☎ 🅿 🛺 AE ① VISA ⨯
 M 17.50/22.00 st. ♪ 4.50 – ⚡ 2.00 – **15 rm** 55.00/95.00 st.
 Spec. Slices of wild duck and foie gras salad (September-February), Tartlet of mushrooms glazed with a veil of
 truffed Sabayon (Sept-Nov), A forbidden melting heart of warm blueberries and clotted cream (July-Oct).

AUSTIN-ROVER-LAND ROVER Burley Rd ☎ 2657

OAKHILL Somerset 403 404 M 30 – see Shepton Mallet.

OAKLEY Hants. 403 404 Q 30 – see Basingstoke.

OBORNE Dorset 403 404 M 31 – see Sherborne.

OCKHAM Surrey 404 ⊛ – pop. 447 – ⊠ Ripley – ☎ 0483 Guildford.
♦London 29 – Guildford 8.

 XXX **Hautboy Inn,** Alms Heath, GU23 6NP, ☎ 225355, Dancing (Friday and Saturday) – 🅿 🛺
 AE ① VISA
 closed Sunday dinner, Monday, last 2 weeks August and Bank Holidays – **M** a la carte
 10.20/13.75 ♪ 2.25.

ODIHAM Hants. 404 R 30 – pop. 4,310 – ECD : Wednesday – ☎ 025 671.
♦London 51 – Reading 16 – Winchester 25.

 XX **Mill House,** North Warnborough, RG25 1ET, NW : 17 m. by A 287 on A 32 ☎ 2953, ≼,
 « Riverside terrace and gardens » – 🅿 🛺 ① VISA
 closed Sunday, Monday and 26 December-14 January – **M** a la carte 11.30/15.65 t. ♪ 3.00.

MERCEDES-BENZ The Square ☎ 2294

ODSTOCK Wilts. 403 404 O 30 – see Salisbury.

OLDHAM Greater Manchester 402 404 N 23 – pop. 105,913 – ECD : Tuesday – ☎ 061 Manches-
ter.
🛅 Lees New Rd ☎ 624 4986 – 🛅 Crompton and Royton, High Barn ☎ 624 2154 – 🛅 Saddleworth,
Uppermill ☎ 045 77 (Saddleworth) 2059, E : 5 m.
🛈 Local Studies Library, 84 Union St. ☎ 678 4654.
♦London 212 – ♦Leeds 36 – ♦Manchester 7 – ♦Sheffield 38.

 🏨 **Bower,** Hollinwood Av., OL9 8DE, SW : 2 ½ m. by A 62 on A 6104 ☎ 682 7254, Telex 666883,
 🐎 – 📺 ⌦wc ⌦wc ☎ 🅿 🏛 🛺 AE ① VISA
 closed 24 to 30 December – **M** (closed Saturday lunch) 6.50/7.50 st. ♪ 3.00 – **50 rm**
 ⚡ 36.00/48.00 st. – SB (weekends only) 47.00/87.00 st.

 🏨 **Belgrade,** Manchester St., OL8 1UZ, ☎ 624 0555, Telex 667782 – 🕭 📺 ⌦wc ☎ 🅿 🏛 🛺
 AE ① VISA ⨯
 M 5.50/9.00 t. ♪ 3.15 – **130 rm** ⚡ 33.00/38.00 t.

RENAULT Manchester Rd, Hollinwood ☎ 624 1979

OLLERTON Notts. 402 403 404 Q 24 – pop. 9,170 – ECD : Thursday – ⊠ Newark – ☎ 0623
Mansfield.
🛅 Woodhouse ☎ 0623 (Mansfield) 33362, SW : 7 m.
♦London 151 – ♦Leeds 53 – Lincoln 25 – ♦Nottingham 19 – ♦Sheffield 27.

 🕭 **Hop Pole,** Main St., NG22 9AD, ☎ 822573 – 🕭 🅿 🛺 VISA ⨯
 M (carving rest.) 3.95/5.20 st. ♪ 2.40 – **12 rm** ⚡ 14.00/27.00 t.

ORFORD Suffolk 404 Y 27 – pop. 673 – ECD : Wednesday – ⊠ Woodbridge – ☎ 039 45.
♦London 93 – ♦Ipswich 20 – ♦Norwich 48.

 🏨 **Crown and Castle** (T.H.F.), Market Hill, IP12 2LJ, ☎ 205, 🐎 – 📺 ⌦wc ☎ 🅿 🛺 AE ①
 VISA
 M (buffet lunch Monday to Saturday) 6.50/8.95 st. ♪ 2.60 – ⚡ 4.75 – **20 rm** 25.00/40.00 st.

Für die 🏰🏰 , 🏰🏰 , 🏰🏰 , geben wir keine Einzelheiten
über die Einrichtung an,
da diese Hotels im allgemeinen jeden Komfort besitzen.

⌦wc 🞀wc

☎

OSWESTRY Salop 402 403 K 25 — pop. 13,000 — ECD : Thursday — ☎ 0691.

🛅 at Llanymynech ℰ 0691 (Llanymynech) 830542, S : 5 m.

🛈 Little Chef rest., A 5, Babbinswood Whittington ℰ 662488 (summer only) — Library, Arthur St. ℰ 662753.

♦London 182 — Chester 28 — Shrewsbury 18.

🏠 **Wynnstay** (T.H.F.), 43 Church St., SY11 2SZ, ℰ 655261, 🚗 — 📺 📠wc 🅿 🛂 🔊 AE ⓞ **VISA**
M *(closed Saturday lunch)* a la carte 8.95/13.20 **st.** 🍷 2.60 — 🖵 4.75 — **31 rm** 26.00/38.00 **st.**

🏚 **Ashfield Country**, Llwyn-y-Maen, Trefonen Rd, SY10 9DD, SW : 1 ½ m. ℰ 655200, ≤, 🚗 — 📠wc 🅿
M *(dinner only)* 10.00 **t.** 🍷 3.50 — **14 rm** 🖵 18.00/32.00 **t.** — SB (except summer) 56.00/64.00 **st.**

at Rhydycroesau W : 3 ½ m. on B 4580 — ⊠ ☎ 0691 Oswestry :

🏠 **Pen-y-Dyffryn Hall** 🌤, SY10 7DT, ℰ 653700, ≤, 🚗 — 🅿. 🔊 **VISA** ⚡
M *(closed Sunday dinner and Monday to non-residents)* a la carte 7.10/10.50 **t.** 🍷 2.30 — **6 rm**
🖵 14.00/25.00 **t.**

ALFA-ROMEO Gobowen ℰ 61233
AUDI, VW Queenshead ℰ 069 188 (Queenshead) 481
AUSTIN-ROVER Lower Brook St. ℰ 652285
BMW Victoria Rd ℰ 652413
FORD Salop Rd ℰ 654141
HONDA ℰ 653491

LANCIA Gobowen ℰ 61233
PEUGEOT-TALBOT Llansantffraid-Ym-Mechain ℰ 069 181 (Llansantffraid) 283
PEUGEOT-TALBOT Willow St. ℰ 652301
VAUXHALL-OPEL Smithfield St. ℰ 652235
VOLVO West Felton ℰ 069 188 (Queens Head) 451

OTTERBURN Northumb. 401 402 N 18 — pop. 564 — ECD : Thursday — ☎ 0830.

♦London 314 — ♦Carlisle 54 — ♦Edinburgh 74 — ♦Newcastle-upon-Tyne 31.

🏠 **Percy Arms**, NE19 1NR, ℰ 20261, Telex 57515, 🐟, 🚗 — 📠wc 🕸 🅿. 🛂 🔊 AE ⓞ **VISA** ⚡
M *(bar lunch)* 12.00 **t.** 🍷 2.00 — **30 rm** 🖵 24.50/44.00 **t.** — SB (weekends only) 50.00/58.00 **st.**

OTTERY ST MARY Devon 403 K 31 The West Country G. — pop. 5,834 — ECD : Wednesday — ☎ 040 481.

See : Site ★ — St. Mary's Church ★★.

♦London 167 — Exeter 12 — Bournemouth 71 — ♦Plymouth 53 — Taunton 23.

XX **The Lodge**, 17 Silver St., EX11 1DB, ℰ 2356 — AE ⓞ **VISA**
closed Sunday dinner and Monday — **M** 15.50 **t.**

OULTON West Yorks. 402 ⑩ — see Leeds.

OULTON Suffolk — see Lowestoft.

OUNDLE Northants. 404 S 26 — pop. 3,739 — ECD : Wednesday — ⊠ Peterborough — ☎ 0832.

♦London 89 — ♦Leicester 37 — Northampton 30.

🏠 **Talbot** (Anchor), New St., PE8 4EA, ℰ 73621, Group Telex 32364, 🚗 — 📺 📠wc 🕸 🅿. 🛂
🔊 AE ⓞ **VISA**
M a la carte 8.10/12.75 **st.** 🍷 2.65 — **38 rm** 🖵 33.00/45.00 **st.** — SB (weekends only) 48.00 **st.**

X **Tyrrells**, 6-8 New St., PE8 4EA, ℰ 72347 — 🔊 AE **VISA**
closed Sunday dinner, Monday lunch and Bank Holidays — **M** a la carte 10.40/12.60 **st.** 🍷 3.00.

AUSTIN-ROVER, FORD 1 Station Rd ℰ 73542   AUSTIN-ROVER 1 Benefield Rd ℰ 73519

OUTLANE West Yorks. — see Huddersfield.

OWERMOIGNE Dorset 403 404 N 32 — see Dorchester.

OWLSWICK Bucks. 404 R 28 — ⊠ Aylesbury — ☎ 084 44 Princes Risborough.

♦London 47 — ♦Oxford 20.

🏠 **Shoulder of Mutton** 🌤, HP17 9RH, ℰ 4304, Telex 837002, 🚗 — 📺 📠wc 🕸 🅿. 🔊 AE ⓞ
VISA ⚡
M *(closed Sunday to non-residents)* (bar lunch) 10.00 **t.** — **20 rm** 🖵 26.00/45.00 **t.** — SB (except Christmas) 42.00/48.00 **st.**

OXFORD Oxon. 403 404 Q 28 — pop. 108,805 — ECD : Thursday — ☎ 0865.

See : Colleges Quarter★★★ : Merton College★, (Old Library★★★, hall★, quadrangle★, chapel windows and glass★)BZ — Christchurch College★ (hall★★, cathedral★, quadrangle★, tower★) BZ — Bodleian Old Library★★ (painted ceiling★★) BZ M2 — Divinity School (carved vaulting★★) BZ M2 — Magdalen College★★ (cloister★★, chapel★) BZ — New College (cloister★, chapel★) BZ Y — All Souls College (chapel★) BZ A — University College (gateway★) BZ V — Corpus Christi College (quadrangle and sundial★) BZ E — Radcliffe Camera★ BZ O — Sheldonian Theatre★ BZ M3 — High Street★ BZ — Ashmolean Museum★★ BY M1.

🛅 Banbury Rd ℰ 54415, N : by A 423 AY.

🛈 St. Aldates Chambers, St. Aldates ℰ 726871 — Erskine Bureaux Ltd., Oxford Railway Station ℰ 242222.

♦London 58 — ♦Birmingham 63 — ♦Brighton 106 — ♦Bristol 73 — ♦Cardiff 103 — ♦Coventry 48 — ♦Southampton 64.

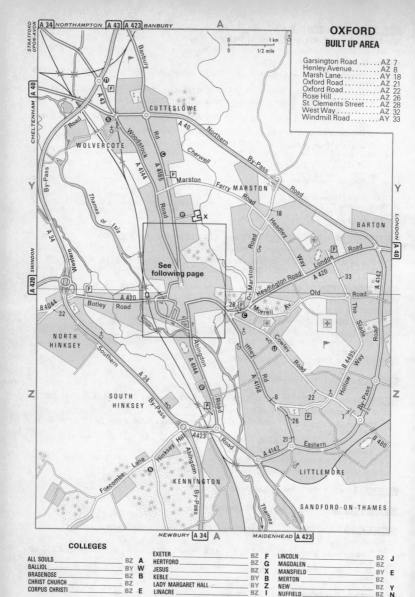

OXFORD
BUILT UP AREA

Garsington Road .... AZ 7
Henley Avenue .... AZ 8
Marsh Lane.............. AY 18
Oxford Road .... AZ 21
Oxford Road .... AZ 22
Rose Hill .... AZ 26
St. Clements Street ...... AZ 28
West Way .... AZ 32
Windmill Road .... AY 33

COLLEGES

ALL SOULS _____ BZ **A**	EXETER _____ BZ **F**	LINCOLN _____ BZ **J**
BALLIOL _____ BY **W**	HERTFORD _____ BZ **G**	MAGDALEN _____ BZ
BRASENOSE _____ BZ **B**	JESUS _____ BZ **X**	MANSFIELD _____ BY **E**
CHRIST CHURCH _____ BZ	KEBLE _____ BY **B**	MERTON _____ BZ
CORPUS CHRISTI _____ BZ **E**	LADY MARGARET HALL _____ BY **Z**	NEW _____ BZ **Y**
	LINACRE _____ BZ **I**	NUFFIELD _____ BZ **N**

🏨 **Randolph** (T.H.F.), Beaumont St., OX1 2LN, ℰ 247481, Telex 83446 – ﹛≡﹜ 📺 ⇦ – 🕍 ⎅ AE ① VISA
　　BZ **n**
　　M 5.75/12.40 **st.** ⌁ 3.15 – ⇆ 5.50 – **109 rm** 42.00/52.50 **st.**

🏨 **Cotswold Lodge,** 66a Banbury Rd, OX2 6JP, ℰ 512120 – 📺 ⎅wc ☎ 🅿 🕍 ⎅ AE ①
　　VISA ❀　　BY **i**
　　closed 26 December-1 January – **M** 8.30/9.80 **t.** ⌁ 2.75 – **52 rm** ⇆ 38.50/49.50 **t.** – SB (week-
　　ends only) 67.50/75.00 **st.**

🏨 **Eastgate** (Anchor), The High, OX1 4BE, ℰ 248244, Group Telex 83302 – ﹛≡﹜ 📺 ⎅wc ☎ 🅿
　　⎅ AE ① VISA　　BZ **z**
　　M (carving lunch) 8.65 **st.** ⌁ 2.65 – **37 rm** ⇆ 40.50/48.00 **st.** – SB 56.00 **st.**

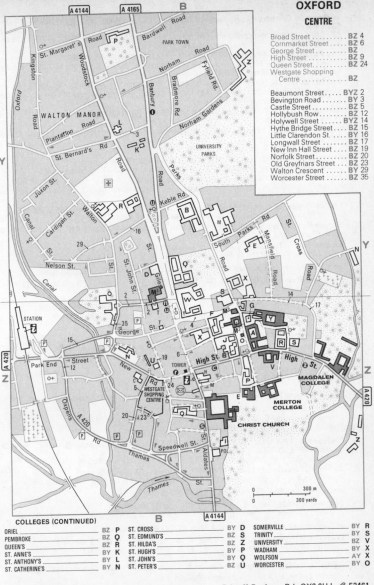

CENTRE

Broad Street . . . . BZ 4
Cornmarket Street . . . . . BZ 6
George Street . . . . BZ
High Street . . . . BZ 9
Queen Street. . . . . BZ 24
Westgate Shopping
Centre . . . . BZ

Beaumont Street . . . . . BYZ 2
Bevington Road . . . . . . BY 3
Castle Street . . . . BZ 5
Hollybush Row . . . . BZ 12
Holywell Street . . . . . BYZ 14
Hythe Bridge Street . . . . BZ 15
Little Clarendon St. . . . . BY 16
Longwall Street . . . . . . BZ 17
New Inn Hall Street . . . BZ 19
Norfolk Street . . . . BZ 20
Old Greyfriars Street . . . BZ 23
Walton Crescent . . . . . . BY 29
Worcester Street . . . . . . BZ 35

COLLEGES (CONTINUED)

ORIEL	BZ P	ST. CROSS	BY D	SOMERVILLE	BY R
PEMBROKE	BZ Q	ST. EDMUND'S	BZ S	TRINITY	BY S
QUEEN'S	BZ R	ST. HILDA'S	BZ Z	UNIVERSITY	BZ V
ST. ANNE'S	BY K	ST. HUGH'S	BY P	WADHAM	BY X
ST. ANTHONY'S	BY L	ST. JOHN'S	BY Q	WOLFSON	AY X
ST. CATHERINE'S	BY N	ST. PETER'S	BZ U	WORCESTER	BY O

🏨 **Ladbroke Linton Lodge** (Ladbroke), 9-13 Linton Rd, off Banbury Rd, OX2 6UJ, 𝓟 53461, Telex 837093, 🍴 – 劇 📺 ⌂wc ☎ ♿ 🅿 🅰 🔼 🔝 AE ⓘ 𝘝𝘐𝘚𝘈   AY **e**
M (bar lunch) 9.00 t. ♨ 3.75 – ⌸ 5.50 – **72 rm** 38.00/49.00 **st.** – SB (weekends only) 38.00/49.00 **st.**

🏨 **Oxford Moat House** (Q.M.H.), Wolvercote Roundabout, OX2 8AL, N : 2 ½ m. at junction A 40 and A 4144 𝓟 59933, Telex 837926 – 📺 ⌂wc ☎ 🅿 🅰 🔼 AE ⓘ 𝘝𝘐𝘚𝘈   AY **s**
M 5.25/7.25 **st.** ♨ 2.50 – **155 rm** ⌸ 38.00/48.00 **st.**

🏨 **TraveLodge** (T.H.F.) without rest., Pear Tree Roundabout, Woodstock Rd, OX2 8JU, N : 3 m. at junction of A 34 and A 43 𝓟 54301, Telex 83202, 🔼 heated – 📺 ⌂wc ♿ 🅰 🅿 🅰 🔼 AE   AY **n**
ⓘ 𝘝𝘐𝘚𝘈 – **100 rm** ⌸ 30.00/40.00 **st.**

Westwood Country 🌿, Hinksey Hill Top, OX1 5BG, ☎ 735408, 🌳 – [TV] 🛁wc 🚿wc ♿ [P]. [CB] [AE] [VISA]. 🚫🐕 AZ **s**
closed 1 to 16 June and Christmas – **M** (bar lunch) (booking essential) 10.00 **t.** 🍷 2.00 – **16 rm** 🛏 23.00/35.00 **t.** – SB (winter only) 42.00 **st.**

Old Parsonage, 1-3 Banbury Rd, OX2 6NN, ☎ 54843, 🌳 – [P]. [CB] [DC] [VISA] BY **u**
closed Christmas – **M** *(closed Sunday dinner)* (dinner only and Sunday lunch) a la carte 4.90/9.30 **t.** 🍷 3.00 – **34 rm** 🛏 16.00/36.00 **t.**

Old Black Horse, 102 St. Clements, OX4 1AR, ☎ 244691 – [TV] 🛁wc 🚿wc [P]. [CB] [DC] [VISA]
closed 23 December-2 January – **M** *(closed Sunday dinner)* (bar lunch) 9.00 **st.** – **8 rm** 🛏 27.50/42.50 **t.** AZ **c**

Earlmont, 322-324 Cowley Rd, OX4 2AF, ☎ 240236 – [TV] 🚿 [P]. 🚫🐕 AZ **u**
11 rm 🛏 9.00/20.00 **st.**

Willow Reaches, 1 Wytham St., via Norrey's Av., OX1 4SU, ☎ 721545 – [TV] 🛁wc. [AE] [DC] [VISA]. 🚫🐕 AZ **e**
closed Christmas – **8 rm** 🛏 12.00/28.00 **st.**

🍴🍴🍴 **Elizabeth,** 84 St. Aldates, OX1 1RA, ☎ 242230 – [CB] [AE] [DC] [VISA] BZ **s**
closed Monday, 5 April and 24 to 31 December – **M** a la carte 14.20/19.50 **st.** 🍷 4.75.

🍴🍴 **Le Petit Blanc,** 272 Banbury Rd, Summertown, OX2 7DY, ☎ 53540, French rest. – [CB] [VISA]
closed Monday lunch, Sunday, first 2 weeks August and 24 December-7 January – **M** (booking essential) 13.50/17.50 **t.** AY **c**

🍴🍴 **La Sorbonne,** 1st floor, 130a High St., OX1 4DH, ☎ 241320, French rest. – [CB] [AE] [DC] [VISA]
closed 10 days at Christmas and New Year – **M** a la carte 6.95/17.30 **st.** 🍷 3.30. BZ **c**

🍴🍴 **Saraceno,** 15 Magdalen St., OX1 3AE, ☎ 249171, Italian rest. – [AE] [DC] [VISA] BZ **u**
closed Sunday and Bank Holidays – **M** a la carte 10.30/13.50 **t.** 🍷 2.80.

🍴 **La Cantina,** 34 Queen St., OX1 1ER, ☎ 247760, Italian rest. – [CB] [DC] [VISA] BZ **r**
closed Monday and 24 December-1 January – **M** a la carte 7.60/14.65 **t.** 🍷 2.65.

at Kidlington N : 4 ½ m. on A 4237 – AY – ✉ Oxford – ☎ 086 75 Kidlington :

Bowood House, 238 Oxford Rd, OX5 1EB, ☎ 2839, 🏊 heated, 🌳 – [TV] 🛁wc 🚿wc [P]. 🚫🐕
9 rm 🛏 11.50/28.00 **t.**

at Cumnor SW : 4 ½ m. by A 420 – AY – off B 4017 – ✉ Oxford – ☎ 0865 Cumnor :

🍴🍴 **Bear and Ragged Staff,** Appleton Rd, OX2 9QH, ☎ 862329 – [P]. [CB] [AE] [DC] [VISA]
closed Sunday dinner – **M** a la carte 10.55/14.45 **t.** 🍷 2.55.

Hotel and restaurant see : Great Milton E : 11 m.

AUDI, VW Abingdon Rd ☎ 242241
AUSTIN-ROVER Oxford Rd, Kidlington ☎ 086 75 (Kidlington) 4363
CITROEN 281 Banbury Rd ☎ 512277
DATSUN 72 Rose Hill ☎ 774696
MERCEDES-BENZ Banbury Rd, Shipton-on-Cherwell ☎ 086 75 (Kidlington) 71011
SAAB 75 Woodstock Rd ☎ 57028
VAUXHALL-OPEL Woodstock Rd ☎ 59955
VOLVO 265 Iffley Rd ☎ 440101

PADSTOW Cornwall [403] F 32 The West Country G. – pop. 2,802 – ECD : Wednesday – ☎ 0841.

See : Site ★.

Envir. : Trevone (Cornwall Coast Path ★★) – Trevose Head ★ (<★★), W : 6 m.

♦London 288 – Exeter 78 – ♦Plymouth 45 – Truro 23.

Metropole (T.H.F.), Station Rd, PL28 8DB, ☎ 532486, < Camel Estuary, 🏊 heated, 🌳 – [lift] [TV] 🛁wc ☎ ♿ [P]. [CB] [AE] [DC] [VISA]
March-October – **M** (bar lunch) 7.95 **st.** 🍷 2.85 – 🛏 5.00 – **44 rm** 29.50/46.00 **st.**

🍴🍴 **Seafood,** Riverside, PL28 8BY, ☎ 532485, Seafood – [CB] [AE] [DC] [VISA]
March-October – **M** *(closed Saturday lunch and Sunday)* a la carte 12.55/14.80 **t.** 🍷 2.60.

at Constantine Bay SW : 4 m. by B 3276 – ✉ ☎ 0841 Padstow :

Treglos 🌿, PL28 8JH, ☎ 520727, <, [🏊], 🌳 – [lift] [TV] ☎ 🚗 [P]
21 March-3 November – **M** 7.00/9.50 **t.** 🍷 2.25 – **43 rm** 🛏 22.50/66.00 **t.** – SB 55.00/79.00 **st.**

at Treyarnon Bay SW : 4 ¾ m. by A 3276 – ✉ ☎ 0841 Padstow :

Waterbeach 🌿, PL28 8JW, ☎ 520292, <, 🌳, 🎾 – 🛁wc 🚿 [P]. [CB] [VISA]. 🚫🐕
Mid May-October – **M** (bar lunch) 9.25 **t.** 🍷 1.50 – **16 rm** 🛏 19.00/42.00 **t.**

PAIGNTON Devon [403] J 32 The West Country G. – pop. 35,100 – ECD : Wednesday – ☎ 0803.

See : Paignton Zoo★★, by A 385 Z – Kirkham House★ Y B.

[i] Festival Hall, Esplanade Rd ☎ 558383.

♦London 226 – Exeter 26 – ♦Plymouth 29.

Plan of Built up Area : see Torbay

Palace (T.H.F.), Esplanade Rd, TQ4 6BJ, ☎ 555121, 🏊 heated, 🌳, 🎾, squash – [lift] [TV] [P]. [CB] [AE] [DC] [VISA] Y **e**
M (buffet lunch) 8.00 **st.** 🍷 2.60 – 🛏 5.00 – **54 rm** 30.50/47.00 **st.**

Redcliffe, 4 Marine Drive, TQ3 2NL, ☎ 526397, < Torbay, 🏊 heated, 🌳 – [lift] [P]. 🏛. [CB] [AE] [VISA] Y **n**
M (buffet lunch in summer) 4.75/7.25 **t.** 🍷 2.95 – **57 rm** 🛏 20.00/54.00 **t.** – SB 44.00/62.00 **st.**

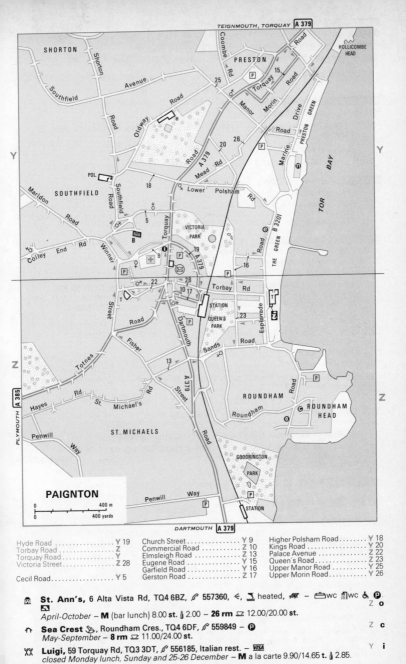

PAIGNTON

0 ———— 400 m
0 ———— 400 yards

🏛 **St. Ann's,** 6 Alta Vista Rd, TQ4 6BZ, 🖉 557360, ≤, 🏊 heated, 🐎 – 🛏wc 🚽wc 🕭 🅿.
        Z **o**
🔲
    April-October – **M** (bar lunch) 8.00 **st.** 🍷 2.00 – **26 rm** 🖃 12.00/20.00 **st.**

⌂ **Sea Crest** 🐾, Roundham Cres., TQ4 6DF, 🖉 559849 – 🅿
        Z **c**
    May-September – **8 rm** 🖃 11.00/24.00 **st.**
        Y **i**

XX **Luigi,** 59 Torquay Rd, TQ3 3DT, 🖉 556185, Italian rest. – 💳
    closed Monday lunch, Sunday and 25-26 December – **M** a la carte 9.90/14.65 **t.** 🍷 2.85.

AUSTIN-ROVER 69 Torquay Rd 🖉 551818
BMW 349 Totnes Rd, Collaton St. Mary 🖉 558567
HONDA Totnes Rd 🖉 554484

MERCEDES-BENZ, COLT Bishop's Pl. 🖉 556234
VOLVO 59 Totnes Rd 🖉 559362

PAINSWICK Glos. [403] [404] N 28 – pop. 2,895 – ECD : Saturday – ✉ Stroud – ✆ 0452.

[i] The Library, Stroud Rd ✆ 812569.

♦London 107 – ♦Bristol 35 – Cheltenham 10 – Gloucester 7.

🏨 **Painswick** 🐦, Kemps Lane, Tibiwell, GL6 6YB, ✆ 812160, Telex 43605, 🌳 – [TV] 🛁wc ☎ [P]. [S] [AE] [O] [VISA]
M *(closed Sunday dinner to non-residents)* (buffet lunch Monday to Saturday) 4.80/12.00 **t.** 🍷 2.50 – **15 rm** ☕ 26.00/50.00 **t.** – SB 45.00/64.00 **st.**

PANGBOURNE Berks. [403] [404] Q 29 – pop. 2,503 – ECD : Thursday – ✆ 073 57.

♦London 56 – ♦Oxford 22 – Reading 6.

🏨 **Copper Inn** (Best Western), 2 Church Rd, RG8 7AR, ✆ 2244, Telex 849041, 🌳 – [TV] 🛁wc ☎ [P]. 🏢. [S] [AE] [O] [VISA]. 🚫
M a la carte 11.50/16.25 **t.** 🍷 3.05 – ☕ 4.75 – **21 rm** 36.50/44.50 **st.** – SB (weekends only) 49.50 **st.**

AUSTIN-ROVER Reading Rd ✆ 2376 MERCEDES-BENZ Station Rd ✆ 3322

PANT MAWR Powys [403] I 26 – ✉ ✆ 055 15 Llangurig.

♦London 219 – Aberystwyth 21 – Shrewsbury 55.

🏨 **Glansevern Arms,** SY18 6SY, on A 44 ✆ 240, ≤, 🎣 – [P]
closed 1 week at Christmas – **M** *(closed Sunday dinner to non-residents)* (booking essential) 7.50/10.00 **t.** 🍷 2.50 – **7 rm** ☕ 17.00/27.50 **t.** – SB (winter only) 34.00 **st.**

PARKGATE Cheshire [402] [403] K 24 – pop. 2,939 (inc. Leighton) – ECD : Wednesday – ✉ Wirral – ✆ 051 Liverpool.

⛳18 Cottage Lane, Gayton, Heswall ✆ 342 2193, NW : 1 ½ m.

♦London 207 – Birkenhead 10 – Chester 11 – ♦Liverpool 12.

🏨 **Ship** (Anchor), The Parade, L64 6SA, ✆ 336 3931 – [TV] 🛁wc ☎ [P]. [S] [AE] [O] [VISA]
M a la carte 8.10/12.75 **st.** 🍷 2.65 – **26 rm** ☕ 31.00/42.00 **st.** – SB (weekends only) 48.00 **st.**

🍴🍴 **Mr Chow's,** The Parade, L64 6SL, ✆ 336 2385, Chinese rest. – [S] [AE] [O] [VISA]
closed 25-26 December – **M** (booking essential)(dinner only) a la carte 6.10/14.20 **t.** 🍷 2.40.

PATELEY BRIDGE North Yorks. [402] O 21 – pop. 2,419 – ✉ ✆ 0423 Harrogate.

Envir. : Brimham Rocks★ E : 4 ½ m.

[i] Southlands Car Park ✆ 711147 (summer only).

♦London 225 – ♦Leeds 28 – ♦Middlesbrough 46 – York 32.

🏠 **Grassfield Country House** 🐦, Ramsgill Rd, HG3 5HL, ✆ 711412, 🌳 – 🛁wc 🚿wc [P]
March-October – **9 rm** ☕ 14.50/30.00 **st.**

at Low Laithe SE : 2 ¾ m. on B 6165 – ✉ ✆ 0423 Harrogate :

🍴🍴 **Dusty Miller,** Main Rd, HG3 4BU, ✆ 780837 – [S] [VISA]
closed Sunday and Monday – **M** (dinner only) a la carte 7.45/15.10 **t.**

at Wath-in-Nidderdale NW : 2 ¼ m. – ✉ ✆ 0423 Harrogate :

🍴🍴 **Sportsman's Arms** 🐦 with rm, HG3 5PP, ✆ 711306, 🌳 – [P]. [S] [AE] [O] [VISA]
M *(closed Sunday dinner)* (bar lunch Monday to Saturday) a la carte 11.35/13.80 **t.** 🍷 2.50 – **6 rm** ☕ 14.00/26.00 **t.**

PATTINGHAM Staffs. [402] [403] [404] N 26 – see Wolverhampton (W. Midlands).

PEASLAKE Surrey [404] S 30 – see Dorking.

PEASMARSH East Sussex [404] W 31 – see Rye.

PEMBROKE (PENFRO) Dyfed [403] F 28 – pop. 14,197 – ECD : Wednesday – ✆ 064 63 (4 fig.) 0646 (6 fig.).

See : Site★ – Castle★★.

Envir. : Lamphey (Bishop's palace★) *AC*, E : 2 m. – Carew (castle★ 13C) *AC*, NE : 4 ½ m.

⛳9 Defensible Barracks, Pembroke Dock ✆ 3817.

⛴ to Ireland (Rosslare) (B & I Line) 1-2 daily (4 h 15 mn).

[i] Pembrokeshire Coast National Park, Drill Hall, Main St. ✆ 2148 (summer only).

♦London 252 – Carmarthen 32 – Fishguard 26.

🏨 **Underdown Country House** 🐦, Grove Hill, SA71 5PR, ✆ 683350, « Antiques and gardens » – [TV] 🛁wc 🚿wc [P]. [S] [VISA]
closed 24 December-2 January – **M** *(Sunday lunch and dinner by arrangement)* (booking essential) a la carte approx. 8.80 **t.** 🍷 2.10 – **6 rm** ☕ 18.50/28.50 **t.** – SB 44.00/54.00 **st.**

🏨 **Old Kings Arms,** 13 Main St., SA72 4UQ, ✆ 3611 – [TV] 🛁wc ☎ [P]. [S] [AE] [VISA]
closed 25-26 December and 1 January – **M** a la carte 8.15/12.20 **st.** 🍷 1.95 – **21 rm** ☕ 18.95/28.00 **st.**

at Lamphey E : 1 ¾ m. on A 4139 – ⊠ Pembroke – ✆ 0646 Lamphey :

🏨 **Court** (Best Western) ⟲, SA71 5NT, 𝄞 672273, ⅃, ▧, ☞ – 📺 ⌂wc ☎ ℗ ⛴ 🅰🄴 ⑩ 𝗩𝗜𝗦𝗔
M (bar lunch) 9.50 **st.** ⋀ 2.85 – ⚍ 3.50 – **22 rm** 23.00/35.50 **st.** – SB 42.00/56.00 **st.**

at Pembroke Dock NW : 2 m. on A 4139 – ⊠ ✆ 0646 Pembroke :

🏨 **Cleddau Bridge,** Essex Rd, SA72 6UT, NE : 1 m. by A 4139 on A 477 (at Toll Bridge)
𝄞 685961, ⅃ heated – 📺 ⌂wc ☎ ℗ ⛴ ⛴ 🅰🄴 ⑩ 𝗩𝗜𝗦𝗔
M a la carte 8.25/11.25 **st.** ⋀ 2.40 – **24 rm** ⚍ 29.50/39.50 **st.**

PEMBROKESHIRE (Coast) ★★ Dyfed 𝟰𝟬𝟯 E 27 28.

See : From Cemaes Head to Strumble Head★★ : Newport (site★) – Bryn Henllan (site★) – Goodwick
⇐★★ – Strumble Head (⇐★★ from the lighthouse). From Strumble Head to Solva★★ : Trevine ⇐★★
– Porthgain (cliffs ☀★★★) – Abereiddy (site★) – St. David's Head★★ – Whitesand Bay★★ – Solva
(site★). From Solva to Dale★★ : Newgale ⇐★★ – Martin's Haven ☀★★ – St. Ann's Head ⇐★★ –
Dale ⇐★. From Dale to Freshwater West★ : Freshwater West (site★). From Freshwater West to
Pendine Sands★★ (Stack Rocks★★) – St. Govan's Chapel (site★) – Freshwater East (site★) –
Manorbier (castle★) – Tenby (site★★) – Amroth (site★) – Pendine Sands★.

PENARTH South Glam. 𝟰𝟬𝟯 K 29 – pop. 22,570 – ECD : Wednesday – ✆ 0222.

🖸 Lavernock Rd 𝄞 707048.

🄱 West House 𝄞 707201 – Piermaster's Office, The Pier 𝄞 706555 (summer only).

♦London 161 – ♦Cardiff 4.

XXX **Caprice,** 1st floor, 1 Beach Cliff, The Esplanade, CF6 2AS, 𝄞 702424, ⇐ – 🄰 🅰🄴 ⑩ 𝗩𝗜𝗦𝗔
closed Sunday and Bank Holidays – **M** a la carte 8.65/13.45 **t.** ⋀ 2.75.

X **Le Gourmand,** 6a Andrew Buildings, Stanwell Rd, CF6 2AA, 𝄞 708742 – 🄰 🅰🄴 ⑩ 𝗩𝗜𝗦𝗔
closed Sunday and Monday – **M** a la carte 7.80/13.50 **t.** ⋀ 3.00.

at Swanbridge S : 2 ½ m. by B 4267 – ⊠ Penarth – ✆ 0222 Sully :

XXX **Sully House** ⟲ with rm, Lavernock Beach Rd, St. Mary's Well Bay, CF6 2XR, 𝄞 530448, ⇐,
☞ – 📺 ⌂wc ℗. 🄰 🅰🄴 ⑩ 𝗩𝗜𝗦𝗔. ☀
M (closed Saturday lunch, Sunday and Bank Holidays) a la carte 12.10/14.60 **t.** ⋀ 3.25 – **4 rm**
⚍ 25.00/35.00 **t.**

AUSTIN-ROVER Windsor Rd 𝄞 703024

PENDOGGETT Cornwall 𝟰𝟬𝟯 F 32 – pop. 60 – ⊠ Bodmin – ✆ 020 888 Port Isaac.

♦London 264 – Newquay 22 – Truro 30.

🏠 Cornish Arms, PL30 3HH, on B 3314 𝄞 263, ☞ – ⌂wc ℗. 🄰 🅰🄴 ⑩ 𝗩𝗜𝗦𝗔. ☀
7 rm.

PENFRO = Pembroke.

PENGETHLEY Heref. and Worc. 𝟰𝟬𝟯 𝟰𝟬𝟰 M 28 – see Ross-on-Wye.

PENMAENHEAD Clwyd – see Colwyn Bay.

PENMAENPOOL Gwynedd 𝟰𝟬𝟮 𝟰𝟬𝟯 I 25 – see Dolgellau.

PENMORFA Gwynedd – see Porthmadog.

PENRITH Cumbria 𝟰𝟬𝟭 𝟰𝟬𝟮 L 19 – pop. 10,590 – ECD : Wednesday – ✆ 0768.

🄱 Robinson's School, Middlegate 𝄞 67466.

♦London 290 – ♦Carlisle 24 – Kendal 31 – Lancaster 48.

🏨 **George,** Devonshire St., CA11 7SO, 𝄞 62696 – ⌂wc 🛏wc ℗. ⛴ 🄰
closed 25-26 December and 1 January – **M** 6.55/8.65 **t.** ⋀ 2.30 – **31 rm** ⚍ 21.50/38.50 **st.** – SB
(winter and spring) (except Bank Holidays) (weekends only) 57.50 **st.**

🏠 **Abbotsford,** Wordsworth St., CA11 7QY, 𝄞 63940, ☞ – 📺 ⌂wc 🛏wc ℗. 🄰 🅰🄴 ⑩ 𝗩𝗜𝗦𝗔
M 5.00/8.00 **t.** ⋀ 2.50 – **11 rm** ⚍ 17.50/35.20 **t.** – SB (weekends only) 41.00/44.00 **st.**

↑ **Limes Country** ⟲, Redhills, Stainton, CA11 0DT, Access off A 592 𝄞 63343, ⇐, ☞ – ℗.
☀
Easter-October – **8 rm** ⚍ 10.00/22.00.

X **Passepartout,** 51 Castlegate, CA11 7HY, 𝄞 65852 – 🄰 𝗩𝗜𝗦𝗔
closed Sunday except Bank Holiday weekends and January-mid February – **M** (dinner only) a
la carte 10.40/13.40 **t.**

AUDI, CITROEN, TALBOT Ullswater Rd 𝄞 64545
AUSTIN-ROVER Victoria Rd 𝄞 63666
FIAT King St. 𝄞 64691
FORD Old London Rd 𝄞 64571

RENAULT 11 King St. 𝄞 62371
TOYOTA 15 Victoria Rd 𝄞 64555
VAUXHALL-OPEL Scotland Rd 𝄞 63756

PENSHURST Kent **404** U 30 – pop. 1,620 – ✪ 0892.

See : Penshurst Place★ (and Tudor gardens★★ 14C) *AC*.

Envir. : Chiddingstone (castle : Egyptian and Japanese collections★ *AC*) NW : 5 m. – Hever Castle★ (13C) *AC*, W : 6 m.

◆London 38 – Maidstone 19 – Royal Tunbridge Wells 6.

🏨 **Leicester Arms,** High St., TN11 8BT, ℰ 870551 – 🖵 ⇌wc 🅿. 🖾 🝙 ⓪ *VISA*
closed 24 to 27 December – **M** 6.50/8.50 t. 🄰 2.00 – **7 rm** ⇌ 22.00/33.00 t. – SB (winter only) 38.50 **st.**

at Chiddingstone NW : 5 m. by B 2176 and B 2027 – ✉ Edenbridge – ✪ 0892 Penshurst :

XX **Castle Inn,** TN8 7AH, ℰ 870247, 🖛 – 🖾 🝙 ⓪ *VISA*
closed Wednesday lunch, Tuesday and January – **M** 16.00 **st.** 🄰 2.50.

PEN-Y-BONT = Bridgend.

PENZANCE Cornwall **403** D 33 The West Country G. – pop. 19,415 – ECD : Wednesday – ✪ 0736.

See : Outlook ★★★ – Western Promenade (⩽★★★) YZ – Chapel St.★ Y – Museum of Nautical Art★ Y M1.

Envir. : St. Michael's Mount★★★, (⩽★★) E : 5 m. by A 30 Y – Trengwainton Garden★★, NW : 2 m. by B 3312 Y – Prussia Cove★, SE : 9 m. by A 30 and A 394 Y – Land's End★ (cliff scenery ★★★), SW : 10 m. by A 30 Z.

Access to the Isles of Scilly by helicopter ℰ 3871.

🚗 ℰ 5831.

⛴ to the Isles of Scilly : Hugh Town, St. Mary's (Isles of Scilly Steamship Co.) summer Monday to Saturday 1-2 daily ; winter 3 weekly (2 h 30 mn).

🄱 Alverton St. ℰ 2207 and 2341 ext 292.

◆London 319 – Exeter 113 – ◆Plymouth 77 – Taunton 153.

Plan opposite

🏩 **Queens,** Promenade, TR18 4HG, ℰ 2371, ⩽ – 🕸 🖵 ⇌wc 🅿
71 rm.   Z u

🏩 **Mount Prospect,** Britons Hill, TR18 3AE, ℰ 3117, ⩽, 🟰 heated, 🖛 – 🖵 ⇌wc 🃏wc ☎ 🅿.
🖾 🖿 ⓪ *VISA*
M 4.50/8.00 🄰 2.95 – **26 rm** ⇌ 25.00/40.00.   Y e

🏨 **Abbey,** Abbey St., TR18 4AR, ℰ 66906, 🖛 – 🖵 🃏wc 🅿   Y u
closed 10 January-1 March – **M** (dinner only) 10.95 **st.** – **6 rm** ⇌ 25.00/55.00 **st.**

🏨 **Sea and Horses,** 6 Alexandra Terr., TR18 4NX, ℰ 61961 – 🃏wc 🅿. 🛇   Z s
M (bar lunch) 5.85 **st.** – **11 rm** ⇌ 10.00/24.00 **st.**

🏨 **Alexandra,** Alexandra Terr., TR18 4NX, ℰ 62644, ⩽ – 🖵 ⇌wc 🃏wc 🕸 🅿. 🖾 🖿 *VISA*
closed Christmas – **M** (bar lunch) 6.00 **st.** 🄰 3.00 – **21 rm** ⇌ 9.00/28.00 – SB (except summer) 28.00/34.00 **st.**   Z a

↑ **Tarbert,** 11 Clarence St., TR18 2NU, ℰ 3758, 🖛 – 🃏wc. 🖾 🖿 *VISA*
12 rm ⇌ 10.50/28.00 **st.**   Y i

↑ **Dunedin,** Alexandra Rd, TR18 4LZ, ℰ 2652 – 🖵   Y r
closed December and January – **9 rm** ⇌ 7.00/17.00 t.

↑ **Kimberley House,** 10 Morrab Rd, TR18 4EZ, ℰ 2727 – 🖾 *VISA*. 🛇   Y s
closed November – **9 rm** ⇌ 8.00/18.00 **st.**

↑ **Carnson House,** 2 East Terr., Market Jew St., TR18 2TD, ℰ 65589 – 🖾 🖿 *VISA*. 🛇   Y c
closed Christmas – **6 rm** ⇌ 8.50/19.00 **st.**

XX **Harris's,** 46 New St., TR18 2LZ, ℰ 4408 – 🖿 ⓪ *VISA*   Y a
closed Monday in winter and Sunday – **M** (bar lunch) a la carte 8.95/14.55 t. 🄰 2.65.

at Newbridge NW : 3 m. on A 3071 – Y – ✉ ✪ 0736 Penzance :

XX **Enzo,** TR20 8QH, ℰ 63777, Italian rest. – 🅿. 🖾 🖿 ⓪
closed Sunday in winter and 25-26 December – **M** (dinner only) (booking essential) a la carte 7.05/10.30 t. 🄰 2.65.

at Newlyn SW : 1 ½ m. on B 3315 – Z – ✉ ✪ 0736 Penzance :

🏩 **Higher Faugan** 🐾, TR18 5NS, SW : ¾ m. on B 3315 ℰ 2076, « Country house atmosphere »,
🟰 heated, 🌳 park, 🛎 – 🖵 ⇌wc 🃏wc 🅿. 🖾 🖿 ⓪. 🛇
March-September – **M** (bar lunch) 9.20 t. 🄰 2.70 – **12 rm** ⇌ 20.50/49.40 t. – SB (spring only) 46.00 **st.**

XX **Tolcarne,** Tolcarne Terr., TR18 5QH, ℰ 66966 – 🖾 ⓪ *VISA*   Z v
closed Sunday and 2 weeks October – **M** (dinner only) a la carte 7.60/12.25 t. 🄰 2.75.

AUSTIN-ROVER Long Rock ℰ 2307
PEUGEOT, TALBOT Hayle Terr. ℰ 753143

PEUGEOT, TALBOT Newlyn ℰ 2038

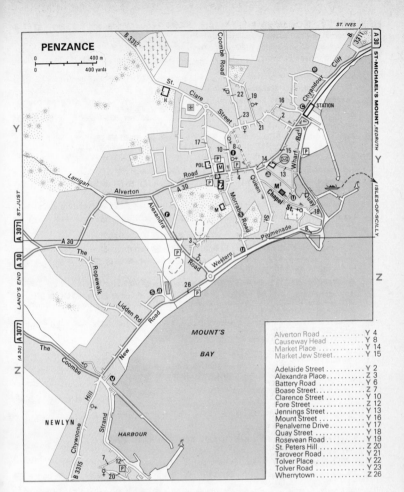

PENZANCE

0   400 m
0   400 yards

MOUNT'S BAY

HARBOUR

NEWLYN

*En saison, surtout dans les stations fréquentées, il est prudent de retenir à l'avance.
Cependant, si vous ne pouvez pas occuper la chambre que vous avez retenue,
prévenez immédiatement l'hôtelier.
Si vous écrivez à un hôtel à l'étranger, joignez à votre lettre
un coupon-réponse international (disponible dans les bureaux de poste).*

PERRANUTHNOE Cornwall **403** D 33 – see Marazion.

PERSHORE Heref. and Worc. **403 404** N 27 – pop. 5,530 – ECD : Thursday – ✆ 038 65 (4 fig.)
0386 (6 fig.).
🇮 Council Offices, 37 High St. ✆ 554711.
♦London 106 – ♦Birmingham 32 – Cheltenham 22 – Stratford-on-Avon 21 – Worcester 9.

  ✗ **Zhivago's,** 22 Bridge St., WR10 1AT, ✆ 553828 – 🅰 AE ⑩ VISA
    closed Sunday dinner, Monday and Bank Holidays – **M** a la carte 7.90/12.75 **st.** ⅃ 3.25.

    at Wyre Piddle NE : 2 m. by B 4082 and B 4083 on B 4084 – ⊠ Pershore – ✆ 0386 Pershore :

  🏠 **Avonside,** Main Rd, WR10 2JB, ✆ 552654, ≼, ⅃ heated, 🐎 – 🆅 🛏wc Ⓟ
    closed November and December – **M** (bar lunch) 9.50 **t.** ⅃ 3.50 – **7 rm** ⇌ 32.00/42.00 **t.** – SB
    (spring and autumn only) 54.00/70.00 **st.**

LOTUS High St. ✆ 555433

PETERBOROUGH Cambs. 402 404 T 26 – pop. 102,500 – ECD : Monday and Thursday – ✆ 0733.
See : Cathedral★★ 12C-13C (nave : painted roof★★★).
Envir. : Crowland : Abbey Church★ (8C ruins), Triangular Bridge★ 13C, NE : 8 m.
🛏 Thorpe Wood, Nene Parkway ✆ 267701, W : 3 m. on A 47 – 🛏 Ramsey ✆ 0487 (Ramsey) 813573, SE : 12 m.
🖪 Central Library, Broadway ✆ 48343 ext 23 – Town Hall, Bridge St. ✆ 63141 or 63396 (Saturday).
◆London 85 – ◆Cambridge 35 – ◆Leicester 41 – Lincoln 51.

🏨 **Peterborough Moat House,** Thorpe Wood, PE3 6SG, SW : 2 ¼ m. at Roundabout 33 ✆ 260000, Telex 32708 – 🛗 📺 🚽wc 🕿 🕹 🅿. 🛆 🛐 🗚 ⓘ 𝘝𝘐𝘚𝘈
M (bar lunch Saturday) 7.10/8.15 t. – 🖵 4.45 – **98 rm** 33.50/42.50 t. – SB (weekends only) 49.00 **st.**

🏨 **Bull,** Westgate, PE1 1RB, ✆ 61364 – 📺 🚽wc 🕿 🅿. 🛆 🛐 🗚 ⓘ 𝘝𝘐𝘚𝘈
M 5.95/6.15 st. 🍷 3.10 – **112 rm** 🖵 32.50/42.00 **st.** – SB (weekends only) 42.00 **st.**

🏠 **Newark,** 239 Eastfield Rd, PE1 4BH, ✆ 69811 – 🚽wc 🎇wc 🅿 – **38 rm**

at Whittlesey SE : 7 m. on A 605 – ✉ ✆ 0733 Peterborough :

🏠 **Falcon,** Paradise Lane, PE7 1BH, ✆ 203247 – 📺 🚽wc 🅿. 🛐 🗚 ⓘ 𝘝𝘐𝘚𝘈. 🎇
M a la carte 8.15/11.95 t. 🍷 2.85 – **8 rm** 🖵 18.00/32.50 t. – SB 43.00/49.00 **st.**

at Norman Cross S : 5 ¾ m. on A 15 at junction with A 1 – ✉ ✆ 0733 Peterborough :

🏨 **Crest** (Crest), Great North Rd, PE7 3TB, ✆ 240209, Telex 32576 – 📺 🚽wc 🕿 🕹 🅿. 🛆 🛐
🗚 ⓘ 𝘝𝘐𝘚𝘈
M (carving lunch) approx. 10.50 **st.** – 🖵 4.95 – **97 rm** 38.50/49.50 **st.**

at Nassington (Northants.) SW : 10 ¾ m. by A 47 – ✉ Peterborough – ✆ 0780 Stamford :

✗✗ **Black Horse Inn,** 2 Fotheringhay Rd, PE8 6QU, ✆ 782324, 🎇 – 🅿. 🛐 🗚 ⓘ 𝘝𝘐𝘚𝘈
M a la carte 9.25/11.45 t. 🍷 3.25.

at Wansford W : 8 ½ m. by A 47 – ✉ Peterborough – ✆ 0780 Stamford :

🏨 **Haycock,** Great North Rd, PE8 6JA, ✆ 782223, 🎇 – 📺 🚽wc 🕿 🅿. 🛆 🛐 🗚 ⓘ 𝘝𝘐𝘚𝘈
M a la carte 10.50/12.50 **st.** 🍷 2.40 – **28 rm** 🖵 24.00/60.00 **st.** – SB (weekends only)(winter only) 38.00/60.00 **st.**

🏠 **Sibson House,** Great North Rd, PE8 6ND, SE : 1 ¾ m. on A 1 ✆ 782227, 🎇 – 📺 🚽wc 🕿
🅿 🛐 🗚 ⓘ 𝘝𝘐𝘚𝘈
M 5.50/15.00 t. 🍷 2.90 – **11 rm** 🖵 27.00/38.00 t.

ALFA-ROMEO, SUZUKI 659 Lincoln Rd ✆ 52141
AUSTIN-ROVER, ROLLS ROYCE-BENTLEY 7 Oundle Rd ✆ 66011
AUSTIN-ROVER-DAIMLER-JAGUAR-LAND ROVER Padholme Rd ✆ 61201
BMW Helpston Rd, Glinton ✆ 253333
FIAT, LANCIA Midland Rd ✆ 314431
FORD 27/53 New Rd ✆ 40104
HYUNDAI, MAZDA, YUGO 50/64 Burghley Rd ✆ 65787

MERCEDES-BENZ High St., Eye ✆ 222363
NISSAN Oxney Rd ✆ 49336
PEUGEOT, TALBOT 343 Eastfield Rd ✆ 64566
PEUGEOT-TALBOT Lincoln Rd ✆ 71739
RENAULT Thorney Rd, Newborough ✆ 073 123 (Newborough) 625
VAUXHALL-OPEL, BEDFORD, RENAULT Sturrock Way ✆ 264981
VW, AUDI Oxney Rd ✆ 312213

PETERSFIELD Hants. 404 R 30 – pop. 10,420 – ECD : Thursday – ✆ 0730.
🛏 The Heath ✆ 3725, E : ½ m.
◆ London 59 – ◆ Brighton 45 – Guildford 25 – ◆ Portsmouth 19 – ◆ Southampton 32 – Winchester 19.

🏨 **Langrish House** 🌲, Langrish, GU32 1RN, W : 3 ½ m. on A 272 ✆ 66941, ≤, 🎇, park – 📺
🚽wc 🕿 🅿. 🛐 🗚 ⓘ 𝘝𝘐𝘚𝘈. 🎇
M *(closed Sunday to non-residents)* (dinner only) a la carte 8.00/11.50 t. 🍷 2.10 – 🖵 2.00 –
12 rm 22.00/35.00 t. – SB (weekends only) 43.00/56.00 **st.**

AUSTIN-ROVER 38 Collace St. ✆ 62206
CITROEN Alton Rd, Froxfield ✆ 073 084 (Hawkley) 200
FORD Station Rd ✆ 62992

NISSAN Alton Rd, Steep ✆ 66341
RENAULT Winchester Rd ✆ 66241
VOLVO 23 London Rd ✆ 64541

PETWORTH West Sussex 404 S 31 – pop. 2,506 – ECD : Wednesday – ✆ 0798.
See : Petworth House★★★ 17C (paintings★★★ and carved room★★★) *AC.*
◆London 54 – ◆Brighton 31 – ◆Portsmouth 33.

✗✗ **Paddington's Table,** East St., GU28 0AB, ✆ 43149 – 🛐 🗚 ⓘ 𝘝𝘐𝘚𝘈
closed Monday lunch, Sunday dinner and 25-26 December – **M** a la carte 8.35/15.95 t. 🍷 3.00.

PEVENSEY East Sussex 404 V 31 – see Eastbourne.

PICKERING North Yorks. 402 R 21 – pop. 4,545 – ECD : Wednesday – ✆ 0751 :
See : SS. Peter and Paul's Church (wall paintings★ 15C) – Norman castle★ (ruins) : ≤★ *AC.*
🖪 The Station, Park St. ✆ 73791.
◆London 237 – ◆Middlesbrough 43 – Scarborough 19 – York 25.

🏠 **Forest and Vale,** Malton Rd, YO18 7DL, ✆ 72722, 🎇 – 🚽wc 🎇wc 🅿. 🛐 🗚 ⓘ 𝘝𝘐𝘚𝘈
M 5.50/9.00 t. 🍷 3.00 – **23 rm** 🖵 18.50/37.00 t. – SB 48.00/50.00 **st.**

364

at Wrelton NW : 2 ½ m. on A 170 – ⊠ ✆ 0751 Pickering :

✗ **Huntsman** with rm, YO18 8PG, ✆ 72530 – Ⓟ
closed last 2 weeks February and 1 week October – **M** *(closed Sunday dinner, Monday and Bank Holidays)* (bar lunch) 9.00/15.00 **st.** ▯ 3.60 – **3 rm** ⊡ 11.50/21.50 **st.** – SB 36.50 **st.**

FORD, MERCEDES-BENZ Eastgate ✆ 72251   FORD Middleton ✆ 72331

PICKHILL North Yorks. ◳◲◱ P 21 – pop. 260 – ⊠ ✆ 0845 Thirsk.
♦London 229 – ♦Leeds 41 – ♦Middlesbrough 30 – York 34.

☆ **Nags Head,** YO7 4JG, ✆ 567391 – ⊡ ⊟wc ⅏wc Ⓟ. ⚞ *VISA*. ⅏
M 8.00/13.50 **t.** ▯ 2.70 – **8 rm** ⊡ 16.00/25.00 **t.**

PICKWORTH Leics. – see Stamford (Lincs.).

PIDDLETRENTHIDE Dorset ◳◲◳ ◳◲◱ M 31 – pop. 610 – ⊠ Dorchester – ✆ 030 04.
♦London 141 – ♦Bristol 54 – Exeter 62 – ♦Southampton 53.

☖ **Old Bakehouse,** DT2 7QR, S : 1 m. on B 3143 ✆ 305, ⚞ heated, ☀ – ⊡ ⊟wc Ⓟ. ⚞ *VISA*.
⅏
M (dinner only) 6.50 **t.** – **9 rm** ⊡ 16.00/30.00 **t.** – SB (except summer) 36.00/39.00 **st.**

PILLATON Cornwall ◳◲◱ H 32 – pop. 334 – ⊠ Saltash – ✆ 0579 St. Dominick.
♦London 254 – ♦Plymouth 11.

☖ **Weary Friar,** PL12 6QS, ✆ 52308, « Part 12C inn » – ⊡ ⊟wc Ⓟ. ⚞ ⚟ ⓪ *VISA*
closed 25 and 26 December – **M** a la carte 5.85/10.00 **t.** ▯ 2.60 – **12 rm** ⊡ 24.00/35.00 **t.**

PIMPERNE Dorset ◳◲◳ ◳◲◱ N 31 – see Blandford Forum.

PINHOE Devon ◳◲◱ J 31 – see Exeter.

PLAYDEN East Sussex – see Rye.

PLYMOUTH Devon ◳◲◱ H 32 The West Country G. – pop. 239,452 – ECD : Wednesday – ✆ 0752.
See : Site ✶✶ – Smeaton's Tower (⩽✶✶) BZ – Royal Citadel✶ (The Ramparts⩽✶✶) BZ – City Museum and Art Gallery✶ BZ **M**.
Envir. : Saltram House✶✶, E : 3 ½ m. BY **A** – Buckland Abbey✶✶, N : 7 m. by A 386 ABY – Antony House✶✶, W : 5 m. by A 374 AY – Yelverton Paperweight Centre✶, N : 9 m. on A 386 ABY.
⛳ Elfordleigh, Plympton, ✆ 336428, E : 6 m. by A 374 BY – ⛳ Whitsand Bay Hotel, Portwrinkle, Torpoint ✆ 0503 (St. Germans) 30470, W : 6 m. by A 374 AY.
✈ Roborough Airport : ✆ 772752, N : 3 ½ m. by A 386 ABY.
⛴ Shipping connections with the Continent : to France (Roscoff) (Brittany Ferries) – to Spain (Santander) (Brittany Ferries).
🛈 Civic Centre, Royal Parade ✆ 264851 and 264849 – 12 The Barbican ✆ 23806 (summer only) – Ferry Terminal, Millbay Docks (summer only).
♦London 242 – ♦Bristol 124 – ♦Southampton 161.

Plans on following pages

🏨 **Holiday Inn,** Armada Way, PL1 2HJ, ✆ 662866, Telex 45637, ⩽ city and Sound, ⚞ – 🗑 ⊡
Ⓖ Ⓟ. ⚐. ⚞ ⚟ ⓪ *VISA*   BZ **e**
M a la carte 8.95/17.85 **st.** – ⊡ 5.25 – **217 rm** 37.50/55.00 **s.**

🏨 **Mayflower Post House** (T.H.F.), Cliff Rd, The Hoe, PL1 3DL, ✆ 662828, Telex 45442, ⩽
Plymouth Sound, ⚞ heated – 🗑 ⊡ ⊟wc ☎ Ⓖ Ⓟ. ⚐. ⚞ ⚟ ⓪ *VISA*   AZ **c**
M *(closed Saturday lunch)* 6.95/10.75 **st.** ▯ 2.65 – ⊡ 5.00 – **104 rm** 39.00/47.00 **st.**

🏨 **Novotel,** Marsh Mills Roundabout, PL6 8HN, ✆ 21422, Telex 45711, ⚞ heated – 🗑 ⊡
⊟wc ☎ Ⓖ Ⓟ. ⚐. ⚞ ⚟ ⓪ *VISA*   BY **i**
M 6.50/8.75 **st.** ▯ 3.00 – ⊡ 4.00 – **100 rm** 34.50/40.60 **st.** – SB (weekends only) 46.00 **st.**

🏨 **Astor,** 14-22 Elliott St., The Hoe, PL1 2PS, ✆ 25511 – 🗑 ⊡ ⊟wc ☎. ⚐. ⚞ ⚟ ⓪ *VISA*. ⅏
closed 25 and 26 December – **M** *(closed Saturday lunch)* 5.15/7.50 **t.** – ⊡ 2.75 – **58 rm**
31.50/45.50 **t.** – SB (weekends only) 44.00/48.00 **st.**   BZ **c**

🏨 **Duke of Cornwall** (Best Western), Millbay Rd, PL1 3LG, ✆ 266256, Telex 45424 – 🗑 ⊡
⊟wc ⅏wc Ⓖ Ⓟ. ⚐. ⚞ ⚟ ⓪ *VISA*   AZ **a**
closed 24 to 27 December – **M** *(closed Saturday lunch)* 5.00/7.50 **t.** ▯ 2.20 – **67 rm**
⊡ 26.00/38.00 **t.** – SB (weekends only) (except summer) 45.00/48.00 **st.**

☖ Grosvenor, 9 Elliott St., The Hoe, PL1 2PP, ✆ 260411 – ⊡ ⊟wc ⅏wc ☎. ⅏   BZ **u**
14 rm.

☖ **Georgian House,** 51 Citadel Rd, The Hoe, PL1 3AU, ✆ 663237 – ⊡ ⊟wc ⅏wc. ⚞ ⚟ *VISA*
M (bar lunch) 6.50 **t.** ▯ 2.25 – **10 rm** ⊡ 16.00/28.00 **t.** – SB (weekends only) 34.00 **st.**   AZ **r**

☖ **Merlin,** 2 Windsor Villas, Lockyer St., The Hoe, PL1 2QD, ✆ 28133 – ⊡ ⅏wc Ⓟ. ⚞ ⚟ ⓪
VISA   BZ **z**
closed 24 December-1 January – **M** *(closed Sunday)* a la carte 5.35/9.55 **st.** ▯ 2.85 – **24 rm**
⊡ 13.75/29.50 **st.**

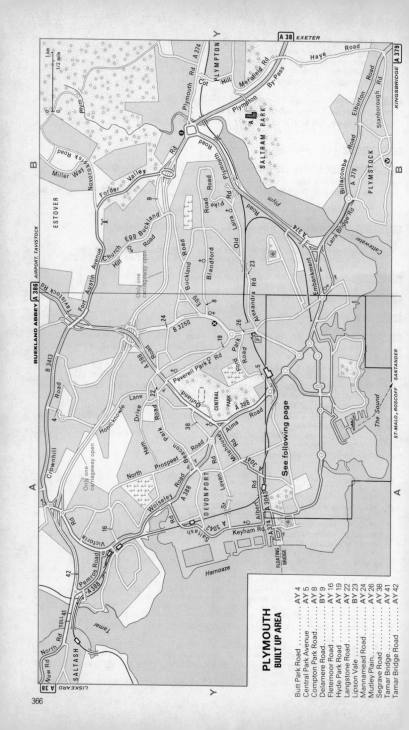

PLYMOUTH
BUILT UP AREA

366

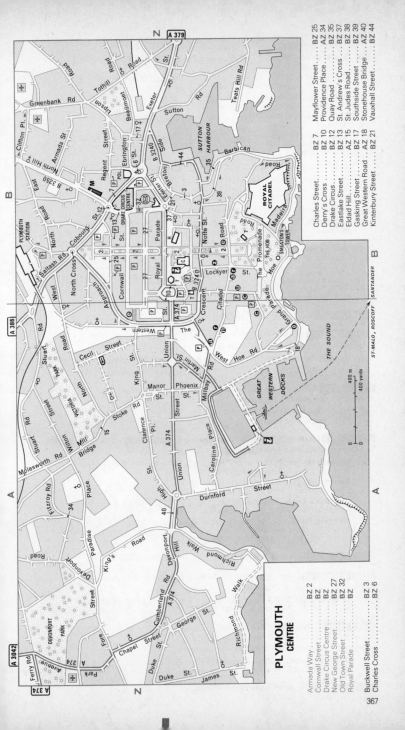

PLYMOUTH
CENTRE

↑ **Mooreton,** 71 Mannamead Rd, PL4 5ST, ℰ 266566 – 📺 🍴wc 🅿. ❀ AY **x**
closed Christmas.

↑ **Sea Breezes,** 28 Grand Par., West Hoe, PL1 3DJ, ℰ 667205 AZ **o**
7 rm ⊊ 7.00/14.00 **st.**

↑ **Cranbourne,** 282 Citadel Rd, The Hoe, PL1 2PZ, ℰ 263858 – 🍴 BZ **r**
closed last 2 weeks December – **10 rm** ⊊ 7.00/14.00 **st.**

↑ **Carnegie,** 172 Citadel Rd, The Hoe, PL1 3BD, ℰ 25158 – 🍴. 🔼 🆎 𝗩𝗜𝗦𝗔 AZ **n**
closed 1 week Christmas – **9 rm** ⊊ 10.50/23.00 **st.**

↑ **Chichester,** 280 Citadel Rd, The Hoe, PL1 2PZ, ℰ 662746 – 𝗩𝗜𝗦𝗔 BZ **a**
10 rm ⊊ 7.50/16.00 **st.**

✕ **Chez Nous,** 13 Frankfort Gate, PL1 1QA, ℰ 266793, French rest. – 🔼 🆎 ⓞ 𝗩𝗜𝗦𝗔 AZ **e**
closed Sunday, Monday, 1 to 10 February, 1 to 10 September and Bank Holidays – **M** a la carte
11.00/19.00 **st.** 🍷 3.20.

at Colebrook E : 6 ½ m. by A 374 – BY – ✉ 🕿 0752 Plymouth :

🏛 **Elfordleigh,** Shaugh Prior Rd, PL7 5EB, N : 1 ½ m. by Boringdon Hill ℰ 336428, ≼, 🔼 heated,
🏊, 🎿, park, ❀, squash – 🛏wc 🍴wc 🅿
closed Christmas – **M** (bar lunch) 6.90 **t.** 🍷 1.65 – **12 rm** ⊊ 19.55/29.90 **t.**

at Plymstock SE : 3 m. on A 379 – ✉ 🕿 0752 Plymouth :

🏛 **Highlands,** Dean Cross Rd, PL9 7AZ, ℰ 43643, 🔼 – 📺 🛏wc 🍴wc 🅿 BY **v**
M *(closed lunch Sunday and Monday)* 5.90 **t.** 🍷 2.50 – **15 rm** ⊊ 16.50/28.00 **st.**

AUSTIN-ROVER Union St. ℰ 263355
BMW Union St. ℰ 669202
CITROEN Colebrook Rd ℰ 336606
CITROEN 87 Crownhill Rd ℰ 772345
FORD Millbay ℰ 668040
HONDA, SAAB Albert Rd ℰ 51810
LANCIA Budshead Rd ℰ 771123
MAZDA Elm Rd, Mannamead ℰ 21594

MERCEDES-BENZ Crown Hill ℰ 785611
NISSAN Colebrook, Plympton ℰ 336462
NISSAN The Crescent ℰ 668332
VAUXHALL-OPEL Normandy Way ℰ 361251
VAUXHALL Bretonside ℰ 667111
VAUXHALL Cobourg St. ℰ 668886
VOLVO Valley Rd, Plympton ℰ 338306

PLYMSTOCK Devon 🟥🟥🟥 H 32 – see Plymouth.

POCKLINGTON Humberside 🟥🟥🟥 R 22 – pop. 4,176 – ✉ York – 🕿 075 92.
♦London 213 – ♦Kingston-upon-Hull 25 – York 13.

🏛 Feathers, 56 Market Pl., YO4 2UN, ℰ 3155 – 🛏wc 🅿. ❀ – **12 rm.**

FORD Hallgate ℰ 2768   RENAULT Kilnwick Rd ℰ 3221

POLKERRIS Cornwall 🟥🟥🟥 F 32 – pop. 75 – ✉ Fowey – 🕿 072 681 Par.
♦London 277 – Newquay 22 – ♦Plymouth 34 – Truro 20.

✕ **Rashleigh Inn,** PL24 2TL, ℰ 3991, ≼ – 🅿
M (buffet lunch) a la carte 8.20/10.50 🍷 1.30.

POLPERRO Cornwall 🟥🟥🟥 G 33 The West Country G. – pop. 1,600 – ✉ Looe – 🕿 0503.
See : Site ★ – ♦London 271 – ♦Plymouth 28.

↑ **Lanhael House,** PL13 2PW, ℰ 72428, ≼, 🔼, 🎿 – 🅿. ❀
March-October – **6 rm** ⊊ 13.50/21.00.

↑ **Claremont,** PL13 2RG, ℰ 72241 – 🍴wc 🅿
Easter-October – **9 rm** ⊊ 11.00/23.00 **t.**

✕ **Captain's Cabin,** Lansallos St., PL13 2QU, ℰ 72292 – 🔼 ⓞ 𝗩𝗜𝗦𝗔
March-October – **M** *(closed Sunday)* a la carte 6.20/15.95 **t.** 🍷 2.95.

✕ **Kitchen,** Fish Na Bridge, The Coombes, PL13 2RQ, ℰ 72780 – 🔼 🆎 ⓞ 𝗩𝗜𝗦𝗔
closed Monday except Bank Holidays and Sunday to Thursday mid November-mid March – **M**
(dinner only) (booking essential) 8.95 **t.** 🍷 2.95.

PONTARFYNACH = Devil's Bridge.

PONT-AR-GOTHI Dyfed 🟥🟥🟥 H 28 – ✉ Carmarthen – 🕿 026 788 Nantgaredig.
♦London 218 – Carmarthen 6 – ♦Swansea 25.

🏯 **Cothi Bridge,** SA32 7NG, ℰ 251, ≼, 🦢 – 🛏wc 🍴wc 🅿. 🔼 🆎 ⓞ 𝗩𝗜𝗦𝗔
M a la carte 6.95/8.90 **st.** 🍷 1.50 – **16 rm** ⊊ 17.00/31.00 **st.** – SB (weekends only) 34.00 **st.**

PONTERWYD Dyfed 🟥🟥🟥 I 26 – pop. 280 – ✉ Aberystwyth – 🕿 097 085.
🅸 Llywernog Silver Lead Mine ℰ 620 (summer only).
♦London 228 – Aberystwyth 12 – Chester 88 – Shrewsbury 64.

🏯 **Dyffryn Castell,** Dyffryn Castell, SY23 3LB, E : 2 m. on A 44 ℰ 237, ≼ – 🅿. 🔼
M *(closed Sunday dinner)* (bar lunch) a la carte 7.70/9.95 **st.** 🍷 2.50 – **7 rm** ⊊ 13.95/25.90 **st.**

PONT-Y-PANT Gwynedd – see Betws-y-Coed.

POOLE Dorset **403 404** O 31 The West Country G. – pop. 107,161 – ECD : Wednesday – ✆ 020 13 (4 and 5 fig.) or 0202 (6 fig.).

See : The Three Museums ★ by A 35 AX.

Envir. : Compton Acres Gardens ★★, SE : 3 m. AX.

🛈 Poole Quay ✆ 673322 – Arndale Centre ✆ 673322.

♦London 116 – Bournemouth 4 – Dorchester 23 – Weymouth 28.

Plan : see Bournemouth

🏥 **Mansion House** (Best Western), 11 Thames St., BH15 1JN, ✆ 685666, Telex 41495 – 📺 ⇌wc ☎ 🅿 🔄 🔌 🆎 ⓪ 𝖵𝖨𝖲𝖠 ❀
by A 35 AX
M 7.50/11.50 **t.** ⌗ 2.75 – **19 rm** ⏄ 35.00/56.00 **t.** – SB (weekends only)(except Bank Holidays) 82.00 **st.**

🏥 Hospitality Inn (Mt. Charlotte), The Quay, BH15 1HD, ✆ 671200, Telex 418374, ⇐ – ⇩ 📺 ⇌wc ☎ 🅿 🔌 🔌 🆎 ⓪ 𝖵𝖨𝖲𝖠 ❀
by A 35 AX
68 rm ⏄ 41.25/49.50 **st.** – SB (weekends only) (except summer) 53.00 **st.**

🏥 **Dolphin,** 180 High St., BH15 1DU, ✆ 673612 – ⇩ 📺 ⇌wc ⇌wc ☎ 🅿 🔄 🔌 🆎 ⓪ 𝖵𝖨𝖲𝖠
M 6.50/8.50 **t.** ⌗ 3.10 – **71 rm** ⏄ 20.00/39.00 **t.** – SB (weekends only) 42.00/46.00 **st.**
by A 35 AX

🏠 Arndale Court, 62-64 Wimborne Rd, BH15 2BY, ✆ 683746 – 📺 ⽊wc 🅿 ❀
18 rm.
by A 3049 AV

↑ Redcroft ⽊, 20 Pinewood Rd, Branksome Park, BH13 6JS, ✆ 763959 – ⇌wc 🅿 ❀
10 rm ⏄ 12.65/27.85 **t.**
BX **e**

↑ Dene ⽊, 16 Pinewood Rd, Branksome Park, BH13 6JS, ✆ 761143 – 📺 ⽊wc 🅿 🔌 🆎 ⓪ 𝖵𝖨𝖲𝖠 ❀
16 rm ⏄ 12.50/33.00 **st.**
BX **c**

✗ **Ca D'Oro Due,** 129 Parkstone Rd, Park Gates, BH15 2PB, ✆ 740223, Italian rest. – 🔌 🆎 ⓪ 𝖵𝖨𝖲𝖠
by A 35 AX
closed Sunday – **M** (dinner only) 11.40/15.20 **t.** ⌗ 3.30.

✗ **John B's,** 20 High St., BH15 1BP, ✆ 672440. 🔌 🆎 ⓪ 𝖵𝖨𝖲𝖠
by A 35 AX
closed Sunday and 25-26 December – **M** (dinner only) 9.75 **t.** ⌗ 2.60.

✗ **Isabel's,** 32 Station Rd, Lower Parkstone, BH14 8UD, ✆ 747885 – 🆎 ⓪ 𝖵𝖨𝖲𝖠
AX **a**
closed Sunday, 17 to 24 February, 1 week October and 25-27 December – **M** (dinner only) a la carte 7.60/12.55 **t.**

✗ **Edelweiss,** 232 Ashley Rd, Upper Parkstone, BH14 9BZ, ✆ 747703, Austrian rest. – 🔌 🆎 ⓪ 𝖵𝖨𝖲𝖠
AX **e**
closed Tuesday dinner – **M** (lunch by arrangement) a la carte 7.30/13.50 **t.** ⌗ 3.95.

at Lilliput SE : 2 ½ m. on B 3369 – ⊠ Poole – ✆ 0202 Canford Cliffs :

✗ **Gullivers,** 292 Sandbanks Rd, BH14 8HX, ✆ 708810 – 🔌 𝖵𝖨𝖲𝖠
AX **i**
closed Sunday dinner and first 3 weeks January – **M** (dinner only and Sunday lunch) a la carte 9.95/12.75 **t.** ⌗ 4.50.

AUDI, VW Station Rd ✆ 745000
AUSTIN-ROVER The Quay ✆ 674187

CITROEN Broadstone ✆ 693501
VAUXHALL-OPEL Poole Rd, Branksome ✆ 763361

POOL IN WHARFEDALE West Yorks. **402** P 22 – pop. 1,672 – ⊠ Otley – ✆ 0532 Arthington.

♦London 204 – Bradford 10 – Harrogate 8 – ♦Leeds 10.

✗✗✗ **Pool Court** with rm, Pool Bank, LS21 1EH, ✆ 842288, 🌳 – ▣ 📺 ⇌wc ☎ 🅿 🔌 🆎 ⓪ 𝖵𝖨𝖲𝖠 ❀
closed Sunday, Monday, 2 weeks July-August and 2 weeks Christmas – **M** (lunch by arrangement) a la carte 16.20/17.95 **t.** ⌗ 4.65 – ⏄ 4.95 – **4 rm** 42.00/67.00 **t.**

POOLEY BRIDGE Cumbria **401 402** L 20 – see Ullswater.

PORLOCK WEIR Somerset **403** J 30 – pop. 95 – ECD : Wednesday – ⊠ Minehead – ✆ 0643 Porlock.

Envir. : Porlock : St. Dubricius Church ★, E : 4 m.

♦London 193 – ♦Bristol 70 – Exeter 49 – Taunton 31.

🏥 **Anchor and Ship,** TA24 8PB, ✆ 862753, ⇐ – 📺 ⇌wc ☎ 🅿 🔌 𝖵𝖨𝖲𝖠
M a la carte 8.75/11.25 **t.** ⌗ 3.15 – **23 rm** ⏄ 17.70/48.50 **st.** – SB (May-October) 48.50/57.90 **st.**

Pour vos déplacements en Grande-Bretagne :

– cinq cartes détaillées n°ˢ **401 402 403 404 405** à 1/400 000

– utilisez-les conjointement avec ce guide,
  un souligné rouge signale toutes les localités citées dans ce guide.

PORT DINORWIC (FELINHELI) Gwynedd **402 403** H 24 – ✪ 0248.

♦London 249 – Caernarfon 4 – Holyhead 23.

✗ **Seahorse,** 20 Snowdon St., LL56 4HQ, ✆ 670546 – ⬛ 𝘝𝘐𝘚𝘈
closed Sunday, 1 week February, 1 week May and 2 weeks October – **M** (dinner only) a la carte
7.35/9.65 ▯ 2.30.

PORTHCAWL Mid Glam. **403** I 29 – pop. 12,520 – ECD : Wednesday – ✪ 065 671.

🛈 The Old Police Station, John St. ✆ 6639 (summer only).

♦London 183 – ♦Cardiff 28 – ♦Swansea 18.

🏨 **Seabank,** The Promenade, CF3 3NU, ✆ 2261, ≼, ☲ heated – ▯ 📺 ☎ 🅿 ⛳ ⬛ 𝖠𝖤 ⓞ 𝘝𝘐𝘚𝘈
❀
M 6.00/7.00 t. ▯ 3.25 – **64 rm** ⛺ 27.50/50.00 t. – SB (weekends only) 48.00/81.00 **st.**

🏨 **Atlantic,** West Drive, Sea Front, CF36 3LT, ✆ 5011, ≼ – ▯ 📺 ⌂wc ☎ 🅿 ⬛ 𝖠𝖤 ⓞ 𝘝𝘐𝘚𝘈
❀
M *(closed Sunday dinner to non-residents)* 6.95/7.95 t. ▯ 3.00 – **18 rm** ⛺ 28.00/38.00 **st.** – SB
42.00 **st.**

🏨 **Seaways,** 26-28 Mary St., CF36 3YA, ✆ 3510 – 📺 ⌂wc 🅵wc. ⬛ 𝖠𝖤 ⓞ 𝘝𝘐𝘚𝘈
M (bar lunch Monday to Saturday) 5.25 t. ▯ 2.20 – **16 rm** ⛺ 14.00/30.00 t. – SB (weekends only) 29.00/38.00 **st.**

at Nottage (Drenewydd yn Notais) N : ¾ m. by A 4229 – ✉ ✪ 065 671 Porthcawl :

🏨 Maid of Sker, West Rd, CF36 3RT, ✆ 2172 – 📺 ⌂wc ⌂ 🅿 ⬛ 𝖠𝖤 𝘝𝘐𝘚𝘈
10 rm ⛺ 25.00/35.00 **st.**

🏨 **Rose and Crown,** Heol-y-Capel, CF36 3ST, ✆ 4850 – 📺 ⌂wc 🅿 ⬛ 𝖠𝖤 ⓞ 𝘝𝘐𝘚𝘈 ❀
M *(closed Sunday dinner)* (bar lunch) a la carte 5.75/8.55 t. ▯ 3.00 – **7 rm** ⛺ 17.00/27.00 t.

PORTHMADOG Gwynedd **402 403** H 25 – pop. 3,840 – ECD : Wednesday – ✪ 0766.

🏌 Morfa Bychan ✆ 2037, W : 2 m.

🛈 High St. ✆ 2981 (summer only).

♦ London 245 – Caernarfon 20 – Chester 70 – Shrewsbury 81.

🏨 **Royal Sportsman** (T.H.F.), High St., LL49 9HA, ✆ 2015 – 📺 ⌂wc ⌂ 🅿 ⬛ 𝖠𝖤 ⓞ 𝘝𝘐𝘚𝘈
M (bar lunch Monday to Saturday) 9.00 **st.** ▯ 2.60 – ⛺ 4.75 – **21 rm** 26.50/39.00 **st.**

at Penmorfa NW : 2 m. on A 487 – ✉ ✪ 0766 Porthmadog :

🏨 **Bwlch-y-Fedwen Country House,** LL49 9RY, ✆ 2975, « Tastefully renovated 17C inn » –
⌂wc 🅿 ❀
April-October – **M** (residents only) (bar lunch) – **5 rm** ⛺ (dinner included) 25.00/46.00 t. – SB
(weekends only) (except summer) 33.00/37.00 **st.**

PORT ISAAC Cornwall **403** F 32 **The West Country** G. – pop. 966 – ECD : Wednesday –
✪ 020 888.

♦London 266 – Newquay 24 – Tintagel 14 – Truro 32.

🏨 **Port Gaverne,** Port Gaverne, PL29 3SQ, S : 1/2 m. ✆ 244 – ⌂wc 🅿 ⬛ 𝖠𝖤 ⓞ 𝘝𝘐𝘚𝘈
closed 13 January-24 February – **M** (buffet lunch) 8.75 **st.** – **18 rm** ⛺ 19.50/43.00 **st.** – SB
(except summer) 50.00/52.00 **st.**

🏠 **Archer Farm** ॐ, Trewetha, PL29 3RU, SE : ½ m. by B 3276 ✆ 522, ≼, ⚘ – 🅵wc 🅿
April-November – **8 rm** ⛺ 10.00/27.00 **st.**

PORTLAND Dorset **403 404** M 32 **The West Country** G. – pop. 9,990 – ECD : Wednesday –
✪ 0305.

See : Site ✶ (vantage point ✶✶).

♦London 149 – Dorchester 14 – Weymouth 6.

🏨 **Portland Heights** (Best Western), Yeates Corner, Wakeham, DT5 2EN, ✆ 821361, Telex
418493, ≼, ☲ heated, squash – ▯ 📺 ⌂wc ☎ 🅿 ⛳ ⬛ 𝖠𝖤 ⓞ 𝘝𝘐𝘚𝘈
closed 24 to 27 December – **M** a la carte 7.10/11.75 **st.** ▯ 2.90 – **68 rm** ⛺ 30.50/55.00 **st.** – SB
(weekends only) 39.90/49.90 **st.**

🏨 **Pennsylvania Castle,** Pennsylvania Rd, Wakeham, DT5 1HT, ✆ 820561, ≼, ⚘ – 📺 ⌂wc
🅵wc 🅿 ⬛ 𝖠𝖤 ⓞ 𝘝𝘐𝘚𝘈
M 6.35 t. ▯ 2.50 – **12 rm** ⛺ 26.00/37.00 t. – SB (weekends only)(except summer) 36.00/42.00 **st.**

FORD Easton Lane ✆ 820483

Pleasant hotels and restaurants
are shown in the Guide by a red sign.

Please send us the names
of any where you have enjoyed your stay.

Your Michelin Guide will be even better.

🏨🏨🏨 ... 🏠

✗✗✗✗✗ ... ✗

PORTLOE Cornwall **403** F 33 – pop. 200 – ⊠ ❀ 0872 Truro.

♦London 296 – St. Austell 15 – Truro 15.

🏠 **Lugger,** TR2 5RD, ✆ 501322, ≼ – ➥wc ⋔wc **P**. **◪ AE ⊙ VISA**. ❀
March-mid November – **M** (bar lunch Monday to Saturday) 5.50/9.50 t. ⬙ 1.40 – **20 rm**
⊠ 20.00/50.00 t.

PORTSCATHO Cornwall **403** F 33 – pop. 800 – ECD : Wednesday and Saturday – ⊠ Truro –
❀ 087 258.

♦London 298 – ♦ Plymouth 55 – Truro 16.

🏠 **Rosevine** ❀, Porthcurnick Beach, TR2 5EW, N : 2 m. by A 3078 ✆ 206, ≼, ✍ – ➥wc ⋔
P. **◪ AE ⊙ VISA**
April-October – **M** (bar lunch) 10.00 t. ⬙ 2.50 – **16 rm** ⊠ (dinner included) 25.00/55.00 t.

🏠 **Gerrans Bay,** Tregassick Rd, TR2 5ED, ✆ 338, ✍ – ➥wc **P**. **◪ AE VISA**
April-October and Christmas – **M** (bar lunch Monday to Saturday) 4.75/8.00 t. ⬙ 2.10 – **15 rm**
⊠ 13.00/29.00 t.

🏠 **Roseland House** ❀, Rosevine, TR2 5EW, N : 2 m. by A 3078 ✆ 644, ≼ Gerrans Bay, ✍ –
➥wc **P**. ❀
March-November – **M** (bar lunch) 7.50 t. ⬙ 2.30 – **19 rm** ⊠ 14.00/48.00 t.

PORTSMOUTH and SOUTHSEA Hants. **403 404** Q 31 – pop. 197,431 – ECD : Monday, Wednesday and Thursday – ❀ 0705.

See : H.M.S. Victory★★★ BY and Victory Museum★ M1 AC – Royal Marines' Museum★, at Eastney
AZ **M2**.

🏌 Great Salterns ✆ 64549 AY – 🏌 Crookhorn Lane, ✆ 070 18 (Cosham) 72210, N : 1 m. off B 2177
AY.

🚢 Shipping connections with the Continent : to France (Cherbourg, Le Havre) (Townsend Thoresen) – to France (Saint-Malo) (Brittany Ferries) – to the Isle of Wight : Fishbourne (Sealink) 19-25
daily (45 mn) – to St. Helier, Jersey (Sealink) summer : 1 daily, winter : 6 weekly (9 h 20 mn) – to
St. Peter Port, Guernsey (Sealink) summer : 1 daily, winter 6 weekly (7 h).

⛴ to the Isle of Wight : Ryde (Sealink from Portsmouth Harbour) 15-24 daily (25 to 30 mn) – from
Southsea to the Isle of Wight : Ryde (Hovertravel from Southsea Clarence Pier) summer frequent
services daily; winter 12 daily (restricted Sundays) (9 mn).

🇧 Civic Offices, Guildhall Sq. ✆ 834092/3 – Castle Buildings, Clarence Esplanade, Southsea ✆ 826722/3/4 –
Continental Ferry Port, Rudmore Roundabout Car Park, Wharf Rd ✆ 698111(summer only).

♦London 78 – ♦Southampton 21.

Plans on following pages

🏨 **Crest** (Crest), Pembroke Rd, PO1 2TA, ✆ 827651, Telex 86397 – ▯ TV ➥wc ☎ **P**. ⛳ **◪ AE**
⊙ **VISA**   BZ **o**
M approx. 12.00 **st.** – ⊠ 5.25 – **169 rm** 43.50/52.50 **st.**

🏨 **Pendragon** (T.H.F.), Clarence Par., Southsea, PO5 2HY, ✆ 823201, Telex 86376 – ▯ TV
➥wc ☎ **P**. ⛳ **◪ AE ⊙ VISA**   BZ **c**
M 6.95/8.00 **st.** ⬙ 3.25 – ⊠ 5.25 – **58 rm** 25.00/40.00 **st.**

🏨 **Hospitality Inn Portsmouth** (Mt. Charlotte), South Parade, Southsea, PO4 0RN, ✆ 731281,
Telex 86719, ≼ – ▯ TV ➥wc ☎ **P**. ⛳ **◪ AE ⊙ VISA**   BZ **r**
108 rm.

🏠 **Keppel's Head** (Anchor), 24-26 The Hard, PO1 3DT, ✆ 833231, Group Telex 858075 – ▯ TV
➥wc ⋔wc ☎ **P**. **◪ AE ⊙ VISA**   BY **a**
M (carving rest.) 8.65 **st.** ⬙ 2.65 – **24 rm** ⊠ 35.00/45.00 **st.** – SB (weekends only) 46.00 **st.**

⟰ **Tudor Court,** 1 Queen's Grove, Southsea, PO5 3HH, ✆ 820174, ✍ – ⋔ **P**   BZ **n**
9 rm ⊠ 12.00/36.00 **st.**

⟰ **Goodwood House,** 1 Taswell Rd, Southsea, PO5 2RG, ✆ 824734 – ⋔. ❀   BZ **e**
closed 23 December-3 January – **8 rm** ⊠ 9.50/21.00 **st.**

✗ **Le Talisman,** 123 High St., Old Portsmouth, PO1 2HW, ✆ 811303 – **◪ ⊙ VISA**   BZ **v**
closed Saturday lunch, Sunday and Monday – **M** a la carte 11.20/15.20 t. ⬙ 2.40.

✗ **Bistro Montparnasse,** 103 Palmerston Rd, Southsea, PO5 3PS, ✆ 816754 – **◪ AE ⊙ VISA**
closed Sunday, 25-26 December and first week January – **M** (dinner only) a la carte 7.95/12.60 t.
⬙ 3.90.   BZ **a**

at Cosham N : 3 ¾ m. by A 3, M 275, M27 and A 27 – ⊠ Portsmouth – ❀ 0705 Cosham :

🏨 **Holiday Inn**, North Harbour, PO6 4SH, ✆ 383151, Telex 86611, ≼, ▣ – ▯ TV ☎ ⛫ **P**. ⛳ **◪**
AE ⊙ VISA   AY **a**
M (buffet lunch) 12.50 t. ⬙ 3.20 – ⊠ 5.95 – **170 rm**.

AUSTIN-ROVER-DAIMLER-JAGUAR   Granada Rd.
Southsea ✆ 735311
AUSTIN-ROVER   Hambledon Rd ✆ 070 14 (Waterlooville) 2641
FIAT 117 Copnor Rd ✆ 691621
FORD Southampton Rd ✆ 370944

NISSAN 135/153 Fratton Rd ✆ 827551
RENAULT 128 Milton Rd ✆ 815151
TALBOT Grove Rd South, Southsea ✆ 823261
TOYOTA Gamble Rd ✆ 660734
VAUXHALL-OPEL London Rd, Hilsea ✆ 661321
VW, AUDI 41/53 Highland Rd ✆ 815111

371

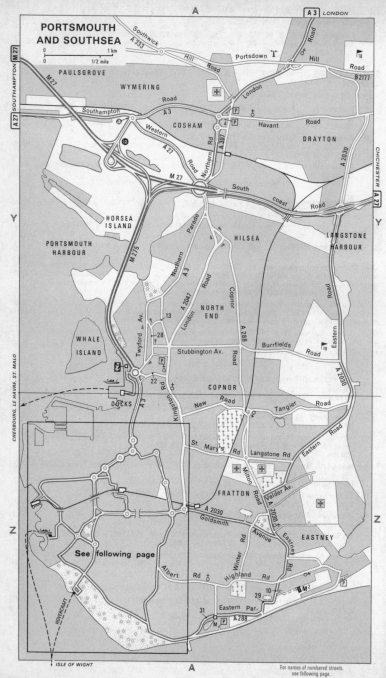

PORTSMOUTH AND SOUTHSEA

0 _____ 1 km
0 _____ 1/2 mile

For names of numbered streets,
see following page.

Arundel Street . . . . BY
Charlotte Street . . . . BY 9
Commercial Road . . . . BY
Palmerston Road . . . . BZ
Tricorn Centre . . . . BY

Alec Rose Lane . . . . BY 2
Alfred Road . . . . BY 5

Anglesea Road . . . . BY 6
Bellevue Terrace . . . . BZ 7
Bradford Road . . . . BY 8
Cromwell Road . . . . AZ 10
Edinburgh Road . . . . BY 12
Gladys Avenue . . . . AY 13
Gordon Road . . . . BZ 14
Grove Road South . . . . BZ 15
Guildhall Walk . . . . BY 16
Gunwharf Road . . . . BZ 17
Hampshire Terrace . . . . BY 18
Hard (The) . . . . BY 19

Isambard Brunel Road . . . . . . BY 20
King's Terrace . . . . BZ 21
Kingston Crescent . . . . AY 22
Landport Terrace . . . . BZ 23
Lennox Road South . . . . BZ 24
Ordnance Row . . . . BY 26
Stamshaw Road . . . . AY 28
St. George's Road . . . . AZ 29
St. Helen's Parade . . . . AZ 31
St. Michael's Road . . . . BY 33
Southsea Terrace . . . . BZ 36
Stanhope Road . . . . BY 37

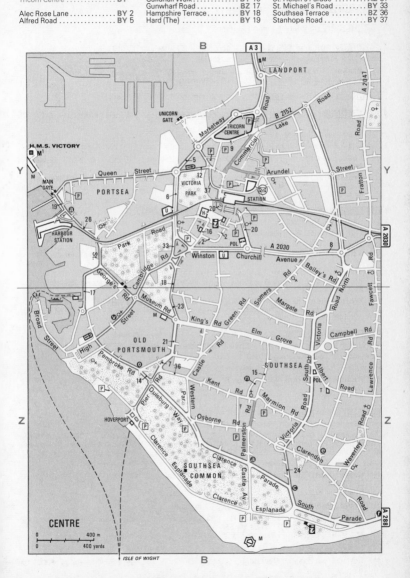

Town plans: roads most used by traffic and those on which guide listed hotels and restaurants stand are fully drawn ; the beginning only of lesser roads is indicated.

PORT TALBOT West Glam. [403] I 29 – pop. 50,729 – ECD : Thursday – ✆ 0639.
♦London 187 – ♦Cardiff 32 – ♦Swansea 9.

🏨 **Twelve Knights** (Ladbroke), Margam Rd, SA13 1DB, SE : 2 m. on A 48 𝒫 882381 – 📺
⇆wc ☎ 🅿. 🔄 *VISA*
closed Christmas – **M** *(closed Saturday lunch)* 7.00 t. 🍷 2.00 – **11 rm** ⇌ 32.00/42.00 t. – SB
(weekends only) 55.00/75.00 **st.**

POUND HILL West Sussex – see Crawley.

POUNDISFORD Somerset – see Taunton.

POWBURN Northumb. [401] [402] O 17 – pop. 233 – ✉ Alnwick – ✆ 066 578.
♦London 312 – ♦Edinburgh 73 – ♦Newcastle-upon-Tyne 36.

🏨 **Breamish House** 🦢, NE66 4LL, 𝒫 266, ≼, 🐎 – 📺 ⇆wc ✄wc 🅿. 🌳
closed January – **M** 8.00/12.00 t. 🍷 2.75 – **10 rm** ⇌ 25.00/40.00 t.

POYNINGS West Sussex [404] T 31 – see Brighton and Hove (East Sussex).

PRAA SANDS Cornwall [403] D 33 The West Country G. – pop. 300 – ✉ Penzance – ✆ 073 676
Germoe.
🏌 Germoe Cross 𝒫 3445, N : 1 m. on A 394.
♦London 321 – Penzance 8 – Truro 24.

🏨 **Lesceave Cliff** 🦢, TR20 9TX, 𝒫 2325, ≼ Mounts Bay, 🐎 – 📺 ⇆wc 🅿. 🔄 🔄 *VISA*
M 5.75/7.50 t. 🍷 3.50 – **26 rm** ⇌ 16.00/52.00 t.

🏠 **Prah Sands,** Chy-an-Dour Rd, TR20 9SY, 𝒫 2438, ≼, 🐎, ✗ – 📺 ⇆wc 🅿. 🔄 *VISA* 🌳
March-October – **M** 4.75/8.50 t. 🍷 2.10 – **22 rm** ⇌ 12.50/36.00 t. – SB (weekends only) 35.00/45.00 **st.**

PRESTBURY Cheshire [402] [403] [404] N 24 – pop. 2,891 – ✆ 0625.
Envir. : Adlington Hall★ (15 C) *AC*, N : 3 ½ m.
♦London 184 – ♦Liverpool 43 – ♦Manchester 17 – ♦Stoke-on-Trent 25.

🏩 **Mottram Hall** 🦢, Wilmslow Rd, Mottram St. Andrew, SK10 4QT, NW : 2 ¼ m. on A 538 𝒫
828135, Telex 668181, ≼, « Part 18C mansion in park », 🐎 – 📺 🅿. 🔄 🔄 🔄 ① *VISA*
M a la carte 10.60/15.60 st. 🍷 3.15 – **72 rm** ⇌ 30.00/55.00 **st.** – SB (weekends only) 62.00/67.00 **st.**

✗✗✗ **Legh Arms and Black Boy,** New Rd, SK10 4DG, 𝒫 829130 – 🅿. 🔄 🔄 ① *VISA*
M a la carte 9.90/16.80 t. 🍷 3.30.

✗✗ **Whitehouse,** The Village, SK10 4OG, 𝒫 829376 – 🅿. 🔄 🔄 ① *VISA*
closed Sunday dinner, Monday, first week February and first two weeks August – **M** a la carte
7.30/9.80 t.

PRESTEIGNE Powys [403] K 27 – pop. 1,213 – ECD : Thursday – ✆ 0544.
See : Church (Flemish Tapestry★) – Envir. : Old Radnor (church★) SW : 7 ½ m.
🏌 at Kington 𝒫 0544 (Kington) 230340, S : 7 m.
♦London 159 – Llandrindod Wells 20 – Shrewsbury 39.

🏨 **Radnorshire Arms** (T.H.F.), High St., LD8 2BE, 𝒫 267406, 🐎 – 📺 ⇆wc ☎ 🅿. 🔄 🔄 ①
VISA
M (bar lunch Monday to Saturday) 6.50/7.50 **st.** 🍷 2.60 – ⇌ 4.50 – **16 rm** 32.00/41.50 **st.**

PRESTON Lancs. [402] L 22 – pop. 98,088 – ECD : Thursday – ✆ 0772.
Envir. : Samlesbury Old Hall★ (14C) *AC*, E : 2 ½ m.
🏌 Ashton and Lea, Lea 𝒫 726480, W : 3 m. – 🏌 Fulwood Hall Lane, Fulwood 𝒫 794234 and 700436
– 🏌 Longridge, Fell Barn, Jeffrey Hill 𝒫 077 478 (Longridge) 3291, NE : 8 m. off B 6243 – 🏌 Fishwick
Hall, Glenluce Drive, Farringdon Park 𝒫 798300 – 🖪 Town Hall, Lancaster Rd 𝒫 53731/54881 ext 211.
♦London 226 – ♦Blackpool 17 – Burnley 22 – ♦Liverpool 30 – ♦Manchester 34 – ♦Stoke-on-Trent 65.

🏨 **Crest** (Crest), The Ring Way, PR1 3AU, 𝒫 59411, Telex 677147 – 🔆 📺 ⇆wc ☎ 🅿. 🔄 🔄
🔄 ① *VISA*
M approx. 10.50 **st.** – ⇌ 5.25 – **132 rm** 42.00/52.00 **st.**

at Broughton N : 3 m. on A 6 – ✉ ✆ 0772 Preston :

🏨 **Broughton Park,** 418 Garstang Rd, PR3 5JB, 𝒫 864087, Group Telex 67180, 🔄, 🐎 – 📺
⇆wc ✄wc 🎾 ♿. 🅿. 🔄 🔄 🔄 ① *VISA*
M 5.50/8.50 t. 🍷 3.00 – **64 rm** ⇌ 32.00/38.00 t. – SB (weekends only) 40.00/45.00 **st.**

at Samlesbury E : 2 ½ m. at junction M 6 and A 59 – ✉ Preston – ✆ 077 477 Samlesbury :

🏨 Tickled Trout, Preston New Rd, PR1 0UJ, 𝒫 671, ≼, 🔄, 🐎 – 📺 ⇆wc ☎ 🅿. 🔄 🔄 🔄 ①
VISA
closed 26 December – **66 rm** ⇌ 34.00/45.00 **st.** – SB (weekends only) 41.00/45.00 **st.**

🏨 **Trafalgar,** Preston New Rd, PR5 0UL, E : 1 m. at junction A 59 and A 677 𝒫 351, Telex
677362, 🔄, squash – 🔆 📺 ⇆wc ☎ 🅿. 🔄 🔄 🔄 ① *VISA* 🌳
M 7.50/10.50 t. 🍷 2.85 – ⇌ 3.50 – **54 rm** 33.00/44.00 **st.** – SB (weekends only) 45.00/55.00 **st.**

at Walton-le-Dale SE : 2 ½ m. on A 6 – ⊠ 🕓 0772 Preston :

🏨 **Vineyard,** Cinnamon Hill, Chorley Rd., 🖋 54646 – ☰ 📺 🚻wc ☎ 🅿 ⬛ 🄰🄴 ⑩ *VISA*. 🎿
M a la carte 4.65/10.70 **t.** ▮ 2.50 – **14 rm** ⌖ 30.00/40.00 **t.** – SB (weekends only) 40.00/52.00 **st.**

MICHELIN Branch, Unit 20, Roman Way, Longridge Rd, Ribbleton, PR2 5BB, 🖋 **651411**

BMW Blackpool Rd, Ashton 🖋 724391
CITROEN Garstang Rd 🖋 718852
COLT Grunsargh Rd 🖋 652323
DAF, VOLVO Emmanuel St. 🖋 21581
FIAT 306/310 Ribbleton Lane 🖋 792823
FORD Penwortham 🖋 744471
FORD Marsh Lane 🖋 54083
HONDA Corporation St. 🖋 58862
LADA Watling Street Rd 🖋 717262
NISSAN Chorley Rd 🖋 53911

MAZDA Leyland Rd, Penwortham 🖋 744312
MERCEDES-BENZ New Hall Lane 🖋 796060
RELIANT Blackpool Rd 🖋 726066
RENAULT Manchester Rd 🖋 704704
SKODA New Hall Lane 🖋 794491
TALBOT Blackpool Rd 🖋 728551
TOYOTA 350 Blackpool Rd 🖋 717750
VAUXHALL Blackpool Rd 🖋 793054
VOLVO Strand Rd 🖋 50501
VW, AUDI 🖋 702288

PRIORS HARDWICK Warw. – pop. 166 – ⊠ Rugby – 🕓 0327 Byfield.

♦London 94 – ♦Coventry 17 – Northampton 26 – Warwick 15.

XXX **Butchers Arms,** CV23 8SN, 🖋 60504, 🎠 – 🅿
closed Saturday lunch and Sunday dinner – **M** a la carte 8.00/13.95 **s.** ▮ 2.75.

PUDDINGTON Cheshire 🔲🔲🔲 K 24 – pop. 348 – ⊠ South Wirral – 🕓 051 Liverpool.

♦London 204 – Birkenhead 12 – Chester 8.

XXX **Craxton Wood** 🦢 with rm, Parkgate Rd, L66 9PB, on A 540 🖋 339 4717, « ≼ picturesque
grounds and gardens », park – 📺 🚻wc 🕮 🅿 ⬛ 🄰🄴 ⑩ *VISA*. 🎿
closed last 2 weeks August and 1 week at Christmas – **M** *(closed Sunday and Bank Holidays)*
a la carte 9.70/12.70 – **12 rm** ⌖ 26.75/41.00.

PULBOROUGH West Sussex 🔲🔲🔲 S 31 – pop. 3,316 – ECD : Wednesday – 🕓 079 82.

Envir. : Hardham (church : wall paintings★ 12C) S : 1 m.

♦London 49 – ♦Brighton 25 – Guildford 25 – ♦Portsmouth 35.

🏨 **Chequers,** Church Pl., RH20 1AD, NE : ¼ m. on A 29 🖋 2486, 🎠 – 🚻wc 🅿 ⬛ 🄰🄴 ⑩ *VISA*
M 4.50/7.50 **st.** ▮ 2.50 – **9 rm** ⌖ 18.75/31.00 **st.** – SB 42.00/44.00 **st.**

XX **Stane Street Hollow,** Codmore Hill, RH20 1BG, NE : 1 m. on A 29 🖋 2819 – 🅿
*closed Tuesday and Saturday lunch, Sunday, Monday, 3 weeks May, 3 weeks October, 24
December-5 January* – **M** (booking essential) a la carte 10.75/12.55 **t.** ▮ 3.00.

AUSTIN-ROVER London Rd 🖋 2407   HONDA London Rd 🖋 079 881 (Bury) 691

PURFLEET Essex 🔲🔲🔲 ⑭ – pop. 430 – ECD : Wednesday – 🕓 040 26.

♦London 17 – Chelmsford 25.

🏨 **Royal,** High St., RM16 1QA, 🖋 5432, ≼ – 📺 🚻wc 🕮 🅿 ⬛ 🄰🄴 ⑩ *VISA*
M (grill rest. only) 9.25 **t.** ▮ 2.75 – **31 rm** ⌖ 30.00/42.00 **t.** – SB 24.00 **st.**

PUTSBOROUGH Devon 🔲🔲🔲 H 30 – pop. 1,342 – ⊠ Braunton – 🕓 0271 Croyde.

♦London 233 – Barnstaple 11 – Exeter 51 – Ilfracombe 9.

🏨 **Putsborough Sands,** EX33 1LB, 🖋 890555, ≼, 🔳, squash – 🚻wc 🅿 ⬛ 🄰🄴 *VISA*
April-September – **M** (bar lunch) 9.00 **t.** ▮ 2.50 – **61 rm** ⌖ 12.00/40.00 **t.** – SB (April-
mid July and September)30.00/37.00 **st.**

QUORN Leics. – see Loughborough.

RADLETT Herts. 🔲🔲🔲 T 28 – pop. 8,180 – ECD : Wednesday – 🕓 092 76.

🏌 at Aldenham, Radlett Rd 🖋 7775, SW : 3 m. BU.

♦London 21 – Luton 15.

Plan : see Greater London (North-West)

🏨 **Red Lion,** Watling St., WD7 7NP, 🖋 5341 – 📺 🚻wc 🕮 🅿 ⬛ 🄰🄴 ⑩ *VISA*   BU **c**
M (grill rest. only) a la carte approx. 7.05 **t.** ▮ 2.70 – **17 rm** ⌖ 25.00/44.00 **t.** – SB (weekends only) 44.00/48.00 **st.**

AUSTIN-ROVER 411 Watling St. 🖋 5681   FORD 203/205 Watling St. 🖋 4851
BMW 74/76 Watling St. 🖋 4802   MAZDA Station Rd 🖋 6711

RAMSBURY Wilts. 🔲🔲🔲 🔲🔲🔲 P 29 – pop. 1,390 – ECD : Wednesday and Saturday – ⊠ 🕓 0672
Marlborough.

♦London 79 – ♦Southampton 51 – Swindon 13.

XX **Bell,** The Square, SN8 2PE, 🖋 20230, 🎠 – 🅿 ⬛ 🄰🄴 ⑩ *VISA*
M 11.50 **t.** ▮ 2.25.

375

RAMSGATE Kent 404 Y 30 – pop. 39,561 – ECD : Thursday – 🕾 0843 Thanet.
See : St. Augustine's Abbey Church (interior★).
Envir. : Minster-in-Thanet (abbey : remains★ 7C-12C) W : 4 ½ m. – Birchington-on-Sea : in Quex
Park (Powell-Cotton Museum★ of African and Asian natural history and ethnology, AC), NW : 9 m.
🚢 Shipping connections with the Continent : to France (Dunkerque) (Sally Viking Line).
🛈 Argyle Centre, Queen St. ✆ 51086.
♦London 77 – ♦Dover 19 – Maidstone 45 – Margate 4.5.

🏨 **Savoy,** 43 Grange Rd, CT11 9NA, ✆ 592637 – 📺 🛏wc 🛊wc 🕾 🅿. 🔼 🗚 ⓞ 🚾
   closed February – **M** (closed Sunday in winter) 6.00/7.00 **st.** ♦ 2.50 – **25 rm** ⌑ 13.50/28.00 **st.**
⌂ **Abbeygail,** 17 Penshurst Rd, East Cliff, CT11 8EG, ✆ 594154 – 🞬
   closed Christmas – **10 rm** ⌑ 7.50/15.00 **st.**

   at Minster-in-Thanet W : 5 ½ m. by A 253 on B 2048 – ✉ 🕾 0843 Thanet :

XX **Old Oak Cottage,** 53 High St., CT12 4BT, ✆ 821229 – 🅿. 🔼 🗚 ⓞ 🚾
   closed Sunday – **M** (dinner only) a la carte 12.00/14.75 **st.** ♦ 2.50.

AUSTIN-ROVER Grange Rd ✆ 583541
FORD Boundary Rd ✆ 53784
RENAULT Margate Rd ✆ 52629

VAUXHALL West Cliff Rd ✆ 53877
VW, AUDI St. Lawrence ✆ 52333

RANGEWORTHY Avon – pop. 318 – ✉ Bristol – 🕾 045 422 Rangeworthy.
♦London 122 – ♦Bristol 13 – Gloucester 30 – Swindon 39.

🏨 **Rangeworthy Court** 🞰, BS17 5ND, ✆ 347, 🏊 heated, 🎾 – 🛊wc 🅿.
   closed 23 December-2 January – **M** (closed Sunday) (bar lunch) 9.50 **t.** ♦ 1.40 – **13 rm**
   ⌑ 18.20/31.00 **t.** – SB (weekends only) 34.00/41.00 **st.**
AUSTIN-ROVER Hatters Lane, Chipping Sodbury
✆ 313181

BEDFORD, VAUXHALL-OPEL West End Garage,
Chipping Sodbury ✆ 318311

RANTON Staffs. 402 403 404 N 25 – see Stafford.

RAVENSCAR North Yorks. 402 S 20 – see Scarborough.

RAVENSTONEDALE Cumbria 402 M 20 – ECD : Thursday – ✉ Kirkby Stephen – 🕾 058 73
Newbiggin-on-Lune.
♦London 280 – ♦Carlisle 43 – Kendal 19 – Kirkby Stephen 5.

🛏 **Black Swan** 🞰, CA17 4NG, ✆ 204 – 🅿. 🗚 ⓞ 🚾
   M (closed Sunday dinner) (bar lunch Monday to Saturday) 8.75 **t.** ♦ 3.25 – **6 rm** ⌑ 18.00/29.00 **t.**
   – SB (winter and spring only) 38.00 **st.**

*In alta stagione, e soprattutto nelle stazioni turistiche,
e prudente prenotare con un certo anticipo.
Avvertite immediatamente l'albergatore se non potete più
occupare la camera prenotata.
Se scrivete ad un albergo all'estero, allegate alla vostra
lettera un tagliando - risposta internazionale (disponibile presso gli uffici postali)*

READING Berks. 403 404 Q 29 – pop. 132,939 – 🕾 0734.
Envir. : Stratfield Saye Park★ AC, S : 7 m. by A 33 X – Mapledurham House★ AC, NW : 3 ½ m. by
A 329 X.
🏌 Hurst, Dinton Pastures, Davis St. ✆ 0734 (Twyford) 345143, NE : 5 m. by A 4 X – 🏌 Bearwood,
Mole Rd, Sindlesham ✆ 760060.
🛈 Civic Offices, Civic Centre ✆ 55911 and 592388.
♦London 43 – ♦Brighton 71 – ♦Bristol 78 – Croydon 47 – Luton 53 – ♦Oxford 28 – ♦Portsmouth 56 – ♦Southampton
46.

Plan opposite

🏨 **Ramada,** Oxford Rd, RG1 7RH, ✆ 586222, Telex 847785, 🔽 – 🛊 📺 🕾 🕹 🅿. 🏛. 🔼 🗚 ⓞ
   🚾   Z i
   M a la carte 7.95/13.00 **st.** ♦ 3.25 – ⌑ 5.25 – **200 rm** 49.50/56.50 **st.** – SB (week-
   ends only) 68.00/90.00 **st.**
🏨 **Post House** (T.H.F.), Basingstoke Rd, RG2 0SL, S : 2 ½ m. on A 33 ✆ 875485, Telex 849160,
   🔽 – 📺 🛏wc 🕾 🅿. 🏛. 🔼 🗚 ⓞ 🚾   X a
   M (closed Saturday lunch) 8.50 **st.** ♦ 2.60 – ⌑ 5.00 – **143 rm** 43.00/50.50 **st.**
🏛 **Ship** (Anchor), 4-8 Duke St., RG1 4RY, ✆ 583455, Group Telex 858875 – 📺 🛏wc 🕾 🅿. 🔼
   🗚 ⓞ 🚾   Z e
   M (carving rest.) 8.65 **st.** ♦ 2.65 – **32 rm** ⌑ 24.50/43.00 **st.** – SB (weekends only) 43.00 **st.**
🏛 **Upcross,** 68 Berkeley Av., RG1 6HY, ✆ 590796, Telex 849021, 🎾 – 📺 🛏wc 🛊wc 🔼 🗚
                                                                                                       Z c
   closed 10 days at Christmas and New Year – **M** (closed Friday, Saturday and Sunday dinner)
   (bar lunch) a la carte 6.25/8.00 **st.** ♦ 2.50 – **29 rm** ⌑ 18.00/33.00 **st.**

376

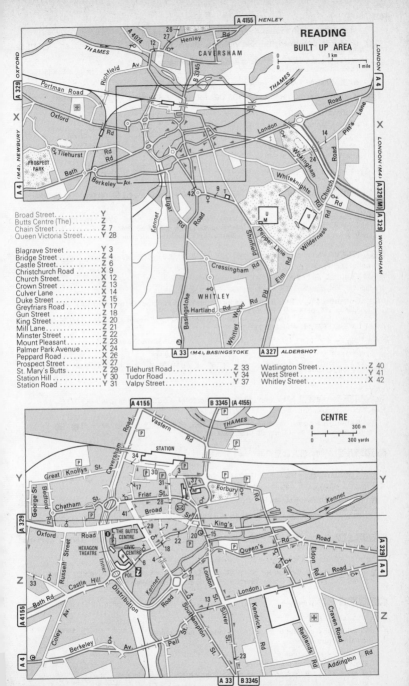

READING
BUILT UP AREA

0 ——— 1 km
0 ——— 1 mile

A 4155 HENLEY

A 4074

THAMES

Henley Rd

CAVERSHAM

B 3345

THAMES

Portman Road

Richfield Av.

Oxford Rd

OXFORD A 329

Tilehurst Rd

PROSPECT PARK

Bath Rd

Berkeley Av.

A 4 (M4) NEWBURY

LONDON A 4

Road

London Rd

Wokingham Rd

Whiteknights

Church Rd

Pitt's Lane

LONDON (M4) A 329(M)

A 329 WOKINGHAM

Kennet

Elgar Rd

Shinfield Rd

Pepper Lane

Wilderness Rd

Elm Rd

Cressingham Rd

WHITLEY

Basingstoke Rd

Hartland Rd

Whitley Wood Rd

A 33 (M4), BASINGSTOKE

A 327 ALDERSHOT

Street	Grid
Broad Street	Y
Butts Centre (The)	Z
Chain Street	Z 7
Queen Victoria Street	Y 28
Blagrave Street	Y 3
Bridge Street	Z 4
Castle Street	Z 6
Christchurch Road	X 9
Church Street	X 12
Crown Street	Z 13
Culver Lane	X 14
Duke Street	Z 15
Greyfriars Road	Y 17
Gun Street	Z 18
King Street	Z 20
Mill Lane	Z 21
Minster Street	Z 22
Mount Pleasant	Z 23
Palmer Park Avenue	X 24
Peppard Road	Z 26
Prospect Street	X 27
St. Mary's Butts	Z 29
Station Hill	Y 30
Station Road	Y 31
Tilehurst Road	Z 33
Tudor Road	Y 34
Valpy Street	Y 37
Watlington Street	Z 40
West Street	Y 41
Whitley Street	X 42

CENTRE

0 ——— 300 m
0 ——— 300 yards

A 4155

B 3345 (A 4155)

THAMES

Vastern Rd

Caversham Road

STATION

Great Knollys St.

George St.

Bedford Rd

Chatham St.

Friar St.

Forbury Rd

Broad St.

King's Rd

Kennet

Oxford Road

THE BUTTS CENTRE

HEXAGON THEATRE

CIVIC CENTRE

POL.

Russell Street

Castle Hill

Bath Rd

Coley Av.

Berkeley Av.

Distribution Road

Kennet

Southampton St.

London St.

Silver St.

Queen's Rd

Eldon Rd

Road

Kendrick Rd

London Rd

Redlands Rd

Craven Road

Addington Rd

A 329

A 329

A 4

A 4155

A 4

A 33

B 3345

at Shinfield S : 4 ¼ m. on A 327 – X – ⊠ ❀ 0734 Reading :

XXX ❀ **Milton Sandford,** The Old Vicarage, Church Lane, RG2 9BY, ✆ 883783, ✿ – ℗. ⬛ Æ ⓞ 𝘝𝘐𝘚𝘈
closed Sunday and first 2 weeks August – **M** (dinner only) 17.25 **st.** ⌂ 2.75
Spec. Artichoke heart filled with mussels, Loin of veal with crab and mushroom sauce, Hot apricot soufflé.

at Burghfield SW : 5 m. by A 4 – X – ⊠ ❀ 0734 Reading :

XX **Knight's Farm,** Berrys Lane, RG3 3XE, NE : 2 m. ✆ 52366, ✿ – ℗. ⬛ Æ ⓞ 𝘝𝘐𝘚𝘈
closed Saturday lunch, Sunday, Monday, last 3 weeks August and 1 week at Christmas – **M**
12.50/16.50 **st.** ⌂ 3.00.

AUSTIN-ROVER-DAIMLER-JAGUAR 38 Portman Rd
✆ 585011
BMW 209/211 Shinfield Rd ✆ 871620
CITROEN 44 George St. ✆ 586425
FIAT Eaton Pl., Chatham St. ✆ 582521
FORD 160 Basingstoke Rd ✆ 875333
PEUGEOT-TALBOT Christchurch Rd ✆ 875242

RENAULT Chatham St. ✆ 583322
RENAULT Wokingham Rd ✆ 669456
TOYOTA 569/575 Basingstoke Rd ✆ 871278
VAUXHALL-OPEL Vastern Rd ✆ 55501
VOLVO 406/412 London Rd ✆ 67321
VW, AUDI Erleigh Rd ✆ 666111
VW, AUDI Oxford Rd ✆ 418181

REDBOURN Herts. 🄌🄌🄌 S 28 – pop. 4,853 – ECD : Wednesday – ⊠ St. Albans – ❀ 058 285.
♦London 31 – Luton 6 – Northampton 42.

🏨 **Aubrey Park** (Best Western), Hemel Hempstead Rd, AL3 7AF, SW : 1 m. on B 487 ✆ 2105,
Telex 825562, ⅃ heated, ✿ – �📺 ⊏⊐wc ☎ ℗. ⩟. ⬛ Æ ⓞ 𝘝𝘐𝘚𝘈
M 5.25/8.00 **st.** ⌂ 2.50 – ⊊ 4.50 – **80 rm** 22.00/50.00 **st.** – SB (weekends only) 45.00/55.00 **st.**

REDDITCH Heref. and Worc. 🄌🄌🄌 🄌🄌🄌 O 27 – pop. 51,800 – ECD : Wednesday – ❀ 0527.
🛇 Pitcheroak, Plymouth Rd ✆ 41054.
🛈 9-11 Royal Square ✆ 60806.
♦London 111 – ♦Birmingham 15 – Cheltenham 33 – Stratford-upon-Avon 15.

🏨 **Southcrest** ♨, Pool Bank off Mount Pleasant, Southcrest District, B97 4JG, ✆ 41511, Telex
338455, ✿, park – �📺 ⊏⊐wc ⫿wc ☎ ℗. ⩟. ⬛ Æ ⓞ 𝘝𝘐𝘚𝘈
closed 25 to 30 December – **M** *(closed Sunday dinner)* 7.50/8.50 **t.** ⌂ 3.25 – **31 rm**
⊊ 33.00/42.00 **t.** – SB 98.00 **st.**

AUSTIN-ROVER Alcester Rd, Studley ✆ 052 785
(Studley) 2297
AUSTIN-ROVER Washford Drive ✆ 25055
CITROEN Birmingham Rd ✆ 63636
PEUGEOT-TALBOT Alcester Rd, Beoley ✆ 056 44
(Tamworth) 2553

FORD Battens Drive ✆ 21212
SKODA 1124 Evesham Rd ✆ 052 789 (Astwood
Bank) 2433
VAUXHALL-OPEL ✆ 052 785 (Studley) 2444
VOLVO Clive Rd ✆ 69111
VW, AUDI 530 Evesham Rd, Crabe Cross ✆ 44554

REDHILL Surrey 🄌🄌🄌 T 30 – pop. 56,223 (inc. Reigate) – ECD : Wednesday – ❀ 0737.
♦London 22 – ♦Brighton 31 – Guildford 20 – Maidstone 34.

⌂ **Ashleigh House,** 39 Redstone Hill, RH1 4BG, ✆ 64763, ⅃ heated, ✿ – ⫿ ℗. ❀
closed Christmas – **9 rm** ⊊ 14.50/27.00 **st.**

REDLYNCH Wilts. 🄌🄌🄌 🄌🄌🄌 O 31 – see Salisbury.

REIGATE Surrey 🄌🄌🄌 T 30 – pop. 56,223 (inc. Redhill) – ECD : Wednesday – ❀ 073 72.
♦London 26 – ♦Brighton 33 – Guildford 20 – Maidstone 38.

🏨 **Bridge House,** Reigate Hill, RH2 9RP, ✆ 46801, Telex 95649, ≤ – �📺 ⊏⊐wc ☎ ℗. ⩟. ⬛ Æ
ⓞ 𝘝𝘐𝘚𝘈. ❀
M *(closed Bank Holiday Mondays)* 8.25/13.50 **t.** ⌂ 2.75 – ⊊ 3.00 – **30 rm** 31.50/43.50 **t.**

RENISHAW Derbs. 🄌🄌🄌 🄌🄌🄌 🄌🄌🄌 P 24 – pop. 1,810 – ⊠ Sheffield (South Yorks.) – ❀ 0246
Eckington.
♦London 157 – Derby 33 – ♦Nottingham 31 – ♦Sheffield 8.

🏨 **Sitwell Arms,** Station Rd, S31 9WE, ✆ 435226 – �📺 ⊏⊐wc ⫿wc ☎ ℗. ⬛ Æ ⓞ 𝘝𝘐𝘚𝘈. ❀
M 9.25 **t.** ⌂ 3.00 – ⊊ 3.50 – **30 rm** 25.50/41.00 **st.** – SB (weekends only) 45.00/55.00 **st.**

RHAEADR = Rhayader.

Gli alberghi o ristoranti ameni sono indicati nella guida
con un simbolo rosso.

🏨🏨🏨 … 🏠

Contribuite a mantenere
la guida aggiornata segnalandoci
gli alberghi ed i ristoranti dove avete soggiornato piacevolmente.

XXXXX … X

RHAYADER (RHAEADR) Powys **403** J 27 – pop. 1,800 – ECD : Thursday – ☎ 0597.
♦London 179 – Aberystwyth 34 – Carmarthen 75 – Shrewsbury 62.

  🏠 **Elan Valley** 🦢, LD6 5HN, ✆ 810448, ≼, 🔧 – 🖦wc 🚗 **P**. 🖭
    closed Christmas – **M** 6.00/6.50 t. – **11 rm** ⌂ 15.00/28.00 t. – SB (winter only) 32.00/34.00 st.

RHOSMAEN Dyfed **403** I 28 – see Llandeilo.

RHOS-ON-SEA (LLANDRILLO-YN-RHOS) Clwyd **402 403** I 24 – see Colwyn Bay.

RHUTHUN = Ruthin.

RHYDAMAN = Ammanford.

RHYDGALED (CHANCERY) Clwyd **403** H 26 – see Aberystwyth (Dyfed).

RHYDYCROESAU Salop – see Oswestry.

RICHMOND North Yorks. **402** O 20 – pop. 7,245 – ECD : Wednesday – ☎ 0748.
See : Castle★ (Norman ruins) *AC*.
Envir. : Bolton Castle★ (15C) *AC*, ≼★, SW : 13 m.
🏌 Bend Hagg ✆ 2457 – 🏌 Catterick Garrison, Leyburn Rd ✆ 0748 (Richmond) 833401, S : 3 m.
🛈 Friary Gardens, Queens Rd ✆ 3525 (summer only).
♦London 243 – ♦Leeds 53 – ♦Middlesbrough 26 – ♦Newcastle-upon-Tyne 44.

  🏠 **Frenchgate**, 59-61 Frenchgate, DL10 7AE, ✆ 2087, 🚗 – 🖵 🖦wc 🛁wc **P**. 🔼 🖭 *VISA*
    closed mid December-mid February – **M** (bar lunch) 7.50 t. ᐟ 2.40 – **12 rm** ⌂ 18.50/35.00 t. –
    SB (except summer) 40.00/42.00 t.

AUSTIN-ROVER Victoria Rd ✆ 2539   CITROEN Darlington Rd ✆ 3014

RINGWOOD Hants. **403 404** O 31 – pop. 7,850 – ECD : Monday and Thursday – ☎ 042 54.
🏌 Ringwood ✆ 042 53 (Burley) 2431, NE : 4 m.
♦London 102 – Bournemouth 11 – Salisbury 17 – ♦Southampton 20.

    at Ibsley N : 2 ½ m. on A 338 – ✉ ☎ 042 54 Ringwood :

  ✗ **Old Beams**, Salisbury Rd, BH23 1AS, ✆ 3387, « 14C thatched cottage » – **P**
    M a la carte 8.00/10.30 st. ᐟ 2.85.

    at Avon S : 4 m. on B 3347 – ✉ Christchurch – ☎ 0425 Bransgore :

  🏠 **Tyrrells Ford** 🦢, BH23 7BH, ✆ 72646, 🚗, park – ⌶ 🖵 🖦wc 🛁wc **P**. 🔼 🖭 ⓪ *VISA* 🦺
    M (bar lunch Monday to Saturday) 6.95/9.95 st. ᐟ 2.25 – **14 rm** ⌂ 20.00/40.00 t. – SB
    (except Bank Holidays) 50.00 st.

FIAT Salisbury Rd ✆ 6111

RIPLEY Surrey **404** S 30 – pop. 2,110 – ECD : Wednesday – ☎ 0483 Guildford.
♦London 28 – Guildford 6.

  ✗✗✗ Clock House, 13 Portsmouth Rd, GU23 6AQ, ✆ 224777, 🚗 .

RIPON North Yorks. **402** P 21 – pop. 10,989 – ECD : Wednesday – ☎ 0765.
See : Cathedral★ 12C-15C.
Envir. : Fountains Abbey★★★ (ruins 12C-13C, floodlit in summer) – Studley Royal Gardens★★ and
Fountains Hall★ (17C) *AC*, SW : 3 m. – Newby Hall★ (18C) *AC* (the tapestry room★★ and gardens★
AC) SE : 3 ½ m.
🏌 Palace Rd ✆ 3640, N : 1 m. on A 6108.
🛈 Wakemans House, Market Pl. ✆ 4625 (summer only).
♦London 222 – ♦Leeds 26 – ♦Middlesbrough 35 – York 23.

  🏨 **Ripon Spa** (Best Western), Park St., HG4 2BU, ✆ 2172, Telex 57780, ≼, 🚗 – ⌶ 🖵 🖦wc
    🛁wc 🚗 **P**. 🔼 🖭 ⓪ *VISA*
    M 7.50/10.50 t. ᐟ 2.85 – **41 rm** ⌂ 27.00/50.00 t. – SB 48.00/58.00 st.

  ✗ **New Hornblower**, Duck Hill, HG4 1BL, ✆ 4841 – 🔼 *VISA*
    closed Sunday, Monday and February – **M** (dinner only) a la carte 7.55/9.65 t. ᐟ 2.90.

FIAT, MERCEDES-BENZ, VAUXHALL Kirkby Rd ✆   RENAULT Water Skellgate ✆ 2083
4491   TALBOT Blossom Gate ✆ 4268
FORD North St. ✆ 2324   VOLVO Palace Rd ✆ 2461

RIPPONDEN West Yorks. **402** O 22 – pop. 4,799 – ✉ ☎ 0422 Halifax.
♦London 210 – Halifax 5 – Huddersfield 9 – ♦Leeds 21.

  ✗✗ **Over the Bridge**, Millfold, HX6 4DJ, off A 58 ✆ 823722 – **P**. 🖭
    closed Sunday – **M** (dinner only)(booking essential) 13.50 t.

ROCHDALE Greater Manchester **402 404** N 23 – pop. 207,430 – ECD : Tuesday – ☺ 0706.

♦London 212 – ♦Blackpool 53 – ♦Leeds 37 – ♦Liverpool 46 – ♦Manchester 13.

  ⌂ Broadfield ⌾, Sparrow Hill, OL16 1AF, ℰ 44085 – ▥ ⌂wc ⽕wc ☏ ℗
  18 rm.

ROCHESTER Kent **404** V 29 – pop. 55,519 – ECD : Wednesday – ✉ Chatham – ☺ 0634 Medway.

See : Castle★, ☆★★ (142 steps) *AC* – Cathedral★ (interior★★) – Eastgate House★ 1590 – Fort Pitt Hill ≤★ – to Brompton : Royal Engineers' Museum★.

Envir. : Cobham Hall (Gilt Hall★) *AC*, W : 4 m.

☶ Deangate Ridge, at Hoo ℰ 0634 (Medway) 251180, NE : 4 m.

🛈 Eastgate Cottage, Eastgate High St. ℰ 43666.

♦London 30 – ♦Dover 45 – Maidstone 8 – Margate 46.

  🏨 **Crest** (Crest), Maidstone Rd, ME5 9SE, SE : 2 ½ m. by A 2 on A 229 ℰ 687111, Telex 965933
  – ⧉ ▥ ⌂wc ☎ ♿ ℗ ⚲ ▥ 🅰 ⑩ 𝗩𝗜𝗦𝗔
  M approx. 12.00 **st**. – ⌸ 5.25 – **106 rm** 42.50/52.50 **st**.

AUSTIN-ROVER-JAGUAR 16 Medway St., Chatham ℰ 41122	RELIANT Gundulph Rd, Chatham ℰ 41857
AUSTIN-ROVER Commercial Rd, Strood ℰ 408451	SKODA Hoath Lane, Wigmore ℰ 31688
FIAT, LANCIA Pier Rd, Gillingham ℰ 52333	TOYOTA High St. ℰ 407788
NISSAN 100 Watling St. ℰ 576741	VAUXHALL Station Rd, Strood ℰ 721021
PEUGEOT, TALBOT High St. ℰ 42231	VOLVO Wood St., Gillingham ℰ 402777
	VW, AUDI 1 Ferndale Rd, Gillingham ℰ 572327

ROCHFORD Essex **404** W 29 – pop. 6,520 – ECD : Wednesday – ✉ ☺ 0702 Southend-on-Sea.

♦London 43 – Southend-on-Sea 4.

  ✗✗ **Renouf's**, 1 South St., SS4 1BL, ℰ 544393 – ▥ 🅰 ⑩ 𝗩𝗜𝗦𝗔
  closed Saturday lunch, Sunday, Monday, 1 to 14 January and 10 to 24 June – **M** a la carte
  10.80/14.80 t. ⓛ 3.00.

ROCK Cornwall **403** F 32 – pop. 350 – ECD : Wednesday – ✉ Wadebridge – ☺ 020 886 Trebetherick.

♦London 288 – Newquay 22 – ♦Plymouth 45 – Truro 30.

  ⌂ **St. Enodoc** ⌾, PL27 6LA, ℰ 2311, ≤, ❀, squash – ▥ ⌂wc ℗ ▥ 🅰 𝗩𝗜𝗦𝗔
  M (bar lunch) a la carte 9.65/16.00 **st**. ⓛ 2.95 – **14 rm** ⌸ 17.50/45.00 **st**. – SB (except summer) 38.00/40.00 **st**.

  ⌂ **Gleneglos**, Trewint Lane, PL27 6LU, ℰ 2369, ❀ – ⌂wc ℗ ▥ 𝗩𝗜𝗦𝗔 ✻
  March-October – **M** (dinner only and Sunday lunch) a la carte 8.50/10.50 t. ⓛ 2.70 – **8 rm**
  ⌸ 12.50/29.00 t.

RODBOROUGH Glos. – see Stroud.

ROEWEN Gwynedd – see Conwy.

ROLLESTON ON DOVE Staffs. **402 403 404** P 25 – see Burton-upon-Trent.

ROMALDKIRK Durham **402** N 20 – see Middleton-in-Teesdale.

ROMSEY Hants. **403 404** P 31 – pop. 10,043 – ECD : Wednesday – ☺ 0794.

See : Abbey Church★ 12C-13C (interior★★).

☶ Dunwood Manor, Shootash Hill ℰ 0794 (Lockerley) 40549, SE : 4 m. on A 27 – ☶ Ampfield Par
Three ℰ 68480, NE : on A 31.

♦London 82 – Bournemouth 28 – Salisbury 16 – ♦Southampton 8 – Winchester 10.

  🏨 **White Horse** (T.H.F.), Market Pl., SO5 8ZJ, ℰ 512431 – ▥ ⌂wc ☏ ♿ ℗ ▥ 🅰 ⑩ 𝗩𝗜𝗦𝗔
  M 5.75/8.95 **st**. ⓛ 2.60 – ⌸ 5.00 – **33 rm** 35.50/46.50 **st**.

  ✗✗ **Old Manor House**, 21 Palmerston St., SO5 8HJ, ℰ 517353 – ℗ ▥ 🅰 ⑩ 𝗩𝗜𝗦𝗔
  closed Sunday dinner, Monday and 24 to 30 December – **M** a la carte 10.60/14.90 t. ⓛ 2.55.

AUSTIN-ROVER Winchester Rd ℰ 512850   VAUXHALL-OPEL 24 Middlebridge St. ℰ 513806
MAZDA, PEUGEOT 45/55 Winchester Hill ℰ 513185

ROSEDALE ABBEY North Yorks. **402** R 20 – ✉ Pickering – ☺ 075 15 Lastingham.

♦London 247 – ♦Middlesbrough 27 – Scarborough 25 – York 36.

  ⌂ **White Horse Farm**, YO18 8SE, ℰ 239, ≤ – ▥ ⌂wc ⽕wc ℗ 🅰 ⑩
  M *(closed Christmas Day)* (bar lunch Monday to Saturday) 5.50/10.00 **st**. ⓛ 3.25 – **12 rm**
  ⌸ 23.50/37.00 **st**. – SB 40.00/49.00 **st**.

  ⌂ **Milburn Arms**, YO18 8RA, ℰ 312 – ℗ ▥ 🅰 ⑩ 𝗩𝗜𝗦𝗔
  M (bar lunch) a la carte 7.60/10.60 **st**. ⓛ 2.25 – **7 rm** ⌸ 24.00/33.00 **st**. – SB (winter only) 39.50 **st**.

ROSSINGTON South Yorks. **402 403 404** Q 23 – see Doncaster.

ROSS-ON-WYE Heref. and Worc. 408 404 M 28 – pop. 6,390 – ECD : Wednesday – ☎ 0989.

Envir. : Goodrich (Castle★ : ruins 12C-14C) *AC*, SW : 3 ½ m. – 🖪 20 Broad St. ☎ 62768.

♦London 118 – Gloucester 15 – Hereford 15 – Newport 35.

🏨 **Chase** (Q.M.H.), Gloucester Rd, HR9 5LH, on A 40 ☎ 63161, 🚗 – 📺 📠wc 🛗wc 🅿 🔌
40 rm.

🏨 **Royal** (T.H.F.), Palace Pound, Royal Par., HR9 5HZ, ☎ 65105, ≤, 🚗 – 📺 📠wc 🛗 🅿 🔌
🔼 🆎 ⓞ *VISA*
M 7.50/10.50 🍸 2.60 – ☲ 5.00 – **31 rm** 35.50/44.50 **st.**

🏠 **Chasedale**, Walford Rd, HR9 5PQ, ☎ 62423, 🚗 – 📠wc 🅿 🔼 *VISA*
M a la carte 8.50/10.00 **st.** – **12 rm** ☲ 16.50/34.00 **st.** – SB 37.00/45.00 **st.**

at Weston-Under-Penyard E : 2 m. on A 40 – ⊠ ☎ 0989 Ross-on-Wye :

🏨 **Wye,** HR9 7NT, ☎ 63541, 🚗, park – 📺 📠wc 🛗 🅿 🔌 🔼 🆎 ⓞ *VISA*
M (bar lunch) 9.50 🍸 2.80 – **41 rm** ☲ 22.00/38.00 **st.** – SB 42.00/46.00 **st.**

🏠 **Hunsdon Manor**, HR9 7PE, ☎ 62748, 🚗 – 📺 📠wc 🛗wc 🅿 🔼 🆎 ⓞ *VISA*
M 7.50/14.00 **st.** 🍸 2.50 – **12 rm** ☲ 19.00/30.00 **st.** – SB 40.00/46.00 **st.**

at Goodrich SW : 5 m. by A 40 on B 4229 – ⊠ Ross-on-Wye – ☎ 0600 Symonds Yat :

🏠 **Ye Hostelrie,** HR9 6HX, ☎ 890241, 🚗 – 🛗wc 🅿
M (closed Sunday dinner) (bar lunch) 9.00 **s.** – **7 rm** ☲ 22.00/34.00 **st.**

at Walford S : 2 m. on B 4228 – ⊠ ☎ 0989 Ross-on-Wye :

XX **Walford House** with rm, HR9 5RY, ☎ 63829, 🚗 – 📺 📠wc 🅿 🔼 🆎 ⓞ *VISA*
M a la carte 9.55/18.00 **st.** 🍸 3.40 – **9 rm** ☲ 25.00/40.00 **st.** – SB 45.00/50.00 **st.**

at Pengethley NW : 4 m. on A 49 – ⊠ Ross-on-Wye – ☎ 098 987 Harewood End :

🏨 **Pengethley** (Best Western) ॐ, HR9 6LL, ☎ 211, ≤, 🔟 heated, 🚗, park – 📺 📠wc 🛗wc
🛗 🔌 🅿 🔼 🆎 ⓞ *VISA*
M 9.50/15.00 **st.** 🍸 4.50 – **20 rm** ☲ 45.00/92.00 **st.** – SB 92.00/108.00 **st.**

AUSTIN-ROVER Cantilupe Rd ☎ 62400
AUSTIN-ROVER High St. ☎ 62447
FORD ☎ 62637

RENAULT Overross St. ☎ 63666
VW, AUDI Whitchurch ☎ 0600 (Monmouth) 890235

ROSTHWAITE Cumbria 402 K 20 – see Keswick.

ROSUDGEON Cornwall – ⊠ Penzance – ☎ 076 676 Germoe.

♦London 321 – Penzance 6 – Truro 24.

X **Trevarrack Cottage,** Helston Rd, TR20 9PA, ☎ 2257 – 🅿 🔼 🆎 ⓞ *VISA*
M a la carte 6.50/15.95 **t.** 🍸 3.00.

ROTHAY BRIDGE Cumbria – see Ambleside.

ROTHBURY Northumb. 401 402 O 18 – pop. 1,694 – ECD : Wednesday – ⊠ Morpeth – ☎ 0669.

♦London 311 – ♦Edinburgh 84 – ♦Newcastle-upon-Tyne 29.

⋔ **Orchard,** High St., NE65 7TL, ☎ 20684, 🚗 – ❄
6 rm ☲ 11.00/19.00 **t.**

ROTHERHAM South Yorks. 402 403 404 P 23 – pop. 248,000 – ECD : Thursday – ☎ 0709.

🏌 Thrybergh Park ☎ 850480, E : 3 m. – 🏌 Sitwell Park, Shrogs Wood Rd ☎ 0709 (Wickersley)
541046, E : 2 ½ m.

♦London 166 – ♦Kingston-upon-Hull 61 – ♦Leeds 36 – ♦Sheffield 6.

🏨 **Carlton Park,** 102-104 Moorgate Rd, S60 2BG, ☎ 64902, Telex 547810 – 📺 🅿 🔌 🔼 🆎 ⓞ
VISA
M (closed Saturday lunch) 5.25/7.95 **st.** – ☲ 4.25 – **62 rm** 35.00/40.00 **st.**

ROTHLEY Leics. 402 403 404 Q 25 – see Leicester.

ROTTINGDEAN East Sussex 404 T 31 – pop. 8,637 – ECD : Wednesday – ⊠ ☎ 0273 Brighton.

♦London 58 – ♦Brighton 4 – Lewes 9 – Newhaven 5.

🏨 **White Horse,** Marine Drive, BN2 7HR, ☎ 31955, ≤ – 📳 📺 📠wc 🛗 🅿 🔼 🆎 ⓞ *VISA*
M 5.95/6.50 **t.** – **18 rm** ☲ 19.50/42.50 **t.**

ROUSDON Devon 403 L 31 – see Lyme Regis.

ROWLEY REGIS West Midlands 403 404 N 26 – pop. 12,753 – ECD : Thursday – ⊠ ☎ 021
Birmingham.

♦London 132 – ♦Birmingham 9 – Wolverhampton 10.

Plan : see Birmingham p. 2

⋔ **Highfield House,** Waterfall Lane, off Holly Rd, B65 0BH, ☎ 559 1066 – 🅿 ❄   BU **a**
12 rm ☲ 12.00/24.00 **st.**

ROWSLEY Derbs. 402 403 404 P 24 – pop. 221 – ECD : Thursday – ✉ Matlock – ☎ 0629 Darley Dale.

♦London 157 – Derby 23 – ♦Manchester 40 – ♦Nottingham 30.

Peacock (Embassy), Bakewell Rd, DE4 2EB, ☎ 733518, « **17C stone house with antiques** », – wc wc P. AE VISA.
M 7.75/14.50 **st.** 4.25 – 4.25 – **20 rm** 23.00/45.00 **st.** – SB (weekends only) 55.00/64.00 **st.**

ROYAL LEAMINGTON SPA Warw. 403 404 P 27 – pop. 45,064 – ECD : Monday and Thursday – ☎ 0926.

Leamington and County, Whitnash ☎ 20298, S : 1 ½ m. by A 452 – Newbold-Comyn, Newbold Terrace East ☎ 21157, off Willes Rd.

Jephson Lodge, The Parade ☎ 311470.

♦London 99 – ♦Birmingham 23 – ♦Coventry 9 – Warwick 3.

Manor House (Anchor), Avenue Rd, CV31 3NJ, ☎ 23251, Telex 311653 – wc wc P. AE VISA **i**
M (carving rest.) 8.65 **st.** 2.65 – **53 rm** 34.00/44.00 – SB (weekends only) 46.00 **st.**

Regent (Best Western), 77 The Parade, CV32 4AX, ☎ 27231 – wc P. **r**
80 rm.

Falstaff, 16-20 Warwick New Rd, CV32 5JQ, ☎ 312044 – wc wc P. AE VISA
M 6.50/7.50 **st.** 3.00 – **53 rm** 27.00/38.00 **st.** – SB (weekends only) 38.00 **st.**
plan of Warwick Z **u**

Lansdowne, 87 Clarendon St., CV32 4PF, ☎ 21313, Telex 337556 – wc P. **a**
M (dinner only) 9.65 **st.** 2.45 – **10 rm** 16.45/32.00 **st.** – SB 42.90/44.90 **st.**

Abbacourt, 40 Kenilworth Rd, CV32 6JF, ☎ 311188, – wc wc P. AE VISA.
M 5.50/6.50 **s.** 4.45 – **22 rm** 15.00/35.00 **s.**
plan of Warwick Z **r**

Angel, 143 Regent St., CV32 4NZ, ☎ 23683 – wc P. AE VISA. **c**
M *(closed Sunday dinner)* a la carte 7.50/11.10 **t.** 2.05 – **17 rm** 21.00/28.00 **t.** – SB (weekends only) 35.00 **st.**

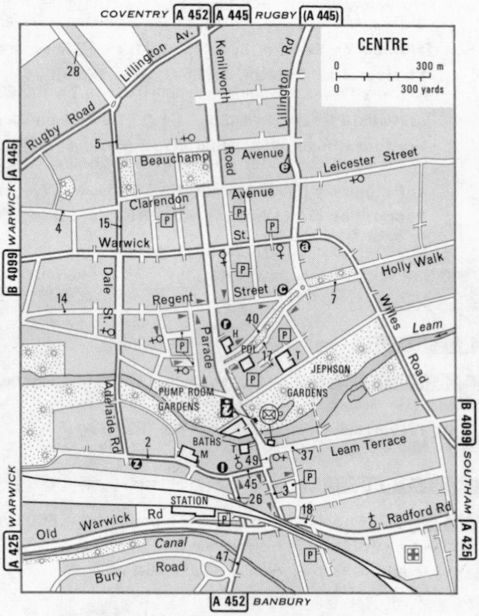

ROYAL LEAMINGTON SPA

Parade
Regent Street
Warwick Street

Avenue Road 2
Bath Street................... 3
Beauchamp Hill 4
Binswood Street............ 5
Brandon Parade 7
Church Hill.................... 14
Clarendon Place 15
Hamilton Terrace 17
High Street 18
Lower Avenue............... 26
Northumberland Road 28
Priory Terrace 37
Regent Grove 40
Spencer Street 45
Tachbrook Road............. 47
Victoria Terrace............ 49

Chesford House, 12 Clarendon St., CV32 5ST, ☎ 20924, – wc wc P **e**
9 rm.

Beech Lodge, 28 Warwick New Rd, CV32 5JJ, ☎ 22227 – wc P.
M (dinner only, residents only) 7.00 **t.** 3.00 – **12 rm** 15.50/28.50 **t.** plan of Warwick Z **s**

Amersham, 34 Kenilworth Rd, CV32 4DF, ☎ 21637, – wc P plan of Warwick Z **e**
13 rm.

Buckland Lodge, 35 Avenue Rd, CV31 3PG, ☎ 23843 – P **z**
closed Christmas and New Year – **11 rm** 9.20/23.00 **st.**

XXX ⚙ **Mallory Court** with rm, Harbury Lane, Bishop's Tachbrook, CV33 9QB, S : 2 m. by A 452 ☎ 30214, Telex 317294, ≤, , , park, squash – wc ☎ P. AE VISA.
closed 24 December-10 January – **M** (booking essential) 14.50/27.00 **st.** – 5.75 – **9 rm** 55.00/90.00 **st.**
see plan of Warwick Z **a**

Spec. Terrine de homard sauce verte, Soufflé de saumon, Gâteau aux fruits de la passion.

AUDI, VW Dormer Pl. ℰ 36511
AUSTIN-ROVER-JAGUAR-RANGE ROVER Station
Approach ℰ 27156
COLT Wood St. ℰ 24681
FORD Sydenham Drive ℰ 29411

PEUGEOT-TALBOT Spencer St. ℰ 30115
RENAULT Russell St. ℰ 21171
SAAB, DAIHATSU Lime Av. ℰ 23221
VAUXHALL-OPEL Old Warwick Rd ℰ 20861
VOLVO Tachbrook Rd ℰ 882111

ROYAL TUNBRIDGE WELLS Kent **404** U 30 – pop. 44,612 – ECD : Wednesday – ✪ 0892.
See : The Pantiles★ (promenade 18C) B – Town Hall Museum (wood-mosaic articles★) B **M**.
Envir. : Scotney Castle Gardens (trees ★, Bastion view ★) AC, SE : 8 m. by B 2169 A.
🛈 Town Hall ℰ 26121 – ◆London 36 – ◆Brighton 33 – Folkestone 46 – Hastings 27 – Maidstone 18.

ROYAL TUNBRIDGE WELLS

Calverley Road	B
High Street	B 14
Mount Pleasant Road	B 25
Pantiles (The)	B 26
Benhall Mill Road	A 3
Bishop's Down	A 4
Calverley Park Gardens	B 7

Clarence Road	B 8
Crescent Road	B 9
Fir Tree Road	A 10
Grosvenor Road	B 12
Hall's Hole Road	A 13
High Rocks Lane	A 16
Hungershall Park Road	A 17
Lansdowne Road	B 18
Lower Green Road	A 20
Major York's Road	A 22

Mount Ephraim	A 23
Mount Ephraim Road	B 24
Prospect Road	A 27
Rusthall Road	A 28
St. John's Road	B 29
Tea Garden Lane	A 30
Upper Grosvenor Road	B 31
Vale Road	B 33
Victoria Road	B 34
Warwick Park	B 35

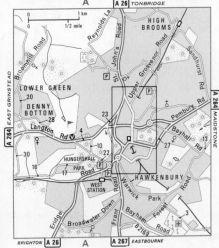

🏨 **Spa,** Mount Ephraim, TN4 8XJ, ℰ 20331, Telex 957188, ≤, 🛲, park, ❤ – 🛗 📺 ☎ 🔧 🔜 🅰🄴
⑩ 𝚅𝙸𝚂𝘼
  A v
M 8.50/9.00 t. ⅄ 3.00 – ☲ 5.50 – **68 rm** 35.00/47.00 st. – SB (weekends only) 50.00/60.00 st.

🏨 **Russell,** 80 London Rd, TN1 1DZ, ℰ 44833 – 📺 ⛌wc 🔧wc ☎ 🄿 🔜 🅰🄴 ⑩ 𝚅𝙸𝚂𝘼 ❤ B a
M (lunch by arrangement) a la carte 8.30/15.80 st. ⅄ 2.50 – **21 rm** ☲ 29.00/40.00 st. – SB
(weekends only) 45.00/55.00 st.

at Southborough N : 2 m. on A 26 – A – ⊠ ✪ 0892 Royal Tunbridge Wells :

XX **Weavers,** London Rd, TN4 0PU, ℰ 29896 – 🄿 🔜 ⑩ 𝚅𝙸𝚂𝘼 ❤
closed Sunday dinner, Monday, 25 to 31 December and Bank Holidays – **M** a la carte
9.90/13.30 t. ⅄ 3.00.

at Frant S : 2 ¼ m. on A 267 – A – ⊠ ✪ 089 275 Frant :

XX **Bassetts,** 35-39 High St., TN3 9DT, ℰ 635 – 🔜 🅰🄴 𝚅𝙸𝚂𝘼
closed Sunday, Monday, Tuesday, 7 to 30 June and 29 September -14 October – **M** (dinner
only) 10.50 t.

at Speldhurst NW : 3 ½ m. by A 26 – A – ⊠ Royal Tunbridge Wells – ✪ 089 286 Langton :

XX **George and Dragon Inn,** Barden Rd, TN3 0NN, ℰ 3125, « 13C inn » – 🄿 🔜 🅰🄴 ⑩ 𝚅𝙸𝚂𝘼
closed Saturday lunch and Sunday dinner – **M** a la carte 11.00/17.00 st. ⅄ 3.00.

AUSTIN-ROVER Crescent Rd ℰ 25266
AUSTIN-ROVER-DAIMLER-JAGUAR Mount Sion ℰ
26463
BMW St. John's Rd ℰ 39355
CITROEN, FIAT, LANCIA 321 St. Johns Rd ℰ 35111
COLT, RELIANT Grosvenor Rd ℰ 27174

FORD Mount Ephraim ℰ 20323
NISSAN 13/17 London Rd ℰ 29292
RENAULT Langton Rd ℰ 39466
PEUGEOT-TALBOT, ALFA-ROMEO 49 Mount Plea-
sant ℰ 27202
VW, AUDI Currie Rd ℰ 44733

RUAN-HIGH-LANES Cornwall **408** F 33 – see Veryan.

RUGBY Warw. **408 404** Q 26 – pop. 59,396 – ECD : Wednesday – ✆ 0788.
Envir. : Stanford-on-Avon (castle 17C : park★ *AC*) NE : 5 m.
🖪 Public Library, St. Matthew's St. ☎ 2687 and 71813.
♦London 88 – ♦Birmingham 33 – ♦Leicester 21 – Northampton 20 – Warwick 17.

🏨 **Three Horse Shoes** (Best Western), Sheep St., CV21 3BX, ☎ 4585 – 📺 ➪wc 🛞 🕾.
🖾 🖾 AE ⓪ VISA
M 6.95/9.50 **st.** ▯ 4.75 – 🖵 5.55 – **32 rm** 38.50/49.00 **st.** – SB 84.00 **st.**

at Kilsby SE : 6 ¼ m. by A 428 on A 5 – ⊠ Rugby – ✆ 0788 Crick :

🞩🞩 **Hunt House,** Main St., CV23 8XR, ☎ 823282, 🐎 – ▤ 🅿 🖾 AE ⓪ VISA
closed Sunday and Monday – **M** (dinner only) 13.25 **t.** ▯ 2.75.

at Crick SE : 6 m. on A 428 – ⊠ ✆ 0788 Rugby :

🏨 **Post House** (T.H.F.), NN6 7XR, W : ½ m. on A 428 ☎ 822101, Telex 311107 – 📺 🅿 🖾 🖾
AE ⓪ VISA
M 6.95/8.25 **st.** ▯ 2.60 – 🖵 5.50 – **96 rm** 38.00/45.50 **st.**

at Stretton Under Fosse NW : 7 ½ m. by A 426 and B 4112 on A 427 – ⊠ ✆ 0788 Rugby :

🏛 **Ashton Lodge** ⚶, CV23 0PJ, N : 1 m. by A 427 on B 4112 ☎ 832278, 🐎 – 📺 ➪wc 🕮wc
🛞 🅿 🖾 AE ⓪. 🞋
M (bar lunch) a la carte 7.65/11.75 **t.** ▯ 2.45 – **10 rm** 🖵 17.00/32.50 **t.** – SB (week-ends only) 37.30/58.50 **st.**

AUSTIN-ROVER Railway Terrace ☎ 3477   NISSAN Temple St. ☎ 3094
CITROEN 339 Hillmorton Rd ☎ 73671   RENAULT 100 Railway Terr. ☎ 2660
HONDA Leicester Rd ☎ 2685

RUGELEY Staffs. **402 408 404** O 25 – pop. 17,240 – ECD : Wednesday – ✆ 088 94.
Envir. : Blithfield Hall★ (Elizabethan) *AC*, N : 5 m.
♦London 135 – ♦Birmingham 23 – Stafford 9 – ♦Stoke-on-Trent 23.

🏛 Eaton Lodge, 118 Wolsley Rd, WS15 2ET, ☎ 3454, 🐎 – 📺 🕮 🅿 🖾 VISA. 🞋
M (bar lunch) 7.00 **st.** ▯ 2.75 – **11 rm**

at Armitage SE : 3 m. on A 513 – ⊠ Rugeley – ✆ 0543 Armitage :

🞩🞩 **Old Farmhouse,** Armitage Rd, WS15 4AT, ☎ 490353, 🐎 – 🅿 🖾 AE ⓪ VISA
*closed Sunday, Monday, 9 April, 28 May-1 June, last 2 weeks July, 25 December-4 January and
Bank Holidays* – **M** 8.75/11.95 **t.** ▯ 2.45.

AUSTIN-ROVER 6 Market St. ☎ 3385   HONDA, SAAB Market St. ☎ 76113

RUNCORN Cheshire **402 408** L 23 – pop. 51,698 – ECD : Wednesday – ✆ 092 85 (5 fig.) or 0928
(6 fig.).
🚆 Highfield Rd, Widnes ☎ 051 (Liverpool) 424 2440, N : 4 m. – 🚆 Dundalk Rd, Widnes ☎ 051
(Liverpool) 424 6230.
🖪 57-61 Church St. ☎ 76776 and 69656.
♦London 202 – ♦Liverpool 14 – ♦Manchester 29.

🏨 **Crest** (Crest), Wood Lane, Beechwood, WA7 3HA, SE : ½ m. off junction 12 of M 56 ☎
714000, Telex 627426 – ▤📺 ➪wc 🛞 🅿 🖾 🖾 AE ⓪ VISA
M approx. 11.00 **st.** – 🖵 5.25 – **130 rm** 42.00/51.00 **st.**

AUSTIN-ROVER Balfour St. ☎ 72271   MAZDA Picow Farm Rd ☎ 63099
FORD Victoria Rd ☎ 74333

RUSHDEN Northants. **404** S 27 – pop. 22,300 – ECD : Thursday – ✆ 0933.
See : Higham Ferrers (St. Mary's Church★ 13C-14C).
♦ London 72 – Bedford 13 – ♦ Cambridge 36 – ♦ Leicester 38 – Northampton 15.

🛖 **Westward,** Shirley Rd, NN10 9BY, ☎ 312376, 🝤 heated – 📺 🕮 🅿. 🞋
26 rm 🖵 15.00/30.00 **t.**

AUSTIN-ROVER High St. South ☎ 59111

RUSHLAKE GREEN East Sussex **404** U 31 – pop. 1,195 (inc. Warbleton) – ⊠ Heathfield –
✆ 0435.
♦London 57 – Eastbourne 14 – Hastings 15 – Royal Tunbridge Wells 21.

🏨 **Priory Country House** ⚶, TN21 9RG, N : 1 m. by Dallington Rd. ☎ 830553, ≼, « 15C priory
with country house atmosphere », 🝤, 🐎, park – 📺 ➪wc 🛞 🅿
closed 24 December-mid January – **M** 10.30/16.05 **t.** ▯ 4.05 – **12 rm** 🖵 33.35/80.50 **t.**

RUSPER West Sussex 🔟🔟🔟 T 30 – pop. 1,100 – ✪ 029 384.

♦London 30 – ♦Brighton 35 – Horsham 6.

   XXX **Ghyll Manor** with rm, High St., RH12 4PX, ℰ 571, ≼, ⣀ heated, 🐾, park, ✵ – 📺 ⌂wc ☎
      🅿. 🔼 🄰🄴 ⑩ 𝑽𝑰𝑺𝑨
      M a la carte 9.90/16.65 t. ⫰ 2.55 – ⊊ 2.50 – **11 rm** 37.50/65.00 t.

RUTHIN (RHUTHUN) Clwyd 🔟🔟🔟 🔟🔟🔟 K 24 – pop. 4,338 – ECD : Thursday – ✪ 082 42.

See : Church★.

🏌 at Pantmywyn ℰ 035 284 (Pantmywyn) 318, NE : 8 m. – 🏌 Pwllglas ℰ 2296, S : 2 ½ m.

🇧 Ruthin Craft Centre ℰ 3992.

♦London 210 – Birkenhead 31 – Chester 23 – Shrewsbury 46.

   🏛 **Ruthin Castle** (Best Western) ⤸, Corwen Rd, LL15 2NU, ℰ 2664, Telex 61169, ≼,
      « Reconstructed medieval castle », ⤸, 🐾, park – 🔳 ⌂wc ⊛ 🅿. 🔼 🄰🄴 ⑩ 𝑽𝑰𝑺𝑨
      M 5.95/7.95 st. ⫰ 3.00 – **58 rm** ⊊ 27.00/51.00 st. – SB 58.00/61.00 st.

   🏛 **Castle**, St. Peter's Sq., LL15 1AA, ℰ 2479, Telex 617074 – 📺 ⌂wc ⊛ 🅿. 🄰. 🔼 🄰🄴 ⑩ 𝑽𝑰𝑺𝑨
      M 3.50/6.90 t. ⫰ 3.40 – **25 rm** ⊊ 20.00/32.00 t. – SB (weekends only) 35.50 st.

AUSTIN-ROVER High St. ℰ 074 578 (Llanynys) 227   VAUXHALL-OPEL Well St. ℰ 2645

RYDAL Cumbria 🔟🔟🔟 L 20 – see Ambleside.

RYDE I.O.W. 🔟🔟🔟 🔟🔟🔟 Q 31 – see Wight (Isle of).

RYE East Sussex 🔟🔟🔟 W 31 – pop. 4,449 – ECD : Tuesday – ✪ 0797.

See : Old Town★ (chiefly : Mermaid Street) – Ypres Tower ≼★.

Envir. : Winchelsea (Church of St. Thomas the Martyr★ 1283 : Tombs★★ 12C) SW : 3 m. – Small
Hythe (Ellen Terry's House★ AC) N : 7 ½ m.

🇧 48 Cinque Ports St., Ferry Rd ℰ 222293.

♦London 61 – ♦Brighton 49 – Folkestone 27 – Maidstone 33.

   🏛 **George** (T.H.F.), High St., TN31 7JP, ℰ 222114 – 📺 ⌂wc 🛆wc ⊛ 🅿. 🄰. 🔼 🄰🄴 ⑩ 𝑽𝑰𝑺𝑨
      M 8.50 st. ⫰ 2.60 – ⊊ 4.50 – **17 rm** 32.50/44.50 st.

   🏛 **Mermaid**, Mermaid St., TN31 7EY, ℰ 223065, Group Telex 957141, « 15C inn » – ⌂wc 🛆wc
      🅿. 🄰🄴 𝑽𝑰𝑺𝑨. ✵
      closed midweek late January-February – **M** 6.50/8.50 t. ⫰ 2.45 – **28 rm** ⊊ 19.00/45.00 t. – SB
      57.50/62.00 st.

   🏛 **Hope Anchor**, Watchbell St., TN31 7HA, ℰ 222216, ≼ – ⌂wc 🅿. 🔼 🄰🄴 ⑩ 𝑽𝑰𝑺𝑨
      M (bar lunch) 7.50 t. – **15 rm** ⊊ 16.00/28.00 t.

   🏠 **Ship Inn**, Strand Quay, TN31 7DB, ℰ 222233, Group Telex 957141 – 📺 ⌂wc. 🔼 🄰🄴 ⑩
      𝑽𝑰𝑺𝑨. ✵
      M (bar lunch Monday to Saturday) a la carte 4.70/5.90 t. ⫰ 2.40 – **12 rm** ⊊ 25.00/32.00 t. – SB
      39.50/42.00 st.

   XX **Flushing Inn**, Market St., TN31 7LA, ℰ 223292, Seafood, « 15C inn with 16C mural » – 🔼
      🄰🄴 ⑩ 𝑽𝑰𝑺𝑨
      closed Monday dinner, Tuesday and 26 December-16 January – **M** a la carte 5.75/11.70 t.
      ⫰ 3.20.

   X **Bistro Down Under**, 1a High St., TN31 7JE, ℰ 222829 – 🔼 🄰🄴 ⑩ 𝑽𝑰𝑺𝑨
      closed Sunday, Monday, first week November, Christmas and first week January – **M** (dinner
      only) a la carte 6.50/10.15 t. ⫰ 1.70.

   at Playden N : 1 m. on A 268 – ✉ ✪ 0797 Rye :

   🏠 **Playden Oasts**, TN31 7UL, on A 268 ℰ 223502, « Former oast house », 🐾 – ⌂wc 🛆wc 🅿
      8 rm.

   at Winchelsea SW : 2 ½ m. on A 259 – ✉ ✪ 0797 Rye :

   X **Manna Plat**, Mill Rd, TN36 4HT, ℰ 226317
      closed lunch Tuesday to Friday, Sunday dinner, Monday, 2 weeks March, 2 weeks November
      and 25-26 December – **M** (booking essential) 6.50/9.25 st. ⫰ 2.40.

   at Peasmarsh NW : 4 m. on A 268 – ✉ Rye – ✪ 079 721 Peasmarsh :

   🏠 **Flackley Ash** (Best Western), London Rd, TN31 6YH, ℰ 381, 🐾 – 📺 ⌂wc 🛆wc 🅿. 🔼 🄰🄴
      ⑩ 𝑽𝑰𝑺𝑨
      M (bar lunch) a la carte 6.95/10.65 t. ⫰ 2.45 – **19 rm** ⊊ 28.00/46.00 st. – SB 55.00/59.00 st.

ALFA-ROMEO, CITROEN Cinque Ports St. ℰ 3196   RENAULT Rye Harbour Rd ℰ 4888
AUSTIN-ROVER-JAGUAR-LAND ROVER Fishmar-
ket Rd ℰ 223334

SAFFRON WALDEN Essex **404** U 27 – pop. 9,971 – ECD : Thursday – **⊙** 0799.

See : Parish Church★ (Perpendicular) – Audley End House★ (Jacobean : interior★★) *AC*.

🛈 Corn Exchange, Market Sq. *⌀* 24282.

♦London 46 – ♦Cambridge 15 – Chelmsford 25.

   🏠 **Saffron,** 10-18 High St., CB10 1AY, *⌀* 22676 – 📺 ⎕wc ⑂ ☎ 🅿. 🔼 *VISA*
      M *(closed Sunday and Bank Holidays)* (bar lunch Saturday) 9.50 **st.** ◊ 2.40 – ⚌ 2.50 – **18 rm**
      13.50/35.00 **st.**

AUSTIN-ROVER High St. *⌀* 27909
AUSTIN-ROVER 66 High St. *⌀* 23597

RENAULT, VAUXHALL-OPEL 13/15 Station St. *⌀* 23238

ST. AGNES Cornwall **403** E 33 The West Country G. – pop. 4,747 – ECD : Wednesday – **⊙** 087 255.

♦London 302 – Newquay 12 – Penzance 26 – Truro 9.

   🏛 **Trevaunance Point** ⌂, Quay Rd, Trevaunance Cove, TR5 0RZ, *⌀* 3235, ≤ bay and cliffs,
      🍴 – ⎕wc 🅿. 🔼 *AE* **①** *VISA*
      M 4.95/8.50 **t.** ◊ 2.75 – **11 rm** ⚌ 17.50/45.00 **t.**

   🏠 **Sunholme** ⌂, Goonvrea Rd, Goonvrea, TR5 0NW, SW : 1 m. by B 3277 *⌀* 2318, 🍴 – 🅿. 🔼
      VISA
      April-October – **11 rm** ⚌ 10.00/29.00 **st.**

      at Mithian E : 2 m. by B 3285 – ✉ **⊙** 087 255 St. Agnes :

   🏠 **Rose-in-Vale** ⌂, TR5 0QD, *⌀* 2202, ≤, 🔼 heated, 🍴 – ⎕wc 🕻wc 🅿
      M (bar lunch) 5.75 **s.** ◊ 1.80 – **14 rm** ⚌ 8.20/36.80 **st.** – SB (except summer) 29.80 **st.**

FORD Trevellas Garage, Trevellas *⌀* 2372

ST. ALBANS Herts. **404** T 28 – pop. 52,174 – ECD : Thursday – **⊙** 0727.

See : Site★★ – Cathedral and Abbey Church★ (Norman Tower★).

Envir. : Hatfield House★★★ *AC* (gardens★ and Old Palace★) E : 6 m. – Verulamium (Roman
remains★ and museum) *AC*, W : 2 m.

🏌 Batchwood Hall *⌀* 52100.

🛈 37 Chequer St. *⌀* 64511 and 66100 ext. 294.

♦London 27 – ♦Cambridge 41 – Luton 10.

   🏨 **St. Michael's Manor** ⌂, Fishpool St., AL3 4RY, *⌀* 64444, « Manor house, lake, ≤ garden »,
      park – 📺 ⎕wc 🕻wc 🅿. 🔼 *AE* **①** *VISA*. ❄
      M 8.00/10.25 **t.** ◊ 3.00 – **26 rm** ⚌ 38.50/52.50 **st.**

   🏨 **Noke Thistle** (Thistle) Watford Rd, AL2 3DS, SW : 2 ½ m. at junction A 405 and B 4630
      ⌀ 54252, Telex 893834 – 📺 ⎕wc ⑂ 🅿. 🔼 *AE* **①** *VISA*. ❄
      M 9.00/10.00 **t.** ◊ 3.45 – ⚌ 4.95 – **57 rm** 38.00/52.00 **st.** – SB (weekends only) 62.00 **st.**

   🏨 **Sopwell House** ⌂, Cottonmill Lane, AL1 2HQ, SE : 1 ½ m. by A 1081 and Mile House Lane
      ⌀ 64477, 🍴, park – 📺 ⎕wc ⑂ 🅿. 🔼 *AE* **①** *VISA*. ❄
      M 8.25/9.75 **t.** – ⚌ 4.50 – **30 rm** 33.50/42.50 **t.** – SB (weekends only) 71.00/73.50 **st.**

   🏠 **Melford House,** 24 Woodstock Rd North, AL1 4QQ, *⌀* 53642 – 🕻wc 🅿
      12 rm ⚌ 14.95/29.90 **t.**

   🏠 **Ardmore House,** 54 Lemsford Rd, AL1 3PR, *⌀* 59313 – 📺 🕻wc 🅿. ❄
      18 rm ⚌ 14.00/28.00 **s.**

   ✗ **La Province,** 13 George St., AL3 4ER, *⌀* 52142, French rest. – 🔼 *AE* **①** *VISA*
      closed Sunday, Monday, 1 week at Easter, last 2 weeks August and 1 week at Christmas – **M** a
      la carte 6.20/13.00 **t.** ◊ 2.75.

   ✗ **Langtry's,** London Rd, AL1 1SP, *⌀* 61848, Seafood – 🔼 *AE* **①** *VISA*
      closed Sunday and 26 December-2 January – **M** a la carte 9.75/14.50 **t.** ◊ 2.30.

AUSTIN-ROVER-DAIMLER-JAGUAR, ROLLS
ROYCE-BENTLEY Acrewood Way, Hatfield Rd *⌀*
66522
AUSTIN-ROVER Park St., Frogmore *⌀* 72626
CITROEN, VAUXHALL-OPEL 66-70 High St., Potters
Bar *⌀* 0707 (Potters Bar) 42391
CITROEN, OPEL, SCIMITAR, VAUXHALL 101 Holy-
well Hill *⌀* 65756

FIAT Beech Rd *⌀* 50871
FORD London Rd *⌀* 59155
HONDA, PEUGEOT Catherine St. *⌀* 54342
PEUGEOT-TALBOT 220 London Rd *⌀* 63377
RENAULT 99/111 London Rd *⌀* 52345
VAUXHALL-OPEL 100 London Rd *⌀* 50601
VW, AUDI Valley Rd *⌀* 36236
VW, AUDI 229/233 Hatfield Rd *⌀* 36366

ST. ASAPH (LLANELWY) Clwyd **402 403** J 24 – pop. 2,910 – ECD : Thursday – **⊙** 0745.

Envir. : Rhuddlan (castle★ 13C) *AC*, NW : 3 m.

🏌 *⌀* 074 571 (Denbigh) 4159, S : 6 m.

♦London 225 – Chester 29 – Shrewsbury 59.

   🏨 Oriel House, Upper Denbigh Rd, LL17 0LW, S : ¾ m. on A 525 *⌀* 582716, 🍴 – 📺 ⎕wc
      🕻wc 🅿. 🔼 – **20 rm**.

ALFA-ROMEO High St. *⌀* 583475
AUSTIN-ROVER Bod Ewr Corner *⌀* 582345

RENAULT The Roe *⌀* 582233

ST. AUSTELL Cornwall 🄰🄾🄳 F 32 The West Country G. – pop. 25,158 – ECD : Thursday – ☎ 0726.
See : Holy Trinity.

Envir. : St. Austell Bay ★★★ (Gribbin Head ★★), E : 3 m. by A 3601 – Wheal Martyn Museum ★★, N : 2 m. on A 391 – Polkerris★, E : 9 m. by A 3082.

🛆 Carlyon Bay ℰ 072 681 (Par) 4250, E : 2 m.

🚗 ℰ 01 (London) 723 7000 ext. 3148.

◆London 281 – Newquay 16 – ◆Plymouth 38 – Truro 14.

  🏨 **White Hart,** Church St., PL25 4AT, ℰ 72100 – 📺 🛏wc 🈲. 🌣 🄰🄴 🅾 💳. ❄
    M 4.50/7.50 t. 🍷 2.40 – **20 rm** ⊆ 17.50/31.00 **st.** – SB (weekends only) (except summer) 35.00 **st.**

    at Tregrehan E : 2 ½ m. by A 390 – ⊠ St. Austell – ☎ 072 681 Par :

  XX **Boscundle Manor** 🌭 with rm, PL25 3RL, ℰ 3557, « Tastefully converted 18C manor »,
    🏊 heated, 🎠 – 📺 🈲wc 🕿 🄿 🌣 🄰🄴 💳. ❄
    closed 23 December-mid February – **M** *(closed Sunday and Bank Holidays)* (restricted lunch
    residents only) 13.50 t. 🍷 2.75 – **6 rm** ⊆ 30.00/45.00 **st.**

    at Carlyon Bay E : 2 ½ m. by A 3601 – ⊠ St. Austell – ☎ 072 681 Par :

  🏨 **Carlyon Bay** 🌭, PL25 3RD, ℰ 2304, ⩽ Carlyon Bay, « Extensive gardens », 🏊 heated, 🌣,
    🛆, park, ❀ – 🛗 📺 🄿. 🌣 🄰🄴 🅾 💳. ❄
    M 6.00/7.00 st. – **72 rm** ⊆ 19.80/27.50 s.

  🏨 **Porth Avallen** 🌭, Sea Rd, PL25 3SG, ℰ 2802, ⩽ Carlyon Bay, 🎠 – 📺 🛏wc 🕿 🄿. 🌤. 🌣
    🄴 🅾 💳. ❄
    closed 2 weeks at New Year – **M** 3.40/7.00 t. 🍷 1.95 – **24 rm** ⊆ 16.50/40.00 t. – SB
    40.50/48.75 **st.**

    at Charlestown SE : 2 m. by A 390 on A 391 – ⊠ ☎ 0726 St. Austell :

  🏠 **Pier House,** Harbour Front, PL25 3NJ, ℰ 5272, ⩽ – 🛏wc 🄿
    M (bar lunch) 6.50 t. 🍷 2.10 – **12 rm** ⊆ 15.00/27.00 t.

AUSTIN-ROVER Carlyon Bay ℰ 072 681 (Par) 2451   PEUGEOT-TALBOT Gwendra, St. Stephen ℰ 822566
CITROEN 77 Fore St. ℰ 850 241   VW, AUDI East Hill ℰ 5624
FORD Slades Rd ℰ 2333

St COLUMB MINOR Cornwall – see Newquay.

☞ *Inclusion in the **Michelin Guide** cannot be achieved by
pulling strings or by offering favours.*

ST. DAVIDS (TYDDEWI) Dyfed 🄰🄾🄳 E 28 – pop. 1,638 – ECD : Wednesday – ☎ 0437.
See : Cathedral★★ 12C (site★) – Bishops Palace★ *AC.*

Envir. : Porthgain (cliffs ☀★★★) NE : 7 m. – Whitesand Bay★★ and St. David's Head★★ NW : 2 m.
– Newgale (⩽★★) by Solva (site★) E : 7 m. – Abereiddy (site★) NE : 5 m.

🛆 ℰ 721570, W : 2 m.

🄱 Pembrokeshire Coast National Park Centre, City Hall ℰ 720392 and 720747 (summer only).

◆London 266 – Carmarthen 46 – Fishguard 16.

  🏨 **Warpool Court** 🌭, SA62 6BN, ℰ 720300, ⩽ sea and countryside, 🌣, 🌭, 🎠 – 📺 🛏wc
    🈲wc 🄿. 🌣 🄰🄴 💳
    closed January – **M** 7.50/12.50 **st.** – **25 rm** ⊆ 25.85/31.90 **st.** – SB (week-
    ends only) (except summer) 49.90 **st.**

  🏨 **St. Non's,** Catherine St., SA62 6RJ, ℰ 720239, 🎠 – 📺 🛏wc 🕿 🄿. 🌣 🄴 🅾 💳
    M *(closed January and February)* (buffet lunch) 9.15 t. 🍷 2.40 – **20 rm** ⊆ 14.75/53.70 t. – SB
    (except August) 38.50/43.50 **st.**

  🏨 **Old Cross,** Cross Sq., SA62 6SP, ℰ 720387, 🎠 – 🛏wc 🄿. ❄
    March-October – **M** (bar lunch) 7.80 t. 🍷 1.80 – **17 rm** ⊆ 16.00/48.00 t. – SB (except sum-
    mer) 34.00/38.00 st.

  🏠 **Belmont,** Cross Sq., SA62 6SE, ℰ 720264, no smoking – 🄿. ❄
    8 rm ⊆ 10.00/19.00 **st.**

ST. HELENS Merseyside 🄰🄾🄴 🄰🄾🄳 L 23 – pop. 104,341 – ECD : Thursday – ☎ 0744.
🛆 Sherdley Park ℰ 813149, E : 2 m. on A 570.

◆London 204 – ◆Liverpool 14 – ◆Manchester 21 – Preston 25.

  🏨 **Fleece,** 15 Church St., WA10 1BA, ℰ 26546, Telex 629811 – 🛗 📺 🛏wc 🕿 🄿. 🌤. 🌣 🄴 🅾
    💳
    M *(closed Sunday and Bank holidays)* 7.50 t. 🍷 3.00 – **73 rm** ⊆ 32.50/44.00 **st.**

AUSTIN ROVER Prescott Rd ℰ 34441   NISSAN, VOLVO Mill Lane, Newton-Le-Willows ℰ
AUSTIN ROVER Elephant Lane ℰ 811565   092 52 (Newton-Le-Willows) 4411
FIAT Gaskell St. ℰ 21961   PEUGEOT-TALBOT, CITROEN Knowsley Rd ℰ 32411
FORD City Rd ℰ 26381   RENAULT East Lancashire Rd ℰ 27373
LADA, NISSAN Jackson St. ℰ 50301   SAAB Aspinal Pl. ℰ 55333
MAZDA, FSO Dentons Green Lane ℰ 24748   VAUXHALL-OPEL Knowsley Rd ℰ 35221

[ST. IVES] Cornwall [403] D 33 The West Country G. – pop. 9,839 – ECD : Thursday – ☎ 0736 Penzance.

See : Site ★★ – Barbara Hepworth Museum★★ Y M1 – St. Ia Church★ Y A – Barnes Museum of Cinematography★ Y M2.

[i] The Guildhall, Street-an-Pol ☎ 796297.

♦London 319 – Penzance 10 – Truro 25.

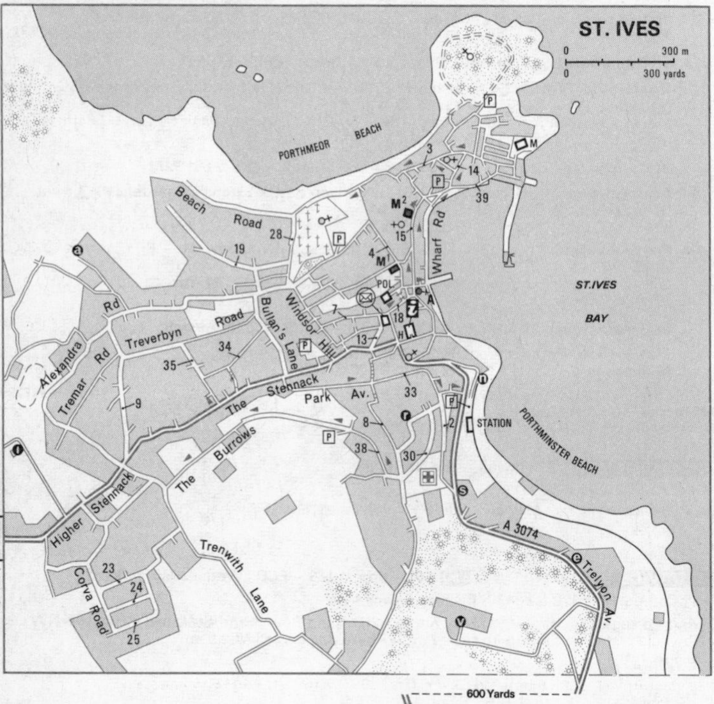

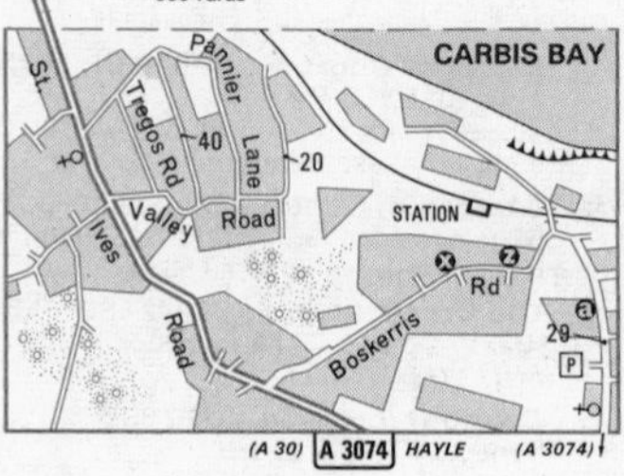

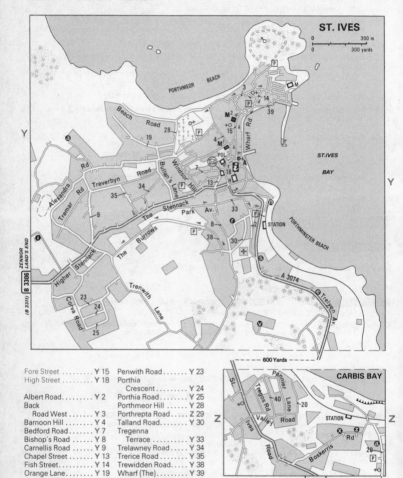

🏨🏨🏨🏨 **Tregenna Castle** 🌳, TR26 2DE, ☎ 795254, Telex 45128, ← St. Ives Bay, 🏊 heated, ⛳18, 🌳, park, 🎾, squash – ⇅ [TV] ♿ [P]. [AE] [AE] [O] [VISA] Y **v**
M (buffet lunch) a la carte 16.00/20.00 **st.** 🍷 3.50 – **80 rm** ☕ 15.50/70.00 **st.** – SB (except summer) 50.00/90.00 **st.**

🏨🏨 **Garrack** 🌳, Burthallan Lane, Higher Ayr, TR26 3AA, ☎ 796199, ←, 🏊, 🌳 – 🛁wc 🚿wc [P]. [AE] [AE] [O] [VISA] Y **a**
March-November – **M** a la carte 6.50/10.10 **t.** 🍷 2.40 – **18 rm** ☕ 14.50/47.00 **t.** – SB (spring only) 34.00 **st.**

🏨🏨 **Porthminster** (Best Western), The Terrace, TR26 2BN, ☎ 795221, ←, 🏊 heated, 🌳 – ⇅ [TV] 🛁wc 🚿wc [P]. [AE] [AE] [O] [VISA] Y **s**
closed mid December-mid January – **M** a la carte 5.95/10.25 **t.** 🍷 2.35 – **50 rm** ☕ 21.00/62.00 **t.** – SB (except summer) 40.00 **st.**

🏠 **Pedn-Olva,** Porthminster Beach, TR26 2EA, ℰ 796222, ≤ coastline – 🛏wc 🕸wc 🅿. 🛇
   M *(closed November-April)* (bar lunch) 7.50 **st.** ♪ 2.40 – **33 rm** ☲ 13.00/50.00 **st.**　　　　Y n

🏠 **Dean Court,** Trelyon Av., TR26 2AD, ℰ 796023, ≤ St. Ives and bay – 📺 🛏wc 🕸wc 🅿. 🛇
   25 March-October – **M** (bar lunch) 5.50 **st.** ♪ 2.30 – **12 rm** ☲ 15.00/43.00 **st.** – SB 42.00/46.00 **st.**
   　　　　Y e

⌂ **Old Vicarage** 🛇, Parc-an-Creet, TR26 2ET, ℰ 796124, 🐾 – 🛏wc 🕸 🅿. 🔼 🆅🆂🅰
   closed 1 week at Christmas – **8 rm** ☲ 10.00/22.00 **t.**　　　　Y i

⌂ **Pondarosa,** 10 Porthminster Terr., TR26 2DQ, ℰ 795875 – 🅿. 🛇
   May-October – **9 rm** ☲ 7.50/22.00 **st.**　　　　Y r

   at Carbis Bay S : 1 ½ m. on A 3074 – ✉ St. Ives – ✆ 0736 Penzance :

🏠 **Boskerris,** Boskerris Rd, TR26 2NQ, ℰ 795295, ≤, 🛋 heated, 🐾 – 🛏wc 🅿 　　　　Z x
   Easter-mid October – **M** (bar lunch) 8.50 **t.** ♪ 2.60 – **20 rm** ☲ 12.00/30.00 **t.** – SB 42.00/55.00 **st.**

🏠 **St. Uny,** Boskerris Rd, TR26 2NQ, ℰ 795011, ≤, 🐾 – 🛏wc 🕸 🅿. 🔼 🆅🆂🅰　　　　Z z
   April-mid October – **M** (bar lunch) 7.00 **st.** ♪ 2.00 – **32 rm** ☲ 14.50/42.00 **st.**

ST. IVES Cambs. 🄬🄬🄬 T 27 – pop. 7,148 – ECD : Thursday – ✆ 0480.

See : Bridge★ 15C.

◆London 75 – ◆Cambridge 14 – Huntingdon 6.

🏨 **Slepe Hall,** Ramsey Rd, PE17 4RB, ℰ 63122, Telex 32339 – 📺 🛏wc 🐜 🅿. 🏌. 🔼 🅰🅴 🄾
   🆅🆂🅰
   closed 25 and 26 December – **M** 9.50 **t.** – **14 rm** ☲ 27.50/44.00 **t.** – SB (week-ends only) 29.00/32.00 **st.**

🏠 **St. Ives Motel,** London Rd, PE17 4EX, S : ¾ m. on A 1096 ℰ 63857 – 📺 🛏wc 🐜 🅿. 🏌.
   🔼 🅰🅴 🄾 🆅🆂🅰
   closed 25 and 26 December – **M** 8.50 **t.** ♪ 2.80 – ☲ 3.75 – **16 rm** 21.00/28.50 **t.** – SB (week-ends only) 40.00 **st.**

AUSTIN-ROVER The Quadrant ℰ 62871　　　　FORD Ramsey Rd ℰ 63184
FIAT, LANCIA Station Rd ℰ 62641

ST. JUST Cornwall 🄬🄬🄬 C 33 – pop. 2,510 – ✆ 0736 Penzance.

◆London 325 – Penzance 7.5 – Truro 35.

🏠 **Boscean** 🛇, TR19 7QP, ℰ 788748, ≤, 🐾 – 🛏wc 🅿. 🛇
   March-October – **M** (bar lunch) 6.00 **st.** – **10 rm** ☲ 9.75/21.50 **t.**

   at Little Kelynack S : 1 ½ m. by A 3071 on B 3306 – ✉ St. Just – ✆ 0736 Penzance :

✕✕ **Old School,** TR19 7RH, ℰ 788911, 🐾 – 🅿. 🔼
   closed Sunday – **M** (dinner only) a la carte 9.35/13.35 **st.** ♪ 2.85.

   at Botallack NW : 2 ¼ m. by B 3306 – ✉ St. Just – ✆ 0736 Penzance :

✕✕ **Count House,** TR19 7QQ, ℰ 788588, ≤ coastline – 🅿. 🔼 🅰🅴 🄾 🆅🆂🅰
   closed Sunday dinner, Monday and Tuesday – **M** (dinner only and Sunday lunch)(booking essential) a la carte 10.25/13.45 **t.** ♪ 2.80.

ST JUST IN ROSELAND Cornwall – see St. Mawes.

ST. KEYNE Cornwall – see Liskeard.

ST LAWRENCE I.O.W. – see Wight (Isle of) : Ventnor.

ST. MARGARET'S BAY Kent 🄬🄬🄬 Y 30 – see Dover.

ST. MARY'S Cornwall 🄬🄬🄬 ⑳ – see Scilly (Isles of).

ST. MAWES Cornwall 🄬🄬🄬 E 33 The West Country G. – pop. 870 – ✉ Truro – ✆ 0326.

See : Site ★★ – Castle★ (≤★).

Envir. : St. Just-in-Roseland ★★★, N : 2 ½ m. by A 3078 – St. Anthony-in-Roseland (≤★★), 8 m. round peninsula.

◆London 299 – ◆Plymouth 56 – Truro 18.

🏨 **Tresanton** 🛇, TR2 5DR, ℰ 270544, ≤ estuary, « Converted cottages », 🐾 – 🛏wc 🅿. 🅰🅴
   🄾 🆅🆂🅰
   M 7.00/15.00 **t.** ♪ 2.20 – **21 rm** ☲ 30.00/73.00 **t.** – SB (weekends only) 42.50/56.00 **st.**

🏨 **Rising Sun,** The Square, TR2 5DJ, ℰ 270233 – 🛏wc 🅿. 🔼 🅰🅴 🄾
   M (bar lunch) 10.00 **t.** ♪ 1.75 – **17 rm** ☲ 17.50/45.00 **t.**

🏨 **Idle Rocks,** Tredenham Rd, TR2 5AN, ℰ 270771, ≤ harbour and estuary – 🛏wc 🕸wc. 🔼
   🅰🅴 🄾 🆅🆂🅰
   27 March-5 November – **M** (bar lunch) 9.50 **t.** – **22 rm** ☲ 20.00/50.00 **t.** – SB (May-September) 60.00 **st.**

389

☆ **St. Mawes,** The Seafront, TR2 5DW, ℰ 270266, ← – ⇔wc. ☒ 𝑉𝐼𝑆𝐴
closed December and January – **M** 8.00/9.00 **st.** ⋔ 3.00 – **8 rm** ⊡ 16.00/36.00 **st.**

XX **Green Lantern** with rm, Marine Par., TR2 5DW, ℰ 270502, ← – ⊡ ⇔wc ⋔wc. ☒ AE ⓞ 𝑉𝐼𝑆𝐴
closed mid December-mid January – **M** (dinner only and Sunday lunch) 5.50/12.00 **t.** ⋔ 4.50 –
10 rm ⊡ 13.50/26.50 **t.**

at St. Just in Roseland N : 2 ½ m. on A 3078 – ⊠ Truro – ✆ 0326 St. Mawes :

🏠 **Rose da Mar** ⋟, TR2 5JB, N : ¼ m. on B 3289 ℰ 270450, ←, ☞ – ⇔wc ℗. ⅍
April-October – **M** (dinner only) 8.00 **st.** ⋔ 2.15 – **9 rm** ⊡ 14.00/34.00 **st.**

ST. MICHAEL'S ON WYRE Lancs. 𝟒𝟎𝟐 L 22 – pop. 529 – ECD : Wednesday – ⊠ Preston –
✆ 099 58.

♦London 234 – ♦Blackpool 11 – Lancaster 14 – Preston 11.

XX **Rivermede** with rm, Garstang Rd, PR3 0UB, ℰ 267, ☜, ☞ – ⊡ ⇔wc ☏ ℗
closed January and February – **M** *(closed Sunday)* (dinner only) 15.00 **t.** ⋔ 2.75 – **3 rm**
⊡ 28.00/40.00 **t.**

ST. NEOTS Cambs. 𝟒𝟎𝟒 T 27 – pop. 10,110 – ✆ 0480 Huntingdon.

See : St. Mary's Church★ 15C.

🏌 Cross Hall Rd ℰ 74311, W : 1 m. – 🏌 Eynesbury Hardwicke, St. Neots Leisure Centre ℰ 215153,
SE : 2 m.

♦London 60 – Bedford 11 – ♦Cambridge 17 – Huntingdon 9.

🏠 **Stephenson's Rocket,** Crosshall Rd ⊠ Huntingdon, NW : 1 m. on A 45 ℰ 72773 – ⊡
⇔wc ☏ ℗. ☒ 𝑉𝐼𝑆𝐴. ⅍
closed Christmas Day – **M** (bar meal only Sunday dinner) a la carte 8.70/18.70 **st.** ⋔ 2.10 –
9 rm ⊡ 28.50/34.00 **st.** – SB (weekdays only) 40.00 **st.**

XX **Chequers Inn,** St. Mary's St., Eynesbury, PE19 2TA, S : ½ m. on B 1043 ℰ 72116 – ℗. ☒ AE
ⓞ 𝑉𝐼𝑆𝐴
M a la carte 11.55/17.00 **t.** ⋔ 3.00.

AUSTIN-ROVER 42 Huntingdon St. ℰ 73237   FORD Cambridge St. ℰ 73321

SALCOMBE Devon 𝟒𝟎𝟑 I 33 The West Country G. – pop. 2,496 – ECD : Thursday – ✆ 054 884.
Envir. : Kingsbridge ★, N : 5 m. by A 381 Y. – 🛈 Main Rd ℰ 2736.

♦London 243 – Exeter 43 – ♦Plymouth 27 – Torquay 28.

Plan opposite

🏨 **Marine,** Cliff Rd, TQ8 8JH, ℰ 2253, Telex 45185, ≤ estuary, ⊼ heated, ⬛, ☞ – ⧈ ⊡ ⅋ ℗.
☒ AE ⓞ 𝑉𝐼𝑆𝐴. ⅍   Y e
M (buffet lunch) 6.80/16.50 **st.** – **51 rm** ⊡ 40.50/81.00 **st.** – SB (winter only) 70.00/100.00 **st.**

🏨 **Tides Reach,** South Sands, TQ8 8LJ, ℰ 3466, ≤, ⬛, ☞, squash – ⧈ ⊡ ⇔wc ☏ ℗. ☒
AE ⓞ 𝑉𝐼𝑆𝐴   Z x
closed January and February – **M** (buffet lunch) 13.50 **t.** – **40 rm** ⊡ (dinner included) 29.00/96.00 **t.**

🏨 **Bolt Head** (Best Western) ⋟, South Sands, TQ8 8LL, ℰ 2780, ≤ estuary, ⊼ heated – ⊡
⇔wc ℗. ☒ AE ⓞ 𝑉𝐼𝑆𝐴   Z z
Easter-October and Christmas – **M** (buffet lunch) 12.50 **t.** ⋔ 2.50 – **28 rm** ⊡ 25.00/64.00 **t.**

🏨 **St. Elmo** ⋟, Sandhills Rd, TQ8 8JR, ℰ 2233, ≤, ☞ – ⊡ ⇔wc ⋔wc ℗. ☒ 𝑉𝐼𝑆𝐴   Z r
Easter-October – **M** (bar lunch) 11.50 ⋔ 3.00 – **25 rm** ⊡ 18.50/54.00 – SB (except summer) 46.00/57.50 **st.**

🏠 **Grafton Towers** ⋟, Moult Rd, TQ8 8LG, ℰ 2882, ≤, ☞ – ⊡ ⇔wc ⋔wc ℗. ☒ 𝑉𝐼𝑆𝐴
April-mid October – **M** (bar lunch) 8.00 **t.** ⋔ 3.00 – **15 rm** ⊡ 10.50/36.00 **t.** – SB
(spring only) 36.00/42.00 **st.**   Z v

🏠 **Castle Point** ⋟, Sandhills Rd, TQ8 8JP, ℰ 2167, ≤ estuary, ☞ – ⊡ ⇔wc ⋔wc ℗. ☒ ⓞ
𝑉𝐼𝑆𝐴. ⅍   Z s
Easter-10 October – **M** (bar lunch) 8.90 **t.** ⋔ 2.40 – **20 rm** ⊡ 12.50/37.00 **t.**

🏠 **Knowle,** Onslow Rd, TQ8 8HY, ℰ 2846, ☞ – ⊡ ⇔wc ⋔wc ℗. ☒ 𝑉𝐼𝑆𝐴   Y a
April-October – **M** (bar lunch) 8.05 **t.** ⋔ 2.30 – **17 rm** ⊡ 12.00/32.00 **t.** – SB (except summer) 36.00/48.00 **st.**

🏠 **Bay View,** Bennett Rd, TQ8 8JJ, ℰ 2238, ≤ estuary – ℗. ⅍   Z o
closed January, February and Christmas – **11 rm** ⊡ 14.00/32.00 **t.**

🏠 **Woodgrange,** Devon Rd, TQ8 8HJ, ℰ 2439, ☞ – ⊡ ⇔wc ℗. ☒ AE 𝑉𝐼𝑆𝐴   Z n
April-September – **11 rm** ⊡ 10.00/20.00 **t.**

🏠 **Penn Torr,** Herbert Rd, TQ8 8HN, ℰ 2234 – ⇔wc ⋔wc ℗. ⅍   Z i
March-October – **9 rm** ⊡ 11.00/22.80.

X **Wellingtons,** 84-86 Fore St., TQ8 8BY, ℰ 3385 – ☒ AE ⓞ 𝑉𝐼𝑆𝐴   Y n
closed Sunday and Monday in January and February and November-26 December – **M** (dinner
only) a la carte 9.55/14.85 **t.** ⋔ 3.50.

SALCOMBE

Fore Street . . . . Y

Allenhayes Road. . . . . Y 2
Bonaventure Road . . . . . . Y 3
Buckley Street. . . . . Y 4
Camperdown Road . . . . . Y 7
Church Street . . . . Y 8
Coronation Road . . . . Y 9
Devon Road. . . . . Y 13
Fortescue Road. . . . . Z 14
Grenville Road. . . . . Y 15
Herbert Road . . . . Z 18
Knowle Road . . . . Y 19
Moult Road . . . . Z 20
Newton Road . . . . Y 23
Sandhills Road . . . . Z 24
Shadycombe Road. . . . . . Y 25

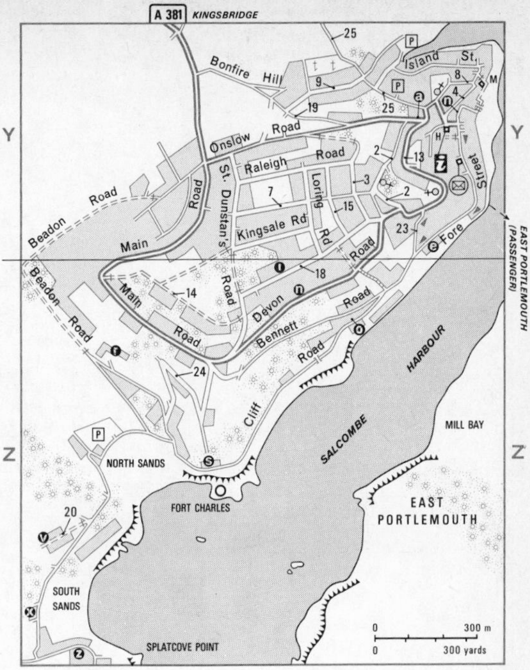

Town plans roads most used by traffic and those on which guide listed hotels and restaurants stand are fully drawn; the beginning only of lesser roads is indicated.

at Soar Mill Cove SW : 3 m. via Cliff Rd – Y – ✉ Malborough – ☎ **0548 Kingsbridge :**

- **Soar Mill Cove** 🐎, TQ7 3DS, ✆ **561566**, ≤, heated, – 📺 wc ♿ **P**. AE VISA
  Mid March-mid October – **M** (bar lunch to non-residents) 5.00/15.50 **t.** 2.70 – **14 rm** 29.00/66.00 **t.**

at Hope Cove W : 4 m. by A 381 – Y – ✉ ☎ **0548 Kingsbridge :**

- **Cottage** 🐎, TQ7 3HJ, ✆ **561555**, ≤ **Bolt Tail and Bigbury Bay**, – wc wc **P**
  closed January – **M** 5.45/9.85 **st.** 3.00 – **36 rm** 10.85/51.35 **st.** – SB 32.60/37.45 **st.**
- **Lantern Lodge** 🐎, TQ7 3HE, ✆ **561280**, ≤, – wc wc **P**. AE VISA.
  March-November and Christmas – **M** (bar lunch) 9.75 **st.** 2.55 – **16 rm** 17.00/49.50 **st.**
- **Port Light** 🐎, **Bolberry Down, TQ7 3DY, SE : 1 ¾ m.** ✆ **561384**, ≤, – wc **P**. VISA
  Easter-October – **M** (bar lunch) 9.50 **t.** 2.80 – **6 rm** 21.25/29.50 **t.** – SB (except summer) 38.70/45.00 **st.**

SALFORDS Surrey **404** T 30 – ✉ ☎ **0737 Redhill.**

♦London 24 – ♦Brighton 29.

- **Mill House,** Brighton Rd, RH1 5BT, ✆ **67277**, – 📺 wc wc ☎ **P**. AE VISA.
  closed 26-28 December – **M** *(closed Saturday lunch)* (carving rest.) 9.75 **t.** 3.50 – 3.50 – **28 rm** 17.50/30.50 **st.**

SALISBURY Wilts. **403** **404** O 30 – pop. 35,302 – ECD : Wednesday – ☎ **0722.**

See : Site ★ – Cathedral ★★★ Z – **The Close★** Z **: Mompesson House★★** Z **A, Military Museum★★** Z **M1, Salisbury and South Wiltshire Museum★★** Z **M2 – Sarum St. Thomas Church ★** Y **B.**

Envir. : Stonehenge★★★, NW : 10 m. by A 345 Y **– Wilton House ★★★, W : 2 ½ m. by A 30** Y **– Old Sarum★ N : 2 m. by A 345** Y **– Wardour Castle★, W : 10 m. by A 30** Y.

18, 9 Salisbury and South Wilts., Netherhampton ✆ **742131, by A 3094** Z – **18 High Post, Great Durnford** ✆ **072 273 (Middle Woodford) 231, N : 4 m. by A 345** Y.

i 10 Endless St. ✆ 334956 – City Hall, Fisherton St. ✆ 27676.

♦London 91 – Bournemouth 28 – ♦Bristol 53 – ♦Southampton 23.

Plan on next page

- **White Hart** (T.H.F.), 1 St. John St., SP1 2SD, ✆ **27476** – 📺 wc ☎ **P**. AE VISA. Z **s**
  M 6.25/8.95 **st.** 2.60 – 5.00 – **72 rm** 26.50/43.50 **st.**

P.T.O. →

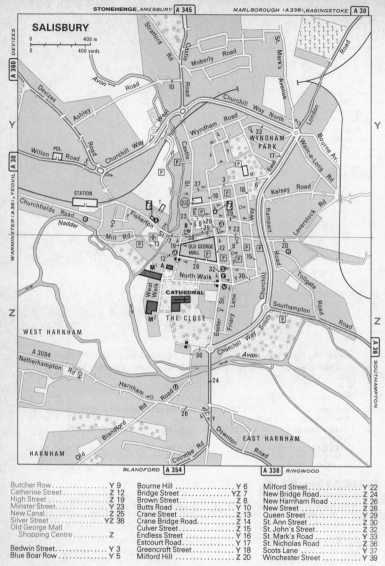

SALISBURY

STONEHENGE, AMESBURY **A 345**   MARLBOROUGH (A338), BASINGSTOKE **A 30**

Old Bell Inn, 2 St. Ann St., SP1 2DN, ℰ 27958, « Converted 14C inn » – ⌷wc ⌷wc 🅰 AE
 ① VISA. ⅍
M (closed Sunday) a la carte 10.50/13.50 t. ⅊ 2.50 – **7 rm** ⊠ 32.00/39.00 st.
Z v

Cathedral, 7 Milford St., SP1 2AJ, ℰ 20144 – ⌷ TV ⌷wc ⌷ 🅰 VISA. ⅍   Y a
M (buffet lunch) a la carte 5.25/9.45 t. ⅊ 3.15 – **30 rm** ⊠ 16.50/39.50 t. – SB (except summer) 35.50/44.50 st.

Kings Arms, 9 St. John's St., SP1 2SB, ℰ 27629, « Part 13C and part 15C inn » – TV ⌷wc
Z r
M 5.50/6.50 st. ⅊ 2.00 – **16 rm** ⊠ 17.35/39.90 st. – SB 33.00/35.00 st.

Byways House, 31 Fowlers Rd, off Milford Hill, SP1 2QP, ℰ 28364, 🚗 – ⌷wc ℗. ⅍
17 rm ⊠ 10.00/23.00 st.
Z e

XX **Crane's,** 90-92 Crane St., SP1 2QD, ℰ 333471, ⅀ – ⬚ 𝔸𝔼 ⓞ 𝑉𝐼𝑆𝐴   Z a
closed Monday dinner in winter, Sunday and Bank Holidays – **M** (restricted lunch) a la carte
7.55/19.20 **st.** ⱡ 1.75.

XX **Dutch Mill,** 58a Fisherton St., SP2 7RB, ℰ 23447 – ⬚ ⓞ 𝑉𝐼𝑆𝐴   Y i
M (lunch by arrangement) a la carte 8.00/10.25 **t.** ⱡ 2.50.

X **Eugene's,** 127 South Western Rd, SP1 1DF, ℰ 331270 – ⬚ 𝔸𝔼 ⓞ 𝑉𝐼𝑆𝐴   Y e
closed August – **M** a la carte 7.00/13.15 **st.** ⱡ 2.45.

    at Redlynch SE : 8 ½ m. by A 338 – Z – off B 3080 – ✉ Salisbury – ☎ 0794 Romsey :

XX **Langley Wood** ⌂ with rm, Hamptworth Rd, SP5 2PB, SE : 1 ½ m. ℰ 390348, ⌖ – ℗. ⬚
𝔸𝔼 ⓞ 𝑉𝐼𝑆𝐴
M (closed Sunday dinner to non-residents) (lunch by arrangement) a la carte 9.50/11.75 **t.**
ⱡ 2.10 – **3 rm** ⥩ 10.00/20.00 **t.**

    at Odstock S : 2 ½ m. by A 338 – Z – ✉ ☎ 0722 Salisbury :

X **Yew Tree Inn,** SP5 4JE, ℰ 29786, ⌖ – ⬚ 𝔸𝔼 ⓞ 𝑉𝐼𝑆𝐴
closed Sunday dinner and Monday – **M** a la carte 5.85/15.50 **t.** ⱡ 3.20.

    at Downton S : 6 m. by A 338 – Z – ✉ ☎ 0725 Downton :

⋔ **Warren,** 15 High St., SP5 3PG, ℰ 20263, ⌖ – ℗
closed mid-December-mid January – **7 rm** ⥩ 16.00/22.00 **st.**

    at Harnham SW : 1 ½ m. by A 3094 – ✉ ☎ 0722 Salisbury :

🏨 **Rose and Crown** (Q.M.H.), Harnham Rd, SP2 8JQ, ℰ 27908, ≼, « Riverside location », ⌖
– 📺 ⌷wc ☎ ⅋ ℗. ⬚ 𝔸𝔼 ⓞ 𝑉𝐼𝑆𝐴 ⚘   Z u
M 7.25/9.50 **st.** ⱡ 2.95 – **27 rm** ⥩ 42.50/57.50 **st.** – SB (weekends only) 65.00 **st.**

    at Barford St. Martin W : 6 m. on A 30 – Y – ✉ Wilton – ☎ 0722 Salisbury :

XX **Michels'** with rm, SP3 4AJ, ℰ 742240 – ℗. ⬚ ⓞ 𝑉𝐼𝑆𝐴 ⚘
closed Sunday – **M** (lunch by arrangement) a la carte 12.25/15.00 **t.** ⱡ 2.50 – **4 rm** ⥩ 9.00/30.00.

AUSTIN-ROVER 41-45 Winchester St. ℰ 336681
AUSTIN-ROVER, ROLLS ROYCE Southampton Rd
ℰ 335251
CITROEN Stephenson Rd ℰ 24136
FORD Castle St. ℰ 28443

PEUGEOT, TALBOT Southampton Rd ℰ 335268
RENAULT 114/120 Wilton Rd ℰ 28328
VAUXHALL-OPEL Brunell Rd ℰ 23522
VOLVO Telford Rd, Churchfields ℰ 333650
VW, AUDI 16 Lower Rd, Churchfields ℰ 27162

🔲 **SAMLESBURY** Lancs. 𝟜𝟘𝟚 M 22 – see Preston.

🔲 **SANDIACRE** Derbs. 𝟜𝟘𝟚 𝟜𝟘𝟛 𝟜𝟘𝟜 Q 25 – see Nottingham (Notts.).

🔲 **SANDOWN** I.O.W. 𝟜𝟘𝟛 𝟜𝟘𝟜 Q 32 – see Wight (Isle of).

🔲 **SANDPLACE** Cornwall – see Looe.

🔲 **SANDWICH** Kent 𝟜𝟘𝟜 Y 30 – pop. 4,490 – ECD : Wednesday – ☎ 030 46 (4 fig.) and 0304 (6 fig.).
⌖⌖, ⌖⌖, ⌖ Prince's, Sandwich Bay ℰ 611147.
♦London 72 – Canterbury 13 – ♦Dover 12 – Maidstone 41 – Margate 9.

🏨 **Bell,** The Quay, CT13 9EF, ℰ 613388 – 📺 ⌷wc ☎ ⅋ ⅍ ⬚ 𝔸𝔼 ⓞ 𝑉𝐼𝑆𝐴
M (bar lunch) 8.50 **t.** ⱡ 3.75 – **33 rm** ⥩ 20.00/45.00 **st.** – SB (weekends only)(except summer) 45.00/55.00 **st.**

ALFA-ROMEO ℰ 611654
FORD New St. ℰ 612308

LANCIA Harnet St. ℰ 613685
RENAULT Woodnesborough ℰ 812349

🔲 **SANDYPARK** Devon 𝟜𝟘𝟛 I 31 – see Chagford.

🔲 **SARISBURY** Hants. 𝟜𝟘𝟛 𝟜𝟘𝟜 Q 31 – pop. 5,682 – ✉ Southampton – ☎ 048 95 Locks Heath.
♦London 90 – ♦Portsmouth 16 – ♦Southampton 6.

⋔ **Dormy House,** 21 Barnes Lane, Sarisbury Green, SO3 6DA, S : 1 m. ℰ 2626, ⌖ – 📺
⌷wc ⍾ ℗
7 rm ⥩ 12.00/22.00 **st.**

🔲 **SAUNDERSFOOT** Dyfed 𝟜𝟘𝟛 F 28 – pop. 3,150 – ECD : Wednesday – ☎ 0834.
♦London 245 – Carmarthen 25 – Fishguard 34 – Tenby 3.

🏨 **St. Brides,** St. Brides Hill, SA69 9NH, ℰ 812304, Telex 48350, ≼ Saundersfoot Bay, ⌇ heated,
⌖ – 📺 ⌷wc ⌗wc ☎ ℗. ⅍ ⬚ 𝔸𝔼 ⓞ 𝑉𝐼𝑆𝐴
M 6.25/8.45 **st.** ⱡ 3.10 – **49 rm** ⥩ 26.50/51.00 **st.** – SB (weekends only) 52.50/56.50 **st.**

🏠 **Glen Beach** ⌂, Swallow Tree Woods, SA69 9DE, S : ½ m. by B 4316 ℰ 813430, ≼, ⌖ –
⌗wc ℗. ⬚ 𝔸𝔼 𝑉𝐼𝑆𝐴
M (bar lunch Monday to Saturday) 6.50/9.00 **st.** ⱡ 3.00 – **12 rm** ⥩ 19.00/46.00 **st.** – SB
50.00/55.00 **st.**

⌂ **Malin House,** St. Brides Hill, SA69 9NP, ℰ 812344, ⌇ heated, ⌖ – 📺 ⌷wc ⌗wc ℗. ⚘
April-October – **M** (bar lunch) 6.00 **st.** ⱡ 1.60 – **11 rm** ⥩ 11.00/24.00 **st.**

SAUNDERTON Bucks. 🗺️404 R 28 – pop. 256 – ✉ Aylesbury – 🕿 084 44 Princes Risborough.
♦London 42 – Aylesbury 9 – ♦Oxford 20.

🏠 **Rose and Crown,** Wycombe Rd, HP17 9NP, N : on A 4010 ℰ 5299 – 📺 ⌂wc ⋔wc 🅿. 🔺
🖦 ① 𝗩𝗜𝗦𝗔 ✻
closed 24 December-1 January – **M** *(closed Saturday lunch and Sunday)* a la carte 9.00/13.30 **t.**
🍴 2.90 – **15 rm** ⊏⊐ 20.00/39.95 **t.** – SB (weekends only) 41.00 **st.**

SAUNTON Devon 🗺️403 H 30 – pop. 200 – ✉ Braunton – 🕿 0271 Croyde.
♦London 230 – Barnstaple 8 – Exeter 48.

🏨 **Saunton Sands,** EX33 1LQ, ℰ 890212, ≤ Saunton Sands, 🔲, 🐎, ✻, squash – 📶 📺 🅿.
🔺 ① 𝗩𝗜𝗦𝗔
M 6.25/9.20 **st.** – **90 rm** ⊏⊐ 27.00/66.00 **s.**
🏠 **Preston House,** EX33 1LG, ℰ 890472, ≤ Saunton Sands, 🐎 – ⌂wc ⋔wc 🅿. ✻
March-mid November – **M** (bar lunch) 8.50 **t.** 🍴 3.10 – **12 rm** ⊏⊐ 16.00/32.00 **t.**

SAWLEY Lancs. 🗺️402 M 22 – ✉ 🕿 0200 Clitheroe.
♦ London 242 – ♦ Blackpool 39 – ♦ Leeds 44 – ♦ Liverpool 54.

🏨 **Spread Eagle** ⤸, BB7 4NH, ℰ 41202, ⤴ – 📺 ⌂wc ⋔wc 🕿 🖐 🅿. 🔺 🖦 ① 𝗩𝗜𝗦𝗔. ✻
M 6.75/10.00 **st.** 🍴 2.50 – **9 rm** ⊏⊐ 18.50/40.00 **st.** – SB (weekends only) 55.00/60.00 **st.**

SCALBY North Yorks. 🗺️402 S 21 – see Scarborough.

*Es ist empfehlenswert, **in der Hauptsaison** und vor allem
in Urlaubsorten, Hotelzimmer im voraus zu bestellen.
Benachrichtigen Sie sofort das Hotel, wenn Sie ein bestelltes
Zimmer nicht belegen können.
Wenn Sie an ein Hotel im Ausland schreiben, fügen Sie Ihrem Brief
einen internationalen Antwortschein bei (im Postamt erhältlich).*

SCARBOROUGH North Yorks. 🗺️402 S 21 – pop. 44,440 – ECD : Monday and Wednesday –
🕿 0723.

See : Castle 12C (≤*) *AC* Y.

🏌 North Cliff, North Cliff Av. ℰ 60786, NW : 2 m. by A 165 Y – 🏌 South Cliff, Deepdale Av., off
Filey Rd ℰ 60522, S : 1 m. by A 165 Z.

🅩 St. Nicholas Cliff ℰ 372261 and 373333.

♦London 253 – ♦Kingston-upon-Hull 47 – ♦Leeds 67 – ♦Middlesbrough 52.

Plan opposite

🏨 **Holbeck Hall** ⤸, Seacliff Rd, YO11 2XX, ℰ 374374, ≤, 🐎 – 📺 🅿. 🔺 🖦 ① 𝗩𝗜𝗦𝗔 ✻
March-October – **M** 6.50/9.95 **t.** 🍴 3.25 – **30 rm** ⊏⊐ 25.30/62.10 **t.** – SB
(spring and autumn only) 30.00/35.00 **st.** by A 165 Z
🏨 **St. Nicholas,** St. Nicholas Cliff, YO11 2EU, ℰ 364101, Telex 52351, ≤ – 📶 📺 ⌂wc 🕾 🅿.
🔺 🖦 ① 𝗩𝗜𝗦𝗔 Z n
M 5.50/9.75 **t.** – **161 rm** ⊏⊐ 20.00/46.00 **t.** – SB 48.00/52.00 **st.**
XX **Lanterna,** 33 Queen St., YO11 1HQ, ℰ 363616, Italian rest. – ① 𝗩𝗜𝗦𝗔 Y a
closed Sunday, Monday and 25-26 December – **M** (dinner only) a la carte 7.15/9.80 **t.** 🍴 2.50.
XX **Grapevine,** 23 Valley Rd, YO11 2LY, ℰ 377088 – 🖦 ① 𝗩𝗜𝗦𝗔 Z a
closed Sunday and 26-30 December – **M** (dinner only) 7.45/14.25 **t.** 🍴 2.95.

at Ravenscar N : 10 m. by A 171 – Z – ✉ 🕿 0723 Scarborough :

🏨 **Raven Hall** ⤸, Raven Hall Rd, YO13 0ET, ℰ 870353, ≤ Robin Hoods Bay, 🔲, 🏌, 🐎, park,
✻ – ⌂wc 🅿. 🔺 🔺 🖦 ① 𝗩𝗜𝗦𝗔
April-November – **M** 6.00/9.00 **t.** 🍴 2.50 – **57 rm** ⊏⊐ 20.00/68.00 **t.**

at Scalby NW : 3 m. by A 171 – Z – ✉ 🕿 0723 Scarborough :

🏨 **Wrea Head** ⤸, YO13 0PB, ℰ 378211, ≤, 🐎, park – 📺 ⌂wc ⋔wc 🅿. 🔺 🖦 ① 𝗩𝗜𝗦𝗔
M 6.25/9.50 **st.** 🍴 2.95 – **20 rm** ⊏⊐ 16.00/36.00 **st.** – SB 42.00/52.00 **st.**

at Hackness NW : 7 m. by A 171 – Z – ✉ 🕿 0723 Scarborough :

🏨 **Hackness Grange** (Best Western) ⤸, YO13 0JW, ℰ 369966, ≤, « 18C house », 🔲, ⤴,
🐎, park, ✻ – 📺 ⌂wc ⋔wc 🕾 🅿. 🔺 🖦 ① 𝗩𝗜𝗦𝗔. ✻
M 7.00/12.50 **t.** 🍴 2.50 – **27 rm** ⊏⊐ 30.00/60.00 **t.** – SB 62.00/72.00 **st.**

AUSTIN-ROVER Valley Bridge Rd ℰ 360221
CITROEN, DATSUN, PEUGEOT, TALBOT Northway
ℰ 363533
FIAT Manor Rd ℰ 364111
FORD Vine St. ℰ 375581
LADA, DAIHATSU Pickering Rd, Westayton ℰ
862880

MAZDA Falconers Rd ℰ 360322
RENAULT Columbus Ravine ℰ 360791
VAUXHALL-OPEL Seamer Rd ℰ 360335
VW, AUDI 60 Ramshill Rd, South Cliff ℰ 362495

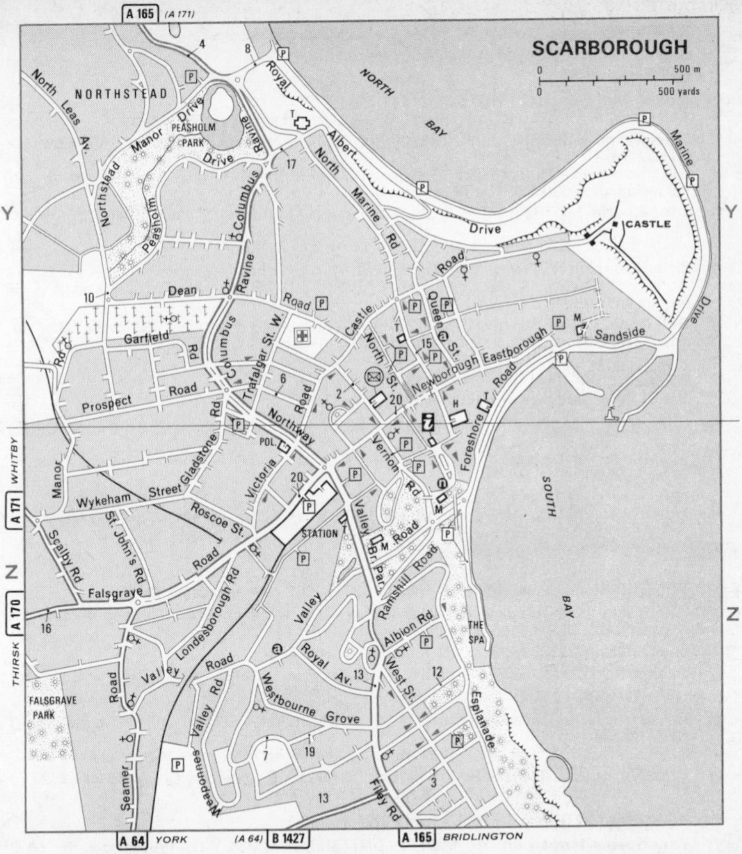

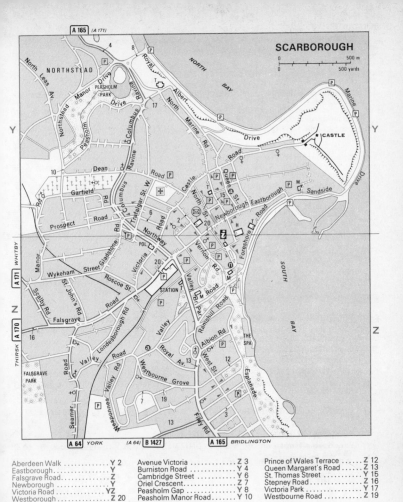

Aberdeen Walk .... Y 2	Avenue Victoria .... Z 3	Prince of Wales Terrace ...... Z 12
Eastborough................ Y	Burniston Road .... Y 4	Queen Margaret's Road ...... Z 13
Falsgrave Road.............. Z	Cambridge Street .... Y 6	St. Thomas Street .... Y 15
Newborough .... Y	Oriel Crescent............... Z 7	Stepney Road .... Z 16
Victoria Road .... YZ	Peasholm Gap .... Y 8	Victoria Park .... Y 17
Westborough .... Z 20	Peasholm Manor Road....... Y 10	Westbourne Road .... Z 19

Town plans : *roads most used by traffic and those on which guide listed hotels and restaurants stand are fully drawn ; the beginning only of lesser roads is indicated.*

SCILLY (ISLES OF) Cornwall **403** ㉚ **The West Country G.** – pop. 2,020.

See : Site ★★. **Envir.** : St. Martin's : Viewpoint ★★ – St. Agnes : Horsepoint ★.

Helicopter service from St. Mary's and Tresco to Penzance : ✆ 0736 (Penzance) 3871.

✈ St. Mary's Airport : ✆ 0720(Scillonia)22677, E : 1 ½ m. from Hugh Town.

⛴ from Hugh Town, St. Mary's to Penzance (Isles of Scilly Steamship Co.) summer Monday/Saturday 1-2 daily; winter 3 weekly (2 h 30 mn).

ℹ Town Hall, St. Mary's ✆ 0720 (Scillonia) 22536.

Bryher – pop. 57 – ✉ ☎ 0720 Scillonia.

See : Village on Watch Hill (≤★) – Hell Bay★.

🏠 **Hell Bay** ⛱, TR23 0PR, ✆ 22947, ☞ – wc. 🅴 VISA. ✕
Mid March-mid October – **M** (bar lunch) a la carte 4.45/7.25 **t.** 🍷 2.30 – **10 rm** ☕ 19.00/38.00 **t.**

16

St. Mary's – pop. 1,958 – ✉ St. Mary's – ✆ 0720 Scillonia.
See : Garrison Walk★ (< ★★) – Peninnis Head ★.
[i] Town Hall, ☎ 22536.

🏨 **Godolphin,** Church St., TR21 0JR, ☎ 22316 – [TV] 🛁wc. 🚫🐕
Mid March-6 October – **M** (bar lunch) 9.00 **t.** 🍷 2.50 – **31 rm** 🛏 13.00/40.00 **st.**

🏨 **Tregarthen's** (Best Western), TR21 0PP, ☎ 22540, < Harbour and islands – [TV] 🛁wc 📞. [S] [AE] [D] [VISA]. 🚫🐕
March-October – **M** (bar lunch Monday to Saturday) 6.50/10.50 **st.** 🍷 3.00 – **33 rm** 🛏 (dinner included) 27.00/73.00 **t.** – SB 65.00 **st.**

🏨 **Star Castle** 🔇, TR21 0JA, ☎ 22317, « Elizabethan fortress », 🏊 heated, 🌳, 🎾 – 🛁wc 🚿wc
April-October – **M** (bar lunch) 8.00 🍷 2.00 – **24 rm** 🛏 21.50/25.00.

🏨 **Atlantic,** Hugh St., TR21 0PL, ☎ 22417, < St. Mary's Harbour – 🛁wc
April-mid October – **M** (bar lunch) 8.50 **st.** – **25 rm** 🛏 20.00/27.00 **st.** – SB (spring and autumn only) 46.00/50.00 **st.**

🏨 **Bell Rock,** Church St., TR21 0JS, ☎ 22575, 🏊 heated – [TV] 🛁wc 🚿wc. [S] [AE] [D] [VISA]
February-October – **M** (bar lunch) 11.45 **t.** 🍷 2.50 – **18 rm** 🛏 13.50/52.00 **t.**

Tresco – pop. 140 – ✉ Tresco – ✆ 0720 Scillonia.
See : Abbey Gardens★ – Lighthouse Way (< ★★).

🏨 **Island** 🔇, TR24 0PU, ☎ 22883, < Islands, « Sub-tropical gardens », 🏊 heated, park – [TV]. 🚫🐕
Mid March-mid October – **M** a la carte 6.15/16.00 **st.** 🍷 4.00 – **35 rm** 🛏 (dinner included) 38.00/70.00 **st.**

🏠 **New Inn** 🔇, TR24 0QQ, ☎ 22844, <, 🌳 – 🛁wc. 🚫🐕
closed November and December – **M** (bar lunch) 9.50 **t.** 🍷 2.20 – **12 rm** 🛏 13.00/17.60 **t.**

SCOLE Norfolk [404] X 26 – see Diss.

SCUNTHORPE Humberside [402] S 23 – pop. 70,907 – ECD : Wednesday – ✆ 0724.
Envir. : Normanby Hall★ (Regency) : Wildlife park★ *AC*, N : 4 m. – Barton-upon-Humber (St. Mary's Church★ 12C, Old St. Peter's Church★ 10C-11C) NE : 13 ½ m.
⛳18 Normanby Hall ☎ 720226, N : 5 m. – ⛳9 Kingsway ☎ 68117.
✈ Humberside Airport : ☎ 0652 (Barnetby) 688456, E : 15 m. by A 18.
♦London 167 – ♦Leeds 54 – Lincoln 30 – ♦Sheffield 45.

🏨 **Royal** (Anchor), Doncaster Rd, DN15 7DE, ☎ 868181, Telex 527479 – [TV] 🛁wc 🚿wc 📞 [P]. [S] [AE] [D] [VISA]
M (carving lunch) 8.65 **st.** 🍷 2.65 – **33 rm** 🛏 33.00/41.30 **st.** – SB (weekends only) 41.00 **st.**

🏨 **Wortley House,** Rowland Rd, DN16 1ST, ☎ 842223 – [TV] 🛁wc 📞 [P]. 🤝. [S] [AE] [D] [VISA]
M a la carte 8.30/12.10 **st.** 🍷 4.60 – **28 rm** 🛏 33.50/40.00 **st.**

at Althorpe W : 4 ½ m. by A 18 – ✉ ✆ 0724 Scunthorpe :

XX **Lansdowne House** with rm, Main St., DN17 3HJ, ☎ 783369, 🌳 – [TV] 🛁wc 📞 [P]. [S] [AE] [D] [VISA]
M (lunch by arrangement) 10.95 **st.** 🍷 2.50 – **6 rm** 🛏 27.00/35.00 **st.**

BMW Normanby Rd ☎ 864251
COLT Doncaster Rd ☎ 860212
FIAT Normanby Rd ☎ 861191
LADA Grange Lane North ☎ 851548
RENAULT 136/144 Ashby High St. ☎ 867474
TALBOT Smith St. ☎ 869323
TOYOTA Brigg Rd ☎ 842011
VAUXHALL-OPEL Moorwell Rd Industrial Estate ☎ 843284
VAUXHALL-OPEL Winterton Rd ☎ 861083

SEACROFT West Yorks. [402] ⑩ – see Leeds.

SEAHOUSES Northumb. [401] [402] P 17 – pop. 1,709 (inc. North Sunderland) – ECD : Wednesday – ✆ 0665.
♦London 328 – ♦Edinburgh 80 – ♦Newcastle-upon-Tyne 46.

🏨 **St. Aidans,** Seafront, ☎ 720355, < – [TV] 🛁wc 🚿wc [P]. [S] [D] [VISA]
Mid February-mid November – **M** (bar lunch) 7.00 **st.** 🍷 3.00 – **10 rm** 🛏 21.00/36.00 **st.** – SB (except summer) 40.00/44.00 **st.**

🏨 **Beach House,** 12a St. Aidens, Seafront, NE68 7SR, ☎ 720337, <, 🌳 – [TV] 🛁wc 🚿wc ♿. [S] [VISA]
April-October – **M** (bar lunch) 7.50 **t.** 🍷 2.80 – **14 rm** 🛏 17.00/34.00 **t.** – SB (April, May and October) 20.00 **st.**

SEALE Surrey [404] R 30 – see Farnham.

SEATON BURN Tyne and Wear [402] P 18 – see Newcastle-upon-Tyne.

SEAVIEW I.O.W. [403] [404] Q 31 – see Wight (Isle of).

SEAVINGTON ST. MARY Somerset **403** L 31 – pop. 212 – ⊠ Ilminster – ✪ 0460 South Pether-ton.

♦London 142 – Taunton 14 – Yeovil 11.

  XX **Pheasant** 🐾 with rm, TA19 0QH, ℰ 40502, 🖾 – 📺 ⌂wc ☎ 📷. 🔼 AE ⓞ VISA. ⬡
     M (dinner only and Sunday lunch) a la carte 9.50/13.50 t. ⓵ 2.30 – **7 rm** ⟷ 35.00/45.00 t. – SB
     50.00 **st.**

SEDBERGH Cumbria **402** M 21 – pop. 3,544 – ECD : Thursday – ✪ 0587.

🏐 The Riggs, S : 1 m.

🅱 National Park Centre, 72 Main St. ℰ 20125 (summer only).

♦London 284 – ♦Carlisle 49 – Kendal 10 – Lancaster 27 – Penrith 30.

  🏠 **Oakdene Country,** Garsdale Rd, LA10 5JN, NE : 1 ½ m. on A 684 ℰ 20280, ≼, 🖾 – 📷. 🔼
     AE VISA
     closed mid January-February – **M** (bar lunch Monday to Saturday) 6.00/10.00 t. – **6 rm**
     ⟷ 12.50/30.00 t.

SEDGEFIELD Durham **401 402** P 20 – pop. 5,337 – ⊠ Stockton-on-Tees (Cleveland) – ✪ 0740.

♦London 261 – Hartlepool 14 – ♦Middlesbrough 13 – ♦Newcastle-upon-Tyne 28.

  🏨 **Hardwick Hall** 🐾, TS21 9EH, W : 1 ½ m. on A 177 ℰ 20253, ≼, 🖾, park – 📺 ⌂wc ☎ 📷.
     ⬡ – **17 rm.**

SEDLESCOMBE East Sussex **404** V 31 – pop. 1,318 – ⊠ Battle – ✪ 042 487.

♦London 56 – Hastings 7 – Lewes 26 – Maidstone 27.

  🏨 **Brickwall,** The Green, TN33 0QA, ℰ 253, 🛋 heated, 🖾 – 📺 ⌂wc 📷. 🔼 AE ⓞ VISA
     M 6.50/8.75 **st.** ⓵ 2.65 – **19 rm** ⟷ 20.00/50.00 t. – SB (summer only) 42.00/45.00 **st.**

  XX **Holmes House,** The Green, TN33 0QA, ℰ 450, 🛋 heated – 🔼 AE ⓞ
     closed Saturday lunch, Sunday dinner and Monday – **M** a la carte 9.00/13.60 **st.** ⓵ 2.50.

SELBY North Yorks. **402** Q 22 – pop. 13,200 – ECD : Thursday – ✪ 0757.

See : Abbey Church★★ 12C-16C.

Envir. : Carlton Towers★ (19C) AC, S : 6 m.

🏐 Mill Lane ℰ 075 782 (Gateforth) 234, SW : 3 m.

♦London 197 – ♦Kingston-upon-Hull 34 – ♦Leeds 21 – York 14.

  🏠 Londesborough Arms, Market Pl., YO8 0NS, ℰ 707355 – 📺 ⌂wc 📷. ⬡ – **34 rm.**

RENAULT Chapel Haddlesey ℰ 075 787 (Burn) 638   VAUXHALL-OPEL Brook St. ℰ 703258

SELMESTON East Sussex **404** U 31 – pop. 187 – ⊠ Polegate – ✪ 032 183 Ripe.

♦London 62 – ♦Brighton 14 – Hastings 23 – Lewes 7.5 – Maidstone 57.

  XX **Corin's,** Church Farm, BN26 6TZ, ℰ 343, « 17C farmhouse », 🖾 – 📷. 🔼 AE ⓞ VISA
     closed Sunday dinner and Monday – **M** (dinner only and Sunday lunch) 6.00/10.00 t. ⓵ 3.00.

SELSEY West Sussex **404** R 31 – pop. 5,650 – ECD : Wednesday – ✪ 024 361 (4 fig.) and 0243 (6 fig.).

♦London 78 – ♦Brighton 40 – Chichester 9.

  🏡 **Thatched House,** 23 Warner Rd, off Clayton Rd, PO20 9DD, ℰ 602207, 🖾 – ⌂wc 📷. 🔼
     AE VISA
     M a la carte 8.00/12.15 t. ⓵ 2.40 – ⟷ 2.75 – **6 rm** 10.00/25.00.

SENNEN Cornwall **403** C 33 The West Country G. – pop. 704 – ⊠ Penzance – ✪ 073 687.

♦London 328 – Penzance 10 – Truro 36.

  🏠 **Tregiffian** 🐾, TR19 7BE, NE : 2 ¼ m. by A 30 ℰ 408, ≼, 🖾 – ⌂wc ⛰wc 📷. 🔼 ⓞ VISA
     March-October – **M** (bar lunch) 7.30 t. ⓵ 3.00 – **7 rm** ⟷ 13.00/34.00 t. – SB
     (spring and autumn only) 37.00 **st.**

SETTLE North Yorks. **402** N 21 – pop. 2,171 – ECD : Wednesday – ✪ 072 92.

🏐 Giggleswick ℰ 3580, off A 65.

🅱 Town Hall, Cheapside ℰ 3617 (summer only).

♦London 238 – Bradford 34 – Kendal 30 – ♦Leeds 41.

  🏨 **Falcon Manor,** Skipton Rd, BD24 9BD, ℰ 2357, ≼, 🖾 – 📺 ⌂wc ⛰wc ☎ 📷. 🔼 ⓞ VISA
     M 3.95/7.90 t. ⓵ 3.00 – **16 rm** ⟷ 25.00/40.00 t. – SB (July-September) 52.00/54.00 **st.**

  🏠 **Royal Oak,** Market Pl., BD24 9ED, ℰ 2561 – 📺 ⌂wc ☎ ⟷ 📷. ⬡
     closed Christmas Night – **M** a la carte 6.00/8.50 **st.** ⓵ 2.75 – **6 rm** ⟷ 20.00/40.00 **st.**

    at Giggleswick NW : ¾ m. on A 65 – ⊠ ✪ 072 92 Settle :

  🏠 **Woodlands** 🐾, The Mains, BD24 0AX, ℰ 2576, ≼, 🖾 – 📷. ⬡
     closed Christmas and New Year – **10 rm** ⟷ 14.75/29.50 t.

AUSTIN-ROVER Station Rd ℰ 2323

SEVENOAKS Kent 404 U 30 – pop. 24,750 – ECD : Wednesday – ✪ 0732.

See : Knole★★ (15C-17C) *AC*.

Envir. : Lullingstone (Roman Villa : mosaic panels★) *AC*, N : 6 m.

☖ Shoreham, Darenth Valley ✆ 095 92 (Otford) 2922, N : 3 m.

🛈 Arthur Barnard Hall, Bradbourne Vale Rd ✆ 459953 (summer only).

♦London 26 – Guildford 40 – Maidstone 17.

🏨 **Moorings** without rest., 97 Hitchen Hatch Lane, TN13 3BE, ✆ 452589, 🚗 – 📺 🗒wc 🅿. 🔄 *VISA*. ❄
  11 rm ⇌ 17.25/26.45 **st.**

XX **Le Chantecler,** 43 High St., TN13 1JF, ✆ 454662
  closed Saturday lunch, Sunday, Monday and 2 weeks in August – **M** a la carte 11.00/12.50 **t.** ▯ 3.25.

  at Ide Hill SW : 4 ¾ m. by A 2028 and A 25 on B 2042 – ⊠ Sevenoaks – ✪ 073 275 Ide Hill :

XX **Churchill,** ✆ 596, 🚗 – 🅿. 🔄 AE ⊙ *VISA*
  closed Sunday dinner – **M** a la carte 10.10/15.95 **t.** ▯ 3.20.

AUSTIN-ROVER, ROLLS ROYCE-BENTLEY London Rd ✆ 458177
BMW London Rd ✆ 450035
CITROEN Tonbridge Rd ✆ 453328
FORD The Vines ✆ 459911
NISSAN London Rd, Dunton Green ✆ 073 273 (Dunton Green) 292

RENAULT 71 St. Johns Hill ✆ 455174
SAAB Borough Green ✆ 883044
SKODA Seal Rd ✆ 454283
TOYOTA Badgers Mount ✆ 095 97 (Badgers Mount) 218
VAUXHALL-OPEL 128 Seal Rd ✆ 451337

SHAFTESBURY Dorset 403 404 N 30 The West Country G. – pop. 3,976 – ECD : Wednesday and Saturday – ✪ 0747.

See : ⩹★ – Gold Hill★ – Local History Museum ★.

Envir. : Wardour Castle★, NE : 5 m.

🛈 County Library, Bell St. ✆ 2256.

♦London 115 – Bournemouth 31 – ♦Bristol 47 – Dorchester 29 – Salisbury 20.

🏨 **Grosvenor** (T.H.F.), The Commons, SP7 8JA, ✆ 2282 – 📺 ⌷wc ☜. 🔼. 🔄 AE ⊙ *VISA*
  M 4.95/5.95 **st.** ▯ 2.60 – ⇌ 4.50 – **47 rm** 29.50/41.00 **st.**

🏨 **Royal Chase** (Best Western), Royal Chase Roundabout, SP7 8DB, junction of A 30 and A 350 ✆ 3355, 🚗 – 📺 ⌷wc 🗒wc ☜ 🅿. 🔄 AE ⊙ *VISA*
  M a la carte 7.45/9.40 **st.** ▯ 3.10 – **18 rm** ⇌ 21.00/52.50 **st.** – SB 48.00/64.00 **st.**

  at Donhead St. Andrew (Wilts.) E : 3 ½ m. on A 30 – ⊠ Shaftesbury – ✪ 074 788 Donhead :

X **Le Radier,** SP8 9LG, ✆ 324, French rest. – 🅿
  closed Sunday, Monday and Bank Holidays – **M** (dinner only) (booking essential) 11.50 **st.**

  at Ludwell (Wilts.) E : 5 m. on A 30 – ⊠ Shaftesbury (Dorset) – ✪ 074 788 Donhead :

🏦 Grove House, SP7 9ND, on A 30 ✆ 365, ⩹, 🚗 – 🗒wc 🅿 – **12 rm**.

  at Fontmell Magna S : 5 ¼ m. on A 350 – ⊠ Shaftesbury – ✪ 0747 Fontmell Magna :

↿ **Estyard House,** SP7 0PB, ✆ 811460, 🚗 – 🅿
  closed November and Christmas – **6 rm** ⇌ 9.75/19.50.

AUSTIN-ROVER Salisbury Rd ✆ 2295

SHALDON Devon 403 J 32 – see Teignmouth.

SHANKLIN I.O.W. 403 404 Q 32 – see Wight (Isle of).

SHAW Wilts. 403 404 N 29 – see Melksham.

SHEDFIELD Hants. 403 404 Q 31 – pop. 2,730 – ⊠ Southampton – ✪ 0329 Wickham.

♦London 75 – ♦Portsmouth 13 – ♦Southampton 10.

🏨 **Meon Valley Golf and Country Club** (Best Western), Sandy Lane, SO3 2HQ, off A 334 ✆ 833455, Telex 86272, ⩹, 🔄, ☖, 🚗, park, ❄ – 📺 ⌷wc ☎ 🅿. 🔼. 🔄 AE ⊙ *VISA*. ❄
  M 6.75/9.00 **st.** ▯ 3.50 – **54 rm** ⇌ 38.00/45.00 **st.** – SB (weekends only) 55.00/58.00 **st.**

SHEEPWASH Devon 403 H 31 – see Hatherleigh.

SHEERNESS Kent 404 W 29 – pop. 13,860 – ✪ 0795.

See : ⩹★ from the pier – Envir. : Minster (abbey : brasses★, effigied tombs★) SE : 2 ½ m.

⚓ Shipping connections with the Continent : to the Netherlands (Vlissingen) (Olau).

🛈 Bridge Rd Car Park ✆ 665324.

♦London 52 – Canterbury 24 – Maidstone 20.

  Hotels and restaurant see : Maidstone SW : 20 m.

AUSTIN-ROVER New Road ✆ 64329   SKODA High St. ✆ 662730

398

SHEFFIELD South Yorks. 402 403 404 P 23 – pop. 520,327 – ECD : Thursday – ☻ 0742.

See : Abbeydale Industrial Hamlet★ (steel and scythe works) *AC*, SW : by A 621 AZ.

🛅 Lees Hall, Hemsworth Rd ℰ 54402, S : 3 ½ m. AZ – 🛅 Beauchief, Abbey Lane ℰ 360648, SW : by
B 6068 AZ – 🛅 Tinsley Park ℰ 442237, E : by A 57 BZ – 🛅 Birley Wood, Birley Lane ℰ 390099, S :
4 m. on A 616 BZ.

🅸 Central Library, Surrey St. ℰ 26444.

♦London 174 – ♦Leeds 36 – ♦Liverpool 79 – ♦Manchester 41 – ♦Nottingham 44.

SHEFFIELD
BUILT UP AREA

Barrow Road	**BY** 4
Bawtry Road	**BY** 5
Bradfield Road	**AY** 7

Brocco Bank	**AZ** 8
Broughton Lane	**BY** 10
Burngreave Road	**AY** 12
Ecclesfield Road	**BY** 17
Handsworth Road	**BZ** 24
Hemsworth Road	**AZ** 27
Hollinsend Road	**BZ** 28
Holywell Road	**BY** 29

Main Road	**BZ** 32
Middlewood Road	**AY** 33
Newhall Road	**BY** 36
Rustlings Road	**AZ** 39
Westbourne Road	**AZ** 47
Western Bank	**AZ** 48
Whitham Road	**AZ** 49
Woodhouse Road	**BZ** 50

🏨 **Hallam Tower Post House** (T.H.F.), Manchester Rd (A 57), S10 5DX, 𝒫 686031, Telex 547293, ⇐ – 🛏 📺 🅿 🏃. 🏊 AE ① 𝘷𝘪𝘴𝘢
AZ **o**
M 5.50/8.00 **st.** ⌀ 2.60 – 🖵 5.25 – **135 rm** 37.50/45.00 **st.**

🏨 **Grosvenor House** (T.H.F.), Charter Sq., S1 3EH, 𝒫 20041, Telex 54312 – 🛏 📺 🅿 🏃. 🏊 AE
① 𝘷𝘪𝘴𝘢
CZ **a**
M (carving rest.) 7.95 **st.** ⌀ 2.85 – 🖵 5.50 – **121 rm** 40.00/46.00 **st.**

SHEFFIELD
CENTRE

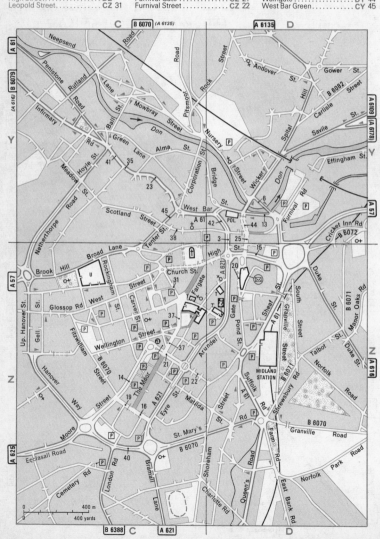

🏨 **St. George** (Swallow) ॐ, Kenwood Rd, S7 1NQ, ℰ 583811, Telex 547030, ≼, 🚗, park – ⛖
📺 ➡wc ☎ & 🅿 🖺 🔼 🆎 ⑩ 𝘝𝘐𝘚𝘈   AZ **r**
M 6.00/7.50 **st.** ⧘ 2.50 – **120 rm** ⊊ 36.00/48.00 **st.** – SB (weekends only) 44.00/46.00 **st.**

🏨 **Rutland,** 452 Glossop Rd, S10 2PY, ℰ 665215, Telex 547500 – ⛖ 📺 ➡wc ☎ 🅿 🖺 🔼 🆎
⑩ 𝘝𝘐𝘚𝘈   AZ **e**
M 3.95/6.25 **st.** ⧘ 2.50 – **90 rm** ⊊ 21.00/38.00 **st.** – SB (weekends only) 38.00/41.00 **st.**

✕✕ **Stirrings,** 141 Oakbrook Rd, S11 7EB, ℰ 305540   by Rustlings Rd   AZ

at Worrall NW : 4 ½ m. by A 61 off A 616 – AY – ✉ Sheffield – ✆ 074 286 Oughtibridge :

🏨 **Middlewood Hall** ॐ, Mowson Lane, S30 3FD, ℰ 3919, ≼, 🚗, park – 📺 ➡wc ▥wc ☎
🅿 🔼 🆎 ⑩ 𝘝𝘐𝘚𝘈 ✀
closed Bank Holidays – **M** *(closed Saturday lunch and Sunday dinner)* a la carte 7.10/11.85 **t.**
– ⊊ 3.00 – **18 rm** 17.00/40.00 **t.** – SB (weekends only) 55.00 **st.**

MICHELIN Branch, 12 Tinsley Park Close, S9 5LX, ℰ **433264**

ALFA-ROMEO Scotland St. ℰ 760567
AUDI-NSU Middlewood Rd ℰ 348807
AUSTIN-ROVER 968 Abbeydale Rd ℰ 362292
AUSTIN-ROVER Ecclesall Rd ℰ 71141
AUSTIN-ROVER 286 Sandygate Rd ℰ 302021
AUSTIN-ROVER Broadfield Rd ℰ 588121
BMW Broad Lane ℰ 25048
CITROEN Suffolk Rd ℰ 21378
DAF, VOLVO Ecclesall Rd ℰ 753151
DATSUN 252 Crookes ℰ 665913
DATSUN 1/7 Meersbrook Rd ℰ 57315
DATSUN 1-7 Allen St. ℰ 750000
FIAT, LANCIA 30/46 Suffolk Rd ℰ 21378
FORD 53/67 London Rd ℰ 751515
FORD 196 Gibraltar St. ℰ 29631
FORD Ecclesall Rd ℰ 686986

FSO Langsutt Rd ℰ 342368
HONDA Bradfield Rd ℰ 344256
LADA Lepping Lane ℰ 345247
MAZDA 850/882 Ecclesall Rd ℰ 662797
MERCEDES-BENZ Hanover Way ℰ 753391
PEUGEOT-TALBOT Halifax Rd ℰ 336191
RENAULT Abbeydale Rd Sth. ℰ 369041
RENAULT Crookes Rd ℰ 669202
ROLLS ROYCE-BENTLEY Tempter St., Bromhill ℰ
71141
TOYOTA Ellin St. ℰ 78717
VAUXHALL Saville St. ℰ 751565
VAUXHALL Ecclesall Rd ℰ 685922
VOLVO Ecclesall Rd ℰ 78739
VW, AUDI 1 Ecclesall Rd South ℰ 668441

SHELDON West Midlands �403 ㉒ �404 ㉖ – see Birmingham.

SHELTON LOCK Derbs. �402 �403 �404 P 25 – see Derby.

SHEPPERTON Surrey �404 S 29 – pop. 10,765 – ✆ 0932 Walton-on-Thames.
♦London 25.

Plan : see Greater London (South-West)

🏨 **Shepperton Moat House** (Q.M.H.), Felix Lane, TW17 8NP, E : 1 ¼ m. on B 375 ℰ 241404,
Telex 928170, 🚗 – ⛖ 📺 ➡wc ☎ 🅿 🖺 🔼 🆎 ⑩ 𝘝𝘐𝘚𝘈   AZ **a**
M 8.00 **st.** ⧘ 4.90 – **179 rm** ⊊ 39.95/49.50 **st.** – SB 44.00 **st.**

✕✕ **Thames Court,** Tow Path, Ferry Lane, TW17 9LJ, W : 1 ¼ m. by B 375 ℰ 221957, ≼ River
Thames, 🚗 – 🅿 🔼 🆎 ⑩ 𝘝𝘐𝘚𝘈   by B 375 AZ
closed Sunday dinner and Monday – **M** a la carte 6.40/12.70 **t.** ⧘ 2.55.

FORD Station Approach ℰ 24811   NISSAN Walton Bridge Rd ℰ 47848
HONDA High St. ℰ 40121

SHEPTON MALLET Somerset �403 �404 M 30 The West Country G. – pop. 5,030 – ECD : Wednesday – ✆ 0749.

See : Site ★ – SS. Peter and Paul's Church ★.
Envir. : Oakhill Manor ★, N : 4 m. off A 37 – Downside Abbey ★, N : 5 m. off A 37 and A 367 –
Nunney ★, W : 9 m. on A 361.
♦London 127 – ♦Bristol 20 – ♦Southampton 63 – Taunton 31.

🏨 **Charlton House,** Charlton Rd, BA4 4PR, E : 1 m. on A 361 ℰ 2008, ≼, 🔼, 🚗, park, ✀ – 📺
➡wc ☎ 🅿 🔼 🆎 ⑩ 𝘝𝘐𝘚𝘈 ✀
M 8.50/11.50 **st.** – **12 rm** ⊊ 27.00/38.00 **st.** – SB 54.00 **st.**

✕✕ **Bowlish House** with rm, Wells Rd, BA4 5JD, W : ½ m. on A 371 ℰ 2022, 🚗 – ➡wc 🅿
closed 24 to 27 December – **M** (lunch by arrangement)(booking essential) 13.00 **t.** – ⊊ 1.50 –
4 rm 20.00/25.00 **t.**

at Oakhill NE : 3 m. by A 37 on A 367 – ✉ ✆ 0749 Shepton Mallet :

✕✕ **Oakhill House** ॐ with rm, Bath Rd, BA3 5AN, ℰ 840180, 🚗 – ➡wc 🅿 🔼 🆎 ⑩ 𝘝𝘐𝘚𝘈 ✀
closed 25 and 26 December – **M** *(closed Bank Holiday lunch and Sunday dinner)* a la carte
8.00/10.15 **t.** ⧘ 2.20 – **3 rm** ⊊ 18.00/27.00 **st.**

HONDA Townsend Rd ℰ 2864   VW, AUDI High St. ℰ 4091

SHERBORNE Dorset 403 404 M 31 – pop. 7,272 – ECD : Wednesday – ☎ 093 581 (4 fig.) or 0935 (6 fig.).

See : Site ★★★ – Abbey ★★★ – Sherborne Castle ★★.

Envir. : Sansford Orcas Manor House★, N : 4 m. by B 3148 – Purse Caundle Manor★, NE : 5 m. by A 30.

🖺 Clatcombe 🖉 2475, N : 1 m.

🛈 Hound St. 🖉 815341 (summer only).

♦London 128 – Bournemouth 39 – Dorchester 19 – Salisbury 36 – Taunton 31.

🏛 **Post House** (T.H.F.), Horsecastles Lane, DT9 6BB, W : 1 m. on A 30 🖉 3191, Telex 46522, 🚗 – 📺 🖴wc ☎ 🕭 🅿 🖳 🔼 🆎 ⓪ 𝒱𝐼𝒮𝒜
   M 7.50/8.95 ♪ 2.60 – ⊊ 5.00 – **60 rm** 33.50/41.00 **st.**

🏛 **Eastbury,** Long St., DT9 3BY, 🖉 3387, 🚗 – 🖴wc 🅿
   M (bar lunch) 7.00 **st.** ♪ 2.60 – **15 rm** ⊊ 15.00/33.00 **st.** – SB (winter only) 31.00/35.00 **st.**

🏛 **Saffron House,** The Avenue, DT9 3AH, 🖉 812734, 🚗 – 🖴wc 🅿
   closed 25 December- 1 January – **M** 8.00 **t.** ♪ 2.60 – **6 rm** ⊊ 18.50/37.00 **t.**

   at Oborne NE : 2 m. by A 30 – ⊠ ☎ 0935 Sherborne :

🗙🗙 **Grange** 🦢 with rm, DT9 4LA, 🖉 813463, ≤, 🚗 – 🖴wc 🅿 🔼 𝒱𝐼𝒮𝒜 🍽
   closed 1 to 10 January and 1 to 10 September – **M** (closed Sunday dinner and Monday) a la carte 7.60/9.95 **t.** ♪ 2.80 – ⊊ 3.00 – **3 rm** 20.00/30.00 **t.**

ALFA-ROMEO, LANCIA Long St. 🖉 3262   MERCEDES-BENZ Yeovil Rd 🖉 3350
AUSTIN-ROVER Digby Rd 🖉 2436

SHERE Surrey 404 S 30 – pop. 3,513 – see Dorking.

   If you find you cannot take up a hotel booking you have made,
   please let the hotel know immediately.

SHERINGHAM Norfolk 404 X 25 – pop. 5,209 – ECD : Wednesday – ☎ 0263 Cromer.

Envir. : Cromer : SS. Peter and Paul's Church (tower ≼★).

♦London 128 – Cromer 4 – ♦Norwich 27.

🏠 **Beacon,** 1 Nelson Rd, NR26 8BT, 🖉 822019, 🚗 – 🅿 🔼 𝒱𝐼𝒮𝒜 🍽
   April-October – **8 rm** ⊊ 12.00/24.00 **st.**

SHIFNAL Salop 402 403 404 M 25 – pop. 5,070 – ECD : Thursday – ⊠ ☎ 0952 Telford.

See : St. Andrew's Church★ 12C-16C.

Envir. : Weston Park★ 17C (paintings★★) AC, NE : 5 m.

♦London 150 – ♦Birmingham 28 – Shrewsbury 16.

🏛 **Park House,** Park St., TF11 9BA, 🖉 460128, 🔲 heated, 🚗 – 📺 🅿 🖳 🔼 🆎 ⓪ 𝒱𝐼𝒮𝒜
   M (bar lunch Saturday) 8.50/12.50 **t.** ♪ 2.60 – **21 rm** ⊊ 28.50/70.00 **t.** – SB (weekends only) 53.00/70.00 **st.**

AUSTIN-ROVER Chepside 🖉 460412   FORD Park St. 🖉 460631

SHINFIELD Berks. 404 R 29 – see Reading.

SHIPDHAM Norfolk 404 W 26 – pop. 1,520 – ⊠ Thetford – ☎ 0362 Dereham.

♦London 102 – East Dereham 5 – ♦Norwich 21 – Watton 6.

🗙🗙 **Shipdham Place** 🦢 with rm, Church Close, IP25 7LX, on A 1075 🖉 820303, 🚗 – 🖴wc ⊛ 🅿 🍽
   closed Tuesday dinner, February and Christmas – **M** (buffet lunch by arrangement to residents only) (booking essential) 16.50 **t.** – **5 rm** ⊊ 30.00/52.50 **t.**

SHIPLEY West Yorks. 402 O 22 – pop. 27,894 – ECD : Wednesday – ☎ 0274 Bradford.

♦London 216 – Bradford 4 – ♦Leeds 12.

🗙 **Aagrah,** 27 Westgate, BD18 3QX, 🖉 594660, Indian rest. – 🔼 🆎 ⓪ 𝒱𝐼𝒮𝒜
   M a la carte 3.95/7.00 **t.** ♪ 1.95.

SHIPSTON-ON-STOUR Warw. 403 404 P 27 – pop. 2,773 – ☎ 0608.

Envir. : Compton Wynyates★ (Tudor Mansion 15C-16C) AC, NE : 4 ½ m.

♦London 85 – ♦Birmingham 34 – ♦Oxford 29.

🗙🗙 **Old Mill** with rm, Mill St., CV36 4AW, on B 4035 🖉 61880, 🚗 – 🖴wc ♒wc 🅿 🔼 🆎 ⓪ 𝒱𝐼𝒮𝒜
   M (closed Sunday dinner) 12.00 **t.** ♪ 2.25 – **5 rm** ⊊ 16.00/29.00 **t.** – SB (winter only) 39.50 **st.**

🗙 **White Bear** with rm, High St., CV36 4AJ, 🖉 61558 – 🖴wc 🅿 🔼 🆎 ⓪ 𝒱𝐼𝒮𝒜
   M (closed Sunday dinner and Bank Holidays) (lunch by arrangement Monday to Saturday) a la carte 8.10/11.75 **t.** ♪ 2.30 – **9 rm** ⊊ 12.00/30.00 **t.** – SB 40.00/60.00 **st.**

AUSTIN-ROVER Church St. 🖉 092 684 (Claverdon)   FORD Church St. 🖉 61425
2208   SUBARU 🖉 61544

♦London 81 – ♦Birmingham 50 – Gloucester 37 – ♦Oxford 25.

  ✕ **Lamb Inn** with rm, High St., OX7 6DQ, ✆ 830465, ♨ – 🚪wc 🅿. 🔼 AE ⑩ VISA. ⨯
    M *(closed Sunday dinner)* (bar lunch Monday to Saturday) 7.00/10.50 **t.** ▯ 2.75 – 🖙 2.50 –
    5 rm 20.00/30.00 **t.** – SB (winter only) 71.00 **st.**

SHORNE Kent 404 V 29 – pop. 2,622 – ✉ Gravesend – ✆ 047 482.

♦London 27 – Gravesend 4 – Maidstone 12 – Rochester 4.

  🏨 **Inn on the Lake,** DA12 3HB, on A 2 ✆ 3333, ≤, 🐦, ♨, park – 📺 🚪wc ☎ 🅿. 🛆. 🔼 AE
    ⑩ VISA. ⨯
    M a la carte 9.95/16.20 **t.** ▯ 2.75 – **78 rm** 🖙 33.00/50.00 **st.**

SHREWSBURY Salop 402 403 L 25 – pop. 56,188 – ECD : Thursday – ✆ 0743.

See : Abbey Church★ 11C-14C **D** – St. Mary's Church★ (Jesse Tree window★) **A** – Grope Lane★ 15C.

Envir. : Wroxeter★ (Roman city and baths) *AC*, SE : 6 m. by A 458 and A 5 – Condover Hall★ (15C) *AC*, S : 5 m. by A 49.

🏌 Meole Brace ✆ 64050, S : by A 49.

🛈 The Square ✆ 52019.

♦London 165 – ♦Birmingham 49 – ♦Cardiff 109 – Chester 43 – Derby 67 – Gloucester 94 – ♦Manchester 68 – ♦Stoke-on-Trent 39 – ♦Swansea 123.

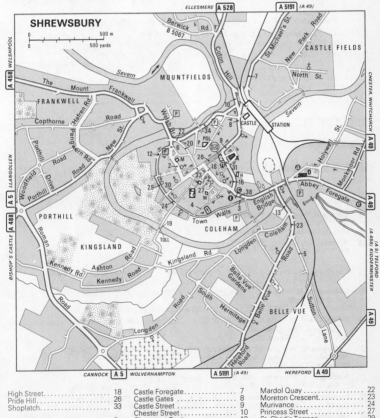

High Street	18	Castle Foregate	7	Mardol Quay	22
Pride Hill	26	Castle Gates	8	Moreton Crescent	23
Shoplatch	33	Castle Street	9	Murivance	24
		Chester Street	10	Princess Street	27
Barker Street	2	Claremont Bank	12	St. Chad's Terrace	29
Beeches Lane	3	Coleham Head	13	St. John's Hill	30
Belmont	4	Dogpole	16	St. Mary's Street	31
Betton Street	5	Kingsland Bridge	19	Smithfield Road	34
Bridge Street	6	Mardol	20	Wyle Cop	38

🏛 **Prince Rupert,** Butcher Row, SY1 1UQ, ℰ 52461, Telex 35100 – 📶 🖥 📺 🛏wc 🛁wc ⚙ 🅿
🔥. 🔼 AE ⓪ VISA
n
M 6.50/8.50 st. ♨ 2.90 – **70 rm** ⊊ 28.00/42.00 st.

🏛 **Lion** (T.H.F.), Wyle Cop, SY1 1UY, ℰ 53107, Telex 35648 – 📶 📺 🛏wc ⚙ 🅿 🔥. 🔼 AE ⓪
VISA
c
M 6.50/9.00 st. ♨ 2.85 – ⊊ 4.75 – **59 rm** 31.00/44.00 st.

🏛 **Lord Hill,** 131 Abbey Foregate, SY2 6AX, ℰ 52601 – 📺 🛏wc 🛁wc ⚙ 🅿 🔥. 🔼 AE ⓪ VISA
closed 26 December – **M** 5.50/6.50 st. ♨ 2.85 – **46 rm** ⊊ 20.00/45.00 st. – SB 54.00 st.   **e**

XX **Penny Farthing,** 23 Abbey Foregate, SY2 6AE, ℰ 56119 – 🔼 AE ⓪ VISA   **a**
closed Saturday lunch, Sunday, Monday, first 2 weeks January and first 2 weeks September –
M a la carte 11.30/13.85 t. ♨ 3.00.

X **Belmont,** Barracks Passage, Wyle Cop, ℰ 246333 – 🔼 AE ⓪ VISA   **i**
closed Sunday, 2 weeks September, 2 weeks Christmas and Bank Holidays – **M** (restricted
lunch) 4.25 a la carte 6.10/13.10 t.

at Albrighton N : 3 m. on A 528 – ✉ Shrewsbury – ☎ 0939 Bomere Heath :

XX **Albright Hussey,** SY4 3AF, ℰ 290523, « 16C timbered manor house with garden » – 🅿
🔼 AE VISA
closed Sunday dinner, Monday and August – **M** a la carte 11.75/16.00 st. ♨ 2.35.

at Atcham SE : 3 ¾ m. by A 5112 on A 5 – ✉ Shrewsbury – ☎ 074 375 Cross Houses :

🏛 **Mytton and Mermaid,** SY5 6QG, ℰ 220, ↘ – 📺 🛏wc 🛁 🅿 🔼 AE ⓪ VISA
M (Dancing Wednesday, Friday and Saturday) 6.00/7.00 t. ♨ 3.00 – **8 rm** ⊊ 14.50/30.00 t. – SB
30.00/40.00 st.

at Dorrington S : 7 m. on A 49 – ✉ Shrewsbury – ☎ 074 373 Dorrington :

XX **Country Friends,** SY5 7JD, ℰ 707, ﷼ – 🅿 AE ⓪ VISA
closed Monday lunch and Sunday – **M** a la carte 9.80/13.50 t.

ALFA-ROMEO, CITROEN   159 Abbey Foregate ℰ
57711
AUSTIN-ROVER   Chester St. ℰ 57231
AUSTIN-ROVER   Harlescott ℰ 52288
BMW   Castle Foregate ℰ 3250
COLT   Harlescott Ind. Est ℰ 64951
FIAT   Wyle Cop ℰ 52471

FORD   Coton Hill ℰ 3631
PEUGEOT-TALBOT   170 Abbey Foregate ℰ 56326
RENAULT   Featherbed Lane ℰ 69611
SAAB   Westbury Garage ℰ 241 445
VAUXHALL-OPEL   Greyfriars ℰ 52321
VOLVO   Featherbed Lane ℰ 51251
VW, AUDI   English Bridge ℰ 52471

SHURDINGTON Glos. 🔢403 🔢404 N 28 – see Cheltenham.

SIDFORD Devon 🔢403 K 31 – see Sidmouth.

SIDMOUTH Devon 🔢403 K 31 The West Country G. – pop. 12,076 – ECD : Thursday – ☎ 039 55.
🏌 Cotmaton Rd ℰ 3023.
🎫 The Esplanade ℰ 6441 (summer only).
♦London 170 – Exeter 14 – Taunton 27 – Weymouth 45.

🏨 **Victoria,** Peak Hill, EX10 8RY, ℰ 2651, ≤, ♨ heated, 🔼, ﷼, 🎾 – 📶 📺 🅿 🔼 AE ⓪ VISA.
🦌
M 6.75/11.00 s. ♨ 2.00 – **62 rm** ⊊ 30.00/72.00 – SB (winter only) 55.20/61.00 st.

🏛 **Riviera,** Esplanade, EX10 8AY, ℰ 5201, ≤ – 📶 📺 🛏wc ⚙ 🍽. AE ⓪
M 7.00/9.00 s. ♨ 2.50 – **34 rm** ⊊ 16.00/55.00 s. – SB (weekends only) (except summer) 49.45/56.35 st.

🏛 **Fortfield,** Station Rd, EX10 8NU, ℰ 2403, 🔼, ﷼ – 📶 📺 🛏wc ♿ 🅿 🔼 ⓪ VISA
M (bar lunch) 6.50 t. ♨ 2.00 – **55 rm** ⊊ 21.00/60.00 t. – SB 38.00/60.00 st.

🏛 **Salcombe Hill House** ⑊, Beatlands Rd, EX10 8JQ, ℰ 4697, ♨ heated, ﷼, 🎾 – 📶 📺
🛏wc 🅿 🔼 VISA
March-October – **M** 5.50/6.50 t. ♨ 2.85 – **33 rm** ⊊ 17.00/52.00 st.

🏛 **Royal Glen,** Glen Rd, EX10 8RW, ℰ 3221, « 17C house furnished with many antiques », ﷼
– 📺 🛏wc 🛁wc 🅿 🔼 VISA
M 4.75/5.00 t. ♨ 2.00 – **37 rm** ⊊ 11.45/45.50 t.

🏠 **Littlecourt,** Seafield Rd, EX10 8HF, ℰ 5279, ♨ heated, ﷼ – 🛏wc 🛁wc 🅿
March-November and Christmas – **M** (bar lunch Monday to Saturday) 6.00/7.50 t. ♨ 2.00 –
20 rm ⊊ 19.00/25.75 t. – SB 36.50/40.00 st.

🏠 **Abbeydale,** Manor Rd, EX10 8RP, ℰ 2060, ﷼ – 📺 🛏wc 🅿 🦌
21 March-5 November – **M** (bar lunch) 7.00 t. ♨ 2.00 – **17 rm** ⊊ 15.50/40.00 t.

🏠 **Mount Pleasant,** Salcombe Rd, EX10 8JA, ℰ 4694, ﷼ – 🛏wc 🛁wc 🅿 🦌
Easter-mid October – **M** (dinner only) 5.50 st. ♨ 2.00 – **15 rm** ⊊ 13.00/13.50 st.

🏠 **Woodlands,** Cotmaton Cross, EX10 8HG, ℰ 3120, ﷼ – 🛏wc ♿ 🅿
M 3.50/4.50 t. ♨ 3.00 – **30 rm** ⊊ 10.50/31.00 – SB (Spring only) 29.90 st.

↑ **Barrington Villa,** Salcombe Rd, EX10 8PU, ℰ 4252, ﷼ – 🅿
closed November – **9 rm** ⊊ 12.00/16.00.

at Sidford N : 2 m. – ✉ ☎ 039 55 Sidmouth :

Applegarth, Church St., EX10 9QP, E : on A 3052 ☎ 3174, « Garden » – P. AE VISA
closed mid October-November – **M** *(closed Tuesday lunch and Sunday dinner to non-residents)* 6.00/9.95 **t.** – **8 rm** 10.00/24.00 **t.** – SB (summer only) 34.00 **st.**

AUSTIN-ROVER Salcombe Rd ☎ 2522
FIAT Crossways, Sidford ☎ 3595
NISSAN Sidford ☎ 3334
PEUGEOT-TALBOT Vicarage Rd ☎ 2433
VOLVO Mill St. ☎ 3433

SILCHESTER Hants. 403 404 Q 29 – pop. 766 – ✉ Reading (Berks.) – ☎ 0734.
♦London 62 – Basingstoke 8 – Reading 14 – Winchester 26.

Romans, Little London Rd, RG7 2PN, ☎ 700421, heated, – TV wc ☎ P. AE VISA
closed last 2 weeks August, Christmas, New Year and Bank Holidays – **M** *(closed Sunday dinner)* 12.00/15.00 **st.** 3.25 – **25 rm** 35.00/50.00 **st.** – SB (weekends only) 60.00/70.00 **st.**

SIMONSBATH Somerset 403 I 30 The West Country G. – pop. 181 – ✉ Minehead – ☎ 064 383 Exford.
♦London 200 – Exeter 40 – Minehead 19 – Taunton 38.

Simonsbath House, TA24 7SH, ☎ 259, ≤, « Tastefully converted 17C country house », squash – TV wc P. AE VISA.
closed Sunday to Thursday January-March – **M** (dinner only) (booking essential) 13.00 **t.** 3.25 – **8 rm** 37.65/68.20 **t.**

SITTINGBOURNE Kent 404 W 29 – pop. 26,450 – ECD : Wednesday – ☎ 0795.
♦London 44 – Canterbury 16 – Maidstone 13.

Coniston, 70 London Rd, ME10 1NT, ☎ 23927 – TV wc P. AE VISA
M 5.55 **t.** 2.50 – **48 rm** 22.50/42.00 **t.**

AUSTIN-ROVER Bapchild ☎ 23085
FORD Canterbury Rd ☎ 70711
MAZDA Newington ☎ 842307
NISSAN St. Michaels Rd ☎ 23422
RENAULT Chalkwell Rd ☎ 76361
TALBOT Teynham ☎ 521286
VAUXHALL-OPEL London Rd, Bapchild ☎ 76222

SIX MILE BOTTOM Cambs. – see Newmarket (Suffolk).

SKEGNESS Lincs. 402 404 V 24 – pop. 12,680 – ECD : Thursday – ☎ 0754.
18 Seacroft ☎ 3020, S : 1 ½ m. – 18 North Shore ☎ 3298.
Embassy Centre, Grand Parade ☎ 4821 and 5441 (summer only).
♦London 145 – Lincoln 41.

Vine, Vine Rd, Seacroft, PE25 3DB, ☎ 3018, – TV wc P. AE VISA.
closed 26 to 28 December – **M** a la carte 6.95/10.25 **st.** – **20 rm** 16.00/34.00 **t.**

County, North Par., PE25 2UB, ☎ 2461, ≤ – TV wc P. AE VISA
M 6.50 **t.** 3.00 – **43 rm** 23.00/36.00 **t.** – SB 44.00/48.00 **st.**

Spinney Lodge, 25 Scarborough Av., PE25 2SZ, ☎ 66466, – P.
closed December – **9 rm** 7.00/22.00 **s.**

AUSTIN-ROVER Roman Bank ☎ 3671
DAIHATSU Burgh Rd ☎ 2244
FIAT, ALFA-ROMEO Beresford Av. ☎ 67131
FORD Wainfleet Rd ☎ 66019
TALBOT Beacon Way ☎ 2556
VAUXHALL-OPEL, YUGO Clifton Grove ☎ 3589

SKELTON North Yorks. 402 Q 22 – see York.

SKELWITH BRIDGE Cumbria 402 K 20 – see Ambleside.

SKIPTON North Yorks. 402 N 22 – pop. 13,220 – ECD : Tuesday – ☎ 0756.
See : Castle★ (14C) *AC*.
18 Short Lee Lane, off Grassington Rd ☎ 3257, NW : 1 m.
High St. Car Park Approach ☎ 2809 (summer only).
♦London 217 – Kendal 45 – ♦Leeds 26 – Preston 36 – York 43.

Unicorn without rest., Keighley Rd, BD23 2LP, ☎ 4146 – TV wc. VISA.
closed 23 December-2 January – **9 rm** 20.50/29.50 **st.**

Highfield, 58 Keighley Rd, BD23 2NB, ☎ 3182 –
closed 2 weeks February, March, Christmas and New Year – **10 rm** 10.25/22.00 **st.**

Oats, Chapel Hill, BD23 1NL, ☎ 3604 – P. AE VISA
closed Sunday and Monday – **M** a la carte 13.55/14.90 **t.** 4.75.

SLAIDBURN Lancs. 🔢🔢🔢 M 22 – pop. 345 – 🎯 020 06.
♦London 249 – Burnley 21 – Lancaster 19 – ♦Leeds 48 – Preston 27.

  🏡 **Parrock Head Farm** 🐾, Near Clitheroe, BB7 3AH, NW : 1 m. 🖉 614, ≤ Bowland Fells, 🚗
    – 📺 🚰wc 🅿. 🅰🅴
    closed 2 weeks mid-January – **M** a la carte 5.70/9.10 **st.** 🍷 2.40 – **7 rm** 🛏 16.00/33.00 **st.**

SLEAFORD Lincs. 🔢🔢🔢 🔢🔢🔢 S 25 – pop. 7,880 – ECD : Thursday – 🎯 0529.
See : St. Denis' Church★ 12C-15C.
🐦 South Rauceby 🖉 052 98 (South Rauceby) 273, W : 1 m. on A 153.
♦London 119 – ♦Leicester 45 – Lincoln 17 – ♦Nottingham 39.

  🍴 **Tally Ho,** Aswarby, NG34 8SA, S : 4 ½ m. on A 15 🖉 205, ≤, 🚗 – 📺 🚰wc 🍴wc 🅿. 🛝
    M (bar lunch) a la carte 3.30/6.80 **t.** 🍷 2.50 – **6 rm** 🛏 14.00/24.00 **t.** – SB 26.00 **st.**

AUSTIN-ROVER Carre St. 🖉 303034
COLT Holdingham 🖉 302545
FORD London Rd 🖉 302921

MAZDA Grantham Rd 🖉 052 98 (Sth. Rauceby) 674
RENAULT 50 Westgate 🖉 305305
TALBOT Boston Rd 🖉 302518

SLOUGH Berks. 🔢🔢🔢 S 29 – pop. 87,075 – ECD : Wednesday – 🎯 0753.
Envir. : Eton (college★★) S : 2 m.
🐦 Farnham Park, Park Rd, Stoke Poges 🖉 028 14 (Farnham Common) 3332, N : 2 m. – 🐦 Wexham
Park, Wexham St. 🖉 028 16 (Fulmer) 3271, N : 2 m.
♦London 29 – ♦Oxford 39 – Reading 19.

  🏨 **Holiday Inn,** Ditton Rd, Langley, SL3 8PT, SE : 2 ½ m. on A 4 🖉 44244, Telex 848646, 🔳, 🛝
    – 🍴 📺 🕿 🕭 🅿. 🔥 🔼 🅰🅴 ⓪ 𝚅𝙸𝚂𝙰
    M 10.50/9.50 **st.** 🍷 4.25 – 🛏 5.65 – **224 rm** 42.50/54.00 **s.**

SAAB Beaconsfield Rd 🖉 028 14 (Farnham Common) 5111
VOLVO Petersfield Av. 🖉 23031

VW, AUDI 57 Farnham Rd 🖉 33917
VW, AUDI-NSU Colnbrook By-Pass 🖉 028 12 (Colnbrook) 2708

SMETHWICK West Midlands 🔢🔢🔢 🔢🔢🔢 O 26 – see Birmingham.

SNAINTON North Yorks. 🔢🔢🔢 S 21 – pop. 652 – ECD : Wednesday – ✉ 🎯 0723 Scarborough.
♦London 240 – Scarborough 10 – York 29.

  🍴 **Coachman Inn,** YO13 9PL, 🖉 85231 – 🚰wc 🍴wc 🅿. 🔼 🅰🅴 ⓪ 𝚅𝙸𝚂𝙰
    M (bar lunch) 8.75 **st.** 🍷 2.75 – **12 rm** 🛏 18.00/33.00 **st.** – SB (winter only) 43.00 **st.**

SNEATON North Yorks. 🔢🔢🔢 S 20 – see Whitby.

SNOWDON (YR WYDDFA) Gwynedd 🔢🔢🔢 🔢🔢🔢 H 24.
See : Ascent and ❄★★★ (1 h 15 mn from Llanberis (Pass★★) by Snowdon Mountain Railway *AC*).
    Hotels and restaurant see : *Beddgelert* S : 4 m., *Caernarfon* NW : 9 m.

SOAR MILL COVE Devon – see Salcombe.

SOLIHULL West Midlands 🔢🔢🔢 🔢🔢🔢 O 26 – pop. 107,095 – ECD : Wednesday – 🎯 021 Birmingham.
🐦 Shirley, Stratford Rd 🖉 744 6001.
🅱 Central Library, Homer Rd 🖉 705 6789 ext 504/5.
♦London 109 – ♦Birmingham 7 – ♦Coventry 13 – Warwick 13.

  🏨 **St. John's** (Swallow), 651 Warwick Rd, B94 6BH, 🖉 705 6777, Telex 339352 – 🍴 📺 🚰wc
    🕭 🅿. 🔼 🅰🅴 ⓪ 𝚅𝙸𝚂𝙰
    M 6.60/8.50 **st.** – **214 rm** 🛏 32.00/44.00 **st.** – SB (weekends only) 50.00 **st.**

  🏨 **George** (Embassy), High St., B91 3RF, 🖉 704 1241 – 📺 🚰wc 🕭 🅿. 🔥 🔼 🅰🅴 ⓪ 𝚅𝙸𝚂𝙰 🛝
    closed 24 December-2 January – **M** 7.40/7.90 **st.** 🍷 4.50 – 🛏 4.25 – **47 rm** 24.00/40.00 **st.** – SB
    (weekends only) 44.00/50.00 **st.**

AUSTIN-ROVER-DAIMLER-JAGUAR-RANGE
ROVER Stratford Rd, Shirley 🖉 745 5855
AUSTIN-ROVER 707 Warwick Rd 🖉 705 3028
AUSTIN-ROVER 301 Warwick Rd 🖉 706 2801
BMW 824 Stratford Rd 🖉 744 4488
COLT 270 Stratford Rd 🖉 744 1033
FIAT The Green 🖉 056 44 (Tanworth) 2218
FORD 361/369 Stratford Rd 🖉 744 4456

HONDA Station Lane 🖉 056 43 (Lapworth) 2933
RENAULT Stratford Rd, Hockley Heath 🖉 056 43 (Lapworth) 2244
TALBOT 270 Stratford Rd, Shirley 🖉 744 1033
TALBOT 386 Warwick Rd 🖉 704 1427
TOYOTA 301 Warwick Rd 🖉 706 2801
VW, AUDI Stratford Rd, Shirley 🖉 745 5811

Pour les 🏨🏨🏨🏨 , 🏨🏨🏨 , 🏨🏨 , nous ne donnons pas
le détail de l'installation,
ces hôtels possèdent, en général, tout le confort.

🚰wc 🍴wc

🕭

406

SONNING-ON-THAMES Berks. 404 R 29 – pop. 1,469 – ECD : Wednesday – ✆ 0734 Reading.

♦London 48 – Reading 4.

🏨 **White Hart,** Thames St., RG4 0UT, ☎ 692277, Telex 849031, ≼, « Rose gardens on river bank » – 📺 ➦wc ☎ 🅿. 🔄 🆎 ① 𝘝𝘐𝘚𝘈
M 9.75/10.50 t. – ⚍ 2.50 – **25 rm** 38.00/48.00 t. – SB (weekends only) 52.50 **st.**

XXX **French Horn** with rm, Thames St., RG4 0TN, ☎ 692204, ≼ River Thames and gardens – 📺 ➦wc 🅿. 🆎 ① 𝘝𝘐𝘚𝘈. ⚘
M a la carte 12.50/20.50 **st.** 🍷 3.50 – **5 rm** ⚍ 50.00/70.00 **st.**

SOUTHAM Glos. 403 404 N 28 – see Cheltenham.

☛ *There is no paid publicity in this Guide.*

SOUTHAMPTON Hants. 403 404 P 31 – pop. 215,118 – ECD : Monday and Wednesday – ✆ 0703.

See : Docks★ AY – Tudor House Museum★ (16C) *AC* AZ **M1** – God's House Tower★ 12C (Museum of Archaeologia) AZ **M2.**

Envir. : Netley (abbey★ ruins 13C) *AC*, SE : 3 m. BZ **A.**

🏌 Stoneham ☎ 768151, N : 2 m. BY – 🏌, 🏌 West Side Basset Av. ☎ 768407 AY – 🏌 Fleming Park ☎ 0703 (Eastleigh) 612797, N : 6 m. by A 33 AY.

✈ Southampton Airport : ☎ 0703 (Eastleigh) 612341, N : 4 m. BY.

🚢 to France (Le Havre) (P & O Ferries : Channel Service) – to America (New York) (Cunard) – to the Isle of Wight : East and West Cowes (Red Funnel Services) 8-18 daily (55 mn to 1 h 10 mn).

🚢 to the Isle of Wight : West Cowes (Red Funnel Services : hydrofoil) Monday/Saturday 14-19 daily ; Sunday 10 daily (20 mn).

🛈 Above Bar Precinct ☎ 21106.

♦London 80 – ♦Bristol 79 – ♦Plymouth 161.

Plans on following pages

🏨 **Polygon** (T.H.F.), Cumberland Pl., SO9 4GD, ☎ 26401, Telex 47175 – 📶 📺 🅿. 🔄 🔄 🆎 ①
𝘝𝘐𝘚𝘈   AZ **n**
M 7.50/10.50 **st.** 🍷 2.95 – ⚍ 5.50 – **119 rm** 41.00/49.50 **st.**

🏨 **Dolphin** (T.H.F.), 35 High St., SO9 2DS, ☎ 26178, Telex 477735 – 📶 📺 ➦wc ☎ 🅿. 🔄
🆎 ① 𝘝𝘐𝘚𝘈   AZ **i**
M (bar lunch Saturday) 5.95/8.50 **st.** 🍷 2.95 – ⚍ 5.00 – **72 rm** 36.50/41.00 **st.**

🏨 **Post House** (T.H.F.), Herbert Walker Av., SO1 0HJ, ☎ 28081, Telex 477368, ≼, ☷ heated –
📶 📺 ➦wc ☎ 🅿 ♿. 🔄 🔄 🆎 ① 𝘝𝘐𝘚𝘈   AZ **o**
M a la carte 9.85/13.20 **st.** 🍷 2.60 – ⚍ 5.50 – **132 rm** 38.00/45.50 **st.**

🏨 **Southampton Park,** Cumberland Pl., SO9 4NY, ☎ 23467, Telex 47439 – 📶 📺 ➦wc ☎.
🔄 🔄 🆎 ① 𝘝𝘐𝘚𝘈   AZ **u**
M 8.25 t. – **77 rm** ⚍ 32.50/39.75 t. – SB (weekends only) 40.00 **st.**

🏨 **Southampton Moat House** (Q.M.H.), 119 Highfield Lane, Portswood Junction, SO9 1YQ,
☎ 559555 – 📺 ➦wc ☎ 🅿. 🔄 🔄 🆎 ① 𝘝𝘐𝘚𝘈   BY **e**
M (closed Saturday lunch) 6.20/7.55 t. 🍷 3.20 – **70 rm** ⚍ 32.45/39.75 t. – SB (weekends only) 36.50 **st.**

🏨 **Star,** High St., SO9 4ZA, ☎ 26199 – 📶 📺 ➦wc 🎞wc ☎ 🅿. 🔄   AZ **z**
31 rm.

🏨 **Northlands,** Northlands Rd, SO9 3ZW, ☎ 333871 – 📺 🎞wc 🅿. 🔄 𝘝𝘐𝘚𝘈   AY **a**
M (closed Saturday and Sunday) 6.00/11.00 t. 🍷 2.30 – **18 rm** ⚍ 16.00/36.00 t.

🏨 **Elizabeth House,** 43-44 The Avenue, SO1 2SX, ☎ 24327 – 📺 ➦wc 🎞wc 🅿. 🔄 🆎 ① 𝘝𝘐𝘚𝘈
closed 22 December-6 January – **M** (dinner only) 6.00 t. 🍷 2.00 – **25 rm** ⚍ 16.00/32.00 t.   AZ **e**

                                                                                              AY **e**
🏨 **Wessex,** 66-68 Northlands Rd, SO1 2LH, ☎ 31744, ☞ – 📺 ➦wc 🎞wc ☎ 🅿. 🔄   AY **r**
M (bar lunch) 6.00 **s.** 🍷 2.30 – **31 rm** ⚍ 16.60/34.20 **st.**

⌂ **Hunters Lodge,** 25 Landguard Rd, SO1 5DL, ☎ 27919 – 🅿. 𝘝𝘐𝘚𝘈. ⚘   AZ **v**
closed 20 December-5 January – **17 rm** ⚍ 10.00/18.00.

⌂ **St. Regulus,** 5 Archers Rd, SO1 2LQ, ☎ 24243, ☞ – ➦wc 🎞wc 🅿. ⚘   AZ **x**
27 rm ⚍ 13.25/29.00 **st.**

⌂ **Earley House,** 46 Pear Tree Av., Bitterne, SO2 7JP, ☎ 448117 – 🅿. ⚘   BY **v**
9 rm ⚍ 14.00/30.00 t.

⌂ **Eaton Court,** 32 Hill Lane, SO1 5AY, ☎ 23081 – 🎞wc 🅿. 🔄 𝘝𝘐𝘚𝘈. ⚘   AZ **r**
closed 1 week at Christmas – **12 rm** ⚍ 10.75/21.50 **st.**

⌂ **Rosida,** 25-27 Hill Lane, SO1 5AB, ☎ 28501, ☷ heated, ☞ – ➦wc 🎞wc 🅿. 🔄 𝘝𝘐𝘚𝘈   AZ **s**
closed 22 December-2 January – **36 rm** ⚍ 15.50/35.00 **st.**

X **La Brasserie,** 33-34 Oxford St., SO1 1DS, ☎ 21046, French rest. – 🔄 🆎 ① 𝘝𝘐𝘚𝘈   AZ **c**
closed Saturday lunch and Sunday – **M** a la carte 7.70/11.25 t. 🍷 2.40.

X **Golden Palace,** 1st Floor, 17 Above Bar St., ☎ 26636, Chinese rest.   AZ **e**

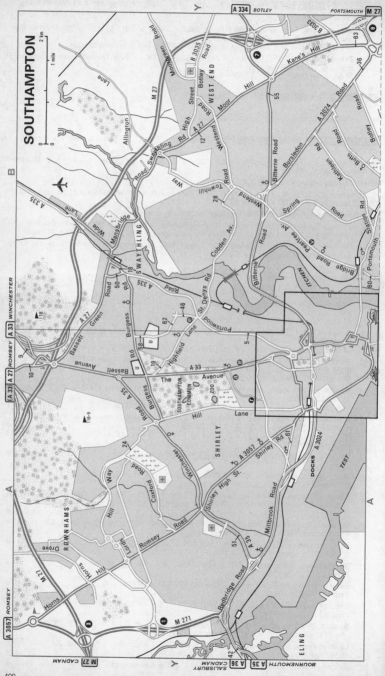

SOUTHAMPTON

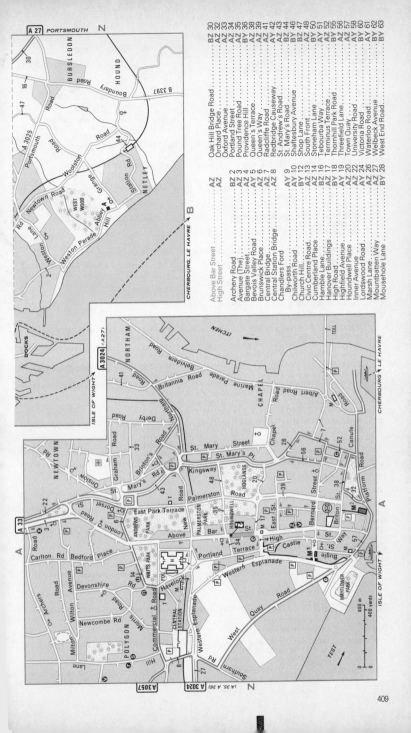

409

MICHELIN Branch, Test Lane, SO1 9JX, ☎ **872344**

AUSTIN-ROVER-DAIMLER-JAGUAR Marsh Lane ☎ 30911
AUSTIN-ROVER The Causeway ☎ 865201
AUSTIN-ROVER High St., West End ☎ 042 18 (West End) 3773
AUSTIN-ROVER 102 High Rd ☎ 554346
AUSTIN-ROVER-DAIMLER-JAGUAR, ROLLS ROYCE The Avenue ☎ 28811
BMW Dorset St. ☎ 29003
COLT 170 Portsmouth Rd ☎ 447761
FIAT 115/125 Lodge Rd ☎ 25518
FORD 362/364 Shirley Rd ☎ 775331
FORD Palmerston Rd ☎ 28331
MAZDA Arundel Towers, Western Esplanade ☎ 38488
NISSAN 21/23 St. Denys Rd ☎ 559533
NISSAN 234 Winchester Rd ☎ 778511
PEUGEOT, TALBOT The Avenue ☎ 28801
RENAULT Portswood Rd ☎ 559902
TALBOT Southampton Rd ☎ 812250
VAUXHALL Portsmouth Rd, Sholing ☎ 449232
VOLVO Millbrook Roundabout ☎ 777616

SOUTHBOROUGH Kent [404] U 30 – see Royal Tunbridge Wells.

SOUTH BRENT Devon [403] I 32 – pop. 1,876 – ECD : Wednesday – ☎ 036 47.
♦London 228 – Exeter 28 – ♦Plymouth 16 – Torquay 17.

- **Brookdale** ⛰, North Huish, TQ10 9NR, S : 3 m. ☎ **054 882 (Gara Bridge) 402**, 🌳 – [TV] 🛁wc [P]. [card] [AE] [D] [VISA]
  closed January – **M** (bar lunch) 7.50 **st.** 🍷 2.05 – **6 rm** 🛏 17.00/31.00 **st.** – SB 19.00/43.00 **st.**
- **Glazebrook House,** Glazebrook, TQ10 9JE, SW : 1 m. ☎ **3322**, 🏊, 🎣, 🌳, **park** – 🛁wc [P]. [card] [AE] [VISA]. 🚫
  M 6.00/15.00 **st.** 🍷 3.00 – **11 rm** 🛏 17.50/30.00 **st.** – SB (except summer) 25.00/30.00 **st.**

SOUTHEND-ON-SEA Essex [404] W 29 – pop. 162,770 – ECD : Wednesday – ☎ 0702.
Envir. : Hadleigh Castle (ruins) ≤★ of Thames *AC*, W : 3 m. – Southend Airport (Historic Aircraft museum) N : 2 m.
⛳18 Belfairs Park, Eastwood Rd, Leigh-on-Sea ☎ 525345.
✈ ☎ 40201/6, N : 2 m.
[i] High St. Precinct ☎ 355120 – Civic Centre, Victoria Av. ☎ 355122.
♦London 39 – ♦Cambridge 69 – Croydon 46 – ♦Dover 85.

- **Balmoral,** 34-36 Valkyrie Rd, Westcliff-on-Sea, SS0 8BU, ☎ **342947**, 🌳 – [TV] 🛁wc 🚿wc ☎ [P]. [card] [VISA]. 🚫
  closed 25 and 26 December – **M** *(closed Sunday dinner and Bank Holidays)* (bar lunch) 7.50 **st.** 🍷 2.50 – **19 rm** 🛏 22.00/34.50 **st.**
- **West Park,** 11 Park Rd, Westcliff-on-Sea, SS0 7PQ, ☎ **330729** – [TV] 🛁wc 🚿wc ☎ [P]. [card] [VISA]
  closed 23 December-1 January – **M** *(closed Sunday dinner)* (bar lunch) 6.50 **st.** 🍷 2.50 – **21 rm** 🛏 18.00/35.00 **st.** – SB (weekends only) 24.50 **st.**
- **Regency,** 18 Royal Terr., SS1 1DU, ☎ **340747**, ≤ – [TV]
  11 rm 🛏 11.00/25.00 **s.**
- **Norman,** 191 Eastern Esplanade, Thorpe Bay, SS1 3AA, ☎ **585212**, 🌳 – [TV]. [card] [VISA]. 🚫
  9 rm 🛏 10.00/18.00 **s.**
- **Strand,** 165 Eastern Esplanade, SS1 2YB, ☎ **586611** – 🚿wc. 🚫
  closed Christmas and New Year – **7 rm** 🛏 9.50/28.00 **s.**
- 🍴🍴 **Petite Fleur,** 96 The Ridgeway, Chalkwell, Westcliffe-on-Sea, SS0 8NU, ☎ **76417** – [card] [AE] [D] [VISA]
  closed Sunday dinner and Monday – **M** a la carte 12.80/18.50 **t.** 🍷 2.55.

AUSTIN-ROVER Priory Crescent ☎ 67766
FIAT 22 Belle Vue Pl. ☎ 610482
LANCIA Station Rd, Thorpe Bay ☎ 588200
NISSAN 661 London Rd, at Westcliff-on-Sea ☎ 351471
PEUGEOT, TALBOT 139/155 West Rd ☎ 347861
RENAULT 536 London Rd, Westcliff-on-Sea ☎ 344940
ROLLS ROYCE-BENTLEY Station Rd, Thorpe Bay ☎ 582233
TOYOTA 57 West Rd ☎ 346288
VW, AUDI 2 Comet Way ☎ 526411

SOUTH MIMMS Herts. [404] T 28 – ECD : Thursday – ✉ ☎ 0707 Potters Bar.
♦London 21 – Luton 17.

- **Crest** (Crest), Bignalls Corner, Potters Bar, EN6 3NH, South Mimms Services, junction of A 1 (M), A 6, M 25 on B 197 ☎ **43311**, Telex **299162** – [TV] 🛁wc ☎ [P]. 🏋. [card] [AE] [D] [VISA]
  M approx. 10.50 **st.** – 🛏 5.25 – **120 rm** 43.50/53.50 **st.**

SOUTH MOLTON Devon [403] I 30 **The West Country G.** – pop. 2,875 – ECD : Wednesday – ✉ ☎ 076 95.
♦London 210 – Exeter 35 – Taunton 39.

- **Marsh Hall Country House** ⛰, EX36 3HQ, N : 1 ¼ m. by North Molton rd ☎ **2666**, ≤, 🌳 – [TV] 🛁wc 🚿wc ☎ [P]. [card] [AE] [VISA]. 🚫
  M (buffet lunch Monday to Saturday residents only) 6.00/11.00 **st.** – **5 rm** 🛏 20.50/40.00 **st.**
- 🍴🍴 **Stumbles** with rm, 131-134 East St., EX36 3BU, ☎ **3683** – [TV] 🛁wc [P]. [card] [AE] [D] [VISA]
  closed Sunday and Christmas – **M** (restricted lunch) a la carte 7.65/10.95 **t.** 🍷 2.95 – **8 rm** 🛏 15.00/23.00 **t.**

at East Buckland NW : 6 ¼ m. by A 361 – ⊠ Barnstaple – ✆ 059 86 Filleigh :

✗ **Lower Pitt** ⌑ with rm, EX32 0TD, ℰ 243, 🛲 – ⓜwc ⓟ. ✻
closed Sunday, Monday, 25-26 December and 1 January – **M** (lunch by arrangement) (booking essential) a la carte 7.00/11.40 ▯ 2.95 – **3 rm** ⊑ 15.00/30.00 t. – SB (not weekends) 44.00/48.00 **st.**

FORD   East St. ℰ 2137

SOUTH NORMANTON Derbs. 402 403 404 Q 24 – pop. 7,045 – ECD : Wednesday – ✆ 0773 Ripley.

♦ London 130 – Derby 17 – ♦ Nottingham 15 – ♦ Sheffield 31.

🏨 **Swallow** (Swallow), Carter Lane East, DE55 2EH, on A 38 ℰ 812000, Telex 377264 – ▤ rest 📺 ☎ & ⓟ. 🅰. ⓣ AE ⓞ 𝘝𝘐𝘚𝘈
M 7.00/8.50 **st.** ▯ 3.40 – **123 rm** ⊑ 39.00/48.75 **st.** – SB (weekends only) 42.50 **st.**

SOUTH PETHERTON Somerset 403 L 31 – pop. 2,549 – ✆ 0460.

♦ London 138 – ♦ Bristol 41 – Exeter 41 – Taunton 19 – Yeovil 7.5.

✗✗✗ **Oaklands** with rm, 8 Palmer St., TA13 5DB, ℰ 40272, 🛲 – 📺 ⓟ. 🅰 AE ⓞ 𝘝𝘐𝘚𝘈. ✻
M *(closed Sunday dinner and Monday)* (bar lunch Monday to Saturday) 6.95/8.75 **t.** ▯ 2.25 – ⊑ 3.25 – **3 rm** 16.00/24.00 **t.** – SB (except summer) 46.50/49.50 **st.**

SOUTHPORT Merseyside 402 K 23 – pop. 84,574 – ECD : Tuesday – ✆ 0704.

Envir. : Rufford Old Hall★ 15C (the Great Hall★★) *AC*, E : 9 m.

📍₁₈ Park Rd ℰ 35286 – 📍₁₈ Hesketh, Cockle Dick's Lane off Cambridge Rd ℰ 30226, N : 1 m. – 📍₁₈ Bradshaws Lane, Ainsdale ℰ 78092, S : 3 m.

🛈 Cambridge Arcade ℰ 33133 and 40404.

♦ London 221 – ♦ Liverpool 20 – ♦ Manchester 38 – Preston 19.

🏨 **Bold,** Lord St., PR9 0BE, ℰ 32578 – 📺 ⌷wc ☎. 🅰. 🅽 AE ⓞ 𝘝𝘐𝘚𝘈
M 4.80/6.50 **st.** ▯ 2.40 – **28 rm** ⊑ 20.00/35.00 **st.**

🏨 **Carlton,** 86-88 Lord St., PR8 1JT, ℰ 35111 – 🕁 📺 ⌷wc ⓜwc ☎ ⓟ. 🅽 AE 𝘝𝘐𝘚𝘈
M (bar lunch Monday to Saturday) 6.95/8.50 **st.** ▯ 1.90 – **25 rm** ⊑ 18.00/35.00 **st.** – SB (weekends only) 40.00 **st.**

🏨 **Club House,** 15 Leicester St., PR9 0ER, ℰ 33745 – ⌷wc ⓜwc ⓟ. 🅽 𝘝𝘐𝘚𝘈
M (bar lunch) 6.75 ▯ 1.90 – **13 rm** ⊑ 17.50/30.00 **t.** – SB (winter only and weekends) 37.50/42.50 **st.**

✗✗ **Squires,** 78-80 King St., PR8 1LG, ℰ 30046 – 🅽 AE ⓞ 𝘝𝘐𝘚𝘈
closed Sunday and Bank Holidays – **M** (dinner only) a la carte 7.55/13.90.

✗✗ **La Terrasse,** 1st. floor, 180 Lord St., PR9 0QG, ℰ 30995.

ALFA-ROMEO, DAIHATSU, LOTUS, SAAB   609 Liverpool Rd ℰ 74114
CITROEN   Liverpool Rd ℰ 74127
COLT   Aughton Rd ℰ 67904
FORD   Virginia St. ℰ 31550
LADA   Liverpool Rd ℰ 77161

PEUGEOT-TALBOT   Albert Rd ℰ 38338
RENAULT   205 Liverpool Rd ℰ 68515
TOYOTA   Tulketh St. ℰ 30909
VAUXHALL-OPEL   89/91 Bath St. North ℰ 35535
VOLVO   51 Weld Rd ℰ 66613
VW, AUDI   Zetland St. ℰ 31091

SOUTHSEA Hants. 403 404 Q 31 – see Portsmouth and Southsea.

SOUTH SHIELDS Tyne and Wear 401 402 P 19 – pop. 100,659 – ECD : Wednesday – ✆ 0632.

📍₁₈ Cleadon Hill ℰ 560475, SE : 3 m.

🛈 Coast Rd, South Foreshore ℰ 557411 and 568841 ext. 284 (summer only).

♦ London 284 – ♦ Newcastle-upon-Tyne 9.5 – Sunderland 6.

🏨 **Sea,** Sea Rd, NE33 2LD, ℰ 566227 – 📺 ⌷wc ⓜwc ☎ ⇐ ⓟ. 🅽 AE ⓞ 𝘝𝘐𝘚𝘈
M 4.95/5.95 **t.** ▯ 2.70 – **29 rm** ⊑ 27.50/37.50 **t.** – SB (weekends only) 39.00 **st.**

SOUTH WALSHAM Norfolk 404 Y 26 – ⊠ Norwich – ✆ 060 549.

♦ London 120 – Great Yarmouth 11 – ♦ Norwich 9.

🏨 **South Walsham Hall H. and Country Club** ⌑, South Walsham Rd, NR13 6DQ, ℰ 378, ≤, ⊃ heated, ⌇, 🛲, park, ✾ – 📺 ⌷wc ☎ ⓟ. 🅽 AE ⓞ 𝘝𝘐𝘚𝘈. ✻
M a la carte 10.20/14.60 **st.** – **18 rm** ⊑ 29.00/40.00 **st.** – SB (weekends only)(except winter) 60.00/70.00 **st.**

SOUTHWELL Notts. 402 403 404 R 24 – pop. 5,129 – ECD : Thursday – ✆ 0636.

See : Minster★ 12C-13C (Chapter house : foliage carving★★ 13C).

♦ London 135 – Lincoln 24 – ♦ Nottingham 14 – ♦ Sheffield 34.

🏨 **Saracen's Head** (Anchor), Market Pl., NG25 0HE, ℰ 812701 – 📺 ⌷wc ☎ ⓟ. 🅰. 🅽 AE ⓞ 𝘝𝘐𝘚𝘈
M a la carte 8.10/12.75 **st.** ▯ 2.65 – **23 rm** ⊑ 34.50/45.00 **st.** – SB (weekends only) 50.00 **st.**

AUSTIN-ROVER   King St. ℰ 812146   FORD   Westgate ℰ 813741

SOUTHWOLD Suffolk 404 Z 27 – pop. 1,998 – ECD : Wednesday – ☻ 0502.

🛈 Town Hall, Market Place ☏ 722366 (summer only).

♦London 108 – Great Yarmouth 24 – ♦Ipswich 35 – ♦Norwich 34.

🏠 **Swan,** Market Pl., IP18 6EG, ☏ 722186, 舟 – ⑂ 📺 ➩wc 🕿 🅿. 🖾 AE ⓪ 𝓥𝓘𝓢𝓐
   M 5.15/8.15 t. – **52 rm** ⥱ 23.25/45.50 t.

🏠 **Crown,** High St., IP18 6DP, ☏ 722275 – 📺 ➩wc 🛏wc 🅿. 🖾 AE ⓪
   M 3.95/7.60 t. ⓵ 2.60 – **21 rm** ⥱ 17.35/38.15 t.

🏡 **Pier Avenue,** Station Rd, IP18 6AY, ☏ 722632 – 📺 ➩wc 🛏wc. 𝓥𝓘𝓢𝓐
   M 4.50/7.50 st. ⓵ 3.00 – **13 rm** ⥱ 14.50/32.00 st.

SOUTH WOODHAM FERRERS Essex 404 V 29 – pop. 7,000 – ⌧ ☻ 0245 Chelmsford

🏠 Oakland, Merchant St., CM3 5XE, ☏ 322811 – 📺 ➩wc 🕿 – **27 rm**.

SOUTH ZEAL Devon 403 I 31 **The West Country** G. – ECD : Thursday – ⌧ Okehampton – ☻ 083 784 Sticklepath.

♦London 218 – Exeter 17 – ♦Plymouth 36 – Torquay 27.

🏠 **Oxenham Arms,** EX20 2JT, ☏ 244, « 12C inn », 舟 – 📺 ➩wc 🅿. 🖾 AE ⓪ 𝓥𝓘𝓢𝓐
   M 7.50/11.00 t. ⓵ 2.45 – **8 rm** ⥱ 18.00/35.00 t. – SB (except summer) 40.00/50.00 **st.**

🏡 **Poltimore,** EX20 2PD, S : 1 m. by A 30 ☏ 0837 (Okehampton) 840209, 舟 – ➩wc 🅿
   7 rm ⥱ 11.00/27.00 st.

SPALDING Lincs. 402 404 T 25 – pop. 15,850 – ECD : Thursday – ☻ 0775.

See : Parish church★ 13C – Ayscoughfee Hall★ 15C.

🌳 Surfleet ☏ 077 585 (Surfleet) 386, N : 4 m. off A 16.

🛈 Ayscoughfee Hall, Churchgate ☏ 5468.

♦London 106 – ♦Leicester 51 – Lincoln 44 – ♦Nottingham 54.

🏠 **White Hart** (T.H.F.), Market Pl., PE11 1SU, ☏ 5668 – 📺 ➩wc 🕿 🅿. ♨. 🖾 AE ⓪ 𝓥𝓘𝓢𝓐
   M 6.00/7.30 st. ⓵ 2.85 – ⥱ 4.75 – **28 rm** 26.00/38.00 **st.**

🏠 **Woodlands,** 80 Pinchbeck Rd, PE11 1QF, N : ½ m. on A 16 ☏ 69933, 舟 – 📺 🛏wc 🕿 🅿. 🖾
   AE ⓪ 𝓥𝓘𝓢𝓐
   M 5.40/7.50 t. – ⥱ 5.00 – **6 rm** 32.50/42.50 **t.** – SB (weekends only) 51.00 **st.**

AUSTIN-ROVER Pinchbeck Rd ☏ 3651
FORD St. Johns Rd ☏ 67651
PEUGEOT Pinchbeck ☏ 3033

VAUXHALL Pinchbeck Rd ☏ 3391
VOLVO High Rd ☏ 0406 (Holbeach) 370307

SPELDHURST Kent 404 U 30 – see Royal Tunbridge Wells.

SPROTBROUGH South Yorks. 402 403 404 Q 23 – see Doncaster.

STAFFORD Staffs. 402 403 404 N 25 – pop. 55,001 – ECD : Wednesday – ☻ 0785.

See : High House★ 16C – St. Mary's Church (Norman font★).

🛈 Civic Offices, Riverside ☏ 3181 ext. 216.

♦London 142 – ♦Birmingham 26 – Derby 32 – Shrewsbury 31 – ♦Stoke-on-Trent 17.

🏠 **Tillington Hall,** Eccleshall Rd, ST16 1JJ, NW : 1 ½ m. on A 5013 ☏ 53531, Telex 36566 – ⑂
   📺 ➩wc 🕿 🅿. ♨. 🖾 AE ⓪ 𝓥𝓘𝓢𝓐
   M 6.00/6.50 st. – **93 rm** ⥱ 37.50/48.00 **st.** – SB (weekends only) 48.00 **st.**

🏠 Swan, 46 Greengate St., ST16 2JA, ☏ 58142 – 📺 ➩wc 🕿 🅿. ✂
   31 rm.

🏡 **Vine,** Salter St., ST16 2JU, ☏ 51071 – 🅿. 🖾 𝓥𝓘𝓢𝓐
   M (closed Sunday dinner) 2.75/5.50 st. ⓵ 2.75 – **26 rm** ⥱ 15.50/22.00 **st.**

   at Ranton W : 7 ¼ m. by A 518 – ⌧ Ranton – ☻ 078 575 Seighford :

XX **Yew Tree,** Long Compton, ST18 9JU, S : 1 m. ☏ 278, 舟 – 🅿. 🖾 AE ⓪ 𝓥𝓘𝓢𝓐
   closed Sunday dinner and Monday – **M** (dinner only and Sunday lunch) a la carte 12.00/16.50 **t.**

AUDI, VW Lichfield Rd ☏ 42367
AUSTIN-ROVER-DAIMLER-JAGUAR Lichfield Rd ☏ 51366
AUSTIN-ROVER Silkmore Lane ☏ 56111
AUSTIN ROVER Friars Terr. ☏ 3131
AUSTIN-ROVER Norton Bridge ☏ 760281
BMW, VAUXHALL-OPEL Walton-on-the-Hill ☏ 661293
CITROEN Astonfields Rd ☏ 3336
DATSUN Lichfield Rd ☏ 59313

FIAT Milford ☏ 661226
FIAT Milford ☏ 661226
FORD Stone Rd ☏ 51331
FSO Little Haywood ☏ 881203
PEUGEOT-TALBOT Newport Rd ☏ 51084
RENAULT Wolverhampton Rd ☏ 52118
SAAB Yarlet Bank ☏ 088 97 (Sandon) 248
VAUXHALL-OPEL Walton ☏ 661293
VOLVO Lichfield Rd ☏ 47221

STAINES Surrey 404 S 29 – pop. 56,712 – ECD : Thursday – ☎ 0784.

♦London 26 – Reading 25.

🏨 **Thames Lodge** (Anchor), Thames St., TW18 4SF, ✆ 54221, Group Telex 858875, ≤ – 📺
⇔wc 🕾 🅿. 👪. 🖾 🖭 ① 𝖵𝖨𝖲𝖠
M *(closed Saturday lunch)* a la carte 8.10/12.75 **st.** ▮ 2.65 – **54 rm** ⊊ 38.50/45.00 **st.** – SB *(weekends only)* 46.00 **st.**

AUSTIN-ROVER 236 Central Trading Estate ✆ 51698   TALBOT Staines Bridge ✆ 55301
PEUGEOT-TALBOT 186 High St., Egham ✆ 38787

STAMFORD Lincs. 402 404 S 26 – pop. 14,662 – ECD : Thursday – ☎ 0780.

See : Burghley House★★ 16C (paintings : Heaven Room★★★) *AC*.

🛱 Luffenham ✆ 720205, W : 5 m.

🖪 6 St. Mary's Hill ✆ 64444.

♦London 92 – ♦Leicester 31 – Lincoln 50 – ♦Nottingham 45.

🏨 **The George of Stamford,** 71 St, Martin's, PE9 2LB, ✆ 55171, Telex 32578, « 17C coaching inn with walled monastic garden » – 📺 🕾 🅿. 👪. 🖾 🖭 ① 𝖵𝖨𝖲𝖠
M a la carte 12.75/17.50 **st.** – **44 rm** ⊊ 36.50/60.00 **st.**

🏨 **Lady Anne's,** 36-38 High St., St. Martin's, ✆ 53175, 🌲 – 📺 ⇔wc 🔐wc 🕾 🅿. 👪. 🖾 🖭
① 𝖵𝖨𝖲𝖠
M 6.50/8.50 **t.** ▮ 3.00 – **30 rm** ⊊ 21.00/40.00 **t.** – SB *(weekends only) (winter only)* 21.00/40.00 **st.**

🏠 **St. Martin's Garden House,** 42 High St., St. Martin's, PE9 2LP, ✆ 63359, 🌲 – 📺 🅿. 🖾
𝖵𝖨𝖲𝖠
10 rm ⊊ 17.00/28.00 **st.**

XX **Candlesticks** with rm, 1 Church Lane, PE9 2JU, ✆ 64033 – 📺 ⇔wc 🅿. 🖾 𝖵𝖨𝖲𝖠. ⚘
closed last week July and first week August – **M** *(closed Tuesday lunch and Monday)*
4.95/7.50 **s.** ▮ 3.00 – **4 rm** 17.50 **st.**

XX **The Courtyard,** 18a Maiden Lane, PE9 2AZ, ✆ 51505 – 🖾 🖭 ① 𝖵𝖨𝖲𝖠 ■ a la carte 9.45/12.80 **t.**
▮ 3.65.

at Collyweston (Northants.) SW : 3 ¾ m. on A 43 – ✉ Stamford – ☎ 078 083 Duddington :

🏠 **Cavalier,** Main Rd, PE9 3PQ, ✆ 288 – 📺 ⇔wc 🅿. 🖾
M *(bar lunch)* a la carte 4.75/11.65 **t.** ▮ 2.25 – **5 rm** ⊊ 11.50/26.50 **t.**

at Pickworth NW : 6 ¾ m. by B 1081 – ✉ Stamford – ☎ 078 081 Castle Bytham :

X **Manor House** 🦌 with rm, PE9 4DJ, ✆ 525, ≤, 🌲 – ⇔ 🅿
closed 25 December-1 January – **M** *(closed Sunday to Wednesday)* (dinner only)(booking essential) 14.50 **st.** ▮ 2.75 – **2 rm** ⊊ 15.00/25.00 **st.**

FORD Wharf Rd ✆ 55151   TOYOTA Collyweston ✆ 078 083 (Duddington) 271
RENAULT Water St. ✆ 3532   VAUXHALL Rock House, Scotgate ✆ 51826

STAMFORD BRIDGE Humberside 402 R 22 – pop. 2,150 – ✉ York – ☎ 0759.

♦London 219 – ♦Kingston-Upon-Hull 35 – York 8.

🏠 **Derwent Hill,** Low Catton Rd, YO4 1DQ, ✆ 72027, 🌲 – ⇔wc 🅿
closed Christmas – **5 rm** ⊊ 13.00/24.00 **st.**

STANDISH Greater Manchester 402 404 M 23 – pop. 11,174 – ECD : Wednesday – ✉ Wigan –
☎ 0257.

♦London 210 – ♦Liverpool 22 – ♦Manchester 21 – Preston 15.

🏨 **Cassinelli's,** Almond Brook Rd, WN6 0SR, W : 1 m. on B 5239 ✆ 425588, Telex 677662 – 📺
⇔wc 🅿. 👪. 🖾 🖭 𝖵𝖨𝖲𝖠. ⚘
M a la carte 5.50/9.65 **st.** ▮ 2.60 – **63 rm** ⊊ 25.00/35.00 **st.**

XX **Beeches** with rm., School Lane, WN6 0TD, on B 5239 ✆ 426432 – 📺 ⇔wc 🔐wc 🅿. 🖾 🖭
① 𝖵𝖨𝖲𝖠. ⚘
M a la carte 8.65/12.95 **st.** ▮ 3.00 – ⊊ 1.95 – **7 rm** 17.00/26.00 **st.**

STANSTEAD ABBOTS Herts. 404 U 28 – pop. 1,882 – ✉ Ware – ☎ 027 979 Roydon.

♦London 22 – ♦Cambridge 37 – Luton 32 – ♦Ipswich 66.

🏨 **Briggens House,** SG12 8LD, E : 2 m. on A 414 ✆ 2416, Telex 817906, ≤, « Arboretum »,
🏊 heated, 🖪, 🌲, park, ⚘ – 🍴 📺 🅿. 👪. 🖾 🖭 ① 𝖵𝖨𝖲𝖠. ⚘
M 8.75/10.75 **t.** ▮ 3.00 – **47 rm** ⊊ 29.00/50.00 **t.** – SB *(weekends only)* 49.00/59.00 **st.**

STAVERTON Devon 403 I 32 – pop. 551 – ✉ Totnes – ☎ 080 426.

♦London 226 – Exeter 26 – ♦Plymouth 24 – Torquay 13.

🏠 **Sea Trout Inn,** TQ9 6PA, ✆ 274 – 🅿. 🖾 🖭 ① 𝖵𝖨𝖲𝖠
M *(bar lunch Monday to Saturday)* a la carte 6.75/10.60 **t.** ▮ 2.30 – **6 rm** ⊊ 14.50/28.00 **t.**

413

STEVENAGE Herts. 𝟒𝟎𝟒 T 28 – pop. 76,000 – ECD : Monday and Wednesday – ☎ 0438.

Envir. : Knebworth House (furniture★) S : 3 m.

🛲 Aston Lane ☞ 043 888 (Shephall) 424.

🇿 Central Library, Southgate ☞ 69441.

♦London 36 – Bedford 25 – ♦Cambridge 27.

🏨 **Stevenage Moat House** (Q.M.H.), High St., Old Town, SG1 3AZ, ☞ 359111, 🛥 – 📺 ⇔wc ☎ 🅿 ⚿ 🔼 🅰🅴 ⓪ 𝘝𝘐𝘚𝘈
   M 7.25 st. ⅃ 3.50 – **60 rm** ⊊ 32.75/41.00 st. – SB (weekends only) 43.40/56.90 st.

⌂ **Northfield,** 15 Hitchin Rd, Old Town, SG1 3BJ, ☞ 314537 – 🛋wc 🅿 ⚿
   closed 24 December-1 January – **10 rm** ⊊ 15.00/26.00 st.

at Broadwater S : 1 ¾ m. by A 602 on B 197 – ⊠ ☎ 0438 Stevenage :

🏨 **Roebuck Inn** (T.H.F.), Old London Rd, SG2 8DS, ☞ 65444, Telex 825505, 🛥 – 📺 ⇔wc ☎ 🅿 ⚿ 🔼 🅰🅴 ⓪ 𝘝𝘐𝘚𝘈
   M 6.00/7.50 st. ⅃ 2.85 – ⊊ 4.95 – **54 rm** 32.00/38.00 st. – SB (weekends only) 43.00 st.

AUDI, VW Lyton Way ☞ 354691
BMW Hertford Rd, Broadwater ☞ 351565

NISSAN Broadwater Crescent ☞ 315555
VAUXHALL-OPEL 124/6 High St. ☞ 51113

Do not look for pleasant and quiet hotels at random,
consult the maps which precede the different sections of this Guide.

STEYNING West Sussex 𝟒𝟎𝟒 T 31 – pop. 7,060 – ECD : Thursday – ☎ 0903.

See : St. Andrew's Church (the nave★ 12C).

♦London 52 – ♦Brighton 12 – Worthing 10.

✗✗ **Springwells** with rm, 9 High St., BN4 3GG, ☞ 812446, ⅃ heated, 🛥 – 📺 ⇔wc ☎ 🅿 🔼 🅰🅴 ⓪ 𝘝𝘐𝘚𝘈 ⚿
   M a la carte 13.00/15.50 t. ⅃ 2.85 – **10 rm** ⊊ 16.00/45.00 t. – SB (weekends only) (winter only) 48.00 st.

at Bramber S : 1 m. by A 283 – ⊠ ☎ 0903 Steyning :

✗ Maharajah, The Street, BN4 3WE, ☞ 814746, Indian rest.

STICKLEPATH Devon 𝟒𝟎𝟑 I 31 The West Country G. – pop. 180 – ⊠ Okehampton – ☎ 083 784.

♦London 219 – Exeter 21 – ♦Plymouth 35.

🏠 **Skaigh House** ⚲, Skaigh, EX20 1RD, S : ¾ m. ☞ 243, ≼, ⅃, 🛥 – ⇔wc 🅿 ⚿
   April-September – **M** (dinner only) 9.80 st. ⅃ 2.30 – **8 rm** ⊊ 18.00/44.00 st.

STOBOROUGH Dorset – see Wareham.

STOCKBRIDGE Hants. 𝟒𝟎𝟑 𝟒𝟎𝟒 P 30 – pop. 431 – ECD : Wednesday – ☎ 0264 Andover.

♦London 75 – Salisbury 14 – Winchester 9.

🏠 **Grosvenor,** High St., SO20 6EU, ☞ 810606, 🛥 – 📺 🅿 🔼 🅰🅴 ⓪ 𝘝𝘐𝘚𝘈
   M 6.00/8.50 st. – **14 rm** ⊊ 20.00/36.00 st. – SB (weekends only) (winter only) 40.00 st.

🏛 **Old Three Cups,** High St., SO20 6HB, ☞ 810527, « 15C inn », 🛥 – ⇔wc. 🔼 𝘝𝘐𝘚𝘈 ⚿
   closed January and Christmas – **M** (closed Sunday evening and Monday to non-residents)
   4.50/5.25 t. ⅃ 2.95 – **8 rm** ⊊ 12.00/30.00.

⌂ **Carbery,** Salisbury Hill, SO20 6EZ, on A 30 ☞ 810771, ⅃, 🛥 – 🅿 ⚿
   closed 2 weeks at Christmas – **11 rm** ⊊ 10.90/21.85 st.

AUSTIN-ROVER High St. ☞ 711

SAAB Middle Wallop ☞ 026 478 (Middle Wallop)
460

STOCKLAND Devon – see Honiton.

STOCKPORT Greater Manchester 𝟒𝟎𝟐 𝟒𝟎𝟑 𝟒𝟎𝟒 N 23 – pop. 139,644 – ECD : Thursday – ☎ 061 Manchester.

Envir. : Lyme Park★ (16C-18C) *AC*, SE : 4 ½ m.

🛲 Heaton Moor, Heaton Mersey ☞ 432 2134 – 🛲 Offerton Rd ☞ 427 2001 – 🛲 Goosehouse Green, Romiley ☞ 430 2392, NE : 2 m.

🇿 9 Princes St. ☞ 480 0315.

♦London 201 – ♦Liverpool 42 – ♦Manchester 6 – ♦Sheffield 37 – ♦Stoke-on-Trent 34.

🏨 **Alma Lodge** (Embassy), 149 Buxton Rd, SK2 6EL, on A 6 ☞ 483 4431 – 📺 ⇔wc ☎ 🅿 ⚿ 🔼 🅰🅴 ⓪ 𝘝𝘐𝘚𝘈
   M 6.75/7.50 st. ⅃ 4.00 – ⊊ 4.25 – **70 rm** 30.00/36.00 st. – SB (weekends only) 40.00/48.00 st.

🏠 **Wycliffe Villa,** 74 Edgeley Rd, Edgeley, SK3 9NQ, ☞ 477 5395 – 📺 ⇔wc 🛋wc ☎ 🅿 🔼 🅰🅴 ⓪ 𝘝𝘐𝘚𝘈 ⚿
   M (closed Saturday lunch, Sunday and Bank Holidays) 3.50/8.00 t. ⅃ 2.70 – **12 rm** ⊊ 24.00/33.00 st.

AUSTIN-ROVER 35 Buxton Rd 📞 480 4244
AUSTIN-ROVER 91 Heaton Moor Rd 📞 432 9416
AUSTIN-ROVER-DAIMLER-JAGUAR Town Hall Sq.
📞 480 7966
AUSTIN-ROVER Wellington Rd North 📞 432 6201
BMW, HONDA, SAAB 31/33 Buxton Rd 📞 483 6271
CITROEN Waterloo Rd 📞 480 4118
COLT School Lane, Heaton Chapel 📞 432 4790
FIAT Heaton Lane 📞 480 6661
FORD Oak St., Haze Grove 📞 483 9431
FORD Adswood Rd 📞 480 0211

MAZDA Wellington Rd North 📞 442 6466
NISSAN 596 Didsbury Rd, Heaton Mersey 📞
442 6050
PEUGEOT-TALBOT 110 Buxton Rd 📞 480 0831
RENAULT 79 Lancashire Hill 📞 480 7476
SAAB 31/33 Buxton Rd 📞 483 6271
VAUXHALL-OPEL Wellington Rd South 📞 480 6146
VAUXHALL-OPEL 398 Wellington Rd North 📞
432 3232
VOLVO Wellington Rd South 📞 429 7099
VW-AUDI Gt. Portwood St. 📞 480 1131

STOCKTON-ON-TEES Cleveland **402** P 20 – pop. 81,274 – ECD : Thursday – ⚙ 0642.

Tees-side Airport : 📞 0325 (Darlington) 332811, SW : 6 m.

♦London 251 – ♦ Leeds 61 – ♦ Middlesbrough 4.

Swallow (Swallow), 10 John Walker Sq., TS18 1AQ, 📞 679721 – 🛗 ▤ 📺 🕭 ᴴ 🅿. 🛗. ◼
🅰🅴 ⓐ *VISA*
M 7.75/9.05 **st.** 🍾 3.00 – **126 rm** 🛏 38.00/50.00 **st.** – SB 40.00 **st.**

at Eaglescliffe S : 3 ½ m. on A 135 – ✉ ⚙ 0642 Stockton-on-Tees :

Parkmore (Best Western), 636 Yarm Rd, TS16 0DH, 📞 786815, 🌿 – 📺 ⇱wc 🏳️wc 📶 🅿.
◼ 🅰🅴 ⓐ *VISA*
M (bar lunch) 7.95 **t.** 🍾 2.95 – **39 rm** 🛏 24.00/33.00 **t.** – SB (weekends only) 38.00/44.00 **st.**

ALFA-ROMEO Norton Av. 📞 531127
AUSTIN-ROVER Church Rd 📞 612621
BMW 45 Norton Rd 📞 675361
CITROEN Yarm Rd 📞 780095
DATSUN Middleway Mandale Industrial Estate 📞
672617
FIAT 318 Bishopton Rd West 📞 675007
FORD 87 Oxbridge Lane 📞 675471

LANCIA Billingham Rd 📞 551542
PEUGEOT, TALBOT Bishop St. 📞 672061
SAAB, SUBARU Chapel St. 📞 679781
TOYOTA 336 Norton Rd 📞 553003
VAUXHALL-OPEL Boathouse Lane 📞 607804
VOLVO Prince Regent St. 📞 673251
VW, AUDI Church Rd 📞 607804

STOKE BRUERNE Northants. **404** R 27 – pop. 342 – ✉ Towcester – ⚙ 0604 Roade.

♦London 70 – ♦Coventry 38 – ♦Leicester 46 – Northampton 7.

✕ **Butty, 5** Canalside, 📞 863654, Italian rest., « Picturesque setting on Grand Union Canal » –
🅿. ◼ *VISA*
closed Saturday lunch, Sunday, Monday, 1 week spring, 1 week summer and 1 week autumn –
M a la carte 10.00/13.90 **st.** 🍾 3.00.

STOKE GABRIEL Devon **403** J 32 – see Totnes.

STOKE MANDEVILLE Bucks. **404** R 28 – see Aylesbury.

During the season, particularly in resorts, it is wise to book in advance.
However, if you find you cannot take up a hotel booking you have made,
please let the hotel know immediately.
If you are writing to a hotel abroad enclose an International Reply Coupon
(available from Post Offices.)

STOKE-ON-TRENT Staffs. **402** **403** **404** N 24 – pop. 265,258 – ECD : Thursday – ⚙ 0782.

See : Gladstone Pottery Museum★ *AC* V.

Envir. : Little Moreton Hall★★ (16C) *AC*, NW : 8 m. on A 34 U.

🛈 Central Library, Bethesda St., Hanley 📞 281242.

♦London 162 – ♦Birmingham 46 – ♦Leicester 59 – ♦Liverpool 58 – ♦Manchester 41 – ♦Sheffield 53.

Plans on following pages

North Stafford (T.H.F.), Station Rd, ST4 2AE, 📞 48501, Telex 36287 – 🛗 📺 🅿. 🛗. ◼ 🅰🅴
ⓐ *VISA*   X a
M (buffet lunch Saturday) 6.95/7.95 **st.** 🍾 3.15 – 🛏 5.50 – **70 rm** 37.50/46.00 **st.**

at Hanley NW : 2 m. by A 5006 – ✉ ⚙ 0782 Stoke-on-Trent :

Stakis Grand (Stakis), 66 Trinity St., ST1 5NB, 📞 22361 – 🛗 📺 ⇱wc 📶 🅿. 🛗. ◼ 🅰🅴 ⓐ
VISA   Y c
M 4.50/8.50 **st.** 🍾 2.80 – **93 rm** 🛏 34.50/44.00 **t.**

at Basford NW : 1 ¾ m. by A 500 off A 53 – ✉ ⚙ 0782 Stoke-on-Trent :

Haydon House, 9 Haydon St., ST4 6JD, 📞 629311 – ▤ rest 📺 ⇱wc 🏳️wc 🕿 🅿. 🛗. ◼ 🅰🅴
ⓐ *VISA*   U a
M 7.50/9.00 **st.** 🍾 3.50 – **24 rm** 🛏 26.00/42.00 **t.** – SB (weekends only) 54.00/75.00 **st.**

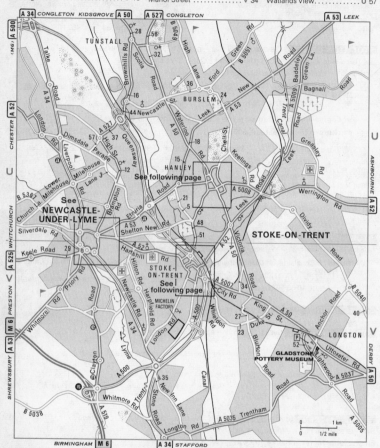

MICHELIN Branch, Jamage Road Industrial Estate, Talke Pits, ST7 1QF, ☎ 078 16 (Kidsgrove) 71211/2/3/4

ALFA ROMEO High St., Tunstall ☎ 89226
AUDI, TOYOTA, VW Leek Rd, Hanley ☎ 274504
AUSTIN-ROVER Leek Rd, Endon ☎ 503160
AUSTIN-ROVER Clough St. ☎ 23841
AUSTIN-ROVER Station Rd, Barlaston ☎ 2014
AUSTIN-ROVER Trentham ☎ 657348
AUSTIN-ROVER Tunstall Rd, Biddulph ☎ 512811
AUSTIN-ROVER Victoria Rd ☎ 45551
AUSTIN-ROVER Sandbach Rd, Cobridge ☎ 85257
AUSTIN-ROVER Broad St. ☎ 29500
AUSTIN-ROVER King St., Longton ☎ 314433
AUSTIN-ROVER Leek New Rd, Hanley ☎ 29985
BMW ☎ 620811
CITROEN Uttoxeter Rd ☎ 312235
DAIHATSU Ashbank ☎ 2426
DATSUN Providence Sq. ☎ 261492

FIAT Lightwood Rd, Longton ☎ 319212
FIAT Leek Rd, Hanley ☎ 30244
FORD Clough St. ☎ 29591
FORD King St. ☎ 317381
FORD Waley St., Biddulph ☎ 513174
F.S.O. Lonsdale St. ☎ 411709
HONDA Sneyd St., Cobridge ☎ 261593
LADA 292 Waterloo Rd, Cobridge ☎ 22210
LADA Congleton Rd, Biddulph ☎ 512250
LANCIA Leek Rd, Hanley ☎ 20244
MAZDA Moorland Rd ☎ 84215
MERCEDES-BENZ Clough St. ☎ 267872
PEUGEOT-TALBOT Leek Rd ☎ 24371
PEUGEOT-TALBOT Bullocks House Rd ☎ 513952
RENAULT Werrington Rd, Bucknall ☎ 25406
RENAULT Blue Gates, Biddulph ☎ 514444

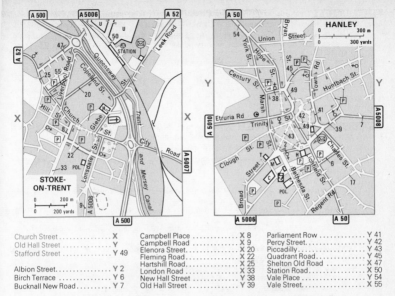

Church Street	X
Old Hall Street	Y
Stafford Street	Y 49

Albion Street	Y 2
Birch Terrace	Y 6
Bucknall New Road	Y 7

Campbell Place	X 8
Campbell Road	X 9
Elenora Street	X 20
Fleming Road	X 22
Hartshill Road	X 25
London Road	X 33
New Hall Street	Y 38
Old Hall Street	Y 39

Parliament Row	Y 41
Percy Street	Y 42
Piccadilly	Y 43
Quadrant Road	Y 45
Shelton Old Road	X 47
Station Road	X 50
Vale Place	X 54
Vale Street	X 55

SAAB Victoria Rd, Fenton ℘ 416666
SAAB Victoria Rd ℘ 415673
SUBARU High St., Tunstall ℘ 88997
TALBOT Lightwood Rd ℘ 317124
TOYOTA Leek Rd ℘ 264888

VAUXHALL-OPEL Victoria Rd, Hanley ℘ 271872
VAUXHALL-OPEL Trent Vale ℘ 613061
VAUXHALL-OPEL Lightwood Rd ℘ 310237
VAUXHALL-OPEL Victoria Rd ℘ 22875
VW, AUDI Leek Rd ℘ 264888

STOKESLEY North Yorks. 402 Q 20 – pop. 3,785 – ECD : Wednesday – ☎ 0642.
♦London 240 – ♦Leeds 59 – ♦Middlesbrough 8 – York 44.

✗ **Jakeman's**, 9 Bridge Rd, TS9 5AA, ℘ 711888 – ⊠ ⓪
closed Sunday – **M** a la carte 7.00/9.95 **t.** ₰ 2.45.

STONE Glos. 403 404 M 29 – pop. 555 (inc. Ham) – ⊠ Berkeley – ☎ 0454 Falfield.
♦London 130 – ♦Bristol 17 – Gloucester 18.

⋔ **Elms**, GL13 9JX, ℘ 260279 – ℗
10 rm ⊊ 11.00/22.00 **st.**

STONE Heref. and Worc. 403 404 N 26 – see Kidderminster.

STONE Staffs. 402 403 404 N 25 – pop. 11,003 – ECD : Wednesday – ☎ 0785.
🛇 Lakeside, Meaford Rd, Barlaston ℘ 078 139 (Barlaston) 3242, N : ¾ m.
♦London 150 – ♦Birmingham 36 – ♦Stoke-on-Trent 9.

🏨 Crown, High St., ST15 8AS, ℘ 813535 – 📺 ⌂wc ⋔wc ☏ ℗. ⊠ ⅀ VISA – **29 rm**.
🏨 Stone House, ST15 0BQ, S : 1 ¼ m. by A 520 on A 34 ℘ 815531, 🚗 – 📺 ⌂wc ☏ ℗. ⊠ ⅀
⓪ VISA ⋘
closed 25 to 27 December – **16 rm** ⊊ 16.50/38.50 **t.**

AUSTIN-ROVER Stafford Rd ℘ 813035   FORD Darlaston Rd ℘ 813332

STON EASTON Somerset – see Farrington Gurney.

STONE CROSS East Sussex – see Eastbourne.

STONEHOUSE Glos. 403 404 N 28 – see Stroud.

STONEY CROSS Hants. 403 404 P 31 – pop. 146 – ⊠ Lyndhurst – ☎ 0703 Southampton.
♦London 94 – Bournemouth 19 – ♦Southampton 12.

🏨 Compton Arms, Ringwood Rd, SO4 7GN, on A 31 ℘ 812134, Telex 477945, 🚗 – 📺 ⌂wc ☏
℗. ⊠ ⅀ ⓪ VISA
18 rm ⊊ 18.00/35.00 **t.** – SB 41.80/48.40 **st.**

STONY STRATFORD Bucks. 404 R 27 – see Milton Keynes.

417

STORRINGTON West Sussex **404** S 31 – pop. 3,277 – ECD : Wednesday – 🕿 090 66.
Envir. : Parham House★ (Elizabethan) *AC*, W : 1 ½ m. – ♦London 54 – ♦Brighton 20 – ♦Portsmouth 36.

🏠 **Little Thakeham** ⚓, Merrywood Lane, RH20 3HE, N : 1 ¾ m. by B 2139 🖉 4416, ≼, « Lutyens house, gardens by Gertrude Jekyll, country house atmosphere », 🏊 heated, 🎾 – 📺 🛏wc
🕿 🅿 🔼 🆎 ⑩ ⋘
closed Christmas and New Year – **M** *(closed Monday lunch and Sunday dinner)* a la carte 14.70/19.50 **s.** 🍷 3.00 – **9 rm** 🖙 50.00/70.00 **s.**

XXX **Manley's,** Manleys Hill, RH20 4BT, 🖉 2331 – 🅿 🔼 🆎 ⑩ **VISA**
closed Sunday dinner, Monday, last week August, first 2 weeks September and first week January – **M** a la carte 11.80/16.60 **s.** 🍷 3.50.

AUSTIN-ROVER The Square 🖉 3282

STOURBRIDGE West Midlands **403 404** N 26 – pop. 54,344 – ECD : Thursday – 🕿 038 43.
♦London 147 – ♦Birmingham 14 – Wolverhampton 10 – Worcester 21.

Plan : see Birmingham p.2

⌂ **Limes,** 260 Hagley Rd, Pedmore, DY9 0RW, SE : 1 ½ m. on A 491 🖉 0562 (Hagley) 882689,
🍴 – 🅿   AU **z**
10 rm 🖙 12.00/20.00 **st.**

at Belbroughton SE : 7 ½ m. by A 491 on B 4188 – AU – ✉ Stourbridge – 🕿 0562 Belbroughton :

XXX **Bell Inn,** Bromsgrove Rd, Bell End, DY9 9XU, E : 1 ½ m. on A 491 🖉 730232 – 🅿 🔼 🆎 ⑩ **VISA**
closed Saturday lunch, Sunday dinner, Monday and 1 to 8 Janaury – **M** a la carte 9.30/17.25 **t.**
🍷 3.00.

at Kinver (Staffs.) W : 5 m. by A 458 – AU – ✉ Stourbridge (West Midlands) – 🕿 0384 Kinver :

XX **Berkley's,** High St., DY7 1BR, 🖉 873679 – 🔼 🆎 ⑩ **VISA**
closed Sunday – **M** (dinner only) 15.00 **t.** 🍷 2.50.

ALFA-ROMEO Hagley Rd 🖉 393031	NISSAN High St 🖉 393231
AUSTIN-ROVER Stourbridge Rd, Lye 🖉 038 482	RENAULT Norton Rd 🖉 396655
(Lye) 2788	TOYOTA 181/183 Bromsgrove Rd, Halesowen 🖉
AUSTIN-ROVER Hagley Rd 🖉 393022	0562 (Romsley) 710243
AUSTIN-ROVER Bridgnorth Rd 🖉 4757	VAUXHALL-OPEL The Hayes, Lye 🖉 038 482 (Lye)
CITROEN Enville St. 🖉 370914	3001
FIAT Clent 🖉 0562 (Belbroughton) 730557	VAUXHALL-OPEL Bridgnorth Rd 🖉 394757
FORD Hagley Rd 🖉 392131	VAUXHALL 131-135 Hagley Rd, Oldswinford 🖉
MERCEDES-BENZ, PORSCHE Grange Lane, Lye	393034
🖉 038 482 (Lye) 5575	VW-AUDI Birmingham St. 🖉 392626

STOURPORT-ON-SEVERN Heref. and Worc. **403 404** N 26 – pop. 14,230 – ECD : Wednesday
– 🕿 029 93.
🅸 Public Library, County Buildings, Worcester St. 🖉 2866.
♦London 137 – ♦Birmingham 21 – Worcester 12.

🏠 **Mount Olympus,** 35 Hartlebury Rd, DY13 9LT, E : 1 ¼ m. on B 4193 🖉 77333, Telex 57515,
🏊 heated, ⛳, park, 🎾, squash – 📺 🛏wc 🍴wc 🕿 🅿 🔼 🔼 🆎 ⑩ **VISA** ⋘
M 5.25/7.50 **st.** 🍷 3.50 – **42 rm** 🖙 29.60/40.00 **st.** – SB (weekends only) 36.00 **st.**

🏠 **Swan (Golden Oak),** 56 High St., DY13 8BX, 🖉 71661 – 📺 🛏wc 🍴wc 🕿 🅿 🔼 🆎 **VISA** ⋘
M *(closed Sunday dinner)* a la carte 5.60/14.50 **t.** 🍷 2.50 – **33 rm**

⌂ **Oakleigh,** 17 York St., DY13 9EE, 🖉 77568, ⛳ – 📺 🍴wc 🅿 ⋘
6 rm 🖙 13.50/22.00 **s.**

XX **Severn Tandoori,** 11 Bridge St., DY13 8UX, 🖉 3090, Indian rest. – 🔼 🆎 ⑩ **VISA**
M a la carte 7.25/10.50 **t.** 🍷 2.40.

COLT Dunley 🖉 3357   VAUXHALL-OPEL Vale Rd 🖉 2760

STOW-ON-THE-WOLD Glos. **403 404** O 28 – pop. 1,737 – ECD : Wednesday – 🕿 0451 Cotswold.
🅸 Public Library, St. Edwards Hall 🖉 30352 (summer only).
♦London 86 – ♦Birmingham 44 – Gloucester 27 – ♦Oxford 30.

🏠 **Unicorn Crest** (Crest), Sheep St., GL54 1HQ, 🖉 30257 – 📺 🛏wc 🕿 🅿 🔼 🆎 ⑩ **VISA**
M approx. 10.50 **st.** – 🖙 4.95 – **20 rm** 37.00/47.50 **st.**

🏠 **Stow Lodge,** The Square, GL54 1AB, 🖉 30485, ⛳ – 📺 🛏wc 🅿 🆎 ⑩ ⋘
closed 17 December-30 January – **M** (bar lunch Monday to Saturday) 6.50/8.00 **t.** 🍷 2.90 –
20 rm 🖙 30.00/50.00 **t.**

🏠 **Fosse Manor,** Fosse Way, GL54 1JX, S : 1 ¼ m. on A 429 🖉 30354, ⛳ – 📺 🛏wc 🍴wc 🅿
🔼 🆎 ⑩ **VISA**
closed 1 week at Christmas – **M** 8.50 **st.** 🍷 2.50 – **22 rm** 🖙 18.50/53.00 **st.** – SB (except summer) 37.00/92.00 **st.**

🏠 **Old Stocks,** The Square, GL54 1AF, 🖉 30666 – 🛏wc 🍴wc. 🔼 **VISA**
closed 25 to 30 December – **M** 7.50 **t.** 🍷 2.75 – **19 rm** 🖙 16.00/31.50 **t.** – SB 32.50/43.00 **st.**

🏠 King's Arms, The Square, GL54 1AF, 🖉 30364 – 📺 🅿 – **9 rm**

X **Rafters,** Park St., GL54 1AG, 🖉 30200 – 🔼 🆎 ⑩ **VISA**
closed Sunday and Monday – **M** a la carte 11.00/13.25 **st.** 🍷 3.75.

at Upper Oddington E : 2 ½ m. by A 436 – ⊠ Moreton-in-Marsh – ☯ 0451 Cotswold :

🏠 **Horse and Groom,** ℰ 30584 – ⋔wc ℗
M (bar lunch) a la carte 6.00/7.70 t. – **5 rm** ⌑ 12.50/25.00 st. – SB (winter only) 35.00 st.

at Lower Slaughter SW : 3 m. by A 429 – ⊠ Bourton-on-the-Water – ☯ 0451 Cotswold :

🏛 **Manor** ⟋, GL54 2HP, ℰ 20456, ⬚, ⟍, ⚘, ※ – �📺 ⋔wc ☎ ℗ ⌧ AE ⓪ VISA
M 6.95/10.00 t. ⅄ 3.65 – **20 rm** ⌑ 36.00/57.00 t. – SB 67.00/75.00 st.

at Upper Slaughter SW : 3 ¼ m. by B 4068 – ⊠ Bourton-on-the-Water – ☯ 0451 Cotswold :

🏛 **Lords of the Manor** ⟋, GL54 2JD, ℰ 20243, « 17C manor house », ⟍, ⚘, park – ⊟wc
☜ ℗ ⌧ AE ⓪ VISA ※
closed 7 to 20 January – **M** a la carte 9.75/17.20 ⅄ 3.25 – ⌑ 4.00 – **15 rm** 35.00/75.00 st. – SB
(winter only) 55.00/60.00 st.

at Lower Swell W : 1 ¼ m. on B 4068 – ⊠ Stow-on-the-Wold – ☯ 0451 Cotswold :

✗ **Old Farmhouse** with rm, GL54 1LF, ℰ 30232, ⚘ – 📺 ⊟wc ℗ ⌧ ⓪ VISA
closed Monday and Tuesday in January – **M** a la carte 6.95/7.50 t. ⅄ 2.35 – **13 rm**
⌑ 20.00/45.00 t. – SB (except winter) 30.00/57.00 st.

SUBARU Stow Rd, near Andoversford ℰ 045 15   VW Oddington, Moreton-in-Marsh ℰ 30422
(Guiting Power) 274

STRATFORD-UPON-AVON Warw. 🔢🔢 🔢🔢 P 27 – pop. 19,452 – ECD : Thursday – ☯ 0789.

See : Shakespeare's birthplace★ (16C) *AC*, AB – Hall's Croft★ (16C) *AC*, A B – Anne Hathaway's
cottage★ *AC*, W : by Shottery Rd A – Holy Trinity Church★ 14C-15C A.

Envir. : Charlecote Park (castle 16C : intérieur★) *AC*, NE : 5 m. by B 4086 B – Wilmcote (Mary
Arden's House★) (16C) *AC*, NW : 5 m. by A 34 A.

🏌 Tiddington Rd ℰ 297296, E : by B 4086 B.

🛈 Judith Shakespeare's House, 1 High St. ℰ 293127.

♦London 96 – ♦Birmingham 23 – ♦Coventry 18 – ♦Oxford 40.

STRATFORD-UPON-AVON

Bridge Street . . . . B 8
Henley Street . . . . A 29
High Street . . . . A 31
Sheep Street . . . . AB 35
Wood Street . . . . A 47

Banbury Road . . . . B 2
Benson Road . . . . B 3
Bridge Foot . . . . B 6
Chapel Lane . . . . A 13
Chapel Street . . . . A 14
Church Street . . . . A 16
Clopton Bridge . . . . B 18
College Lane . . . . A 19
Ely Street . . . . A 22
Evesham Place . . . . A 24
Great William Street . . . . A 25
Greenhill Street . . . . A 27
Guild Street . . . . A 28
Scholars Lane . . . . A 33
Tiddington Road . . . . B 38
Trinity Street . . . . A 40
Warwick Road . . . . B 42
Waterside . . . . A 43
Windsor Street . . . . A 45

*Town plans : the names of
main shopping streets are
indicated in red at the
beginning of the list of streets.*

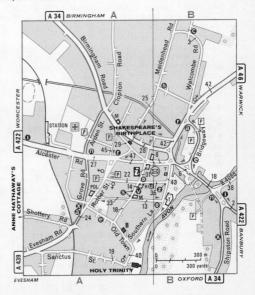

🏩 **Welcombe** ⟋, Warwick Rd, CV37 0NR, NE : 1 ½ m. on A 46 ℰ 295252, Telex 31347, ≤,
« 19C mansion in grounds », 🏌, ⚘, park – 📺 ℗ ⌧ ⌧ AE ⓪ VISA   on A 46   B
closed 29 December-3 January – **M** 9.50/12.50 st. ⅄ 4.30 – **84 rm** ⌑ 39.50/69.50 st. – SB
(winter only)(except Tuesday and Wednesday) 69.50 st.

🏩 **Moat House International** (Q.M.H.), Bridgefoot, CV37 6YR, ℰ 67511, Telex 311127, ⚘ –
⌧ 📺 ☎ ⅋ ℗ ⌧ ⌧ AE ⓪ VISA   B e
M 7.20/8.40 t. ⅄ 3.15 – ⌑ 5.30 – **249 rm** 42.00/54.00 t. – SB (weekends only) 62.00/70.00 st.

P.T.O. →

🏨 **Shakespeare** (T.H.F.), Chapel St., CV37 6ER, ℰ 294771, Telex 311181, « 16C timbered inn »
– 🛗 📺 🅿. 🔬. 🔝 AE ⓞ 𝘝𝘐𝘚𝘈   A **v**
M 7.00/10.50 **st.** ░ 2.60 – � 5.50 – **66 rm** 41.50/56.00 **st.**

🏨 **Alveston Manor** (T.H.F.), Banbury Rd, CV37 7HP, ℰ 204581, Telex 31324, 🐎 – 📺 ☎ 🅿.
🔬. 🔝 AE 𝘝𝘐𝘚𝘈   B **i**
M 8.50/9.75 **st.** ░ 2.20 – �
桌 5.50 – **108 rm** 35.50/46.50 **st.**

🏨 **Falcon** (Q.M.H.), Chapel St., CV37 6HA, ℰ 205777, Telex 312522 – 🛗 📺 ⇌wc ☏ 🅿. 🔬. 🔝
AE ⓞ 𝘝𝘐𝘚𝘈   A **s**
M 6.75/8.50 **st.** ░ 2.80 – **73 rm** ⌑ 30.00/54.00 **st.** – SB 55.00/70.00 **st.**

🏨 **White Swan** (T.H.F.), Rother St., CV37 6NH, ℰ 297022 – 📺 ⇌wc ☏. 🔬. 🔝 AE ⓞ 𝘝𝘐𝘚𝘈
M 5.50/8.50 **st.** ░ 2.60 – ⌑ 4.75 – **47 rm** 26.00/41.00 **st.**   A **r**

🏨 **Arden,** 44 Waterside, CV37 6BA, ℰ 294949, 🐎 – 📺 ⇌wc ㎡wc ☏ 🅿. 🔬. 🔝 AE ⓞ 𝘝𝘐𝘚𝘈
M (carving lunch) 6.00/11.25 **t.** ░ 3.25 – **59 rm** ⌑ 21.50/46.00 **t.** – SB 44.00/60.00 **st.**   B **o**

🏨 **Grosvenor House** (Best Western), 12-14 Warwick Rd, CV37 6YT, ℰ 69213, Telex 311699,
🐎 – 📺 ⇌wc ㎡wc ☏ 🅿. 🔬. 🔝 AE ⓞ 𝘝𝘐𝘚𝘈 ❄   B **r**
closed 24 to 28 December – **M** a la carte 7.30/9.90 **t.** – **57 rm** ⌑ 19.00/39.00 **st.** – SB
39.00/48.00 **st.**

🏨 **Swan's Nest** (T.H.F.), Bridgefoot, CV37 7LT, ℰ 66761, 🐎 – 📺 ⇌wc ㎡wc ☏ 🅑 🅿. 🔬. 🔝 AE
ⓞ 𝘝𝘐𝘚𝘈   B **n**
M 6.50/8.50 **st.** ░ 2.60 – ⌑ 4.50 – **68 rm** 29.50/44.50 **st.**

🏨 **Stratford House** without rest., Sheep St., CV37 6EF, ℰ 68288 – 📺 ⇌wc ㎡wc ☏. 🔝 AE
ⓞ 𝘝𝘐𝘚𝘈   A **u**
closed 1 week at Christmas – **9 rm** ⌑ 32.50/45.00 **st.**

🏠 **Haytor** ⌚, Avenue Rd, CV37 6UX, ℰ 297799, 🐎 – 📺 ⇌wc ㎡wc 🅿
M (buffet lunch) 8.00 **st.** ░ 3.00 – **15 rm** ⌑ 22.00/45.00 **st.**   B **c**

🏠 **Hylands** without rest., Warwick Rd, CV37 6YW, ℰ 297962, 🐎 – 📺 ㎡wc 🅿. 🔝. ❄
closed Christmas and New Year – **15 rm** ⌑ 25.00/34.00 **st.**   B **a**

🏠 **Bancroft Garden** without rest., Waterside, CV37 6EF, ℰ 69196 – ⇌wc ㎡wc ☏. 🔝 AE ⓞ
𝘝𝘐𝘚𝘈   B **z**
closed 25 and 26 December – ⌑ 2.95 – **16 rm** 16.50/33.50 **st.**

↟ **Moonraker House,** 40 Alcester Rd, CV37 9DB, ℰ 67115 – 📺 ⇌wc ㎡wc 🅿
closed 25-26 December, 31 December and 1 January – **15 rm** ⌑ 12.00/20.00 **st.**   A **i**

↟ **Hardwick House,** 1 Avenue Rd, CV37 6UY, ℰ 204307 – 📺 🅿. ❄
closed Christmas – **12 rm** ⌑ 9.50/24.00 **st.**   B **s**

↟ **Stratheden,** 5 Chapel St., CV37 6EP, ℰ 297119 – ⇌wc ㎡wc. ❄
closed last 2 weeks February, last 2 weeks November and Christmas – **10 rm** ⌑ 10.35/30.00 **t.**   A **s**

↟ **Melita,** 37 Shipston Rd, CV37 7LN, ℰ 292432, 🐎 – ⇌wc 🅿. ❄
closed Christmas – **13 rm** ⌑ 13.00/34.00 **st.**   B **x**

↟ **Marlyn,** 3 Chestnut Walk, CV37 6HG, ℰ 293752 – ❄
closed Christmas – **8 rm** ⌑ 8.50/19.90 **st.**   A **e**

↟ **Virginia Lodge,** 12 Evesham Pl., CV37 6HT, ℰ 292157 – 🅿. ❄
closed 23 December-4 January – **7 rm** ⌑ 7.50/18.00 **st.**   A **x**

↟ **Grosvenor Villa,** 9 Evesham Pl., CV37 6HT, ℰ 66192 – 🅿. ❄
8 rm ⌑ 7.00/17.00 **st.**   A **a**

✕✕ **Marlowe's Elizabethan Room,** 18 High St., CV37 6AU, ℰ 204999 – 🔝 AE 𝘝𝘐𝘚𝘈   A **o**
M (lunch by arrangement) a la carte 12.00/19.00 **t.** ░ 2.75.

✕✕ **Hill's,** 3 Greenhill St., CV37 6LF, ℰ 293563 – 🔝 AE ⓞ 𝘝𝘐𝘚𝘈   A **n**
closed Sunday, Monday and first week August – **M** a la carte 11.00/13.00 **t.**

at Charlecote E : 4 ¾ m. by B 4086 – B – on B 4088 – ✉ Warwick – ☎ 0789 Stratford-
upon-Avon :

🏨 **Charlecote Pheasant,** CV35 9EW, ℰ 840649, 🐎, ❄ – 📺 ⇌wc ㎡wc 🅿. 🔬. 🔝 AE ⓞ
M (carving rest.) 6.20/7.60 **st.** ░ 3.40 – **16 rm** ⌑ 24.00/34.00 **st.** – SB 50.00 **st.**

at Wellesbourne E : 6 m. by B 4086 – B – on A 429 – ✉ Wellesbourne – ☎ 0789 Stratford-
upon-Avon :

🏛 **King's Head,** CV35 9LT, on A 429 ℰ 840206 – ⇌wc ㎡wc 🅿. 🔝 AE ⓞ 𝘝𝘐𝘚𝘈
M (bar lunch) a la carte 6.25 **t.** – **11 rm** ⌑ 16.00/35.00 **t.** – SB (except Bank Holidays) 30.50/38.50 **st.**

at Ettington SE : 6 ½ m. on A 422 – B – ✉ ☎ 0789 Stratford-upon-Avon :

✕✕ **The Chase Country House** ⌚ with rm, CV37 7NZ, ℰ 740000, ⩽, 🐎, park – 📺 ⇌wc ☏
🅿. 🔝 AE ⓞ 𝘝𝘐𝘚𝘈. ❄
closed 24 December-21 January – **M** (closed Saturday lunch and Sunday dinner to non-
residents) 10.00/16.00 **t.** ░ 2.95 – **11 rm** ⌑ 23.00/42.00 **t.**

at Billesley NW : 4 m. by A 422 – B – ✉ ☎ 0789 Stratford-upon-Avon :

🏨 **Billesley Manor** ⌚, B49 6NF, ℰ 763737, Telex 312599, ⩽, 🔝, 🐎, park, ✕ – 📺 ☎ 🅿. 🔬.
🔝 AE ⓞ 𝘝𝘐𝘚𝘈
M 10.00/18.50 **st.** ░ 4.50 – **28 rm** ⌑ 41.00/75.00 **st.** – SB 74.50/85.00 **st.**

at Wilmcote NW : 4 m. by A 34 – A – ⊠ ✆ 0789 Stratford-upon-Avon :

🏨 **Swan House,** The Green, CV37 9XJ, ✆ 67030, 🍴 – 📺 ⌷wc Ⓟ. 🔲 🅰🅴 VISA. 𝒮𝒳
M *(closed Sunday dinner to non-residents)* (bar lunch) 8.00 **t.** ⋀ 3.60 – **11 rm** ⊆ 19.00/33.00 **st.**
– SB (weekends only) 36.00/60.00 **st.**

AUDI, VW Western Rd ✆ 294477
AUSTIN-ROVER-DAIMLER-JAGUAR Birmingham Rd ✆ 67555
BEDFORD, VAUXHALL-OPEL Rother St. ✆ 66254
CITROEN 23 Weston Rd ✆ 293577

FIAT, LANCIA Western Rd ✆ 68913
PEUGEOT, TALBOT Alderminster ✆ 078 987 (Alderminster) 331
RENAULT Western Rd ✆ 67911
VOLVO Western Rd ✆ 292468

STRATTON Glos. 📗 📗 O 28 – see Cirencester.

STRATTON ST. MARGARET Wilts. 📗 📗 O 29 – see Swindon.

STREATLEY Berks. 📗 📗 Q 29 – pop. 986 – ⊠ ✆ 0491 Goring.
♦ London 56 – ♦ Oxford 16 – Reading 11.

🏨 **Swan,** High St., RG8 9HR, ✆ 873737, « ≤ Thameside setting », 🍴 – 📺 ⌷wc 🐕 Ⓟ. 🔲 🅰🅴 ⓞ VISA. 𝒮𝒳
M 17.50 **t.** ⋀ 2.50 – ⊆ 5.75 – **24 rm** 34.00/55.00 **t.** – SB 60.00/70.00 **st.**

STREET Somerset 📗 L 30 The West Country G. – pop. 7,550 – ECD : Wednesday – ✆ 0458.
♦London 138 – ♦Bristol 28 – Taunton 20.

🏨 **Wessex,** High St., BA16 0EF, ✆ 43383, Telex 57515 – 📲 📺 ⌷wc 🐕 Ⓟ. 🔼 🔲 🅰🅴 ⓞ VISA
M (grill rest. only) a la carte 5.10/9.70 **st.** ⋀ 2.30 – **50 rm** ⊆ 25.80/35.80 **st.** – SB (weekends only) 36.00 **st.**

AUSTIN-ROVER Creeches Lane, Walton ✆ 42735   FORD 189 High St. ✆ 47147

STREETLY West Midlands 📗 📗 O 26 – see Birmingham.

STRETE Devon – see Dartmouth.

STRETTON Cheshire 📗 📗 📗 M 23 – see Warrington.

STRETTON UNDER FOSSE Warw. 📗 📗 Q 26 – see Rugby.

STROUD Glos. 📗 📗 N 28 – pop. 25,580 – ECD : Thursday – ✆ 045 36.
Envir. : Severn Wildfowl Trust★ *AC*, W : 11 m.
🏌, 🏌 Minchinhampton ✆ 045 383 (Nailsworth) 2642 (Old Course) and 3866 (New Course), E : 3 m. and 5 m.
🛈 Council Offices, High St. ✆ 4252.
♦London 113 – ♦Bristol 30 – Gloucester 9.

🏨 **London,** 30-31 London Rd, GL5 2AJ, ✆ 79992 – 📺 ⌷wc ⋔wc Ⓟ. 🔲 ⓞ VISA. 𝒮𝒳
M *(closed Sunday to non-residents)* 6.00/7.25 **t.** ⋀ 2.65 – **10 rm** ⊆ 15.00/40.00 **t.** – SB 40.00 **st.**

↑ **Downfield,** 134 Cainscross Rd, GL5 4HN, ✆ 4496 – ⌷wc ⋔wc Ⓟ
closed 23 December-4 January – **21 rm** ⊆ 11.00/22.00 **st.**

XX **Mr Baillie's,** 56 Westward Rd, Cainscross, GL5 4JA, W : 1 ½ m. on A 419 ✆ 79111 – 🔲 ⓞ
closed Sunday and Monday except Bank Holidays – **M** (dinner only)(booking essential) 9.45 **st.**

at Brimscombe SE : 2 ¼ m. on A 419 – ⊠ Stroud – ✆ 0453 Brimscombe :

🏨 **Burleigh Court** ⤵, Burleigh Hill, GL5 2PF, SW : ½ m. off Burleigh Rd ✆ 883804, ≤, ⊒ heated, 🍴 – 📺 ⌷wc ⋔wc Ⓟ. 🔲 🅰🅴 VISA. 𝒮𝒳
closed 1 week at Christmas – **M** (buffet Sunday dinner) 7.00/12.00 **st.** ⋀ 2.40 – **11 rm** ⊆ 30.00/50.00 **st.** – SB 55.00/60.00 **st.**

at Rodborough S : ¾ m. by A 46 – ⊠ Stroud – ✆ 045 387 Amberley :

🏨 **Bear of Rodborough** (Anchor), Rodborough Common, GL5 5DE, E : 1 ½ m. ✆ 3522, 🍴 – 📺 ⌷wc 🐕 Ⓟ. 🔼 🔲 🅰🅴 ⓞ VISA
M a la carte 8.10/12.75 **st.** ⋀ 2.65 – **48 rm** ⊆ 36.00/47.00 **st.** – SB (weekends only) 50.00 **st.**

at Stonehouse W : 2 m. on A 419 – ⊠ Stroud – ✆ 045 382 Stonehouse :

🏨 **Stonehouse Court,** Bristol Rd, GL10 3RA, ✆ 5155, Telex 437244, 🍴, park – 📺 ⌷wc ⋔wc 🐕 Ⓟ. 🔼 🔲 🅰🅴 ⓞ VISA. 𝒮𝒳
closed 2 weeks after Christmas – **M** 8.95/10.25 **t.** ⋀ 2.75 – **10 rm** ⊆ 32.00/43.00 **t.** – SB (weekends only) 59.00 **st.**

ALFA ROMEO Lansdown Rd ✆ 4845
AUSTIN-ROVER Caincross Rd ✆ 3671
CITROEN London Rd ✆ 2861
FIAT Stratford Rd ✆ 4007
FORD London Rd ✆ 71341
NISSAN Westward Rd, Ebley ✆ 2000

PEUGEOT-TALBOT Rodborough Common ✆ 045 387 (Amberley) 3559
RENAULT London Rd ✆ 4203
TALBOT Stonehouse ✆ 045 382 (Stonehouse) 2139
VAUXHALL-OPEL Westward Rd ✆ 5522

STUBBINGTON Hants. 🅰️🅾️🅾️ Q 31 – pop. 5,396 – ✆ 0329.

◆London 89 – ◆Portsmouth 15 – ◆Southampton 12.

🏠 Crofton Manor, off Titchfield Rd, PO14 3NA, 🏠 662014, 🚗 – ▥wc ℗
7 rm.

STUCKTON Hants. – see Fordingbridge.

STUDLAND Dorset 🅰️🅾️🅾️ O 32 The West Country G. – pop. 620 – ECD : Thursday – ✉ Swanage – ✆ 092 944.

🗼 Isle of Purbeck 🏠 210.

◆London 130 – Bournemouth 22 – Dorchester 26.

🏨 **Knoll House**, BH19 3AH, 🏠 251, 🏊 heated, 🗼, 🚗, park, 💥 – ▤wc 🅿 ℗
April-October – **M** 7.00/7.50 t. 🍷 3.00 – **111 rm** ⇌ 22.00/72.00 **st.**

🏨 **Manor House** 🏊, Beach Rd, Studland Bay, BH19 3AU, 🏠 288, ≤ Old Harry rocks and Poole Bay, 🚗, park – 📺 ▤wc ▥wc ℗
Easter-October – **M** (bar lunch) 10.50 🍷 2.50 – **18 rm** ⇌ (dinner included) 20.00/54.00 – SB 44.00/60.00 **st.**

STURMINSTER NEWTON Dorset 🅰️🅾️🅾️ N 31 – pop. 2,111 – ✆ 0258.

◆London 123 – Bournemouth 30 – ◆Bristol 49 – Salisbury 28 – Taunton 41.

XXX **Plumber Manor** 🏊 with rm, Hazelbury Bryan Rd, DT10 2AF, SW : 1 ¾ m. 🏠 72507, ≤, « 18C manor house », 🚗, park, 💥 – 📺 ▤wc 🅿. 💥
closed February and first 2 weeks November – **M** *(closed Sunday November-March to non-residents and Monday)* (dinner only) 14.00 t. 🍷 2.80 – **12 rm** ⇌ 30.00/50.00 **st.**

LADA, MAZDA Station Rd 🏠 72155

GREEN TOURIST GUIDES

Picturesque scenery, buildings

Attractive routes

Touring programmes

Plans of towns and buildings.

SUDBURY Derbs. 🅰️🅾️🅾️🅾️ O 25 – pop. 868 – ✉ Derby – ✆ 028 372 Marchington.
See : Sudbury Hall★★ (17C) *AC.*

◆London 138 – ◆Birmingham 33 – Derby 13 – ◆Stoke-on-Trent 23.

Hotel and restaurant see : **Tutbury** SE : 6 m., **Uttoxeter** W : 4 ½ m.

SUDBURY Suffolk 🅾️🅾️ W 27 – pop. 8,166 – ECD : Wednesday – ✆ 0787.

🅱 Public Library, Market Hill 🏠 72092.

◆London 59 – ◆Cambridge 37 – Colchester 15 – ◆Ipswich 21.

🏨 **Mill**, Walnut Tree Lane, CO10 0BD, 🏠 75544, ≤, 🛶 – 📺 ▤wc 🅿 ℗. 🏌 🔄 🆎 🅾 VISA
M 6.50/8.75 t. 🍷 3.60 – **45 rm** ⇌ 29.50/45.00 t. – SB 50.00/70.00 **st.**

🏠 **Hill Lodge**, 8 Newton Rd, 🏠 77568 – 📺 ▥wc ℗. 💥
closed 1 week at Christmas – **16 rm** ⇌ 10.00/18.50 **s.**

VAUXHALL-OPEL Cornard Rd 🏠 72301

SUNDERLAND Tyne and Wear 🅰️🅾️🅾️ P 19 – pop. 217,079 – ECD : Wednesday – ✆ 0783.

🗼 Wearside, Coxgreen 🏠 078 324 (Hylton) 2518, W : 2 m. by A 183 A – 🗼 Whitburn, Lizard Lane 🏠 0783 (Whitburn) 292144, N : 2 m. by A 183 A.

◆London 272 – ◆Leeds 92 – ◆Middlesbrough 29 – ◆Newcastle-upon-Tyne 12.

Plan opposite

🏨 **Seaburn** (Swallow), Queen's Par., SR6 8DB, N : 2 ½ m. on A 183 🏠 292041, Group Telex 53168, ≤, – ▤📺 ▤wc 🅿 ℗. 🏌 🔄 🆎 🅾 VISA
M 5.75/6.50 **st.** 🍷 2.90 – **82 rm** ⇌ 33.00/39.50 **st.** – SB (weekends only) 44.00/49.50 **st.**
A c

ALFA-ROMEO 🏠 487722
AUSTIN-ROVER, DAIMLER-JAGUAR 190 Roker Av.
🏠 656221
AUSTIN-ROVER Allison Rd, West Boldon 🏠 362726
AUSTIN-ROVER Warwick 🏠 210838
BMW Ryhope Rd 🏠 657631
CITROEN Durham Rd 🏠 57191
COLT Nth. Bridge St. 🏠 659252
FIAT Durham Rd 🏠 657191
FIAT Newcastle Rd 🏠 673204

FORD Trimdon St. 🏠 40311
HONDA Toward Rd, Doker 🏠 40898
LADA High St. West 🏠 40337
RENAULT High St. West 🏠 43441
SAAB 🏠 77538
TALBOT Newcastle Rd 🏠 488811
VAUXHALL Paley St. 🏠 42841
VOLVO Nth. Hylton Rd 🏠 491277
YUGO Boldon Lane 🏠 365313

SUNDERLAND

Central Area	....	B
Fawcett Street	....	B
High Street West	....	B 15
Holmeside	....	B 16
John Street	....	B

Albion Place	....	B 2
Barnes Park Road	....	A 3
Bedford Street	....	B 4
Borough Road	....	B 5
Bridge Street	....	B 6
Chariton Road	....	B 8
Chester Road	....	B 10
Derwent Street	....	B 12
Green Terrace	....	B 13
Harbour View	....	A 14
Kayll Road	....	A 17
Livingstone Road	....	B 18
New Durham Road	....	B 19
Northern Way	....	A 20
Ormonde Street	....	A 21
Pallion Road	....	A 22
Park Lane	....	B 23
Roker Terrace	....	A 24
St. Luke's Terrace	....	A 26
St. Mary's Way	....	B 27
Shields Road	....	A 29
Southwick Road	....	B 30
Station Road	....	A 32
Sunderland Road	....	A 33
Trimdon Street	....	A 35
Vine Place	....	B 36
Wessington Way	....	A 38

Plans de villes :
Les principales voies
commerçantes figurent
en rouge au début
de la liste des rues
des plans de villes.

CENTRE

A 183

B

A 1018

North Bridge

Wear

B 1289

Roker Avⁿ

Dame Dorothy St.

Fawcett St.

Crowtree Rd

CENTRAL AREA

CROWTREE LEISURE CENTRE

POL

Low Row

Silksworth Row

STATION

Holmeside

Stockton Rd

Toward Rd

MOWBRAY PARK

Burdon Rd

Ryhope Rd

Park Rd

Belvedere Rd

Tunstall Rd

Derby St.

Thornhill Rex

Thornhill

A 1290 (A 1231)

A 183

A 690

300 m
300 yards

BUILT UP AREA

1 km
1/2 mile

NEWCASTLE-UPON-TYNE A 184

A 1018 SOUTH SHIELDS

A 183 WHITBURN

WHITBURN

Whitburn Road

Sea Road

MONKWEARMOUTH

Fulwell

Dame Dorothy St.

Roker Rd

Thompson Rd

North Hylton Rd

Southwick Rd

SOUTHWICK

Wear

Pallion

New Rd

A 1280

Hylton Rd

St. Luke's Rd

Northern Way

Front Rd

Holborn Rd

Broadway

Chester Rd

The Springwell Rd

Durham Rd

Durham Rd

High St. East

Hendon Rd

Commercial Rd

Ocean Rd

Grey Rd

Ryhope Rd

Alexandra Rd

Queen Alexandra

Leechmere Rd

Tunstall

Lane

Silksworth

Premier Rd

A 1018

MIDDLESBROUGH

A 690 (A 1 : M), DURHAM

A 1231 WASHINGTON

A 183 CHESTER-LE-STREET

Newcastle

423

SUTTON BENGER Wilts. 403 404 N 29 – pop. 840 – ⊠ Chippenham – ☎ 0249 Seagry.
♦London 92 – ♦Bristol 26 – Chippenham 4.5 – Swindon 16.

🏨 **Bell House,** High St., SN15 4RH, ℰ 720401, ☞ – ▤ rest 📺 ⇔wc ☜ Ⓟ. 🏄. 🔼 ⒶⒺ ⓪ 𝘝𝘐𝘚𝘈. ❄️
M (grill rest. only) a la carte 5.80/11.00 **t.** ♦3.00 – ⇌ 4.50 – **14 rm** 19.00/39.00 **st.** – SB (weekends only) 68.00/90.00 **st.**

SUTTON COLDFIELD West Midlands 403 404 O 26 – see Birmingham.

SWAFFHAM Norfolk 404 W 26 – pop. 4,280 – ECD : Thursday – ☎ 0760.
Envir. : Oxburgh Hall (15C) : Gate house★ *AC*, SW : 7 ½ m.
♦London 97 – ♦Cambridge 46 – King's Lynn 16 – ♦Norwich 27.

🏠 **George,** Station St., PE37 7LJ, ℰ 21238 – 📺 ⇔wc ☜ Ⓟ. 🔼 ⒶⒺ ⓪ 𝘝𝘐𝘚𝘈. ❄️
M a la carte 6.00/9.75 **t.** – **32 rm** ⇌ 22.00/38.50 **t.** – SB (weekends only) 54.00/63.00 **st.**

FORD London St. ℰ 21239

SWANAGE Dorset 403 404 O 32 The West Country G. – pop. 7,860 – ECD : Thursday – ☎ 092 92 (4 fig.) or 0929 (6 fig.).
See : Site ★ – Durlston Country Park (≤★★) – The Great Globe★.
Envir. : St. Aldhelm's Head★★ (≤★★★), SW : 4 m. by B 3069 – Corfe Castle★★ (≤★★), NW : 6 m. – Old Harry Rocks★★ (Studland Village - St. Nicholas Church★) N : 4 ½ m. – Studland Beach (≤★), N : 5 m.

🚩 The White House, Shore Rd ℰ 422885.
♦London 130 – Bournemouth 22 – Dorchester 26 – ♦Southampton 52.

🏨 **The Pines,** Burlington Rd, BH19 1LT, ℰ 425211, Telex 418297, ≤, ☞ – 🛗 📺 ⇔wc ☎ Ⓟ. 🔼 𝘝𝘐𝘚𝘈
M 5.50/8.00 ♦2.10 – **43 rm** ⇌ 17.00/40.00 – SB (winter only) 43.00 **s.**

🏠 Ship Inn, 23 High St., BH19 2LR, ℰ 422078 – ☜ Ⓟ
18 rm.

☝ **Boyne,** 1 Cliff Av., BH19 1LX, ℰ 422939 – Ⓟ
April-September – **15 rm** ⇌ 9.50/19.00 **st.**

☝ **Suncliffe,** 1 Burlington Rd, BH19 1LR, ℰ 423299, ☞ – ▥wc Ⓟ. ❄️
Easter-22 September – **13 rm** ⇌ 16.25/26.00 **st**

☝ **Eversden,** 5 Victoria Rd, BH19 1LY, ℰ 423276 – ⇔wc ▥wc Ⓟ. 𝘝𝘐𝘚𝘈. ❄️
12 rm ⇌ 8.50/19.30 **t.**

☝ **Havenhurst,** 3 Cranborne Rd, BH19 1EA, ℰ 424224 – ▥wc Ⓟ. ❄️
March-October – **16 rm** ⇌ 10.00/26.00 **t.**

FORD 281 High St. ℰ 422877   MAZDA Victoria Av. ℰ 422888

SWANBRIDGE South Glam. 403 K 29 – see Penarth.

SWANSEA (ABERTAWE) West Glam. 403 I 29 – pop. 173,413 – ECD : Thursday – ☎ 0792.
Envir. : Cefn Bryn (❈★★★ from the reservoir) W : 12 m. by A 4118 A.
Exc. : Rhosili (site and ≤★★★) W : 18 m. by A 4118 A.

🏌 Morriston ℰ 71079, N : 4 m. by A 48 A – 🏌 Langland Bay ℰ 66023, W : 6 m. by A 4067 A.
🚩 Crymlyn Burrows, Jersey Marine ℰ 462403 (summer only) – Singleton St. ℰ 468321 – Ty Croeso, Gloucester Pl. ℰ 465204 – Oystermouth Sq., The Mumbles ℰ 61302 (summer only).
♦London 191 – ♦Birmingham 136 – ♦Bristol 82 – ♦Cardiff 40 – ♦Liverpool 186 – ♦Stoke-on-Trent 175.

Plan opposite

🏨🏨 **Dragon** (T.H.F.), 39 The Kingsway, SA1 5LS, ℰ 51074, Telex 48309 – 🛗 📺 👤 Ⓟ. 🏄. 🔼 ⒶⒺ ⓪ 𝘝𝘐𝘚𝘈
M 6.95/8.50 **st.** ♦2.60 – ⇌ 5.50 – **118 rm** 40.00/49.50 **st.**
B **a**

🏠 **Windsor Lodge,** 15 Mount Pleasant, SA1 6EG, ℰ 42158 – 📺 ⇔wc ▥wc Ⓟ. 🔼 ⒶⒺ 𝘝𝘐𝘚𝘈
closed 25 and 26 December – **M** (booking essential) 8.00/12.00 **t.** ♦2.40 – **18 rm** ⇌ 20.00/35.00 **t.** – SB (weekends only) 47.00/57.00 **st.**
B **r**

🏠 **Llwyn Helyg,** Ffynone Rd, Ffynone, SA1 6BT, ℰ 465735, ☞ – 📺 ⇔wc ▥wc ☜ Ⓟ. 🔼 ⒶⒺ ⓪ 𝘝𝘐𝘚𝘈
M 4.50/7.00 **st.** – **11 rm** ⇌ 19.00/28.00 **st.**
A **a**

🏠 **Alexander,** 3 Sketty Rd, Uplands, SA2 0EU, ℰ 470045 – 📺 ⇔wc ▥wc. 🔼 ⒶⒺ ⓪ 𝘝𝘐𝘚𝘈. ❄️
closed Christmas and New Year – **M** (dinner only) 6.00 **t.** – **7 rm** ⇌ 12.00/24.00 **t.**
A **c**

🍴🍴 **Drangwy,** 66 Wind St., SA1 1UQ, ℰ 461397 – 🔼 ⒶⒺ ⓪ 𝘝𝘐𝘚𝘈
closed Sunday and Monday – **M** a la carte 12.85/18.85 **t.** ♦3.25.
B **c**

🍴 Jasmine, 326 Oystermouth Rd, SA1 3UL, ℰ 52912, Chinese rest. – 🔼 ⒶⒺ ⓪ 𝘝𝘐𝘚𝘈
A **e**

AUSTIN-ROVER-DAIMLER-JAGUAR 511 Carmarthen Rd ℰ 588141
FORD Garngoch ℰ 893041
HONDA, SAAB Llangyfelach ℰ 71960
NISSAN Sway Rd ℰ 75271
PEUGEOT, TALBOT Neath Rd ℰ 73391

RENAULT Eaton Rd, Manselton ℰ 53125
VAUXHALL William St. ℰ 41311
VAUXHALL Neath Rd, Morriston ℰ 75101
VW, AUDI-NSU Gorseinon Rd ℰ 0792 (Gorseinon) 894951

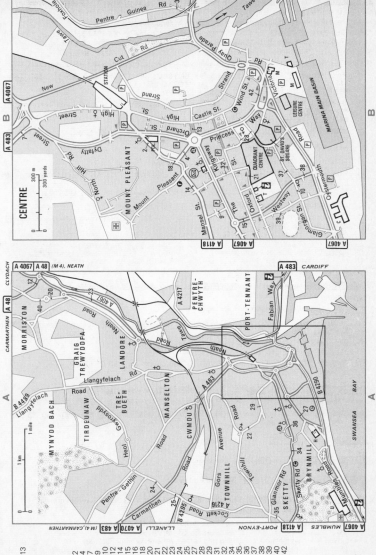

SWANSEA

SWAY Hants. 403 404 P 31 — see Lymington.

SWINDON Wilts. 403 404 O 29 The West Country G. — pop. 91,033 — ECD : Wednesday — ✆ 0793.

See : Great Western Railway Museum★ — Railway Village Museum★.

🏌 Bremhill Park, ✆ 782946, E : 4 m. — 🏌 Ogbourne St. George ✆ 067 284 (Ogbourne St. George) 217, S : 7 m. on A 345 — 🏌, 🏌 Broome Manor, Pipers Way ✆ 32403, 2 m. from centre.

🖪 32 The Arcade, David Murray John Building, Brunel Centre ✆ 30328 and 26161 ext. 3056.

♦London 83 — Bournemouth 69 — ♦Bristol 40 — ♦Coventry 66 — ♦Oxford 29 — Reading 40 — ♦Southampton 65.

🏨 **Post House** (T.H.F.), Marlborough Rd, SN3 6AQ, SE : 2 ¾ m. on A 345 ✆ 24601, Telex 444464, ♨ heated — 📺 ➱wc ☎ 🅿. 🏌. 🔼 AE ① VISA
   M 6.50/8.50 st. ▮ 2.60 — ☲ 5.00 — **103 rm** 39.00/45.50 st.

🏨 **Goddard Arms** (Anchor), High St., Old Town, SN1 3EW, ✆ 692313, Telex 444764 — 📺 ➱wc ☎ 🅿. 🏌. 🔼 AE ① VISA
   M 10.00 t. — **65 rm** ☲ 44.00/50.00 t. — SB (weekends only) 52.00 st.

🏨 **Wiltshire,** Fleming Way, SN1 1TN, ✆ 28282, Telex 444250 — 📢 📺 ➱wc ☎. 🏌. 🔼 AE ① VISA
   M 8.00 st. ▮ 3.00 — **85 rm** ☲ 40.00/50.00 st. — SB (weekends only) 46.00 st.

   at Blunsdon N : 4 ½ m. on A 419 — ✉ ✆ 0793 Swindon :

🏨 **Blunsdon House** (Best Western), The Ridge, SN2 4AD, ✆ 721701, Telex 444491, ♨ — 📢 📺 ☎ & 🅿. 🏌. 🔼 AE ① VISA. ❄
   M 6.50/8.00 st. ▮ 2.80 — **92 rm** ☲ 35.00/49.00 st. — SB (weekends only) 52.00/54.50 st.

   at Stratton St. Margaret NE : 2 m. on A 420 — ✉ ✆ 0793 Swindon :

🏨 **Crest** (Crest), Oxford Rd, SN3 4TL, NE : 1 ½ m. on A 420 ✆ 822921, Telex 444456 — ▦ rest 📺 ➱wc ☎ & 🅿. 🏌. 🔼 AE ① VISA
   M approx. 10.50 st. — ☲ 5.25 — **98 rm** 42.00/53.00 st.

AUSTIN-ROVER Dorkan Way ✆ 612091
BEDFORD, FIAT, VAUXHALL Drove Rd ✆ 20971
BMW High St. at Wroughton ✆ 812387
FORD 30 Marlborough Rd ✆ 20002

RENAULT Elgin Drive ✆ 693841
VAUXHALL 13/21 The Street, Moredon ✆ 23457
VW, AUDI-NSU Eldene Drive ✆ 31333

SYMONDS YAT Heref. and Worc. 403 404 M 28 — pop. 807 — ✉ Ross-on-Wye — ✆ 0600.

See : Symond's Yat Rock ⇐★★.

♦London 126 — Gloucester 23 — Hereford 17 — Newport 31.

   at Symonds Yat (West) SW : 7 ½ m. by A 40 on B 4164 — ✉ Ross-on-Wye — ✆ 0600 Symonds Yat :

🛏 **Woodlea** ❧, HR9 6BL, ✆ 890206, ♨, ♨ — ▥wc 🅿
   closed Christmas — **10 rm** ☲ 11.50/23.50 t.

✕✕ **Gallery,** Wayside, Whitchurch, HR9 6DJ, ✆ 890408, ♨ — 🅿. 🔼 AE ① VISA
   closed Sunday and first 2 weeks November — **M** a la carte 11.95/17.35 st.

TADCASTER North Yorks. 402 Q 22 — pop. 5,910 — ECD : Wednesday — ✆ 0937.

♦London 176 — Harrogate 16 — ♦Kingston-upon-Hull 47 — ♦Leeds 16 — York 10.

🏨 **Shann House** without rest., 47 Kirkgate, LS24 9AQ, ✆ 833931 — 📺 ➱wc ▥wc 🅿. 🔼 VISA
   8 rm ☲ 12.00/22.00 st.

TALKIN Cumbria 401 402 L 19 — see Brampton.

TALLAND BAY Cornwall 403 G 32 — see Looe.

TAL-Y-BONT Gwynedd 402 403 I 24 — see Conwy.

TAL-Y-LLYN Gwynedd 402 403 I 25 — pop. 620 — ✉ Tywyn — ✆ 065 477 Abergynolwyn.

♦London 224 — Dolgellau 9 — Shrewsbury 60.

🏨 **Minffordd,** LL36 9AJ, NE : 2 ¾ m. on A 487 ✆ 065 473 (Corris) 665, ⇐, « Converted 18C farmhouse and inn », ♨ — ➱wc ▥wc 🅿. 🔼 ① VISA. ❄
   closed weekdays March, November and December and January-February — **M** *(closed Sunday to non-residents)* (buffet lunch residents only) 9.50 st. ▮ 3.95 — **7 rm** ☲ 20.00/40.80 st. — SB (except summer) 39.00 st.

🏨 **Tynycornel,** LL36 9AJ, on B 4405 ✆ 282, ⇐ lake and mountains, ❧, ♨ — ➱wc ▥wc ☎ 🅿. 🔼 ① VISA
   restricted opening in winter — **M** a la carte 6.95/9.15 t. ▮ 1.75 — **16 rm** ☲ (dinner included) 27.00/58.00 t. — SB (except summer) 45.00/55.00 st.

TAMWORTH Staffs. 402 403 404 O 26 — pop. 64,315 — ✆ 0827.

♦London 118 — ♦Birmingham 12 — ♦Leicester 32 — ♦Nottingham 35 — ♦Stoke on Trent 37.

✕✕ **Kealey's,** 36, Market St., B79 7LR, ✆ 55444 — 🔼 AE ① VISA
   closed Wednesday lunch, Saturday lunch, Sunday and Monday — **M** 6.50/10.95 t.

MICHELIN

THE BEST TYRES IN THE WORLD

The story of Michelin is the history of the motor vehicle. Most of the important developments in tyre technology have been originated by Michelin: this started with the first detachable cycle tyre in 1892. In 1948 the introduction of the first radial, Michelin X, heralded a concept that inside two decades was to change the standards of tyre performance for ever.

In earlier days the introduction of new types was uncommon. Today, with more rigorous demands from both manufacturer and driver, there is something new from Michelin nearly every year. Family cars, fast cars, exotic cars, ordinary roads, motorways, off-the-road, winter roads: there is a Michelin for every driver in every condition.

The MX Range

The car tyre range today is bigger than ever before. In 1983 a whole new range was launched: MX for family cars, MXL low profile for the sport derivatives, MXV for performance cars.

MX

MX was introduced as a replacement for the world famous XZX and is made in 80 series. The multi-siped tread pattern ensures rapid water dispersal, providing excellent grip, particularly in wet conditions. No compromises have been made in the design so the long mileage associated with Michelin radials is maintained. With MX the advantages of previous Michelin radials have been maintained, including the retention of low rolling resistance providing excellent fuel economy.

MXL

MXL was developed as a tyre for the sportier saloon. Many top of the range cars and sports derivatives are fitted with low profile tyres as original equipment. MXL will out perform other tyres of this type. Sizes are available in 60, 65 and 70 Series and either S rated (180 km/h: 113 mph) or T rated (190 km/h: 120 mph).

MXL give superb grip in all conditions; broad grooves lead from the tread centre to the shoulders, ensuring efficient water clearance for good wet road grip. The tyre has the usual Michelin attributes of long life, coupled with excellent fuel economy.

MXV

MXV tyres have been designed specifically for many of the truly fast sports cars that require low profile, high performance tyres. After a short period the MXV has already gained an enviable reputation with manufacturers, tyre dealers and motorists.

To give positive grip at high speeds great attention has been paid to tread design: broad, deep circumferential grooves ensure excellent water dispersal and transverse grooves link the crown to the shoulder to give extra clearance. As with all Michelin radials, MXV tyres have a low rolling resistance and therefore save fuel.

MXV will progressively replace most XAS and XVS sizes and are available in 60, 65, 70 and 80 series.

TRX AND TDX TYRES

A further development in radial tyre technology came in the mid '70s with the launch of Michelin TRX. Because there are certain inherent disadvantages with the conventional design of tyre and rim, Michelin returned to basics and redesigned the tyre/wheel assembly as a unit. With standard profile rims the near vertical flange imposes stresses to the sidewall which results in a reversal of the direction in sidewall movement above the top edge of the flange. This results in an awkward 'S' shaped distortion of the sidewall. The TR rim has a gently sloping flange that allows the casing to adopt a natural 'C' curve. With the TR concept, stresses

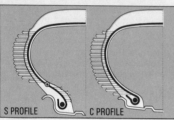

S PROFILE   C PROFILE

within the tyre are equalised; performance is enhanced, mileage increased due to more even wear and fuel

economy improved. And even though TRX tyres are all low profile tyres there is no reduction in comfort compared with more conventional tyres because there is a longer sidewall flexing area.

In 1983 an additional development to the TR principle was announced; this is called TDX. This new tyre takes the TRX concept further with changes to the bead area. The bead has an extended toe which locates in a channel in the rim base. With this development of the TR design a limited run-on capability is added to the already considerable advantages of the TRX tyre: the tyre

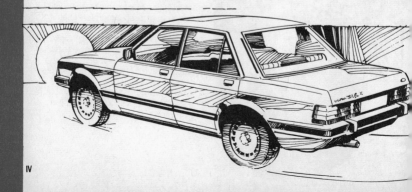

cannot leave the rim after a sudden deflation because the bead toe cannot be dislodged, so the car can always be brought to a safe stop. TDX is the great new tyre for the future and means total safety, security and peace of mind.

OTHER TYRES IN THE RANGE

The comparatively new MX Series, plus TRX and TDX, represent the great bulk of Michelin car tyres sold today. Nevertheless there are of course many other types of tyre for every possible type of application in the total Michelin car tyre range.

   Although the great mass of drivers seldom use their cars on anything other than tarmac roads, wet or dry, there are still those people that need extra traction. Service engineers for water, gas, electricity and land line authorities, rally enthusiasts, drivers operating in areas of heavy snowfalls, including mountain rescue teams and even certain types of farm representative, all these need something extra that conventional tread patterns cannot give. Then there are the out and out racing cars on which Michelin has been so successful in recent years.

   The list is endless, and all are catered for by Michelin. The Michelin car tyre range taken in its entirety must offer the widest choice in the world today.

Conventional tyre on rim

V

MICHELIN MAPS & GUIDES

At the end of the last century motor cars were still a rarity, horse power still meant a flying mane, steel-bound wheels and a hard ride. But if motor cars were rare, route maps were almost unheard of and guide books with hotels and restaurants just didn't exist.

The development of the pneumatic tyre was the one factor without which the motor car would have remained a noisy, slow and cumbersome toy with little future. The tyre gave life to the motor car and provided fast long-distance travel to the masses in a relatively short space of time. André Michelin, one of the Company's founders, sensed the need for accurate information and in 1900 published the first Hotel and Restaurant Guide for France. The whole vast Michelin range of maps and guides available today stems from this first publication.

HOTEL & RESTAURANT GUIDES

This Hotel and Restaurant Guide to Great Britain and Ireland is one of a world famous range of similar publications. The complete list is: Benelux, France, Germany, Great Britain and Ireland, Italy, Main Cities Europe and Spain and Portugal.

The guides are all prepared to the same standards and updated annually. Easy to understand (and to remember) symbols give details of the size and grade of the hotel or restaurant and the varying facilities available (see the reference pages at the front of this guide).

There is also another special guide for the visitor to France who prefers the open air life, also revised annually – this is Camping and Caravaning in France.

GREEN TOURIST GUIDES

The first touring guides appeared before the First World War. In those days they did not have a standard format; the shape and binding varied from guide to guide. Some of the earliest guides were of places that even today a visit is still an adventure. The guide of the Sunny Countries featured parts of North Africa as well as Southern Europe.

Within a year of Armistice Day a special series of tourist books was published that today are collector's pieces; these are the Guides to the Battlefields. In words and pictures the horror and destruction at Amiens and Arras, Lille, the Marne Campaigns and Rheims, Soissons, the Somme, Verdun Ypres and Yser helped a multitude of visitors to fully appreciate what had happened.

Today there are guides to important cities: Paris, London, Rome, New York; to countries: Canada, Portugal, Spain, Austria, Germany, Greece, Italy, Belgium-Luxembourg, Switzerland and to regions of France (in 19 books), South West England and New England. And of course all the Guides are to the same standard and with the familiar green covers.

All Green Tourist Guides are revised and updated regularly (but not necessarily annually).

MAPS

The Michelin archives contain many maps produced by the Company shortly after the first Michelin red guide, in other words some 80 years ago. Like the Guide, the early maps were of France. However as the coverage of the guides spread to cover the Mediterranean area and the British Isles so did the maps. Indeed in those areas that have never been blessed with motorways an old Michelin map is still quite usable (if you ignore the size of the towns and villages) because they were produced to such accuracy.

The range and scope of Michelin maps increases all the time and today covers the whole of Europe and Africa. Indeed the Michelin Africa maps are the only truly motoring maps of that vast continent.

Setting aside the rather special maps; of specific areas, geologic regions of France, city environs, historic events etc., the map range divides into three categories: main roads, regional maps and detailed maps. A one sheet map covers Europe from east to west and as far north as Bergen. There are main road maps of the whole of western Europe. The biggest expansion in new Michelin maps at this time is of the regional maps. The British Isles are covered completely by five maps; there is a regional map for each significant part of France so that the whole country is covered. Spain and Portugal, the Benelux countries, Western Germany,

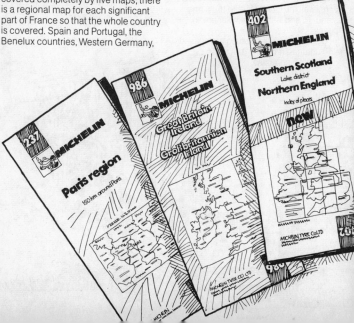

Switzerland and Austria are already in the series and the next country to be tackled will be Italy. The detailed maps are primarily of France and the country is in 37 sheets.

We have said that the Michelin maps are for motorists; we believe that they are the only maps designed and produced with the driver in mind. They are famous not only for what they include but also for what is omitted. There is none of the clutter so often associated with some other maps which can make reference so difficult. On regional maps there is a handsome overlap from sheet to sheet so that no town or place is on the join.

Motorist does of course mean every type of driver from tourist to businessman and we are all both at some time or another. And truck drivers need good maps too. Because Michelin maps set out to cater for all drivers, the extra references are for all sorts of people. You will find a cross reference against any place where we recommend a hotel or restaurant in our appropriate hotel guide, and equally detail a place of natural beauty or other tourist attraction.

We could go on, but it is sufficient to say that we believe that, like our tyres, our maps and guides are the best too. Changes are never made for cosmetic reasons but rather because our constant reviews, our research and the help we get from our customers keep us up to date and on our toes.

EUROPE
BRITISH ISLES
FRANCE
AUSTRIA
BENELUX
GERMANY
GREECE
ITALY
PORTUGAL
SPAIN
SWITZERLAND
YUGOSLAVIA
AFRICA

The Race & Rally Scene

Let us look back just 100 years to 1884. Karl Benz was just about to patent his first motor vehicle. The age of the motor car was about to begin. In just two decades from this date the advances were enormous. From a slow, cumbersome, erratic and unreliable alternative to the horse drawn carriage came the monsters and the landaulets, the sport and the elegance, that were Edwardian motoring. It is hard to believe that so much could have happened so quickly, from nothing to 10 litres of thundering Delage or 12 litres of Itala and many many more.

Without the pneumatic tyre none of this could have happened. Cars would have remained slow and heavy to withstand the shocks transmitted from the road.

But something was needed to get through to ordinary people. Sport was the answer and motor sport was to capture the imagination in a couple of

years. Artists like Montaut saw the thrills and recorded them on canvas, and today we can see the fear on the face of the mechanic. Gordon Bennett of other adventures and sporting fame presented a cup for his own race and all the long distance events of those early years, culminating in the Paris-Madrid, were organised. You can see many of those races recorded on the tile frieze that graces the walls of Michelin House in London's Chelsea, the Michelin commercial offices in the U.K. since 1910.

In those early days, like today, Michelin was the world's leading tyre manufacturer. So we were into racing in a very serious way. In fact we remained involved until the 1920s, by which time it was decided that at least for the present competition involvement was no longer appropriate.

However, 40 years on a decision was made to re-enter competitive sport. The time was ripe to show the world

that Michelin radials would more than hold their own in the toughest rallies and the most severe test of all, the Formula 1 race circuits. And so it was proved.

Between 1978 and 1984 Michelin radials chalked up 59 Formula 1 wins and Michelin equipped cars won the Constructors' and Drivers' Championships outright in 1979, 1983 and 1984. A super start for the new arrival. The year 1983 was more to Michelin than the Formula 1 Championship, indeed much more. In that year every major championship went to Michelin: the list is a manufacturer's dream.

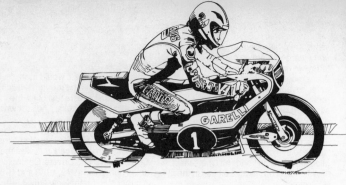

1983

FORMULA 1

There were nine Michelin victories out of 15 races. The champion was Nelson Piquet in a Brabham BMW.

FORMULA 2

There were 11 victories out of 12 races. The champion was Jonathan Palmer in a Ralt Honda.

FORMULA 3

There were 11 Michelin victories out of 14 races. The champion was Pier Lúigi Martini in a Ralt Alfa Romeo.

WORLD RALLY CHAMPIONSHIP

Here again Michelin tyres were supreme, with an outright win for Mikkola's Audi on Michelin. Five rallies were won by cars on Michelin.

MOTORCYCLE

To cap all this, Michelin tyres were chosen for all the winning motorcycles too:
500cc: Freddie Spencer/Honda;
250cc: Carlos Lavado/Yamaha;
125cc: Angel Nieto/Garelli;
50cc: Stefan Dorflinger/Kreidler; and
Trials: Eddie Lejeune/Honda

1984

On September 24 1984, Michelin announced that it intended to withdraw from Formula 1 racing to concentrate all the efforts into successful rallying. The objective in Formula 1 participation was to test the versatility of the radial technology and this had been fully achieved. 1984 was a good time to retire: the results are their own testimony.

FORMULA 1

Niki Lauda won the Formula 1 Championship and Alain Prost was the runner-up. Both drove McLaren on Michelin. There were 16 races, Michelin were on 14 of the winners' cars. McLaren won the Constructors' Championship.

WORLD RALLY CHAMPIONSHIP

The choice of Michelin by the leading drivers again proved to be the right decision. The World Rally Championship was a win for Audi driven by Stig Blomqvist and of course on Michelin. Blomqvist is the 1984 World Rally Champion.

MOTORCYCLE

1984 was almost a repeat of 1983. Honda, with Michelin, won the World 500cc Constructors' Championship, Christian Sarron won the 250cc on Yamaha, Angel Nieto the 125cc on Garelli and Stefan Dorflinger the 50cc on Zündapp. And as if to underline all this Eddie Lejeune with Michelin won the World Trials Championship again.

TANKERTON Kent — see Whitstable.

TARRANT MONKTON Dorset — see Blandford Forum.

TAUNTON Somerset **408** K 30 The West Country G. — pop. 37,444 — ECD : Thursday — ☎ 0823.
See : Site★★ — St. Mary Magdalene's Church★★ — Museum★ — St. James Church★ — Hammett St.★ — The Crescent★ — Bath Alley★.
Envir. : Muchelney★★ (Parish Church★★), E : 14 ½ m. — Trull : Church★, S : 2 m.
🖪 Public Library, Corporation St. ℰ 74785.
◆London 168 — Bournemouth 69 — ◆Bristol 50 — Exeter 37 — ◆Plymouth 76 — ◆Southampton 93 — Weymouth 50.

🏰 ✿ **Castle,** Castle Green, TA1 1NF, ℰ 72671, Telex 46488, « Part 12C castle with Norman garden » — 📶 🖵 🐕 ⇐ 🅿 🏛 🔌 AE ⓞ VISA ✻
  M a la carte 22.10/24.80 **t.** ⒩ 3.40 — ⬷ 5.75 — **40 rm** 38.50/85.00 **t.** — SB (except summer) 79.00 **st.**
  Spec. Braised fillet of red mullet with French bean purée and vinaigrette, Loin of Lamb with a parcel of sweetbreads and rosemary sauce, Fig and Armagnac ice cream with hazelnut biscuits.

🏨 **County** (T.H.F.), East St., TA1 3LT, ℰ 87651, Telex 46484 — 📶 🖵 ⬷wc ☎ 🅿 🏛 🔌 AE ⓞ VISA
  M 6.25/8.75 **st.** ⒩ 2.60 — ⬷ 5.00 — **68 rm** 25.00/42.00 **st.**

🏠 **Corner House,** Park St., TA1 4DQ, ℰ 84683 — 🖵 ⬷wc 🅿 🔌 AE ⓞ VISA ✻
  M (closed dinner Sunday and Bank Holidays) a la carte 6.15/11.25 **st.** ⒩ 3.05 — **22 rm** ⬷ 19.55/39.50 **st.**

  at Henlade E : 3 ½ m. on A 358 — ⊠ Taunton — ☎ 0823 Henlade :

🏠 **Falcon,** TA3 5DH, on A 358 ℰ 442502, 🐕 — 🖵 ⬷wc ⊪wc 🅿 🔌 VISA ✻
  closed 1 to 13 January — **M** (closed Sunday to non-residents) (bar lunch) a la carte 6.75/9.25 **t.** ⒩ 2.75 — **9 rm** ⬷ 24.75/38.00 **t.** — SB (weekends only) 45.00 **st.**

  at Hatch Beauchamp SE : 6 m. on A 358 — ⊠ Taunton — ☎ 0823 Hatch Beauchamp :

XXX **Farthings Country House** with rm, TA3 6SG, ℰ 480664, « Tastefully decorated country house », 🐕 — ⬷wc ☎ 🅿 🔌 VISA ✻
  closed first 2 weeks January — **M** (lunch residents only) a la carte 11.00/13.00 **t.** ⒩ 3.00 — **6 rm** ⬷ 34.00/60.00 **t.** — SB (except summer and Bank Holidays) 65.00/74.00 **t.**

  at Poundisford S : 3 ¾ m. by B 3170 — ⊠ Taunton — ☎ 082 342 Blagdon Hill :

XX **Well House,** Poundisford Park, TA3 7AF, ℰ 566, 🐕 — 🅿 🔌 VISA
  closed Sunday dinner and Monday — **M** a la carte 7.70/9.80 **t.** ⒩ 2.00.

  at Bradford-on-Tone W : 4 m. on A 38 — ⊠ Taunton — ☎ 082 346 Bradford-on-Tone :

🏠 **Heatherton Grange,** Wellington Rd, TA4 1ET, ℰ 777 — 🖵 ⊪wc 🅿 🔌 AE ⓞ VISA
  M 7.50 **t.** ⒩ 2.50 — **18 rm** ⬷ 19.50/30.00 **t.**

AUDI, MERCEDES-BENZ, VW Silver St. ℰ 88371
AUSTIN-ROVER, DAIMLER-JAGUAR South St. ℰ 88991
FORD 151/6 East Reach ℰ 85481

LADA 16 Kingston Rd ℰ 88288
RENAULT 138 Bridgwater Rd, Bathpool ℰ 412559
SAAB 60 East Reach ℰ 88351
VAUXHALL-OPEL Priory Av. ℰ 87611

TAVISTOCK Devon **408** H 32 The West Country G. — pop. 6,720 — ECD : Wednesday — ☎ 0822.
Envir. : Dartmoor National Park★★ — Morwellham★, W : 4 m.
🛝 Down Rd ℰ 2049, SW : 1 m.
🖪 Guildhall, Bedford Sq. ℰ 2938 (summer only).
◆London 239 — Exeter 38 — ◆Plymouth 15.

🏨 **Bedford** (T.H.F.), 1 Plymouth Rd, PL19 8BB, ℰ 3221 — 🖵 ⬷wc ☎ ⇐ 🏛 🔌 AE ⓞ VISA
  M a la carte 10.60/12.70 **st.** ⒩ 2.70 — ⬷ 4.75 — **31 rm** 32.50/44.50 **st.**

  at Gulworthy W : 3 m. on A 390 — ⊠ Tavistock — ☎ 0822 Gunnislake :

XX **Horn of Plenty,** PL19 8JD, ℰ 832528, ≼ Tamar Valley and Bodmin Moor, 🐕 — 🅿
  closed Friday lunch, Thursday and Christmas Day — **M** a la carte 11.45/19.85 **t.** ⒩ 3.00.

  at Mary Tavy N : 4 ½ m. by A 386 — ⊠ Tavistock — ☎ 082 281 Mary Tavy :

🏠 **Moorland Hall** 🐾, Brentor Rd, PL19 9PY, ℰ 466, « Country house atmosphere », 🐕 — ⬷wc ⊪wc 🅿 🔌 VISA
  Mid March-mid November — **M** (restricted lunch to residents only) 4.00/8.50 **t.** ⒩ 3.50 — **10 rm** ⬷ 16.00/30.00 **t.** — SB (winter only) 39.00/41.00 **t.**

AUSTIN-ROVER Plymouth Rd ℰ 2301

FORD Vigo Bridge ℰ 3735

TEDBURN ST. MARY Devon **408** I 31 — pop. 586 — ECD : Thursday — ⊠ Exeter — ☎ 064 76.
◆London 209 — Exeter 8.5 — ◆Plymouth 51.

🏯 **King's Arms Inn,** EX6 6EG, ℰ 224, 🐕 — 🖵 🅿
  M a la carte 6.30/8.50 **st.** ⒩ 2.50 — **6 rm** ⬷ 12.00/22.50 **st.**

TEESSIDE AIRPORT Durham **402** P 20 — see Darlington.

TEIGNMOUTH Devon 403 J 32 **The West Country G.** – pop. 12,575 – ECD : Thursday – ☎ 062 67.

🛈 The Den, Sea Front ✆ 6271 ext 207/258.

♦London 216 – Exeter 16 – Torquay 8.

🏨 **London**, 24 Bank St., TQ14 8AW, ✆ 2776, ⤢ heated – 🛗 📺 ➾wc ♒wc 🅿. ⚠ AE VISA
M 5.00/8.00 t. 🍷 2.80 – **26 rm** ☵ 18.00/38.00 t. – SB (except summer and Bank Holidays) 39.00/44.00 st.

🏨 **Venn Farm Country House** (Best Western) ⌁, Higher Exeter Rd, TQ14 9PB, ✆ 2196, ≼, 🌣 – 📺 ➾wc ♒wc 🅿. ⚠ AE ⓄVISA
M (bar lunch) 8.00 t. 🍷 3.00 – **10 rm** ☵ 22.00/40.00 t. – SB 47.00/55.00 st.

⌂ **Belvedere**, 19 Barnpark Rd, TQ14 8PJ, ✆ 4561 – 🅿. ⚠
14 rm ☵ 11.00/25.20 st.

at Shaldon S : 1 m. on A 379 – ✉ Teignmouth – ☎ 062 687 Shaldon :

⌂ **Glenside**, Ringmore Rd, TQ14 0EP, W : ½ m. on B 3195 ✆ 2448 – 📺 ♒wc 🅿. ⚠ VISA
March to October – **10 rm** ☵ 8.50/23.00 st.

NISSAN 106 Bitton Park Rd ✆ 2501

TELFORD Salop 402 403 404 M 25 – pop. 96,700 – ☎ 0952.

Envir. : Ironbridge Gorge Museum★ (Iron Bridge★★) *AC*, S : 5 m. – Buildwas Abbey★ (ruins 12C) S : 7 m.

♦London 152 – ♦Birmingham 33 – Shrewsbury 12 – ♦Stoke-on-Trent 29.

🏨 **Buckatree Hall** (Best Western) ⌁, Ercall Lane, The Wrekin, Wellington, TF6 5AL, S : 1 m. off M 54 junction 7 ✆ 51821, 🌣, park – 📺 ➾wc ☎ ᵭ 🅿. 🖾 ⚠ AE ⓄVISA
M a la carte 11.40/17.40 t. 🍷 3.50 – **37 rm** ☵ 32.00/45.00 t. – SB (weekends only) 48.00 st.

🏨 **Telford Hotel, Golf and Country Club**, Great Hay, Sutton Hill, TF7 4DT, S : 5 m. by A 442 ✆ 585642, Telex 35481, ≼, 🏊, ⛳, squash – 📺 ➾wc ☎ ᵭ 🅿. 🖾 ⚠ AE ⓄVISA 🦌
M 6.90/7.90 st. 🍷 3.00 – **58 rm** ☵ 35.00/42.50 st. – SB (weekends only) 57.00/67.00 st.

🏨 **Charlton Arms**, Church St., Wellington, TF1 1DG, ✆ 51351 – 📺 ➾wc ⊕ 🅿. 🖾
27 rm

AUSTIN-ROVER-VANDEN PLAS Market St., Wellington ✆ 44896
CITROEN Holyhead Rd ✆ 617273
FIAT Trench Rd ✆ 605301

FORD Haygate Rd ✆ 42433
RENAULT Watling St. ✆ 53221
TOYOTA Wellington Rd ✆ 605616
VAUXHALL-OPEL Holyhead Rd ✆ 618081

TEMPLE SOWERBY Cumbria 401 402 M 20 – pop. 279 – ECD : Thursday – ✉ Penrith – ☎ 0930 Kirkby Thore.

♦London 297 – ♦Carlisle 31 – Kendal 38.

🏨 **Temple Sowerby House**, CA10 1RZ, ✆ 61578, 🌣 – ➾wc ☎ ᵭ 🅿. ⚠ VISA 🦌
closed 25 December to 1 January – **M** *(closed Sunday dinner to non-residents)* (dinner only and Sunday lunch) 9.50 t. 🍷 1.95 – **12 rm** ☵ 24.00/34.00 t.

🕯 **King's Arms**, CA10 1SB, ✆ 61211, ⌁, 🌣 – ➾wc
M 5.50/7.50 st. – **10 rm** ☵ 12.00/19.00 st

TENBY (DINBYCH-Y-PYSGOD) Dyfed 403 F 28 – pop. 4,994 – ECD : Wednesday – ☎ 0834.

See : Site★★.

⛳ The Burrows ✆ 2787.

🛈 Guildhall, The Norton ✆ 2402 and 3510.

♦London 247 – Carmarthen 27 – Fishguard 36.

🏨 **Imperial** (Best Western), The Paragon, SA70 7HR, ✆ 3737, ≼ sea and bay – 🛗 📺 ➾wc ♒wc ⊕ ⟷ ⚠ AE ⓄVISA
M (bar lunch Monday to Saturday) a la carte 9.00/12.50 t. – **46 rm** ☵ 26.00/65.00 t. – SB 42.00/57.00 t.

🏨 **Fourcroft**, Croft Terr., SA70 8AP, ✆ 2516, ≼, ⤢ heated, 🌣 – 🛗 📺 ➾wc. ⚠ VISA
Easter-mid October – **M** (bar lunch) 7.50 st. 🍷 2.00 – **38 rm** ☵ 14.00/34.00 st. – SB 39.00/43.00 st.

🏨 **Royal Lion**, 1 High St., SA70 7EX, ✆ 2127 – 🛗 📺 ➾wc. ⚠ VISA
closed January and February – **M** (bar lunch Monday to Saturday) 6.00 st. 🍷 3.00 – **36 rm** ☵ 14.00/23.00 st.

🏨 **Harbour Heights**, 11 Croft Terrace, SA70 8AP, ✆ 2132, ≼ – 📺 ➾wc. ⚠ AE ⓄVISA 🦌
closed December and January – **M** (bar lunch) 6.00 st. 🍷 2.20 – **10 rm** ☵ 16.75/30.00 st.

🏨 **Buckingham**, Esplanade, SA70 7DU, ✆ 2622, ≼ – ➾wc ♒wc. ⚠ AE ⓄVISA
March-October – **M** (bar lunch) 8.00 t. 🍷 2.00 – **22 rm** ☵ 11.00/31.00 t. – SB 36.00/46.00 st.

⌂ **Heywood Lodge**, Heywood Lane, SA70 8BN, ✆ 2684, 🌣 – ➾wc 🅿
Easter-October – **14 rm** ☵ 9.50/23.00 s.

AUSTIN-ROVER Greenhill Rd ✆ 2459

TENTERDEN Kent **404** W 30 – pop. 5,800 – ECD : Wednesday – ✆ 058 06.

🗓 Town Hall, High St. ☎ 3572 (summer only).

◆ London 57 – Folkestone 26 – Hastings 21 – Maidstone 19.

🏨 **White Lion,** High St., TN30 6BD, ☎ 2921 – 📺 ➪wc ℗. 🔺 AE ⑩ VISA
M 6.50/10.50 t. ⅃ 3.20 – **12 rm** ⊊ 28.75/43.00 **st.** – SB 39.50/49.50 **st.**

XX **Hookstead House** with rm, Durrant Green, High Halden, TN26 3NE, N : 3 m. on A 28 ☎ 023 385 (High Halden) 612, ⌇ heated, 🚗 – 📺 ➪wc ℗. 🔺 AE ⑩ VISA 🍴
M (booking essential) 11.50 **t.** – **4 rm** ⊊ 20.00/35.00 **t.** – SB (except summer) 40.00 **st.**

AUSTIN-ROVER High St. ☎ 4444   NISSAN St. Michaels ☎ 3413

TERN HILL Salop **402 403 404** M 25 – ✉ Market Drayton – ✆ 063 083.

◆London 161 – ◆Birmingham 44 – Chester 30 – Shrewsbury 16 – ◆Stoke-on-Trent 19.

🏨 **Tern Hill Hall** ⤫, TF9 3PU, on A 53 ☎ 310, ≼, 🚗 – 📺 ➪wc 🅗 ℗. 🔺 AE ⑩ VISA 🍴
M (closed Sunday dinner to non-residents) a la carte 6.05/10.90 **st.** ⅃ 2.10 – **11 rm** ⊊ 16.00/28.00 **st.**

In July and August, hotels are often overcrowded and staff overworked.
You will be more satisfied if you go in other months.

TETBURY Glos. **403 404** N 29 – pop. 3,461 – ECD : Thursday – ✆ 0666.

Envir. : Westonbirt Arboretum★ *AC*, SW : 3 ½ m.

⛳ Westonbirt 066 66 (Westonbirt) 242, S : 3 m.

🗓 The Old Court House, Long St. ☎ 53552 (summer only).

◆London 113 – ◆Bristol 27 – Gloucester 19 – Swindon 24.

🏨 **Snooty Fox,** Market Pl., GL8 8DD, ☎ 52436, Telex 449848 – 📺. 🔺 AE ⑩ VISA. 🍴
M 6.75/10.75 t. ⅃ 2.75 – ⊊ 3.50 – **12 rm** 35.00/60.00 **t.** – SB 57.50/65.00 **st.**

XXX **The Close** with rm, 8 Long St., GL8 8AQ, ☎ 52272, Group Telex 43232, 🚗 – 📺 ➪wc 🅗wc ⊛ ℗. 🔺 AE ⑩ VISA. 🍴
M a la carte 12.60/15.65 **st.** ⅃ 2.50 – ⊊ 3.50 – **12 rm** 30.00/69.00 **st.** – SB 61.00/80.00 **st.**

at Westonbirt SW : 2 ½ m. on A 433 – ✉ Tetbury – ✆ 066 688 Westonbirt :

🏨 **Hare and Hounds** (Best Western), GL8 8QL, ☎ 233, 🚗, park, 🍴, squash – 📺 ➪wc ⊛ ⇦℗. ⚒. 🔺 AE VISA
M 7.00/9.50 **st.** ⅃ 2.50 – **27 rm** ⊊ 20.00/47.00 **st.** – SB (except summer) 51.00/57.00 **st.**

at Calcot W : 3 ½ m. on A 4135 – ✉ Tetbury – ✆ 066 689 Leighterton :

🏨 **Calcot Manor** ⤫, GL8 8YJ, ☎ 355, ⌇ heated, 🚗 – 📺 ➪wc ☎ ℗. 🔺 AE ⑩ VISA. 🍴
M (closed Sunday dinner to non-residents) 10.50/18.50 **st.** ⅃ 2.50 – **7 rm** ⊊ 27.50/85.00 **st.** – SB (September-April) 60.00/88.00 **st.**

VW, AUDI London Rd ☎ 52473

TEWKESBURY Glos. **403 404** N 28 – pop. 8,749 – ECD : Thursday – ✆ 0684.

See : Abbey Church★ 12C-14C.

🗓 Tewkesbury Museum, 64 Barton St. ☎ 295027 (summer only).

◆London 108 – ◆Birmingham 39 – Gloucester 11.

🏨 **Royal Hop Pole** (Crest), Church St., GL20 5RT, ☎ 293236, Telex 437176, 🚗 – 📺 ➪wc ⊛ ℗. ⚒. 🔺 AE ⑩ VISA. 🍴
M approx. 13.50 **st.** – ⊊ 5.25 – **29 rm** 40.00/53.00 **st.**

🏨 **Tewkesbury Park Hotel, Golf and Country Club** ⤫, Lincoln Green Lane, GL20 7DN, S : 1 ¼ m. by A 38 ☎ 295405, Telex 43563, ≼, 📕, ⌇, park – 📺 ➪wc ☎ ℗. ⚒. 🔺 AE ⑩ VISA closed 3 days after Christmas – **M** (closed Saturday lunch) (carving lunch) 6.50/8.75 **st.** – **52 rm** ⊊ 36.00/45.00 **st.** – SB (weekends only)(except Easter and Christmas) 54.00/58.00 **st.**

🏨 **Tudor House,** 51 High St., GL20 5BH, ☎ 297755, 🚗 – 📺 ➪wc 🅗wc ⊛. 🔺 ⑩ VISA. 🍴
M (bar lunch) 7.50 t. ⅃ 2.90 – **16 rm** ⊊ 22.00/38.00 **st.**

at Corse Lawn SW : 6 m. by A 38 and A 438 on B 4211 – ✉ Gloucester – ✆ 045 278 Tirley :

XXX **Corse Lawn House** with rm, GL19 4LZ, ☎ 479, 🚗 – 📺 ➪wc ℗. 🔺 ⑩ VISA
M (closed Sunday dinner and Monday) 8.50/11.75 **st.** ⅃ 2.30 – **4 rm** ⊊ 18.50/32.50 **st.**

ALFA-ROMEO Shuthonger ☎ 293448   NISSAN Bredon ☎ 72333
AUSTIN-ROVER Gloucester Rd ☎ 293122   PEUGEOT-TALBOT Bredon Rd ☎ 297575
FORD Ashchurch Rd ☎ 292398   TALBOT Bredon Rd ☎ 293071

THAME Oxon. **404** R 28 – pop. 5,948 – ECD : Wednesday – ✆ 084 421.

See : St. Mary's Church★ 13C.

Envir. : Rycote Chapel★ (15C) *AC*, W : 3 ½ m.

🗓 Town Hall ☎ 2834.

◆London 48 – Aylesbury 9 – ◆Oxford 13.

🏨 **Spread Eagle** (Best Western), 16 Cornmarket, OX9 2BR, ℰ 3661 – 📺 ⇔wc ☎ 🅿 🛠 🔌
🝰 ⑩ 𝘝𝘐𝘚𝘈 ✄
   closed 29 and 30 December – **M** *(closed Saturday lunch)* 8.20/9.85 **st.** ⌀ 2.75 – ⇌ 3.75 –
26 rm 36.75/47.25 **st.** – SB (weekends only) 60.00 **st.**

🏚 **Jolly Sailor**, 14 Wellington St., OX9 3BN, ℰ 2682 – 📺 🅿. ✄
16 rm.

✗ **Thatchers** with rm, 29-30 Lower High St., OX9 2AA, ℰ 2146 – ⇔wc ⋔wc. 🔌 𝘝𝘐𝘚𝘈
   closed Monday lunch and Sunday – **M** a la carte 10.50/15.70 **t.** ⌀ 2.75 – **6 rm** ⇌ 29.50/39.50 **st.**

PEUGEOT-TALBOT North St. ℰ 2921   VAUXHALL-OPEL Park St. ℰ 2505

THETFORD Norfolk 𝟰𝟬𝟰 W 26 – pop. 13,727 – ECD : Wednesday – ✆ 0842.
🏌 Brandon Rd ℰ 2258.
🮲 Ancient House Museum, 21 White Hart St. ℰ 2599.
♦London 83 – ♦Cambridge 32 – ♦Ipswich 33 – King's Lynn 30 – ♦Norwich 29.

🏨 **Bell** (T.H.F.), King St., IP24 2AZ, ℰ 4455, Telex 818868 – 📺 🅿 🛠 🔌 🝰 ⑩ 𝘝𝘐𝘚𝘈
   M 6.50/8.50 **st.** ⌀ 2.60 – ⇌ 5.00 – **42 rm** 40.00/54.50 **st.**

🏛 **The Historical Thomas Paine** (Best Western), White Hart St., IP24 1AA, ℰ 5631 – 📺
⇔wc ⋔wc ☎ 🅿. 🔌 🝰 ⑩ 𝘝𝘐𝘚𝘈
   M 5.50/8.50 **st.** – **14 rm** ⇌ 25.95/37.00 **st.** – SB 44.00/48.00 **st.**

🏚 **Anchor**, Bridge St., IP24 3AE, ℰ 63925 – 📺 ⇔wc ☎ 🅿. ✄
19 rm.

AUSTIN-ROVER, LAND-ROVER Guildhall St. ℰ 4427

THIRSK North Yorks. 𝟰𝟬𝟮 P 21 – pop. 5,820 – ECD : Wednesday – ✆ 0845.
See : St. Mary's Church★ (Gothic).
Envir. : Sutton Bank (≤★★) E : 6 m. on A 170.
🮲 Thirsk Museum, 16 Kirkgate ℰ 22755 (summer only).
♦London 227 – ♦Leeds 37 – ♦Middlesbrough 24 – York 24.

🏛 **Golden Fleece** (T.H.F.), Market Pl., Y07 1LL, ℰ 23108 – 📺 ⇔wc ☎ 🅿. 🛠 🔌 🝰 ⑩ 𝘝𝘐𝘚𝘈
   M 4.25/8.50 **st.** ⌀ 2.60 – ⇌ 4.50 – **22 rm** 29.50/44.00 **st.**

AUSTIN-ROVER Long St. ℰ 23152   PEUGEOT Station Rd ℰ 22370

THORNABY-ON-TEES Cleveland 𝟰𝟬𝟮 Q 20 – pop. 4,025 – ✉ Middlesbrough.
♦London 250 – ♦Leeds 62 – ♦Middlesbrough 3 – York 49.

🏨 **Post House** (T.H.F.), Low Lane, Stainton Village, TS17 9LW, SE : 3 ½ m. by A 1045 on A 1044
   ℰ 0642 (Middlesbrough) 591213, Telex 58426 – 📺 ⇔wc ☎ 🅖. 🛠 🔌 🝰 ⑩ 𝘝𝘐𝘚𝘈
   M *(closed Sunday dinner)* a la carte 13.30/17.70 **st.** ⌀ 2.60 – ⇌ 5.00 – **136 rm** 32.00/39.50 **st.**

🏨 **Golden Eagle Thistle** (Thistle), Trenchard Av., TS17 0DA, ℰ 0642 (Stockton-on-Tees) 766511
   – 🛗 📺 ⇔wc ☎ 🅿. 🛠 🔌 🝰 ⑩ 𝘝𝘐𝘚𝘈. ✄
   ⇌ 4.75 – **54 rm** 27.00/42.00 **t.** – SB (weekends only) 44.00 **st.**

MAZDA Thornaby Pl. ℰ 63513   VAUXHALL Acklam Rd ℰ 593333

THORNAGE Norfolk – see Holt.

THORNBURY Avon 𝟰𝟬𝟯 𝟰𝟬𝟰 M 29 The West Country G. – pop. 9,900 – ECD : Thursday –
✉ Bristol – ✆ 0454.
♦London 128 – ♦Bristol 12 – Gloucester 23 – Swindon 43.

🏰 **Thornbury Castle** 🍃, Castle St., BS12 1HH, ℰ 412647, Telex 449986, « 16C castle », 🐎,
   park – 📺 ☎ 🅿. 🔌 🝰 ⑩ 𝘝𝘐𝘚𝘈 ✄
   closed 5 days at Christmas – **M** 17.50/a la carte 21.00/23.00 **st.** ⌀ 3.00 – ⇌ a la carte approx.
   3.50 – **12 rm** 40.00/115.00 **st.**

THORNTON West Yorks. 𝟰𝟬𝟮 O 22 – see Bradford.

THORNTON HOUGH Merseyside 𝟰𝟬𝟮 𝟰𝟬𝟯 K 24 – ✉ Wirral – ✆ 051 Liverpool.
♦London 208 – Chester 12 – ♦Liverpool 13.

🏨 Thornton Hall, Neston Rd, Wirral, L63 1JF, ℰ 336 3938, 🐎 – 📺 ⇔wc ☎ 🅿. ✄
36 rm.

This Guide is not a comprehensive list of all hotels and restaurants,
nor even of all good hotels and restaurants in Great Britain and Ireland.

Since our aim is to be of service to all motorists,
we must show establishments in all categories and so we have made a
selection of some in each.

THORPE Derbs. 402 403 404 O 24 – pop. 161 – ⊠ Ashbourne – ✪ 033 529 Thorpe Cloud.

Envir. : N : Dovedale (valley)⋆⋆ – Ashbourne (St. Oswald's Church⋆ 13C) SE : 3 m.

🅂 at Ashbourne ☞ 0335 (Ashbourne) 42078, SE : 5 m.

♦London 151 – Derby 16 – ♦Sheffield 33 – ♦Stoke-on-Trent 26.

 🏨 **Izaak Walton** ⤳, Dovedale, DE6 2AY, W : 1 m. ☞ 261, ≤ Dovedale, ⤳, 🚗 – 📺 🛏wc ☏
  🅿 🅐 🔼 AE VISA
  M 7.80/10.50 st. ⏱ 3.00 – **27 rm** � 32.00/49.50 st. – SB 56.00/65.00 st.

 🏨 **Peveril of the Peak** (T.H.F.) ⤳, Dovedale, DE6 2AW, ☞ 333, ≤, 🚗, ⅌ – 📺 🛏wc ☏ 🅿.
  🅐 🔼 AE ① VISA
  M 6.95/8.75 st. ⏱ 2.60 – ⊒ 5.00 – **41 rm** 32.50/42.00 st.

THORPE LE SOKEN Essex 404 X 28 – pop. 1,666 – ⊠ ✪ 0255 Clacton-on-Sea.

♦London 68 – Colchester 13 – ♦Ipswich 28.

 ✗ **Loblollies,** High St., CO16 0DY, ☞ 861616 – 🅿 🔼 VISA
  closed 25 and 26 December – **M** a la carte 8.75/13.00 t. ⏱ 3.00.

THORPE ST. ANDREW Norfolk 404 Y 26 – see Norwich.

THORVERTON Devon 403 J 31 – pop. 709 – ⊠ ✪ 0392 Exeter.

♦London 200 – Exeter 9 – Taunton 33.

 ☝ **Berribridge House** ⤳, EX5 5JR, S : ½ m. ☞ 860259, 🚗 – 🛏wc 🅿. ⅌
  M approx. 8.50 t. ⏱ 3.50 – **6 rm** ⊒ 18.00/40.00 t. – SB (July-October) 40.00/48.00 st.

THREE COCKS (ABERLLYNFI) Powys 403 K 27 – pop. 221 – ⊠ Brecon – ✪ 049 74 Glasbury.

♦London 184 – Brecon 11 – Hereford 25 – ♦Swansea 55.

 ✗✗ **Three Cocks** with rm, LD3 0SL, on A 438 ☞ 215, 🚗 – 🅿 🔼 AE ① VISA
  closed January – **M** (dinner only) 12.75 ⏱ 3.55 – **7 rm** ⊒ 15.50/31.00 st. – SB 25.50/26.75 st.

THURLESTONE Devon 403 I 33 – see Kingsbridge.

THURSTASTON Merseyside 402 403 K 23 – pop. 15,196 – ⊠ West Kirby – ✪ 051 Liverpool.

♦London 226 – Birkenhead 6 – Chester 15 – ♦Liverpool 9 – ♦Manchester 51.

 ✗✗ Cottage Loaf, Telegraph Rd, LA8 0RB, on A 540 ☞ 648 1635 – 🅿.

TICKTON Humberside – see Beverley.

TILBURY Essex 404 V 29 – pop. 11,130 – ✪ 037 52.

⛴ Shipping connections with the Continent : to USSR (Leningrad) via Norway (Oslo) and Denmark (Copenhagen) (Baltic Shipping Co.).

⛴ to Gravesend (Sealink) frequent services daily (5 mn).

♦London 24 – Southend-on-Sea 20.

  Hotels and restaurants see : London W : 24 m.

TIMPERLEY Greater Manchester 402 ② 403 ③ 404 ⑨ – see Altrincham.

TINTAGEL Cornwall 403 F 32 The West Country G. – pop. 1,372 – ECD : Wednesday except summer – ✪ 0840 Camelford.

See : Arthur's Castle : site⋆⋆⋆ – Tintagel Church⋆ – Old Post Office⋆.

Envir. : Delabole Quarry⋆, SE : 4 m. by B 3263 – Camelford⋆, SE : 6 m. by B 3263 and B 3266.

♦London 264 – Exeter 63 – ♦Plymouth 49 – Truro 41.

 🏨 **Atlantic View,** Treknow, PL34 0EJ, S : 1 m. by B 3263 ☞ 770221, ≤, ⤲ heated, 🚗 – 🛏wc
  🛏wc 🅿 🔼 AE ① VISA
  April-September – **M** (bar lunch) 9.00 st. ⏱ 3.20 – **10 rm** ⊒ 18.00/34.00 st. – SB (except summer) 40.00/46.00 st.

 🏨 **Bossiney House,** Bossiney, PL34 0AX, NE : ½ m. on B 3263 ☞ 770240, 🔲, 🚗 – 🛏wc
  🛏wc 🅿. AE ①
  Easter-October – **M** (bar lunch) 7.00 st. ⏱ 1.50 – **20 rm** ⊒ 13.65/33.00 st. – SB 38.00/41.00 st.

 ☝ **Trewarmett Lodge,** Trewarmett, PL34 0ET, SW : 1 ½ m. on B 3263 ☞ 770460, ≤, 🚗 – 🅿.
  🔼 ① VISA
  M 6.50/7.50 st. ⏱ 2.70 – **6 rm** ⊒ 11.00/24.00 t. – SB 31.00/36.00 st.

 ✗ **Mill House Inn** with rm, Trebarwith, PL34 0HD, S : 1 ¼ m. by B 3263 via Treknow ☞ 770200,
  « Former corn mill » – 📺 🛏wc 🛏wc 🅿
  closed 24 December-2 January – **M** (bar lunch) a la carte 7.40/11.00 t. ⏱ 2.25 – **9 rm** ⊒ 17.00/34.20 t. – SB (spring only) 36.00 st.

TINTERN (TYNDYRN) Gwent 403 404 L 28 – pop. 647 – ECD : Wednesday – ⊠ Chepstow – ☏ 029 18.

See : Abbey★★ (ruins) *AC*.

🛈 Tintern Abbey ⌀ 431 (summer only).

◆London 137 – ◆Bristol 23 – Gloucester 40 – Newport 22.

- 🏨 **Beaufort** (Embassy), NP6 6SF, ⌀ 202, ⇗ – 📺 ⇱wc �wc ☎ 🅿. 🅰. 🔼 ᴀᴇ ⓞ 𝗩𝗜𝗦𝗔. ℅
  M 6.25/8.50 **st.** ⓐ 4.00 – **25 rm** ⇌ 28.00/44.00 **st.** – SB 40.00/50.00 **st.**

- 🏨 **Royal George**, NP6 6SF, ⌀ 205, ⇗ – 📺 ⇱wc ☜ 🅿. 🔼 ᴀᴇ 𝗩𝗜𝗦𝗔
  M (buffet lunch) 6.50/8.25 **st.** ⓐ 2.50 – **19 rm** ⇌ 26.00/54.00 **t.** – SB 57.00 **st.**

- ⌂ **Parva Farmhouse**, NP6 6SQ, on A 466 ⌀ 411 – ⇱wc 🅿
  7 rm ⇌ 12.50/24.00 **st.**

TITCHWELL Norfolk 404 V 25 – pop. 131 – ⊠ King's Lynn – ☏ 048 521 Brancaster.

◆London 124 – ◆Cambridge 66 – ◆Norwich 41.

- 🏠 **Titchwell Manor** (Best Western), PE31 8BB, on A 149 ⌀ 210221, ⇗ – ⇱wc 🅿. 🔼 ᴀᴇ ⓞ 𝗩𝗜𝗦𝗔
  closed 24 to 30 December – **M** (booking essential)(bar lunch) a la carte 6.35/9.65 **t.** ⓐ 2.70 –
  10 rm ⇌ 17.75/39.40 **t.**

Red Lion	If the name of the hotel is not in bold type, on arrival ask the hotelier his prices.

TIVERTON Devon 403 J 31 The West Country G. – pop. 15,566 – ECD : Thursday – ☏ 0884.

See : Museum★.

Envir. : Knightshayes Court★, N : 2 m. on A 396 – Coldharbour Mill, Uffculme★, W : 11 m. by A 373.

🛈 Tiverton Museum, St. Andrew's St. ⌀ 256295 and 255446.

◆London 190 – Exeter 14 – Taunton 23.

- 🏨 **Tiverton**, Blundells Rd, EX16 4DB, E : ½ m. on A 373 ⌀ 256120 – 🍽 rest 📺 ⇱wc ☜ 🅿. 🅰. 🔼 ᴀᴇ ⓞ 𝗩𝗜𝗦𝗔
  M 4.95/7.75 **st.** ⓐ 2.95 – **29 rm** ⇌ 18.00/40.00 **st.** – SB (June to September) 42.00/48.00 **st.**

- ✗ **Hendersons**, 18 Newport St., EX16 6NL, ⌀ 254256 – 🔼 ᴀᴇ 𝗩𝗜𝗦𝗔
  closed Sunday and 4 days at Christmas – **M** a la carte 9.65/13.60 **t.** ⓐ 3.00.

  at Oakfordbridge NW : 9 m. on A 396 – ⊠ Tiverton – ☏ 039 85 Oakford :

- 🏠 Bark House, EX16 9HZ, ⌀ 236 – ⇱wc 填wc 🅿. 🔼 ᴀᴇ ⓞ 𝗩𝗜𝗦𝗔
  closed January and February – ⇌ 2.00 – **6 rm** 16.00/26.00 **st.**
  ⓐ 3.00.

CITRÖEN 31 Leat St. ⌀ 252170

TONBRIDGE Kent 404 U 30 – pop. 32,890 – ECD : Wednesday – ☏ 0732.

See : Tonbridge School★ (1553).

Envir. : Ightham Mote★ (Manor House 14C-15C) *AC*, site★ N : 7 m.

🛅 Poult Wood, Higham Lane ⌀ 364039, N : 2 m. by A 227.

◆London 33 – ◆Brighton 37 – Hastings 31 – Maidstone 14.

- 🏨 **Rose and Crown** (T.H.F.), 125 High St., TN9 1DD, ⌀ 357966, ⇗ – 📺 ⇱wc ☜ 🅿. 🅰. 🔼 ᴀᴇ ⓞ 𝗩𝗜𝗦𝗔
  M 6.75/7.25 **st.** ⓐ 2.60 – ⇌ 4.50 – **52 rm** 32.50/44.50 **st.**

- ✗✗ **Winch**, 160 High St., TN9 1BB, ⌀ 366755 – 🔼 ᴀᴇ ⓞ 𝗩𝗜𝗦𝗔
  closed Sunday, first week January, 9 to 31 August and Bank Holidays – **M** a la carte 9.40/14.65 **t.**
  ⓐ 3.00.

ALFA-ROMEO, PEUGEOT-TALBOT Sovereign Way ⌀ 350288
AUSTIN-ROVER, DAIMLER-JAGUAR Cannon Lane ⌀ 364444
FORD Avebury Av. ⌀ 356301

RENAULT London Rd, Hildenborough ⌀ 832022
VAUXHALL Waterloo Rd ⌀ 354035
VOLVO Hildenborough ⌀ 832424
VW, AUDI-NSU, MERCEDES-BENZ Vale Rd ⌀ 355822

TORQUAY Devon 403 J 32 The West Country G. – pop. 109,257 (inc Brixham and Paignton) – ECD : Wednesday and Saturday – ☏ 0803.

See : Kent's Cavern★ CX A.

⛴ to Channel Islands : Alderney (Torbay Seaways) summer only 1 weekly (5 h) – to Channel Islands : St. Peter Port, Guernsey (Torbay Seaways) summer only 2 weekly (5-8 h).

🛈 Vaughan Parade ⌀ 27428.

◆London 223 – Exeter 23 – ◆Plymouth 32.

Plans on following pages

Imperial (T.H.F.), Park Hill Rd, TQ1 2DG, ☏ 24301, Telex 42849, ≤ Torbay, ⤳ heated, ☒, ⇛, ⋇ – 🛗 TV ☎ ⅙ ⟵ 🅿 🏠 ☒ AE ① VISA — CZ **a**
M 13.00/19.00 st. ⅙ 3.50 – ⌷ 6.00 – **164 rm** 43.50/87.00 st.

Palace, Babbacombe Rd, TQ1 3TG, ☏ 22271, Telex 42606, ⤳ heated, ☒, ⅌, ⇛, ⋇, squash – 🛗 TV ⟵ 🅿 🏠 ☒ AE ① VISA — CX **u**
M 6.00/12.00 st. ⌷ 32.00/68.00 st. – SB (except Bank Holidays) 52.00/58.00 st.

Homers, Warren Rd, TQ2 5TN, ☏ 213456, ≤ Torbay – TV ⇌wc 🍽wc ☎. ☒ AE ① VISA
closed January and February – **M** 8.00/13.00 t. ⅙ 2.95 – **14 rm** ⌷ 23.00/39.00 t. – SB 48.00/56.00 st. — CZ **n**

Livermead House (Best Western), Sea Front, TQ2 6QJ, ☏ 24361, Telex 42918, ≤, ⤳ heated, ⇛, ⋇, squash – 🛗 🍽 rest TV ⇌wc 🍽wc 🅿 🏠 ☒ AE ① VISA ⅌ — BZ **e**
M 5.50/8.00 st. ⅙ 2.95 – **72 rm** ⌷ 15.50/48.00 st. – SB 27.00/34.00 st.

Livermead Cliff (Best Western), Sea Front, TQ2 6RQ, ☏ 22881, Telex 42918, ≤, ⤳ heated, ⇛ – 🛗 🍽 rest TV ⇌wc 🅿 🏠 ☒ AE ① VISA ⅌ — BX **r**
M 5.50/8.00 st. ⅙ 2.95 – **62 rm** ⌷ 15.50/49.00 st. – SB 27.50/35.00 st.

Toorak, Chestnut Av., TQ2 5JS, ☏ 211866, ⤳ heated, ⇛, ⋇ – TV ⇌wc 🅿 🏠 ☒ — BY **v**
M 6.00/9.50 st. ⅙ 1.95 – **41 rm** ⌷ 16.50/32.50 st. – SB 23.50/38.75 st.

Kistor, Belgrave Rd, TQ2 5HF, ☏ 23219, ☒, ⇛ – 🛗 TV ⇌wc 🅿 🏠 ☒ AE ① VISA — CY **r**
M (buffet lunch) 5.15/8.00 st. ⅙ 2.40 – **52 rm** ⌷ 18.00/48.00 st. – SB 41.00/56.00 st.

Belgrave, Seafront, Belgrave Rd, TQ2 5HE, ☏ 28566, ⤳ heated, ⇛ – 🛗 🍽 rest TV ⇌wc ☎ 🅿 🏠 ☒ AE ① VISA — CZ **c**
M (buffet lunch) 6.50 t. – **54 rm** ⌷ 18.50/49.00 t.

Nepaul, 27 Croft Rd, TQ2 5UD, ☏ 28457, ≤, ☒, ⇛, ⋇ – 🛗 TV ⇌wc 🍽wc ⟵ 🅿 ☒ AE ① VISA — CY **v**
M 4.50/8.50 st. ⅙ 2.80 – **41 rm** ⌷ 16.50/44.00 st. – SB (except summer) 38.00/45.00 st.

Gleneagles, Asheldon Rd, Wellswood, TQ1 2QS, ☏ 23637, ≤, ⤳ heated, ⇛ – ⇌wc 🅿 ☒ AE ① VISA — CX **n**
May-October – **M** (bar lunch) 8.50 t. ⅙ 2.30 – **40 rm** ⌷ 17.00/38.00 t. – SB (spring and autumn only) 39.00/43.00 st.

Glenorleigh, 26 Cleveland Rd, TQ2 5BE, ☏ 22135, ⤳ heated, ⇛ – 🍽wc 🅿 ⅌ — BY **n**
closed Christmas – **M** (bar lunch Monday to Friday) 4.50 t. ⅙ 2.75 – **16 rm** ⌷ 11.50/34.50 st. – SB (winter only) 20.70 st.

Nethway, Falkland Rd, TQ2 5JR, ☏ 27630, ⤳ heated, ⇛ – ⇌wc 🍽wc 🅿 VISA — BY **u**
April-October and Christmas – **M** (bar lunch) 5.95 t. ⅙ 1.95 – **26 rm** ⌷ 12.85/35.40 t. – SB (except summer) 31.40/35.60 st.

Fairmount House ⌂, Herbert Rd, Chelston, TQ2 6RW, ☏ 605446, ⇛ – ⇌wc 🍽wc 🅿 AE VISA — AX **a**
March-mid November – **7 rm** ⌷ 10.00/24.00 t.

Clevedon, Meadfoot Sea Rd, TQ1 2LQ, ☏ 24260, ⇛ – 🅿 ⅌ — CX **v**
April-October – **16 rm** ⌷ 8.75/28.00 st.

Cranborne, 58 Belgrave Rd, TQ2 5HY, ☏ 28046 – ⇌wc 🍽 ☒ VISA ⅌ — BY **i**
15 rm ⌷ 6.50/23.00 st.

Concorde, 26 Newton Rd, TQ2 5BZ, ☏ 22330, ⤳ heated – 🍽 🅿 — BY **e**
Easter-mid October – **16 rm** ⌷ 7.50/15.00 st.

Elmsdale, 70 Avenue Rd, TQ2 5LF, ☏ 25929 – 🍽wc 🅿 VISA — BY **a**
7 rm ⌷ 7.00/15.00 s.

Mount Nessing, St. Lukes Rd North, TQ2 5PD, ☏ 22970 – 🅿 ⅌ — CZ **i**
Easter-October and Christmas – **13 rm** ⌷ 7.00/14.00 t.

at **Maidencombe** N : 3 ½ m. on A 379 – BX – ✉ ☎ 0803 Torquay :

Orestone House ⌂, Rockhouse Lane, TQ1 4SX, ☏ 38099, ≤, ⤳ heated, ⇛ – TV ⇌wc 🍽wc 🅿 ☒ AE ① VISA ⅌
March-November and Christmas – **M** 4.95/7.95 t. ⅙ 2.60 – **20 rm** ⌷ 22.00/55.00 t. – SB (except summer) 43.00/49.00 st.

at **Babbacombe** NE : 1 ½ m. – ✉ ☎ 0803 Torquay :

Norcliffe, 7 Babbacombe Downs Rd, TQ1 3LF, ☏ 38456, ≤, ⇛ – TV ⇌wc 🍽 🅿 ☒ VISA — CX **r**
M (bar lunch) 7.00 ⅙ 1.45 – **22 rm** ⌷ 10.50/31.00 st.

Green Mantle, 135 Babbacombe Rd, TQ1 3SR, ☏ 34292 – AE ① VISA — CX **a**
closed Sunday dinner and 2 weeks November – **M** (dinner only) a la carte 8.00/12.00 t. ⅙ 2.25.

AUDI, VW Torwood St. ☏ 24347
AUSTIN-ROVER Lawes Bridge ☏ 62781
CITROEN Walnut Rd ☏ 605858
FORD Lawes Bridge, Newton Rd ☏ 62021
NISSAN 50 Torwood St. ☏ 28555

PEUGEOT-TALBOT 141 Newton Rd ☏ 63626
ROLLS ROYCE-BENTLEY, FERRARI, SAAB Lisburne Sq. ☏ 24321
VAUXHALL Brunswick Sq., Torre ☏ 22287

Do not lose your way in Europe, use the Michelin
Main Road maps, scale : 1 inch : 16 miles.

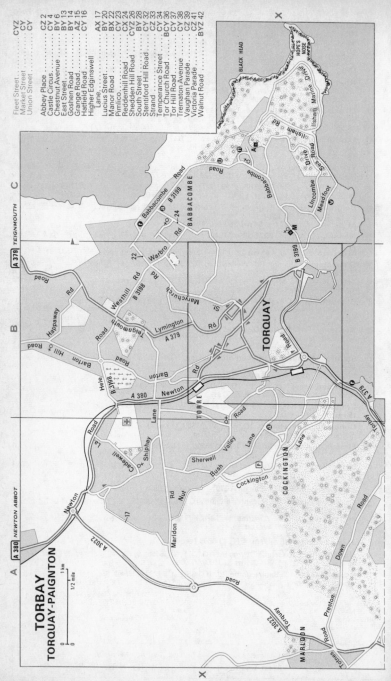

TORBAY
TORQUAY-PAIGNTON

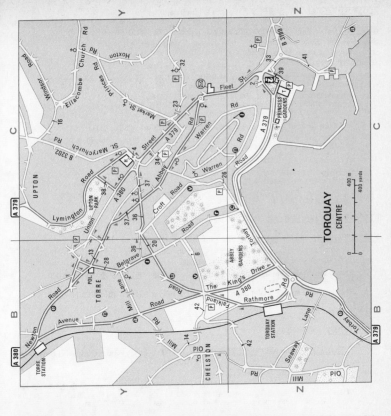

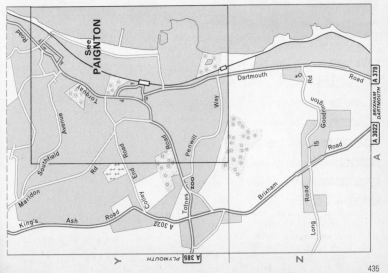

TOTLAND BAY I.O.W. 403 404 P 31 – see Wight (Isle of).

TOTNES Devon 403 I 32 **The West Country G.** – pop. 5,772 – ECD : Thursday – ✆ 0803.
See : Site★★ – St. Mary's Church★ – Butterwalk★ – Castle (≤ ★★★).
🛈 The Plains ℘ 863168 (summer only).
◆London 224 – Exeter 24 – ◆Plymouth 23 – Torquay 9.

- 🏨 **Royal Seven Stars,** The Plains, TQ9 5DD, ℘ 862125 – 📺 ⌂wc 🅿 🔌 🅰🅴 ⓓ 𝘝𝘐𝘚𝘈
  M 6.00/9.00 t. 🍷 2.50 – **18 rm** ⱬ 20.00/38.00 t.
- ✕✕ **Elbow Room,** 6 North St., TQ9 5NZ, ℘ 863480 – 🅰🅴 𝘝𝘐𝘚𝘈
  closed Saturday lunch, Tuesday dinner, Sunday, Monday, 2 weeks February, 2 weeks November
  and Bank Holidays – **M** (restricted lunch) a la carte 10.30/13.65 t.

  at Stoke Gabriel SE : 4 m. by A 385 – ⌧ Totnes – ✆ 080 428 Stoke Gabriel :

- 🏨 **Gabriel Court** 🕭, TQ9 6SF, ℘ 206, 🌊 heated, 🐾, 🎾 – ⌂wc 🎇wc 🅿 🔌 🅰🅴 ⓓ 𝘝𝘐𝘚𝘈
  M 5.50/10.50 st. 🍷 3.00 – **24 rm** ⱬ 19.50/39.00 st.

  at Dartington NW : 2 m. by A 385 – ⌧ ✆ 0803 Totnes :

- ⚐ **Cott Inn,** TQ9 6HE, ℘ 863777 – 🅿 🔌 🅰🅴 ⓓ 𝘝𝘐𝘚𝘈
  M (buffet lunch) a la carte 6.75/8.55 t. – **6 rm** ⱬ 25.00/32.00 t. – SB 42.50 **st.**

AUSTIN-ROVER Station Rd ℘ 862404
FORD North St. ℘ 862196   VAUXHALL-OPEL The Plains ℘ 862247

TOTON Notts. 402 403 404 Q 25 – see Nottingham.

TOWCESTER Northants. 403 404 R 27 – pop. 3,768 – ✆ 0327.
🏌 Woodlands, Farthingstone ℘ 36291, W : 6 m. M 1 Junction 16.
◆London 70 – ◆Birmingham 50 – Northampton 9 – ◆Oxford 36.

- ⚐ **Brave Old Oak,** Watling St. East, NN12 7BT, ℘ 50533 – 📺 🎇 ☎ 🅿 🔌 🅰🅴 ⓓ 𝘝𝘐𝘚𝘈
  M (carving lunch) 8.00 **t.** – **12 rm** ⱬ 17.50/38.00 **t.**
- ⚐ **Saracen's Head,** 219 Watling St. West, NN12 7BX, ℘ 50414 – 🅿 🔌 🅰🅴 ⓓ 𝘝𝘐𝘚𝘈
  M 4.75/6.75 t. 🍷 2.60 – **12 rm** ⱬ 17.00/26.00 t.

AUSTIN-ROVER Quinbury End ℘ 0327 (Blakesley) 860208

TRALLWNG = Welshpool.

TREARDDUR BAY Gwynedd 402 403 G 24 – pop. 1,000 – ECD : Wednesday – ⌧ Holyhead –
✆ 0407.
See : Site★ – ◆London 270 – Holyhead 2.

- 🏨 **Trearddur Bay,** LL65 2UN, ℘ 860301, Telex 61609, 🏊, 🐾 – 📺 ⌂wc ☎ 🅿 🔌 🅰🅴 ⓓ 𝘝𝘐𝘚𝘈
  M (bar lunch Monday to Saturday in winter) 5.50/7.50 **st.** 🍷 3.00 – ⱬ 4.00 – **28 rm** 14.00/34.00 **st.**
  – SB (weekends only)(except Easter, August and Christmas) 35.00/50.00 **st.**

TREBETHERICK Cornwall 403 F 32 – pop. 510 – ECD : Wednesday – ⌧ Wadebridge –
✆ 020 886.
◆London 286 – Newquay 22 – ◆Plymouth 46 – Truro 32.

- 🏨 **Bodare** 🕭, Daymer Lane, PL27 6SA, ℘ 3210, 🐾 – ⌂wc 🎇wc 🅿 🔌 𝘝𝘐𝘚𝘈
  April-mid October – **M** (buffet lunch) 7.00 **s.** – **19 rm** ⱬ 12.50/39.50 **s.**

TREDETHY Cornwall – see Bodmin.

TREFDRAETH = Newport (Dyfed).

TREFFYNNON = Holywell.

TREFYNWY = Monmouth.

TREGREHAN Cornwall 403 F 32 – see St. Austell.

TRESCO Cornwall 403 ㉚ – see Scilly (Isles of).

TREYARNON BAY Cornwall 403 E 32 – see Padstow.

TRING Herts. 404 S 28 – pop. 7,790 – ECD : Wednesday – ✆ 044 282.
See : Church of St. Peter and St. Paul (interior : stone corbels★).
◆London 38 – Aylesbury 7 – Luton 14.

- 🏨 **Rose and Crown,** High St., HP23 5AH, ℘ 4071 – 📺 ⌂wc ☎ 🅿 🦽 🔌 🅰🅴 ⓓ 𝘝𝘐𝘚𝘈
  M 4.30/9.80 t. – **16 rm** ⱬ 25.00/43.00 **st.** – SB (weekends only) 40.00/44.00 **st.**

HONDA, RELIANT 110 Western Rd ℘ 4144   MAZDA 22 Western Rd ℘ 3027

TROTTON West Sussex – see Midhurst.

TROUTBECK Cumbria 402 L 20 – see Windermere.

TROWBRIDGE Wilts. 403 404 N 30 – pop. 23,123 – ECD : Wednesday – ✆ 022 14.
♦London 115 – ♦Bristol 27 – ♦Southampton 55 – Swindon 32.

　🏨 **Hilbury Court,** Hilperton Rd, BA14 7JW, ✆ 2949, 🚗 – 📺 🛁wc 🅿. 🔼 VISA 🛇
　　closed 25 and 26 December – **M** *(closed Saturday, Sunday and Bank Holidays)* (bar lunch)
　　7.50 **st.** 🍸 2.20 – **12 rm** ⌚ 17.00/29.00 **st.**

TRURO Cornwall 403 E 33 The West Country G. – pop. 14,849 – ECD : Thursday – ✆ 0872.
See : Cornwall Country Museum★.
Envir. : Trewithen★★★, NE : 7 ½ m. by A 390 – Trelissick garden★★, S : 8 m. by A 39 and B 3289.
🛝 Treliske ✆ 2640, W : 2 m. on A 390.
🮲 Municipal Building, Boscawen St. ✆ 74555.
♦London 295 – Exeter 87 – Penzance 26 – ♦Plymouth 52.

　🏨 **Royal,** Lemon St., TR1 2QB, ✆ 70345 – 📺 🛁wc 🅿. 🏌 🔼 VISA
　　closed Christmas – **M** *(closed Sunday lunch)* (grill rest. only) 4.75 **st.** 🍸 2.80 – **34 rm**
　　⌚ 21.50/38.50 **st.** – SB (weekends only) 39.50 **st.**

　🏨 **Brookdale,** Tregolls Rd, TR1 1JZ, ✆ 73513 – 📺 🛁wc 🚿wc 🅿. 🔼 AE ⓞ VISA
　　closed Christmas – **M** 5.00/9.50 **st.** 🍸 2.25 – **43 rm** ⌚ 17.00/38.00 **s.**

　🏨 **Carlton,** 49 Falmouth Rd, TR1 2HL, ✆ 72450 – 📺 🛁wc 🚿wc 🅿. 🔼 VISA
　　closed 20 December to 5 January – **M** *(closed Sunday dinner)* (dinner only) 4.95 **st.** 🍸 2.30 –
　　25 rm ⌚ 14.75/28.60 **st.**

　　at Deveron SW : 4 ½ m. by A 39 – ✉ ✆ 0872 Truro :

　↑ **Driffold** 🌭, 8 Deveron Lane, TR3 6PA, ✆ 863314, 🚗 – 🚿wc 🅿. 🛇
　　7 rm ⌚ 8.00/31.00 **t.**

AUSTIN-ROVER Newquay Rd ✆ 72581　　　　　TALBOT Bissoe ✆ 0872 (Devoran) 863073
FORD Lemon Quay ✆ 73933　　　　　　　　　VAUXHALL Fairmantle St. ✆ 76231
RENAULT Lemon Quay ✆ 74321　　　　　　　　VW, AUDI Three Milestone ✆ 79301

TUDWEILIOG Gwynedd 402 403 G 25 – ✉ Pwllheli – ✆ 075 887.
♦London 267 – Caernarfon 25.

　✗ **Dive Inn,** LL53 8PB, W : 2 m. by B 4417 ✆ 246, Seafood – 🅿
　　closed Sunday and Monday to Friday from November to Easter – **M** (bar lunch) 13.50 **t.** 🍸 2.75.

TUNBRIDGE WELLS Kent 404 U 30 – see Royal Tunbridge Wells.

TURVEY Beds. 404 S 27 – see Bedford.

TUTBURY Staffs. 402 403 404 O 25 – pop. 3,025 – ECD : Wednesday – ✉ ✆ 0283 Burton-
upon-Trent.
♦London 132 – ♦Birmingham 33 – Derby 11 – ♦Stoke-on-Trent 27.

　🏨 **Ye Olde Dog and Partridge Inn,** High St., DE13 9LS, ✆ 813030, « Part 15C timbered inn »,
　　🚗 – 📺 🛁wc 🚿wc ☎ 🅿. 🔼 AE VISA 🛇
　　closed 25-26 December and 1 January – **M** (carving lunch Monday, Saturday and Sunday)
　　7.00/12.00 **t.** 🍸 3.30 – **18 rm** ⌚ 30.00/40.00 **t.**

TUXFORD Notts. 402 404 R 24 – pop. 2,145 – ECD : Wednesday – ✉ Newark – ✆ 0777.
♦London 141 – ♦Leeds 53 – Lincoln 18 – ♦Nottingham 26 – ♦Sheffield 29.

　🏨 **Newcastle Arms,** Market Place, NG22 0LA, ✆ 870208 – 📺 🛁wc 🚿wc 🍽 🅿. 🔼 AE ⓞ
　　VISA
　　M a la carte 8.40/12.00 **t.** 🍸 3.00 – **14 rm** ⌚ 28.00/40.00 **t.** – SB 42.00 **st.**

TWEMLOW GREEN Cheshire 402 403 404 N 24 – see Holmes Chapel.

TWO BRIDGES Devon 403 I 32 The West Country G. – pop. 30 – ✉ Yelverton – ✆ 0822 Tavistock.
♦London 226 – Exeter 25 – ♦Plymouth 17.

　↑ **Cherrybrook** 🌭, PL20 6SP, NE : 1 m. on B 3212 ✆ 88260, ≤, 🚗 – 🚿wc 🅿
　　closed Christmas and New Year – **8 rm** ⌚ 11.00/25.00 **st.**

TYDDEWI = St. David's.

TYNDYRN = Tintern.

TYNEMOUTH Tyne and Wear **401 402** P 18 – pop. 69,338 – ECD : Wednesday – ✆ 0632 North Shields.

See : Priory and castle : ruins★ (11C) *AC* – ◆London 290 – ◆Newcastle-upon-Tyne 8 – Sunderland 7.

🏨 **Park,** Grand Par., NE30 4JQ, ℘ 571406, ≼ – 📺 ➡wc ➥ ➋ 👍 🔼 🅰🅴 ⓞ 𝘝𝘐𝘚𝘈.
M 6.65/7.40 st. ⅄ 2.65 – **27 rm** ⴻ 19.50/36.50 **st.** – SB (weekends only)(summer only) 44.00 **st.**

VAUXHALL Tynemouth Rd ℘ 570346

UCKFIELD East Sussex **404** U 31 – pop. 5,973 – ECD : Wednesday – ✆ 0825.
Envir. : Sheffield Park Gardens★★ *AC*, W : 6 m.

◆London 45 – ◆Brighton 17 – Eastbourne 20 – Maidstone 34.

🏨 **Ye Maiden's Head,** High St., ℘ 2019, Telex 957141 – 📺 ➡wc ➋. 🔼 🅰🅴 ⓞ 𝘝𝘐𝘚𝘈. ⚘
M (buffet lunch) 5.00/7.00 **t.** ⅄ 2.30 – **13 rm** ⴻ 15.50/35.00 **t.** – SB 39.50/42.00 **st.**

at Framfield SE : 1 ¾ m. on B 2102 – ✉ Uckfield – ✆ 082 582 Framfield :

✗ **Coach House,** The Street, TN22 5NL, ℘ 636, 🔥 heated – ➋. 🔼 🅰🅴 ⓞ
closed Tuesday lunch, Sunday dinner and Monday – **M** a la carte 9.60/13.10 **t.** ⅄ 3.60.

AUSTIN-ROVER 84/86 High St. ℘ 4255
FORD 143/145 High St. ℘ 4722
PEUGEOT-TALBOT Five Ash Down ℘ 082 581 (Buxted) 3220

RENAULT Blackboys ℘ 082 582 (Framfield) 317
VAUXHALL-OPEL Maresfield ℘ 2477

ULLSWATER Cumbria **402** L 20 – ✉ Penrith – ✆ 085 36 Pooley Bridge.
See : Lake★.

🛈 Main Car Park, Glenridding ℘ 085 32 (Glenridding) 414 (summer only) – at Pooley Bridge, Eusemere Car Park ℘ 530 (summer only).

◆London 296 – ◆Carlisle 25 – Kendal 31 – Penrith 6.

at Pooley Bridge on B 5320 – ✉ Penrith – ✆ 085 36 Pooley Bridge :

🏨 **Howtown** ⌛, CA10 2ND, S : 4 m. ℘ 514, ≼, ⋈ – ➋. ⚘
26 March-October – **M** (buffet lunch Monday to Saturday) 4.75/6.75 **t.** ⅄ 2.00 – **16 rm** ⴻ 15.00/30.00 **t.**

✗✗✗ **Sharrow Bay Country House** ⌛ with rm, CA10 2LZ, S : 2 m. on Howtown Rd ℘ 301, ≼ lake and hills, « Lake-side setting, tasteful decor », ⋈ – 📺 ➡wc ☎ ➋. ⚘
7 March-November – **M** 16.50/23.50 **st.** – **29 rm** ⴻ (dinner included) 50.00/144.00 **st.**

at Watermillock on A 592 – ✉ Penrith – ✆ 085 36 Pooley Bridge :

🏛 **Leeming on Ullswater Country House** ⌛, CA11 0JJ, on A 592 ℘ 622, ≼ lake, hills and gardens, « Elegant installation and gardens », park – ➓. ➋. 🔼 🅰🅴 ⓞ 𝘝𝘐𝘚𝘈. ⚘
closed January and February – **M** (buffet lunch Monday to Saturday) 6.00/16.75 **t.** – ⴻ 4.00 – **25 rm** 30.00/64.00 **t.**

at Glenridding on A 592 – ✉ Penrith – ✆ 085 32 Glenridding :

🏨 **Glenridding** (Best Western), CA11 0PB, on A 592 ℘ 228, ≼, ⋈ – ➡wc 🔥wc ➋. 🔼 🅰🅴 ⓞ 𝘝𝘐𝘚𝘈
M (buffet lunch) 9.00 **st.** ⅄ 2.85 – **42 rm** ⴻ 16.50/43.00 **st.** – SB 46.00/52.00 **st.**

ULVERSTON Cumbria **402** K 21 – pop. 10,710 – ECD : Wednesday – ✆ 0229.
Envir. : Furness Abbey★ (ruins 13C-15C) *AC*, SW : 6 ½ m.

🛫 Barrow, Rakesmoor, Hawcoat ℘ 0229 (Barrow-in-Furness) 25444, SW : 7 m. – 🛫 Furness, Walney Island ℘ 0229 (Barrow-in-Furness) 41232 – 🛫 Dunnerholme, Askam-in-Furness ℘ 0229 (Barrow-in-Furness) 62675 – 🛈 Renaissance Centre, 17 Fountain St. ℘ 52299.

◆London 278 – Kendal 25 – Lancaster 36.

🏨 **Lonsdale House,** 11 Daltongate, LA12 7BD, ℘ 52598, ⋈ – 📺 ➡wc ➥ 🔼 🅰🅴
closed 25-31 December – **M** (closed Sunday dinner) (bar lunch) a la carte 6.75/8.15 **st.** ⅄ 2.40 – **22 rm** ⴻ 20.55/34.20 **st.**

at Lowick Green NE : 5 m. by A 590 on A 5092 – ✉ Ulverston – ✆ 022 986 Greenodd :

🏨 **Farmers Arms,** LA12 8DT, ℘ 376 – ➋. 🔼 🅰🅴 𝘝𝘐𝘚𝘈
M (closed Saturday lunch) a la carte 6.50/9.70 **t.** ⅄ 2.60 – **13 rm** 12.50/26.50 **t.** – SB 36.00 **st.**

FORD Argyle St. ℘ 53209

UMBERLEIGH Devon **403** I 31 – ✆ 0769 High Bickington.
◆London 215 – Exeter 33 – ◆Plymouth 59 – Taunton 47.

🏨 **Rising Sun,** EX37 9DU, ℘ 60447, ⌛ – ➡wc ➋. 🔼 ⓞ 𝘝𝘐𝘚𝘈
March-October – **M** (bar lunch Monday to Saturday) 8.00 **st.** ⅄ 2.45 – **8 rm** ⴻ 18.00/38.00 **st.**

UNDERBARROW Cumbria **402** L 21 – see Kendal.

UPLYME Devon **403** L 31 – see Lyme Regis.

UPPER ODDINGTON Glos. – see Stow-on-the-Wold.

UPPER SLAUGHTER Glos. 403 404 O 28 – see Stow-on-the-Wold.

UPPINGHAM Leics. 404 R 26 – pop. 3,250 – ECD : Thursday – ✆ 0572.
Envir. : Kirkby Hall★ (ruins 16 C), SE : 8 m.
♦London 101 – ♦Leicester 19 – Northampton 28 – ♦Nottingham 35.

  ♙ **Central,** 16 High St. West, LE15 9QD, ℰ 822352, 舟 – ⊟wc. 🔼 VISA
      closed 2 weeks January – **M** *(closed Wednesday dinner)* 6.50 t. ⅃ 2.50 – **12 rm** ⌷ 17.00/30.00 t.
      – SB (October-March) 36.00 **st.**

  ✗ **Lake Isle** with rm, 16 High St. East, LE15 9PZ, ℰ 822951 – 📺 ⋔wc. 🔼 AE VISA. 彩
      closed Sunday dinner and Monday – **M** 6.50/12.50 t. ⅃ 2.75 – **2 rm** ⌷ 18.00/36.00 **st.**

    at Lyddington SE : 2 m. by A 6003 – ⊠ Oakham – ✆ 0572 Uppingham :

  🏠 **Marquess of Exeter** ⤸, 52 Main St., LE15 9LT, ℰ 822477 – 📺 ⊟wc ⋔wc ☎ 🅿. 🔼 AE ①
      VISA. 彩
      M *(closed Sunday dinner to non-residents)* a la carte 9.15/12.65 t. ⅃ 2.95 – **15 rm**
      ⌷ 28.50/46.50 **st.**

UPTON ST. LEONARDS Glos. – see Gloucester.

UPTON UPON SEVERN Heref. and Worc. 403 404 N 27 – pop. 2,048 – ECD : Thursday –
✆ 068 46.
🛈 Church St. ℰ 068 45 (Malvern) 2700.
♦London 116 – Hereford 25 – Stratford-upon-Avon 29 – Worcester 11.

  🏠 **White Lion,** High St., WR8 0HJ, ℰ 2551 – 📺 ⊟wc 🅿. 🔼 VISA
      M a la carte 8.25/14.50 t. ⅃ 2.95 – **10 rm** ⌷ 27.50/39.50 t. – SB 51.50 **st.**

  ⌂ **Pool House,** Hanley Rd, WR8 0PA, NW : ½ m. on B 4211 ℰ 2151, ⩽, ⤸, 舟 – ⊟wc 🅿. 🔼.
      彩
      closed December and January – **9 rm** ⌷ 13.00/28.00 **st.**

USK (BRYNBUGA) Gwent 403 L 28 – pop. 2,060 – ECD : Wednesday – ✆ 029 13.
See : Valley★.
🛈₈ at Pontypool ℰ 049 55 (Pontypool) 3655, W : 7 m.
♦London 144 – ♦Bristol 30 – Gloucester 39 – Newport 10.

  🏠 **Glen-yr-Afon House,** Pontypool Rd, NP5 1SY, ℰ 2302, 舟 – ⋔wc 🅿
      M 9.00/12.00 t. ⅃ 3.50 – **15 rm** ⌷ 19.90/28.75 t. – SB (weekends only) 41.00 **st.**

AUSTIN-ROVER ℰ 2136   AUSTIN-ROVER ℰ 2014

UTTOXETER Staffs. 402 403 404 O 25 – pop. 8,430 – ECD : Thursday – ✆ 088 93.
Envir. : Alton Towers (gardens★★) *AC* NW : 7 ½ m.
🛈₈ Wood Lane ℰ 4844.
♦London 145 – ♦Birmingham 33 – Derby 19 – Stafford 13 – ♦Stoke-on-Trent 16.

  🏠 **White Hart,** Carter St., ST14 8EU, ℰ 2437 – ⊟wc ⋔wc ☎ 🅿. 🔼 AE ① VISA. 彩
      M a la carte 5.45/9.80 t. ⅃ 3.30 – **24 rm** ⌷ 22.30/33.60 **st.**

AUSTIN-ROVER 20/24 Carter St. ℰ 2255   FORD, VAUXHALL Derby Rd ℰ 2301
FIAT Smithfield Rd ℰ 3838   PEUGEOT-TALBOT Market St. ℰ 2858

VELINDRE (FELINDRE FARCHOG) Dyfed 403 F 27 – see Newport (Dyfed).

VENN OTTERY Devon 403 K 31 – pop. 120 – ⊠ ✆ 040 481 Ottery St. Mary.
♦London 209 – Exeter 11 – Sidmouth 5.

  ⌂ **Venn Ottery Barton** ⤸, EX11 1RZ, ℰ 2733, ⤸, 舟 – ⊟wc ⋔wc 🅿
      April-October – **14 rm** ⌷ 12.50/30.00 t.

VENTNOR I.O.W. 403 404 Q 32 – see Wight (Isle of).

VERYAN Cornwall 403 F 33 The West Country G. – pop. 876 – ⊠ ✆ 0872 Truro.
See : Site★★.
♦London 291 – St. Austell 13 – Truro 13.

  🏦 **Nare** ⤸, Carne Beach, TR2 5PF, SW : 1 ¼ m. ℰ 501279, ⩽ Carne Bay, ♨ heated, 舟, ✗ –
      ⊟wc 🅿. ♨. 🔼 AE ① VISA. 彩
      M (bar lunch) 10.25 t. ⅃ 2.20 – **37 rm** ⌷ 13.00/52.50 **st.** – SB 70.00 **st.**

  🏠 **Elerkey House,** TR2 5QA, ℰ 501261, 舟 – ⊟wc ⋔ 🅿. 🔼 VISA
      closed January and February – **M** (bar lunch) 9.00 t. ⅃ 2.80 – **9 rm** ⌷ 14.00/36.50 **st.** – SB
      40.00/47.00 **st.**

  ✗ **Treverbyn House,** with rm, Pendower Rd, TR2 5QL, ℰ 501201 – 🅿. 彩
      closed November and December – **M** (dinner only) 9.50 t. ⅃ 2.80 – **4 rm** ⌷ (dinner included)
      20.00/40.00 **t.**

at Ruan High Lanes W : 1 ¼ m. on A 3078 – ✉ ☎ 0872 Truro :

Polsue Manor 🌿, TR2 5LU, ☎ 501270, ≤, 🌳 – 🛁wc [P]
M *(closed Sunday dinner to non-residents)* (bar lunch) 7.50 **st.** 🍷 2.40 – **13 rm** ☕ 14.00/38.00 **st.** – SB 46.85/48.85 **st.**

Hundred House, TR2 5JR, ☎ 501336, 🌳 – [TV] 🛁wc 🚿 [P]. [S] [AE] [VISA]
closed January and February – **M** (bar lunch) 9.50 **st.** 🍷 2.25 – **8 rm** ☕ 13.50/35.00 **st.**

WADDESDON Bucks. [404] R 28 – pop. 1,939 – ECD : Thursday – ☎ 029 665.
See : Waddesdon Manor (Rothschild Collection★★★) *AC*.
♦London 52 – Aylesbury 6 – ♦Birmingham 66 – ♦Oxford 25.

Hotels see : Aylesbury E : 5 m.

WADHURST East Sussex [404] U 30 – ☎ 0580 Ticehurst.
♦ London 44 – Hastings 21 – Maidstone 24 – Royal Tunbridge Wells 6.

XX **Spindlewood** 🌿 with rm, Wallcrouch, TN5 7JG, SE : 2 ¼ m. on B 2099 ☎ 200430, ≤, 🌳, 🍴 – [TV] 🛁wc ☎ [P]. [S] [AE] [VISA]. ✂
M 14.50 **t.** 🍷 2.70 – **9 rm** ☕ 25.00/56.00 **t.** – SB (except summer) 48.00/56.00 **st.**

WAKEFIELD West Yorks. [402] P 22 – pop. 59,590 – ECD : Wednesday – ☎ 0924.
Envir. : Pontefract (castle★ : ruins 12C-13C) *AC*, E : 9 m.
⛳18 Woodthorpe ☎ 255104, S : 3 m. – ⛳18 Lupset Park, Horbury Rd ☎ 374316 – ⛳9 Painthorpe House, Painthorpe Lane ☎ 255083, near junction 39 on M 1.
[i] Town Hall, Wood St. ☎ 370211 and 370700 (evenings and weekends).
♦London 188 – ♦Leeds 9 – ♦Manchester 38 – ♦Sheffield 23.

Post House (T.H.F.), Queen's Drive, Ossett, WF5 9BE, W : 2 ½ m. on A 638 ☎ 276388, Telex 53168, 🌳 – [lift] [TV] 🛁wc ☎ ♿ [P]. 🏫. [S] [AE] [O] [VISA]
M *(closed Saturday lunch)* 5.75/8.25 **st.** 🍷 2.85 – ☕ 5.25 – **96 rm** 39.00/46.00 **st.**

Swallow (Swallow), Queen St., WF1 1JU, ☎ 372111, Telex 53168 – [lift] [TV] 🛁wc ☎ [P]. 🏫. [S] [AE] [O] [VISA]
M 5.95/7.25 **st.** 🍷 3.40 – **62 rm** ☕ 35.00/45.00 **st.** – SB (weekends only) (except July-August) 40.00 **st.**

AUSTIN-ROVER Ings Rd ☎ 370100
AUSTIN-ROVER 509 Leeds Rd ☎ 0532 (Leeds) 822254
BMW Ings Rd ☎ 363796
FIAT, CITROEN, PEUGEOT-TALBOT Ings Rd ☎ 376771
FORD Barnsley Rd ☎ 370551
NISSAN Barnsley Rd ☎ 255904
RENAULT 129 New Rd, Middlestown ☎ 272087
TOYOTA Stanley Rd ☎ 373493
VAUXHALL 68 Ings Rd ☎ 372812
VAUXHALL-OPEL Westgate ☎ 366261
VOLVO Barnsley Rd ☎ 255126
VW-AUDI Ings Rd ☎ 375588

WALBERSWICK Suffolk [404] Y 27 – pop. 423 – ECD : Wednesday – ✉ ☎ 0502 Southwold.
♦London 106 – Great Yarmouth 28 – ♦Ipswich 33 – ♦Norwich 32.

Anchor, Main St., IP18 6UA, ☎ 2112, 🌳 – [TV] 🛁wc [P]. [S] [AE] [O] [VISA]
April-October – **M** 5.50/8.50 **t.** 🍷 3.75 – **14 rm** ☕ 17.90/39.50 **t.** – SB 40.15/42.05 **st.**

WALBERTON West Sussex – see Arundel.

WALFORD Heref. and Worc. – see Ross-on-Wye.

WALL Northumb. [401] [402] N 18 – see Hexham.

WALLASEY Merseyside [402] [403] K 23 – pop. 90,680 – ☎ 051 Liverpool.
⛳18 Bayswater Rd ☎ 639 3630 – ⛳9 Warren, Grove Rd ☎ 639 5730.
⛴ to Liverpool (Merseyside Transport) frequent services daily (7-8 mn).
♦ London 226 – Birkenhead 3.5 – ♦ Liverpool 4.

Grove House, Grove Rd, L45 3HF, ☎ 639 3947, 🌳 – [TV] ☎ [P]. 🏫 – **14 rm**.

WALLINGFORD Oxon. [403] [404] Q 29 – pop. 6,182 – ECD : Wednesday – ☎ 0491.
[i] 9 St. Martin's St. ☎ 35351 ext. 3810.
♦London 54 – ♦Oxford 12 – Reading 16.

George, 66 High St., OX10 0BS, ☎ 36665 – [TV] 🛁wc 🚿wc ☎ [P]. 🏫. [S] [AE] [O] [VISA]
M 7.25 **t.** 🍷 3.00 – **18 rm** ☕ 27.00/42.00 **t.** – SB (weekends only) 46.00 **st.**

Shillingford Bridge, OX10 8LZ, N : 2 m. on A 329 ☎ 086 732 (Warborough) 8567, Telex 837763, 🏊 heated, 🎣, 🌳 – [TV] 🛁wc 🚿wc ☎ [P]. 🏫. [S] [AE] [O] [VISA]. ✂
M 9.00 **t.** 🍷 2.50 – **31 rm** ☕ 30.00/45.00 **t.**

at North Stoke S : 2 ¾ m. by A 4130 and A 4074 on B 4009 – ✉ ✆ 0491 Wallingford :

🏨 **Springs** 🦢, Wallingford Rd, OX9 6BE, ℰ 36687, Telex 849794, ≼, ⨀ heated, ⌗, ✗ – 📺 ☎
   ℙ 🔥 🅰 ⒶⒺ *VISA*
   M (buffet lunch Sunday) 9.75/14.00 t. ⌕ 3.75 – **28 rm** ⊑ 44.00/137.50 t. – SB (weekends only) 85.00 t.

WALMLEY West Midlands 🄴🄾🄸 🄴🄾🄸 O 26 – see Birmingham.

WALSALL West Midlands 🄴🄾🄸 🄴🄾🄸 O 26 – pop. 184,734 – ECD : Thursday – ✆ 0922.
🄸 Calderfields, Aldridge Rd ℰ 32243, N : 1 m. CT.
♦London 126 – ♦Birmingham 9 – ♦Coventry 29 – Shrewsbury 36.

Plan of Enlarged Area : see Birmingham pp. 2 and 3

🏨 **Crest** (Crest), Birmingham Rd, WS5 3AB, SE : 1 ½ m. on A 34 ℰ 33555, Telex 335479 – 📶
   ▤ rest 📺 ➟wc ☎ ⅋ ℙ 🔥 🅰 ⒶⒺ ⑩ *VISA*   CT **e**
   M approx. 10.50 **st.** – ⊑ 5.25 – **100 rm** 40.00/50.00 **st.**

at Walsall Wood NE : 3 ½ m. on A 461 – CT – ✉ Walsall – ✆ 0543 Brownhills :

🏨 **Barons Court** (Best Western), Walsall Rd, WS9 9AH, ℰ 376543, Telex 338212 – 📶 📺
   ➟wc ☎ ℙ 🔥 🅰 ⒶⒺ ⑩ *VISA* ✗
   M *(closed Sunday dinner to non-residents)* 6.50/8.50 t. ⌕ 3.25 – **76 rm** ⊑ 30.00/43.00 t. – SB (weekends only) 42.00/52.00 **st.**

CITROEN Hatherton Rd ℰ 32911
FORD Wolverhampton St. ℰ 21212
LADA 152 Green Lane ℰ 645347
RENAULT Day St. ℰ 613232
SAAB West Bromwich Rd ℰ 22695

TALBOT, RELIANT Charlotte St. ℰ 21723
TALBOT Stafford Rd ℰ 76366
TOYOTA Lichfield Rd, Willenhall ℰ 0922 (Bloxwich) 76484
VAUXHALL-OPEL Broadway ℰ 614336

WALSGRAVE ON SOWE West Midlands – see Coventry.

WALTON LE DALE Lancs. 🄴🄾🄸 L 22 – see Preston.

WANSFORD Cambs. 🄴🄾🄸 S 26 – see Peterborough.

WANTAGE Oxon. 🄴🄾🄸 🄴🄾🄸 P 29 – pop. 7,200 – ECD : Thursday – ✆ 023 57.
Envir. : White Horse ≼ ∗.
♦London 75 – ♦Bristol 58 – ♦Oxford 15 – Reading 25.

🏨 **Bear**, Market Pl., OX12 8AB, ℰ 66366 – 📺 ➟wc ▥wc ☎. 🅰 ⒶⒺ ⑩ *VISA*. ✗
   M a la carte 6.75/12.45 t. ⌕ 3.25 – **25 rm** ⊑ 31.50/45.75 t. – SB (weekends only) 46.00 **st.**

AUSTIN-ROVER Wallingford St. ℰ 3355
PEUGEOT-TALBOT, SAAB East Hanney ℰ 023 587 (West Hanney) 257

VW, AUDI Grove Rd ℰ 65511

WARE Herts. 🄴🄾🄸 T 28 – pop. 13,740 – ECD : Thursday – ✆ 0920.
♦London 24 – ♦Cambridge 30 – Luton 22.

🏨 **Ware Moat House** (Q.M.H.), Baldock St., SG12 9DR, N : ½ m. on A 1170 ℰ 5011 – 📶 📺
   ➟wc ▥wc ☎ ℙ 🔥 🅰 ⒶⒺ ⑩ *VISA*
   M 7.50 t. – **50 rm** ⊑ 33.00/47.00 t.

WAREHAM Dorset 🄴🄾🄸 🄴🄾🄸 N 31 The West Country G. – pop. 4,368 – ECD : Wednesday – ✆ 092 95.
See : Site∗ – St. Martin's Church∗∗.
Envir. : Blue Pool∗, S : 3 m. on A 351 – Smedmore∗, S : 7 m. by A 351 – Bovington : Tank Museum∗, W : 7 m. on A 352 – Lulworth Cove∗, SW : 11 m. by A 352.
♦London 123 – Bournemouth 13 – Weymouth 19.

🏨 **Priory** 🦢, Church Green, BH20 4ND, ℰ 2772, « Tastefully renovated part 16C priory with gardens », ⚲ – 📺 ➟wc ▥wc ☎ ℙ 🔥 🅰 ⒶⒺ ⑩ *VISA*. ✗
   M 6.95/12.50 t. ⌕ 2.75 – **15 rm** ⊑ 25.00/85.00 t. – SB (except summer) 50.00/100.00 **st.**

🏨 **Kemps Country House**, East Stoke, W : 2 ¾ m. on A 352 ℰ 0929 (Bindon Abbey) 462563, ⌗ – 📺 ➟wc ▥wc ℙ. 🅰 ⒶⒺ ⑩ *VISA*. ✗
   closed Christmas – **M** a la carte 9.25/14.20 t. – **10 rm** ⊑ 25.00/50.00 t. – SB 47.00/52.00 **st.**

🏨 **Worgret Manor**, Worgret Rd, BH20 5AL, W : 1 m. on A 352 ℰ 2957, ⌗ – 📺 ▥wc ℙ. 🅰
   ⒶⒺ ⑩ *VISA*
   closed 25 to 27 December – **M** 4.95/7.25 **st.** ⌕ 2.90 – **9 rm** ⊑ 18.00/36.50 **st.** – SB (except summer) 34.00/38.00 **st.**

at Stoborough S : ½ m. on A 351 – ✉ ✆ 092 95 Wareham :

🏨 **Springfield Country,** Grange Rd, BH20 5AL, ℰ 2177, ⨀ heated, ⌗, ✗ – 📺 ➟wc ℙ. 🅰
   ⑩ *VISA*
   M (bar lunch) 7.75 t. – **30 rm** ⊑ 28.50/67.80 t.

WARMINSTER Wilts. 🗺️ 403 404 N 30 The West Country G. – pop. 16,000 – ECD : Wednesday – ✆ 0985.

Envir. : Westbury Hill (White Horse★, ≼★) N : 6 m.

🛈 Old Bell Hotel, Market Pl. ✆ 216611.

♦London 111 – ♦Bristol 29 – Exeter 74 – ♦Southampton 47.

🏛 **Bishopstrow House** 🦢, Boreham Rd, BA12 9HH, SE : 1 ½ m. on A 36 ✆ 212312, ≼, « Tastefully furnished country house », 🏊 heated, 🐟, 🎣, park, 🎾 – 📺 🅿 🔊 AE ① VISA 🦢
   M (lunch by arrangement) (booking essential) 16.50/19.50 **st.** 🍷 4.00 – 🖙 5.00 – **15 rm** 55.00/110.00 **st.**

🏨 **Old Bell,** 42 Market Pl., BA12 9AN, ✆ 216611 – 📺 📶wc 🔊 AE ① VISA 🦢
   M (grill rest. only) a la carte 6.40/9.70 **st.** 🍷 2.65 – **16 rm** 🖙 18.00/30.00 **st.**

✗ **Coopers,** 28 High St., BA12 9AF, ✆ 216911 – 🔊 ① VISA
   closed Sunday and Monday – **M** (bar lunch) 7.05/12.50 **t.** 🍷 2.00.

AUSTIN-ROVER George St. ✆ 212808

WARREN ROW Berks – see Knowl Hill.

WARRINGTON Cheshire 402 403 404 M 23 – pop. 133,400 – ECD : Thursday – ✆ 0925.

See : St. Elphin's Church (chancel★ 14C).

🏌 Hill Warren ✆ 61620, S : 3 m. – 🏌 Walton Hall, Warrington Rd ✆ 66775, S : 2 m. – 🏌 Kelvin Close, Birchwood ✆ 0925 (Padgate) 818819.

🛈 80 Sankey St. ✆ 36501 and 35961 ext. 90.

♦London 195 – Chester 20 – ♦Liverpool 18 – ♦Manchester 21 – Preston 28.

🏨 **Patten Arms,** Parker St. (Bank Quay Station), WA1 1LS, ✆ 36602 – 📺 📶wc 🛗wc ☎ 🅿. 🔊 AE ① VISA
   closed 25 and 26 December – **M** (closed Sunday) 12.00 **st.** 🍷 3.10 – **43 rm** 🖙 28.00/40.00 **st.**

🏨 **Hill Cliffe,** London Rd, WA4 5BS, S : 2 m. on A 49 ✆ 63638, 🌳 – 📺 📶wc 🅿. 🔊 VISA 🦢
   closed Bank Holidays – **M** (closed Sunday dinner) (carving rest.) 7.50 **t.** 🍷 2.75 – **11 rm** 🖙 19.95/30.45 **t.**

🏨 **Birchdale** 🦢, Birchdale Rd, Stockton Heath, WA4 5AW, S : 1 ¾ m. by A 49 ✆ 63662, 🌳 – 🅿
   closed 24 December-2 January – **M** (closed Saturday, Sunday and Bank Holidays) 4.00/6.00 **st.** 🍷 2.75 – **20 rm** 🖙 15.00/23.00 **st.**

   at Grappenhall SE : 2 m. by A 50 – ✉ ✆ 0925 Warrington :

🏛 **Fir Grove Inn,** Knutsford Old Rd, WA4 2LD, ✆ 67471, Telex 628117 – 📺 📶wc 🛗wc ☎ 🅿. 🏌. 🦢
   M 7.50/8.00 **st.** 🍷 2.90 – **38 rm** 🖙 28.00/38.00 **st.**

   at Stretton S : 3 ½ m. by A 49 on B 5356 – ✉ Warrington – ✆ 092 573 Norcott Brook :

🏨 **Old Vicarage,** Stretton Rd, WA4 4NS, ✆ 238, 🌳, 🎾 – 🛗 📺 📶wc 🛗wc 🅿. 🔊 VISA
   closed Bank Holidays – **M** 6.50/8.50 **st.** 🍷 3.35 – **36 rm** 🖙 27.00/39.50 **st.**

AUSTIN-ROVER Winwick St. ✆ 50011
BMW Farrell St. ✆ 35987
CITROEN 194/196 Knutsford Rd ✆ 68444

FORD Winwick Rd ✆ 51111
RENAULT Farrell St. ✆ 30448
VW, AUDI 101 Knutsford Rd ✆ 65265

WARWICK Warw. 403 404 P 27 – pop. 18,296 – ECD : Thursday – ✆ 0926.

See : Castle★★ (14C) AC Y – St. Mary's Church★ 12C-18C Y A – Lord Leycester's Hospital★ Y B.

🏌 Warwick Golf Centre ✆ 44316 Y.

🛈 The Court House, Jury St. ✆ 492212.

♦London 96 – ♦Birmingham 20 – ♦Coventry 11 – ♦Oxford 43.

Plan opposite

🏨 **Woolpack,** Market Pl., CV34 4SD, ✆ 496191 – 📺 📶wc 🛗wc ☎. 🔊 AE ① VISA   Y **a**
   M (bar lunch) 6.00 **t.** 🍷 2.40 – **29 rm** 🖙 15.00/34.00 **t.**

🏠 **Cambridge Villa,** 20a Emscote Rd, CV34 4PL, ✆ 491169 – 📺 🅿. 🦢   Z **a**
   12 rm 🖙 9.00/18.00 **s.**

🏠 **Avon,** 7 Emscote Rd, CV34 4PH, ✆ 491367, 🌳 – 🅿. 🦢   Z **v**
   closed Christmas Day – **7 rm** 🖙 15.00/17.00 **st.**

✗✗✗ **Westgate Arms,** 3 Old Bowling Green St., CV34 4DD, ✆ 492362, 🌳 – 🅿. 🔊 AE ① VISA   Y **u**
   closed Sunday, 25 and 26 December and Bank Holiday Mondays – **M** a la carte 15.35/23.15 **st.** 🍷 2.75.

✗✗ **Randolph's,** 19-21 Coten End, CV34 4NT, ✆ 491292 – 🔊 VISA   Y **i**
   closed Sunday and 25 to 30 December – **M** (dinner only) (booking essential) a la carte 14.30 **t.** 🍷 2.50.

✗✗ **Aylesford,** 1 High St., CV34 4AP, ✆ 492799, Italian rest. – 🔊 AE ① VISA   Y **e**
   closed Monday dinner, Sunday, last 3 weeks in July and 1 week at Christmas – **M** a la carte 9.05/15.45 **st.** 🍷 3.60.

*Les plans de villes
sont disposés le Nord en haut.*

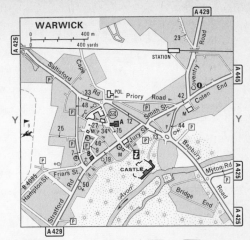

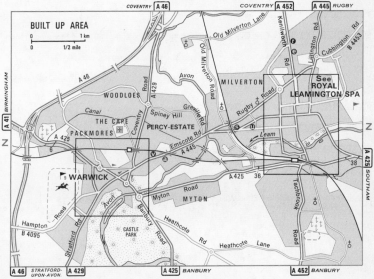

at Longbridge SW : 2 m. on A 429 – Z – ⊠ ✆ 0926 Warwick :

🏛 **Ladbroke** (Ladbroke), CV34 6RE, junction of A 429, A 46 and A 41 ✆ 499555, 🔲 – 🔳 📺
🛏wc ✆ 🔥 🅿. 🔏. 🔲 AE ⓞ VISA
M *(closed Saturday lunch)* (carving rest.) 8.50/10.50 **t.** ▮ 3.65 – 🍽 5.75 – **126 rm** 40.00/50.00 **t.**
– SB (weekends only) 60.00/64.00 **st.**

FIAT Wharf St. ✆ 496231
PORSCHE Birmingham Rd ✆ 491731

VOLVO Millers Rd ✆ 491377

WASDALE HEAD Cumbria 🔢 K 20 – see Gosforth.

WASHINGTON Tyne and Wear 🔢 🔢 P 19 – pop. 41,000 – ECD : Wednesday – ⊠ ✆ 091
Tyneside.

🏌 Stone Cellar Rd ✆ 472626.

♦London 278 – Durham 13 – ♦Middlesbrough 32 – ♦Newcastle-upon-Tyne 7.

🏨 **Post House** (T.H.F.), Emerson, District 5, NE37 1LB, Junction A 1 (M) and A 1231 ℰ 416 2264, Telex 537574 – ⚙ 📺 ⌷wc ☎ **ℙ** ▲ 🄰 🄰🄴 🅞 𝚅𝙸𝚂𝙰
M *(closed Saturday lunch)* 6.95/8.75 **st.** 🍷 2.65 – ⤶ 5.00 – **138 rm** 34.00/41.50 **st.**

🏨 **George Washington** (Best Western), Stone Cellar Rd, District 12, NE37 1PH, ℰ 4172626, Telex 537143, 🛏 – 📺 ⌷wc ☎ **ℙ** ▲ 🄰 🄰🄴 🅞 𝚅𝙸𝚂𝙰
M 7.50/15.00 **t.** 🍷 2.50 – ⤶ 4.85 – **70 rm** 34.50/39.50 **t.** – SB (weekends only) 56.00/64.00 **st.**

AUSTIN-ROVER Village Lane ℰ 4160607
FORD Parsons Rd ℰ 4167700

RENAULT Waterloo Rd ℰ 416 1655
VAUXHALL Waterloo Rd ℰ 4173565

WATCHET Somerset �403 J 30 The West Country G. – pop. 2,900 – ECD : Wednesday – ✪ 0984.
Envir. : Cleeve Abbey★★, SW : 2 m.
🔰 2 Market St. ℰ 31824 (summer only).
♦London 180 – ♦Bristol 57 – Taunton 18.

🏨 **Downfield,** 16 St. Decumans Rd, TA23 0HR, ℰ 31267, 🚗 – 📺 ⌷wc 🍽wc **ℙ** ▲ 🄰🄴 🅞 𝚅𝙸𝚂𝙰
M 8.00/8.50 **st.** 🍷 2.60 – **6 rm** ⤶ 24.15/35.65 **st.** – SB 44.00 **st.**

WATERGATE BAY Cornwall �403 E 32 – ✉ Newquay – ✪ 0637 St. Mawgan.
♦London 293 – Newquay 2 – Padstow 8.

🏨 **Tregurrian,** TR8 4AB, ℰ 860280, ⤒ heated – 🍽wc **ℙ**
Mid May-September – **M** (bar lunch) 4.75 **st.** 🍷 1.70 – **28 rm** ⤶ 9.75/34.00 **st.** – SB 22.00/36.50 **st.**

WATERHEAD Cumbria �402 L 20 – see Ambleside.

WATERHOUSES Staffs. �402 �403 �404 O 24 – pop. 836 (inc. Waterfall) – ✉ Stoke-on-Trent – ✪ 053 86.
♦London 115 – ♦Birmingham 63 – Derby 23 – ♦Manchester 39 – ♦Stoke-on-Trent 17.

XX **Old Beams,** Leek Rd, ST10 3HW, ℰ 254, 🚗 – **ℙ** 🄰🄴 🅞 𝚅𝙸𝚂𝙰
closed Sunday dinner, Monday, first week in January and first week in October – **M** a la carte 10.50/15.70 **t.**

WATERLOO Merseyside �402 ✪ �403 ② – see Liverpool.

WATERMILLOCK Cumbria �402 L 20 – see Ullswater.

WATFORD Herts. �404 S 29 – pop. 78,465 – ECD : Wednesday – ✪ 0923.
🔰 High St., Bushey ℰ 01 (London) 950 2283.
♦London 21 – Aylesbury 23.

Plan : see Greater London (North-West)

🏨🏨 **Ladbroke** (Ladbroke), Elton Way, WD2 8HA, Watford By-Pass E : 3 ½ m. on A 41 at junction A 4008 ℰ 35881, Telex 923422 – ⚙ 📺 ☎ **ℙ** ▲ 🄰 🄰🄴 🅞 𝚅𝙸𝚂𝙰 ✳ BU **e**
M (carving rest.)(bar lunch Saturday) 9.50/11.00 **t.** – ⤶ 5.50 – **155 rm** 40.00/47.00 **t.**

AUSTIN-ROVER Pinner Rd ℰ 28680
HONDA, MERCEDES-BENZ High Rd at Bushey Heath ℰ 01 (London) 950 3311
OPEL 6/10 High Rd at Bushey Heath ℰ 01 (London) 950 6146
PEUGEOT, TALBOT 16 St. Albans Rd ℰ 25283

PEUGEOT-TALBOT Aldenham ℰ 092 76 (Radlett) 2177
VAUXHALL-OPEL 6/10 High Rd at Bushey Heath ℰ 01 (London) 950 6146
VAUXHALL-OPEL, VOLVO 329 St. Albans Rd ℰ 31716

WATH-IN-NIDDERDALE North Yorks. – see Pateley Bridge.

WDIG (GOODWICK) Dyfed – see Fishguard.

WEEDON BEC Northants. �403 �404 Q 27 – pop. 2,361 – ECD : Wednesday – ✉ Northampton – ✪ 0327.
♦London 74 – ♦Birmingham 54 – ♦Leicester 39 – ♦Oxford 40 – Northampton 8.5.

🏨 **Crossroads** (Best Western), High St., NN7 4PX, at junction A 5 and A 45 ℰ 40354 – 📺 ⌷wc ☎ **ℙ** ▲ 🄰 🄰🄴 🅞 𝚅𝙸𝚂𝙰 ✳
closed 25 and 26 December – **M** a la carte 7.90/13.20 **t.** 🍷 2.80 – **28 rm** ⤶ 30.00/46.00 **st.** – SB (weekends only) 58.00/65.00 **st.**

WELLAND Heref. and Worc. �403 �404 N 27 – see Great Malvern.

WELLESBOURNE Warw. �403 �404 P 27 – see Stratford-upon-Avon.

WELLINGBOROUGH Northants. 404 R 27 – pop. 27,540 – ECD : Thursday – ☎ 0933.

♦London 73 – ♦Cambridge 43 – ♦Leicester 34 – Northampton 10.

- **Hind** (Q.M.H.), Sheep St., NN8 1BY, ☎ 222827 – TV wc ☎ P. AE VISA
closed 23 December-1 January – **M** 5.45/7.45 **t.** 2.50 – **32 rm** 35.05/44.10 **t.** – SB (weekends only) 49.00/51.00 **st.**
- **High View,** 156 Midland Rd, NN8 1NG, ☎ 226060 – TV wc P. AE VISA
16 rm 14.50/29.00 **st.**

AUSTIN-ROVER Finedon Rd ☎ 76651
SKODA 51-55 Broad Green ☎ 223924
VAUXHALL-OPEL Oxford St. ☎ 223252

WELLINGTON HEATH Heref. and Worc. – see Ledbury.

WELLS Somerset 403 404 M 30 The West Country G. – pop. 8,604 – ECD : Wednesday – ☎ 0749.

See : Site★★★ – Cathedral★★★ – Vicar's Close★ – Bishop's Palace★ (≤★★ of east end of cathedral).

Envir. : Wookey Hole★★ (Caves ★, Papermill ★, Fairground collection ★) NW : 2 m.

9 ☎ 72868, E : Horrington Rd.

Town Hall, Market Sq. ☎ 72552.

♦London 132 – ♦Bristol 20 – ♦Southampton 68 – Taunton 28.

- **Swan** (Best Western), Sadler St., BA5 2RX, ☎ 78877, Telex 449658 – TV wc wc ☎ P. AE VISA
M 6.95/8.95 **t.** 3.00 – **26 rm** 30.00/45.00 **t.** – SB 60.00/65.00 **t.**
- **Crown,** Market Pl., BA5 2RP, ☎ 73457 – TV wc wc ☎ P. AE VISA
M 6.95/10.50 **t.** 3.50 – **14 rm** 18.00/41.00 **t.** – SB (except Bank Holidays) 43.00/49.00 **st.**
- Star, The High St., BA5 2SQ, ☎ 73055 – TV wc. AE VISA.
2.00 – **16 rm** 13.00/29.00 **t.**
- **White Hart,** 19 Sadler St., BA5 2RR, ☎ 72056 – wc P. AE VISA.
M 4.00/6.60 **st.** 2.50 – **15 rm** 19.50/32.50 **st.** – SB (January-June) 34.00/37.50 **st.**

AUSTIN-ROVER-DAIMLER-JAGUAR Glastonbury Rd ☎ 72626
TALBOT Priory Rd ☎ 73834
VAUXHALL New St. ☎ 72099

WELLS-NEXT-THE-SEA Norfolk 404 V 25 – pop. 2,389 – ECD : Thursday – ☎ 0328 Fakenham.

Envir. : Holkam Hall★★ (18C) *AC*, W : 3 m.

♦London 121 – King's Lynn 31 – ♦Norwich 36.

- **Mill House,** Northfield Lane, NR23 1JZ, ☎ 710739, – P
closed December – **7 rm** 9.00/16.00 **st.**

WELSHPOOL (TRALLWNG) Powys 402 403 K 26 – pop. 7,030 – ECD : Thursday – ☎ 0938.

18 Golfa Hill ☎ 093 883 (Castle Caereinion) 249.

Vicarage Garden Car Park ☎ 2043.

♦London 182 – ♦Birmingham 64 – Chester 45 – Shrewsbury 19.

- **Royal Oak,** The Cross, SY21 7RF, ☎ 2217 – wc P. VISA
M a la carte 6.35/11.50 **st.** – **26 rm** 14.50/35.00 **st.** – SB (weekends only)(late October-April) 38.00 **st.**

AUSTIN-ROVER Union St. ☎ 3152
HONDA ☎ 3503
PEUGEOT-TALBOT ☎ 069 181 (Llansantffraid) 283
PEUGEOT-TALBOT Forden ☎ 093 876 (Forden) 203
PEUGEOT-TALBOT Salop Rd ☎ 2391
VAUXHALL-OPEL Newtown Rd ☎ 4444

WELWYN Herts. 404 T 28 – pop. 6,890 – ECD : Wednesday – ☎ 043 871.

♦London 30 – Bedford 31 – ♦Cambridge 32.

- **Heath Lodge,** Danesbury Park Rd, AL6 9SL, NE : 1 ¼ m. by B 197 ☎ 7064, , park – TV wc ☎ P. AE VISA
M *(closed Sunday dinner)* 10.00 **t.** 3.10 – **28 rm** 30.00/43.70 **t.** – SB (weekends only) 60.00/80.00 **st.**

COLT 54 Great North Rd ☎ 5911
FORD By Pass Rd ☎ 6123

WELWYN GARDEN CITY Herts. 404 T 28 – pop. 40,000 – ECD : Wednesday – ☎ 070 73 Welwyn Garden.

18 Panshanger ☎ 33350.

The Campus ☎ 31212.

♦London 28 – Bedford 34 – ♦Cambridge 34.

- **Crest** (Crest), Homestead Lane, AL7 4LX, ☎ 24336, Telex 261523, – TV wc ☎ P. AE VISA.
M (carving lunch) approx. 10.00 **st.** – 5.25 – **58 rm** 42.00/51.00 **st.**

AUSTIN-ROVER-DAIMLER-JAGUAR Stanborough Rd ☎ 35131
RENAULT Great North Rd ☎ 070 72 (Hatfield) 64567

WENTBRIDGE West Yorks. 💽💽💽 Q 23 – pop. 130 – ✉ 🏵 0977 Pontefract.
♦London 183 – ♦Leeds 19 – ♦Nottingham 55 – ♦Sheffield 28.

   🏨 **Wentbridge House,** WF8 3JJ, ℰ 620444, 🐎 – 📺 ⌂wc ⓜwc ☎ 🄿 🛴 🔼 🄰🄴 ⓞ 𝘝𝘐𝘚𝘈 ⚡
      closed Christmas Day – **M** a la carte 12.35/16.10 **st.** 🍸 3.70 – ⌷ 2.50 – **20 rm** 28.00/49.00 **st.**

     at Barnsdale Bar S : 2 m. on A 1 – ✉ 🏵 0977 Pontefract :

   🏨 **Doncaster Travelodge** (T.H.F.) without rest., Trunk Rd, WF8 3JB, on A 1 ℰ 620711, Telex
     557457 – 📺 ⌂wc ☎ 🄿 🔼 🄰🄴 ⓞ 𝘝𝘐𝘚𝘈
     72 rm 25.00/36.00 **st.**

WEOBLEY Heref. and Worc. 💽💽💽 L 27 – pop. 881 – ECD : Wednesday – ✉ Hereford – 🏵 054 45.
♦London 145 – Brecon 30 – Hereford 12 – Leominster 9.

   🏠 **Red Lion,** Broad St., HR4 8SE, ℰ 220 – 📺 ⌂wc ⓜwc ☎ 🄿 🔼 🄰🄴 ⓞ 𝘝𝘐𝘚𝘈
     M a la carte 10.00/16.00 **st.** 🍸 3.50 – **7 rm** ⌷ 26.00/33.00 **st.**

WEST BAY Dorset 💽💽💽 L 31 – see Bridport.

WEST BEXINGTON Dorset – see Bridport.

WEST BRIDGFORD Notts. 💽💽💽💽 Q 25 – see Nottingham.

WEST BROMWICH West Midlands 💽💽💽💽 O 26 – see Birmingham.

WEST CHILTINGTON West Sussex 💽💽💽💽 S 31 – pop. 1,765 – ECD : Wednesday and Thursday –
✉ Pulborough – 🏵 079 83.
♦London 50 – ♦Brighton 22 – Worthing 12.

   🏨 **Roundabout** (Best Western), Monkmead Lane, RH20 2PF, S : 1 ¼ m. ℰ 3838, 🐎 – 📺
     ⌂wc ⓜwc ☎ 🄿 🛴 🔼 🄰🄴 ⓞ 𝘝𝘐𝘚𝘈
     closed 3 to 23 January – **M** 6.95/9.25 **st.** 🍸 2.95 – **20 rm** ⌷ 27.75/45.00 **st.** – SB 50.00/60.00 **st.**

WEST CLANDON Surrey – see Guildford.

WEST COKER Somerset 💽💽💽💽 M 31 – see Yeovil.

WESTERHAM Kent 💽💽💽💽 U 30 – pop. 4,641 – ECD : Wednesday – 🏵 0959.
Envir. : Chartwell★ (Sir Winston Churchill's country home, Museum) *AC*, S : 2 m.
♦London 24 – ♦Brighton 45 – Maidstone 22.

   🏨 **Kings Arms,** Market Sq., TN16 1AN, ℰ 62990 – 📺 ⌂wc ☎ 🄿 🔼 🄰🄴 ⓞ 𝘝𝘐𝘚𝘈 ⚡
     M 8.90 **t.** – **12 rm** ⌷ 32.00/44.00 **st.**

   XXX **Montmorency,** Quebec Sq., TN16 1AN, on A 25 ℰ 62139, 🐎 – 🄿 🔼 🄰🄴 ⓞ 𝘝𝘐𝘚𝘈
     M a la carte 12.25/15.75 **st.** 🍸 2.95.

ALFA-ROMEO London Rd ℰ 64333   RENAULT London Rd ℰ 64001
AUSTIN-ROVER High St. ℰ 62212   VW, AUDI London Rd ℰ 64333

WEST HUNTSPILL Somerset 💽💽💽 L 30 – see Bridgwater.

WEST LULWORTH Dorset 💽💽💽💽 N 32 – pop. 1,003 – ECD : Wednesday – ✉ Wareham –
🏵 092 941.
See : Lulworth Cove★.
♦London 129 – Bournemouth 21 – Dorchester 17 – Weymouth 19.

   🌊 **Mill House,** BH20 5RQ, ℰ 404, 🐎 – ⌂wc ⓜwc. 🔼 🄰🄴 ⓞ 𝘝𝘐𝘚𝘈
     M 3.80/7.45 **t.** 🍸 2.65 – **10 rm** ⌷ 9.50/23.00 **t.** – SB (except summer) 31.00/37.00 **st.**

   ↑ **Cromwell House,** Main Rd, BH20 5RJ, ℰ 253, ≤, 🛀, 🐎 – 📺 ⌂wc ⓜwc 🄿
     closed Christmas – **7 rm** ⌷ 11.00/26.00 **st.**

   ↑ Lulworth, Main Rd, BH20 5RJ, ℰ 230 – 📺 🄿 ⚡ – **8 rm**

   ↑ **Gatton House,** Main Rd, BH20 5RU, ℰ 252, 🐎 – ⌂wc ⓜwc 🄿
     closed January and February – **9 rm** ⌷ 10.00/28.00 **st.**

WEST MALVERN Heref. and Worc. 💽💽💽💽 M 27 – see Great Malvern.

WEST MERSEA Essex 💽💽💽💽 W 28 – pop. 6,170 – ✉ Colchester – 🏵 0206.
♦ London 58 – Chelmsford 27 – Colchester 9.5.

   XX **Blackwater** with rm, 20-22 Church Rd, CO5 8QH, ℰ 383338 – 📺 ⓜwc 🄿 🔼 🄰🄴. ⚡
     closed 8 to 22 January – **M** *(closed Tuesday lunch and Sunday dinner)* a la carte 10.00/14.65 **t.**
     – **7 rm** ⌷ 15.00/33.00 **t.** – SB (except Bank Holidays) 36.00/40.50 **st.**

WESTONBIRT Glos. 408 404 N 29 – see Tetbury.

WESTON-FAVELL Northants. 404 R 27 – see Northampton.

WESTON-ON-THE-GREEN Oxon. 408 404 Q 28 – pop. 460 – ⊠ ✪ 0865 Oxford.
◆London 65 – ◆Birmingham 61 – Northampton 33 – ◆Oxford 8.

🏨 **Weston Manor** (Best Western) ⏎, on A 43, OX6 8QL, ℰ 50621, ⊥ heated, ⚞, park, squash – 📺 ⊆wc ☎ 🅿 🅰 🖭 ⓞ 𝘝𝘐𝘚𝘈 ⚸
M (bar lunch) 15.00 **st.** ⅊ 3.50 – **23 rm** ⊇ 37.50/60.00 **st.** – SB 55.00/65.00 **st.**

🚩 *To go a long way quickly, use Michelin maps at a scale of 1:1 000 000.*

WESTON-SUPER-MARE Avon 408 K 29 The West Country G. – pop. 50,894 – ECD : Thursday –
✪ 0934.
See : Sea front ≤ ★★.
📇 Worlebury ℰ 23214, 2 m. from station BY – 🅿 Beach Lawns ℰ 26838.
◆London 147 – ◆Bristol 24 – Taunton 32.

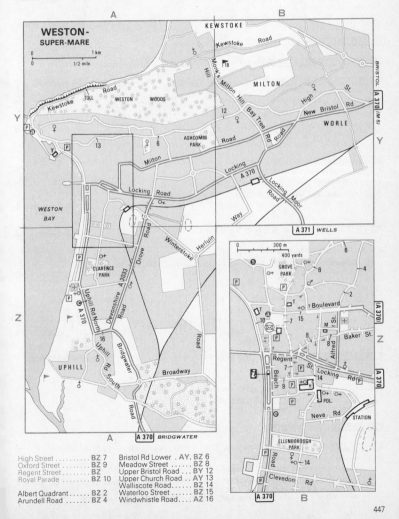

High Street .... BZ 7	Bristol Rd Lower . AY, BZ 6	
Oxford Street .... BZ 9	Meadow Street ...... BZ 8	
Regent Street .... BZ	Upper Bristol Road .. BY 12	
Royal Parade .... BZ 10	Upper Church Road .. AY 13	
	Walliscote Road..... BZ 14	
Albert Quadrant ...... BZ 2	Waterloo Street ...... BZ 15	
Arundell Road .... BZ 4	Windwhistle Road.... AZ 16	

447

🏨 **Grand Atlantic** (T.H.F.), Beach Rd, BS23 1BA, ✆ 26543, ≤, ⤳ heated, ⛱, ✗ – 🛗 📺 🅿
🍴 🔽 AE ⓞ VISA
BZ **e**
M 6.50/9.00 st. ⅃ 2.50 – 🍽 5.00 – **79 rm** 31.50/48.00 st.

🏨 **Royal Pier**, 55-57 Birnbeck Rd, BS23 2EJ, ✆ 26644, ≤ – 🛗 📺 ⌂wc ⛽ 🅿 🍴 🔽 AE VISA
AY **a**
M 6.50/8.00 t. ⅃ 2.95 – **42 rm** 🍽 19.25/46.20 st.

🏨 **Berni Royal**, South Par., BS23 1JN, ⛱ – 🛗 📺 ⌂wc ⛽ 🅿 🍴 🔽 AE ⓞ VISA
BZ **a**
M 6.00/8.00 t. ⅃ 3.00 – **36 rm** 🍽 23.00/40.00 t.

🏨 **Queenswood**, Victoria Park, BS23 2HZ, ✆ 21759, ≤ – ⌂wc 🛁wc. 🔽 AE ⓞ VISA
BZ **s**
M 5.50/8.00 st. ⅃ 2.50 – **19 rm** 🍽 12.50/33.00 st. – SB 38.00/44.00 st.

🏠 **Beachlands**, 17 Uphill Rd North, BS23 4NG, ✆ 21401, ⛱ – ⌂wc 🛁wc ₰ 🅿 🔽 AE ⓞ VISA ✗
AZ **c**
closed January and February – **M** (bar lunch) 5.95 t. ⅃ 2.25 – **19 rm** 🍽 11.50/29.90 t. – SB (except summer)(not Bank Holidays) 32.00/36.00 st.

AUSTIN-ROVER Alfred St. ✆ 21451
CITROEN Baker St. ✆ 23995
DAIHATSU, SAAB Bridgwater Rd ✆ 813012
DAIHATSU, SAAB Main Rd ✆ 0934 (Bleadon) 812546
FORD Locking Rd ✆ 28291
HONDA Bridgwater Rd ✆ 812244
PEUGEOT-TALBOT Broadway ✆ 0934 (Bleadon) 812479

RENAULT Locking Rd ✆ 414007
SUBARU 62 Knightston Rd ✆ 21161
TALBOT 264 Milton Rd ✆ 25707
VAUXHALL-OPEL, BEDFORD Winterstoke Rd ✆ 23904

WESTON TURVILLE Bucks. 🗾 R 28 – see Aylesbury.

WESTON-UNDER-PENYARD Heref. and Worc. 🗾 🗾 M 28 – see Ross-on-Wye.

WESTON-UNDER-REDCASTLE Salop 🗾 🗾 🗾 M 25 – pop. 245 – ✉ Shrewsbury – ☎ 093 924 Lee Brockhurst.
🏌, 🏌 Hawkstone Park ✆ 611.
♦London 165 – Chester 31 – ♦Birmingham 48 – Shrewsbury 12 – ♦Stoke-on-Trent 25.

🏨 **Hawkstone Park** (Best Western) ⌖, SY4 5UY, ✆ 611, ≤, ⤳, 🏌, 🔌, ⛱, park, ✗ – 📺 ⌂wc ₰ ₰ 🅿 🍴 🔽 AE VISA
M 5.45/7.50 st. – **59 rm** 🍽 25.00/46.00 st. – SB (January-March) 39.50 st.

WEST RUNTON Norfolk 🗾 X 25 – pop. 1,467 – ECD : Wednesday – ✉ Cromer – ☎ 026 375.
🏌 Links Country Park Hotel ✆ 691.
♦London 135 – King's Lynn 42 – ♦Norwich 24.

✗✗ **Mirabelle**, 7 Station Rd, NR27 9QD, ✆ 396 – 🅿 🔽 AE ⓞ VISA
closed Sunday dinner in winter, Monday, first 2 weeks November and Christmas Day – **M** a la carte 12.50/16.50 t. ⅃ 2.40.

WESTWARD HO Devon 🗾 H 30 The West Country G. – pop. 2,203 – ECD : Tuesday – ✉ ☎ 023 72 Bideford.
♦London 235 – Bideford 4 – Exeter 47 – ♦Plymouth 62.

🏠 **Buckleigh Grange** ⌖, Buckleigh Rd, EX39 3PU, ✆ 4468, ⛱, ✗ – 🛁wc 🅿
closed January and February – **M** (bar lunch) 6.30 st. ⅃ 2.30 – **11 rm** 🍽 10.50/27.00 st. – SB (weekends only) 29.00/38.50 st.

WEST WITTON North Yorks. 🗾 O 21 – pop. 324 – ✉ Leyburn – ☎ 0969 Wensleydale.
♦London 241 – Kendal 39 – ♦Leeds 60 – York 53.

🏠 **Wensleydale Heifer**, Main St., DL8 4LS, ✆ 22322 – 📺 ⌂wc 🛁wc 🅿 🔽 VISA
M (bar lunch Monday to Saturday) 6.00/11.25 t. ⅃ 3.25 – **13 rm** 🍽 25.00/38.00 t. – SB (November-May) 45.00/55.00 st.

WEST WOODBURN Northumb. 🗾 🗾 N 18 – pop. 425 – ECD : Thursday – ✉ Hexham – ☎ 0660 Bellingham.
🏌 Bellingham ✆ 20530, SW : 4 ½ m.
♦ London 316 – ♦ Carlisle 49 – ♦ Edinburgh 78 – Hawick 35 – ♦ Newcastle-upon-Tyne 35.

🏠 **Bay Horse Inn**, NE48 2RX, ✆ 60218, ⛱ – 🅿
4 rm 🍽 12.00/20.00 st.

WETHERAL Cumbria 🗾 🗾 L 19 – see Carlisle.

WETHERBY West Yorks. 🗾 P 22 – pop. 5,900 – ECD : Wednesday – ☎ 0937.
🅱 Council Offices, 24 Westgate ✆ 62706/7.
♦London 208 – Harrogate 8 – ♦Leeds 13 – York 14.

🏨 **Ladbroke** (Ladbroke), Leeds Rd, Wetherby Roundabout, LS22 5HE, junction A 661 and A 1 ✆ 63881 – 📺 ⌂wc ⛽ 🅿 🍴 🔽 AE ⓞ VISA
M 6.50/8.50 t. – 🍽 5.25 – **72 rm** 36.50/44.50 t. – SB (weekends only) 33.00 st.

XXX **Linton Spring,** Sicklinghall Rd, LS22 9XX, W : 1 ¾ m. ✐ 65353, 🌳, park – **🅿 🔼 AE ① VISA**
closed Sunday dinner, Monday and 1 week January – **M** a la carte 11.30/16.35 **t.** ⓘ 2.75.

XX **L'Escale,** 16 Bank St., LS22 4NQ, ✐ 63613 – **🅿 🔼 AE ① VISA**
closed Sunday, Monday, 1 to 16 January and 1 to 14 August – **M** (dinner only) a la carte
10.00/18.25 **t.**

AUSTIN-ROVER North St. ✐ 62623

WETHERINGSETT Suffolk – pop. 1,594 – ✉ Stowmarket – ✆ 044 94 Mendlesham

🏠 **Wetheringsett Manor** ⌖, IP14 5PP, ✐ 545, 🌳, park – 🍴 📺 ➘wc **🅿 🔼 VISA**
M a la carte 10.70/14.00 **t.** ⓘ 2.55 – **9 rm** ⌑ 22.00/37.50 **t.** – SB 50.00/56.00 **st.**

WEYBOURNE Norfolk 404 X 25 – pop. 430 – ✉ Holt – ✆ 026 370.

♦London 128 – Cromer 7.5 – ♦Norwich 26.

🏠 **Maltings,** The Street, NR25 6SY, on A 149 ✐ 275, 🌳 – 📺 ➘wc **🅿 🔼 AE ① VISA**
M 7.30/10.50 **st.** ⓘ 2.90 – **22 rm** ⌑ 20.00/40.00 **st.** – SB (November-May) 29.50/34.50 **st.**

XX **Gasché's Swiss,** The Street, NR25 7SY, on A 149 ✐ 220 – **🅿 🔼 AE ① VISA**
closed Sunday dinner and Monday – **M** a la carte 13.35/18.05 **t.** ⓘ 1.50.

WEYBRIDGE Surrey 404 S 29 – pop. 51,134 (inc. Walton-on-Thames) – ECD : Wednesday –
✆ 0932 – ♦London 23.

Plan : see Greater London (South-West)

🏠 **Ship Thistle** (Thistle), Monument Green, High St., KT13 8BQ, ✐ 48364, Telex 894271 – 📺
➘wc ☎ **🅿** ⌖. **🔼 VISA**   by A 3050   AZ
M a la carte 12.50/15.00 **t.** ⓘ 3.45 – ⌑ 4.75 – **39 rm** 42.00/55.00 **t.** – SB (weekends only) 58.00 **st.**

XXX **Casa Romana,** 2 Temple Hall, Monument Hill, KT13 8RH, ✐ 43470, Italian rest. – **🅿 🔼 AE**
VISA   by A 3050   AZ
closed Saturday lunch and Monday – **M** a la carte 9.95/15.70 **t.**

AUSTIN-ROVER Woodham Lane, New Haw ✐
093 23 (Byfleet) 42870
AUSTIN-ROVER 30 Queens Rd ✐ 42233
FIAT, LANCIA Brooklands Rd ✐ 093 23 (Byfleet)
52941
FORD Monument Hill ✐ 46231

RENAULT 51/59 Baker St. ✐ 48247
SAAB Spinney Hill, Addlestone ✐ 093 287 (Otter-
shaw) 3726
VAUXHALL-OPEL New Haw Rd ✐ 53101
VOLVO 168 Oatlands Drive ✐ 54422

WEYMOUTH Dorset 403 404 M 32 The West Country G. – pop. 42,349 (inc. Melcombe Regis) –
ECD : Wednesday – ✆ 030 57 (5 fig.) or 0305 (6 fig.).

See : Boat Trip★ (Weymouth Bay and Portland Harbour).

Envir. : Abbotsbury★★, NW : 9 m. by B 3157.

🚢 Shipping connections with the Continent : to France (Cherbourg) (Sealink) – to Channel
Islands : St. Peter Port, Guernsey (Sealink) summer 1-3 daily ; winter 2 weekly (4 h 30 mn day, 10 h
night) – to Channel Islands : St. Helier, Jersey (Sealink) summer 2 daily ; winter 2 weekly (5 h
45 mn-7 h 30 mn).

🛈 Pavilion Complex, The Esplanade ✐ 72444 – King's Statue, The Esplanade ✐ 785747 (summer only).

♦London 141 – Bournemouth 35 – ♦Bristol 68 – Exeter 59 – Swindon 94.

🏠 **Streamside,** Preston Rd, Overcombe, DT3 6PX, NE : 2 m. on A 353 ✐ 833121, 🌳 – 📺
➘wc 🍴 **🅿. 🔼 AE ① VISA**
closed 25 and 26 December – **M** (dinner only and Sunday lunch) 5.50/8.00 **t.** ⓘ 3.00 – **19 rm**
⌑ 25.00/36.80 **t.**

🏠 **Glenburn,** 42 Preston Rd, Overcombe, DT3 6PZ, NE : 2 m. on A 353 ✐ 832353 – 📺 ➘wc
🍴wc **🅿. 🔼 AE VISA.** ⌖
M a la carte 8.30/10.30 **t.** ⓘ 2.50 – **13 rm** ⌑ 18.50/37.00 **t.** – SB (except summer) 52.00/60.00 **st.**

🏠 **Rex,** 29 The Esplanade, DT4 8DN, ✐ 773485 – 🍴 📺 ➘wc 🍴wc. **🔼 VISA**
closed 25 and 26 December – **M** (lunch by arrangement) 4.50/6.00 **t.** ⓘ 1.60 – **21 rm**
⌑ 15.00/34.00 – SB 36.80/41.40 **st.**

⌂ **Ellendale,** 88 Rodwell Av., DT4 8SQ, ✐ 786650 – **🅿.** ⌖
18 rm ⌑ 9.50/15.00 **st.**

FORD Dorchester Rd ✐ 782222   TALBOT 172 Dorchester Rd ✐ 786311

WHALLEY Lancs. 402 M 22 – pop. 3,449 – ✉ Blackburn – ✆ 025 482.

♦London 233 – ♦Blackpool 32 – Burnley 12 – ♦Manchester 28 – Preston 15.

XXX **Foxfields,** Whalley Rd, Billington, BB6 9HY, SW : 1 m. on A 59 ✐ 2556 – **🅿. 🔼 AE VISA**
closed Saturday lunch, Monday and Bank Holidays – **M** a la carte 11.45/15.95 **t.** ⓘ 3.00.

WHETSTONE Leics. – see Leicester.

WHIMPLE Devon 403 J 31 – see Exeter.

WHIPPINGHAM I.O.W. 403 404 Q 31 – see Wight (Isle of).

449

WHITBY North Yorks. 402 S 20 – pop. 12,150 – ECD : Wednesday – ✆ 0947.
See : Abbey ruins★ (13C) *AC*, Old St. Mary's Church★ 12C, East Terrace ≤★.
🛏 Low Straggleton ✆ 602768 – 🛱 New Quay Rd ✆ 602674.
◆London 257 – ◆Middlesbrough 31 – Scarborough 21 – York 45.

🏨 **Stakesby Manor,** High Stakesby, YO21 1HL, ✆ 602773, ☎ – 📺 🛏wc ⋔wc 🅿. ✖
M (dinner only and bar lunch Monday to Friday) 6.50 **t.** 🍷 2.75 – **8 rm** ☲ 17.50/29.50 **t.** – SB
(except summer and Bank Holidays) 39.00 **t.**

⋔ **Hudsons,** 24 Hudson St., YO21 3EP, ✆ 605277 – 📺 ⋔
6 rm ☲ 11.00/22.00 **st.**

at Sneaton S : 3 m. by A 171 on B 1416 – ⊠ ✆ 0947 Whitby :

🏨 **Sneaton Hall,** YO22 5HP, ✆ 605929, ☎ – 🛏wc ⋔wc 🅿. ⦿
M (bar lunch Monday to Saturday) approx. 7.50 **t.** – **8 rm** ☲ 15.50/31.00 **t.**

AUSTIN-ROVER – DAIMLER-JAGUAR 6 Upgang
Lane ✆ 603321
DATSUN Castle Park ✆ 602841

FORD Silver St. ✆ 602237
RENAULT 18 Silver St. ✆ 602093
VAUXHALL Argyle Rd ✆ 602898

WHITCHURCH Salop 402 403 404 L 25 – pop. 7,360 – ECD : Wednesday – ✆ 0948.
🛏 Hill Valley, Terrick Rd ✆ 3584, N : 1 m. – 🛱 Civic Centre, High St. ✆ 4577.
◆London 171 – ◆Birmingham 54 – Chester 22 – ◆Manchester 43 – Shrewsbury 20.

🏨 **Redbrook Hunting Lodge,** Wrexham Rd, SY13 3ET, W : 2 ½ m. on A 525 ✆ 094 873 (Redbrook Maelor) 204, ☎ – 🛏wc 🅿. 🖭 🅰🅴 🆅🆂🅰
M 7.00 **t.** 🍷 2.95 – **12 rm** ☲ 19.75/29.75 **t.** – SB (weekends only) 41.40/42.60 **st.**

AUSTIN-ROVER Brownlow St. ✆ 2826
AUSTIN-ROVER, LAND-ROVER Newport Rd ✆ 3333

FORD Dodington ✆ 4471
RENAULT Wrexham Rd ✆ 2257

WHITEBROOK Gwent – see Monmouth.

WHITFIELD Kent 404 X 30 – see Dover.

WHITLAND (HENDY-GWYN) Dyfed 403 G 28 – pop. 1,350 – ✆ 0994.
◆London 235 – Carmarthen 15 – Haverfordwest 17.

🏨 **Waungron Farm** ⚘, SA34 0QX, SW : 1 m. ✆ 240682, « Converted farm buildings », park –
📺 🛏wc ⋔wc 🅿. ✖ – **13 rm**

⋔ **Cilpost Farm** ⚘, SA34 4RP, N : 1 ¼ m. by North Rd ✆ 240280, ≤, ☎ – 🛏wc 🅿. ✖
April-September – **7 rm** ☲ 12.00/36.00 **st.**

WHITLEY BAY Tyne and Wear 401 402 P 18 – pop. 37,817 – ECD : Wednesday – ✆ 091 Tyneside.
Envir. : Seaton Delaval Hall★ (18C) *AC*, NW : 6 m.
🛱 Central Promenade. ✆ 524494 and 513131 (summer only).
◆London 293 – ◆Newcastle-upon-Tyne 10 – Sunderland 10.

🏨 **Ambassador,** 38-42 South Par., NE26 2RQ, ✆ 253 1218 – 📺 🛏wc ☎ 🅿. 🅰🅴 ⦿ 🆅🆂🅰
closed Christmas Day – **M** 5.50/8.00 **t.** 🍷 2.80 – **28 rm** ☲ 21.00/33.00 **t.** – SB (weekends only) 44.00/52.00 **st.**

ALFA-ROMEO ✆ 521848
AUSTIN-ROVER Cauldwell Lane ✆ 522231
AUSTIN-ROVER Links Rd, Seaton Sluice ✆ 371844
CITROEN Claremont Rd ✆ 525909
FIAT Claremont Rd ✆ 523347

FORD Whitley Rd ✆ 522225
LADA Fox Hunters Rd ✆ 528282
VAUXHALL Earsdon Rd, West Monkseaton ✆
523355
VW, AUDI-NSU Hillheads Rd ✆ 528225

WHITSTABLE Kent 404 X 29 – pop. 21,950 – ECD : Wednesday – ✆ 0227.
Envir. : Herne Bay : Reculver (church twin towers★ *AC*), E : 8 ½ m.
🛱 1 Tankerton Rd ✆ 272233.
◆London 59 – ◆Dover 22 – Maidstone 28 – Margate 19.

XXX **Giovanni's,** 49-55 Canterbury Rd, CT5 4HH, ✆ 273034, Italian rest. – 🅿. 🅰 🅰🅴 ⦿ 🆅🆂🅰
closed Monday and 26-27 December – **M** a la carte 8.00/13.40 **t.** 🍷 2.50.

at Tankerton E : ¾ m. on B 2205 – ⊠ ✆ 0227 Whitstable :

✗ Le Pousse Bedaine, 101 Tankerton Rd, CT5 2AJ, ✆ 272056, Bistro.

AUSTIN-ROVER Tankerton Rd ✆ 264614
COLT Swale Cliffe ✆ 0246 (Chesterfield) 2396

FORD Tankerton Rd ✆ 265613
RENAULT Tower Parade ✆ 261477

WHITTLESEY Cambs. 404 T 26 – see Peterborough.

WHITWELL-ON-THE-HILL North Yorks. 402 R 21 – ⊠ York – ✆ 065 381.
◆London 223 – Malton 5 – York 12.

🏨 **Whitwell Hall Country House** ⚘, YO6 7JJ, ✆ 551, ≤, ☎, park, ✗ – 🛏wc ⋔wc ☎ 🅿.
🛎 🅰🅴 ⦿ 🆅🆂🅰 ✖
M (lunch by arrangement) 8.00/15.00 **st.** 🍷 2.80 – **20 rm** ☲ 25.00/57.00 **st.**

WICKHAM Hants. 000 000 Q 31 – pop. 3,896 – ECD : Wednesday – ✆ 0329.
◆London 74 – ◆Portsmouth 12 – ◆Southampton 11 – Winchester 16.

🏨 **Old House,** The Square, PO17 5JG, ☎ 833049, « Tastefully renovated Queen Anne house », 🛋 – 📺 ⇄wc ☜ 🅿. 🆘 🆎 ⑩ 𝘝𝘐𝘚𝘈 ❄
closed 2 weeks Easter, 2 weeks July-August and 10 days at Christmas – **M** (closed lunch Saturday and Monday, Sunday and Bank Holidays) a la carte 13.30/15.50 **st.** ⊥ 3.45 – **10 rm** ⊐ 38.00/50.00 **st.**

WIGAN Greater Manchester 000 000 M 23 – pop. 81,147 – ECD : Wednesday – ✆ 0942.
🅱 Haigh Hall Park ☎ 42050, NW : 3 m. – 🅱 Arley Hall, Haigh ☎ 0257 (Standish) 421360, N : 4 m. – 🅱 Pennington Recreation Area, ☎ 672823.
◆London 206 – ◆Liverpool 19 – ◆Manchester 18 – Preston 18.

🏨 **Brocket Arms,** Mesnes Rd, WN1 2DD, ☎ 46283 – 📺 ⇄wc ⧎wc ☜ 🅿. 🔺. 🆘 🆎 ⑩ 𝘝𝘐𝘚𝘈 ❄
M (closed Sunday dinner) (bar lunch only Saturday and Sunday) 7.50 **st.** ⊥ 2.75 – **27 rm** ⊐ 25.00/36.00 **st.**

AUSTIN-ROVER, DAIMLER-JAGUAR Wallgate ☎ 44977	RELIANT Cerrell Post ☎ 214437
FIAT Miry Lane ☎ 39107	TALBOT Nicol Rd, Bryn ☎ 0942 (Ashton in Makerfield) 78588
FORD Wallgate ☎ 41393	VAUXHALL-OPEL Warrington Rd ☎ 494848
LADA Chapel St., Pemberton ☎ 214028	VOLVO Platt Bridge ☎ 866594
NISSAN Woodhouse Lane ☎ 34141	VW, AUDI Crompton St. ☎ 42281
PEUGEOT-TALBOT 32, Whelly ☎ 41493	

WIGHT (Isle of) 000 000 PQ 31 32 – pop. 109,512.
⛴ from East to West Cowes to Southampton (Red Funnel Services) 8-18 daily (55 mn to 1 h 10 mn) – from Yarmouth to Lymington (Sealink) 24-30 daily (30 mn) – from Fishbourne to Portsmouth (Sealink) 19-25 daily (45 mn).
⛴ From West Cowes to Southampton (Red Funnel Services : hydrofoil) Monday to Saturday 14-19 daily ; Sunday 10 daily (20 mn) – from Ryde to Southsea (Hovertravel to Southsea Clarence Pier) summer frequent services daily ; winter 8-12 daily (restricted Sundays) (9 mn) – from Ryde to Portsmouth (Sealink to Portsmouth Harbour) 15-24 daily (25-30 mn).

Bembridge – pop. 3,272 – ✉ ✆ 0983 Isle of Wight – Newport 14.

🏨 **Highbury,** Lane End Rd, PO35 5SU, ☎ 872838, ⴲ heated, 🛋 – 📺 ⇄wc ⧎wc ☜ 🅿. 🆘 🆎 ⑩ 𝘝𝘐𝘚𝘈 ❄
closed 3 weeks October and 24 to 27 December – **M** 5.00/9.00 **t.** ⊥ 2.85 – **9 rm** ⊐ 17.00/38.50 **st.** – SB 44.00 **st.**

🏨 **Elms Country** ⚲, Swaines Rd, PO35 5XS, ☎ 872248, 🛋 – 📺 ⇄wc ⧎wc 🅿
March-mid October – **M** (closed lunch to non-residents) 6.00/11.00 **t.** ⊥ 3.50 – **12 rm** ⊐ 16.00/32.00 **st.**

PEUGEOT Church Rd ☎ 2121

Chale – pop. 537 – ECD : Thursday – ✉ Ventnor – ✆ 0983 Isle of Wight.
Newport 9.

🏨 **Clarendon,** Newport Rd, PO38 2HA, ☎ 730431, ≼, 🛋 – ⇄wc ⧎wc 🅿
M (bar lunch) a la carte 4.75/8.05 **t.** – **13 rm** ⊐ (dinner included) 18.00/36.00 – SB (except summer) 32.00/36.00 **st.**

Cowes – pop. 17,260 – ECD : Wednesday – ✉ ✆ 0983 Isle of Wight.
Envir. : Osborne House* (19C) AC, E : 1 m.– 🅱 Crossfield Av. ☎ 293529.
Newport 4.

🏨 **Holmwood,** Egypt Point, 65 Queens Rd, PO30 8BW, ☎ 292508, ≼ – 📺 ⇄wc ⧎wc ☜ 🅿. 🆘 🆎 ⑩ 𝘝𝘐𝘚𝘈
closed Christmas and New Year – **M** 7.50/9.00 **t.** – **18 rm** ⊐ 18.00/40.00 **t.**

🏨 **Cowes,** 260 Artic Rd, PO31 7RJ, ☎ 291541, ⴲ – 📺 ⇄wc ☜ 🅿. 🆘 🆎 ⑩ 𝘝𝘐𝘚𝘈
closed Christmas – **M** 8.00 **t.** ⊥ 1.85 – **14 rm** ⊐ 19.50/29.50 **t.**

✗ **G's,** 10 Bath Rd, PO31 7QN, ☎ 297021 – 🆘 🆎 ⑩ 𝘝𝘐𝘚𝘈
closed Sundays except Bank Holidays, 25 to 27 December, 1 to 3 January and February – **M** (lunch by arrangement) a la carte 8.25/13.20 **t.** ⊥ 3.95.

Freshwater Bay – pop. 5,570 – ECD : Thursday – ✉ ✆ 0983 Isle of Wight.
🅱 ☎ 752955.
Newport 13.

🏨 **Albion,** PO40 9RA, ☎ 753631, ≼ – 📺 ⇄wc ☜ 🅿. 🆘 𝘝𝘐𝘚𝘈
April-October – **M** 5.00/8.25 **st.** – **43 rm** ⊐ 13.50/33.75 **st.**

↑ **Blenheim House,** Gate Lane, PO40 9QD, ☎ 752858, ⴲ heated – ⧎wc 🅿. ❄
May-October – **8 rm** ⊐ 13.50/23.40 **st.**

[Newport] – pop. 22,309 – ECD : Thursday – ✉ ⊕ 0983 Isle of Wight.

Envir. : Shorwell (St. Peter's Church★ 15C) SW : 5 m – Carisbrooke Castle★★ 12C-16C (keep <★) *AC* SW : 1 ½ m.

⛳9 St. George's Down, Shide ℘ 525076, SE : 1 m.

[i] 21 High St. ℘ 524343.

🏨🏨🏨 **Bugle,** 117 High St., PO30 1TP, ℘ 522800 – [TV] 🛁wc ☎ [P]. 👥. 💳 [AE] ◐ [VISA]
M (grill rest. only) a la carte 5.90/9.80 **st.** – **26 rm** ☕ 27.50/36.00 **st.**

AUDI, MERCEDES-BENZ, VW Medina Avenue ℘ 523232
BMW Blackwater ℘ 523684

[Ryde] – pop. 23,204 – ECD : Thursday – ✉ ⊕ 0983 Isle of Wight.

⛳9 Ryde House Park ℘ 62088.

[i] Western Gardens, Esplanade ℘ 62905 (summer only).

Newport 7.5.

🏨🏨🏨 **Yelf's** (T.H.F.), Union St., PO33 2LG, ℘ 64062 – [TV] 🛁wc ☎. 👥. 💳 [AE] ◐ [VISA]
M 7.00/8.00 **st.** 🍾 2.60 – ☕ 5.00 – **21 rm** 30.50/41.00 **st.**

AUSTIN-ROVER Elmfield ℘ 62717
FORD Gorfield Rd ℘ 62281
HONDA Brading Rd ℘ 64166
LANCIA Victoria St. ℘ 63661
SKODA Havenstreet ℘ 0983 (Wootton Bridge) 882455
VW, AUDI-NSU Fishbourne Lane ℘ 0983 (Wootton Bridge) 882465

[Sandown] – pop. 4,593 – ECD : Wednesday – ✉ ⊕ 0983 Isle of Wight.

⛳18 Shanklin and Sandown ℘ 403170.

[i] The Esplanade ℘ 403886.

Newport 9.

🏨 **St. Catherine's,** 1 Winchester Park Rd, PO36 8HJ, ℘ 402392 – 🛁wc 🚿wc [P]. 💳 [VISA]. 🐕
closed Christmas – **M** (dinner only) 5.00 **t.** 🍾 1.75 – **18 rm** ☕ 12.00/35.00 **t.** – SB 35.00/40.00 **st.**

CITROEN Avenue Rd ℘ 402189

[Seaview] – ✉ ⊕ 098 371 Seaview

🏨 **Seaview,** High St., PO34 5EX, ℘ 2711 – 🛁wc [P]. 💳 [AE] [VISA]
M 5.95/6.95 **t.** 🍾 2.50 – **14 rm** ☕ 15.00/34.00 **t.** – SB 35.00/38.00 **st.**

[Shanklin] – pop. 7,240 – ECD : Wednesday – ✉ ⊕ 0983 Isle of Wight.

See : Old Village (thatched cottages)★ – The Chine★ *AC*.

Envir. : Brading (Roman Villa : mosaics★ *AC*) N : 3 ½ m.

[i] 67 High St. ℘ 862942.

Newport 9.

🏨🏨🏨🏨 Cliff Tops, 1-5 Park Rd, PO37 6BB, ℘ 863262, <, 🏊 heated, 🌳 – ⇅ [TV] ☎ [P]. 👥 – **106 rm**.

🏨🏨🏨 **Hartland,** 41 Victoria Av., PO37 6LT, ℘ 863123, [🏊], 🌳 – [TV] 🛁wc 🚿wc [P]. 💳 [VISA]. 🐕
M *(closed Sunday dinner and Monday)* 5.50/14.00 **st.** 🍾 1.80 – **24 rm** ☕ 17.85/46.00 **st.**

🏨 Carlton 🐦, Eastcliff Promenade, PO37 6AY, ℘ 862517, <, 🌳 – 🛁wc [P]. 🐕
April-September – **12 rm** ☕ 13.50/36.00 **st.**

🏨 **Bourne Hall Country** 🐦, Luccombe Rd, PO37 6RR, ℘ 862820, 🏊 heated, [🏊], 🌳, 🎾 – [TV] 🛁wc [P]. 💳 [AE] ◐ [VISA]. 🐕
March-October – **M** (bar lunch) 7.00 **t.** 🍾 2.50 – **23 rm** ☕ 17.50/43.00 **t.**

🏨 **Queensmead,** 12 Queens Rd, PO37 6AN, ℘ 862342, 🏊 heated, 🌳 – 🛁wc 🚿wc. 🐕
April-October – **M** (bar lunch) 6.00 **st.** 🍾 2.00 – **26 rm** ☕ 12.70/34.70 **st.** – SB 21.85/24.15 **st.**

🏠 **Delphi Cliff,** 7 St. Boniface Cliff Rd, PO37 6ET, ℘ 862179, <, 🌳 – 🛁wc [P]. 🐕
Easter-October – **11 rm** ☕ 9.80/27.50 **st.**

🏠 **Overstrand,** Howard Rd, PO37 6HD, ℘ 862100, <, 🌳, 🎾 – 🛁wc 🚿wc [P]. 💳. 🐕
March-October – **15 rm** ☕ 10.00/23.00 **t.**

🍴 **Cottage,** 8 Eastcliff Rd, PO37 6AA, ℘ 862504 – [VISA]
closed Sunday lunch in summer, Sunday dinner, Monday except summer, mid February-mid March and October – **M** (restricted lunch)(booking essential) a la carte 8.90/12.10 **t.**

[Totland Bay] – pop. 1,724 – ECD : Wednesday – ✉ ⊕ 0983 Isle of Wight.

Envir. : Alum Bay (coloured sands★) and the Needles★ SW : 1 m.

Newport 13.

🏨🏨🏨 **Country Garden,** Church Hill, PO39 0ET, on B 3322 ℘ 754521, <, 🌳 – [TV] 🛁wc ☎ [P]. 💳 [AE] ◐ [VISA]
closed 25 and 26 December – **M** 6.00/8.50 **st.** 🍾 2.60 – **16 rm** ☕ 23.00/36.00 **t.** – SB 42.00/45.00 **st.**

🏨 Sentry Mead, Madeira Rd, PO39 0BJ, ℘ 753212, 🌳 – 🛁wc [P]. 🐕 – **13 rm**.

🏠 **Nodes Country** 🐦, Alum Bay, Old Road, PO39 0HZ, SW : 1 ½ m. by B 3322 ℘ 752859, 🌳 – 🛁wc 🚿wc [P]
April-October – **11 rm** ☕ 14.00/28.00 **st.**

Ventnor – pop. 6,931 – ECD : Wednesday – ✉ ✪ 0983 Isle of Wight.
Envir. : St. Catherine's Point (≤★ from the car-park) W : 5 m.
🖥 Steephill Down Rd ✆ 853326.
🛈 34 High St. ✆ 853625 (summer only).
Newport 10.

🏨 **Ventnor Towers,** 54 Madeira Rd, PO38 1QT, ✆ 852277, ≤, ⊒ heated, ⚓, ✵ – 📺 ⌂wc
☎ 🅿. ⚡ ⒶⒺ ⑩ 𝒱𝒮𝒜
M 5.00/8.00 **st.** ⓘ 3.50 – **30 rm** ⊆ 16.50/53.00 **st.** – SB (weekends only)(except summer) 40.00/44.00 **st.**

🏨 **Royal** (T.H.F.), Belgrave Rd, PO38 1JJ, ✆ 852186, ⊒ heated, ⚓ – ⧉ 📺 ⌂wc ☎ 🅿. ⚡ ⒶⒺ
⑩ 𝒱𝒮𝒜
March-October – **M** (buffet lunch) 7.50 **st.** ⓘ 2.60 – ⊆ 5.00 – **55 rm** 28.50/42.00 **st.**

↖ **Madeira Hall** ⟋, Trinity Rd, PO38 1NS, ✆ 852624, ⊒ heated, ⚓ – ⌂wc 🅿. ⚡ ⒶⒺ 𝒱𝒮𝒜
mid March-mid October – **12 rm** ⊆ 12.00/28.50 **st.**

↖ **Channel View,** Hambrough Rd, PO38 1SQ, ✆ 852230, ≤ – 🔥. 𝒱𝒮𝒜 ✵
April-October – **14 rm** ⊆ 13.00/24.00 **st.**

at Bonchurch – ✉ ✪ 0983 Isle of Wight :

🏨 **Winterbourne** ⟋, PO38 1RQ, ✆ 852535, ≤ gardens and sea, « Country house and gardens », ⊒ heated – 📺 ⌂wc 🔥wc 🅿. ⚡ ⒶⒺ 𝒱𝒮𝒜
February-November – **M** (buffet lunch) 12.75 **t.** ⓘ 2.50 – **19 rm** ⊆ (dinner included) 28.00/76.00 **t.** – SB (spring and autumn only) 48.00/57.00 **st.**

🏨 **Bonchurch Manor** ⟋, Bonchurch Shute, PO38 1NU, ✆ 852868, ≤, ⚡, ⚓ – 📺 ⌂wc
🔥wc 🅿. ⚡ 𝒱𝒮𝒜
closed January – **M** (dinner only and Sunday lunch) 5.25/8.25 **t.** ⓘ 2.40 – **11 rm** ⊆ 26.00/52.00 **st.** – SB (October-April) 46.00 **st.**

🏨 **Highfield,** Leeson Rd, Upper Bonchurch, PO38 1PU, on A 3055 ✆ 852800, ≤, ⚓ – 📺 ⌂wc
🅿. ⚡ 𝒱𝒮𝒜 – **8 rm.**

🏨 **Lake** ⟋, Shore Rd, PO38 1RF, ✆ 852613, ⚓ – 🔥wc 🅿
April-October – **M** (bar lunch) 3.00/4.50 **t.** ⓘ 2.25 – **23 rm** ⊆ 8.50/26.50 **t.** – SB 23.00/30.50 **st.**

↖ **Under Rock** ⟋, Shore Rd, PO38 1RF, ✆ 852714, « Gardens » – 📺 🅿. ⚡ ⒶⒺ ⑩ 𝒱𝒮𝒜
March-October – **7 rm** ⊆ 14.00/28.00 **s.**

↖ **Horseshoe Bay** ⟋, Shore Rd, PO38 1RN, ✆ 852487, ≤ – ⌂wc 🅿. ⚡
Easter-October – **7 rm** ⊆ 9.00/28.00 **t.**

✗✗ **Peacock Vane** ⟋ with rm, Bonchurch Village Rd, PO38 1RG, ✆ 852019, ≤, « Country house atmosphere », ⊒ heated, ⚓ – 📺 ⌂wc 🅿 – **9 rm.**

at St. Lawrence – ✉ ✪ 0983 Ventnor :

↖ **Woody Bank,** Undercliff Drive, PO38 1XF, ✆ 852610, ≤, ⚓ – 🔥wc 🅿
March-October – **9 rm** ⊆ 11.50/30.00 **st.**

AUSTIN-ROVER Victoria St. ✆ 852650

Whippingham – ✉ ✪ 0983 Isle of Wight.
Newport 3.5.

🏨 **Padmore House** ⟋, Beatrice Av., PO32 6LP, ✆ 293210, ⚓ – 📺 ⌂wc 🔥 ☎ 🅿. ⚡ ⒶⒺ ⑩
𝒱𝒮𝒜
closed 25 to 28 December – **M** (closed Saturday lunch) 7.60/10.00 **st.** ⓘ 2.75 – **11 rm**
⊆ 18.75/49.80 **t.** – SB (weekends only) 42.00/50.00 **st.**

Yarmouth – pop. 984 – ECD : Wednesday – ✉ ✪ 0983 Isle of Wight.
🛈 Quay Rd ✆ 760015 (summer only).
Newport 10.

🏨 Bugle, St. James Sq., PO41 0NS, ✆ 760272 – ⌂wc 🅿 – **10 rm.**

AUSTIN-ROVER Mill Rd ✆ 760436

☛ *Inclusion in the Michelin Guide cannot be achieved by pulling strings or by offering favours.*

WILLENHALL West Midlands �403 �404 N 26 – see Coventry.

WILLERBY Humberside �402 S 22 – see Kingston-upon-Hull.

WILLERSEY Heref. and Worc. �403 �404 O 27 – see Broadway.

WILLERSEY HILL Glos. �403 �404 O 27 – see Broadway (Heref. and Worc.).

WILLINGDON East Sussex �404 U 31 – see Eastbourne.

WILLITON Somerset 408 K 30 The West Country G. – pop. 2,948 – ECD : Saturday – 🕾 0984.
♦London 177 – Minehead 8 – Taunton 16.

   🏠 **White House,** 11 Long St., TA4 4QW, ℰ 32306 – 🚻wc ℗
      11 May-October – **M** (dinner only) 13.50 t. ‖ 3.00 – **13 rm** ⚏ 19.00/38.00 t. – SB 50.00/55.00 **st.**

AUSTIN-ROVER West Quantoxhead ℰ 32437   PEUGEOT, TALBOT High St. ℰ 32761

WILMCOTE Warw. 408 404 O 27 – see Stratford-upon-Avon.

WILMINGTON Devon 408 K 31 – see Honiton.

WILMINGTON East Sussex 404 U 31 – see Eastbourne.

WILMSLOW Cheshire 402 408 404 N 24 – pop. 27,220 – ECD : Wednesday – 🕾 0625.
🅶 Great Warford ℰ 056 587 (Mobberley) 2579, SW : 1 ½ m.
♦London 189 – ♦Liverpool 38 – ♦Manchester 12 – ♦Stoke-on-Trent 27.

   🏯 **Stanneylands,** Stanneylands Rd, SK9 4EY, N : 1 m. by A 34 ℰ 525225, Telex 666358, « Gardens » – 📺 ☎ & ℗ 🚗 🅰 🆎 ⑩ VISA ⁂
      closed 5 April, 26 December and 1 January – **M** *(closed Sunday dinner)* 6.00/12.50 **st.** ‖ 2.60 –
      ⚏ 4.50 – **34 rm** 18.00/42.00 **st.** – SB (weekends only)(except Christmas and New Year) 75.00 **st.**

   🏠 Valley Lodge, Oversley Ford, Altrincham Rd, SK9 4LR, NW : 2 ¾ m. on A 538 ℰ 529201, Telex
      666401 – ♨ 📺 🚻wc ☎ ℗ 🚗 ⁂ – **87 rm.**

      at Handforth N : 3 m. on A 34 – ✉ Wilmslow :

   🏯 **Belfry,** Stanley Rd, SK9 3LD, ℰ 061 (Manchester) 437 0511, Telex 666358, 🎘 – ♨ 📺 & ℗.
      🚗 🅰 🆎 ⑩ VISA ⁂
      M 7.75/8.95 **t.** ‖ 3.75 – ⚏ 5.00 – **92 rm** 35.25/45.00 **t.**

   🏠 **Pinewood,** 180 Wilmslow Rd, SK9 3LG, ℰ 0625 (Wilmslow) 529211, 🎘 – ♨ 📺 🚻wc ☎
      ℗ 🚗 🅰 🆎 ⑩ VISA ⁂
      M 6.50/9.50 **st.** – ⚏ 3.95 – **64 rm** 33.00/39.00 **st.**

BMW Manchester Rd ℰ 523542   RENAULT Station Rd ℰ 527356
NISSAN ℰ 524145   RENAULT Knutsford Rd ℰ 523669
PORSCHE Green Lane ℰ 526392   VAUXHALL-OPEL Water Lane ℰ 527311

WIMBORNE MINSTER Dorset 408 404 O 31 The West Country G. – pop. 7,400 – ECD : Wednesday – 🕾 0202 Wimborne.
See : Site★.
🅶 Ashley Wood ℰ 025 82 (Blandford) 52253, NW : 8 m.
🎫 The Quarter Jack, 6 Cook Row. ℰ 886116.
♦London 112 – Bournemouth 10 – Dorchester 23 – Salisbury 27 – ♦Southampton 30.

   🏠 **King's Head** (T.H.F.), The Square, BH21 1JA, ℰ 880101 – ♨ 📺 🚻wc ☎ ℗ 🚗 🅰 🆎 ⑩
      VISA
      M 5.50/9.75 **st.** ‖ 2.85 – ⚏ 4.75 – **28 rm** 29.50/44.00 **st.**

   XXX **Antiqua,** Allendale House, Hanham Rd, BH21 1AS, ℰ 881666 – ℗ 🅰 ⑩ VISA
      closed Sunday and Bank Holidays – **M** a la carte 9.50/20.10 **t.** ‖ 3.00.

   XX **Old Town House,** 9 Church St., BH21 1JH, ℰ 888227 – VISA
      closed Sunday, Monday, first week January and 2 weeks at Easter – **M** (dinner only) a la carte
      9.85/12.80.

      at Horton N : 6 m. on B 3078 – ✉ Wimborne Minster – 🕾 0258 Witchampton :

   🏠 **Horton Inn,** Cranborne Rd, BH21 5AD, ℰ 840252 – 📺 🚻wc ℗ 🅰 🆎 ⑩ VISA ⁂
      M *(closed Sunday dinner)* a la carte 7.80/11.55 **st.** ‖ 1.75 – ⚏ 2.50 – **5 rm** 17.50/28.00 **st.**

      at Broadstone S : 3 ¼ m. by A 349 on B 3074 – ✉ Poole – 🕾 0202 Broadstone :

   ↥ **Fairlight** ⏚, 1 Golf Links Rd, BH18 8BE, ℰ 694316, 🎘 – 🚻wc ♨wc ℗
      10 rm ⚏ 13.00/28.00 **st.**

AUSTIN-ROVER West St. ℰ 882261   OPEL Walford Bridge ℰ 884211
FORD Poole Rd ℰ 886211   VOLVO 41 Leigh Rd ℰ 887163

WINCANTON Somerset 408 404 M 30 – pop. 2,576 – ECD : Thursday – 🕾 0963.
🅶 Tower Hill ℰ 074 981 (Bruton) 3233, N : 5 m. on A 359.
🎫 Public Library, 7 Carrington Way ℰ 32173.
♦London 119 – ♦Bristol 37 – Taunton 34 – Yeovil 16.

   🏠 **Holbrook House** ⏚, Holbrook, BA9 8BS, W : 1 ½ m. on A 371, ℰ 32377, ≤, « Country
      mansion », ⊒ heated, 🎘, park, ⁒ – 🚻wc ♨wc ℗ 🅰 🆎 VISA
      M 5.50/7.50 **t.** ‖ 2.50 – **20 rm** ⚏ 16.50/37.00 **t.** – SB (except Christmas) 40.00/45.00 **st.**

AUSTIN-ROVER Station Rd ℰ 32021

WINCHELSEA East Sussex 404 W 31 – see Rye.

454

See : Cathedral★★★ 11C-13C B – Winchester College★★ 14C B B – Pilgrim's Hall★ 14C B E – St. Cross Hospital★ 12C-15C A.

Envir. : Marwell Zoological Park★★ *AC*, SE : 5 m. on A 333 A.

🚺 The Guildhall, The Broadway ℰ 68166 and 65406 (weekends).

◆London 72 – ◆Bristol 76 – ◆Oxford 52 – ◆Southampton 12.

WINCHESTER

High Street . . . . **B**	City Road . . . . **B** 10	Petersfield Road . . . . **A** 28
	Clifton Terrace . . . . **B** 12	Quarry Road . . . . **A** 29
Alresford Road . . . . **A** 2	East Hill . . . . **B** 15	St. George's Street . . . . **B** 32
Andover Road . . . . **B** 3	Eastgate Street . . . . **B** 16	St. Paul's Hill . . . . **B** 33
Bereweeke Road . . . . **A** 5	Easton Lane . . . . **A** 18	St. Peter's Street . . . . **B** 34
Bridge Street . . . . **B** 6	Friarsgate . . . . **B** 19	Southgate Street . . . . **B** 35
Broadway (The) . . . . **B** 8	Garnier Road . . . . **A** 20	Stoney Lane . . . . **B** 36
Chilbolton Avenue . . . . **A** 9	Kingsgate Road . . . . **A** 22	Stockbridge Road . . . . **B** 37
	Magdalen Hill . . . . **B** 23	Sussex Street . . . . **B** 38
	Middle Brook Street . . . . **B** 25	Union Street . . . . **B** 39
	Park Road . . . . **A** 26	Upper High Street . . . . **B** 40

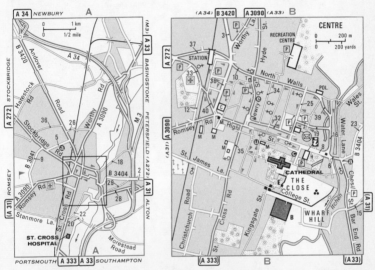

🏨🏨 **Wessex** (T.H.F.), Paternoster Row, SO23 9LQ, ℰ 61611, Telex 47419, ≤ – 📳 📺 🅿 🏂 🌃
AE ① VISA
B c
M 8.50/11.50 **st.** 🍴 2.60 – ⬜ 5.50 – **94 rm** 41.50/50.00 **st.**

🏨🏨 **Lainston House** ⤸, Sparsholt, SO21 2LT, NW : 3 ½ m. by A 272 ℰ 63588, Telex 477375, ≤,
« 17C manor house », 🌹, park, 🎾 – 📺 🕿 🔥 🅿 🖾 AE ① VISA 🌠 by A 272 A
M 12.50/20.00 **t.** 🍴 3.50 – ⬜ 5.50 – **32 rm** 42.00/75.00 **t.** – SB (September-March) 85.00 **st.**

🏠 **Chantry Mead,** 22 Bereweeke Rd, SO22 6AJ, ℰ 52767, 🌹 – 📺 ⊟wc 🐾 🅿 🖾 A a
closed 24 December to 1 January – **M** (closed Sunday dinner) (dinner only and Sunday lunch)
4.50/6.50 🍴 2.95 – **17 rm** ⬜ 16.20/42.35 **t.**

🗙🗙 **Old Chesil Rectory,** Chesil St., SO23 8HU, ℰ 53177, French rest. – 🖾 AE ① VISA B a
closed Sunday, 23 December-23 January and Bank Holidays – **M** (dinner only) 12.95 **t.** 🍴 2.75.

🗙🗙 **Cellar Peking,** 32-33 Jewry St., SO23 8RY, ℰ 64178, Chinese-Peking and Szechuan – 🖾
① VISA B e
M a la carte 6.20/12.20 **t.**

🗙 **Splinters,** 9 Great Minster St., SO23 9AP, ℰ 64004 – 🖾 AE ① VISA B u
closed Sunday – **M** (dinner only) a la carte 15.50/19.40 **t.** 🍴 2.45.

ASTON-MARTIN Hursley ℰ 75218
AUSTIN-ROVER St. Swithun St. ℰ 68461
AUSTIN-ROVER Easton Lane, The By-pass ℰ 69182
FORD Bar-End Rd ℰ 62211
NISSAN Gordon Rd ℰ 69544

RENAULT Stockbridge Rd ℰ 63344
TALBOT, CITROEN 2/4 St. Cross Rd ℰ 61855
VOLVO Kingsworthy ℰ 881414
VW, AUDI St. Cross Rd ℰ 66331

WINDERMERE Cumbria [402] L 20 – pop. 7,140 – ECD : Thursday – ☎ 096 62.
See : Lake★ – **Envir.** : Kirkstone Pass (on Windermere ←★) N : 7 m. by A 592 Y.
Cleabarrow ✆ 3123 by A 5074 Z and B 5284 – Victoria St. ✆ 4561.
♦London 274 – ♦Blackpool 55 – ♦Carlisle 46 – Kendal 10.

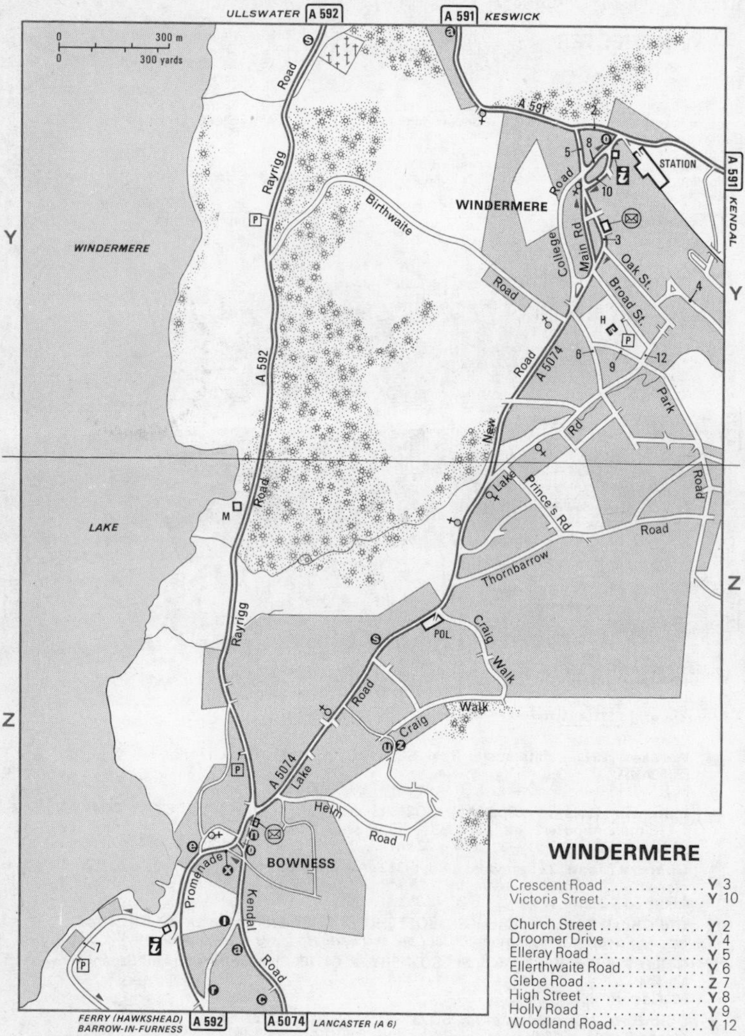

WINDERMERE

Crescent Road . . . . **Y** 3
Victoria Street. . . . . **Y** 10

Church Street . . . . **Y** 2
Droomer Drive . . . . **Y** 4
Elleray Road . . . . **Y** 5
Ellerthwaite Road. . . . . **Y** 6
Glebe Road . . . . **Z** 7
High Street . . . . **Y** 8
Holly Road . . . . **Y** 9
Woodland Road. . . . . **Y** 12

Langdale Chase, LA23 1LW, NW : 3 m. on A 591 ✆ 0966 (Ambleside) 32201, ← Lake Windermere and mountains, « Extensive grounds with lake frontage », park, – rest [TV] [P]. [AE] [VISA] — on A 591 Y
M 7.25/13.25 **st.** 2.75 – **35 rm** 26.50/65.00 **st.** – SB (except summer) 52.00/58.00 **st.**

Wild Boar (Best Western), Crook Rd, LA23 3NF, SE : 4 m. by A 5074 on B 5284 ✆ 5225, – [TV] wc wc ☎ [P]. [AE] [VISA] — by A 5074 Z
M 7.00/12.25 **st.** 2.80 – **38 rm** 24.75/49.50 **st.** – SB 42.00/45.00 **st.**

Priory, Rayrigg Rd, LA23 1EX, NW : ¾ m. by A 591 on A 592 ✆ 4377, ←, – [TV] wc ☎ [P] **15 rm**. — by A592 Y

🏠 **Holbeck Ghyll Country House** 🍴, Holbeck Lane, LA23 1LU, NW : 3 ½ m. by A 591
  ℘ 0966 (Ambleside) 32375, ≤, « Country house atmosphere », 🌳 – ➔wc **P**. 🔂
  March-November – **M** (bar lunch) 8.50 **st**. ⓝ 2.50 – **11 rm** ⊑ 20.00/42.00 **st**. – SB
  (spring and November) 36.00/40.00 **st**.   by A 591   Y

🏠 **Willowsmere,** Ambleside Rd, LA23 1ES, ℘ 3575, 🌳 – ➔wc **P**. 🔂 🅰🅴 ⓞ 🆅🅸🆂🅰   Y **a**
  Easter-November – **14 rm** ⊑ 12.75/25.50 **t**.

XX **Miller Howe** with rm, Rayrigg Rd, LA23 1EY, ℘ 2536, ≤ Lake Windermere and mountains,
  🌳 – 🍽 rest ➔wc 🚿wc **P**. 🔂 🅰🅴 ⓞ 🆅🅸🆂🅰   Y **s**
  closed 2 January-7 March – **M** (dinner only) 18.25 **t**. ⓝ 3.60 – **13 rm** ⊑ (dinner included)
  65.00/150.00 **t**.

XX **Roger's,** 4 High St., LA23 1AF, ℘ 4954 – 🔂 🅰🅴 ⓞ 🆅🅸🆂🅰   Y **o**
  closed Monday lunch, Monday dinner January-March and Sunday – **M** a la carte 9.30/12.65 **t**.
  ⓝ 3.25.

  at Bowness-on-Windermere S : 1 m. – 🖂 ⊛ 096 62 Windermere :

🏨 **Old England** (T.H.F.), LA23 3DF, ℘ 2444, Telex 65194, ≤ Lake Windermere and mountains,
  🎐 heated, 🌳 – 🛗 📺 **P**. 🔂 🅰🅴 ⓞ 🆅🅸🆂🅰   Z **e**
  M (buffet lunch Monday to Saturday) 6.75/11.50 **st**. ⓝ 2.85 – ⊑ 5.50 – **82 rm** 38.00/51.50 **st**.

🏨 **Belsfield** (T.H.F.), Kendal Rd, LA23 3EL, ℘ 2448, Telex 65238, ≤ Lake Windermere and
  mountains, 🎐, 🌳 – 🛗 📺 ⓖ. **P**. 🔂 🅰🅴 ⓞ 🆅🅸🆂🅰   Z **i**
  M (bar lunch) 12.50 **st**. ⓝ 2.60 – ⊑ 5.50 – **64 rm** 25.00/45.50 **st**.

🏛 **Linthwaite** 🍴, Crook Rd, LA23 3JA, S : ¾ m. by A 5074 on B 5284 ℘ 3688, ≤ Belle Isle,
  Lake Windermere and mountains, « Extensive grounds and private lake », 🍴, 🌳, park – 📺
  ➔wc **P**. 🎾   by A 5074   Z
  Easter-October – **M** (dinner only) 9.00 **st**. ⓝ 2.40 – **11 rm** ⊑ (dinner included) 28.00/60.00 **st**.

🏛 **Burnside,** Kendal Rd, LA23 3EP, ℘ 2211, ≤, 🌳 – 📺 ➔wc 🚿wc ⊛ **P**. 🔂 🅰🅴 ⓞ 🆅🅸🆂🅰
  M (bar lunch Monday to Saturday) 6.50/9.50 **t**. ⓝ 2.50 – **31 rm** ⊑ 24.00/50.00 **t**. – SB
  48.00/66.00 **st**.   Z **c**

🏠 **Lindeth Fell Country House** 🍴, Kendal Rd, LA23 3NH, S : 1 m. on A 5074 ℘ 3286, ≤ Lake
  Windermere and mountains, 🍴, 🌳, park, 🎾 – 📺 ➔wc 🚿wc **P**. 🔂 🅰🅴 ⓞ 🆅🅸🆂🅰. 🎾
  April-October – **M** (bar lunch) 9.50 **st**. ⓝ 2.90 – **13 rm** ⊑ 25.95/55.90 **st**.   by A 5074   Z

🏠 **Cranleigh,** Kendal Rd, LA23 3EW, ℘ 3293 – ➔wc 🚿 **P**. 🎾   Z **a**
  March-November – **M** (dinner only) 7.75 **st**. ⓝ 2.80 – **11 rm** ⊑ 12.50/33.00 **st**. – SB
  39.00/47.00 **st**.

🏠 **St. Martin's,** Lake Rd, LA23 3DE, ℘ 3731 – ➔wc 🚿wc **P**. 🔂 🅰🅴 ⓞ 🆅🅸🆂🅰   Z **x**
  closed mid December-mid January – **M** (bar lunch) 7.50 **t**. ⓝ 2.85 – **17 rm** ⊑ 15.50/35.00 **t**.

🏠 **Burn How Motel,** Back Belsfield Rd, LA23 3HH, ℘ 6226, 🌳 – 📺 ➔wc **P**. 🔂 🅰🅴 ⓞ 🆅🅸🆂🅰.
  🎾   Z **r**
  closed January – **M** (bar lunch) 12.00 **st**. ⓝ 2.80 – ⊑ 4.50 – **18 rm** 25.00/45.00 **st**. – SB
  (except summer) 45.00/55.00 **st**.

🏠 **Quarry Garth** 🍴, LA23 1LF, N : 1 ¾ m. on A 591 ℘ 3761, 🌳 – **P**   by A 591   Y
  Mid March-mid November – **M** 6.00/10.50 **t**. – **7 rm** ⊑ (dinner included) 26.00/52.00 **t**.

🏠 **Craig Foot,** Lake Rd, LA29 2JF, ℘ 3902, ≤, 🌳 – ➔wc 🚿wc **P**. 🎾   Z **s**
  Mid March-mid November – **12 rm** ⊑ 13.00/31.00 **st**.

🏠 **Westbourne,** Biskey Howe Rd, LA23 2JR, ℘ 3625 – **P**. 🔂 🆅🅸🆂🅰   Z **z**
  closed January and February – **9 rm** ⊑ 11.75/25.50 **st**.

🏠 **Eastbourne,** Biskey Howe Rd, LA23 2JR, ℘ 3525 – **P**. 🔂 🆅🅸🆂🅰   Z **u**
  9 rm ⊑ 10.50/19.90 **st**.

XX **La Silhouette,** Ash St., LA23 3EB, ℘ 5663 – 🔂 🅰🅴 ⓞ 🆅🅸🆂🅰   Z **o**
  closed Monday – **M** (dinner only) a la carte 10.00/16.25 **t**. ⓝ 2.90.

XX **Porthole Eating House,** 3 Ash St., LA23 3EB, ℘ 2793, Italian rest. – 🔂 🅰🅴 ⓞ 🆅🅸🆂🅰   Z **n**
  closed Tuesday and mid December-mid February – **M** (dinner only) a la carte 11.30/15.00 **t**.
  ⓝ 3.00.

  at Troutbeck N : 4 m. by A 592 – Y – 🖂 Windermere – ⊛ 096 63 Ambleside :

🏠 **Mortal Man** 🍴, LA23 1PL, ℘ 3193, ≤, 🌳 – ➔wc **P**
  Mid February-mid November – **M** (bar lunch Monday to Saturday) approx. 11.00 **st**. ⓝ 2.75 –
  12 rm ⊑ 27.00/32.00 **st**. – SB 50.00/60.00 **st**.

AUSTIN-ROVER College Rd ℘ 2451   TALBOT Main Rd ℘ 2441
HONDA, VAUXHALL Kendal Rd ℘ 2000

  When travelling for business or pleasure
  in England, Wales, Scotland and Ireland :

  — use the series of five maps
    (nos **401**, **402**, **403**, **404** and **405**) at a scale of 1:400 000

  — they are the perfect complement to this Guide
    as towns underlined in red on the maps will be found in this Guide.

WINDSOR

North is at the top
on all town plans.

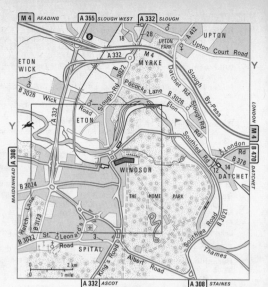

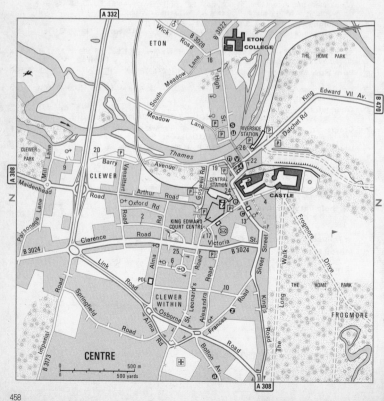

CENTRE

WINDSOR Berks. 404 S 29 – pop. 30,114 – ECD : Wednesday – ☎ 075 35.

See : Castle★★★ (St. George's Chapel★★★) Z.

Envir. : Eton (College★★) N : 1 m. Z – Runnymede (signing of the Magna Carta, 1215, museum) AC, SE : 4 m. by A 308 Y.

🇮 Central Station ✆ 52010.

♦London 28 – Reading 19 – ♦Southampton 59.

Plan opposite

🏨 **Oakley Court** ♨, Windsor Rd, Water Oakley, SL4 5UR, W : 3 m. on A 308 ✆ 0628 (Maidenhead) 74141, Telex 849958, ≼, « Part Gothic mansion on banks of River Thames », 🐎, park –
📺 ☎ ℗. 🏄 🛤 ⬤ 𝘝𝘐𝘚𝘈 ⌘
by A 308 Y
M 11.00/17.00 st. – **90 rm** ⇌ 48.00/110.00 st.

🏨 **Castle** (T.H.F.), High St., SL4 1LJ, ✆ 51011, Telex 849220 – 🛗 📺 ☎ ℗. 🏄. 🛤 🛤 ⬤ 𝘝𝘐𝘚𝘈
M 9.50/11.50 st. 🍷 2.60 – ⇌ 5.50 – **85 rm** 42.00/50.00 st.
Z c

🏨 **Wren's Old House**, Thames St., SL4 1PX, ✆ 61354, Telex 847938, ≼, « Former residence of Sir Christopher Wren », 🐎 – 📺 ⊟wc 🗍wc ☎ ℗. 🛤 🛤 ⬤ 𝘝𝘐𝘚𝘈
Z v
closed Christmas – **M** (closed Saturday lunch) 9.00/10.00 st. 🍷 2.90 – ⇌ 3.00 – **39 rm** 40.00/59.00 st. – SB (weekends only) 52.50/58.00 st.

🏨 **Aurora Garden**, 14 Bolton Av., SL4 3JF, ✆ 58838, 🐎 – 📺 🗍wc ☎ ℗. 🏄. 🛤 🛤 ⬤ 𝘝𝘐𝘚𝘈
M (lunch by arrangement) 8.00 st. 🍷 3.80 – ⇌ 3.00 – **13 rm** 25.00/37.50 st. – SB (summer only) 42.00/49.00 st.
Z a

🏨 **Ye Harte and Garter**, 21 High St., SL4 1LR, ✆ 63426 – 🛗 📺 ⊟wc 🗍wc ☎ ℗. 🛤 🛤 ⬤ 𝘝𝘐𝘚𝘈.
⌘
Z e
closed 25 and 26 December – **M** (grill rest. only) – **48 rm**.

🏠 **Fairlight Lodge**, 41 Frances Rd, SL4 3AQ, ✆ 61207 – ⌘
Z z
closed 1 week at Christmas – **8 rm** ⇌ 13.50/23.00 st.

XX **Don Peppino**, 30 Thames St., SL4 1PR, ✆ 60081, Italian rest. – 🛤 🛤 ⬤ 𝘝𝘐𝘚𝘈
Z x
closed Sunday and 25-26 December – **M** a la carte 6.95/11.50 t.

X **La Taverna**, 2 River St., SL4 1QT, ✆ 63020, Italian rest. – 🛤 🛤 ⬤ 𝘝𝘐𝘚𝘈
Z n
closed Sunday.

at Eton – ✉ ☎ 075 35 Windsor :

🏨 **Christopher**, 110 High St., SL4 6AN, ✆ 52359 – 📺 🗍wc ☎ ℗. 🛤 🛤 ⬤ 𝘝𝘐𝘚𝘈
Z r
M (closed Sunday dinner) (bar lunch Monday) 5.50/8.50 st. 🍷 2.40 – ⇌ 3.55 – **21 rm** 25.30/40.25 st. – SB (weekends only) 52.00 st.

XX **Antico**, 42 High St., SL4 6BD, ✆ 63977, Italian rest. – 🛤 🛤 ⬤ 𝘝𝘐𝘚𝘈
Z s
closed Saturday lunch, Sunday and Bank Holidays – **M** a la carte 12.00/17.50 st. 🍷 3.20.

VAUXHALL-OPEL 72-74 Arthur Rd ✆ 60131

During the season, particularly in resorts, it is wise to book in advance.
However, if you find you cannot take up a hotel booking you have made,
please let the hotel know immediately.

If you are writing to a hotel abroad enclose an International Reply Coupon
(available from Post Offices.)

WINKLEIGH Devon 403 I 31 – pop. 1,093 – ☎ 083 783.

♦London 214 – Barnstaple 20 – Exeter 22 – ♦Plymouth 41.

XX **Kings Arms**, The Square, EX19 8HQ, ✆ 384 – ▤. 🛤 🛤 ⬤ 𝘝𝘐𝘚𝘈
closed dinner Sunday and Monday, February and November – **M** (dinner only)(booking essential) 15.00 st. 🍷 2.30.

WINSFORD Somerset 403 J 30 **The West Country G.** – pop. 294 – ECD : Thursday – ✉ Minehead – ☎ 064 385.

♦London 194 – Exeter 31 – Minehead 10 – Taunton 32.

🏠 **Royal Oak Inn**, TA24 7JE, ✆ 232 – 📺 ⊟wc ℗. 🛤 🛤 ⬤ 𝘝𝘐𝘚𝘈
M (bar lunch Monday to Saturday) 9.50 t. 🍷 2.75 – **12 rm** ⇌ 25.00/50.00 st. – SB 66.00 st.

WINTERBOURNE Avon 403 404 M 29 – see Bristol.

WISBECH Cambs. 402 404 U 25 – pop. 17,016 – ECD : Wednesday – ☎ 0945.

Envir. : St. Wendreda's Church 15C : the Angel roof★) SW : 10 m – Long Sutton (St. Mary's Church★ : Gothic) NW : 10 m.

♦London 106 – ♦Cambridge 47 – ♦Leicester 62 – ♦Norwich 57.

🏠 **White Lion**, 5 South Brink, PE13 1JD, ✆ 584813 – 📺 ⊟wc ℗. 🏄. 🛤 🛤 ⬤ 𝘝𝘐𝘚𝘈
M 6.75 t. 🍷 2.95 – **18 rm** ⇌ 18.50/32.95 st.

AUSTIN-ROVER 46 Norwich Rd ✆ 584342
FIAT Harecroft Rd ✆ 65131
FORD Elm Rd ✆ 582681

RENAULT Old Lynn Rd ✆ 582662
VAUXHALL-OPEL Elm High Rd ✆ 582471
VOLVO Sutton Rd ✆ 583082

WITHAM Essex **404** V 28 – pop. 8,060 – ECD : Wednesday – ✆ 0376.
◆London 42 – ◆Cambridge 46 – Chelmsford 9 – Colchester 13.

🏠 **White Hart,** 39 Newland St., CM8 2AF, ☎ 512245 – 📺 ➰wc 🅿️ 🔼 🅰🅴 ⓪ 𝚅𝙸𝚂𝙰 ✂
M (carving rest.) 5.50 **t.** ▯ 2.80 – **13 rm** ⌷ 18.75/28.50 **st.**

🏠 **Batsford Court,** 100 Newland St., CM8 1AH, ☎ 517777 – 📺 ⌁wc 🅿️ 🔼 𝚅𝙸𝚂𝙰
M 7.50 **st.** ▯ 2.40 – ⌷ 2.50 – **22 rm** 18.50/28.50 **st.** – SB (weekends only) 35.00 **st.**

AUSTIN-ROVER Newland St. ☎ 513272
FORD Colchester Rd ☎ 513496

NISSAN London Rd ☎ 515575

WITHERSLACK Cumbria – see Grange-over-Sands.

WITHYPOOL Somerset **403** J 30 **The West Country G.** – pop. 199 – ECD : Thursday – ✉
✆ 064 383 Exford.
◆London 204 – Exeter 34 – Taunton 36.

🏠 **Royal Oak Inn,** TA24 7QP, ☎ 236, ➘ – 📺 ➰wc ⌁wc 🅿️ 🔼 🅰🅴 ⓪ 𝚅𝙸𝚂𝙰
M (closed Monday and Tuesday in winter) (bar lunch) 11.00 **t.** ▯ 2.75 – **8 rm** ⌷ 16.50/36.00 **t.**

🏠 **Westerclose Country House** ⬥, TA24 7QR, NW : ¼ m. ☎ 302, 🐎 – ⌁wc 🅿️
M (lunch by arrangement) 6.50/7.50 **t.** ▯ 2.80 – **10 rm** ⌷ 14.00/30.00 **t.**

GRÜNE REISEFÜHRER

Landschaften, Baudenkmäler
Sehenswürdigkeiten
Fremdenverkehrsstraßen
Tourenvorschläge
Stadtpläne und Übersichtskarten.

WITNEY Oxon. **403 404** P 28 – pop. 14,985 – ECD : Tuesday – ✆ 0993.
◆London 69 – ◆Birmingham 63 – ◆Oxford 12 – Swindon 24.

⌂ **Greystones,** 34 Tower Hill, OX8 5ES, ☎ 71898, ⌧ heated, 🐎 – 🅿️ ✂
10 rm ⌷ 14.00/28.00 **s.**

WIVELISCOMBE Somerset **403** K 30 **The West Country G.** – pop. 1,300 – ECD : Thursday –
✆ 0984.
◆ London 185 – Barnstaple 38 – Exeter 37 – Taunton 14.

🏠 **Langley House** ⬥, Langley Marsh, TA4 2UF, NW : ½ m. ☎ 23318, « Country house atmos-
phere », 🐎 – 📺 ➰wc ⌁wc 🅿️
March-October – **M** (dinner only) (booking essential) 13.50 **st.** ▯ 3.50 – **6 rm** ⌷ 19.90/38.80 **st.**
– SB 52.00/62.00 **st.**

WOBURN Beds. **404** S 28 – pop. 796 – ECD : Wednesday – ✉ Milton Keynes – ✆ 052 525.
See : Woburn Abbey★★★ (18C) *AC*, Wild Animal Kingdom★★ *AC*.
◆London 49 – Bedford 13 – Luton 13 – Northampton 24.

🏨 **Bedford Arms,** 1 George St., MK17 9PX, ☎ 441, Telex 825205 – 📺 ➰wc ☎ 🅿️ 🔼 🔼 🅰🅴
⓪ 𝚅𝙸𝚂𝙰
M 7.95/8.95 **st.** ▯ 2.50 – **55 rm** ⌷ 41.00/54.00 **st.** – SB (weekends only) 46.00 **st.**

XXX ⊛ **Paris House,** Woburn Park, MK17 9QP, SE : 2 ¼ m. on B 528 ☎ 692, « Reproduction
timbered house in Park », 🐎 – 🅿️ 🔼 🅰🅴 ⓪ 𝚅𝙸𝚂𝙰
closed Sunday dinner, Monday and February – **M** a la carte 13.80/19.40 **s.**
Spec. Hure de saumon sauce aux concombres, Filet de garenne au cidre et raisins, Tulipe en fantaisie.

WOLF'S CASTLE (CAS-BLAIDD) Dyfed **403** F 28 – ✉ Haverfordwest – ✆ 043 787 Treffgarne.
◆London 258 – Fishguard 7 – Haverfordwest 8.

XX **Wolfscastle Country** with rm, SA62 5LZ, on A 40 ☎ 225, 🐎, ✵, squash – 📺 ➰wc 🅿️
🔼 𝚅𝙸𝚂𝙰
closed 5 days at Christmas – **M** (bar lunch) a la carte 8.30/13.20 **st.** ▯ 2.65 – **12 rm**
⌷ 12.95/29.90 **st.** – SB (except summer) 40.00/54.00 **st.**

WOLVERHAMPTON West Midlands **402 403 404** N 26 – pop. 269,112 – ECD : Thursday –
✆ 0902.
See : St. Peter's Church★ 15C B A.

⛳ Oxley Park, Bushbury, ☎ 20506, N : 1 ½ m. A – ⛳ Blackhill Wood, Bridgnorth Rd ☎ 892279, S :
5 m. by A 449 A.

◆London 132 – ◆Birmingham 15 – ◆Liverpool 89 – Shrewsbury 30.

Plan of Enlarged Area : see Birmingham pp. 2 and 3

WOLVERHAMPTON

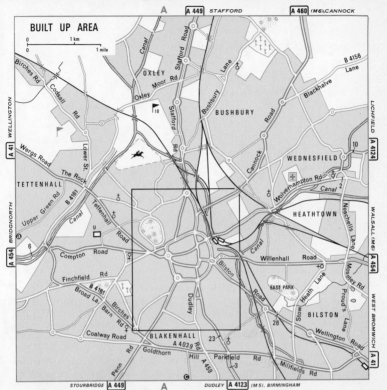

🏛 **Goldthorn,** 126 Penn Rd, WV3 0ER, ℰ 29216 – 📺 ⇌wc ⊛ 🅿. ⚗. 🔼 🆎 *VISA*   B **i**
closed 25 and 26 December – **M** 7.75 **t.** – **86 rm** ⚏ 21.00/48.00 t.

🏛 **Park Hall** (Embassy) ৯, Park Drive, off Ednam Rd, Goldthorn Park, WV4 5AJ, S : 2 m. by A
449 ℰ 331121, 🐎, – 📺 ⇌wc ☎ 🅿. ⚗. 🔼 🆎 ⓪ *VISA*. ⋇   A **c**
M *(closed Saturday lunch and Sunday dinner to non-residents)* 7.25 **st.** ⅄ 4.50 – ⚏ 4.25 –
57 rm 22.00/38.00 **st.** – SB *(weekends only)* 41.00/48.00 **st.**

🏛 **Mount** (Embassy) ৯, Mount Rd, Tettenhall Wood, WV6 8HL, W : 2 ½ m. by A 454
ℰ 752055, 🐎, – 📺 ⇌wc ⊛ 🅿. ⚗. 🔼 🆎 ⓪ *VISA*. ⋇   A **a**
M *(bar lunch Saturday)* 6.75/7.75 **st.** ⅄ 5.00 – ⚏ 4.25 – **63 rm** 23.00/38.00 **st.** – SB *(week-
ends only)* 45.00/48.00 **st.**

XX **Tandoor,** 46 Queen St., WV1 3BJ, ℰ 20747, Indian rest. – 🔼 🆎 ⓪ *VISA*   B **o**
closed lunch Sunday and Bank Holidays and Christmas Day – **M** 3.55/8.05 **t.** ⅄ 2.75.

at Pattingham (Staffs.) W : 6 ¼ m. by A 454 – A – ⊠ ✆ 0902 Pattingham :

🏛 **Lakeside Lodge** ৯, Patshull Park, WV6 7HR, W : 1 ¾ m. by Patshull Rd ℰ 700100, ≤, ⛳,
⬤, park – 📺 ⇌wc 🅿. ⚗. 🔼 🆎 ⓪ *VISA*
M *(closed Sunday dinner)* (bar lunch) a la carte 7.20/12.50 **t.** ⅄ 3.00 – ⚏ 3.75 – **28 rm**
23.50/28.50 **t.** – SB *(weekends only)* 39.40 **st.**

ALFA-ROMEO, CITROEN Merridale Lane ℰ 23295
AUSTIN ROVER-DAIMLER-JAGUAR Stafford St. ℰ
29122
AUSTIN-ROVER Chapel Ash ℰ 26781
AUSTIN-ROVER Wolverhampton Rd, Wednesfield
ℰ 731372

BMW, VW, AUDI Rabey St. ℰ 54602
COLT Lichfield Rd ℰ 731689
FIAT Warstones Rd ℰ 339104
FORD Bilston Rd ℰ 51515
LADA 372 Penn Rd, Penn ℰ 335570
MERCEDES-BENZ Penn Rd ℰ 27897

P.T.O. →

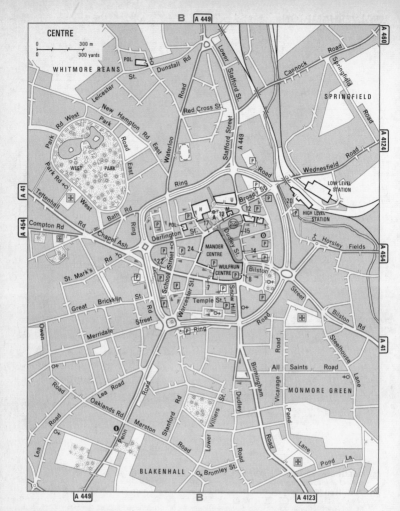

CENTRE

0   300 m
0   300 yards

WHITMORE REANS

WEST PARK

SPRINGFIELD

LOW LEVEL STATION

HIGH LEVEL STATION

Horsley Fields

MANDER CENTRE

WULFRUN CENTRE

MONMORE GREEN

BLAKENHALL

RENAULT Bilston Rd ℰ 53111
SKODA Vulcan Rd, Bilston ℰ 402222
TOYOTA Wolverhampton Rd East ℰ 333131
VAUXHALL-OPEL Dudley Rd ℰ 58000

VAUXHALL-OPEL 67/71 Bilston Rd ℰ 52611
VOLVO Parkfield Rd ℰ 333211
VW-AUDI Raby St. ℰ 54602

For maximum information from town plans : consult the conventional signs key, p. 19.

WOODBRIDGE Suffolk 𝟜𝟘𝟜 X 27 – pop. 8,660 – ECD : Wednesday – ✪ 039 43.

⌐₁₈, ⌐₁₉ Bromeswell Heath ℰ 2038, E : 2 m.

♦London 81 – Great Yarmouth 45 – ♦Ipswich 8 – ♦Norwich 47.

🏛 **Seckford Hall** ⤳, IP13 6NU, SW : 1 ¼ m. by A 12 ℰ 5678, Telex 987446, ≤, « Part Tudor country house », 굧, 🛋, park – 🖵 🛏wc 🕿 🅿 🛗 🔼 AE ⓪ VISA
closed Christmas Day – **M** a la carte 8.95/12.45 **st.** ∦ 2.50 – **24 rm** ⊏⊐ 34.00/48.00 **st.**

🏠 **Crown** (T.H.F.), Thoroughfare, IP12 1AD, ℰ 4242 – 🖵 🛏wc 🕿 🅿 🔼 AE ⓪ VISA
M a la carte 9.25/11.90 **st.** ∦ 2.60 – ⊏⊐ 4.75 – **24 rm** 29.00/41.00 **st.**

AUSTIN-ROVER, LAND-ROVER Melton Rd ℰ 3456
FORD 96 Thorough Fare ℰ 3333

FORD Bawdsey ℰ 039 441 (Shottisham) 1368

462

WOODHALL SPA Lincs. 402 404 T 24 – pop. 2,261 – ECD : Wednesday – ✆ 0526.

Envir. : Tattershall Castle★ (15C Keep) *AC*, SE : 3 ½ m – ⛳ ✆ 52511.

🛈 Jubilee Park, Stixwould Rd ✆ 52448 and 52461.

♦London 138 – Lincoln 18.

🏠 **Golf** (Best Western), The Broadway, LN10 6SG, ✆ 53535, 🚗 – 📺 ⌂wc ▥wc ☎ 🅿. 🔥. 🔽
   AE ⓪ VISA
   M (lunch by arrangement) a la carte 10.25/14.20 **t.** – **51 rm** ⚏ 28.00/38.00 **t.** – SB 49.00/52.00 **st.**

🏠 **Dower House** 🦢, Manor Estate, off Spa Rd, LN10 6PY, ✆ 52588, 🚗 – ⌂wc 🅿. 🔽 AE
   VISA. ⚘
   M (closed Sunday lunch) 7.50/8.50 **st.** ᛫ 2.75 – **7 rm** ⚏ 18.00/35.00 **st.** – SB (week-
   ends only)(winter only) 40.00/46.00 **st.**

↗ **Dunns,** The Broadway, LN10 6SQ, ✆ 52969 – 🅿
   6 rm ⚏ 8.00/15.00 **st.**

WOODLANDS Hants. – see Lyndhurst.

WOODSTOCK Oxon. 403 404 P 28 – pop. 1,961 – ECD : Wednesday – ✆ 0993.

See : Blenheim Palace★★★ 18C (park and gardens★★★) *AC*.

Envir. : Rousham (Manor House gardens : statues★) NE : 5 m. – Ditchley Park★ (Renaissance) *AC*,
NW : 6 m.

🛈 Hensington Rd Car Park ✆ 811038 and 812231 (summer only).

♦London 65 – Gloucester 47 – ♦Oxford 8.

🏨 **Bear,** Park St., OX7 1SZ, ✆ 811511, Telex 837921, « Tastefully converted part 16C inn » – 📺
   ☎ 🅿. 🔥. 🔽 AE ⓪ VISA
   M 8.95/12.50 **st.** ᛫ 2.65 – ⚏ 6.50 – **45 rm** 28.50/69.50 **st.** – SB (weekends only) 63.00/105.00 **st.**

🏠 **Feathers,** Market St., OX7 2SX, ✆ 812291, Telex 83138, « Tastefully furnished » – 📺 ⌂wc
   ▥wc ☎. 🔥. 🔽 AE ⓪ VISA. ⚘
   M 9.50/14.50 **st.** ᛫ 3.25 – **14 rm** ⚏ 32.00/78.00 **st.** – SB (except summer) 72.00/82.00 **st.**

AUSTIN-ROVER 2 Oxford St. ✆ 811286

WOODY BAY Devon 403 I 30 – see Lynton.

WOOLACOMBE Devon 403 H 30 The West Country G. – pop. 809 – ECD : Wednesday – ✆ 0271.

Envir. : Mortehoe★★ – Morte Point (vantage point ★) – Mortehoe Church ★.

🛈 Hall 70, Beach Rd ✆ 870553 (summer only).

♦London 237 – Barnstaple 15 – Exeter 55.

🏠 **Little Beach,** The Esplanade, EX34 7DJ, ✆ 870398, ≤ – ⌂wc ▥wc 🅿. 🔽 VISA
   February-October – **M** (bar lunch residents only) 9.25 **t.** ᛫ 2.50 – **10 rm** ⚏ 14.50/41.00 **st.** – SB
   40.00/52.00 **st.**

🏠 **Water's Fall,** Beach Rd, EX34 7AD, ✆ 870365, ≤ Woolacombe Bay, 🚗 – ⌂wc 🅿
   closed November-1 March except Christmas – **M** (bar lunch Monday to Saturday) 5.50/7.50 **t.**
   ᛫ 2.10 – **17 rm** ⚏ 12.00/30.00 **t.** – SB (spring and October) 33.00 **st.**

   at Mortehoe N : ½ m. – ✉ ✆ 0271 Woolacombe :

🏠 **Watersmeet,** The Esplanade, EX34 7EB, ✆ 870333, ≤, ⤓ heated, ⚘ – ⌂wc 🅿. 🔽 ⓪. ⚘
   Easter-October – **M** 9.50/11.50 **st.** ᛫ 2.25 – **36 rm**

🏠 **Sunnycliffe,** Chapel Hill, EX34 7EB, ✆ 870597, ≤ – 📺 ⌂wc ▥wc 🅿. ⚘
   closed December and January – **M** (residents only)(bar lunch) 7.00 **st.** – **8 rm** ⚏ 14.00/44.00 **st.**
   – SB 36.00/40.00 **st.**

WOOLER Northumb. 401 402 N 17 – pop. 1,833 – ECD : Thursday – ✆ 0668.

🛈 Bus Station Car Park, High St. ✆ 81602 (summer only).

♦London 332 – ♦Edinburgh 62 – ♦Newcastle-upon-Tyne 46.

↗ **Tankerville Arms,** 22 Cottage Rd, NE71 6AD, on A 697 ✆ 81581, 🚗 – ⌂wc 🅿
   M (bar lunch) 8.00 **st.** ᛫ 2.50 – **17 rm** – SB (except July and August) 35.00/37.00 **st.**

↗ **Ryecroft,** 28 Rycroft Way, NE71 6AB, ✆ 81459 – 🅿
   11 rm ⚏ 11.00/27.00 **st.**

ALFA-ROMEO ✆ 81836
AUSTIN-ROVER, JAGUAR South Rd ✆ 81267

FORD Haughead ✆ 81316
RENAULT South Rd ✆ 81472

WOOLVERTON Somerset – see Bath.

WORCESTER Heref. and Worc. 403 404 N 27 – pop. 73,452 – ECD : Thursday – ✆ 0905.

See : Cathedral★★ 13C-15C (crypt★★ 11C) – The Commandery★ (15C) *AC* B.

Envir. : Great Witley : Witley Court (ruins) and the Parish Church of St. Michael and All Saints
(Baroque interior★★) NW : 12 m. by A 443.

🛈 Guildhall, High St. ✆ 23471.

♦London 124 – ♦Birmingham 26 – ♦Bristol 61 – ♦Cardiff 74.

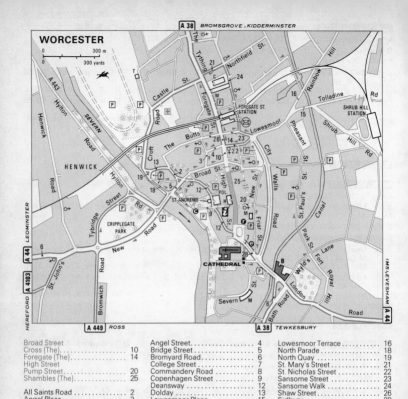

WORCESTER

A 38 BROMSGROVE, KIDDERMINSTER

Broad Street	Angel Street	4	Lowesmoor Terrace	16
Cross (The)	10	Bridge Street	5	North Parade	18
Foregate (The)	14	Bromyard Road	6	North Quay	19
High Street	College Street	7	St. Mary's Street	21
Pump Street	20	Commandery Road	8	St. Nicholas Street	22
Shambles (The)	25	Copenhagen Street	9	Sansome Street	23
	Deansway	12	Sansome Walk	24
All Saints Road	2	Dolday	13	Shaw Street	26
Angel Place	3	Lowesmoor Place	15	Sidbury	28

🏨 **Giffard** (T.H.F.), High St., WR1 2QR, ☎ 27155, Telex 338869 – 🛗 📺 🆓 🔼 AE ⓞ VISA   **r**
   M 6.95/9.50 st. 🍴 3.40 – 🖙 5.50 – **104 rm** 37.50/43.50 st.

🏨 **Ye Olde Talbot,** Friar St., WR1 2NA, ☎ 23573 – 📺 🛏️wc ☎. 🔼 AE ⓞ VISA. 🦌   **e**
   M 4.95/6.95 t. – **17 rm** 🖙 30.00/40.00 t.

🏠 **Park House,** 12 Droitwich Rd, WR3 7LJ, ☎ 21816 – ℗   by A 38
   6 rm 🖙 10.50/18.00 st.

XX **Brown's,** 24 Quay St., WR1 2JN, ☎ 26263, « Converted corn mill » – 🔼 AE VISA   **c**
   closed Saturday lunch, Sunday, 25-26 and 31 December, 1 January and Bank Holiday Mondays
   – M 11.95/14.95 t. 🍴 3.75.

MICHELIN Branch, Blackpole Trading Estate, WR3 8TJ, ☎ 55626

ALFA-ROMEO, HONDA Pershore Rd, Stoulton ☎ 840661
BEDFORD, VAUXHALL-OPEL Brook St. ☎ 27781
AUSTIN-ROVER, DAIMLER-JAGUAR Castle St. ☎ 27100
AUSTIN-ROVER 49 Friar St. ☎ 26988
COLT Hallow ☎ 640294
DAIHATSU Ombersley Rd ☎ 52730
FIAT Powick ☎ 830361
FORD Bath Rd ☎ 352123
LADA College St. ☎ 27500

MERCEDES-BENZ Cranham Drive ☎ 57219
NISSAN Bransford Rd ☎ 428101
PEUGEOT, TALBOT Bath Rd ☎ 820777
RENAULT St. Martins Gate ☎ 21215
RENAULT The Butts ☎ 24252
SUBARU, YUGO Pierpoint St. ☎ 25786
TOYOTA Bromyard Rd ☎ 422029
VAUXHALL-OPEL Hallow ☎ 640228
VAUXHALL-OPEL Brook St. ☎ 27781
VOLVO Farrier St. ☎ 23338
VW, AUDI Hallow Rd ☎ 640512

WORFIELD Salop – see Bridgnorth.

> Bitte beachten Sie die Geschwindigkeitsbeschränkungen in Großbritannien
>
> – 60 mph (= 96 km/h) außerhalb geschlossener Ortschaften
>
> – 70 mph (= 112 km/h) auf Straßen mit getrennten Fahrbahnen und Autobahnen.

WORKINGTON Cumbria 401 402 J 20 – pop. 28,431 – ECD : Thursday – ✆ 0900.

🛥 Bankend, Maryport ✆ 090 081 (Maryport) 2605, N : 7 m. on A 596.

◆London 314 – ◆Carlisle 33 – Keswick 21.

🏨 Westland, Branthwaite Rd, CA14 4SS, S : 2 m. by A 596 ✆ 4544 – 📺 ⇌wc 🚿wc ☎ 🅿. 🏊
48 rm.

AUSTIN-ROVER Central Sq. ✆ 2113
DATSUN Guard St. ✆ 64455
FORD Washington St. ✆ 3740

RENAULT Clay Flatts Estate ✆ 4542
TOYOTA Finkle St. ✆ (0946) 830247

WORRALL South Yorks. – see Sheffield.

LES GUIDES VERTS MICHELIN

Paysages, monuments
Routes touristiques
Géographie, Économie
Histoire, Art
Itinéraires de visite
Plans de villes et de monuments.

WORTHING West Sussex 404 S 31 – pop. 88,407 – ECD : Wednesday – ✆ 0903.

Envir. : Shoreham-by-Sea (St. Mary of Haura's Church★ 12C-13C – St. Nichola's Church carved arches★ 12C) E : 5 m. by A 259 BY.

🛝, 🛝 Links Rd ✆ 60801 AY – 🛝 Worthing Hill Barn, Hill Barn Lane ✆ 37301 BY.

✈ Shoreham Airport : ✆ 079 17 (Shoreham-by-Sea) 2304, E : 4 m. by A 27 BY.

🛈 Town Hall, Chapel Rd ✆ 39999 ext 132/3 – Marine Parade ✆ 210022 (summer only).

◆London 59 – ◆Brighton 11 – ◆Southampton 50.

Plan on next page

🏨 **Beach,** Marine Par., BN11 3QJ, ✆ 34001, ← – ▐ 📺 🅿. 🏊 ◪ AE Ⓞ VISA. ❄︎   AZ **e**
M 6.75/8.50 **st.** – **91 rm** ⇌ 25.00/46.25 **st.** – SB (weekends only)(except summer) 45.15/52.35 **st.**

🏨 **Chatsworth,** Steyne Gdns, BN11 3DU, ✆ 36103, Telex 877046 – ▐ 📺 ⇌wc ☎. 🏊. ◪ VISA   BZ **x**
M 6.50/6.95 **t.** § 1.95 – **90 rm** ⇌ 23.10/48.40 **t.** – SB (weekends only) 44.00/52.00 **st.**

🏨 **Eardley,** 3-10 Marine Par., BN11 3PW, ✆ 34444, Group Telex 877046, ← – ▐ 📺 ⇌wc ☎ 🅿.
🏊. ◪ VISA   BZ **u**
M (carving lunch) 5.75/6.50 **t.** § 2.50 – **83 rm** ⇌ 21.00/48.00 **t.** – SB (weekends only) 42.00/65.00 **st.**

🏠 **Beechwood Hall,** Wykeham Rd, BN11 4AH, ✆ 32872, ☞ – 📺 ⇌wc 🅿. ◪ VISA   AZ **a**
M (closed Sunday dinner to non-residents) (bar lunch) 6.75 **t.** § 2.50 – **14 rm** ⇌ 19.00/33.00 **t.** – SB (except summer) 33.00/38.00 **st.**

🏠 **Ardington,** Steyne Gdns, BN11 3DZ, ✆ 30451 – 📺 ⇌wc 🚿wc. 🏊 ◪ AE Ⓞ VISA   BZ **s**
closed Christmas – **M** (bar lunch) 6.50 **t.** § 3.00 – **51 rm** ⇌ 16.50/40.00 **t.**

🏡 **Wansfell,** 49 Chesswood Rd, BN11 2AA, ✆ 30612, ☞ – 📺 ⇌wc 🚿wc 🅿. ❄︎   BY **a**
12 rm ⇌ 11.50/32.50 **t.**

🏡 **Ainslea Court,** Abbey Rd, BN11 3RW, ✆ 30442   AZ **r**
8 rm ⇌ 8.50/17.00 **s.**

XX **Manor House** with rm, Durrington Hill, BN13 2PX, ✆ 60795 – 🅿. ◪ AE Ⓞ VISA. ❄︎   AY **e**
M a la carte 7.95/13.75 **t.** § 3.25 – **4 rm** ⇌ 25.00/45.00 **st.**

XX **Paragon,** 9-10 Brunswick Rd, BN11 3NG, ✆ 33367 – ◪ AE Ⓞ VISA   AZ **c**
closed Sunday and Bank Holidays – **M** a la carte 11.40/15.35 **st.** § 2.75.

X **La Gondola,** 121 Rectory Rd, BN14 7PH, ✆ 66384, Italian rest. – ◪ AE Ⓞ VISA   AY **e**
closed Sunday and Monday – **M** (booking essential) a la carte 6.40/11.20 **t.** § 2.85.

at Findon N : 4 m. by A 24 – AY – ✉ Worthing – ✆ 090 671 Findon :

🏠 **Village House,** The Square, BN14 0TE, ✆ 3350, ☞ – 🅿. ◪ AE Ⓞ VISA
M 5.50/7.00 **st.** § 2.00 – **9 rm** ⇌ 13.50/22.00 **t.**

at East Preston W : 6 ½ m. by A 259 – AY – off B 2225 – ✉ Littlehampton – ✆ 0903 Rustington :

XX **Old Forge,** The Street, BN16 1JJ, ✆ 782040, « 17C cottage » – 🅿. ◪ AE Ⓞ VISA
closed Sunday dinner and Monday – **M** a la carte 6.70/18.15 **t.** § 2.50.

ALFA-ROMEO Lancing ✆ 766981
AUSTIN-ROVER 55 Broadwater Rd ✆ 31111
BMW Angermering ✆ 090 62 (Rushington) 4147
CITROEN 28 Broadwater Rd ✆ 39573
FIAT 123 Upper Brighton Rd ✆ 36065
NISSAN Broadwater Rd ✆ 206091
RENAULT Portland Rd ✆ 200820

SAAB, PEUGEOT-TALBOT St. Lawrence Av. ✆ 207703
SKODA Tarring ✆ 34363
TALBOT Broadwater Rd ✆ 262338
TOYOTA 93 Rowlands Rd ✆ 32571
VAUXHALL-OPEL Goring Rd ✆ 42389
VOLVO 187 Findon Rd ✆ 090 671 (Findon) 3022

WORTHING

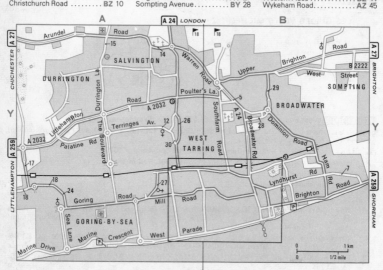

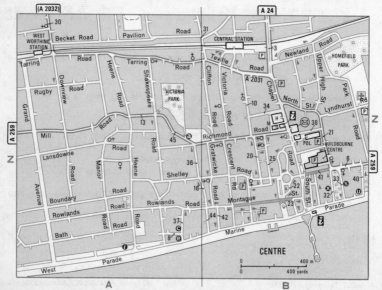

CENTRE

WRAFTON Devon 🔢🔢🔢 H 30 – ✉ 🕻 0271 Braunton.
♦London 227 – Barnstaple 5 – Exeter 45 – Ilfracombe 9.

🏠 **Poyers,** EX33 2DN, 🕾 812149, 🐴 – 🛁wc 🛁wc 🅿. 🔳 ⑩ 𝘝𝘐𝘚𝘈
  closed 24 December-7 January – **M** *(closed lunch and Sunday dinner to non-residents)* a la
  carte 10.65/12.60 t. 🍷 2.75 – **10 rm** 🛏 19.50/29.00 t. – SB 44.60/54.60 **st.**

WRELTON North Yorks. 🔢🔢🔢 R 21 – see Pickering.

WRENTHAM Suffolk 🔢🔢🔢 Z 26 – pop. 910 – ECD : Wednesday – ✉ Beccles – 🕻 050 275.
♦London 110 – Great Yarmouth 17 – ♦Ipswich 37 – ♦Norwich 26.

XX **Quiggins,** 2 High St., NR34 7HB, 🕾 397, « Tasteful decor » – 🅿. 🔳 𝘝𝘐𝘚𝘈
  closed Sunday dinner and Monday – **M** (booking essential) a la carte 10.95/13.50 t. 🍷 3.00.

WREXHAM (WRECSAM) Clwyd 🔢🔢🔢 🔢🔢🔢 L 24 – pop. 39,052 – ECD : Wednesday – 🕻 0978.
See : St. Giles' Church (tower★) – Envir. : Erddig★ (17C-18C) *AC*, SW : 2 m.
🅱 Guildhall Car Park, Town Centre 🕾 357845 (summer only) – ♦London 192 – Chester 12 – Shrewsbury 28.

🏨 **Crest** (Crest), Yorke St., LL13 8LP, 🕾 353431, Telex 61674 – 🎿 🍽 rest 📺 🛁wc 📞 🅿. 🚗.
  🔳 🅰🅴 𝘝𝘐𝘚𝘈 🐕
  M approx. 10.00 **st.** – 🛏 5.25 – **80 rm** 36.00/46.00 **st.** – SB (weekends only) 49.00 **st.**

AUSTIN-ROVER Hightown Rd 🕾 364151
CITROEN Holt Rd 🕾 356707
FORD Holt Rd 🕾 351001
NISSAN 🕾 757838
RENAULT, NISSAN Regent St. 🕾 356822

SKODA Wrexham Rd 🕾 263438
TOYOTA Wrexham Rd 🕾 840578
VAUXHALL-OPEL Mold Rd 🕾 263777
VOLVO Hill St. 🕾 262685
VW-AUDI Wrexham Rd 🕾 355777

WROTHAM HEATH Kent – pop. 1,669 – ✉ 🕻 0732 Sevenoaks.
♦London 35 – Maidstone 10.

🏨 **Post House,** London Rd, TN15 1RS, 🕾 883311, Telex 957309, 🔲, 🐴 – 📺 📞 🅿. 🚗. 🔳 🅰🅴
  ⑩ 𝘝𝘐𝘚𝘈
  M 8.95/12.90 **st.** 🍷 2.60 – 🛏 5.50 – **119 rm** 37.50/45.00 **st.**

  at Ightham W : 2 ½ m. by A 25 on A 227 – ✉ Sevenoaks – 🕻 0732 Borough Green :

XX **Town House,** The Street, TN15 9HH, 🕾 884578, « 15C medieval hall », 🐴 – 🅿. 🔳 🅰🅴 ⑩
  𝘝𝘐𝘚𝘈
  *closed Sunday, Monday, 2 weeks Easter, 2 weeks August-September and 25 December-
  8 January* – **M** (lunch by arrangement) (booking essential) 13.00/20.50 **st.** 🍷 3.75.

WROXHAM Norfolk 🔢🔢🔢 Y 25 – pop. 1,254 – ECD : Wednesday – ✉ Norwich – 🕻 060 53.
♦London 118 – Great Yarmouth 21 – ♦Norwich 7.

🏠 **Wroxham,** Broads Centre, NR12 8AJ, 🕾 2061, ≼ – 📺 🛁wc 🅿. 🔳 🅰🅴 ⑩ 𝘝𝘐𝘚𝘈
  M 5.50/6.00 **t.** 🍷 2.95 – **18 rm** 🛏 19.50/41.00 **t.** – SB (weekends only) 38.00/47.00 **st.**

WROXTON Oxon. 🔢🔢🔢 🔢🔢🔢 P 27 – see Banbury.

WYCH CROSS East Sussex 🔢🔢🔢 U 30 – see Forest Row.

WYE Kent 🔢🔢🔢 W 30 – pop. 2,028 – ECD : Wednesday – ✉ Ashford – 🕻 0233.
♦London 61 – Folkestone 21 – Maidstone 24 – Margate 28.

XX **Wife of Bath,** 4 Upper Bridge St., TN25 5AW, 🕾 812540 – 🅿. 🔳 🅰🅴
  closed Sunday and Monday – **M** a la carte approx. 13.30 **t.** 🍷 3.50.

AUSTIN-ROVER Bridge St. 🕾 812331   RENAULT Bramble Lane 🕾 812270

WYMONDHAM Norfolk 🔢🔢🔢 X 26 – pop. 9,811 – ECD : Wednesday – 🕻 0953.
♦London 110 – ♦Cambridge 53 – ♦Norwich 9.

X **Adlards,** 16 Damgate St., NR18 0BQ, 🕾 603533 – 🔳 𝘝𝘐𝘚𝘈
  closed Sunday, Monday and Tuesday – **M** (dinner only) (booking essential) 12.50 **t.**

WYNDS POINT Heref. and Worc. 🔢🔢🔢 🔢🔢🔢 M 27 – see Great Malvern.

WYRE PIDDLE Heref. and Worc. – see Pershore.

YARCOMBE Devon 🔢🔢🔢 K 31 – pop. 418 – 🕻 040 486 Upottery.
♦London 157 – Exeter 25 – Taunton 12 – Weymouth 42.

🏚 Yarcombe Inn, 🕾 218 – 🅿 – **7 rm.**

YARM Cleveland 🔢🔢🔢 P 20 – pop. 6,900 – 🕻 0642 Middlesbrough.
♦ London 242 – Middlesbrough 8.

🏨 **Crathorne Hall** 🐾, Crathorne, TS15 0AR, S : 3 ½ m. by A 67 🕾 700398, « Converted Edwardian mansion house », 🐴, park – 📺 🅿. 🚗. 🔳 🅰🅴 ⑩ 𝘝𝘐𝘚𝘈 🐕
  closed 1 to 5 January – **M** 6.50/9.50 **t.** – **31 rm** 🛏 30.75/52.00 **t.** – SB (weekends only) 65.00 **st.**

YARMOUTH I.O.W. **403 404** P 31 — see Wight (Isle of).

YATTENDON Berks. **403 404** Q 29 — pop. 240 — ECD : Saturday — ✉ Newbury — ☎ 0635 Hermitage.

♦London 62 — Newbury 8 — Reading 12.

🍽 **Royal Oak** with rm, The Square, RG16 0UF, ☏ 201325, 🌿 — TV 🛏wc 🕾 🅿. 🔥 AE ⓞ VISA. 🎿
M a la carte 10.95/15.55 🍷 2.70 — **5 rm** 🛏 32.50/48.50 t. — SB (weekends only) 50.00 st.

YELVERTON Devon **403** H 32 — ☎ 0822.

♦London 234 — Exeter 33 — ♦Plymouth 9.

🏨 **Moorland Links** 🐾, PL20 6DA, S : 2 m. on A 386 ☏ 852245, ≼, 🌿, park, 🎿 — TV 🛏wc 🕾 🅿. 🔥 AE ⓞ VISA
M a la carte 8.95/16.15 t. 🍷 4.45 — **23 rm** 🛏 29.50/42.00 t. — SB (weekends only) 52.00/55.00 st.

↟ **Overcombe** 🐾, Horrabridge, PL20 7RN, N : 1 ¼ m. on A 386 ☏ 853501, ≼, 🌿 — 🛏wc 🅿. 🔥 AE VISA
7 rm 🛏 12.25/26.50 st.

↟ **Retreat,** Tavistock Rd, PL20 6ED, N : ½ m. on A 386 ☏ 852099, ≼, 🌿 — 🅿
9 rm 🛏 11.50/23.00 st.

YEOVIL Somerset **403 404** M 31 The West Country G. — pop. 25,503 — ECD : Monday and Thursday — ☎ 0935.

See : St. John the Baptist Church★.

Envir. : Montacute House★★★, W : 4 m. on A 3088 — Fleet Air Museum★★, NW : 8 m. by A 37 — Long Sutton★ (Church★★), NW : 10 m. — Huish Episcopi : Church Tower★★, NW : 13 m. — Martock : All Saints Church★★, W : 7 m. — Cadbury Castle (≼★★), NE : 11 m. by A 359.

🏌 Sherborne Rd ☏ 75949.

🛈 Johnson Hall, Hendford ☏ 22884.

♦London 136 — Exeter 48 — ♦Southampton 72 — Taunton 26.

🏨 **Manor Crest** (Crest), Hendford Rd, BA20 1TG, ☏ 353431, Telex 46580, 🌿 — ▦ rest TV 🛏wc 🕾 🅿. 🔥 AE ⓞ VISA 🎿
M approx. 12.00 st. — 🛏 5.25 — **42 rm** 40.00/50.00 st.

↟ **Preston,** 64 Preston Rd, BA20 2DL, ☏ 74400 — TV 🛏wc 🅿. 🔥 VISA
11 rm 🛏 12.00/29.00 t.

at Barwick S : 2 m. by A 30 off A 37 — ✉ ☎ 0935 Yeovil :

🍽🍽 **Little Barwick House** 🐾 with rm, BA22 9TD, ☏ 23902, ≼, 🌿 — TV 🛏wc 🅿. 🔥 AE ⓞ VISA
closed 25 and 26 December — **M** *(closed Sunday to non-residents)* (dinner only) 11.80 t. 🍷 2.50 — **3 rm** 🛏 28.50 st. — SB 42.00 st.

at West Coker SW : 3 ½ m. on A 30 — ✉ Yeovil — ☎ 093 586 West Coker :

🏨 **Four Acres,** High St., BA22 9AJ, ☏ 2555, 🌿 — TV 🛏wc 🕾 🅿. 🔥 AE ⓞ VISA
M *(closed Sunday lunch in summer)* a la carte 7.90/10.60 t. — **18 rm** 🛏 30.00/38.50 t.

at East Chinnock SW : 5 m. on A 30 — ✉ Yeovil — ☎ 093 586 West Coker :

↟ **Barrows Country House** 🐾, Weston St., BA22 9EJ, ☏ 2390, 🌿 — 🅿. 🎿
closed 24 December-1 January — **6 rm** 🛏 9.00/20.00.

at Montacute W : 4 m. on A 3088 — ✉ ☎ 0935 Yeovil :

🏠 **Kings Arms,** Bishopston, TA15 6UU, ☏ 822513, 🌿 — TV 🛏wc 🕾 🅿. 🔥 AE ⓞ VISA. 🎿
M *(closed Sunday dinner to non-residents)* (buffet lunch) a la carte 8.80/13.55 🍷 2.50 — **10 rm** 🛏 27.50/40.00 t. — SB 57.50 st.

🍽🍽 **Milk House,** 17 The Borough, TA15 6XB, ☏ 823823 — 🔥 AE ⓞ VISA
closed Saturday lunch, Sunday and Monday — **M** a la carte 9.20/12.55 st. 🍷 2.20.

Y-FENNI = Abergavenny.

YORK North Yorks. **402** Q 22 — pop. 104,782 — ECD : Wednesday — ☎ 0904.

See : Minster★★★ 13C-15C (Chapter House★★★, 🔭★★ from tower, AC, 275 steps) CDY — National Railway Museum★★★ CY — Castle Museum★★ AC DZ **M2** — Clifford's Tower★ (13C) AC DYZ **B** — Art Gallery★ CX **M3** — Treasurer's House★ (14C) AC DX **E** — City Walls★ 14C — The Shambles★ DY.

🏌 Lords Moor Lane, Strensall ☏ 490304, NE : 6 m. by Huntington Rd BY.

🛈 De Grey Rooms, Exhibition Sq. ☏ 21756/7 — 3 Lendal ☏ 641551.

♦London 204 — ♦Kingston-upon-Hull 38 — ♦Leeds 26 — ♦Middlesbrough 51 — ♦Nottingham 88 — ♦Sheffield 62.

YORK

469

🏨 **Royal York,** Station Rd, YO2 2AA, ℰ 53681, Telex 57912, 🚗 – ⬚ 📺 🅿. 🏧. 🔊 🆎 ⓞ 𝒱𝐼𝑆𝐴
M (bar lunch) 9.00 **st.** – **130 rm** ⫌ 37.00/60.00 **st.** – SB 37.00 **st.**   CY **e**

Annex : 🏠 Friars Garden, Station Rd, YO2 2AA, ℰ 53681, Telex 57912, 🚗 – 📺 🖵wc 🅿
🅿   CY **e**
M (see Royal York H.) – **22 rm**.

🏨 **Middlethorpe Hall** ⟲, Bishopthorpe Rd, YO2 1QP, ℰ 641 241, Telex 57802, ≼, « Tastefully
decorated Queen Anne house », 🚗, park – 🖵 📺 ☎ 🅿. 🔊 🆎 ⓞ 𝒱𝐼𝑆𝐴. ℀   by A 19   BZ
M 12.00/14.50 **st.** ◊ 3.50 – ⫌ 4.50 – **31 rm** 50.00/70.00 **st.**

🏨 **Viking** (Q.M.H.), North St., YO1 1JF, ℰ 59822, Telex 57937, ≼ – ⬚ 📺 ☎ 🅿. 🏧. 🔊 🆎 ⓞ
𝒱𝐼𝑆𝐴   CY **n**
M (carving lunch) 7.25/12.95 **st.** ◊ 2.85 – **187 rm** ⫌ 45.60/68.70 **st.** – SB (week-
ends only) 52.00/56.00 **st.**

🏨 **Judges' Lodging,** 9 Lendal, YO1 2AQ, ℰ 38733, « Tastefully restored 18C Judges' lod-
gings » – 📺 ☎ 🅿. 🆎 ⓞ 𝒱𝐼𝑆𝐴   CY **x**
M (bar lunch) 16.50 **st.** ◊ 4.75 – **12 rm** ⫌ 35.00/80.00 **st.** – SB (winter
and spring only) 65.00/85.00 **st.**

🏨 **Post House** (T.H.F.), Tadcaster Rd, YO2 2QF, SW : 1 ¾ m. on A 64 ℰ 707921, Telex 57798,
🚗 – ⬚ 📺 🖵wc ☜ ♿ ◊. 🔊 🆎 ⓞ   AZ **r**
M 4.50/9.45 **st.** ◊ 2.60 – ⫌ 5.00 – **147 rm** 39.00/48.00 **st.**

🏨 **Mount Royale,** 119 The Mount, YO2 2DA, ℰ 28856, ⌱ heated, 🚗 – 📺 🖵wc 🍴wc 🅿.
🔊 🆎 ⓞ 𝒱𝐼𝑆𝐴. ℀   AZ **s**
closed 24 December-7 January – **M** (bar lunch residents only) 16.00 **t.** ◊ 3.30 – **19 rm**
⫌ 29.50/55.00 **t.** – SB 60.00/65.00 **st.**

🏨 **Dean Court** (Best Western), Duncombe Pl., YO1 2EF, ℰ 25082 – ⬚ 📺 🖵wc ☎. 🔊 🆎 ⓞ
𝒱𝐼𝑆𝐴. ℀   CY **a**
M 8.00/13.00 **st.** – **35 rm** ⫌ 36.00/66.00 **st.** – SB 76.00 **st.**

🏨 **Hill,** 60 York Rd, Acomb, YO2 5LW, W : 2 m. by A 59 on B 1224 ℰ 790777, 🚗 – 📺 🖵wc ☎
🅿. 🔊 🆎 ⓞ 𝒱𝐼𝑆𝐴. ℀   AZ **v**
closed mid December-mid January – **M** (bar lunch) a la carte approx. 9.00 **t.** ◊ 3.00 – **10 rm**
⫌ 28.00/53.00 **st.**

🏨 **Town House,** 98-104 Holgate Rd, YO2 4BB, ℰ 36171, 🚗 – 📺 🖵wc 🍴wc 🅿. 🔊 🆎 ⓞ 𝒱𝐼𝑆𝐴
closed 24 December-1 January – **M** (bar lunch) 6.50 **t.** ◊ 2.60 – **23 rm** ⫌ 15.00/35.00 **t.**   AZ **z**

🏨 **Hudsons,** 58-60 Bootham, YO3 7BZ, ℰ 21267 – 📺 🖵wc 🍴wc 🅿. 🔊 🆎 ⓞ 𝒱𝐼𝑆𝐴. ℀
M 5.00/8.00 **st.** ◊ 4.00 – **13 rm** ⫌ 33.00/44.00 **st.** – SB 41.00/60.00 **st.**   CX **u**

🏨 **Sheppard,** 63 Blossom St., YO2 2BD, ℰ 20500 – 📺 🖵wc 🍴 ☜. 🔊 𝒱𝐼𝑆𝐴
M (closed Sunday lunch) 5.00/6.50 **t.** ◊ 2.40 – **19 rm** ⫌ 19.50/40.00 **st.** – SB 35.00/44.00 **st.**   CZ **i**

🏨 **Grasmead House** without rest., 1 Scarcroft Hill, YO2 1DF, ℰ 29996 – 📺 🖵wc. 𝒱𝐼𝑆𝐴. ℀
6 rm ⫌ 35.00 **st.**   CZ **a**

🏨 **Field House,** 2 St. Georges Pl., YO2 2DR, ℰ 39572, 🚗 – 📺 🍴wc 🅿. 🔊 🆎 𝒱𝐼𝑆𝐴   AZ **e**
closed Christmas – **M** (bar lunch) 8.00 **st.** ◊ 2.75 – **16 rm** ⫌ 17.50/40.00 **st.** – SB 42.00/52.00 **st.**

🏠 **Priory,** 126 Fulford Rd, YO1 4BE, ℰ 25280, 🚗 – 🍴wc 🅿. 🔊 🆎 ⓞ 𝒱𝐼𝑆𝐴. ℀   DZ **r**
closed Christmas – **19 rm** ⫌ 11.00/24.00 **s.**

✗ **Jeeves,** 39 Tanner Row, YO1 1JP, ℰ 59622 – 🆎 ⓞ   CY **s**
closed Monday in winter, Sunday, 2 weeks July and 23 December-2 January – **M** (dinner only)
a la carte 9.90/14.80 **t.** ◊ 2.95.

at Skelton NW : 3 m. on A 19 – AY – ✉ ✆ 0904 York :

🏨 **Fairfield Manor,** Shipton Rd, YO3 6XW, ℰ 25621, 🚗 – 📺 🖵wc 🍴wc 🅿. 🔊 🆎 ⓞ
𝒱𝐼𝑆𝐴. ℀
closed 2 to 13 January – **M** a la carte 8.90/12.70 **t.** ◊ 3.05 – **25 rm** ⫌ 35.00/50.00 **t.** – SB
(except Bank Holidays) 60.00 **st.**

ALFA-ROMEO Leeman Rd ℰ 22772
AUSTIN-ROVER, FORD, VAUXHALL-OPEL 117 Long
St. ℰ 0347 (Easingwold) 21694
AUSTIN-ROVER Gladstone St. ℰ 58781
CITROEN Lowther St. ℰ 22064
COLT Fulford ℰ 33139
FORD Piccadilly ℰ 25371
LADA Leeman Rd ℰ 59241
LANCIA Piccadilly ℰ 34321

NISSAN 21-27 Layerthorpe ℰ 58809
PEUGEOT, TALBOT The Stonebow ℰ 55118
RENAULT Layerthorpe ℰ 58252
RENAULT Clifton ℰ 58647
SAAB 223 Malton Rd ℰ 55787
TOYOTA 172 Fulford Rd ℰ 52947
VAUXHALL-OPEL Rougier St. ℰ 25444
VAUXHALL-OPEL 100 Layerthorpe ℰ 56671
VOLVO 88/96 Walmgate ℰ 53798

YOXFORD Suffolk 🏼🏼🏼 Y 27 – pop. 693 – ✉ Saxmundham – ✆ 072 877.
♦London 95 – ♦Ipswich 25 – ♦Norwich 55.

✗ **Jacey's,** Blythburgh House, High St., IP17 3EU, ℰ 298 – 𝒱𝐼𝑆𝐴
closed Sunday – **M** (dinner only) a la carte 9.00/12.05 **t.** ◊ 2.00.

YR WYDDFA = Snowdon.

YR WYDDGRUG = Mold.

Y WAUN = Chirk.

Scotland

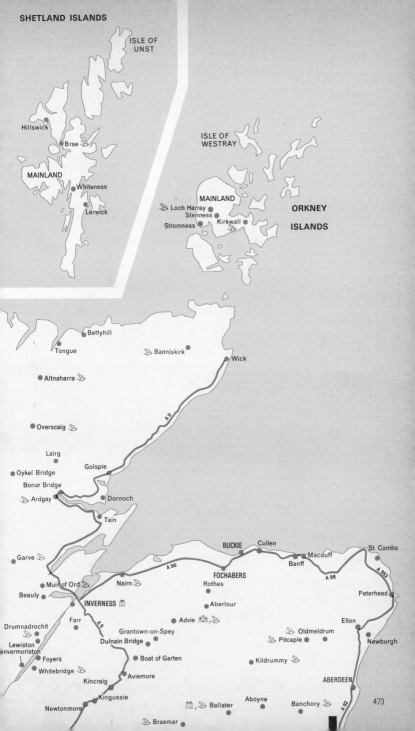

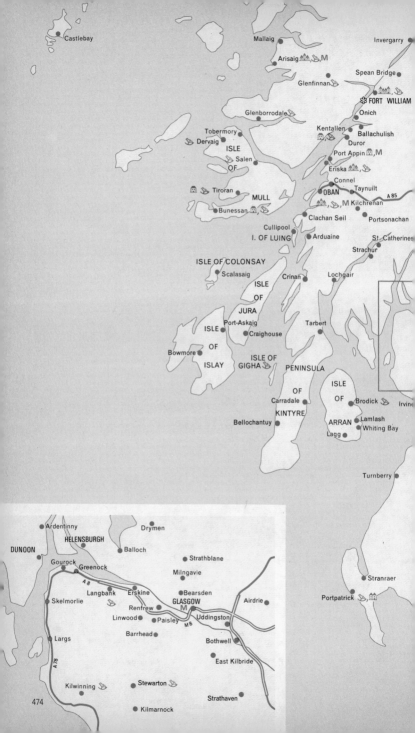

SCOTLAND

Towns

ABERDEEN Aberdeen. (Grampian) **401** N 12 – pop. 182,071 – ECD : Wednesday and Saturday – ✆ 0224.

See : Marischal College★ Y **U** – Art Gallery and Museum★ Y **M** – ≼★ from the lighthouse X – St. Machar's Cathedral★ X **B** – King's College Chapel★ (Crown Tower) X **U**.

⛳ King's Links, 19 Golf Rd ✆ 21464 X – ⛳, ⛳ Hazlehead ✆ 35747, W : 3 m. by King's Gate X – ⛳ St. Fittick's Rd, Balnagask ✆ 871286 X.

✈ Aberdeen Airport ✆ 722331 NW : 7 m. by A 96 X – **Terminal :** Bus Station, Guild St. (adjacent to Railway Station).

🚗 ✆ 22005.

⛴ by P & O Ferries : Orkney & Shetland Services : to Shetland Islands : Lerwick 3 weekly (14 h).

🛈 St. Nicholas House, Broad St. ✆ 23456 (Saturdays ✆ 24890/21814/21810), Telex 73366 – Information Caravan, Stonehaven Rd ✆ 873030 (summer only).

◆Edinburgh 130 – ◆Dundee 67.

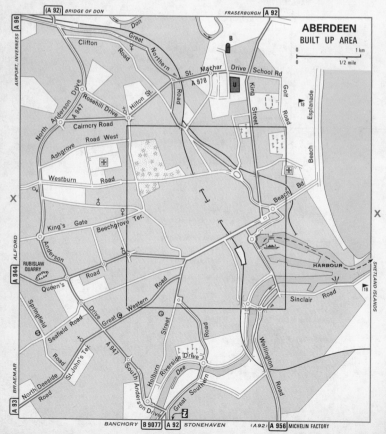

ABERDEEN

Station, 78 Guild St., AB9 2DN, ℰ 587214, Telex 73161 – 🛗 📺 ☎ Ⓟ 🕭 🔺 🔼 ᴬᴱ ⓪ 𝘝𝘐𝘚𝘈 🍽
closed 24 to 26 December and 31 December-3 January – **M** 7.55/9.25 **t.** – 🍽 4.55 – **60 rm**
25.50/52.50 **st.** – SB 60.00/90.50 **st.**   Z **o**

Stakis Tree Tops (Stakis), 161 Springfield Rd, AB9 2QM, ℰ 33377, Telex 73794 – 🛗 📺
🍽wc 🕭 Ⓟ 🔺 🔼 ᴬᴱ ⓪ 𝘝𝘐𝘚𝘈 🍽
M 6.50/9.95 **st.** ⌀ 3.20 – **92 rm** 🍽 44.50/50.00 **t.**   X **s**

Caledonian Thistle (Thistle), 10-14 Union Terr., AB9 1HE, ℰ 640233, Telex 73758 – 🛗 📺
🍽wc 🕭 Ⓟ 🔼 ᴬᴱ ⓪ 𝘝𝘐𝘚𝘈 🍽
M a la carte 13.50/16.00 **t.** ⌀ 3.45 – 🍽 4.75 – **75 rm** 41.00/55.00 **t.** – SB (weekends only) 52.00 **st.**   Z **i**

Royal, 1-3 Bath St., AB1 2HY, ℰ 585152 – 🛗 📺 🍽wc 🕅wc 🕭 Ⓟ   Z **a**
43 rm.

Bracklinn, 348 Great Western Rd, AB1 6LX, ℰ 37060   X **c**
6 rm 🍽 15.00/25.00 **st.**

Russell, 50 St. Swithin St., AB1 6XJ, ℰ 323555 – Ⓟ. 🍽   Z **c**
9 rm 🍽 13.50/27.00 **st.**

ABERDEEN

XX Atlantis, 145 Crown St., AB1 2HR, *℘* 591403, Seafood – **ℙ**. **⚃ AE ① VISA**　　　　Z　**r**
closed Saturday lunch, Sunday, Christmas and New Year – **M** a la carte 12.25/20.90 **t**. ⌂ 3.00.

XX Aberdeen Rendezvous, 218-222 George St., AB1 1BS, *℘* 633610, Chinese rest. – **⚃ AE ①**
VISA　　　　　　　　　　　　　　　　　　　　　　　　　　　　　　　　　　　　　Y　**c**
closed Sunday lunch and 1 January – **M** a la carte 10.50/15.00 **t**. ⌂ 3.50.

XX Nargile, 77-79 Skene St., AB1 1QD, *℘* 636 093, Turkish rest. – **⚃ AE ① VISA**　　Y　**a**
M (closed Sunday lunch) a la carte 7.00/13.00 **t**. ⌂ 3.40.

X Poldino's, 7 Little Belmont St., AB1 1JG, *℘* 647777, Italian rest. – **⚃ AE ① VISA**　　YZ　**u**
closed Christmas Day and New Years Day – **M** a la carte 8.40/11.70 **st**. ⌂ 3.00.

　　at Altens S : 3 m. on A 956 – X – ⊠ ✿ 0224 Aberdeen :

🏨 Skean Dhu Altens, Souterhead Rd, AB1 4LF, *℘* 877000, Telex 739631, ⊐ heated – 🛗
🍽 rest **TV** ☎ &. **ℙ**. ⚱. **⚃ AE ① VISA**
M 6.95/8.25 **st**. ⌂ 3.25 – ⊊ 3.25 – **221 rm** 41.95/46.95 **st**. – SB (weekends only) 56.00 **st**.

　　at Banchory-Devenick SW : 4 ½ m. on B 9077 – X – ⊠ ✿ 0224 Aberdeen :

🏨 Ardoe House ⌂, South Deeside Rd, AB1 5YP, *℘* 867355, ≼, ⌂, ⌂, park – **TV** ⌂wc 🛗
⌂ **ℙ**. ⚱. **⚃** *VISA*. ⌂
M 12.50 **st**. ⌂ 3.50 – **20 rm** ⊊ 22.00/50.00 **st**.

　　at Westhill W : 6 ½ m. by A 944 – X – ⊠ ✿ 0224 Aberdeen :

🏨 Westhill Inn, Westhill Drive, AB3 6TT, *℘* 740388, Telex 739925 – 🛗 **TV** ⌂wc 🛗wc **ℙ**.
⚱. **⚃ AE ① VISA**
closed 1 and 2 January – **M** 6.25/8.25 **st**. ⌂ 3.00 – **52 rm** ⊊ 33.00/45.00 **st**. – SB (weekends only) 50.50 **st**.

　　at Aberdeen Airport NW : 6 m. by A 96 – X – ⊠ ✿ 0224 Aberdeen :

🏨 Holiday Inn, Riverview Drive, Farburn, Dyce, AB2 0AZ, *℘* 770011, Telex 739651, ⊐ – **TV** ☎
&. **ℙ**. ⚱. **⚃ AE ① VISA**
M (buffet lunch) 10.50 **st**. ⌂ 6.25 – ⊊ 5.65 – **154 rm** 48.00/56.00 **s**. – SB (weekends only) 70.00/80.00 **st**.

🏨 Aberdeen Airport Skean Dhu, Argyll Rd, AB2 0DU, *℘* 725252, Telex 739239, ⊐ heated –
🍽 rest **TV** ☎ &. **ℙ**. ⚱. **⚃ AE ① VISA**
M (coffee shop and bar lunch) a la carte 10.00/15.55 **st**. ⌂ 2.95 – ⊊ 3.95 – **148 rm** 45.95/50.95 **st**.
– SB (weekends only) 56.00 **st**.

　　at Bucksburn NW : 4 m. by A 96 – X – on A 947 – ⊠ ✿ 0224 Aberdeen :

🏨 Holiday Inn, Oldmeldrum Rd, AB2 9LN, *℘* 713911, Telex 73108, ⊐ – 🛗 **TV** ☎ **ℙ**. ⚱. **⚃ AE**
① VISA
M 9.50 **t**. – ⊊ 4.50 – **98 rm** 42.50/49.75 **s**. – SB (weekends only) 54.00 **st**.

🏨 Craighaar, Waterton Rd, AB2 9HS, *℘* 712275 – **TV** 🛗wc ☎ **ℙ** – **44 rm**.

　　at Dyce NW : 6 ½ m. by A 96 – X – on A 947 – ⊠ ✿ 0224 Aberdeen :

🏨 Skean Dhu, Farburn Terr., AB2 0DW, *℘* 723101, Telex 73473, squash – **TV** &. **ℙ**. ⚱. **⚃ AE**
① VISA. ⌂
M 6.75/8.75 **st**. ⌂ 3.00 – ⊊ 3.95 – **222 rm** 42.50/45.50 **st**. – SB (weekends only) 45.00/55.00 **st**.

MICHELIN Branch, Wellington St., AB9 2JZ, *℘* 875075

ALFA-ROMEO 542 Gt Western Rd *℘* 30181
AUSTIN-ROVER 92 Crown St. *℘* 50381
AUSTIN-ROVER, ROLLS ROYCE 19 Justice Mill Lane
℘ 56151
BMW Grey St. *℘* 33355
NISSAN 78 Powis Terr. *℘* 41313
FIAT 870 Gt Northern Rd *℘* 695573
FORD Menzies Rd *℘* 879024

FORD 29 Union Glen *℘* 29022
LANCIA 3 Whitehall Rd *℘* 641349
MERCEDES-BENZ, OPEL 366 King St. *℘* 634211
RENAULT Lang Stracht *℘* 683181
SUBARU 16/22 Mid Stocket Rd *℘* 631950
VAUXHALL-OPEL 16 Dee St. *℘* 29216
VW, AUDI 94 Hilton Drive *℘* 43327

ABERDOUR Fife. (Fife) **401** K 15 – pop. 1,576 – ECD : Wednesday – ✿ 0383.
See : ≼ ★★ from the harbour – ⌂ Dodhead, Burntisland *℘* 0592 (Burntisland) 873247, E : 5 m. on A 92.
♦Edinburgh 17 – Dunfermline 7.

🏨 Woodside, High St., KY3 9SW, *℘* 860328 – **TV** 🛗wc 🛗wc ☎ **ℙ**. **⚃ AE ① VISA**
closed 25 December and 1 January – **M** a la carte 5.75/13.00 **t**. ⌂ 3.95 – **12 rm** ⊊ 18.00/40.00 **t**.

ABERFELDY Perth. (Tayside) **401** I 14 – pop. 1,537 – ECD : Wednesday – ✿ 0887.
Envir. : Loch Tay ★ W : 6 m – ⌂ District Tourist Association, 8 Dunkeld St. *℘* 20276 (summer only).
♦Edinburgh 74 – ♦Glasgow 72 – ♦Oban 77 – Perth 32.

🏨 Cruachan Country House, Kenmore St., PH15 2BL, *℘* 20545, ≼, ⌂ – 🛗wc **ℙ**
M (bar lunch) a la carte 7.65/12.20 **t**. ⌂ 4.00 – **9 rm** ⊊ 12.50/33.00 – SB (except summer) 45.00/60.00 **st**.

🏨 Balnearn, Crieff Rd, PH15 2BJ, *℘* 20431, ⌂ – **ℙ**
13 rm ⊊ 10.35/20.70 **t**.

AUSTIN-ROVER, FORD Dunkeld St. *℘* 20254

ABERFOYLE Perth. (Central) **401** G 15 – pop. 593 – ECD : Wednesday – ⊠ Stirling – ☎ 087 72.
Envir. : Loch Ard★★ W : 3 ½ m. – Loch Chon★★ NW : 8 m. – Loch Arklet Reservoir★ NW : 11 m.
🏌₉ Braeval ✐ 493.
� Main St. ✐ 352 (Easter-September).
♦Edinburgh 55 – ♦Glasgow 27.

  Hotels see : *Callander* NE : 10 ½ m., *Drymen* SW : 11 ½ m.

ABERLADY E. Lothian (Lothian) **401** L 15 – pop. 737 – ECD : Wednesday – ☎ 087 57.
🏌₁₈ Kilspindie, ✐ 216.
♦Edinburgh 16 – Haddington 5 – North Berwick 7.

  🏠 **Kilspindie House,** Main St., EH32 0RE, ✐ 319 – ⊟wc **℗**. 🖭 *VISA*
  M (bar lunch) 6.80 **st.** – **12 rm** ⊿ 14.00/28.00 **st.** – SB (weekends only) 38.00/41.60 **st.**

ABERLOUR Banff. (Grampian) **401** K 11 – pop. 763 – ECD : Wednesday – ☎ 034 05.
♦Edinburgh 187 – ♦Aberdeen 63 – ♦Inverness 54.

  🏠 **Dowans,** AB3 9LS, SW : ¾ m. by A 95 ✐ 488, ≤, 🐾, 🌳 – ⊟wc **℗**
  March to November – **M** 4.00/7.00 – **13 rm** ⊿ 12.00/24.00.

AUSTIN-ROVER-LAND ROVER-RANGE ROVER 15-19 High St. ✐ 505

ABOYNE Aberdeen. (Grampian) **401** L 12 – pop. 1,040 – ECD : Thursday – ☎ 0339.
Envir. : Craigievar Castle★ (17C) *AC*, NE : 12 m.
🏌₁₈ Formaston Park ✐ 2328, E : end of Village – 🏌₉ Tarland ✐ 033 981 (Tarland) 413, NW : 5 m.
♦Edinburgh 137 – ♦Aberdeen 31 – ♦Dundee 80.

  🏠 **Birse Lodge** 🐾, Charleston Rd, AB3 5EL, ✐ 2253, 🌳 – ⊟wc **℗**. 🖭 ⓞ
  Mid March-mid October – **M** (bar lunch) 11.00 **t.** – **16 rm** ⊿ 19.00/38.00 **t.**

AUSTIN-ROVER Main Rd ✐ 2440

ACHILTIBUIE Ross and Cromarty (Highland) **401** D 9 – pop. 300 – ☎ 085 482.
♦Edinburgh 243 – ♦Inverness 84 – Ullapool 25.

  🏠 **Summer Isles** 🐾, IV26 2YG, ✐ 282, ≤ Summer Isles, 🐾 – ⊟wc **℗**
  Easter-September – **M** (dinner only) 16.00 **st.** ⍾ 5.00 – **16 rm** ⊿ 15.00/50.00 **st.**

ACHNASHEEN Ross and Cromarty (Highland) **401** E 11 – pop. 100 – ECD : Wednesday –
☎ 044 588.
Envir. : Glen Docherty★★ W : 6 m. – Glen Carron★ SW : 8 m.
♦Edinburgh 202 – ♦Inverness 43.

  🏠 **Ledgowan Lodge** (Best Western) 🐾, IV22 2EJ, on A 890 ✐ 252, ≤, 🐾, 🌳 – ⊟wc **℗**. 🖭
  🖭 ⓞ *VISA*
  April-October – **M** 6.00/12.00 **t.** ⍾ 2.00 – **18 rm** ⊿ 17.45/40.00 **t.**

ADVIE Moray. (Highland) **401** J 11 – ⊠ Grantown-on-Spey – ☎ 080 75.
♦Edinburgh 153 – ♦Inverness 46.

  🏛 Tulchan Lodge 🐾, PH26 3PW, on B 9102 ✐ 200, Telex 75405, ≤ Spey Valley, « Tasteful
  decor », 🐾, 🌳, park – ☎ **℗**. 🎾
  closed February and March – **11 rm**.

AIRDRIE Lanark. (Strathclyde) **401** **402** I 16 – pop. 37,740 – ECD : Wednesday – ☎ 023 64.
♦Edinburgh 32 – ♦Glasgow 14 – Motherwell 6.5 – Perth 53.

  🏠 **Staging Post,** 8-10 Anderson St., ML6 0BZ, ✐ 67525 – 📺 ⊟wc 🏧 **℗**. 🖭 🖭 ⓞ *VISA*. 🎾
  closed New Year's Day – **M** *(closed Saturday lunch)* a la carte 5.60/14.85 **t.** ⍾ 3.05 – **8 rm**
  ⊿ 25.00/35.00 **st.**

FORD South Biggar Rd ✐ 64702

AIRTH Stirling. (Central) **401** I 15 – pop. 1,027 – ⊠ Falkirk – ☎ 032 483.
♦Edinburgh 27 – Dunfermline 14 – Falkirk 6 – Stirling 8.

  🏛 **Airth Castle** 🐾, FK2 8JF, ✐ 411, Telex 777975, ≤, « Former castle in extensive grounds »,
  🌳, park – ☎ **℗**. 🖭 🖭 *VISA*. 🎾
  closed 27 to 29 December and 2 to 4 January – **M** 8.75 **st.** ⍾ 3.20 – **23 rm** ⊿ 42.00/58.00 **st.** –
  SB (weekends only) 56.50/64.50 **st.**

ALLOWAY Ayr (Strathclyde) **401** **402** G 17 – see Ayr.

ALTENS Aberdeen. (Grampian) – see Aberdeen.

479

ALTNAHARRA Sutherland (Highland) **401** G 9 – ⊠ Lairg – ☎ 054 981.
◆Edinburgh 282 – ◆Inverness 123 – Thurso 60.

  🏠 **Altnaharra** ॐ, IV27 4UE, ℰ 222, ≤, ↘, ⚞ – ⌂wc ℗
    closed 20 December-7 January – **M** (bar lunch) 9.50 **t.** ₰ 2.25 – **15 rm** ⊊ 14.00/36.00 **t.**

ALYTH Perth. (Tayside) **401** K 14 – pop. 1,701 – ECD : Wednesday – ☎ 082 83.
Envir. : Reekie Linn (waterfall)★ N : 5 ½ m. – ᵢᵢᵢᵢ Pitcrocknie ℰ 2268, E : 1 ½ m.
◆Edinburgh 63 – ◆Aberdeen 69 – ◆Dundee 16 – Perth 21.

  🏠 **Lands of Loyal** ॐ, Loyal Rd, PH11 8JQ, N : ½ m. by B 954 ℰ 2481, ≤, « Victorian country
    house », ⚞, park – ⌂wc ℗. ◪ ⊙ 𝚅𝙸𝚂𝙰
    closed 10 days at Christmas and New Year – **M** 6.00/11.00 **st.** ₰ 2.75 – **14 rm** ⊊ 15.50/40.00 **st.**
    – SB 49.00/63.00 **st.**

ANSTRUTHER Fife. (Fife) **401** L 15 – pop. 3,037 (inc. Kilrenny) – ECD : Wednesday – ☎ 0333 -
ᵢ₉ – See : Harbour★.
Envir. : St. Monance (church★) SW : 3 m. – Elie (site and ≤★) SW : 5 ½ m. – Kellie Castle★
(16C-17C) *AC,* W : 5 m.
🛈 Scottish Fisheries Museum, St. Ayles ℰ 310628.
◆Edinburgh 46 – ◆Dundee 23 – Dunfermline 34.

  🏠 **Craw's Nest,** Bankwell Rd, KY10 3DR, ℰ 310691, ⚞ – 📺 ⌂wc ☜ ℗. ◪. ◪ ◪ ⊙ 𝚅𝙸𝚂𝙰
    🌤
    M 6.00/10.50 **t.** ₰ 2.55 – **31 rm** ⊊ 22.00/42.00 **t.** – SB (October-March) 54.00/60.00 **st.**
  🍴 **Smugglers Inn,** High St., KY10 3DQ, ℰ 310506 – ᵢᵢwc ℗. ◪ ◪ 𝚅𝙸𝚂𝙰
    M a la carte 9.00/12.50 **t.** ₰ 3.00 – **9 rm** ⊊ 15.00/32.00 **t.**

ARBROATH Angus (Tayside) **401** M 14 – pop. 22,586 – ECD : Wednesday – ☎ 0241.
See : Cliffs★★ (nature trail) – Abbey★ *AC* – ᵢᵢᵢ Elliot ℰ 72272, S : 1 m.
🛈 Angus District Council, 105 High St., ℰ 72609/76680.
◆Edinburgh 72 – ◆Aberdeen 51 – ◆Dundee 16.

  Hotel see :, Montrose NE : 13 ½ m.

AUSTIN-ROVER 1 Burnside Drive ℰ 72921   FORD Millgate ℰ 73051
BMW Montrose Rd ℰ 72919

ARDENTINNY Argyll. (Strathclyde) **401** F 15 – pop. 150 – ECD : Wednesday – ⊠ Dunoon –
☎ 036 981.
◆Edinburgh 107 – Dunoon 13 – ◆Glasgow 64 – ◆Oban 71.

  🏠 **Ardentinny** ॐ, PA23 8TR, ℰ 209, ≤ Loch Long, ⚞ – ⌂wc ᵢᵢwc ℗. ◪ ◪ ⊙ 𝚅𝙸𝚂𝙰
    March-October – **M** (bar lunch) 14.00 **st.** ₰ 2.85 – **11 rm** ⊊ 18.00/29.50 **st.**

ARDEONAIG Perth. (Central) – see Killin.

ARDGAY Ross and Cromarty (Highland) **401** G 10 – ☎ 086 32.
◆Edinburgh 204 – ◆Inverness 49 – ◆Wick 77.

  ↑ **Croit Mairi** ॐ, Kincardine Hill, IV24 3DJ, S : 1 ¼ m. off A 9 ℰ 504, ≤ Dornoch Firthland
    hills, ⚞ – ℗. ◪ ◪ ⊙ 𝚅𝙸𝚂𝙰 🌤
    closed first 2 weeks November – **5 rm** ⊊ 11.00/16.00 **st.**

ARDROSSAN Ayr. (Strathclyde) **401 402** F 17 – pop. 10,562 – ECD : Wednesday – ☎ 0294.
⚓ by Isle of Man Steam Packet Co. : to the Isle of Man : Douglas June-September 1-3 weekly
(6 h) – by Caledonian MacBrayne : to the Isle of Arran : Brodick 2-6 daily (1 h).
◆Edinburgh 75 – ◆Ayr 18 – ◆Glasgow 32.

  Hotels see : Kilmarnock SE : 11 ½ m., *Largs* N : 11 ½ m.

ARDUAINE Argyll. (Strathclyde) **401** D 15 – ECD : Wednesday – ⊠ Oban – ☎ 085 22 Kilmelford.
Envir. : Loch Craignish (site★★) S : 6 m.
◆Edinburgh 142 – ◆Oban 20.

  🏠 **Loch Melfort** ॐ, PA34 4XG, ℰ 233, ≤ Sound of Jura, ⚞ – ⌂wc ℗. ◪
    Easter-mid October – **M** (buffet lunch) 12.50 **t.** – ⊊ 2.50 – **26 rm** 22.00/50.00 **t.**

ARISAIG Inverness. (Highland) **401** C 13 – pop. 177 – ECD : Thursday – ☎ 068 75.
See : Sound of Arisaig★.
◆Edinburgh 172 – ◆Inverness 102 – ◆Oban 88.

  🏠 **Arisaig House** ॐ, Beasdale, PH39 4NR, SE : 3 ¼ m. on A 830 ℰ 622, ≤ Loch Nan Uamh
    and Roshven Mountains, ⚞, park – 📺 ☎ ℗. ◪ ◪ 𝚅𝙸𝚂𝙰 🌤
    April-October – **M** (booking essential) (restricted lunch residents only) 17.50 **st.** ₰ 4.50 –
    16 rm ⊊ 26.50/85.00 **st.** – SB (except summer) 81.75/115.75 **st.**
  🏠 **Arisaig,** PH39 4NH, ℰ 210, ≤ – ⌂wc ℗
    March-October – **M** (bar lunch) 14.00 **t.** ₰ 2.50 – **13 rm** ⊊ 20.00/38.50 **t.**

480

ARMADALE Inverness. (Highland) **401** C 12 – Shipping Services : see Skye (Isle of).

ARRAN (Isle of) Bute. (Strathclyde) **401** **402** DE 16 17 – pop. 3,576.

See : W : Kilbrannan Sound★★ – N : Sound of Bute★ – Lochranza (site★) – Catacol Bay★.

🚢 by Caledonian MacBrayne : from Brodick to Ardrossan 2-6 daily (1 h) – from Lochranza to Claonaig (Kintyre Peninsula) summer only : 6-7 daily (30 mn).

     Brodick – pop. 630 – ECD : Wednesday – ⊠ 🕓 0770 Brodick.

     See : Brodick Bay★★.

     🏌 *ℰ* 2349, ½ m. from Pier.

     🛈 The Pier *ℰ* 2401/2140.

↑   **Auchrannie** ⤳, KA27 8BZ, *ℰ* 2234, 🐎 – 🛁wc 🅿
     April-September – **16 rm** ⌁ 10.00/24.00 **st.**

↑   **Altanna,** KA27 8DW, *ℰ* 2232 – 🅿
     closed October and 23 December-5 January – **11 rm** ⌁ 10.00/35.00 **st.**

     Lagg – ⊠ Kilmory – 🕓 077 087 Sliddery.

🏛   **Lagg,** KA27 8PQ, *ℰ* 255, 🐎 – 🛁wc 🅿
     7 March-28 October – **M** 5.00/11.00 **t.** – **17 rm** ⌁ 15.00/30.00 **t.**

     Lamlash – pop. 613 – ECD : Wednesday except summer – ⊠ Brodick – 🕓 077 06 Lamlash.

     See : Lamlash Bay★★.

     🏌 *ℰ* 296.

↑   **Glenisle,** Shore Rd, KA27 8LY, *ℰ* 559, ≤, 🐎 – 🛁wc 🅿
     April-October – **16 rm** ⌁ 7.20/22.00 **t.**

     Whiting Bay – pop. 352 – ECD : Wednesday except summer – ⊠ Brodick – 🕓 077 07 Whiting Bay.

     🏌.

🏮   **Cameronia,** Shore Rd, *ℰ* 254 – 🅿. 🍴
     M (bar lunch) a la carte 3.70/12.00 **t.** �🍷 2.25 – **6 rm** ⌁ 13.50/27.00 **t.**

AUCHENCAIRN Kirkcudbright. (Dumfries and Galloway) **401** **402** I 19 – pop. 215 – ⊠ Castle Douglas – 🕓 055 664.

♦Edinburgh 98 – ♦Dumfries 21 – Stranraer 62.

  🏨   **Balcary Bay** ⤳, Balcary, DG7 1QZ, SE : 2 m. by A 711 *ℰ* 217, ≤ Auchencairn bay, hills and countryside, 🐎 – 🛁wc 📶 🅿. 🖧 AE ⓞ VISA
     M a la carte 7.40/13.15 **st.** ⍾ 3.00 – **11 rm** ⌁ 17.00/44.00 **st.**

AUCHTERARDER Perth. (Tayside) **401** I 15 – pop. 2,446 – ECD : Wednesday – 🕓 076 46.

🏌 Orchil Rd *ℰ* 2804, SW : 1 m. – 🏌, 🏌, 🏌, 🏌 Gleneagles *ℰ* 3543.

♦Edinburgh 55 – ♦Glasgow 45 – Perth 14.

  🏰   **Gleneagles,** PH3 1NF, SW : 1 ½ m. by A 9 *ℰ* 2231, Telex 76105, ≤, 🔲, 🏌, 🎣, 🐎, park, 🎾, squash – 🛗 📺 ☎ 🅫 🖧. 🖧 AE ⓞ VISA
     M 14.00/17.50 **t.** ⍾ 3.75 – ⌁ 7.25 – **254 rm** 45.00/100.00 **t.** – SB (spring only) 99.00 **st.**

  🏠   **Collearn House,** PH3 1DF, *ℰ* 3553, 🐎 – 📺 🛁wc 📶 🅿. 🖧 AE ⓞ VISA
     M a la carte 8.10/15.20 **t.** ⍾ 2.45 – **8 rm** ⌁ 20.00/40.00 **t.** – SB 46.00/66.00 **st.**

  🏠   Ruthven Tower, Abbey Rd, PH3 1DN, *ℰ* 2578, 🐎 – 🛁wc 🅿
     19 rm.

AUCHTERHOUSE Angus. (Tayside) **401** K 14 – ⊠ Dundee – 🕓 082 626.

♦Edinburgh 69 – ♦Dundee 7 – Perth 24.

  XXX   **Old Mansion House** ⤳ with rm, DD3 0QN, *ℰ* 366, ≤, « 15-17C country house », 🏊 heated, 🐎, park, 🎾 – 📺 🛁wc 📶 🅿. 🖧 AE ⓞ VISA
     closed 31 December-7 January – **M** 7.50/a la carte 17.70 **t.** – **6 rm** ⌁ 36.00/55.00 **t.**

AULTBEA Ross and Cromarty (Highland) **401** D 10 – pop. 150 – ECD : Wednesday – 🕓 044 582.

♦Edinburgh 234 – ♦Inverness 79 – Kyle of Lochalsh 80.

  🏠   **Aultbea,** IV22 2HX, *ℰ* 201, ≤ – 🅿. 🖧 VISA
     April-October – **M** a la carte 2.30/7.50 **t.** ⍾ 2.10 – **9 rm** ⌁ 15.00/35.00 **t.**

AVIEMORE Inverness. (Highland) **401** I 12 – pop. 1,224 – ECD : Wednesday – Winter Sports – ✪ 0479.

Envir. : Cairngorm Mountains ❄****** from the summit (alt. 4084 ft) SE : 8 ½ m. and by chairlift (*AC*) 40 mn Rtn and 45 mn on foot Rtn.

🛈 Main Rd ℰ 810363, Telex 75127.

♦Edinburgh 127 – ♦Inverness 32 – Perth 85.

🏨 **Stakis Coylumbridge** (Stakis), PH22 1QH, SE : 1 ¾ m. by B 970 ℰ 810661, Telex 75272, ≤, 🔦, 🔧, 🚗, 🎣 – 🔟 ☎ ⏥ 🅿. 🔼 🔼 AE ⑩ VISA
M (buffet lunch) 5.00/10.00 **st.**, ⌂ 3.75 – **153 rm** ⊠ 37.00/52.00 **t.** – SB 52.00/64.00 **st.**

🏨 Strathspey Thistle (Thistle), Aviemore Centre, PH22 1PF, ℰ 810681, Telex 75213, ≤ Cairngorms – ⏺ 🔟 🅿. 🔼 AE VISA
88 rm ⊠ 49.50 **t.** – SB (weekends only) 47.00 **st.**

🏨 **Post House** (T.H.F.), Aviemore Centre, PH22 1PJ, ℰ 810771, Telex 75597, ≤ – ⏺ 🔟 ⌷wc ☏ ⏥ 🅿. 🔼 🔼 AE ⑩ VISA
M a la carte 9.75/14.50 **st.** ⌂ 2.60 – ⊠ 5.25 – **103 rm** 30.50/44.00 **st.**

🏨 **Badenoch** (Osprey), Aviemore Centre, PH22 1PH, ℰ 810261, ≤ – ⏺ 🔟 ⌷wc ⏥ 🅿. 🔼 AE ⑩ VISA
M (bar lunch) 8.50 **st.** ⌂ 3.00 – **77 rm** ⊠ 15.00/39.70 **st.** – SB 32.00/44.00 **st.**

🏠 **Lynwilg**, PH22 1QB, S : 2 ¼ m. on A 9 ⊠ Loch Alvie ℰ 810207, ≤, 🚗 – ⌷wc 🅿. 🔼 AE VISA
M (bar lunch) 6.95 **t.** ⌂ 1.95 – **12 rm** ⊠ 12.00/25.00 **t.** – SB 33.00/37.00 **st.**

AUSTIN-ROVER Main Rd ℰ 810492   FORD 115 Grampian Rd ℰ 810232

If you write to a hotel abroad,
enclose an International Reply Coupon
(available from Post Offices).

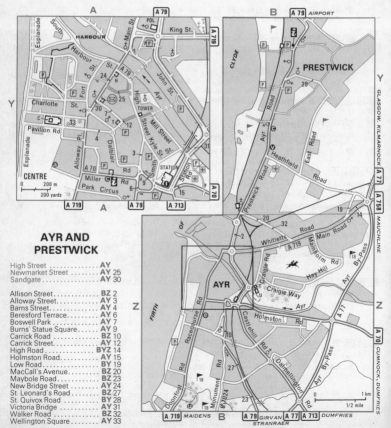

AYR AND PRESTWICK

AYR Ayr. (Strathclyde) **401 402** G 17 – pop. 47,896 – ECD : Wednesday – ☎ 0292.

See : Harbour★ AY.

Envir. : Culzean Castle 18C (site★★, interior★) *AC*, SW : 14 ½ m. by A 719 BZ – Alloway★ (Burn's Museum *AC*, Burn's birthplace *AC*, Auld brig) S : 2 ½ m. by B 7024 BZ.

🛦 Belleisle ☎ 0292 (Alloway) 41258 BZ – 🛦 Dalmilling, Westwood Av., Whitletts ☎ 263893 BZ.

🛿 30 Miller Rd ☎ 68077.

◆Edinburgh 81 – ◆Glasgow 35.

Plan opposite

🏛 **Stakis Station** (Stakis), Burns Statue Sq., KA7 3AT, ☎ 263268 – 🕮 🗹 ⇔wc ☜ 🅿 🛦 🔼 🎿 🔘 *VISA*
AY i
M a la carte 8.15/8.50 **t.** ⅃ 3.25 – **73 rm** � 32.00/44.00 t. – SB 36.00/50.00 st.

🏛 **Pickwick,** 19 Racecourse Rd, KA7 2TD, ☎ 260111, ♠ – 🗹 ⇔wc ⋔wc ☜ 🅿 *VISA* 🎿
BZ e
M 7.00/10.00 **t.** ⅃ 3.00 – **15 rm** ⊐z 25.00/40.00 t.

🏛 **Belleisle House** ⬎, Doonfoot Rd, Belleisle Park, KA7 4DU, S : 1 ½ m. on A 719 ☎ 42331, ⟨
– 🗹 ⇔wc ⋔wc 🅿 🎿 🔼 🆑 🅿 🎿
BZ u
M 5.95/10.95 **t.** ⅃ 2.30 – **16 rm** ⊐z 27.50/37.50 st. – SB 37.50/42.50 st.

🏛 **Marine Court,** 12 Fairfield Rd, KA7 2AR, ☎ 267461, 🔼 – 🗹 ⇔wc ⋔wc ☜ 🅿 🛦 🔼 🆎
🔘 *VISA*
AY a
M 6.50/10.50 **st.** ⅃ 2.25 – **27 rm** ⊐z 32.00/50.00 st. – SB 60.00/80.00 st.

⌂ **Clifton,** 19 Miller Rd, KA7 2AX, ☎ 264521 – ⋔wc 🅿 🆎 *VISA* 🎿
AY c
11 rm ⊐z 10.50/23.00 t.

at Alloway S : 3 m. on A 719 – BZ – ✉ ☎ 0292 Ayr :

🏛 Balgarth, Dunure Rd, KA7 4HR, on A 719 ☎ 42441, ♠ – 🗹 ⇔wc ⋔wc ☜ 🅿 – **15 rm**

at Hollybush SE : 6 m. on A 713 – BZ – ✉ Ayr – ☎ 029 256 Dalrymple :

🏛 **Hollybush House** ⬎, KA8 7EA, ☎ 214, ⟨, ♘, ♠, park – ⇔wc 🅿 🔼 🆎 *VISA* 🎿
April-December – **M** (bar lunch) 12.00 **t.** ⅃ 3.40 – **12 rm** ⊐z 15.00/40.00 t.

ALFA-ROMEO, FIAT Galloway Av. ☎ 260416
AUSTIN-ROVER, DAIMLER-JAGUAR 18 Holmston Rd ☎ 266944
MERCEDES-BENZ, PORSCHE Heathfield Industrial Estate ☎ 282727
NISSAN Alloway Pl. ☎ 263140

SAAB Cambuslea Rd ☎ 266146
TOYOTA 65 Peebles St. ☎ 267606
VAUXHALL 196 Prestwick Rd ☎ 261631
VOLVO Burn's Statue Sq. ☎ 282711
VW, AUDI 24 Dalblair Rd ☎ 269522
YUGO 49 New Rd ☎ 266261

AYTON Berwick. (Borders) **401 402** N 16 – pop. 418 – ECD : Thursday – ☎ 039 02.

🛦 at Eyemouth, Gunsgreen House ☎ 0390 (Eyemouth) 50551, N : 3 m. by A 6355.

◆ Edinburgh 48 – Berwick-upon-Tweed 8.

🏠 **Red Lion,** High St., TD14 5QP, ☎ 400 – 🅿 🎿
M 5.50/a la carte 8.40 **st.** ⅃ 2.50 – **10 rm** ⊐z 10.00/18.00 st.

BALLACHULISH Argyll. (Highland) **401** E 13 – pop. 1,089 – ECD : Wednesday – ☎ 085 52.

Envir. : Glen Coe★★ (glen and waterfall) E : 6 m.

🛿 ☎ 296 (summer only).

◆Edinburgh 117 – ◆ Inverness 80 – Kyle of Lochalsh 90 – ◆ Oban 38.

⌂ **Lyn Leven,** White St., PA39 4JW, ☎ 392, ⟨ – ⋔wc 🅿 🎿
closed December – **8 rm** ⊐z 8.50/20.00.

BALLATER Aberdeen. (Grampian) **401** K 12 – pop. 982 – ECD : Thursday – ☎ 0338.

Envir. : NW : Lecht Road ⟨★★ of the Grampian Mountains – Balmoral Castle★ (not open) and park★ *AC*, W : 9 m.

🛦 ☎ 55200.

🛿 Station Sq. ☎ 55306 (summer only).

◆Edinburgh 109 – ◆Aberdeen 41 – ◆Inverness 69 – Perth 67.

🏛 **Tullich Lodge** ⬎, AB3 5SB, E : 1 ½ m. on A 93 ☎ 55406, ⟨ Dee valley and Grampians, « Country house atmosphere », ♠ – ⇔wc ☜ 🅿 🆎
April-November – **M** (bar lunch) (booking essential) 14.00 **st.** ⅃ 3.00 – **9 rm** ⊐z 36.00/72.00 st.

🏛 **Darroch Learg,** Braemar Rd, AB3 5UX, ☎ 55443, ⟨ Dee Valley and Grampians, ♠ – ⇔wc ⋔wc 🅿 🎿
February-October – **M** 5.00/8.00 **st.** ⅃ 3.00 – **23 rm** ⊐z 13.00/34.00 st.

🏠 **Alexandra,** 12 Bridge Sq., AB3 6QJ, ☎ 55376 – 🗹 ⋔wc 🅿 🔼 🔘 *VISA*
M (bar lunch) 15.00 **st.** ⅃ 2.00 – **6 rm** ⊐z 12.00/25.00 st. – SB 34.00/44.00 st.

⌂ **Moorside House,** 26 Braemar Rd, AB3 5RL, ☎ 55492, ♠ – ⋔wc 🅿 🎿
April-November – **8 rm** ⊐z 11.00/20.00 st.

🏠 **Glen Lui** ⬎, 14 Invercauld Rd, AB3 5RP, ☎ 55402, ⟨, ♠ – ⋔wc 🅿
April-November – **M** (bar lunch) 10.00 **t.** – **10 rm** ⊐z 20.00/36.00 st.

⌂ **Morvada,** Braemar Rd, AB3 5RL, ☎ 55501, ♠ – ⋔wc 🅿 🎿
April-October – **6 rm** ⊐z 12.00/20.00 st.

BALLOCH Dunbarton (Strathclyde) – ✪ 038 985 Arden.

♦Edinburgh 62 – ♦Glasgow 18 – Helensburgh 7.

🏨 **Lomond Castle** ॐ, G83 8RB, N : 2 m. on A 82 ℰ 681, ≼, 🖼, 🖎, 🖎, park – 📺 ☎ 🅿 🏊
⊠ 🗚 *VISA* 🕸
M 7.50/9.00 t. – **21 rm** ヱ 30.00/50.00 t. – SB 47.00/55.00 st.

BALMACARA Ross and Cromarty (Highland) **401** D 12 – pop. 107 – ECD : Wednesday – ⊠ Kyle
of Lochalsh – ✪ 059 986.

♦Edinburgh 197 – Kyle of Lochalsh 4.5.

🏨 **Balmacara,** IV40 8DH, ℰ 283, ≼ coast and mountains – 🛏wc 🅿 🗚 *VISA*
M (bar lunch) 9.00 st. ⓵ 3.00 – **29 rm** ヱ 19.50/32.00 st. – SB (winter only) 45.00 st.

BALNAKEIL Sutherland (Highland) **401** F 8.
See : Balnakeil Bay★★ – Envir. : Smoo Cave★ SE : 3 ½ m. – SW : Dionard Valley★.

♦Edinburgh 294 – Durness 2 – ♦Inverness 135 – Thurso 83.

BALQUHIDDER Perth. (Central) **401** G 14 – see Lochearnhead.

BANAVIE Inverness. (Highland) **401** E 13 – see Fort William.

BANCHORY Kincardine. (Grampian) **401** M 12 – pop. 2,355 – ECD : Thursday – ✪ 033 02.
🏌 Kinneskie ℰ 2365 – 🏌 Torphins ℰ 033 982 (Torphins) 493, NW : 6 m.
🛈 Dee St. Car Park ℰ 2000 (summer only).

♦Edinburgh 125 – ♦Aberdeen 17 – ♦Dundee 66 – ♦Inverness 92.

🏨 **Banchory Lodge** ॐ, Dee St., AB3 3HS, ℰ 2625, ≼, « Part 18C house on River Dee », 🖎,
🌲 – 📺 🛏wc 🅿 ⊠ 🗚 ⓪ *VISA*
closed 12 December-28 January – **M** 6.95/15.00 st. ⓵ 2.85 – **25 rm** ヱ 40.00/70.00 s.

🏨 **Raemoir House** ॐ, AB3 4ED, N : 2 ½ m. on A 980 ℰ 2622, ≼, « 18C mansion in extensive
grounds », 🌲, park – 📺 🛏wc 🅿 ⊠ 🗚 ⓪
M (bar lunch Monday to Saturday) 7.00/12.50 t. ⓵ 3.20 – **24 rm** ヱ 25.00/48.00 t.

🏨 **Tor-Na-Coille** ॐ, Inchmarlo Rd, AB3 4AB, ℰ 2242, 🌲, park – 🍴 📺 🛏wc 🍴wc 🕸 🅿.
🏊 . ⊠ 🗚 ⓪ *VISA*
closed 3 days at Christmas – **M** (bar lunch) 10.50 st. ⓵ 3.00 – **25 rm** ヱ 28.00/40.00 st. – SB
(weekends only) 50.00/60.00 st.

AUSTIN-ROVER High St. ℰ 2293   RENAULT North Deeside Rd ℰ 2847
AUSTIN-ROVER North Deeside Rd ℰ 2255

BANCHORY-DEVENICK Aberdeen. (Grampian) – see Aberdeen.

BANFF Banff. (Grampian) **401** M 10 – pop. 3,723 – ECD : Wednesday – ✪ 026 12.
See : Duff House★ – Envir. : Gardenstown (site★) E : 8 m.
🏌 Royal Tarlair, Macduff ℰ 0261 (Macduff) 32548 – 🛈 Collie Lodge ℰ 2419 (summer only).

♦Edinburgh 170 – ♦Aberdeen 46 – Fraserburgh 26 – ♦Inverness 74.

🏨 **Banff Springs,** Golden Knowes Rd, AB4 2JE, W : ¾ m. on A 98 ℰ 2881, Telex 57515, ≼ –
📺 🛏wc 🍴wc 🕸 🅿 🏊 ⊠ 🗚 ⓪ *VISA* 🕸
M (bar lunch) 8.50 t. ⓵ 2.95 – **30 rm** ヱ 27.60/34.00 t. – SB (weekends only) 40.00 st.

🏠 **County,** 32 High St., AB4 1AE, ℰ 5353, ≼, 🌲 – 📺 🛏wc 🕸 🅿 ⊠ 🗚 ⓪ *VISA*
M 2.70/11.50 st. ⓵ 4.25 – **6 rm** ヱ 26.00/44.00 st.

🏠 **Carmelite House,** 40 Low St., AB4 1AY, ℰ 2152 – 🅿
8 rm ヱ 9.50/19.00 st.

AUSTIN-ROVER Castle St. ℰ 2473   FORD Bridge Rd ℰ 2673

BANNISKIRK Caithness (Highland) – ⊠ ✪ 084 783 Halkirk.

♦Edinburgh 282 – Thurso 8 – ♦Wick 18.

🏠 **Banniskirk House** ॐ, KW12 6XA, on A 895 ℰ 609, 🌲, park – 🅿
(booking essential in winter) – **8 rm** ヱ 7.50/16.00 st.

BARRA (Isle of) Inverness. (Outer Hebrides) (Western Isles) **401** X 12 13 – pop. 1,147.
✈ at North Bay ℰ 041 889 1311.
🚢 by Caledonian MacBrayne : from Castlebay to Oban 3-4 weekly (5-8 h) – to Lochboisdale
(South Uist) 1-3 weekly (2 h).
🚢 by Western Isles Council : to Vatersay Monday/Saturday 4 daily (5 mn).

Castlebay – ⊠ ✪ 087 14 Castlebay.
🛈 ℰ 336 (May-September).

🏨 **Isle of Barra** ॐ, Tangusdale Beach, PA80 5XW, NW : 2 m. on A 888 ℰ 383, ≼ sea and
mountains – 🛏wc 🅿 ⊠ 🗚 ⓪ *VISA*
March-October – **M** (bar lunch) 9.50 st. ⓵ 2.50 – **14 rm** ヱ 21.50/37.00 st. – SB 44.00/58.00 st.

BARRHEAD Renfrew. (Strathclyde) **401 402** G 16 – pop. 18,289 – ECD : Tuesday – ✉ 🕿 041 Glasgow.

♦Edinburgh 51 – ♦Ayr 30 – ♦Glasgow 8.

🏠 **Dalmeny Park,** Lochlibo Rd, G78 1LG, SW : ½ m. on A 736 🖉 881 9211, « Gardens » – 📺 🎞wc ☜ **P** 🔏 ☒ 🆑 ⑩ *VISA*
 closed 26 December and 1-2 January – **M** 6.25/8.75 t. 🍷 3.40 – **18 rm** 🖙 25.50/38.00 t.

BATHGATE W. Lothian (Lothian) **401** J 16 – pop. 14,224 – ECD : Wednesday – 🕿 0506.
Envir. : Cairnpapple Hill (burial cairn★ *AC*, ≼ ★) N : 3 m.
🛆 Edinburgh Rd 🖉 52232.

♦Edinburgh 19 – ♦Glasgow 26.

🏠 **Golden Circle** (Swallow), Blackburn Rd, EH48 2EL, S : 1 ¾ m. on B 792 🖉 53771, Telex 72606 – 🔋 📺 🎞wc **P** 🔏 ☒ 🆑 ⑩ *VISA*
 M 5.50/8.25 st. 🍷 1.70 – **74 rm** 🖙 33.00/44.00 st. – SB (weekends only) 38.00/44.00 st.

FORD Linlithgow Rd 🖉 56685   VW, AUDI Blackburn Rd 🖉 52948

BEARSDEN Dunbarton. (Strathclyde) **401** G 16 – pop. 25,013 – ECD : Tuesday and Saturday – ✉ 🕿 041 Glasgow.

♦Edinburgh 49 – ♦Glasgow 6.

🏠 **Stakis Burnbrae** (Stakis), Milngavie Rd, G61 3TA, NE : 1 m. on A 81 🖉 942 5951 – 📺 🎞wc ☜ **P** 🔏 ☒ 🆑 ⑩ *VISA*
 M 11.70 t. 🍷 2.80 – **16 rm** 🖙 35.50/46.00 t. – SB 46.00/54.00 st.
✗ **La Bavarde,** 9 New Kirk Rd, G61 9JS, 🖉 942 2202 – ☒ 🆑 ⑩ *VISA*
 closed Sunday, Monday, last 3 weeks July and 24 December-8 January – **M** a la carte 9.90/11.00 t. 🍷 2.50.

PEUGEOT-TALBOT, VOLVO Bearsden Cross 🖉   PORSCHE Maxwell Av. 🖉 943 1155
942 2225

BEATTOCK Dumfries. (Dumfries and Galloway) **401 402** J 18 – pop. 309 – ✉ Moffat – 🕿 068 33.
♦Edinburgh 58 – ♦Carlisle 40 – ♦Dumfries 19 – ♦Glasgow 55.

🏠 **Auchen Castle** 🦢, DG10 9SH, N : 2 m. by A 74 🖉 407, ≼, 🐾, 🖼, park – 📺 🎞wc 🎞wc
 P ☒ 🆑 ⑩ *VISA*
 closed December and January – **M** (bar lunch) 10.50 st. 🍷 2.90 – **26 rm** 🖙 24.00/39.00 st. – SB 42.00/58.00 st.
🏠 **Beattock House,** DG10 9QB, 🖉 403, 🖼 – 🎞wc **P**
 M 5.50/8.50 t. 🍷 3.10 – **7 rm** 🖙 14.50/29.00 t.

BEAULY Inverness. (Highland) **401** G 11 – pop. 1,141 – ECD : Thursday – 🕿 0463.
Envir. : Channory Point ≼★ NE : 16 m.
♦Edinburgh 171 – ♦Inverness 12 – ♦Wick 111.

🏠 **Priory,** The Square, IV4 7BX, 🖉 782309 – 🎞wc. ☒ 🆑 ⑩ *VISA*
 M (bar lunch) 9.25 st. 🍷 – **12 rm** 🖙 15.50/27.50 t. – SB 27.00/35.00 st.

SUBARU High St. 🖉 782266

BELLOCHANTUY Argyll. (Strathclyde) **401** C 17 – see Kintyre (Peninsula).

BENBECULA Inverness. (Western Isles) **401** X 11 – see Uist (Isles of).

BETTYHILL Sutherland (Highland) **401** H 8 – pop. 177 – ✉ Thurso – 🕿 064 12.
See : Cliffs★.
Envir. : Strathy Point★★★ NE : 12 m. – Torrisdale Bay★★ W : 2 m. – Mellvich Bay ≼★ (cliffs) E : 13 ½ m.
🛈 🖉 342 (June-September).
♦Edinburgh 299 – ♦Inverness 140 – Thurso 32.

🏠 Bettyhill, KW14 7SP, 🖉 352, ≼, 🐾 – 🎞wc **P** – **22 rm**.

BIRSAY Orkney (Orkney Islands) **401** K 6 – see Orkney Islands (Mainland).

BLACKFORD Perth. (Tayside) **401** I 15 – pop. 529 – ECD : Wednesday – ✉ Auchterarder – 🕿 076 482.
♦Edinburgh 51 – ♦Glasgow 41 – Perth 18.

✗ **Blackford,** Moray St., PH4 1QF, 🖉 246 – 🎞wc **P**
 M a la carte 3.20/7.75 t. 🍷 3.15 – **5 rm** 🖙 15.00/27.00 t.

BLAIRGOWRIE Perth (Tayside) **401** J 14 – pop. 6,122 – ✿ 0250.

🖪 Wellmeadow ℰ 2960 (summer) 2258 (winter) (visitors summer only) – Upper Allan St. ℰ 2785.
◆Edinburgh 59 – ◆Dundee 19 – Perth 16.

    🏠 **Kinloch House** ❧, PH10 6SG, W : 3 m. on A 923 ℰ 025 084 (Essendy) 237, ≤, « Country house atmosphere », 🐎, park – 🛏wc 🛊wc **P**. 🔄 🖭 ⓞ
    M (bar lunch) 10.25 t. – **9 rm** ⊊ 22.00/37.00 **st.**

    🏠 **Altamount House** ❧, Coupar Angus Rd, PH10 6JN, ℰ 3512, 🐎, park – 🛏wc **P**. 🔄 🖭
    ⓞ 𝗩𝗜𝗦𝗔. 🌭
    closed Monday from mid October-Easter, 4 January-18 February and 1 week October – **M** (bar lunch Monday to Saturday) 6.50/10.50 t. – **7 rm** ⊊ 19.50/47.00 **t.**

    🏠 **Rosemount Golf,** Golf Course Rd, SE : 1 ¾ m. off A 923 ℰ 2604, 🐎 – 🖵 🛏wc 🛊wc **P**.
    🌭
    M a la carte 3.00/7.35 t. ▯ 2.75 – **12 rm** ⊊ 14.00/24.00 **t.**

BLAIRLOGIE Stirling. (Central) – see Stirling.

BOAT OF GARTEN Inverness. (Highland) **401** I 12 – pop. 322 – ECD : Thursday – ✿ 047 983.
🏌ᴵ₈ ℰ 282.
◆Edinburgh 160 – ◆Inverness 28 – ◆Perth 92.

    🏨 **The Boat,** PH24 3BH, ℰ 258, 🐎 – 🖵 🛏wc 🛊wc **P**. 🔄 🖭 ⓞ 𝗩𝗜𝗦𝗔
    closed 1 November-22 December – **M** 5.00/9.50 t. ▯ 2.85 – **36 rm** ⊊ 28.75/56.00 **t.**

    ⋂ **Moorfield House,** PH24 3BN, ℰ 983646, 🐎 – **P**
    closed November – **6 rm** ⊊ 10.00/23.00 **t.**

BONAR BRIDGE Sutherland (Highland) **401** G 10 – pop. 519 – ECD : Wednesday – ✿ 086 32 Ardgay.

See : Site★.
🏌ₐ.
🖪 ℰ 333 (June-September).
◆Edinburgh 206 – ◆Inverness 50 – ◆Wick 76.

    🏠 **Bridge,** Dornoch Rd, IV24 3EB, ℰ 204, ≤ Kyle of Sutherland and Bonar Bridge – 🖵 🛏wc
    🛊wc 🕿 **P**. 🔄 🖭 ⓞ 𝗩𝗜𝗦𝗔
    M (bar lunch) a la carte 6.10/14.35 t. ▯ 2.20 – **16 rm** ⊊ 16.50/38.00 t. – SB (week-
    ends only) 36.00 **st.**

    🏠 **Caledonian,** Dornoch Rd, IV24 3EB, ℰ 214, ≤ Kyle of Sutherland and Bonar Bridge, 🐎 –
    🛏wc 🛊wc **P**. 🔄 🖭 ⓞ 𝗩𝗜𝗦𝗔
    M (closed dinner in winter) 6.50/8.75 st. ▯ 2.40 – **15 rm** ⊊ 12.50/28.00 **st.**

BONNYRIGG Midlothian (Lothian) **401 402** K 16 – see Edinburgh.

BOTHWELL Lanark. (Strathclyde) **401 402** H 16 – pop. 4,840 – ✿ 0698.
◆Edinburgh 38 – ◆Glasgow 8.5.

    🏨 **Silvertrees,** 27 Silverwells Crescent, G71 8DP, ℰ 852311, 🐎 – 🖵 🛏wc 🕿 **P**. 🏛. 🔄 🖭
    ⓞ 𝗩𝗜𝗦𝗔
    M (closed Sunday dinner) 6.35/7.50 t. ▯ 3.50 – **24 rm** ⊊ 33.00/40.00 **t.**

BOWMORE Argyll. (Strathclyde) **401** B 16 – see Islay (Isle of).

BRAE Shetland (Shetland Islands) **401** P 2 – see Shetland Islands (Mainland).

BRAEMAR Aberdeen. (Grampian) **401** J 12 – pop. 394 – ECD : Thursday except summer –
✿ 033 83.
Envir. : NW : Cairngorm Mountains ❄★★★ from the summit (alt. 4084 ft) by chairlift from Aviemore,
AC, 40 mn Rtn and 45 mn on foot Rtn – Linn of Dee ★ W : 6 m.
🏌ᴵ₈ ℰ 618, S : ½ m.
🖪 Information Caravan ℰ 600 (May-October).
◆Edinburgh 92 – ◆Aberdeen 58 – ◆Dundee 52 – Perth 50.

    🏨 Mar Lodge ❧, AB3 5YJ, W : 4 m. ℰ 216, ≤, « Former royal hunting lodge », ❧, 🐎, park –
    🛏wc **P**. 🔄 🖭
    May-October – **12 rm** ⊊ 30.00/60.00.

    ⋂ **Callater Lodge,** 9 Glenshee Rd, AB3 5YQ, ℰ 275, 🐎 – **P**
    closed mid October-26 December – **9 rm** ⊊ 11.10/22.20 **st.**

AUSTIN-ROVER Ballater Rd ℰ 301

BRESSAY (Isle of) Shetland (Shetland Islands) **401** Q 3 – Shipping services : see Shetland Islands.

BRIDGE OF ALLAN Stirling. (Central) 🗺️ I 15 – pop. 4,314 – ECD : Wednesday – ☎ 0786.
See : Wallace Monument ≼★.
♦Edinburgh 39 – ♦Dundee 52 – ♦Glasgow 30.

🏨 **Royal** (Best Western), 55 Henderson St., FK9 4HG, 𝒫 832284, Telex 778982, 🍴 – 📶 🚻wc
☎ 🅿 🏧 🔼 🅰🅴 ⑩ 𝘝𝘐𝘚𝘈
M (bar lunch) 8.50 **st.** 🍷 2.90 – **32 rm** ⭐ 15.00/40.00 **t.**

BRIDGE OF CALLY Perth. (Tayside) 🗺️ J 14 – ✉ Blairgowrie – ☎ 025 086.
♦Edinburgh 63 – ♦Dundee 23 – Perth 21.

🏠 **Bridge of Cally,** PH10 7JJ, on A 93 𝒫 231, 🎣, 🍴 – 🚻wc 🛏wc 🅿 🔼 ⑩ 𝘝𝘐𝘚𝘈
closed November – **M** 4.55/9.25 **t.** 🍷 2.55 – **9 rm** ⭐ 20.00/29.00 **st.** – SB 22.50/23.50 **st.**

BRIDGE OF EARN Perth. (Tayside) 🗺️ J 14 – see Perth.

BROADFORD Inverness. (Highland) 🗺️ C 12 – see Skye (Isle of).

BRODICK Bute. (Strathclyde) 🗺️ 🗺️ E 17 – see Arran (Isle of).

BROUGHTON Peebles. (Borders) 🗺️ 🗺️ J 17 – pop. 182 – ECD : Wednesday – ✉ Biggar
(Lanark) – ☎ 089 94.
🏌️ Broughton Rd, Biggar 𝒫 0899 (Biggar) 20618, W : 6 m.
♦Edinburgh 30 – Moffat 24 – Peebles 12.

🏠 **Greenmantle,** ML12 6HQ, 𝒫 302, 🍴 – 🅿 🔼 🅰🅴 ⑩ 𝘝𝘐𝘚𝘈
closed 10 January-25 February – **M** 5.95/8.95 **t.** 🍷 3.00 – **6 rm** ⭐ 18.00/35.00 **t.** – SB
(except summer) 35.00/50.00 **st.**

BROUGHTY FERRY Angus (Tayside) 🗺️ L 14 – see Dundee.

BUCKIE Banff. (Grampian) 🗺️ L 10 – pop. 7,919 – ECD : Wednesday – ☎ 0542.
🏌️ Buckpool, Barrhill Rd 𝒫 32236 – 🏌️ Strathlene 𝒫 31798, E : ½ m.
♦Edinburgh 184 – ♦Aberdeen 60 – ♦Inverness 53.

🏠 **Cluny,** 2 High St., AB5 1AL, 𝒫 32922 – 🚻wc 🅿 🔼 🅰🅴 ⑩ 𝘝𝘐𝘚𝘈
M 3.50/12.00 **t.** 🍷 2.50 – **16 rm** ⭐ 12.00/35.00 **t.** – SB 38.00/50.00 **st.**

at Drybridge S : 2 m. by A 942 – ✉ Drybridge – ☎ 0542 Buckie :

XX **Old Monastery,** AB5 2JB, SW : 2 m. 𝒫 32660 – 🅿
closed Sunday, Monday, 3 weeks January, 2 weeks October and 3 days at Christmas – **M** a la
carte 8.45/10.70 **t.** 🍷 2.30.

BUCKSBURN Aberdeen. (Grampian) 🗺️ N 12 – see Aberdeen.

BUNESSAN Argyll. (Strathclyde) 🗺️ B 15 – see Mull (Isle of).

BUSBY Lanark. (Strathclyde) 🗺️ 🗺️ H 16 – see Glasgow.

BUTE (Isle of) Bute. (Strathclyde) 🗺️ 🗺️ E 16 – pop. 1,834.
See : N : Kyles of Bute★★ – S : Sound of Bute★★.
Envir. : Rothesay : site★ – Rothesay Castle★ (13C) *AC*.
🚢 by Caledonian MacBrayne : from Rothesay to Wemyss Bay summer 5-18 daily ; winter 6-14
daily (30 mn) – from Rhubodach to Colintraive frequent services daily (5 mn).
🛈 Rothesay : The Pier 𝒫 0700 (Rothesay) 2151.

CAIRNGORM (Mountains) Inverness. (Highland) 🗺️ J 12.
See : ❄★★★ from the summit (alt. 4084 ft) by chairlift *AC*, 40 mn Rtn and 45 mn on foot Rtn.
Hotels see : **Aviemore** NW, **Braemar** SE.

CAIRNRYAN Wigtown. (Dumfries and Galloway) 🗺️ 🗺️ E 19.
🚢 by Townsend Thoresen : to Larne 2-5 daily (2 to 2 h 30 mn).
♦ Edinburgh 70 – ♦ Ayr 47 – Stranraer 6,5.
Hotel see : **Stranraer** S : 6 ½ m.

CALLANDER Perth. (Central) **401** H 15 – pop. 1,768 – ECD : Wednesday except summer – ☎ 0877.

Envir. : The Trossachs★★ and Loch Katrine★★ W : 8 ½ m. – Loch Venacher★ W : 4 m.

🏌18 ♟ 30090.

🖪 Leny Rd ♟ 30342 (Easter-September).

♦Edinburgh 51 – ♦Glasgow 43 – ♦Oban 70 – Perth 40.

🏛 **Roman Camp** ♨, Main St., FK17 8BG, ♟ 30003, ≼, « 17C hunting lodge in extensive gardens », 🦯, park – 📺 🛏wc 🕎wc ☜ 🅿
mid February-mid November – **M** 10.50/15.50 **st.** ♨ 3.15 – **11 rm** ☲ 30.00/60.00. **st.**

🏠 **Bridgend,** Bridgend, FK17 8AA, ♟ 30130, 🚗 – 📺 🛏wc 🕎wc ☜ 🅿. 🔼 AE ① VISA
closed January – **M** a la carte 6.20/11.20 **t.** ♨ 2.20 – **7 rm** ☲ 12.00/34.00 **t.**

🏠 **Lubnaig,** Leny Feus, FK17 8AS, ♟ 30376, 🚗 – 🕎wc 🅿. 🧇
10 rm.

↑ **Highland House,** 8 South Church St, FK17 8BN, ♟ 30269 – 🕎wc
April-October – **10 rm** ☲ 10.00/23.00 **st.**

↑ **Glenorchy,** Leny Rd, FK17 8AL, ♟ 30329 – 🛏wc 🕎wc 🅿. VISA. 🧇
14 rm ☲ 10.00/24.00 **t.**

PEUGEOT 124/126 Main St. ♟ 30022

CANNA (Isle of) Inverness. (Highland) **401** A 12 – Shipping Services : see Mallaig.

CANONBIE Dumfries (Dumfries and Galloway) **401 402** L 18 – pop. 1,303 – ☎ 054 15 Canonbie.

♦Edinburgh 80 – ♦Carlisle 15 – ♦Dumfries 34.

XX **Riverside Inn** with rm, DG14 0UX, ♟ 295 – 🛏wc 🅿. 🔼 VISA. 🧇
closed last 2 weeks January – **M** (closed Sunday dinner) (booking essential)(bar lunch Monday to Saturday) 6.50/12.50 **t.** ♨ 2.25 – **6 rm** ☲ 28.00/36.00 **t.** – SB (except summer) 46.00 **st.**

CARFRAEMILL Berwick (Borders) **401 402** L 16 – see Lauder.

CARRADALE Argyll. (Strathclyde) **401** D 17 – see Kintyre (Peninsula).

CASTLEBAY Inverness. (Outer Hebrides) (Western Isles) **401** X 13 – see Barra (Isle of).

CASTLE DOUGLAS Kirkcudbright. (Dumfries and Galloway) **401 402** I 19 – pop. 3,331 – ECD : Thursday – ☎ 0556.

🏌9 ♟ 2801.

🖪 Markethill ♟ 2611 (summer only).

♦Edinburgh 95 – ♦Ayr 50 – ♦Dumfries 18 – Stranraer 58.

🏛 **Douglas Arms,** King St., DG7 1DB, ♟ 2231 – 🛏wc ☜ 🅿. 🔼 AE ① VISA
M (bar lunch) 10.50 **st.** – **26 rm** ☲ 16.00/34.00 **st.**

🏠 **King's Arms,** St. Andrew St., DG7 1EL, ♟ 2626 – 🛏wc 🅿. 🔼 AE ① VISA
M (bar lunch, residents only) 10.00 **st.** ♨ 3.00 – **15 rm** ☲ 15.50/40.00 **st.**

AUSTIN-ROVER Morris House ♟ 2560
FORD Oakwell Rd ♟ 2805

VAUXHALL-OPEL King St. ♟ 2038

CATTERLINE Kincardine (Grampian) **401** N 13 – see Stonehaven.

CLACHAN SEIL Argyll. (Strathclyde) **401** D 15 – ECD : Wednesday – ⊠ Oban – ☎ 085 23 Balvicar.

♦Edinburgh 133 – ♦Oban 11.

☝ **Willowburn** ♨, Isle of Seil, PA34 4TJ, ♟ 276, ≼ – 🕎wc 🅿. 🔼 AE ① VISA
M (lunch by arrangement in winter) 12.00/13.45 **st.** ♨ 3.60 – **6 rm** ☲ 13.00/29.80 **t.** – SB (except summer) 40.00/63.00. **st.**

CLAONAIG (Cap) Argyll. (Strathclyde) **401 402** D 16 – Shipping Services : see Kintyre (Peninsula).

CLEISH Fife. (Tayside) **401** J 15 – see Kinross.

CLOCHAN Banff. (Grampian) – see Fochabers.

CLOVA Angus (Tayside) **401** K 13 – ⊠ Kirriemuir – ☎ 057 55.
See : Glen★★.

♦Edinburgh 86 – ♦Dundee 31 – Perth 44.

🏠 **Rottal Lodge** ♨, DD8 4QT, SE : 3 ¾ m. off B 955 ♟ 224, ≼, 🚗, park – 🛏wc 🕎 🅿
June-November – **M** 6.00/10.75 ♨ 1.75 – **12 rm** ☲ 21.50/43.00.

COLINTRAIVE Argyll. (Strathclyde) **401** **402** E 16 – pop. 104 – ✪ 070 084.
See : Kyles of Bute★★.
🚢 by Caledonian MacBrayne : to Rhubodach (Isle of Bute) frequent services daily (5 mn).
♦Edinburgh 121 – ♦Glasgow 78 – ♦Oban 80.

COLL (Isle of) Argyll. (Strathclyde) **401** A 14 – pop. 153.
🚢 by Caledonian MacBrayne : from Arinagour to Oban 3-4 weekly (3 h 30 mn) – from Arinagour to Tobermory (Isle of Mull) 3 weekly (1 h 30 mn) – from Arinagour to Lochaline May to September 2 weekly (2 h 30 mn) – from Arinagour to Gott Bay (Isle of Tiree) 3 weekly (1 h).

COLONSAY (Isle of) Argyll. (Strathclyde) **401** B 15 – pop. 349 – ✪ 095 12 Colonsay.
🏠₁₈ ✆ 316.
🚢 by Caledonian MacBrayne : from Scalasaig to Oban 3 weekly (2 h 30 mn).

    Scalasaig – ECD : Wednesday – ✉ ✪ 095 12 Colonsay.
  🏠 **Isle of Colonsay** ⚓, PA61 7YP, ✆ 316, ≤, 🚗 – **P**. 🔺 AE ⓞ VISA
    M (bar lunch) 10.00 **st.** 🍸 2.50 – **11 rm** �æ 20.00/40.00 **st.** – SB (except summer) 37.00/40.00 **st.**

COMRIE Perth. (Tayside) **401** I 14 – pop. 1,119 – ECD : Wednesday – ✪ 0764 – 🏠.
♦Edinburgh 58 – ♦Glasgow 49 – ♦Oban 70 – Perth 23.
  🏠 **Royal,** Melville Sq., PH6 2DN, ✆ 70200, 🚗 – 📺 🛁wc 🖨 **P**. 🔺 AE VISA
    M a la carte 8.60/13.85 **t.** 🍸 2.70 – **16 rm** �æ 16.50/33.00 **t.** – SB (except Easter, Christ-mas and New Year) 48.00/50.00 **st.**
  🏠 **Comrie,** Drummond St., PH6 2DY, ✆ 70239 – 🛁wc 🚿wc **P**
    Easter-October – **M** 3.85/8.00 **st.** 🍸 1.30 – **12 rm** �æ 10.50/30.00 **st.**

CONNEL Argyll. (Strathclyde) **401** D 14 – pop. 300 – ECD : Wednesday – ✪ 063 171.
Envir. : Loch Creran★ N : 7 m.
♦Edinburgh 117 – ♦Glasgow 88 – ♦Inverness 109 – ♦Oban 5.
  🏠 **Lochnell Arms,** North Connel, PA37 1RF, ✆ 408, ≤, 🚗 – 🛁wc **P**. 🔺 AE ⓞ VISA
    closed January and February – **M** 6.00/10.00 **st.** 🍸 2.50 – **11 rm** �æ 12.00/26.00 **st.** – SB 34.00/40.00 **st.**
  🏠 **Ossian's** ⚓, Bonawe Rd, North Connel, PA37 1RB, ✆ 322, ≤, 🚗 – 🛁wc **P**. AE VISA
    April-first week October – **M** (bar lunch) 8.50 **t.** 🍸 2.00 – **14 rm** ⊆ 14.95/31.90 **t.**

CRAIGHOUSE Argyll. (Strathclyde) **401** C 16 – see Jura (Isle of).

CRAIL Fife. (Fife) **401** M 15 – pop. 1,075 – ECD : Wednesday – ✪ 033 35.
🏠₁₈ Balcomie Clubhouse ✆ 278.
♦Edinburgh 52 – ♦Dundee 24 – Dunfermline 39.
  🏛 **Marine,** 54 Nethergate South, KY10 3TZ, ✆ 207, ≤, 🚗
    12 rm.

CRIEFF Perth. (Tayside) **401** I 14 – pop. 5,603 – ECD : Wednesday – ✪ 0764.
Envir. : Drummond Castle Gardens★★ *AC*, S : 3 ½ m.
🏠 Peat Rd, Muthill, S : 3 m. on A 822.
🛈 James Sq. ✆ 2578 (summer only).
♦Edinburgh 58 – ♦Glasgow 48 – ♦Oban 76 – Perth 17.
  🏠 **Murraypark** ⚓, Connaught Terr., PH7 3DJ, ✆ 3731, 🚗 – 🛁wc 🖨 **P**. ⓞ
    M 9.00/15.00 **t.** 🍸 3.00 – **15 rm** ⊆ 16.00/48.00 **t.**
  🏠 **Gwydyr House,** Comrie Rd, PH7 4BP, ✆ 3277, ≤, 🚗 – **P**
    April-October – **M** (bar lunch) 6.60 **t.** 🍸 2.40 – **10 rm** ⊆ 10.50/21.00 **t.**
  🏠 **Leven House,** Comrie Rd, PH7 4BA, ✆ 2529
    13 rm ⊆ 8.50/17.00 **st.**

    at Sma'Glen NE : 4 m. by A 85 on A 822 – ✉ ✪ 0764 Crieff :
  🏛 **Foulford Inn** ⚓, PH7 3LN, ✆ 2407, ≤ – **P**
    closed February – **M** *(closed Sunday dinner)* (lunch by arrangement) a la carte 6.40/9.25 **t.** 🍸 2.40 – **11 rm** ⊆ 10.00/25.00 **t.**

AUSTIN-ROVER Comrie Rd ✆ 2125   VAUXHALL-OPEL ✆ 2147

Per i 🏨 , 🏨 , 🏨 , non diamo il dettaglio delle installazioni, poichè questi alberghi dispongono di ogni confort.

    🛁wc 🚿wc
    🖨

CRINAN Argyll. (Strathclyde) 401 D 15 – ⊠ Lochgilphead – ☎ 054 683.

See : Site★★ – Crinan Canal★.

Envir. : Tayvallich (harbour★) SW : 7 m. – Keills (site and ≤★) SW : 13 m.

♦Edinburgh 132 – ♦Glasgow 89 – ♦Oban 34.

    🏠 **Crinan,** PA31 8SR, ♟ 235, ≤ Loch Crinan and Sound of Jura, « Tasteful decor », 🐎 – ⬚
    ⬚wc ☎ ❷ ⬛ AE ⬥ *VISA*
    April-October – **M** (buffet lunch) 5.00/14.00 **t.** (rest. see also **Lock 16** below) – **22 rm**
    ⬚ 28.50/58.00 **t.**

    XX **Lock 16** (at Crinan H.), PA31 8SR, ♟ 235, ≤ Loch Crinan and Sound of Jura, Seafood – ❷.
    ⬛ AE ⬥ *VISA*
    April-October – **M** (booking essential) a la carte 8.20/13.00 **t.**

CROCKETFORD Kirkcudbright. (Dumfries and Galloway) 401 402 I 18 – pop. 102 – ⊠ Dumfries
– ☎ 055 669.

♦Edinburgh 86 – ♦Dumfries 9 – Stranraer 67.

    🏠 **Galloway Arms,** DG2 8RA, ♟ 240 – 📺 ⬚wc ❷ ⬛ ⬥ *VISA*
    closed November – **M** 5.50/10.00 **t.** ♦ 3.50 – **11 rm** ⬚ 15.00/40.00 **t.** – SB 40.00/48.00 **st.**

CULLEN Banff. (Grampian) 401 L 10 – pop. 1,207 – ECD : Wednesday – ☎ 0542.

See : Cullen Bay★.

🏌 The Links ♟ 40685.

🎫 20 Seafield St. ♟ 40757 (summer only).

♦Edinburgh 184 – ♦Aberdeen 60 – Banff 14 – ♦Inverness 60.

    🏠 **Seafield Arms,** Seafield St., AB5 2SG, ♟ 40791 – 📺 ⬚wc ☎ ❷ ⬛ AE ⬥ *VISA*
    M 5.00/8.50 **t.** ♦ 3.25 – **24 rm** ⬚ 18.00/40.00 **t.** – SB 48.00 **st.**

CULLIPOOL Argyll. (Strathclyde) 401 D 15 – see Luing (Isle of).

CULLODEN MOOR Inverness. (Highland) 401 H 11 – see Inverness.

CUPAR Fife. (Fife) 401 K 15 – pop. 6, 603 – ECD : Thursday – ☎ 0334.

♦Edinburgh 45 – ♦Dundee 14 – Perth 21.

    X **Ostler's Close,** 25 Bonnygate, KY15 4BU, ♟ 55574 – ⬛ *VISA*
    closed Monday lunch, Sunday, 25-26 December and 1 to 3 January – **M** a la carte 10.25/12.95 **t.**
    ♦ 3.20.

DALIBURGH Inverness. (Outer Hebrides) (Western Isles) 401 X 12 – see Uist (South) (Isles of).

DALRY Kirkcudbright. (Dumfries and Galloway) 401 402 H 18 – pop. 432 – ⊠ Castle Douglas –
☎ 064 43.

♦Edinburgh 83 – ♦Dumfries 27 – ♦Glasgow 65 – Stranraer 48.

    🏠 **Lochinvar,** 3 Main St., DG7 3UP, on A 713 ♟ 210 – ⬚wc ❷
    M (bar lunch) 7.00 **st.** ♦ 1.95 – **15 rm** ⬚ 13.45/28.90 **st.**

DERVAIG Argyll. (Strathclyde) 401 B 14 – see Mull (Isle of).

DIRLETON E. Lothian (Lothian) 401 402 L 15 – see Gullane.

DORNIE Ross and Cromarty (Highland) 401 D 12 – pop. 127 – ⊠ Kyle of Lochalsh – ☎ 059 985.

♦Edinburgh 191 – ♦Inverness 74 – Kyle of Lochalsh 8.

    🏠 Loch Duich, IV40 1DY, ♟ 213, ≤ Eilean Donan Castle and hills, ♞, 🐎 – ❷
    18 rm.

DORNOCH Sutherland. (Highland) 401 H 10 – pop. 838 – ECD : Thursday – ☎ 0862.

Envir. : Dunrobin Castle gardens★ *AC*, NE : 11 m.

🏌, 🏌 Royal Dornoch, Golf Rd ♟ 219.

🎫 The Square, ♟ 400.

♦Edinburgh 220 – ♦Inverness 61 – ♦Wick 64.

    🏠 **Royal Golf** ♦, Grange Rd, IV25 3LG, ♟ 810283, Group Telex 779713, ≤, 🐎 – 📺 ⬚wc ☎
    ❷ ⬛ AE ⬥ *VISA*
    April-October – **M** 5.75/8.50 **t.** ♦ 4.50 – **32 rm** ⬚ 33.00/60.00 **t.**

    🏠 **Dornoch Castle,** Castle St., IV25 3SD, ♟ 810216, « Former bishop's palace, part 16C », 🐎
    – ⬚ ⬚wc ❷ ⬛ *VISA*
    Easter-October – **M** 4.50/10.00 **st.** ♦ 2.05 – **20 rm** ⬚ 14.00/33.50 **st.**

TALBOT St. Gilbert St. ♟ 810255

DOUNE Perth. (Central) **401** H 15 – pop. 3,977 – ECD : Wednesday – ✆ 078 684.

See : Doune Castle★ (stronghold 15C) *AC*.

♦Edinburgh 45 – ♦Glasgow 33 – Perth 32 – Stirling 8.

🏠 **Woodside,** Stirling Rd, FK16 6AB, on A 84 ℰ 841237, ☞ – ⇌wc **P**. ⚊
M *(closed Sunday dinner to non-residents)* (bar lunch) a la carte 6.25/13.30 t. ⬩ 3.75 – **14 rm**
⊐ 19.00/32.00 t.

DRUMNADROCHIT Inverness. (Highland) **401** G 11 – pop. 359 – ⊠ Milton – ✆ 045 62.

Envir. : Loch Ness★★ E : 1 ½ m. – Urquhart Castle (site★) *AC*, E : 1 ½ m. – Glencannich★ and Glen
Affric★ W : 12 m. by Cannich.

♦Edinburgh 174 – ♦Inverness 15 – Kyle of Lochalsh 67.

🏛 **Polmaily House** ⚘, IV3 6XT, W : 2 m. on A 831 ℰ 343, ⚒, ☞ – ⇌wc **P**. ⚊ 🅰🅴 ① 🆅🆂🅰
⚘
Easter-mid October – **M** (bar lunch, residents only) a la carte 8.00/10.20 t. ⬩ 2.95 – **9 rm**
⊐ 20.00/45.00 t.

DRYBRIDGE Banff. (Grampian) – see Buckie.

DRYMEN Stirling. (Central) **401** G 15 – pop. 659 – ECD : Wednesday – ✆ 0360.

Envir. : Loch Lomond★★, W : 3 m.

♦Edinburgh 60 – ♦Glasgow 17 – Stirling 21.

🏛 **Buchanan Arms,** Main St., G63 0BQ, ℰ 60588, ☞ – 📺 ⇌wc ☜ **P**. ⚫. ⚊ 🅰🅴 ①
. 🆅🆂🅰 ⚘
M 6.80/10.50 t. ⬩ 3.00 – **35 rm** ⊐ 34.00/52.00 t.

DULNAIN BRIDGE Inverness. (Highland) **401** J 12 – ECD : Wednesday – ⊠ Grantown-on-Spey
– ✆ 047 985.

♦Edinburgh 166 – ♦Inverness 31 – Perth 98.

🏠 **Muckrach Lodge,** PH26 3LY, W : ½ m. on A 938 ℰ 257, ≤, ☞ – **P**. ⚘
M (bar lunch) (booking essential) 12.50 t. ⬩ 3.50 – **9 rm** ⊐ 16.90/36.80 t.

🏠 **Skye of Curr,** Skye of Curr Rd, PH26 3PA, ℰ 345, ≤, ☞ – **P**. ⚊ 🅰🅴 ① 🆅🆂🅰
M (bar lunch) 8.75 t. – **8 rm** ⊐ 13.50/22.00 st.

Pleasant hotels and restaurants
are shown in the Guide by a red sign.
Please send us the names
of any where you have enjoyed your stay.
Your Michelin Guide will be even better.

🏛🏛 ... 🏠

XXXXX ... X

DUMFRIES Dumfries. (Dumfries and Galloway) **401** **402** J 18 – pop. 29,382 – ECD : Thursday –
✆ 0387.

Envir. : Ruthwell Cross★ 8C, SE : 11 m. by B 725 B – Caerlaverock Castle★ (medieval) *AC*, SE :
7 ½ m. by B 725 B – New Abbey★ *AC*, S : 6 m. by A 710 A.

🏌 Laurieston Av. ℰ 3582 A – 🏌 Lochmaben ℰ 552, NE : 8 m. by A 709 B.

🎫 Whitesands ℰ 3862 (April-September).

♦Edinburgh 80 – ♦Ayr 59 – ♦Carlisle 34 – ♦Glasgow 79 – ♦Manchester 155 – ♦Newcastle-upon-Tyne 91.

Plan on next page

🏛🏛 **Cairndale,** 138 English St., DG1 2DF, ℰ 54111 – 📳 📺 ⇌wc ☎ **P**. ⚊ 🅰🅴 ① 🆅🆂🅰   B c
M 5.00/9.25 t. – **44 rm** ⊐ 19.00/38.00 st. – SB (weekends only) 40.00 st.

🏛🏛 **Station,** 49 Lovers Walk, DG1 1LT, ℰ 54316 – 📳 📺 ⇌wc 🍴wc ☜ **P**. ⚊ 🅰🅴 ① 🆅🆂🅰   B e
closed 1 January – **M** 4.25/8.00 t. ⬩ 2.80 – **30 rm** ⊐ 26.50/35.00 t. – SB (weekends only) 32.00 st.

↑ **Dalston,** 5 Laurieknowe, DG2 7AJ, ℰ 54422 – **P**   A n
closed 25-26 December and 1-2 January – **7 rm** ⊐ 10.50/21.00 st.

X **Bruno's,** 3 Balmoral Rd, DG1 3BE, ℰ 55757, Italian rest.   B i
closed Tuesday – **M** (dinner only) a la carte 9.10/14.00 t. ⬩ 3.00.

AUSTIN-ROVER-DAIMLER-JAGUAR   Charlotte St.
ℰ 4301
CITROEN, VAUXHALL York Pl. ℰ 5291
FIAT   123 Whitesands ℰ 64875
FORD   Main Rd ℰ 038771 (Amisfield) 710491
LANCIA   St. Michaels St. ℰ 63733
OPEL   York Pl. ℰ 5291

PEUGEOT-TALBOT   St. Mary's Industrial Estate ℰ
63076
PEUGEOT-TALBOT Terregles St. ℰ 61997
RENAULT 33/35 Glasgow St. ℰ 3430
VOLVO   Annan Rd ℰ 61437
VW, AUDI-NSU   English St. ℰ 5111

DUMFRIES

High Street . . . . A 18

Aldermanhill Road . . . . B 2
Bank Street . . . . A 3
Buccleuch Street . . . . A 4
Cardoness Street . . . . B 5
Cassalands . . . . A 6
Castle Street . . . . A 7
Castle Douglas Road . . . . A 8
Catherine Street . . . . B 9
Corberry Avenue . . . . A 10
Eastfield Road . . . . B 12
Friars Vennel . . . . A 13
Galloway Street . . . . A 14
Glebe Street . . . . B 15
Great King Street . . . . A 16
Hermitage Drive . . . . A 17
Laurieknowe . . . . A 20
Loreburn Street . . . . A 21
Nith Street . . . . AB 22
Queen Street . . . . B 23
Queensberry Street . . . . A 24
Rae Street . . . . B 26
St. Mary's Street . . . . B 27
St. Michael Street . . . . B 28
St. Michael's Bridge Road . . . . A 30
Shakespeare Street . . . . B 31
Union Street . . . . A 32
Whitesands . . . . A 34

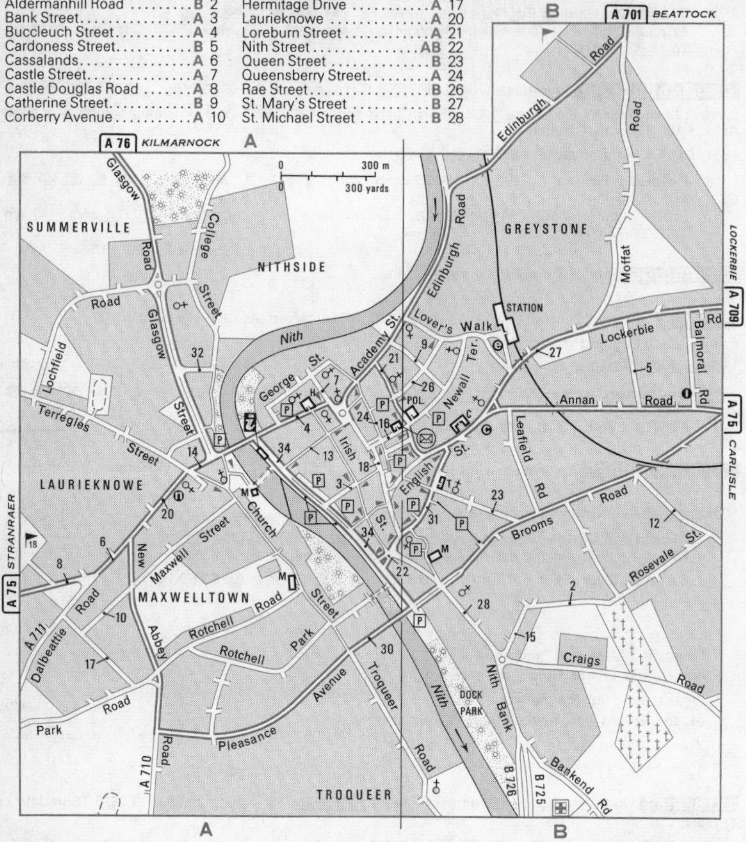

DUNAIN PARK Inverness. (Highland) – see Inverness.

DUNBAR E. Lothian (Lothian) [401] M 15 – pop. 4,611 – ECD : Wednesday – ✆ 0368.
See : Site★.
⛳ Winterfield, Back Rd ☎ 62280 – ⛳ ☎ 62317, S : ½ m – ℹ Town House, High St. ☎ 63353.
♦Edinburgh 30 – ♦Newcastle-upon-Tyne 91.

🏠 **Marine,** 7 Marine Rd, EH42 1AR, ☎ 63315
9 rm ☕ 8.50/17.00 **st.**

DUNBLANE Perth. (Central) [401] I 15 – pop. 4,497 – ECD : Wednesday – ✆ 0786.
See : Cathedral★.
ℹ Stirling Rd ☎ 824428 (Easter, May-mid October).
♦Edinburgh 41 – ♦Glasgow 31 – Perth 28.

🏰 **Cromlix House** 🐎, FK15 9JT, N : 3 ¼ m. by A 9 on B 8033 ☎ 822125, <, « Antique furnishings », 🎣, 🌳, park, 🎾 – [TV] [P]. [AE] [VISA]
M (restricted lunch Monday to Saturday)(booking essential) 15.00/26.00 **st.** – **11 rm** ☕ 45.00/110.00 **st.**

AUSTIN-ROVER High St. ☎ 823271

See : Dundee Law ≤★★ Z – Museum and Art Gallery★ Y **M**.

Envir. : Affleck Castle★ (15C) NE : 11 ½ m. by B 961 Z.

🛅, 🛅 Caird Park 🖋 453606 off Kingsway Bypass at Mains Loan Z – 🛅 Camperdown Park 🖋 645450, NW : 2 m. by A 923 Z.

✈ Dundee Airport : 🖋 643242, SW : 1 ½ m. Z.

🛈 16 City Sq. 🖋 27723.

♦Edinburgh 63 – ♦Aberdeen 67 – ♦Glasgow 83.

DUNDEE

Commercial Street	Y 8
High Street	Y 16
Murraygate	Y 25
Nethergate	Y 26
Overgate Centre	Y
Reform Street	Y 35
Wellgate Centre	Y
Albert Street	Z 2
Allan Street	Y 4
Ancrum Road	Z 5
Bell Street	Y 6
Coupar Angus Road	Z 9
Douglas Road	Z 10
Drumgeith Road	Z 12
Dudhope Terrace	Z 13
East Dock Street	Z 14
Greendykes Road	Z 15
Logie Street	Z 18
Longtown Road	Z 20
Mains Road	Z 21
Marketgait	Y 22
Meadowside	Y 23
Moncur Crescent	Z 24
Old Glamis Road	Z 32
Provost Road	Z 34
St. Andrews Street	Z 36
Seagate	Y 38
South Union Street	Z 39
Strathmartine Road	Z 40
Trades Lane	Y 41
Ward Road	Y 42
West Bell Street	Y 43

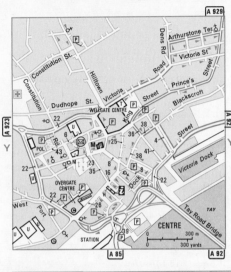

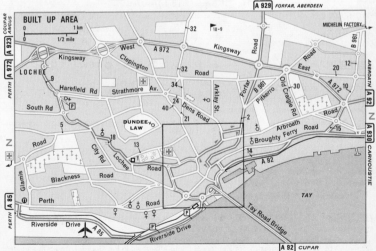

🏛 **Angus Thistle** (Thistle), 101 Marketgait, DD1 1QU, 🖋 26874, Telex 76456 – 🛗 📺 ⌷wc 📞 🅿. 🔬. 🔲 ⅍ **VISA**
M 6.50/8.50 **t.** ⅍ 3.45 – 🍽 4.75 – **57 rm** 32.00/52.00 **t.** – SB (weekends only) 52.00 **st.**
Y c

🏛 **Invercarse**, 371 Perth Rd, DD2 IPG, W : 2 m. on B 911 🖋 69231, Telex 76608, 🍴 – 📺 ⌷wc ⅍wc 📞 🅿. 🔬. 🔲 ⅍ 🅿 🔲
M 6.00/8.50 **t.** ⅍ 2.75 – 🍽 3.95 – **27 rm** 30.00/36.00 **t.**
Z n

🏠 **Queen's**, 160 Nethergate, DD1 4DU, 🖋 22515 – 🛗 📺 ⌷wc 📞 🅿. 🔬. – **56 rm**.
Y e

at Broughty Ferry E : 4 ½ m. by A 930 – Z – (Dundee Road) – ✉ ☎ 0382 Dundee :

🏨 **Tayview** without rest., 71-73 St. Vincent St., DD5 2EZ, ☎ 79438, 🌳 – ✗
11 rm ☕ 25.00/35.00 **t.**

at Invergowrie W : 4 ¾ m. by A 85 on A 872 – Z – ✉ ☎ 0382 Dundee :

🏨 **Swallow** (Swallow), Kingsway West (Dundee Ring Road), DD2 5JT, ☎ 641122, Telex 76694, 🏊, 🌳 – ▤ [TV] 🛁wc ☎ ♿ [P]. [S] [AE] [O] [VISA]
M 4.95/8.70 **st.** 🍷 3.40 – **69 rm** ☕ 22.00/50.00 **st.** – SB (weekends only) 44.00 **st.**

ALFA-ROMEO, HONDA Queen St., Broughty Ferry ☎ 77257
AUSTIN-ROVER 64 Ward Rd ☎ 24013
CITROEN 3 Roseangle ☎ 28483
DAIHATSU, PEUGEOT 25 Rosebank St. ☎ 25406
FIAT, LADA, LANCIA MacAlpine Rd ☎ 818004
FORD Balfield Rd ☎ 60191
MAZDA 166 Seagate ☎ 25007
RENAULT Riverside Drive ☎ 644401
TOYOTA East Kingsway ☎ 41715
VAUXHALL East Dock St. ☎ 26521
VOLVO Riverside Drive ☎ 643295
VW, AUDI 45/53 Gellatly St. ☎ 24251

DUNDONNELL Ross and Cromarty (Highland) [401] E 10 – pop. 120 – ✉ Garve – ☎ 085 483.

Envir. : Little Loch Broom★ NW : 7 m.

♦Edinburgh 218 – ♦ Inverness 59.

🏨 **Dundonnell,** IV23 2QS, ☎ 204, ≤ Dundonnell Valley – [TV] 🛁wc [P]. [S] [VISA]
April-October – **M** (bar lunch) 10.00 **t.** 🍷 2.50 – **24 rm** ☕ 17.50/39.00 **t.** – SB 46.00/58.00 **st.**

DUNFERMLINE Fife. (Fife) [401] J 15 – pop. 49,897 – ECD : Wednesday – ☎ 0383.

See : Abbey★ *AC.*

⛳18 Canmore, Venturefair ☎ 24969, N : 1 m. – ⛳18 Pitreavie, Queensferry Rd ☎ 22591 – ⛳9 Saline, Kinneddar Hill ☎ 038 384 (Saline) 591, NW : 5 m.

[i] Glen Bridge Car Park ☎ 20999 (Easter-September) – District Council Offices, 3 New Row ☎ 36321 (October-March).

♦Edinburgh 16 – ♦ Dundee 48 – Motherwell 39.

🏨 **Keavil House** 🐦, KY12 8QW, ☎ 736258, Telex 728227, 🌳 – [TV] 🛁wc 🚿wc ☎ ♿ [P]. [S] [AE] [O] [VISA]. ✗
M a la carte 5.60/10.65 **t.** 🍷 2.80 – **32 rm** ☕ 22.00/36.00 **t.** – SB (weekends only) 46.00/72.00 **st.**

🏨 King Malcolm Thistle (Thistle), West Pitcothrie, KY11 5DS, S : 1 m. on A 823 ☎ 722611, Telex 727721 – [TV] 🛁wc ☎ [P]. 🏃. [S] [AE] [O] [VISA]. ✗
☕ 4.75 – **48 rm** 34.00/42.00 **t.** – SB (weekends only) 50.00 **st.**

MICHELIN Branch, Taxi Way, Hillend Industrial Estate, Hillend, Dunfermline, KY11 5JT, ☎ 822961

AUSTIN-ROVER 18 Halbeath Rd ☎ 31041
FIAT 128/138 Pittencrieff St. ☎ 22565
PEUGEOT Headwell Av. ☎ 21914
TALBOT 45/47 Baldridgeburn ☎ 31821
TOYOTA Bruce St. ☎ 23675
VAUXHALL 3 Carnock Rd ☎ 21511

DUNKELD Perth. (Tayside) [401] J 14 – pop. 273 – ECD : Thursday – ☎ 035 02.

See : Cathedral★.

⛳9 ☎ 524, N : 1 m. on A 923.

[i] The Cross ☎ 688 (summer only).

♦Edinburgh 57 – ♦ Aberdeen 85 – ♦ Inverness 102 – Perth 15.

🏨 **Dunkeld House** 🐦, PH8 0HX, ☎ 243, ≤, « Country house in extensive grounds on banks of river Tay », 🎣, 🌳, park, 🎾 – [TV] 🛁wc [P]. [VISA]. ✗
closed November-mid January – **M** 8.25/11.50 **t.** 🍷 3.00 – **31 rm** ☕ 20.00/78.00 **t.**

DUNNET HEAD Caithness. (Highland) [401] J 7.

See : ※★★★ (sea birds' nests) and cliffs.

♦Edinburgh 303 – ♦Wick 23.

Hotel see : Wick SE : 23 m.

DUNOON Argyll. (Strathclyde) [401] F 16 – pop. 9,718 – ECD : Wednesday – ☎ 0369.

⛳18 Cowal, Ardenslate Rd ☎ 2216, NE : boundary – ⛳9 Innellan ☎ 3546, S : 4 m.

⛴ by Caledonian MacBrayne : from Dunoon Pier to Gourock Railway Pier frequent services daily (20 mn) – by Western Ferries : from Hunters Quay to McInroy's Point, Gourock frequent services daily (20 mn).

[i] Pier Esplanade ☎ 3785.

♦Edinburgh 69 – ♦Glasgow 26 – ♦Oban 79.

at Kirn N : 1 m. on A 815 – ✉ ☎ 0369 Dunoon :

🏨 **Enmore,** Marine Par., PA23 8HH, ☎ 2230, ≤ Firth of Clyde, 🌳, squash – [TV] 🛁wc 🚿wc [P]. [O] [VISA]
April-October – **M** (bar lunch) 10.00 **t.** 🍷 2.95 – **16 rm** ☕ 16.00/38.00 **st.** – SB 50.00 **st.**

DUNOON

at Sandbank N : 2 ½ m. on A 815 – ⊠ ⊛ 0369 Dunoon :

🏠 **Firpark,** Shore Rd, PA23 8QG, ✆ 6506, ≼ Holy Loch, 🚗 – 📺 📞wc 🅿 VISA
M 6.50/12.50 **st.** ░ 2.45 – **6 rm** ⊑ 15.00/30.00 **t.**

FIAT Wellington St. ✆ 3931   RENAULT Shore St., Inverary ✆ 0499 (Inverary) 2271
FORD George St. ✆ 3234

DUNVEGAN Inverness. (Highland) 401 A 11 – see Skye (Isle of).

DUROR Argyll. (Strathclyde) 401 E 14 – pop. 102 – ⊠ Appin – ⊛ 063 174.
♦Edinburgh 125 – Fort William 19 – ♦Oban 28.

🏠 **Stewart** (Best Western) ⚓, Glen Duror, PA38 4BW, ✆ 268, ≼, 🚗, park – 📺 📞wc 🅿 🔄
AE ① VISA
15 March-15 October – **M** (bar lunch) 11.50 **t.** ░ 2.45 – **26 rm** ⊑ 25.00/40.00 **t.** – SB
(except summer) 51.00/60.00 **st.**

DYCE Aberdeen. (Grampian) 401 N 12 – see Aberdeen.

EAST KILBRIDE Lanark. (Strathclyde) 401 402 H 16 – pop. 63,502 – ECD : Wednesday –
⊛ 035 52.

🚩 Torrance House, Strathaven Rd ✆ 48638.
♦Edinburgh 44 – ♦Ayr 34 – ♦Glasgow 8.

🏨 **Bruce** (Swallow), Cornwall St., G74 1AF, ✆ 29771, Telex 778428 – ▤ 📺 🅿 ⚐ 🔄 AE ① VISA
M (closed Sunday lunch) 5.00/8.50 **st.** ░ 3.40 – **84 rm** ⊑ 37.25/46.50 **st.**

🏨 **Stuart Thistle** (Thistle), 2 Cornwall Way, G74 1JR, ✆ 21161, Telex 778504 – ▤ 📺 📞wc ⚐
⚙ ⚐ 🔄 AE ① VISA ⚸
⊑ 4.75 – **30 rm** 30.00/38.00 **t.**

🏠 **Crutherland Country House** ⚓, Strathaven Rd, G75 0QZ, SE : 2 m. on A 726 ✆ 37633, ⚹, 🚗,
park – 📺 📞wc ▦wc ⚐ 🅿 – **21 rm**

🏠 Torrance, Main St., G74 4LN, ✆ 25241 – 📺 📞wc ▦wc ☎ 🅿 – **26 rm**

AUSTIN-ROVER Telford Rd ✆ 23455

EAST LINTON E. Lothian (Lothian) 401 M 16 – pop. 880 – ECD : Wednesday – ⊛ 0620.
♦Edinburgh 24 – ♦Newcastle-upon-Tyne 96.

🏨 Harvesters (Best Western), Station Rd, EH40 3DP, ✆ 860395, 🚗 – 📞wc 🅿 🔄 AE ① VISA
closed 25 December-January – **M** 5.00/10.00 **t.** ░ 3.50 – **10 rm.**

EDAY (Isle of) Orkney (Orkney Islands) 401 L 6 – Shipping Services : see Orkney Islands (Mainland : Kirkwall).

EDDLESTON Peebles. (Borders) 401 402 K 16 – see Peebles.

En saison, surtout dans les stations fréquentées, il est prudent de retenir à l'avance.
Cependant, si vous ne pouvez pas occuper la chambre que vous avez retenue,
prévenez immédiatement l'hôtelier.
Si vous écrivez à un hôtel à l'étranger, joignez à votre lettre
un coupon-réponse international (disponible dans les bureaux de poste).

EDINBURGH Midlothian (Lothian) 401 K 16 – pop. 453,584 – ⊛ 031.

See : Castle★ (site★, ≼★★, Regalia★, Scottish United Services Museum★, Scottish National War
Memorial) *AC* DZ – National Museum of Antiquities★★ EY **M1** – National Gallery★★ DY **M2** – St.
Giles' Cathedral★ EYZ – Charlotte Square★ CY – National Portrait Gallery★ *AC* EY **M1** – Royal
Scottish Museum★ EZ **M3** – Old houses and closes near Lawnmarket, Grassmarket★ DEYZ –
Abbey of Holyrood★ *AC* BV – Royal Botanic Gardens★ ABV – Princes Street ≼★★ DY – Palace of
Holyrood (State apartments★, historic apartments★★) *AC* BV A – Calton Hill ≼★ EY – Arthur's Seat
≼★ BV – Drama and Music Festival in summer.

Envir. : Roslyn Chapel★★ (15C) *AC*, S : 6 ½ m. by A 701 BX – Leith ≼★ of the firth of Forth, NE :
2 ½ m. BV – Craigmillar Castle★ (stronghold) 14C, *AC*, SE : 3 m. BX D – Crichton Castle★ (16C) *AC*,
SE : 13 m. by A 7 BX.

🚩 Liberton, Kingston Grange, 297 Gilmerton Rd ✆ 664 8580, SE : 3 ½ m. BX – 🚩 Silverknowes,
Silverknowes Parkway, ✆ 336 3843, W : 4 m. AV – 🚩 Craigmillar Park, Observatory Rd ✆ 667 2837
BX – 🚩 Carrick Knowe, Glendevon Park ✆ 337 1096, W : 5 m. AX.

✈ ✆ 333 1000, Telex 727615, W : 6 m. by A 8 AV – **Terminal :** Waverley Bridge.

🚆 ✆ 556 5633.

🄷 5 Waverley Bridge ✆ 226 6591 – Edinburgh Airport ✆ 333 2167 and 344 3125.

♦Glasgow 46 – ♦Newcastle-upon-Tyne 105.

495

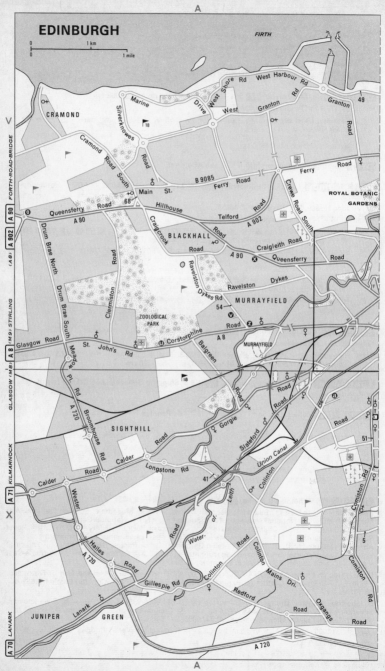

EDINBURGH

0 ____ 1 km
0 ____ 1 mile

A

FIRTH

V

CRAMOND

Marine Drive

West Shore Rd

West Harbour Rd

Granton

49

Silverknowes

West Granton Road

Granton Road

FORTH-ROAD-BRIDGE

Cramond Road South

Cramond Road

Ferry Road

B 9085

Ferry Road

ROYAL BOTANIC GARDENS

(A 8)   A 902   A 90

Queensferry Road

Main St.

68

Hillhouse

Telford Road

Crewe Road South

A 90

A 902

Drum Brae North

Craigcrook Road

BLACKHALL

Road

Craigleith Road

Queensferry

Road

Clermiston Road

Craigcrook Road

A 90

Queensferry

GLASGOW (M8)   A 8 (M9) STIRLING

Drum Brae South

Ravelston Dykes

Ravelston Dykes Rd

Ravelston Dykes

MURRAYFIELD

54

ZOOLOGICAL PARK

Road

V

Z

A 8

MURRAYFIELD

KILMARNOCK   A 71

Glasgow Road

St. John's Rd

Corstorphine

Meadow Pl. Rd

Balgreen

Road

18

Road

Road

Road

A 720

Broomhouse Rd

SIGHTHILL

Gorgie

Road

Stateford

Road

51

Road

Calder

Road

Calder   Road

Longstone Rd

41

Union Canal

Colinton

Road

X

Wester

Water-

Leith

or

Colinton

Road

Colinton

Road

Road

Comiston Rd

5

A 71

Hailes

Road

Road

Gillespie Rd

Colinton

Colinton Mains Dri.

Redford

Road

Oxgangs

Comiston Rd

LANARK

A 70

JUNIPER GREEN

Lanark

Road

Road

Road

A 720

A

496

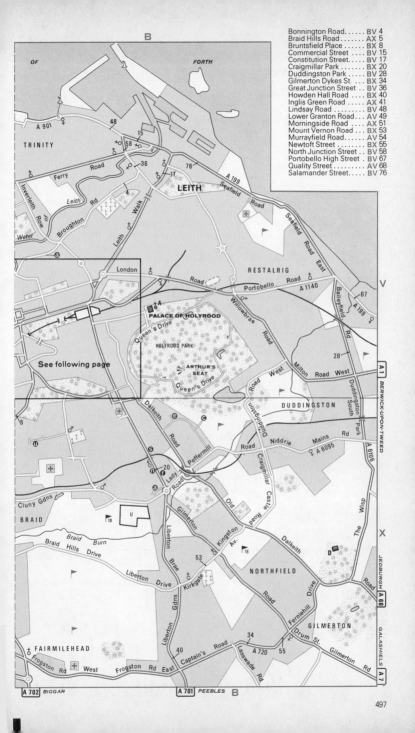

EDINBURGH
CENTRE

Caledonian, Princes St., EH1 2AB, ℰ 225 2433, Telex 72179 – 🛗 📺 ☎ 🄿. 🍴. 🔦 🆎 ⑩ 𝗩𝗜𝗦𝗔. ❀
CY **n**
M (rest. see **Pompadour** below) – ⊆ 6.50 – **254 rm** 38.00/85.00 **st.** – SB (weekends only) (winter only) 75.00 **st.**

George (Inter-Con), 19-21 George St., EH2 2PB, ℰ 225 1251, Telex 72570 – 🛗 🍴 rest 📺 ☎ ⴕ. 🄿. 🔦 🆎 ⑩ 𝗩𝗜𝗦𝗔. ❀
DY **z**
M 9.25/9.75 **t.** ⁹ 3.00 – ⊆ 6.00 – **196 rm** 38.00/80.00 **t.** – SB (weekends only) 56.50/63.50 **st.**

Ladbroke Dragonara (Ladbroke), Bells Mills, 69 Belford Rd, EH4 3DG, ℰ 332 2545, Telex 727979 – 🛗 📺 ☎ ⴕ. 🄿. 🔦 🆎 ⑩ 𝗩𝗜𝗦𝗔. ❀
CY **i**
M 8.95/10.95 **t.** ⁹ 3.50 – ⊆ 5.75 – **145 rm** 55.00/85.00 **t.** – SB (weekends only) 58.00/70.00 **st.**

Roxburghe (Best Western), 38 Charlotte Sq., EH2 4HG, ℰ 225 3921, Telex 727054 – 🛗 📺. 🔦 🆎 ⑩ 𝗩𝗜𝗦𝗔
DY **o**
M 8.00/11.00 **st.** ⁹ 3.00 – ⊆ 5.00 – **72 rm** 40.00/90.00 **st.**

Royal Scot (Swallow), 111 Glasgow Rd, EH12 8NF, W : 4 ½ m. on A 8 ℰ 334 9191, Telex 727197 – 🛗 📺 ☎ ⴕ. 🄿. 🔦 🆎 ⑩ 𝗩𝗜𝗦𝗔
by A 8   AV
M (carving rest.) 9.50 **st.** ⁹ 3.50 – ⊆ **252 rm** 44.00/56.00 **st.** – SB (weekends only) 50.00 **st.**

Post House (T.H.F.), Corstorphine Rd, EH12 6UA, W : 3 m. on A 8 ℰ 334 8221, Telex 727103, ≤ – 🛗 📺 ⇌wc 🅿 ⴕ. 🄿. 🔦 🆎 ⑩ 𝗩𝗜𝗦𝗔
AV **u**
M a la carte 10.65/16.15 **st.** ⁹ 2.45 – ⊆ 5.00 – **208 rm** 39.00/48.00 **st.**

Crest (Crest), Queensferry Rd, EH4 3HL, NW : 2 m. on A 90 ℰ 332 2442, Telex 72541 – 🛗 🍴 rest 📺 ⇌wc ☎ 🄿. 🔦 🆎 ⑩ 𝗩𝗜𝗦𝗔. ❀
AV **x**
M approx. 12.00 **st.** – ⊆ 5.25 – **120 rm** 43.50/56.00 **st.**

King James Thistle (Thistle), 7 St. James Centre, Leith St., EH1 3SW, ℰ 556 0111, Telex 727200 – 🛗 📺 ⇌wc 🛁wc 🅿 🄿. 🔦 🆎 ⑩ 𝗩𝗜𝗦𝗔. ❀
EY **u**
M 9.00/12.50 ⁹ 3.45 – ⊆ 4.75 – **141 rm** 45.00/70.00 **st.** – SB (weekends only) 66.00 **st.**

Stakis Grosvenor (Stakis), Grosvenor St., EH12 5EF, ℰ 226 6001, Telex 72445 – 🛗 📺 ⇌wc 🛁wc ☎ ⴕ. 🄿.
CZ **a**
130 rm.

Howard, 32-36 Gt. King St., EH3 6QH, ℰ 557 3500, Telex 727887 – 🛗 📺 ⇌wc 🛁wc ☎ 🄿. 🔦 🆎 ⑩ 𝗩𝗜𝗦𝗔
DY **s**
closed 24 to 26 December and 31 December-2 January – **M** 6.50/13.50 **t.** ⁹ 3.00 – **25 rm** ⊆ 37.50/59.00 **t.**

Ellersly House, 4 Ellersly Rd, EH12 6HZ, W : 2 ½ m. by A 8 ℰ 337 6888, Telex 76357, 🐎 – 🛗 📺 ⇌wc 🅿 🄿. 🔦 🆎 ⑩ 𝗩𝗜𝗦𝗔
AV **v**
M a la carte 8.50/12.50 **t.** ⁹ 3.00 – **57 rm** ⊆ 34.00/49.00 **t.**

Bruntsfield (Best Western), 69-74 Bruntsfield Pl., EH10 4HH, ℰ 229 1393, Telex 727897 – 🛗 📺 ⇌wc 🅿 🄿. 🔦 🆎 ⑩ 𝗩𝗜𝗦𝗔
DZ **e**
closed 24 to 29 December – **M** 6.50/9.00 **st.** ⁹ 2.50 – **54 rm** ⊆ 22.00/49.00 **st.** – SB 39.50/55.00 **st.**

Albany (Best Western), 39-43 Albany St., EH1 3QY, ℰ 556 0397, Telex 727079 – 📺 ⇌wc 🛁wc 🅿
EY **v**
21 rm.

Barnton Thistle (Thistle), 562 Queensferry Rd, EH4 6AS, NW : 4 ¾ m. on A 90 ℰ 339 1144, Telex 727928 – 🛗 📺 ⇌wc 🛁wc 🅿 🄿. 🔦 🆎 ⑩ 𝗩𝗜𝗦𝗔. ❀
AV **o**
M 7.00/8.50 ⁹ 3.45 – ⊆ 4.75 – **50 rm** 36.00/55.00 **t.** – SB (weekends only) 56.00 **st.**

Old Waverley, 43 Princes St., EH2 2BY, ℰ 556 4648, Group Telex 778215 – 🛗 📺 ⇌wc 🛁wc 🅿. ❀
EY **r**
66 rm.

St. Andrew, 8-10 South Saint Andrew St., EH2 2AZ, ℰ 556 8774 – 🛗 ⇌wc 🅿. 🔦 🆎 ⑩ 𝗩𝗜𝗦𝗔. ❀
EY **s**
M 4.50/5.50 **t.** – **40 rm** ⊆ 19.00/44.00 **t.** – SB (winter only) 44.00/48.00 **st.**

Murrayfield, 18 Corstorphine Rd, EH12 6HN, W : 2 ½ m. on A 8 ℰ 337 1844 – 📺 ⇌wc 🅿 🄿
AV **z**
M (grill rest. only) – **36 rm.**

Iona, 17 Strathearn Pl., EH9 2AL, ℰ 447 6264 – 🛁 🄿. 🔦 𝗩𝗜𝗦𝗔
BX **v**
M 4.50/9.50 **t.** ⁹ 3.00 – **21 rm** ⊆ 19.00/39.00 **t.** – SB (weekends only)(except summer) 44.00/48.00 **st.**

Kildonan Lodge, 27 Craigmillar Park, EH16 5PE, ℰ 667 2793 – 🄿. 🆎
BX **r**
closed January – **M** (lunch by arrangement) a la carte 6.70/10.00 **t.** ⁹ 2.80 – **8 rm** ⊆ 9.50/23.00 **t.**

Glenisla, 12 Lygon Rd, EH16 5QB, ℰ 667 4098 – 🄿
BX **a**
closed 3 weeks at Christmas and New Year – **9 rm** ⊆ 11.00/20.00 **st.**

International, 37 Mayfield Gdns, EH9 2BX, ℰ 667 2511 – ⇌wc. ❀
BX **s**
7 rm ⊆ 9.00/22.00 **st.**

Quinton Lodge, 24 Polwarth Terr., EH11 1NA, ℰ 229 4100, 🐎 – 📺 🄿
AX **a**
7 rm ⊆ 10.50/17.00 **st.**

Dorstan, 7 Priestfield Rd, EH16 5HJ, ℰ 667 6721 – ⇌wc 🛁 🄿
BX **e**
closed Christmas and New Year – **14 rm** ⊆ 9.75/27.00 **st.**

Southdown, 20 Craigmillar Park, EH16 5PS, ℰ 667 2410 – 📺 🛁 🄿. 🆎
BX **n**
8 rm ⊆ 10.50/19.00 **st.**

XXXX **Pompadour** (at Caledonian H.), Princes St., EH1 2AB, $\mathcal{C}$ 225 2433, Telex 72179 – 🅿. 🔄 🇦🇪 ⓪ 𝘝𝘐𝘚𝘈   CY **n**
closed lunch Saturday and Sunday – **M** a la carte 9.30/20.50 **st.** ♨ 3.25.

XXX **Prestonfield House** 🦢 with rm, Priestfield Rd, EH16 5UT, SE : 2 ½ m. off A 68 $\mathcal{C}$ 667 8000, Telex 727396, ≼, « Elegant 17C mansion », ☞, park – 📶 🍴 🅿. 🔄 🇦🇪 ⓪ 𝘝𝘐𝘚𝘈   BX **c**
M a la carte 9.00/14.50 **t.** ♨ 2.50 – **5 rm** ⊊ 40.00/52.50 **t.**

XXX **Howtowdie**, 27a Stafford St., EH3 7BJ, $\mathcal{C}$ 225 6291 – 🔄 🇦🇪 ⓪ 𝘝𝘐𝘚𝘈   CY **u**
closed Sunday, 25-26 December and 1-2 January – **M** a la carte 19.55/27.85 **t.** ♨ 4.50.

XX **Cosmo**, 58a North Castle St., EH2 3LU, $\mathcal{C}$ 226 6743, Italian rest. – 🔄 𝘝𝘐𝘚𝘈   DY **r**
closed Saturday lunch, Sunday and Monday – **M** a la carte 8.85/12.90 **t.** ♨ 2.75.

XX **Raffaelli**, 10-11 Randolph Pl., EH3 7TA, $\mathcal{C}$ 225 6060, Italian rest. – 🔄 🇦🇪 ⓪ 𝘝𝘐𝘚𝘈   CY **c**
closed Saturday lunch and Sunday – **M** a la carte 7.00/12.05 **t.** ♨ 2.40.

XX **Ristorante Milano**, 7 Victoria St., EH1 2HE, $\mathcal{C}$ 226 5260, Italian rest. – 🔄 🇦🇪 ⓪ 𝘝𝘐𝘚𝘈   EZ **a**
closed Saturday, 25-26 December and 1-3 Janaury – **M** a la carte 6.30/14.50 **t.** ♨ 3.00.

XX **Handsel**, 22 Stafford St., EH3 7BD, $\mathcal{C}$ 225 5521 – 🔄 🇦🇪 ⓪ 𝘝𝘐𝘚𝘈   CY **e**
closed Saturday lunch and Sunday – **M** a la carte 8.90/12.25 **t.** ♨ 2.30.

XX **Shamiana**, 14 Brougham St., Tollcross, EH3 9JH, $\mathcal{C}$ 228 2265, Indian rest. – 🔄 🇦🇪 ⓪ 𝘝𝘐𝘚𝘈
closed Sunday, Christmas Day and New Years Day – **M** (dinner only) a la carte 9.35/11.90 **t.**
♨ 2.85.   DZ **a**

X **L'Auberge**, 56 St. Mary's St., EH1 1SX, $\mathcal{C}$ 556 5888, French rest. – 🔄 🇦🇪 𝘝𝘐𝘚𝘈   EYZ **v**
M a la carte 9.20/13.60 **t.** ♨ 3.50.

X **Mermans**, 8-10 Eyre Pl., EH3 5EP, $\mathcal{C}$ 556 1177, Seafood – 🔄 🇦🇪 ⓪ 𝘝𝘐𝘚𝘈   BV **a**
closed Sunday, Christmas, New Year and Bank Holidays – **M** (dinner only) a la carte 6.05/13.75 **t.**
♨ 2.60.

X **Vito's**, 55a Frederick St., EH2 1LH, $\mathcal{C}$ 225 5052, Italian rest. – 🔄 🇦🇪 ⓪ 𝘝𝘐𝘚𝘈   DY **i**
closed Sunday and 1 January – **M** a la carte 7.30/14.60 **t.**

X **Verandah**, 17 Dalry Rd, EH11 2BQ, $\mathcal{C}$ 337 5828, Indian rest. – 🔄 🇦🇪 ⓪ 𝘝𝘐𝘚𝘈   CZ **z**
M a la carte 5.15/8.35 **t.** ♨ 3.25.

X **Alp-Horn**, 167 Rose St., EH2 4LS, $\mathcal{C}$ 225 4787, Swiss rest. – 🔄   DY **x**
closed Sunday, Monday, first 3 weeks July and 2 weeks at Christmas – **M** a la carte 5.90/10.60 **t.**
♨ 3.20.

at Bonnyrigg S : 8 m. by A 7 – BX – on A 6094 – ✉ Bonnyrigg – 🕓 0875 Gorebridge :

🏰 **Dalhousie Castle** 🦢, EH19 3JB, SE : 1 ¼ m. on B 704 $\mathcal{C}$ 20153, Telex 72380, ≼, « Converted 12C castle », 🔄, park – 📺 🅿. 🛎. 🔄 🇦🇪 ⓪ 𝘝𝘐𝘚𝘈. 🍴
M a la carte 12.75/21.95 **t.** – **24 rm** ⊊ 53.00/97.50 **t.**

EDZELL Angus (Tayside) 🔟🔟🔟 M 13 – pop. 658 – ECD : Thursday – 🕓 035 64.

See : Castle★ (16C) AC (Walled garden).

Envir. : Brechin (Cathedral : round tower★) S : 6 ½ m. – Glen Esk★ NW : 11 m.

🟦 $\mathcal{C}$ 235 – 🟦 at Brechin $\mathcal{C}$ 035 62 (Brechin) 2383, S : 5 ½ m.

♦Edinburgh 91 – ♦Aberdeen 36 – ♦Dundee 32.

🏠 Glenesk, High St., DD9 7TF, $\mathcal{C}$ 319, ⟍, ☞ – 📺 ⌁wc 📶wc 🍴 🅿. 🛎. 🇦🇪 ⓪
24 rm ⊊ 21.00/44.00 **t.**

EGILSAY (Isle of) Orkney (Orkney Islands) 🔟🔟🔟 L 6 – Shipping Services : see Orkney Islands (Mainland : Kirkwall).

EIGG (Isle of) Inverness. (Highland) 🔟🔟🔟 B 13 – Shipping Services : see Mallaig.

EUROPE on a single sheet
Michelin map no **🟥🟥🟥**.

ELGIN Moray. (Grampian) **401** K 11 – pop. 16,407 – ECD : Wednesday – ✆ 0343.

See : Cathedral★.

Envir. : Burghead (❄✳✳ from the lighthouse) NW : 10 m. – Findhorn (site★) W : 12 m.

🅡 Hardhillock, Birnie Rd ✆ 2338, S : 1 m. – 🅡 Hopeman ✆ 034 383 (Hopeman) 578, N : 7 m.

🅉 17 High St. ✆ 3388 (summer only).

♦Edinburgh 191 – ♦Aberdeen 67 – Fraserburgh 61 – ♦Inverness 39.

Hotels see : Fochabers E : 9 ½ m.

AUSTIN ROVER-DAIMLER-JAGUAR Station Rd ✆ 48444
CITROEN 27 Greyfriars St. ✆ 7416
FORD East Rd ✆ 2176
MAZDA, RELIANT Sheriff Mill ✆ 7121

NISSAN Borough Briggs Rd ✆ 7473
RENAULT Edgar Rd ✆ 7688
VAUXHALL-OPEL, VOLVO South College St. ✆ 7561
VW, AUDI Blackfriars Rd ✆ 44977

ELLON Aberdeen. (Grampian) **401** N 11 – pop. 2,263 – ECD : Wednesday – ✆ 0358.

🅡 McDonald ✆ 20576.

🅉 Market St. Car Park ✆ 20730 (summer only).

♦Edinburgh 140 – ♦Aberdeen 16 – Fraserburgh 26.

🏨 **Ladbroke Mercury** (Ladbroke), AB4 9NP, ✆ 20666, Telex 739200 – 📺 ➾wc ☏ 🅿. 🔬. 🔊 🅰🅴 ⓘ 𝚅𝙸𝚂𝙰
   M (bar lunch) 8.50 t. ≬ 3.45 – **40 rm** ⊏⊐ 32.00/42.00 t. – SB (summer only) 59.00 **st.**

ERIBOLL (Loch) ★★★ Sutherland (Highland) **401** F 8.

♦Edinburgh 276 – Tongue 21.

Hotel see : Tongue E : 21 m.

ERISKA (Isle of) Argyll. (Strathclyde) **401** D 14 – ✉ Oban – ✆ 063 172 Ledaig.

🏚 **Isle of Eriska** ⌕, PA37 1SD, ✆ 371, ≤ Lismore and mountains, « Country house atmosphere », 🛵, park, ⚒ – ➾wc ☏ 🅘 🅿. 🔊. 🛥
   April-November – **M** (buffet lunch) 18.50 ≬ 3.10 – **21 rm** ⊏⊐ (dinner included) 60.00/130.00.

ERSKINE Renfrew. (Strathclyde) **401 402** G 16 – pop. 3,300 – ✆ 041 Glasgow.

♦Edinburgh 56 – ♦Glasgow 13.

🏨 **Crest** (Crest) ⌕, Erskine Bridge, PA8 6AN, on A 726 ✆ 812 0123, Telex 777713, ≤, 🛵 – 🛗
   🍽 rest 📺 ➾wc ☏ ⅙ 🅿. 🔬. 🔊 🅰🅴 ⓘ 𝚅𝙸𝚂𝙰
   M approx. 11.00 **st.** – ⊏⊐ 5.25 – **200 rm** 43.00/52.00 **st.**

ETTRICKBRIDGE Selkirk. (Borders) **401 402** L 17 – see Selkirk.

FALKIRK Stirling. (Central) **401** I 16 – pop. 37,579 – ECD : Wednesday – ✆ 0324.

🅡 Grangemouth ✆ 0324 (Polmont) 711500, E : 3 m.

♦Edinburgh 26 – Dunfermline 18 – ♦Glasgow 25 – Motherwell 27 – Perth 43.

🏨 **Stakis Park** (Stakis), Camelon Rd, Arnothill, FK1 5RY, ✆ 28331, Telex 776502 – 🛗 📺 ➾wc ☏ 🅿. 🔬. 🔊 🅰🅴 ⓘ 𝚅𝙸𝚂𝙰
   M a la carte 5.30/12.45 **t.** ≬ 2.80 – **55 rm** ⊏⊐ 34.00/44.00.

✗ **Pierre's,** 140 Grahams Rd, FK2 7BQ, ✆ 35843, French rest. – 🔊 🅰🅴 ⓘ 𝚅𝙸𝚂𝙰
   closed Saturday lunch, Sunday, Monday, 25-26 December and 1 to 17 January – **M** a la carte 9.20/13.75 **t.** ≬ 2.75.

at Polmont SE : 3 m. on A 803 – ✉ ✆ 0324 Polmont :

🏨 **Inchyra Grange,** Grange Rd, FK2 0YB, ✆ 711911, Telex 777693, 🛵 – 📺 ➾wc ☏ ⅙ 🅿. 🔬. 🔊 🅰🅴 ⓘ 𝚅𝙸𝚂𝙰
   M 6.50/8.50 **st.** ≬ 2.50 – **30 rm** ⊏⊐ 32.00/49.00 **t.** – SB (weekends only) 40.00/44.00 **st.**

AUSTIN-ROVER Main St. ✆ 22584
FIAT Callendar Rd ✆ 24204
FORD Callendar Rd ✆ 21511
HYUNDAI High Station Rd ✆ 24221
MAZDA Victoria Rd ✆ 37921

PEUGEOT, TALBOT 95 Glasgow Rd ✆ 22571
TOYOTA Lady'smill ✆ 35935
TOYOTA Winchester Ave., Denny ✆ 824387
VAUXHALL 76/86 Grahams Rd ✆ 21234
VOLVO West End ✆ 23042

FALKLAND Fife. (Fife) **401** K 15 – pop. 896 – ✆ 033 75.

See : Palace★ (16C) *AC.*

🅉 ✆ 397.

♦Edinburgh 36 – ♦Dundee 23 – Perth 18.

✗ **Covenanter** with rm, High St., KY7 7BU, ✆ 224 – 🅰🅴 ⓘ 𝚅𝙸𝚂𝙰
   closed Monday – **M** a la carte 9.80/11.60 **st.** ≬ 3.00 – **4 rm** ⊏⊐ 10.00/16.00 **st.**

FARR Inverness. (Highland) **401** H 11 – ✆ 080 83.

♦Edinburgh 154 – ♦Inverness 10.

✗✗ **Grouse and Trout,** Flichity, IV1 2XE, S : 4 m. by B 851 ✆ 314, ≤, 🛵, ⚒ – 🅿. 🔊 🅰🅴 ⓘ 𝚅𝙸𝚂𝙰
   M (bar lunch) a la carte 8.80/11.85 **t.** ≬ 3.00.

501

FEOLIN Argyll. (Strathclyde) **401** B 16 – Shipping Services : see Jura (Isle of).

FETLAR (Isle of) Shetland (Shetland Islands) **401** R 2 – Shipping Services : see Shetland Islands.

FIONNPHORT Argyll. (Strathclyde) **401** A 15 – Shipping Services : see Mull (Isle of).

FISHNISH Argyll. (Strathclyde) **401** C 14 – Shipping Services : see Mull (Isle of).

FLOTTA (Isle of) Orkney (Orkney Islands) **401** K 7 – Shipping Services : see Orkney Islands.

FOCHABERS Moray. (Grampian) **401** K 11 – pop. 1238 – ECD : Wednesday – ✪ 0343.
🖪 Spey Bay ✆ 820424, N : 5 m. – 🖪 Garmouth ✆ 034 387 (Spey Bay) 388.
♦Edinburgh 182 – ♦Aberdeen 58 – Fraserburgh 52 – ♦Inverness 48.

  🏠 **Gordon Arms,** 89 High St., IV32 7DH, ✆ 820508 – 📺 🛏wc ☎ 🅿 🖭 AE ⓞ VISA
     M 3.50/9.00 t. 🍷 2.50 – **12 rm** ⒔ 18.00/24.00 t. – SB 40.00/50.00 st.

     at Clochan NE : 3 ½ m. on A 98 – ✉ Fochabers – ✪ 054 27 Clochan :

  🏠 **Mill,** AB5 2HJ, on A 98 ✆ 233 – 📺 🛏wc 🛏wc 🅿 🖭 AE ⓞ VISA
     M *(closed Sunday dinner)* 3.75/8.50 t. 🍷 2.50 – **15 rm** ⒔ 20.00/34.00 t. – SB (week-
     ends only) 50.00 **st.**

FORFAR Angus (Tayside) **401** L 14 – pop. 10,499 – ECD : Thursday – ✪ 0307.
Envir. : Glamis (castle ★) *AC,* SW : 5 ½ m.
♦Edinburgh 72 – ♦Aberdeen 52 – ♦Dundee 13 – Perth 30.

  🏠 **Royal,** 31-33 Castle St., DD8 3AE, ✆ 62691 – 🛏wc 🅿 🖭 AE ⓞ VISA
     M *(closed dinner Friday, Saturday and Sunday)* (bar lunch) 10.00 t. 🍷 3.00 – **21 rm**
     ⒔ 24.00/37.00 t.

  🏠 **Benholm,** 78 Glamis Rd, DD8 1DS, SW : ½ m. on A 94 ✆ 64281, 🚗 – 📺 🛏wc ☎ 🅿 🖭 AE
     ⓞ VISA
     M 5.00/9.00 t. 🍷 2.50 – ⒔ 3.00 – **7 rm** 17.50/34.00 t. – SB 60.00/79.00 **st.**

AUSTIN-ROVER 128 Castle St. ✆ 62542   VW, AUDI Kirriemuir Rd ✆ 62347
TALBOT Lochside Rd ✆ 62676

FORTINGALL Perth. (Tayside) **401** H 14 – see Kenmore.

FORT WILLIAM Inverness. (Highland) **401** E 13 – pop. 4,214 – ECD : Wednesday except summer
– ✪ 0397.
Envir. : SE : Glen Nevis★ – 🖪 Torlundy ✆ 4464, N : 3 m. on A 82 – 🛈 Area Tourist Officer ✆ 3581.
♦Edinburgh 131 – ♦Glasgow 102 – ♦Inverness 66 – ♦Oban 51.

  🏰 ✿ **Inverlochy Castle** 🦢, Inverlochy, PH33 6SN, NE : 3 m. on A 82 ✆ 2177, ≼ garden, loch
     and mountains, « Victorian castle in extensive grounds », 🐾, 🚗, park, 🎾 – 📺 ☎ 🅿 🖭
     VISA 🦌
     Mid March-mid November – **M** (restricted lunch) (booking essential) 23.00 – **16 rm**
     ⒔ 72.00/125.00
     Spec. Grilled prawns with pernod butter, Traditional roast grouse, Coulibiac of salmon.

  🏨 **Ladbroke Mercury** (Ladbroke), Achintore Rd, PH33 6RW, on A 82 ✆ 3117, ≼ – 📺 🛏wc
     ☎ 🅿 🖭 AE ⓞ VISA 🦌
     M a la carte 7.30/12.75 t. – ⒔ 5.00 – **61 rm** 25.00/44.00 t. – SB 55.00/59.00 **st.**

  🏠 **Nevis Bank,** Belford Rd, PH33 6BY, ✆ 2595 – 🛏wc 🅿 🖭 VISA
     M 4.50/9.50 t. 🍷 2.75 – **20 rm** ⒔ 13.50/35.00 t.

  ⌂ **Guisachan,** Alma Rd, PH33 6HA, ✆ 3797, ≼ – 🅿 🦌
     15 rm ⒔ 8.00/19.00 t.

     at Banavie N : 3 m. by A 82 and A 830 on B 8004 – ✉ Fort William – ✪ 039 77 Corpach :

  🏠 **Moorings,** PH33 7LY, ✆ 550, ≼, 🚗 – 🛏wc 🛏wc 🅿 ⓞ VISA 🦌
     M *(closed in winter)* 9.75/10.50 **st.** 🍷 2.00 – **14 rm** ⒔ 12.00/36.00 **st.**

AUSTIN-ROVER Gordon Sq. ✆ 2345   PEUGEOT-TALBOT Canaghael ✆ 4141

FOYERS Inverness. (Highland) **401** G 12 – ✪ 045 63 Gorthleck.
Envir. : SE : Loch Knockie ≼ ★★from Glendoebeg by A 862 – ♦Edinburgh 168 – ♦Inverness 18.

  🏠 **Foyers,** IV1 2XT, N : ½ m. on B 852 ✆ 216, ≼ Loch Ness and mountains, 🐾, 🚗 – 🛏 🅿
     M 4.50/5.00 **st.** 🍷 2.10 – **9 rm** ⒔ 9.50/19.00 **st.**

GAIRLOCH Ross and Cromarty (Highland) **401** C 10 – pop. 125 – ECD : Wednesday except
summer – ✪ 0445.
Envir. : NE : Gruinard Bay★★★ – Inverewe gardens★ (rhododendrons) NE : 6 m. – SE : Loch Maree★.
🛈 Area Tourist Officer, Achtercairn ✆ 2130.
♦Edinburgh 230 – ♦Inverness 71 – Kyle of Lochalsh 65.

502

🏛 **Gairloch,** IV21 2BL, ℰ 2001, ⩽ Gair Loch and Isle of Skye, ⌇, ✵ – ⧗ ⌂wc ⋔wc 🅿. ◪ 🆎 ① *VISA*
April-October – **M** (bar lunch) 8.50 **t.** ▯ 3.50 – **50 rm** ⊡ 25.00/46.00 **t.** – SB 46.00/58.00 **st.**

🏛 **Shieldaig Lodge** ⌇, IV21 2AW, S : 4 m. by A 832 on B 8056 ℰ 044 583 (Badachro) 250, ⩽ Gair Loch, « Former hunting lodge on lochside », ⌇, ⌇ – ⌂wc 🅿. ◪ *VISA*
May-October – **M** *(closed Sunday lunch)* 3.00/9.25 **t.** ▯ 3.00 – **14 rm** ⊡ 21.50/45.00 **t.**

🏠 Creag Mor, Charlestown, IV21 2AH, S : 2 m. on A 832 ℰ 2068, ⌇ – ⌂wc 🅿. ✾
closed November – **9 rm** ⊡ 14.50/29.00 **st.**

GALASHIELS Selkirk. (Borders) 🗺️ 🗺️ L 17 – pop. 12,609 – ECD : Wednesday – ☎ 0896.
⒕ Ladhope, ℰ 3724, NE : ¼ m. – ⒕ Torwoodlee, ℰ 2260, N : 1 m. on A 7.
🛈 Bank St. ℰ 55551 (Easter and mid May-October).
♦Edinburgh 34 – ♦Carlisle 61 – ♦Glasgow 71 – ♦Newcastle-upon-Tyne 74.

🏛 **Kingsknowes,** Selkirk Rd, TD1 3HY, ℰ 3478, ⩽, 🌳, ✵ – 📺 ⌂wc 🅿. ◪ 🆎 ① *VISA*
M 7.00 **t.** ▯ 2.40 – **10 rm** ⊡ 23.00/40.00 **t.** – SB (winter only) 42.00/46.00 **st.**

🏛 **Woodlands House,** Windyknowe Rd, TD1 1RQ, ℰ 4722, 🌳 – ⌂wc ☎ 🅿. ◪ 🆎 ① *VISA*
M (buffet lunch) a la carte 6.40/12.00 **t.** ▯ 3.00 – **9 rm** ⊡ 23.50/42.00 **t.** – SB 57.50/65.00 **st.**

GARVE Ross and Cromarty (Highland) 🗺️ F 11 – pop. 200 – ECD : Thursday – ☎ 099 74.
Envir. : SE : Blackwater Valley (Falls of Rogie★).
♦Edinburgh 186 – ♦Inverness 27 – ♦Wick 116.

🏛 **Strathgarve Lodge** ⌇, IV23 2PU, N : 2 ¾ m. by A 832 off A 835 ℰ 204, ⩽, ⌇, 🌳, park – 📺 ⌂wc ☜ 🅿 – **15 rm**.

GATEHOUSE OF FLEET Kirkcudbright. (Dumfries and Galloway) 🗺️ 🗺️ H 19 – pop. 837 –
ECD : Thursday – ☎ 055 74 – ⒕.
🛈 Car Park ℰ 212 (summer only).
♦Edinburgh 109 – ♦Dumfries 32 – Stranraer 44.

🏛 **Cally Palace** ⌇, DG7 2DL, S : 1 ½ m. by A 75 ℰ 341, ⩽, ⊿ heated, ⌇, 🌳, park, ✵ – ⧗ 📺 ⌂wc 🅿. ▯
M 4.00/8.25 **st.** ▯ 2.10 – **60 rm** ⊡ 28.50/57.00 **st.**

🏛 **Murray Arms** (Best Western), High St., DG7 2HY, ℰ 207, ⌇, 🌳, ✵ – ⌂wc ☜ 🅿. ◪ 🆎 ① *VISA*
M (bar lunch) 9.50 **st.** ▯ 2.90 – **19 rm** ⊡ 21.00/48.00 **st.** – SB 44.00/54.00 **st.**

GIFFNOCK Renfrew. (Strathclyde) 🗺️ ④ 🗺️ ⑨ – see Glasgow.

GIFFORD E. Lothian (Lothian) 🗺️ L 16 – pop. 575 – ECD : Monday and Wednesday – ✉ Haddington – ☎ 062 081.
♦Edinburgh 20 – Hawick 50.

🏠 **Tweeddale Arms,** High St., EH41 4PR, ℰ 240 – 📺 ⌂wc ⋔wc. 🆎 *VISA*
M (bar lunch Monday to Saturday) 5.95/8.50 **t.** ▯ 2.50 – **10 rm** ⊡ 16.00/30.00 **t.**

GIGHA (Isle of) Argyll. (Strathclyde) 🗺️ C 16 – pop. 171 – ☎ 058 35.
See : Sound of Gigha★.
⛴ by Caledonian MacBrayne : from Ardminish to Tayinloan Monday/Saturday 5-7 daily ; Sunday 2 May-30 September only 4 daily (20 mn).

🏠 **Gigha** ⌇, PA41 7AD, ℰ 254, ⩽ Sound of Gigha and Kintyre Peninsula, « Tastefully renovated farmhouse », ⌇, 🌳 – ⌂wc 🅿. ◪ *VISA*
April-October – **M** 6.00/10.00 **t.** – **9 rm** ⊡ 17.50/40.00 **t.**

GLASGOW Lanark. (Strathclyde) 🗺️ 🗺️ H 16 – pop. 897,483 – ☎ 041.
See : St. Mungo Cathedral★★★ DYZ – Art Gallery and Museum★★ CY – Provand's Lordship★ DZ D
– Pollock House★ (Spanish paintings) AX E.
⒕ Linn Park, Simshill Rd ℰ 637 5871, S : 4 m. BX – ⒕ Lethamhill, Cumbernauld Rd ℰ 770 6220 BV –
⒕ Knightswood, Lincoln Av. ℰ 959 2131, W : 4 m. AV – ⒕ Ruchill, Brassey St. ℰ 946 9728 BV.
Access to Oban by helicopter.
✈ Glasgow Airport : ℰ 887 1111, Telex 778219, W : 8 m. by M 8 AV – Terminal : Coach service from Glasgow Central and Queen Street main line Railway Stations and from Anderston Cross and Buchanan Bus Stations – ✈ see also Prestwick.
🛈 George Sq. ℰ 221 6136/7 or 221 7371/2. Telex 779504.
♦Edinburgh 46 – ♦Manchester 221.

GLASGOW
BUILT UP AREA

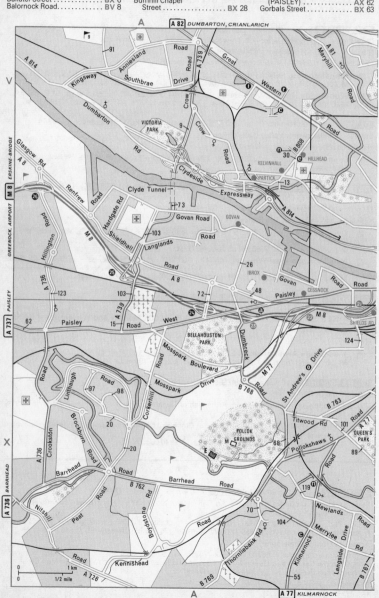

For Street Index see Glasgow p. 6

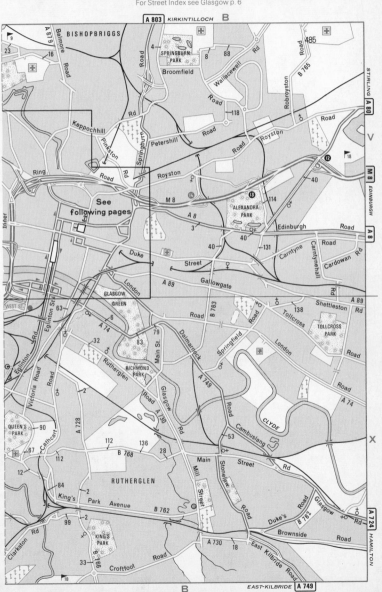

505

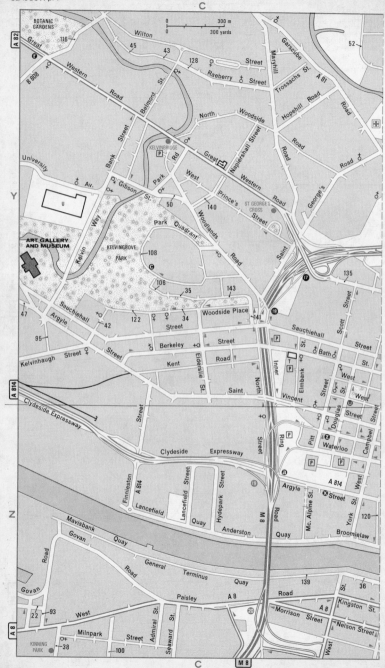

GLASGOW
CENTRE

For Street Index
see Glasgow p. 6

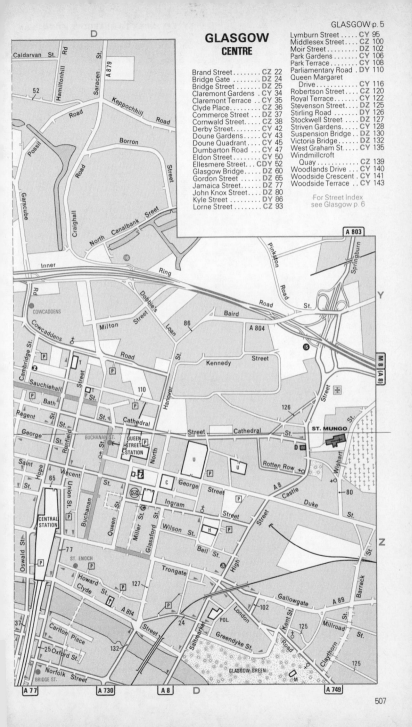

507

STREET INDEX TO GLASGOW TOWN PLAN

Holiday Inn, Argyle St., Anderston, G3 8RR, ✆ 226 5577, Telex 776355, ⊠ – 🛗 ▤ 📺 ☎ 👐
🅿 🛂 🔼 🝕 ⓞ *VISA*   CZ **a**
M 11.50/9.95 **st.** – ⋍ 5.65 – **296 rm** 46.00/82.00 **s.**

Albany (T.H.F.), Bothwell St., G2 7EN, ✆ 248 2656, Telex 77440, ⪡ – 🛗 📺 ☎ 🅿 🛂 🔼 🝕
ⓞ *VISA*   CZ **z**
M 9.95 **st.** 🍷 2.85 – ⋍ 5.50 – **251 rm** 45.00/57.50 **st.**

Glasgow Skean Dhu (Mt. Charlotte), 36 Cambridge St., G2 3HN, ✆ 332 3311, Telex 777334
– 🛗 🔼 🅿 🛂 🔼 🝕 ⓞ *VISA*   DY **z**
M 8.50/13.00 **st.** 🍷 2.75 – ⋍ 3.95 – **320 rm** 39.50/50.00 **st.** – SB (weekends only) 49.00 **st.**

Stakis Grosvenor (Stakis), Grosvenor Terr., Great Western Rd, G12 0TA, ✆ 339 8811, Telex
776247 – 🛗 📺 ☎ 🅿 🛂 🔼 🝕 ⓞ *VISA*   CY **r**
M 7.00/11.00 **t.** 🍷 3.30 – **95 rm** ⋍ 48.50/60.00 **t.** – SB (weekends only) 50.00/54.00 **st.**

White House ⚘ without rest., 11-14 Cleveden Cres., G12 0PA, ✆ 339 9375 – 📺 🛂 🔼 🝕
ⓞ *VISA*   AV **r**
M (room service only) a la carte approx. 10.75 **t.** – ⋍ 4.40 – **32 rm** 30.00/60.00 – SB (week-
ends only) 56.70 **st.**

Stakis Ingram (Stakis), 201 Ingram St., G1 1DQ, ✆ 248 4401 – 🛗 📺 🖚wc ☎ 🅿 🛂 🔼 🝕
ⓞ *VISA*   DZ **c**
M (bar lunch) a la carte 6.95/9.85 **st.** 🍷 3.25 – **90 rm** ⋍ 40.00/55.00 **st.** – SB 46.00/64.00 **st.**

Bellahouston Swallow (Swallow), 517 Paisley Rd West, G51 1RW, ✆ 427 3146, Telex
778795 – 🛗 📺 🖚wc �⛨wc 🅿 🛂 🔼 🝕 ⓞ *VISA*   AX **a**
M (buffet lunch Saturday) 5.50/7.50 **st.** 🍷 3.25 – **122 rm** ⋍ 38.00/46.00 – SB 40.00 **st.**

Crest (Crest), Argyle St., G2 8LL, ✆ 248 2355, Telex 779652 – 🛗 📺 🖚wc ☎ 🛂 🔼 🝕
VISA. ⚘   CZ **x**
M approx. 11.00 **st.** – ⋍ 4.95 – **123 rm** 37.50/46.50 **st.**

Tinto Firs Thistle (Thistle), 470 Kilmarnock Rd, G43 2BB, ✆ 637 2353, Telex 778329 – 📺
🖚wc 🅿 🛂 🔼 🝕 ⓞ *VISA*. ⚘   AX **c**
M 6.00/10.00 🍷 3.45 – ⋍ 4.75 – **28 rm** 39.00/44.00 **t.**

Stakis Pond (Stakis), Great Western Rd, G12 0XP, ✆ 334 8161, Telex 776573 – 🛗 📺 🖚wc
🕭 🅿 🛂 🔼 🝕 ⓞ *VISA*   AV **i**
M a la carte 6.95/13.50 **st.** 🍷 3.00 – **133 rm** ⋍ 36.50/44.00 **st.** – SB 48.00/52.00 **st.**

Beacons, 7 Park Terr., G3 6BY, ✆ 332 9438 – 🛗 📺 🖚wc 🕭 – **35 rm**   CY **c**

Stakis Burnside (Stakis), East Kilbride Rd, Rutherglen, G73 5EA, ✆ 634 1276 – 📺 🖚wc
🕭 🅿 🛂 🔼 🝕 ⓞ *VISA*   by A 749   BX
M a la carte 5.35/9.20 **t.** 🍷 2.00 – **16 rm** ⋍ 25.00/39.50 **t.** – SB 54.00/78.00 **st.**

Kings Park, Mill St., Rutherglen, G73 2LX, ✆ 647 5491 – 📺 🖚wc 🕭 🅿 🛂 🔼 🝕 ⓞ *VISA*
M 4.50/8.50 **t.** 🍷 3.80 – **24 rm** ⋍ 22.00/35.00 **t.** – SB (weekends only) 21.50/27.50 **st.**   BX **e**

Newlands, 290 Kilmarnock Rd, G43 2XS, ✆ 632 9171 – 📺 🖚wc 🕭 🔼 🝕 ⓞ *VISA*   AX **n**
M a la carte 6.95/9.05 **t.** 🍷 2.70 – **17 rm** ⋍ 22.00/42.00 **t.**

Dalmeny, 62 St. Andrews Drive, Nithsdale Cross, Pollokshields, G41 5EZ, ✆ 427 1106 – 📺
🖚wc �⛨wc 🅿   AX **o**
12 rm ⋍ 18.40/34.50 **st.**

Kirklee, 11 Kensington Gate, G12 9LG, ✆ 334 5555 – 🖚wc. ⚘   AV **c**
11 rm ⋍ 19.00/28.50 **st.**

Malmaison (at Central H.), Gordon St., G1 3SF, ✆ 221 9680, Telex 777771, French rest. – 🔼
🝕 ⓞ *VISA*   DZ **e**
closed Saturday lunch, Sunday and 2 weeks July – **M** a la carte 15.50/20.50 **t.** 🍷 3.00.

Ambassador, 19-20 Blythswood Sq., G2 4AS, ✆ 221 2034, Dancing (Tuesday-Saturday) –
🔼 🝕 ⓞ *VISA*   CY **u**
closed Sunday and Bank Holidays – **M** (bar lunch Saturday) a la carte 12.20/18.90 **t.** 🍷 3.50.

Colonial, 25 High St., G1 1LX, ✆ 552 1923 – 🔼 🝕 ⓞ *VISA*   DZ **a**
closed Sunday and Monday – **M** a la carte 7.80/13.30 **t.** 🍷 2.95.

Poacher's, Ruthven Lane, off Byres Rd, G12 9BG, ✆ 339 0932 – 🅿 🔼 🝕 🔼 *VISA*   AV **n**
closed Sunday, 25 December and 1-3 January – **M** a la carte 9.00/12.75 **t.** 🍷 2.70.

Kensingtons, 164 Darnley St., G41 2LL, ✆ 424 3662   BX **c**

Ubiquitous Chip, 12 Ashton Lane, off Byres Rd, G12 8SJ, ✆ 334 5007, Bistro – 🔼 🝕 ⓞ
VISA   AV **e**
closed Sunday, Christmas Day and New Year – **M** a la carte 5.15/15.60 **t.**

at Busby S : 5 ½ m. by A 727 – AX – on A 726 – ✉ ☼ 041 Glasgow :

Busby, 1 Field Rd, Clarkston, G76 8RX, ✆ 644 2661 – 🛗 📺 🖚wc 🇛⛨wc 🕭 🅿 🔼 🝕 ⓞ *VISA*.
⚘
M *(closed 25 December and 1 January)* (bar lunch) 6.50 **t.** – **14 rm** ⋍ 23.00/31.00 **t.**

at Giffnock (Renfrew.) (Strathclyde) S : 5 ¼ m. by A 77 – AX – ✉ ☼ 041 Glasgow :

MacDonald Thistle (Thistle), Eastwood Toll, G46 6RA, at intersection of A 77 and A 726 ✆
638 2225, Telex 779138 – 📺 🖚wc 🕭 🅿 🛂 🔼 🝕 ⓞ *VISA*
M 7.00/10.00 **t.** 🍷 3.45 – ⋍ 4.75 – **58 rm** 35.00/48.00 **t.** – SB (weekends only) 54.00 **st.**

Stakis Redhurst (Stakis), 27 Eastwoodmains Rd, G46 6QE, ✆ 638 6465 – 📺 🖚wc 🕭 🅿
🛂 🔼 🝕 ⓞ *VISA*
M (grill rest. only) 4.40/8.95 **st.** 🍷 2.80 – **16 rm** ⋍ 37.50/46.00 **st.** – SB (week-
ends only) 37.00/50.00 **st.**

at Glasgow Airport Renfrew. (Strathclyde) W : 8 m. by M 8 – AV – ✉ ⊛ 041 Glasgow :

🏨 **Excelsior** (T.H.F.), Abbotsinch, PA3 2TR, ☎ 887 1212, Telex 777733 – ⇅ [TV] ♿ [P]. ⛹. [A] [AE] [D] VISA
M 5.25/7.95 **st.** 🍷 2.75 – ☕ 5.50 – **305 rm** 43.00/53.50 **st.**

MICHELIN Branch, 60 Cunningham Rd, Rutherglen, G73 1PP, ☎ **647 9516**

AUSTIN-ROVER, HONDA 198 Maxwell Rd ☎ 429 4298
AUSTIN-ROVER 55 Hamilton Rd ☎ 778 8383
AUSTIN-ROVER 215 Queensborough Gardens ☎ 357 1234
AUSTIN-ROVER, MAZDA, TOYOTA 470 Royston Rd ☎ 552 4718
AUSTIN-ROVER Vineycombe St. ☎ 334 4761
BMW 10 Abbey Drive ☎ 959 1272
FORD 1009 Gallowgate ☎ 554 4321
FORD Temple Industrial Estate, Anniesland ☎ 954 1500
FORD 34 Fenwick Rd ☎ 637 7161
FORD 370 Pollokshaws Rd ☎ 423 6644
HONDA Maxwell Rd ☎ 429 4298
NISSAN 77/81 Dumbarton Rd ☎ 334 1241
OPEL-VAUXHALL 10 Holmbank Av. ☎ 649 9321
OPEL-VAUXHALL 712 Edinburgh Rd ☎ 774 2791
PEUGEOT-TALBOT 100 Minerva St. ☎ 248 2345
RENAULT 64 Kirkintilloch Rd ☎ 772 6481
SAAB 162 Crow Rd ☎ 334 4661
VAUXHALL-OPEL 640 Pollokshaws Rd ☎ 423 3074
VAUXHALL-OPEL Grand St. ☎ 332 2626
VOLVO 2413/2493 London Rd ☎ 778 8501
VOLVO 136 Merrylee Rd ☎ 633 0500
VW-AUDI Barrhead Rd ☎ 882 4601
VW, AUDI 512 Kilmarnock Rd ☎ 637 2241

GREEN TOURIST GUIDES

Picturesque scenery, buildings
Attractive routes
Touring programmes
Plans of towns and buildings.

GLENBORRODALE Argyll. (Highland) [401] C 13 – ✉ Acharacle – ⊛ 097 24.
♦Edinburgh 153 – ♦Inverness 104 – ♦Oban 70.

🏨 **Glenborrodale Castle** (T.H.F.) 🔇, Ardnamurchan, PH36 4JP, ☎ 266, ⩽ Loch Sunart and gardens, « Victorian castle in extensive gardens », park – [TV] 🛁wc ☏ [P]. [A] [AE] [D] VISA
Mid March-October – **M** (bar lunch) 11.00 **st.** 🍷 2.85 – **22 rm** ☕ (dinner included) 35.00/84.00 **st.**

GLENCARSE Perth. (Tayside) [401] K 14 – see Perth.

GLENFINNAN Inverness. (Highland) [401] D 13 – pop. 70 – ✉ Fort William – ⊛ 039 783 Kinlocheil.
See : Glenfinnan Monument ⩽★.
[i] ☎ 250 (summer only).
♦Edinburgh 149 – ♦Inverness 80 – Kyle of Lochalsh 89 – ♦Oban 66.

🏨 **Glenfinnan House** 🔇, PH37 4LT, ☎ 235, ⩽ Loch Shiel and Ben Nevis, 🎣, 🌳, park – 🚿wc [P]
Mid April-mid October – **M** (bar lunch) 9.00 **st.** – **19 rm** ☕ 13.00/39.00 **st.**

GLENROTHES Fife. (Fife) [401] K 15 – pop. 27,335 – ECD : Tuesday – ⊛ 0592.
⛳18 Golf Course Rd ☎ 758686 – ⛳18 Thornton ☎ 771111, S : 3 m. – ⛳9 Leslie, W : 3 m. on A 911.
[i] Information Kiosk ☎ 754 954.
♦Edinburgh 31 – ♦Dundee 23 – Stirling 35.

🏨 Balgeddie House 🔇, Leslie Rd, KY6 3ET, W : 2 m. by A 911 ☎ 742511, ⩽, 🌳 – [TV] 🛁wc ☏ [P]. [A] [AE] VISA. 🚫🐕
closed 1 and 2 January – **18 rm**.

🏨 Stakis Albany (Stakis), North St., KY7 5NA, ☎ 752292 – ⇅ [TV] 🛁wc 🚿wc ☏ [P]. ⛹
29 rm.

🏨 **Forum,** 3 North St., KY7 5NA, ☎ 755340 – 🚿wc ☏. [A] [AE] [D] VISA. 🚫🐕
closed 25 December and 1 January – **M** *(closed Sunday lunch)* (bar lunch) 9.90 **t.** 🍷 3.50 – ☕ 2.50 – **11 rm** 16.00/28.00 **t.**

VW, AUDI North St. ☎ 752262

GLENSHEE Perth. (Tayside) [401] J 13 – see Spittal of Glenshee.

GOLSPIE Sutherland (Highland) [401] I 10 – pop. 1,374 – ECD : Wednesday – ✉ ⊛ 040 83.
⛳18 ☎ 3266.
♦Edinburgh 228 – ♦Inverness 72 – ♦Wick 54.

🏨 **Golf Links,** Church St., KW10 6TT, ☎ 3408, ⩽, 🌳 – 🛁wc [P]. [A] [AE] [D] VISA
M (bar lunch) 8.00 **st.** 🍷 2.75 – **9 rm** ☕ 13.50/33.00 **st.**

AUSTIN-ROVER Station Rd ☎ 3205
RENAULT Old Bank Rd ☎ 3411

GOUROCK Renfrew. (Strathclyde) 401 F 16 – pop. 10,922 – ECD : Wednesday – ✆ 0475.

🚢 by Caledonian MacBrayne : from Railway Pier to Dunoon Pier frequent services daily (20 mn) – by Western Ferries : from McInroy's Point to Hunters Quay, Dunoon frequent services daily (20 mn).

🚢 by Caledonian MacBrayne : to Kilcreggan Monday/Saturday 4-8 daily (10 mn) – to Helensburgh summer only Monday/Saturday 4-5 daily (40 mn).

🛈 Information Centre, Municipal Buildings ✆ 31126.

◆Edinburgh 69 – ◆Ayr 43 – ◆Glasgow 26.

🏨 **Stakis Gantock** (Stakis), Cloch Rd, PA15 1AR, SW : 2 m. on A 78 ✆ 34671, ≤ Firth of Clyde – 📺 ⌂wc 🅿 🖻 🛦 📶 AE ① VISA
M 4.50/8.50 t. ₫ 2.80 – **63 rm** ⌸ 36.00/50.00 t.

🏠 **Claremont,** 34 Victoria Rd, PA19 1DF, ✆ 31687, ≤ Firth of Clyde – 📺 🅿
6 rm ⌸ 9.00/18.00.

CITROEN Manor Crescent ✆ 32356

GRAEMSAY (Isle of) Orkney (Orkney Islands) 401 K 7 – Shipping Services : see Orkney Islands.

GRANTOWN-ON-SPEY Moray. (Highland) 401 J 12 – pop. 1,600 – ECD : Thursday – ✆ 0479.

Envir. : Tomintoul (site★) SE : 13 ½ m.

🏌 ✆ 2079, East town boundary.

🛈 54 High St. ✆ 2773 (summer only).

◆Edinburgh 142 – ◆Inverness 35 – Perth 100.

🏨 **Garth,** Castle Rd, PH26 3HN, ✆ 2836, 🌴 – ⌂wc 🚿wc 🅿 ① VISA
M (bar lunch) 10.00 t. ₫ 2.75 – **18 rm** ⌸ 12.50/39.00 t.

🏠 **Dunachton,** Coppice Close, off Grant Rd, PH26 3LD, ✆ 2098, 🌴 – 🅿
7 rm ⌸ 6.90/14.50 st.

AUSTIN-ROVER Chapel Rd ✆ 2037   FORD Woodland Service Centre ✆ 2289

GREAT CUMBRAE ISLAND Bute (Strathclyde) 401 402 F 16 – pop. 56 – ✆ 047 553 Millport.

🏌 at Millport ✆ 311.

🚢 by Caledonian MacBrayne : from Cumbrae Slip to Largs frequent services every day (10 mn).

🚢 by Caledonian MacBrayne : from Millport to Largs summer only 3-6 daily (30 mn).

GREENLAW Berwick. (Borders) 401 402 M 16 – pop. 601 – ✆ 089 084 Leitholm.

◆ Edinburgh 39 – ◆ Newcastle-upon-Tyne 70.

🏨 **Purves Hall** 🦢, TD10 6UJ, SE : 4 m. by A 697 ✆ 558, 🏊 heated, 🌴, park, 🎾 – ⌂wc 🚿wc
🅿
closed February – **M** 5.50/10.50 t. ₫ 2.75 – **7 rm** ⌸ 22.00/40.00 t. – SB 46.00/55.00 st.

GREENOCK Renfrew. (Strathclyde) 401 F 16 – pop. 69,502 – ECD : Wednesday – ✆ 0475.

🏌 Whinhill, Beith Rd ✆ 24694, S : 2 m.

🛈 Municipal Buildings ✆ 24400.

◆Edinburgh 70 – ◆Ayr 52 – ◆Glasgow 24 – ◆Oban 98.

🏨 **Tontine** (Best Western), 6 Ardgowan Sq., PA16 8NG, ✆ 23316, Telex 779801 – 📺 ⌂wc 🖻
🅿 🛦 📶 AE ① VISA
closed 25-26 December and 1-3 January – **M** a la carte 10.00/17.50 st. – ⌸ 3.50 – **32 rm**
25.00/38.00 st. – SB (weekends only) 38.00 st.

NISSAN, PEUGEOT-TALBOT 1 Campbell St. ✆ 24355   VOLVO 46 Campbell St. ✆ 21610 and 23107
VAUXHALL-OPEL Port Glasgow Rd ✆ 42511   VW, AUDI 60 East Hamilton St. ✆ 83535

GRETNA Dumfries. (Dumfries and Galloway) 401 K 19 – pop. 2809 (inc. Springfield) – ECD : Wednesday – ✆ 046 13.

🛈 Annan Rd ✆ 834 (summer only).

◆Edinburgh 91 – ◆Carlisle 10 – ◆Dumfries 24.

🏨 **Gretna Chase,** CA6 5JB, S : ¼ m. on B 721 ✉ Carlisle (Cumbria) ✆ 517, 🌴 – 🚿wc 🅿 🛦
AE ① VISA ✀
M a la carte 6.90/10.00 t. ₫ 1.80 – **9 rm** ⌸ 18.00/40.00 t.

GRUINARD BAY ★★★ Ross and Cromarty (Highland) 401 D 10.

Pour les 🏨🏨🏨 , 🏨🏨 , 🏨 , nous ne donnons pas
le détail de l'installation,
ces hôtels possédant, en général, tout le confort.

⌂wc 🚿wc

🖻

GULLANE E. Lothian (Lothian) 🗺️**401** L 15 – pop. 1,701 – ECD : Wednesday – ✆ 0620.
Envir. : Dirleton : Castle★ (gardens★) *AC*, NE : 2 m – ⏸️, ⏸️, ⏸️ ✆ 843115.
♦Edinburgh 19 – North Berwick 5.

🏛️   **Greywalls** ⚲, Muirfield,Duncar Rd, EH31 2EG, ✆ 842144, ≤ gardens and golf course,
« Edwardian country house with fine walled gardens », ✗ – 🚪wc 🕾 🅿. ☒ 🆎 ⑩ 𝘝𝘐𝘚𝘈
April-December – **M** 9.50/17.50 t. ₰ 3.75 – **22 rm** ⊐ 36.00/72.00 t.

✗   **La Potinière,** Main St., EH31 2AA, ✆ 843214 – 🅿
closed Wednesday and Saturday lunch, 1 week June and October – **M** (lunch only and
Saturday dinner) (booking essential) 10.00/14.00 t. ₰ 2.80.

   at Dirleton NE : 2 m. by A 198 – ✉ ✆ 062 085 Dirleton :

🏛️   **Open Arms** (Best Western), EH39 5EG, ✆ 241, 🛋 – 📺 🚪wc 🕾 🅿. ☒ 🆎 ⑩ 𝘝𝘐𝘚𝘈
M (restricted lunch) 12.50 t. ₰ 3.50 – **7 rm** ⊐ 37.50/50.00 t. – SB (except summer) 51.00 st.

HADDINGTON E. Lothian (Lothian) 🗺️**401** L 16 – pop. 6,502 – ECD : Thursday – ✆ 062 082.
⏸️ Amisfield Park, ✆ 3627.
♦ Edinburgh 17 – Hawick 53 – ♦ Newcastle-upon-Tyne 103.

✗✗   **Brown's** with rm, 1 West Rd, EH41 3RD, ✆ 2254 – 📺 🚪wc 🅿
M (dinner only) (booking essential) 13.50 st. ₰ 2.45 – **6 rm** ⊐ 16.50/38.00 st.

HARRIS (Isle of) Inverness. (Outer Hebrides) (Western Isles) 🗺️**401** Z 10 – pop. 2,879.
🛳️ by Caledonian MacBrayne : from Kyles Scalpay to the Isle of Scalpay : Monday/Saturday 5-10
daily (restricted in winter) (10 mn) – from Tarbert to Uig (Isle of Skye) Monday/Saturday 6 weekly
(2 h - 2 h 30 mn) – from Tarbert to Lochmaddy (Isle of Uist) Monday/Saturday 3-6 weekly (2 h
direct - 5 h 30 mn via Uig).

   Scarista – ✉ ✆ 085 985 Scarista.

🏛️   **Scarista House** ⚲, PA85 3HX, ✆ 238, ≤ beach and mountains, 🛋 – 🚪wc 🅿
Easter-mid October – **M** (closed lunch and Sunday to non-residents) (buffet lunch) (booking
essential) 14.00 t. ₰ 2.50 – **7 rm** ⊐ 27.50/45.00 t.

   Tarbert – pop. 479 – ECD : Thursday – ✉ ✆ 0859 Harris.
See : Site★ – **Envir. :** Loch Seaforth★ NE : 6 m.
Exc. : Golden Road★ from Tarbert to Rodel – Rodel (site★) S : 21 ½ m.
🛈 ✆ 2011 (summer only).

🏛️   **Harris,** PA85 3DJ, ✆ 2154, ≤, ⚲, 🛋 – 🚪wc 🅿
April-October – **M** 5.70/8.20 st. ₰ 2.45 – **25 rm** ⊐ 14.50/31.50 st.

HAWICK Roxburgh. (Borders) 🗺️**401** **402** L 17 – pop. 16,286 – ECD : Tuesday – ✆ 0450.
Envir. : Jedburgh Abbey★★ *AC*, NE : 10 ½ m. – Hermitage (castle★ : Stronghold 14C) *AC*, S : 15 m.
⏸️ Vertish Hill ✆ 2293, S : 1 ½ m – 🅱 Common Haugh, Car Park ✆ 2547 (summer only).
♦Edinburgh 51 – ♦Ayr 122 – ♦Carlisle 44 – ♦Dumfries 63 – Motherwell 76 – ♦Newcastle-upon-Tyne 62.

🏛️   **Mansfield House,** Weensland Rd, TD9 9EL, NE : 1 m. on A 698 ✆ 73988, 🛋, park – 📺
🚪wc 🅿. ☒ 🆎 ⑩ 𝘝𝘐𝘚𝘈
closed January and February – **M** (closed Sunday lunch) a la carte 6.35/10.90 ₰ 2.75 – ⊐ 2.75
– **10 rm** 18.50/27.00 t.

🏛️   **Kirklands,** West Stewart Pl., TD9 8BH, ✆ 72263 – 📺 🚪wc 🕿 🅿
closed 1 week at Christmas – **M** (closed Sunday to non-residents) a la carte 8.20/11.50 t. ₰ 2.75
– **6 rm** ⊐ 19.50/35.00 t. – SB (except summer) 36.00/38.00 st.

FORD Earl St. ✆ 73316
NISSAN Weensland ✆ 72256
PEUGEOT, TALBOT 61 High St. ✆ 72287

VAUXHALL-OPEL Bridge St. ✆ 72179
VW, AUDI Commercial Rd ✆ 73211

HEITON Roxburgh (Borders) – see Kelso.

HELENSBURGH Dunbarton. (Strathclyde) 🗺️**401** F 15 – pop. 12,870 – ECD : Wednesday – ✆ 0436.
🛳️ to Gourock summer only Monday/Saturday 4-5 daily (40 mn).
🅱 Pier Head Car Park, ✆ 2642 (summer only).
♦Edinburgh 65 – ♦Glasgow 22.

🏛️   **Commodore** (Osprey), 112 West Clyde St., G84 8ER, ✆ 6924, ≤ – 🛌 📺 🚪wc 🕿 🅿. 🏊
   ☒ 🆎 ⑩ 𝘝𝘐𝘚𝘈
M 5.00/8.00 t. – **45 rm** ⊐ 29.00/40.00 t. – SB 42.00/60.00 st.

   at Rhu NW : 2 m. on A 814 – ✉ ✆ 0436 Rhu :

🏛️   **Rosslea Hall** ⚲, Ferry Rd, G84 8NF, ✆ 820684, ≤, 🛋 – 📺 🚪wc 🚪wc 🕿 🅿. 🏊 ☒ 🆎
   ⑩ 𝘝𝘐𝘚𝘈
M 5.75/10.50 st. ₰ 2.50 – **16 rm** ⊐ 31.00/45.00 st. – SB (weekends only) 28.00 st.

AUSTIN-ROVER 135 East Clyde St. ✆ 3344
RENAULT 103 East Clyde St. ✆ 6021
TOYOTA 5/7 John St. ✆ 2779

VW, AUDI Waterside Rd, Kirkintilloch ✆ 041 (Glasgow) 776 7771
VW, AUDI 15/27 East Clyde St. ✆ 2233

HILLSWICK Shetland (Shetland Islands) **401** P 2 – see Shetland Islands (Mainland).

HOLLYBUSH Ayr. (Strathclyde) **401 402** G 17 – see Ayr.

HOWGATE Midlothian (Lothian) **401 402** K 16 – ⊠ ✆ 0968 Penicuik.
♦Edinburgh 11 – Peebles 11.

    ✗ **Old Howgate Inn,** 7 Wester Howgate, EH26 8QB, ☎ 74244, Smörrebrod – **℗**. △ ⒶⒺ 𝗩𝗜𝗦𝗔
    closed Sunday dinner, Christmas Day and 1-2 January – **M** a la carte 6.25/11.30 **t.** ⌖ 3.50.

HOY (Isle of) Orkney (Orkney Islands) **401** K 7 – see Orkney Islands.

INCHNADAMPH Sutherland. (Highland) **401** F 9 – ⊠ Lairg – ✆ 057 12 Assynt.
See : ≤★.
♦Edinburgh 244 – ♦Inverness 85.

    🏠 **Inchnadamph** ॐ, IV27 4HL, ☎ 202, ≤ Loch Assynt and mountains, ॐ – ⌂wc **℗**. △ ⓞ
    𝗩𝗜𝗦𝗔
    Mid March-October – **M** 4.50/6.50 **t.** – **28 rm** ⊆ 15.25/32.50 **st.**

INNERLEITHEN Peebles. (Borders) **401 402** K 17 – ✆ 0896.
⌖₉·
♦Edinburgh 30 – Galashiels 12 – ♦Glasgow 59 – Hawick 25.

    ↟ **Tighnuilt House,** Peebles Rd, EH44 6RD, W : ½ m. on A 72 ☎ 830491, ≤, ॐ – **℗**. ✗
    6 rm ⊆ 10.50/15.00.

INVERGARRY Inverness. (Highland) **401** F 12 – pop. 178 – ✆ 080 93.
Envir. : Loch Garry (⁂★★ from the A 87) W : 3 m.
♦Edinburgh 148 – ♦Inverness 41 – Kyle of Lochalsh 51 – ♦Oban 73.

    🏠 **Inn on the Garry,** PH35 4HJ, on A 87 ☎ 206, ☀ – ⌂wc **℗**
    April-October – **M** (bar lunch) 10.00 **st.** ⌖ 3.00 – **10 rm** ⊆ 17.00/40.00 **st.**

INVERGOWRIE Perth. (Tayside) **401** K 14 – see Dundee.

INVERMORISTON Inverness. (Highland) **401** G 12 – pop. 114 – ✆ 0320 Glenmoriston.
See : Loch Ness★★.
♦Edinburgh 162 – ♦Inverness 27 – Kyle of Lochalsh 55.

    🏠 **Glenmoriston Arms,** IV3 6YA, ☎ 51206, ॐ – ⌂wc **℗**. △ ⒶⒺ ⓞ 𝗩𝗜𝗦𝗔
    April-mid November – **M** (bar lunch) a la carte 7.70/15.00 **t.** ⌖2.60 – ⊆ 3.00 – **8 rm**
    25.00/37.00 **t.**

INVERNESS Inverness. (Highland) **401** H 11 – pop. 34,839 – ECD : Wednesday – ✆ 0463.
See : Tomnahurich cemetery★ – ≤★ from the Castle Terrace.
Envir. : Culloden Battlefield, site of the defeat (1746) of Bonnie Prince Charlie, E : 5 m. by Culcabock
Rd.
⌖ˢ ☎ 33422, S : 1 m. by Culcabock Rd.
✈ Dalcross Airport : ☎ 32471, NE : 8 m. by A 96.
🚗 ☎ 232471.
🖪 23 Church St. ☎ 34353.
♦Edinburgh 156 – ♦Aberdeen 107 – ♦Dundee 134.

Plan on next page

    🏨 **Kingsmills** (Best Western), Culcabock Rd, IV2 3LP, ☎ 237166, Telex 75566, ☀ – 📺 ☎ **℗**.
    △ ⒶⒺ ⓞ 𝗩𝗜𝗦𝗔   **s**
    M 7.00/9.95 **t.** ⌖ 2.90 – **60 rm** ⊆ 35.75/64.00 **t.** – SB (weekends only) 51.00/67.00 **st.**

    🏨 **Station,** Academy St., IV1 1LG, ☎ 231926, Telex 75275 – 📲 📺 ⌂wc 🚿wc ☎. △. △ ⒶⒺ ⓞ
    𝗩𝗜𝗦𝗔   **a**
    closed Christmas and New Year – **M** (buffet lunch) 9.75 **st.** ⌖ 3.50 – **64 rm** ⊆ 23.50/58.00 **st.**

    🏨 **Ladbroke** (Ladbroke), Nairn Rd, IV2 3TR, E : by A 96 at junction A 9 and A 96 ☎ 239666,
    Telex 75377 – 📲 📺 ⌂wc ☀ **℗**. △. △ ⒶⒺ ⓞ 𝗩𝗜𝗦𝗔
    M (buffet lunch) 9.50 **t.** ⌖ 4.45 – ⊆ 5.00 – **108 rm** 29.00/47.00 **t.** – SB 47.00/59.00 **st.**

    🏨 **Craigmonie,** 9 Annfield Rd, IV2 3HX, ☎ 231649 – 📲 📺 ⌂wc ☎ **℗**. △. △ ⒶⒺ ⓞ 𝗩𝗜𝗦𝗔   **e**
    M 6.50/9.00 **t.** ⌖ 3.25 – **30 rm** ⊆ 25.50/44.00 **t.** – SB (weekends only) 46.00 **st.**

    🏠 **Glen Mhor,** 9-10 Ness Bank, IV2 4SG, ☎ 234308 – 📺 ⌂wc 🚿wc ☎ **℗**. △ ⒶⒺ ⓞ 𝗩𝗜𝗦𝗔   **i**
    closed 31 December-4 January – **M** 6.70/15.20 **t.** ⌖ 3.00 – **22 rm** ⊆ 16.50/60.00 **t.**

    🏠 **Glenmoriston,** 20 Ness Bank, IV3 6YB, ☎ 223777, ☀ – 📺 ⌂wc 🚿wc **℗**. △ 𝗩𝗜𝗦𝗔. ✗   **x**
    M 6.50/14.00 **t.** – **21 rm** ⊆ 16.00/36.00 **t.**

    ↟ **Felstead,** 18 Ness Bank, IV2 4SF, ☎ 231634 – **℗**   **u**
    May-September – **7 rm** ⊆ 9.00/18.00 **st.**

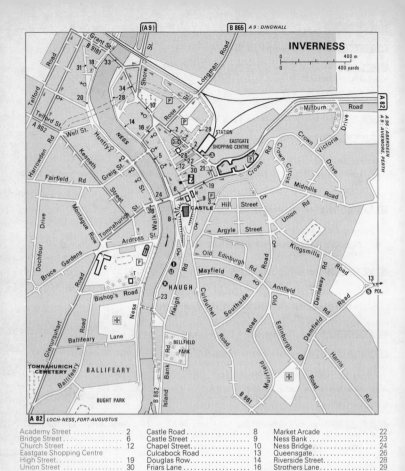

INVERSCESS

at Culloden Moor E : 3 m. by A 96 – ⊠ ✆ 0463 Inverness :

Culloden House ⟫, IV1 2NZ, ✆ 790461, Telex 75402, ≤, ☞, park – 📺 🅿. 🔼 🗚 ① 𝗩𝗜𝗦𝗔. ⬥
M approx. 20.50 t. ↥ 3.50 – **20 rm** ⊊ 54.00/109.00 t.

at Dunain Park SW : 2 ½ m. on A 82 – ⊠ ✆ 0463 Inverness :

Dunain Park ⟫, IV3 6JN, ✆ 230512, ≤, « Country house and gardens », park – ⌂wc 🅿
April–mid October – **M** (bar lunch) 17.00 t. ↥ 3.80 – **8 rm** ⊊ 66.00 t.

AUSTIN-ROVER-DAIMLER-JAGUAR-LAND ROVER-
RANGE ROVER, ROLLS ROYCE Harbour Rd ✆
220011
BMW Harbour Rd ✆ 236566
FIAT, LANCIA 8 Tomnahurich St. ✆ 235777
FORD Harbour Rd ✆ 238001
LADA Harbour Rd ✆ 222841

MAZDA Harbour Rd ✆ 230777
PEUGEOT, TALBOT Harbour Rd ✆ 231536
RENAULT 16 Telford St. ✆ 222848
VAUXHALL-OPEL 112 Academy St. ✆ 234311
VOLVO Harbour Rd ✆ 230885
VW, AUDI Harbour Rd ✆ 231313

IONA (Isle of) Argyll. (Strathclyde) 👪👪👪 A 15 – ✆ 068 17.

See : Site★ – MacLean's Cross★ – St. John's Cross★.

⛴ by Caledonian MacBrayne : to Fionnphort (Isle of Mull) frequent services daily in summer,
restricted service in winter (5 mn).

IRVINE Ayr (Strathclyde) 401 402 F 17 – ✪ 0294.

♦Edinburgh 75 – Ayr 14 – ♦Glasgow 29.

🏨 Skean Dhu (Mt. Charlotte), Roseholm, Annick Water, E : ¾ m. on A 71 ℰ 74272, Telex 777097, 🔲 – 🗐 📺 ☎ ৬ 🅿. 🏊 – **128 rm**.

ISLAY (Isle of) Argyll. (Strathclyde) 401 B 16 – pop. 3,837.

See : Machir Bay★.

🗻 Port Ellen ℰ 0496 (Port Ellen) 2310.

✈ Glenegedale Airport : ℰ 0496 (Port Ellen) 2361.

🚢 by Western Ferries : from Port Askaig to Feolin (Isle of Jura) Monday/Saturday 8-10 daily ; Sunday 2-4 daily (5 mn) – by Caledonian MacBrayne : from Port Ellen to Kennacraig (Kintyre Peninsula) 1-2 daily (2 h) – from Port Askaig to Kennacraig (Kintyre Peninsula) Monday/Saturday 1 daily (1 h 45 mn).

🛈 at Bowmore ℰ 049 681 (Bowmore) 254 (summer only).

Bowmore – ⊠ ✪ 049 681 Bowmore.

♨ **Lochside**, Shore St., PA43 7LB, ℰ 244, ≤, ⌇ – 📺 🗖wc ☜. 🔃 🖭 𝘝𝘐𝘚𝘈
M 6.00/9.00 **st.** ⓘ 2.75 – **7 rm** ⊆ 19.00/42.00 **st.**

Port Askaig – ECD : Tuesday – ⊠ ✪ 049 684 Port Askaig.

🏠 **Port Askaig**, PA46 7RD, ℰ 245, ≤ Sound of Islay and Jura, ⍟ – 🗖wc 🗐wc 🅿. ✵
M (bar lunch) 9.00 **st.** ⓘ 3.95 – ⊆ 4.00 – **9 rm** 14.50/50.00 **st.** – SB (summer only) 46.00/52.00 **st.**

ISLEORNSAY Inverness. (Highland) 401 C 12 – see Skye (Isle of).

JOHN O'GROATS Caithness. (Highland) 401 K 8 – Shipping Services : see Orkney Islands.

JURA (Isle of) Argyll. (Strathclyde) 401 C 15 – pop. 349.

🚢 by Western Ferries : from Feolin to Port Askaig (Isle of Islay) Monday/Saturday 8-10 daily ; Sunday 2-4 daily (5 mn).

Craighouse – ECD : Tuesday – ⊠ ✪ 049 682 Jura.

🏠 **Jura** ⌇, PA60 7XU, ℰ 243, ≤ Small Isles Bay, ⌇, ⍟ – 🗖wc 🅿. 🔃 🖭 ⓞ 𝘝𝘐𝘚𝘈
M (bar lunch) 8.50 **st.** ⓘ 2.50 – **18 rm** ⊆ 16.50/36.00 **st.**

KELSO Roxburgh. (Borders) 401 402 M 17 – pop. 4,852 – ECD : Wednesday – ✪ 0573.

🗻 ℰ 23009.

🛈 66 Woodmarket ℰ 23464 (Easter and May-September).

♦Edinburgh 44 – Hawick 22 – ♦Newcastle-upon-Tyne 67.

🏨 **Cross Keys**, 36-37 The Square, TD5 7HL, ℰ 23303 – 🕅 📺 🗖wc 🗐wc ☎ ৬ 🅿. 🏊 🔃 🖭 ⓞ 𝘝𝘐𝘚𝘈
M (bar lunch) 11.00 **st.** ⓘ 2.50 – **26 rm** ⊆ 16.00/34.00 **st.** – SB 44.00/50.00 **st.**

🏨 **Ednam House**, Bridge St., TD5 7HT, ℰ 24168, ≤, ⍟ – 🗖wc 🗐wc ☜ 🅿. 🏊
32 rm.

at Heiton SW : 3 m. by A 698 – ⊠ Kelso – ✪ 057 35 Roxburgh :

🏨 **Sunlaws House** ⌇, TD5 8JZ, ℰ 331, ≤, « Victorian country house », ⌇, ⍟, park, ✵ –
📺 🗖wc 🅿. 🏊 🔃 🖭 ⓞ 𝘝𝘐𝘚𝘈
M a la carte 8.55/13.35 **t.** ⓘ 3.30 – **14 rm** ⊆ 40.00/60.00 **st.** – SB (winter only) 60.00/66.00 **st.**

AUSTIN-ROVER-JAGUAR Bridge St. ℰ 24345   TALBOT Sheddon Par. Rd ℰ 24488
RENAULT Golf Course Rd ℰ 24720

KENMORE Perth. (Tayside) 401 I 14 – pop. 211 – ECD : Thursday except summer – ⊠ Aberfeldy – ✪ 088 73.

🗻 Taymouth Castle ℰ 228.

♦Edinburgh 80 – ♦Dundee 60 – ♦Oban 71 – Perth 38.

🏨 **Kenmore**, PH15 2NU, ℰ 205, 🗻, ⌇, ⍟ – 🕅 🗖wc 🅿. 🔃 🖭 𝘝𝘐𝘚𝘈 ✵
M (bar lunch) 10.50 **t.** ⓘ 3.25 – **38 rm** ⊆ 19.00/50.00 **t.** – SB 54.00/66.00 **st.**

at Fortingall NW : 6 m. by A 827 – ⊠ Aberfeldy – ✪ 088 73 Kenmore :

🏠 Fortingall ⌇, PH15 2NQ, ℰ 367, ≤, ⌇, ⍟ – 🅿
17 rm.

KENNACRAIG Argyll. (Strathclyde) 401 D 16 – Shipping Services : see Kintyre (Peninsula).

KENSALEYRE Inverness. (Highland) 401 B 11 – see Skye (Isle of).

KENTALLEN Argyll. (Highland) **401** E 14 – ⊠ Kentallen – ☎ 063 174 Duror.
♦Edinburgh 123 – Fort William 32 – ♦Oban 30.

🏛 **Ardsheal House** 🐾, PA38 4BX, SW : ¾ m. by A 828 ℰ 227, ≤, « Country house in lochside setting », ☞, park, ✖ – ⇔wc ▥wc Ⓟ
April-October – **M** 9.00/17.50 st. – **12 rm** ⚏ 30.00/64.00 st.

✕ **Holly Tree,** Kentallen Pier, PA38 4BY, ℰ 292, ≤ Loch Linnhe and mountains – Ⓟ. ◳ ◷
VISA
closed Monday, Tuesday, 6 to 30 January and 17 November-19 December – **M** *(closed lunch Thursday to Saturday during February and March and Wednesday except summer)* a la carte 9.20/12.05 t.

KILCHOAN Argyll. (Highland) **401** B 13 – pop. 349 – ⊠ Acharacle – ☎ 097 23.
⛴ by Caledonian MacBrayne : to Tobermory (Isle of Mull) summer only Monday/Saturday 4-5 daily (35 mn).
♦Edinburgh 163 – ♦Inverness 114 – ♦Oban 80.

KILCHRENAN Argyll. (Strathclyde) **401** E 14 – pop. 109 – ⊠ Taynuilt – ☎ 086 63.
See : Loch Awe★.
♦Edinburgh 116 – ♦Glasgow 88 – ♦Oban 19.

🏛 **Ardanaiseig** 🐾, NE : 4 m. by B 845 ℰ 333, ≤ gardens and Loch Awe, « Country house in extensive informal gardens on Loch Awe », ☜, park, ✖ – ▥ ☎ Ⓟ. ◳ ◷ **VISA**
Easter-October – **M** 7.70/20.00 t. ⓝ 3.10 – **14 rm** ⚏ (dinner included) 58.00/126.00 st.

🏛 **Taychreggan** 🐾, Lochaweside, PA35 1HQ, SE : 1 ¼ m. ℰ 211, ≤ Loch Awe, « Lochside setting », ☜, ☞, park – ⇔wc Ⓟ. ◳ ◭ ◷ **VISA**
Easter-mid October – **M** (buffet lunch) 11.00 t. ⓝ 3.00 – **17 rm** ⚏ 20.00/60.00 t.

KILCREGGAN Dunbarton. (Strathclyde) **401** F 16 – Shipping Services : see Gourock.

KILDRUMMY Aberdeen. (Grampian) **401** L 12 – pop. 175 – ⊠ Alford – ☎ 033 65.
Envir. : Kildrummy Castle gardens ★ *AC*, SW : 2 m.
♦Edinburgh 136 – ♦Aberdeen 35.

🏛 **Kildrummy Castle** (Best Western) 🐾, AB3 8RA, S : 1 ¼ m. on A 97 ℰ 288, ≤ gardens and Kildrummy Castle, « 19C mansion in extensive park », ☜ – ▥ ⇔wc ☎ Ⓟ. ◳ ◭ ◷ **VISA**
closed January and February – **M** 7.50/12.00 t. ⓝ 2.75 – **15 rm** ⚏ 19.50/52.00 t. – SB (except summer) 48.00/58.00 st.

KILLIECRANKIE Perth. (Tayside) **401** I 13 – see Pitlochry.

KILLIN Perth. (Central) **401** H 14 – pop. 600 – ECD : Wednesday – ☎ 056 72.
Envir. : N : Glen Lyon★.
🛆 ℰ 312.
🛈 Main St. ℰ 254 (summer only).
♦Edinburgh 72 – ♦Dundee 65 – Perth 43 – ♦Oban 54.

🏛 **Bridge of Lochay,** FK21 8TS, N : ½ m. on A 827 ℰ 272 – ⇔wc ▥wc Ⓟ
closed January – **M** 4.95/7.75 t. ⓝ 2.55 – **17 rm** ⚏ 12.25/29.50 t.

⌂ **Dall Lodge,** FK21 8TN, N : ¼ m. on A 827 ℰ 217, ☜ – ⇔wc Ⓟ
April-October – **9 rm** ⚏ 9.60/25.00 t.

at Ardeonaig NE : 7 ¼ m. – ⊠ ☎ 056 72 Killin :

🏛 **Ardeonaig** 🐾, South Loch Tayside, FK21 2IV, ℰ 400, Telex 76163, ☜, ☞, park – ⇔wc ▥wc Ⓟ. ✖
April-October – **M** (bar lunch) 12.75 st. ⓝ 3.40 – **14 rm** ⚏ 17.50/38.00 st.

AUSTIN-ROVER The Garage, Main St. ℰ 319

KILMARNOCK Ayr. (Strathclyde) **401 402** G 17 – pop. 48,787 – ECD : Wednesday – ☎ 0563.
🛇 Annanhill, Irvine Rd ℰ 21644, W : 1 m. – 🛇 Caprington, Ayr Rd ℰ 21915.
♦Edinburgh 64 – ♦Ayr 14 – ♦Dumfries 58 – ♦Glasgow 21.

🏛 **Howard Park** (Swallow), 136 Glasgow Rd, KA3 1UT, N : 2 m. on B 7038 ℰ 31211 – 🕍 ▥
⇔wc ⓝ Ⓟ. ◮ ◳ ◭ ◷ **VISA**
closed 25-26 December and 1-2 January – **M** (bar lunch Saturday and Sunday) 6.00/8.50 st.
ⓝ 2.25 – **45 rm** ⚏ 31.50/42.50 st. – SB 36.00 st.

KILNINVER Argyll. (Strathclyde) **401** D 14 – see Oban.

KILWINNING Ayr. (Strathclyde) **401 402** F 17 – pop. 11,000 – ☎ 0294.
♦Edinburgh 77 – ♦Ayr 16 – ♦Glasgow 30.

🏛 **Montgreenan Mansion House** 🐾, Montgreenan Estate, KA13 7QL, NE : 3 m. by B 785 ℰ
57733, ≤, ☞, park, ✖ – ▥ ☎ Ⓟ. ◳ ◭ ◷ **VISA**. ✖
M 7.50/12.50 t. ⓝ 3.00 – **11 rm** ⚏ 25.00/75.00 t. – SB (weekends only) (October-April) 75.00 st.

KINCLAVEN Perth. (Tayside) [401] J 14 – pop. 560 – ✉ Stanley – ☎ 025 083 Meikleour.

♦Edinburgh 54 – Perth 12.

🏨 **Ballathie House** 🐦, PH1 4QN, ✆ 268, ≤, « Country house in extensive grounds on banks of river Tay », 🎣, 🌳, park, 🎾 – [TV] 🛁wc ☎ [P]. [BC] [AE] [DC]. 🐕
M (bar lunch Monday to Saturday) 6.75/12.00 **t.** – **33 rm** 🛏 20.00/68.00 **t.**

KINCRAIG Inverness. (Highland) [401] I 12 – pop. 106 – ECD : Wednesday – ✉ Kingussie – ☎ 054 04.

♦Edinburgh 121 – ♦Inverness 38 – Perth 79.

🏨 **Ossian,** PH21 1NA, by A 9 ✆ 242, ≤, 🎣, 🌳 – [P]. [DC] [VISA]
closed November and January – **M** (dinner only) 9.00 **st.** 🍷 3.00 – **6 rm** 🛏 14.00/28.00 **st.**

KINGUSSIE Inverness. (Highland) [401] H 12 – pop. 1,104 – ECD : Wednesday – ☎ 054 02.

⛳18 ✆ 374, ½ m. from town shops off A 9.

[i] Caledonia Buildings, King St. ✆ 297 (June-September).

♦Edinburgh 115 – ♦Inverness 44 – Perth 73.

🏨 **Osprey,** Ruthven Rd, PH21 1EN, ✆ 510 – [BC] [AE] [DC] [VISA]
closed November and December – **M** (dinner only) 9.00 **st.** 🍷 2.75 – **9 rm** 🛏 10.00/24.00 **st.**

🏠 **Columba House,** Manse Rd, PH21 1JF, ✆ 402, 🌳 – 🚿wc [P]
closed 1 November-27 December – **7 rm** 🛏 10.50/23.00 **t.**

🍴 **The Cross,** 25-27 High St., PH21 1HX, ✆ 762
closed Monday and Tuesday in winter – **M** *(dinner only)* 12.50 **t.** 🍷 1.75.

KINLOCHBERVIE Sutherland (Highland) [401] E 8 – pop. 450 – ECD : Wednesday – ☎ 097 182.

See : Site★.

♦Edinburgh 282 – Thurso 101 – Ullapool 64.

🏨 **Kinlochbervie** 🐦, IV27 4RP, ✆ 275, ≤ Loch Inchard and sea – [TV] 🛁wc [P]. [BC] [AE] [DC] [VISA]
M (bar lunch) (booking essential in winter) 14.95 **st.** 🍷 3.00 – **10 rm** 🛏 30.00/60.00 **st.** – SB 79.00/89.00 **st.**

KINLOCHEWE Ross and Cromarty (Highland) [401] E 11 – ✉ Achnasheen – ☎ 044 584.

♦Edinburgh 207 – ♦Inverness 52.

🏨 Kinlochewe, IV22 2PA, ✆ 253, ≤, 🎣, 🌳 – [P]. [BC] [VISA]
April-mid November – **10 rm** 🛏 16.00/33.00 **t.**

KINLOCH RANNOCH Perth. (Tayside) [401] H 13 – pop. 241 – ECD : Wednesday except summer – ☎ 088 22.

See : Loch★★.

♦Edinburgh 88 – ♦Inverness 92 – Perth 46.

KINROSS Kinross. (Tayside) [401] J 15 – pop. 2,418 – ECD : Thursday – ☎ 0577.

See : Loch Leven★.

⛳18 Green Hotel, Beeches Park ✆ 63467 – ⛳9 Bishopshire, Kinnesswood, E : 3 m. – ⛳9 Milnathort, N : 2 m.

[i] Turfhills (off Junction 6, M 90) ✆ 63680.

♦Edinburgh 25 – Dunfermline 12 – Perth 17 – Stirling 23.

🏨 **Green** (Best Western), 2 The Muirs, KY13 7AS, ✆ 63467, Telex 76684, « Gardens », 🏊, ⛳18, 🎣 – [TV] 🛁wc ☎ [P]. 🎪. [BC] [AE] [DC] [VISA]
M 7.00/11.00 **t.** 🍷 3.50 – **46 rm** 🛏 30.00/45.00 **t.** – SB 63.00/70.00 **st.**

🏨 Croft Bank, Station Rd, KY13 7TG, ✆ 63819 – [TV] 🛁wc 🚿wc [P] – **7 rm**.

🍴🍴 **Windlestrae** with rm, The Muirs, KY13 7AS, ✆ 63217, Telex 76168, 🌳 – [TV] 🛁wc ☎ [P]. [BC] [AE] [DC] [VISA]. 🐕
M a la carte 8.20/16.10 **t.** 🍷 2.20 – **4 rm** 🛏 26.00/38.00 **t.**

at Cleish SW : 4 ½ m. by B 996 and B 9097 – ✉ Kinross – ☎ 057 75 Cleish Hills :

🍴🍴 **Nivingston House** 🐦 with rm, KY13 7LS, ✆ 216, ≤, 🌳 – [P]. [BC] [AE] [DC] [VISA]
closed January – **M** 9.50/13.50 **t.** 🍷 3.50 – **4 rm** 🛏 35.00/47.50 **t.** – SB (weekends only) 55.00 **st.**

FORD High St. ✆ 62424

KINTYRE (Peninsula) Argyll. (Strathclyde) [401] D 16 17 – pop. 6,051.

See : SW : Machrihanish Bay★ – SE : Black Bay★ – Ugadale Bay★ – Saddell Bay★ – Campbeltown : Site★.

✈ at Campbeltown (Machrihanish Airport) : ✆ 0586 (Campbeltown) 53021.

⛴ by Caledonian MacBrayne : from Claonaig to Lochranza (Isle of Arran) summer only 6-7 daily (30 mn) – from Kennacraig to Port Ellen (Isle of Islay) 1-2 daily (2 h) – from Kennacraig to Port Askaig (Isle of Islay) Monday/Saturday 1 daily (1 h 45 mn).

KINTYRE (Peninsula)

Bellochantuy – ✉ Campbeltown – ☎ 058 32 Glenbarr.

🏛 Putechan Lodge, PA28 6QE, on A 83 ℰ 266, ⪻ – 🚽wc ℗ – **12 rm**.

Carradale – pop. 262 – ECD : Wednesday – ✉ ☎ 058 33 Carradale.
See : Site★, ⪻★ over Kilbrannan Sound★★, harbour★, Carradale Bay★.
🏌9 ℰ 624.
♦Edinburgh 164 – ♦Glasgow 121 – ♦Oban 74.

🏛 **Carradale,** PA28 6RY, ℰ 223, ⪻, 🍴, – 🚽wc ℗ 🔍 ⱽⁱˢᵃ
M 4.00/9.00 **st.** ₰2.50 – **22 rm** ⱼ 13.00/30.00 **st.** – SB (except Christmas
and New Year) 42.00/48.00 **st.**

Tarbert – pop. 1,391 – ECD : Wednesday – ✉ ☎ 088 02 Tarbert.
See : West Loch Tarbert★.
🏌9 ℰ 565, W : 1 m – 🇿 ℰ 429 (summer only).
♦Edinburgh 139 – ♦Glasgow 96 – ♦Oban 49.

✕ **West Loch** with rm, West Tarbert, PA29 6YF, SW : 1 m. on A 83 ℰ 283, ⪻ – ℗. 🔍
closed November – **M** 10.50/12.50 **t.** ₰3.00 – **6 rm** ⱼ 18.00/27.00 **t.** – SB (weekends only) (winter only) 52.00 **st.**

KIRKCALDY Fife. (Fife) 401 K 15 – pop. 50,360 – ECD : Wednesday – ☎ 0592.
🏌18 Balwearie ℰ 260370 – 🏌18 Dunnikier Park, Dunnikier Way ℰ 61599, North boundary – 🏌9 Auchter-
derran, Cardenden ℰ 721547, N : 5 m.
🇿 Esplanade ℰ 267775 (summer only).
♦Edinburgh 26 – ♦Dundee 28 – ♦Glasgow 52.

at West Wemyss NE : 4 ½ m. by A 955 – ✉ ☎ 0592 Kirkcaldy :

🏛 **Belvedere,** Coxstool, KY1 4SN, ℰ 54167, ⪻ – 📺 🚽wc ☎ ℗ 🔍 ⱽⁱˢᵃ
closed Sunday – **M** 8.00/11.00 **t.** ₰3.90 – **5 rm** ⱼ 25.30/36.80 **st.**

AUSTIN-ROVER 39 Rosslyn St. ℰ 51997
CITROEN, VAUXHALL-OPEL 24 Victoria Rd ℰ 264755
FORD Forth Av. ℰ 261199
NISSAN Meldrum Rd ℰ 200354

PEUGEOT, TALBOT Bennochy Rd ℰ 262191
RENAULT 15 Esplanade ℰ 263123
SAAB 180/186 St. Clair St. ℰ 52291
VOLVO Wemyssfield ℰ 262141

KIRKCUDBRIGHT Kirkcudbright. (Dumfries and Galloway) 401 402 H 19 – pop. 2,502 – ECD :
Thursday – ☎ 0557.
🏌18 – 🇿 Harbour Sq. ℰ 30494 (summer only).
♦Edinburgh 105 – ♦ Dumfries 28 – Stranraer 52.

🏛 **Selkirk Arms,** 123 High St., DG6 4JG, ℰ 30402, 🚗 – 🚽wc ℗. 🔍 ᴬᴱ ⓞ ⱽⁱˢᵃ
M 4.75/8.95 **t.** – **26 rm** ⱼ 13.65/34.95 **t.** – SB (winter only) 39.90/43.50 **t.**
AUSTIN-ROVER Mews Lane ℰ 30412   LADA ℰ 055 77 (Borgue) 227

KIRKMICHAEL Perth. (Tayside) 401 J 13 – pop. 100 – ✉ Blairgowrie – ☎ 025 081 Strathardle.
♦Edinburgh 70 – Perth 28 – Pitlochry 12.

🏛 **Log Cabin** 📞, PH10 7NB, W : 1 m. ℰ 288, ⪻, « Scandinavian pine chalet », 📞 – 🚽wc ℗.
🔍 ᴬᴱ ⓞ ⱽⁱˢᵃ
M (bar lunch) 12.00 **st.** ₰3.00 – **13 rm** ⱼ 16.00/44.00 **st.** – SB 50.00 **st.**

KIRKWALL Orkney (Orkney Islands) 401 L 7 – see Orkney Islands (Mainland).

KIRN Argyll. (Strathclyde) 401 402 F 16 – see Dunoon.

KYLEAKIN Inverness. (Highland) 401 C 12 – Shipping Services : see Skye (Isle of).

KYLE OF LOCHALSH Ross and Cromarty (Highland) 401 C 12 – pop. 687 – ECD : Thursday –
☎ 0599.
See : Loch★.
🚢 by Caledonian MacBrayne : to Kyleakin (Isle of Skye) frequent services daily (5 mn).
🚢 by Caledonian MacBrayne : to Mallaig summer only 3 weekly (2 h).
🇿 ℰ 4276 (summer only).
♦Edinburgh 204 – ♦ Dundee 182 – ♦Inverness 82 – ♦Oban 125.

🏛 **Lochalsh,** Ferry Rd, IV40 8AF, ℰ 4202, Telex 75318, ⪻ Skye Ferry and hills – 🏛 📺 ℗. 🔍 ᴬᴱ
ⓞ ⱽⁱˢᵃ
closed 19 to 29 December – **M** (buffet lunch) 10.50 **st.** ₰3.50 – **45 rm** ⱼ 17.50/64.00 **st.** – SB
(winter only) 50.00 **st.**

AUSTIN-ROVER The Garage ℰ 4210   FORD Main Rd ℰ 4329
518

KYLES SCALPAY Inverness. (Western Isles) (Highland) **401** Z 10 – Shipping Services : see Harris (Isle of).

LAGG Bute. (Strathclyde) – see Arran (Isle of).

LAIDE Ross and Cromarty (Highland) **401** D 10 – ⊠ Achnasheen – ✆ 044 582 Aultbea.
See : Gruinard Bay★★★.
♦Edinburgh 243 – ♦Inverness 84.

  ↱ **Ocean View,** Sand Passage Rd, Sand, IV22 2ND, ✆ 385, ⩽ sea and Summer Isles – **❷**. ⁕
    8 rm ⊊ 8.50/19.00 t.

LAIRG Sutherland (Highland) **401** G 9 – pop. 572 – ECD : Wednesday – ✆ 0549.
🛈 ✆ 2160 (summer only).
♦Edinburgh 218 – ♦Inverness 61 – ♦Wick 72.

  🏨 **Sutherland Arms,** IV27 4AT, ✆ 2291, ⩽, ⬿, 🚗 – 🚪wc **❷**. 🔼 **AE ①** **VISA**
    April-mid October – **M** (bar lunch) 9.00 t. – **24 rm** ⊊ 25.00/46.00 t. – SB (except summer) 23.00/29.00 st.

LAMLASH Bute. (Strathclyde) **401** E 17 – see Arran (Isle of).

LANARK Lanark. (Strathclyde) **401 402** I 16 – pop. 8,700 – ECD : Thursday – ✆ 0555.
🛅 Douglas Water ✆ 055 588 (Douglas Water) 460, SW : 7 m.
♦Edinburgh 33 – ♦Carlisle 76 – ♦ Glasgow 28.

  🏨 **Cartland Bridge** ⤬, ML11 9UF, NW : ¾ m. on A 73 ✆ 4426, 🚗 – ☎ **❷**. 🏧. 🔼 **AE ①** **VISA**
    M 5.50/8.50 st. ⧍ 3.35 – **15 rm** ⊊ 17.50/35.00 st.

AUSTIN-ROVER 17/19 Bloomgate ✆ 2371   FORD 144 Hyndford Rd ✆ 4431
CITROEN 30 West Port ✆ 2581   VAUXHALL St. Leonard St. ✆ 2185

LANGBANK Renfrew. (Strathclyde) **401** G 16 – pop. 375 – ECD : Saturday – ✆ 047 554.
♦Edinburgh 59 – ♦ Glasgow 16 – Greenock 7.

  🏰 **Gleddoch House** ⤬, PA14 6YE, SE : 1 m. by B 789 ✆ 711, Telex 779801, ⩽ Clyde and countryside, « Tastefully furnished », 🛅, ⬿, 🚗, park – 📺 ☎ **❷**. 🔼 **AE ①** **VISA**
    closed 1 and 2 January and 26 and 27 December – **M** 8.50/16.50 st. ⧍ 3.25 – **18 rm** ⊊ 49.00/83.00 st. – SB (weekends only) 35.00 st.

LARGS Ayr. (Strathclyde) **401 402** F 16 – pop. 9,771 – ECD : Wednesday – ✆ 0475.
See : Skelmorlie Aisle★ in old churchyard.
🛅 Irvine Rd ✆ 673594 S : 1 m. – **🛅** Routenburn, ✆ 673230.
🚢 by Caledonian MacBrayne : to Cumbrae Slip (Great Cumbrae Island) frequent services daily (10 mn).
🚢 by Caledonian MacBrayne : to Millport (Great Cumbrae Island) summer only 3-6 daily (30 mn).
🛈 Pierhead ✆ 673765.
♦Edinburgh 72 – ♦Ayr 30 – ♦Glasgow 29.

  🏠 **Glen Eldon,** 2 Barr Cres., KA30 8PX, ✆ 673381 – 🚪wc ▥wc **❷**. ⁕
    closed February – **M** (bar lunch) 7.00 t. ⧍ 2.70 – **9 rm** ⊊ 15.00/30.00 t.

  ↱ **Haylie,** 108 Irvine Rd, KA30 8EY, ✆ 673207, ⩽ Firth of Clyde and Islands, 🚗 – ▥wc **❷**. 🔼 **AE ①** **VISA**. ⁕
    8 rm ⊊ 12.00/28.00 st.

LAUDER Berwick. (Borders) **401 402** L 16 – pop. 604 – ECD : Thursday – ✆ 057 82.
🛅 ✆ 381, W : ½ m.
♦Edinburgh 27 – Hawick 31 – ♦Newcastle-upon-Tyne 78.

  🏨 **Black Bull,** Market Pl., ✆ 208 – 🚪wc **❷**
    M 4.50/7.50 st. ⧍ 3.00 – **13 rm** ⊊ 18.00/23.00 st.

    at Carfraemill N : 4 m. on A 68 – ⊠ Lauder – ✆ 057 85 Oxton :

  🏨 Carfraemill, TD2 6RA, ✆ 200 – 📺 🚪wc ☎ **❷** – **10 rm**.

LERWICK Shetland (Shetland Islands) **401** Q 3 – see Shetland Islands (Mainland).

LETHAM Fife. (Fife) **401** K 15 – pop. 170 – ⊠ Ladybank – ✆ 033 781.
♦Edinburgh 41 – ♦Dundee 14 – Perth 18.

  🏰 **Fernie Castle** ⤬, KY7 7RU, NE : ½ m. on A 914 ✆ 381, 🚗, park – 📺 🚪wc ▥wc ☎ **❷**. 🔼 **AE ①**
    M 6.25/15.00 t. – **11 rm** ⊊ 25.00/50.00 t.

LEVEN Fife. (Fife) **401** K 15 – pop. 9,472 – ECD : Thursday – ✆ 0333.

�▯ Leven Links – �▯ Leven Municipal.

🛈 South St. ✆ 29464.

♦Edinburgh 34 – ♦Dundee 23 – ♦Glasgow 61.

    at Lundin Links E : 2 m. on A 915 – ✉ ✆ 0333 Lundin Links :

🏛 **Old Manor,** Leven Rd, KY8 6AJ, ✆ 320368, ≤, 🍴 – ▯tv ⊟wc 🅿 ▯ AE ⓘ *VISA*, ✖
    M 6.15/16.95 **t.** ▮ 3.00 – **12 rm** ⊡ 19.50/35.00 **t.** – SB (weekends only) 52.00/55.00 **st.**

🏠 **Lundin Links,** Leven Rd, KY8 6AP, ✆ 320207, 🍴 – ▯tv ⊟wc ▯wc 🅿 ▯ ⚷ ▯ AE ⓘ
    VISA
    M 4.50/7.50 **st.** ▮ 2.50 – **15 rm** ⊡ 16.50/29.50 **st.** – SB 35.00/39.00 **st.**

AUSTIN-ROVER The Promenade ✆ 23449   FIAT Scoonie Rd ✆ 27003

LEWIS (Isle of) Ross and Cromarty (Outer Hebrides) (Western Isles) **401** Z 8 – pop. 15,174.

⛴ by Caledonian MacBrayne : from Stornoway to Ullapool Monday/Saturday 1-2 daily (3 h 30 mn).

    Stornoway – pop. 5,152 – ECD : Wednesday – ✉ ✆ 0851 Stornoway.

See : Broad Bay★★.

Envir. : Tiumpan Head ≤★★ NE : 11 m. – Loch Erisort★★ SW : 12 m. – Callanish Standing Stones★★ W : 16 m. – East Loch Roag★ W : 13 ½ m. – Tolsta (site★) NE : 13 m.

Exc. : Dun Carloway★ (stone fort) W : 21 m. – Port of Ness★ NE : 25 ½ m. – Valtos★ W : 32 m.

✈ Stornoway Airport : ✆ 2256, Telex 75495, E : 2 ½ m. – **Terminal :** British Airways, Cromwell St.

🛈 Area Tourist Officer, 4 South Beach St. ✆ 3088.

🏠 Royal, Cromwell St., PA87 2DG, ✆ 2109, ≤
    22 rm.

AUSTIN-ROVER 11-16 Bayhead St. ✆ 3246   VAUXHALL-OPEL Bayhead St. ✆ 2888
FORD 80 Keith St. ✆ 3225   VW, AUDI Sandwick Rd ✆ 2956

LEWISTON Inverness. (Highland) **401** G 12 – ✆ 045 62 Drumnadrochit.

♦Edinburgh 175 – ♦Inverness 16.

⚘ **Lewiston Arms,** IV3 6UN, ✆ 225, 🍴 – 🅿 *VISA*
    M (bar lunch) a la carte 7.75 **t.** ▮ 3.00 – **8 rm** ⊡ 11.00/22.00 **t.**

LINWOOD Renfrew. (Strathclyde) **401 402** G 16 – pop. 10,510 – ECD : Tuesday – ✆ 0505 John-stone.

♦Edinburgh 54 – ♦Glasgow 11 – Greenock 13.

🏠 **Golden Pheasant,** 1 Moss Rd, PA3 3HP, ✆ 21266 – ▯tv ⊟wc ▯ ▯ AE ⓘ *VISA*
    M (bar lunch) 8.25 **t.** ▮ 2.15 – **12 rm** ⊡ 18.50/29.45 **t.**

LISMORE (Isle of) Argyll. (Strathclyde) **401** D 14.

⛴ by Caledonian MacBrayne : from Achnacroish to Oban Monday/Saturday 2-3 daily (1 h).

⛴ to Port Appin summer 8-9 daily ; winter 3 daily (10 mn).

    Hotels see : Oban.

LOCHALINE Argyll. (Highland) **401** C 14 – pop. 213.

⛴ by Caledonian MacBrayne : to Fishnish (Isle of Mull) May-October Monday/Saturday 13-17 daily (15 mn) – to Tobermory (Isle of Mull) May-September 2 weekly (1 h) – to Arinagour (Isle of Coll) May-September 2 weekly (2 h 30 mn) – to Gott Bay (Isle of Tiree) (via Coll and Tobermory) May-September 2 weekly (3 h 50 mn) – to Oban May-September 2 weekly (1 h 10 mn).

♦Edinburgh 129 – ♦Inverness 105 – Kyle of Lochalsh 115 – ♦Oban 7.

    Hotels see : Mull (Isle of).

LOCHBOISDALE Inverness. (Western Isles) **401** Y 12 – Shipping Services : see Uist (South) (Isles of).

LOCHCARRON Ross and Cromarty (Highland) **401** D 11 – pop. 204 – ECD : Thursday – ✆ 052 02
- ▯9 .

♦Edinburgh 223 – ♦Inverness 64 – Kyle of Lochalsh 23.

⚘ **Lochcarron,** IV54 8YS, ✆ 226, ≤ Loch Carron – ⊟wc 🅿 ▯ *VISA*
    closed Christmas and New Year – **M** (bar lunch Monday to Saturday) 8.50 **t.** ▮ 2.00 – **7 rm**
    ⊡ 13.00/32.00 **t.**

LOCHEARNHEAD Perth. (Central) 401 H 14 – pop. 175 – ECD : Wednesday – ☎ 056 73.
♦Edinburgh 65 – ♦Glasgow 56 – ♦Oban 57 – Perth 36.

⌂ **Mansewood Country House,** FK19 8NS, S : ½ m. on A 84 ℰ 213, 🚗 – ⌷wc 🅿. ✖
closed January and February – **6 rm** ⛱ 12.75/23.50 **st.**

at Balquhidder SW : 4 ½ m. by A 84 – ✉ Lochearnhead – ☎ 087 74 Strathyre :

XX **Ledcreich** 🐾 with rm, FK19 8PQ, W : 1 ¾ m. ℰ 230, ≤, 🐾, 🚗 – ⌷wc 🏮 🅿. 🔝 AE ⓞ VISA
✖
closed 2 weeks April and 2 weeks October – **M** (closed Tuesday to non-residents) (bar lunch
Monday to Saturday) 9.00/15.50 **t.** ⑄ 3.50 – **4 rm** ⛱ 20.00/40.00 **t.**

LOCHGAIR Argyll. (Strathclyde) 401 D 15 – pop. 100 – ☎ 054 682.
Envir. : Inveraray (site★, castle★ 18C) NE : 18 m.
♦Edinburgh 119 – ♦Glasgow 76 – ♦Oban 43.

🏠 Lochgair, PA31 8SA, on A 83 ℰ 233, 🐾, 🚗 – ⌷wc 🅿
18 rm.

LOCHGILPHEAD Argyll. (Strathclyde) 401 D 15 – pop. 1,184 – ECD : Tuesday – ☎ 0546.
Envir. : Loch Fyne★★ E : 4 m. – Crarae Lodge gardens★ AC, NE : 12 m.
🅱 Lochnell St. ℰ 2344 (summer only).
♦Edinburgh 126 – ♦Glasgow 83 – ♦Oban 36.

Hotel and restaurant see : Crinan NW : 4 ½ m.

LOCH HARRAY Orkney (Orkney Islands) 401 K 6 – see Orkney Islands (Mainland).

LOCHINVER Sutherland (Highland) 401 E 9 – pop. 283 – ECD : Tuesday – ✉ Lairg – ☎ 057 14.
See : Site★.
Envir. : E : Inver Valley★.
🅱 ℰ 330 (summer only).
♦Edinburgh 259 – ♦Inverness 100 – ♦Wick 118.

🏛 **Culag** (Best Western), IV27 4LF, ℰ 209, ≤, 🐾, 🚗 – 🈁 ⌷wc 🅿. 🔝 AE ⓞ VISA
mid April-mid October – **M** (bar lunch Monday to Saturday) 7.00/10.00 **t.** ⑄ 3.00 – **38 rm**
⛱ 22.00/47.00 **t.**

⌂ **Ardglas** 🐾, IV27 4LI, ℰ 257, ≤ Loch Inver – 🅿
8 rm ⛱ 8.00/16.00 **st.**

LOCHMADDY Inverness. (Outer Hebrides) (Western Isles) 401 Y 11 – see Uist (North) (Isles of).

LOCHRANZA Bute (Strathclyde) 401 402 E 16 – Shipping Services : see Arran (Isle of).

LOCKERBIE Dumfries. (Dumfries and Galloway) 401 402 J 18 – pop. 2,999 – ECD : Tuesday –
☎ 057 62.
🅵 Corrie Rd ℰ 3363.
♦Edinburgh 72 – ♦Carlisle 26 – ♦Dumfries 13 – ♦Glasgow 69.

🏠 **Dryfesdale** 🐾, Dryfe Rd, DG11 2JF, NW : 1 m. off A 74 ℰ 2427, ≤, 🚗 – 📺 ⌷wc 🐾 🅿.
🔝 AE ⓞ VISA
closed first week January – **M** 7.50/11.50 **st.** ⑄ 2.85 – **11 rm** ⛱ 16.00/34.00 **st.** – SB
(except summer) 24.00 **st.**

FORD Caledonia Pl. ℰ 3240

LOSSIEMOUTH Moray. (Grampian) 401 K 10 – pop. 5,678 (inc. Branderburgh) – ECD : Thursday
– ☎ 034 381.
See : Site★★.
🅸, 🅸 Stotfield Rd, Moray ℰ 2018.
♦Edinburgh 196 – ♦Aberdeen 72 – Fraserburgh 66 – ♦Inverness 44.

Hotels see : Fochabers SE : 14 ½ m.

LUING (Isle of) Argyll. (Strathclyde) 401 D 15 – pop. 183.

Cullipool – ✉ Oban – ☎ 085 24 Luing

X **Longhouse Buttery,** PA34 4TX, ℰ 209, ≤ – 🅿
Easter-mid October – **M** (closed Sunday) (lunch only and dinner Thursday to Saturday July-
August by arrangement) a la carte 3.05/9.05 **t.** ⑄ 3.25.

LUNDIN LINKS Fife. (Fife) 401 L 15 – see Leven.

MACDUFF Banff. (Grampian) **401** M 10 − ECD : Wednesday − ✆ 0261.
🛏 Royal Tarlair ✆ 32548.
♦ Edinburgh 170 − ♦ Aberdeen 46 − Fraserburgh 24 − ♦ Inverness 76.

   🏛 **Deveron House,** 25 Union Rd, AB4 1UD, ✆ 32309 − 📺 ➡wc 🚿wc 🅿. 🅰. 🔼 AE ⓪ VISA
   M (bar lunch) 4.50/7.50 t. ⅃ 3.00 − **17 rm** � 16.00/39.00 t. − SB 36.00/48.00 st.

MAINLAND Orkney (Orkney Islands) **401** KL 6 − see Orkney Islands.

MAINLAND Shetland (Shetland Islands) **401** PQ 3 − see Shetland Islands.

MALLAIG Inverness. (Highland) **401** C 12 − pop. 903 − ECD : Wednesday − ✆ 0687.
See : Site★ − Harbour★ − Sound of Sleat ★★ − Envir. : Sound of Arisaig ★ S : 9 m.
🛏 Traigh ✆ 068 75 (Arisaig) 2126, S : 9 m.
⚓ by Caledonian MacBrayne : to Armadale (Isle of Skye) summer only Monday/Saturday 3-5 daily (30 mn).
⚓ by Caledonian MacBrayne : to Isles of Eigg, Muck, Rhum, Canna, return Mallaig Monday/Saturday 3-4 weekly (7 h) − to Kyle of Lochalsh summer only 3 weekly (2 h) − to Armadale (Isle of Skye) Monday/Saturday 10 weekly (30 mn).
🛈 Station Buildings ✆ 2170 (summer only).
♦ Edinburgh 181 − ♦ Inverness 111 − ♦ Oban 97.

   🏛 **Marine,** 10 Railway Rd, PH41 4PY, ✆ 2217 − ➡wc. AE
   M (bar lunch) 9.00 st. ⅃ 2.50 − **21 rm** ⊏ 12.00/28.00 st.

MEIGLE Perth. (Tayside) **401** K 14 − pop. 375 − ✆ 082 84.
See : Museum (Crosses)★.
♦ Edinburgh 60 − ♦ Dundee 13 − Perth 18.

   🏠 **Kings of Kinloch** ≫ , Coupar Angus Rd, PH12 8QX, W : 1 m. on A 94 ✆ 273, ≼, 🐎 − 🅿.
   🔼 ✺
   closed January − **M** (closed Sunday dinner) 11.30/15.00 t. ⅃ 3.40 − **7 rm** ⊏ 16.00/30.00 t.

MELROSE Roxburgh. (Borders) **401 402** L 17 − pop. 2,185 − ECD : Thursday − ✆ 089 682.
See : Abbey★ AC − Envir. : Scotts View★ NE : 3 m. − Dryburgh (abbey★ AC) SE : 4 ½ m. − Abbotsford House★ (Sir Walter Scott's home) AC, W : 2 m.
🛏 Dingleton ✆ 2855, South boundary − 🛈 Priorwood, near Abbey ✆ 2555 (April-December).
♦ Edinburgh 37 − Hawick 21 − ♦ Newcastle-upon-Tyne 69.

   🏠 **Burts,** Market Sq., TD6 9PN, ✆ 2285, 🐎 − ➡wc 🚿wc 🅿. 🔼 AE ⓪ VISA
   M 7.00/13.00 t. ⅃ 2.50 − **22 rm** ⊏ 14.50/32.00 t. − SB 38.00/42.00 st.

AUSTIN-ROVER Palma Pl. ✆ 2048

MILLPORT Bute (Strathclyde) **401 402** F 16 − Shipping Services : see Great Cumbrae Island.

MILNGAVIE Dunbarton. (Strathclyde) **401** H 16 − pop. 10,741 − ECD : Tuesday and Saturday − ✉ ✆ 041 Glasgow.
🛏 Dougalston ✆ 956 5750 − ♦ Edinburgh 50 − ♦ Glasgow 7.

   🏨 **Black Bull Thistle** (Thistle), Main St., G62 6BH, ✆ 956 2291, Telex 778323 − 📺 ➡wc 🚿wc
   ◑ 🅿. 🅰. 🔼 AE ⓪ VISA. ✻
   M 5.00/12.00 t. ⅃ 3.45 − ⊏ 4.75 − **27 rm** 33.30/41.30 t. − SB (weekends only) 52.00 st.

AUSTIN-ROVER Main St. ✆ 956 2255   VAUXHALL-OPEL Glasgow Rd ✆ 956 1126

MOFFAT Dumfries. (Dumfries and Galloway) **401 402** J 17 − pop. 2,031 − ECD : Wednesday − ✆ 0683.
Envir. : E : Moffatwater Valley★ − Grey Mare's Tail Waterfall★ NE : 11 m.
🛈 Church Gate ✆ 20620 (summer only).
♦ Edinburgh 58 − ♦ Dumfries 21 − ♦ Carlisle 42 − ♦ Glasgow 54.

   🏨 **Ladbroke Mercury Motor Inn** (Ladbroke), Church St., DG10 9EL, ✆ 20464 − 📺 ➡wc 🅿.
   🔼 AE ⓪ VISA
   M (bar lunch) 9.00 t. ⅃ 3.25 − ⊏ 5.00 − **51 rm** 25.00/37.00 t. − SB (summer only) 59.00 st.
   🏠 **Beechwood Country House** ≫, up Harthope Pl., off Academy Rd, DG10 9RS, ✆ 20210,
   🐎 − ➡wc 🚿wc ◑ 🅿. 🔼 AE ⓪ VISA. ✻
   closed January − **M** (bar lunch) 10.00 t. ⅃ 2.30 − **8 rm** ⊏ 15.50/36.00 t. − SB 49.00/53.00 st.
   🏠 **Moffat House,** High St., DG10 9HL, ✆ 20039, 🐎 − ➡wc 🚿wc 🅿. AE ⓪ VISA
   Mid March-October − **M** 6.00/9.75 t. ⅃ 3.40 − **14 rm** ⊏ 20.00/35.00 t.
   ↑ **Hartfell House,** Hartfell Cres., DG10 9AL, ✆ 20153, 🐎 − 🅿
   closed January and February − **9 rm** ⊏ 9.10/18.20 t.
   ↑ **Arden House,** High St., DG10 9HG, ✆ 20220 − 🚿wc 🅿
   March-October − **8 rm** ⊏ 9.50/18.00 st.

MONTROSE Angus (Tayside) 🏙 M 13 – pop. 9,959 – ECD : Wednesday – ☎ 0674.

🏌 Broomfield ✆ 2634 E : 1 m. off A 92.

🛈 212 High St ✆ 2000.

◆Edinburgh 85 – ◆Aberdeen 38 – ◆Dundee 29.

🏨 **Park,** John St., DD10 8RJ, ✆ 73415, Telex 76367, 🚗 – 📺 🏠wc 🏠wc ☎ 🅿 🏛 🔌 🆎 ⑩ *VISA*

M 5.50/7.50 **st.** 🛆 2.65 – **59 rm** 🖙 20.00/40.00 **st.** – SB (weekends only) 42.00/52.00 **st.**

AUSTIN-ROVER, FORD Craigo ✆ 067 483 (Hillside)   NISSAN New Wynd ✆ 3606 374/5

MUCK (Isle of) Inverness. (Highland) 🏙 B 13 – Shipping Services : see Mallaig.

MUIR OF ORD Ross and Cromarty (Highland) 🏙 G 11 – pop. 1,339 – ECD : Thursday – ☎ 0463.

🏌 – 🛈 ✆ 870433 and 870525.

◆Edinburgh 174 – ◆Inverness 14 – ◆Wick 122.

🏨 **Ord House** 🦢, off A 832 ✆ 870492, ≤, 🏊, 🚗, park – 🏠wc 🅿
April-October – **M** (bar lunch) 10.00 **t.** 🛆 2.50 – **14 rm** 🖙 13.75/33.00 **t.** – SB 42.00 **st.**

MULL (Isle of) Argyll. (Strathclyde) 🏙 C 14 – pop. 1,569.

See : Coast★.

🚢 by Caledonian MacBrayne : from Craignure to Oban summer 4-7 daily, winter Monday/Saturday 1-3 daily (45 mn) – from Fishnish to Lochaline May-October Monday-Saturday 13-17 daily (15 mn) – from Tobermory to Arinagour (Isle of Coll) 3 weekly (1 h 30 mn) – from Tobermory to Gott Bay (Isle of Tiree) 2-3 weekly (2 h 45 mn) – from Tobermory to Lochaline May-September 2 weekly (1 h) – from Tobermory to Oban 2-3 weekly (2 h direct).

🚢 by Caledonian MacBrayne : from Fionnphort to Isle of Iona frequent services daily in summer, restricted service in winter (5 mn) – from Tobermory to Kilchoan summer only Monday/Saturday 4-5 daily (35 mn).

🛈 48 Main St. at Tobermory ✆ 0688 (Tobermory) 2182.

Bunessan – ECD : Wednesday – ✉ Bunessan – ☎ 068 17 Fionnphort.
Envir. : NE : Loch Scridain★ – Fionnphort (site★) W : 6 m.

🏠 **Ardfenaig House** 🦢, PA67 6DX, W : 3 m. by A 849 ✆ 210, ≤, 🚗, park – 🅿
May-September – **M** *(closed Sunday dinner to non-residents)* (dinner only) (booking essential) 12.50 **st.** 🛆 1.50 – **5 rm** 🖙 (dinner included) 40.00/80.00 **st.**

Dervaig – ✉ Tobermory – ☎ 068 84 Dervaig.

🏠 **Druimnacroish** 🦢, PA75 6QW, SE : 2 m. by B 8073 ✆ 274, ≤ Bellart Glen, « Converted steading », 🚗 – 📺 🏠wc 🛆 🅿 🔌 🆎 ⑩ *VISA*
April-October – **M** (dinner only) (booking essential) 15.00 **st.** – **7 rm** 🖙 28.00/56.00.

Salen – pop. 181 – ECD : Wednesday – ✉ Salen – ☎ 068 03 Aros.
See : Sound of Mull★★.
Envir. : Loch Na Keal★★ SW : 2 ½ m.

🏠 **Glenforsa** 🦢, PA72 6JN, E : 1 ¼ m. by A 849 ✆ 377, ≤ Sound of Mull, « Norwegian wood chalet », 🏊, park – 🏠wc 🅿
Easter-October – **M** (bar lunch) 9.50 **t.** 🛆 2.50 – **14 rm** 🖙 16.00/35.00 **st.**

Tiroran – ✉ ☎ 068 15 Tiroran.

🏠 **Tiroran House** 🦢, PA69 6ES, ✆ 232, ≤, « Country house atmosphere », 🚗, park – 🏠wc 🅿. 🎾
April-September – **M** (bar lunch, residents only) (booking essential) 5.50/14.50 **st.** 🛆 2.50 – **8 rm** 🖙 26.00/63.00 **st.**

Tobermory – pop. 641 – ECD : Wednesday – ✉ ☎ 0688 Tobermory.
See : Site★ – Envir. : Calgary Bay★★ SW : 14 m. – Loch Tuath★★ SW : 17 m.
🏌 .

↑ **Tobermory,** 53 Main St., PA75 6NT, ✆ 2091, ≤
April-October – **14 rm** 🖙 13.00/44.00 **st.**

↑ **Suidhe,** 59 Main St., PA75 6NT, ✆ 2209, ≤ – 🎾
April-October – **9 rm** 🖙 11.00/28.00 **t.**

NAIRN Nairn. (Highland) 🏙 I 11 – pop. 8,037 – ECD : Wednesday – ☎ 0667.
See : ≤★ from the harbour.
Envir. : Fort George★ (Museum of the Queen's Own Highlanders★) W : 8 ½ m. – Sveno's Stone★ E : 11 m.

🏌, 🏌 ✆ 52103 – 🏌 Nairn Dunbar, ✆ 52741.

🛈 King St ✆ 52753 (summer only).

◆Edinburgh 175 – ◆Aberdeen 91 – ◆Inverness 16.

🏨 **Newton** 🦢, Inverness Rd, IV12 4RX, off A 96 ✆ 53144, ≼, « Country house in extensive grounds », 🚗, park, 🍽 – 📶 📺 🅿. 🏌. 🔄 AE ⓪ *VISA*
M 5.00/12.00 t. 🍷 3.00 – **44 rm** 🛏 28.00/60.00 t. – SB 70.00/80.00 **st.**

🏨 **Golf View,** Seabank Rd, IV12 4HD, ✆ 52301, ≼, 🔄 heated, 🚗, 🍽 – 📶 📺 🅿. 🏌. 🔄 AE ⓪ *VISA*
M 6.00/12.50 t. 🍷 3.00 – **55 rm** 🛏 30.00/54.00 t. – SB (weekends only) 50.00/66.00 **st.**

🏠 **Clifton** 🦢, Viewfield St., IV12 4HW, ✆ 53119, ≼, « Tasteful decor », 🚗 – 🚻wc 🅿. 🔄 AE ⓪ *VISA*
April-October – **M** (booking essential) a la carte 8.60/12.50 t. 🍷 4.00 – **16 rm** 🛏 28.00/55.00 t.

🍴 **Carnach Country House,** Inverness Rd, IV12 5NT, W : 2 m. on A 96 ✆ 52094, 🚗 – 🅿. 🔄 *VISA*
M *(dinner only)* 7.50 **st.** 🍷 2.00.

AUSTIN-ROVER   King St. ✆ 52304.   TALBOT   Inverness Rd ✆ 52335

NETHERLEY Kincardine (Grampian) **401** N 12 – see Stonehaven.

NEWBURGH Aberdeen. (Grampian) **401** N 12 – pop. 447 – ✆ 035 86.
♦Edinburgh 137 – ♦Aberdeen 13 – Fraserburgh 31.

🏠 **Udny Arms,** Main St., AB4 0BL, ✆ 444 – 📺 🚻wc 🛁wc ☎ 🅿. 🔄 AE *VISA*
M 13.50 t. – 🛏 4.00 – **25 rm** 27.50/37.50 t. – SB (weekends only) 55.00 **st.**

NEW SCONE Perth. (Tayside) **401** J 14 – see Perth.

NEWTONMORE Inverness. (Highland) **401** H 12 – pop. 894 – ECD : Wednesday – ✆ 054 03.
🏌 Golf Course Rd ✆ 328.
🛈 Perth Rd ✆ 253 (summer only).
♦Edinburgh 112 – ♦Inverness 47 – Perth 70.

🏠 **Ard-na-Coille,** Kingussie Rd, PH20 1AY, ✆ 214, ≼, 🚗 – 🛁wc 🅿
Mid February-October – **M** (dinner only) 8.25 **st.** 🍷 2.20 – **10 rm** 🛏 10.50/29.00 **st.**

🏠 **Coig-na-Shee,** Fort William Rd, PH20 1DG, ✆ 216, 🚗 – 🅿
closed December and January – **6 rm** 🛏 9.50/21.00 **st.**

NEWTON STEWART Wigtown. (Dumfries and Galloway) **401** **402** G 19 – pop. 1,883 – ECD : Wednesday – ✆ 0671.
🏌 Kirroughtree Av., Minnigaff ✆ 2172.
🛈 Dashwood Sq. ✆ 2431 (summer only).
♦Edinburgh 127 – ♦Dumfries 50 – ♦Glasgow 84 – Stranraer 26.

🏨 **Kirroughtree** 🦢, DG8 6AN, N : 1 ½ m. on A 712 ✆ 2141, ≼ woodland and river Cree, « Country house and gardens », park – 📺 ☎ 🅿. 🔄 AE ⓪ *VISA*. 🦌
March-November – **M** a la carte 9.00/13.50 t. 🍷 3.30 – **24 rm** 🛏 24.00/56.00 t. – SB (except summer) 70.00/74.00 **st.**

🏠 **Bruce,** 88 Queen St., DG8 6JL, ✆ 2294 – 📺 🚻wc 🐾 🅿. 🔄 AE ⓪ *VISA*
closed December and January – **M** 6.00/13.50 **st.** – **17 rm** 🛏 21.00/38.00 st. – SB (winter only) 48.00 **st.**

🏠 **Crown,** 101 Queen St., DG8 6JP, ✆ 2727 – 🚻wc 🛁 🅿. 🔄 AE ⓪ *VISA*
M a la carte 7.05/9.20 **t.** – **9 rm** 🛏 12.50/29.00 t. – SB 39.00/47.80 **st.**

FORD   Queen St. ✆ 2112   VOLVO ✆ 3101
RENAULT   Duncan Park, Wigtown ✆ 098 84 (Wigtown) 3287

NEWTON WAMPHRAY Dumfries. (Dumfries and Galloway) **401** **402** J 18 – ECD : Wednesday – ✉ Moffat – ✆ 057 64 Johnstone Bridge.
♦Edinburgh 62 – ♦Carlisle 35 – ♦Dumfries 22 – ♦Glasgow 58.

🏠 **Red House,** DG10 9NF, off A 74 ✆ 214, ≼, 🚗 – 🅿. ⓪
Easter-15 November – **M** (residents only) 4.50/6.75 **t.** – **6 rm** 🛏 13.50/27.00 t.

NORTH BERWICK E. Lothian (Lothian) **401** L 15 – pop. 4,414 – ECD : Thursday – ✆ 0620.
See : Site*.
Envir. : Tantallon Castle* (ruins 14C), site* *AC,* E : 2 ½ m.
🏌 Burgh Links, East Links ✆ 2726 – 🏌 West Links, Beach Rd ✆ 2135.
🛈 Quality St. ✆ 2197.
♦Edinburgh 24 – ♦Newcastle-upon-Tyne 101.

🏨 **Marine** (T.H.F.), Cromwell Rd, EH39 4LZ, ℰ 2406, Telex 727363, ≤, ⤓ heated, 🐾, ⋇ – 🛗
📺 🅿 🚶 🔳 🅰🅴 ⑩ 𝘷𝘪𝘴𝘢
M (buffet lunch) 9.50 **st.** 🍴 2.85 – �🍽 5.00 – **85 rm** 29.50/54.00 **st.**

🏨 **Nether Abbey,** 20 Dirleton Av., EH39 4BQ, ℰ 2802, 🐾 – �🚪wc 🎬wc 🅿 🔳 𝘷𝘪𝘴𝘢
M (bar lunch)(restricted dinner during winter) 7.50 **t.** 🍴 3.00 – **17 rm** �⊐ 13.00/29.50 **t.**

🏨 **Blenheim House,** 14 Westgate, EH39 4AF, ℰ 2385, ≤ – ⚬wc 🅿
M 5.00/8.00 **t.** – **11 rm** �⊐ 13.00/30.00 **t.**

🏨 **Point Garry,** 20 West Bay Rd, EH39 4AW, ℰ 2380 – ⚬wc 🎬wc 🅿
April-October – **M** (bar lunch) 7.50 **t.** 🍴 2.85 – **15 rm** �⊐ 16.50/35.00 **t.**

AUSTIN-ROVER 18/24 High St. ℰ 2304   FORD 52 Dunbar Rd ℰ 2232

NORTH RONALDSAY (Isle of) Orkney (Orkney Islands) 🟦🟦🟦 M 5 – Shipping Services : see
Orkney Islands (Mainland : Kirkwall).

OBAN Argyll. (Strathclyde) 🟦🟦🟦 D 14 – pop. 6,897 – ECD : Thursday – ☏ 0631.
See : Site★.
🏌 Glencruitten ℰ 62868, E : 1 m.
Access to Glasgow by helicopter.
🚢 by Caledonian MacBrayne : to Craignure (Isle of Mull) summer 4-7 daily ; winter Monday/Saturday 1-3 daily (45 mn) – to Castlebay (Isle of Barra) 3-4 weekly (5 h to 8 h) – to Lochboisdale (South Uist) 3-6 weekly (6 h direct ; 8 h via Castlebay) – to Arinagour (Isle of Coll) 3-4 weekly (3 h 15 mn to 5 h 45 mn) – to Gott Bay (Isle of Tiree) 3-4 weekly (4 to 5 h) – to Scalasaig (Isle of Colonsay) 3 weekly (2 h 30 mn) – to Achnacroish (Isle of Lismore) Monday/Saturday 2-3 daily (1 h) – to Tobermory (Isle of Mull) 2-3 weekly (1 h 45 mn to 2 h 15 mn) – to Lochaline May-September 2 weekly (1 h 5 mn).
🛈 Argyll Sq. ℰ 63122/63551.
♦Edinburgh 123 – ♦Dundee 116 – ♦Glasgow 93 – ♦Inverness 118.

🏨 **Alexandra,** Corran Esplanade, PA34 5AA, ℰ 62381, Telex 778215, ≤ – 🛗 ⚬wc 🅿 🔳 🅰🅴
⑩ 𝘷𝘪𝘴𝘢
April-mid October – **M** (bar lunch) 9.00 **t.** 🍴 3.50 – **56 rm** ⍊ 28.00/48.00 **t.**

🏨 **Regent,** The Esplanade, PA34 5PZ, ℰ 62341, ≤ – 🛗 ⚬wc 🎬wc ⧫ 🔳 🅰🅴 ⑩ 𝘷𝘪𝘴𝘢
M (bar lunch) 10.00 **st.** 🍴 2.40 – **75 rm** ⍊ 13.00/36.00 **st.** – SB 36.00/54.00 **st.**

🏨 **Great Western,** Corran Esplanade, PA34 5PP, ℰ 63101, Group Telex 778215, ≤ – 🛗 ⚬wc
🅿 🚶 🔳 🅰🅴 ⑩ 𝘷𝘪𝘴𝘢
Mid April-mid October – **M** (bar lunch) 8.50 **t.** 🍴 3.20 – **74 rm** ⍊ 25.00/46.00 **t.** – SB (summer only) 46.00/58.00 **st.**

🏨 **Soroba House,** Soroba Rd, PA34 4SB, S : 1 ¼ m. on A 816 ℰ 62628, 🐾, ⋇ – 📺 ⚬wc 🅿
⑩ 𝘷𝘪𝘴𝘢
M 4.50/7.90 **t.** 🍴 2.25 – **14 rm** ⍊ 22.00/28.00 **t.**

🏨 **Manor House,** Gallanach Rd, PA34 4LS, ℰ 62087, ≤ – ⚬wc 🎬wc 🅿 🔳 ⑩ 𝘷𝘪𝘴𝘢
M (bar lunch) 9.00 **t.** 🍴 2.50 – **11 rm** ⍊ 24.00/38.00 **t.**

🏨 **Rowan Tree,** George St., PA34 5NX, ℰ 62954 – 📺 ⚬wc 🅿 🔳 🅰🅴 ⑩ 𝘷𝘪𝘴𝘢
M (bar lunch) 8.00 **t.** 🍴 2.50 – **24 rm** ⍊ 15.50/17.50 **t.**

🏨 **Corriemar,** PA34 5AQ, ℰ 62476, ≤ – 🎬wc 🅿
March-mid October – **16 rm** ⍊ 12.00/30.00 **st.**

at Kilninver SW : 8 m. on A 816 – ✉ Oban – ☏ 085 26 Kilninver :

🏨 **Knipoch,** PA34 4QT, NE : 1 ½ m. on A 816 ℰ 251, ≤, « Tastefully furnished », 🐾 – 📺 🅿
🔳 🅰🅴 ⑩ 𝘷𝘪𝘴𝘢 ⋇
M (bar lunch) a la carte 13.50/23.50 **t.** 🍴 3.00 – **21 rm** ⍊ 40.00/70.00 **t.**

AUSTIN-ROVER Airds Pl. ℰ 63173   VOLVO, OPEL, BEDFORD Breadalbane Pl. ℰ 63066
FORD Soroba Rd ℰ 63061

OLDMELDRUM Aberdeen. (Grampian) 🟦🟦🟦 N 11 – pop. 1,085 – ECD : Wednesday – ☏ 065 12.
Envir. : Pitmedden gardens★ *AC*, E : 6 m. – Tolquhon Castle★ (16C) *AC*, E : 7 ½ m.
🏌.
♦Edinburgh 142 – ♦Aberdeen 18 – Fraserburgh 29 – ♦Inverness 89.

⋇⋇ **Meldrum House** 🌲 with rm, AB5 0AE, N : 1 ½ m. by A 947 ℰ 2294, ≤, 🏌, 🐾, park – 📺
⚬wc 🅿 🅰🅴 ⑩ ⋇
Mid March-mid December – **M** (bar lunch Monday to Saturday) 12.00 🍴 2.75 – **9 rm**
⍊ 30.00/44.00 – SB (weekends only) 60.00/70.00 **st.**

ONICH Inverness. (Highland) 🟦🟦🟦 E 13 – pop. 280 – ECD : Saturday except summer – ✉ Fort
William – ☏ 085 53.
♦Edinburgh 122 – ♦Glasgow 93 – ♦Inverness 75 – ♦Oban 39.

🏨 **Creag Dhu,** PH33 6RY, on A 82 ℰ 238, ≤ Loch Linnhe and mountains, 🐾 – ⚬wc 🎬wc 🅿
🔳 🅰🅴 ⑩ 𝘷𝘪𝘴𝘢
March-October – **M** (bar lunch) 9.00 **t.** 🍴 2.40 – **20 rm** ⍊ 20.50/41.00 **t.**

🏨 **Onich,** PH33 6RY, on A 82 ℰ 214, ≤ Loch Linnhe and mountains, 🐾 – 🅿 🔳 🅰🅴 ⑩ 𝘷𝘪𝘴𝘢
M 6.50/8.50 **st.** 🍴 2.45 – **24 rm** ⍊ 12.00/35.00 **st.** – SB (winter only) 35.00/45.00 **st.**

ORKNEY ISLANDS Orkney (Orkney Islands) **401** KL 6 and 7 – pop. 17,077.

🚢 see Mainland : Kirkwall.

🚢 🚢 see Mainland : Kirkwall and Stromness – by Orkney Islands Shipping Co. : service between Longhope (Isle of Hoy), Lyness (Isle of Hoy), Flotta (Isle of), Houton, Graemsay (Isle of), Stromness and return, daily itinerary varies consult operator.

🚢 by Thomas & Bews : from Burwick (South Ronaldsay) to John O'Groats summer only 2-4 daily (45 mn).

HOY

Old Man of Hoy .
See : Rock Spike***.

MAINLAND

Birsay – ✉ ✆ 085 672 Birsay.
See : Brough of Birsay (site and ≤★★) *AC*.
Envir. : Kitchener Memorial ※★★★ (birds' nests) S : 5 m. – Skara Brae (prehistoric village★★ *AC*) S : 7 ½ m. – Yesnaby (cliffs★★ : birds' nests) S : 11 m. – Broch of Gurness★ E : 12 m.

Kirkwall – pop. 4,617 – ECD : Wednesday – ✉ ✆ 0856 Kirkwall.
See : Site★ – St. Magnus Cathedral★★.
Envir. : Wideford Hill cairn (Megalithic cairn★, ≤★) W : 2 m.
🏠 Grainbank ✆ 2457, W : 1 m.
🚉 Kirkwall Airport : ✆ 2421, Telex 75473, S : 3 ½ m.
🚢 by Orkney Islands Shipping Co. : to Westray via Eday, Stronsay, Sanday and Papa Westray 3 weekly (2 to 6 h) – to North Ronaldsay 1 weekly (2 h 30 mn) – to Wyre via Rousay and Egilsay 1 weekly (1 to 4 h) – to Shapinsay 9 weekly (25 mn).
🛈 Broad St. ✆ 2856.

🏨 **Kirkwall**, Harbour St., KW15 1LF, ✆ 2232, ≤ – 🔌 🛏wc
M 2.50/8.00 st. ⏷ 2.80 – **40 rm** ☳ 18.00/46.00 st.

🏨 **Lynnfield** 🍴, KW15 1RX, S : 1 ¼ m. by A 961 ✆ 2505, 🌳 – 📺 ☵ 🅿 🔀 *VISA*
M 4.50/11.20 t. ⏷ 2.50 – **6 rm** ☳ 22.00/44.00 t.

🏨 **Ayre**, Ayre Rd, KW15 1QX, ✆ 2197 – 🛏wc ☵ 🅿 🔀 *VISA*
M 3.00/10.00 st. ⏷ 2.60 – ☳ 2.50 – **30 rm** 13.50/34.00 st.

🏠 **Bellavista** 🍴, Carness Rd, KW15 1TB, N : 1 m. via Cromwell Rd ✆ 2306 – 🅿 ⚘
closed October and 21 December-7 January – **8 rm** ☳ 8.00/16.00 st.

XX **Foveran** with rm, St. Ola, KW15 1SF, SW : 3 m. on A 964 ✆ 2389, ≤ Scapa Flow – 🛏wc
☵wc 🅿 🔀 🆎 *VISA*
closed October – **M** *(closed to non-residents Sunday and Monday)* (bar lunch) a la carte 7.80/12.50 t. ⏷ 2.85 – **8 rm** ☳ 17.50/30.00 st.

AUSTIN-ROVER 25 Broad St. ✆ 2785
COLT, TALBOT Gt Western Rd ✆ 2805
FIAT Junction Rd ✆ 2158

FORD Castle St. ✆ 3212
RENAULT Gt Western Rd ✆ 2601
VAUXHALL Burnmouth Rd ✆ 2950

Loch Harray – ✉ Loch Harray – ✆ 085 677 Harray.

🏨 **Merkister** 🍴, KW17 2LF, ✆ 366, ≤, 🐟, 🌳 – ☵wc 🅿
M 5.50/9.75 t. ⏷ 2.30 – **18 rm** ☳ 15.00/32.00 t.

Stenness – ✉ ✆ 0856 Stromness.
Envir. : Maes Howe Cairn★★ (Neolithic chambered cairn) *AC*, NE : 1 ½ m. – Ring of Brodgar (stone circle)★ NW : 2 ½ m.

🏨 **Standing Stones** 🍴, KW16 3JX, ✆ 850 449, ≤ Loch Stenness and Standing Stones – 🅿
20 rm ☳ 11.75/20.00.

Stromness – pop. 1,646 – ECD : Thursday – ✉ ✆ 0856 Stromness.
See : Site★.
🏠 Ness ✆ 850593.
🚢 by P & O Ferries : Orkney and Shetland Services : to Scrabster Monday/Saturday 1-3 daily (2 h).
🚢 to Moaness (Isle of Hoy) 2-3 daily (25 mn).
🛈 Ferry Terminal Building, Pierhead ✆ 850716 (summer only).

🏨 **Stromness**, 108 Victoria St., KW16 3AA, ✆ 850298, 🌳 – ☵ 🛏wc ☵wc. *VISA*
closed 1 to 5 January – **M** a la carte 4.40/11.60 st. ⏷ 2.70 – **39 rm** ☳ 17.25/32.20 st. – SB 25.00/48.00 st.

Do not use yesterday's maps for today's journey.

OUT SKERRIES Shetland (Shetland Islands) 401 R 2 – Shipping Services : see Shetland Islands (Mainland : Lerwick).

OVERSCAIG Sutherland (Highland) 401 F 9 – ⊠ Lairg – ✪ 054 983 Merkland.
♦Edinburgh 235 – ♦Inverness 76.

   🏠 Overscaig ⌕, Loch Shin, IV27 4NY, ✆ 203, ≼ Loch Shin and mountains, ⌇, park – ⌷wc 🅿
        10 rm.

OYKEL BRIDGE Sutherland. (Highland) 401 F 10 – ⊠ Lairg – ✪ 054 984 Rosehall.
♦Edinburgh 225 – ♦Inverness 66 – Lochinver 31.

   🏨 **Oykel Bridge** ⌕, IV27 4HE, ✆ 218, ≼, ⌇, 🚗 – ⌷wc 🅿
        March-September – **M** *(bar lunch)* 11.00 st. ⌑ 4.00 – **16 rm** ⌷ 34.00/68.00 **st.**

PAISLEY Renfrew. (Strathclyde) 401 402 G 16 – pop. 95,357 – ECD : Tuesday – ✪ 041 Glasgow.
🏌 Barshaw Park ✆ 889 2908, E : 1 m. of Paisley Cross off A 737.
♦Edinburgh 50 – ♦Ayr 36 – ♦Glasgow 7 – Greenock 16.

   🏨 **Stakis Watermill** (Stakis), Lonend, PA1 1SR, ✆ 889 3201 – 🛗 📺 ⌷wc 🕿 🅿 🔉 AE ①
        VISA
        M a la carte 5.35/10.00 st. ⌑ 2.80 – **51 rm** ⌷ 33.75/44.00 **st.** – SB 38.00/46.00 **st.**

   🏠 **Rockfield,** 125 Renfrew Rd, PA3 4BL, ✆ 889 6182 – 📺 ⌷wc 🛗wc 🕿 🅿 🔉 🔉 ① VISA
        ⌖
        closed 1 week at Christmas – **M** *(closed Sunday dinner to non-residents) (bar lunch)* a la carte
        5.55/12.15 **t.** – **20 rm** ⌷ 26.25/31.25 **t.**

AUSTIN-ROVER 46 New Sneddon St. ✆ 889 7882	NISSAN 11/17 Weir St. ✆ 889 6866
AUSTIN-ROVER 92 Glasgow Rd ✆ 889 8526	PEUGEOT, TALBOT 7 West St. ✆ 889 0011
FIAT 4/8 Lochfield Rd ✆ 884 2281	VAUXHALL-OPEL 69 Espedair St. ✆ 889 5254
FORD 37/41 Lonend ✆ 887 0191	VAUXHALL-OPEL 15/17 St. James St. ✆ 887 7951

PAPA WESTRAY (Isle of) Orkney (Orkney Islands) 401 L 5 – Shipping Services : see Orkney Islands (Mainland : Kirkwall).

PEAT INN Fife. (Fife) 401 L 15 – ⊠ Cupar – ✪ 033 484.
♦Edinburgh 44 – Dundee 21 – Perth 28.

   XX **The Peat Inn,** KY15 5LH, ✆ 206 – 🅿 AE ① VISA
        closed Sunday, Monday, 1 week January, 1 week April and 1 week October – **M** (booking
        essential)(restricted lunch) 9.00/a la carte 13.25/15.30 st. ⌑ 3.50.

PEEBLES Peebles. (Borders) 401 402 K 17 – pop. 5,884 – ECD : Wednesday – ✪ 0721.
Envir. : Neidpath Castle (site*) W : 1 m. – Traquair House★ *AC*, SE : 7 ½ m.
🏌 Kirkland St. ✆ 20197 – 🏌 West Linton ✆ 096 86 (West Linton) 589.
🛈 High St. ✆ 20138 (Easter and May-mid October).
♦Edinburgh 23 – Hawick 32 – ♦Glasgow 52.

   🏩 **Peebles Hydro,** Innerleithen Rd, EH45 8LX, ✆ 20602, Telex 72568, ≼, 🔲, 🚗, park, ⌘,
        squash – 🛗 📺 🅿 🔉 🔉 AE ① VISA ⌖
        M 6.25/10.50 st. ⌑ 3.00 – **135 rm** ⌷ 31.00/68.00 **st.** – SB 63.50/82.50 **st.**

   🏨 **Tontine** (T.H.F.), 39 High St., EH45 8AJ, ✆ 20892 – 📺 ⌷wc 🕿 🅿 🔉 AE ① VISA
        M 5.00/8.50 st. ⌑ 2.60 – ⌷ 4.50 – **37 rm** 29.50/40.00 **st.**

   🏨 **Park** (Swallow), Innerleithen Rd, EH45 8BA, ✆ 20451, Group Telex 53168, 🚗 – 📺 ⌷wc 🕿
        🅿 🔉 AE ① VISA
        M (buffet lunch) 6.50/8.50 st. ⌑ 3.40 – **26 rm** ⌷ 27.50/45.00 **st.** – SB 52.00/58.00 **st.**

   🏨 **Cringletie House** ⌕, EH45 8PL, N : 3 m. on A 703 ✆ 072 13 (Eddleston) 233, ≼, « Country
        house in extensive grounds », 🚗, park, ⌘ – 🛗 ⌷wc 🅿
        3 March-27 December – **M** (bar lunch Monday to Saturday) 8.50/13.00 **t.** ⌑ 3.00 – **16 rm**
        ⌷ 19.00/44.00 **t.**

        at Eddleston N : 4 ½ m. on A 703 – ⊠ Peebles – ✪ 072 13 Eddleston :

   XX **Horse Shoe Inn,** EH45 8QP, ✆ 225 – 🅿 🔉 AE ① VISA
        closed 25 December and 1 January – **M** a la carte 10.70/18.00 **t.** ⌑ 2.85.

AUSTIN-ROVER Innerleithen Rd ✆ 20627	VAUXHALL-OPEL St. Andrews Rd ✆ 20886
LANCIA George St. ✆ 20545	

PERTH Perth. (Tayside) 401 J 14 – pop. 43,030 – ECD : Wednesday – ✪ 0738.
Envir. : Scone Palace★ (furniture) *AC*, N : 4 m. by A 93 Y.
🏌 Craigie Hill, Cherrybank ✆ 24377, West boundary, by A 9 Z.
🛈 The Round House, Marshall Pl. ✆ 22900.
♦Edinburgh 44 – ♦Aberdeen 86 – ♦Dundee 22 – Dunfermline 29 – ♦Glasgow 64 – ♦Inverness 112 – ♦Oban 94.

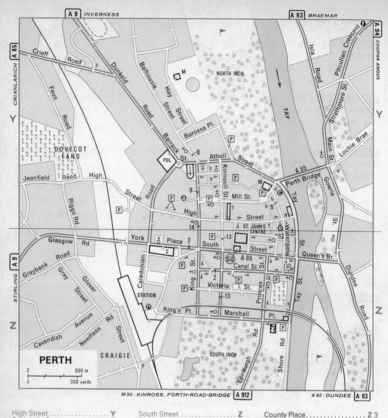

CRIANLARICH | A 85   Crieff   Road

Feus   Road

Dunkeld   Road

Balhousie

Hay   Street

Street

NORTH INCH

Isla   Road

Pitcullen   Crescent

Strathmore St.

Lochie Brae

Y

DOVECOT LAND

Jeanfield   Road   High

Barossa Pl.

Barrack   St.

POL   St.

8

Atholl   Street

A 85

Perth Bridge

Gowrie

Main St.

St.

Y

Glasgow   Rd

Riggs Rd

Street   Road

Kinnoull St.

9

High

Mill St.

Street

M

P

Perth Bridge

Graybank   Road

Gray   Street

Glover   Street

Needless   Rd

York   Place

Caledonian

3

14

South

ST. JOHN'S CENTRE

13

Street

Watergate

12

Queen's Br.

Dundee

Z

Cavendish   Avenue

STATION

King's Pl.

Canal St.

A 85

2

Victoria   St.

King   St.

Princes   St.

Tay   St.

Marshall   Pl.

Road

13

CRAIGIE

SOUTH INCH

Edinburgh   Rd

Shore   Rd

PERTH

0   300 m
0   300 yards

M 90 : KINROSS - FORTH-ROAD-BRIDGE   A 912   A 85 : DUNDEE   A 93

High Street .... Y	South Street .... Z	County Place .... Z 3
St. John's Centre .... Z	South Methven Street ..... Y 14	George Street .... Y 5
St. John Street .... Z 12		Melville Street .... Y 8
Scott Street .... Z 13	Charterhouse Lane .... Z 2	North Methven Street ..... Y 9

🏨 **Royal George** (T.H.F.), Tay St., PH1 5LD, ℘ 24455 – 📺 ⇔wc ☎ 🅿 🔒 🔊 🅰🅴 ⓓ 𝑉𝐼𝑆𝐴   Y c
  M 6.50/8.50 **st.** ⓪ 2.60 – 🖙 5.00 – **43 rm** 29.50/43.50 **st.**

🏨 **Stakis City Mills** (Stakis), West Mill St., PH1 5QP, ℘ 28281 – 📺 ⇔wc ☎ 🅿 🔒 🔊 🅰🅴 ⓓ 𝑉𝐼𝑆𝐴   Y a
  M a la carte 6.00/15.00 **st.** ⓪ 2.80 – **78 rm** 🖙 33.75/44.00 **st.**

🏨 **Station,** Leonard St., PH2 8HE, ℘ 24141, Telex 76481, 🚗 – 🛗 📺 ⇔wc ☎ 🅿 🔒 🔊 🅰🅴 ⓓ 𝑉𝐼𝑆𝐴   Z n
  M 5.00/6.95 – **54 rm** 🖙 19.25/46.20 **st.** – SB 50.00 **st.**

⤴ **Pitcullen,** 17 Pitcullen Cresent, PH2 7HT, NE : ¾ m. on A 94 ℘ 26506 – 🅿   Y r
  6 rm 🖙 10.00/16.00 **st.**

✗✗ **Huntingtower** ⤶ with rm, Crieff Rd, PH1 3JT, W : 3 ½ m. on A 85 ℘
  073 883 (Almond Bank) 241, ≤, 🚗 – ⇔wc 🅿   on A 85   Y
  4 rm.

✗ **Timothy's,** 24 St. John St., PH1 5SP, ℘ 26641, Smörrebrod – 🔊 𝑉𝐼𝑆𝐴   Y e
  closed Sunday, Monday and 14 July-4 August – **M** a la carte 3.00/6.15 **t.** ⓪ 2.80.

  at New Scone NE : 2 ½ m. on A 94 – Y – ✉ ☎ 0738 Perth :

🏨 **Balcraig House** ⤶, E : 1 ½ m. by A 94 ℘ 51123, ≤, 🚗, park, ✗ – ⇔wc ☎ 🅿 🔊 🅰🅴 ⓓ
  𝑉𝐼𝑆𝐴
  closed 7 to 11 January – **M** (lunch by arrangement) 17.50 **st.** – **10 rm** 🖙 38.50/77.50 **st.** – SB
  (weekends only)(winter only) 99.50 **st.**

🏨 **Murrayshall House** ⤶, PH2 7PH, E : 1 ½ m. by A 94 ℘ 51171, ≤, 🛝, 🚗, park – 📺 ⇔wc
  🛗wc ☎ 🅿 🔊 🅰🅴 ⓓ 𝑉𝐼𝑆𝐴 ⓪
  M 7.50/15.00 **t.** ⓪ 1.75 – **9 rm** 🖙 25.00/36.00 **t.** – SB 52.50/70.00 **st.**

528

at Glencarse E : 6 ½ m. by A 85 – Z – ⊠ Perth – ☻ 073 886 Glencarse :

XX **Newton House** with rm, PH2 7LX, ☞ 250, ☞ – 📺 ⊟wc �🚿wc ☎ Ⓟ 🅰 ⓪ 𝗩𝗜𝗦𝗔
　　M a la carte 8.35/14.25 **t.** ⍭ 2.50 – **5 rm** �🛏 28.00/38.00 **t.**

at Bridge of Earn S : 4 m. by A 90 and A 912 – Z – ⊠ ☻ 073 881 Bridge of Earn :

☝ **Moncreiffe Arms,** Main St., PH2 9PJ, ☞ 2931, ☞ – ⊟wc Ⓟ 🅰 🅰🅴 ⓪ 𝗩𝗜𝗦𝗔
　　M a la carte 8.10/10.55 **t.** ⍭ 3.00 – **12 rm** ⍁ 18.00/30.00 **t.**

AUSTIN-ROVER-JAGUAR Glenearn Rd ☞ 20811
BMW, ROLLS ROYCE 50/56 Leonard St. ☞ 25481
CITROEN 60 South St. ☞ 23335
DATSUN, MERCEDES-BENZ, SAAB 172 Dunkeld Rd
☞ 28211
FIAT, LOTUS 2 Dunkeld Rd ☞ 28211

FORD Riggs Rd ☞ 25121
VAUXHALL Dunkeld Rd ☞ 26241
VOLVO Arran Rd, North Muirton ☞ 22156
VW, AUDI, RENAULT Dunkeld Rd ☞ 25252
VW, AUDI 58/68 Perth Rd, Scone ☞ 0738 (Scone)
51276

PETERHEAD Aberdeen. (Grampian) 𝟰𝟬𝟭 O 11 – pop. 14,160 – ECD : Wednesday – ☻ 0779.

Envir. : Bullers of Buchan (cliffs★★) S : 6 m. – Cruden Bay (site★) SW : 8 m.

🆗, 🆗 Craigewan ☞ 2149.

♦Edinburgh 158 – ♦Aberdeen 34 – Fraserburgh 18.

🏨 **Waterside Inn,** 1 Fraserburgh Rd, AB4 7BN, NW : 2 m. on A 952 ☞ 71121, Telex 739413 –
　　📺 Ⓟ 🕮 🅰 🅰🅴 ⓪ 𝗩𝗜𝗦𝗔
　　M 4.75/12.00 **t.** ⍭ 3.00 – **114 rm** ⍁ 35.50/45.00 **st.** – SB (weekends only) 44.00/55.00 **st.**

🏨 **Palace,** Prince St., AB4 6RE, ☞ 4821 – 🛗 📺 ⊟wc �🚿wc ☎ Ⓟ 🅰 ⓪ 𝗩𝗜𝗦𝗔
　　M *(closed Sunday dinner)* 4.75/6.00 **st.** ⍭ 3.00 – **93 rm** ⍁ 25.30/29.90 **st.**

PITCAPLE Aberdeen. (Grampian) 𝟰𝟬𝟭 M 12 – ☻ 046 76.

♦Edinburgh 145 – ♦Aberdeen 21.

🏨 **Pittodrie House** ⌂, AB5 9HS, SW : 1 ¾ m. off A 96 by Chapel of Garioch rd ☞ 202, Telex
　　739935, ≤, « Country house with many antiques », ☞, park, ☞ squash – 📺 ⊟wc ☎ ⟺
　　Ⓟ 🅰 ⓪ 𝗩𝗜𝗦𝗔
　　M 9.00/18.00 **st.** ⍭ 2.50 – **12 rm** ⍁ 32.00/50.00 **st.** – SB (weekends only) (win-
　　ter only) 70.00/80.00 **st.**

PITLOCHRY Perth. (Tayside) 𝟰𝟬𝟭 I 13 – pop. 2,599 – ECD : Thursday – ☻ 0796.

Envir. : Blair Castle (interior★★) *AC*, NW : 7 ½ m. – Linn of Tummel★ NW : 4 m. – Queen's View
(≤★ of Loch Tummel) NW : 6 m.

🆗 ☞ 2792.

🇮 22 Atholl Rd ☞ 2215.

♦Edinburgh 68 – ♦Inverness 91 – Perth 26.

🏨 **Atholl Palace** (T.H.F.) ⌂, PH16 5LY, ☞ 2400, Telex 76406, ≤, ⌇ heated, ☞, park, ☞ – 🛗
　　📺 Ⓟ 🕮 🅰 🅰🅴 ⓪ 𝗩𝗜𝗦𝗔
　　M (bar lunch) 9.95 **st.** ⍭ 2.85 – ⍁ 5.00 – **92 rm** 29.50/46.00 **st.**

🏨 **Green Park,** Clunie Bridge Rd, PH16 5JY, ☞ 2537, ≤ Loch Tummel and Mountains, ☞ –
　　⊟wc �🚿wc Ⓟ ☞
　　Mid March-October – **M** 4.50/9.00 **st.** ⍭ 2.60 – **37 rm** ⍁ 18.00/48.00 **st.** – SB 50.00/64.00 **st.**

🏨 **Pine Trees** ⌂, Strathview Terr., PH16 5QR, ☞ 2121, ≤, ☜, ☞ – ⊟wc �🚿wc ⟺ Ⓟ 🅰 🅰🅴
　　⓪ 𝗩𝗜𝗦𝗔
　　April-December – **M** 5.50/9.50 **t.** ⍭ 2.25 – **27 rm** ⍁ 13.00/52.00 **t.**

🏨 **Burnside,** 19 West Moulin Rd, PH16 5EA, on A 924 ☞ 2203, ☞ – 📺 ⊟wc �🚿wc Ⓟ 🅰🅴 ⓪
　　𝗩𝗜𝗦𝗔
　　Late March-October – **M** (bar lunch) 8.50 **t.** ⍭ 2.75 – **22 rm** ⍁ 17.10/35.80 **t.**

🏨 Fisher's, 75-79 Atholl Rd, PH16 5BN, ☞ 2000, ☞ – 🛗 ⊟wc Ⓟ ☞ – **77 rm**.

🏠 **Craigard** ⌂, Strathview Terr., PH16 5AZ, ☞ 2592, ≤, ☞ – ⊟wc �🚿wc Ⓟ
　　April-October – **M** (bar lunch) 8.60 **st.** ⍭ 2.50 – **10 rm** ⍁ 14.25/34.00 **st.** – SB 40.50/49.00 **st.**

🏠 **Port-an-Eilean** ⌂, Strathtummel, PH16 5RU, NW : 10 m. by A 9 on B 8019 ☞ 088 24 (Tum-
　　mel Bridge) 233, ≤ Loch Tummel and mountains, « Victorian shooting lodge on banks of
　　Loch Tummel », ☜, ☞, park – ⊟wc Ⓟ
　　Mid April-mid October – **M** (bar lunch) 8.00 **t.** ⍭ 2.80 – **11 rm** ⍁ 14.00/33.00 **t.**

🏠 **Queen's View** ⌂, Strathtummel, PH16 5NR, NW : 6 ½ m. by A 9 on B 8019 ☞ 3291, ≤ Loch
　　Tummel and mountains, ☜, ☞ – ⊟wc Ⓟ
　　(booking essential November-February) – **M** a la carte 7.90/18.50 **t.** ⍭ 2.80 – **12 rm**
　　⍁ 13.65/32.60 **t.**

🏠 **Moulin,** 11-13 Kirkmichael Rd, PH16 5EH, N : 1 m. on A 924 ☞ 2196, ☞ – ⊟wc Ⓟ 🅰 🅰🅴
　　⓪
　　M (bar lunch) a la carte 6.40/12.70 **t.** ⍭ 3.90 – **22 rm** ⍁ 13.50/51.50 **t.**

🏠 **Acarsaid,** 8 Atholl Rd, PH16 5BX, ☞ 2389 – ⊟wc �🚿wc Ⓟ 🅰 𝗩𝗜𝗦𝗔 ☞
　　Easter-October – **M** (bar lunch) 9.00 **t.** – **19 rm** ⍁ 16.00/32.00 **t.**

🏠 **Castlebeigh** ⌂, 10 Knockard Rd, PH16 5HJ, off A 924 ☞ 2925, ≤, ☞ – ⊟wc Ⓟ
　　April-October – **M** (bar lunch) 8.50 **s.** ⍭ 3.50 – **18 rm** ⍁ 15.50/30.00 **st.** – SB 39.00/43.00 **st.**

  🏛 **Airdaniar,** 160 Atholl Rd, PH16 5AR, 𝒫 2266, ☞ – ℗
    April-October – **M** (bar lunch) 8.50 **st.** ⓘ 1.75 – **10 rm** �745 18.75/31.50 **st.**

  🏛 **Claymore,** 162 Atholl Rd, PH16 5AR, 𝒫 2888, ☞ – ⌂wc ℗. 🖭 *VISA*
    April-October – **M** (bar lunch) 8.50 **t.** ⓘ 2.50 – **12 rm** �745 14.50/36.50 **t.**

  ↑ **Craig Urrard,** 10 Atholl Rd, PH16 5BX, 𝒫 2346, ☞ – ⋔wc ℗. 🖭 AE ⓪ *VISA*
    10 rm �745 11.40/18.90 **st.**

    at Killiecrankie NW : 3 ¾ m. by A 9 on B 8079 – ✉ Pitlochry – ☎ 079 684 Killiecrankie :

  🏛 **Killiecrankie,** PH16 5LG, on A 9 𝒫 3220, ☞ – ⌂wc ⋔wc ℗
    Easter-mid October – **M** (bar lunch) 13.00 **t.** ⓘ 2.10 – **12 rm** �745 13.80/38.50 **t.**

 FORD Pitlochry Garage, Perth Rd 𝒫 2316

POLMONT Stirling. (Central) **401 402** I 16 – see Falkirk.

PORT APPIN Argyll. (Strathclyde) **401** D 14 – pop. 100 – ECD : Thursday – ☎ 063 173 Appin.
 🛳 to Lismore (Isle of) summer 8-9 daily ; winter 3 daily (10 mn).
 ♦Edinburgh 136 – Ballachulish 20 – ♦Oban 24.

  🏛 **Airds** ⌖, PA38 4DF, 𝒫 236, ≤ Loch Linnhe and hills of Kingairloch, « Former ferry inn on
    lochside » – ⌂wc ⋔wc ℗
    April-October – **M** (bar lunch) 15.00 **t.** ⓘ 3.20 – **15 rm** �745 (dinner included) 36.00/76.00 **t.**

PORT ASKAIG Argyll. (Strathclyde) **401** B 16 – see Islay (Isle of).

PORTPATRICK Wigtown. (Dumfries and Galloway) **401 402** E 19 – pop. 643 – ECD : Thursday
 – ✉ Stranraer – ☎ 077 681.
 Envir. : Logan gardens★ *AC*, SE : 13 m.
 Exc. : Mull of Galloway (site and ≤★★) SE : 24 ½ m. by Drummore – 🛝 𝒫 273.
 ♦Edinburgh 138 – ♦Ayr 61 – ♦Dumfries 80 – Stranraer 8.

  🏛 **Knockinaam Lodge** ⌖, DG9 9AD, SE : 3 ¼ m. off A 77 𝒫 471, ≤ garden and sea, « Country
    house atmosphere », ⌖, park – ⌂wc ℗. AE ⓪ *VISA*
    closed January and February – **M** (bar lunch) 13.50 **t.** ⓘ 3.55 – **10 rm** �745 (dinner included)
    40.00/100.00 – SB (except summer) (except Bank Holidays) 60.00 **st.**

  🏛 **Fernhill,** Heugh Rd, DG9 8TD, 𝒫 220, ≤, ☞ – ⌂wc ⋔wc ℗. 🖭 ⓪ *VISA*
    M a la carte 8.35/13.15 **t.** ⓘ 2.50 – **15 rm** �745 16.50/36.00 **t.** – SB 46.00/49.00 **st.**

PORTREE Inverness. (Highland) **401** B 11 – see Skye (Isle of).

PORTSONACHAN Argyll. (Strathclyde) **401** E 14 – ✉ Dalmally – ☎ 086 63 Kilchrenan.
 ♦ Edinburgh 108 – ♦ Glasgow 72 – ♦ Oban 30 – Perth 80.

  🏛 **Portsonachan** ⌖, Lochaweside, PA33 1BL, 𝒫 224, ≤ Loch Awe and Ben Cruachan, ⌖, ☞
    – ⌂wc. 🖭 *VISA*
    closed 5 January-1 March – **M** (buffet lunch) 10.50 **t.** ⓘ 2.00 – **18 rm** �745 15.00/41.50 **t.**

PRESTWICK Ayr. (Strathclyde) **401 402** G 17 – pop. 13,437 – ECD : Wednesday – ☎ 0292.
 ✈ 𝒫 79822, Telex 77209 – Glasgow Terminal : Stand no. 23, Anderston Cross Bus Station, Blythswood St – ✈ see also Glasgow.
 🅱 2 The Cross, Station Rd 𝒫 79234 – Prestwick Airport 𝒫 77309.
 ♦Edinburgh 73 – ♦Ayr 4 – ♦Glasgow 30.

                Plan of Built up Area : see Ayr

  🏛 **Carlton** (Osprey), 187 Ayr Rd, KA9 1TP, 𝒫 76811 – 📺 ⌂wc ⚙ ℗. 🖭 AE ⓪ *VISA*   BY **v**
    M (bar lunch) 8.50 **t.** ⓘ 3.25 – **34 rm** �745 23.00/40.00 **t.** – SB 40.00/44.00 **st.**

  ↑ **Kincraig,** 39 Ayr Rd, KA9 1SY, 𝒫 79480 – ℗. ⌀   BY **c**
    6 rm �745 8.50/16.00 **st.**

 AUSTIN-ROVER 1 Monkton Rd 𝒫 77415   VAUXHALL-OPEL 97/99 Main St. 𝒫 70545

QUOTHQUAN Lanark. (Strathclyde) **401 402** J 17 – pop. 73 – ✉ ☎ 0899 Biggar.
 ♦Edinburgh 30 – ♦Carlisle 72 – ♦Glasgow 37.

  🏛 **Shieldhill House** ⌖, ML12 6NA, NE : 1 m. 𝒫 20035, ≤, ☞ – ⌂wc ⋔wc ℗. 🖭 AE ⓪
    M (bar lunch) 10.00 **st.** ⓘ 2.75 – **20 rm** �745 12.00/30.00 **st.** – SB 30.00/35.00 **st.**

RAASAY (Isle of) Inverness. (Highland) **401** B 11.
 🛳 by Caledonian MacBrayne : to Isle of Skye : Sconser Monday/Saturday 3-4 daily (15 mn).

    Raasay – ✉ Kyle of Lochalsh – ☎ 047 862 Raasay.

  🏛 **Isle of Raasay** ⌖, IV40 8PB, 𝒫 222, ≤ Narrows of Raasay and Skye, ☞ – 📺 ⌂wc ⚙ ℗.
    ⌀
    April-September – **M** (bar lunch) 9.50 **t.** – **12 rm** �745 12.00/24.00 **t.**

RENFREW Renfrew. (Strathclyde) **401** G 16 – pop. 18,595 – ECD : Wednesday – ✆ 041 Glasgow.
♦Edinburgh 50 – ♦Glasgow 7.

🏨 **Stakis Normandy** (Stakis), Inchinnan Rd, PA4 9EJ, ✆ 886 4100, Telex 778897 – 🛗 📺
⌷wc ☎ 🕭 🅿 🔄 🔊 AE ⓪ VISA
M 7.00/9.00 t. – **142 rm** ⬜ 41.00/49.00 t. – SB (weekends only) 46.00 **st.**

🏨 **Dean Park,** 91 Glasgow Rd, PA4 8YB, ✆ 886 3771, Telex 779032, 🍴 – 📺 ⌷wc ☎ 🅿 🔄
🔊 AE ⓪ VISA
M 6.50/7.50 t. 🍷 2.50 – **120 rm** ⬜ 34.00/42.00 t. – SB (weekends only) 54.00/60.00 **st.**

XX **Piccolo Mondo,** 63 Hairst St., PA4 8QY, ✆ 886 3055, Italian rest. – 🅿 🔊 AE ⓪ VISA
closed Sunday, New Year's day and Bank Holidays – **M** a la carte 7.65/13.25 t. 🍷 2.85.

PEUGEOT, TALBOT 18/20 Fulbar St. ✆ 886 3354   VAUXHALL-OPEL Porterfield Rd ✆ 886 2777

RHU Dunbarton. (Strathclyde) **401 402** F 15 – see Helensburgh.

RHUBODACH Bute. (Strathclyde) **401 402** E 16 – Shipping Services : see Bute (Isle of).

RHUM (Isle of) Inverness. (Highland) **401** B 13 – Shipping Services : see Mallaig.

ROCKCLIFFE Kirkcudbright. (Dumfries and Galloway) **401 402** I 19 – pop. 170 – ✉ Dalbeattie
– ✆ 055 663.
See : Site★.
🐚 Dalbeattie, N : 6 m. on A 710.
♦Edinburgh 95 – ♦Dumfries 18 – Stranraer 69.

🏨 **Baron's Craig** ⚓, DG5 4QF, ✆ 225, ≤, 🍴, park – ⌷wc 🅿
April-mid October – **M** 6.00/11.00 t. 🍷 2.50 – **25 rm** ⬜ 23.25/64.00 t. – SB 60.00/80.00 **st.**

ROTHES Moray. (Grampian) **401** K 11 – pop. 1,204 – ECD : Wednesday – ✆ 034 03.
♦Edinburgh 185 – ♦Aberdeen 61 – Fraserburgh 59 – ♦Inverness 49.

🏨 **Rothes Glen** ⚓, IV33 7AH, N : 3 m. on A 941 ✆ 254, ≤, « Country house atmosphere », 🍴,
park – ⌷wc ☎ 🅿 🔊 AE ⓪ VISA
March-mid November – **M** 6.00/12.75 t. 🍷 3.30 – **16 rm** ⬜ 27.00/50.00 t.

ROUSAY (Isle of) Orkney (Orkney Islands) **401** K 6 – Shipping Services : see Orkney Islands
(Mainland : Kirkwall).

ST. ANDREWS Fife. (Fife) **401** L 14 – pop. 11,630 – ECD : Thursday – ✆ 0334.
See : Cathedral★ (St. Rule's tower and Museum AC).
Envir. : Leuchars (church★) NW : 6 m.
🐚 Eden Course, St. Andrews Links ✆ 74296 – 🐚 Jubilee Course, St. Andrews Links ✆ 73938 – 🐚
New Course, St. Andrews Links, ✆ 73938 – 🐚 St. Michaels ✆ 033 483 (Leuchars) 365, N : 5 m.
🛈 South St. ✆ 72021.
♦Edinburgh 49 – ♦Dundee 14 – Stirling 51.

🏨 **Old Course Golf and Country Club** ⚓, Old Station Rd, KY16 9SP, ✆ 74371, Telex 76280,
≤ – 🛗 📺 🕭 🅿 🔄 🔊 AE ⓪ VISA
M 9.00/14.50 t. 🍷 3.50 – **146 rm** ⬜ 68.00/98.00 t.

🏨 Rusacks Marine, 16 Pilmour Links, KY16 9JQ, ✆ 74321, ≤ – 🛗 📺 🅿
50 rm.

🏨 **Rufflets** ⚓, Strathkinness Low Rd, KY16 9TX, W : 1 ½ m. on B 939 ✆ 72594, ≤, « Country
house, gardens » – 📺 ⌷wc ☎ 🅿 🔊 AE ⓪ VISA 🍴
closed 6 January-4 February – **M** 6.00/11.00 t. 🍷 4.00 – **21 rm** ⬜ 29.00/50.00 t. – SB
(except summer) 23.00/25.00 **st.**

🏨 **St. Andrews Golf,** 40 The Scores, KY16 9AS, ✆ 72611, ≤ – 🛗 📺 ⌷wc ☎ 🔄 🔊 AE ⓪
VISA
M a la carte 11.25/15.50 t. 🍷 3.00 – **22 rm** ⬜ 29.50/49.00 st. – SB (summer only) 63.00/73.00 **st.**

AUSTIN-ROVER West Port ✆ 72101

ST. BOSWELLS Roxburgh. (Borders) [401] [402] L 17 – pop. 1,002 – ☎ 0835.
⛳9 ℘ 2359, off A 68 at St. Boswells Green.
♦Edinburgh 39 – ♦ Glasgow 79 – Hawick 17 – ♦Newcastle-upon-Tyne 66.

🏨 **Dryburgh Abbey** (Best Western) 🌙, TD6 0RQ, N : 3 ½ m. by B 6404 on B 6356 ℘ 22261, ⩽, 🎣, 🌳, park – 🛁wc [P]. 🧒. [EN] [AE] [①] [VISA]
M (buffet lunch) 11.00 **t.** 🍷 3.00 – **27 rm** 🛏 21.00/48.80 **t.** – SB (weekends only) (except summer) 55.00/60.00 **st.**

ST. CATHERINES Argyll. (Strathclyde) [401] E 15 – ✉ Cairndow – ☎ 0499 Inveraray.
♦Edinburgh 96 – ♦Glasgow 53 – ♦Oban 53.

🏠 **Thistle House,** PA25 6AZ, on A 815 ℘ 2209, ⩽, 🌳 – [P]. 🚫🐕
April-October – **6 rm** 🛏 10.50/21.00.

ST. COMBS Aberdeen. (Grampian) [401] O 11 – pop. 738 – ECD : Wednesday – ✉ Fraserburgh – ☎ 034 65 Inverallochy.
♦Edinburgh 166 – ♦Aberdeen 42 – Fraserburgh 6.

🏨 **Tufted Duck** 🌙, AB4 5YS, ℘ 2481, ⩽, 🌳 – [TV] 🛁wc 🚿wc 📞 [P]. [EN] [AE] [①] [VISA]
M (lunch by arrangement) a la carte 10.50/14.00 **t.** 🍷 3.00 – **18 rm** 🛏 18.95/31.95 **t.**

ST. FILLANS Perth. (Tayside) [401] H 14 – pop. 160 – ECD : Wednesday – ☎ 076 485.
⛳9 ℘ 312.
♦Edinburgh 65 – ♦Glasgow 55 – ♦Oban 64 – Perth 29.

🏨 **Four Seasons,** PH6 2NF, ℘ 333, ⩽ Loch Earn and mountains, 🌳 – [TV] 🛁wc 📞 [P]. [EN] [AE]
April-October – **M** 7.50/11.00 **t.** 🍷 3.00 – **18 rm** 🛏 32.00/54.00 **st.**

SALEN Argyll. (Strathclyde) [401] C 13 – see Mull (Isle of).

SANDAY (Isle of) Orkney (Orkney Islands) [401] M 6 – Shipping Services : see Orkney Islands (Mainland : Kirkwall).

SANDBANK Argyll. (Strathclyde) [401] [402] F 16 – see Dunoon.

SCALASAIG Argyll. (Strathclyde) [401] B 15 – see Colonsay (Isle of).

SCALLOWAY Shetland (Shetland Islands) [401] Q 3 – see Shetland Islands (Mainland).

SCALPAY (Isle of) Inverness. (Highland) [401] A 10 – Shipping Services : see Harris (Isle of).

SCARISTA Inverness. (Outer Hebrides) (Western Isles) – see Harris (Isle of).

SCOURIE Sutherland (Highland) [401] E 8 – pop. 250 – ✉ Lairg – ☎ 0971.
See : Site★.
♦Edinburgh 261 – ♦Inverness 102.

🏨 **Scourie** 🌙, IV27 4SX, ℘ 2396, ⩽, 🎣 – 🛁wc [P]. [EN] [①] [VISA]
Mid March-mid October – **M** (bar lunch Monday to Saturday) 5.50/7.50 **t.** 🍷 2.50 – **21 rm** 🛏 15.70/39.40 **t.**

🏠 **Eddrachilles** 🌙, Badcall Bay, IV27 4TH, S : 2½ m. on A 894 ℘ 2080, ⩽ Badcall Bay and islands, 🌳 – 🛁wc 🚿wc [P]
closed 10 to 24 November, Christmas Day and New Year's Day – **M** (lunch by arrangement) 5.95 **t.** 🍷 2.30 – **11 rm** 🛏 19.15/34.30 **t.**

SCRABSTER Caithness. (Highland) [401] J 8 – Shipping Services : see Thurso.

SELKIRK Selkirk. (Borders) [401] [402] L 17 – pop. 5,417 – ☎ 0750.
Envir. : St. Mary's Loch★ SW : 17 m.
⛳9 ℘ 20621, S : 1 m – [i] Town Centre ℘ 20054 (Easter and mid May-mid October).
♦Edinburgh 40 – ♦Glasgow 74 – Hawick 11 – ♦Newcastle-upon-Tyne 62.

🏨 **Philipburn House** 🌙, TD7 5LS, W : 1 m. at junction A 707 and A 708 ℘ 20747, 🏊 heated, 🌳 – [TV] 🛁wc [P]. [EN] [AE] [①] [VISA]. 🚫🐕
closed January – **M** 8.50/13.50 **t.** 🍷 3.15 – **16 rm** 🛏 20.00/48.00 **t.** – SB (weekends only) (except summer) 60.00/74.00 **st.**

at Ettrickbridge SW : 7 m. on B 7009 – ✉ ☎ 075 05 Ettrickbridge :

🏨 **Ettrickshaws** 🌙, TD7 5HW, SW : 1 m. by B 7009 ℘ 52229, ⩽, 🌳 – [TV] 🛁wc [P]. 🚫🐕
closed 22 December-22 February – **M** *(closed Monday lunch)* (bar lunch) 11.00 **t.** – **6 rm** 🛏 26.00/55.00 **t.** – SB (winter only) 44.00/46.00 **st.**

SHAPINSAY (Isle of) Orkney (Orkney Islands) [401] L 6 – Shipping Services : see Orkney Islands (Mainland : Kirkwall).

SHETLAND ISLANDS Shetland (Shetland Islands) **401** PQ 3 – pop. 17,327.

✈ see Mainland : Lerwick and Sumburgh.

✈ Unst Airport : at Baltasound ℰ 095 781 (Baltasound) 404/7.

🚢 Shipping connections with the Continent : from Lerwick to Faroe Islands (Thorshavn) (Smyril Line) – to Norway (Bergen) (Smyril Line) – to Iceland (Seydisfjordur via Thorshavn) (Smyril Line) – by P & O Ferries : Orkney and Shetland Services : from Lerwick to Aberdeen 3 weekly (14 h) – by Shetland Islands Council : from Lerwick (Mainland) to Bressay 11-13 daily (10 mn) – from Laxo (Mainland) to Symbister (Isle of Whalsay) 5-7 daily (25 mn) – from Toft (Mainland) to Ulsta (Isle of Yell) 16-20 daily (22 mn) – from Gutcher (Isle of Yell) to Belmont (Isle of Unst) 11-17 daily (10 mn) – to Oddsta (Isle of Fetlar) 2-3 daily (25 mn).

🚢 by J.W. Stout : from Fair Isle to Sumburgh (Gruntness) 2 weekly (2 h 45 mn) – by Shetland Islands Council : from Lerwick (Mainland) to Skerries 2 weekly (3 h).

MAINLAND

Brae – ⊠ ✆ 080 622 Brae

🏠 **Busta House** ⌖, ZE9 9QN, SW : 1½ m. ℰ 506, ≤, « Part 16C and 18C country house », ✿ – ▭ 🖵wc 🛁wc ☎ ℗
closed mid December-mid January – **M** (bar lunch) 13.50 **st.** ⅄ 2.75 – **21 rm** ⊂⊃ 20.00/54.00 **st.** – SB 50.00/70.00 **st.**

Hillswick – ⊠ ✆ 080 623 Hillswick.
See : Site★.
Envir. : Esha Ness (St. Magnus Bay★★★) W : 8 m. – E : Sullom Voe★★.

🏠 **St. Magnus Bay** ⌖, ZE2 9RW, ℰ 209, ≤, ✿ – ▭ 🛁wc ℗. ◪
M 4.50/7.70 t. ⅄ 3.25 – **26 rm** ⊂⊃ 15.40/34.00 t.

Lerwick – pop. 6,127 – ECD : Wednesday – ⊠ ✆ 0595 Lerwick.
See : Site★ – Harbour★ – Clickhimin Broch★.
Envir. : W : The Deeps (cliff)★★★ – Loch of Tingwall★ NW : 5 m. – Gulberwick (wick ≤★) SW : 5 m.
🟦 Dale ℰ 059 584 (Gott) 369, N : 3 ½ m.
✈ Tingwall Airport : ℰ 3535/2024, NW : 6 ½ m. by A 971.
🅑 Market Cross ℰ 3434.

🏠 **Shetland**, Holmsgarth Rd, ZE1 0PW, ℰ 5515, Telex 75432, ≤, ◪ – 🛗 ▭ 🛁wc ☎ 👤 ℗. 🏌.
◪ 🅰🅴 ⓪ 𝘝𝘐𝘚𝘈
M a la carte 4.50/11.25 **st.** ⅄ 2.50 – **67 rm** ⊂⊃ 44.00/52.00 **st.**

🏠 **Lerwick Thistle** (Thistle), 15 South Rd, ZE1 0RB, ℰ 2166, Telex 75128, ≤ – ▭ 🛁wc ✆ ℗.
◪ 🅰🅴 ⓪ 𝘝𝘐𝘚𝘈
⊂⊃ 4.75 – **55 rm** 35.00/42.00 t. – SB 44.00 **st.**

🏠 **Kveldsro House**, Greenfield Pl., ZE1 0AN, ℰ 2195 – ▭ 🛁wc ℗. ✎
closed Christmas and New Year – **M** 6.00/9.00 ⅄ 2.60 – **14 rm**.

AUSTIN-ROVER-LAND ROVER Commercial Rd ℰ   PEUGEOT-TALBOT, RENAULT North Rd ℰ 3315
3313
MAZDA, PEUGEOT-TALBOT 20 Commercial Rd ℰ
2896

Scalloway – pop. 896 – ECD : Thursday – ⊠ ✆ 059 588 Scalloway.
See : Site and ≤★★.
🟦 Berry Farm ℰ 219.

Sumburgh – ⊠ ✆ 0950 Sumburgh.
See : Jarlshof (prehistoric village★★, site★).
Envir. : St. Ninian's Isle★★ NW : 9 m. – Levenwick ≤★ N : 9 m.
✈ ℰ 60654, Telex 75451.

Voe – pop. 220 – ⊠ ✆ 080 68 Voe.
See : Site★.
Envir. : Dales Voe★ N : 5 m. – Walls (site★) SW : 18 ½ m.
Exc. : W : Voe of Snarraness★★ – Swarbacks Minn (from B 9071 ≤★★) – Sound of Papa★★ – The Rona Aith Voe (from B 9071 ≤★★).

Whiteness – ⊠ Whiteness – ✆ 059 584 Gott.
🏠 Westings, Wormadale, ZE2 9LJ, ℰ 242, ≤ The Deeps and Islands – ▭ 🛁wc ℗. ◪ ✎
closed January – **9 rm** ⊂⊃ 16.50/25.00.

SHIEL BRIDGE Ross and Cromarty (Highland) 📖 D 12 – ✉ ✆ 059 981 Glenshiel.

◆Edinburgh 187 – ◆Inverness 63 – Kyle of Lochalsh 15.

🏨 **Kintail Lodge,** IV40 8HL, 🖉 275, ≤ Loch Duich and mountains, 🛲 – 🛏wc 🅿. 🔼 𝐕𝐈𝐒𝐀
closed November, Christmas and New Year – **M** (bar lunch) 8.80 **st.** �⅃ 2.60 – **11 rm** ⯐ (dinner included) 30.00/60.00 **st.**

SHIELDAIG Ross and Cromarty (Highland) 📖 D 11 – pop. 90 – ✉ Strathcarron – ✆ 052 05.
See : Site★.

◆Edinburgh 226 – ◆ Inverness 71 – Kyle of Lochalsh 67.

🍴 **Tigh-An-Eilean,** IV54 8XN, 🖉 251, ≤ Shieldaig Islands and Loch – 🅿. �
April-October – **M** (buffet lunch) 7.50 **t.** ⅃ 2.25 – **13 rm** ⯐ 19.50/44.00 **t.**

SKEABOST Inverness. (Highland) 📖 B 11 – see Skye (Isle of).

SKELMORLIE Ayr. (Strathclyde) 📖 F 16 – pop. 1,535 – ECD : Wednesday – ✆ 0475 Wemyss Bay.

◆Edinburgh 73 – ◆Ayr 36 – ◆Glasgow 30.

🏨 **Manor Park** ⚘, PA17 5HE, S : 2 ¾ m. on A 78 🖉 520832, ≤ gardens and Firth of Clyde, « Extensive well kept gardens », park – 📺 🛏wc 🍴wc ⊛ 🅿. �
closed 3 January-mid February – **M** a la carte 11.60/16.85 **t.** ⅃ 2.75 – **18 rm** ⯐ 27.50/50.00 **t.** – SB 60.00 **st.**

🏠 **Redcliffe,** 25 Shore Rd, PA17 5EH, on A 78 🖉 521036, ≤, 🛲 – 📺 🍴wc ⊛ 🅿. 🔼 🅰🅴 ⓞ
M 10.00/20.00 **st.** ⅃ 3.50 – **5 rm** ⯐ 23.50/39.00 **st.**

SKYE (Isle of) Inverness. (Highland) 📖 B 11 and 12 – pop. 7,364.
See : East coast scenery and Cuillin Hills★★★.
✈ at Broadford : 🖉 047 12 (Broadford) 202.
🚢 by Caledonian MacBrayne : from Kyleakin to Kyle of Lochalsh : frequent services daily (5 mn) – from Armadale to Mallaig summer only Monday/Saturday 3-5 daily (30 mn) – from Uig to Tarbert (Isle of Harris) Monday/Saturday 6 weekly (2 h 30 mn direct - 4 h 45 mn via Lochmaddy) – from Uig to Lochmaddy (North Uist) Monday/Saturday 6-9 weekly (2 h - 2 h 30 mn direct - 4 h 45 mn via Tarbert) – from Sconser to Isle of Raasay ; Monday/Saturday 3-4 daily (15 mn).
🚢 by Caledonian Mac Brayne : from Armadale to Mallaig Monday/Saturday 10 weekly (30 mn).

Broadford – pop. 310 – ECD : Wednesday – ✉ ✆ 047 12 Broadford.
See : Broadford Bay★★ – Red Hills★★.
Envir. : Elgol (site★★★) SW : 13 ½ m. – Kyleakin (site★) E : 8 m.
🛈 🖉 361 and 463 (summer only).

VW, AUDI 🖉 225

Dunvegan – pop. 301 – ✉ ✆ 047 022 Dunvegan.
See : Loch★★ – Dunvegan Castle★ AC.

Isleornsay – ✉ ✆ 047 13 Isleornsay.
Envir. : Armadale Castle (site★★) SW : 7 m.

🏨 **Kinloch Lodge** ⚘, IV43 8QY, N : 3 ½ m. by A 851 🖉 333, ≤ Loch Na Dal, ⚲, 🛲 – 🛏wc 🅿
closed 20 January-28 February – **M** (bar lunch residents only) 15.40 **st.** ⅃ 3.20 – **9 rm** ⯐ 28.00/66.00 **st.**

🏠 **Toravaig House,** IV44 8RJ, SW : 3 m. on A 851 🖉 231, 🛲 – 🛏wc 🍴wc 🅿. 🅰🅴 ⓞ 𝐕𝐈𝐒𝐀
March-October – **M** 5.00/9.00 **t.** ⅃ 2.50 – **10 rm** ⯐ 13.00/32.00 **t.**

Kensaleyre – ✉ Portree – ✆ 047 032 Skeabost Bridge.

🏠 **MacDonald** ⚘, IV51 9XE, 🖉 339, ≤ Loch Snizort Beag, 🛲 – 🍴wc 🅿. 🅰🅴. �
10 May-September – **11 rm** ⯐ 14.00/34.00 **st.**

Portree – pop. 1,374 – ECD : Wednesday – ✉ ✆ 0478 Portree.
See : Site★ – Sound of Raasay★★★.
Envir. : Old Man of Storr★★ N : 7 m. – Loch Bracadale★★ SW : 9 m.
Exc. : Kilt Rock (≤★★★), Staffin Bay and Quiraing★★★ N : 18 m.
🛈 Meall House 🖉 2137.

🏠 **Rosedale,** Beaumont Cres., IV51 9DB, 🖉 2531, ≤ harbour – 🛏wc 🍴wc 🅿
May-September – **M** (bar lunch) 8.50 **t.** – **20 rm** ⯐ 18.50/36.00 **t.**

🍴 **Kings Haven** with rm, 11 Bosville Terr., IV51 9DJ, 🖉 2290 – 🍴wc. 🔼 𝐕𝐈𝐒𝐀. �
April-October – **M** (bar lunch) 10.50 **t.** – **6 rm** ⯐ 23.00/33.00 **t.**

███ Skeabost ███ – ECD : Wednesday – ✉ ☎ 047 032 Skeabost Bridge.

🏨 **Skeabost House** ⌂, IV51 9NP, 𝒫 202, ≤ Loch Snizort Beag, « Country house in grounds bordering loch », ⌷, 🦌, park – 🚾wc ☎
May-12 October – **M** (buffet lunch) 9.50 **st.** 🍷 3.00 – **21 rm** ⊡ 16.50/44.00 **st.**

███ Sligachan ███ – ✉ ☎ 047 852 Sligachan.
See : Site★★★ – Loch★★.
Envir. : Loch Harport★★ W : 6 m.

🏨 Sligachan, IV47 8SW, 𝒫 204, ≤, ⌷ – 🚾wc 🚗 ☎
23 rm.

███ Uig ███ – pop. 103 – ECD : Wednesday – ✉ ☎ 047 042 Uig.
See : Loch Snizort★★.
Envir. : Score Bay★ N : 8 m.

███ SLIGACHAN ███ Inverness. (Highland) 🗺 B 12 – see Skye (Isle of).

███ SMA'GLEN ███ Perth. (Tayside) 🗺 I 14 – see Crieff.

███ SOUTH QUEENSFERRY ███ W. Lothian (Lothian) 🗺 J 16 – pop. 5,056 – ECD : Wednesday – ☎ 031 Edinburgh.
See : Forth Bridge★★ *AC*.
Envir. : Hopetoun House★★ *AC*, W : 3 m. – Blackness Castle★ (15C) *AC*, W : 8 ½ m.
♦Edinburgh 9 – Dunfermline 7 – ♦Glasgow 40.

🏨 **Forth Bridges Moat House** (Q.M.H.), EH30 9SF, junction A 90 and Forth Bridge 𝒫 331 1199, Telex 727430, ≤ Firth of Forth and Bridges, squash – 📺 🚾wc 🅿 ☎. 🎿. 🔼 AE ① 𝒱𝐼𝒮𝒜
M 6.95/8.00 **st.** – ⊡ 4.25 – **108 rm** 34.50/42.50 **st.** – SB (weekends only) 48.00 **st.**

███ SPEAN BRIDGE ███ Inverness. (Highland) 🗺 F 13 – pop. 235 – ECD : Thursday – ☎ 039 781.
Envir. : N : Loch Lochy★★ – Clunes Forest (waterfall)★ NW : 3 ½ m.
♦Edinburgh 133 – ♦Inverness 56 – Kyle of Lochalsh 66 – ♦Oban 58 – Perth 91.

🏨 **Letterfinlay Lodge**, PH34 4DZ, N : 7 ½ m. on A 82 𝒫 039 784 (Invergloy) 222, ≤ Loch Lochy and mountains, ⌷, 🦌 – 🚾wc 📶wc ☎. 🔼 AE ① 𝒱𝐼𝒮𝒜
March-October – **M** (buffet lunch) 8.00 **st.** – **15 rm** ⊡ 11.00/32.00 **st.**

🏨 **Spean Bridge**, PH34 4ES, 𝒫 250, ⌷ – 🚾wc ☎. 🔼 ① 𝒱𝐼𝒮𝒜
April-October – **M** (bar lunch) 8.00 **t.** 🍷 2.50 – **24 rm** ⊡ 11.50/29.00 **t.**

███ SPITTAL OF GLENSHEE ███ Perth. (Tayside) 🗺 J 13 – Winter Sports – ✉ Blairgowrie – ☎ 025 085 Glenshee.
Envir. : Devil's Elbow★★ N : 6 m. – S : Glenshee (❄★★ by chairlift 15 mn, *AC*).
♦Edinburgh 76 – ♦Dundee 36 – Perth 34.

🏨 **Dalmunzie House** ⌂, PH10 7QG, NW : 1 ½ m. 𝒫 224, ≤, ⌷, 🦌, park, ⛳ – ╞ 🚾wc ☎. 🔼 ①
January-23 October – **M** (bar lunch) 12.00 **st.** 🍷 3.50 – **16 rm** ⊡ 20.00/50.00 **st.**

███ STENNESS ███ Orkney (Orkney Islands) 🗺 K 7 – see Orkney Islands (Mainland).

███ STEWARTON ███ Ayr. (Strathclyde) 🗺 🗺 G 16 – pop. 4,492 – ECD : Wednesday and Saturday – ☎ 0560.
♦Edinburgh 60 – ♦Ayr 21 – ♦Glasgow 19.

XXX **Chapeltoun House** ⌂ with rm, KA3 3ED, SW : 2 ½ m. by B 769 𝒫 82696, ≤, « Country house in extensive grounds », ⌷, 🦌, park – 📺 🚾wc 📶wc ☎ ☎. 🔼 AE ① 𝒱𝐼𝒮𝒜 ⛳
closed 1 to 8 January, 14 July-6 August and 25-26 December – **M** (booking essential) a la carte 12.20/17.30 **t.** 🍷 3.80 – **6 rm** ⊡ 40.00/65.00 **t.**

Per viaggiare in Europa, utilizzate :
Le carte Michelin scala 1/1 000 000 **Le Grandi Strade ;**
Le carte Michelin dettagliate ;
Le guide Rosse Michelin (alberghi e ristoranti) :
   Benelux, Deutschland, España Portugal, Main Cities **Europe, France, Italia.**
Le Guide Verdi Michelin che descrivono
   le curiosità e gli itinerari di visita :
   musei, monumenti, percorsi turistici interessanti.

Stirling. (Central) **401** I 15 – pop. 29,776 – ECD : Wednesday – ✆ 0786.

See : Stirling Castle★★ *AC* B – Church of the Holy Rude★ B **A**.

Envir. : Bannockburn (battlefield) *AC*, S : 3 m. by Glasgow Rd A – Doune Castle★ (stronghold 15C) *AC*, NW : 8 m. by A 84 A.

🏌 Tillicoultry ✆ 0259 (Tillicoultry) 50741, E : 9 m. by A 9 A.

🚗 ✆ 3085.

🛈 Dumbarton Rd ✆ 5019 – Bannockburn ✆ 814026 (summer only).

♦Edinburgh 37 – Dunfermline 23 – Falkirk 14 – ♦Glasgow 28 – Greenock 52 – Motherwell 30 – ♦Oban 87 – Perth 35.

STIRLING

Dumbarton Road	B 9	Barnton Street	B 2	Park Place
Murray Place	B 15	Borestone Crescent	A 3	Queen Street
Port Street	B	Causewayhead Road	A, B 4	Randolph Terrace
Thistle Centre	B	Corn Exchange Road	B 5	Seaforth Place
Upper Craigs	B 29	Cornton Road	A 7	Shirra's Brae Road

Barnton Street .... B 2
Borestone Crescent .... A 3
Causewayhead Road ...... A, B 4
Corn Exchange Road........ B 5
Cornton Road .... A 7
Coxithill Road .... A 8
Goosecroft Road .... B 12
King Street .... B 13
Newhouse .... A 16

Park Place .... A 18
Queen Street .... B 20
Randolph Terrace .... A 22
Seaforth Place .... B 24
Shirra's Brae Road........... A 26
Southfield Crescent.......... B 27
Union Street .... B 28
Victoria Square.............. B 30
Weaver Row .... A 31

🏨 **Park Lodge** without rest., 32 Park Terr., FK8 2JS, ✆ 74862, « Tasteful decor », 🌲 – 📺 🛁wc 🅿. 🔟 💳 ⚡ B a
9 rm ⊇ 25.00/50.00 **st.**

🏨 **Stakis Station** (Stakis), 56 Murray Pl., FK8 2BX, ✆ 72017 – 📺 🛁wc 🚿wc ☎ 🅿. 🔟 AE ⓞ 💳 B n
M 4.40/8.95 **t.** 🍷 2.80 – **25 rm** ⊇ 26.75/35.00 **t.** – SB 39.00 **st.**

🏨 King Robert, Glasgow Rd, FK7 0LJ, ✆ 811666 – 📺 🛁wc ☎ 🅿 A c
21 rm.

XX **Heritage** with rm, 16 Allan Park, FK8 2QG, ✆ 73660, French rest. – 📺 🛁wc 🅿. 🔟 ⓞ 💳 B e
M 3.80/8.50 🍷 2.50 – **4 rm** ⊇ 18.00/25.00.

at Blairlogie E : 4 ½ m. by A 9 and A 91 – A – ✉ Stirling – ✆ 0259 Alva :

🏨 **Blairlogie House**, FK9 5QE, ✆ 61441, 🌲 – 🛁wc 🚿wc 🅿. 💳
closed Sunday dinner and Bank Holidays – **M** a la carte 9.30/12.50 **t.** 🍷 3.30 – **6 rm** ⊇ 23.00/36.00 **t.** – SB (weekends only) 27.30/35.50 **t.**

ALFA-ROMEO, COLT, DAIHATSU, JEEP, RENAULT
Kerse Rd 🖉 62618
AUSTIN-ROVER-DAIMLER-JAGUAR,   ROLLS
ROYCE-BENTLEY Wallace St. 🖉 62821
CITROEN, VAUXHALL-OPEL 119/139 Glasgow Rd
🖉 0786 (Bannockburn) 811234
FIAT 44 Causeway Head Rd 🖉 62426

FORD Drip Rd 🖉 70519
MAZDA, DAIHATSU Kildean Market 🖉 2162
OPEL Birkhill Rd, Cambusbarron 🖉 71300
TALBOT, BMW Goosecroft Rd 🖉 4477
VW, AUDI-NSU Borestone Crescent, St. Ninians
🖉 5101

STONEHAVEN Kincardine. (Grampian) 401 N 13 – pop. 4,730 – ECD : Wednesday – ☎ 0569.
See : Site★.
Envir. : Dunnottar Castle (site★★, ruins★) *AC*, S : 1 ½ m.
🛅 Cowie 🖉 62124, N : 1 m. on Aberdeen Rd.
🛈 The Square 🖉 62806 (summer only).
♦Edinburgh 109 – ♦Aberdeen 15 – ♦Dundee 50.

　　at Netherley N : 6 m. on B 979 – ✉ Netherley – ☎ 0569 Stonehaven :

　✗　Lairhillock, AB3 2QS, 🖉 30682 – 🅿.

　　at Catterline S : 6 m. by A 92 – ✉ Stonehaven – ☎ 056 95 Catterline :

　✗　**Creel Inn,** S : 6 m. by A 92, AB3 2UL, 🖉 254, Seafood – 🅿. 🆎 ⓞ 𝘝𝘐𝘚𝘈
　　closed Monday, January and February – **M** a la carte 10.40/27.45 **t.**

AUSTIN-ROVER-LAND ROVER-RANGE ROVER　　　FORD 110 Barclay St. 🖉 63666
64/74 Barclay St. 🖉 62077

STORNOWAY Ross and Cromarty (Outer Hebrides) (Western Isles) 401 A 9 – see Lewis (Isle of).

STRACHUR Argyll. (Strathclyde) 401 E 15 – pop. 700 – ECD : Wednesday – ✉ Cairndow – ☎ 036 986.
Envir. : Glen Coe★ NE : 15 m.
♦Edinburgh 99 – ♦Glasgow 56 – ♦Oban 60.

　🏨　**Creggans Inn,** PA27 8BX, on A 815 🖉 279, ≤ Loch Fyne, 🍴 – 🛏wc 📺 ᓀ 🅿. 🔼 🆎 ⓞ
　　𝘝𝘐𝘚𝘈. ⚱
　　M a la carte 5.60/13.00 **t.** ᓵ 3.00 – **22 rm** ⚏ 27.50/55.00 **t.**

STRANRAER Wigtown. (Dumfries and Galloway) 401 402 E 19 – pop. 9,853 – ECD : Wednesday
– ☎ 0776.
Envir. : Kennedy Castle gardens★ *AC*, E : 3 ½ m.
🛅 Creachmore, Leswalt 🖉 87245, SW : 2 m.
🚢 by Sealink : to Larne 3-8 daily (2 h 15 mn).
🛈 Port Rodie 🖉 2595.
♦Edinburgh 132 – ♦Ayr 51 – ♦Dumfries 75.

　🏨　**North West Castle,** Royal Cres., DG9 8EH, 🖉 4413, Telex 777088, 🔲 – ᖶ 📺 🛏wc 📺 🅿.
　　⚱
　　M 5.00/10.00 **t.** – **78 rm** ⚏ 25.00/42.00 **t.** – SB (except weekends) 24.75/27.00 **st.**

COLT 🖉 87634　　　　　　　　　　　　　VOLVO Hanover Sq. 🖉 3939
NISSAN North Strand St. 🖉 2561

STRATHAVEN Lanark. (Strathclyde) 401 402 H 16 – pop. 4,207 – ECD : Wednesday – ☎ 0357.
♦Edinburgh 46 – ♦Ayr 29 – ♦Glasgow 16.

　✗✗　**Waterside,** 31 Waterside St., ML10 2AW, 🖉 22588 – 🆎 ⓞ 𝘝𝘐𝘚𝘈
　　closed dinner Sunday and Monday and 1 to 14 January – **M** 5.00/7.50 **t.**

STRATHBLANE Stirling. (Central) 401 H 16 – pop. 755 – ECD : Wednesday – ✉ Glasgow –
☎ 0360 Blanefield.
♦Edinburgh 48 – ♦Glasgow 11 – Stirling 25.

　🏨　**Country Club** ⚲, 41 Milngavie Rd, G63 9AH, S : ¾ m. on A 81 🖉 70491, 🍴, park – 📺
　　🛏wc 📺wc 📺 🅿. 🔼 🆎 ⓞ 𝘝𝘐𝘚𝘈
　　closed 1 to 3 January – **M** 8.00/12.50 **st.** ᓵ 3.50 – **10 rm** ⚏ 30.00/40.00 **st.** – SB (week-
　　ends only) 50.00 **st.**
　🏨　**Kirkhouse Inn,** Glasgow Rd, G63 9AA, 🖉 70621 – 📺 🛏wc 📺 🅿. 🔼 🆎 ⓞ 𝘝𝘐𝘚𝘈
　　M 5.25/9.25 **t.** ᓵ 3.00 – **17 rm** ⚏ 22.00/34.00 **t.** – SB (weekends only) 41.00/44.00 **st.**

Ensure that you have up to date **Michelin maps** in your car.

STRATHCONON Ross and Cromarty (Highland) – ✉ Muir of Ord – ☎ 099 77 Strathconon.
♦Edinburgh 187 – ♦Inverness 28.

   ⌂ East Lodge ⌖, IV6 7QQ, 𝒫 222, ≤, ⟍, ☞ – ⇥wc �456wc 🅿. 🅰 ⓞ 𝘝𝘐𝘚𝘈
   M (bar lunch) 9.50 t. ⫶ 2.05 – **10 rm**.

STRATHY Sutherland (Highland) 𝟜𝟘𝟙 I 8 – ☎ 064 14.
Envir. : Strathy Point★★★ N : 3 ½ m.
♦Edinburgh 301 – ♦Inverness 142 – Thurso 21 – Tongue 23.

   *Hotel see : **Bettyhill** SW : 12 m.*

STROMNESS Orkney (Orkney Islands) 𝟜𝟘𝟙 K 7 – see Orkney Islands (Mainland).

STRONSAY (Isle of) Orkney (Orkney Islands) 𝟜𝟘𝟙 M 6 – Shipping Services : see Orkney Islands (Mainland : Kirkwall).

SUMBURGH Shetland (Shetland Islands) 𝟜𝟘𝟙 Q 4 – see Shetland Islands (Mainland).

TAIN Ross and Cromarty (Highland) 𝟜𝟘𝟙 H 10 – pop. 1,942 – ECD : Thursday – ☎ 0862.
Envir. : Portmahomack (≤★) E : 10 m.
🐟₁₈ 𝒫 2314.
♦Edinburgh 191 – ♦Inverness 35 – ♦Wick 91.

   ⌂ **Royal,** High St., IV19 1AB, 𝒫 2013 – 📺 ⇥wc �456wc ☎ 🅿. 🄰. 🅰 🄰🄴 ⓞ 𝘝𝘐𝘚𝘈
   M a la carte 7.45/17.25 t. – **25 rm** ☲ 16.00/35.00 t.

TOYOTA Knockbreck Rd 𝒫 2175

TARBERT Argyll. (Strathclyde) 𝟜𝟘𝟙 D 16 – see Kintyre (Peninsula).

TARBERT Inverness. (Outer Hebrides) (Western Isles) 𝟜𝟘𝟙 Z 10 – see Harris (Isle of).

TAYINLOAN Argyll. (Strathclyde) 𝟜𝟘𝟙 D 16 – Shipping Services : see Gigha (Isle of).

TAYNUILT Argyll. (Strathclyde) 𝟜𝟘𝟙 E 14 – pop. 672 – ECD : Wednesday – ☎ 086 62.
♦Edinburgh 109 – ♦Glasgow 79 – ♦Oban 11.

   ⌂ **Polfearn** ⌖, PA35 1JQ, N : 1 m. 𝒫 251, ≤, ☞ – 🅿
   March-October – **M** 5.00/9.00 t. ⫶ 2.75 – **15 rm** ☲ 13.00/28.00 t.

THORNHILL Dumfries. (Dumfries and Galloway) 𝟜𝟘𝟙 𝟜𝟘𝟚 I 18 – pop. 1,510 – ECD : Thursday – ☎ 0848.
Envir. : Drumlanrig Castle★ NW : 2 ½ m.
🐟₁₈ 𝒫 30546.
♦Edinburgh 62 – ♦Ayr 44 – ♦Dumfries 15 – ♦Glasgow 59.

   ⌂ **Buccleuch and Queensberry,** 112 Drumlanrig St., DG3 5LU, 𝒫 30215 – ⇥wc ⇔ 🅿. 🅰 𝘝𝘐𝘚𝘈
   M a la carte 6.35/10.00 t. ⫶ 2.85 – **11 rm** ☲ 12.75/30.00 st.

THURSO Caithness. (Highland) 𝟜𝟘𝟙 J 8 – pop. 9,087 – ECD : Thursday – ☎ 0847.
Envir. : Dunnet Head★★★ (sea birds' nests) NE : 13 m. – Dunnet Bay★★ NE : 9 m.
🐟₁₈ 𝒫 63807, 2 m. from railway station.
🚢 by P & O Ferries : Orkney and Shetland Services : from Scrabster to Stromness (Orkney Islands) Monday/Saturday 1-3 daily (2 h).
🅱 Car Park, Riverside 𝒫 2371 (summer only).
♦Edinburgh 289 – ♦Inverness 133 – ♦Wick 21.

   *Hotel see : **Wick** SE : 21 m.*

CITROEN Couper Sq. Riverside 𝒫 62778   RENAULT Bridgend 𝒫 4622
FORD Mansons Lane 𝒫 63101

TIREE (Isle of) Argyll. (Strathclyde) 𝟜𝟘𝟙 Z 14 – pop. 1,019.
✈ 𝒫 087 92 (Scarinish) 456.
🚢 by Caledonian MacBrayne : from Gott Bay to Arinagour (Isle of Coll) 3 weekly (1 h) – from Gott Bay to Tobermory (Isle of Mull) 2-3 weekly (2 h 45 mn) – from Gott Bay to Lochaline (via Coll and Tobermory) May-September 2 weekly (3 h 50 mn) – from Gott Bay to Oban 3-4 weekly (4 h 30 mn-5 h.)

TIRORAN Argyll. (Strathclyde) 𝟜𝟘𝟙 B 14 – see Mull (Isle of).

TOBERMORY Argyll. (Strathclyde) 𝟜𝟘𝟙 B 14 – see Mull (Isle of).

538

TONGUE Sutherland (Highland) **401** G 8 – pop. 129 – ECD : Saturday – ✉ Lairg – ☎ 080 05.
Envir. : Tongue Bay (≤★ from Coldbackie) N : 2 ½ m.
Exc. : Loch Eriboll★★★ W : 21 m. – SW : Ben Loyal and Ben Hope (≤★) : road from Tongue to Durness.
♦Edinburgh 255 – ♦Inverness 96 – Thurso 44.

🏠 **Ben Loyal,** Main St., IV27 4XE, ℰ 216, ≤ – 🛏wc 🅿. 🔼 𝗩𝗜𝗦𝗔
    M (bar lunch) 7.00 **t.** – **19 rm** ☞ 19.75/23.75 **t.**

TORRIDON Ross and Cromarty (Highland) **401** D 11 – ☎ 044 587.
♦Edinburgh 220 – ♦Inverness 61 – Kyle of Lochalsh 41.

🏠 Loch Torridon ⚓, IV22 2EY, ℰ 242, ≤ Loch Torridon and mountains, ✑, 🚏, park – 🛏wc
    ☎ 🅿
    19 rm

TROON Ayr. (Strathclyde) **401 402** G 17 – pop. 11,318 – ECD : Wednesday – ☎ 0292.
🏌, 🏌, 🏌 ℰ 312464.
🅱 Municipal Buildings, South Beach ℰ 315131.
♦Edinburgh 72 – ♦Ayr 7 – ♦Glasgow 29.

🏨 **Marine,** 8 Crosbie Rd, KA10 6HE, ℰ 314444, Telex 778215, ≤, 🚏 – 🛗 📺 🅿. 🏋. 🔼 🅰🅴 ⓪
    𝗩𝗜𝗦𝗔
    M (closed lunch in winter) 7.50/12.00 **t.** ⛊ 3.30 – **70 rm** ☞ 37.00/58.00 **t.** – SB 29.00/36.00 **t.**
🏠 **Sun Court,** 19 Crosbie Rd, KA10 6HF, ℰ 312727, ≤, 🚏, ℀ – 📺 🛏wc ☎ 🅿. 🏋. 🔼 🅰🅴 ⓪
    M 7.00/11.00 **st.** ⛊ 2.00 – **20 rm** ☞ 31.00/50.00 **st.** – SB 31.00/34.00 **st.**
🏠 **Piersland House,** 17 Craigend Rd, KA10 6HD, ℰ 314747, 🚏, ℀ – 📺 🛏wc 🍴wc ☎ 🅿
    M 10.50 **t.** ⛊ 3.00 – **12 rm** ☞ 25.00/40.00 **t.**
🏠 **Craiglea,** 78-80 South Beach, KA10 6EG, ℰ 311366, 🚏 – 📺 🛏wc ☎ 🅿. 🔼 🅰🅴 ⓪ 𝗩𝗜𝗦𝗔. ℀
    M 7.00/9.00 **t.** ⛊ 2.85 – **21 rm** ☞ 19.50/38.00 **t.**
🏠 **Ardneil,** 51 St. Meddans St., KA10 6NU, ℰ 311611 – 🛏wc 🅿. 🔼 🅰🅴. ℀
    M 3.15/8.00 **st.** ⛊ 2.25 – **7 rm** ☞ 11.00/31.00 **st.**

AUSTIN-ROVER Dundonald Rd ℰ 314141   FORD 72-76 Portland St. ℰ 312312
DAIHATSU St. Meddans St. ℰ 312099

   Sie suchen ein angenehmes, ruhiges Hotel ?
   Blättern Sie nicht wahllos im Führer, sondern benutzen Sie die Karten,
   die den verschiedenen Regionen vorangestellt sind.

TURNBERRY Ayr. (Strathclyde) **401 402** F 18 – pop. 164 – ECD : Wednesday – ✉ Girvan –
☎ 065 53.
🏌, 🏌 Turnberry Hotel ℰ 202.
♦Edinburgh 93 – ♦Ayr 18 – ♦Glasgow 50 – Stranraer 35.

🏨 **Turnberry** ⚓, Maidens Rd, KA26 9LT, on A 719 ℰ 202, Telex 777779, ≤ golf course and bay,
    🔼, 🏌, 🚏, ℀ – 🛗 📺 ⛊ 🅿. 🏋. 🔼 🅰🅴 ⓪ 𝗩𝗜𝗦𝗔
    closed 6 January-28 February – **M** a la carte approx. 18.50 **st.** ⛊ 5.50 – **120 rm** ☞ 45.00/120.00 **st.**

TWEEDSMUIR Lanark (Strathclyde) **401 402** J 17 – ✉ Biggar – ☎ 089 97.
♦Edinburgh 38 – ♦Carlisle 58 – ♦Dumfries 57 – ♦Glasgow 37.

XX **Crook Inn** with rm, ML12 6QN, N : 1 m. on A 107 ℰ 272, ✑, 🚏 – 🛏wc 🅿
    closed 25-26 December – **M** (bar lunch) a la carte 8.70/13.00 **t.** ⛊ 2.50 – **8 rm** ☞ 19.00/38.00 **t.**
    – SB 50.00/54.00 **st.**

UDDINGSTON Lanark. (Strathclyde) **401 402** H 16 – pop. 5,278 – ECD : Wednesday – ✉ Glasgow – ☎ 0698.
♦Edinburgh 38 – ♦Glasgow 7.5.

🏠 Redstones, 8-10 Glasgow Rd, G71 7AS, ℰ 813774 – 📺 🛏wc 🍴wc ☎ 🅿. ℀
    13 rm

UIG Inverness. (Highland) **401** A 11 – see Skye (Isle of).

UIST (Isles of) Inverness. (Western Isles) **401** XY 11 and 12 – pop. 5,105.
See : Benbecula (≤ ★ From Peinavalla, South Nunton).
🏌 see Benbecula.
🚢 by Caledonian MacBrayne from Lochboisdale : to Oban 3-6 weekly (5 h 30 mn direct ; 7 h 30 mn via Castle Bay) – to Castlebay (Isle of Barra) 1-3 weekly (1 h 30 mn-2 h) – from Lochmaddy to Uig (Isle of Skye) Monday/Saturday 6-9 weekly (2 h direct - 4 h 45 mn via Tarbert) – from Lochmaddy to Tarbert (Isle of Harris) Monday/Saturday 3-6 weekly (2 h direct - 4 h 45 mn via Uig).

Benbecula – ⊠ Liniclate – ✪ 0870 Benbecula.
⤴ Benbecula Airport : ℰ 2051.

🏨 **Dark Island** ⟨⟩, PA88 5PJ, ℰ 2414, ≼ – ⇔wc ⋔wc 🅿 *VISA*
M 5.15/30.00 t. �ℓ 2.75 – **22 rm** ⥖ 20.00/30.00 t.

Daliburgh (South Uist) – pop. 261 – ⊠ ✪ 087 84 Lochboisdale.

🏠 **Borrodale**, PA81 5SS, ℰ 444, ≼, ⟨⟩ – ⇔wc 🅿 *VISA*
M 4.20/8.50 t. – **12 rm** ⥖ 14.55/34.15 st. – SB (weekends only) 29.10/34.15 st.

Lochboisdale (South Uist) – pop. 382 – ECD : Thursday – ⊠ ✪ 087 84 Lochboisdale.
Envir. : Sound of Eriskay (≼★ from Ludac) S : 9 m. by A 865 and B 888.
🛆 Askernish, N : 5 m.
🅘 ℰ 286 (summer only).

Lochmaddy (North Uist) – pop. 307 – ECD : Thursday – ⊠ ✪ 087 63 Lochmaddy.
See : Site★.
Envir. : Sound of Berneray★★ NE : 8 m. by A 865 – Vallay Strand★ NW by A 865.
🅘 ℰ 321 (summer only).

🏠 **Lochmaddy**, PA28 5AA, ℰ 331, ≼ harbour and mountains, ⟨⟩ – ⇔wc ⋔wc 🅿
M *(closed Sunday in winter)* (bar lunch) 9.50 st. ⓛ 2.50 – **15 rm** ⥖ 14.50/33.00 st.

*During the season, particularly in resorts, it is wise to book in advance.
However, if you find you cannot take up a hotel booking you have made,
please let the hotel know immediately.
If you are writing to a hotel abroad enclose an International Reply Coupon
(available from Post Offices.)*

ULLAPOOL Ross and Cromarty (Highland) **401** E 10 – pop. 807 – ECD : Tuesday except summer
– ✪ 0854.
See : Site★.
Envir. : Corrieshalloch Gorge★, Falls of Measach★ SE : 12 m. – Strath More (≼★ from the A 832)
SE : 10 m.
⤴ by Caledonian MacBrayne : to Stornoway (Isle of Lewis) Monday/Saturday 1-2 daily (3 h
30 mn).
🅘 ℰ 2135 (Easter and May-September).
✦Edinburgh 218 – ✦Inverness 59.

🏨 **Royal** (Best Western), Garve Rd, IV26 2SY, ℰ 2181, ≼ Loch Broom, ⟨⟩, ⟨⟩, park – ⇔wc
⟨⟩ 🅿 🅰 🅰🅴 🅞 *VISA*
closed 24 December-5 January – M (bar lunch) 10.50 t. ⓛ 3.75 – **54 rm** ⥖ 13.50/45.00 t.

🏨 **Ladbroke Mercury Motor Inn** (Ladbroke), North Rd, IV26 2UD, ℰ 2314, ≼ – 📺 ⇔wc
🅿 🅰 🅰🅴 🅞 *VISA*
April-October – M (bar lunch) 9.50 st. – ⥖ 5.25 – **60 rm** 23.00/32.00 st.

🏠 **Ceilidh Place,** 14 West Argyle St., IV26 2TY, ℰ 2103, « Tasteful decor, gaelic art, musical
theatrical exhibitions » – ⇔wc 🅿 🅞
March-October – M (buffet lunch) a la carte 7.25/11.60 t. ⓛ 2.50 – **15 rm** ⥖ 19.50/42.00 t.

🏠 Harbour Lights Motel, Garve Rd, ℰ 2222, ≼ Loch Broom, ⟨⟩ – ⇔wc ⋔wc 🅿
22 rm.

🏮 **Ferry Boat Inn,** Shore St., ℰ 2366 – 🅰
M (bar lunch) 10.50 st. ⓛ 2.75 – **12 rm** ⥖ 14.75/23.50 st.

UNST Shetland (Shetland Islands) **401** R 1 – Shipping Services : see Shetland Islands.

UPHALL W. Lothian (Lothian) **401** J 16 – pop. 3,035 – ECD : Wednesday – ✪ 0506 Broxburn.
🛆 ℰ 856404.
✦Edinburgh 11 – ✦Glasgow 32.

🏨 **Houstoun House** ⟨⟩, EH52 6JS, ℰ 853831, Telex 727148, ≼, « Gardens », park – 📺 ⇔wc
⋔wc ⟨⟩ 🅿 🅰 🅰🅴 🅞
closed 1 to 3 January – M 10.00/14.50 st. ⓛ 4.00 – ⥖ 2.00 – **29 rm** 36.00/64.00 st.

VATERSAY Inverness (Western Isles) **401** X 13 – Shipping Services : see Barra (Isle of).

VOE Shetland (Shetland Islands) **401** Q 2 – see Shetland Islands (Mainland).

WALKERBURN Peebles. (Borders) 401 402 K 17 – pop. 842 – ✆ 089 687.

See : Tweed Valley★.

♦Edinburgh 32 – Galashiels 9 – Peebles 9.

   🏨 **Tweed Valley** 🦢, Galashiels Rd, EH43 6AA, ✆ 220, ≤, 🦢, 🍴 – 📺 🛏wc 🛏wc 🅿. 🔄 AE
      ① *VISA*
      M 4.50/9.50 **st.** ▯ 3.50 – **14 rm** ⌷ 13.00/45.00 **st.** – SB (January-October) 19.50/25.00 **st.**

WEMYSS BAY Renfrew. (Strathclyde) 401 402 F 16 – pop. 323 – ECD : Wednesday – ✆ 0475.
🛳 by Caledonian MacBrayne : to Rothesay (Isle of Bute) summer 5-18 daily ; winter 6-14 daily
(30 mn).

    Hotels see : Largs S : 4 ½ m., *Skelmorlie* S : 1 ½ m.

WESTHILL Aberdeen. (Grampian) 401 N 12 – see Aberdeen.

WESTRAY (Isle of) Orkney (Orkney Islands) 401 KL 6 – Shipping Services : see Orkney Islands
(Mainland : Kirkwall).

WEST WEMYSS Fife. (Fife) – see Kirkcaldy.

WHALSAY (Isle of) Shetland (Shetland Islands) 401 R 2 – Shipping Services : see Shetland
Islands.

WHITEBRIDGE Inverness (Highland) 401 G 12 – ✆ 045 63 Gorthleck.

♦Edinburgh 164 – ♦Inverness 23 – Kyle of Lochalsh 67 – ♦Oban 89.

   🏨 **Knockie Lodge** 🦢, IV1 2UP, SW : 3 ½ m. by A 862 ✆ 276, ≤ Loch Nanlann and mountains,
      « Tastefully converted hunting lodge », 🦢, 🍴, park – 🅿. 🔄 AE *VISA*
      April-October – **M** (bar lunch) – **10 rm** ⌷ 32.00/70.00 **st.**

   🏨 **Whitebridge**, IV1 2UN, ✆ 226, ≤, 🦢, 🍴 – 🛏wc 🛏wc 🅿. 🔄 AE ① *VISA*
      closed January and February – **M** 6.00/8.50 **t.** – **12 rm** ⌷ 13.50/32.00 **t.**

WHITENESS Shetland (Shetland Islands) 401 Q 3 – see Shetland Islands (Mainland).

WHITING BAY Bute (Strathclyde) 401 402 E 17 – see Arran (Isle of).

WHITHORN (Isle of) Wigtown. (Dumfries and Galloway) 401 402 G 19 – pop. 222 – ECD :
Wednesday – ✆ 098 85.

See : Harbour★.

♦Edinburgh 149 – ♦Ayr 74 – ♦Dumfries 72 – Stranraer 32.

   🏨 **Queens Arms**, 22 Main St., DG8 8LF, ✆ 369 – 🛏wc 🅿. 🔄 AE ① *VISA*
      M 6.50/8.95 **t.** ▯ 2.50 – **10 rm** ⌷ 11.50/27.00 **t.** – SB (winter only) 32.00/36.00 **st.**

WICK Caithness. (Highland) 401 K 8 – pop. 7,617 – ECD : Wednesday – ✆ 0955.

See : ≤★ of Orkney.

Envir. : Skirza Head (cliffs : birds' nests★) N : 12 m. – Duransby Head (cliffs : birds' nests ★) N :
15 m.

📷 Reiss ✆ 2726, N : 3 m.

✈ ✆ 2215, N : 1 m.

🛈 Caithness Tourist Organisation, Whitechapel Rd off High St. ✆ 2596.

♦Edinburgh 282 – ♦Inverness 126.

   🏨 **Ladbroke Mercury Motor Inn** (Ladbroke), Riverside, KW1 4NL, ✆ 3344 – 📺 🛏wc 📶 🅿. 🔄
      AE ① *VISA*
      closed 1 week at Christmas – **M** *(closed Sunday lunch)* (bar lunch) 9.00 **t.** – ⌷ 5.00 – **48 rm**.

AUSTIN-ROVER Bridge St. ✆ 2195   FORD Francis St. ✆ 2103
DATSUN, VAUXHALL Francis St. ✆ 4123   TALBOT George St. ✆ 2321

When travelling for business or pleasure
in England, Wales, Scotland and Ireland :

  – use the series of five maps
    (nos 401, 402, 403, 404 and 405) at a scale of 1:400 000
  – they are the perfect complement to this Guide
    as towns underlined in red on the maps will be found in this Guide.

WIGTOWN Wigtown. (Dumfries and Galloway) 🗺️ G 19 – pop. 1,020 – ECD : Wednesday – ✉️ Newton Stewart – 🕿 098 886 Mochrum.

♦Edinburgh 133 – ♦Ayr 57 – ♦Dumfries 57 – Stranraer 30.

🏨 **Corsemalzie House** 🏠, DG8 9RL, SW : 6 ½ m. by A 714 on B 7005 ☎ 254, « Country house atmosphere », 🐟, 🎾, park – 🚾wc 🛁wc 🅿️. 🅰️ 🆎 ⑩ 𝘝𝘐𝘚𝘈
closed 20 January-1 March – **M** 6.50/9.50 **t.** 🍷 2.50 – **15 rm** 🛏️ 25.00/42.00 **t.** – SB (except winter) 47.50/55.00 **st.**

WORMIT Fife. (Fife) 🗺️ L 14 – pop. 3,750 – ECD : Wednesday – ✉️ 🕿 0382 Newport-on-Tay.

♦Edinburgh 53 – ♦Dundee 4 – St. Andrews 12.

🏨 **Sandford Hill** 🏠, DD6 8RG, S : 2 m. junction A 914 and B 946 ☎ 541802, ≼, 🎾 – 📺 🚾wc 🕿 🅿️. 🅰️ 🆎 ⑩ 𝘝𝘐𝘚𝘈
closed 1 and 2 January – **M** 6.50/9.50 **t.** 🍷 3.50 – **15 rm** 🛏️ 24.70/38.80 **t.** – SB (weekends only) 39.50/44.00 **st.**

WYRE (Isle of) Orkney (Orkney Islands) 🗺️ L 6 – Shipping Services : see Orkney Islands (Mainland : Kirkwall).

YELL (Isle of) Shetland (Shetland Islands) 🗺️ Q 2 – Shipping Services : see Shetland Islands.

Northern Ireland

Towns

ANTRIM (Coast Road) Antrim 📖📖📖 O 3.
See : Road★★★ (A 2) from Larne to Portrush.

BALLYCASTLE Antrim 📖📖📖 N 2 – 💠 026 57.
See : Site★★.

Envir. : Giant's Causeway★★★ (Chaussée des Géants) basalt formation (from the car-park *AC*, ½ h Rtn on foot) NW : 12 m. – White Park Bay★★ NW : 8 ½ m. – Carrick-a-Rede (≤★★ of Rathlin Island) NW : 5 ½ m.

📇₁₈ 🖉 62536.

🆔 Sheskburn House, 7 Mary St. 🖉 62024.

◆Belfast 60 – Ballymena 28 – Larne 40.

  🏨   **Antrim Arms**, 75 Castle St., BT54 6AS, 🖉 62284 – 🛏wc 🅿
      closed first 2 weeks October and 25-26 December – **M** 5.50/10.00 t. 🍷 4.25 – **11 rm**
      🛏 12.50/27.00 t. – SB (spring and autumn) 33.00/36.00 **st**.

  ⌂   Mount Pleasant, 30 Quay Rd, BT54 6BH, 🖉 62118 – 🛏wc 🅿 – **7 rm**.

BALLYGALLEY Antrim 📖📖📖 O 3 – pop. 487 – ✉ Larne – 💠 057 483.

◆Belfast 27 – Ballymena 24 – Larne 4.

  🏨   Ballygally Castle, 274 Coast Rd, BT40 2QX, 🖉 212, ≤, 🐴, 🍽 – 📺 🛏wc 📞 🅿
      30 rm.

BALLYMENA Antrim 📖📖📖 N 3 – pop. 16,487 – 💠 0266.

Envir. : Glen of Glenariff★★★ – Glenariff (or Waterfoot) site★ NE : 19 m.

📇₁₈ Broughshane 🖉 026 686 (Broughshane) 487, E : 2 m. on A 42.

🆔 2 Ballymoney Rd 🖉 46043.

◆Belfast 28 – ◆Dundalk 78 – Larne 21 – ◆Londonderry 51 – ◆Omagh 53.

  🏨   Adair Arms, 1-5 Ballymoney Rd, BT43 5BS, 🖉 3674 – 📺 🛏wc 📞 🅿. 🧖. 🍽
      40 rm.

ALFA-ROMEO, TALBOT, LOTUS   Broadway Av. 🖉
2161
AUSTIN-ROVER   Waveney Av. 🖉 3557

RENAULT   120 Antrim Rd 🖉 2650
VW, AUDI   1/5 Railway St. 🖉 46014

BELFAST Antrim 📖📖📖 O 4 – pop. 360,150 – 💠 0232.

See : City Hall★★ 1906 BZ – Queen's University★★ 1906 AZ **U** – Ulster Museum★ AZ **M** – Church House★ 1905 BZ **B** – Botanic Gardens (hot houses★) AZ – Bellevue Zoological Gardens (site★, ≤★) *AC*, by A 6 AY.

Envir. : Stormont (Parliament House★ 1932, terrace : vista★★) E : 4 m. by Belmont Rd AZ – The Giant's Ring★ (prehistoric area) S : 5 m. by Malone Rd AZ – Lisburn (Castle gardens ≤★) SW : 8 m. by A 1 AZ.

📇₁₈ Balmoral, Lisburn Rd 🖉 668540 AZ – 📇₁₈ Fortwilliam, Downview Av. 🖉 771770, N : 2 m. AY – 📇₁₈, 📇₉ 240 Upper Malone Rd, Dunmurry 🖉 612695 by A 55 AZ – 📇₁₈ Shandon Park 🖉 793730, E : 3 m. by A 55 AZ.

✈   Belfast Airport : 🖉 229271, NW : 12 m. by M 2 Motorway AY – **Terminal :** Coach service (Ulsterbus Ltd.) from Great Victoria Street Station (40 mn).

⛴ to Liverpool (Belfast Car Ferries) 1 daily (9 h) – to Isle of Man : Douglas (Isle of Man Steam Packet Co.) June-September 1-2 weekly (4 h 30 mn).

🆔 River House, 48-52 High St. BT1 2DS 🖉 246609, Telex 748087 – Belfast Airport, Aldergrove 🖉 084 94 (Crumlin) 52103 – Larne Harbour, Terminal Building, Larne 🖉 0574 (Larne) 2270 (Easter-September).

◆Dublin 103 – ◆Londonderry 70.

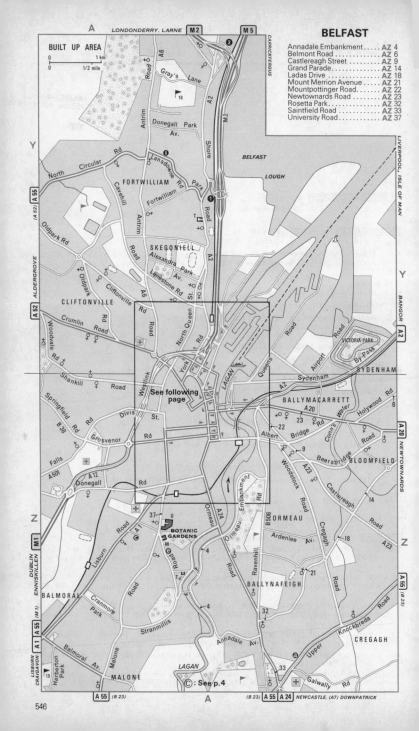

BELFAST

BUILT UP AREA
0 ___ 1 km
0 ___ 1/2 mile

LONDONDERRY, LARNE M2   M5   CARRICKFERGUS

BELFAST LOUGH

LIVERPOOL, ISLE OF MAN

Gray's Lane

Donegall Park Av.

FORTWILLIAM

Fortwilliam Road

SKEGONIELL

Alexandra Park

Limestone Rd.

CLIFTONVILLE

Cliftonville Rd

Crumlin Road

Shankill Road

Springfield Rd

Grosvenor Rd

Falls

Donegall Rd

North Queen St.

Westlink

York St.

Divis St.

See following page

LAGAN

VICTORIA PARK

Airport

SYDENHAM

BALLYMACARRETT
A20

Colin's Water

Holywood Rd

Albert Bridge

BLOOMFIELD

Beersbridge Road

Woodstock Road

A23

Castlereagh Road

Ormeau Embankment Rd

BOTANIC GARDENS

Malone Road

Lisburn Road

Ormeau Road

Ravenhill Road

ORMEAU

Ardenlee Av.

Creagh Road

BALLYNAFEIGH

CREGAGH

Cranmore Park

Stranmillis

MALONE

Balmoral Av.

BALMORAL

Annadale Av.

LAGAN

Knockbreda Road

Upper Galwally Rd

©: See p.4

A55 (B23)   (B23) A55 A24 NEWCASTLE, (A7) DOWNPATRICK

BELFAST

CENTRE

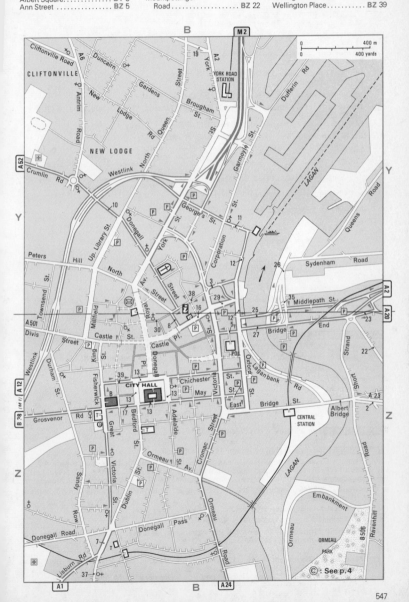

See p. 4

547

🏨 **Forum** (Forum), Great Victoria St., BT2 7AP, ℰ 245161, Telex 74491, ⇐ – 🛓 TV ☎ 🄿 🅪 🔼
🅰🅔 ⓪ 𝚅𝙸𝚂𝙰 ✵
BZ **e**
closed Christmas – **M** (carving rest.) 9.25 **st.** ⅜ 3.25 – ⬛ 4.50 – **200 rm** 44.50/58.00 **st.** – SB
(weekends only) 48.00/58.00 **st.**

🏨 **Stormont,** 587 Upper Newtownards Rd, BT4 3LP, E : 4 ½ m. by A 2 on A 20 ℰ 658621 – 🛓
TV ➡wc ☎ 🄿 🅪 🔼 🅰🅔 ⓪
on A 20 AZ
closed Christmas Day – **M** 8.00 **t.** ⅜ 3.00 – **67 rm** ⬛ 34.50/46.00 **t.** – SB (weekends only) 42.50 **st.**

🏨 **Drumkeen,** Upper Galwally, off Upper Knockbreda Rd, BT8 4TL, SE : 3 m. by A 24 off A 55
ℰ 645321 – TV ➡wc ☎ 🄿 🔼 𝚅𝙸𝚂𝙰 ✵
AZ **a**
M 5.50/9.00 **t.** ⅜ 2.50 – **28 rm** ⬛ 33.00/50.00 **t.**

↑ **Camera House,** 44 Wellington Park, BT9 6DP, ℰ 660026 – ➡wc 𝚅𝙸𝚂𝙰
AZ **c**
11 rm ⬛ 14.40/23.00 **st.**

↑ **Somerton,** 22 Lansdowne Rd, BT15 4DB, ℰ 778717 – TV
AY **i**
8 rm ⬛ 11.00/20.00 **t.**

✗ **Strand,** 12 Stranmillis Rd, BT9 5AA, ℰ 682266, Bistro
AZ **e**
M (booking essential).

at Dunmurry SW : 5 ½ m. on A 1 – AZ – ✉ 🕸 0232 Belfast :

🏨 **Conway** (T.H.F.), Kingsway, BT17 9ES, ℰ 612101, Telex 74281, ⬛ heated, ☞ – 🛓 TV ☎ 🄿.
🅪 🔼 🅰🅔 ⓪ 𝚅𝙸𝚂𝙰
M 8.50/9.50 **st.** ⅜ 2.90 – ⬛ 5.50 – **76 rm** 39.00/47.00 **st.**

MICHELIN Branch, 101/3 Limestone Rd, BT15 3AB, ℰ 748255

AUSTIN-ROVER-DAIMLER-JAGUAR   Saintfield Rd
ℰ 649774
AUSTIN-ROVER   3 Diamond St., Shankil Rd ℰ
242456
AUSTIN-ROVER-DAIMLER-JAGUAR   10/18 Adelaide
St. ℰ 230566
AUSTIN-ROVER   Upper Newtownards Rd, Dundo-
nald ℰ 2651
BEDFORD, OPEL-VAUXHALL   17/29 Ravenhill Rd ℰ
51422
BEDFORD, OPEL-VAUXHALL   101 Kingsway, Dun-
murry ℰ 614211
CITROEN   118/124 Donegall Pass ℰ 223441
FIAT   45/47 Rosetta Rd ℰ 648049

FORD   Lislea Drive ℰ 662231
FORD   58/82 Antrim Rd ℰ 744744
HYUNDAI   27, Pakenham St., Donegal Pass ℰ 232111
NISSAN   226 York St. ℰ 747133
NISSAN   397 Upper Newtownards Rd ℰ 654687
RENAULT   Boucher Rd ℰ 681721
SAAB, FIAT   250/252 Donegall St. ℰ 221019
TOYOTA   269/285 Upper Newtownards Rd ℰ 655208
TOYOTA   39/49 Adelaide St. ℰ 228225
VAUXHALL-OPEL   46 Florenceville Av. ℰ 641350
VAUXHALL-OPEL   83/87 York Rd ℰ 744869
VOLVO   59/75 Ladas Drive ℰ 703666
VW, AUDI   318a Sandown Rd ℰ 653082

CARNLOUGH Antrim 𝟺𝟶𝟻 0 3 – pop. 2,280 – ✉ Ballymena – 🕸 0574.
🄿 Post Office, Harbour Rd ℰ 85210.
♦Belfast 37 – Ballymena 16 – Larne 14.

🏠 **Londonderry Arms,** Harbour Rd, BT44 0EU, ℰ 85255 – ▦ TV ➡wc ➡wc ⊛ 🄿 🔼 🅰🅔 ⓪
𝚅𝙸𝚂𝙰 ✵
M 6.50/8.95 **t.** ⅜ 2.85 – **12 rm** ⬛ 15.00/28.00 **t.** – SB (except summer) 40.00/45.00 **st.**

CARRICKFERGUS Antrim 𝟺𝟶𝟻 0 3 – pop. 15,162 – 🕸 096 03.
See : Castle★★ (13C) *AC* – Sea Front★ – St. Nicholas' Church★ 12C-18C.
Envir. : Island Magee Peninsula (Port Muck★, Isle of Muck★, Power Station ⇐★) NE : 9 m.
🟦 North Rd ℰ 62203.
🄿 Castle Green ℰ 63604 (Mid June-August).
♦Belfast 10 – Larne 14.

🏠 Coast Road, 28 Scotch Quarter, BT38 7DP, ℰ 61021 – TV ➡wc ➡wc ⊛. ✵ – **20 rm**.
PEUGEOT, TALBOT   72 Belfast Rd ℰ 62299
RENAULT   Larne Rd ℰ 63516

CASTLEROCK Londonderry – see Coleraine.

COLERAINE Londonderry 𝟺𝟶𝟻 L 2 – pop. 14,871 – 🕸 0265.
Envir. : Giant's Causeway★★★ (Chaussée des Géants) basalt formation (from the car-park *AC*, ½ h
Rtn on foot) NE : 9 m. – Downhill Castle (Mussenden Temple★ 18C : ⇐★★★ *AC*) NW : 7 m. –
Portrush (site★, ⇐★) N : 6 m. – Dunluce Castle (site★, ⇐★) NE : 8 m. – W : Benevenagh Mountain★.
🟦 Castlerock ℰ 026 584 (Castlerock) 314, W : 5 m. – 🟦, 🟦, 🟦 Royal Portrush, Dunluce Rd, Portrush
ℰ 0265 (Portrush) 822311.
🄿 Swimming Pool, Main St., Castlerock ℰ 884258.
♦Belfast 53 – Ballymena 25 – ♦Londonderry 31 – ♦Omagh 65.

↑ **Greenhill House** ⑤, 24 Greenhill Rd, Aghadowey, BT51 4EU, S : 9 m. by A 29 on B 66
ℰ 026 585 (Aghadowey) 241, ☞ – ➡wc 🄿 🔼. ✵
March-October – **7 rm** ⬛ 11.00/21.00 **st.**

✗✗ **MacDuffs,** Blackheath House, 112 Killeague Rd, Blackhill, BT51 4HH, S : 8 m. by A 29 on
Macosquin Rd ℰ 026 585 (Aghadowey) 433 – 🄿
closed Sunday, last 2 weeks October and 25-26 December – **M** (dinner only) a la carte
9.50/12.10 **t.** ⅜ 2.75.

at Castlerock NW : 6 m. by A 2 off B 119 – ⊠ 🏢 0265 Castlerock :

↥ **Maritima**, 43 Main St., BT51 4RA, 🟰 848388, ← – 🛏wc 🅿
6 rm 🖙 10.00/20.00 **st.**

FORD 30-32 Church St. 🟰 2361   VAUXHALL-OPEL Hanover Pl. 🟰 2386

CRAIGAVON Armagh **405** M 4 – pop. 12,594 – ⊠ 🏢 0762 Portadown.
Envir. : Ardress House★ 17C (site★, drawing-room plasterwork★★) *AC*, W : 11 m. – Rich Hill (site★, church : scenery★) SW : 9 ½ m.
🏌 The Demesne, Lurgan 🟰 076 22 (Lurgan) 22087, NE : 3 m.
♦Belfast 28 – Armagh 13.

🏨 Seagoe, Upper Church Lane, BT53 5QS, 🟰 333076, 🟰 – 📺 🛏wc ☎ 🅿. 🅰. 🛇
38 rm.

CRAWFORDSBURN Down **405** O 4 – pop. 487 – 🏢 0247 Helen's Bay.
🏌 Carnalea 🟰 0247 (Bangor) 65004 – 🏌, 🏌 Clandeboye, Conlig 🟰 0247 (Bangor) 65767.
♦Belfast 10 – Bangor 3.

🏨 Old Inn, 15 Main St., BT19 1JH, 🟰 853255, 🟰 – 📺 🛏wc 🕾 🅿. 🛇 – **25 rm**.

DOWNPATRICK Down **405** O 5 – pop. 3,377 – 🏢 0396.
Envir. : Saul (St. Patrick's Memorial Church : site★, ←★) NE : 3 m. – Castle Ward 1765 (great hall★) NE : 6 m. – Portaferry : Strangford (site★, Audley's Castle : top ⅜★★, 44 steps) NE : 8 m.
🏌 Saul Rd 🟰 2152 – 🏌 Castle Pl., Ardglass 🟰 0396 (Ardglass) 841219, SE : 7 m.
⛴ to Portaferry, frequent services daily (5 mn).
🅸 Strangford Rd 🟰 2641.
♦Belfast 22 – Bangor 27.

🏨 Abbey Lodge, 38 Belfast Rd, BT30 9AV, NW : 1 m. on A 7 🟰 4511 – 📺 🛏wc 🕾 🅿. 🅰. 🛇
21 rm.

AUSTIN-ROVER St. Patrick's Av. 🟰 2215   FIAT, FORD Church St. 🟰 2777

DUNADRY Antrim **405** N 3 – 🏢 084 94 Templepatrick.
Envir. : Antrim (round tower★ 10C) NW : 5 m. – Shane's Castle★ (16C ruins) *AC*, NW : 5 ½ m. (access by miniature railway).
♦Belfast 15 – Larne 18 – ♦Londonderry 56.

🏨 **Dunadry Inn**, 2 Islandreagh Drive, BT41 2HA, 🟰 32474, Telex 747245, 🟰 – 📺 ☎ 🅿. 🅰. 🅽
🅰🅴 ① 𝕍𝕀𝕊𝔸. 🛇
closed 24 to 27 December – **M** *(closed Saturday lunch and Sunday dinner)* 6.50/10.50 **t.** 🍷 3.00
– **77 rm** 🖙 40.00/50.00 **t.** – SB 46.00/70.00 **st.**

DUNMURRY Antrim **405** N 4 – see Belfast.

ENNISKILLEN Fermanagh **405** J 4 – pop. 6,558 – 🏢 0365.
See : Lough Erne★★★ (Upper and Lower) – On Lower Lough Erne, by boat *AC* : Devenish Island (site★★, monastic ruins : scenery★) and White Island★.
Envir. : Castle Coole★ 18C (site★) E : 1 m. – Florence Court (site★, park★) *AC*, SW : 8 m.
🏌 Castlecoole 🟰 22900.
🅸 Lakeland Visitor Centre, Shore Rd 🟰 23110 and 25050.
♦Belfast 87 – ♦Londonderry 59.

🏨 Killyhevlin, Dublin Rd, BT74 6DX, SE : 1 ¾ m. on A 4 🟰 23481, ←, 🟰, park – 📺 🛏wc
🛏wc ☎ 🅿. 🅰. 🅽 🅰🅴 ① 𝕍𝕀𝕊𝔸. 🛇
M a la carte 7.25/11.20 **st.** 🍷 3.75 – **23 rm** 🖙 27.00/48.00 **st.** – SB (weekends only)(summer only) 47.50/50.00 **st.**

🏨 Fort Lodge, Forthill St., 🟰 23275 – 🛏wc 🛏wc 🕾 🅿
12 rm.

↥ Willoughby, 24 Willoughby Pl., BT74 7EX, 🟰 25275 – 🅿. 🅽 𝕍𝕀𝕊𝔸. 🛇
closed Christmas Day – **13 rm** 🖙 8.50/16.00 **st.**

AUSTIN-ROVER Dublin Rd 🟰 3475   VAUXHALL-OPEL Tempo Rd 🟰 4366

In addition to establishments indicated by
〰〰〰 … ✗ ,
many hotels possess
good class restaurants.

GLENGORMLEY Antrim **405** O 3 – ✉ Newtownabbey – ☎ 023 13.
✦Belfast 6 – Larne 15.

🏨 **Chimney Corner,** 630 Antrim Rd, BT36 8RH, NW : 2 m. on A 6 ✆ 44925, Telex 748158, ⟋,
✗ – 🔟 📺 ☎ 🅿. 🚗, 🅰🅴 🅾 𝗩𝗜𝗦𝗔 – ✗
closed 7 to 23 July and 1 week at Christmas – **M** (closed Sunday to non-residents) 5.45/9.00 **st.**
🍷 3.00 – **63 rm** 🛏 28.00/38.00 **st.**

✗✗ **Sleepy Hollow,** 15 Kiln Rd, BT36 8SU, N : 2 m. by B 56 ✆ 44042 – 🅿. ✗
closed Sunday to Tuesday – **M** (dinner only) 13.50 **st.** 🍷 2.25.

HILLSBOROUGH Down **405** N 4 – pop. 780 – ☎ 0849.
See : Government House★ 18C – the Fort★ 17C.
Envir. : Legananny Dolmen ⪦★ S : 16 m.
🖈 Eglantine Rd, Lisburn ✆ 023 82 (Lisburn) 2186, N : 5 m.
✦Belfast 13.

🏨 White Gables, 14 Dromore Rd, BT26 6PE, ✆ 682755 – 🔟 🚻wc ☎ 🅿. ✗ – **25 rm**.
TOYOTA 23 Lisburn Rd ✆ 682188

HOLYWOOD Down **405** O 4 – pop. 5,078 – ☎ 023 17.
Envir. : Craigavad : Ulster Folk and Transport Museum★ (Cultra Manor) AC, NE : 3 m.
🖈 Nuns Walk, Demesne Rd ✆ 2138.
✦Belfast 5 – Bangor 6.

🏨🏨 Culloden 🦢, 142 Bangor Rd, BT18 0EX, E : 1½ m. on A 2 ✆ 5223, Telex 74617, ⪦, ⟋, park,
✗, squash – 🛏 🔟 🅱 ♿ 🅿. 🎱 – **74 rm**.
FIAT 36/38 Shore Rd ✆ 5636

IRVINESTOWN Fermanagh **405** J 4 – pop. 785 – ☎ 036 56.
✦Belfast 78 – ✦Dublin 132 – Donegal 27.

⛢ **Mahon's,** Mill St., BT74 9XX, ✆ 21656 – 🚻wc 🆗 🅿. 𝗔𝗘 𝗩𝗜𝗦𝗔
M 4.50/7.00 **t.** 🍷 2.50 – **18 rm** 🛏 11.00/23.00 **t.** – SB (weekends only) 23.00 **st.**

LARNE Antrim **405** O 3 – pop. 18,242 – ☎ 0574.
Exc. : Antrim Coast Road★★★ (A 2) from Larne to Portrush.
🖈 Cairndhu, 192 Coast Rd ✆ 057 483 (Ballygally) 248, N : 4 m.
🚢 to Stranraer (Sealink) 3-8 daily (2 h 15 mn) – to Cairnryan (Townsend Thoresen) 2-5 daily (2 h
to 2 h 30 mn).
🛈 Sir Thomas Dixon Buildings, Victoria Rd ✆ 2313 – Car Park, Murrayfield Shopping Centre, Broadway ✆ 2313
(June-August).
✦Belfast 23 – Ballymena 20.

⛢ **Derrin House,** 2 Prince's Gdns, BT40 1RQ, off Glenarm Rd (A 2) ✆ 73269 – 🅿
7 rm 🛏 8.00/18.00 **st.**

AUSTIN-ROVER Point St. ✆ 2071   FORD 39 Glynn Rd ✆ 5411

LONDONDERRY Londonderry **405** K 2-3 – pop. 31,437 – ☎ 0504.
See : City Walls★★ 17C – Guildhall★ 1908 – Memorial Hall★.
Envir. : Grianan of Aileach★ (Republic of Ireland) (stone fort) ❋★★★ NW : 5 m. – Dungiven (priory :
site★) SE : 18 m.
🖈 City of Derry, Victoria Rd, Prehen ✆ 42610.
✈ Eglinton Airport : ✆ 810784, E : 6 m.
🛈 Foyle St. ✆ 269501.
✦Belfast 70 – ✦Dublin 146.

🏨🏨 **Everglades,** Prehen Rd, BT47 2PA, S : 1 ½ m. on A 5 ✆ 46722, Telex 748005 – 🔟 ☎ ♿ 🅿.
🚗 𝗔𝗘 𝗔𝗘 🅾 𝗩𝗜𝗦𝗔. ✗
closed 25 and 26 December – **M** 6.50/10.50 **st.** 🍷 2.00 – 🛏 4.25 – **38 rm** 25.00/35.00 **st.** – SB
(weekends only) 36.50 **st.**

🏨 **White Horse Inn,** 68 Clooney Rd, BT47 3PA, NE : 5 ¼ m. on A 2 ✆ 0504 (Campsie) 860606 –
🔟 🚻wc ☎ 🅿. 𝗔𝗘 𝗔𝗘 🅾 𝗩𝗜𝗦𝗔 ✗
closed Christmas Day – **M** 5.00/10.00 **st.** – 🛏 2.75 – **44 rm** 20.00/40.00 **st.**

BEDFORD, VAUXHALL-OPEL Maydown ✆ 860601   PEUGEOT, TALBOT Campsie ✆ 860588
FORD 173 Strand Rd ✆ 67613   VW, AUDI 24 Buncrana Rd ✆ 65985

LOUGHGALL Armagh **405** M 4 – pop. 2,899 – ☎ 076 289.
✦Belfast 38 – Armagh 5 – ✦Dublin 89.

✗✗ Bramley Apple, Old Cope School, 1 Main St., ✆ 318 – 🅿.

NEWCASTLE Down **405** O 5 – pop. 4,621 – ✪ 039 67.

Envir.: Tollymore Forest Park★ *AC*, NW : 2 m. by B 180 – Dundrum (castle★ 13C ruins : top ❄★★, 70 steps) NE : 3 m. – Loughinisland (the 3 churches★ : 1000-1547-1636) NE : 8 m.

Exc. : SW : Mourne Mountains★★ (Slieve Donard★, Silent Valley★, Lough Shannagh★ : reservoir 1948).

🛈 61 Central Promenade ☎ 22222 (July-August).

♦Belfast 30 – ♦Londonderry 101.

🏨 Enniskeen ♨, 98 Bryansford Rd, BT33 0LF, NW : 1 m. ☎ 22392, ≤, ☞, park – 📺 ⇱wc ☜ 🅿. ✻

  12 rm.

🏨 Burrendale, Castlewellan Rd, BT33 0JZ, N : 1 m. on A 50 ☎ 22599, ☞ – 📺 ⇱wc ☜ 🅿. ⚘.

  🖭 ⑩ 𝘝𝘐𝘚𝘈

  M (bar lunch Monday to Saturday) a la carte 7.50/12.80 **t.** ⚗ 3.00 – **12 rm** – SB (weekends only) 36.00 **st.**

NEWRY Down **405** M N 5 – pop. 11,393 – ✪ 0693.

Envir.: Slieve Gullion★★, Ring of Gullion : Ballitemple viewpoint★★, Bernish Rock viewpoint★★, – Cam Lough★, Killevy Churches (site★) SW : 5 m. – Derrymore House (site★) *AC*, NW : 2 ½ m. – Rostrevor (Fairy Glen★) SE : 8 ¾ m. – Carlingford Lough★ SE : 10 m.

🖈 Warrenpoint ☎ 069 372 (Warrenpoint) 2219, S : 5 m.

🛈 Arts Centre, Bank Parade ☎ 66232.

♦Belfast 39 – Armagh 20 – ♦Dundalk 13.

AUSTIN-ROVER Railway Av. ☎ 2201
PEUGEOT, TALBOT 18 Edward St. ☎ 2877

RENAULT 49/53 Merchants Quay ☎ 3626

NEWTOWNARDS Down **405** O 4 – pop. 15,387 – ✪ 0247.

Envir.: Scrabo Tower (site★) SW : 1 m. – Mount Stewart Gardens★ *AC* – Temple of the Winds ≤ ★ *AC*, SE : 5 ½ m. – Grey Abbey★ (Cistercian ruins 12C) *AC*, SW : 7 m.

🖈 Kirkstown Castle, Cloughey ☎ 024 77 (Portavogie) 353.

♦Belfast 10 – Bangor 5.

🏨 **Strangford Arms,** 92 Church St., BT23 4AL, ☎ 814141 – 📺 ⇱wc ☎ 🅿. ⚘. 🖭 🗚🗉 ⑩ 𝘝𝘐𝘚𝘈.

  ✻

  closed 8-9 April and Christmas Day – **M** 6.50/8.50 **t.** ⚗ 3.00 – ⇆ 3.75 – **36 rm** 31.00/41.50 **t.**

FORD Regent St. ☎ 812626
VAUXHALL-OPEL Portaferry Rd ☎ 813376

VW, AUDI Portaferry Rd ☎ 815505

OMAGH Tyrone **405** K 4 – pop. 27,998 – ✪ 0662.

Envir.: Gortin Glen Forest Park★, Gortin Gap★ (on B 48) NE : 9 m. – Glenelly Valley★ NE : 17 m. by Plumbridge.

🖈 Dublin Rd ☎ 3160 – 🖈 Fintona ☎ 0662 (Fintona) 841480, S : 5 ½ m.

♦Belfast 68 – ♦Dublin 112 – ♦Dundalk 64 – ♦Londonderry 34 – ♦Sligo 69.

FORD Derry Rd ☎ 2788
RENAULT Cookstown Rd ☎ 3451

VW-AUDI, VAUXHALL-OPEL 60 Dublin Rd ☎ 3116

PORTAFERRY Down **405** P 4 – pop. 1,592 – ✪ 024 77.

⛴ to Downpatrick, frequent services daily (5 mn).

♦ Belfast 29 – Bangor 24.

🏨 **Portaferry,** 10 The Strand, BT22 1PE, ☎ 28231, ≤ – ⇱wc 🛉wc. 🖭 🗚🗉 ⑩ 𝘝𝘐𝘚𝘈. ✻

  closed 25 and 26 December – **M** (closed Sunday dinner to non-residents) a la carte 7.50/14.95 **t.** ⚗ 2.80 – **6 rm** ⇆ 14.50/26.00 **t.**

PORT BALLINTRAE Antrim **405** M 2 – ✉ ✪ 026 57 Bushmills.

♦Belfast 68 – Coleraine 15.

🏨 Bayview, 2 Bayhead Rd, ☎ 31453, ≤ – 📺 ⇱wc ☎ 🅿

  16 rm.

When visiting London use the Green Guide **"London"**

  – Detailed descriptions of places of interest

  – Useful local information

  – A section on the historic square-mile of the
    City of London with a detailed fold out plan

  – The lesser known London boroughs — their people,
    places and sights

  – Plans of selected areas and important buildings.

PORTSTEWART Londonderry 405 L 2 – pop. 4,975 – ✆ 026 583.

🏌, 🏌 Strand Head ✆ 2015, West boundary.

🛈 Town Hall ✆ 2286 (July-August).

♦Belfast 67 – Coleraine 6.

🏠 **Edgewater,** 88 Strand Rd, BT55 7LZ, ✆ 3314, ≤ – 📺 🛏wc 🚿wc ⏣ 🅿. 🔼 ⓪ *VISA*. 🎿
　 M 5.00/6.50 **t.** – **30 rm** ⭤ 17.00/32.50 **t.**

↑ **The Links,** 103 Strand Rd, BT55 7LZ, ✆ 2580 – 🅿. 🎿
　 April-October – **14 rm** ⭤ 9.00/18.00 **st.**

STRABANE Tyrone 405 J 3 – pop. 10,748 – ✆ 0504.

🏌 Bally Colman ✆ 882271.

🛈 Lifford Rd ✆ 883735 (June-mid September).

♦Belfast 87 – Donegal 34 – ♦Dundalk 98 – ♦Londonderry 14.

🏨 **Fir Trees Lodge,** Omagh Rd, BT82 9JT, ✆ 883003 – 📺 🛏wc ⏣ 🅿. 🔼 🅰🅴 ⓪
　 M 5.75/10.00 **st.** – **26 rm** ⭤ 19.50/29.00 **st.**

WHITEHEAD Antrim 405 O 3 – pop. 1,403 – ✉ Carrickfergus – ✆ 096 03.

♦Belfast 16 – Larne 8.5.

🏠 **Dolphin,** 16 Marine Par., BT38 9QD, ✆ 72481, ≤ – 🛏wc 🅿
　 closed 24 December-10 January – **M** a la carte 7.80/9.40 **st.** 🍷 2.50 – **19 rm** ⭤ 14.50/28.00 **st.**

552

Channel

Islands

Place with at least :

one hotel or restaurant .... ● Herm
one pleasant hotel .... 🏠, ✕ with rm
one quiet, secluded hotel .... ⬧
one restaurant with .... ❀, ❀❀, ❀❀❀ M
See this town for establishments
 located in its vicinity .... GOREY

La località possiede come minimo :

una risorsa alberghiera .... ● Herm
un albergo ameno .... 🏠, ✕ with rm
un albergo molto tranquillo, isolato .... ⬧
un'ottima tavola con .... ❀, ❀❀, ❀❀❀ M
La località raggruppa nel suo testo
 le risorse dei dintorni .... GOREY

Localité offrant au moins :

une ressource hôtelière .... ● Herm
un hôtel agréable .... 🏠, ✕ with rm
un hôtel très tranquille, isolé .... ⬧
une bonne table à .... ❀, ❀❀, ❀❀❀ M
Localité groupant dans le texte
 les ressources de ses environs .... GOREY

Ort mit mindestens :

einem Hotel oder Restaurant .... ● Herm
einem angenehmen Hotel .... 🏠, ✕ with rm
einem sehr ruhigen und abgelegenen Hotel ..... ⬧
einem Restaurant mit .... ❀, ❀❀, ❀❀❀ M
Ort mit Angaben über Hotels und Restaurants
 in seiner Umgebung .... GOREY

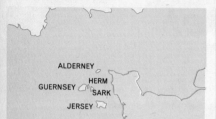

ALDERNEY

554

CHANNEL ISLANDS

Towns

ALDERNEY 403 Q 33 and 230 ⑨ – pop. 1,686 – ECD : Wednesday – ✪ 048 182.
See : Telegraph Bay★ (cliffs★) – Clonque Bay★ – Braye Bay★.
✈ ✆ 2711 - Booking Office : Aurigny Air Services ✆ 2889 Air Ferries ✆ 2993.
⛴ to Torquay (Torbay Seaways) summer only 1 weekly (5 h).
⛴ Shipping connections with the Continent : to France (Saint-Malo) (via Guernsey, Sark and Jersey) (Condor : hydrofoil) – to Jersey (St. Helier) (Condor : hydrofoil) 3 weekly summer only (2 h 30 mn) – to Guernsey (St. Peter Port) (Condor : hydrofoil) summer only 2 weekly (45 mn) – to Sark (Condor : hydrofoil) summer only 2 weekly (1 h 30 mn).
🛈 States Office ✆ 2994.

St. Anne – ✉ St. Anne – ✪ 048 182 Alderney.
🛈 ✆ 2835, E : 1 m.
🏠 Chez André, Victoria St., ✆ 2777 – ⌷wc – **14 rm**.
🏠 **Town House**, 10 High St., ✆ 2330 – �
closed 2 weeks at Christmas – **11 rm** ⌷ 11.00/22.00 **s.**

GUERNSEY 403 OP 33 230 and 230 ⑨ ⑩ – pop. 51,458 – ✪ 0481.
See : Icart Point ≤★★★ – Cobo Bay★★ – Fort Pézéries ≤★★ – Fort Doyle ≤★ – Fort Saumarez ≤★ – Moulin Huet Bay★ – Rocquaine Bay★ – Moye Point (Le Gouffre★).
✈ La Villiaze, Forest ✆ 37766.
⛴ Shipping connections with the Continent : to France (Saint-Malo) (Commodore Shipping Co.) cars only (passengers travel by hydrofoil) – to Portsmouth (Sealink) summer 1 daily ; winter 6 weekly (6 h 35 mn) – to Weymouth (Sealink) summer 1-3 daily ; winter 2 weekly (4 h 30 mn day, 11 h 30 mn night) – to Jersey (St. Helier) (Sealink) 1-2 daily (2 h) – to Torquay (Torbay Seaways) summer only 2 weekly (5-8 h).
⛴ Shipping connections with the Continent : to France (Saint-Malo) (Condor : hydrofoil) summer only – to France (Carteret) (Service Maritime) – to Jersey (St. Helier) (Condor : hydrofoil) 2-3 daily in summer (1 h) – to Alderney (Condor : hydrofoil) summer only 2 weekly (45 mn) – to Herm (Herm Seaway) summer, (Trident Charter Co.) winter 1-6 daily (25 mn) – to Sark (Isle of Sark Shipping Co.) Monday/Saturday 7 daily (35 mn to 1 h).
🛈 Crown Pier, St. Peter Port ✆ 23552 – The Airport, La Villiaze ✆ 37267.

L'Ancresse – ✪ 0481 Guernsey
🏠 **Lynton** ⋙, Hacse Lane, ✆ 45418, ⋈ – ⌷wc ⋔wc 🅿. �
May-September – **14 rm** ⌷ 14.00/33.00.

Fermain Bay – ✉ St. Peter Port – ✪ 0481 Guernsey.
🏨 **La Favorita** ⋙, Fermain Lane, ✆ 35666, ⋈ – 📺 ⌷wc ☎ 🅿. 𝘝𝘐𝘚𝘈. �
closed January – **M** (bar lunch) 5.00 **s.** ▯ 1.50 – **31 rm** ⌷ 13.50/47.00 **s.** – SB (winter only) 54.00/64.00 **s.**
🏨 **Le Chalet** ⋙, Fermain Lane, ✉ St. Martin, ✆ 35716, ≤ – 📺 ⌷wc ⋔wc ☜ 🅿. 🔌 ⍰ ⓞ
𝘝𝘐𝘚𝘈
April-October – **M** 4.50/5.50 **s.** ▯ 1.50 – **50 rm** ⌷ 16.75/36.60 **s.**

St. Martin – pop. 6,161 – ECD : Thursday – ✉ St. Martin – ✪ 0481 Guernsey.
See : Church★ 11C.
St. Peter Port 2.
🏨 **Green Acres** ⋙, Les Hubits, ✆ 35711, ⟰ heated, ⋈ – 📺 ⌷wc ☜ 🅿. �
M (bar lunch) 6.00 ▯ 1.65 – **48 rm** ⌷ (dinner included) 46.00.
🏨 **Bella Luce**, La Fosse, Moulin Huet, ✆ 38764, ⟰ heated, ⋈ – 📺 ⌷wc ⋔wc 🅿
closed 2 weeks January – **M** (bar lunch Monday to Saturday) 4.50/7.75 ▯ 1.75 – **31 rm** ⌷ 14.50/46.00.
🏨 **St. Margaret's Lodge**, Forest Rd, ✆ 35757, ⟰ heated, ⋈ – 📺 ⌷wc ☜ 🅿. 🔌 ⍰ ⓞ
𝘝𝘐𝘚𝘈 �
M (bar lunch) 6.75 ▯ 2.25 – **43 rm** ⌷ 13.50/40.00 – SB (except summer) 35.00/45.00.
🏨 **La Trelade**, Forest Rd, ✆ 35454, ⟰ heated – ▮ 📺 ⌷wc ☎ 🅿. 🔌 𝘝𝘐𝘚𝘈
M (bar lunch) 9.00 **s.** ▯ 1.80 – **45 rm** ⌷ 28.00/45.00 **s.**

GUERNSEY-St. Martin

La Cloche ⌂, Les Traudes, 🖉 35421, ⊒ heated, 🚗 – 📺 🛏wc 📶wc ☎ 🅿. 🛇
March-October – **M** (bar lunch)(residents only) 6.00 **s.** 🍷 1.60 – **10 rm** 🛏 (dinner included) 21.00/45.00 **s.**

Windmill, Rue Poudreuse, 🖉 37402, ⊒ heated, 🚗 – 📺 🛏wc 📶wc 🅿. 🛇
March-October – **M** (residents only) 6.00 **s.** 🍷 1.60 – **19 rm** 🛏 20.00/39.00.

Captain's, La Fosse, Moulin Huet, 🖉 38990 – 🅿 – **11 rm.**

Wellesley, Sausmarez Rd, 🖉 38028, 🚗 – 🛏wc 📶wc 🅿
May-October – **9 rm** 🛏 11.50/23.00.

ALFA ROMEO, FERRARI, FIAT Forest Rd 🖉 35753   AUSTIN-ROVER Ville au Roi 🖉 37661

☞ *Michelin puts no plaque or sign*
on the hotels and restaurants mentioned in this Guide.

St. Peter Port – pop. 16,303 – ECD : Thursday – ✉ St. Peter Port – ☎ 0481 Guernsey.

See : St. Peter's Church★ 14C Z – Castle Cornet★ (❋★) *AC* Z – Hauteville House (Victor Hugo Museum★ : 5 pearl-embroidered tapestries★★) *AC* Z – Victoria Tower : top ❋★★, 100 steps Y.

Envir. : Les Vauxbelets (Little Chapel★) SW : 2 ½ m. by Mount Durand Z – Saumarez Park★ W : 2 ½ m. by Grange Rd Z – Vale (castle ≼ ★) NW : 4 ½ m. by St. Georges Esplanade Y.
🛈 Crown Pier 🖉 23552.

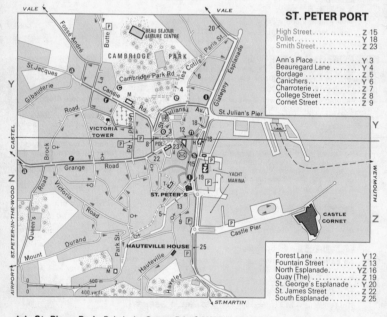

ST. PETER PORT

High Street . . . . Z 15
Pollet . . . . Y 18
Smith Street . . . . Z 23

Ann's Place . . . . Y 3
Beauregard Lane . . . . Y 4
Bordage . . . . Z 5
Canichers . . . . Y 6
Charroterie . . . . Y 7
College Street . . . . Z 8
Cornet Street . . . . Z 9

Forest Lane . . . . Y 12
Fountain Street . . . . Z 13
North Esplanade . . . . YZ 16
Quay (The) . . . . Z 19
St. George's Esplanade . . . Y 20
St. James Street . . . . Z 22
South Esplanade . . . . Z 25

St. Pierre Park, Rohais, by Grange Rd, 🖉 28282, Telex 4191662, ≼, 🔲, ⛳, 🚗, park, ❀ – 📶 📺 ☎ & 🅿. 🟥. 🔬 🖭 ⓪ 𝘝𝘐𝘚𝘈. 🛇
M 5.50/8.00 **s.** 🍷 2.10 (see also rest. **Victor Hugo**) – **131 rm** 🛏 30.25/70.00 **s.**

Old Government House, Ann's Pl., 🖉 24921, Telex 4191144, ⊒ heated, 🚗 – 📶 📺 ☎. 🟥. 🔬 🖭 ⓪ 𝘝𝘐𝘚𝘈
M 5.00/7.50 🍷 2.00 – **73 rm** 🛏 21.50/66.00.

Duke of Richmond, Cambridge Park, 🖉 26221, Telex 4191462, ⊒ heated – 📶 🍽 rest 📺 ☎. 🔬 🖭 ⓪ 𝘝𝘐𝘚𝘈
M 5.50/9.00 🍷 1.80 – **75 rm** 🛏 22.50/60.00 **s.** – SB (weekends only) 40.00/60.00 **s.**

Royal, Glategny Esplanade, 🖉 23921, Telex 4191221, ≼, ⊒ heated, 🚗 – 📶 📺 🅿. 🟥. 🔬 🖭 ⓪ 𝘝𝘐𝘚𝘈
M 5.00/5.50 🍷 1.75 – **79 rm** 🛏 17.50/55.00.

La Collinette, St. Jacques, 🖉 22585, ⊒ heated, 🚗 – 📺 🛏wc 📶 🅿. 🔬 🖭 ⓪ 𝘝𝘐𝘚𝘈. 🛇
M 4.00/5.00 🍷 1.80 – **27 rm** 🛏 12.00/48.00.

556

🏠 **Dunchoille,** Guelles Rd, ℰ 22912, 🗻 heated, 🛏 – ⌷wc 🛁wc 🅿. ⚅ N : by la Butte Y
24 rm.

🏠 **Grange Lodge,** The Grange, ℰ 25161, 🗻 heated, 🛏 – 📺 ⌷wc 🅿. 🔤 𝗩𝗜𝗦𝗔 Z r
closed December-February – **M** (bar lunch) 3.50 ⵜ 2.75 – **33 rm** 🖙 (dinner included) 14.00/36.00.

🏠 **Moore's Central,** Le Pollet, ℰ 24452 – ⫿ 📺 ⌷wc 🚗. 🔤 𝖠𝖤 ⓞ 𝗩𝗜𝗦𝗔 Y n
M 4.00/5.50 **s.** ⵜ 1.50 – **40 rm** 🖙 16.00/36.50 **s.**

⌂ **Midhurst House,** Candie Rd, ℰ 24391, 🛏 – 📺 🛁wc. 🕸 Y r
March-October – **7 rm** 🖙 13.75/26.00 **s.**

⌂ **Baltimore House,** Les Gravées, ℰ 23641, 🛏 – 🛁wc. 🔤 𝖠𝖤 ⓞ 𝗩𝗜𝗦𝗔 Z a
March-October – **12 rm** 🖙 7.50/25.50 **s.**

XXXX **Victor Hugo** (at St. Pierre Park H.), Rohais, by Grange Rd, ℰ 28282 – 🅿. 🔤 𝖠𝖤 ⓞ 𝗩𝗜𝗦𝗔
closed Saturday lunch and Sunday dinner – **M** a la carte 10.75/15.25 ⵜ 2.10. Z

XXX **La Frégate** 🐦 with rm, Les Côtils, ℰ 24624, ≤ town and harbour, « Country house atmosphere », 🛏 – 🍽 rest ⌷wc 🚗 🅿. 🔤 𝖠𝖤 𝗩𝗜𝗦𝗔. 🕸 Y e
M (booking essential) 7.00/9.50 **s.** ⵜ 2.00 – 🖙 5.00 – **13 rm** 17.00/50.00 **s.**

XX **Le Nautique,** Quay Steps, ℰ 21714, ≤ – 🔤 𝖠𝖤 ⓞ 𝗩𝗜𝗦𝗔 Z s
closed Sunday and 1 to 21 January – **M** (booking essential) a la carte 7.40/10.00 ⵜ 1.90.

XX **Steak and Stilton,** The Quay, ℰ 23080 – 🔤 𝖠𝖤 𝗩𝗜𝗦𝗔 Z i
closed 23 December-23 January – **M** a la carte 6.25/10.75 ⵜ 1.95.

ASTON-MARTIN, LANCIA, NISSAN, PEUGEOT-
TALBOT, ROLLS ROYCE Rue du Pré ℰ 24261
BMW, MERCEDES-BENZ 16 Glategny Esplanade
ℰ 23916

FORD Les Banques ℰ 24774
HONDA Doyle Rd ℰ 24025
RENAULT Upland Rd ℰ 26846

St. Sampson – pop. 6,534 – ✉ St. Sampson's – ☎ 0481 Guernsey.
St. Peter Port 3.5.

⌂ **Pinetops** 🐦, Pointues Rocques, Delancey, off Vale Rd, ℰ 44020 – 📺 ⌷wc 🅿. 🕸
15 rm 🖙 10.20/31.90 **s.**

St. Saviour – pop. 2,116 – ✉ St. Saviour – ☎ 0481 Guernsey.
St. Peter Port 4.

🏨 **L'Atlantique,** Perelle Bay, ℰ 64056, ≤, 🗻 heated, 🛏 – 📺 ⌷wc ☎ 🅿. 🔤 𝖠𝖤 ⓞ 𝗩𝗜𝗦𝗔. 🕸
closed January and February – **M** (bar lunch in winter) 5.00/7.25 ⵜ 1.80 – **21 rm** 🖙 13.00/40.00.

🏨 **La Hougue Fouque Farm,** Route-des-Bas-Courtil, ℰ 63800 – ⌷wc 🛁wc 🅿. 𝗩𝗜𝗦𝗔. 🕸
M 5.00/7.00 **s.** ⵜ 1.30 – **16 rm** 🖙 20.50/35.00 **s.**

🏠 **La Girouette Country House** 🐦, ℰ 63269, 🛏 – 📺 ⌷wc 🛁wc ☎ 🅿. 🔤 𝖠𝖤 𝗩𝗜𝗦𝗔. 🕸
closed December and January – **M** (dinner only and Sunday lunch) 4.00/5.00 **s.** ⵜ 2.00 – **14 rm**
🖙 11.00/30.00 **s.**

HERM ISLAND 𝟜𝟘𝟛 P 33 𝟚𝟛𝟘 and 𝟚𝟛𝟘 ⑩ – pop. 30 – ☎ 0481 Guernsey.
🛳 to Guernsey (Herm Seaway) summer, (Trident Charter Co.) winter, 1-6 daily (25 mn).
🄱 Administrative Office ℰ 22377.

Herm – ✉ Herm – ☎ 0481 Guernsey.

🏨 **White House** 🐦, ℰ 22159, ≤, 🗻, 🛏, park, ✗ – ⌷wc. 𝗩𝗜𝗦𝗔. 🕸
April-October – **M** 4.75/8.00 ⵜ 1.90 – **30 rm** 🖙 (dinner included) 25.50/46.00.

JERSEY 𝟜𝟘𝟛 OP 33 𝟚𝟛𝟘 and 𝟚𝟛𝟘 ⑪ – pop. 72,629 – ☎ 0534.
See : Devil's Hole★ (site★★) *AC* private access, ¾ h Rtn on foot by a steep road – Grosnez Castle
≤★ – La Hougue Bie Tumulus★ (prehistoric tomb) *AC* – St. Catherine's Bay★ – Fliquet Bay (St.
Catherine's Breakwater ≤★★) – Sorel Point ≤★ – Noirmont Point ≤★ – Jersey zoo (site★) *AC*.

✈ States of Jersey Airport ℰ 41272.

🛥 Shipping connections with the Continent : to France (Saint-Malo) (Emeraude Ferries) – to
France (Saint-Malo) (Commodore Shipping Co.) cars only (passengers travel by hydrofoil) – to
Portsmouth (Sealink) summer 1 daily ; winter 6 weekly (8 h 50 mn) – to Weymouth (Sealink)
summer 2 daily ; winter 2 weekly (5 h 45 mn) – to Guernsey (St. Peter Port) (Sealink) 1-2 daily (1 h
45 mn).

🛥 Shipping connections with the Continent : to France (Saint-Malo) (Condor : hydrofoil) (Vedettes
Blanches, summer only) (Vedettes Armoricaines) – to France (Granville) (Vedettes Armoricaines
and Vedettes Vertes Granvillaises) - from Gorey to France (Carteret) (Service Maritime Carteret
and Hovercross) – from Gorey to France (Port Bail) (Compagnie Côte des Isles) – to Sark (Condor :
hydrofoil) summer Monday/Saturday 1-2 daily (45 mn-1 h 30 mn) – to Guernsey (St. Peter Port)
(Condor : hydrofoil) 2-3 daily in summer (1 h) – to Alderney (Condor : hydrofoil) summer 3 weekly
(2 h 5 mn).

🄱 Weighbridge, St. Helier ℰ 78000 and 24779.

[Archirondel] – ✉ Gorey – ☎ 0534 Jersey.
St. Helier 5.

🏨 **Les Arches,** ✆ 53839, Telex 4192085, <, 🏊 heated, 🌳 – 🛁wc 🚿wc ☏ [P]. ♿. 💳 VISA
M 15.00/20.00 **s.** 🍷 2.50 – **54 rm** ☕ 15.50/44.50 **s.**

[Bonne Nuit Bay] – ✉ St. John – ☎ 0534 Jersey.
St. Helier 6.

🏨 **Cheval Roc** 🔇, ✆ 62865, < Bonne Nuit Bay, 🏊 heated – 🛁wc 🚿wc [P]. 💳 VISA
May-October – **M** 3.50/5.50 **s.** 🍷 2.20 – **45 rm** ☕ 15.00/50.00 **s.**

🏨 **Bonne Nuit,** ✆ 61644, < Bonne Nuit Bay, 🌳 – 🛁wc 🚿wc ☏ [P]. 💳 [AE] [D] VISA. 🚫🐕
March-October – **M** (seafood rest.) a la carte 5.90/12.50 🍷 1.75 – **30 rm** ☕ 20.00/40.00 **s.**

[Bouley Bay] – ✉ Trinity – ☎ 0534 Jersey.
St. Helier 5.

🏨 Water's Edge 🔇, ✆ 62777, Group Telex 4191462, < Bouley Bay, 🏊 heated, 🌳 – 🛗 [TV] [P].
💳 [AE] [D] VISA
Mid April-mid October – **M** 8.00/11.00 🍷 2.50 – **56 rm**.

[Corbiere] – ✉ St. Brelade – ☎ 0534 Jersey.
St. Helier 8.

🍴🍴 **Sea Crest,** with rm, Petit Port, ✆ 42687, <, 🏊, 🌳 – [TV] 🛁wc ☏ [P]. 💳 [AE] VISA. 🚫🐕
April-October – **M** a la carte 7.20/15.00 🍷 1.80 – **7 rm** ☕ 44.00.

[Gorey] – ✉ St. Martin – ☎ 0534 Jersey.
See : Mont Orgueil Castle★ (<★★, paintings★) *AC*.
St. Helier 4.

🏨 Old Court House, Gorey Village, ✆ 54444, Telex 4192032, 🏊 heated, 🌳 – 🛗 [TV] 🛁wc ☏ [P].
🚫🐕 – **58 rm**.

🏨 **Trafalgar Bay,** Gorey Village, ✆ 53216, Telex 4192349, 🏊 heated, 🌳 – 🛁wc [P]. 💳 VISA.
🚫🐕
June-September – **M** (bar lunch) 5.75 **s.** 🍷 1.70 – **37 rm** ☕ 11.25/32.00 **s.**

at Gorey Pier – ✉ St. Martin – ☎ 0534 Jersey :

🏨 **Moorings,** ✆ 53633 – ▤ rest [TV] 🛁wc 🚿wc ☏ [P]. 💳 VISA. 🚫🐕
M a la carte 9.40/13.00 🍷 1.95 – **16 rm** ☕ 17.50/53.00.

🏠 **Seascale,** ✆ 54395 – 🛁wc 🚿wc. 💳 VISA
closed 2 January-28 February – **M** 15.00/20.00 **s.** 🍷 1.90 – **10 rm** ☕ 12.50/32.00 **s.**

🏠 **Dolphin,** ✆ 53370, Group Telex 4192085 – 🚿wc ☏. 💳 [AE] VISA. 🚫🐕
M 4.50/8.50 **st.** 🍷 1.80 – **17 rm** ☕ 14.00/36.00 **s.**

[La Haule] – ✉ St. Brelade – ☎ 0534 Jersey.

🏨 La Place 🔇, Route du Coin, by B 25 on B 43 ✆ 44261, Telex 4191462, 🏊 heated – [TV] [P]. 💳
[AE] [D] VISA
M 6.50/8.50 🍷 3.00 – **40 rm**.

[Portelet Bay] – ✉ St. Brelade – ☎ 0534 Jersey.
St. Helier 5.

🏨 **Portelet** 🔇, ✆ 41204, Telex 4192039, <, 🏊 heated, 🌳, 🎾 – [TV] [P]. 💳 [AE] [D] VISA. 🚫🐕
May-September – **M** 4.00 **s.** 🍷 2.95 – **86 rm** ☕ 21.50/61.00 **s.**

[La Pulente] – ✉ St. Brelade – ☎ 0534 Jersey.
St. Helier 7.

🏨 **Atlantic** 🔇, La Moye, ✆ 44101, Telex 4192405, <, 🏊 heated, 🌳, 🎾 – 🛗 [TV] ☏ [P]. ♿. 💳
[AE] [D] VISA. 🚫🐕
closed January and February – **M** 6.50/9.50 🍷 2.00 – **46 rm** ☕ 33.25/77.50.

[Rozel Bay] – ✉ St. Martin – ☎ 0534 Jersey.
St. Helier 6.

🏨 **Le Couperon de Rozel,** ✆ 62190, 🏊 heated – 🛁wc [P]. 💳 [AE] [D] VISA. 🚫🐕
April-November – **M** 6.00/7.50 🍷 1.80 – **24 rm** ☕ 14.00/50.00 **s.**

[St. Aubin] – ✉ St. Aubin – ☎ 0534 Jersey.
St. Helier 4.

🍴🍴 **Portofino,** High St., ✆ 42100, Italian rest. – 💳 VISA
closed Wednesday – **M** a la carte 7.00/12.50 🍷 1.95.

🍴 **Old Court House Inn** with rm, St. Aubin's Harbour, ✆ 41156 – [TV] 🛁wc ☏. 🚫🐕
closed 25 and 26 December – **M** a la carte 5.00/12.00 **s.** 🍷 1.90 – **9 rm** ☕ 15.00/75.00 **s.**

St. Brelade's Bay – pop. 8,224 – ⊠ St. Brelade – ✆ 0534 Jersey.
See : Site★.
St. Helier 6.

🏨 **L'Horizon,** ℰ 43101, Telex 4192281, ≤ St. Brelades Bay, ⬚ – 🕮 📺 ☎ 👍 🅿 🏛 ⬚ 🆎 ⓪ 𝘝𝘐𝘚𝘈 ⚘
   M a la carte 10.40/16.50 **s.** (see also rest. **Star Grill** below) – **104 rm** 🚬 27.50/88.00 **s.**

🏨 **St. Brelade's Bay,** ℰ 43281, ≤, ⤳ heated, ➾, ⚘ – 🕮 📺 ☎ 🅿 ⬚ 🆎 ⓪ 𝘝𝘐𝘚𝘈 ⚘
   Mid April-October – **M** 6.00/9.50 ♠ 2.10 – **79 rm** 🚬 23.50/49.50.

🏨 **Chateau Valeuse,** rue de la Valeuse, ℰ 43476, ⤳ heated, ➾ – 🛁wc 🛁wc 🅿 ⬚ 🆎 𝘝𝘐𝘚𝘈 ⚘
   March-October – **M** 5.50/8.50 ♠ 1.70 – **26 rm** 🚬 19.00/48.00.

XXX **Star Grill,** (at L'Horizon H.), ℰ 43101, Telex 4192281, ≤ St. Brelades Bay – 🅿 ⬚ 🆎 ⓪ 𝘝𝘐𝘚𝘈
   M *(closed Monday except Bank Holidays)* (booking essential) a la carte 13.00/17.00 ♠ 1.90.

FORD Airport Rd ℰ 43222   HONDA Route de Noirmont ℰ 41911

St. Clement – pop. 5,329 – ⊠ St. Clement – ✆ 0534 Jersey.
St. Helier 2.

🏨 **Ambassadeur,** St. Clement's Coast Rd, ℰ 24455, Group Telex 4192296, ≤, ⤳ heated – 🕮 📺 🛁wc 🅿 ⬚ ⓪ 𝘝𝘐𝘚𝘈 ⚘
   closed 2 January-1 March – **M** 8.00 ♠ 1.90 – **41 rm** 🚬 13.00/49.00 **s.**

🏨 **Shakespeare,** Samares, St. Clement's Coast Rd, ℰ 51915 – 📺 🛁wc ☎ 🅿 ⬚ 🆎 𝘝𝘐𝘚𝘈
   closed 2 January-26 February – **M** 6.00/8.80 **s.** ♠ 1.75 – **26 rm** 🚬 17.00/36.00 **s.**

In alta stagione, e soprattutto nelle stazioni turistiche,
e prudente prenotare con un certo anticipo.
Avvertite immediatamente l'albergatore se non potete più
occupare la camera prenotata.
Se scrivete ad un albergo all'estero, allegate alla vostra
lettera un tagliando - risposta internazionale (disponibile presso gli uffici postali)

St. Helier – pop. 28,135 – ECD : Thursday and Saturday – ⊠ St. Helier – ✆ 0534 Jersey.
See : Fort Regent ☀★★★ (Militia Museum) *AC* Z – Elizabeth Castle ☀★ *AC* Z – Rocher des Proscrits (au Havre des Pas) Z.
🛈 Weighbridge ℰ 78000 and 24779.
Plan on next page

🏨 **De la Plage,** Havre des Pas, ℰ 23474, Telex 4192328, ≤ – 🕮 📺 🅿 ⬚ 🆎 ⓪ 𝘝𝘐𝘚𝘈 ⚘   Z **s**
   April-October – **M** 5.75/7.00 ♠ 1.50 – **96 rm** 🚬 18.50/57.00 **s.**

🏨 **Beaufort,** Green St., ℰ 32471, Telex 4192160 – 🕮 📺 🅿 ⬚ 🆎 ⓪ 𝘝𝘐𝘚𝘈 ⚘   Z **r**
   M 5.50/7.00 ♠ 1.40 – **54 rm** 🚬 19.50/25.50 **s.**

🏨 **Pomme d'Or,** The Esplanade, ℰ 78644, Telex 4192309 – 🕮 🍽 📺 🛁wc ☎ 🏛 ⬚ 🆎 ⓪ 𝘝𝘐𝘚𝘈 ⚘   Z **u**
   M 6.05/8.25 **s.** ♠ 1.80 – **151 rm** 🚬 22.00/46.00 **s.** – SB (weekends only)(winter only) 36.00/45.00 **s.**

🏨 **Savoy,** Rouge Bouillon, ℰ 30012, ⤳ heated – 🕮 📺 🛁wc 🛁wc 🅿 ⬚ ⚘   Y **i**
   March-November – **M** 4.00/6.00 **s.** ♠ 1.30 – **61 rm** 🚬 12.00/36.00 **s.**

🏨 **Apollo,** 9 St. Saviour's Rd, ℰ 25441, Telex 4192086 – 🕮 📺 🛁wc ☎ 🅿 ⬚ 🆎 ⓪ 𝘝𝘐𝘚𝘈 ⚘   Z **e**
   M 5.00/6.50 **s.** ♠ 1.40 – **53 rm** 🚬 18.50/24.50 **s.**

🏨 **Royal Yacht,** Weighbridge, ℰ 20511, Telex 4192085 – 🕮 📺 🛁wc 🛁wc ☎ ⬚ 𝘝𝘐𝘚𝘈 ⚘   Z **c**
   M 5.50/9.00 **s.** ♠ 2.50 – **45 rm** 🚬 18.50/37.00 **s.**

🏨 **Uplands,** St. John's Rd, ℰ 70460, ⤳ heated, ➾ – 📺 🛁wc 🅿 ⚘   Y **a**
   April-October – **M** (bar lunch) (residents only) 6.00 **s.** ♠ 1.40 – **28 rm** 🚬 10.00/28.00 **s.**

🏨 **Mountview,** 46 New St. John's Rd, ℰ 78887, Telex 4192341 – 🕮 📺 🛁wc 🛁wc 🅿 ⬚ 𝘝𝘐𝘚𝘈   Y **e**
   April-November – **M** (bar lunch) 6.00 **s.** ♠ 1.75 – **36 rm** 🚬 16.50/44.00 **s.**

🏨 **Almorah,** 1 Almorah Cres., La Pougelaye, ℰ 21648, ➾ – 🛁wc 🅿 ⚘   Y **o**
   April-October – **16 rm** 🚬 10.00/30.00 **s.**

XX **La Capannina,** 67 Halkett Pl., ℰ 34602, Italian rest. – ⬚ ⓪ 𝘝𝘐𝘚𝘈   Z **n**
   closed Sunday and Bank Holidays – **M** (booking essential) a la carte 5.90/12.20 ♠ 1.95.

XX **Mauro's,** 37 La Motte St., ℰ 20147 – 🍽 ⬚ 🆎 𝘝𝘐𝘚𝘈   Z **a**
   closed Sunday, January and Bank Holidays – **M** a la carte 10.60/14.00 **s.** ♠ 1.70.

X **La Buca,** The Parade, ℰ 34283, Italian rest.   Y **n**

ASTON-MARTIN, AUSTIN-ROVER, ROLLS ROYCE-   CITROEN 50 New St. ℰ 24541
BENTLEY 33-35 Lamotte St. ℰ 31341   NISSAN 1/2 Victoria St. ℰ 37357
AUSTIN-ROVER Havre des Pas ℰ 33233   PEUGEOT 17 Esplanade ℰ 33623

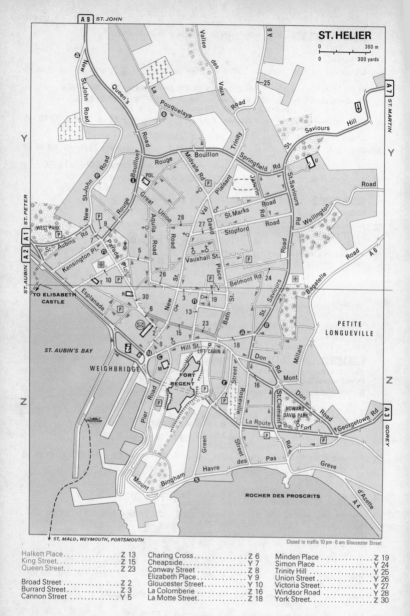

ST. HELIER

0   300 m
0   300 yards

Closed to traffic 10 pm - 6 am Gloucester Street

↘ ST. MALO, WEYMOUTH, PORTSMOUTH

🖝   *To go a long way quickly, use* **Michelin maps** *at a scale of 1:1 000 000.*

St. Lawrence – pop. 2,437 – ⊠ St. Lawrence – 🕿 0534 Jersey.

See : German Military Underground Hospital★ *AC* Y – St Helier 3.

🏯 **Little Grove** ⤳, Rue de Haut, by A 11 🖉 25321, ⌿ heated, 🚗 – 📺 🅿 🄿 🄰🄴 🅾 𝘝𝘐𝘚𝘈
   M 4.50/7.00 🍴 1.60 – **14 rm** ⊊ 23.50/47.00 **s.**

St. Martin – pop. 2,626 – ⊠ St. Martin – ✆ 0534 Jersey.
St. Helier 4.

↰ **St. Martin's House,** ℰ 53271, ⊥, 🌳 – 🛏wc ⋔wc **P**. ❀
April-December – **11 rm** ⊇ 10.00/35.00 **s.**

St. Peter – pop. 4,000 – ⊠ St. Peter – ✆ 0534 Jersey.
Envir. : St. Ouen Manor★ *AC*, NW : 2 m.
St. Helier 5.

🏨 **Mermaid,** Airport Rd, on B 36, ℰ 41255, Telex 4192249, ≼, ⊥ heated, 🌳 – 📺 **P**. ⚶. 🔂 🖭
    ⓪ 𝘃𝘐𝘚𝘈
    M 5.50/6.50 ⋔ 1.75 – **68 rm** ⊇ 18.00/48.00 **s.**

🏨 **Greenhill Country,** Coin Varin, Mont de l'Ecole, on C 112 ℰ 81042, Telex 4192249, ⊥ heated
    – 📺 🛏wc ⋔wc 📶 **P**. 🔂 🖭 ⓪ 𝘃𝘐𝘚𝘈 ❀
    closed mid December-mid February – **M** 4.50/8.00 ⋔ 1.50 – **18 rm** ⊇ 20.00/50.00.

St. Saviour – pop. 11,064 – ECD : Thursday – ⊠ St. Saviour – ✆ 0534 Jersey.
St. Helier 1.

🏨 **Longueville Manor,** Longueville Rd, on A 3 ℰ 25501, Telex 4192306, ⊥ heated, 🌳, park –
    💈 🗐 rest 📺 ☎ **P**. 🔂 🖭 ⓪ 𝘃𝘐𝘚𝘈
    M a la carte 19.00/24.00 ⋔ 1.75 – **33 rm** ⊇ 36.50/93.00 **s.** – SB (weekends only)(win-
    ter only) 66.00/84.00 **s.**

PORSCHE Five Oaks ℰ 26156   RENAULT Bagot Rd ℰ 36471

SARK 🄳🄳🄳 P 33 and 🄳🄳🄳 – pop. 590 – ✆ 048 183.
See : La Coupée★★★ (isthmus) – Port du Moulin★★ – Creux Harbour★ – Happy Valley★ – Little
Sark★ – La Seigneurie★ (manor 18C, Residence of the Seigneur of Sark).

🚢 Shipping connections with the Continent : to France (Saint-Malo) (Condor : hydrofoil) – to
Jersey (St. Helier) (Condor : hydrofoil) summer Monday/Saturday 1-2 daily (1 h 15 mn-2 h) – to
Guernsey (St. Peter Port) (Isle of Sark Shipping Co.) Monday/Saturday 7 daily (35 mn to 1 h) – to
Alderney (Condor : hydrofoil) summer only 2 weekly (1 h 45 mn).

🛈 ℰ 2262.

🏠 **Petit Champ** ❀, ℰ 2046, ≼ coast, Herm, Jetou and Guernsey, « Country house atmos-
    phere », ⊥ heated, 🌳 – 🛏wc ⋔wc. 🔂 ⓪ 𝘃𝘐𝘚𝘈 ❀
    May-September – **M** (buffet Sunday dinner) (booking essential to non-residents) 9.00/9.50 **s.**
    ⋔ 1.75 – **16 rm** ⊇ 11.50/28.60 **s.**

🏠 **Stocks** ❀, ℰ 2001, ⊥, 🌳 – ⋔wc. ❀
    April-7 October – **M** 10.00/11.00 ⋔ 1.75 – **24 rm** ⊇ (dinner included) 20.50/48.00.

XX **Aval du Creux** with rm, Harbour Hill, ℰ 2036, 🌳 – ⋔wc. 𝘃𝘐𝘚𝘈 ❀
    May-September – **M** (booking essential) 5.00/8.00 **s.** ⋔ 1.60 – **7 rm** ⊇ (dinner inclu-
    ded) 19.00/38.00 **s.**

Isle
of Man

Place with at least :

one hotel or restaurant _____ ● Douglas

one pleasant hotel _____ 🏠 . ✗ with rm

one quiet, secluded hotel _____ ॐ

one restaurant with _____ ✿, ✿✿, ✿✿✿, M

See this town for establishments
located in its vicinity _____

Localité offrant au moins :

une ressource hôtelière _____ ● Douglas

un hôtel agréable _____ 🏠 . ✗ with rm

un hôtel très tranquille, isolé _____ ॐ

une bonne table à _____ ✿, ✿✿, ✿✿✿, M

Localité groupant dans le texte
les ressources de ses environs _____

La località possiede come minimo :

una risorsa alberghiera _____ ● Douglas

un albergo ameno _____ 🏠 . ✗ with rm

un albergo molto tranquillo, isolato _____ ॐ

un'ottima tavola con _____ ✿, ✿✿, ✿✿✿, M

La località raggruppa nel suo testo
le risorse dei dintorni _____

Ort mit mindestens :

einem Hotel oder Restaurant _____ ● Douglas

einem angenehmen Hotel _____ 🏠 . ✗ with rm

einem sehr ruhigen und abgelegenen Hotel _____ ॐ

einem Restaurant mit _____ ✿, ✿✿, ✿✿✿, M

Ort mit Angaben über Hotels und Restaurants
in seiner Umgebung _____

ISLE OF MAN

ISLE OF MAN

Towns

BALLAUGH 402 G 21 – pop. 524 – ✉ Kirkmichael – 🕿 062 489 Sulby.
Envir. : Curraghs Wildlife Park★ *AC*, NE : 1 ½ m.
Douglas 18.

🏠 **Ravensdale Castle** ॐ, Glen Rd, Ballaugh Glen, S : 1 ¼ m. ℰ 7330, 🍴, park – 🚪wc 🅿.
🄰 𝖵𝖨𝖲𝖠
M a la carte 3.80/9.20 **t.** ⬩ 3.25 – ☲ 4.00 – **10 rm** 10.00/25.00 **st.** – SB (winter only) 46.00/56.00 **st.**

CASTLETOWN 402 G 21 – pop. 2,820 – ECD : Thursday – 🕿 0624.
See : Rushen Castle★★ (13C) *AC* : Keep ⁂★ – Port Erin (site★) W : 4 ½ m.
🏌 Fort Island ℰ 822201, E : 2 m.
🅱 Commissioner's Office, Parliament Sq. ℰ 823518 and 822041.
Douglas 10.

🏨 **Castletown Golf Links** ॐ, Fort Island, E : 2 m. ℰ 822201, Telex 627636, ≤ sea and golf
links, ⴽ heated, 🏌, ✗ – 🚪wc 🁢wc 🕾 🅿. 🄰 𝖵𝖨𝖲𝖠
Easter-October – **M** 6.50/7.75 **t.** ⬩ 2.75 – **65 rm** ☲ 23.00/45.00 **t.**

DOUGLAS 402 G 21 – pop. 21,100 – ECD : Thursday – ✆ 0624.

See : Manx Museum★★ – The Promenades★ – A 18 Road★★ From Douglas to Ramsey.

Envir. : Snaefell ❄★★★ (by electric railway from Laxey) *AC*, NE : 7 m. – Laxey (waterwheel★ · Lady Isabella) NE : 6 m. – St. John's (Tynwald Hill) NW : 8 m. – Peel : Castle★ (ruins 13C-16C) *AC*, NW : 11 ½ m.

ᴳ Pulrose Park ✆ 5952, 1 m. from Douglas Pier – ᴳ Howstrake at Onchan ✆ 24299, N : 1 m.

✈ Ronaldsway Airport, ✆ 0624 (Castletown) 823311, SW : 7 m. – **Terminal** : Coach service from Lord St.

⛴ by Isle of Man Steam Packet Co. to Ardrossan : June-September 1-3 weekly (6 h) – to Belfast : June-September 1-2 weekly (4 h 30 mn) – to Dublin : June-September 1-3 weekly (4 h 30 mn) – to Fleetwood : June-September 2-3 weekly (3 h) – to Liverpool : 1-5 daily (4 h 15 mn) – to Heysham (Sealink) summer 2 daily ; winter 6 weekly (4 h).

🛈 13 Victoria St. ✆ 4323 – Public Library, 10 Elm Tree Rd at Onchan ✆ 22311 and 21228.

🏨 **Palace,** Central Promenade, ✆ 4521, Telex 627742, ≼, ⍓ – 🛗 📺 ⌷wc ☎ Ⓟ. 🅐. 🅽 🅰🅴 ⓪ *VISA*
   M 5.50/6.95 t. ⌷ 3.00 – ⌸ 4.50 – **135 rm** 27.50/57.50 t. – SB (weekends only) 45.50 **st.**

🏨 **Springfield Mansion House** 🦢, New Castletown Rd., SW : 2 m. on Airport Rd ✆ 21752, « Country house », 🍴 – 📺 ⌷wc 🍴wc ☎ Ⓟ. 🅽 🅰🅴 ⓪ *VISA*
   M (bar lunch) 6.50 **s.** ⌷ 2.75 – **5 rm** ⌸ 22.00/38.00 **s.**

✕ **L'Expérience,** Summerhill, ✆ 23103
   closed 25-26 December, 1 January and last 2 weeks January – **M** *(closed Sunday and Tuesday except dinner May-October)* 6.35/13.00 t. ⌷ 2.50.

AUSTIN-ROVER Westmoreland Rd ✆ 23481
BMW Castle Mona Av. ✆ 3380
CITROEN Kingswood Grove ✆ 24114
DAIHATSU Victoria Rd ✆ 5039
FIAT Station Rd ✆ 832021
FORD Douglas ✆ 3211
MERCEDES-BENZ Douglas Rd ✆ 822884
PEUGEOT-TALBOT Peel Rd ✆ 24519

RENAULT Peel Rd ✆ 3342
SAAB West St. ✆ 813350
TOYOTA Westmoreland Rd ✆ 5556
VAUXHALL-OPEL The Milestone, Peel Rd ✆ 3781
VOLVO New Castletown Rd ✆ 4683
YUGO Derby Rd, Kirk Michael ✆ 062 487 (Kirk Michael) 577

Republic

of Ireland

Prices quoted in this section of the guide are in " Punts "

Dans cette partie du guide, les prix sont indiqués en monnaie irlandaise " Punts "

In questa parte della guida, i prezzi sono indicati in lire irlandesi " Punts "

In diesem Teil des Führers sind die Preise in irländischer Währung " Punts " angegeben

567

REPUBLIC OF IRELAND

Towns

ABBEYLEIX Laois **405** J 9 – pop. 1,033 – ECD : Wednesday – ✆ 0502 Portlaoise – ⓕ.
Envir. : Dunamase Rock (castle★★ 13C-16C ruins), site★★, ⚘★★ NE : 13 ½ m.
♦Dublin 64 – Kilkenny 21 – ♦Limerick 65 – ♦Tullamore 30.

  🏨 **Hibernian House,** Lower Main St., ✆ 31252 – 🛏wc. ◪ _VISA_. ❀
      M 5.50/10.00 **st.** ⓙ 3.50 – **13 rm** ⊊ 10.00/24.00 **t.** – SB 36.00/44.00 **st.**

FORD Market Sq. ✆ 31125

ACHILL ISLAND Mayo **405** B 6 – pop. 1,163.
See : Achill Sound★ – The Atlantic Drive★★★ SW : Coast Rd from Cloghmore to Dooega – Keel : (the strand★) – Lough Keel★.
ⓕ Achill Sound, Westport, in Keel.
🛈 ✆ Achill Sound 51 (July-August).

ADARE Limerick **405** F 10 – pop. 545 – ✆ 061 Limerick.
See : ≼★ from the bridge of the River Maigue.
ⓕ ✆ 94204.
🛈 ✆ 94255 (June-August).
♦Dublin 131 – ♦Killarney 59 – ♦Limerick 10.

  🏨 **Dunraven Arms,** Main St., ✆ 94209, Telex 70202, ⚘ – 🛏wc �🛁wc ☏ ⒫ ◪ ᴁ ⓞ _VISA_. ❀
      M 6.50/13.50 **t.** ⓙ 3.50 – ⊊ 6.00 – **23 rm** 28.00/48.00 **t.** – SB 50.40/86.40 **st.**
  ✗ Cottage, Main St., ✆ 94520.

ANNAMOE Wicklow **405** N 8 – ⊠ ✆ 0404 Wicklow.
Envir. : Glendalough (ancient monastic city★★ : site★★★, St. Kervin's Church★) and Upper Lake★ in Glendalough Valley★★★ SW : 5 m.
♦Dublin 29 – Wexford 72.

  ✗✗ **Armstrong's Barn,** ✆ 5194, ⚘ – ⒫ ᴁ _VISA_
      closed Sunday, Monday and Christmas-17 March – **M** (dinner only) (booking essential) 17.50 **t.**
      ⓙ 4.20.

ANNESTOWN Waterford **405** K 11 – ✆ 051 Waterford.
♦Dublin 119 – ♦Cork 66 – ♦Killarney 108 – ♦Waterford 14.

  ✗✗ Annestown House, ✆ 96160, ⚘ – ⒫.

ARAN ISLANDS ★★ Galway **405** CD 8.
See : Inishmore Island (Kilronan harbour★).
Access by boat or aeroplane from Galway City or by boat from Kilkieran, or Fisherstreet (Clare).
      Hotels see : Galway.

ARDARA Donegal **405** G 3 – pop. 640.
♦Dublin 188 – Donegal 24 – ♦Londonderry 58.

  ↑ Bay View House ⌂, Portnoo Rd, N : ¾ m. ✆ 45, ≼ Loughros Bay and hills, ⚘ – �🛁wc ⒫ –
      7 rm.

ATHLONE Westmeath **405** I 7 – pop. 9,825 – ECD : Thursday – ✆ 0902.
Envir. : Clonmacnoise★★ (medieval ruins) SW : 8 m. – N : Lough Ree★.
🛈 17 Church St. ✆ 2866.
♦Dublin 75 – ♦Galway 57 – ♦Limerick 75 – Roscommon 20 – ♦Tullamore 24.

  🏨 **Prince of Wales,** Church St., ✆ 72626, Telex 25368 – 📺 🛏wc ☏ ⒫ ⚠ ◪ ᴁ ⓞ _VISA_
      M 8.00/11.00 **st.** – **42 rm** ⊊ 19.50/35.00 **st.**
  ✗✗ **Le Chateau,** Abbey Lane, ✆ 4517 – ◪ _VISA_
      closed Sunday and 24 December-31 January – **M** (dinner only)(booking essential) a la carte
      9.50/14.75 **t.**

FORD Dublin Rd ✆ 75426

AVOCA Wicklow **405** N 9 – pop. 2,266 – ✪ 0402 Arklow.

See : Vale of Avoca★ from Arklow to Rathdrum on T 7.

♦Dublin 47 – ♦Waterford 72 – Wexford 55.

  🏠 Vale View, Kilcashel, N : 1 ¾ m. on T 7 ℰ 5236, ≤ – 📺 ⌂wc 🕿 **🅿**. ⇗
      10 rm.

BALLINA Mayo **405** E 5 – pop. 6,063 – ECD : Thursday – ✪ 096.

Envir. : Rosserk Abbey★ (Franciscan Friary 15C) N : 4 m. – Ballycastle (cliffs★) NW : 3 m. near
Downpatrick Head★ NW : 18 m.

🛫 ℰ 21050, E : 1 m. – 🛫 Belmullet ℰ Belmullet 28.

🛈 ℰ 21544 (July-August).

♦Dublin 150 – ♦Galway 73 – Roscommon 64 – ♦Sligo 37.

  🏠 **Downhill**, Sligo Rd, ℰ 21033, Telex 33796, 🏊, 🐎, squash – 📺 ⌂wc 🛏wc 🕿 **🅿**. 🏊 **AE**
      ① VISA 🍽
      closed 13 to 26 December – **M** 10.00/17.60 **st.** ₰ 6.50 – **55 rm** ⇌ 55.00/70.00 **st.** – SB (week-
      ends only)(except summer) 100.00/120.00 **st.**

  🏠 **Mount Falcon Castle** ⌂, Foxford Rd, S : 4 m. on Foxford-Ballina rd (T 40/N 57) ℰ 21172,
      Telex 33149, ≤, « Country house atmosphere », 🐟, park, 🍽 – ⌂wc **🅿**. 🏊 **AE ① VISA**
      closed February and March – **M** (buffet lunch) 13.00 **t.** ₰ 4.50 – **11 rm** ⇌ 25.00/50.00 **t.**

RENAULT Lord Edward St. ℰ 21037

BALLINASCARTY Cork **405** F 12 – ⊠ Clonakilty – ✪ 023 Bandon.

♦Dublin 188 – ♦Cork 27.

  🏠 **Ardnavaha House** ⌂, SE : 2 m. by L 63 ℰ 49135, ≤, 🏊 heated, 🐟, 🐎, park, 🍽 – ⌂wc
      🕿 **🅿**. 🏊 **AE ① VISA** 🍽
      Easter-September – **M** 10.00/14.00 **t.** ₰ 4.10 – **36 rm** ⇌ 26.50/42.00 **t.** – SB (not week-
      ends) 58.00/66.00 **st.**

BALLINASLOE Galway **405** H 8 – pop. 5,969 – ECD : Thursday – ✪ 0905.

🛫 ℰ 2126.

🛈 ℰ 2332 (July-August).

♦Dublin 91 – ♦Galway 41 – ♦Limerick 66 – Roscommon 36 – ♦Tullamore 34.

  🏠 Hayden's, Dunlo St., ℰ 42347, Telex 33147, 🐎 – 📶 📺 ⌂wc 🕿 **🅿**
      55 rm.

FORD Kilmartins ℰ 42204   RENAULT Brackernagh ℰ 42420
PEUGEOT Dunlo St. ℰ 42290

BALLYBOFEY Donegal **405** I 3 – pop. 2,214 – ECD : Wednesday – ✪ 074 Letterkenny.

🛈 ℰ 93.

♦Dublin 148 – ♦Londonderry 30 – ♦Sligo 58.

  🏠 **Jackson's**, Glenfinn St., ℰ 49296, 🐎 – 📺 ⌂wc 🛏wc 🕿 **🅿**. 🏊 **AE VISA**
      closed Christmas Day – **M** 5.30/8.50 **st.** ₰ 2.75 – **44 rm** ⇌ 15.00/26.20 **st.** – SB (week-
      ends only) 24.20/26.00 **st.**

BALLYDUFF Waterford **405** H 11 – pop. 406 – ⊠ Fermoy.

♦Dublin 150 – ♦Cork 30 – ♦Waterford 51.

  🏠 **Blackwater Lodge** ⌂, Upper Ballyduff, SW : 1 ½ m. ℰ 35, ≤, 🐟 – ⌂wc **🅿**. 🏊 **VISA** 🍽
      27 February-September – **M** (bar lunch) 14.00 **t.** ₰ 5.00 – **10 rm** ⇌ 18.00/32.00 **t.**

BALLYLICKEY Cork **405** D 12 – pop. 350 – ⊠ ✪ 027 Bantry.

♦Dublin 216 – ♦Cork 55 – ♦Killarney 45.

  🏠 Sea View House ⌂, ℰ 50462, ≤, 🐎 – ⌂wc 🛏wc 🕿 **🅿**
      10 rm.

  XX **Ballylickey House** ⌂ with rm, ℰ 50071, ≤, 🏊 heated, 🐟, 🐎, park – ⌂wc 🕿 **🅿**. **AE**
      VISA 🍽
      Mid March-October – **M** *(closed Thursday lunch)* (restricted lunch) a la carte 11.60/17.00 **t.**
      ₰ 5.00 – ⇌ 6.50 – **9 rm** 25.00/38.00 **t.**

BALLYLIFFIN Donegal **405** J 2 – ⊠ ✪ Clonmany.

Envir. : Carndonagh (Donagh Cross★) SE : 6 m. – Lough Naminn★ S : 6 m.

🛈 Lifford ℰ 19.

♦Dublin 180 – Donegal 83 – ♦Londonderry 35.

  🏠 **Strand**, ℰ 7, 🐎 – 📺 ⌂wc 🛏wc 🕿 **🅿**. 🏊 **VISA** 🍽
      closed Christmas – **M** 6.50/9.00 **t.** ₰ 3.95 – **10 rm** ⇌ 20.00/28.00 **t.** – SB (week-
      ends only) 48.00/56.00 **st.**

BALLYNAHINCH Galway [405] C 7 – ✆ 095 Clifden.
See : Lake★.
♦Dublin 140 – ♦Galway 41 – Westport 49.

🏨 **Ballynahinch Castle** 🌿, ☎ 21269, Telex 28809, ≤ Cranmore river, 🐟, 🌳, park, 🎾 – 🛁wc [P]. 🚗 [AE] [D] [VISA]. 🚫🐕
Mid March-mid November – **M** 9.60/17.50 **st.** 🕯 5.00 – **20 rm** ☕ 44.50/77.00 **st.**

BALLYVAUGHAN Clare [405] E 8 – pop. 116 – ✆ 065 Ennis.
Envir. : SW : Coast road L 54 from Ailladie to Fanore : Burren District (Burren limestone terraces★★) – Corcomroe Abbey★ (or Abbey of St. Maria de Petra Fertilis : 12C Cistercian ruins) NE : 6 m.
♦Dublin 149 – Ennis 34 – ♦Galway 29.

🏨 **Gregans Castle** 🌿, SW : 3 ¼ m. on T 69 ☎ 77005, Telex 70130, ≤ Countryside and Galway Bay, 🌳 – 🛁wc [P]. [VISA]. 🚫🐕
March-October – **M** a la carte 5.50/16.50 **t.** 🕯 5.00 – **16 rm** ☕ 28.00/49.00 **t.**

BANAGHER Offaly [405] I 8 – pop. 1,052.
See : ≤★ from the bridge of Shannon.
Envir. : Clonfert (St. Brendan's Cathedral : west door★ 12C, east windows★ 13C) NW : 4 ½ m. – Birr : Castle Demesne (arboretum★, gardens★, telescope of Lord Rosse) *AC*, SE : 8 m.
♦Dublin 83 – ♦Galway 54 – ♦Limerick 56 – ♦Tullamore 24.

⌂ Brosna Lodge, Main St., ☎ 50, 🌳 – 🛁wc [P]. 🚫🐕 – **12 rm**.

BANTRY Cork [405] D 12 – pop. 2,579 – ECD : Wednesday – ✆ 027.
See : Bantry Bay★★ – Bantry House (interior★★, ≤★) *AC*.
Envir. : Glengarrif (site★★★) NW : 8 m. – NE : Shehy Mountains★★.
⛳9 Donemark ☎ 579, on Glengariff Rd – [i] ☎ 50229 (July-August).
♦Dublin 218 – ♦Cork 57 – ♦Killarney 48.

RENAULT Barrack St. ☎ 50092 VAUXHALL-OPEL The Square ☎ 50023

BARNA Galway [405] E 8 – pop. 560 – ✆ 091 Galway.
♦Dublin 135 – ♦Galway 3.

🍴 **Ty Ar Mor,** Sea Point, ☎ 69186, ≤, Seafood – [P]
closed Sunday – **M** (dinner only) a la carte 11.10/20.30 **t.** 🕯 4.05.

BETTYSTOWN Meath [405] N 6 – ✉ ✆ 041 Drogheda.
⛳18 ☎ 27534.
♦Dublin 28 – Drogheda 6.

🍴🍴 **Coastguard Inn,** ☎ 27115, ≤ – [P]. [AE] [D] [VISA]
closed Sunday, Monday, Christmas and Bank Holidays – **M** (dinner only) a la carte 13.00/17.95 **t.**

BIRR Offaly [405] I 8 – pop. 3,689 – ✆ 0509.
Athlone 28 – ♦Dublin 87 – Kilkenny 49 – ♦Limerick 49.

🏨 **County Arms,** Railway Rd, ☎ 20191, 🌳, squash – [TV] 🛁wc ☎ [P]. 🚗 [AE] [D] [VISA]. 🚫🐕
M 6.00/12.00 **t.** 🕯 3.00 – ☕ 4.50 – **18 rm** 16.00/32.00 **t.** – SB 44.00/50.00 **st.**

BLARNEY Cork [405] G 11 – pop. 1,128 – ✉ ✆ 021 Cork.
See : Castle★ 15C (top ✳★, 112 steps) *AC*.
♦Dublin 167 – ♦Cork 6.

🏨 Blarney, ☎ 85281, 🌳 – [TV] 🛁wc 🚿wc ☎ ♿ [P]. 👥 – **76 rm**.

BLESSINGTON Wicklow [405] M 8 – pop. 637 – ✆ 045 Naas.
Envir. : Lackan ≤★ SE : 4 ½ m. – SE : Poulaphuca Lake★ (reservoir).
♦Dublin 20.

🏨 **Downshire House,** Main St., ☎ 65199, 🌳, 🎾 – 🛁wc ☎ [P]
closed mid December-mid January – **M** 8.50/15.00 **t.** 🕯 5.25 – ☕ 4.50 – **25 rm** 15.00/30.00 **t.**

BOYLE Roscommon [405] H 16 – pop. 1,727 – ✆ 079.
See : Cistercian Abbey★ 12C – **Envir.** : NE : Lough Key★.
⛳9 Roscommon Rd.
[i] ☎ 145 (June-August).
♦Dublin 107 – Ballina 40 – ♦Galway 74 – Roscommon 26 – ♦Sligo 24.

🏨 **Forest Park,** Dublin Rd, E : ½ m. on T 3 ☎ 62229, 🌳 – [TV] 🛁wc ☎ [P]. 🚗 [AE] [VISA]. 🚫🐕
closed 24 to 26 December – **M** 6.50/11.00 **st.** 🕯 3.50 – **12 rm** ☕ 18.00/32.00 **st.**

FORD Elphin St. ☎ 22

BRAY Wicklow **405** N 8 – pop. 14,467 – ECD : Wednesday – ✪ 01 Dublin.

🛇 Woodbrook ✆ 824799, N : 1 m. – 🛇 Ravenswell Rd ✆ 862484.

🛇 ✆ 867128/9 (July-August).

♦Dublin 13 – Wicklow 20.

🏛 **Esplanade,** Sea Front, Strand Rd, ✆ 862056 – ℗. 🔼 ㏂ ⑩ 𝑉𝐼𝑆𝐴. ✹
closed 25 to 29 December – **M** (closed Sunday) 7.00/11.00 **st.** ⚱ 3.75 – **40 rm** ⚏ 12.00/26.00 **t.**

🗙🗙 **Tree of Idleness,** Seafront, ✆ 863498, Greek-Cypriot rest. – 🔼 ㏂ ⑩ 𝑉𝐼𝑆𝐴
closed Monday, Christmas and Bank Holidays – **M** (dinner only) a la carte 10.70/17.00 **t.** ⚱ 3.50.

BUNRATTY Clare **405** F 9 – pop. 274 – ✉ ✪ 061 Limerick.

See : Castle (Great Hall★) *AC* – Folk Park★ *AC.*

♦Dublin 129 – Ennis 14 – ♦Limerick 8.

🏛🏛 Fitzpatrick's Shannon Shamrock Inn, ✆ 61177, Telex 26214, 🔲, 🐎 – ▤ rest 📺 ⇨wc ☎ &
℗ ≜ 🔼 ㏂ ⑩ 𝑉𝐼𝑆𝐴
closed Christmas Day – **103 rm.**

🗙🗙 **MacCloskey's,** Bunratty House Mews, ✆ 74082 – ℗. 🔼 ㏂ ⑩ 𝑉𝐼𝑆𝐴
closed Sunday, Monday and January – **M** (dinner only) 18.00 **t.** ⚱ 5.00.

CAHERDANIEL Kerry **405** B 12 – pop. 357.

Envir. : Sheehan's Point ≼★★★ W : 5 m. – Staigue Fort★ (prehistoric stone fort : site★, ≼★) *AC*,
NE : 5 m.

♦Dublin 238 – ♦Killarney 48.

CAHIR Tipperary **405** I 10 – pop. 1,747 – ECD : Thursday – ✪ 052.

See : Castle★ (12C-15C) the most extensive mediaeval castle in Ireland.

🛇 Cahir Park, ✆ 41474, S : 1 m. – 🛇 ✆ 41453 (July-August).

♦Dublin 112 – ♦Cork 49 – Kilkenny 41 – ♦Limerick 38 – ♦Waterford 39.

🗙🗙 Earl of Glengall, The Square, ✆ 41505 – 🔼 𝑉𝐼𝑆𝐴
closed Sunday.

SAAB Dublin Rd ✆ 41432

CAPPOQUIN Waterford **405** I 11 – pop. 950 – ✉ Lismore – ✪ 058 Dungarvan.

♦Dublin 136 – ♦Cork 31 – ♦Waterford 40.

🛖 **Richmond House** ⌂, SE : ½ m. on N 72, ✆ 54278, 🐎, park – ⇨wc ℗. ✹
February-October – **9 rm** ⚏ 10.00/22.00 **t.**

CARAGH LAKE Kerry **405** C 11 – ✪ 066 Tralee.

See : Lough Caragh★.

♦Dublin 212 – ♦Killarney 22 – Tralee 25.

🏛🏛 **Caragh Lodge** ⌂, ✆ 61570, ≼, « Country house atmosphere, fine gardens », ⬲, park, ✹
– ⇨wc ℗. 🔼 𝑉𝐼𝑆𝐴. ✹
April-mid September – **M** (dinner only) 14.00 **t.** ⚱ 4.20 – **10 rm** ⚏ 22.00/45.00 **t.**

🏛🏛 Ard-na-Sidhe ⌂, ✆ 69105, ≼, « Country house atmosphere », ⬲, 🐎, park – ⇨wc ℗
18 rm.

CARLINGFORD Louth **405** N 5 – pop. 631 – ✪ 042.

♦Dublin 66 – ♦Dundalk 13.

🗙🗙 **Oscar's,** The Square, ✆ 73162 – ℗. 🔼 ⑩ 𝑉𝐼𝑆𝐴
closed Sunday dinner, Monday September-May and 24-26 December – **M** (dinner only and
Sunday lunch) 7.50/14.50 **t.** ⚱ 3.50.

CARLOW Carlow **405** L 9 – pop. 9,588 – ECD : Thursday – ✪ 0503.

🛇 Oak Park ✆ 31695 – 🛇 ✆ 31554 (July-August).

♦Dublin 52 – Kilkenny 25 – ♦Tullamore 44 – Wexford 46.

🏛 **Carlow Lodge,** Kilkenny Rd, S : 2 m. on N 9 ✆ 42002, 🐎 – ⇨wc ☎ ℗. 🔼 ㏂ ⑩ 𝑉𝐼𝑆𝐴. ✹
closed 5 April and 25 December – **M** 7.00/10.95 **st.** ⚱ 3.50 – ⚏ 3.50 – **10 rm** 13.50/25.00 **st.** –
SB 45.00/50.00 **st.**

AUSTIN-ROVER Pollerton Rd ✆ 31141
BMW, TOYOTA Dublin Rd ✆ 31572
FIAT, LANCIA Tullow Rd ✆ 31955
FORD Court Place ✆ 31665

OPEL Tullow Rd ✆ 31303
PEUGEOT-TALBOT Tullow Rd ✆ 31391
VW, AUDI, MAZDA, MERCEDES-BENZ Green Lane
✆ 31047

CARRICKMACROSS Monaghan **405** L 6 – pop. 2,100 – ECD : Wednesday – ✪ 042.

🛇 Nuremore H. ✆ 61438.

♦Dublin 97 – ♦Dundalk 14.

🏛🏛 Nuremore ⌂, SE : 1 m. on N 2 ✆ 61438, ≼, 🔲, 🛇, ⬲, 🐎, park, squash – 📺 ⇨wc 🎏wc ☎
℗. ≜. ✹ – **39 rm.**

CARRICK-ON-SHANNON Leitrim **405** H 6 – pop. 1,854 – ECD : Wednesday – ⊙ 078.

⛳ ℰ 157 – 🖬 ℰ 170 (June-September).

♦Dublin 97 – Ballina 50 – Roscommon 26 – ♦Sligo 34.

🏛 County, Bridge St., ℰ 20550 – ⛝wc ⛝wc ⊛ ℗. ⚄ – **17 rm**.

AUSTIN-ROVER Cartober ℰ (078) 20080

CASHEL Tipperary **405** I 10 – pop. 2,692 – ECD : Wednesday – ⊙ 062.

See : St. Patrick's Rock★★★ (or Rock of Cashel) : site and ecclesiastical ruins 12C-15C (⚄★★) *AC* – Hore Abbey★ ruins 13C – St. Dominick's Abbey★ ruins 13C.

Envir. : Holycross Abbey★★ (12C) *AC*, N : 9 m.

🖬 Town Hall ℰ 61333.

♦Dublin 101 – ♦Cork 60 – Kilkenny 34 – ♦Limerick 36 – ♦Waterford 44.

🏛 **Cashel Palace** ⚓, Main St., ℰ 61411, Telex 26938, « Former Archbishop's palace, gardens » – ℗. ⚖. ⚄ Æ ⓪ *VISA*. ⚄.
M 9.00/19.00 **st.** ⅙ 6.00 – ⚄ 7.00 – **20 rm** 45.00/80.00 **t.** – SB (winter only) 54.00 **st.**

XX **Chez Hans**, Rockside, ℰ 61177, « Converted 19C church »
closed Sunday November-March, Monday, 3 weeks November and 4 days at Christmas – **M** (dinner only) a la carte 11.50/18.00 **t.** ⅙ 4.00.

PEUGEOT-TALBOT Ladyswell St. ℰ 61155

CASHEL BAY Galway **405** C 7.

Envir. : SE : Kilkieran Peninsula★★.

♦Dublin 173 – Galway 41.

🏛 **Cashel House** ⚓, ℰ 095 (Cashel Bay) 21252, Telex 28812, ≼, « Country house set in attractive grounds », ⚘, ⚐, ⚄ – ⛝wc ℗. ⚄ Æ ⓪ *VISA*
March-October – **M** (bar lunch) 17.95 **t.** ⅙ 4.25 – **30 rm** ⚄ 25.50/59.00 **t.**

🏛 **Zetland** ⚓, ℰ 8, Telex 28853, ≼, ⚘, ⚐ – ⛝wc ℗. ⚄ Æ ⓪ *VISA*
April-October – **M** 12.00/17.00 **t.** ⅙ 5.00 – **16 rm** ⚄ 23.00/50.00 **t.**

CASTLEBAR Mayo **405** E 6 – pop. 5,979 – ECD : Thursday – ⊙ 094.

Envir. : Ballintuber Abbey★ (13C-15C) S : 7 m. – Pontoon (⚄★, moraines★) NE : 10 m.

⛳ Rocklands ℰ 21649 – 🖬 ℰ 21207 (July-August).

♦Dublin 152 – Ballina 25 – ♦Galway 48 – ♦Sligo 54.

🏛 **Breaffy House** (Best Western) ⚓, SE : 2 ¾ m. on T 39 ℰ 22033, Telex 33790, ⚘, park – 🖿 �📺 ⛝wc ⊛ ℗. ⚖. ⚄ Æ ⓪ *VISA*
M 7.25/12.25 **t.** ⅙ 4.25 – **40 rm** ⚄ 29.45/58.90 **t.**

CITROEN Breaffy Rd ℰ 21975   RENAULT Spencer St. ℰ 21355

CASTLEDERMOT Kildare **405** L 9 – pop. 535 – ⊙ 0503 Carlow.

Envir. : Baltinglass (abbey ruins : scenery★) NE : 7 m.

♦Dublin 44 – Kilkenny 33 – Wexford 54.

🏛 Kilkea Castle (Best Western) ⚓, Kilkea, NW : 3 ½ m. ℰ 45156, Telex 25388, ≼, « 12C castle », ⚄ heated, ⚘, park, ⚄ – ⛝wc ⊛ ℗. ⚖. ⚄ – **50 rm**.

AUSTIN-ROVER, CITROEN ℰ 44114

CAVAN Cavan **405** J 6 – pop. 3,240 – ⊙ 049.

♦Dublin 71 – Drogheda 58 – Enniskillen 40.

🏛 Kilmore, Dublin Rd, E : 2 m. on N 3 ℰ 32288, Group Telex 33676 – 📺 ⛝wc ☎ ⚖ ℗. ⚖ – **40 rm**.

CHARLEVILLE (RATH LUIRC) Cork **405** F 12 – pop. 2,232 – ECD : Thursday – ⊙ 063.

Envir. : Kilmallock (Dominican Friary ruins 13C, SS. Peter and Paul church 14C : scenery★) NE : 6 m. – Kilfinnane (site★) E : 11 m.

⛳ ℰ 257.

♦Dublin 138 – ♦Cork 38 – ♦Killarney 57 – ♦Limerick 24.

🏛 **Deerpark**, Limerick Rd, N : ½ m. on N 20 ℰ 581, ⚘ – ⛝wc ⊛ ℗. ⚄ *VISA*
M 4.65/7.50 **t.** ⅙ 3.50 – ⚄ 4.20 – **20 rm** 10.75/19.45 **t.**

FORD Limerick Rd ℰ 561

CLIFDEN Galway **405** B 7 – pop. 790 – ECD : Thursday – ⊙ 095.

Envir. : E : Connemara★★ : The Twelve Pins★ (mountains), Lough Inagh★ – Cleggan (site★★) NW : 6 m. – Streamstown Bay★ NW : 2 m.

⛳ Connemara, Ballyconneely ℰ Ballyconneely 5, W : 8 m..

🖬 ℰ 103 (June-September).

♦Dublin 181 – Ballina 77 – ♦Galway 49.

🏨 **Abbeyglen House** ⚶, Sky Rd, W : ½ m. ℘ 21070, Telex 28366, ≤, ⻌ heated, ⚐, ✗ – 📺 ⚌wc ☏ ☎. 🖿 🄰🄴 ① 𝘝𝘐𝘚𝘈
closed 10 January-5 March and 10 November-18 December – **M** (bar lunch Monday to Saturday) 12.00/17.00 t. ⧅ 5.50 – ⯑ 6.00 – **40 rm** 20.00/40.00 t. – SB (except summer) 80.00/90.00 st.

🏠 **Rock Glen Country House** ⚶, S : 1 ¼ m. by L 102 ℘ 21035, Telex 28989 – ⚌wc ☎. 🖿 🄰🄴 ① 𝘝𝘐𝘚𝘈. ⛭
Mid March-October – **M** (bar lunch) 14.00 t. ⧅ 4.50 – **30 rm** ⯑ 16.00/38.00 t.

🏠 **Ardagh** ⚶, Ardbear Bay, S : 1 ¾ m. on L 102 ℘ 234, ≤ Ardbear Bay, ⟋ – ⚌wc ☎. 🖿 🄰🄴 𝘝𝘐𝘚𝘈. ⛭
Easter-October – **M** 6.00/12.50 t. ⧅ 3.50 – **22 rm** ⯑ 10.00/30.00 t.

🏠 Clifden Bay, Main St., ℘ 21167 – ⚌wc – **40 rm**.

CLONMEL Tipperary 🛆🄾🄵 I 10 – pop. 11,622 – ECD : Thursday – ✿ 052.
See : The Main Guard★ 1674.
Envir. : Ahenny (2 high crosses★) NE : 16 m. – S : Nire Valley★ (≤★★).
🛇 Lyreanearla, ℘ 21138.
🖪 ℘ 22960 (July-August).
♦Dublin 108 – ♦Cork 59 – Kilkenny 31 – ♦Limerick 48 – ♦Waterford 29.

🏨 **Clonmel Arms,** Sarsfield St., ℘ 21233, Telex 80263 – 🕮 📺 ⚌wc 🕮wc ☎. 🖿 🄰🄴 ①
𝘝𝘐𝘚𝘈
M 7.50/13.00 st. ⧅ 3.50 – ⯑ 5.00 – **33 rm** 22.00/38.00 st.

AUDI, MAZDA, MERCEDES-BENZ, VW Upper Irish-town ℘ 22199
FIAT Parnell St. ℘ 21615
FORD Davis Rd ℘ 21199
NISSAN, RENAULT Dungarvon Rd ℘ 22399
RENAULT Thomas St. ℘ 22430
TOYOTA Cashel Rd ℘ 21652

CONG Mayo 🛆🄾🄵 E 7 – pop. 208 – ✿ 094 Castlebar.
See : Ashford Castle (site ★).
Envir. : Ross Abbey★★, Franciscan Friary (tower ⚘★, 80 steps) SE : 9 m.
♦Dublin 160 – Ballina 49 – ♦Galway 28.

🏰 **Ashford Castle** ⚶, ℘ 22644, Telex 24749, ≤ Lough Corrib and countryside, « Tastefully converted castle », 🛇, ⟋, ⚐, park, ✗ – 🕮 ☎ ☏. 🖿 🄰🄴 ① 𝘝𝘐𝘚𝘈. ⛭
April-December – **M** 14.00/24.00 t. ⧅ 6.00 – ⯑ 6.50 – **78 rm** 50.00/127.00 t.

COOTEHILL Cavan 🛆🄾🄵 K 5 – pop. 1,415 – ECD : Tuesday – ✿ 049 Cavan.
Envir. : Bellamont Forest★ N : 1 ½ m.
♦Dublin 68 – ♦Dundalk 33.

🏠 **White Horse,** Market St., ℘ 52124 – ⚌wc 🕮wc ☏. ☎. 🖿 𝘝𝘐𝘚𝘈
M 5.95/9.95 t. – **30 rm** ⯑ 17.00/32.00 t.

CORK Cork 🛆🄾🄵 G 12 – pop. 128,645 – ✿ 021.
See : St. Patrick's Street★ YZ – St. Ann's Shandon Church★ 18C (steeple ⚘★ AC, 134 steps) Y A – University College★ 1845 X U – The Marina ≤★ X.
🛇 Little Island ℘ 953263, E : 5 m. by N 25 X – 🛇 Monkstown ℘ 841225, S : 7 m. by L 66 X.
✈ ℘ 965388, S : 4 m. by L 42 X – Terminal : Bus Station, Parnell Pl.
⛴ Shipping connections with the Continent : to France (Roscoff) (Brittany Ferries) – to France (Le Havre) (Irish Continental Line).
🖪 Cork City, Tourist House, Grand Parade ℘ 23251 – Cork Airport ℘ 964347 (July-August).
♦Dublin 154.

Plan on next page

🏰 **Jury's,** Western Rd, ℘ 966377, Telex 26073, ⻌ heated, ⚐, squash – 📺 ☎ ⧅ ☏. 🖿 🄰🄴 ① 𝘝𝘐𝘚𝘈. ⛭   Z v
M 10.50/12.00 t. – ⯑ 5.50 – **144 rm** 53.50/62.50 t.

🏨 **Imperial,** South Mall, ℘ 965333, Telex 75126 – 🕮 📺 ☎. 🖿. ⛭   Z n
85 rm.

🏨 **Silver Springs,** Tivoli, E : 2 ½ m. on N 25 ℘ 507533, Telex 26111, ⚐, ✗ – 🕮 📺 ☎ ☏. 🖿. 🖿 🄰🄴 ① 𝘝𝘐𝘚𝘈. ⛭   X c
M 6.70/12.00 t. ⧅ 4.50 – **72 rm** ⯑ 40.25/51.75 t.

🏨 **Arbutus Lodge,** Middle Glanmire Rd, Montenotte, ℘ 501237, Telex 75079, ≤, ⚐ – 🞗 rest 📺 ⚌wc 🕮wc ☎ ☏. 🖿 🄰🄴 ① 𝘝𝘐𝘚𝘈. ⛭   Y a
closed 24 to 30 December – **M** (closed Sunday) 14.50/18.50 st. ⧅ 4.05 – **20 rm** ⯑ 35.90/63.80 st. – SB (weekends only) 56.00/70.00 st.

🏠 **Lotamore House** without rest., Tivoli, E : 3 ¼ m. on N 25 ℘ 822344, ≤, ⚐, park – 📺 ⚌wc ☎ ☏. 🖿 🄰🄴 𝘝𝘐𝘚𝘈   X a
20 rm ⯑ 16.00/30.00 st.

🍴🍴🍴 **Lovett's,** Churchyard Lane, off Well Rd, Douglas, ℘ 294909 – ☏. 🖿 🄰🄴 ① 𝘝𝘐𝘚𝘈   X s
closed Saturday lunch and Sunday – **M** a la carte 14.75/19.25 st. ⧅ 4.00.

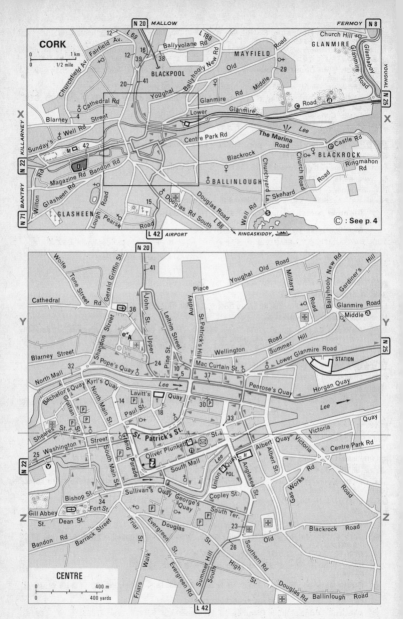

CORK

at Glounthaune E : 7 m. on N 25 – ✕ – ✉ ☏ 021 Cork :

🏨 **Ashbourne House,** ☎ 953319, « Extensive gardens », 🏊 heated, 🎾 – [TV] 🛁wc 🚿wc ☎ [P]. [EC] [AE] [DC] [VISA]. 🚫🐕
M 6.00/11.50 **t.** – **26 rm** 🍳 28.00/40.00 **t.** – SB (weekends only) 40.00 **st.**

FIAT 24 Watercourse Rd ☎ 503228
FIAT 11 South Terr. ☎ 507344
FORD Dennehys Cross ☎ 42846
OPEL 26 St. Patricks Quay ☎ 26657
RENAULT Tivoli ☎ 503397
RENAULT ☎ 44655
TALBOT Mallow Rd ☎ 503271

COURTMACSHERRY Cork [405] F 13 – pop. 210 – ✉ ☏ 023 Bandon.

Envir. : Timoleague (Franciscan Abbey★ 16 C) W : 1 ½ m.

◆Dublin 190 – ◆Cork 29.

🏨 **Courtmacsherry** 🪑, ☎ 46198, <, 🌳, park, 🎾 – 🛁wc [P]
April-September – **M** (bar lunch Monday to Saturday) 7.00/12.50 **t.** 🍷 3.90 – **16 rm** 🍳 14.50/32.00 **t.** – SB 52.80/58.30 **st.**

🏨 **Lislee House** 🪑, SW : 2 m. ☎ 40126, <, « Country house atmosphere », 🌳 – 🛁wc [P]. 🚫🐕
M (dinner only) 13.00 **st.** – 🍳 3.00 – **7 rm** 16.50/37.00 **st.**

COURTOWN Wexford [405] N 10 – pop. 291 – ☏ 055 Gorey.

⛳18 Courtown Harbour ☎ 21566.

◆Dublin 62 – ◆Waterford 59 – Wexford 42.

🏨 **Courtown,** ☎ 25108, 🏊 – 🛁wc 🚿wc [P]. [EC] [AE] [DC] [VISA]. 🚫🐕
Easter-October – **M** 7.50/12.50 **t.** – **28 rm** 🍳 15.00/30.00 **t.** – SB (except summer) 52.00/60.00 **st.**

CROSSHAVEN Cork [405] H 12 – pop. 1,222 – ✉ ☏ 021 Cork.

◆Dublin 173 – ◆Cork 12.

🏨 **Whispering Pines,** ☎ 831843, <, 🎣 – 🛁wc 🚿wc [P]. [EC] [AE] [DC] [VISA]. 🚫🐕
closed 21 to 31 December – **M** (bar lunch) 11.00 **st.** 🍷 4.00 – **15 rm** 🍳 16.00/28.00 **st.** – SB 40.00/44.00 **st.**

DALKEY Dublin [405] N 8 – ☏ 01 Dublin.

◆Dublin 11.

🍴🍴 **Guinea Pig,** 17-18 Railway Rd, ☎ 859055, Seafood – [EC] [AE] [DC] [VISA]
closed Sunday, 1 week April, 2 weeks August and 1 week Christmas – **M** (dinner only) (booking essential) a la carte 16.35/22.90 **t.** 🍷 4.00.

DELGANY Wicklow [405] N 8 – pop. 1,205 – ✉ Bray – ☏ 01 Dublin.

⛳18 ☎ 874645.

◆Dublin 19.

🏨 **Glenview** 🪑, Glen of the Downs, NW : 2 m. on N 11 by L 164 ☎ 862896, <, 🌳, park – [P]. 🎪. [AE]. 🚫🐕
closed 23 to 27 December – **M** 9.00/17.00 **t.** 🍷 5.50 – 🍳 6.00 – **23 rm** 25.00/38.00 **t.** – SB 45.00 **st.**

🏨 Delgany Inn, ☎ 875701 – 🛁wc ☎. 🚫🐕 – **10 rm**.

DINGLE Kerry [405] B 11 – pop. 1,401 – ECD : Thursday – ☏ 066.

See : Dingle Bay★.

Envir. : NE : Conair Pass ✳★ – Fahan : Belvedere (coast road) <★ SW : 7 ½ m. – Kilmakedar (church★ 12C), Gallarus Oratory★ 8C, NW : 5 m.

[i] ☎ 51188 (July-August).

◆Dublin 216 – ◆Killarney 51 – ◆Limerick 95.

⌂ **Milltown House** 🪑, W : ¾ m. ☎ 51372, < – 🛁wc 🚿wc [P]. 🚫🐕
Easter-September – **7 rm** 🍳 10.00/20.00 **st.**

⌂ **Alpine House,** Mail Rd, ☎ 51250, 🌳 – 🚿wc [P]. 🚫🐕
March-October – **15 rm** 🍳 18.00/20.00 **st.**

🍴 **Half Door,** John St., ☎ 51600, Seafood – [EC] [AE] [DC] [VISA]
Mid March-mid November – **M** *(closed Tuesday)* a la carte 9.30/12.00 **st.** 🍷 5.00.

🍴 **Doyle's Seafood Bar,** 4 John St., ☎ 51174 – [EC] [AE] [DC] [VISA]
Mid March-mid November – **M** *(closed Sunday)* a la carte 10.25/12.50 **t.** 🍷 5.00.

Do not lose your way in Europe, use the Michelin
Main Road maps, scale : 1 inch : 16 miles.

DONEGAL Donegal **405** H 4 – pop. 1,725 – ECD : Wednesday – ✆ 073.

See : Franciscan Priory (site★, ←★).

🏌 Murvagh ⌘ Ballintra 54, S : 8 m.

🛈 ⌘ 148 (June-September).

◆Dublin 164 – ◆Londonderry 48 – ◆Sligo 40.

  🏨 **Hyland Central** (Best Western), The Diamond, ⌘ 21027, Telex 40522, 🚗 – 📶 📺 🖿wc
    🖿wc ☎ 🅿. 🔄 🏧 <u>VISA</u>. ⚡
    closed 24 to 29 December – **M** 7.50/13.50 t. 🍷 4.00 – **58 rm** ⇌ 22.00/37.00 t. – SB (week-
    ends only)(except summer) 45.00/50.00 **st.**

    at St. Ernan's Island SW : 2 ¼ m. by T 18 – ✉ ✆ 073 Donegal :

  XX **Ernan Park** 🦢 with rm, ⌘ 21065, ←Donegal Bay, park – 🅿 – **10 rm**.

AUSTIN-ROVER Quay St. ⌘ 073 21039
FORD The Glebe ⌘ 073 21017
NISSAN Dunkineely ⌘ 14

NISSAN Kerrykell ⌘ 3
RENAULT ⌘ 073 21117

DROGHEDA Louth **405** M 6 – pop. 19,762 – ECD : Wednesday – ✆ 041.

See : St. Lawrence's Gate ★ 13C.

Envir. : Mellifont Abbey★★★ (Cistercian ruins 1142) NW : 4 ½ m. – Monasterboice (3 tall crosses★★
10C) NW : 5 ½ m. – Dowth Tumulus ⚞⚟ W : 4 m. – Duleek (priory★ 12C ruins) SW : 5 m. –
Newgrange Tumulus★ (prehistoric tomb) AC, SW : 7 m.

🏌 County Louth, Baltray ⌘ 22329, E : 3 m.

🛈 ⌘ 7070 (July-August).

◆Dublin 31 – ◆Dundalk 22 – ◆Tullamore 69.

  🏨 **Boyne Valley**, SE : 1 ½ m. on T 1 ⌘ 7737, 🚗, park – 📺 🖿wc 🖿wc ☜ 🅿. ⚖. ⚡ – **20 rm**.

  🏨 **Glenside**, Smithstown, SE : 3 m. on N 1 ⌘ 29049, 🚗 – 📺 🖿wc 🖿wc ☎ 🅿. 🔄 🏧 ① <u>VISA</u>
    closed 20 to 31 December – **M** 7.50/12.50 st. 🍷 3.95 – **14 rm** ⇌ 24.00/36.00 **st.**

FIAT, LANCIA North Rd ⌘ 37920
FORD North Rd ⌘ 31106

NISSAN North Rd ⌘ 38566
PEUGEOT Palace St. ⌘ 37303

DROICHEAD NUA = Newbridge.

DROMAHAIR Leitrim **405** H 5 – pop. 273 – ✆ 071 Sligo.

◆Dublin 141 – ◆Sligo 8.

  🏨 **Drumlease Glebe House** 🦢, NE : 2 ¼ m. ⌘ 64141, ←, « Country house atmosphere », ⚒, 🎣,
    🚗 – 🖿wc 🅿
    M (booking essential) – **9 rm**.

DUBLIN Dublin **405** N 7 – pop. 567,866 – ✆ 01.

See : National Gallery★★★ BY – Castle (State apartments★★★ AC) BY – Christ Church Cathedral★★
12C BY – National Museum (Irish antiquities, Art and Industrial)★★ BY M2 – Trinity College★
(Library★★) BY – National Museum (Zoological Collection)★ BY M1 – Municipal Art Gallery★ BX M3
– O'Connell Street★ (and the General Post Office) BXY – St. Stephen's Green★ BZ – St. Patrick's
Cathedral (interior★) BZ – Phoenix Park (Zoological Gardens★) AY.

Envir. : St. Doolagh's Church★ 13C (open Saturday and Sunday, afternoon only) NE : 7 m. by L 87
AY.

🏌 Edmondstown, Rathfarnham ⌘ 907461, S : 3 m. by N 81 AZ – 🏌 Elm Park, Nutley House,
Donnybrook ⌘ 693438, S : 3 m. AZ – 🏌 Lower Churchtown Rd, Milltown ⌘ 977060, S : by T 43 AZ.

✈ ⌘ 379900, N : 5 ½ m. by N 1 AY – Terminal : Busaras (Central Bus Station) Store St.

🚢 to Liverpool (B & I Line) 1 nightly (8 h) – to Holyhead (B & I Line) 1 daily (3 h 30 mn) – to the
Isle of Man : Douglas (Isle of Man Steam Packet Co.) June to September 1-3 weekly (4 h 30 mn).

🛈 14 Upper O'Connell St. ⌘ 747733 – Dublin Airport ⌘ 376387 and 375533.

◆Belfast 103 – ◆Cork 154 – ◆Londonderry 146.

Plans on following pages

  🏨 **Berkeley Court,** Lansdowne Rd, Ballsbridge, ⌘ 601711, Telex 30554, 🔲 – 📶 📺 ☎ 🚗 🅿.
    ⚖. 🔄 🏧 ① <u>VISA</u>. ⚡   AZ **c**
    M 12.75/16.50 t. 🍷 4.50 – ⇌ 6.00 – **210 rm** 68.00/82.00 t.

  🏨 **Jury's,** Pembroke Rd, Ballsbridge, ⌘ 605000, Telex 25304, ⚒ heated, 🔲 – 📶 📺 ☎ ♿ 🅿.
    🔄 🏧 ① <u>VISA</u>   AZ **c**
    M 12.00/15.00 t. 🍷 7.50 – ⇌ 7.50 – **314 rm** 69.50/77.50 t.

  🏨 **Shelbourne** (T.H.F.), 27 St. Stephen's Green, ⌘ 766471, Telex 25184 – 📶 📺 ☎. ⚖. 🔄 🏧
    ① <u>VISA</u>   BZ **s**
    M 15.50/18.00 t. 🍷 4.00 – ⇌ 7.50 – **167 rm** 70.00/110.00 t.

  🏨 **Blooms,** Anglesea St., ⌘ 715622, Telex 31688 – 📶 📺 ☎ 🅿. 🔄 🏧 ① <u>VISA</u>. ⚡   BY **e**
    M 9.00/11.50 t. 🍷 4.25 – ⇌ 5.50 – **86 rm** 60.00/70.00 t.

576

🏨 **Tara Tower,** Merrion Rd, SE : 4 m. on T 44 ℰ 694666, Group Telex 90790 – 🛗 📺 🛏wc ⊞ **P.**   on T 44 AZ
  🏰. ℅
  M (coffee shop) – **83 rm**.

🏨 **Skylon,** Upper Drumcondra Rd, N : 2 ½ m. on N 1 ℰ 379121, Group Telex 90790 – 🛗 📺
  🛏wc ⊞ **P.** 🏰. ℅ AY **e**
  M (coffee shop) – **88 rm**.

🏨 **Buswells,** 25-26 Molesworth St., ℰ 764013, Telex 90622 – 🛗 📺 🛏wc ☎. 🏰. 🔽 🆎 ⓪ 𝘝𝘐𝘚𝘈
  ℅ BY **u**
  70 rm.

🏨 **Ashling,** Parkgate St., Kingsbridge, ℰ 772324, Telex 32802 – 🛗 📺 🛏wc ⊞ ⟻ 🏰. 🔽
  🆎 ⓪ 𝘝𝘐𝘚𝘈. ℅ AY **r**
  closed 24 to 26 December – **M** 9.00/14.00 st. ▯ 3.50 – **56 rm** � 35.00/54.00 st.

🏠 **Ariel House,** 52 Lansdowne Rd, ℰ 685512, ☞ – 📺 🛏wc ▥wc ⊞ **P.** ℅ AZ **e**
  closed 18 to 31 December – **M** 7.50/12.50 t. ▯ 3.80 – **15 rm** ⊊ 25.00/40.00 t.

🏠 **Maples,** 79-81 Iona Rd, Glasnevin, ℰ 728382 – ▤ rest ▥wc ⊞. 🔽 🆎 ⓪ 𝘝𝘐𝘚𝘈. ℅ AY **c**
  M (closed Sunday and Bank Holidays for lunch) (bar lunch Monday to Saturday) 15.00 st.
  ▯ 3.75 – **25 rm** ⊊ 20.00/28.00 t.

⋔ **Kilronan House,** 70 Adelaide Rd, ℰ 755266 – 🛏wc ⊞. ℅ BZ **r**
  closed 23 to 30 December – **11 rm** ⊊ 20.00/36.00 st.

⋔ **Egans House,** 7-9 Iona Park, Glasnevin, ℰ 303611 – 🛏wc ▥wc ⊞ ⅚ **P.** ℅ AY **a**
  ⊊ 4.50 – **25 rm** 12.00/24.00 st.

⋔ **Abrae Court,** 9 Zion Rd, Rathgar, ℰ 979944 – ▥ **P.** ℅ AZ **i**
  10 rm ⊊ 15.00/24.00 st.

⋔ **St. Aidan's,** 32 Brighton Rd, Rathgar, ℰ 970559 – 🛏wc ▥wc. 🔽 🆎 ⓪ AZ **r**
  13 rm ⊊ 13.00/26.00 st.

XXX **Le Coq Hardi,** 35 Pembroke Rd, ℰ 689070 – **P.** 🆎 ⓪ 𝘝𝘐𝘚𝘈 AZ **n**
  closed Saturday lunch, Sunday, 2 weeks August, 2 weeks Christmas and Bank Holidays – **M** a
  la carte 17.00/27.50 t. ▯ 5.00.

XXX **Patrick Guilbaud,** 46 St. James's Pl., St. James St., off Lower Baggot St., ℰ 764192,
  French rest. – **P.** 🔽 🆎 ⓪ 𝘝𝘐𝘚𝘈 BZ **n**
  closed Saturday lunch, Sunday and Bank Holidays – **M** a la carte 14.95/27.15 t.

XXX **Bailey,** 2-4 Duke St., ℰ 770600. 🔽 🆎 ⓪ 𝘝𝘐𝘚𝘈 BY **a**
  closed Saturday lunch, Sunday, 2 weeks Easter and 2 weeks Christmas – **M** a la carte
  17.50/26.00 t. ▯ 5.95.

XX **Locks,** 1 Windsor Terr., Portobello, ℰ 752025 – 🆎 ⓪ 𝘝𝘐𝘚𝘈 BZ **u**
  closed Saturday lunch, Sunday, 25 December-3 January and Bank Holidays – **M** a la carte
  13.95/17.35 t. ▯ 3.75.

XX **Old Dublin,** 90-91 Francis St., ℰ 751173, Scandinavian rest. – 🔽 🆎 ⓪ 𝘝𝘐𝘚𝘈 BY **i**
  closed Saturday lunch, Sunday and Bank Holidays – **M** 8.50/13.95 t. ▯ 4.25.

XX **Lord Edward,** 23 Christchurch Pl., ℰ 752557, Seafood – 🔽 🆎 ⓪ 𝘝𝘐𝘚𝘈 BY **c**
  closed Saturday lunch, Sunday, 1 week at Christmas and Bank Holidays – **M** a la carte
  16.25/30.75 t.

XX **Celtic Mews,** 109a Lower Baggot St., ℰ 760796 – 🔽 🆎 ⓪ 𝘝𝘐𝘚𝘈 BZ **z**
  closed Sunday and last 2 weeks July – **M** (dinner only) a la carte 21.00/25.00 t.

XX **Small Home,** 41-43 Shelbourne Rd, Ballsbridge, ℰ 608087 – 🔽 🆎 ⓪ 𝘝𝘐𝘚𝘈 AZ **u**
  closed Saturday lunch, Sunday, Easter, Christmas and Bank Holidays – **M** a la carte
  11.25/15.25 t. ▯ 4.00.

X **Dobbin's,** 15 Stephen's Lane, ℰ 764679, Bistro – 🔽 🆎 ⓪ 𝘝𝘐𝘚𝘈 AZ **s**
  closed lunch Saturday and Bank Holidays, Monday dinner and Sunday – **M** a la carte
  10.95/15.90 t. ▯ 3.75.

X **Mitchell's Cellars,** 21 Kildare St., ℰ 680367 – 🔽 🆎 𝘝𝘐𝘚𝘈 BZ **x**
  closed Sunday, 25 December-2 January and Bank Holiday weekends – **M** (lunch only)
  a la carte/8.60 t. ▯ 3.75.

  at Dublin Airport N : 6 ½ m. by N 1 – AY – ✉ ✆ 01 Dublin :

🏨 **Dublin International** (T.H.F.), ℰ 379211, Telex 24612 – 📺 🛏wc ☎ ⅚ **P.** 🏰. 🔽 🆎 ⓪
  𝘝𝘐𝘚𝘈
  M 14.00/17.00 st. ▯ 4.75 – ⊊ 6.00 – **195 rm** 52.00/75.00 st.

MICHELIN Branch, 4 Spilmak Pl., Bluebell Industrial Estate, Naas Rd, Dublin 12, ℰ 509096

ALFA-ROMEO, PEUGEOT, SAAB Maxwell Rd
ℰ 973338
AUSTIN-ROVER Temple Rd ℰ 885085
AUSTIN-ROVER, NISSAN 48-52 New St. ℰ 780033
AUSTIN-ROVER Northbrook Rd ℰ 970811
AUSTIN-ROVER Richmond Rd ℰ 379162
BMW, ROLLS ROYCE-BENTLEY, VOLVO Townsend
St. ℰ 779177
BMW Ballygall Rd East ℰ 342577
BMW, TOYOTA Rathgar Av. ℰ 979456
CITROEN Buckingham St. ℰ 745821
FIAT Milltown Rd ℰ 698577

FIAT, LANCIA Dublin Rd, Bray ℰ 822433
FIAT, LANCIA 56 Howth Rd ℰ 332301
FIAT Church Pl. ℰ 973999
FIAT North Rd ℰ 342977
FIAT, LANCIA 84 Prussia St. ℰ 791722
FIAT Taney Rd ℰ 987166
FIAT, LANCIA Herberton Rd ℰ 754216
FORD 172/175 Parnell St. ℰ 747831
FORD Naas Rd ℰ 505721
FORD Stillorgan Rd ℰ 886821
FORD Upper Rathmines Rd ℰ 971227
MERCEDES-BENZ 54 Glasnevin Hill ℰ 373771

DUBLIN

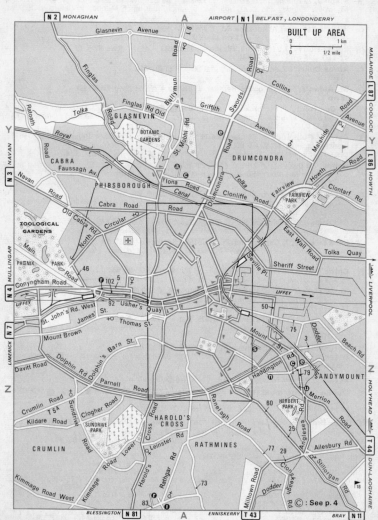

DUBLIN

MITSUBISHI Swords Rd &º 379933
NISSAN, VOLVO Howth Rd &º 314066
NISSAN Bluebell Av. &º 507887
OPEL Beach Rd &º 686011
OPEL 146 Cabra Rd &º 301222
OPEL Emmet Rd, Inchicore &º 755535
OPEL New Rd &º 592438
PEUGEOT-TALBOT North Rd &º 343033
PEUGEOT-TALBOT, CITROEN 23 Parkgate St.
&º 710333
RENAULT 232 North Circular Rd, Grangegorman
&º 300799
RENAULT 19 Conyngnam Rd &º 775677
RENAULT 27 Upper Drumcondra Rd &º 373706

RENAULT Newlands Cross &º 593751
RENAULT Malahide Rd &º 339948
RENAULT Merrion Rd &º 693911
RENAULT Crumlin Rd &º 752297
TALBOT 10 b Russel St. &º 723833
TOYOTA Smithfield Market &º 721222
TOYOTA Kilbarrack Rd &º 322701
VW, AUDI, MAZDA, MERCEDES-BENZ 218/224
North Circular Rd &º 792011
VW, AUDI-NSU, MAZDA, MERCEDES-BENZ Bally-
bough Rd &º 723033
VW, AUDI-NSU, MAZDA, MERCEDES-BENZ Ha-
rolds Cross Rd &º 975757

DUNDALK Louth 405 M 5 – pop. 25,610 – ECD : Thursday – ✪ 042.

Ⓖ Blackrock &º 35379, S : 3 m – 🇮 &º 35484 (July-August).

♦Dublin 53 – Drogheda 22.

🏛 **Ballymascanlon House** 🦌, N : 3 ½ m. by N 1 &º 71124, 🔲, 🛥, park, 🎾, squash – 📺
▭wc ▥wc ☎ Ⓟ. 🅰. 🔳 🆎 ⑨ 🆅🆂🅰
M 9.00/13.50 t. 🍷 4.00 – **36 rm** 🖙 26.00/40.00 t. – SB 48.00/50.00 **st.**

DUNDERRY Meath – see Navan.

DUNFANAGHY Donegal 405 I 2 – pop. 303 – ✉ ✪ 074 Letterkenny.

Envir. : Doe Castle★ 16 C ruins (site★, ≼ ★) SE : 7 ½ m. – SW : Bloody Foreland Head★.

Ⓖ – 🇮 &º 63 (June-August).

♦Dublin 172 – Donegal 54 – ♦Londonderry 43.

🏨 **Carrig Rua**, Main St., &º 36133, ≼ – ▭wc Ⓟ. 🔳 🆅🆂🅰
Easter-September – **M** 5.50/11.50 t. – **23 rm** 🖙 13.50/32.00 t. – SB 40.00/46.00 **st.**

at Port-na-Blagh E : 1 ½ m. on T 72 – ✉ ✪ 074 Letterkenny :

🏛 Shandon 🦌, Marble Hill Strand, NE : 2 ½ m. &º 36137, ≼ bay and hills, 🌴, 🛥, 🎾 – 🛝
▭wc ☎ Ⓟ
season – **55 rm**.

🏠 **Port-na-Blagh**, &º 36129, ≼ Sheephaven Bay and harbour, 🌴, 🛥, 🎾 – ▭wc Ⓟ
Easter-24 September – **M** 9.00/12.00 t. 🍷 3.90 – **59 rm** 🖙 15.50/39.00 t. – SB 55.00/63.00 **st.**

DUNGARVAN Waterford 405 J 11 – pop. 5,583 – ECD : Thursday – ✪ 058.

Ⓖ Ballinacourty, &º 41605 – 🇮 &º 41741 (July-August).

♦Dublin 124 – ♦Cork 48 – ♦Killarney 90 – ♦Waterford 29.

✗ **Seanachie**, SW : 5 ½ m. by N 25, &º 46285 – Ⓟ
17 March-October – **M** (closed Sunday) a la carte approx. 15.00 t. 🍷 6.50.

DUN LAOGHAIRE Dublin 405 N 8 – pop. 53,171 – ✪ 01 Dublin.

See : Windsor Terrace ≼★ over Dublin Bay.

Ⓖ Eglinton Park &º 801055.

⛴ to Holyhead (Sealink) summer 2-4 daily; winter 2 daily (3 h 30 mn).

🇮 St. Michaels Wharf &º 805760, 806547 and 806984/5/6.

♦Dublin 9.

XXX **na Mara**, 1 Harbour Rd, &º 806767, Seafood – 🔳 🆎 ⑨ 🆅🆂🅰   i
closed Sunday, Monday, Easter and Christmas – **M** a la carte 16.10/22.50 t. 🍷 4.25.

XX **Digby's**, 5 Windsor Terr., &º 804600, ≼ – 🔳 🆎 ⑨ 🆅🆂🅰   a
closed lunch Saturday and Bank Holidays, Sunday, Easter and 25-26 December – **M** (restricted
lunch) a la carte 15.70/18.70 t. 🍷 4.20.

XX **The Abbot of Monkstown**, Monkstown Cres., N : ¾ m. on T 44 &º 805174 – 🔳 🆎 ⑨ 🆅🆂🅰
closed Saturday lunch, Sunday, 24 December-1 January and Bank Holidays – **M** a la carte
13.00/24.00 t. 🍷 4.50.   v

✗ **Trudi's**, 107 Lower George's St., &º 805318, Bistro – 🔳 🆎 ⑨ 🆅🆂🅰   u
closed Sunday, Monday and 1 week Easter – **M** (dinner only) a la carte 10.10/14.35 t. 🍷 5.35.

✗ **Salty Dog**, 3a Haddington Terr. off Adelaide St., &º 808015, Indonesian rest. – 🔳 🆎 ⑨   s
🆅🆂🅰
M (dinner only) a la carte 7.85/11.90 t. 🍷 3.50.

✗ **Russell's**, 56 Glasthule Rd, Sandycove, &º 808878
closed Sunday, Good Friday and 25-26 December – **M** a la carte 8.70/10.00 t.

OPEL Crofton Pl. &º 800341
PEUGEOT Glenageary Rd &º 850011

RENAULT Rochestown Av. &º 852555
TOYOTA Glasthule Rd &º 802991

580

DUN LAOGHAIRE

Georges Street
Mulgrave Street
Patrick Street

Cumberland Street 2

Dunleary Hill 4
Longford Place 5
Marine Road 7
Monkstown Avenue 8
Monkstown
   Crescent 9
Mount Town Upper 10
Pakenham Road 13

HOLYHEAD, FISHGUARD

WEST PIER

EAST PIER

Longford Terrace

Dunleary Road

Crofton

STATION

Carrickbrennan Rd

DUBLIN T 44

The Slope

Knapton Rd

York

George St. Lower

George St. Upper

Patrick St.

Mulgrave St.

Corrig Av.

Tivoli

Corrig

Corrig Rd

Clarinda Park Rd

Queen's Rd

SHOPPING CENTRE

POL.

Park Rd

Windsor Ter.

Summerhill Rd

Marine

Parade

STATION

Eden Road

Hudson Road

Glasthule Rd

T 44 DALKEY

Oliver Plunkett Road

Mount Town Lower

Kill Avenue

Glenageary Road

Silchester Road

Glenageary Road

Upper

Adelaide Road

Albert Road

Station Road

STATION

© : See p. 4

(N 11) WICKLOW

DURRUS Cork **405** D 13 – ⊠ – ❸ 027 Bantry.

♦Dublin 210 – ♦Cork 56 – ♦Killarney 53.

XX **Blairs Cove,** SW : 1 m. on L 56 ℰ 61127, « Converted barn », 🍴 – **P**. 🔁 AE ⓞ *VISA*
closed Monday to Friday mid October-Easter, January and February – **M** (closed Sunday dinner) (dinner only and Sunday lunch) (booking essential) 9.00/17.00 **t.** ▯ 4.00.

EMO Laois **405** K 8 – pop. 200 – ⊠ ❸ 0502 Portlaoise.

♦Dublin 49 – ♦Limerick 74 – ♦Tullamore 20.

🏨 Montague, E : 1 ¾ m. on N 7 ℰ 26154, 🍴 – ⇌wc ☎ ₷ **P** – **20 rm**.

ENNIS Clare **405** F 9 – pop. 5,972 – ECD : Thursday – ❸ 065.

See : Franciscan Friary★ (13C ruins).

Envir. : Tulla (site★, ancient church ⁂ ★★) E : 10 m. – Killone Abbey (site★) S : 4 m. – Dysert O'Dea (site★) NW : 6 ½ m. – Kilmacduagh monastic ruins★ (site★) NE : 16 ½ m.

🖪 Drumbiggle Rd ℰ 21070 – 🛈 Bank Pl. ℰ 21366.

♦Dublin 142 – ♦Galway 42 – ♦Limerick 22 – Roscommon 92 – ♦Tullamore 93.

🏨 **Old Ground** (T.H.F.), O'Connell St., ℰ 28127, Telex 28103, 🍴 – 🆀 ⇌wc ☎ **P**. 🔁 🔁 AE
ⓞ *VISA* ⌇⌇
   M 8.50/15.50 **st.** – ⊆ 6.00 – **60 rm** 40.00/55.00 **st.** – SB 54.00/96.00 **st.**

🏨 **Auburn Lodge,** Galway Rd, N : 1 ½ m. on N 18 ℰ 21247, 🍴, squash – 🆀 ⇌wc ₷ **P**. 🔁
AE ⓞ *VISA* ⌇⌇
   closed 24 to 28 December – **M** 6.00/12.00 **st.** ▯ 4.00 – **22 rm** ⊆ 28.00/38.00 **st.**

FORD Lifford ℰ 21035
RENAULT Tulla Rd ℰ 22758

TOYOTA Gort Rd ℰ 21904
VW, AUDI, MAZDA Mill Rd ℰ 21505

ENNISCORTHY Wexford **405** M 10 – pop. 5,704 – ECD : Thursday – 🕾 054.

🏌 Bloomfield ☎ 33191.

♦Dublin 77 – Kilkenny 36 – ♦Waterford 36 – Wexford 14.

🏨 **Murphy Floods,** 24 Main St., Market Sq., ☎ 33413 – ⇔wc ⩎wc ☎. 🔼 ⒶⒺ 𝑽𝑰𝑺𝑨. ⋇
closed Christmas Day – **M** 6.50/11.50 **st.** ⓐ 3.20 – **22 rm** ⊊ 16.00/30.00 **st.** – SB (weekends only) 45.00/50.00 **st.**

FIAT Temple Shannon ☎ 33742   FORD Dublin Rd ☎ 33606

ENNISKERRY Wicklow **405** N 8 – pop. 772 – 🕾 01 Dublin.

See : Site★ – Powerscourt Demesne (gardens★★★, Araucaria Walk★) *AC*.

Envir. : Powerscourt Waterfall★ *AC*, S : 4 m. – Lough Tay★★ SW by T 43, T 61, L 161.

♦Dublin 17 – ♦Waterford 100.

🏨 Summerhill ⤬, ☎ 867928, ℐ – �🺛 ⇔wc ☎ Ⓟ
10 rm.

FAHAN Donegal **405** J 2 – pop. 332 – ⊠ Lifford – 🕾 077 Buncrana.

🏌 North West, Lisfannon, ☎ Buncrana 12.

♦Dublin 156 – ♦Londonderry 11 – ♦Sligo 95.

XX **St. John's,** ☎ 60289, « Lough-side setting » – Ⓟ. 🔼 ⒶⒺ ⒪ 𝑽𝑰𝑺𝑨
closed Monday except Bank Holidays, Good Friday and Christmas Day – **M** (dinner only) a la
carte 9.45/17.00 **t.** ⓐ 3.25.

FEAKLE Clare **405** G 9.

♦Dublin 125 – ♦Galway 36 – ♦Limerick 25.

🏨 **Smyth's Village** ⤬, ☎ 2, ⬟, park, ⋇ – ⇔wc ⩎wc Ⓟ. ⒶⒺ 𝑽𝑰𝑺𝑨. ⋇
April-October – **M** (lunch by arrangement)(booking essential) 4.00/6.00 ⓐ 4.00 – **12 rm**
⊊ 11.00/22.00.

GALWAY Galway **405** E 8 – pop. 27,726 – ECD : Monday – 🕾 091.

See : Lynch's Castle★ 16C.

Envir. : NW : Lough Corrib★★★ – Claregalway (Franciscan Friary★ 13C) NE : 7 m. – Abbeyknockmoy
(Cistercian Monastery★ 12C ruins) NE : 18 m. – Tuam (St. Mary's Cathedral : chancel arch★ 12C)
NE : 20 m.

🏌 Blackrock, Salthill ☎ 21827, W : 3 m.

✈ ☎ 84300, Telex 28323, NE : 4 m.

🅱 Aras Failte, Eyre Sq. ☎ 63081.

♦Dublin 135 – ♦Limerick 64 – ♦Sligo 90.

🏩 Great Southern, Eyre Sq., ☎ 64041, Telex 28364, 🖾 – 🛗 🺛 ☎. 🚗. 🔼 ⒶⒺ ⒪ 𝑽𝑰𝑺𝑨
120 rm.

🏨 Ardilaun House ⤬, Taylor's Hill, ☎ 21433, Telex 28873, 🌿 – 🛗 🺛 ⇔wc ⩎wc ☎ Ⓟ. 🚗. 🔼
ⒶⒺ ⒪ 𝑽𝑰𝑺𝑨
closed 2 weeks at Christmas – **M** 7.50/14.00 ⓐ 3.75 – **72 rm**.

🏨 **Galway Ryan,** Dublin Rd, E : 1 ¼ m. on N 6 ☎ 53181, Telex 28349, 🌿 – 🛗 ⇔wc ☎ Ⓟ. 🔼
ⒶⒺ ⒪ 𝑽𝑰𝑺𝑨. ⋇
closed 24 and 25 December – **M** (bar lunch) 12.50 **st.** ⓐ 5.95 – ⊊ 4.75 – **96 rm** 25.00/42.50 **st.**
– SB (weekends only) 38.00/55.00 **st.**

↑ **Adare House,** 9 Father Griffin Pl., Lower Salthill, ☎ 62638 – Ⓟ. 🔼 ⒶⒺ 𝑽𝑰𝑺𝑨. ⋇
10 rm ⊊ 10.00/22.00 **st.**

at Salthill SW : 2 m. – ⊠ Salthill – 🕾 091 Galway :

🏨 Warwick, 150 Lower Salthill, ☎ 21244 – ⇔wc ☎ Ⓟ. ⋇
50 rm.

🏨 Anno Santo, Threadneedle Rd, ☎ 22110 – ⇔wc ☎ Ⓟ. ⋇ – **13 rm**.

🏨 **Rockbarton Park,** 5-7 Rockbarton Pk., ☎ 22018 – ⇔wc ⩎wc ☎ Ⓟ. 🔼 ⒶⒺ ⒪ 𝑽𝑰𝑺𝑨
closed 23 December-1 January – **M** *(closed October-May)* (bar lunch) 11.50 **t.** ⓐ 4.40 – **11 rm**
⊊ 15.10/30.00 **t.** – SB 48.70 **st.**

🏨 **Lochlurgain,** 22 Monksfield, Upper Salthill, ☎ 22884 – 🔼 ⒶⒺ 𝑽𝑰𝑺𝑨. ⋇
6 April-September – **M** (bar lunch) 7.75 **st.** ⓐ 4.00 – **19 rm** ⊊ 12.85/38.10 **st.** – SB (Easter
and summer only) 49.90/60.65 **st.**

BMW, DATSUN, TALBOT Headford Rd ☎ 65296   VW, AUDI, MAZDA, MERCEDES-BENZ Lower Sal-
PEUGEOT, SAAB Spanish Par. ☎ 62167   thill ☎ 62583
TOYOTA Bohermore ☎ 63664

GARRYVOE STRAND Cork **405** H 12 – ⊠ Castlemartyr – 🕾 021 Cork.

♦Dublin 161 – ♦Cork 23 – ♦Waterford 62.

🏨 **Garryvoe,** Castlemartyr, ☎ 646718 – ⇔wc ⩎wc ☎ Ⓟ. 🔼 ⒶⒺ ⒪ 𝑽𝑰𝑺𝑨. ⋇
closed Christmas Day – **M** 7.00/a la carte 7.15/14.95 **t.** ⓐ 3.75 – ⊊ 3.00 – **19 rm** 10.00/22.00 **t.**

GLENCAR Kerry 405 C 11.
◆Dublin 215 – ◆Cork 80 – ◆Killarney 25.

  🏠 **Glencar** 🏊, 𝒫 102, ≤, 🎣, 🚗, park, 🍴 – ⌷wc 🅿. 🖽 –
    February-September – **M** (bar lunch) 11.00 t. ♦ 4.00 – **29 rm** 🖙 17.00/38.00 t.

GLENDALOUGH Wicklow 405 MN 8 – pop. 184 – ✆ 0404.
See : Ancient monastic city★★ (site★★★, St. Kervin's Church★) and Upper Lake★ in Glendalough
Valley★★★.
◆Dublin 34 – Wexford 71.

  🏠 **Royal,** 𝒫 5135 – ⌷wc 🅿. 🖎 VISA 🛇
    Mid March-October – **M** 8.60/15.75 t. ♦ 4.30 – **13 rm** 🖙 25.00/42.00 t. – SB 30.00/33.00 st.

GLENGARRIFF Cork 405 D 12 – pop. 244 – ✆ 027.
See : Site★★★.
Envir. : S : Garinish Island (20 mn by boat *AC*) : Italian gardens★ – Martello Tower 🌲★★ *AC*.
🏌 𝒫 150, E : 1 m.
🅸 𝒫 63084 (July-August).
◆Dublin 224 – ◆Cork 63 – ◆Killarney 37.

  🏠 Casey's, 𝒫 63010, 🚗 – ⌷wc 🅿
    20 rm.

GLEN OF AHERLOW Tipperary 405 H 10 – ⊠ ✆ 062 Tipperary.
See : Glen of Aherlow★ (statue of Christ the King★★).
◆Dublin 118 – Cahir 6 – Tipperary 9.

  🏠🏠 **Glen,** 𝒫 56146, 🚗 – ⌷wc 🕾 🅿. 🖎 🖽 VISA. 🛇
    M 6.50/12.00 st. ♦ 3.75 – **24 rm** 🖙 17.00/32.00 t. – SB (weekends only) 35.00/38.00 st.

GLOUNTHAUNE Cork – see Cork.

GOREY Wexford 405 N 9 – pop. 2,946 – ECD : Wednesday – ✆ 055.
🅸 𝒫 21248 (July-August).
◆Dublin 58 – Waterford 55 – Wexford 38.

  XXX Marlfield House 🏊 with rm, Courtown Rd, E : 1 m. 𝒫 21124, ≤, « Regency house and
    conservatory », 🚗, park – 📺 ⌷wc 🕾 🅿. 🛇
    M (booking essential) a la carte – **12 rm**.

GOUGANE BARRA Cork 405 D 12 – ⊠ ✆ Ballingeary.
See : Lake (site★).
◆Dublin 206 – ◆Cork 45.

  🏠 **Gougane Barra** 🏊, 𝒫 69, ≤ lough and mountains, 🎣 – ⌷wc 🅿. 🖎 VISA. 🛇
    April-September – **M** 7.00/10.00 t. – **32 rm** 🖙 10.00/24.00 t. – SB (weekends only) (sum-
    mer only) 41.50 st.

HOWTH Dublin 405 N 7 – pop. 3,146 – ⊠ ✆ 01 Dublin.
See : Howth Summit ≤★★ – Cliff Walk ≤★★ – Harbour★ – St Mary's Abbey★ (ruins 13C, 15C),
site★ – Howth Gardens (rhododendrons★, site★, ≤★) *AC*.
🏌 Deer Park Hotel 𝒫 322624.
◆Dublin 10.

  XX **King Sitric,** Harbour Rd, East Pier, 𝒫 325235, Seafood – 🖎 🖽 ① VISA
    closed Saturday lunch, Sunday, 2 weeks Easter, 10 days at Christmas and Bank Holidays – **M**
    (booking essential in winter) a la carte 14.60/21.20 t. ♦ 4.60.
  XX Abbey Tavern, 19 Abbey St., 𝒫 322006, Seafood.

INNISHANNON Cork 405 G 12 – pop. 190 – ✆ 021 Cork.
🏌 Bandon 𝒫 41111, SW : 5 m.
◆Dublin 175 – ◆Cork 14 – ◆Killarney 46 – Bandon 4.5.

  🏠 **Innishannon,** S : ¾ m. on L 41 𝒫 75121, Telex 75398, 🎣, 🚗 – 📺 ⌷wc 🕾 🅿. 🖎 ① VISA
    March-October – **M** 8.95/12.95 st. ♦ 4.50 – **13 rm** 🖙 22.50/35.00 st. – SB (except sum-
    mer) 50.00/60.00 st.

FIAT, LANCIA 𝒫 023 (Bandon) 41514   NISSAN, OPEL Irishtown 𝒫 023 (Bandon) 41264
FORD 72 Main St. 𝒫 023 (Bandon) 41522   RENAULT Clonakilty Rd 𝒫 023 (Bandon) 41617

KANTURK Cork 405 F 11 – pop. 1,524 – ECD : Wednesday – ✆ 029.
◆Dublin 161 – ◆Cork 33 – ◆Killarney 31 – ◆Limerick 44.

  🏠 Assolas Country House 🏊, E : 3 ¼ m. by L 38 on L 186 𝒫 50015, ≤, « Country house
    atmosphere », 🎣, 🚗, park, 🍴 – ⌷wc 🅿. ①. 🛇
    April-September – **M** (dinner only) – **7 rm** 🖙 19.50/45.00 t.

AUDI, MAZDA 𝒫 12

KELLS Kilkenny 🔢 K 10 – pop. 2,391.

See : Augustinian Priory★★ 14C.

Envir. : Kilree's Church (site★, round tower★) S : 2 m.

♦Dublin 86 – Kilkenny 9 – ♦Waterford 23.

Hotels and restaurant see : Kilkenny N : 9 m.

KENMARE Kerry 🔢 D 12 – pop. 903 – ECD : Thursday – ✪ 064 Killarney.

Envir. : Kenmare River Valley★★ E : by L 62.

🔂 ✗ 41291.

🔋 ✗ 41233 (July-August).

♦Dublin 210 – ♦Cork 58 – ♦Killarney 20.

   🏨 ✿ **Park** ⬡, ✗ 41200, Telex 70005, ≼, « Antiques, paintings », 🌳, park, ✗ – 🛗 ☎ 👤 👤. 🔲
   🆎 🆎 𝕍𝕊𝔸. ✾
   closed 4 January-mid April – **M** 12.00/23.00 **st.** 🍷 6.00 – **50 rm** ⬓ 48.00/104.00 **st.**
   Spec. Aiguillettes de caneton en sauce de mûres, Grand pot aux fruits de mer - sauce d'oursins, Soufflé Irish
   mist.

   ✗ **Remy's House** with rm, Main St., ✗ 41589, French rest. – 📺 ⬚wc ☎. 🆎 🆎 ⓞ 𝕍𝕊𝔸
   Mid March-mid October – **M** *(closed Tuesday)* (dinner only) a la carte 9.35/12.25 **t.** 🍷 5.00 –
   3 rm ⬓ 13.00/23.00 **t.**

FORD Henry St. ✗ 41166   DATSUN Shelbourne St. ✗ 41355

KILKENNY Kilkenny 🔢 K 10 – pop. 9,838 – ECD : Thursday – ✪ 056.

See : St. Canice's Cathedral★★ 13C – Grace's Castle (Courthouse)★ – Castle (park★, ≼★).

Envir. : Jerpoint Abbey★★ (ruins 12C-15C) SE : 12 m. – Callan (St. Mary's Church★ 13C-15C) SW :
13 m.

🔂 Glendine ✗ 22125, N : 1 m.

🔋 Rose Inn St. ✗ 21755.

♦Dublin 71 – ♦Cork 86 – ♦Killarney 115 – ♦Limerick 69 – ♦Tullamore 52 – ♦Waterford 29.

   🏨 **Newpark**, Castlecomer Rd, N : ¾ m. on N 77 ✗ 22122, Telex 80080, 🌳, ✗ – 📼 rest 📺
   ⬚wc 🅜wc ☎ 👤. 🏊. 🆎 🆎 ⓞ 𝕍𝕊𝔸. ✾
   M 8.50/14.00 **st.** 🍷 4.00 – ⬓ 5.00 – **43 rm** 27.00/42.00 **t.** – SB 60.00 **st.**

   🏨 **Springhill Court**, Waterford Rd, S : 2 m. on N 10 ✗ 21122 – 📺 ⬚wc 🅜wc ☎ 👤. 🆎 🆎
   𝕍𝕊𝔸. ✾
   M (buffet lunch) 14.00 **st.** 🍷 3.50 – **44 rm** ⬓ 21.00/34.00 **st.** – SB (weekends only) 50.00/53.00 **st.**

   ✗✗ **Lacken House** with rm, Dublin Rd, ✗ 61085, 🌳 – 👤
   closed Sunday and Monday – **M** (dinner only) a la carte 13.50/15.25 **t.** 🍷 4.25 – **9 rm**
   ⬓ 13.00/28.00 **st.** – SB 40.00 **st.**

   at Knocktopher S : 13 m. on N 10 – ✉ ✪ 056 Kilkenny :

   ✗✗ **Knocktopher Abbey**, ✗ 28618, ≼, 🌳 – 👤. 🆎 🆎 ⓞ 𝕍𝕊𝔸
   closed Sunday – **M** (dinner only) a la carte 10.75/18.25 **t.**

FORD Patrick St. ✗ 21016   OPEL Green St. ✗ 21304
NISSAN Hebron Rd ✗ 22185   RENAULT Irishtown ✗ 21494

KILLALOE Clare 🔢 G 9 – pop. 871 – ECD : Wednesday – ✪ 061.

See : Site★.

Envir. : N : Lough Derg Coast Road★★ (L 12) to Tuamgraney, Lough Derg★★★ (Holy Island : site★★)
– Nenagh : Butler Castle (keep★ 13C) NE : 9 m.

♦Dublin 109 – Ennis 32 – ♦Limerick 13 – ♦Tullamore 58.

KILLARNEY Kerry 🔢 D 11 – pop. 7,184 – ECD : Thursday – ✪ 064.

Envir. : SW : Killarney District, Ring of Kerry : Lough Leane★★★, Muckross House (gardens★★★) –
Muckross Abbey★ (ruins 13C), Tork Waterfall (Belvedere : ≼★★, 251 steps), Lady's View Belve-
dere★★ – Gap of Dunloe★★.

🔂, 🔂 Mahoney's Point ✗ 31034, W : 3 m.

🔋 Town Hall ✗ 31633.

♦Dublin 189 – ♦Cork 54 – ♦Limerick 69 – ♦Waterford 112.

   🏨 **Europe** ⬡, Fossa, W : 3 ½ m. on T 67 ✗ 31900, Telex 28213, ≼ lake and mountains, 🔲, ⬡,
   🌳, park – 🛗 ☎ 👤 👤. 🏊. 🆎 🆎 ⓞ 𝕍𝕊𝔸. ✾
   March-October – **M** (restricted lunch) 11.00/17.50 **st.** 🍷 7.00 – **175 rm** ⬓ 28.00/65.00 **st.**

   🏨 Aghadoe Heights ⬡, NW : 3 ½ m. by N 22 ✗ 31766, Telex 26942, ≼ countryside, lake and
   mountains, 🌳, ✗ – 📺 ☎ 👤 👤. 🏊
   55 rm.

   🏨 **Cahernane** ⬡, Muckross Rd, S : 1 m. on N 71 ✗ 31895, Telex 28123, ≼, ⬡, 🌳, ✗ – ⬚wc
   ☎ 👤. 🆎 🆎 ⓞ 𝕍𝕊𝔸. ✾
   April-October – **M** (bar lunch) 16.00 **t.** 🍷 4.50 – **37 rm** ⬓ 32.00/55.00 **t.**

   🏨 Castlerosse (Best Western) ⬡, W : 2 m. on T 67 ✗ 31144, Telex 70010, ≼ lake and mountains,
   🔲, ⬡, 🌳, ✗ – ⬚wc ☎ 👤. ✾ – **40 rm**.

🏠 **Linden House,** New Rd, ℰ 31379 – 🛏wc 🛁wc 🅿. 🛇
   closed December and January – **M** (dinner only) 10.00 **t.** 🍷 3.60 – **11 rm** ⧄ 9.00/18.00 **t.**

⌂ Carriglea Farmhouse 📞, Muckross Rd, S : 1 ½ m. on N 71 ℰ 31116, ≼, 🚗 – 🛏wc 🛁wc 🅿
   9 rm.

⌂ **Gardens,** Countess Rd, off Muckross Rd, ℰ 31147, 🚗 – 🛏wc 🛁wc 🅿. 🛇
   17 March-1 November – **22 rm** ⧄ 12.00/20.00 **st.**

⌂ **Loch Lein Farm** 📞, Fossa, W : 4 m. on T 67 ℰ 31260, ≼, 🚗 – 🛏wc 🛁wc 🅿. 🛇
   10 March-October – **12 rm** ⧄ 9.00/11.50 **t.**

⌂ **Castle Lodge,** Muckross Rd, ℰ 31545 – 🛁wc 🅿. VISA
   March-November – **16 rm** ⧄ 8.50/20.00.

✗ **Gaby's,** 17 High St., ℰ 32519, Seafood bistro – 🖃 AE ① VISA
   Mid March-November – **M** *(closed Monday lunch and Sunday)* a la carte 13.65/18.80 **t.** 🍷 4.20.

AUDI, MAZDA, MERCEDES-BENZ, VW   Park Rd ℰ
31355
AUSTIN-ROVER   Muckross Rd ℰ 31237

FORD   New Rd ℰ 31087
RENAULT   Ballycasheen ℰ 31416

KILLINEY Dublin ④⓪⑤ N 8 – 🕿 01 Dublin.

See : Killiney Bay★★.

🛆 ℰ 851983.

♦Dublin 12.

🏨 **Court,** Station Rd, Killiney Bay, ℰ 851622, Telex 33244, ≼, 🚗 – 🛗 📺 🕿 🅿. ⚗. 🖃 AE VISA
   closed Christmas Day – **M** 7.25/12.00 **t.** – ⧄ 5.40 – **32 rm** 30.00/48.00 **t.** – SB (week-ends only) 60.00 **st.**

KILLYBEGS Donegal ④⓪⑤ G 4 – pop. 1,094.

See : Fishing harbour★ – Carpet factory.

Envir. : NW : Glen Bay★★ – Glencolumbkille (site★★, folk village) NW : 14 m. – Portnoo (site★).

♦Dublin 181 – ♦Londonderry 65 – ♦Sligo 57.

KILTIMAGH Mayo ④⓪⑤ F 6 – pop. 1,145 – ECD : Monday – 🕿 094 Castlebar.

♦Dublin 140 – ♦Sligo 52.

🏠 **Westway,** James St., ℰ 81145 – 🛏wc 🅿. 🖃 VISA
   closed 24 to 30 December – **M** *(closed Sunday and Bank Holidays)* (bar lunch) 13.75 **t.** 🍷 4.00 –
   20 rm ⧄ 15.00/30.00 **t.** – SB 50.00 **st.**

KINSALE Cork ④⓪⑤ G 12 – pop. 1,622 – ECD : Thursday – 🕿 021 Cork.

See : St. Multose's Church★ 12C.

🛆 Ringnanean, Belgooley ℰ 72197.

🛈 ℰ 72234 (July-August).

♦Dublin 178 – ♦Cork 17.

🏨 **Acton's** (T.H.F.), Pier Rd, ℰ 72135, Telex 75443, ≼, ⤢, 🚗 – 🛗 📺 🅿. ⚗. 🖃 AE ① VISA
   closed 3 January-5 March – **M** (bar lunch) 12.00 **st.** 🍷 3.75 – **58 rm** ⧄ 24.00/54.00 – SB
   46.00/64.00 **st.**

⌂ **Old Presbytery,** Cork St., ℰ 72027 – 🛇
   5 rm ⧄ 14.00/27.00 **st.**

✗✗ **Bawnleigh House,** N : 5 ½ m. on Old Cork Rd ℰ 71333 – 🅿. 🖃 VISA
   closed Sunday, Monday and 10 days at Christmas – **M** (dinner only) a la carte 10.45/15.95 **t.**
   🍷 3.95.

✗✗ **Blue Haven** with rm, 3 Pearse St., ℰ 72209, Seafood – 🛁wc. 🖃 AE ① VISA. 🛇
   closed January and February – **M** (bar lunch) a la carte 12.50/16.90 **t.** 🍷 3.90 – **10 rm**
   ⧄ 18.00/38.00 **t.** – SB (weekends only) 46.00/50.00 **st.**

✗✗ **Vintage,** 50 Main St., ℰ 72502 – 🖃 AE ① VISA 🛇
   closed Sunday – **M** (dinner only) a la carte 12.50/17.50 **st.** 🍷 4.00.

✗ **Man Friday,** Scilly, SE : ½ m. ℰ 72260 – 🖃 VISA
   closed Sunday, Monday in winter and 2 weeks January – **M** (dinner only) a la carte 11.55/16.65 **t.**
   🍷 4.50.

✗ **Le Toucan,** Milk Market, ℰ 72233 – 🖃 AE ① VISA
   closed Monday dinner, 3 weeks February and 3 weeks October – **M** (dinner only) a la carte
   10.00/16.50 **t.** 🍷 4.50.

✗ **Cottage Loft,** Castlepark, SW : 1 ¾m. by L 42 ℰ 72803, Seafood – 🅿. 🖃 AE ① VISA
   M (dinner only and Sunday lunch) a la carte 11.90/15.50 **st.** 🍷 4.25.

KNOCKTOPHER Kilkenny – see Kilkenny.

L'EUROPE en une seule feuille
Carte Michelin n° ⑨②⓪

LAHINCH Clare 405 D 9 – pop. 455 – ✪ 065.

Envir. : Cliffs of Moher★★★ (O'Brien's Tower ☀★★ N : 1 h Rtn on foot) NW : 5 ½ m.

🏌, 🏌 ♟ Lahinch 3.

♦Dublin 162 – ♦Galway 49 – ♦Limerick 41.

   🏨 **Aberdeen Arms,** ♟ 81100, Telex 70132 – 🛏wc 🅿 ☎. 🔼 AE ① VISA
      April-mid October – **M** (bar lunch) 16.50 t. ⍭ 3.00 – **48 rm** 🖙 23.00/40.00 t.

LEENANE Galway 405 C 7.

See : ≼★ on Killary Harbour★.

Exc. : SE : Joyces Country : by road L 100 from Leenane to Clonbur : Lough Nafooey★, – ☀★ from the bridge on Lough Mask★★.

♦Dublin 173 – Ballina 56 – ♦Galway 41.

   Hotels see : **Clifden** SW : 19 m.

LETTERFRACK Galway 405 C 7 – ✪ Moyard.

Envir. : Kylemore Abbey (site★★) and Kylemore Lake★, E : 4 m. – Renvyle (castle ≼★) NW : 5 m.

♦Dublin 189 – Ballina 69 – ♦Galway 57.

   🏨 **Rosleague Manor** 🦢, W : 1 ½ m. on T 71 ♟ 7, ≼ Ballynakill harbour and Tully mountain,
      🚗 – 🛏wc 🅿. 🔼 VISA. ✂
      Easter-October – **M** (bar lunch) 15.50 t. ⍭ 5.00 – **15 rm** 🖙 20.00/50.00 t. – SB (except Easter) 60.00/75.00 **st.**

LETTERKENNY Donegal 405 I 3 – pop. 4,930 – ECD : Monday – ✪ 074.

See : St. Eunan's Cathedral ≼★.

Envir. : Grianan of Aileach★ (stone fort) ☀★★★ NE : 18 m. – Gartan Lake★ NW : 8 ½ m.

🏌 Barnhill ♟ 21150, NE : 1 m.

🚩 Derry Rd ♟ 21160.

♦Dublin 150 – ♦Londonderry 21 – ♦Sligo 72.

   🏨 **Gallagher's,** 100 Upper Main St., ♟ 22066 – 📺 🛏wc ☎ 🅿. 🔼 AE VISA. ✂
      closed 25 to 30 December – **M** 7.50/11.00 **st.** ⍭ 3.50 – **26 rm** 🖙 13.50/32.00 **st.**

*If you write to a hotel abroad,
enclose an International Reply Coupon
(available from Post Offices).*

LIMERICK Limerick 405 G 9 – pop. 57,161 – ECD : Thursday – ✪ 061.

Envir. : Monasteranenagh Abbey★ (ruins 12C) S : 14 m. by N 20 Z.

🏌 Ballyclough ♟ 44083, S : 3 m. by N 20 Z.

✈ Shannon Airport : ♟ 061 (Shannon) 61444, Telex 26222, W : 16 m. by N 18 Y – **Terminal :** Limerick Railway Station.

🚩 The Granary, Michael St. ♟ 317522.

♦Dublin 120 – ♦Cork 58.

Plan opposite

   🏩 **Limerick Inn,** Ennis Rd, NW : 4 m. on N 18 ♟ 51544, Telex 28121, ✂ – ▤ rest 📺 ☎ �‌ 🅿.
      🏊. 🔼 AE ① VISA. ✂   on N 18   Y
      M 8.50/16.00 **st.** ⍭ 3.50 – 🖙 5.75 – **133 rm** 30.00/50.00 **st.** – SB (except summer) 70.00/84.00 **st.**

   🏩 **Jury's,** Ennis Rd, ♟ 55266, Telex 28266, 🚗 – 📺 ☎ ᗌ 🅿   Y z
      96 rm.

   🏨 **Two Mile Inn,** Ennis Rd, NW : 3 ½ m. on N 18 ♟ 53122, Telex 70157, 🚗 – 📺 🛏wc ☎ ᗌ 🅿.
      🏊   on N 18   Y
      125 rm.

   🏨 **New Greenhills,** Ennis Rd., NW : 2 ¼ m. on N 18 ♟ 53033, Telex 70246 – 📺 🛏wc ☎ 🅿. ✂
      55 rm.   on N 18   Y

   🏨 **Limerick Ryan,** Ennis Rd, NW : 1 ¼ m. on N 18 ♟ 53922, Telex 26920 – ⬆ 📺 🛏wc ☎ 🅿.
      🏊. 🔼 AE ① VISA. ✂   on N 18   Y
      M (bar lunch Monday to Saturday) 7.00/10.00 **st.** ⍭ 4.00 – 🖙 4.50 – **181 rm** 22.00/35.00 **st.** – SB (weekends only) 29.00/45.00 **st.**

   🏨 **Cruise's Royal,** 4-7 O'Connell St., ♟ 44977, Telex 70088 – ⬆ 📺 🛏wc ☎. 🏊. 🔼 AE ①
      VISA. ✂   Z a
      M 7.50/12.00 t. ⍭ 3.75 – **73 rm** 🖙 21.50/39.00 t.

   🏨 **Royal George,** O'Connell St., ♟ 44566, Telex 26910 – ⬆ 📺 🛏wc ☎. 🏊. 🔼 AE ① VISA
      M a la carte 6.45/8.45 **t.** ⍭ 3.50 – **60 rm** 🖙 21.75/39.00 t.   Z c

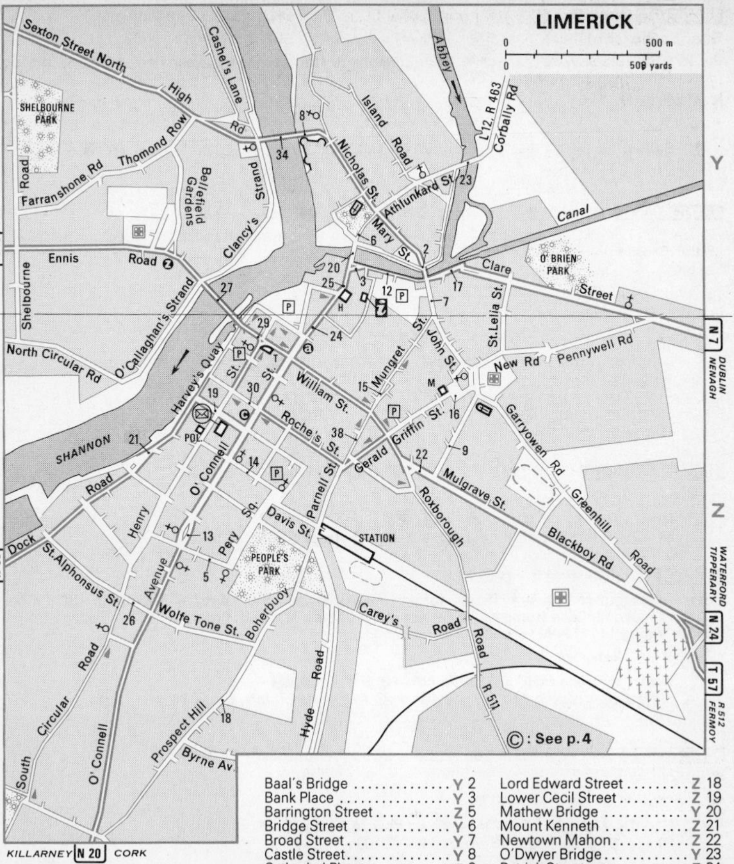

Mary Street .... Y
O'Connell Street .... Z
Roches Street .... Z
Shannon Street .... Z 30
William Street .... Z

Baal's Bridge .... Y 2
Bank Place .... Y 3
Barrington Street .... Z 5
Bridge Street .... Y 6
Broad Street .... Y 7
Castle Street .... Y 8
Cathedral Place .... Z 9
Charlotte's Quay .... Y 12
Crescent (The) .... Z 13
Glentworth Street .... Z 14
High Street .... Z 15
John Square .... Z 16
Lock Quay .... Y 17

Lord Edward Street .... Z 18
Lower Cecil Street .... Z 19
Mathew Bridge .... Y 20
Mount Kenneth .... Z 21
Newtown Mahon .... Z 22
O'Dwyer Bridge .... Y 23
Patrick Street .... Z 24
Rutland Street .... Y 25
St. Gerard Street .... Z 26
Sarsfield Bridge .... Y 27
Sarsfield Street .... Z 29
Thomond Bridge .... Y 34
Wickham Street .... Z 38

***En saison,** surtout dans les stations fréquentées, il est prudent de retenir à l'avance. Cependant, si vous ne pouvez pas occuper la chambre que vous avez retenue, prévenez immédiatement l'hôtelier.*
Si vous écrivez à un hôtel à l'étranger, joignez à votre lettre un coupon-réponse international (disponible dans les bureaux de poste).

LISCANNOR Clare **405** D 9 – ✆ 065 Lahinch.
♦Dublin 164 – ♦Galway 51 – ♦Limerick 43.

- **Liscannor Golf,** ✆ 81186, ≤ Liscannor harbour, – wc ✆ **P**. AE VISA.
  M (bar lunch) 8.00/15.00 **st.** – **26 rm** 25.00/38.00 **st.**

LISDOONVARNA Clare **405** E 8 – pop. 249 – ✆ 065 Ennis.
Envir. : Cliffs of Moher★★★ (O' Brien's Tower ※★★ N : 1 h Rtn on foot) SW : 8 m.
✆ 62 (June-September).
♦Dublin 167 – ♦Galway 39 – ♦Limerick 47.

- **Sheedy's Spa View,** ✆ 74026, – wc wc **P**. VISA.
  March-October – **M** (bar lunch) 10.00 **t.** – **10 rm** 14.00/29.00 **t.**

LISMORE Waterford **405** I 11 – pop. 884 – ECD : Thursday – ✪ 058 Dungarvan.

See : Castle (site★).

Envir. : SE : Blackwater Valley★★ (from Lismore to the mouth, by a scenic road along the right bank of the River Blackwater).

🏌 ✐ 54026, N : 1 m.

◆Dublin 143 – ◆Cork 37 – ◆Killarney 74 – ◆Waterford 44.

   🏠 Ballyrafter House 🍸, N : ¾ m. by T 30 on T 34 ✐ 54002, 🚗, park – 🚻wc 🅿. 🎿 – **14 rm**.

TOYOTA Lismore ✐ 54147

LONGFORD Longford **405** I 6 – pop. 3,876 – ECD : Thursday – ✪ 043.

Envir. : SE : Lough Derravaragh★ – Lough Owel★ – Multyfarnan (Franciscan College park : Stations of the Cross★) – Lough Lene★ – Fore (St. Feichin's Church and ruined priory 13C★) – Lough Ennell★.

🏌 Dublin Rd ✐ 6310.

🅱 ✐ 6566 (May-September).

◆Dublin 74 – Roscommon 19 – ◆Sligo 57 – ◆Tullamore 47.

   🏠 Longford Arms, Main St., ✐ 46296 – 🚻wc 🍽wc 🕾 🅿. 🏋. 🎿 – **51 rm**.

FORD Dublin Rd ✐ 46421
MAZDA, VW, AUDI Dublin Rd ✐ 46321
MAZDA, VW Dublin Rd ✐ 46496
NISSAN Drumlish ✐ 24104

RENAULT Athlone Rd ✐ 46615
TOYOTA Lanesboro ✐ 21159
TOYOTA Athlone Rd ✐ 45621

LOUGH GOWNA Cavan **405** J 6 – pop. 125 – ✪ 043 Cavan.

◆Dublin 81 – ◆Tullamore 54.

   🏨 **Robin Hill** 🍸, ✐ 83121, 🚗 – 🅿. 🎿
      M *(closed Monday)* (dinner only) 9.00 **st.** – **5 rm** ⌿ 9.50/20.00 **st.**

LUCAN Dublin **405** M 7 – ✪ 01 Dublin.

Envir. : Castletown House★ 18C (Georgian mansion) *AC*, SW : 4 m. – Maynooth (St. Patrick's College : museum Ecce Homo★ 12C, leaf of ivory diptych Northern French★ 14C) – College Chapel : interior wainscots★) NW : 5 ½ m.

◆Dublin 9 – ◆Tullamore 50.

   XX **Henri's,** 4 The Mall, ✐ 280319, 🚗 – 🅿. 🔟 🗛🗀 ⓪ 𝗩𝗜𝗦𝗔
      closed Saturday lunch, Sunday and 23 December-2 January – **M** a la carte 18.20/21.40 **t.**
      🍷 4.75.

MACROOM Cork **405** F 12 – pop. 2,256 – ECD : Wednesday – ✪ 026.

🏌 Lackadove ✐ 72.

◆Dublin 186 – ◆Cork 25 – ◆Killarney 30.

   🏠 **Castle,** Main St., ✐ 41074 – 🚻wc 🍽wc. 🗛 ⓪ 𝗩𝗜𝗦𝗔. 🎿
      M 4.50/8.50 **t.** 🍷 3.00 – **18 rm** ⌿ 11.00/22.00 **t.**

FORD Main St. ✐ 29

MALAHIDE Dublin **405** N 7 – pop. 3,834 – ✪ 01 Dublin.

Envir. : Swords (St. Columba's Church : towers★) W : 2 ½ m. – Lusk (church : round towers★) NW : 8 m.

🏌 ✐ 450245.

◆Dublin 9 – Drogheda 24.

   XX **Johnny's,** 9 St. James's Terr., ✐ 450314 – 🔟 🗛🗀 ⓪ 𝗩𝗜𝗦𝗔
      closed Sunday, Monday, 1 week at Easter, September-mid October and 1 week at Christmas –
      M (dinner only) a la carte 12.60/24.95 **t.** 🍷 3.90.

MALLOW Cork **405** F 11 – pop. 5,901 – ECD : Wednesday – ✪ 022.

🏌 Balleyellis ✐ 21145, SE : 1 ½ m. from Mallow Bridge.

◆Dublin 149 – ◆Cork 21 – ◆Killarney 40 – ◆Limerick 41.

   🏨 **Longueville House** 🍸, W : 3 ½ m. by N 27 ✐ 27156, ≼, « Georgian mansion in extensive
      grounds », 🔍, 🚗, park – 🚻wc 🍽wc 🅿. 🗛🗀 ⓪ 𝗩𝗜𝗦𝗔. 🎿
      Easter-October – **M** (bar lunch and Sunday and Monday dinner, residents only) (book-
      ing essential) 18.00 **st.** 🍷 5.00 – **17 rm** ⌿ 28.00/66.00 **st.** – SB (weekends only) 85.00/96.00 **st.**

OPEL Buttevant ✐ 23338

MAYNOOTH Kildare **405** M 7 – pop. 3,388 – ECD : Wednesday – ✪ 01 Dublin

   XXX **Moyglare Manor** 🍸 with rm, Moyglare, N : 2 m. ✐ 286351, ≼, « Georgian country house »,
      🚗, park – 🚻wc 🕾 🅿. 🗛🗀 ⓪ 𝗩𝗜𝗦𝗔. 🎿
      M a la carte 14.70/23.15 **st.** 🍷 4.50 – **11 rm** ⌿ 35.00/60.00 **st.**

MOYARD Galway **405** C 7 – pop. 382.
♦Dublin 187 – ♦Galway 55.

🏠 **Crocnaraw Country House** ⟨⟩, 🌡 9, ≼, « Country house atmosphere », 🐾, 🚲, park –
⌷wc 🅿. *VISA*. 🍴
April-October – **M** (booking essential) 8.50/15.00 t. 🍴 4.50 – **10 rm** ⤶ 25.00/45.00 t. – SB
(not weekends) (April-June) 60.00/65.00 **st.**

MOYCULLEN Galway **405** E 9 – pop. 3,260 – ✉ Rosscahill – ⚙ 091 Galway.
♦Dublin 139 – ♦Galway 7.

⚓ **Knockferry Lodge** ⟨⟩, Knockferry (on Lough Corrib), NE : 6 ½ m. 🌡 80122, 🐾 – ⌷wc 🅿.
AE ⓪ *VISA*. 🍴
Easter-October – **M** (bar lunch) (booking essential) 8.75 **st.** – **12 rm** ⤶ 11.25/21.00 **st.**

XX **Drimcong House**, NW : 1 m. on N 59 🌡 85115, 🚲 – 🅿. 🔟 **AE** ⓪ *VISA*
closed Sunday, Monday and 1 week at Christmas – **M** (dinner only) a la carte 11.20/17.45 **st.**
🍴 3.50.

NAVAN Meath **405** L 7 – pop. 4,605 – ECD : Thursday – ⚙ 046.
Envir. : Bective Abbey★ (12C ruins) S : 3 m.
🏌 Royal Tara, Bellinter Park 🌡 25244.
♦Dublin 30 – Drogheda 16 – ♦Dundalk 34.

at Dunderry SW : 5 ½ m. by N 51 on L 23 – ✉ ⚙ 046 Navan :

XXX **Dunderry Lodge**, W : ¾ m. 🌡 31671, « Converted farm buildings » – 🅿. 🔟 **AE** ⓪ *VISA*
closed Sunday, Monday, 1 to 9 April, 11 August-5 September and 20 December-3 January – **M**
(dinner only) (booking essential) a la carte 13.50/16.10 t. 🍴 4.25.

AUSTIN-ROVER-DAIMLER-JAGUAR-LAND ROVER
Dublin Rd 🌡 21929
FORD Dublin Rd 🌡 21212

PEUGEOT Castlemartin 🌡 21949
RENAULT Cannon Row 🌡 21312
TOYOTA Kells Rd 🌡 21336

NEWBAWN Wexford **405** L 10 – see New Ross.

NEWBRIDGE (DROICHEAD NUA) Kildare **405** L 8 – pop. 5,053 – ECD : Tuesday – ⚙ 045 Naas.
Envir. : Kildare (St. Brigid's Cathedral★ 13C-19C and round tower★ 9C-10C) SW : 5 m. – Tully
(National Stud★, Japanese gardens★ *AC*) SW : 6 m. via Kildare – Old Kilcullen (site★, ⚜★).
🏌 Cill-Dara, 🌡 045 (Kildare) 21433, Kildare Town, SW : 5 m. – 🏌 Curragh 🌡 045 (Curragh) 41238,
S : 3 m.
♦Dublin 28 – Kilkenny 57 – ♦Tullamore 36.

🏨 Keadeen, Ballymany, SW : 1 m. on N 7 🌡 31666, Telex 24326, 🚲 – 📺 ⅗ 🅿. 🏊
36 rm.

FIAT Moorefield 🌡 31725
NISSAN, TOYOTA Dublin Rd 🌡 31281

NEWMARKET-ON-FERGUS Clare **405** F 7 – pop. 1,000 – ⚙ 061 Shannon.
♦Dublin 136 – Ennis 8 – ♦Limerick 15.

🏨 **Dromoland Castle** ⟨⟩, NW : 1½ m. on T 11 🌡 71144, Telex 26854, ≼, « Converted castle »,
🏌9, ⚐, park, ⚜ – ☎ 🅿. 🏊 🔟 **AE** ⓪ *VISA*. 🍴
April-October – **M** 14.00/24.40 **t.** 🍴 4.60 – ⤶ 8.50 – **67 rm** 62.00/94.00 **t.**

NEWPORT Mayo **405** D 6 – pop. 420 – ⚙ 098.
See : St. Patrick's Church★, modern Irish-Romanesque style (site★).
Envir. : Burrishoole Abbey (site★) NW : 2 m.
♦Dublin 164 – Ballina 37 – ♦Galway 60.

🏨 **Newport House** ⟨⟩, 🌡 41222, Telex 53740, « Country house atmosphere, antiques », 🐾,
🚲, park – ⌷wc 🅿. **AE** ⓪ *VISA*. 🍴
April-September – **M** 10.00/15.00 **st.** 🍴 4.50 – **20 rm** ⤶ 20.00/50.00 **st.** – SB 60.00/72.00 **st.**

NEW ROSS Wexford **405** L 10 – pop. 4,775 – ECD : Wednesday – ⚙ 051.
Envir. : St. Mullins Monastery (site★) N : 9 m. – John F. Kennedy Memorial Park★ 1968 (arboretum,
≼★) S : 7 ½ m. – SW : River Barrow Valley★.
🏌 Tinneranny 🌡 21433.
🛈 🌡 21857 (July-August).
♦Dublin 88 – Kilkenny 27 – ♦Waterford 15 – Wexford 23.

🏠 **Inishross House**, 96 Mary St., 🌡 21335 – 🅿. 🍴
closed 1 week at Christmas – **6 rm** ⤶ 9.00/17.00 **st.**

at Newbawn E : 8 m. by N 25 and L 160 – ✉ ⚙ 051 New Ross :

XX **Cedar Lodge** with rm, Carrigbyrne, N : 1 ½ m. on N 25 🌡 24386 – 📺 ⌷wc ☎ 🅿. 🔟 *VISA*.
🍴
M a la carte 11.40/16.50 **t.** – **14 rm** ⤶ 25.00/38.00 **t.**

FIAT Rosebercon 🌡 21122
FORD Waterford Rd 🌡 21403

OUGHTERARD Galway **405** E 7 – pop. 628 – ✿ 091 Galway.

See : The northern scenic road (cul-de-sac) ≼✶✶ on Lough Corrib✶✶✶.

Envir. : Aughnanure Castle✶ (16C) SE : 3 m. – Leckavrea Mountain✶ NW : 13 m. – Gortmore (≼✶✶ S : on Kilkieran Bay, ≼✶ NW : on the Twelve Pins) SW : 16 m.

🇫🇸 Gurteeva ℰ 82131.

◆Dublin 149 – ◆Galway 17.

🏠 **Currarevagh House** 🦢, NW : 4 m. ℰ 82313, ≼, « Country house atmosphere », 🦢, 🌲, park, 🎾 – ➭wc ➮wc. ❀
   4 April-3 October – **M** (closed lunch to non-residents)(booking essential) 6.20/13.00 t. 🍸 3.50 – **15 rm** ⟷ 22.50/48.00 t.

🏠 **Sweeney's Oughterard House** 🦢, W : ½ m. on T 71 ℰ 82207, 🌲 – 🛏 ➭wc ☎ Ⓟ. 💳 ⓪ 𝘝𝘐𝘚𝘈
   M a la carte 8.25/17.25 t. 🍸 3.50 – **21 rm** ⟷ 35.00/66.00 t.

PARKNASILLA Kerry **405** C 12 – pop. 250 – ✿ 064 Sneem.

🇫🇸 Parknasilla ℰ 45122.

◆Dublin 224 – ◆Cork 72 – ◆Killarney 34.

🏛 **Great Southern** 🦢, ℰ 45122, Telex 26899, ≼ Kenmare river, bay and mountains, 🏊, 🇫🇸, 🦢, 🌲, park, 🎾 – 📺 Ⓟ. 🦽 💳 🆎 ⓪ 𝘝𝘐𝘚𝘈
   4 April-1 November and Christmas – **M** approx. 15.00 t. 🍸 5.00 – ⟷ 6.50 – **59 rm** 37.00/64.00 t.

PORTLAOISE Laois **405** K 8 – pop. 4,346 – ✿ 0502.

🇫🇸 Heath ℰ 21322, E : 4 m.

🅱 ℰ 21178 (July-August).

◆ Dublin 54 – Kilkenny 31 – ◆Limerick 67.

🏨 Killeshin, Dublin Rd, E : 1 m. on N 7 ℰ 21663, Telex 33272 – 📺 ➭wc ➮wc ☎ Ⓟ. 🦽 ❀
   44 rm.

PORT NA BLAGH Donegal **405** I 2 – see Dunfanaghy.

PUCKANE Tipperary **405** H 9 – pop. 253 – ✉ ✿ 067 Nenagh.

◆Dublin 98 – ◆Limerick 28.

🏠 **St. David's Country House** 🦢, Ballycommon, W : 2 ½ m. ℰ 24237, Group Telex 26807, ≼, 🦢, 🌲 – ➮wc Ⓟ. 🆎
   closed Christmas Day – **M** 10.00/15.00 t. 🍸 5.00 – **6 rm** ⟷ 23.00/40.00 t.

RAPHOE Donegal **405** J 3 – pop. 945 – ✿ 074.

Envir. : Beltany Stone Circle✶ (site✶) from the road 10 mn on foot, S : 2 m.

◆Dublin 139 – Donegal 29 – ◆Londonderry 20 – ◆Sligo 69.

🍴 **Central,** The Diamond, ℰ 45126 – ➮wc. ❀
   closed 23 to 31 December – **M** *(closed Sunday lunch)* 5.50/8.00 **st.** 🍸 3.00 – ⟷ 3.50 – **10 rm** 7.00/15.00 **st.**

RATH LUIRC = Charleville.

RATHMULLAN Donegal **405** J 2 – pop. 486 – ✉ ✿ 074 Letterkenny.

Envir. : Mulroy Bay ✶✶ NW : 8 m. – Fanad Head ≼✶ N : 20 m – 🇫🇸 Otway, Saltpans ℰ 108.

◆Dublin 165 – ◆Londonderry 36 – ◆Sligo 87.

🏛 **Rathmullan House** 🦢, N : ½ m. on L 77 ℰ 58188, ≼ Lough Swilly and hills, « Country house atmosphere », 🦢, park, 🎾 – ➭wc ➮wc. 🦽 🆎 ⓪ 𝘝𝘐𝘚𝘈
   Easter-8 October – **M** (restricted lunch) 8.50/14.50 t. 🍸 3.50 – **21 rm** ⟷ 16.00/58.00 **st.** – SB 58.00/80.00 **st.**

🏠 **Fort Royal** 🦢, N : 1 m. off L 77 ℰ 58100, ≼ Lough Swilly, 🇫🇸, 🦢, 🌲, park, 🎾, squash – ➮wc Ⓟ. 💳 🆎 𝘝𝘐𝘚𝘈
   April-September – **M** (bar lunch Monday to Saturday) 14.00 **st.** 🍸 4.00 – **21 rm** ⟷ 22.00/50.00 **st.** – SB (weekends only)(summer only) 60.00/70.00 **st.**

RATHNEW Wicklow **405** N 8 – pop. 954 – ✉ ✿ 0404 Wicklow.

◆Dublin 31 – ◆Waterford 82 – Wexford 65.

🏛 **Tinakilly House** 🦢, ℰ 9274, Telex 32227, ≼, « Victorian country house », 🌲, park – ➭wc ☎ Ⓟ. 🦽 🆎 𝘝𝘐𝘚𝘈 ❀
   Mid March-October – **M** (restricted lunch Monday to Saturday) 12.00/19.50 **st.** 🍸 4.25 – **10 rm** ⟷ 28.00/65.00 **st.**

🏛 Hunter's, N : ¾ m. on L 29 ℰ 4106, « Inn in attractive gardens », 🦢, 🌲 – ➭wc Ⓟ. 🆎 ❀ – **17 rm**.

REDCASTLE Donegal **405** K 2 – pop. 467 – ✉ ✿ Moville.

◆Dublin 162 – ◆Londonderry 17.

🏛 Redcastle, ℰ 243, ≼, 🇫🇸, 🦢, park, 🎾, squash – 📺 ➭wc ☎ Ⓟ. ❀ – **14 rm**.

ROSCOMMON Roscommon **405** H 7 – pop. 1, 673 – ECD : Thusrday – ✆ 0903.
◆Dublin 95 – ◆Galway 50 – ◆Sligo 51.

  🏨 **Abbey,** ✆ 6015, Telex 33116, 🚗 – 📺 🛏wc 📶 & ℗. 🔼 🅰🅴 𝗩𝗜𝗦𝗔 . ❀
    closed Christmas Day – **M** 7.50/12.50 **st.** ▮ 4.50 – ⛛ 4.00 – **25 rm** 20.00/36.00 **t.** – SB (week-
    ends only) 55.00/60.50 **st.**

ROSSES POINT Sligo **405** G 5 – see Sligo.

ROSSLARE Wexford **405** M 11 – pop. 588 – ✆ 053 Wexford.
📸 ✆ 32113 – ◆Dublin 104 – ◆Waterford 50 – Wexford 12.

  🏨 Kelly's Strand, Strand Rd, ✆ 32114, 🏊 heated, 🔼, 🚗, ❀ – 🈁 ☎ ℗. ❀ – **97 rm**.
  🏨 **Casey's Cedars,** Strand Rd, ✆ 32124, Telex 80237, 🚗 – 📺 🛏wc 📶 & ℗. 🔼 🅰🅴 ⓞ 𝗩𝗜𝗦𝗔
    ❀
    closed January – **M** (booking essential in winter) 7.50/14.50 **t.** – **35 rm** ⛛ 28.00/44.00 **t.** – SB
    51.00/65.00 **t.**

ROSSLARE HARBOUR Wexford **405** N 11 – pop. 725 – ✆ 053 Wexford.
⚓ Shipping connections with the Continent : to France (Cherbourg), (Le Havre) (Irish Continental
Line) – to Fishguard (Sealink) 1-2 daily (3 h 30 mn) – to Pembroke (B & I Line) 7-11 weekly (4 h).
🛈 ✆ 33232.
◆Dublin 105 – ◆Waterford 51 – Wexford 13.

  🏨 **Rosslare,** ✆ 33110, Telex 80772, ≤ – 📺 🛏wc ☎ ℗. 🔼 🅰🅴 𝗩𝗜𝗦𝗔
    closed Christmas Day – **M** a la carte 7.30/9.70 **t.** – **25 rm** ⛛ 16.50/45.00 **t.** – SB 45.00/60.00 **st.**
  🏠 Tuskar House, St. Martins Rd, ✆ 33363, ≤, 🚗 – 🛏wc 📶 ℗. ❀ – **15 rm**.

ROSSNOWLAGH Donegal **405** H 4 – ✆ 072 Bundoran.
◆Dublin 157 – Donegal 9 – ◆Sligo 33.

  🏨 **Sand House** 🌲, ✆ 51777, Telex 40460, ≤ bay, beach and mountains, 🛥, 🎾, ❀ – ℗. 🔼
    🅰🅴 ⓞ . ❀
    Easter-September – **M** 8.00/15.00 **t.** ▮ 4.75 – **40 rm** ⛛ 20.00/52.00 **t.**

ST ERNAN'S ISLAND Donegal – see Donegal.

SALTHILL Galway **405** E 8 – see Galway.

SCHULL (SKULL) Cork **405** D 13 – pop. 457 – ✆ 028 Skibbereen.
Envir. : E : Roaringwater Bay★ – ◆Dublin 226 – ◆Cork 65 – ◆Killarney 64.

  ✗ **Ard-na-Greine Inn** 🌲 with rm, SW : 1 ¾ m. by L 57 ✆ 28181, 🚗 – 🛏wc ℗. 🅰🅴 ⓞ 𝗩𝗜𝗦𝗔 .
    ❀
    Easter-September – **M** (bar lunch) (booking essential) 16.00 **t.** ▮ 4.25 – **7 rm** ⛛ 26.00/46.00 **t.**
  ✗ **Courtyard,** Main St., ✆ 28209 – 🔼 🅰🅴 𝗩𝗜𝗦𝗔
    closed Sunday, Monday to Wednesday during October-May, and February – **M** (bar
    lunch)(booking essential) 17.00 **st.**

SHANAGARRY Cork **405** H 12 – ✉ ✆ 021 Cork.
◆Dublin 163 – ◆Cork 25 – ◆Waterford 64.

  ✗✗ **Ballymaloe House** 🌲 with rm, NW : 1 ¾ m. on L 35 ✆ 652531, Telex 75208, ≤, « Country
    house atmosphere », 🏊 heated, 🎾, 🚗, park, ❀ – 🛏wc 🛏wc 📶 & ℗. 🔼 🅰🅴 ⓞ 𝗩𝗜𝗦𝗔 .
    closed 24 to 26 December – **M** (buffet lunch) 19.00 **t.** ▮ 4.00 – ⛛ 4.00 – **25 rm** 21.15/50.60 **t.**

SHANNON AIRPORT Clare **405** F 9 – pop. 3,657 – ✆ 061 Limerick.
📸 ✆ Shannon 61020.
✈ ✆ 61444, Telex 26222 – Terminal : Limerick Railway Station ✆ 42433.
🛈 ✆ 61664 and 61604 – ◆Dublin 136 – Ennis 16 – ◆Limerick 15.

  🏨 **Shannon International,** ✆ 61122, Telex 24018 – 📺 ☎ ℗. 🔼 🅰🅴 ⓞ 𝗩𝗜𝗦𝗔
    14 March-December – **M** (buffet lunch) 16.00 **t.** – ⛛ 6.50 – **117 rm** 25.00/50.00 **t.**

SKIBBEREEN Cork **405** E 13 – pop. 2,130 – ✆ 028.
◆Dublin 205 – ◆Cork 51 – ◆Killarney 68.

  ✗✗ **Mill House,** Rineen, E : 5 m. by L 60 on Union Hall rd ✆ 36299, 🚗 – ℗. 🔼 🅰🅴 ⓞ 𝗩𝗜𝗦𝗔
    closed Sunday and Monday from October-May – **M** (dinner only)(booking essential) 14.50 **t.**

SKULL = Schull.

SLANE Meath **405** M 6 – pop. 483 – ✆ 041 Drogheda.
See : Hill of Slane (site★, ≤★).
◆Dublin 42 – Drogheda 8 – ◆Dundalk 26.

  ✗✗ **Slane Castle,** W : 1 m. on N 51 ✆ 24207 – ℗. 🔼 🅰🅴 ⓞ 𝗩𝗜𝗦𝗔
    closed Sunday and Monday – **M** (dinner only) a la carte 12.55/17.50 **t.** ▮ 3.50.

SLIEVERUE Waterford – see Waterford.

SLIGO Sligo 🅐🅑🅔 G 5 – pop. 14,080 – ✪ 071.

See : Sligo Abbey★ (13C ruins) – Court House★.

Envir. : E : Lough Gill★★★ (Innisfree★) Park's Castle (site★★), Lough Colgagh★★, Drumcliff (High Cross) ≤★ on Benbulbin Moutains N : 4 m. – Glencar Lough★ NE : 6 m. – Carrowmore (Megalithic cemetery★) SW : 2 m.

🏌 Strandhill ✆ 78188, W : 8 m.

🖪 Aras Reddan, Temple St. ✆ 61201.

♦Dublin 133 – ♦Belfast 126 – ♦Dundalk 106 – ♦Londonderry 86.

🏨 Sligo Park, Pearse Rd, S : 1 m. on N 4 ✆ 60291, ≤, 🐎 – 📺 ⅙ ℗. 🏖
60 rm.

🏨 **Ballincar House** ⬓, Rosses Point Rd, NW : 2 ½ m. on L 16 ✆ 5362, ≤, 🐎, ⅙, squash – ➡wc ⃑wc ℗ 🅝 🅰🅴 𝖵𝖨𝖲𝖠 ⅍
closed Christmas and first 3 weeks January – **M** 6.50/13.50 t. ⅙ 4.00 – **20 rm** ☑ 20.00/48.00 t. – SB (weekends only)(except summer) 60.00/70.00 **st.**

at Strandhill W : 7 m. on L 132 – ✉ ✪ 071 Sligo :

✗✗ **Knockmuldowney,** ✆ 68122, 🐎 – ℗. 🅝 🅰🅴 🅞 𝖵𝖨𝖲𝖠
closed Sunday, Monday except Bank Holidays, Good Friday, Christmas Day and February – **M** (dinner only) (booking essential) a la carte 11.10/13.00 **t.** ⅙ 3.40.

at Rosses Point NW : 5 m. on L 16 – ✉ ✪ 071 Sligo :

✗ **Moorings,** ✆ 77112, Seafood – ℗. 🅰🅴 🅞 𝖵𝖨𝖲𝖠
closed Sunday – **M** (bar lunch June-August only) a la carte 14.00/24.00 **st.** ⅙ 3.00.

AUSTIN-ROVER, PEUGEOT-TALBOT Bridge St. ✆ 2091
FIAT, LANCIA Ballinode ✆ 2188
FORD Bundoran Rd ✆ 2610
VW Ballisodare ✆ 67291

SPIDDLE Galway 🅐🅑🅔 E 8 – pop. 145 – ✪ 091 Galway.

♦Dublin 143 – ♦Galway 11.

🏨 **Bridge House,** Main St., ✆ 83118, 🐎 – ➡wc ⃑wc ℗. 🅝 𝖵𝖨𝖲𝖠 ⅍
closed 23 December-6 January – **M** 10.00/16.00 **st.** ⅙ 5.00 – **14 rm** ☑ 18.00/45.00 **st.** – SB 50.00/55.00 **st.**

🏨 **Park Lodge,** E : 1 ¾ m. on L 100 ✆ 83159 – ➡wc ⃑wc ☎ ℗. 🅝 🅰🅴 𝖵𝖨𝖲𝖠 ⅍
Easter and April-October – **M** (closed Saturday) 7.25/10.75 **st.** ⅙ 3.50 – **25 rm** ☑ 15.50/29.00 **st.**

STRANDHILL Sligo 🅐🅑🅔 G 5 – see Sligo.

TEMPLEGLANTINE Limerick 🅐🅑🅔 E 10 – ✪ 069 Newcastle West.

♦Dublin 154 – ♦Killarney 36 – ♦Limerick 33.

🏨 Devon Inn, on N 21 ✆ 62811, 🐎 – 📺 ➡wc ☎ ℗. ⅍
18 rm.

THURLES Tipperary 🅐🅑🅔 I 9 – pop. 7,356 – ✪ 0504.

See : Catholic Cathedral (interior)★.

🏌 Turtula ✆ 21983.

♦Dublin 93 – Kilkenny 29 – ♦Limerick 39.

🏨 **Hayes,** Liberty Sq., ✆ 22122 – ➡wc ℗. 🏖 🅝 𝖵𝖨𝖲𝖠
closed 10 days at Christmas – **M** 8.25/12.00 **st.** ⅙ 3.50 – **38 rm** ☑ 22.00/42.00 **st.**

TIPPERARY Tipperary 🅐🅑🅔 H 10 – pop. 4,631 – ECD : Wednesday – ✪ 062.

Envir. : S : Glen of Aherlow★ (statue of Christ the King ≤★★).

🏌 Rathanny ✆ 51119, S : 1 m.

♦Dublin 113 – ♦Cork 57 – ♦Limerick 24 – ♦Waterford 53.

⋔ **Ach-na-Sheen House,** Waterford Rd, ✆ 51298 – ➡wc ℗. 𝖵𝖨𝖲𝖠
13 rm ☑ 9.00/19.00 **st.**

TRALEE Kerry 🅐🅑🅔 C 11 – pop. 12,287 – ECD : Wednesday – ✪ 066.

🏌 Mount Hawke ✆ 21150.

🖪 32 The Mall ✆ 21288.

♦Dublin 185 – ♦Killarney 20 – ♦Limerick 64.

🏨 **Ballygarry House,** SE : 1 ½ m. on N 21 ✆ 21233, 🐎 – 📺 ➡wc ⃑wc ☎ ℗. 🅝 🅰🅴 𝖵𝖨𝖲𝖠
M (bar lunch Monday to Saturday) 8.00/14.95 **st.** – **16 rm** ☑ 20.00/40.00 **st.** – SB 57.00/65.95 **st.**

🏨 Mount Brandon, Princes St., ✆ 21311, Telex 28130 – 🛗 📺 ➡wc ☎ ℗. 🏖 – **162 rm**.

AUSTIN-ROVER 100 Rock St. ✆ 21113
FIAT Ashe St. ✆ 21124
FORD Edward St. ✆ 21555
MAZDA, VW, AUDI-NSU The Market and Rock St. ✆ 21193
TOYOTA Denny St. ✆ 21688

TRAMORE Waterford 405 K 11 – pop. 3,792 – ⊠ ✪ 051 Waterford.
ᔆ ✆ 81247.
🎌 ✆ 81572 (July-August).
♦Dublin 107 – ♦Cork 72 – ♦Waterford 8.

🏨 Grand (Best Western), Market Sq., ✆ 81414, ≤ – 🛗 ⇔wc ⑁wc 🕾 ℗ – **50 rm**.

TRIM Meath 405 L 7 – pop. 1,700 – ECD : Thursday – ✪ 046.
ᔆ ✆ 31463, SW : 2 ½ m.
♦Dublin 28 – Drogheda 25 – ♦Dundalk 43.

🏨 Wellington Court, Summerhill Rd, ✆ 31516 – 📺 ⇔wc 🕾 ℗. ⁒
18 rm.

VIRGINIA Cavan 405 K 6 – pop. 583 – ✪ 049 Cavan.
Envir. : Kells : St. Columba's House★ 9C – St. Columba's Church : old tower★ 1783 – Churchyard
(high crosses★) SE : 11 m.
ᔆ ✆ 35.
♦Dublin 52 – ♦Dundalk 39 – Roscommon 56 – ♦Tullamore 59.

🏨 Park ⟋, ✆ 47235, ≤, ᔆ, ⟍, ⚘, park, ⁒ – ⇔wc ⑁wc 🕾 ℗. 🔃 🅰🅴 ⓞ 𝑽𝑰𝑺𝑨. ⁒
closed January and February – **M** 7.00/14.00 **st**. ⏐5.90 – **27 rm** ⊆ 24.00/30.50 **st**. – SB
(weekends only) 50.75 **st**.

WATERFORD Waterford 405 K 11 – pop. 31,968 – ✪ 051.
See : Franciscan ruins of the French Church★ 13C-16C (Grey Friars Street).
ᔆ Newrath ✆ 74182.
⤳ Waterford Airport : ✆ 75589, S : 6 m.
🎌 41 The Quay ✆ 75788.
♦Dublin 96 – ♦Cork 73 – ♦Limerick 77.

🏨🏨 Granville, Meagher Quay, ✆ 55111, Telex 80188 – 🛗 📺 ☎. 🔃. 🔃 🅰🅴 ⓞ 𝑽𝑰𝑺𝑨. ⁒
closed 25 and 26 December – **M** 7.25/12.75 **st**. ⏐4.75 – **60 rm** ⊆ 25.00/48.00 **st**. – SB
(weekends only) 58.00/60.00 **st**.

🏨 Tower, The Mall, ✆ 75801, Telex 80699 – 🛗 📺 ⇔wc 🕾. 🔃. ⁒
82 rm.

at Slieverue N : 2 m. on N 25 – ⊠ ✪ 051 Waterford :

↟ Diamond Hill, SW : ½ m. on N 25 ✆ 32855, ⚘ – ⑁wc ℗. ⁒
10 rm.

NISSAN, RENAULT 3 Michael St. ✆ 76181
OPEL Catherine St. ✆ 74988
PEUGEOT Morgan St. ✆ 74232

RENAULT Lady Lane Rd ✆ 75831
TOYOTA William St. ✆ 74037

WATERVILLE Kerry 405 B 12 – pop. 547 – ✪ 0667 Waterville.
Envir. : Sheehan's Point ≤★★★ S : 6 m. – Remains of Carhan House (birthplace of Daniel O'Connell)
N : 11 m. – Ballinskelligs (Augustinian Monastery ≤★) W : 9 m.
♦Dublin 238 – ♦Killarney 48.

🏨 Butler Arms, ✆ 4144, Telex 26826, ⟍, ⚘, ⁒ – ⇔wc ⑁wc ℗. 🔃 🅰🅴 ⓞ 𝑽𝑰𝑺𝑨
Easter-mid October – **M** (bar lunch) 15.40 **st**. ⏐4.25 – **37 rm** ⊆ 12.00/40.00 **st**.

✗ Huntsman, ✆ 4124, ≤, Seafood – 🔃 🅰🅴 ⓞ 𝑽𝑰𝑺𝑨
closed Monday to Wednesday during winter – **M** a la carte 9.20/16.45 **t**. ⏐4.00.

WESTPORT Mayo 405 D 6 – pop. 3,023 – ECD : Wednesday.
See : Westport House★ AC.
Envir. : Croagh Patrick Mountain★ (statue of St. Patrick ≤★, pilgrimage) SW : 6 m. – Roonah Quay
≤★ on Clare Island W : 15 m.
ᔆ Carrowholly ✆ 547.
🎌 The Mall ✆ 098 (Newport) 25711.
♦Dublin 163 – ♦Galway 50 – ♦Sligo 65.

Hotel see : Newport N : 8 m.

WEXFORD Wexford 405 M 10 – pop. 11,849 – ECD : Thursday – ☺ 053.

Envir. : Johnstown Castle (the park-arboretum★) SW : 4 m.

🛝 Mulgannon ✏ 22238, SE : 1 m.

🛈 Crescent Quay ✏ 23111.

♦Dublin 88 – Kilkenny 49 – ♦Waterford 38.

🏨 **Talbot,** Trinity St., ✏ 22566, Telex 80658, 🔄, squash – 🛗 📺 ⟂wc ☎ 🅿 🔄 🔄 AE ⑩ VISA ✂
M 9.50/15.00 t. ⓵ 3.60 – ⟂ 5.50 – **105 rm** 28.60/50.00 t.

🏨 **Ferrycarrig** 🏊, Ferrycarrig Bridge, NW : 2 ¾ m. on N 11 ✏ 22999, Telex 91880, ≼, 🌿, ✂ – 🛗 ⟂wc 🅿 🔄 AE ⑩ VISA
Easter-October – **M** (bar lunch Monday to Saturday) a la carte 7.90/11.65 t. ⓵ 5.00 – ⟂ 4.00 – **40 rm** 18.50/37.00 t. – SB 45.00/60.00 st.

🏠 **Whitford House,** New Line Rd, SW : 2 m. on L 159 ✏ 24673, 🔄, 🌿 – ⟂wc 🅿 VISA ✂
closed 15 December-1 January – **20 rm** ⟂ 12.50/24.50 st.

FORD Ferrybank ✏ 23329
OPEL Ferrybank ✏ 22107
PEUGEOT, VOLVO ✏ 22998

RENAULT Redmond Rd ✏ 23133
TOYOTA Carriglawn, Newtown Rd ✏ 23788
VW, AUDI, MAZDA Drinagh ✏ 22377

WICKLOW Wicklow 405 N 9 – pop. 3,786 – ECD : Thursday – ☺ 0404.

Envir. : Ashford (Mount Usher or Walpole's Gardens★) *AC*, NW : 4 m.

🛝 Blainroe ✏ 2675, S : 3½ m.

🛈 ✏ 2904.

♦Dublin 33 – ♦Waterford 84 – Wexford 67.

%% **Old Rectory** with rm, ✏ 2048, 🌿 – ⟂wc ☎ 🅿 ✂
April-October – **M** (dinner only)(booking essential) a la carte 16.30/21.30 st. ⓵ 4.50 – **5 rm** ⟂ 24.50/49.00 st.

FIAT Bollarney ✏ 2212
FORD Whitegates ✏ 2331

VW, AUDI-NSU The Glebe ✏ 2126

YOUGHAL Cork 405 I 12 – pop. 5,445 – ECD : Wednesday – ☺ 024.

See : St. Mary's Collegiate Church★ 13C.

Envir. : Ardmore (site★, round tower★ 10C, cathedral ruins★ 12C, ≼★) E : 5 ½ m.

🛝 Knockaverry ✏ 2787.

🛈 ✏ 2390 (July-August).

♦Dublin 146 – ♦Cork 30 – ♦Waterford 47.

%% **Aherne's Seafood Bar,** 163 North Main St., ✏ 92424 – 🅿 🔄 AE ⑩ VISA
closed Sunday lunch, Monday dinner except July and August and 5 days at Christmas – **M** a la carte 11.00/16.50 t. ⓵ 3.55.

RENAULT North Abbey ✏ 2019

MAJOR
HOTEL GROUPS

**Abbreviations used in the Guide
and central reservation telephone
numbers**

PRINCIPALES
CHAINES HOTELIÈRES

Abréviations utilisées dans nos
textes et centraux téléphoniques
de réservation

PRINCIPALI
CATENE ALBERGHIERE

**Abbreviazioni utilizzate nei nostri testi
e centrali telefoniche di
prenotazione**

DIE WICHTIGSTEN
HOTELKETTEN

Im Führer benutzte Abkürzungen der Hotel-
ketten und ihre Zentralen für telefonische
Reservierung

ANCHOR HOTELS LTD	ANCHOR	0252 (Farnborough) 517517
BEST WESTERN HOTELS...................	BEST WESTERN	01 (London) 940 9766
CREST HOTELS LTD	CREST	01 (London) 236 3242
DE VERE HOTELS PLC.....................	DE VERE	01 (London) 404 0991
EMBASSY HOTELS	EMBASSY	01 (London) 581 3466
FORUM HOTELS	FORUM	01 (London) 491 7181
GOLDEN OAK INNS LTD	GOLDEN OAK	021 (Birmingham) 356 9177
INTER-CONTINENTAL HOTELS LTD.........	INTER-CON	01 (London) 491 7181
LADBROKE HOTELS	LADBROKE	01 (London) 734 6000
MOUNT CHARLOTTE HOTELS LTD	MT. CHARLOTTE	0532 (Leeds) 444866
NORFOLK CAPITAL HOTELS LTD	NORFOLK CAP.	01 (London) 589 7000
OSPREY HOTELS	OSPREY	041 (Glasgow) 552 7788
QUEENS MOAT HOUSES PLC	Q.M.H.	02934 (Horley) 75321
RANK HOTELS LTD	RANK	01 (London) 262 2893
STAKIS HOTELS	STAKIS	041 (Glasgow) 332 4343 and 01 (London) 222 4081
SWALLOW HOTELS PLC	SWALLOW	0783 (Sunderland) 294666
THISTLE HOTELS LTD	THISTLE	01 (London) 937 8033
TRUSTHOUSE FORTE HOTELS LTD	T.H.F.	01 (London) 567 3444

TRAFFIC SIGNS
A few important signs

SIGNALISATION ROUTIÈRE
Quelques signaux routiers importants

SEGNALETICA STRADALE
Alcuni segnali importanti

VERKEHRSZEICHEN
Die wichtigsten Straßenverkehrszeichen

Please note: The maximum speed limits in Great Britain are 70 mph (112 km/h) on motorways and dual carriageways and 60 mph (96 km/h) on all other roads, except where a lower speed limit is indicated.

N.B. N'oubliez pas qu'il existe des limitations de vitesse en Grande-Bretagne: 70 mph (112 km/h) sur routes à chaussée séparée et autoroutes, 60 mph (96 km/h) sur autres routes, sauf indication d'une vitesse inférieure.

N.B. In Gran Bretagna esistono dei limiti di velocità: 70 mph (112 km/h) sulle strade a doppia carreggiata e autostrade, 60 mph (96 km/h) sulle altre strade, salvo che sia indicata una velocità inferiore.

Zur Beachtung: In Großbritannien gelten folgende Geschwindigkeitsbegrenzungen: 70 mph (112 km/h) auf Autobahnen und Straßen mit getrennten Fahrbahnen, 60 mph (96 km/h) auf allen anderen Straßen, wenn keine niedrigere Geschwindigkeit angezeigt ist.

Warning signs — *Signaux d'avertissement*
Segnali di avvertimento — *Warnzeichen*

 T junction
Jonction avec autre route
Confluenza con altra strada
Straßeneinmündung

 Roundabout
Sens giratoire
Senso rotatorio
Kreisverkehr

 Dual carriageway ends

Fin de chaussée à deux voies

Fine di doppia carreggiata

Ende der zweispurigen Fahrbahn

 Change to opposite carriageway

Déviation sur chaussée opposée

Deviazione sulla carreggiata opposta

Überleitung auf Gegenfahrbahn

 Distance to give way sign ahead
Cédez le passage à 50 yards
Dare la precedenza a 50 iarde
Vorfahrt gewähren in 50 yards Entfernung

 Ralentir maintenant
Rallentare subito
Geschwindigkeit verringern

 Right-hand lane closed
Voie de droite barrée
Corsia di destra sbarrata
Rechte Fahrbahn gesperrt

 Quayside or river bank
Débouché sur un quai ou une berge
Banchina o argine senza sponda
Ufer

 Two-way traffic crosses one-way road
Voie à deux sens croisant voie à sens unique
Strada a due sensi che incrocia una strada a senso unico
Straße mit Gegenverkehr kreuzt Einbahnstraße

 Level crossing with automatic half barriers ahead
Passage à niveau automatique
Passaggio a livello automatico con semi-barriere
Bahnübergang mit automatischen Halbschranken

 Height limit
Hauteur limitée (en pieds et pouces)
Altezza limitata (piedi e pollici)
Maximale Höhe (in Fuß und Zoll)

 Opening or swing bridge
Pont mobile
Ponte mobile
Bewegliche Brücke

Signs giving orders

Signaux de prescriptions absolues
Segnali di prescrizione (di divieto o d'obbligo)
Gebots- und Verbotszeichen

End of speed limit
Fin de limitation de vitesse
Fine di limitazione di velocità
Ende der Geschwindigkeitsbeschränkung

School crossing patrol
Sortie d'école
Uscita di scolari
Achtung Schule

No stopping (« clearway »)

Arrêt interdit

Fermata vietata

Halteverbot

All vehicles prohibited
(plate gives details)
Circulation interdite à tous véhicules
(plaque donnant détails)
Divieto di transito a tutti i veicoli (la
placca sottostante fornisce dei dettagli)
Verkehrsverbot für Fahrzeuge aller Art
(näherer Hinweis auf Zusatzschild)

Give priority to vehicles from opposite
direction
Priorité aux véhicules venant de face
Dare la precedenza ai veicoli che proven-
gono dal senso opposto
Dem Gegenverkehr Vorrang gewähren

Voie à stationnement réglementé

Sosta regolamentata

Fahrbahn mit zeitlich begrenzter
Parkerlaubnis

Width limit
Largeur limitée (en pieds et pouces)
Larghezza limitata (piedi e pollici)
Breite begrenzt (in Fuß und Zoll)

Plate below sign at end of prohibition
Fin d'interdiction
Fine del divieto posta sotto il segnale
Ende einer Beschränkung

Information signs

Signaux de simple indication
Segnali di indicazione
Hinweiszeichen

One-way street
Rue à sens unique
Via a senso unico
Einbahnstraße

No through road
Voie sans issue
Strada senza uscita
Sackgasse

Accès à une chaussée à deux voies

Accesso ad una carreggiata a due corsie

Zufahrt zu einer zweispurigen Fahrbahn

Ring road
Voie de contournement
Strada di circonvallazione
Ringstraße

Warning signs on rural motorways

Signaux d'avertissement sur autoroutes
Segnali di avvertimento su autostrade
Warnzeichen auf Autobahnen

Maximum advised speed
Vitesse maximum conseillée
Velocità massima consigliata
Empfohlene Höchstgeschwindigkeit

1 Lane closed
1 voie barrée
1 Corsia sbarrata
1 Fahrstreifen gesperrt

Count-down markers at exit from motorway or primary route
Balises situées sur autoroute ou route principale et annonçant une sortie
Segnali su autostrada annuncianti un'uscita
Hinweise auf Abfahrten an Autobahnen und Hauptverkehrsstraßen

 Road clear

Route libre

Strada libera

Straße frei

Direction to service area, with fuel, parking, cafeteria and restaurant facilities.

Indication d'aire de service avec carburant, parc à voitures, cafeteria et restaurant.

Indicazione di area di servizio con carburante, parcheggio, bar e ristorante

Hinweis auf Tankstelle, Parkplatz, Cafeteria und Restaurant

Warning signs on urban motorways
Signaux d'avertissement sur autoroutes urbaines
Segnali di avvertimento su autostrade urbane
Warnzeichen auf Stadtautobahnen

_1_   _2_   _3_

The insets show (flashing amber lights) (1) advised maximum speed, (2) lane to be used; (3) (flashing red lights), you must stop.

L'ensemble de ces panneaux indique : (1) la vitesse maximale conseillée, (2) la voie à utiliser (signaux lumineux jaunes) ; (3) l'arrêt obligatoire (signaux lumineux rouges).

L'insieme di questi segnali indica : (1) la velocità massima consigliata, (2) la corsia da imboccare (segnali luminosi gialli) ; (3) la fermata obbligatoria (segnali luminosi rossi).

Diese Schilder (mit blinkenden Ampeln) weisen hin auf : 1. die empfohlene Höchstgeschwindigkeit, 2. die zu befahrende Fahrbahn (gelbes Licht) und 3. Halt (rotes Licht).

In town — *En ville*
In città — *in der Stadt*

SIGNALISATION SHOWN ON OR ALONG KERBS

SIGNALISATION MATÉRIALISÉE SUR OU AU LONG DES TROTTOIRS

SEGNALI TRACCIATI SOPRA O LUNGO I MARCIAPIEDI

ZEICHEN AUF ODER AN GEHWEGEN

OTHER ROAD SIGNS

AUTRES PANNEAUX

ALTRI CARTELLI INDICATORI

ZUSÄTZLICHE VERKEHRSZEICHEN

No waiting during every working day
Stationnement interdit tous les jours ouvrables
Sosta vietata nei giorni feriali con indicazioni complementari
Parkverbot an Werktagen

Stationnement interdit de 8 h 30 à 18 h 30 du lundi au samedi
Sosta vietata da lunedi a sabato dalle 8,30 alle 18,30
Parkverbot Montag bis Samstag von 8.30 bis 18.30 Uhr

No loading or unloading during every working day

Livraisons interdites tous les jours ouvrables

Carico e scarico vietato nei giorni feriali con indicazioni complementari

Be- und Entladen verboten an allen Werktagen

Livraisons interdites de 8 h 30 à 18 h 30 du lundi au samedi
Carico e scarico vietato da lunedi a sabato dalle 8,30 alle 18,30
Be- und Entladen verboten von Montag bis Samstag von 8.30 bis 18.30 Uhr

---

No waiting during every working day and additional times as indicated
Stationnement interdit tous les jours ouvrables plus autres périodes indiquées sur panneaux
Divieto di sosta tutti i giorni feriali e negli altri periodi indicati sul cartello
Parkverbot an Werktagen und den auf Zusatz- schildern angegebenen Zeiten

Stationnement interdit en permanence

Divieto permanente di sosta

Parkverbot zu jeder Zeit

No loading or unloading during every working day and additional times as indicated
Livraisons interdites tous les jours ouvrables plus autres périodes indiquées sur panneaux
Divieto di carico e scarico tutti i giorni feriali e negli altri periodi indicati sul cartello
Be- und Entladen verboten an Werktagen und den auf Zusatzschildern angegebenen Zeiten

No loading at any time

Livraisons interdites en permanence

Divieto permanente di carico e scarico

Be- und Entladeverbot zu jeder Zeit

No waiting during any other periods
Stationnement interdit à toute autre période
Sosta vietata in determinate ore
Parkverbot zu bestimmten Zeiten

Waiting Limited 8 am-6 pm 20 minutes in any hour

Stationnement limité à 20 mn de 8 h à 18 h
Sosta limitata a 20 mn dalle 8 alle 18
Höchstparkdauer 20 min. in der Zeit von 8.00 bis 18.00 Uhr

No loading or unloading during any other periods

Livraisons interdites à toute autre période

Divieto di carico e scarico in determinate ore

Be- und Entladeverbot zu bestimmten Zeiten

No loading Mon-Fri 8.00-9.30 am 4.30-6.30 pm

Livraisons interdites du lundi au vendredi de 8 h à 9 h 30 et de 16 h 30 à 18 h 30
Carico e scarico vietato da lunedi a venerdi dalle 8 alle 9,30 e dalle 16,30 alle 18,30
Be- und Entladeverbot Montag bis Freitag von 8.00 bis 9.30 und von 16.30 bis 18.30 Uhr

---

Remember : speed limit in Great Britain 70 mph and in Eire 60 mph.

Direction signs on the road network
Panneaux de direction sur le réseau routier
Cartelli direzionali sulla rete stradale
Richtungsschilder auf den Straßen

Motorways and A (M) class roads
Sur autoroutes et routes classées A (M)
Sulle autostrade e strade classificate A (M)
Autobahn M und Schnellstraße A (M)

Primary routes
Apart from motorways, « Primary routes » provide the major road network linking towns of local and national traffic importance

Sur grands itinéraires routiers « Primary routes »
En complément du système autoroutier, les grands itinéraires constituent un réseau de routes recommandées reliant les villes selon leur importance dans le trafic national

Sui principali itinerari stradali (Primary routes)
I principali itinerari, unitamente alle autostrade, costituiscono una rete di strade consigliate che collegano le città secondo la loro importanza nel traffico nazionale

Empfohlene Fernverkehrsstraßen (Primary routes)
Sie bilden ein überregionales Straßennetz, das verkehrswichtige Orte verbindet ; sie ergänzen das Autobahnnetz

Other A class roads
Sur autres routes classées A
Sulle altre strade classificate A
Andere Straße der Kategorie A

B class roads
Sur routes classées B
Sulle strade classificate B
Straße der Kategorie B

Unclassified roads — Local direction sign
Sur routes non classées — Signalisation locale
Sulle strade non classificate — Segnaletica locale
Nicht klassifizierte Straßen — Örtliche Richtungsschilder

ADDRESSES OF SHIPPING COMPANIES AND THEIR PRINCIPAL AGENTS

ADRESSES DES COMPAGNIES DE NAVIGATION ET DE LEURS PRINCIPALES AGENCES

INDIRIZZI DELLE COMPAGNIE DI NAVIGAZIONE E DELLE LORO PRINCIPALI AGENZIE

ADRESSEN DER SCHIFFAHRTSGESELLSCHAFTEN UND IHRER WICHTIGSTEN AGENTUREN

BALTIC SHIPPING CO.

5 Mezhevoi Canal, Leningrad L35, USSR.

Agents : C.T.C. Lines (UK), 1-3 Lower Regent St., London, SW1Y 4NN, ☏ (01) 930 5833, Telex 917193.

Heitmann & Son A/S, Prinsensgt 3A, P.O. Box 378, Oslo 1, ☏ 334 180, Telex 16481.

Baltic Shipping Co, 35 Hertzen St., Leningrad 190000, U.S.S.R. ☏ 211 7776, Telex 551.

Transtours, 49 Avenue de l'Opéra, 75067 Paris, France, ☏ 251.58.28, Telex 230732

B & I LINE

16 Westmoreland St., Dublin 2, Eire, ☏ 724711, Telex 25651.

Agents : 155 Regent St., London, W1R 7FD, ☏ (01) 734 4681, Telex 23523.

42 Grand Par., Cork, Eire, ☏ (021) 23024, Telex 26137.

Reliance House, Water St., Liverpool, L2 8TP, ☏ (051) 227 3131, Telex 627839.

BRITISH RAIL see SEALINK and HOVERSPEED

BRITTANY FERRIES

BAI Brittany Ferries, Gare Maritime Roscoff, Port du Bloscon 29211, France, ☏ (98) 61.22.11, Telex 940360.

Agents : Millbay Docks, Plymouth, PL1 3EW, Devon, ☏ (0752) 21321, Telex 45380.

The Brittany Centre, Wharf Rd, Portsmouth, PO2 8RU, Hampshire. ☏ (0705) 827701, Telex 86878.

Gare Maritime, 35400 St-Malo, France, ☏ (99) 56.68.40, Telex 950487.

Tourist House, 42 Grand Parade, Cork, Eire, ☏ (021) 507666, Telex 75088.

Modesto Pineiro & Co., 27 Paseo de Pereda, Santander, Spain, ☏ (042) 214500, Telex 35913.

CALEDONIAN MACBRAYNE LTD.

Ferry Terminal, Gourock, PA19 1QP, Renfrewshire, Scotland, ☏ (0475) 33755, Telex 779318.

COMMODORE SHIPPING SERVICES AND CONDOR LTD.

Commodore House, Bulwer Av., St. Sampsons, Guernsey, Channel Islands, ☏ (0481) 46841.

Condor Ltd, 4 North Quay, P.O. Box 33, St. Peter Port, Guernsey, Channel Islands, ☏ (0481) 24604, Telex 419 1275.

Agents : Commodore Travel Ltd., 28 Conway St., St. Helier, Jersey, Channel Islands, ☏ (0534) 71263, Telex 419 2079.

Condor Ltd., Morvan Fils, 2 Place du Poids du Roi, 35402 St. Malo, France, ☏ 564229, Telex 950486 TRANSIT F.

CUNARD LINE LTD.

South Western House, Canute Rd, Southampton, Hampshire, SO9 1ZA, ☏ (0703) 29933, Telex 477577.

Agents : 8 Berkeley St., London W1X 6NR, ☏ (01) 491 3930, Telex 295483.

555 Fifth Av., New York, NY 10017, USA, ☏ (212) 880 7500, Telex 220436.

American Express Co. Inc., 11 rue Scribe, Paris 75009, France, ☏ 266 0999, Telex 210718.

DFDS PRINS FERRIES

Agents : Latham House, 16 Minories, London EC3N 1AD, ☏ (01) 481 3211, Telex 883049.

DFDS Prinzenlinien, Jessenstrasse 4, 2000 Hamburg 50, West Germany, ☏ (040) 389030, Telex 2161759.

DFDS SEAWAYS

Sankt Annae Plads 30, DK-1295 Copenhagen K, Denmark, ✆ (01) 11 22 55, Telex 19416.

Agents : DFDS (UK) Ltd., Tyne Commission Quay, North Shields, NE29 6EE, Tyne and Wear, ✆ (0632) 575655, Telex 537285.
DFDS Seaways, Bruksgaten 1, S-21120 Malmo, Sweden, ✆ (40) 10 30 10, Telex 32888.
A/S Danske-Batene, Karl Johansgate 1, Oslo 1, Norway, ✆ 330700, Telex 18129.

DFDS TOR LINE

Skandiahamnen, P.O. Box 8895, S-40272 Gothenburg 8, Sweden, ✆ (031) 54 03 00, Telex 20688.

Agent : Anzani House, Trinity Av., Felixstowe, Suffolk, IP11 8XE, ✆ (03942) 73131.
Scandia Terminal, Suezhaven, P.O. Box 8238, 1005 AE Amsterdam, ✆ 117005, Telex 11257.

EMERAUDE FERRIES

Agents : Marine Management Ltd., 17a York St., St. Helier, Jersey, Channel Islands, ✆ (0534) 74458 and 74467, Telex 419 2029 MARMAN.
Emeraude Ferries, Albert Quay, St. Helier, Jersey, Channel Islands, ✆ (0534) 74458, Telex 4192311 SEACAR.
Gare Maritime du Naye, 35400 St-Malo, France, ✆ (99) 81.61.46, Telex 950271.

FRED, OLSEN-BERGEN LINE

11 Conduit St., London W1R 0LS, ✆ (01) 491 3760, Telex 263670.

Agents : DFDS, Tyne Commission Quay, Tyne and Wear, NE29 6EE, ✆ (0632) 575655, Telex 537285.
Consignataria Fred Olsen S.A., c/o Maestro Valle 22, Ciudad Jardin, P.O. Box 252, Las Palmas, Canary Islands, ✆ 232166, Telex 95020 NAFOL.
Consignataria Fred Olsen S.A., Calle Dr. Zerolo 14, Santa Cruz de Tenerife, ✆ 287250, Telex 92590 CMHN.
Joao, de Freitas Martins Lda, Avenida do Mar 15/16, Funchal, Madeira, ✆ 21106/07, Telex 72173 JFMART.
VCK-Zeereisen, P.O. Box 561, De Ruijterkade 139, 1000 AM Amsterdam, Netherlands, ✆ 262216, Telex 14561.

HERM SEAWAY

Guernsey Motors Ltd., Picquet House, St. Peter Port, Guernsey, Channel Islands, ✆ (0481) 24161 and 24677.

HOVERCROSS LTD

P.O. Box 31, Templar House, Don Rd, St. Helier, Jersey, Channel Islands, ✆ (0534) 275111.

Agents : Hovercross Office, Gorey Harbour, Jersey, Channel Islands, ✆ (0534) 54495.
Gare Maritime, Barneville, Carteret, France, ✆ 54.70.50, Telex 171935 PEQUEEN.

HOVERSPEED

International Hoverport, Ramsgate, Kent, CT12 5HS, ✆ (0843) 594881, Telex 96323. Reservations : General (0843) 595555, London (01) 554 7061, Birmingham (021) 236 2190, Manchester (061) 228 1321.

Agents : International Hoverport, Boulogne, France, ✆ (21) 30.27.26, Telex 110008.
International Hoverport, Calais, France, ✆ (21) 96.65.70, Telex 810856.

HOVERTRAVEL LTD.

Quay Road, Ryde, Isle of Wight, P033 2HB.
Agent : Clarence Pier, Southsea, Portsmouth, PO5 3AD, Hampshire, ✆ (0705) 829988.

IRISH CONTINENTAL LINE LTD.

19/21 Aston Quay, Dublin 2, Eire, ✆ (01) 774331, Telex 30355.

Agent : Transport et Voyages, 2 Rue de la Paix, 75002 Paris, France, ✆ (514) 261.58.04, Telex 042-230970 TOUVOYA.

ISLE OF MAN STEAM PACKET CO. LTD.

P.O. Box 5, Imperial Buildings, Douglas, Isle of Man, ✆ (0624) 3824, Telex 629414.

Agents : Caledonian MacBrayne Ltd., Buchanan Bus Station, Killermont St., Glasgow, Scotland, ✆ 041 (Glasgow) 332 4451, Telex 778177.
W.E. Williames & Co. Ltd., 35/39 Middlepath St., Belfast, Northern Ireland, ✆ (0232) 55411, Telex 747166.
B & I Line, 16 Westmoreland St., Dublin 2, Eire ✆ (01) 724711, Telex 002725651.
India Buildings, 40 Brunswick St., Liverpool, ✆ (051) 236 3214, Telex 629415.
Queens Terr., Fleetwood, Lancashire, ✆ (039 17) 6263 (summer), ✆ 0624 (Douglas I.O.M.) 3824 (winter).

ISLE OF SARK SHIPPING CO. LTD.

White Rock, St. Peter Port, Guernsey, Channel Islands, ✆ (0481) 24059, Telex 419 1549.

ISLES OF SCILLY STEAMSHIP CO. LTD.

Hugh Town, St. Mary's, Isles of Scilly, TR21 OLJ, ✆ 0720 (Scillonia) 22357/8.

Agent : 16 Quay St., Penzance, TR18 4BD, Cornwall, ✆ (0736) 2009/4013.

LUNDY CO.

Lundy via Ilfracombe, Devon, EX34 8LA, ✆ (0271) 870870.

MERSEYSIDE PASSENGER TRANSPORT EXECUTIVE

24, Hatton Garden, Liverpool L3 2AN, Merseyside, ✆ (051) 227 5181.

NORFOLK LINE BV

Kranenburgweg 207, Postbus 84214, 2508 Ae Den Haag, Netherlands, ✆ (070) 514601, Telex 31515.

Agent : Atlas House, Southgates Rd, Great Yarmouth, Norfolk, ✆ (0493) 56133, Telex 97449.

NORTH SEA FERRIES LTD.

Noordzee Veerdiensten, Beneluxhaven, Europoort, P.O. Box 1123, 3180 AC Rozenburg Z.H., Netherlands, ✆ (01819) 62077, Telex 26571.

Agents : King George Dock, Hedon Rd, Hull, HU9 5QA, Humberside, ✆ (0482) 795141, Telex 52349.

Prins Filipsdock, Lancelot Blondeellaan, 8380 Zeebrugge, Belgium, ✆ (050) 545601, Telex 81469.

OLAU-LINE LTD.

Sheerness, Kent, ME12 1SN, ✆ (0795) 666666 and 663355, Telex 965605.

Agents : Olau-Line Terminal, Buitenhaven, Postbus 231, Vlissingen, Netherlands, ✆ (01184) 65400, Telex 37817.

ORKNEY ISLANDS SHIPPING CO. LTD.

4 Ayre Road, Kirkwall, Orkney Islands, Scotland, ✆ (0856) 2044.

ORWELL & HARWICH NAVIGATION CO. LTD.

The Quay, Harwich, Essex, ✆ (025 55) 2004.

P & O FERRIES : CHANNEL SERVICES

Arundel Towers, Portland Terrace, Southampton, SO9 4AE, Hampshire, ✆ (0703) 34141, Telex 47485. London Reservations : ✆ (01) 623 1505.

Agents : Eastern Docks, Dover, Kent, ✆ (0304) 203399, Telex 965726.

9 Place de la Madeleine, 75008 Paris, France, ✆ 265.22.16, Telex 660144.
Route du Môle Central, Port du Havre, 76600 Le Havre 76, France, ✆ (35) 26.57.26, Telex 190736.
Gare Maritime, Quai Chanzy BP 312, 62204 Boulogne-sur-Mer, ✆ 31.78.00, Telex 130187.

P & O FERRIES : ORKNEY & SHETLAND SERVICES

P.O. Box 5, P & O Ferry Terminal, Jamieson's Quay, Aberdeen, AB9 8DL, Scotland, ✆ (0224) 572615, Telex 73344.

Agents : Terminal Building, Scrabster, Caithness, KW14 7UJ, Scotland, ✆ (0847) 62052.
Harbour Street, Kirkwall, Orkney Islands, KW15 1LE, Scotland, ✆ (0856) 3330, Telex 75296.
Holmsgarth Terminal, Lerwick, Shetland Islands, ZE1 0PW, Scotland, ✆ (0595) 5252, Telex 75294.
Terminal Bldg., Stromness, Orkney Islands, KW16 3AA, Scotland, ✆ (0856) 850 655, Telex 75221.

POLISH OCEAN LINES

P.O. Box 265, 10 Lutego 24, 81-364 Gdynia, Poland, ✆ 20-19-01, Telex 054-231.

Agents : Gdynia America Shipping Lines (London) Ltd, 238 City Rd, London, EC1V 2QL, ✆ 01-251 3389, Telex 884477.
Riodan's Travel, 111 Lower Baggot St., Dublin 2, Eire, ✆ 62434, Telex 5163.
Hamburg Süd Reiseagentur GmbH, 59 Ostwest Strasse, P.O. Box 1661, 2, Hamburg 11, West Germany, ✆ 37051, Telex 02-14991.
McLean Kennedy Ltd., 410 St. Nicolas St., P.O. Box 1086, Montreal H2Y 2P5, Canada, ✆ (514) 849 6111.
HAL Zeereizen B.V., Postbus 791, Wilhelminakade 86, Rotterdam 3020, Netherlands, ✆ (010) 392213, Telex 288-76.
Franck and Tobiesen, 10 Strandagervg, Copenhagen DK 2900 Hellerup, Denmark, ✆ 13-02-55, Telex 275-15.

RED FUNNEL SERVICES

12 Bugle St., Southampton, SO9 4LJ, Hampshire, ✆ (0703) 26211.

Agents : Fountain Pier, West Cowes, Isle of Wight, ✆ (098 382) 292101 and 292704.

THE SALLY LINE LTD

54 Harbour Parade, Ramsgate, Kent, CT11 8LN ✆ (0843) 55522, Telex 96352 SALLY.

Agents : 81 Piccadilly, London W1, ✆ (01) 409 2240, Telex 291860.

Sally Viking Line, Dunkerque Port-Ouest, 59279 Loon Plage, France, ✆ (28) 68.43.44, Telex 820055.

SEALINK U.K. LTD. (British Rail)

Sealink UK Ltd., 163/203 Eversholt St., London, NW1 1BG, ✆ (01) 387 1234, Telex 269295 BRSLIN G.

SNCF, 88 Rue Saint-Lazare, 75436 Paris Cedex 09, France.

RTM Belgian Maritime Transport Authority, 30 Rue Belliard, B.1040 Brussels, Belgium, ✆ 230 0180, Telex 23851.

Zeeland Steamship Co., Hook of Holland, Netherlands, ✆ 47 39 44, Telex 31272 ZLDHK NL.

A.L.A. Steamship Co., Gare Maritime, Dunkirk West, France, ✆ 66 80 01, Telex 160247.

Agents : Sealink UK Ltd., Southern House, Lord Warden Square, Dover, CT17 9DH, Kent, ✆ (0304) 203203 Ext. 3187.

Sealink UK Ltd., Fishguard Harbour, Dyfed, Wales, SA64 0BX, ✆ (0348) 872881, Telex 48167.

Sealink UK Ltd., Car Ferry Terminal, Folkestone Harbour, Kent, CT20, 1QH, ✆ (0303) 53949, Telex 965136.

Sealink UK Ltd., Parkeston Quay, Harwich, Essex, CO12 4SR, ✆ (025 55) 7022, Telex 98235.

Sealink UK Ltd., Sea Terminal, Heysham, Lancashire, LA3 2XF, ✆ (0524) 53802, Telex 65260 MANXL G.

Sealink UK Ltd., Car Ferry Booking Office, Lymington Pier, Lymington, Hampshire, SO4 8ZE, ✆ (0590) 73301.

Sealink UK Ltd., Newhaven Harbour, East Sussex, BN9 0BG, ✆ (0273) 514131, Telex 87151.

Sealink UK Ltd., Channel Islands Services, Norman House, Continental Ferry Terminal, Portsmouth, Hampshire, PO2 7AE, ✆ (0705) 811315.

Sealink UK Ltd., Isle of Wight Ferry Services, P.O. Box 59, Portsmouth, Hampshire, PO1 2XB, ✆ (0705) 827744, Telex 86440.

Sealink, Isle of Man, Ladywell House, Marsh Lane, Preston, Lancashire, PR2 2TT, ✆ (0772) 24220, Telex 677398.

Sealink UK Ltd., Car Ferry Office, The Slipway, Fishbourne Lane, Cowes, Isle of Wight, PO33 4EU, ✆ (0983) 882432.

Sealink UK Ltd., Weymouth Quay, Weymouth, Dorset, DT4 8DY, ✆ (030 57) 86363, Telex 41245.

Sealink UK Ltd., Car Ferry Office, The Slipway Quay Street, Yarmouth, Isle of Wight, PO41 0PB, ✆ (0983) 760213.

Sealink Travel Centre, Victoria Station, London SW1, ✆ (01) 834 3838/8511, Telex 22708.

Sealink (Scotland) Ltd., Stranraer Harbour, Wigtownshire, DG9 8EJ, ✆ (0776) 2262, Telex 778125.

Sealink UK Ltd., 24 Donegall Place., Belfast, BT1 5BH, Northern Ireland, ✆ (0232) 227525.

Sealink UK Ltd., The Jetty, St Peter Port, Guernsey, Channel Islands, ✆ (0481) 24742, Telex 4191249.

Sealink UK Ltd., Wests Centre, St Helier, Jersey, Channel Islands, ✆ (0534) 77122, Telex 4192262.

Sealink Isle of Man, Sea Terminal, Douglas, Isle of Man, ✆ (0624) 24241.

Sealink UK Ltd., 15 Westmoreland St., Dublin 2, Eire, ✆ 714455, Telex 30847.

Manager British Rail, Rue de la Montagne 52, B-1000 Brussels, Belgium, ✆ 511 6685, Telex 23108 GB RAIL B .

Manager British Rail, Montergade 5, DK 1116 Kobenhavn K, Denmark, ✆ 12 64 60, Telex 15370.

Armement Naval SNCF, Gare Maritime BP 27, F-62201 Boulogne-sur-Mer, France, ✆ 30.25.11, Telex 110908.

Armement Naval SNCF, Terminal TNM, Gare Maritime, F-62100 Calais, France, ✆ 96.70.70, Telex 130086.

Agence Maritime Tellier, Gare Maritime, F-50100 Cherbourg, France, ✆ (33) 53.24.27, Telex 170684.

Armement Naval SNCF, Gare Maritime BP 85, F-76203 Dieppe, France, ✆ 82.24.87, Telex 770924.

Armement Naval SNCF, Gare Maritime, Dunkerque Ouest, ✆ 66.80.01, Telex 160247.

Armement Naval SNCF, 3 Rue Ambroise-Paré, 75010 Paris, France, ✆ 280 4848, Telex 280549.

Manager British Rail, Boulevard de la Madeleine, F-75009 Paris, ✆ 266.90.53, Telex 210774.

Manager British Rail, Neue Mainzer Strasse 22, D-6000 Frankfurt/Main, Germany, ✆ 23.23.81, Telex 416421.

Manager British Rail, Via Pirelli 11, 20124 Milan, Italy, ✆ 661 683, Telex 310412.

Manager British Rail, Leidseplein 5, Amsterdam, Netherlands, ✆ 234 133, Telex 13395.

Manager British Rail, Centralbahnplatz 9, 4002 Basel, Switzerland, ✆ 23 14 04, Telex 62739.

ERVICE MARITIME CARTERET-JERSEY

BP 15, 50270 Barneville-Carteret, France, ✆ (33) 54.87.21 and 54.80.72, Telex 170477.
Agent : CNTM Ltd., Gorey, Jersey, Channel Islands, ✆ (0534) 53757.

HETLAND ISLANDS COUNCIL

Grantfield, Lerwick, Shetland, ZE1 ONT, ✆ (0595) 2024, Telex 75218.

MYRIL LINE

P.O. Box 370, Jonas Broncksgoeta 25, 3800 Thorshavn, Faroe Islands, ✆ (042) 15900, Telex 81295.
Agent : P & O Ferries, Orkney & Shetland Services, P.O. Box 5, P & O Ferry Terminal, Aberdeen, AB9 8DL, Scotland, ✆ (0224) 572615, Telex 73344.
Urval Travel Bureau, Posthusstraeti 9, Reykjavik, Iceland, ✆ (01) 26900, Telex 2187
Korsør-Kiel Linien, Yderhavnsvej, 4420 Korsør, Denmark, ✆ (03) 576 100, Telex 45830.

HOMAS & BEWS FERRIES

Ferry Office, John O'Groats, Caithness, Scotland, ✆ (095 581) 353 (summer).
Windieknap, Brough, Thurso, Caithness, Scotland, ✆ (084 785) 619 (winter).

ORBAY SEAWAY

Beacon Quay, Torquay, Devon, ✆ (0803) 211974.

OWNSEND THORESEN

Agents : 127 Regent Street, London, W1R 8LB, ✆ (01) 734 4431 and 473 7800, Telex 23802.
Main Reservation Centre, Enterprise Hse., Channel View Rd Dover, CT16 1LD, Kent, ✆ (0304) 223000 Reservations : ✆ 203388.
Car Ferry House, Canute Road, Southampton, SO9 5GP, Hampshire, ✆ (0703) 34488.
Continental Ferry Port, Mile End, Portsmouth Hants, ✆ (0705) 815231.
European House, The Docks, Felixstowe, IP11 8TS, Suffolk, ✆ (039 42) 78711, Telex 98236.
Cairnryan, Stranraer, Wigtownshire, Scotland, ✆ (058 12) 276 and 277.
Larne Harbour, Larne, Co. Antrim, Northern Ireland, ✆ (0574) 4321, Telex 74528.
Car Ferry Terminal, Doverlaan 7, B-8380 Zeebrugge, Belgium, ✆ (050) 54-48.73.
41 place d'Armes, 62226 Calais, France, ✆ 34.41.90, Telex 810750.
41 boulevard des Capucines, 75002 Paris, France, ✆ 261.51.75, Telex 210679.
Gare Maritime, 50101 Cherbourg, France, ✆ (33) 44.20.13.
90 rue de Paris, 59000 Lille, ✆ (20) 57.74.65, Telex 120311
Quai de Southampton, 76600 Le Havre, France, ✆ (35) 21.36.50.
Leidsestraat 32, Amsterdam, Netherlands, ✆ (020) 223832, Telex 14601.

RIDENT CHARTER CO. LTD.

Las Vegas, L'Ancresse, Vale, Guernsey, Channel Islands, ✆ (0481) 21379.

EDETTES ARMORICAINES S.A.

Gare Maritime de la Bourse, B.P. 180, 35049 St-Malo, France, ✆ (99) 56.48.88, Telex 950196 NAVIPAX.
Agents : Vedettes Armoricaines, Albert Pier, St. Helier, Jersey, ✆ 20361, Telex 4192131 NAVIEX.
Boutins Travel Bureau, Library Pl., St. Helier, Jersey, ✆ 21532/3/4, Telex 4192149.
12 rue Georges-Clemenceau, B.P. 24, 50400 Granville, France, ✆ (33) 50.77.45, Telex 170449 F.
1er Bassin, Port de Commerce, BP 88, 29268 Brest, France, ✆ (98) 44.44.04, Telex 940210 NAVIPAMF.

VEDETTES BLANCHES

Les Vedettes Blanches, Gare Maritime, 35400 St-Malo, France, ✆ 566321, Telex 740906.
Agent : Marine Management Ltd., Albert Quay, St. Helier, Jersey, ✆ (0534) 71896, Telex 4192311 SEACAR.

VEDETTES VERTES GRANVILLAISES

1-3 rue Le Campion, 50400 Granville, France, ✆ (33) 50.16.36, Telex 170002.
Agent : Marine Management Ltd., Albert Quay, St. Helier, Jersey, ✆ (0534) 74458, Telex 4192311 SEACAR.

WESTERN FERRIES ARGYLL LTD.

16 Woodside Crescent, Glasgow, Scotland, G3 7UT, ✆ (041) 332 9766, Telex 77203 CLYDE-BUILT.
Agent : Hunters Quay, Dunoon, Argyll, Scotland, ✆ (0369) 4452.

NOTES

MANUFACTURE FRANÇAISE DES PNEUMATIQUES MICHELIN

Société en commandite par actions au capital de 700 000 000 de francs

Place des Carmes-Déchaux - 63 Clermont-Ferrand (France)

R.C.S. Clermont-Fd B 855 200 507

© Michelin et Cie, Propriétaires-Éditeurs 1985

Dépôt légal 2-85 — ISBN 2.06.006.555-0

Printed in France — 12-84-62

Photocomposition : S.C.I.A., La Chapelle d'Armentières - Impression : Tardy Quercy, Bourges n° 11942